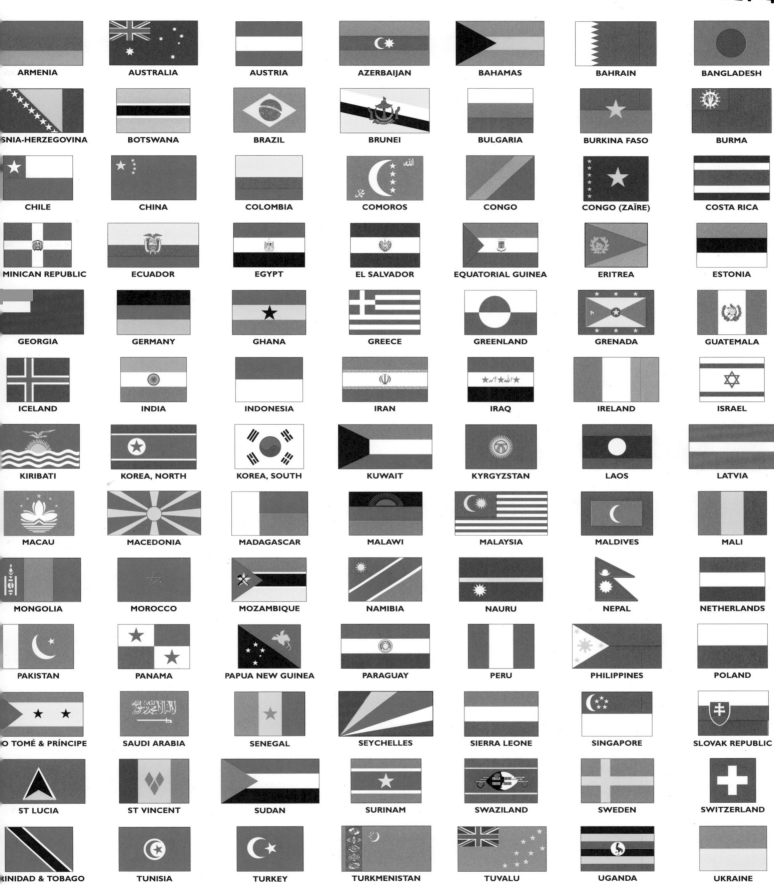

ARMENIA	AUSTRALIA	AUSTRIA	AZERBAIJAN	BAHAMAS	BAHRAIN	BANGLADESH
SNIA-HERZEGOVINA	BOTSWANA	BRAZIL	BRUNEI	BULGARIA	BURKINA FASO	BURMA
CHILE	CHINA	COLOMBIA	COMOROS	CONGO	CONGO (ZAÏRE)	COSTA RICA
MINICAN REPUBLIC	ECUADOR	EGYPT	EL SALVADOR	EQUATORIAL GUINEA	ERITREA	ESTONIA
GEORGIA	GERMANY	GHANA	GREECE	GREENLAND	GRENADA	GUATEMALA
ICELAND	INDIA	INDONESIA	IRAN	IRAQ	IRELAND	ISRAEL
KIRIBATI	KOREA, NORTH	KOREA, SOUTH	KUWAIT	KYRGYZSTAN	LAOS	LATVIA
MACAU	MACEDONIA	MADAGASCAR	MALAWI	MALAYSIA	MALDIVES	MALI
MONGOLIA	MOROCCO	MOZAMBIQUE	NAMIBIA	NAURU	NEPAL	NETHERLANDS
PAKISTAN	PANAMA	PAPUA NEW GUINEA	PARAGUAY	PERU	PHILIPPINES	POLAND
O TOMÉ & PRÍNCIPE	SAUDI ARABIA	SENEGAL	SEYCHELLES	SIERRA LEONE	SINGAPORE	SLOVAK REPUBLIC
ST LUCIA	ST VINCENT	SUDAN	SURINAM	SWAZILAND	SWEDEN	SWITZERLAND
RINIDAD & TOBAGO	TUNISIA	TURKEY	TURKMENISTAN	TUVALU	UGANDA	UKRAINE
VENEZUELA	VIETNAM	WESTERN SAMOA	YEMEN	YUGOSLAVIA	ZAMBIA	ZIMBABWE

OXFORD

CONCISE
ATLAS
OF THE
WORLD

FIFTH EDITION

Contents

The World In Focus
Cartography by Philip's

Picture Acknowledgements
Page 14 Science Photo Library/NOAA

Illustrations
Stefan Chabluk

CONSULTANTS
The publishers are grateful to the following people who acted
as specialist geography consultants on "The World In Focus"
front section:

Professor D. Brunsden, Kings College, University of London, UK
Dr C. Clarke, Oxford University, UK
Dr. I. S. Evans, Durham University, UK
Professor P. Haggett, University of Bristol, UK
Professor K. McLachlan, University of London, UK
Professor M. Monmonier, Syracuse University, New York, USA
Professor M-L. Hsu, University of Minnesota, Minnesota, USA
Professor M. J. Tooley, University of St Andrews, UK
Dr T. Unwin, Royal Holloway, University of London, UK

George Philip Limited,
a division of Octopus Publishing Group Limited,
2–4 Heron Quays, London E14 4JP

Cartography by Philip's

Published in North America by
Oxford University Press, Inc.,
198 Madison Avenue,
New York, N.Y. 10016

Oxford is a registered trademark of Oxford University Press

Library of Congress Cataloging-in-Publication Data available

ISBN 0–19–521564–8

Printing (last digit):
9 8 7 6 5 4 3 2 1

Printed in China

World Statistics: Countries

This alphabetical list includes all the countries and territories of the world. If a territory is not completely independent, then the country it is associated with is named. The area figures give the total area of land, inland water and ice. The population figures are 1998 estimates. The annual income is the Gross National Product per capita in US dollars. The figures are the latest available, usually 1997.

Country/Territory	Area km² Thousands	Area miles² Thousands	Population Thousands	Capital	Annual Income US $
Adélie Land (France)	432	167	0.03	–	–
Afghanistan	652	252	24,792	Kabul	600
Albania	28.8	11.1	3,331	Tirana	750
Algeria	2,382	920	30,481	Algiers	1,490
American Samoa (US)	0.20	0.08	62	Pago Pago	2,600
Andorra	0.45	0.17	75	Andorra La Vella	16,200
Angola	1,247	481	11,200	Luanda	340
Anguilla (UK)	0.1	0.04	11	The Valley	6,800
Antigua & Barbuda	0.44	0.17	64	St John's	7,330
Argentina	2,767	1,068	36,265	Buenos Aires	8,750
Armenia	29.8	11.5	3,422	Yerevan	530
Aruba (Netherlands)	0.19	0.07	69	Oranjestad	15,890
Ascension Is. (UK)	0.09	0.03	1.5	Georgetown	–
Australia	7,687	2,968	18,613	Canberra	20,540
Austria	83.9	32.4	8,134	Vienna	27,980
Azerbaijan	86.6	33.4	7,856	Baku	510
Azores (Portugal)	2.2	0.87	238	Ponta Delgada	–
Bahamas	13.9	5.4	280	Nassau	11,940
Bahrain	0.68	0.26	616	Manama	7,840
Bangladesh	144	56	125,000	Dhaka	270
Barbados	0.43	0.17	259	Bridgetown	6,560
Belarus	207.6	80.1	10,409	Minsk	2,150
Belgium	30.5	11.8	10,175	Brussels	26,420
Belize	23	8.9	230	Belmopan	2,700
Benin	113	43	6,101	Porto-Novo	380
Bermuda (UK)	0.05	0.02	62	Hamilton	31,870
Bhutan	47	18.1	1,908	Thimphu	390
Bolivia	1,099	424	7,826	La Paz/Sucre	950
Bosnia-Herzegovina	51	20	3,366	Sarajevo	300
Botswana	582	225	1,448	Gaborone	4,381
Brazil	8,512	3,286	170,000	Brasília	4,720
British Indian Ocean Terr. (UK)	0.08	0.03	0	–	–
Brunei	5.8	2.2	315	Bandar Seri Begawan	15,800
Bulgaria	111	43	8,240	Sofia	1,140
Burkina Faso	274	106	11,266	Ouagadougou	240
Burma (= Myanmar)	677	261	47,305	Rangoon	1,790
Burundi	27.8	10.7	5,531	Bujumbura	180
Cambodia	181	70	11,340	Phnom Penh	300
Cameroon	475	184	15,029	Yaoundé	650
Canada	9,976	3,852	30,675	Ottawa	19,290
Canary Is. (Spain)	7.3	2.8	1,494	Las Palmas/Santa Cruz	–
Cape Verde Is.	4	1.6	399	Praia	1,010
Cayman Is. (UK)	0.26	0.10	35	George Town	20,000
Central African Republic	623	241	3,376	Bangui	320
Chad	1,284	496	7,360	Ndjaména	240
Chatham Is. (NZ)	0.96	0.37	0.05	Waitangi	–
Chile	757	292	14,788	Santiago	5,020
China	9,597	3,705	1,236,915	Beijing	860
Christmas Is. (Australia)	0.14	0.05	2	The Settlement	–
Cocos (Keeling) Is. (Australia)	0.01	0.005	1	West Island	–
Colombia	1,139	440	38,581	Bogotá	2,280
Comoros	2.2	0.86	545	Moroni	450
Congo	342	132	2,658	Brazzaville	660
Congo (= Zaïre)	2,345	905	49,001	Kinshasa	110
Cook Is. (NZ)	0.24	0.09	20	Avarua	900
Costa Rica	51.1	19.7	3,605	San José	2,640
Croatia	56.5	21.8	4,672	Zagreb	4,610
Cuba	111	43	11,051	Havana	1,300
Cyprus	9.3	3.6	749	Nicosia	13,420
Czech Republic	78.9	30.4	10,286	Prague	5,200
Denmark	43.1	16.6	5,334	Copenhagen	32,500
Djibouti	23.2	9	650	Djibouti	850
Dominica	0.75	0.29	78	Roseau	3,090
Dominican Republic	48.7	18.8	7,999	Santo Domingo	1,670
Ecuador	284	109	12,337	Quito	1,590
Egypt	1,001	387	66,050	Cairo	1,180
El Salvador	21	8.1	5,752	San Salvador	1,810
Equatorial Guinea	28.1	10.8	454	Malabo	530
Eritrea	94	36	3,842	Asmara	570
Estonia	44.7	17.3	1,421	Tallinn	3,330
Ethiopia	1,128	436	58,390	Addis Ababa	110
Falkland Is. (UK)	12.2	4.7	2	Stanley	–
Faroe Is. (Denmark)	1.4	0.54	41	Tórshavn	23,660
Fiji	18.3	7.1	802	Suva	2,470
Finland	338	131	5,149	Helsinki	24,080
France	552	213	58,805	Paris	26,050
French Guiana (France)	90	34.7	162	Cayenne	10,580
French Polynesia (France)	4	1.5	237	Papeete	7,500
Gabon	268	103	1,208	Libreville	4,230
Gambia, The	11.3	4.4	1,292	Banjul	320
Georgia	69.7	26.9	5,109	Tbilisi	840
Germany	357	138	82,079	Berlin/Bonn	28,260
Ghana	239	92	18,497	Accra	370
Gibraltar (UK)	0.007	0.003	29	Gibraltar Town	5,000
Greece	132	51	10,662	Athens	12,010
Greenland (Denmark)	2,176	840	59	Nuuk (Godthåb)	15,500
Grenada	0.34	0.13	96	St George's	2,880
Guadeloupe (France)	1.7	0.66	416	Basse-Terre	9,200
Guam (US)	0.55	0.21	149	Agana	6,000
Guatemala	109	42	12,008	Guatemala City	1,500
Guinea	246	95	7,477	Conakry	570
Guinea-Bissau	36.1	13.9	1,206	Bissau	240
Guyana	215	83	820	Georgetown	690
Haiti	27.8	10.7	6,781	Port-au-Prince	330
Honduras	112	43	5,862	Tegucigalpa	700
Hong Kong (China)	1.1	0.40	6,707	–	22,990
Hungary	93	35.9	10,208	Budapest	4,430
Iceland	103	40	271	Reykjavik	26,580
India	3,288	1,269	984,000	New Delhi	390
Indonesia	1,905	735	212,942	Jakarta	1,110
Iran	1,648	636	64,411	Tehran	4,700
Iraq	438	169	21,722	Baghdad	2,000
Ireland	70.3	27.1	3,619	Dublin	18,280
Israel	27	10.3	5,644	Jerusalem	15,810
Italy	301	116	56,783	Rome	20,120
Ivory Coast (Côte d'Ivoire)	322	125	15,446	Yamoussoukro	690
Jamaica	11	4.2	2,635	Kingston	1,560
Jan Mayen Is. (Norway)	0.38	0.15	1	–	–
Japan	378	146	125,932	Tokyo	37,850
Johnston Is. (US)	0.002	0.0009	1	–	–
Jordan	89.2	34.4	4,435	Amman	1,570
Kazakstan	2,717	1,049	16,847	Astana	1,340
Kenya	580	224	28,337	Nairobi	330
Kerguelen Is. (France)	7.2	2.8	0.7	–	–
Kermadec Is. (NZ)	0.03	0.01	0.1	–	–
Kiribati	0.72	0.28	85	Tarawa	920
Korea, North	121	47	21,234	Pyŏngyang	1,000
Korea, South	99	38.2	46,417	Seoul	10,550
Kuwait	17.8	6.9	1,913	Kuwait City	17,390
Kyrgyzstan	198.5	76.6	4,522	Bishkek	440
Laos	237	91	5,261	Vientiane	400
Latvia	65	25	2,385	Riga	2,430
Lebanon	10.4	4	3,506	Beirut	3,350
Lesotho	30.4	11.7	2,090	Maseru	670
Liberia	111	43	2,772	Monrovia	770
Libya	1,760	679	4,875	Tripoli	6,510
Liechtenstein	0.16	0.06	32	Vaduz	33,000
Lithuania	65.2	25.2	3,600	Vilnius	2,230
Luxembourg	2.6	1	425	Luxembourg	45,360
Macau (China)	0.02	0.006	429	Macau	7,500
Macedonia	25.7	9.9	2,009	Skopje	1,090
Madagascar	587	227	14,463	Antananarivo	250
Madeira (Portugal)	0.81	0.31	253	Funchal	–
Malawi	118	46	9,840	Lilongwe	220
Malaysia	330	127	20,993	Kuala Lumpur	4,680
Maldives	0.30	0.12	290	Malé	1,080
Mali	1,240	479	10,109	Bamako	260
Malta	0.32	0.12	379	Valletta	12,000
Marshall Is.	0.18	0.07	63	Dalap-Uliga-Darrit	1,890
Martinique (France)	1.1	0.42	407	Fort-de-France	10,000
Mauritania	1,030	412	2,511	Nouakchott	450
Mauritius	2.0	0.72	1,168	Port Louis	3,800
Mayotte (France)	0.37	0.14	141	Mamoundzou	1,430
Mexico	1,958	756	98,553	Mexico City	3,680
Micronesia, Fed. States of	0.70	0.27	127	Palikir	2,070
Midway Is. (US)	0.005	0.002	2	–	–
Moldova	33.7	13	4,458	Chişinău	540
Monaco	0.002	0.0001	32	Monaco	25,000
Mongolia	1,567	605	2,579	Ulan Bator	390
Montserrat (UK)	0.10	0.04	12	Plymouth	4,500
Morocco	447	172	29,114	Rabat	1,250
Mozambique	802	309	18,641	Maputo	90
Namibia	825	318	1,622	Windhoek	2,220
Nauru	0.02	0.008	12	Yaren District	10,000
Nepal	141	54	23,698	Katmandu	210
Netherlands	41.5	16	15,731	Amsterdam/The Hague	25,820
Netherlands Antilles (Neths)	0.99	0.38	210	Willemstad	10,400
New Caledonia (France)	18.6	7.2	192	Nouméa	8,000
New Zealand	269	104	3,625	Wellington	16,480
Nicaragua	130	50	4,583	Managua	410
Niger	1,267	489	9,672	Niamey	200
Nigeria	924	357	110,532	Abuja	260
Niue (NZ)	0.26	0.10	2	Alofi	–
Norfolk Is. (Australia)	0.03	0.01	2	Kingston	–
Northern Mariana Is. (US)	0.48	0.18	50	Saipan	11,500
Norway	324	125	4,420	Oslo	36,090
Oman	212	82	2,364	Muscat	4,950
Pakistan	796	307	135,135	Islamabad	490
Palau	0.46	0.18	18	Koror	5,000
Panama	77.1	29.8	2,736	Panama City	3,080
Papua New Guinea	463	179	4,600	Port Moresby	940
Paraguay	407	157	5,291	Asunción	2,010
Peru	1,285	496	26,111	Lima	2,460
Philippines	300	116	77,736	Manila	1,220
Pitcairn Is. (UK)	0.03	0.01	0.05	Adamstown	–
Poland	313	121	38,607	Warsaw	3,590
Portugal	92.4	35.7	9,928	Lisbon	10,450
Puerto Rico (US)	9	3.5	3,860	San Juan	7,800
Qatar	11	4.2	697	Doha	11,600
Queen Maud Land (Norway)	2,800	1,081	0	–	–
Réunion (France)	2.5	0.97	705	Saint-Denis	4,500
Romania	238	92	22,396	Bucharest	1,420
Russia	17,075	6,592	146,861	Moscow	2,740
Rwanda	26.3	10.2	7,956	Kigali	210
St Helena (UK)	0.12	0.05	7	Jamestown	–
St Kitts & Nevis	0.36	0.14	42	Basseterre	5,870
St Lucia	0.62	0.24	150	Castries	3,500
St Pierre & Miquelon (France)	0.24	0.09	7	Saint Pierre	–
St Vincent & Grenadines	0.39	0.15	120	Kingstown	2,370
San Marino	0.06	0.02	25	San Marino	20,000
São Tomé & Príncipe	0.96	0.37	150	São Tomé	330
Saudi Arabia	2,150	830	20,786	Riyadh	6,790
Senegal	197	76	9,723	Dakar	550
Seychelles	0.46	0.18	79	Victoria	6,850
Sierra Leone	71.7	27.7	5,080	Freetown	200
Singapore	0.62	0.24	3,490	Singapore	32,940
Slovak Republic	49	18.9	5,393	Bratislava	3,700
Slovenia	20.3	7.8	1,972	Ljubljana	9,680
Solomon Is.	28.9	11.2	441	Honiara	900
Somalia	638	246	6,842	Mogadishu	500
South Africa	1,220	471	42,835	C. Town/Pretoria/Bloem.	3,400
South Georgia (UK)	3.8	1.4	0.05	–	–
Spain	505	195	39,134	Madrid	14,510
Sri Lanka	65.6	25.3	18,934	Colombo	800
Sudan	2,506	967	33,551	Khartoum	800
Surinam	163	63	427	Paramaribo	1,000
Svalbard (Norway)	62.9	24.3	4	Longyearbyen	–
Swaziland	17.4	6.7	966	Mbabane	1,210
Sweden	450	174	8,887	Stockholm	26,220
Switzerland	41.3	15.9	7,260	Bern	44,220
Syria	185	71	16,673	Damascus	1,150
Taiwan	36	13.9	21,908	Taipei	12,400
Tajikistan	143.1	55.2	6,020	Dushanbe	330
Tanzania	945	365	30,609	Dodoma	210
Thailand	513	198	60,037	Bangkok	2,800
Togo	56.8	21.9	4,906	Lomé	330
Tokelau (NZ)	0.01	0.005	2	Nukunonu	–
Tonga	0.75	0.29	107	Nuku'alofa	1,790
Trinidad & Tobago	5.1	2	1,117	Port of Spain	4,230
Tristan da Cunha (UK)	0.11	0.04	0.33	Edinburgh	–
Tunisia	164	63	9,380	Tunis	2,090
Turkey	779	301	64,568	Ankara	3,130
Turkmenistan	488.1	188.5	4,298	Ashkhabad	630
Turks & Caicos Is. (UK)	0.43	0.17	16	Cockburn Town	5,000
Tuvalu	0.03	0.01	10	Fongafale	600
Uganda	236	91	22,167	Kampala	320
Ukraine	603.7	233.1	50,125	Kiev	1,040
United Arab Emirates	83.6	32.3	2,303	Abu Dhabi	17,360
United Kingdom	243.3	94	58,970	London	20,710
United States of America	9,373	3,619	270,290	Washington, DC	28,740
Uruguay	177	68	3,285	Montevideo	6,020
Uzbekistan	447.4	172.7	23,784	Tashkent	1,010
Vanuatu	12.2	4.7	185	Port-Vila	1,290
Vatican City	0.0004	0.0002	1	–	–
Venezuela	912	352	22,803	Caracas	3,450
Vietnam	332	127	76,236	Hanoi	320
Virgin Is. (UK)	0.15	0.06	13	Road Town	–
Virgin Is. (US)	0.34	0.13	118	Charlotte Amalie	12,000
Wake Is.	0.008	0.003	0.3	–	–
Wallis & Futuna Is. (France)	0.20	0.08	15	Mata-Utu	–
Western Sahara	266	103	280	El Aaiún	300
Western Samoa	2.8	1.1	224	Apia	1,170
Yemen	528	204	16,388	Sana	270
Yugoslavia	102.3	39.5	10,500	Belgrade	2,000
Zambia	753	291	9,461	Lusaka	380
Zimbabwe	391	151	11,044	Harare	750

World Statistics: Physical Dimensions

Each topic list is divided into continents and within a continent the items are listed in order of size. The bottom part of many of the lists is selective in order to give examples from as many different countries as possible. The order of the continents is the same as in the atlas, beginning with Europe and ending with South America. The figures are rounded as appropriate.

World, Continents, Oceans

	km²	miles²	%
The World	509,450,000	196,672,000	–
Land	149,450,000	57,688,000	29.3
Water	360,000,000	138,984,000	70.7
Asia	44,500,000	17,177,000	29.8
Africa	30,302,000	11,697,000	20.3
North America	24,241,000	9,357,000	16.2
South America	17,793,000	6,868,000	11.9
Antarctica	14,100,000	5,443,000	9.4
Europe	9,957,000	3,843,000	6.7
Australia & Oceania	8,557,000	3,303,000	5.7
Pacific Ocean	179,679,000	69,356,000	49.9
Atlantic Ocean	92,373,000	35,657,000	25.7
Indian Ocean	73,917,000	28,532,000	20.5
Arctic Ocean	14,090,000	5,439,000	3.9

Ocean Depths

Atlantic Ocean	m	ft
Puerto Rico (Milwaukee) Deep	9,220	30,249
Cayman Trench	7,680	25,197
Gulf of Mexico	5,203	17,070
Mediterranean Sea	5,121	16,801
Black Sea	2,211	7,254
North Sea	660	2,165

Indian Ocean	m	ft
Java Trench	7,450	24,442
Red Sea	2,635	8,454

Pacific Ocean	m	ft
Mariana Trench	11,022	36,161
Tonga Trench	10,882	35,702
Japan Trench	10,554	34,626
Kuril Trench	10,542	34,587

Arctic Ocean	m	ft
Molloy Deep	5,608	18,399

Mountains

Europe		m	ft
Elbrus	Russia	5,642	18,510
Mont Blanc	France/Italy	4,807	15,771
Monte Rosa	Italy/Switzerland	4,634	15,203
Dom	Switzerland	4,545	14,911
Liskamm	Switzerland	4,527	14,852
Weisshorn	Switzerland	4,505	14,780
Taschorn	Switzerland	4,490	14,730
Matterhorn/Cervino	Italy/Switzerland	4,478	14,691
Mont Maudit	France/Italy	4,465	14,649
Dent Blanche	Switzerland	4,356	14,291
Nadelhorn	Switzerland	4,327	14,196
Grandes Jorasses	France/Italy	4,208	13,806
Jungfrau	Switzerland	4,158	13,642
Grossglockner	Austria	3,797	12,457
Mulhacén	Spain	3,478	11,411
Zugspitze	Germany	2,962	9,718
Olympus	Greece	2,917	9,570
Triglav	Slovenia	2,863	9,393
Gerlachovka	Slovak Republic	2,655	8,711
Galdhöpiggen	Norway	2,468	8,100
Kebnekaise	Sweden	2,117	6,946
Ben Nevis	UK	1,343	4,406

Asia		m	ft
Everest	China/Nepal	8,848	29,029
K2 (Godwin Austen)	China/Kashmir	8,611	28,251
Kanchenjunga	India/Nepal	8,598	28,208
Lhotse	China/Nepal	8,516	27,939
Makalu	China/Nepal	8,481	27,824
Cho Oyu	China/Nepal	8,201	26,906
Dhaulagiri	Nepal	8,172	26,811
Manaslu	Nepal	8,156	26,758
Nanga Parbat	Kashmir	8,126	26,660
Annapurna	Nepal	8,078	26,502
Gasherbrum	China/Kashmir	8,068	26,469
Broad Peak	China/Kashmir	8,051	26,414
Xixabangma	China	8,012	26,286
Kangbachen	India/Nepal	7,902	25,925
Trivor	Pakistan	7,720	25,328
Pik Kommunizma	Tajikistan	7,495	24,590
Demavend	Iran	5,604	18,386
Ararat	Turkey	5,165	16,945
Gunong Kinabalu	Malaysia (Borneo)	4,101	13,455
Fuji-San	Japan	3,776	12,388

Africa		m	ft
Kilimanjaro	Tanzania	5,895	19,340
Mt Kenya	Kenya	5,199	17,057
Ruwenzori (Margherita)	Ug./Congo (Z.)	5,109	16,762
Ras Dashan	Ethiopia	4,620	15,157
Meru	Tanzania	4,565	14,977
Karisimbi	Rwanda/Congo (Zaïre)	4,507	14,787
Mt Elgon	Kenya/Uganda	4,321	14,176
Batu	Ethiopia	4,307	14,130
Toubkal	Morocco	4,165	13,665
Mt Cameroon	Cameroon	4,070	13,353

Oceania		m	ft
Puncak Jaya	Indonesia	5,029	16,499
Puncak Trikora	Indonesia	4,750	15,584

		m	ft
Puncak Mandala	Indonesia	4,702	15,427
Mt Wilhelm	Papua New Guinea	4,508	14,790
Mauna Kea	USA (Hawaii)	4,205	13,796
Mauna Loa	USA (Hawaii)	4,170	13,681
Mt Cook (Aoraki)	New Zealand	3,753	12,313
Mt Kosciuszko	Australia	2,237	7,339

North America		m	ft
Mt McKinley (Denali)	USA (Alaska)	6,194	20,321
Mt Logan	Canada	5,959	19,551
Citlaltepetl	Mexico	5,700	18,701
Mt St Elias	USA/Canada	5,489	18,008
Popocatepetl	Mexico	5,452	17,887
Mt Foraker	USA (Alaska)	5,304	17,401
Ixtaccihuatl	Mexico	5,286	17,342
Lucania	Canada	5,227	17,149
Mt Steele	Canada	5,073	16,644
Mt Bona	USA (Alaska)	5,005	16,420
Mt Whitney	USA	4,418	14,495
Tajumulco	Guatemala	4,220	13,845
Chirripó Grande	Costa Rica	3,837	12,589
Pico Duarte	Dominican Rep.	3,175	10,417

South America		m	ft
Aconcagua	Argentina	6,960	22,834
Bonete	Argentina	6,872	22,546
Ojos del Salado	Argentina/Chile	6,863	22,516
Pissis	Argentina	6,779	22,241
Mercedario	Argentina/Chile	6,770	22,211
Huascaran	Peru	6,768	22,204
Llullaillaco	Argentina/Chile	6,723	22,057
Nudo de Cachi	Argentina	6,720	22,047
Yerupaja	Peru	6,632	21,758
Sajama	Bolivia	6,542	21,463
Chimborazo	Ecuador	6,267	20,561
Pico Colon	Colombia	5,800	19,029
Pico Bolivar	Venezuela	5,007	16,427

Antarctica		m	ft
Vinson Massif		4,897	16,066
Mt Kirkpatrick		4,528	14,855

Rivers

Europe		km	miles
Volga	Caspian Sea	3,700	2,300
Danube	Black Sea	2,850	1,770
Ural	Caspian Sea	2,535	1,575
Dnepr (Dnipro)	Black Sea	2,285	1,420
Kama	Volga	2,030	1,260
Don	Black Sea	1,990	1,240
Petchora	Arctic Ocean	1,790	1,110
Oka	Volga	1,480	920
Dnister (Dniester)	Black Sea	1,400	870
Vyatka	Kama	1,370	850
Rhine	North Sea	1,320	820
N. Dvina	Arctic Ocean	1,290	800
Elbe	North Sea	1,145	710

Asia		km	miles
Yangtze	Pacific Ocean	6,380	3,960
Yenisey–Angara	Arctic Ocean	5,550	3,445
Huang He	Pacific Ocean	5,464	3,395
Ob–Irtysh	Arctic Ocean	5,410	3,360
Mekong	Pacific Ocean	4,500	2,795
Amur	Pacific Ocean	4,400	2,730
Lena	Arctic Ocean	4,400	2,730
Irtysh	Ob	4,250	2,640
Yenisey	Arctic Ocean	4,090	2,540
Ob	Arctic Ocean	3,680	2,285
Indus	Indian Ocean	3,100	1,925
Brahmaputra	Indian Ocean	2,900	1,800
Syrdarya	Aral Sea	2,860	1,775
Salween	Indian Ocean	2,800	1,740
Euphrates	Indian Ocean	2,700	1,675
Amudarya	Aral Sea	2,540	1,575

Africa		km	miles
Nile	Mediterranean	6,670	4,140
Congo	Atlantic Ocean	4,670	2,900
Niger	Atlantic Ocean	4,180	2,595
Zambezi	Indian Ocean	3,540	2,200
Oubangi/Uele	Congo (Zaïre)	2,250	1,400
Kasai	Congo (Zaïre)	1,950	1,210
Shaballe	Indian Ocean	1,930	1,200
Orange	Atlantic Ocean	1,860	1,155
Cubango	Okavango Swamps	1,800	1,120
Limpopo	Indian Ocean	1,600	995
Senegal	Atlantic Ocean	1,600	995

Australia		km	miles
Murray–Darling	Indian Ocean	3,750	2,330
Darling	Murray	3,070	1,905
Murray	Indian Ocean	2,575	1,600
Murrumbidgee	Murray	1,690	1,050

North America		km	miles
Mississippi–Missouri	Gulf of Mexico	6,020	3,740
Mackenzie	Arctic Ocean	4,240	2,630
Mississippi	Gulf of Mexico	3,780	2,350
Missouri	Mississippi	3,780	2,350
Yukon	Pacific Ocean	3,185	1,980
Rio Grande	Gulf of Mexico	3,030	1,880
Arkansas	Mississippi	2,340	1,450
Colorado	Pacific Ocean	2,330	1,445

		m	ft
Red	Mississippi	2,040	1,270
Columbia	Pacific Ocean	1,950	1,210
Saskatchewan	Lake Winnipeg	1,940	1,205

South America		km	miles
Amazon	Atlantic Ocean	6,450	4,010
Paraná–Plate	Atlantic Ocean	4,500	2,800
Purus	Amazon	3,350	2,080
Madeira	Amazon	3,200	1,990
São Francisco	Atlantic Ocean	2,900	1,800
Paraná	Plate	2,800	1,740
Tocantins	Atlantic Ocean	2,750	1,710
Paraguay	Paraná	2,550	1,580
Orinoco	Atlantic Ocean	2,500	1,550
Pilcomayo	Paraná	2,500	1,550
Araguaia	Tocantins	2,250	1,400

Lakes

Europe		km²	miles²
Lake Ladoga	Russia	17,700	6,800
Lake Onega	Russia	9,700	3,700
Saimaa system	Finland	8,000	3,100
Vänern	Sweden	5,500	2,100

Asia		km²	miles²
Caspian Sea	Asia	371,800	143,550
Lake Baykal	Russia	30,500	11,780
Aral Sea	Kazakstan/Uzbekistan	28,687	11,086
Tonlé Sap	Cambodia	20,000	7,700
Lake Balqash	Kazakstan	18,500	7,100

Africa		km²	miles²
Lake Victoria	East Africa	68,000	26,000
Lake Tanganyika	Central Africa	33,000	13,000
Lake Malawi/Nyasa	East Africa	29,600	11,430
Lake Chad	Central Africa	25,000	9,700
Lake Turkana	Ethiopia/Kenya	8,500	3,300
Lake Volta	Ghana	8,500	3,300

Australia		km²	miles²
Lake Eyre	Australia	8,900	3,400
Lake Torrens	Australia	5,800	2,200
Lake Gairdner	Australia	4,800	1,900

North America		km²	miles²
Lake Superior	Canada/USA	82,350	31,800
Lake Huron	Canada/USA	59,600	23,010
Lake Michigan	USA	58,000	22,400
Great Bear Lake	Canada	31,800	12,280
Great Slave Lake	Canada	28,500	11,000
Lake Erie	Canada/USA	25,700	9,900
Lake Winnipeg	Canada	24,400	9,400
Lake Ontario	Canada/USA	19,500	7,500
Lake Nicaragua	Nicaragua	8,200	3,200

South America		km²	miles²
Lake Titicaca	Bolivia/Peru	8,300	3,200
Lake Poopo	Peru	2,800	1,100

Islands

Europe		km²	miles²
Great Britain	UK	229,880	88,700
Iceland	Atlantic Ocean	103,000	39,800
Ireland	Ireland/UK	84,400	32,600
Novaya Zemlya (N.)	Russia	48,200	18,600
Sicily	Italy	25,500	9,800
Corsica	France	8,700	3,400

Asia		km²	miles²
Borneo	Southeast Asia	744,360	287,400
Sumatra	Indonesia	473,600	182,860
Honshu	Japan	230,500	88,980
Sulawesi (Celebes)	Indonesia	189,000	73,000
Java	Indonesia	126,700	48,900
Luzon	Philippines	104,700	40,400
Hokkaido	Japan	78,400	30,300

Africa		km²	miles²
Madagascar	Indian Ocean	587,040	226,660
Socotra	Indian Ocean	3,600	1,400
Réunion	Indian Ocean	2,500	965

Oceania		km²	miles²
New Guinea	Indonesia/Papua NG	821,030	317,000
New Zealand (S.)	Pacific Ocean	150,500	58,100
New Zealand (N.)	Pacific Ocean	114,700	44,300
Tasmania	Australia	67,800	26,200
Hawaii	Pacific Ocean	10,450	4,000

North America		km²	miles²
Greenland	Atlantic Ocean	2,175,600	839,800
Baffin Is.	Canada	508,000	196,100
Victoria Is.	Canada	212,200	81,900
Ellesmere Is.	Canada	212,000	81,800
Cuba	Caribbean Sea	110,860	42,800
Hispaniola	Dominican Rep./Haiti	76,200	29,400
Jamaica	Caribbean Sea	11,400	4,400
Puerto Rico	Atlantic Ocean	8,900	3,400

South America		km²	miles²
Tierra del Fuego	Argentina/Chile	47,000	18,100
Falkland Is. (E.)	Atlantic Ocean	6,800	2,600

User Guide

Organization of the atlas

Prepared in accordance with the highest standards in cartography to provide accurate and detailed representation of the earth, the atlas is made up of four separate sections and is organized with ease of use in mind.

The first section of the atlas consists of up-to-date geographical and demographical statistics for all the countries in the world, and this user guide.

The second section of the atlas, the 34-page United States Maps section, has blue page borders and offers comprehensive coverage of the United States and its outlying areas, with climate and agricultural maps, politically colored maps with some topographical detail, maps of major urban areas, and a 16-page index with latitude and longitude coordinates.

The third section of the atlas, the informative 32-page The World In Focus section, consists of thematic maps, graphs, tables, and charts on a wide range of geographical and demographical topics, followed by a subject index.

The fourth and final section of the atlas, the 96-page World Maps section, covers the earth continent by continent in the classic sequence adopted by cartographers since the 16th century. This section begins with Europe, then Asia, Africa, Australia and Oceania, North America, and South America. For each continent, there are maps at a variety of scales: first, physical relief maps and political maps of the whole continent, then large-scale maps of the most important or densely populated areas.

The governing principle is that by turning the pages of the World Maps section, the reader moves steadily from north to south through each continent, with each map overlapping its neighbors. Immediately following the maps in the World Maps section is the comprehensive index to the maps, which contains 35,000 entries of both place names and geographical features. The index provides the latitude and longitude coordinates as well as letters and numbers, so that locating any site can be accomplished with speed and accuracy.

Map presentation

All of the maps in the atlas are drawn with north at the top (except for two maps: the map of the Arctic Ocean and the map of Antarctica). The maps in the United States Maps section and the World Maps section all contain the following information in their borders: the map title; scale; the projection used; the degrees of latitude and longitude; and on the physical relief maps, a height and depth reference panel identifying the colors used for each layer of contouring. In addition to this information, the maps in the World Maps section also contain locator diagrams which show the area covered, the page numbers for adjacent maps, and the letters and numbers used in the index for locating place names and geographical features.

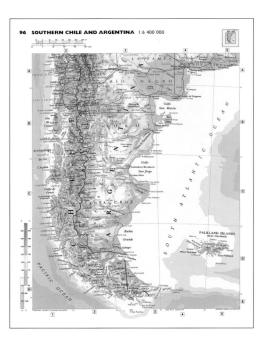

Map symbols

Each map contains a vast amount of detail which is conveyed clearly and accurately by the use of symbols. Points and circles of varying sizes locate and identify the relative importance of towns and cities; different styles of type are employed for administrative, geographical and regional place names. A variety of pictorial symbols denote landscape features such as glaciers, marshes and reefs, and man-made structures including roads, railroads, airports and canals. International borders are shown by red lines. Where neighboring countries are in dispute, the maps show the *de facto* boundary between nations, regardless of the legal or historical situation. The symbols are explained on the first page of each of the map sections.

Map scales

The scale of each map is given in the numerical form known as the representative fraction. The first figure is always one, signifying one unit of distance on the map; the second figure, usually in millions, is the number by which the map unit must be multiplied to give the equivalent distance on the earth's surface. Calculations can easily be made in centimeters and kilometers, by dividing the earth units figure by 100 000 (i.e. deleting the last five 0s). Thus 1:1 000 000 means 1 cm = 10 km. The calculation for inches

LARGE SCALE

1:1 000 000	1 cm = 10 km	1 inch = 16 miles
1:2 500 000	1 cm = 25 km	1 inch = 39.5 miles
1:5 000 000	1 cm = 50 km	1 inch = 79 miles
1:6 000 000	1 cm = 60 km	1 inch = 95 miles
1:8 000 000	1 cm = 80 km	1 inch = 126 miles
1:10 000 000	1 cm = 100 km	1 inch = 158 miles
1:15 000 000	1 cm = 150 km	1 inch = 237 miles
1:20 000 000	1 cm = 200 km	1 inch = 316 miles
1:50 000 000	1 cm = 500 km	1 inch = 790 miles

SMALL SCALE

and miles is more laborious, but 1 000 000 divided by 63 360 (the number of inches in a mile) shows that 1:1 000 000 means about 1 inch = 16 miles.

Measuring distances

Although each map is accompanied by a scale bar, distances cannot always be measured with confidence because of the distortions involved in portraying the curved surface of the earth on a flat page. As a general rule, the larger the map scale (i.e. the lower the number of earth units in the representative fraction), the more accurate and reliable will be the distance measured. On small scale maps such as those of the world and of entire continents, measurement may only be accurate along the standard parallels, or central axes, and should not be attempted without considering the map projection.

Latitude and longitude

Accurate positioning of individual points on the earth's surface is made possible by reference to the geometrical system of latitude and longitude. Latitude parallels are drawn west–east around the earth and numbered by degrees north and south of the Equator, which is designated 0° of latitude. Longitude meridians are drawn north–south and numbered by degrees east and west of the Prime Meridian, 0° of longitude, which passes through Greenwich in England. By referring to these coordinates and their subdivisions of minutes ($^1/_{60}$th of a degree) and seconds ($^1/_{60}$th of a minute), any place on earth can be located to within a few hundred yards. Latitude and longitude are indicated by blue lines on the maps; they are straight or curved according to the projection employed. Reference to these lines is the easiest way of determining the relative positions of places on different maps, and for plotting compass directions.

Name forms

For ease of reference, both English and local name forms appear in the atlas. Oceans, seas and countries are shown in English throughout the atlas; country names may be abbreviated to their commonly accepted form. English conventional forms are also used for place names on the continental maps. However, local name forms are used on all large scale and regional maps, with the English form given in brackets only for important cities – the large-scale map of Russia and Central Asia thus shows Moskva (Moscow). For countries which do not use a Roman script, place names have been transcribed according to the systems adopted by the British and US Geographic Names Authorities. For China, the Pin Yin system has been used, with some more widely known forms appearing in brackets, as with Beijing (Peking). Both English and local names appear in the index.

UNITED STATES MAPS

SETTLEMENTS

◯ WASHINGTON D.C.   ◼ Tampa   ◉ Fresno   ◉ Waterloo   ◎ *Ventura*   ○ *Barstow*   ○ *Blythe*   ○ *Hope*

Settlement symbols and type styles vary according to the scale of each map and indicate the importance of towns on the map rather than specific population figures

ADMINISTRATION

———— International Boundaries

·········· Internal Boundaries

National Parks, Recreation Areas and Monuments

Country Names

CANADA

Administrative Area Names

MICHIGAN

COMMUNICATIONS

═══ Major Highways

⌒ Other Principal Roads

⨝ Passes

✈ ✛ ✧ Airports and Airfields

⌒ Principal Railroads

···· Railroads Under Construction

⌒ Other Railroads

⌐---⌐ Railroad Tunnels

⊣⊣⊣⊣ Principal Canals

PHYSICAL FEATURES

⌒ Perennial Streams

······ Intermittent Streams

◯ Perennial Lakes and Reservoirs

◌ Intermittent Lakes and Salt Flats

Swamps and Marshes

Permanent Ice and Glaciers

▲ 8848 Elevations in meters

▼ 8050 Sea Depths in meters

1134 Height of Lake Surface Above Sea Level in meters

1 meter is approx. 3.3 feet

CITY MAPS

In addition to, or instead of, the symbols explained above, the following symbols are used on the city maps between pages 22-31

Urban Areas

⌒ Limited Access Roads

Aqueducts

Woodland and Parks

⌒ Secondary Roads

···· Ferry Routes

State Boundaries

✕ Airports

⌒ Canals

County Boundaries

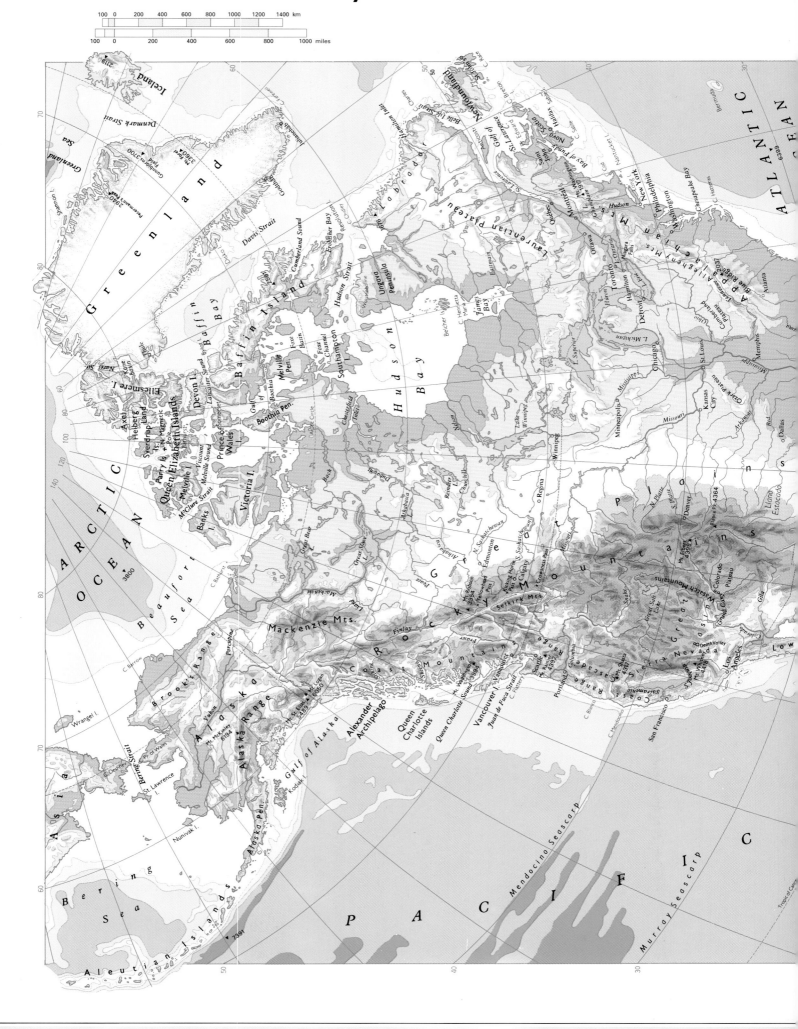

100 0 200 400 600 800 1000 1200 1400 km

100 0 200 400 600 800 1000 miles

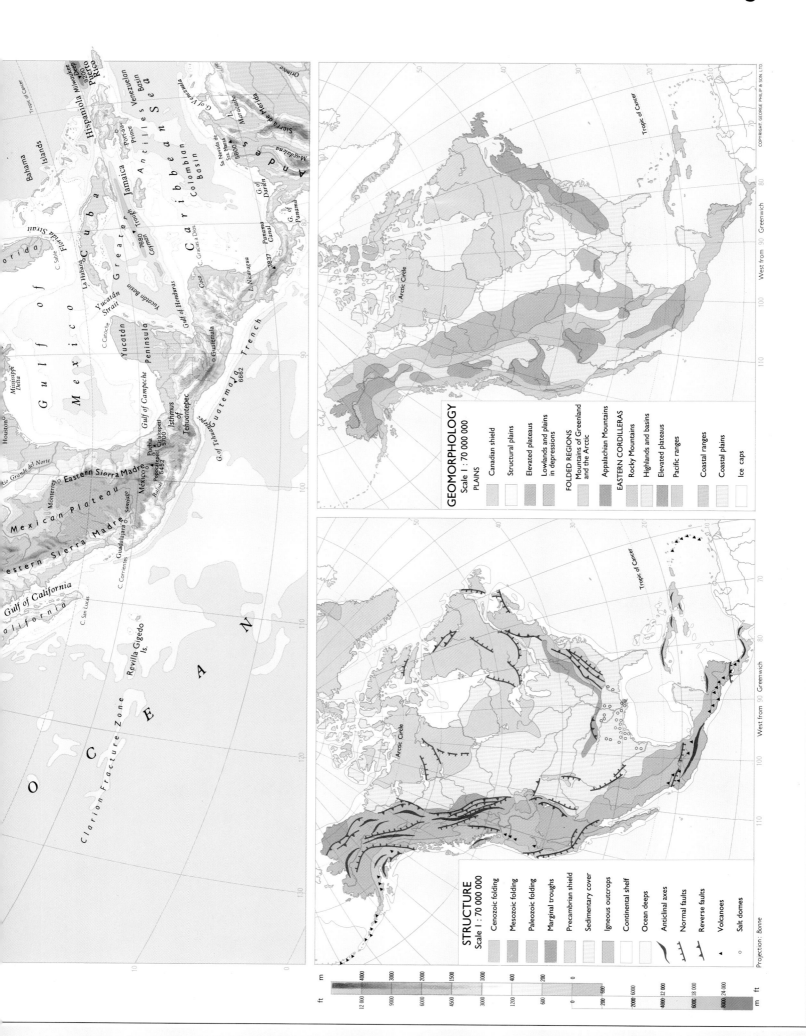

3

COPYRIGHT GEORGE PHILIP & SON LTD

Tropic of Cancer

Arctic Circle

West from 90 Greenwich

GEOMORPHOLOGY
Scale 1 : 70 000 000

PLAINS
- Canadian shield
- Structural plains
- Elevated plateaus
- Lowlands and plains in depressions

FOLDED REGIONS
- Mountains of Greenland and the Arctic
- Appalachian Mountains

EASTERN CORDILLERAS
- Rocky Mountains
- Highlands and basins
- Elevated plateaus
- Pacific ranges
- Coastal ranges
- Coastal plains
- Ice caps

STRUCTURE
Scale 1 : 70 000 000

- Cenozoic folding
- Mesozoic folding
- Paleozoic folding
- Marginal troughs
- Precambrian shield
- Sedimentary cover
- Igneous outcrops
- Continental shelf
- Ocean deeps
- Anticlinal axes
- Normal faults
- Reverse faults
- Volcanoes
- Salt domes

Projection: Bonne

Tropic of Cancer

Arctic Circle

West from 90 Greenwich

Bahama
Islands

Tropic of Cancer

Milwaukee
Deep
Puerto
Rico

Hispaniola

Port-au-Prince

Venezuelan
Basin

Anegada

Sierra de Merida

5800

Maracaibo

Antilles Sea

Greater Antilles

Jamaica

Colombian
Basin

Cuba

Florida Strait

La Habana

C. Sable

7680 Trough
Cayman
3837

C. Gracias à Dios

G. of Venezuela

G. of
Darién

G. of
Panamá

Panamá
Canal

Caribbean

Florida

Gulf of
Mexico

Mississippi
Delta

Houston

Yucatán
Strait

Yucatán basin

Yucatán
Peninsula

C. Catoche

Gulf of Honduras

Guatemala

L. Nicaragua

Coco

6662
Guatemala Trench

G. of Tehuantepec

Gulf of Campeche

Rio Grande del Norte

Eastern Sierra Madre

Monterrey

Mexican Plateau

Guadalajara

México

Puebla
Popocatépetl
5465

Citlaltepec

Isthmus
of
Tehuantepec

Western Sierra Madre

Gulf of California

C. Corrientes

C. San Lucas

California

Revilla Gigedo
Is.

Clarion Fracture Zone

PACIFIC

OCEAN

Ortoco

m | ft
4000 | 12 000
3000 | 9000
2000 | 6000
1500 | 4500
1000 | 3000
400 | 1200
200 | 600
0 | 0
200 | 600
2000 | 6000
4000 | 12 000
6000 | 18 000
8000 | 24 000
m | ft

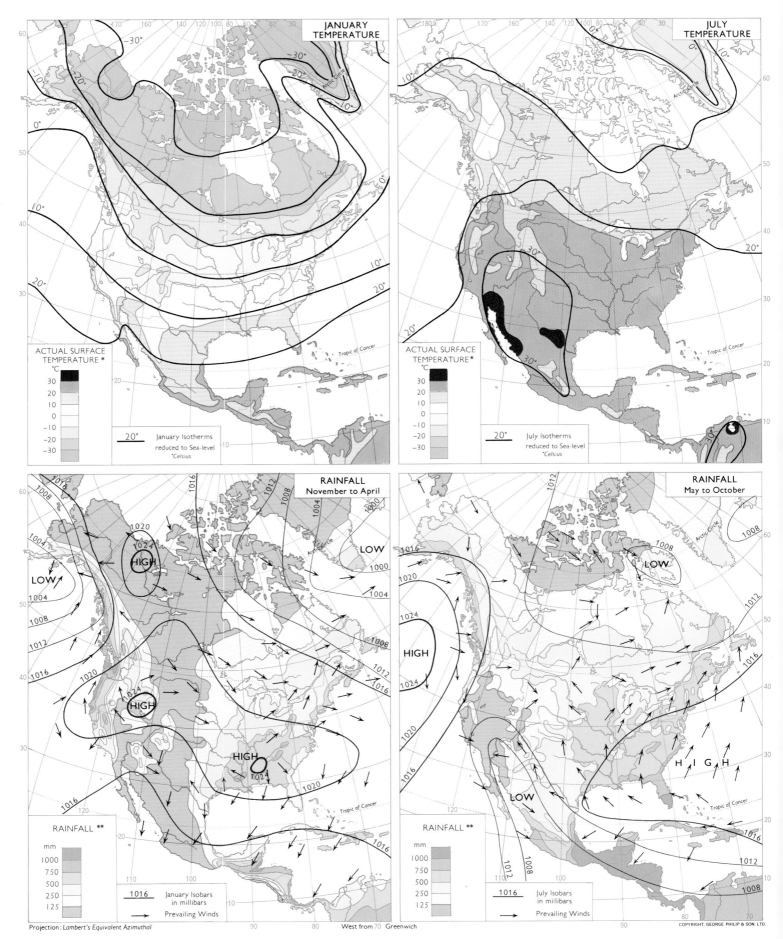

JANUARY TEMPERATURE

ACTUAL SURFACE TEMPERATURE *
°C
30
20
10
0
-10
-20
-30

20° January Isotherms reduced to Sea-level °Celsius

JULY TEMPERATURE

ACTUAL SURFACE TEMPERATURE *
°C
30
20
10
0
-10
-20
-30

20° July Isotherms reduced to Sea-level °Celsius

RAINFALL November to April

RAINFALL **
mm
1000
750
500
250
125

1016 January Isobars in millibars
→ Prevailing Winds

RAINFALL May to October

RAINFALL **
mm
1000
750
500
250
125

1016 July Isobars in millibars
→ Prevailing Winds

Projection: Lambert's Equivalent Azimuthal   West from 70 Greenwich   COPYRIGHT. GEORGE PHILIP & SON. LTD.

*To convert °C to °F, multiply by 1.8, then add 32   **1 in equals 25.4mm

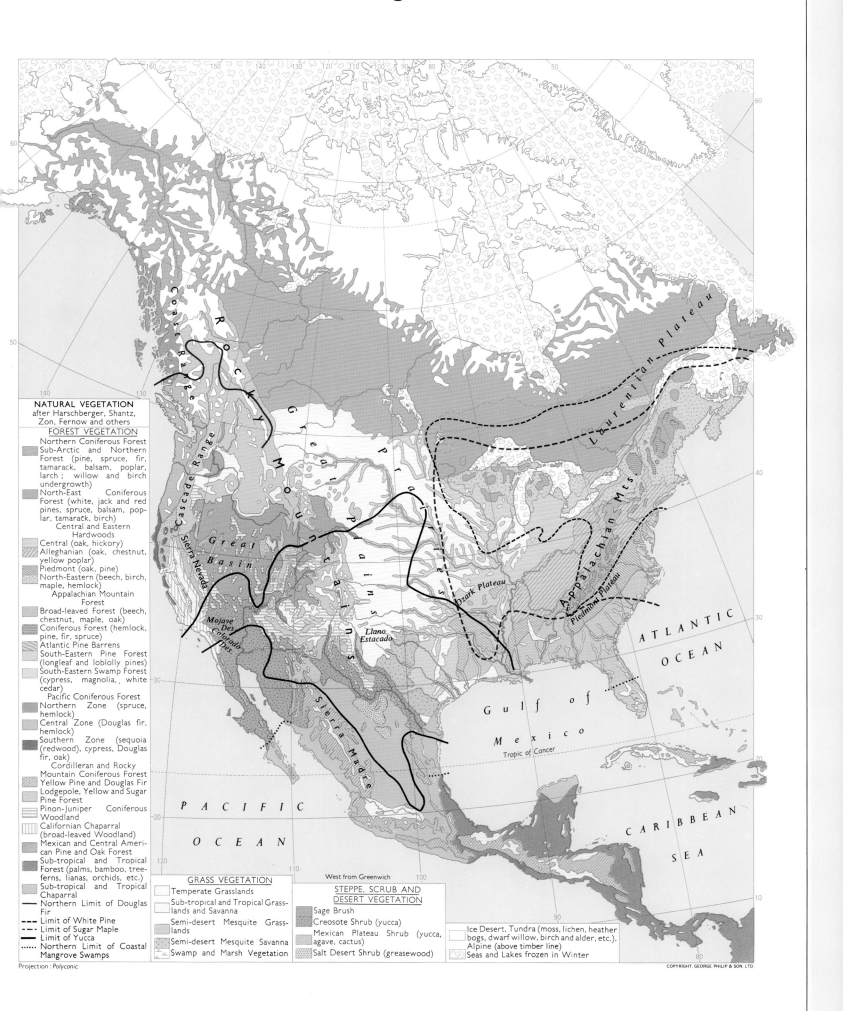

NATURAL VEGETATION
after Harschberger, Shantz, Zon, Fernow and others

FOREST VEGETATION

Northern Coniferous Forest
Sub-Arctic and Northern Forest (pine, spruce, fir, tamarack, balsam, poplar, larch ; willow and birch undergrowth)
North-East Coniferous Forest (white, jack and red pines, spruce, balsam, poplar, tamarack, birch)

Central and Eastern Hardwoods
Central (oak, hickory)
Alleghanian (oak, chestnut, yellow poplar)
Piedmont (oak, pine)
North-Eastern (beech, birch, maple, hemlock)

Appalachian Mountain Forest
Broad-leaved Forest (beech, chestnut, maple, oak)
Coniferous Forest (hemlock, pine, fir, spruce)
Atlantic Pine Barrens
South-Eastern Pine Forest (longleaf and loblolly pines)
South-Eastern Swamp Forest (cypress, magnolia, white cedar)

Pacific Coniferous Forest
Northern Zone (spruce, hemlock)
Central Zone (Douglas fir, hemlock)
Southern Zone (sequoia (redwood), cypress, Douglas fir, oak)

Cordilleran and Rocky Mountain Coniferous Forest
Yellow Pine and Douglas Fir
Lodgepole, Yellow and Sugar Pine Forest
Pinon-Juniper Coniferous Woodland
Californian Chaparral (broad-leaved Woodland)
Mexican and Central American Pine and Oak Forest
Sub-tropical and Tropical Forest (palms, bamboo, tree-ferns, lianas, orchids, etc.)
Sub-tropical and Tropical Chaparral

— Northern Limit of Douglas Fir
--- Limit of White Pine
— Limit of Sugar Maple
— Limit of Yucca
..... Northern Limit of Coastal Mangrove Swamps

GRASS VEGETATION
Temperate Grasslands
Sub-tropical and Tropical Grasslands and Savanna
Semi-desert Mesquite Grasslands
Semi-desert Mesquite Savanna
Swamp and Marsh Vegetation

STEPPE, SCRUB AND DESERT VEGETATION
Sage Brush
Creosote Shrub (yucca)
Mexican Plateau Shrub (yucca, agave, cactus)
Salt Desert Shrub (greasewood)

Ice Desert, Tundra (moss, lichen, heather bogs, dwarf willow, birch and alder, etc.).
Alpine (above timber line)
Seas and Lakes frozen in Winter

West from Greenwich

Projection: *Polyconic*

National Capital ⊛
State Capital ■ ● ● ● ●

Projection: Albers' Equal Area with two standard parallels

HAWAII 1:10 000 000

West from Greenwich

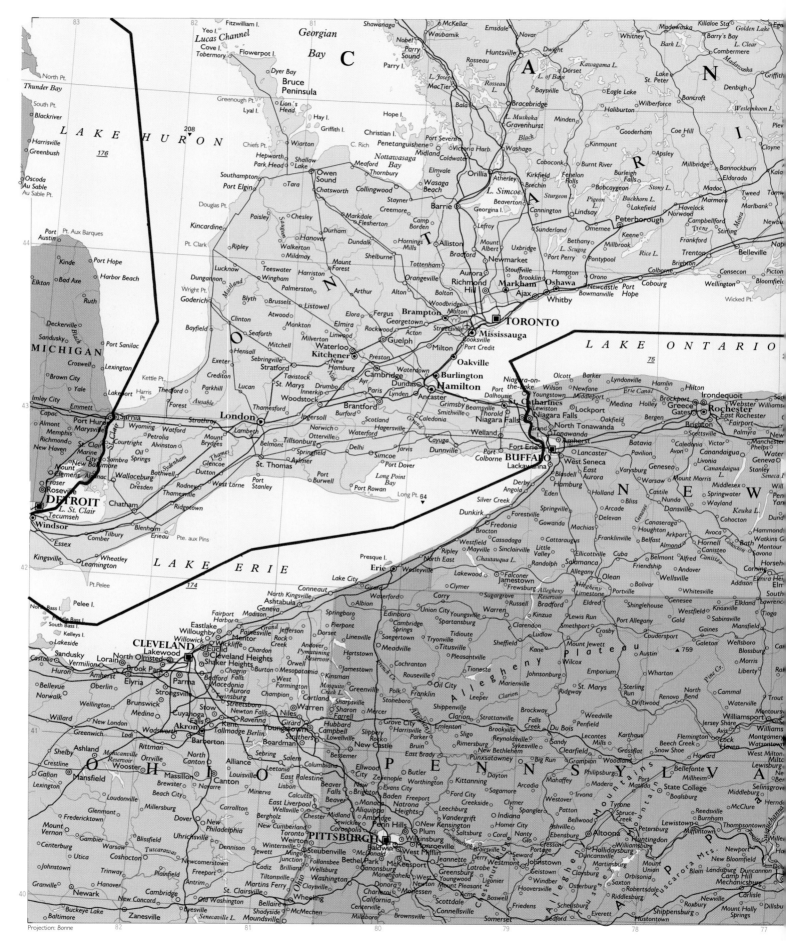

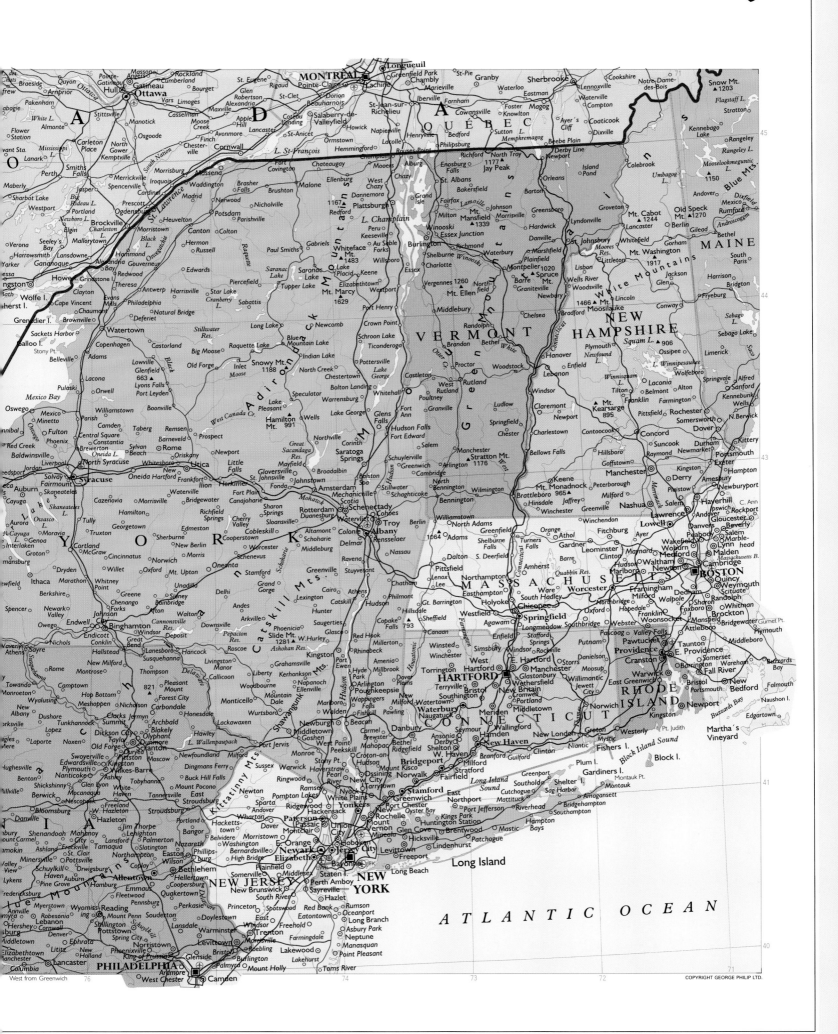

COPYRIGHT GEORGE PHILIP LTD.

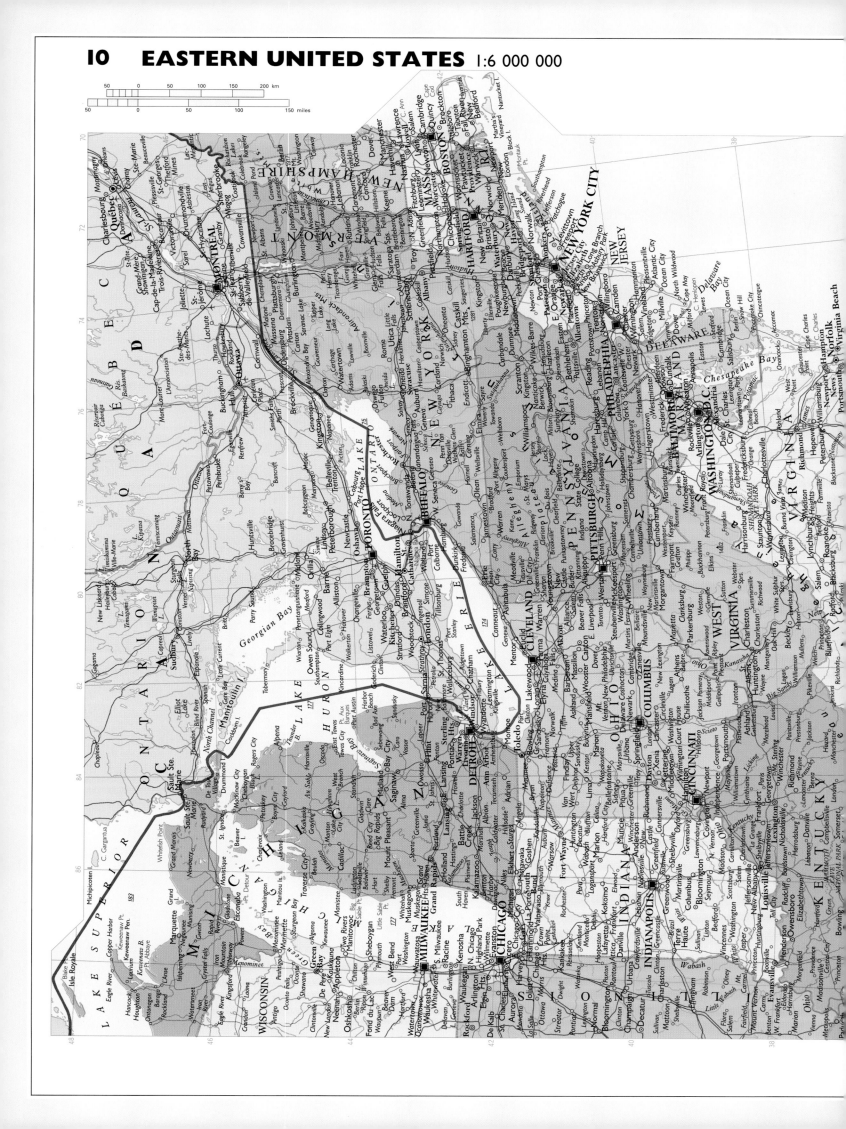

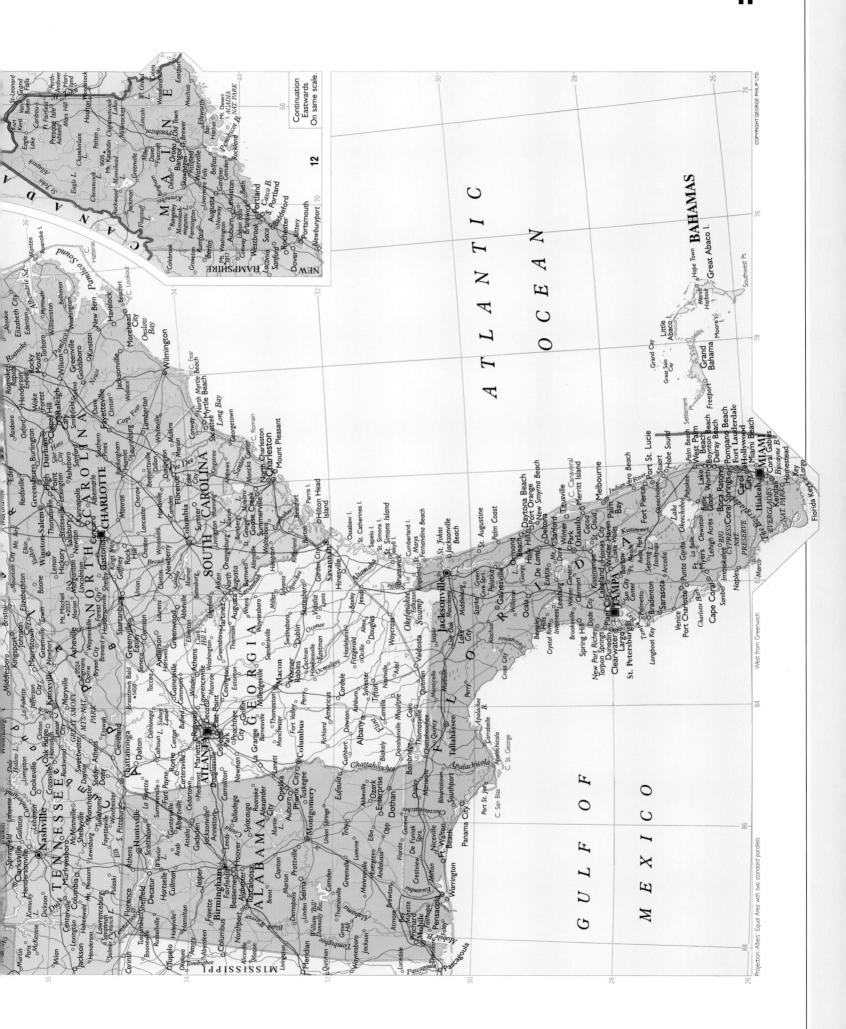

CANADA

MAINE

NEW HAMPSHIRE

Continuation
Eastwards
On same scale.

12

COPYRIGHT GEORGE PHILIP LTD.

TENNESSEE

NORTH CAROLINA

CHARLOTTE

SOUTH CAROLINA

GEORGIA

ALABAMA

MISSISSIPPI

ATLANTIC

OCEAN

FLORIDA

GULF OF

MEXICO

BAHAMAS

BAHAMA

Great Abaco I.

Grand Bahama

ATLANTA

Montgomery

Tallahassee

Jacksonville

TAMPA

MIAMI

Birmingham

Nashville

Chattanooga

Columbus

Macon

Savannah

Charleston

Wilmington

Raleigh

Columbia

Augusta

Orlando

EVERGLADES
NAT. PARK

Florida Keys

Projection: Albers' Equal Area with two standard parallels

West from Greenwich

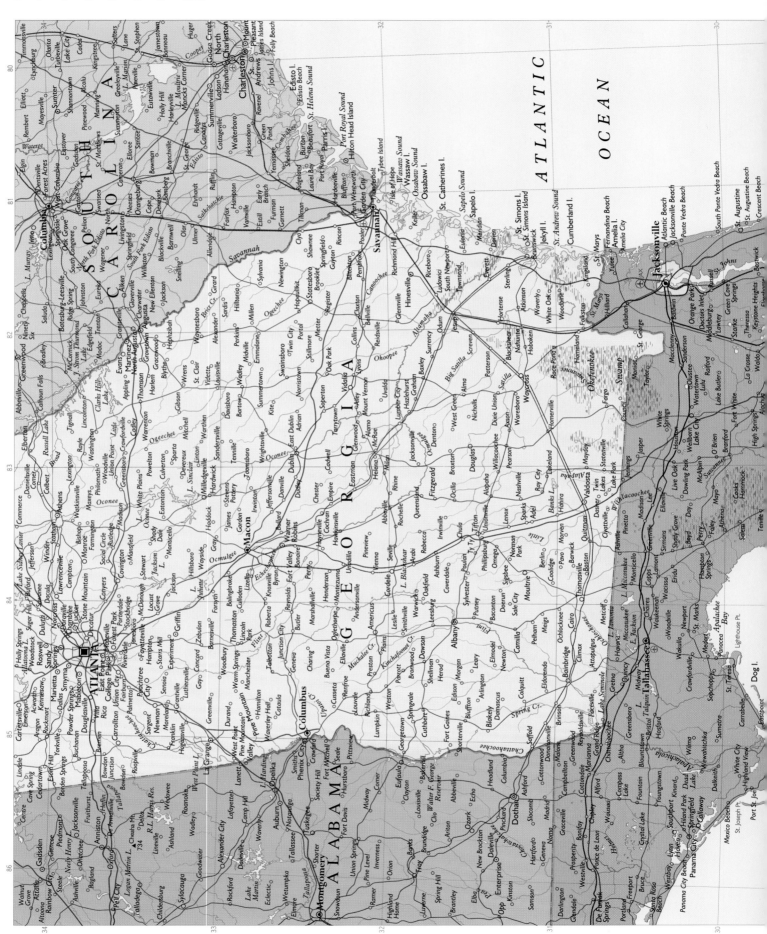

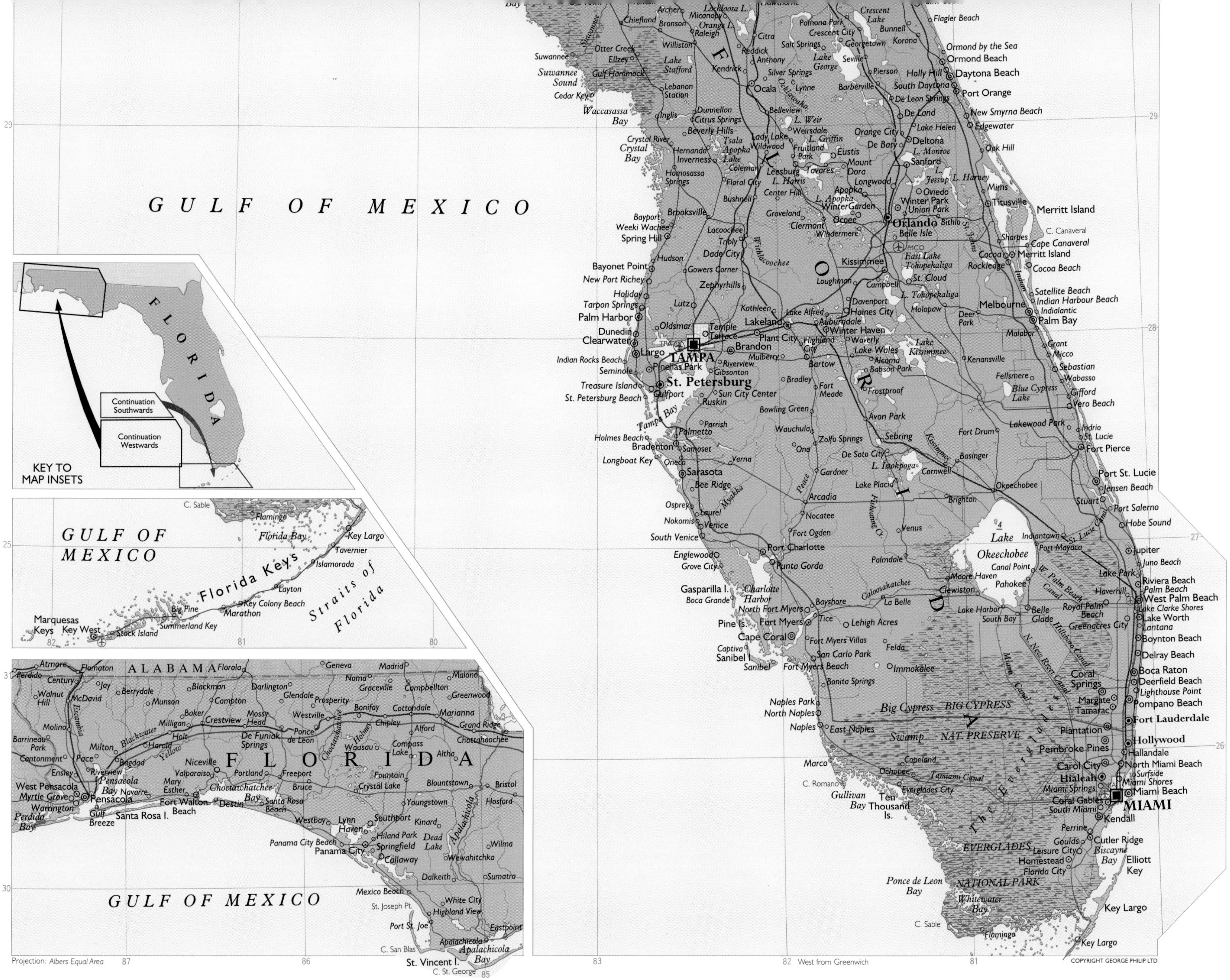

GULF OF MEXICO

F L O R I D A

Lake Okeechobee

BIG CYPRESS NAT. PRESERVE

EVERGLADES NATIONAL PARK

MIAMI

TAMPA

St. Petersburg

Orlando

West from Greenwich

Straits of Florida

Florida Keys

GULF OF MEXICO

A L A B A M A

F L O R I D A

GULF OF MEXICO

Apalachicola Bay

St. Vincent I.   C. St. George

KEY TO MAP INSETS

FLORIDA

Continuation Southwards

Continuation Westwards

Projection: Albers Equal Area

50 0 50 100 150 200 km
50 0 50 100 150 miles

CANADA

LAKE SUPERIOR

LAKE MICHIGAN

MICHIGAN

WISCONSIN

MINNESOTA

NORTH DAKOTA

SOUTH DAKOTA

NEBRASKA

KANSAS

IOWA

MISSOURI

ILLINOIS

COLORADO

WYOMING

MONTANA

MILWAUKEE · CHICAGO · MINNEAPOLIS · ST. PAUL · ST. LOUIS · KANSAS CITY · DENVER

Isle Royale Nat. Park · Voyageurs Nat. Park · Theodore Roosevelt Nat. Park · Badlands Nat. Park

Thunder Bay · Duluth · Superior · Fargo · Grand Forks · Bismarck · Rapid City · Sioux Falls · Sioux City · Omaha · Lincoln · Des Moines · Cedar Rapids · Davenport · Madison · Green Bay · Springfield · Colorado Springs · Pueblo · Boulder

Lake Superior · Lake Michigan · Lake of the Woods · Rainy Lake · Red Lake · Mille Lacs L. · Lake Oahe · Lake Francis Case · Missouri River · Mississippi River · Coteau des Prairies · Sand Hills · Smoky Hills · Black Hills · Mt. Rushmore · Harney Peak 2207 · Laramie Mountains · Pikes Peak 4301

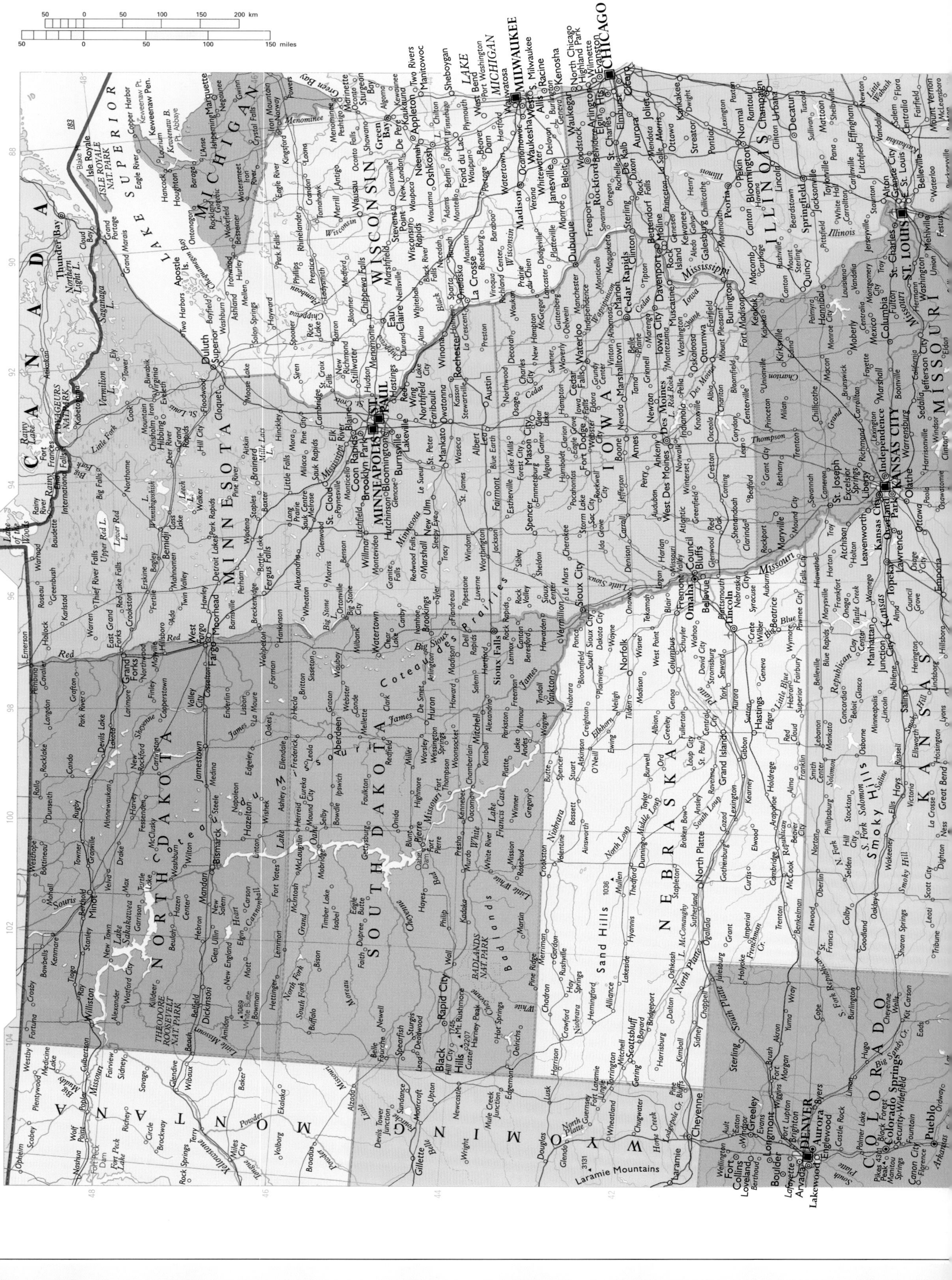

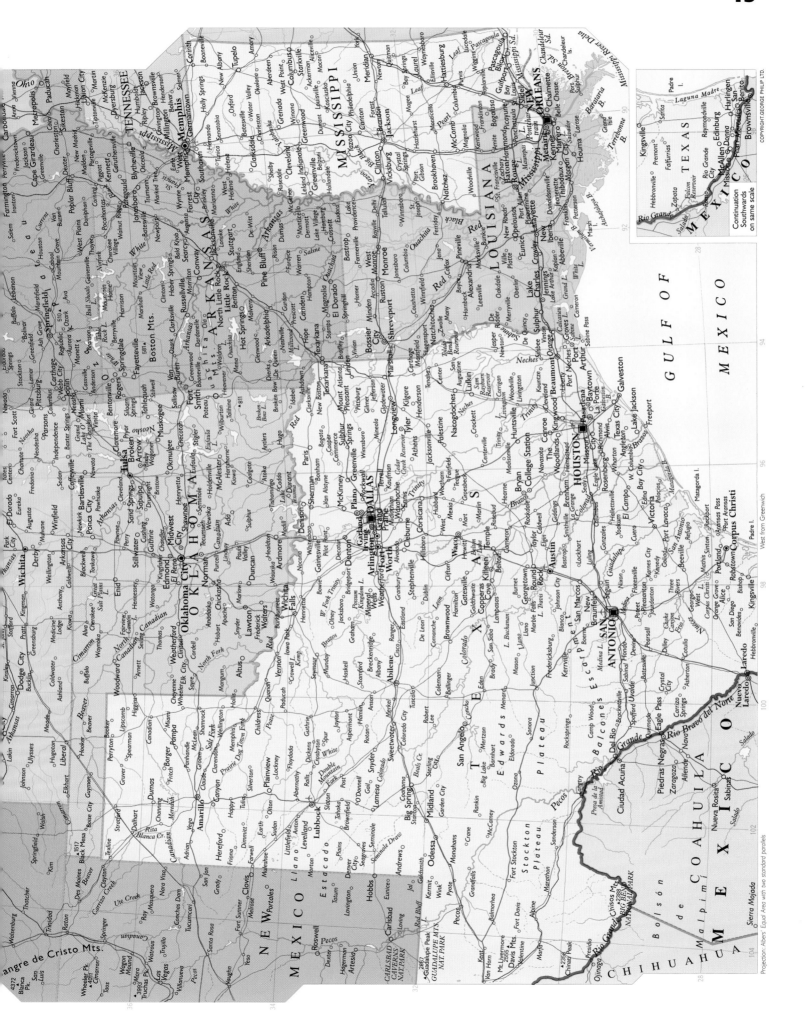

Projection: Albers' Equal Area with two standard parallels

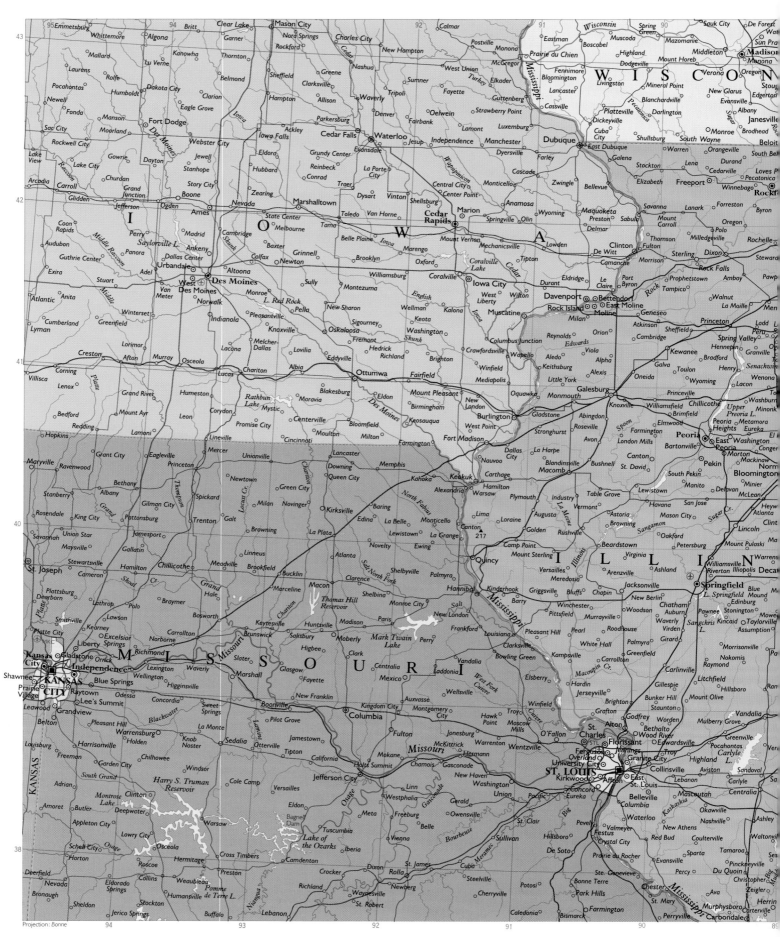

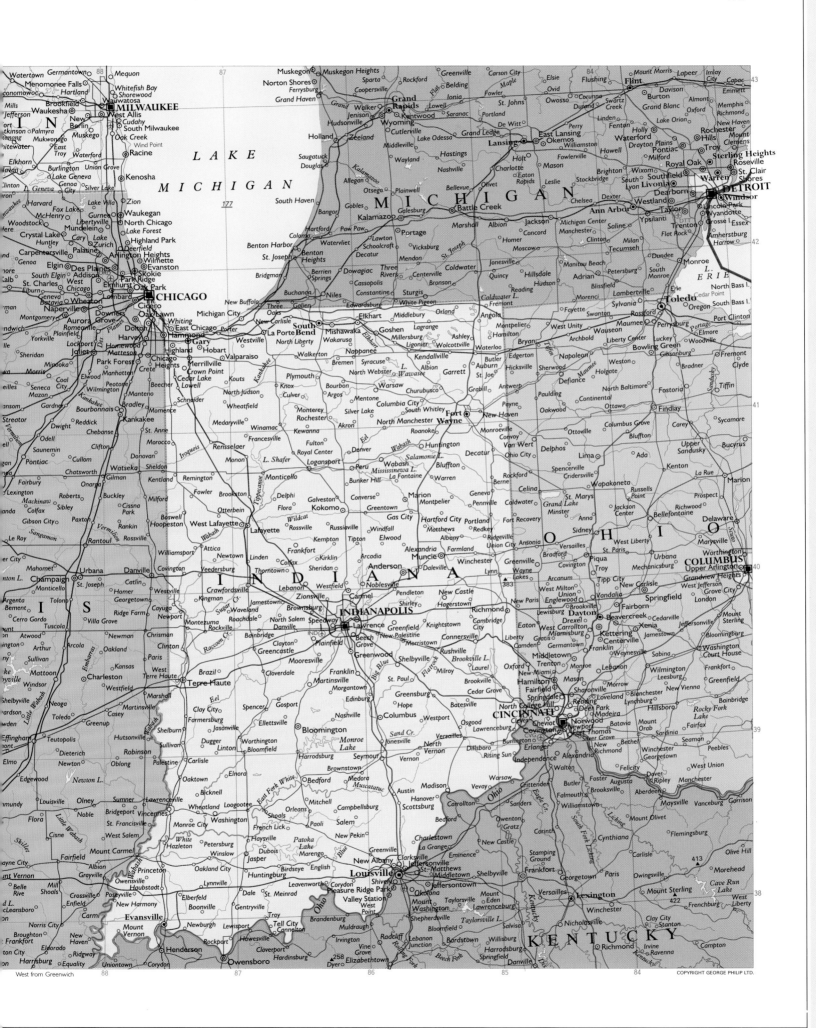

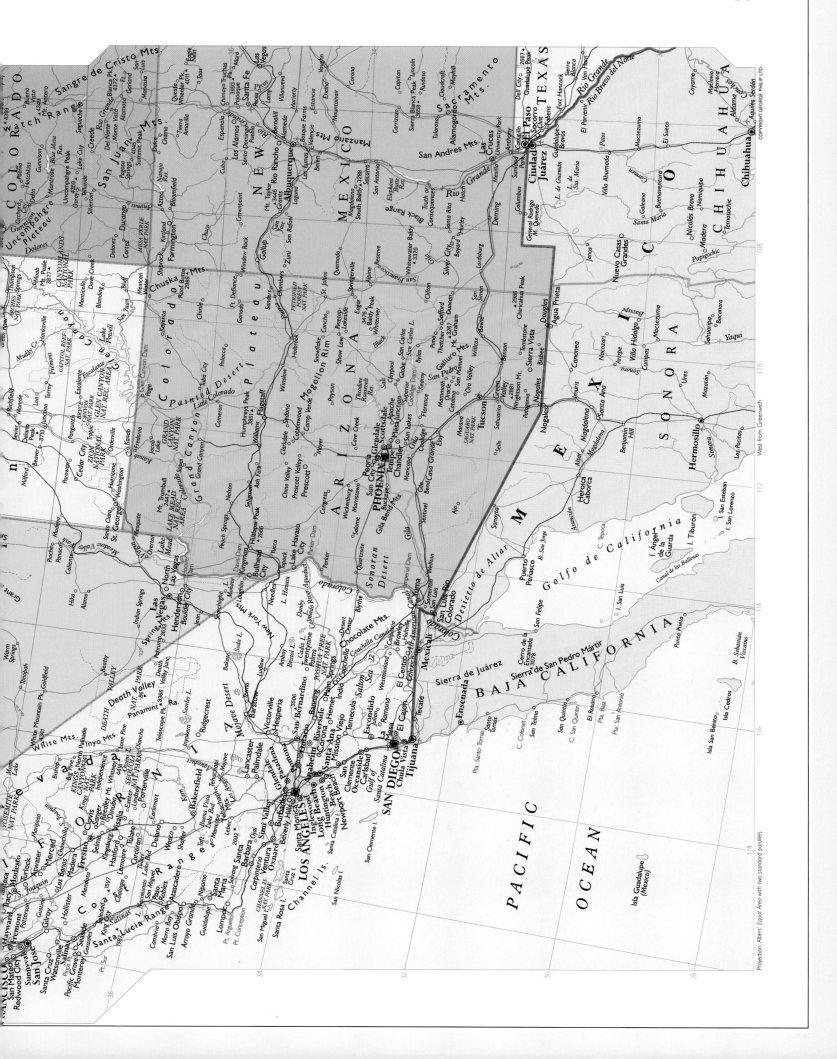

PACIFIC

OCEAN

Projection: Albers' Equal Area with two standard parallels

West from Greenwich

WESTERN WASHINGTON REGION
On same scale

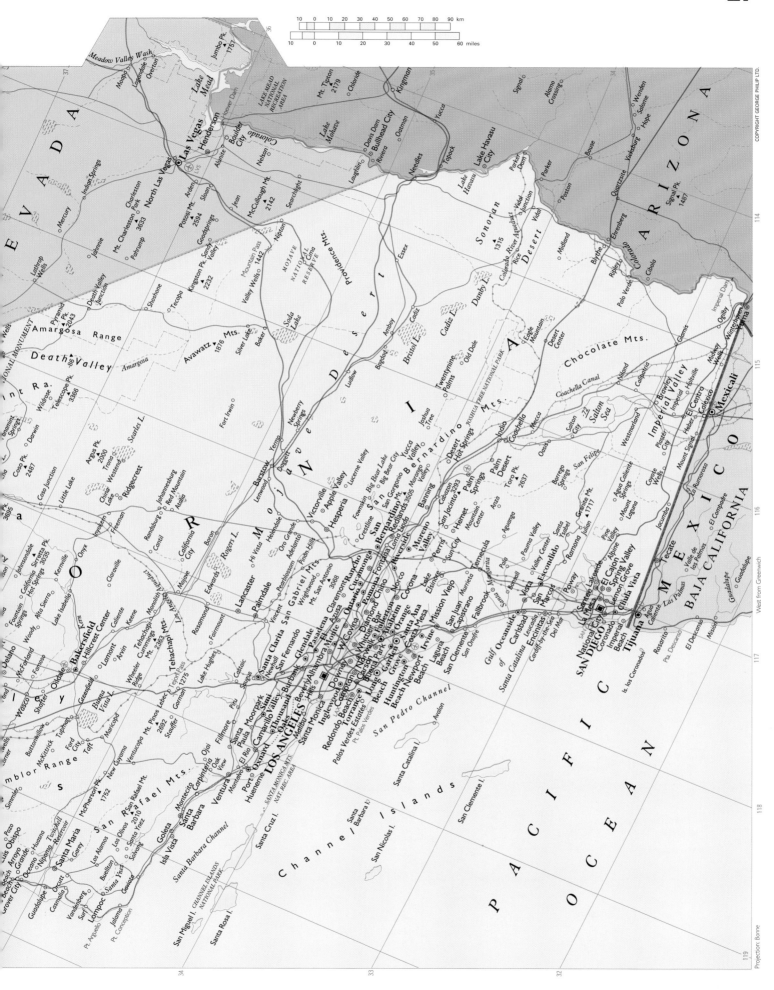

10 0 10 20 30 40 50 60 70 80 90 km

10 0 10 20 30 40 50 60 miles

NEVADA

Meadow Valley Wash

Jumbo Pk. 1757

Moapa
Overton

Lake Mead

Henderson

Las Vegas

LVS

Boulder City

LAKE MEAD NATIONAL RECREATION AREA

Nelson

Colorado

Davis Dam

Bullhead City

Riviera

Laughlin

Needles

Mt. Tipton 2179

Chloride

Oatman

Kingman

Yucca

Signal

Alamo Crossing

Wenden
Hope

A R I Z O N A

North Las Vegas

Arden
Sloan

McCullough Mt. 2142

Searchlight

Lake Mohave

Topock

Lake Havasu City

Parker Dam

Vidal Junction

Vidal

Parker

Bouse

Vicksburg

Quartzsite

Signal Pk. 1487

114

Indian Springs

Mercury

Charleston Park

Mt. Charleston Pk. 3663

Potosi Mt. 2594

Goodsprings

Jean

Nipton

S o n o r a n

1315

Colorado River Aqueduct

Midland

Ehrenberg
Blythe

Ripley

Cibola

Palo Verde

Ehrenberg

115

Johnnie

Pahrump

D e s e r t

Midway Wells

NATIONAL MONUMENT

Lathrop Wells

Death Valley Junction

Shoshone

Tecopa

Kingston Pk. 2232

Sentinel 1442

Valley Wells

M O J A V E

NATIONAL RESERVE

Cima

Essex

Danby L.

Eagle Mountain

Desert Center

Chocolate Mts.

Glamis

Imperial Dam

Ogilby

Yuma

Pyramid Pk. 2043

Amargosa Range

Amargosa

Death Valley

-86

Avawatz Mts. 1876

Silver Lake

Soda Lake

Baker

Ludlow

Bagdad

Cadiz

Cadiz L.

Amboy

Bristol L.

Old Dale

Twentynine Palms

JOSHUA TREE NATIONAL PARK

Coachella Canal

Niland

Calipatria

Westmorland

Brawley

Imperial Valley

Holtville

El Centro

Heber

Calexico

Mexicali

Telescope Pk. 3366

Darwin

Coso Pk. 2487

Panamint Springs

Argus Pk. 2000

Trona

Searles L.

Westend

Red Mountain

California City

Boron

Rogers L.

Mojave

M O J A V E

Daggett

Yermo

Newberry Springs

D e s e r t

Joshua Tree

Desert Hot Springs

Indio

Coachella

Mecca

Salton Sea

Salton City

Mecca

Oasis

Plaster City

Mount Signal

B A J A   C A L I F O R N I A

M E X I C O

Coso Junction

Little Lake

Inyokern

Randsburg
Johannesburg

Atolia

Hinkley

Barstow

Lenwood

Victorville

Hesperia

Apple Valley

Lucerne Valley

Big Bear Lake
Big Bear City

Yucca Valley

Morongo Valley

Banning

Cabazon

Palm Springs

Palm Desert

Toro Pk. 2637

Borrego Springs

San Felipe

Agua Caliente Springs

Coyote Wells

Tecate

Valle de las Palmas

El Compadre

Sierra Nevada 3695

C A L I F O R N I A

Cantil

Red Mountain

Edwards

Adelanto

Hi Vista

Oro Grande

Pinon Hills

Crestline

San Bernardino

Redlands

Loma Linda

Moreno Valley

Perris

Sun City

Hemet

San Jacinto Mt. 3505

Idyllwild

Anza

Aguanga

Warner Springs

Santa Ysabel

Ranchita

Julian

Granite Mt. 1717

Pine Valley

Jacumba

La Rumorosa

Rosarito

El Descanso

Guadalupe

Darwin

Olancha

Little Lake

Ridgecrest

California Hot Springs 3035

Lake Isabella

Onyx

Kernville

Woody

Glennville

Caliente

Keene

Tehachapi Mts. 2363

Monolith

Rosamond

Lancaster

Palmdale

Littlerock

Wrightwood

Mt. San Antonio 3068

Rancho Cucamonga

Ontario

Pomona

Fontana

Chino

Riverside

Corona

Norco

Lake Elsinore

Temecula

Murrieta

Fallbrook

Valley Center

Ramona

Poway

Lakeside

El Cajon

Alpine

Spring Valley

Lemon Grove

Chula Vista

Tijuana

Agua Caliente

Valle de las Palmas

S a n   G a b r i e l   M t s.

Redmond

Delano

McFarland

Wasco

Shafter

Oildale

Bakersfield

Hillcrest Center

Lamont

Arvin

Wheeler Ridge

Mt. Pinos 2692

Lebec

Gorman 1275

Frazier Park

Castaic

Santa Clarita

Newhall

Vincent

Pasadena

Glendale

Monrovia

Azusa

Claremont

Covina

West Covina

Diamond Bar

Fullerton

Anaheim

Orange

Santa Ana

Costa Mesa

Irvine

Mission Viejo

San Juan Capistrano

San Clemente

San Onofre

Oceanside

Carlsbad

Encinitas

Leucadia

Cardiff-by-the-Sea

Del Mar

Escondido

San Marcos

Vista

San Diego

National City

Coronado

Imperial Beach

Tijuana

Taft

Maricopa

New Cuyama

Ventucopa

Cuyama

Ojai

Fillmore

Piru

Simi Valley

Thousand Oaks

Moorpark

Camarillo

Santa Paula

Ventura

Oxnard

El Rio

Montalvo

Port Hueneme

SANTA MONICA MTS. NAT. REC. AREA

S a n   R a f a e l   M t s.

LOS ANGELES

Santa Monica

Malibu

Beverly Hills

Burbank

Inglewood

Downey

Norwalk

Whittier

La Habra

Buena Park

Garden Grove

Cerritos

Lakewood

Long Beach

Carson

Torrance

Redondo Beach

Palos Verdes Estates

Pt. Palos Verdes

Huntington Beach

Newport Beach

Laguna Beach

Santa Maria

Santa Barbara

Goleta

Isla Vista

Montecito

Carpinteria

McPherson Pk. 1752

San Rafael Mt. 2010

S a n t a   Y n e z   M t s.

Santa Ynez Reservoir

San Miguel I.

CHANNEL ISLANDS NATIONAL PARK

Santa Rosa I.

Santa Cruz I.

Santa Barbara I.

C h a n n e l   I s l a n d s

San Nicolas I.

San Clemente I.

Avalon

Santa Catalina I.

San Pedro Channel

Is. los Coronados

P A C I F I C   O C E A N

Los Osos

San Luis Obispo

Pismo Beach

Arroyo Grande

Oceano

Grover City

Nipomo

Guadalupe

Los Alamos

Buellton

Solvang

Los Olivos

Lompoc

Vandenberg

Pt. Arguello

Pt. Conception

Gulf of Santa Catalina

West from Greenwich

116

117

118

119

Projection: Bonne

34

33

32

35

36

37

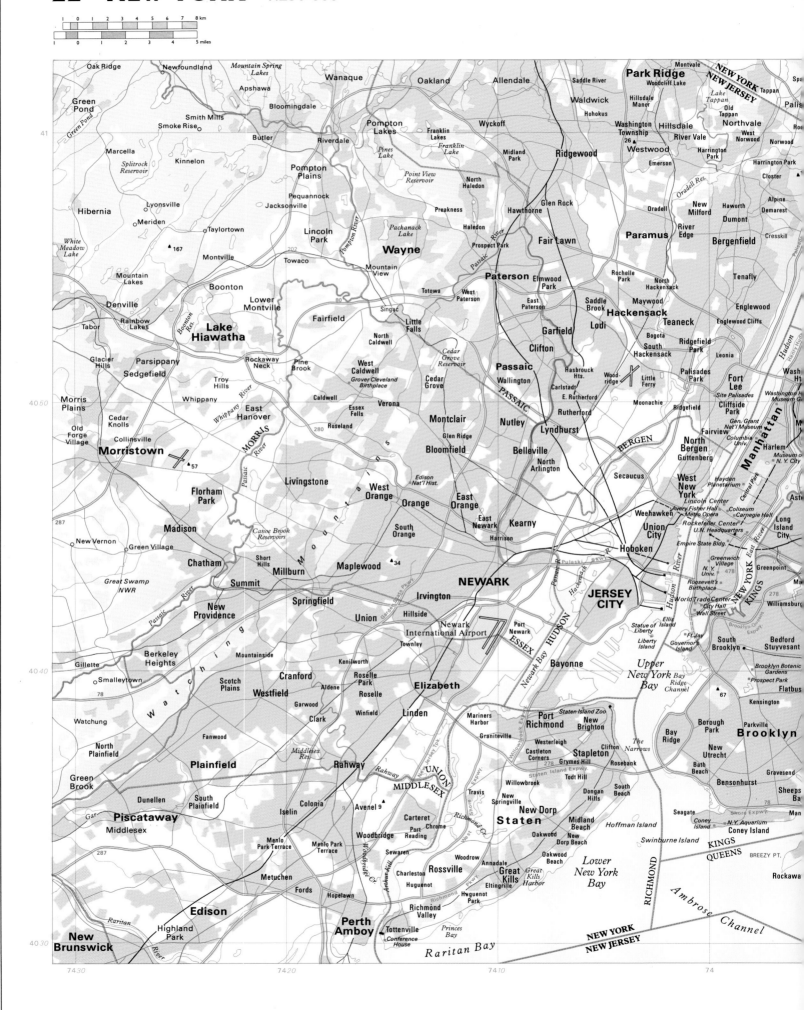

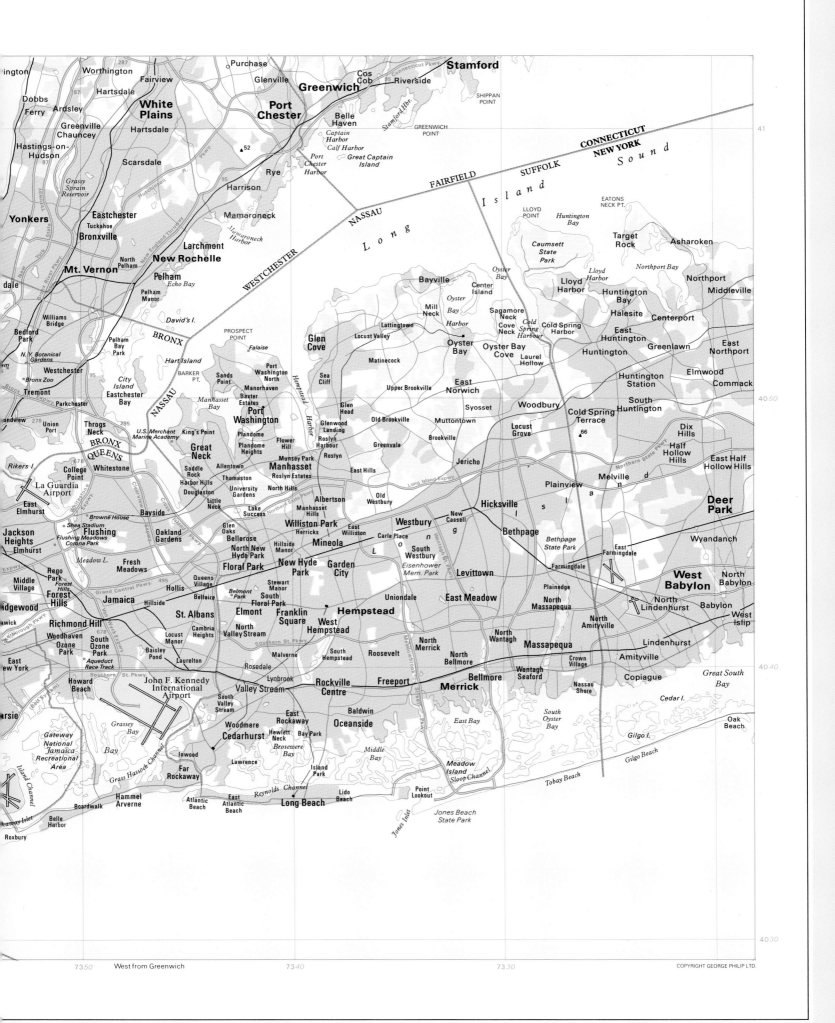

Purchase · Glenville · Cos Cob · Riverside · **Stamford**
Fairview · **Greenwich** · Port Chester · Belle Haven · SHIPPAN POINT
Worthington · Hartsdale
White Plains · Hartsdale
Dobbs Ferry · Ardsley · Greenville · Chauncey
Hastings-on-Hudson · Scarsdale · Captain Harbor · Calf Harbor · Great Captain Island
Port Chester Harbor · **GREENWICH POINT**

CONNECTICUT · **NEW YORK**
FAIRFIELD · SUFFOLK · S o u n d

L o n g   I s l a n d

Yonkers · Eastchester · Tuckahoe · Bronxville
Rye · Harrison
Mamaroneck · Mamaroneck Harbor
North Pelham · **New Rochelle** · Larchmont
Mt. Vernon · Pelham · Echo Bay
Pelham Manor
David's I.
BRONX · WESTCHESTER · NASSAU

EATONS NECK PT.
LLOYD POINT · Huntington Bay
Caumsett State Park · **Target Rock** · Asharoken
Northport Bay
Bayville · Center Island · Oyster Bay · Lloyd Harbor · Lloyd Harbor · Northport · Middleville
Mill Neck · Oyster Bay · Sagamore Neck · Cold Spring Harbour · Cold Spring Harbor · Huntington Bay · Halesite · Centerport
Lattingtown · Locust Valley · Harbor · Cove Neck · East Huntington · Greenlawn · East Northport

Bedford Park · N.Y. Botanical Gardens
Westchester · Bronx Zoo · Tremont
Hart Island · BARKER PT. · Falaise
Sands Point · Port Washington North · Manorhaven · Baxter Estates
Manhasset Bay · **Port Washington** · Plandome · Plandome Heights
Glen Head · Glenwood Landing · Roslyn Harbour · Roslyn
Greenvale · East Hills
Flower Hill · Munsey Park · Roslyn

Glen Cove
Sea Cliff
Matinecock
Upper Brookville · Old Brookville
East Norwich
Syosset · Woodbury · Cold Spring Terrace
Muttontown · Brookville
Jericho · Locust Grove
66

City Island · Eastchester Bay
Parkchester · 95
Union Port · 278 · 295
Throgs Neck · U.S. Merchant Marine Academy · King's Point
Saddle Rock · Harbor Hills · Thomaston · Douglaston
Great Neck · Allentown · **Manhasset** · Roslyn Estates · Manhasset Hills
University Gardens · North Hills
Little Neck · Lake Success · Old Westbury
Albertson · New Cassell
Williston Park · Herricks · East Williston · Carle Place
Hicksville · Plainview · Melville · d · Dix Hills · Half Hollow Hills · East Half Hollow Hills
Deer Park
Wyandanch

Rikers I.
College Point · Whitestone · **La Guardia Airport**
East Elmhurst · Browne House · Bayside · Oakland Gardens
Shea Stadium · Flushing Meadows Corona Park
Jackson Heights · Elmhurst · **Flushing** · Meadow L. · Fresh Meadows
Glen Oaks · Bellerose · North New Hyde Park · Hillside Manor · **Mineola** · **Westbury** · South Westbury · Bethpage · Bethpage State Park · East Farmingdale
West Babylon · North Babylon
Middle Village · Rego Park · Forest Hills · **Floral Park** · **New Hyde Park** · Garden City · Eisenhower Mem. Park · Levittown · Plainedge · Farmingdale
North Lindenhurst · Babylon · West Islip

Ridgewood · **Forest Hills** · Queens Village · Bellaire · Stewart Manor · South Floral Park
Jamaica · Hollis · Hillside · Belmont Park
St. Albans · Elmont · Franklin Square · West Hempstead · **Hempstead** · Uniondale · **East Meadow** · North Massapequa · North Amityville · Lindenhurst · Amityville
Cambria Heights · North Valley Stream

Richmond Hill · Woodhaven · South Ozone Park · Locust Manor · Baisley Pond · Laurelton
Rosedale · Malverne · South Hempstead · Roosevelt · North Merrick · North Bellmore · North Wantagh · **Massapequa** · Crown Village · Copiague
East New York · Aqueduct Race Track
Lynbrook · **Rockville Centre** · **Freeport** · **Bellmore** · Wantagh Seaford · Nassau Shore · **Amityville**

John F. Kennedy International Airport
Howard Beach
Gateway National Jamaica Recreational Area · Grassey Bay
Valley Stream · South Valley Stream · East Rockaway · Baldwin · **Oceanside** · **Merrick** · South Oyster Bay · Cedar I. · Oak Beach
Woodmere · Cedarhurst · Hewlett Neck · Bay Park · East Bay
Broseure Bay
Lawrence · Inwood · Island Park · Middle Bay · Meadow Island Sloop Channel · Gilgo I. · South Oyster Bay · Gilgo Beach

Far Rockaway · Reynolds Channel · Lido Beach · Point Lookout · Tobay Beach · Gilgo Beach
Roxbury · Belle Harbor · Hammel · Arverne · Boardwalk · Atlantic Beach · East Atlantic Beach · **Long Beach**
Jones Inlet · Jones Beach State Park

LAKE

MICHIGAN

Potawatomi Woods
Wheeling
208 ▲
Chipilly Woods
Chicago Botanic Garden
Glencoe
Northbrook
Techny
Skokie Lagoons
Winnetka
Prospect Heights
Northfield
Kenilworth
Arlington Heights
Glenview N.A.S.
Lake Avenue Woods
Beck Lake
Glenview Woods
Wilmette Harbor
Baha'i Temple
Wilmette
Northwestern University
Mount Prospect
Glenview
Glenview Countryside
Evanston
Des Plaines
Morton Grove
Skokie
Weller Cr
Niles
Lincolnwood
Rogers Park
Edison Park
Loyola University
Park Ridge
Smith Forest Preserve
Edens Expwy
North Shore Channel
Rosemont
Norwood Park
North Branch Chicago River
Uptown
Chicago-O'Hare International Airport
Jefferson Park
Lake O'Hare
Schiller Woods
Norridge
Harwood Heights
Irving Park
Lincoln Park
Bensenville
Schiller Park
Dunning
Portage Park
Avondale
Lakeview
Belmont Harbor
Des Plaines R
Westdale
Franklin Park
Elmwood Park
Belmont Cragin
John F. Kennedy Expwy
Logan Square
Lake Shore Drive
River Grove
Northlake
▲ 198
Stone Park
Humboldt Park
Old Town
John Hancock Center
Water Tower
Elmhurst
Melrose Park
Frank Lloyd Wright Home
Austin
West Town
Northwestern Station
Art Institute
Berkeley
River Forest
Garfield Park
Sears Tower
Chicago Harbor
Bellwood
Oak Park
Dwight D. Eisenhower Expwy
La Salle St. Station
Chicago Fire Marker
The Loop
Grant Park
Hillside
Maywood
S. Branch Chicago R
Adler Planetarium
Broadview
Miller Meadow
Douglas Park
Burnham Park Harbor
Westchester
Forest Park
Cicero
Lawndale
Bridgeport
CHICAGO
Sailt Creek
North Riverside
Berwyn
Dan Ryan Expressway
Bemis Woods
La Grange Park
Riverside
Stickney
Chicago Sanitary and Ship Canal
Michigan Ave
La Grange
Brookfield
Lyons
Forest View
A. E. Stevenson Expwy
Brighton Park
Western Springs
Chicago Portage National Historical Site
MaCook
Clearing
Gage Park
Washington Park
Hyde Park
Museum of Science and Industry
Hinsdale
Countryside
University of Chicago
La Grange Highlands
Summit
Chicago-Midway Airport
Chicago Lawn
Englewood
Jackson Park
Burr Ridge
Bedford Park
Hodgkins
Marquette Park
South Shore
Bridgeview
Ashburn
Hayford
Chatham
COOK COUNTY
LAKE COUNTY
Des Plaines R
Justice
Burbank
Hometown
Dan Ryan Woods
South Chicago
Willow Springs
Calumet Harbor
Hickory Hills
Oak Lawn
Evergreen Park
Beverley
Roseland
South Deering
Calumet Harbor
▲ 185
Palos Hills
Mount Greenwood
Chicago Ridge
Jackson Park
Maple Lake
Longjohn Slough
Palos Park
Merrionette Park
Morgan Park
Lake Calumet
Whiting
Sag Bridge
Saganashkee Slough
Worth
Alsip
Stony Creek
Blue Island
Calumet Park
Calumet Skyway
Robertsdale
Indiana Harbor
Palos Hills Forest
Calumet Sag Channel
Tri State Tollway
Calumet River
ILLINOIS
Indiana
Wolf Lake
Tampier Slough
Palos Park
Palos Heights
Robbins
Riverdale
Hegewisch
Powderhorn Lake
East Chicago
Orland Lake
221 ▲
Tinley Creek
Rubio Woods
Crestwood
Posen
Little Calumet River
Burnham
Grand Calumet River
180 ▲
Orland Park
Tinley Creek Woods
Midlothian
Dixmoor
Dolton
Calumet City
Goeselville
Little Calumet River
Phoenix
Indiana Harbor Canal
Oak Forest
Harvey
South Holland
Shabbona Woods
Hammond
Gary
Tinley Park
Markham

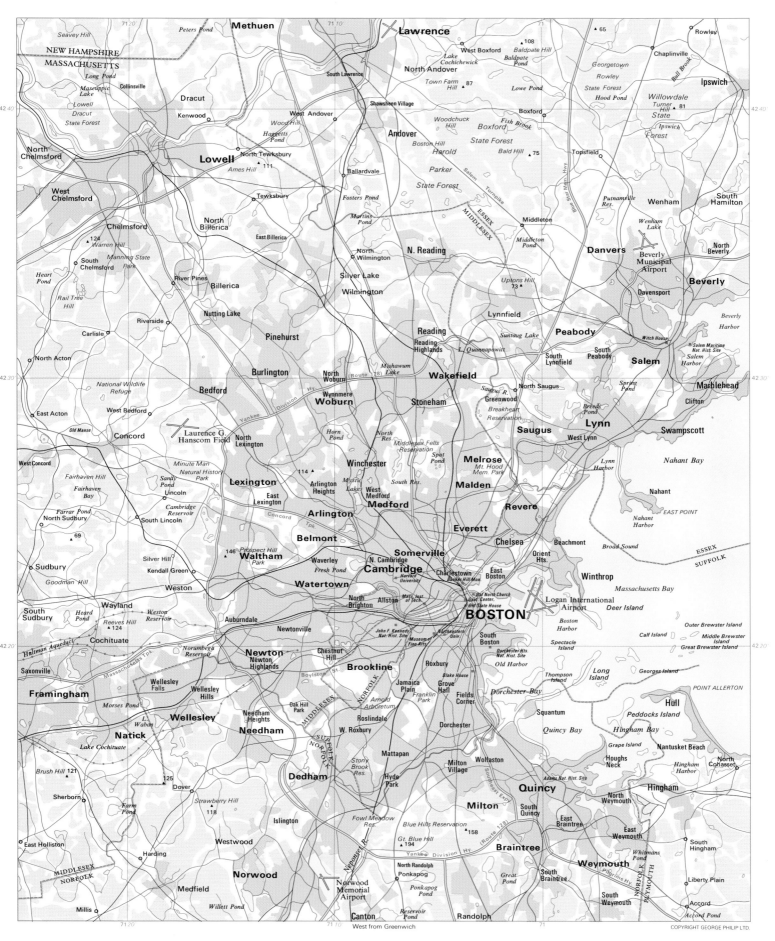

NEW HAMPSHIRE
MASSACHUSETTS

Peters Pond

Seavey Hill

Lawrence

West Boxford · ▲108
Lake Cochichewick · Baldpate Hill
North Andover · Baldpate Pond

· 65

Rowley

Chaplinville

Georgetown
Rowley

Ipswich

Long Pond
Masauppic Lake · Collinsville
Lowell Dracut State Forest

Dracut

Town Farm Hill · 87

Lowe Pond

State Forest
Hood Pond

Kenwood

West Andover

Shawsheen Village

Boxford

Willowdale
Turner Hill ▲ 81
State

North Chelmsford

Lowell

North Tewksbury

Ames Hill · 111

Andover

Boston Hill
Harold

Woodchuck Hill
Boxford State Forest

Fish Brook

Bald Hill ▲ 75

Topsfield

Ipswich Forest

West Chelmsford

Ballardvale

Parker State Forest

Tewksbury

Fosters Pond

Salem R.

Middleton

Putnamville Res.

Wenham

South Hamilton

Chelmsford · ▲124
Warren Hill

North Billerica

East Billerica

Martins Pond

ESSEX
MIDDLESEX

Middleton Pond

Wenham Lake

Danvers

Beverly Municipal Airport

North Beverly

South Chelmsford · Manning State Park

River Pines

Billerica

North Wilmington

N. Reading

Uptons Hill 73 ▲

Davensport

Beverly

Heart Pond

Rail Tree Hill

Riverside

Nutting Lake

Silver Lake

Wilmington

Lynnfield

Suntaug Lake

Peabody

South Lynnfield

South Peabody

Witch House

Beverly Harbor

Salem Maritime Nat. Hist. Site
Salem Harbor

Carlisle

Pinehurst

Reading
Reading Highlands

L. Quannapowitt

Salem

North Acton

Burlington

North Woburn

Mishawum Lake
Route 128

Wakefield

North Saugus

Spring Pond

Marblehead

National Wildlife Refuge

Bedford

Wynnmere

Woburn

Stoneham

Saugus R.
Greenwood
Breakheart Reservation

Breeds Pond

Clifton

East Acton

West Bedford

Horn Pond

North Res.

Middlesex Fells Reservation

Spot Pond

Saugus

West Lynn

Lynn

Swampscott

Laurence G. Hanscom Field

North Lexington

Winchester

▲114

Mystic Lakes

South Res.

Melrose

Mt. Hood Mem. Park

Lynn Harbor

Nahant Bay

Old Manse

Minute Man Natural History Park

Lexington

Arlington Heights

West Medford

Malden

Nahant

Concord

West Concord

Fairhaven Hill
Fairhaven Bay

Sandy Pond

East Lexington

Medford

Revere

Nahant Harbor

EAST POINT

Lincoln

Cambridge Reservoir

Arlington

Everett

Chelsea

Beachmont

Broad Sound

Farrar Pond
North Sudbury

South Lincoln

South Lincoln

Concord Tpk.

Belmont

Orient Hts.

Winthrop

ESSEX
SUFFOLK

· 69

▲146 Prospect Hill

N. Cambridge
Fresh Pond

Somerville

Charlestown
Bunker Hill Mon.
Harvard University

East Boston

Massachusetts Bay

Sudbury

Silver Hill

Waltham Park

Waverley

Cambridge

Old North Church
Govt. Center
Old State House

Logan International Airport

Deer Island

Goodman Hill

Kendall Green

Watertown

Mass. Inst. of Tech.

Weston

North Brighton

Allston

BOSTON

Boston Harbor

Wayland

Heard Pond

Weston Reservoir

Auburndale

John F. Kennedy Nat. Hist. Site

Northeastern Univ.
Museum of Fine Arts

South Boston

Dorchester Hts. Nat. Hist. Site

Spectacle Island

Calf Island

Outer Brewster Island
Middle Brewster Island
Great Brewster Island

South Sudbury

Reeves Hill ▲124

Newtonville

Chestnut Hill

Roxbury

Old Harbor

Thompson Island

Long Island

Georges Island

POINT ALLERTON

Halfman Aqueduct

Cochituate

Massachusetts Tpke.

Norumbega Reservoir

Newton
Newton Highlands

Boylston St.

Brookline

Blake House
Grove Hall

Dorchester Bay

Hull

Framingham

Wellesley Falls

Wellesley Hills

Morses Pond

Oak Hill Park

Jamaica Plain
Arnold Arboretum

Franklin Park

Fields Corner

Squantum

Peddocks Island

Saxonville

Wellesley

NORFOLK

Roslindale

W. Roxbury

Dorchester

Quincy Bay

Hingham Bay

Grape Island

Nantasket Beach

Waban

Natick

Needham Heights

Needham

SUFFOLK
NORFOLK

Mattapan

Wollaston

Houghs Neck

Hingham Harbor

North Cohasset

Lake Cochituate

Stony Brook Res.

Hyde Park

Milton Village

Adams Nat. Hist. Site

Brush Hill 121

· 125

Dedham

Quincy

North Weymouth

Hingham

Sherborn

Dover

Strawberry Hill · 118

Islington

Fowl Meadow Res.

Milton

South Quincy

East Braintree

East Weymouth

South Hingham

East Holliston

Harding

Westwood

Blue Hills Reservation
· 158

Southeast Expy. (Route 128)

South Braintree

Whitmans Pond

MIDDLESEX
NORFOLK

Gt. Blue Hill ▲194

Yankee Division Hwy.

Braintree

Weymouth

Pilgrims Hwy.

Liberty Plain

Millis

Norwood

Medfield

Willett Pond

North Randolph

Ponkapog

Norwood Memorial Airport

Ponkapog Pond

Great Pond

South Braintree

South Weymouth

Accord

Canton

Reservoir Pond

Randolph

NORFOLK
PLYMOUTH

Accord Pond

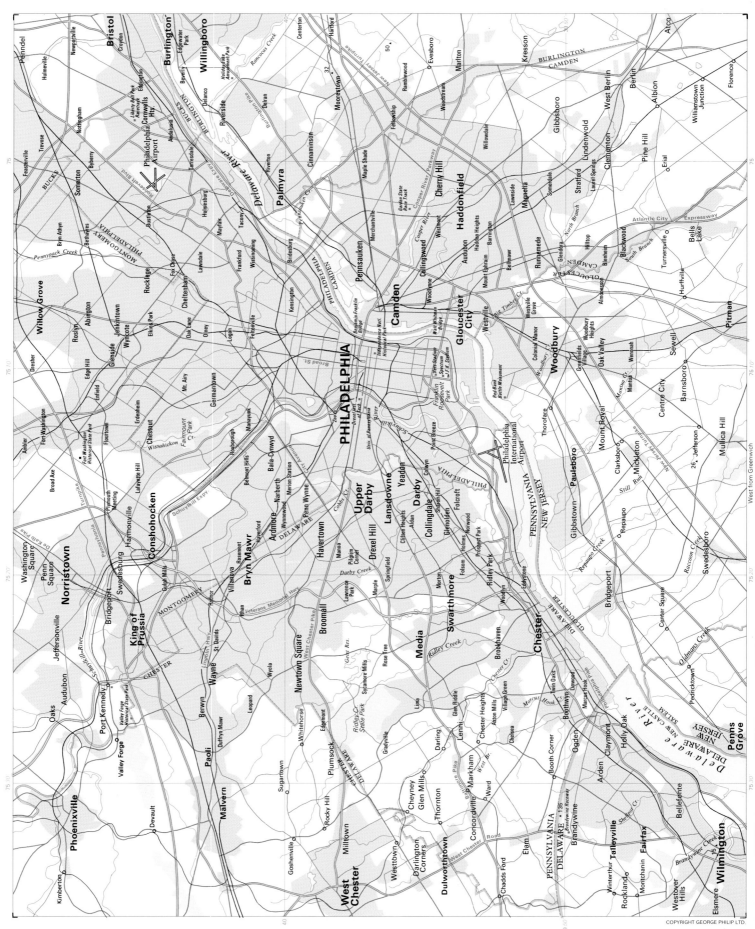

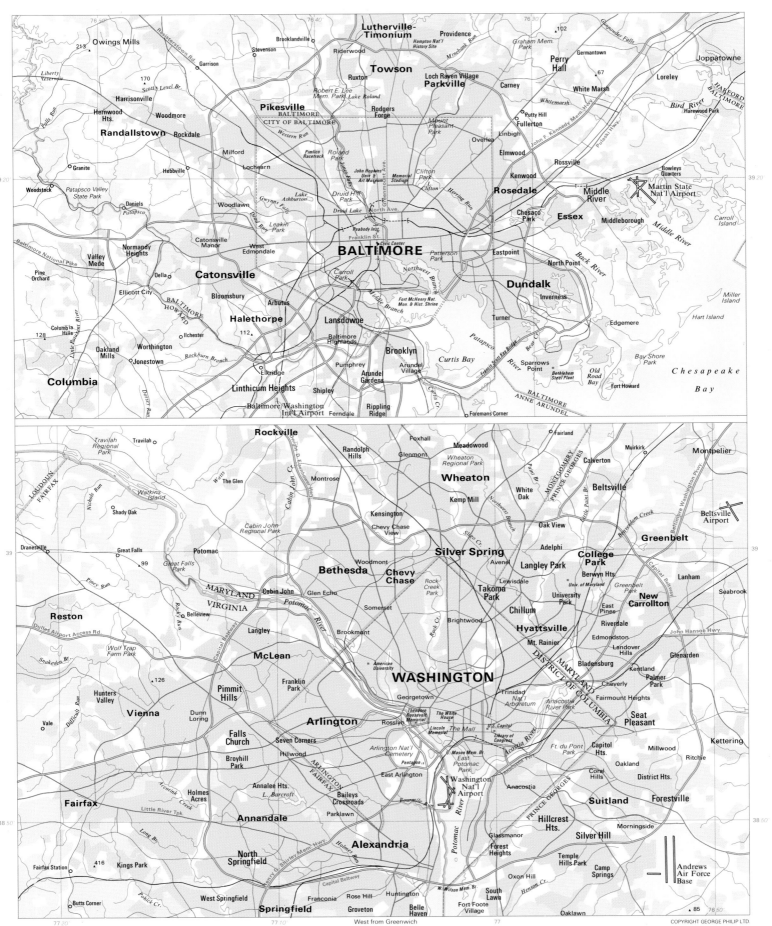

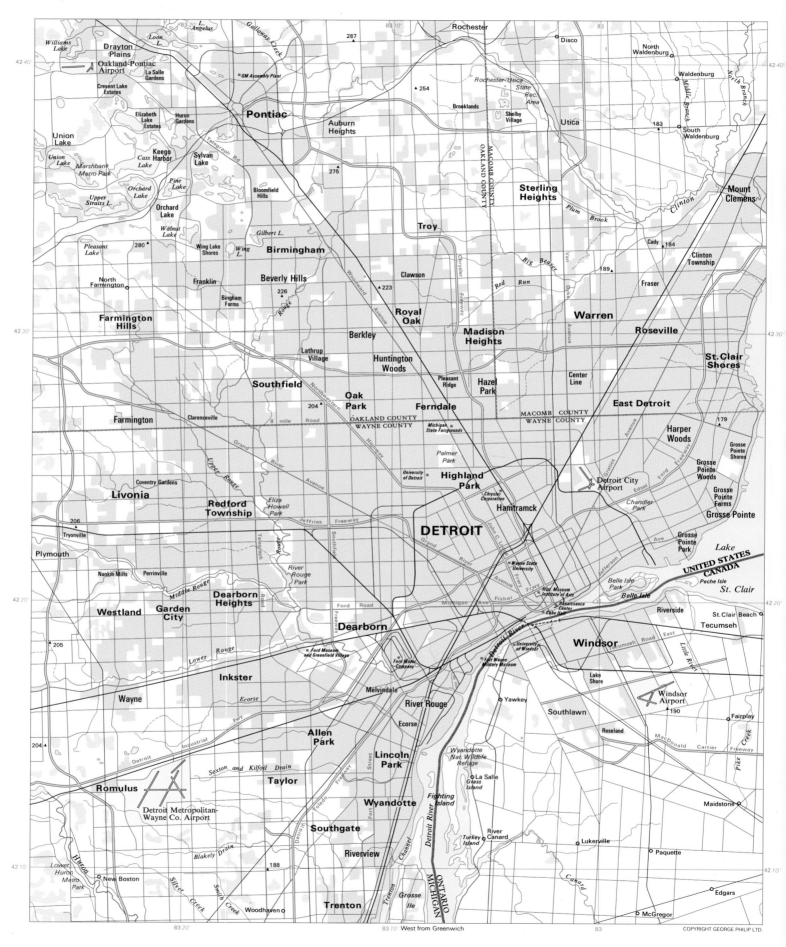

Williams Lake
Drayton Plains
Oakland-Pontiac Airport
La Salle Gardens
Cresent Lake Estates
Union Lake
Elizabeth Lake Estates
Huron Gardens
Union Lake
Marshbank Metro Park
Keego Harbor
Cass Lake
Sylvan Lake
Upper Straits L.
Orchard Lake
Pine Lake
Orchard Lake
Walnut Lake
Bloomfield Hills
Pleasant Lake
280
Gilbert L.
Wing Lake Shores
Wing L.
Birmingham
North Farmington
Franklin
Beverly Hills
Bingham Farms
226
Farmington Hills
Farmington
Clarenceville
Coventry Gardens
Livonia
204
Redford Township
Eliza Howell Park
206
Tryonville
Plymouth
Nankin Mills
Perrinville
Dearborn Heights
River Rouge Park
Westland
Garden City
205
Inkster
Wayne
204
Romulus
Detroit Metropolitan-Wayne Co. Airport
Taylor
Southgate
New Boston
Woodhaven
Trenton
Riverview
Wyandotte
Allen Park
Lincoln Park
Melvindale
River Rouge
Ecorse
Ecorse

Loon L.
L. Angelus
Galloway Creek
287
Rochester
Disco
North Waldenburg
Waldenburg
GM Assembly Plant
254
Pontiac
Auburn Heights
Brooklands
Rochester-Utica State Rec. Area
Shelby Village
Utica
183
South Waldenburg
275
Sterling Heights
Mount Clemens
Troy
Big Beaver
Plum Brook
Clinton
Clawson
Cady
184
Clinton Township
189
Fraser
223
Royal Oak
Red Run
Warren
Roseville
Berkley
Madison Heights
St. Clair Shores
Lathrup Village
Huntington Woods
Pleasant Ridge
Hazel Park
Center Line
179
Southfield
Oak Park
Ferndale
East Detroit
8 mile Road
OAKLAND COUNTY
WAYNE COUNTY
Michigan State Fairgrounds
MACOMB COUNTY
WAYNE COUNTY
Harper Woods
Grosse Pointe Shores
Palmer Park
Grosse Pointe Woods
University of Detroit
Highland Park
Detroit City Airport
Chandler Park
Grosse Pointe Farms
Chrysler Corporation
Hamtramck
Grosse Pointe
DETROIT
Grosse Pointe Park
Wayne State University
Lake St. Clair
Hist. Museum Institute of Arts
UNITED STATES
CANADA
Belle Isle Park
Peche Isle
St. Clair
Belle Isle
Jeffries Freeway
Ford Road
Dearborn
Renaissance Center
Cobo Hall
Riverside
St. Clair Beach
Tecumseh
Ford Museum and Greenfield Village
Ford Motor Company
University of Windsor
Fort Wayne Military Museum
Windsor
Lake Shore
Yawkey
Windsor Airport
190
Fairplay
Southlawn
Roseland
Wyandotte Nat. Wildlife Refuge
La Salle
Grass Island
MacDonald Cartier Freeway
Maidstone
Fighting Island
River Canard
Turkey Island
Lukerville
Paquette
Grosse Ile
Detroit River
ONTARIO
MICHIGAN
Canard
Edgars
McGregor

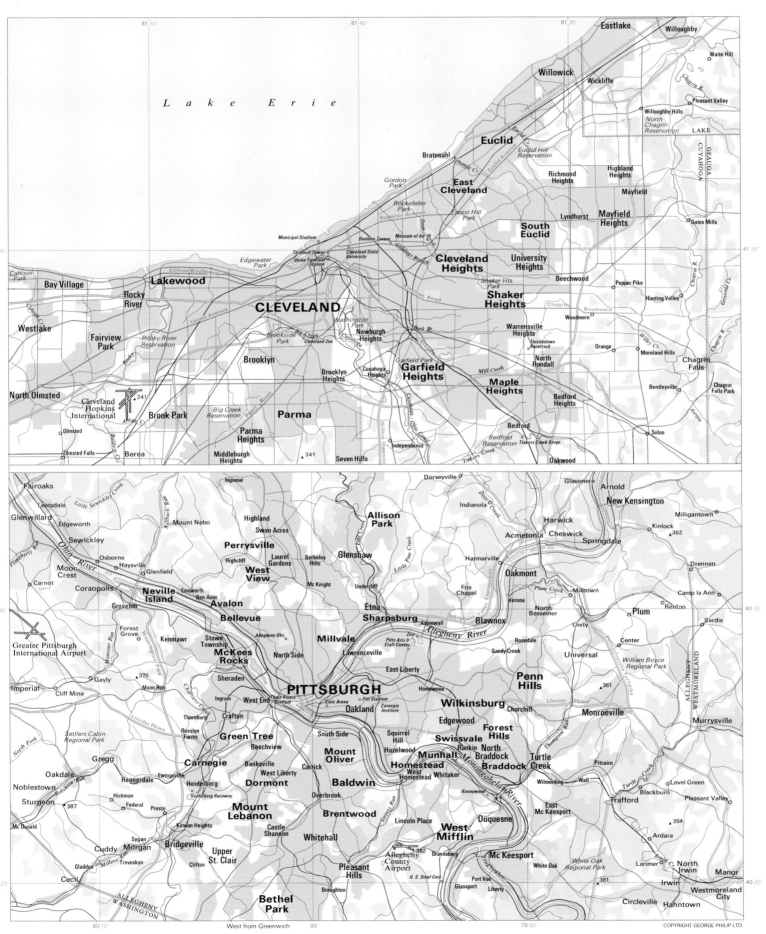

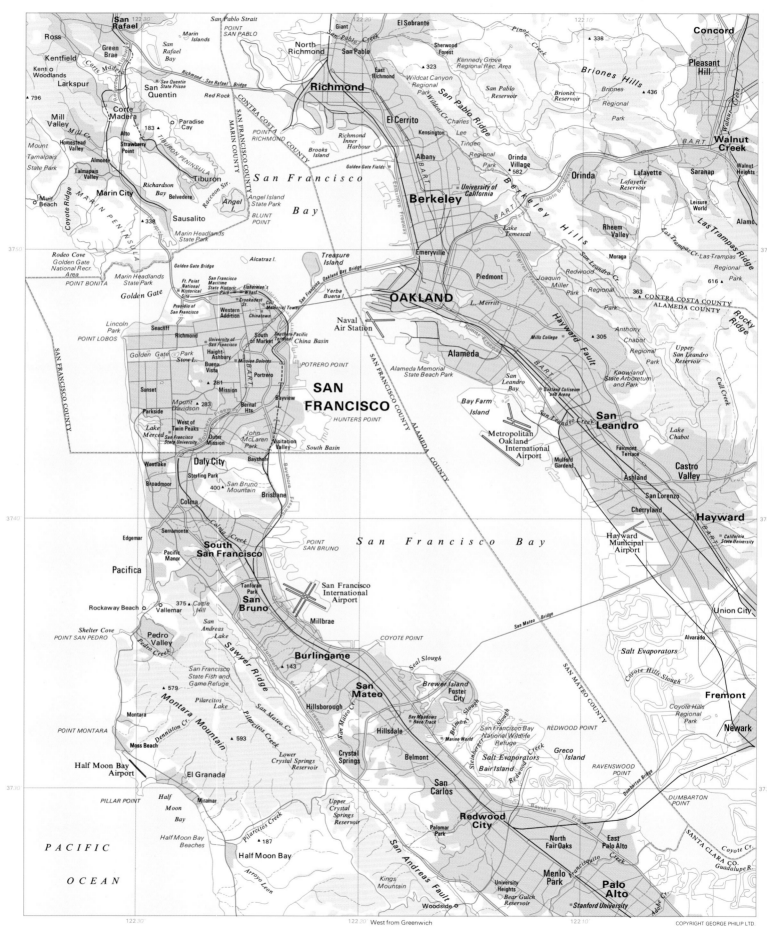

San Rafael 122 30
Ross
Kentfield
Green Brae
Kent o Woodlands
Larkspur
Mill Valley
Corte Madera
San Quentin
Alto 183
Strawberry Point
▲ 796
Mount Tamalpais State Park
Homestead Valley
Almonte
Talmalpais Valley
Marin City
Richardson Bay
Belvedere
Tiburon
Muir Beach
Coyote Ridge
Sausalito
▲ 338
Marin Headlands State Park
San Pablo Strait
POINT SAN PABLO
North Richmond
San Pablo
Giant
San Pablo Creek
El Sobrante
Sherwood Forest
Kennedy Grove Regional Rec. Area
▲ 338
Concord
▲ 323
East Richmond
Wildcat Canyon Regional Park
Richmond
El Cerrito
Kensington
Tilden Regional Park
Charles
Lee
San Pablo Ridge
San Pablo Reservoir
Briones Reservoir
Briones Hills
Briones Regional Park
▲ 436
Pleasant Hill
Richmond - San Rafael Bridge
Red Rock
San Quentin State Prison
Paradise Cay
Richmond Inner Harbour
Brooks Island
Albany
Berkeley
University of California
Orinda Village
582
Walnut Creek
BART
Orinda
Lafayette
Lafayette Reservoir
Saranap
Walnut Heights
San Rafael Bay
Marin Islands
Marin County
San Francisco Bay
Angel Island State Park
BLUNT POINT
Golden Gate Fields
Emeryville
Piedmont
Diablo Boulevard
Moraga
Berkeley Hills
Rheem Valley
Leisure World
Alamo
Las Trampas Regional Park

POINT BONITA
Rodeo Cove
Golden Gate National Recr. Area
Marin Headlands State Park
Golden Gate
Golden Gate Bridge
Alcatraz I.
Treasure Island
Oakland Bay Bridge
Yerba Buena I.
San Francisco
OAKLAND
Naval Air Station
L. Merritt
Hayward Fault
363
CONTRA COSTA COUNTY
ALAMEDA COUNTY
616
Rocky Ridge
Cull Creek
3750
POINT LOBOS
Lincoln Park
Seacliff
Richmond
University of San Francisco
Golden Gate Park
Stow L.
Haight-Ashbury
Buena Vista
Western Addition
Chinatown
South of Market
China Basin
POTRERO POINT
Mills College
Anthony Chabot Regional Park
Upper San Leandro Reservoir
Knowland State Arboretum and Park
Alameda
▲ 305
Sunset
Parkside
Mount Davidson
▲ 281
283
Mission
Portrero
Bernal Hts.
Bayview
SAN FRANCISCO
HUNTERS POINT
Alameda Memorial State Beach Park
Bay Farm Island
San Leandro Bay
Oakland Coliseum and Arena
San Leandro
Lake Chabot
San Francisco County
ALAMEDA COUNTY
Lake Merced
West of Twin Peaks
San Francisco State University
John McLaren Park
Visitacion Valley
Metropolitan Oakland International Airport
Mulford Gardens
Fairmont Terrace
Castro Valley
Daly City
Bayshore
South Basin
Ashland
San Lorenzo
Westlake
Broadmoor
Sterling Park
400
San Bruno Mountain
Brisbane
Cherryland
Hayward
3740
Colma
Serramonte
Edgemar
Canada Creek
POINT SAN BRUNO
San Francisco Bay
Hayward Municipal Airport
California State University
Pacifica
Pacific Manor
South San Francisco
Bayshore Freeway
Union City
Tanforan Park
San Bruno
San Francisco International Airport
Millbrae
Coyote Point
Salt Evaporators
Alvarado
Rockaway Beach
375 Cattle Hill
Vallemar
San Andreas Lake
Sawyer Ridge
San Mateo Bridge
Coyote Hills Slough
Shelter Cove
POINT SAN PEDRO
Pedro Valley
Pedro Creek
San Francisco State Fish and Game Refuge
Burlingame
▲ 143
Seal Slough
Brewer Island
Foster City
San Mateo County
Fremont
Montara
Pilarcitos Lake
▲ 579
Montara Mountain
Hillsborough
San Mateo
Bay Meadows Race Track
Marine World
Belmont Slough
San Francisco Bay National Wildlife Refuge
REDWOOD POINT
Coyote Hills Regional Park
Newark
POINT MONTARA
Moss Beach
▲ 593
Hillsdale
Steinberger Slough
Salt Evaporators
Bair Island
Greco Island
RAVENSWOOD POINT
Half Moon Bay Airport
El Granada
Lower Crystal Springs Reservoir
Crystal Springs
Belmont
San Carlos
Dumbarton Bridge
DUMBARTON POINT
37.30
PILLAR POINT
Half Moon Bay
Miramar
Upper Crystal Springs Reservoir
Palomar Park
Redwood City
North Fair Oaks
East Palo Alto
SANTA CLARA CO.
PACIFIC
OCEAN
Half Moon Bay Beaches
Pilarcitos Creek
▲ 187
Half Moon Bay
Arroyo Leon
San Andreas Fault
Kings Mountain
University Heights
Bear Gulch Reservoir
Woodside
Menlo Park
Palo Alto
Stanford University
Coyote Cr.
Guadalupe R.

122.30   122.20 West from Greenwich   122.10

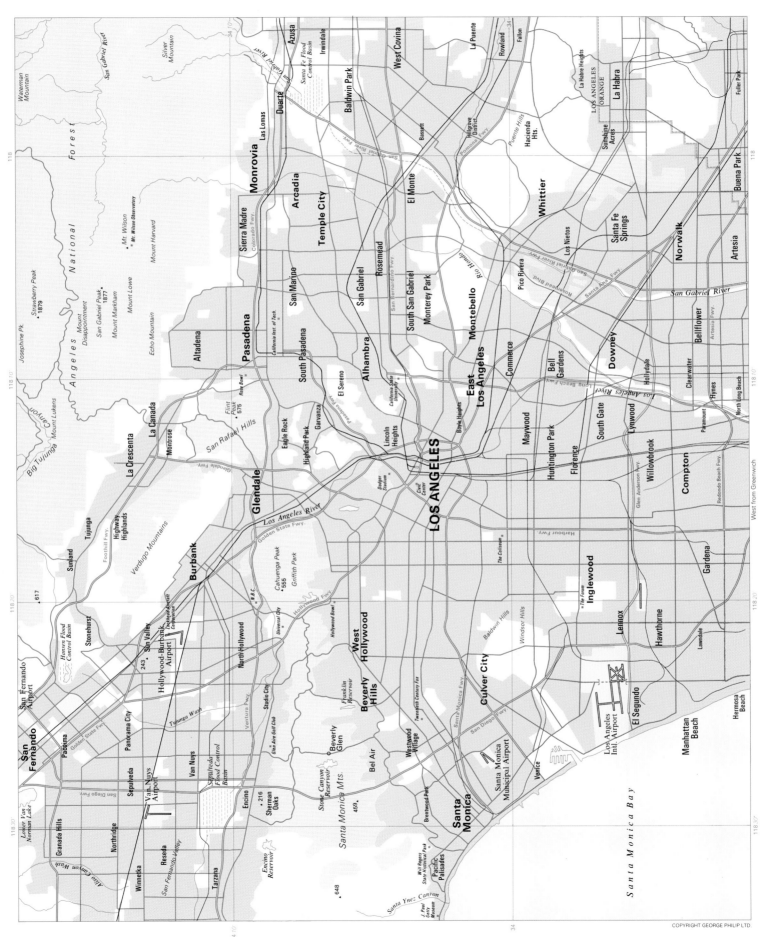

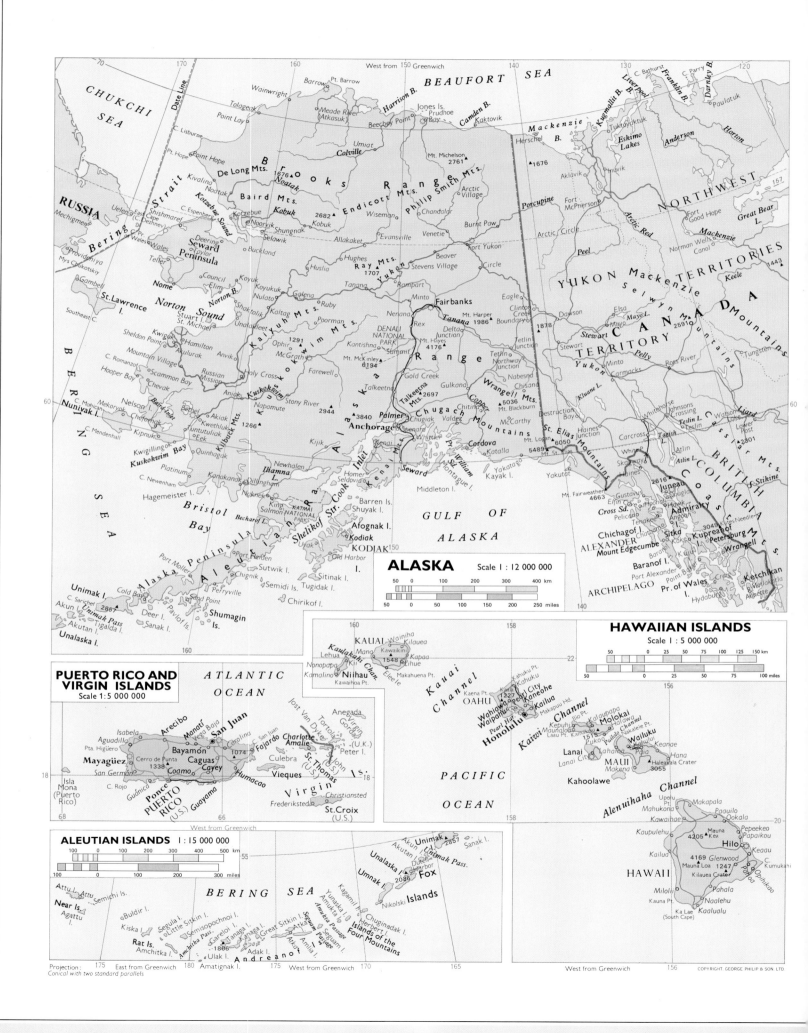

ALASKA Scale 1 : 12 000 000

HAWAIIAN ISLANDS Scale 1 : 5 000 000

PUERTO RICO AND VIRGIN ISLANDS Scale 1:5 000 000

ALEUTIAN ISLANDS 1 : 15 000 000

Projection: East from Greenwich
Conical with two standard parallels

West from Greenwich

COPYRIGHT GEORGE PHILIP & SON. LTD

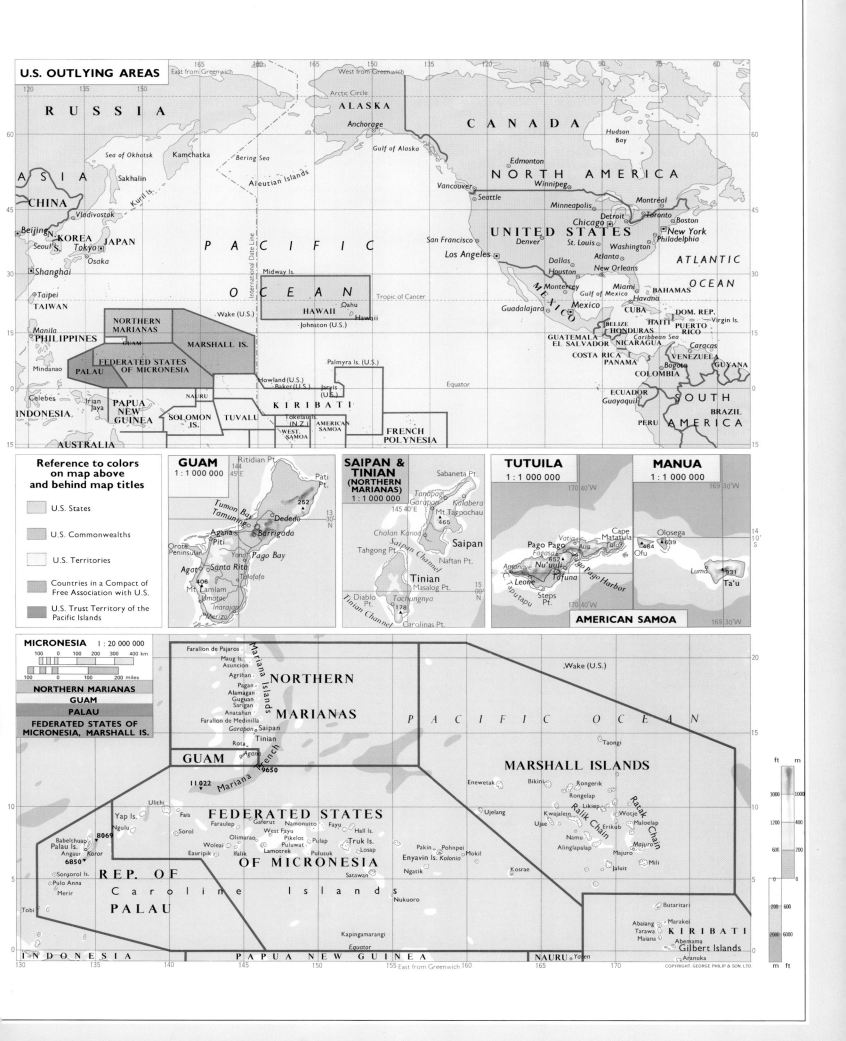

U.S. OUTLYING AREAS

RUSSIA

ALASKA
Anchorage

CANADA

Sea of Okhotsk Kamchatka

Bering Sea

Gulf of Alaska

Hudson
Bay

NORTH AMERICA

ASIA

Sakhalin

Aleutian Islands

Edmonton

CHINA
Vladivostok

Kuril Is.

Vancouver
Seattle

Winnipeg

Montreal

N. KOREA JAPAN
Beijing
Seoul Tokyo
S.
Osaka

Minneapolis
San Francisco

Detroit
Chicago
Denver St. Louis

Toronto
Boston
New York
Philadelphia

Shanghai

Los Angeles

Washington
Atlanta

ATLANTIC

Taipei
TAIWAN

Midway Is.
Oahu

Dallas
Houston
Monterrey

New Orleans

OCEAN

PACIFIC

Tropic of Cancer

Miami
Gulf of Mexico BAHAMAS
Havana

OCEAN

Manila
PHILIPPINES

NORTHERN
MARIANAS

Wake (U.S.)

HAWAII
Hawaii

Guadalajara

Mexico

CUBA
DOM. REP.
Virgin Is.
HAITI PUERTO
RICO

Mindanao

GUAM

MARSHALL IS.

Johnston (U.S.)

GUATEMALA
EL SALVADOR

BELIZE
HONDURAS
NICARAGUA

Caribbean Sea

Caracas

FEDERATED STATES
OF MICRONESIA
PALAU

Palmyra Is. (U.S.)

COSTA RICA
PANAMA

VENEZUELA
Bogota GUYANA

COLOMBIA

Celebes
Irian
Jaya

PAPUA
NEW
GUINEA

NAURU

Howland (U.S.)
Baker (U.S.)

Jarvis
(U.S.)

Equator

ECUADOR
Guayaquil

SOUTH

INDONESIA

SOLOMON
IS.

TUVALU

KIRIBATI

Tokelau Is.
(N.Z.)
WEST.
SAMOA

AMERICAN
SAMOA

FRENCH
POLYNESIA

PERU

BRAZIL
AMERICA

AUSTRALIA

Reference to colors on map above and behind map titles

- U.S. States
- U.S. Commonwealths
- U.S. Territories
- Countries in a Compact of Free Association with U.S.
- U.S. Trust Territory of the Pacific Islands

GUAM
1 : 1 000 000

Ritidian Pt.
Pati
Pt.

Tumon Bay
Tamuning
252
Dededo

Agana
Piti
Barrigada
Orote
Peninsular
Yona
Pago Bay
Agat Santa Rita
Talofofo
406
Mt. Lamlam
Umatac
Inarajan
Merizo

SAIPAN & TINIAN
(NORTHERN MARIANAS)
1 : 1 000 000

Sabaneta Pt.
Tanapag
Garapan Kalabera
Mt. Tagpochau
465

Chalan Kanoa
Saipan
Tahgong Pt.
Saipan Channel
Naftan Pt.

Tinian
Masalog Pt.
Diablo
Pt.
Tachungnya
178
Tinian Channel
Carolinas Pt.

TUTUILA
1 : 1 000 000

Pago Pago
Vatia
Cape
Matatula
Fagasa Aua Tula
Amanave Nu'uuli
Ofu
652
Leone Tafuna
Pago Pago Harbor
Taputapu
Steps
Pt.

MANUA
1 : 1 000 000

Olosega
484 639
Lumā
931
Ta'u

AMERICAN SAMOA

MICRONESIA 1 : 20 000 000

100 0 100 200 300 400 km
100 0 100 200 miles

NORTHERN MARIANAS
GUAM
PALAU
FEDERATED STATES OF MICRONESIA, MARSHALL IS.

Farallon de Pajaros
Maug Is.
Asuncion
Agrihan
Pagan
Alamagan
Guguan
Sarigan
Anatahan
Farallon de Medinilla
Garapan Saipan
Tinian
Rota
Agana

NORTHERN

MARIANAS

PACIFIC OCEAN

Wake (U.S.)

GUAM
Mariana Trench
9650
11 022

MARSHALL ISLANDS

Taongi

Ulithi
Yap Is.
Ngulu
8069
Babelthuap
Palau Is.
Angaur Koror
6850
Sonsorol Is.
Pulo Anna
Merir
Tobi

Fais
Sorol

FEDERATED STATES

Faraulep
Gaferut Namonuito Fayu
Olimarao West Fayu
Woleai Pikelot Pulap
Ifalik Puluwat Pulusuk
Eauripik Lamotrek Satawan

OF MICRONESIA

Hall Is.
Truk Is.
Losap

Enewetak
Bikini
Rongerik
Rongelap
Likiep
Ujelang
Kwajalein
Ujae Namu
Alinglapalap

Ratak Chain
Wotje Maloelap
Erikub
Majuro
Mili

Caroline Islands

Pakin Pohnpei
Enyavin Is. Kolonia
Ngatik
Nukuoro

Mokil
Kosrae

Jaluit

REP. OF
PALAU

Satawan

Kapingamarangi

Equator

Butaritari

Abaiang Marakei
Tarawa KIRIBATI
Maiana
Abemama
Gilbert Islands
Aranuka

INDONESIA PAPUA NEW GUINEA NAURU Yaren

East from Greenwich

COPYRIGHT. GEORGE PHILIP & SON. LTD.

ft m
3000 1000
1200 400
600 200
0 0
200 600
2000 6000
m ft

INDEX

UNITED STATES & OUTLYING AREAS

This index lists all the place names which appear on the large scale maps of the United States and outlying areas (pages which precede this index). Place names for the rest of the world can be found in the World Maps Index at the end of the atlas.

The number in dark type which follows each name in the index refers to the page number on which the place or feature is located. The geographical coordinates which follow the page number give the latitude and longitude of each place. The first coordinate indicates the latitude – the distance north or south of the Equator. The second coordinate indicates the longitude – the distance east or west of the Greenwich Meridian. Both latitude and longitude are measured in degrees and minutes (there are 60 minutes in a degree). Rivers are indexed to their mouths or confluences. A solid square ■ follows the name of a country, while an open square □ signifies that the name is a state. An arrow → follows the name of a river.

The alphabetic order of names composed of two or more words is governed by the first word and then by the second. Names composed of a proper name (Alaska) and a description (Gulf of) are positioned alphabetically by the proper name. All names beginning St. are alphabetized under Saint and those beginning Mc under Mac.

Abbreviations used in the index

Ala. — Alabama
Amer. — America, American
Ariz. — Arizona
Ark. — Arkansas
B. — Bay
C. — Cape
Calif. — California
Chan. — Channel
Colo. — Colorado
Conn. — Connecticut
Cr. — Creek
D.C. — District of Columbia
Del. — Delaware
Dist. — District
E. — East, Eastern
Fla. — Florida
G. — Gulf
Ga. — Georgia
Gt. — Great
I.(s) — Island(s)
Ill. — Illinois
Ind. — Indiana
Kans. — Kansas
Ky. — Kentucky
L. — Lake
La. — Louisiana
Ld. — Land
Mass. — Massachusetts
Md. — Maryland
Mich. — Michigan
Minn. — Minnesota
Miss. — Mississippi
Mo. — Missouri
Mont. — Montana
Mt.(s) — Mountain(s)
N. — North, Northern
N.B. — New Brunswick
N.C. — North Carolina
N. Dak. — North Dakota
N.H. — New Hampshire
N.J. — New Jersey
N. Mex. — New Mexico
N.Y. — New York
Nat. Mon. — National Monument
Nat. Park — National Park
Nat. Rec. Area. — National Recreation Area
Nebr. — Nebraska
Nev. — Nevada
Okla. — Oklahoma
Oreg. — Oregon
Pa. — Pennsylvania
Pac. Oc. — Pacific Ocean
Pass. — Passage
Pen. — Peninsula
Pk. — Peak
Pt. — Point
R. — Rio, River
R.I. — Rhode Island
Ra.(s) — Range(s)
Res. — Reserve, Reservoir, Reservation
S.C. — South Carolina
S. Dak. — South Dakota
Sa. — Serra, Sierra
Sd. — Sound
St. — Saint
Ste. — Sainte
Str. — Strait
Tenn. — Tennessee
Tex. — Texas
U.S.A. — United States of America
Va. — Virginia
Vt. — Vermont
Wash. — Washington
W. — West, Western
W. Va. — West Virginia
Wis. — Wisconsin
Wyo. — Wyoming

A

Abbaye, Pt. ... **10** 46 58N 88 8W
Abbeville, *Ala.* . **12** 31 34N 85 15W
Abbeville, *Ga.* . **12** 31 59N 83 18W
Abbeville, *La.* . **15** 29 58N 92 8W
Abbeville, *S.C.* **12** 34 11N 82 23W
Aberdeen, *Ala.* **11** 33 49N 88 33W
Aberdeen, *Idaho* **18** 42 57N 112 50W
Aberdeen, *Md.* **10** 39 31N 76 10W
Aberdeen, *Ohio* **17** 38 39N 83 46W
Aberdeen, *S. Dak.* **14** 45 28N 98 29W
Aberdeen, *Wash.* **20** 46 59N 123 50W
Abernathy **15** 33 50N 101 51W
Abert, L. **18** 42 38N 120 14W
Abilene, *Kans.* . **14** 38 55N 97 13W
Abilene, *Tex.* .. **15** 32 28N 99 43W
Abingdon, *Ill.* . **16** 40 48N 90 24W
Abingdon, *Va.* . **11** 36 43N 81 59W
Abington **26** 40 7N 75 7W
Absaroka Range **18** 44 45N 109 50W
Acadia National Park **11** 44 20N 68 13W
Accomac **10** 37 43N 75 40W
Accord **25** 42 10N 70 52W
Accord Pond .. **25** 42 10N 70 53W
Ackerman **15** 33 19N 89 11W
Ackley **16** 42 33N 93 3W
Acme **8** 40 8N 79 26W
Acworth **12** 34 4N 84 41W
Ada, *Minn.* **14** 47 18N 96 31W
Ada, *Ohio* **17** 40 46N 83 49W
Ada, *Okla.* **15** 34 46N 96 41W
Adams, *Mass.* . **9** 42 38N 73 7W
Adams, *N.Y.* .. **9** 43 49N 76 1W
Adams, *Wis.* .. **14** 43 57N 89 49W
Adams Mt. **20** 46 12N 121 30W
Adams Nat. Hist. Site ... **25** 42 15N 71 0W
Addison, *Ill.* ... **17** 41 55N 88 0W
Addison, *N.Y.* . **8** 42 1N 77 14W
Addyston **17** 39 8N 84 43W
Adel, *Ga.* **12** 31 8N 83 25W
Adel, *Iowa* **16** 41 37N 94 1W
Adelanto **21** 34 35N 117 22W
Adelphi **27** 39 0N 76 58W
Adirondack Mts. **9** 44 0N 74 0W
Adler Planetarium . **24** 41 52N 87 36W
Admiralty I. ... **32** 57 30N 134 30W
Adrian, *Ga.* ... **12** 32 33N 82 35W
Adrian, *Mich.* . **17** 41 54N 84 2W
Adrian, *Mo.* ... **16** 38 24N 94 21W
Adrian, *Tex.* ... **15** 35 16N 102 40W
Affton **16** 38 33N 90 20W
Afognak I. **32** 58 15N 152 30W
Afton, *N.Y.* **9** 42 14N 75 32W
Afton, *Wyo.* ... **18** 42 44N 110 56W
Agana .... **33** 13 28N 144 45 E
Agattu I. ...... **32** 52 25N 172 30 E
Agawam **9** 42 5N 72 37W
Agua Caliente Springs **21** 32 56N 116 19W
Aguadilla **32** 18 26N 67 10W
Aguanga **21** 33 27N 116 51W
Ahoskie **11** 36 17N 76 59W
Aiken **12** 33 34N 81 43W
Ailey **12** 32 11N 82 34W
Ainsworth **14** 42 33N 99 52W
Aitkin **14** 46 32N 93 42W
Ajo **19** 32 22N 112 52W
Akiak **32** 60 55N 161 13W
Akron, *Colo.* .. **14** 40 10N 103 13W
Akron, *Ind.* **17** 41 2N 86 1W
Akron, *Ohio* ... **8** 41 5N 81 31W
Akulurak **32** 62 40N 164 35W
Akun I. **32** 54 11N 165 32W
Akutan I. **32** 54 7N 165 55W
Alabama □ ... **11** 33 0N 87 0W
Alabama → . **2** 31 8N 87 57W
Alabaster **11** 33 15N 86 49W
Alachua **12** 29 47N 82 30W
Alameda, *Calif.* **30** 37 46N 122 15W
Alameda, *N. Mex.* **19** 35 11N 106 37W
Alameda Memorial State Beach Park **30** 37 45N 122 16W
Alamo, *Calif.* .. **30** 37 51N 122 2W
Alamo, *Ga.* ... **12** 32 9N 82 47W
Alamo, *Nev.* .. **21** 37 22N 115 10W
Alamo Crossing **21** 34 16N 113 33W
Alamogordo .. **19** 32 54N 105 57W
Alamosa **19** 37 28N 105 52W
Alapaha **12** 31 23N 83 13W
Alaska □ **32** 64 0N 154 0W
Alaska, G. of .. **32** 58 0N 145 0W
Alaska Peninsula ... **32** 56 0N 159 0W
Alaska Range . **32** 62 50N 151 0W
Alava, C. **18** 48 10N 124 44W
Albany, *Calif.* .. **30** 37 53N 122 17W
Albany, *Ga.* ... **12** 31 35N 84 10W
Albany, *Ind.* ... **17** 40 18N 85 14W
Albany, *Mo.* ... **16** 40 15N 94 20W
Albany, *N.Y.* .. **9** 42 39N 73 45W
Albany, *Oreg.* . **18** 44 38N 123 6W
Albany, *Tex.* .. **15** 32 44N 99 18W
Albany, *Wis.* .. **16** 42 43N 89 26W
Albemarle **11** 35 21N 80 11W
Albemarle Sd. . **11** 36 5N 76 0W
Albert Lea **14** 43 39N 93 22W
Albertson **23** 40 46N 73 38W
Albertville **11** 34 16N 86 13W
Albia **16** 41 2N 92 48W
Albion, *N.J.* ... **26** 39 46N 74 57W
Albion, *Ill.* **17** 38 23N 88 4W
Albion, *Ind.* ... **17** 41 24N 85 25W
Albion, *Mich.* .. **17** 42 15N 84 45W
Albion, *Nebr.* .. **14** 41 42N 98 0W
Albion, *Pa.* **8** 41 53N 80 22W
Albuquerque .. **19** 35 5N 106 39W
Alburg **9** 44 59N 73 18W
Alcatraz I. **30** 37 49N 122 25W
Alcoma **13** 27 54N 81 29W
Alcova **18** 42 34N 106 43W
Aldan **26** 39 55N 75 17W
Aldene **22** 40 39N 74 17W
Alder Pk. **20** 35 53N 121 22W
Aledo **16** 41 12N 90 45W
Alenuihaha Channel **32** 20 30N 156 0W
Aleutian Is. ... **32** 52 0N 175 0W
Aleutian Ra. ... **32** 55 0N 155 0W
Alexander, *Ga.* **12** 33 1N 81 53W
Alexander, *N. Dak.* **14** 47 51N 103 39W
Alexander Arch. **32** 56 0N 136 0W
Alexander City **12** 32 56N 85 58W
Alexandria, *Ind.* **17** 40 16N 85 41W
Alexandria, *Ky.* **17** 38 58N 84 23W
Alexandria, *La.* **15** 31 18N 92 27W
Alexandria, *Minn.* **14** 45 53N 95 22W
Alexandria, *Mo.* **16** 40 27N 91 28W
Alexandria, *S. Dak.* **14** 43 39N 97 47W
Alexandria, *Va.* **27** 38 49N 77 5W
Alexandria Bay **9** 44 20N 75 55W
Alexis **16** 41 4N 90 33W
Alford **12** 30 42N 85 24W
Alfred, *Maine* . **9** 43 29N 70 43W
Alfred, *N.Y.* ... **8** 42 16N 77 48W
Algoma **10** 44 36N 87 26W
Algona **16** 43 4N 94 14W
Algonac **8** 42 37N 82 32W
Alhambra, *Calif.* **31** 34 5N 118 7W
Alhambra, *Ill.* . **16** 38 52N 89 45W
Alice **15** 27 45N 98 5W
Aliceville **11** 33 8N 88 9W
Aliquippa **8** 40 37N 80 15W
All American Canal **19** 32 45N 115 15W
Allagash → .. **11** 47 5N 69 3W
Allakaket **32** 66 34N 152 39W
Allatoona L. ... **12** 34 10N 84 44W
Allegan **17** 42 32N 85 51W
Allegany **8** 42 6N 78 30W
Allegheny → **8** 40 27N 80 1W
Allegheny Mts. **2** 38 15N 80 10W
Allegheny Reservoir ... **8** 41 50N 79 0W
Allen Park **28** 42 14N 83 12W
Allendale, *N.J.* **22** 41 1N 74 9W
Allendale, *S.C.* **12** 33 1N 81 18W
Allentown, *N.Y.* **23** 40 47N 73 43W
Allentown, *Pa.* . **9** 40 37N 75 29W
Allerton, Pt. ... **25** 42 18N 70 52W
Alliance, *Nebr.* **14** 42 6N 102 52W
Alliance, *Ohio* . **8** 40 55N 81 6W
Allison **16** 42 45N 92 48W
Allison Park ... **29** 40 33N 79 56W
Allston **25** 42 21N 71 7W
Alma, *Ga.* **12** 31 33N 82 28W
Alma, *Kans.* ... **14** 39 1N 96 17W
Alma, *Mich.* ... **10** 43 23N 84 39W
Alma, *Nebr.* ... **14** 40 6N 99 22W
Almanor, L. ... **18** 40 14N 121 9W
Almon **12** 33 37N 83 56W
Almond **8** 42 19N 77 44W
Almonesson .. **26** 39 48N 75 5W
Almont **8** 42 55N 83 3W
Almonte **30** 37 53N 122 31W
Alpaugh **20** 35 53N 119 29W
Alpena **10** 45 4N 83 27W
Alpha **16** 41 12N 90 23W
Alpine, *N.J.* ... **22** 40 57N 73 57W
Alpine, *Ariz.* ... **19** 33 51N 109 9W
Alpine, *Calif.* .. **21** 32 50N 116 46W
Alpine, *Tex.* ... **15** 30 22N 103 40W
Alsip **24** 41 40N 87 44W
Alta Sierra **21** 35 42N 118 33W
Altadena **31** 34 11N 118 8W
Altamaha → . **12** 31 20N 81 20W
Altamont, *Ill.* .. **17** 39 4N 88 45W
Altamont, *N.Y.* **9** 42 43N 74 3W
Altavista **10** 37 6N 79 17W
Altha **12** 30 34N 85 8W
Alto **30** 37 54N 122 30W
Alton, *Ill.* **16** 38 53N 90 11W
Alton, *N.H.* **9** 43 27N 71 13W
Altoona, *Ala.* .. **12** 34 2N 86 20W
Altoona, *Iowa* . **16** 41 39N 93 28W
Altoona, *Pa.* ... **8** 40 31N 78 24W
Alturas **18** 41 29N 120 32W
Altus **15** 34 38N 99 20W
Alunite **21** 35 59N 114 55W
Alva **15** 36 48N 98 40W
Alvarado, *Calif.* **30** 37 35N 122 4W
Alvarado, *Tex.* . **15** 32 24N 97 13W
Alvin, *S.C.* **12** 33 22N 79 48W
Alvin, *Tex.* **15** 29 26N 95 15W
Alvord Desert . **18** 42 30N 118 25W
Alzada **14** 45 2N 104 25W
Amagansett ... **9** 40 59N 72 9W
Amanda Park . **20** 47 28N 123 55W
Amargosa → **21** 36 14N 116 51W
Amargosa Range **21** 36 20N 116 45W
Amarillo **15** 35 13N 101 50W
Amatignak I. .. **32** 51 16N 179 6W
Ambler **26** 40 9N 75 13W
Amboy, *Calif.* . **21** 34 33N 115 45W
Amboy, *Ill.* **16** 41 44N 89 20W
Ambridge **8** 40 36N 80 14W
Ambrose **12** 31 36N 83 1W
Ambrose Channel **22** 40 31N 73 50W
Amchitka I. ... **32** 51 32N 179 0 E
Amchitka Pass. **32** 51 30N 179 0W
Amelia City ... **12** 30 35N 81 28W
Amelia I. **12** 30 40N 81 25W
Amenia **9** 41 51N 73 33W
American Falls **18** 42 47N 112 51W
American Falls Reservoir ... **18** 42 47N 112 52W
American Fork **18** 40 23N 111 48W
American Samoa ■ ... **33** 14 20S 170 40W
Americus **12** 32 4N 84 14W
Ames **16** 42 2N 93 37W
Ames Hill **25** 42 38N 71 13W
Amesbury **9** 42 51N 70 56W
Amherst, *Mass.* **9** 42 23N 72 31W
Amherst, *N.Y.* . **8** 42 59N 78 48W
Amherst, *Ohio* **8** 41 24N 82 14W
Amidon **14** 46 29N 103 19W
Amite **15** 30 44N 90 30W
Amityville **23** 40 40N 73 23W
Amlia I. **32** 52 4N 173 30W
Ammon **18** 43 28N 111 58W
Amoret **16** 38 15N 94 35W
Amory **11** 33 59N 88 29W
Amsterdam ... **9** 42 56N 74 11W
Amukta I. **32** 52 30N 171 16W
Anaconda **18** 46 8N 112 57W
Anacortes **20** 48 30N 122 37W
Anacostia **27** 38 51N 76 59W
Anacostia River Park **27** 38 54N 76 57W
Anadarko **15** 35 4N 98 15W
Anaheim **21** 33 50N 117 55W
Anamosa **16** 42 7N 91 17W
Anchor Bay ... **20** 38 48N 123 34W
Anchorage **32** 61 13N 149 54W
Andalusia, *Pa.* . **26** 40 4N 74 58W
Andalusia, *Ala.* **11** 31 18N 86 29W
Anderson, *Calif.* **18** 40 27N 122 18W
Anderson, *Ind.* **17** 40 10N 85 41W
Anderson, *Mo.* **15** 36 39N 94 27W
Anderson, *S.C.* **11** 34 31N 82 39W
Andersonville . **12** 32 12N 84 9W
Andes **9** 42 12N 74 47W
Andover, *Mass.* **25** 42 39N 71 7W
Andover, *Maine* **9** 44 38N 70 45W
Andover, *N.J.* . **9** 40 59N 74 45W
Andover, *N.Y.* . **8** 42 10N 77 48W
Andover, *Ohio* **8** 41 36N 80 34W
Andreanof Is. . **32** 51 30N 176 0W
Andrews, *S.C.* . **11** 33 27N 79 34W
Andrews, *Tex.* . **15** 32 19N 102 33W
Andrews Air Force Base .. **27** 38 48N 76 52W
Androscoggin → **9** 43 58N 70 0W
Anegada I. **32** 18 45N 64 20W
Angel I. **30** 37 52N 122 25W
Angel Island State Park .. **30** 37 52N 122 25W
Angels Camp . **20** 38 4N 120 32W
Angleton **15** 29 10N 95 26W
Angola, *Ind.* ... **17** 41 38N 85 0W
Angola, *N.Y.* .. **8** 42 38N 79 2W
Angoon **32** 57 30N 134 35W
Aniak **32** 61 35N 159 32W
Animas → ... **19** 36 43N 108 13W
Anita **16** 41 27N 94 46W
Ankeny **16** 41 44N 93 36W
Ankona **13** 27 21N 80 17W
Ann, C. **9** 42 38N 70 35W
Ann Arbor **17** 42 17N 83 45W
Anna, *Ill.* **15** 37 28N 89 15W
Anna, *Ohio* ... **17** 40 24N 84 11W
Annadale **22** 40 32N 74 10W
Annalee Heights **27** 38 51N 77 10W
Annandale **27** 38 50N 77 11W
Annapolis **10** 38 59N 76 30W
Annette **32** 55 2N 131 35W
Anniston **12** 33 39N 85 50W
Annville **9** 40 20N 76 31W
Ansley **14** 41 18N 99 23W
Anson **15** 32 45N 99 54W
Ansonia, *Conn.* **9** 41 21N 73 5W
Ansonia, *Ohio* . **17** 40 13N 84 38W
Antero, Mt. ... **19** 38 41N 106 15W
Anthony, *Fla.* .. **13** 29 18N 82 7W
Anthony, *Kans.* **15** 37 9N 98 2W
Anthony, *N. Mex.* **19** 32 0N 106 36W
Anthony Chabot Regional Park **30** 37 46N 122 7W
Antigo **14** 45 9N 89 9W
Antioch **20** 38 1N 121 48W
Antlers **15** 34 14N 95 37W
Anton **15** 33 49N 102 10W
Antrim **8** 40 7N 81 21W
Antwerp, *N.Y.* . **9** 44 12N 75 37W
Antwerp, *Ohio* **17** 41 11N 84 45W
Anvik **32** 62 39N 160 13W
Anza **21** 33 35N 116 39W
Apache **15** 34 54N 98 22W
Apache Junction **19** 33 25N 111 33W
Apalachee B. .. **12** 30 0N 84 0W
Apalachicola .. **12** 29 43N 84 59W
Apalachicola → **12** 29 43N 84 58W
Apalachicola B. **12** 29 40N 85 0W
Apalachicola National Forest **12** 30 10N 85 0W
Apopka **13** 28 40N 81 31W
Apopka L. **13** 28 38N 81 38W
Apostle Is. **14** 47 0N 90 40W
Appalachian Mts. **2** 38 0N 80 0W
Apple Valley .. **21** 34 32N 117 14W
Appleton **10** 44 16N 88 25W
Appleton City . **16** 38 11N 94 2W
Appling **12** 33 33N 82 19W
Apshawa **22** 41 1N 74 22W
Arab **11** 34 19N 86 30W
Arabi **12** 31 50N 83 44W
Aragon **12** 34 2N 85 3W
Aransas Pass .. **15** 27 55N 97 9W
Arapahoe **14** 40 18N 99 54W
Arbuckle **20** 39 1N 122 3W
Arbuckle L. ... **13** 27 42N 81 24W
Arbutus **27** 39 15N 76 41W
Arcade, *Calif.* .. **21** 34 2N 118 15W
Arcade, *Ga.* ... **12** 34 5N 83 34W
Arcade, *N.Y.* .. **8** 42 32N 78 25W
Arcadia, *Calif.* . **31** 34 7N 118 1W
Arcadia, *Fla.* .. **11** 27 13N 81 52W
Arcadia, *Ind.* .. **17** 40 11N 86 1W
Arcadia, *Iowa* . **16** 42 5N 95 3W
Arcadia, *La.* ... **15** 32 33N 92 55W
Arcadia, *Pa.* ... **8** 40 47N 78 51W
Arcanum **17** 39 59N 84 33W
Arcata **18** 40 52N 124 5W
Archbald **9** 41 30N 75 32W
Archbold **17** 41 31N 84 18W
Archer **13** 29 32N 82 32W
Arches National Park **19** 38 45N 109 25W
Arco **18** 43 38N 113 18W

Bogota

Arcola 17 39 41N 88 19W
Arctic Village 32 68 8N 145 32W
Arden, Del. 26 39 48N 75 29W
Arden, Calif. 20 38 36N 121 33W
Arden, Nev. 21 36 1N 115 14W
Ardmore, Pa. 26 40 0N 75 17W
Ardmore, Okla. 15 34 10N 97 8W
Ardsley 23 41 0N 73 50W
Arecibo 32 18 29N 66 43W
Arena, Pt. 20 38 57N 123 44W
Arenzville 16 39 53N 90 22W
Argenta 17 39 59N 88 49W
Argonne Forest 24 41 42N 87 53W
Argos 17 41 14N 86 15W
Arguello, Pt. 21 34 35N 120 39W
Argus Pk. 21 35 52N 117 26W
Ariton 12 31 36N 85 43W
Arizona □ 19 34 0N 112 0W
Arkadelphia 15 34 7N 93 4W
Arkansas □ 15 35 0N 92 30W
Arkansas —► 2 33 47N 91 4W
Arkansas City 15 37 4N 97 2W
Arkport 8 42 24N 77 42W
Arkville 9 42 9N 74 37W
Arlington, Mass. 25 42 24N 71 10W
Arlington, Ga. 12 31 26N 84 44W
Arlington, N.Y. 9 41 42N 73 54W
Arlington, Oreg. 18 45 43N 120 12W
Arlington, S. Dak. 14 44 22N 97 8W
Arlington, Tex. 15 32 44N 97 7W
Arlington, Vt. 9 43 5N 73 9W
Arlington, Wash. 20 48 12N 122 8W
Arlington, Va. 27 38 53N 77 7W
Arlington Heights, Mass. 25 42 25N 71 10W
Arlington Heights, Ill. 24 42 5N 87 55W
Arlington Nat. Cemetery 27 38 52N 77 4W
Armour 14 43 19N 98 21W
Arnett 15 36 8N 99 46W
Arnold 20 38 15N 120 20W
Arnold Arboretum 25 42 18N 71 8W
Arrowhead, L. 21 34 16N 117 10W
Arroyo Grande 21 35 7N 120 35W
Artesia, Calif. 31 33 51N 118 4W
Artesia, N. Mex. 15 32 51N 104 24W
Arthur 17 39 43N 88 28W
Arundel Gardens 27 39 12N 76 37W
Arundel Village 27 39 13N 76 35W
Arvada, Colo. 14 39 48N 105 5W
Arvada, Wyo. 18 44 39N 106 8W
Arvin 21 35 12N 118 50W
Asbury Park 9 40 13N 74 1W
Ash Fork 19 35 13N 112 29W
Ash Grove 15 37 19N 93 35W
Asharoken 23 40 55N 73 21W
Ashburn, Ill. 24 41 45N 87 43W
Ashburn, Ga. 12 31 43N 83 39W
Ashburton, L. 27 39 19N 76 40W
Ashdown 15 33 40N 94 8W
Asheboro 11 35 43N 79 49W
Asherton 15 28 27N 99 46W
Asheville 11 35 36N 82 33W
Ashford 12 31 11N 85 14W
Ashland, Calif. 30 37 41N 122 7W
Ashland, Ala. 12 33 16N 85 50W
Ashland, Ill. 16 39 53N 90 1W
Ashland, Kans. 15 37 11N 99 46W
Ashland, Ky. 10 38 28N 82 38W
Ashland, Mont. 18 45 36N 106 16W
Ashland, Ohio 8 40 52N 82 19W
Ashland, Oreg. 18 42 12N 122 43W
Ashland, Pa. 9 40 45N 76 22W
Ashland, Va. 10 37 46N 77 29W
Ashland, Wis. 14 46 35N 90 53W
Ashley, Ill. 16 38 20N 89 11W
Ashley, Ind. 17 41 32N 85 4W
Ashley, N. Dak. 14 46 2N 99 22W
Ashley, Pa. 9 41 12N 75 55W
Ashokan Reservoir 9 41 56N 74 13W
Ashtabula 8 41 52N 80 47W
Ashton 18 44 4N 111 27W
Ashville, Ala. 12 33 50N 86 15W
Ashville, Fla. 12 30 37N 83 39W
Ashville, Pa. 8 40 34N 78 33W
Aspen 19 39 11N 106 49W
Aspermont 15 33 8N 100 14W
Assumption 16 39 31N 89 3W
Astatula 13 28 43N 81 44W
Aston Mills 26 39 52N 75 26W
Astoria, N.Y. 22 40 46N 73 55W
Astoria, Ill. 16 40 14N 90 21W
Astoria, Oreg. 20 46 11N 123 50W
Atascadero 20 35 29N 120 40W
Atchafalaya B. 15 29 25N 91 25W
Atchison 14 39 34N 95 7W
Atco 26 39 46N 74 53W
Athena 12 29 59N 83 30W
Athens, Ala. 11 34 48N 86 58W
Athens, Ga. 12 33 57N 83 23W
Athens, N.Y. 9 42 16N 73 49W
Athens, Ohio 10 39 20N 82 6W
Athens, Pa. 9 41 57N 76 31W
Athens, Tenn. 11 35 27N 84 36W
Athens, Tex. 15 32 12N 95 51W
Athol 9 42 36N 72 14W
Atka 32 52 5N 174 40W
Atkasuk 32 70 30N 157 20W
Atkinson, Ga. 12 31 13N 81 47W
Atkinson, Ill. 16 41 25N 90 1W
Atkinson, Nebr. 14 42 32N 98 59W
Atlanta, Ga. 12 33 45N 84 23W
Atlanta, Ill. 16 40 16N 89 14W
Atlanta, Mo. 16 39 54N 92 29W
Atlanta, Tex. 15 33 7N 94 10W
Atlantic 14 41 24N 95 1W
Atlantic Beach, N.Y. 23 40 35N 73 44W
Atlantic Beach, Fla. 12 30 20N 81 24W
Atlantic City 10 39 21N 74 27W
Atmore 11 31 2N 87 29W
Atoka 15 34 23N 96 8W
Atolia 21 35 19N 117 37W
Attalla 12 34 1N 86 6W
Attapulgus 12 30 45N 84 29W
Attica, Ind. 17 40 18N 87 15W
Attica, Ohio 8 41 4N 82 53W
Attleboro 9 41 57N 71 17W
Attu 32 52 56N 173 15 E
Atwater 20 37 21N 120 37W
Atwood 14 39 48N 101 3W
Au Sable 8 44 25N 83 20W
Au Sable —► 10 44 25N 83 20W
Au Sable Forks 9 44 27N 73 41W
Au Sable Pt. 8 44 20N 83 20W
Auberry 20 37 7N 119 29W
Auburn, Ala. 12 32 36N 85 29W
Auburn, Calif. 20 38 54N 121 4W
Auburn, Ill. 16 39 36N 89 45W
Auburn, Ind. 17 41 22N 85 4W
Auburn, Maine 11 44 6N 70 14W
Auburn, N.Y. 9 42 56N 76 34W
Auburn, Nebr. 14 40 23N 95 51W
Auburn, Pa. 9 40 36N 76 6W
Auburn, Wash. 20 47 18N 122 14W
Auburndale 25 42 20N 71 14W
Aucilla —► 12 30 5N 83 59W
Audubon, Pa. 26 40 7N 75 25W
Audubon, Iowa 16 41 43N 94 56W
Augusta, Ark. 15 35 17N 91 22W
Augusta, Ga. 12 33 28N 81 58W
Augusta, Ill. 16 40 14N 90 57W
Augusta, Kans. 15 37 41N 96 59W
Augusta, Ky. 17 38 47N 84 0W
Augusta, Maine 11 44 19N 69 47W
Augusta, Mont. 18 47 30N 112 24W
Aukum 20 38 34N 120 43W
Ault 14 40 35N 104 44W
Aurora, Colo. 14 39 44N 104 52W
Aurora, Ill. 17 41 45N 88 19W
Aurora, Mo. 15 36 58N 93 43W
Aurora, N.Y. 9 42 45N 76 42W
Aurora, Nebr. 14 40 52N 98 0W
Aurora, Ohio 8 41 21N 81 20W
Austin, Ill. 24 41 53N 87 45W
Austin, Ind. 17 38 45N 85 49W
Austin, Minn. 14 43 40N 92 58W
Austin, Nev. 18 39 30N 117 4W
Austin, Pa. 8 41 38N 78 6W
Austin, Tex. 15 30 17N 97 45W
Auxvasse 16 39 1N 91 54W
Ava, Ill. 16 37 53N 89 30W
Ava, Mo. 15 36 57N 92 40W
Avalon, Pa. 29 40 30N 80 4W
Avalon, Calif. 21 33 21N 118 20W
Avawatz Mts. 21 35 40N 116 30W
Avenal 20 36 0N 120 8W
Avenel, N.J. 22 40 34N 74 16W
Avenel, Md. 27 38 59N 76 59W
Avera 12 33 12N 82 32W
Avery 18 47 15N 115 49W
Avila Beach 21 35 11N 120 44W
Avis 8 41 11N 77 19W
Aviston 16 38 36N 89 36W
Avoca 8 42 25N 77 25W
Avon, Ill. 16 40 40N 90 26W
Avon, N.Y. 8 42 55N 77 45W
Avon Park 13 27 36N 81 31W
Avondale 24 41 56N 87 41W
Axson 12 31 17N 82 44W
Ayer 9 42 34N 71 35W
Aztec 19 36 49N 107 59W
Azusa 31 34 7N 117 54W

B

Babb 18 48 51N 113 27W
Babson Park 13 27 49N 81 32W
Babylon 23 40 42N 73 19W
Baconton 12 31 23N 84 10W
Bad —► 14 44 21N 100 22W
Bad Axe 8 43 48N 83 0W
Bad Lands 14 43 40N 102 10W
Baden 8 40 38N 80 14W
Badger 20 36 38N 119 1W
Badlands National Park 14 43 38N 102 56W
Bagdad, Calif. 21 34 35N 115 53W
Bagdad, Fla. 13 30 36N 87 2W
Baggs 18 41 2N 107 39W
Bagley 14 47 32N 95 24W
Bagnell Dam 16 38 14N 92 36W
Baha'i Temple 24 42 4N 87 41W
Bahamas ■ 2 24 0N 75 0W
Baileys Crossroads 27 38 50N 77 6W
Bainbridge, Ga. 12 30 55N 84 35W
Bainbridge, Ind. 17 39 46N 86 49W
Bainbridge, N.Y. 9 42 18N 75 29W
Bainbridge, Ohio 17 39 14N 83 16W
Bair I. 30 37 30N 122 13W
Baird Inlet 32 60 50N 164 18W
Baird Mts. 32 67 0N 160 0W
Baisley Pond 23 40 40N 73 47W
Baker, Calif. 21 35 16N 116 4W
Baker, Fla. 13 30 48N 86 41W
Baker, Mont. 14 46 22N 104 17W
Baker City 18 44 47N 117 50W
Baker Hill 12 31 47N 85 18W
Baker Mt. 18 48 50N 121 49W
Bakersfield, Calif. 21 35 23N 119 1W
Bakersfield, Vt. 9 44 45N 72 48W
Bala-Cynwyd 26 40 0N 75 15W
Balcones Escarpment 15 29 30N 99 15W
Bald Hill 25 42 38N 71 0W
Bald Knob 15 35 19N 91 34W
Baldpate Hill 25 42 42N 71 0W
Baldpate Pond 25 42 41N 71 0W
Baldwin, N.Y. 23 40 38N 73 37W
Baldwin, Pa. 29 40 23N 79 58W
Baldwin, Fla. 12 30 18N 81 59W
Baldwin, Mich. 10 43 54N 85 51W
Baldwin Hills 31 34 0N 118 21W
Baldwin Park 31 34 5N 117 57W
Baldwinsville 9 43 10N 76 20W
Baldy Mt. 18 48 9N 109 39W
Baldy Peak 19 33 54N 109 34W
Ballardvale 25 42 37N 71 9W
Ballinger 15 31 45N 99 57W
Ballston Spa 9 43 0N 73 51W
Balmorhea 15 30 59N 103 45W
Balston Spa 9 43 0N 73 52W
Baltimore, Md. 10 39 17N 76 37W
Baltimore, Ohio 8 39 51N 82 36W
Baltimore Highlands 27 39 14N 76 38W
Baltimore-Washington Int. Airport 27 39 11N 76 39W
Bamberg 12 33 18N 81 2W
Bangor, Maine 11 44 48N 68 46W
Bangor, Mich. 17 42 18N 86 7W
Bangor, Pa. 9 40 52N 75 13W
Banks 12 31 49N 85 51W
Banks L. 12 31 2N 83 6W
Banning 21 33 56N 116 53W
Bar Harbor 11 44 23N 68 13W
Baraboo 14 43 28N 89 45W
Baraga 14 46 47N 88 30W
Baranof I. 32 57 0N 135 0W
Barataria B. 15 29 20N 89 55W
Barberton 8 41 0N 81 39W
Barberville 13 29 11N 81 26W
Barbourville 11 36 52N 83 53W
Barcroft, L. 27 38 50N 77 9W
Bardstown 17 37 49N 85 28W
Baring 16 40 15N 92 12W
Barker 8 43 20N 78 33W
Barker Pt. 23 40 50N 73 44W
Barkley, L. 11 37 1N 88 14W
Barnesville 12 33 3N 84 9W
Barneveld 9 43 16N 75 14W
Barney 12 31 1N 83 31W
Barnhart 15 31 8N 101 10W
Barnsboro 26 39 45N 75 9W
Barnsville 14 46 43N 96 28W
Barnwell 12 33 15N 81 23W
Barques, Pt. Aux 8 44 4N 82 58W
Barre, Mass. 9 42 25N 72 6W
Barre, Vt. 9 44 12N 72 30W
Barren Is. 32 58 45N 152 0W
Barrineau Park 13 30 42N 87 26W
Barrington, N.J. 26 39 52N 75 3W
Barrington, R.I. 9 41 44N 71 18W
Barron 14 45 24N 91 51W
Barrow 32 71 18N 156 47W
Barrow Pt. 32 71 24N 156 29W
Barry 16 39 42N 91 2W
Barstow 21 34 54N 117 1W
Bartlesville 15 36 45N 95 59W
Bartlett 20 36 29N 118 2W
Barton 9 44 45N 72 11W
Bartonville 16 40 39N 89 39W
Bartow, Fla. 11 27 54N 81 50W
Bartow, Ga. 12 32 53N 82 29W
Barwick 12 30 54N 83 44W
Basin 18 44 23N 108 2W
Basinger 13 27 23N 81 2W
Bassett, Calif. 31 34 3N 117 59W
Bassett, Nebr. 14 42 35N 99 32W
Bastrop, La. 15 32 47N 91 55W
Bastrop, Tex. 15 30 7N 97 19W
Batavia, Ill. 17 41 51N 88 19W
Batavia, N.Y. 8 43 0N 78 11W
Batavia, Ohio 17 39 5N 84 11W
Batesburg 12 33 54N 81 33W
Batesville, Ark. 15 35 46N 91 39W
Batesville, Ind. 17 39 18N 85 13W
Batesville, Miss. 15 34 19N 89 57W
Batesville, Tex. 15 28 58N 99 37W
Bath, Maine 11 43 55N 69 49W
Bath, N.Y. 8 42 20N 77 19W
Bath, S.C. 12 33 31N 81 51W
Bath Beach 22 40 36N 74 0W
Baton Rouge 15 30 27N 91 11W
Battle Creek 17 42 19N 85 11W
Battle Ground 20 45 47N 122 32W
Battle Lake 14 46 17N 95 43W
Battle Mountain 18 40 38N 116 56W
Baudette 14 48 43N 94 36W
Baxley 12 31 47N 82 21W
Baxter, Iowa 16 41 49N 93 9W
Baxter, Minn. 14 46 21N 94 17W
Baxter Estates 23 40 50N 73 42W
Baxter Springs 15 37 2N 94 44W
Bay City, Mich. 10 43 36N 83 54W
Bay City, Tex. 15 28 59N 95 58W
Bay Farm I. 30 37 44N 122 14W
Bay Meadows Race Track 30 37 32N 122 17W
Bay Minette 11 30 53N 87 46W
Bay Park 23 40 37N 73 39W
Bay Ridge 22 40 37N 74 1W
Bay Ridge Channel 22 40 39N 74 1W
Bay St. Louis 15 30 19N 89 20W
Bay Shore Park 27 39 13N 76 25W
Bay Springs 15 31 59N 89 17W
Bay Village 29 41 29N 81 53W
Bayamón 32 18 24N 66 10W
Bayard, N. Mex. 19 32 46N 108 8W
Bayard, Nebr. 14 41 45N 103 20W
Bayfield 14 46 49N 90 49W
Bayonne 22 40 40N 74 6W
Bayou George 12 30 16N 85 33W
Bayport 13 28 32N 82 39W
Bayshore, Calif. 30 37 42N 122 24W
Bayshore, Fla. 13 26 43N 81 50W
Bayside 23 40 45N 73 46W
Baytown 15 29 43N 94 59W
Bayview 30 37 44N 122 23W
Bayville 23 40 54N 73 33W
Beach 14 46 58N 104 0W
Beach City 8 40 39N 81 35W
Beachmont 25 42 23N 70 59W
Beacon 9 41 30N 73 58W
Beacon Hill 12 29 55N 85 23W
Beals Cr. —► 15 32 10N 100 51W
Bear —►, Calif. 20 38 56N 121 36W
Bear —►, Utah 6 41 30N 112 8W
Bear Gulch Res. 30 37 26N 122 13W
Bear L. 18 41 59N 111 21W
Beardstown 16 40 1N 90 26W
Bearpaw Mts. 18 48 12N 109 30W
Beatrice 14 40 16N 96 45W
Beatty 20 36 54N 116 46W
Beaufort, N.C. 11 34 43N 76 40W
Beaufort, S.C. 12 32 26N 80 40W
Beaufort Sea 2 72 0N 140 0W
Beaumont 15 30 5N 94 6W
Beaver, Alaska 32 66 22N 147 24W
Beaver, Okla. 15 36 49N 100 31W
Beaver, Pa. 8 40 42N 80 19W
Beaver, Utah 19 38 17N 112 38W
Beaver —► 15 36 35N 99 30W
Beaver City 14 40 8N 99 50W
Beaver Dam 14 43 28N 88 50W
Beaver Falls 8 40 46N 80 20W
Beaver I. 10 45 40N 85 33W
Beavercreek 17 39 43N 84 11W
Beaverton 20 45 29N 122 48W
Beaverville 17 40 57N 87 39W
Becharof L. 32 57 56N 156 23W
Beck L. 24 42 4N 87 52W
Beckley 10 37 47N 81 11W
Bedford, Mass. 25 42 27N 71 15W
Bedford, Ind. 17 38 52N 86 29W
Bedford, Iowa 16 40 40N 94 44W
Bedford, Ky. 17 38 36N 85 19W
Bedford, Ohio 8 41 23N 81 32W
Bedford, Pa. 8 40 1N 78 30W
Bedford, Va. 10 37 20N 79 31W
Bedford Park, Ill. 24 41 46N 87 46W
Bedford Park, N.Y. 23 40 52N 73 52W
Bedford Stuyvesant 22 40 41N 73 56W
Bee Ridge 13 27 17N 82 29W
Beech Creek 8 41 5N 77 36W
Beech Fork —► 17 37 46N 85 41W
Beech Grove 17 39 44N 86 3W
Beecher 17 41 21N 87 38W
Beechey Point 32 70 27N 149 18W
Beeville 15 28 24N 97 45W
Bel Air 31 34 4N 118 27W
Belden 20 40 2N 121 17W
Belen 19 34 40N 106 46W
Belfair 20 47 27N 122 50W
Belfast, Maine 11 44 26N 69 1W
Belfast, N.Y. 8 42 21N 78 7W
Belfield 14 46 53N 103 12W
Belfry 18 45 9N 109 1W
Belgrade 18 45 47N 111 11W
Belhaven 11 35 33N 76 37W
Bell 12 29 45N 82 52W
Bell Gardens 31 33 58N 118 9W
Bellaire, N.Y. 23 40 42N 73 44W
Bellaire, Ohio 8 40 1N 80 45W
Belle 16 38 17N 91 43W
Belle-Chasse 15 29 51N 89 59W
Belle Fourche 14 44 40N 103 51W
Belle Fourche —► 14 44 26N 102 18W
Belle Glade 11 26 41N 80 40W
Belle Harbour 23 40 34N 73 51W
Belle Haven, Conn. 23 41 0N 73 37W
Belle Haven, Va. 27 38 46N 77 3W
Belle Isle 13 28 27N 81 21W
Belle Plaine 16 41 54N 92 17W
Belle Rive 17 38 14N 88 45W
Bellefontaine 17 40 22N 83 46W
Bellefonte, Del. 26 39 45N 75 30W
Bellefonte, Pa. 8 40 55N 77 47W
Bellerose 23 40 44N 73 42W
Belleview, Fla. 13 29 4N 82 3W
Belleview, Va. 27 38 57N 77 14W
Belleville, N.J. 22 40 48N 74 8W
Belleville, Ill. 16 38 31N 89 59W
Belleville, Kans. 14 39 50N 97 38W
Belleville, N.Y. 9 43 46N 76 10W
Bellevue, Pa. 29 40 29N 80 3W
Bellevue, Idaho 18 43 28N 114 16W
Bellevue, Iowa 16 42 16N 90 26W
Bellevue, Mich. 17 42 27N 85 1W
Bellevue, Nebr. 14 41 8N 95 53W
Bellevue, Ohio 8 41 17N 82 51W
Bellevue, Wash. 20 47 37N 122 12W
Bellflower, Calif. 31 33 53N 118 7W
Bellflower, Mo. 16 39 0N 91 21W
Bellingham 20 48 46N 122 29W
Bellmawr 26 39 52N 75 5W
Bellmore 23 40 39N 73 31W
Bellows Falls 9 43 8N 72 27W
Bells Lake 26 39 45N 75 3W
Bellville 13 32 9N 81 59W
Bellwood, Ill. 24 41 52N 87 53W
Bellwood, Pa. 8 40 36N 78 20W
Belmond 16 42 51N 93 37W
Belmont, Mass. 25 42 23N 71 10W
Belmont, Calif. 30 37 31N 122 17W
Belmont, N.Y. 8 42 14N 78 2W
Belmont Cragin 24 41 56N 87 45W
Belmont Harbor 24 41 56N 87 38W
Belmont Hills 26 40 1N 75 15W
Belmont Slough 30 37 32N 122 15W
Beloit, Kans. 14 39 28N 98 6W
Beloit, Wis. 16 42 31N 89 2W
Belpre 10 39 17N 81 34W
Belt 18 47 23N 110 55W
Belton 15 31 3N 97 28W
Belton L. 15 31 8N 97 32W
Beltsville 27 39 2N 76 54W
Beltsville Airport 27 39 1N 76 49W
Belvedere 30 37 52N 122 27W
Belvidere, Ill. 17 42 15N 88 50W
Belvidere, N.J. 9 40 50N 75 5W
Belzoni 15 33 11N 90 29W
Bement 17 39 55N 88 34W
Bemidji 14 47 28N 94 53W
Bemis Woods 24 41 49N 87 54W
Benavides 15 27 36N 98 25W
Bend 18 44 4N 121 19W
Benevolence 12 31 53N 84 44W
Benicia 20 38 3N 122 9W
Benjamin Franklin Br. 26 39 57N 75 8W
Benkelman 14 40 3N 101 32W
Bennettsville 11 34 37N 79 41W
Bennington, N.H. 9 43 0N 71 55W
Bennington, Vt. 9 42 53N 73 12W
Bensenville 24 41 57N 87 56W
Benson, Ariz. 19 31 58N 110 18W
Benson, Minn. 14 45 19N 95 36W
Bensonhurst 22 40 35N 73 59W
Benton, Ark. 15 34 34N 92 35W
Benton, Calif. 20 37 48N 118 32W
Benton, Ill. 16 38 0N 88 55W
Benton, Pa. 9 41 12N 76 23W
Benton Harbor 17 42 6N 86 27W
Bentonville 15 36 22N 94 13W
Berea 10 37 34N 84 17W
Beresford 14 43 5N 96 47W
Bergen 8 43 5N 77 57W
Bergenfield 22 40 55N 73 59W
Bergholz 8 40 31N 80 53W
Bering Sea 32 58 0N 171 0 E
Bering Strait 32 65 30N 169 0W
Berkeley, Ill. 24 41 53N 87 54W
Berkeley, Calif. 30 37 51N 122 16W
Berkeley Heights 22 40 40N 74 26W
Berkeley Hills 30 37 51N 122 14W
Berkley 28 42 29N 83 11W
Berkshire 9 42 19N 76 11W
Berlin, N.J. 26 39 47N 74 55W
Berlin, Ga. 12 31 4N 83 37W
Berlin, Md. 10 38 20N 75 13W
Berlin, N.H. 9 44 28N 71 11W
Berlin, N.Y. 9 42 42N 73 23W
Berlin, Wis. 10 43 58N 88 57W
Berlin L. 8 41 3N 81 0W
Bermuda ■ 2 32 45N 65 0W
Bernal Heights 30 37 44N 122 24W
Bernalillo 19 35 18N 106 33W
Bernardsville 9 40 43N 74 34W
Berne 17 40 39N 84 57W
Berrien Springs 17 41 57N 86 20W
Berry 17 38 31N 84 23W
Berrydale 13 30 53N 87 3W
Berryessa L. 20 38 31N 122 6W
Berryville 15 36 22N 93 34W
Berthold 14 48 19N 101 44W
Berthoud 14 40 19N 105 5W
Berthpage 23 40 45N 73 29W
Berwick 9 41 3N 76 14W
Berwyn, Ill. 24 41 50N 87 47W
Berwyn, Pa. 26 40 2N 75 26W
Berwyn Heights 27 38 59N 76 55W
Bessemer, Ala. 11 33 24N 86 58W
Bessemer, Mich. 14 46 29N 90 3W
Bessemer, Pa. 8 40 59N 80 30W
Bethany, Ill. 17 39 39N 88 45W
Bethany, Mo. 16 40 16N 94 2W
Bethayres 26 40 7N 75 4W
Bethel, Alaska 32 60 48N 161 45W
Bethel, Conn. 9 41 22N 73 25W
Bethel, Maine 9 44 25N 70 47W
Bethel, Ohio 17 38 58N 84 5W
Bethel, Vt. 9 43 50N 72 38W
Bethel Park 29 40 19N 80 1W
Bethera 12 33 12N 79 47W
Bethesda 27 38 59N 77 6W
Bethlehem 9 40 37N 75 23W
Bethlehem Steel Plant 27 39 13N 76 29W
Bethpage State Park 23 40 45N 73 25W
Bettendorf 16 41 32N 90 30W
Beulah, Mich. 10 44 38N 86 6W
Beulah, N. Dak. 14 47 16N 101 47W
Beverley 24 41 42N 87 39W
Beverley Hills 13 28 56N 82 28W
Beverly, Mass. 25 42 34N 70 53W
Beverly, N.J. 26 40 3N 74 55W
Beverly Glen 31 34 6N 118 26W
Beverly Harbor 25 42 32N 70 51W
Beverly Hills, Calif. 31 34 5N 118 24W
Beverly Hills, Mich. 28 42 31N 83 15W
Beverly Municipal Airport 25 42 36N 70 55W
Bicknell 17 38 47N 87 19W
Biddeford 11 43 30N 70 28W
Bieber 18 41 7N 121 8W
Big —► 16 38 28N 90 37W
Big Bear City 21 34 16N 116 51W
Big Bear Lake 21 34 15N 116 56W
Big Belt Mts. 18 46 30N 111 25W
Big Bend National Park 15 29 20N 103 5W
Big Black —► 15 32 3N 91 4W
Big Blue —►, Ind. 17 39 12N 85 56W
Big Blue —►, Kans. 14 39 35N 96 34W
Big Creek 20 37 11N 119 14W
Big Cypress Indian Reservation 13 26 20N 81 10W
Big Cypress National Preserve 13 26 0N 81 10W
Big Cypress Swamp, Fla. 11 26 12N 81 10W
Big Cypress Swamp, Fla. 13 26 15N 81 30W
Big Falls 14 48 12N 93 48W
Big Fork —► 14 48 31N 93 43W
Big Horn Mts. = Bighorn Mts. 18 44 30N 107 30W
Big Lake 15 31 12N 101 28W
Big Moose 9 43 49N 74 58W
Big Muddy —► 16 38 0N 89 0W
Big Muddy Cr. —► 14 48 8N 104 36W
Big Pine, Calif. 20 37 10N 118 17W
Big Pine, Fla. 13 24 40N 81 21W
Big Piney 18 42 32N 110 7W
Big Rapids 10 43 42N 85 29W
Big Run 8 40 57N 78 55W
Big Sable Pt. 10 44 3N 86 1W
Big Sandy 18 48 11N 110 7W
Big Sandy —► 10 38 25N 82 36W
Big Sandy Cr. —► 14 38 7N 102 29W
Big Satilla —► 12 31 27N 82 3W
Big Sioux —► 14 42 29N 96 27W
Big Spring 15 32 15N 101 28W
Big Stone City 14 45 18N 96 28W
Big Stone Gap 11 36 52N 82 47W
Big Stone L. 14 45 30N 96 35W
Big Sur 20 36 15N 121 48W
Big Timber 18 45 50N 109 57W
Biggs 20 39 25N 121 43W
Bighorn 18 46 10N 107 27W
Bighorn —► 18 46 10N 107 28W
Bighorn L. 18 44 55N 108 15W
Bighorn Mts. 18 44 30N 107 30W
Bikini Atoll 33 12 0N 167 30 E
Billerica 25 42 33N 71 16W
Billings 18 45 47N 108 30W
Biloxi 15 30 24N 88 53W
Bingham 11 45 3N 69 53W
Binghamton 9 42 6N 75 55W
Birds 17 38 50N 87 40W
Birdseye 17 38 19N 86 42W
Birmingham, Mich. 28 42 33N 83 13W
Birmingham, Ala. 11 33 31N 86 48W
Birmingham, Iowa 16 40 53N 91 57W
Bisbee 19 31 27N 109 55W
Biscayne B. 11 25 40N 80 12W
Biscayne National Park 13 25 25N 80 12W
Bishop, Calif. 20 37 22N 118 24W
Bishop, Ga. 12 33 49N 83 26W
Bishop, Tex. 15 27 35N 97 48W
Bismarck, Mo. 16 37 46N 90 38W
Bismarck, N. Dak. 14 46 48N 100 47W
Bison 14 45 31N 102 28W
Bithlo 13 28 33N 81 6W
Bitter Creek 18 41 33N 108 33W
Bitterroot —► 18 46 52N 114 7W
Bitterroot Range 18 46 0N 114 20W
Bitterwater 20 36 23N 121 0W
Biwabik 14 47 32N 92 21W
Bixby 15 35 57N 95 53W
Black —►, Ariz. 19 33 44N 110 13W
Black —►, Ark. 15 35 38N 91 20W
Black —►, Mich. 8 42 59N 82 27W
Black —►, N.Y. 9 43 59N 76 4W
Black —►, Wis. 14 43 57N 91 22W
Black Forest 14 39 0N 104 43W
Black Hills 14 44 0N 103 45W
Black L., Mich. 10 45 28N 84 16W
Black L., N.Y. 9 44 31N 75 36W
Black Mesa 15 36 58N 102 58W
Black Range 19 33 15N 107 50W
Black River Falls 14 44 18N 90 51W
Black Warrior —► 11 32 32N 87 51W
Blackburn, Mt. 32 61 44N 143 26W
Blackfoot 18 43 11N 112 21W
Blackfoot —► 18 46 52N 113 53W
Blackfoot River Reservoir 18 43 0N 111 43W
Blackman 13 30 56N 86 38W
Blackriver 8 44 46N 83 17W
Blacksburg 10 37 14N 80 25W
Blackshear 12 31 18N 82 14W
Blackshear L. 12 31 51N 83 56W
Blackstone 10 37 4N 78 0W
Blackville 12 33 22N 81 16W
Blackwater —►, Fla. 13 30 36N 87 2W
Blackwater —►, Mo. 16 38 59N 92 59W
Blackwell 15 36 48N 97 17W
Blackwells Corner 21 35 37N 119 47W
Blackwood 26 39 47N 75 4W
Bladensburg 27 38 55N 76 55W
Blain 8 40 20N 77 31W
Blaine, Minn. 14 45 10N 93 13W
Blaine, Wash. 20 48 59N 122 45W
Blair 14 41 33N 96 8W
Blairsden 20 39 47N 120 37W
Blairsville 8 40 26N 79 16W
Blake Pt. 14 48 11N 88 25W
Blakely, Ga. 12 31 23N 84 56W
Blakely, Pa. 9 41 28N 75 37W
Blakesburg 16 40 58N 92 38W
Blanca Peak 2 37 35N 105 29W
Blanchardville 16 42 49N 89 52W
Blanchester 17 39 17N 83 59W
Blanco 15 30 6N 98 25W
Blanco, C. 2 42 51N 124 34W
Blanding 19 37 37N 109 29W
Blandinsville 16 40 33N 90 52W
Blasdell 8 42 48N 78 50W
Blenheim 26 39 48N 75 4W
Bliss, Idaho 18 42 56N 114 57W
Bliss, N.Y. 8 42 34N 78 15W
Blissfield, Mich. 17 41 50N 83 52W
Blissfield, Ohio 8 40 24N 81 58W
Blitchton 12 32 12N 81 26W
Block I. 9 41 11N 71 35W
Block Island Sd. 9 41 15N 71 40W
Blockton 16 40 37N 94 29W
Bloomer 14 45 6N 91 29W
Bloomfield, N.J. 22 40 48N 74 12W
Bloomfield, Ind. 17 39 1N 86 57W
Bloomfield, Iowa 16 40 45N 92 25W
Bloomfield, Ky. 17 37 55N 85 19W
Bloomfield, N. Mex. 19 36 43N 107 59W
Bloomfield, Nebr. 14 42 36N 97 39W
Bloomingburg 17 39 36N 83 24W
Bloomingdale 22 41 0N 74 19W
Bloomington, Ill. 16 40 28N 89 0W
Bloomington, Ind. 17 39 10N 86 32W
Bloomington, Minn. 14 44 50N 93 17W
Bloomington, Wis. 16 42 53N 90 55W
Bloomsburg 9 41 0N 76 27W
Bloomsbury 27 39 15N 76 44W
Blossburg 8 41 41N 77 4W
Blountstown 12 30 27N 85 3W
Blue —► 17 38 11N 86 19W
Blue Cypress L. 13 27 44N 80 45W
Blue Earth 14 43 38N 94 6W
Blue Hills Reservation 25 42 13N 71 5W
Blue Island 24 41 40N 87 40W
Blue Mesa Reservoir 19 38 28N 107 20W
Blue Mound 16 39 42N 89 7W
Blue Mountain Lake 9 43 52N 74 30W
Blue Mts., Maine 9 44 50N 70 35W
Blue Mts., Oreg. 18 45 15N 119 0W
Blue Mts., Pa. 9 40 30N 76 30W
Blue Rapids 14 39 41N 96 39W
Blue Ridge Mts. 2 36 30N 80 15W
Blue Springs 16 39 1N 94 17W
Bluefield 10 37 15N 81 17W
Bluff 19 37 17N 109 33W
Bluffs 16 39 45N 90 32W
Bluffton, Ga. 12 31 31N 84 52W
Bluffton, Ind. 17 40 44N 85 11W
Bluffton, Ohio 17 40 54N 83 54W
Bluffton, S.C. 12 32 14N 80 52W
Bluford 17 38 20N 88 45W
Blunt 14 44 31N 99 59W
Blunt Pt. 30 37 51N 122 25W
Bly 18 42 24N 121 3W
Blythe, Calif. 21 33 37N 114 36W
Blythe, Ga. 12 33 17N 82 12W
Blytheville 15 35 56N 89 55W
Boalsburg 8 40 46N 77 47W
Boardman 8 41 2N 80 40W
Boardwalk 23 40 34N 73 49W
Boca Grande 13 26 45N 82 16W
Boca Raton 11 26 21N 80 5W
Bodega Bay 20 38 20N 123 3W
Boerne 15 29 47N 98 44W
Bogalusa 15 30 47N 89 52W
Bogota 15 33 28N 95 13W
Bogota 22 40 52N 74 2W

Boise

Boise 18 43 37N 116 13W
Boise City 15 36 44N 102 31W
Bolingbroke . . . 12 32 57N 83 48W
Bolivar, *Mo.* . . . 15 37 37N 93 25W
Bolivar, *N.Y.* . . 8 42 4N 78 10W
Bolivar, *Tenn.* . 15 35 12N 89 0W
Bolton Landing 9 43 32N 73 35W
Bonaire 12 32 33N 83 36W
Bonham 15 33 35N 96 11W
Bonifay 12 30 47N 85 41W
Bonita, Pt. 30 37 48N 122 31W
Bonita Springs 13 26 21N 81 47W
Bonne Terre . . 16 37 55N 90 33W
Bonneau 12 33 16N 79 58W
Bonners Ferry . 18 48 42N 116 19W
Bonsall 21 33 16N 117 14W
Booker 15 36 27N 100 32W
Boone, *Iowa* . . 16 42 4N 93 53W
Boone, *N.C.* . . . 11 36 13N 81 41W
Booneville, *Ark.* 15 35 8N 93 55W
Booneville,
Miss. 11 34 39N 88 34W
Boonton 22 40 54N 74 24W
Boonton Res. . . 22 40 53N 74 24W
Boonville, *Calif.* 20 39 1N 123 22W
Boonville, *Ind.* . 17 38 3N 87 16W
Boonville, *Mo.* . 16 38 58N 92 44W
Boonville, *N.Y.* . 9 43 29N 75 20W
Booth Corner . 26 39 50N 75 29W
Boothwyn 26 39 49N 75 26W
Borah Peak . . . 18 44 8N 113 47W
Borden Springs 12 33 56N 85 28W
Borger 15 35 39N 101 24W
Boron 21 35 0N 117 39W
Borough Park . 22 40 38N 73 59W
Borrego Springs 21 33 15N 116 23W
Boscobel 16 43 8N 90 42W
Bosque Farms . 19 34 53N 106 40W
Bossier City . . . 15 32 31N 93 44W
Boston, *Ga.* . . . 12 30 47N 83 47W
Boston, *Mass.* . 9 42 22N 71 4W
Boston B. 25 42 22N 70 55W
Boston Harbor 25 42 20N 70 58W
Boston Hill 25 42 38N 71 5W
Boston Mts. . . . 15 35 42N 93 15W
Bostwick, *Fla.* . 12 29 46N 81 38W
Bostwick, *Ga.* . 12 33 44N 83 31W
Boswell, *Ind.* . . 17 40 31N 87 23W
Boswell, *Pa.* . . . 8 40 10N 79 2W
Bosworth 16 39 28N 93 20W
Bottineau 14 48 50N 100 27W
Boulder, *Colo.* . 14 40 1N 105 17W
Boulder, *Mont.* 18 46 14N 112 7W
Boulder City . . 21 35 59N 114 50W
Boulder Creek . 20 37 7N 122 7W
Boulder Dam =
Hoover Dam 21 36 1N 114 44W
Boundary 32 64 4N 141 6W
Boundary Peak 20 37 51N 118 21W
Bountiful 18 40 53N 111 53W
Bourbeuse → . 16 38 24N 90 53W
Bourbon 17 41 18N 86 7W
Bouse 21 33 56N 114 0W
Bovill 18 46 51N 116 24W
Bowbells 14 48 48N 102 15W
Bowdle 14 45 27N 99 39W
Bowdon 12 33 32N 85 15W
Bowdon
Junction 12 33 40N 85 9W
Bowie, *Ariz.* . . . 19 32 19N 109 29W
Bowie, *Tex.* . . . 15 33 34N 97 51W
Bowleys
Quarters 27 39 20N 76 24W
Bowling Green,
Fla. 13 27 38N 81 50W
Bowling Green,
Ky. 10 36 59N 86 27W
Bowling Green,
Mo. 16 39 21N 91 12W
Bowling Green,
Ohio 17 41 23N 83 39W
Bowman,
N. Dak. 14 46 11N 103 24W
Bowman, *S.C.* . 12 33 21N 80 41W
Boxford State
Forest 25 42 39N 71 2W
Boyce 15 31 23N 92 40W
Boyd 12 30 11N 83 37W
Boykin 12 31 6N 84 41W
Boyle Heights . 31 34 1N 118 12 E
Boyne City 10 45 13N 85 1W
Boynton Beach 11 26 32N 80 4W
Boysen
Reservoir . . . 18 43 25N 108 11W
Bozeman 18 45 41N 111 2W
Brackettville . . 15 29 19N 100 25W
Braddock 29 40 24N 79 51W
Bradenton 11 27 30N 82 34W
Bradford, *Ill.* . . 16 41 11N 89 39W
Bradford, *Ohio* 17 40 8N 84 27W
Bradford, *Pa.* . . 8 41 58N 78 38W
Bradford, *Vt.* . . 9 43 59N 72 9W
Bradley, *Ark.* . . 15 33 6N 93 39W
Bradley, *Calif.* . 20 35 52N 120 48W
Bradley, *Fla.* . . 13 27 48N 81 59W
Bradley, *Ill.* . . . 17 41 9N 87 52W
Brady 15 31 9N 99 20W
Brainerd 14 46 22N 94 12W
Braintree 25 42 12N 71 0W
Branchville . . . 12 33 15N 80 49W
Brandenburg . . 17 38 0N 86 10W
Brandon, *Fla.* . . 13 27 56N 82 17W
Brandon, *Vt.* . . 9 43 48N 73 4W
Brandywine . . 26 39 49N 75 32W
Branford, *Conn.* 9 41 17N 72 49W
Branford, *Fla.* . 12 29 58N 82 56W
Branson 15 36 39N 93 13W
Brantley 12 31 35N 86 16W
Brasher Falls . . 9 44 49N 74 47W
Brasstown Bald 11 34 53N 83 49W
Bratt 13 30 58N 87 26W
Brattleboro . . . 9 42 51N 72 34W
Bravo del Norte,
Rio = Grande,
Rio → 2 25 58N 97 9W
Brawley 21 32 59N 115 31W
Braymer 16 39 35N 93 48W
Brazil 17 39 32N 87 8W
Brazos → 15 28 53N 95 23W
Breakheart
Reservation . 25 42 28N 71 1W
Breckenridge,
Colo. 18 39 29N 106 3W
Breckenridge,
Minn. 14 46 16N 96 35W
Breckenridge,
Mo. 16 39 46N 93 48W
Breckenridge,
Tex. 15 32 45N 98 54W
Breeds Pond . . 25 42 28N 70 58W
Breezy Pt. 22 40 33N 73 56W
Bremen 12 33 43N 85 9W
Bremerton 20 47 34N 122 38W
Brenham 15 30 10N 96 24W
Brent 11 32 56N 87 10W
Brentwood, *Pa.* 29 40 22N 79 59W
Brentwood,
Calif. 20 37 56N 121 42W
Brentwood, *N.Y.* 9 40 47N 73 15W
Brentwood Park 31 34 3N 118 29W
Breton Sd. 15 29 35N 89 15W
Brevard 11 35 14N 82 44W
Brewer 11 44 48N 68 46W
Brewer, Mt. . . . 20 36 44N 118 28W
Brewer I. 30 37 33N 122 16W
Brewster, *N.Y.* . 9 41 23N 73 37W
Brewster, *Ohio* 8 40 43N 81 36W
Brewster, *Wash.* 18 48 6N 119 47W
Brewton, *Ala.* . . 11 31 7N 87 4W
Brewton, *Ga.* . . 12 32 36N 82 48W
Bridesburg 26 39 59N 75 4W
Bridgeboro 12 31 24N 83 59W
Bridgehampton 9 40 56N 72 19W
Bridgeport, *Ill.* . 24 41 50N 87 38W
Bridgeport, *Pa.* 26 40 6N 75 21W
Bridgeport,
Calif. 20 38 15N 119 14W
Bridgeport,
Conn. 9 41 11N 73 12W
Bridgeport,
Nebr. 14 41 40N 103 6W
Bridgeport, *Tex.* 15 33 13N 97 45W
Bridger 18 45 18N 108 55W
Bridgeton 10 39 26N 75 14W
Bridgeview . . . 24 41 45N 87 48W
Bridgeville 29 21 0N 80 6W
Bridgewater,
Mass. 9 41 59N 70 58W
Bridgewater,
N.Y. 9 42 53N 75 15W
Bridgman 17 41 57N 86 33W
Bridgton 9 44 3N 70 42W
Brier Cr. → . . . 12 32 44N 81 26W
Brigham City . . 18 41 31N 112 1W
Brighton, *Colo.* 14 39 59N 104 49W
Brighton, *Fla.* . 13 27 14N 81 6W
Brighton, *Ill.* . . 16 39 2N 90 8W
Brighton, *Iowa* 16 41 10N 91 49W
Brighton, *N.Y.* . 8 43 8N 77 34W
Brighton Park . 24 41 48N 87 41W
Brighton
Seminole
Indian
Reservation . 13 27 0N 81 15W
Brightwood . . . 27 38 57N 77 1W
Brilliant 8 40 15N 80 39W
Brimfield 16 40 50N 89 53W
Brinkley 15 34 53N 91 12W
Brinnon 20 47 41N 122 54W
Brinson 12 30 59N 84 44W
Briones Hills . . 30 37 56N 122 8W
Briones
Regional Park 30 37 55N 122 8W
Briones Res. . . 30 37 55N 122 11W
Brisbane 30 37 40N 122 23W
Bristol, *Pa.* . . . 26 40 6N 74 53W
Bristol, *Conn.* . 9 41 40N 72 57W
Bristol, *Fla.* . . 12 30 26N 84 59W
Bristol, *R.I.* . . . 9 41 40N 71 16W
Bristol, *Tenn.* . . 11 36 36N 82 11W
Bristol B. 32 58 0N 160 0W
Bristol L. 19 34 23N 116 50W
Bristow 15 35 50N 96 23W
Britt 16 43 6N 93 48W
Britton 14 45 48N 97 45W
Broad →, *Ga.* 12 33 59N 82 39W
Broad →, *S.C.* 11 34 1N 81 4W
Broad Axe 26 40 8N 75 14W
Broad Sd. 25 42 23N 70 56W
Broadalbin 9 43 4N 74 12W
Broadhurst . . . 12 31 28N 81 55W
Broadmoor . . . 30 37 41N 122 29W
Broadus 14 45 27N 105 25W
Broadview 24 41 51N 87 52W
Brockport 8 43 13N 77 56W
Brockton 9 42 5N 71 1W
Brockway, *Mont.* 14 47 18N 105 45W
Brockway, *Pa.* . 8 41 15N 78 47W
Brocton 8 42 23N 79 26W
Brodhead 16 42 37N 89 22W
Brodhead, Mt. . 8 41 39N 77 47W
Brogan 18 44 15N 117 31W
Broken Arrow . 15 36 3N 95 48W
Broken Bow,
Nebr. 14 41 24N 99 38W
Broken Bow,
Okla. 15 34 2N 94 44W
Broken Bow
Lake 15 34 9N 94 40W
Bronaugh 16 37 41N 94 28W
Bronson, *Fla.* . . 13 29 27N 82 39W
Bronson, *Mich.* 17 41 52N 85 12W
Bronwood 12 31 50N 84 22W
Bronx Zoo 23 40 50N 73 51W
Bronxville 23 40 56N 73 49W
Brook Park . . . 29 41 24N 81 48W
Brookfield, *Ill.* . 24 41 48N 87 50W
Brookfield, *Mo.* 16 39 47N 93 4W
Brookhaven, *Pa.* 26 39 52N 75 23W
Brookhaven,
Miss. 15 31 35N 90 26W
Brookings, *Oreg.* 18 42 3N 124 17W
Brookings,
S. Dak. 14 44 19N 96 48W
Brooklandville . 27 39 25N 76 40W
Brooklet 12 32 23N 81 40W
Brookline 25 42 19N 71 8W
Brooklyn, *Md.* . 27 39 13N 76 36W
Brooklyn, *N.Y.* . 22 40 37N 73 57W
Brooklyn, *Ohio* 29 41 26N 81 44W
Brooklyn, *Iowa* 16 41 44N 92 27W
Brooklyn Park . 16 45 6N 93 23W
Brookmont 27 38 57N 77 7W
Brooks I. 30 37 53N 122 21W
Brooks Range . 32 68 0N 152 0W
Brookston 17 40 36N 86 52W
Brooksville, *Fla.* 11 28 33N 82 23W
Brooksville, *Ky.* 17 38 41N 84 4W
Brookville, *N.Y.* 23 40 48N 73 33W
Brookville, *Ind.* 17 39 25N 85 1W
Brookville, *Pa.* . 8 41 10N 79 5W
Broomall 26 39 58N 75 22W
Brosewere B. . . 23 40 37N 73 40W
Brothers 18 43 49N 120 36W
Broughton 17 37 56N 88 27W
Brown City 8 43 13N 82 59W
Brownfield 15 33 11N 102 17W
Browning, *Ill.* . . 16 40 8N 90 22W
Browning, *Mo.* . 16 40 3N 93 12W
Browning, *Mont.* 18 48 34N 113 1W
Brownsburg . . 17 39 51N 86 24W
Brownstown . . 17 38 53N 86 3W
Brownsville,
Oreg. 18 44 24N 122 59W
Brownsville, *Pa.* 8 40 1N 79 53W
Brownsville,
Tenn. 15 35 36N 89 16W
Brownsville,
Tex. 15 25 54N 97 30W
Brownville 9 44 0N 75 59W
Brownwood . . . 15 31 43N 98 59W
Broxton 12 31 38N 82 53W
Broyhill Park . . 27 38 52N 77 12W
Bruce 12 30 28N 85 58W
Bruin 8 41 3N 79 43W
Brundidge 12 31 43N 85 49W
Bruneau 18 42 53N 115 48W
Bruneau → . . . 18 42 56N 115 57W
Brunswick, *Ga.* 12 31 10N 81 30W
Brunswick,
Maine 11 43 55N 69 58W
Brunswick, *Md.* 10 39 19N 77 38W
Brunswick, *Mo.* 16 39 26N 93 8W
Brunswick, *Ohio* 8 41 14N 81 51W
Brush 14 40 15N 103 37W
Brush Hill 25 42 15N 71 22W
Brushton 9 44 50N 74 31W
Bryan, *Ohio* . . . 17 41 28N 84 33W
Bryan, *Tex.* . . . 15 30 40N 96 22W
Bryce Canyon
National Park 19 37 30N 112 10W
Bryn Athyn . . . 26 40 8N 75 3W
Bryn Mawr . . . 26 40 1N 75 19W
Bryson City . . . 11 35 26N 83 27W
Buchanan, *Ga.* . 12 33 48N 85 11W
Buchanan, *Mich.* 17 41 50N 86 22W
Buchanan, L. . . 15 30 45N 98 25W
Buchon, Pt. . . . 20 35 15N 120 54W
Buck Hill Falls . 9 41 11N 75 16W
Buckeye 19 33 22N 112 35W
Buckeye Lake . 8 39 55N 82 29W
Buckhannon . . 10 39 0N 80 8W
Buckland,
Alaska 32 65 59N 161 8W
Buckland, *Ohio* 17 40 37N 84 16W
Buckley 17 40 36N 88 2W
Bucklin, *Kans.* . 15 37 33N 99 38W
Bucklin, *Mo.* . . 16 39 47N 92 53W
Bucks L. 20 39 54N 121 12W
Bucyrus 17 40 48N 82 59W
Buellton 21 34 37N 120 12W
Buena Park . . . 31 33 51N 118 1W
Buena Vista,
Calif. 30 37 45N 122 26W
Buena Vista,
Colo. 19 38 51N 106 8W
Buena Vista, *Ga.* 12 32 19N 84 31W
Buena Vista, *Va.* 10 37 44N 79 21W
Buena Vista
Lake Bed . . . 21 35 12N 119 18W
Buffalo, *Mo.* . . 16 37 39N 93 6W
Buffalo, *N.Y.* . . 8 42 53N 78 53W
Buffalo, *Okla.* . 15 36 50N 99 38W
Buffalo, *S. Dak.* 14 45 35N 103 33W
Buffalo, *Wyo.* . 18 44 21N 106 42W
Buford 11 34 10N 84 0W
Buhl 18 42 36N 114 46W
Buldir I. . . . . . . 32 52 21N 175 56 E
Bull Shoals L. . . 15 36 22N 92 35W
Bullard 12 32 38N 83 30W
Bullhead City . . 21 35 8N 114 32W
Bunker Hill, *Ill.* . 16 39 3N 89 57W
Bunker Hill, *Ind.* 17 40 40N 86 6W
Bunkie 15 30 57N 92 11W
Burbank, *Ill.* . . 24 41 44N 87 46W
Burbank, *Calif.* 31 34 12N 118 18W
Burien 20 47 28N 122 21W
Burkburnett . . . 15 34 6N 98 34W
Burkettsville . . 18 42 32N 113 48W
Burlingame . . . 30 37 34N 122 20W
Burlington,
Mass. 25 42 30N 71 13W
Burlington, *N.J.* 26 40 4N 74 53W
Burlington
Colo. 14 39 18N 102 16W
Burlington, *Ill.* . 17 42 3N 88 33W
Burlington, *Iowa* 16 40 49N 91 14W
Burlington,
Kans. 14 38 12N 95 45W
Burlington, *Ky.* 17 39 2N 84 43W
Burlington, *N.C.* 11 36 6N 79 26W
Burlington, *Vt.* . 9 44 29N 73 12W
Burlington,
Wash. 20 48 28N 122 20W
Burlington, *Wis.* 10 42 41N 88 17W
Burnet 15 30 45N 98 14W
Burney 18 40 53N 121 40W
Burnham, *Ill.* . . 24 41 38N 87 32W
Burnham, *Pa.* . 8 40 38N 77 34W
Burnham Park
Harbor 24 41 51N 87 36W
Burns 18 43 35N 119 3W
Burnsville 14 44 47N 93 17W
Burnt Paw 32 67 2N 142 43W
Burr Ridge 24 41 46N 87 54W
Burton, *Mich.* . 17 43 0N 83 40W
Burton, *Ohio* . . 8 41 28N 81 8W
Burton, *S.C.* . . . 11 32 25N 80 45W
Burwell 14 41 47N 99 8W
Bushnell 13 28 40N 82 7W
Bushwick 23 40 41N 73 54W
Bustleton 26 40 4N 75 2W
Butler, *N.J.* . . . 22 40 59N 74 20W
Butler, *Ga.* 12 32 33N 84 14W
Butler, *Ind.* . . . 17 41 26N 84 52W
Butler, *Ky.* 17 38 47N 84 22W
Butler, *Mo.* . . . 16 38 16N 94 20W
Butler, *Pa.* 8 40 52N 79 54W
Butte, *Mont.* . . 18 46 0N 112 32W
Butte, *Nebr.* . . . 14 42 58N 98 51W
Butte Creek → 20 39 12N 121 56W
Buttonwillow . . 21 35 24N 119 28W
Butts Corner . . 27 38 46N 77 19W
Buzzards B. . . . 9 41 45N 70 37W
Buzzards Bay . . 9 41 44N 70 37W
Byberry 26 40 6N 74 59W
Byers 14 39 43N 104 14W
Byesville 8 39 58N 81 32W
Bylas 19 33 8N 110 7W
Byron, *Ga.* 12 32 39N 83 46W
Byron, *Ill.* 16 42 8N 89 15W

C

Cabazon 21 33 55N 116 47W
Cabery 17 41 0N 88 12W
Cabin John . . . 27 38 58N 77 10W
Cabin John
Regional Park 27 39 0N 77 10W
Cabinet Mts. . . 18 48 0N 115 30W
Cabool 15 37 7N 92 6W
Cabot, Mt. 9 44 30N 71 25W
Cache Cr. → . . 20 38 42N 121 42W
Caddo 15 34 7N 96 16W
Cades 12 33 47N 79 47W
Cadillac 10 44 15N 85 24W
Cadiz, *Calif.* . . . 21 34 30N 115 28W
Cadiz, *Ohio* . . . 8 40 22N 81 0W
Cadiz L. 19 34 18N 115 24W
Cadley 12 33 32N 82 40W
Cadwell 12 32 20N 83 3W
Caguas 32 18 14N 66 2W
Cahuenga Pk. . 31 34 8N 118 19 E
Cairo, *Ga.* 12 30 52N 84 13W
Cairo, *Ill.* 15 37 0N 89 11W
Cairo, *N.Y.* 9 42 18N 74 0W
Calais 11 45 11N 67 17W
Calcasieu L. . . . 15 29 55N 93 18W
Calcutta 8 40 40N 80 34W
Caldwell, *N.J.* . 22 40 50N 74 19W
Caldwell, *Idaho* 18 43 40N 116 41W
Caldwell, *Kans.* 15 37 2N 97 37W
Caldwell, *Tex.* . 15 30 32N 96 42W
Caledonia, *Mo.* 16 37 45N 90 46W
Caledonia, *N.Y.* 8 42 58N 77 51W
Calexico 21 32 40N 115 30W
Calf Harbour . . 23 40 59N 73 37W
Calf I. 25 42 20N 70 53W
Calhoun 11 34 30N 84 57W
Calhoun Falls . 12 34 6N 82 36W
Caliente 19 37 37N 114 31W
California, *Mo.* 16 38 38N 92 34W
California, *Pa.* . 8 40 4N 79 54W
California □ . . . 20 37 30N 119 30W
California, Univ.
of 30 37 52N 122 16W
California City . 21 35 10N 117 55W
California Hot
Springs 21 35 51N 118 41W
California Inst.
of Tech. 31 34 8N 118 8W
California State
Univ., *Calif.* . 31 34 4N 118 10W
California State
Univ., *Calif.* . 30 37 39N 122 6W
Calipatria 21 33 8N 115 31W
Calistoga 20 38 35N 122 35W
Callahan 12 30 34N 81 50W
Callaway 12 30 8N 85 36W
Callender 16 42 22N 94 17W
Callicoon 9 41 46N 75 3W
Calmar 16 43 11N 91 52W
Caloosahatchee →
. . . . 13 26 31N 82 1W
Calpella 20 39 14N 123 12W
Calpine 20 39 40N 120 27W
Calumet, L. . . . 24 41 40N 87 35W
Calumet City . . 24 41 36N 87 32W
Calumet Harbor 24 41 43N 87 30W
Calumet Park . . 24 41 40N 87 39W
Calverton 27 39 3N 76 56W
Calwa 20 36 42N 119 46W
Camak 12 33 27N 82 39W
Camanche 16 41 47N 90 15W
Camanche
Reservoir . . . 20 38 14N 121 1W
Camarillo 21 34 13N 119 2W
Camas 20 45 35N 122 24W
Camas Valley . . 18 43 2N 123 40W
Cambria 20 35 34N 121 5W
Cambria Heights 23 40 41N 73 44W
Cambridge,
Mass. 25 42 23N 71 7W
Cambridge, *Ill.* . 16 41 18N 90 12W
Cambridge,
Iowa 16 41 54N 93 32W
Cambridge,
Minn. 14 45 34N 93 13W
Cambridge, *N.Y.* 9 43 2N 73 22W
Cambridge,
Nebr. 14 40 17N 100 10W
Cambridge,
Ohio 8 40 2N 81 35W
Cambridge City 17 39 49N 85 10W
Cambridge Res. 25 42 24N 71 16W
Cambridge
Springs 8 41 48N 80 4W
Camden, *N.J.* . . 26 39 56N 75 7W
Camden, *Ala.* . . 11 31 59N 87 17W
Camden, *Ark.* . . 15 33 35N 92 50W
Camden, *Maine* 11 44 13N 69 4W
Camden, *N.Y.* . . 9 43 20N 75 45W
Camden, *Ohio* . 17 39 38N 84 39W
Camden, *S.C.* . . 11 34 16N 80 36W
Camden, B. . . . 32 70 30N 145 0W
Camdenton . . . 16 38 1N 92 45W
Cameron, *Ariz.* . 19 35 53N 111 25W
Cameron, *La.* . . 15 29 48N 93 20W
Cameron, *Mo.* . 16 39 44N 94 14W
Cameron, *S.C.* . 12 33 34N 80 43W
Cameron, *Tex.* . 15 30 51N 96 59W
Camilla 12 31 14N 84 12W
Camino 20 38 44N 120 41W
Cammal 8 41 24N 77 28W
Camp Hill, *Ala.* . 12 32 48N 85 39W
Camp Hill, *Pa.* . 8 40 14N 76 55W
Camp Nelson . 21 36 8N 118 39W
Camp Pendleton 21 33 16N 117 23W
Camp Point . . . 16 40 3N 91 4W
Camp Springs . 27 38 48N 76 55W
Camp Verde . . 19 34 34N 111 51W
Camp Wood . . 15 29 40N 100 1W
Campbell, *Calif.* 20 37 17N 121 57W
Campbell, *Ohio* 8 41 5N 80 37W
Campbellsburg 17 38 39N 86 16W
Campbellsville 10 37 21N 85 20W
Campbellton . . 12 30 57N 85 24W
Campton, *Fla.* . 13 30 53N 86 31W
Campton, *Ga.* . . 12 33 52N 83 43W
Campton, *Ky.* . . 17 37 44N 83 33W
Camptonville . . 20 39 27N 121 3W
Camptown 9 41 44N 76 14W
Campville 12 29 40N 82 7W
Canaan 9 42 2N 73 20W
Canadian 15 35 55N 100 23W
Canadian → . . 15 35 28N 95 3W
Canadys 12 33 3N 80 37W
Canajoharie . . . 9 42 54N 74 35W
Canal Point . . . 13 26 52N 80 38W
Canandaigua . . 8 42 54N 77 17W
Canandaigua L. 8 42 47N 77 19W
Canarsie 23 40 38N 73 53W
Canaseraga . . . 8 42 27N 77 45W
Canaveral, C. . . 11 28 27N 80 32W
Canaveral
National
Seashore . . . 13 28 28N 80 34W
Canby, *Calif.* . . 18 41 27N 120 52W
Canby, *Minn.* . . 14 44 43N 96 16W
Canby, *Oreg.* . . 20 45 16N 122 42W
Cando 14 48 32N 99 12W
Canisteo 8 42 16N 77 36W
Canisteo → . . . 8 42 7N 77 8W
Cannelton 17 37 55N 86 45W
Cannon Ball → 14 46 20N 100 38W
Cannonsville
Reservoir . . . 9 42 4N 75 22W
Canoe Brook
Res. 22 40 45N 74 21W
Canon City . . . 14 38 27N 105 14W
Canoochee → . 12 31 59N 81 19W
Cantil 21 35 18N 117 58W
Canton, *Mass.* . 25 42 10N 71 8W
Canton, *Ga.* . . . 11 34 14N 84 29W
Canton, *Ill.* . . . 16 40 33N 90 2W
Canton, *Miss.* . . 15 32 37N 90 2W
Canton, *Mo.* . . . 16 40 8N 91 32W
Canton, *N.Y.* . . . 9 44 36N 75 10W
Canton, *Ohio* . . 8 40 48N 81 23W
Canton, *Pa.* . . . 8 41 39N 76 51W
Canton, *S. Dak.* 14 43 18N 96 35W
Canton L. 15 36 6N 98 35W
Cantonment . . 13 30 37N 87 20W
Canutillo 19 31 55N 106 36W
Canyon 15 34 59N 101 55W
Canyonlands
National Park 19 38 15N 110 0W
Canyonville . . . 18 42 56N 123 17W
Capac 8 43 1N 82 56W
Cape Canaveral 13 28 24N 80 36W
Cape Charles . . 10 37 16N 76 1W
Cape Coral 11 26 33N 81 57W
Cape Fear → . . 11 33 53N 78 1W
Cape Girardeau 15 37 19N 89 32W
Cape May 10 38 56N 74 56W
Cape May Point 10 38 56N 74 58W
Cape Vincent . . 9 44 8N 76 20W
Capitan 19 33 35N 105 35W
Capitol Heights 27 38 52N 76 55W
Capitol Reef
National Park 19 38 15N 111 10W
Capitola, *Calif.* . 20 36 59N 121 57W
Capitola, *Fla.* . . 12 30 27N 84 5W
Captain Harbour 23 40 59N 73 37W
Captiva 13 26 31N 82 11W
Carbondale,
Colo. 18 39 24N 107 13W
Carbondale, *Ill.* 16 37 44N 89 13W
Carbondale, *Pa.* 9 41 35N 75 30W
Cardiff-by-the-
Sea 21 33 1N 117 17W
Carey, *Idaho* . . 18 43 19N 113 57W
Carey, *Ohio* . . . 17 40 57N 83 23W
Caribou 11 46 52N 68 1W
Carle Place . . . 23 40 44N 73 35W
Carlin 18 40 43N 116 7W
Carlinville 16 39 17N 89 53W
Carlisle, *Mass.* . 25 42 31N 71 20W
Carlisle, *Ky.* . . . 17 38 19N 84 1W
Carlisle, *Pa.* . . . 8 40 12N 77 12W
Carlsbad, *Calif.* 21 33 10N 117 21W
Carlsbad,
N. Mex. 15 32 25N 104 14W
Carlsbad
Caverns
National Park 15 32 10N 104 35W
Carlstadt 22 40 50N 74 6W
Carlyle Res. . . . 16 38 37N 89 21W
Carmel, *Ind.* . . . 17 39 59N 86 8W
Carmel, *N.Y.* . . . 9 41 26N 73 41W
Carmel-by-the-
Sea 20 36 33N 121 55W
Carmel Valley . 20 36 29N 121 43W
Carmi 17 38 5N 88 10W
Carmichael . . . 20 38 38N 121 19W
Carnation 20 47 39N 121 55W
Carnegie, *Pa.* . . 29 40 24N 80 5W
Carnegie, *Ga.* . . 12 31 39N 84 47W
Carnegie Hall . 22 40 45N 73 59W
Carney 27 39 23N 76 31W
Caro 10 43 29N 83 24W
Carol City 11 25 56N 80 16W
Caroline Is. . . . 33 8 0N 150 0 E
Carpentersville 17 42 6N 88 17W
Carpinteria . . . 21 34 24N 119 31W
Carrabelle 12 29 51N 84 40W
Carrington 14 47 27N 99 8W
Carrizo Cr. → . 15 36 55N 103 55W
Carrizo Springs 15 28 31N 99 52W
Carrizozo 19 33 38N 105 53W
Carroll 16 42 4N 94 52W
Carroll I. 27 39 19N 76 20W
Carroll Park . . 27 39 16N 76 38W
Carrollton, *Ga.* . 12 33 35N 85 5W
Carrollton, *Ill.* . 16 39 18N 90 24W
Carrollton, *Ky.* . 17 38 41N 85 11W
Carrollton, *Mo.* 16 39 22N 93 30W
Carrollton, *Ohio* 8 40 34N 81 5W
Carson, *Calif.* . . 31 33 48N 118 17W
Carson, *N. Dak.* 14 46 25N 101 34W
Carson → 20 39 45N 118 40W
Carson City,
Mich. 17 43 11N 84 51W
Carson City,
Nev. 20 39 10N 119 46W
Carson Sink . . . 18 39 50N 118 25W
Carteret 22 40 34N 74 13W
Cartersville . . . 12 34 10N 84 48W
Carthage, *Ark.* . 16 37 46N 89 5W
Carthage, *Ill.* . . 16 40 25N 91 8W
Carthage, *Mo.* . 15 37 11N 94 19W
Carthage, *N.Y.* . 10 43 59N 75 37W
Carthage, *Tex.* . 15 32 9N 94 20W
Caruthersville . 15 36 11N 89 39W
Cary 11 35 47N 78 46W
Casa Grande . . 19 32 53N 111 45W
Cascade, *Idaho* 18 44 31N 116 2W
Cascade, *Iowa* . 16 42 18N 91 1W
Cascade, *Mont.* 18 47 16N 111 42W
Cascade Locks 20 45 40N 121 54W
Cascade Ra. . . . 2 47 0N 121 30W
Cascade
Reservoir . . . 18 44 32N 116 3W
Casco B. 11 43 45N 70 0W
Casmalia 21 34 50N 120 32W
Casper 18 42 51N 106 19W
Cass Lake 14 47 23N 94 37W
Cassadaga 8 42 20N 79 19W
Casselton 14 46 54N 97 13W
Cassopolis 17 41 55N 86 1W
Cassville, *Mo.* . . 15 36 41N 93 52W
Cassville, *Wis.* . 16 42 43N 90 59W
Castaic 21 34 30N 118 38W
Castalia 8 41 24N 82 49W
Castile 8 42 38N 78 3W
Castle Dale . . . 18 39 13N 111 1W
Castle Rock,
Colo. 14 39 22N 104 51W
Castle Rock,
Wash. 20 46 17N 122 54W
Castleton 9 43 37N 73 11W
Castleton
Corners 22 40 36N 74 8W
Castorland 9 43 53N 75 31W
Castro Valley . . 30 37 41N 122 5W
Castroville 20 36 46N 121 45W
Catalina 19 32 30N 110 50W
Cataula 12 32 39N 84 52W
Cathlamet 20 46 12N 123 23W
Catlettsburg . . 10 38 25N 82 36W
Catlin 17 40 4N 87 42W
Catonsville 27 39 16N 76 43W
Catonsville
Manor 27 39 17N 76 44W
Catskill 9 42 14N 73 52W
Catskill Mts. . . 9 42 10N 74 25W
Cattaraugus . . . 8 42 22N 78 52W
Cattle Hill 30 37 36N 122 27W
Caumsett State
Park 23 40 55N 73 27W
Cavalier 14 48 48N 97 37W
Cave Creek . . . 19 33 50N 111 57W
Cave Spring . . . 12 34 6N 85 20W
Cayce 12 33 59N 81 4W
Cayey 32 18 7N 66 10W
Cayuga, *Ind.* . . . 17 39 57N 87 28W
Cayuga, *N.Y.* . . 9 42 54N 76 44W
Cayuga L. 9 42 41N 76 41W
Cazenovia 9 42 56N 75 51W
Cecil 12 31 3N 83 24W
Cedar → 16 41 17N 91 21W
Cedar City 19 37 41N 113 4W
Cedar Creek
Reservoir . . . 15 32 11N 96 4W
Cedar Falls,
Iowa 16 42 32N 92 27W
Cedar Falls,
Wash. 20 47 25N 121 45W
Cedar Grove,
N.J. 22 40 50N 74 13W
Cedar Grove,
Ind. 17 39 22N 84 56W
Cedar Grove
Res. 22 40 51N 74 12W
Cedar I. 23 40 38N 73 22W
Cedar Knolls . . 22 40 49N 74 27W
Cedar Lake . . . 17 41 22N 87 26W
Cedar Point . . . 17 41 44N 83 21W
Cedar Rapids . . 16 41 59N 91 40W
Cedarhurst 23 40 37N 73 43W
Cedartown 12 34 1N 85 15W
Cedarville, *Ill.* . . 16 42 23N 89 38W
Cedarville, *Ohio* 17 39 44N 83 49W
Celina 17 40 33N 84 35W
Center, *Ga.* 12 34 3N 83 23W
Center, *N. Dak.* 14 47 7N 101 18W
Center, *Tex.* . . . 15 31 48N 94 11W
Center Hill 13 28 38N 82 3W
Center Point . . . 12 32 12N 91 46W
Center Square . 26 39 46N 75 22W
Centerburg 8 40 18N 82 42W
Centerport 23 40 53N 73 22W
Centerton 26 39 59N 74 53W
Centerville,
Calif. 20 36 44N 119 30W
Centerville, *Iowa* 16 40 44N 92 52W
Centerville,
Mich. 17 41 55N 85 32W
Centerville, *Pa.* 8 40 3N 79 59W
Centerville,
Tenn. 11 35 47N 87 28W
Centerville, *Tex.* 15 31 16N 95 59W
Central City,
Colo. 18 39 48N 105 31W
Central City, *Ky.* 10 37 18N 87 7W
Central City,
Nebr. 14 41 7N 98 0W
Central Park . . 22 40 47N 73 58W
Central Point . . 18 42 23N 122 55W
Central Square 9 43 17N 76 9W
Centralhatchee 12 33 22N 85 6W
Centralia, *Ill.* . . 16 38 32N 89 8W
Centralia, *Mo.* . 16 39 13N 92 8W
Centralia, *Wash.* 20 46 43N 122 58W
Centre 12 34 9N 85 41W
Centre City . . . 26 39 46N 75 31W
Centre I. 23 40 54N 73 31W
Century 13 30 58N 87 16W
Ceres 20 37 35N 120 57W
Cerro de Punta,
Mt. 32 18 10N 67 0W
Cerro Gordo . . 17 39 53N 88 44W
Chabot, L. 30 37 43N 122 6W
Chaco → 19 36 46N 108 39W
Chadds Ford . . 26 39 52N 75 35W
Chadron 14 42 50N 103 0W
Chagrin Falls . . 8 41 26N 81 24W
Chaires 12 30 26N 84 7W
Chalfant 20 37 32N 118 21W
Challis 18 44 30N 114 14W
Chalmette 15 29 56N 89 58W
Chama 19 36 54N 106 35W
Chamberlain . . 14 43 49N 99 20W
Chamberlain L. . 11 46 14N 69 19W
Chambers 19 35 11N 109 26W
Chambersburg 10 39 56N 77 40W

Custer

Chamblee 12 33 53N 84 18W
Chamois 16 38 41N 91 46W
Champaign ... 17 40 7N 88 15W
Champion 8 41 19N 80 51W
Champlain 9 44 59N 73 27W
Champlain, L. . 9 44 40N 73 20W
Chandalar 32 67 30N 148 35W
Chandeleur Is. . 15 29 55N 88 57W
Chandeleur Sd. 15 29 55N 89 0W
Chandler, *Ariz.* 19 33 18N 111 50W
Chandler, *Okla.* 15 35 42N 96 53W
Channel Is. ... 21 33 40N 119 15W
Channel Islands National Park 21 33 30N 119 0W
Channing 15 35 41N 102 20W
Chanute 15 37 41N 95 27W
Chapel Hill 11 35 55N 79 4W
Chapin 16 39 46N 90 24W
Chaplinville ... 25 42 42N 70 54W
Chappell 14 41 6N 102 28W
Chappells 12 34 11N 81 52W
Chardon 8 41 35N 81 12W
Charing 12 32 28N 84 22W
Chariton 16 41 1N 93 19W
Chariton → ... 16 39 19N 92 58W
Charleroi 8 40 9N 79 57W
Charles 12 32 8N 84 50W
Charles, C. ... 2 37 7N 75 58W
Charles City ... 16 43 4N 92 41W
Charles Lee Tinden Regional Park 30 37 53N 122 14W
Charles Town . 10 39 17N 77 52W
Charleston, *N.Y.* 22 40 32N 74 14W
Charleston, *Ill.* . 17 39 30N 88 10W
Charleston, *Miss.* 15 34 1N 90 4W
Charleston, *Mo.* 15 36 55N 89 21W
Charleston, *S.C.* 12 32 46N 79 56W
Charleston, *W. Va.* 10 38 21N 81 38W
Charleston Peak 21 36 16N 115 42W
Charlestown, *Mass.* 25 42 22N 71 4W
Charlestown, *Ind.* 17 38 27N 85 40W
Charlestown, *N.H.* 9 43 14N 72 25W
Charlevoix 10 45 19N 85 16W
Charlotte, *Mich.* 17 42 34N 84 50W
Charlotte, *N.C.* 11 35 13N 80 51W
Charlotte, *Vt.* .. 9 44 19N 73 14W
Charlotte Amalie 32 18 21N 64 56W
Charlotte Harbor 11 26 50N 82 10W
Charlottesville . 10 38 2N 78 30W
Charlton 14 40 59N 93 20W
Chateaugay 9 44 56N 74 5W
Chatham, *Ill.* .. 24 41 45N 87 36W
Chatham, *N.J.* . 22 40 44N 74 23W
Chatham, *Alaska* 32 57 30N 135 0W
Chatham, *Ill.* .. 16 39 40N 89 42W
Chatham, *N.Y.* . 9 42 21N 73 36W
Chatsworth 17 40 45N 88 18W
Chattahoochee 12 30 42N 84 51W
Chattahoochee → 12 30 54N 84 57W
Chattanooga .. 11 35 3N 85 19W
Chaumont 9 44 4N 76 8W
Chautauqua L. . 8 42 10N 79 24W
Chazy 9 44 53N 73 26W
Cheaha Mt. ... 12 33 29N 85 49W
Chebanse 17 41 0N 87 54W
Cheboygan ... 10 45 39N 84 29W
Checotah 15 35 28N 95 31W
Chefornak 32 60 13N 164 12W
Chehalis 20 46 40N 122 58W
Chehalis → .. 20 46 57N 123 50W
Chelan 18 47 51N 120 1W
Chelan, L. 18 48 11N 120 30W
Chelmsford ... 25 42 35N 71 20W
Chelsea, *Mass.* 25 42 23N 71 1W
Chelsea, *Pa.* ... 26 39 51N 75 27W
Chelsea, *Mich.* 17 42 19N 84 1W
Chelsea, *Vt.* ... 9 43 59N 72 27W
Cheltenham ... 26 40 3N 75 6W
Chemult 18 43 14N 121 47W
Chenango Forks 9 42 15N 75 51W
Cheney 18 47 30N 117 35W
Chenoa 17 40 45N 88 43W
Chequamegon B. 14 46 40N 90 30W
Cheraw 11 34 42N 79 53W
Cherokee, *Iowa* 14 42 45N 95 33W
Cherokee, *Okla.* 15 36 45N 98 21W
Cherokee Village 15 36 17N 91 30W
Cherokees, Grand Lake O' The 15 36 28N 95 2W
Cherry Hill 26 39 54N 75 1W
Cherry Valley, *Calif.* 21 33 59N 116 57W
Cherry Valley, *N.Y.* 9 42 48N 74 45W
Cherryland 30 37 40N 122 7W
Chesaco Park . 27 39 18N 76 30W
Chesapeake .. 10 36 50N 76 17W
Chesapeake B. 2 38 0N 76 10W
Chester, *Pa.* ... 26 39 50N 75 23W
Chester, *Calif.* . 18 40 19N 121 14W
Chester, *Ga.* .. 12 32 24N 83 9W
Chester, *Ill.* ... 16 37 55N 89 49W
Chester, *Mont.* 18 48 31N 110 58W
Chester, *S.C.* .. 11 34 43N 81 12W
Chester, *Vt.* ... 9 43 16N 72 36W
Chester, *W. Va.* 8 40 37N 80 34W
Chester Heights 26 39 53N 75 27W
Chestertown ... 9 43 40N 73 48W
Chestnut 26 40 4N 75 13W
Chestnut Hill .. 25 42 19N 71 10W
Chestnut Ridge 8 40 20N 79 10W
Chesuncook L. 11 46 0N 69 21W
Cheverly 27 38 55N 76 54W
Cheviot 17 39 10N 84 37W
Chevy Chase .. 27 38 59N 77 4W
Chevy Chase View 27 39 0N 77 4W
Chewelah 18 48 17N 117 43W
Cheyenne, *Okla.* 15 35 37N 99 40W
Cheyenne, *Wyo.* 14 41 8N 104 49W
Cheyenne → . 14 44 41N 101 18W
Cheyenne Wells 14 38 49N 102 21W
Cheyney 26 39 55N 75 31W
Chicago 17 41 53N 87 38W
Chicago, Univ. of 24 41 47N 87 35W
Chicago Harbor 24 41 52N 87 36W
Chicago Heights 17 41 30N 87 38W
Chicago Lawn . 24 41 47N 87 40W
Chicago-Midway Airport 24 41 47N 87 45W
Chicago-O'Hare Int. Airport .. 24 41 58N 87 53W
Chicago Ridge . 24 41 41N 87 46W
Chicago Sanitary and Ship Canal .. 24 41 49N 87 45W
Chickasha 15 35 3N 97 58W
Chico 20 39 44N 121 50W
Chicopee 9 42 9N 72 37W
Chiefland 13 29 29N 82 52W
Chignik 32 56 18N 158 24W
Childersburg .. 12 33 16N 86 21W
Childress 15 34 25N 100 13W
Chilhowee 16 38 36N 93 51W
Chillicothe, *Ill.* . 16 40 55N 89 29W
Chillicothe, *Mo.* 16 39 48N 93 33W
Chillicothe, *Ohio* 10 39 20N 82 59W
Chillum 27 38 57N 76 58W
Chilton 10 44 2N 88 10W
Chimayo 19 36 0N 105 56W
China Basin ... 30 37 46N 122 22W
China Lake ... 21 35 44N 117 37W
Chinati Peak .. 15 29 57N 104 29W
Chincoteague . 10 37 56N 75 23W
Chinle 19 36 9N 109 33W
Chino 21 34 1N 117 41W
Chino Valley .. 19 34 45N 112 27W
Chinook 18 48 35N 109 14W
Chipilly Woods 24 42 8N 87 48W
Chipley 12 30 47N 85 32W
Chipola → .. 12 30 1N 85 5W
Chippewa → . 14 44 25N 92 5W
Chippewa Falls 14 44 56N 91 24W
Chiputneticook Lakes 11 45 35N 67 35W
Chiricahua Peak 19 31 51N 109 18W
Chirikof I. 32 55 50N 155 40W
Chisholm 14 47 29N 92 53W
Chisos Mts. ... 15 29 5N 103 15W
Chitina 32 61 31N 144 26W
Chloride 21 35 25N 114 12W
Chocolate Mts. 21 33 15N 115 15W
Choctawatchee → 12 30 25N 86 8W
Choke Canyon L. 15 28 30N 98 20W
Chokoloskee .. 13 25 49N 81 22W
Cholame 20 35 44N 120 18W
Choteau 18 47 49N 112 11W
Chowchilla ... 20 37 7N 120 16W
Chrisman 17 39 48N 87 41W
Chrome 22 40 34N 74 13W
Chubbuck 18 42 55N 112 28W
Chugach Mts. . 32 60 45N 147 0W
Chugiak 32 61 24N 149 29W
Chuginadak I. . 32 52 50N 169 45W
Chugwater ... 14 41 46N 104 50W
Chula, *Ga.* ... 12 31 33N 83 32W
Chula, *Mo.* ... 16 39 55N 93 29W
Chula Vista .. 21 32 39N 117 5W
Churdan 16 42 9N 94 29W
Churubusco .. 17 41 14N 85 19W
Chuska Mts. .. 19 36 15N 108 50W
Cibola 21 33 17N 114 42W
Cicero 24 41 51N 87 44W
Cima 21 35 14N 115 30W
Cimarron, *Kans.* 15 37 48N 100 21W
Cimarron, *N. Mex.* 15 36 31N 104 55W
Cimarron → . 15 36 10N 96 17W
Cincinnati, *Iowa* 16 40 38N 92 56W
Cincinnati, *Ohio* 17 39 6N 84 31W
Cincinnatus .. 9 42 33N 75 54W
Cinnaminson .. 26 39 59N 74 59W
Circle, *Alaska* . 32 65 50N 144 4W
Circle, *Mont.* .. 14 47 25N 105 35W
Circleville ... 10 39 36N 82 57W
Cisco 15 32 23N 98 59W
Cisne 17 38 31N 88 26W
Cissna Park .. 17 40 34N 87 54W
Citra 13 29 25N 82 7W
Citrus Heights 20 38 42N 121 17W
Citrus Springs . 13 29 2N 82 27W
City I. 23 40 50N 73 47W
Clairton 8 40 18N 79 53W
Clallam Bay .. 20 48 15N 124 16W
Clanton 11 32 51N 86 38W
Claraville 21 35 24N 118 20W
Clare 10 43 49N 84 46W
Claremont, *Calif.* 21 34 6N 117 43W
Claremont, *N.H.* 9 43 23N 72 20W
Claremore 15 36 19N 95 36W
Clarence 16 39 45N 92 16W
Clarendon, *Pa.* 8 41 47N 79 6W
Clarendon, *Tex.* 15 34 56N 100 53W
Clarinda 14 40 44N 95 2W
Clarion, *Iowa* . 16 42 44N 93 44W
Clarion, *Pa.* .. 8 41 13N 79 23W
Clarion → .. 8 41 7N 79 41W
Clark, *N.J.* ... 22 40 38N 74 18W
Clark, *S. Dak.* . 14 44 53N 97 44W
Clark Fork ... 18 48 9N 116 11W
Clark Fork → . 18 48 9N 116 15W
Clark Hill L. .. 12 33 40N 82 12W
Clarkdale ... 19 34 46N 112 3W
Clark's Fork → 18 45 39N 108 43W
Clarks Summit 9 41 30N 75 42W
Clarksboro .. 26 39 48N 75 13W
Clarksburg .. 10 39 17N 80 30W
Clarksdale ... 15 34 12N 90 35W
Clarksville, *Ark.* 15 35 28N 93 28W
Clarksville, *Iowa* 16 42 47N 92 40W
Clarksville, *Mich.* 17 42 50N 85 15W
Clarksville, *Ohio* 17 39 24N 83 59W
Clarksville, *Tenn.* 11 36 32N 87 21W
Clarksville, *Tex.* 15 33 37N 95 3W
Clatskanie ... 20 46 6N 123 12W
Claude 15 35 7N 101 22W
Claxton 12 32 10N 81 55W
Clay 20 38 17N 121 10W
Clay Center .. 14 39 23N 97 8W
Clay City, *Ind.* . 17 39 17N 87 7W
Clay City, *Ky.* .. 17 37 52N 83 55W
Claymont 26 39 48N 75 27W
Claypool 19 33 25N 110 51W
Claysburg ... 8 40 17N 78 27W
Claysville ... 8 40 7N 80 25W
Clayton, *Ala.* .. 12 31 53N 85 27W
Clayton, *Ind.* .. 17 39 41N 86 31W
Clayton, *N. Mex.* 15 36 27N 103 11W
Clayton, *N.Y.* .. 9 44 14N 76 5W
Clear L. 20 39 2N 122 47W
Clear Lake, *Iowa* 16 43 8N 93 23W
Clear Lake, *S. Dak.* 14 44 45N 96 41W
Clear Lake Reservoir ... 18 41 56N 121 5W
Clearfield, *Iowa* 16 40 48N 94 29W
Clearfield, *Pa.* . 8 41 2N 78 27W
Clearfield, *Utah* 18 41 7N 112 2W
Clearing 24 41 47N 87 45W
Clearlake 18 38 57N 122 38W
Clearlake Highlands ... 20 38 57N 122 38W
Clearwater, *Calif.* 31 33 52N 118 10W
Clearwater, *Fla.* 11 27 58N 82 48W
Clearwater Mts. 18 46 5N 115 20W
Cleburne 15 32 21N 97 23W
Clem 12 33 32N 85 1W
Clementon ... 26 39 48N 74 59W
Clemson 11 34 41N 82 50W
Clermont 13 28 33N 81 46W
Cleveland, *Miss.* 15 33 45N 90 43W
Cleveland, *Ohio* 8 41 30N 81 42W
Cleveland, *Okla.* 15 36 19N 96 28W
Cleveland, *Tenn.* 11 35 10N 84 53W
Cleveland, *Tex.* 15 30 21N 95 5W
Cleveland, Mt. . 18 48 56N 113 51W
Cleveland Heights 29 41 29N 81 35W
Cleveland Hopkins International Airport 29 41 24N 81 51W
Cleves 17 39 10N 84 45W
Clewiston 11 26 45N 80 56W
Cliffdell 20 46 56N 121 5W
Cliffside Park . 22 40 49N 73 59W
Clifton, *Mass.* . 25 42 29N 70 52W
Clifton, *N.Y.* .. 22 40 37N 74 4W
Clifton, *N.J.* .. 22 40 51N 74 7W
Clifton, *Ariz.* .. 19 33 3N 109 18W
Clifton, *Colo.* .. 19 39 7N 108 25W
Clifton, *Ill.* 17 40 56N 87 56W
Clifton, *Tex.* ... 15 31 47N 97 35W
Clifton, L. 27 39 19N 76 35W
Clifton Heights 26 39 55N 75 17W
Clifton Park .. 27 39 20N 76 35W
Climax 12 30 53N 84 26W
Clinch → ... 11 35 53N 84 29W
Clingmans Dome 11 35 34N 83 30W
Clint 19 31 35N 106 14W
Clinton, *Ark.* .. 15 35 36N 92 28W
Clinton, *Conn.* . 9 41 17N 72 32W
Clinton, *Ill.* ... 14 40 9N 88 57W
Clinton, *Ind.* .. 17 39 40N 87 24W
Clinton, *Iowa* . 16 41 51N 90 12W
Clinton, *Mass.* . 9 42 25N 71 41W
Clinton, *Miss.* . 15 32 20N 90 20W
Clinton, *Mo.* .. 16 38 22N 93 46W
Clinton, *N.C.* .. 11 35 0N 78 22W
Clinton, *Okla.* . 15 35 31N 98 58W
Clinton, *S.C.* .. 11 34 29N 81 53W
Clinton, *Tenn.* . 11 36 6N 84 8W
Clinton, *Wash.* 20 47 59N 122 21W
Clinton, *Wis.* . 17 42 34N 88 52W
Clintonville .. 14 44 37N 88 46W
Clio 12 31 43N 85 37W
Cloquet 14 46 43N 92 28W
Closter 22 40 58N 73 57W
Cloud Peak .. 18 44 23N 107 11W
Cloudcroft .. 19 32 58N 105 45W
Cloverdale, *Calif.* 20 38 48N 123 1W
Cloverdale, *Ind.* 17 39 31N 86 48W
Cloverport ... 17 37 50N 86 38W
Clovis, *Calif.* .. 20 36 49N 119 42W
Clovis, *N. Mex.* 15 34 24N 103 12W
Clyattville ... 12 30 42N 83 19W
Clyde 8 43 5N 76 52W
Clymer, *N.Y.* .. 8 42 1N 79 37W
Clymer, *Pa.* ... 8 40 40N 79 1W
Clyo 12 32 29N 81 16W
Coachella 21 33 41N 116 10W
Coachella Canal 21 32 43N 114 57W
Coahoma 15 32 18N 101 18W
Coal City 17 41 17N 88 17W
Coalgate 15 34 32N 96 13W
Coalinga 20 36 9N 120 21W
Coalville 18 40 55N 111 24W
Coamo 32 18 5N 66 22W
Coast Ranges . 2 39 0N 123 0W
Coatesville ... 10 39 59N 75 50W
Cobleskill 9 42 41N 74 29W
Cochichewick, L. 25 42 42N 71 5W
Cochituate ... 25 42 20N 71 21W
Cochituate, L. . 25 42 16N 71 21W
Cochran 12 32 23N 83 21W
Cochranton ... 8 41 31N 80 3W
Coco → 2 15 0N 83 8W
Cocoa 11 28 21N 80 44W
Cocoa Beach . 13 28 19N 80 37W
Cod, C. 2 42 5N 70 10W
Cody 18 44 32N 109 3W
Cœur d'Alene . 18 47 45N 116 51W
Cœur d'Alene L. 18 47 32N 116 48W
Coffeyville ... 15 37 2N 95 37W
Cogdell 12 31 10N 82 43W
Cohocton 8 42 30N 77 30W
Cohocton → . 8 42 9N 77 6W
Cohoes 9 42 46N 73 42W
Cokeville 18 42 5N 110 57W
Colbert 12 34 2N 83 13W
Colby 14 39 24N 101 3W
Cold Spring Harbor 23 40 52N 73 27W
Cold Spring Terrace 23 40 49N 73 25W
Coldwater, *Kans.* 15 37 16N 99 20W
Coldwater, *Mich.* 17 41 57N 85 0W
Coldwater, *Ohio* 17 40 29N 84 38W
Coldwater, L. .. 17 41 48N 84 59W
Cole Camp ... 16 38 28N 93 12W
Colebrook ... 9 44 54N 71 30W
Coleman, *Fla.* . 13 28 48N 82 4W
Coleman, *Ga.* . 12 31 40N 84 54W
Coleman, *Tex.* . 15 31 50N 99 26W
Colesburg ... 16 42 38N 91 12W
Coleville 20 38 34N 119 30W
Colfax, *Calif.* .. 20 39 6N 120 57W
Colfax, *Ill.* 17 40 34N 88 37W
Colfax, *Ind.* ... 17 40 12N 86 40W
Colfax, *La.* 15 31 31N 92 42W
Colfax, *Wash.* . 18 46 53N 117 22W
College Park, *Fla.* 12 29 53N 81 21W
College Park, *Ga.* 12 33 40N 84 27W
College Park, *Md.* 27 38 59N 76 55W
College Point . 23 40 47N 73 50W
College Station 15 30 37N 96 21W
Collingdale ... 26 39 54N 75 17W
Collingswood . 26 39 55N 75 5W
Collins, *Ga.* ... 12 32 11N 82 7W
Collins, *Mo.* ... 16 37 54N 93 37W
Collinsville, *Mass.* 25 42 40N 71 20W
Collinsville, *N.J.* 22 40 48N 74 26W
Collinsville, *Ill.* . 16 38 40N 89 59W
Colma 30 37 40N 122 27W
Coloma 20 38 48N 120 53W
Colombian Basin 2 14 0N 76 0W
Colonia 22 40 35N 74 18W
Colonial Beach 10 38 15N 76 58W
Colonial Manor 26 39 51N 75 9W
Colonie 9 42 43N 73 50W
Colorado □ ... 19 39 30N 105 30W
Colorado →, *N. Amer.* 2 31 45N 114 40W
Colorado →, *Tex.* 15 28 36N 95 59W
Colorado City . 15 32 24N 100 52W
Colorado Plateau 2 37 0N 111 0W
Colorado River Aqueduct .. 21 34 17N 114 10W
Colorado Springs 14 38 50N 104 49W
Colquitt 12 31 10N 84 44W
Colstrip 18 45 53N 106 38W
Colton 9 44 33N 74 56W
Columbia, *Md.* 27 39 12N 76 50W
Columbia, *Ala.* . 12 31 18N 85 7W
Columbia, *Ill.* .. 16 38 27N 90 12W
Columbia, *Ky.* . 10 37 6N 85 18W
Columbia, *La.* . 15 32 6N 92 5W
Columbia, *Miss.* 15 31 15N 89 50W
Columbia, *Mo.* . 16 38 57N 92 20W
Columbia, *Pa.* . 9 40 2N 76 30W
Columbia, *S.C.* 12 34 0N 81 2W
Columbia, *Tenn.* 11 35 37N 87 2W
Columbia → . 2 46 15N 124 5W
Columbia, District of □ . 10 38 55N 77 0W
Columbia Basin 18 46 45N 119 5W
Columbia Falls 18 48 23N 114 11W
Columbia Hills 27 39 14N 76 51W
Columbia Plateau 18 44 0N 117 30W
Columbia Univ. 22 40 48N 73 58W
Columbiana ... 8 40 53N 80 42W
Columbus, *Ga.* 12 32 28N 84 59W
Columbus, *Ind.* 17 39 13N 85 55W
Columbus, *Kans.* 15 37 10N 94 50W
Columbus, *Miss.* 11 33 30N 88 25W
Columbus, *Mont.* 18 45 38N 109 15W
Columbus, *N. Mex.* 19 31 50N 107 38W
Columbus, *Nebr.* 14 41 26N 97 22W
Columbus, *Ohio* 17 39 58N 83 0W
Columbus, *Tex.* 15 29 42N 96 33W
Columbus Grove 17 40 55N 84 4W
Columbus Junction 16 41 17N 91 22W
Colusa 20 39 13N 122 1W
Colville 18 48 33N 117 54W
Colville → ... 32 70 25N 150 30W
Colwyn 26 39 54N 75 14W
Comanche 15 31 54N 98 36W
Combahee → . 11 32 30N 80 31W
Comer, *Ala.* .. 12 32 2N 85 23W
Comer, *Ga.* .. 12 34 4N 83 8W
Commack 23 40 50N 73 19W
Commerce, *Calif.* 31 34 0N 118 9W
Commerce, *Ga.* 11 34 12N 83 28W
Commerce, *Tex.* 15 33 15N 95 54W
Compass Lake . 12 30 36N 85 24W
Compton 31 33 53N 118 14W
Conception, Pt. 21 34 27N 120 28W
Conchas Dam . 15 35 22N 104 11W
Concho 19 34 28N 109 36W
Concho → ... 15 31 31N 99 43W
Concord, *Mass.* 25 42 27N 71 20W
Concord, *Calif.* 30 37 58N 122 3W
Concord, *Ga.* .. 12 33 5N 84 27W
Concord, *Mich.* 17 42 11N 84 38W
Concord, *N.C.* . 11 35 25N 80 35W
Concord, *N.H.* . 9 43 12N 71 32W
Concordia, *Kans.* 14 39 34N 97 40W
Concordia, *Mo.* 16 38 59N 93 34W
Concordville .. 26 39 53N 75 31W
Concrete 18 48 32N 121 45W
Conde 14 45 9N 98 6W
Condon 18 45 14N 120 11W
Coney Island .. 22 40 34N 74 0W
Congaree → . 12 33 44N 80 38W
Congress 19 34 9N 112 51W
Conklin 9 42 2N 75 49W
Conneaut 8 41 57N 80 34W
Connecticut □ . 9 41 30N 72 45W
Connecticut → 9 41 16N 72 20W
Connell 18 46 40N 118 52W
Connellsville .. 8 40 1N 79 35W
Connemaugh → 8 40 28N 79 19W
Connersville .. 17 39 39N 85 8W
Conrad, *Iowa* .. 16 42 14N 92 52W
Conrad, *Mont.* . 18 48 10N 111 57W
Conroe 15 30 19N 95 27W
Conshohocken 26 40 4N 75 18W
Constantia ... 9 43 15N 76 1W
Constantine .. 17 41 50N 85 40W
Contact 18 41 46N 114 45W
Continental .. 17 41 6N 84 16W
Contoocook ... 9 43 13N 71 45W
Converse 17 40 35N 85 52W
Convoy 17 40 55N 84 43W
Conway, *Ark.* .. 15 35 5N 92 26W
Conway, *Fla.* .. 13 28 28N 81 22W
Conway, *N.H.* . 9 43 59N 71 7W
Conway, *S.C.* .. 11 33 51N 79 3W
Conyers 12 33 40N 84 1W
Cook 14 47 49N 92 39W
Cook Inlet 32 60 0N 152 0W
Cookeville 11 36 10N 85 30W
Cooks Hammock 12 29 56N 83 17W
Coolidge, *Ariz.* 19 32 59N 111 31W
Coolidge, *Ga.* . 12 31 1N 83 52W
Coolidge Dam . 19 33 0N 110 20W
Coon Rapids, *Iowa* 16 41 53N 94 41W
Coon Rapids, *Minn.* 14 45 9N 93 19W
Cooper 15 33 23N 95 42W
Cooper → ... 12 32 50N 79 56W
Cooperstown, *N. Dak.* 14 47 27N 98 8W
Cooperstown, *N.Y.* 9 42 42N 74 56W
Coopersville .. 17 43 4N 85 57W
Coos Bay 18 43 22N 124 13W
Coosa → 11 32 30N 86 16W
Copake Falls . 9 42 7N 73 31W
Cope, *Colo.* .. 14 39 40N 102 51W
Cope, *S.C.* ... 12 33 23N 81 0W
Copeland 13 25 57N 81 22W
Copenhagen .. 9 43 54N 75 41W
Copiague 23 40 39N 73 23W
Coplay 9 40 44N 75 29W
Copper → ... 32 60 18N 145 3W
Copper Center . 32 61 58N 145 18W
Copper Harbor 10 47 28N 87 53W
Copperas Cove 15 31 8N 97 54W
Copperopolis .. 20 37 58N 120 38W
Coquille 18 43 11N 124 11W
Coral 8 40 29N 79 10W
Coral Gables . 11 25 45N 80 16W
Coral Hills ... 27 38 51N 76 55W
Coral Springs . 11 26 16N 80 13W
Coralville 16 41 40N 91 35W
Coralville Res. . 16 41 50N 91 40W
Coraopolis ... 8 40 31N 80 10W
Corbin 10 36 57N 84 6W
Corcoran 20 36 6N 119 33W
Cordele 12 31 58N 83 47W
Cordell 15 35 17N 98 59W
Cordova, *Alaska* 32 60 33N 145 45W
Cordova, *Ill.* .. 16 41 41N 90 19W
Corinth, *Ga.* .. 12 33 14N 84 57W
Corinth, *Ky.* .. 17 38 30N 84 34W
Corinth, *Miss.* . 11 34 56N 88 31W
Corinth, *N.Y.* .. 9 43 14N 73 49W
Corinth, *N.Y.* .. 9 43 15N 73 49W
Cornell 17 41 0N 88 44W
Corning, *Ark.* . 15 36 25N 90 35W
Corning, *Calif.* 18 39 56N 122 11W
Corning, *Iowa* . 16 40 59N 94 44W
Corning, *N.Y.* . 8 42 9N 77 3W
Cornwall 9 40 17N 76 25W
Cornwell 13 27 23N 81 6W
Cornwells Heights 26 40 4N 74 57W
Corona, *Calif.* . 21 33 53N 117 34W
Corona, *N. Mex.* 19 34 15N 105 36W
Coronado 21 32 41N 117 11W
Coronados, Is. los 21 32 25N 117 15W
Corpus Christi . 15 27 47N 97 24W
Corpus Christi, L. 15 28 2N 97 52W
Corrigan 15 31 0N 94 52W
Corry 8 41 55N 79 39W
Corsicana ... 15 32 6N 96 28W
Corte Madera . 30 37 55N 122 30W
Cortez 19 37 21N 108 35W
Cortland, *N.Y.* . 9 42 36N 76 11W
Cortland, *Ohio* 8 41 20N 80 44W
Corunna 17 42 59N 84 7W
Corvallis 18 44 34N 123 16W
Corydon, *Ind.* . 17 38 13N 86 7W
Corydon, *Iowa* 16 40 46N 93 19W
Corydon, *Ky.* . 17 37 44N 87 43W
Cos Cob 23 41 1N 73 36W
Coshocton ... 8 40 16N 81 51W
Coso Junction . 21 36 3N 117 57W
Coso Pk. 21 36 13N 117 44W
Costa Mesa .. 21 33 38N 117 55W
Cosumnes → 20 38 16N 121 26W
Coteau des Prairies 14 45 20N 97 50W
Coteau du Missouri 14 47 0N 100 0W
Cottage Grove . 18 43 48N 123 3W
Cottageville .. 12 32 56N 80 29W
Cotton 12 31 10N 84 4W
Cottondale ... 12 30 48N 85 23W
Cottonwood, *Ala.* 12 31 3N 85 18W
Cottonwood, *Ariz.* 19 34 45N 112 1W
Cotulla 15 28 26N 99 14W
Coudersport . 8 41 46N 78 1W
Coulee City .. 18 47 37N 119 17W
Coulterville, *Calif.* 20 37 43N 120 12W
Coulterville, *Ill.* 16 38 11N 89 36W
Council, *Alaska* 32 64 55N 163 45W
Council, *Ga.* .. 12 30 37N 82 31W
Council, *Idaho* 18 44 44N 116 26W
Council Bluffs . 14 41 16N 95 52W
Council Grove . 14 38 40N 96 29W
Countryside .. 24 41 47N 87 52W
Coupeville ... 20 48 13N 122 41W
Courtland ... 20 38 20N 121 34W
Coushatta ... 15 32 1N 93 21W
Cove Neck ... 23 40 52N 73 29W
Coverdale ... 12 31 38N 83 58W
Covington, *Ga.* 12 33 36N 83 51W
Covington, *Ind.* 17 40 9N 87 24W
Covington, *Ky.* 17 39 5N 84 31W
Covington, *Ohio* 17 40 7N 84 21W
Covington, *Okla.* 15 36 18N 97 35W
Covington, *Tenn.* 15 35 34N 89 39W
Covington, *Va.* 10 37 47N 79 59W
Coward 12 33 58N 79 45W
Cowden 17 39 15N 88 52W
Cowlitz → .. 20 46 6N 122 55W
Cox 12 31 27N 81 34W
Coyote Hills Regional Park 30 37 32N 122 7W
Coyote Hills Slough 30 37 33N 122 7W
Coyote Pt. ... 30 37 35N 122 18W
Coyote Ridge . 30 37 51N 122 33W
Coyote Wells .. 21 32 44N 115 58W
Cozad 14 40 52N 99 59W
Craig, *Alaska* .. 32 55 29N 133 9W
Craig, *Colo.* .. 18 40 31N 107 33W
Cranberry L. .. 9 44 11N 74 50W
Crandon 14 45 34N 88 54W
Crane, *Oreg.* .. 18 43 25N 118 35W
Crane, *Tex.* ... 15 31 24N 102 21W
Cranford 22 40 39N 74 19W
Cranston 9 41 47N 71 26W
Crater L. 18 42 56N 122 6W
Crater Lake National Park 18 42 55N 122 10W
Crawford, *Ala.* . 12 32 27N 85 11W
Crawford, *Nebr.* 14 42 41N 103 25W
Crawfordsville . 17 40 2N 86 54W
Crawfordville, *Fla.* 12 30 11N 84 23W
Crawfordville, *Ga.* 12 33 33N 82 54W
Crazy Mts. ... 18 46 12N 110 20W
Creede 19 37 51N 106 56W
Creekside ... 8 40 40N 79 11W
Creighton ... 14 42 28N 97 54W
Crescent Beach 12 29 46N 81 15W
Crescent City, *Calif.* 18 41 45N 124 12W
Crescent City, *Fla.* 13 29 26N 81 31W
Crescent L. .. 13 29 28N 81 30W
Cresskill 22 40 56N 73 57W
Cresson 8 40 28N 78 36W
Crestline, *Calif.* 21 34 14N 117 18W
Crestline, *Ohio* 8 40 47N 82 44W
Creston, *Calif.* . 20 35 32N 120 33W
Creston, *Iowa* . 16 41 4N 94 22W
Crestview, *Calif.* 20 37 46N 118 58W
Crestview, *Fla.* 11 30 46N 86 34W
Crestwood ... 24 41 38N 87 43W
Crete 14 40 38N 96 58W
Cridersville .. 17 40 39N 84 9W
Crittenden ... 17 38 47N 84 36W
Crocker 16 37 57N 92 16W
Crockett 15 31 19N 95 27W
Cromwell 9 41 36N 72 39W
Crooked → .. 18 44 32N 121 16W
Crooked L. .. 13 27 48N 81 35W
Crookston, *Minn.* 14 47 47N 96 37W
Crookston, *Nebr.* 14 42 56N 100 45W
Crosby, *N. Dak.* 14 48 55N 103 18W
Crosby, *Pa.* .. 8 41 45N 78 23W
Crosbyton ... 15 33 40N 101 14W
Cross City ... 13 29 38N 83 7W
Cross Sound .. 32 58 0N 135 0W
Cross Timbers . 16 38 1N 93 14W
Crossett 15 33 8N 91 58W
Crossville, *Ill.* . 17 38 10N 88 4W
Crossville, *Tenn.* 11 35 57N 85 2W
Croswell 8 43 16N 82 37W
Croton-on-Hudson 9 41 12N 73 55W
Crow Agency . 18 45 36N 107 28W
Crowell 15 33 59N 99 43W
Crowley 15 30 13N 92 22W
Crowley, L. .. 20 37 35N 118 42W
Crown Point, *Ind.* 17 41 25N 87 22W
Crown Point, *N.Y.* 9 43 57N 73 26W
Crown Village . 23 40 40N 73 26W
Crownpoint .. 19 35 41N 108 9W
Crows Landing 20 37 23N 121 6W
Croydon 26 40 5N 74 54W
Crystal B. ... 13 28 50N 82 45W
Crystal Bay .. 20 39 15N 120 0W
Crystal City, *Mo.* 16 38 13N 90 23W
Crystal City, *Tex.* 15 28 41N 99 50W
Crystal Falls .. 10 46 5N 88 20W
Crystal Lake, *Fla.* 12 30 26N 85 42W
Crystal Lake, *Ill.* 17 42 14N 88 19W
Crystal River .. 11 28 54N 82 35W
Crystal Springs, *Calif.* 30 37 31N 122 20W
Crystal Springs, *Miss.* 15 31 59N 90 21W
Cuba, *Mo.* ... 16 38 4N 91 24W
Cuba, *N. Mex.* . 19 36 1N 107 4W
Cuba, *N.Y.* .. 8 42 13N 78 17W
Cuba City ... 16 42 36N 90 26W
Cudahy 17 42 58N 87 52W
Cuero 15 29 6N 97 17W
Cuivre → ... 16 38 55N 90 44W
Cuivre, West Fork → 16 39 2N 90 58W
Culbertson ... 14 48 9N 104 31W
Culebra, Isla de 32 18 19N 65 18W
Cull Creek ... 30 37 45N 122 2W
Cullman 11 34 11N 86 51W
Culloden 12 32 52N 84 6W
Cullom 17 40 53N 88 16W
Culpeper 10 38 30N 78 0W
Culver 17 41 13N 86 25W
Culver City .. 31 34 1N 118 24W
Culverton ... 12 33 19N 82 54W
Cumberland, *Iowa* 16 41 16N 94 52W
Cumberland, *Md.* 10 39 39N 78 46W
Cumberland → 11 36 15N 87 0W
Cumberland, L. 11 36 57N 84 55W
Cumberland I. 12 30 50N 81 25W
Cumberland I. Nat. Seashore 12 30 12N 81 24W
Cumberland Plateau 2 36 0N 85 0W
Cummings ... 12 32 47N 80 59W
Cummings Mt. 21 35 2N 118 34W
Currant 18 38 51N 115 32W
Current → .. 15 36 15N 90 55W
Currie 18 40 16N 114 45W
Curtis 14 40 38N 100 31W
Curtis B. ... 27 39 13N 76 34W
Cushing 15 35 59N 96 46W
Cusseta 12 32 18N 84 47W
Custer 14 43 46N 103 36W

Cut Bank

Cut Bank 18 48 38N 112 20W
Cutchogue 9 41 1N 72 30W
Cuthbert 12 31 46N 84 48W
Cutler 20 36 31N 119 17W
Cutler Ridge 13 25 35N 80 20W
Cuyahoga Falls 8 41 8N 81 29W
Cynthiana 17 38 23N 84 18W

D

Dacula 12 33 59N 83 54W
Dade City 11 28 22N 82 11W
Dadeville 12 32 50N 85 46W
Daggett 21 34 52N 116 52W
Dahlgren 17 38 12N 88 41W
Dahlonega 11 34 32N 83 59W
Dakota City, *Iowa* 16 42 43N 94 12W
Dakota City, *Nebr.* 14 42 25N 96 25W
Dale 17 38 10N 86 59W
Dale City 10 38 38N 77 18W
Dale Hollow L. 11 36 32N 85 27W
Daleville, *Ala.* 12 31 19N 85 43W
Daleville, *Ind.* 17 40 7N 85 33W
Dalhart 15 36 4N 102 31W
Dalkeith 12 30 0N 85 9W
Dallas, *Ga.* 12 33 55N 84 51W
Dallas, *Oreg.* 18 44 55N 123 19W
Dallas, *Tex.* 15 32 47N 96 49W
Dallas Center 16 41 41N 93 58W
Dallas City 16 40 38N 91 10W
Dalton, *Ga.* 11 34 46N 84 58W
Dalton, *Mass.* 9 42 28N 73 11W
Dalton, *Nebr.* 14 41 25N 102 58W
Daly City 30 37 42N 122 27W
Damascus 12 31 18N 84 43W
Dan Ryan Woods 24 41 44N 87 40W
Dana, Mt. 20 37 54N 119 12W
Danbury 9 41 24N 73 28W
Danby L. 19 34 13N 115 5W
Daniel 18 42 52N 110 4W
Daniels 27 39 19N 76 48W
Danielson 9 41 48N 71 53W
Danielsville 12 34 8N 83 13W
Dannemora 9 44 43N 73 44W
Dansville 8 42 34N 77 42W
Danvers 25 42 34N 70 56W
Danville, *Ga.* 12 32 37N 83 15W
Danville, *Ill.* 17 40 8N 87 37W
Danville, *Ind.* 17 39 46N 86 32W
Danville, *Ky.* 17 37 39N 84 46W
Danville, *Pa.* 9 40 58N 76 37W
Danville, *Va.* 11 36 36N 79 23W
Danville, *Vt.* 9 44 25N 72 9W
Darby 26 39 55N 75 15W
Dardanelle, *Ark.* 15 35 13N 93 9W
Dardanelle, *Calif.* 20 38 20N 119 50W
Darien 12 31 23N 81 26W
Darién, G. del 2 9 0N 77 0W
Darling 26 39 54N 75 28W
Darlington, *Fla.* 12 30 57N 86 3W
Darlington, *S.C.* 11 34 18N 79 52W
Darlington, *Wis.* 16 42 41N 90 7W
Darlington Corners 26 39 55N 75 34W
Darrington 18 48 15N 121 36W
Darwin 21 36 15N 117 35W
Dasher 12 30 45N 83 13W
Dauphin 8 40 22N 76 56W
Davenport, *Calif.* 20 37 1N 122 12W
Davenport, *Fla.* 13 28 10N 81 36W
Davenport, *Iowa* 16 41 32N 90 35W
Davenport, *Wash.* 18 47 39N 118 9W
Davensport 25 42 33N 70 54W
David City 14 41 15N 97 8W
David's I. 23 40 53N 73 46W
Davidson, Mt. 30 37 44N 122 27W
Davis 20 38 33N 121 44W
Davis Dam 21 35 11N 114 34W
Davis Mts. 15 30 50N 103 55W
Davis Str. 2 65 0N 58 0W
Davisboro 12 32 59N 82 36W
Dawson 12 31 46N 84 27W
Day 12 30 12N 83 17W
Dayton, *Iowa* 16 42 14N 94 6W
Dayton, *Ky.* 17 39 47N 84 28W
Dayton, *Nev.* 20 39 14N 119 36W
Dayton, *Ohio* 10 39 45N 84 12W
Dayton, *Pa.* 8 40 53N 79 15W
Dayton, *Tenn.* 11 35 30N 85 1W
Dayton, *Wash.* 18 46 19N 117 59W
Dayton, *Wyo.* 18 44 53N 107 16W
Daytona Beach 11 29 13N 81 1W
Dayville 18 44 28N 119 32W
De Armanville 12 33 38N 85 45W
De Bary 13 28 54N 81 18W
De Forest 16 43 15N 89 20W
De Funiak Springs 12 30 43N 86 7W
De Kalb 17 41 56N 88 46W
De Land 11 29 2N 81 18W
De Leon 15 32 7N 98 32W
De Leon Springs 13 29 7N 81 21W
De Long Mts. 32 68 30N 163 0W
De Pere 10 44 27N 88 4W
De Queen 15 34 2N 94 21W
De Quincy 15 30 27N 93 26W
De Ridder 15 30 51N 93 17W
De Smet 14 44 23N 97 33W
De Soto 16 38 8N 90 34W
De Soto City 13 27 27N 81 24W
De Tour Village 10 46 0N 83 56W
De Witt, *Ark.* 15 34 18N 91 20W
De Witt, *Iowa* 16 41 49N 90 33W
De Witt, *Mich.* 17 42 51N 84 34W
Dead L. 12 30 10N 85 10W
Deadman B. 13 29 30N 83 30W
Deadwood 14 44 23N 103 44W
Dearborn, *Mich.* 28 42 19N 83 10W
Dearborn, *Mo.* 16 39 32N 94 46W
Dearborn Heights 28 42 20N 83 17W
Death Valley 2 36 15N 116 50W
Death Valley Junction 21 36 20N 116 25W
Death Valley National Park 21 36 45N 117 15W
Decatur, *Ala.* 11 34 36N 86 59W
Decatur, *Ga.* 12 33 47N 84 18W
Decatur, *Ill.* 16 39 51N 88 57W
Decatur, *Ind.* 17 40 50N 84 56W
Decatur, *Mich.* 17 42 7N 85 58W
Decatur, *Tex.* 15 33 14N 97 35W
Deckerville 8 43 32N 82 44W
Decorah 14 43 18N 91 48W
Dedham 25 42 15N 71 10W
Deep River 16 41 35N 92 22W
Deepstep 12 33 1N 82 58W
Deepwater 16 38 16N 93 47W
Deer I., *Mass.* 25 42 21N 70 57W
Deer I., *Alaska* 32 54 55N 162 18W
Deer Lodge 18 46 24N 112 44W
Deer Park, *N.Y.* 23 40 46N 73 19W
Deer Park, *Fla.* 13 28 6N 80 54W
Deer Park, *Ohio* 17 39 13N 84 23W
Deer Park, *Wash.* 18 47 57N 117 28W
Deer River 14 47 20N 93 48W
Deerfield Beach 13 26 19N 80 6W
Deering 32 66 4N 162 42W
Deferiet 9 44 2N 75 41W
Defiance 17 41 17N 84 22W
Del Mar 21 32 58N 117 16W
Del Norte 19 37 41N 106 21W
Del Rio 15 29 22N 100 54W
Delanco 26 40 2N 74 57W
Delano 21 35 46N 119 15W
Delano Peak 19 38 22N 112 22W
Delavan, *Ill.* 16 40 22N 89 33W
Delavan, *Wis.* 17 42 38N 88 39W
Delaware 17 40 18N 83 4W
Delaware □ 10 39 0N 75 20W
Delaware → 9 39 15N 75 20W
Delaware B. 10 39 0N 75 10W
Delevan 8 42 29N 78 29W
Delhi, *La.* 15 32 28N 91 30W
Delhi, *N.Y.* 9 42 17N 74 55W
Dell City 19 31 56N 105 12W
Dell Rapids 14 43 50N 96 43W
Delmar, *Iowa* 16 42 0N 90 37W
Delmar, *N.Y.* 9 42 37N 73 47W
Delphi 17 40 36N 86 41W
Delphos 17 40 51N 84 21W
Delran 26 40 0N 74 57W
Delray Beach 11 26 28N 80 4W
Delta, *Ala.* 12 33 26N 85 42W
Delta, *Colo.* 19 38 44N 108 4W
Delta, *Utah* 18 39 21N 112 35W
Deltona 13 28 54N 81 16W
Demarest 22 40 57N 73 57W
Deming, *N. Mex.* 19 32 16N 107 46W
Deming, *Wash.* 20 48 50N 122 13W
Demopolis 11 32 31N 87 50W
Denair 20 37 32N 120 48W
Denali National Park and Preserve 32 63 30N 150 0W
Denison, *Iowa* 14 42 1N 95 21W
Denison, *Tex.* 15 33 45N 96 33W
Denmark 12 33 19N 81 9W
Denmark Str. 2 66 0N 30 0W
Dennison 8 40 24N 81 19W
Denton, *Ga.* 12 31 44N 82 42W
Denton, *Mont.* 18 47 19N 109 57W
Denton, *Tex.* 15 33 13N 97 8W
Dentsville 12 34 4N 80 58W
Denver, *Colo.* 14 39 44N 104 59W
Denver, *Ind.* 17 40 52N 86 5W
Denver, *Iowa* 16 42 40N 92 20W
Denver, *Pa.* 9 40 14N 76 8W
Denver City 15 32 58N 102 50W
Denville 22 40 53N 74 28W
Deposit 9 42 4N 75 25W
Derby, *Conn.* 9 41 19N 73 5W
Derby, *Kans.* 15 37 33N 97 16W
Derby, *N.Y.* 8 42 41N 78 58W
Derby Line 9 45 0N 72 6W
Dermott 15 33 32N 91 26W
Derry, *N.H.* 9 42 53N 71 19W
Derry, *Pa.* 8 40 20N 79 18W
Des Moines, *Iowa* 16 41 35N 93 37W
Des Moines, *N. Mex.* 15 36 46N 103 50W
Des Moines → 14 40 23N 91 25W
Des Plaines 24 42 2N 87 54W
Des Plaines → 17 41 23N 88 15W
Deschutes → 18 45 38N 120 55W
Desert Center 21 33 43N 115 24W
Desert Hot Springs 21 33 58N 116 30W
Destin 13 30 24N 86 30W
Detour, Pt. 10 45 40N 86 40W
Detroit 17 42 20N 83 3W
Detroit City Airport 28 42 24N 83 0W
Detroit Lakes 14 46 49N 95 51W
Detroit-Wayne Airport 28 42 13N 83 20W
Devault 26 40 4N 75 32W
Devereux 12 33 13N 83 5W
Devils Den 20 35 46N 119 58W
Devils Lake 14 48 7N 98 52W
Devils Tower Junction 14 44 31N 104 57W
Devine 15 29 8N 98 54W
Dewy Rose 12 34 10N 82 57W
Dexter, *Ga.* 12 32 27N 83 4W
Dexter, *Maine* 11 45 1N 69 18W
Dexter, *Mich.* 17 42 20N 83 53W
Dexter, *Mo.* 15 36 48N 89 57W
Dexter, *N. Mex.* 15 33 12N 104 22W
Diablo, Mt. 20 37 53N 121 56W
Diablo Range 20 37 20N 121 25W
Diagonal 16 40 49N 94 20W
Diamond Bar 21 34 1N 117 48W
Diamond Mts. 18 39 50N 115 30W
Diamond Springs 20 38 42N 120 49W
Dickens 15 33 37N 100 50W
Dickeyville 16 42 38N 90 36W
Dickinson 14 46 53N 102 47W
Dickson 11 36 5N 87 23W
Dickson City 9 41 29N 75 40W
Dierks 15 34 7N 94 1W
Dieterich 17 39 4N 88 23W
Dighton 14 38 29N 100 28W
Dillard 16 37 44N 91 13W
Dilley 15 28 40N 99 10W
Dillingham 32 59 3N 158 28W
Dillon, *Mont.* 18 45 13N 112 38W
Dillon, *S.C.* 11 34 25N 79 22W
Dillsboro 17 39 1N 85 4W
Dillsburg 8 40 7N 77 2W
Dimmitt 15 34 33N 102 19W
Dingmans Ferry 9 41 13N 74 55W
Dinosaur National Monument 18 40 30N 108 45W
Dinuba 20 36 32N 119 23W
Disappointment, C. 18 46 18N 124 5W
Disappointment, Mt. 31 34 15N 118 7W
District Heights 27 38 51N 76 53W
Divide 18 45 45N 112 45W
Dix → 17 37 49N 84 43W
Dix Hills 23 40 48N 73 21W
Dixie Mt. 20 39 55N 120 16W
Dixie Union 12 34 20N 82 28W
Dixmoor 24 41 37N 87 40W
Dixon, *Calif.* 20 38 27N 121 49W
Dixon, *Ill.* 16 41 50N 89 29W
Dixon, *Iowa* 16 41 45N 90 47W
Dixon, *Mo.* 16 37 59N 92 6W
Dobbs 23 41 1N 73 52W
Doctors Inlet 12 30 6N 81 47W
Dodge City 15 37 45N 100 1W
Dodger Stadium 31 34 4N 118 14W
Dodgeville 16 42 58N 90 8W
Dodson 18 48 24N 108 15W
Doerun 12 31 19N 83 55W
Dog I. 12 29 48N 84 36W
Dog L. 12 31 42N 83 53W
Dolores 19 37 28N 108 30W
Dolores → 19 38 49N 109 17W
Dolton 24 41 37N 87 35W
Donaldsonville 15 30 6N 90 59W
Donalsonville 12 31 3N 84 53W
Dongan Hills 22 40 35N 74 5W
Doniphan 15 36 37N 90 50W
Donna 15 26 9N 98 4W
Donora 8 40 11N 79 52W
Doraville 12 33 54N 84 17W
Dorchester 25 42 17N 71 4W
Dorchester B. 25 42 18N 71 1W
Dorchester Heights Nat. Hist. Site 25 42 19N 71 2W
Dormont 29 40 23N 80 2W
Dorris 18 41 58N 121 55W
Dorset 8 41 40N 80 40W
Dos Palos 20 36 59N 120 37W
Dothan 12 31 13N 85 24W
Doty 20 46 38N 123 17W
Double Mountain Fork → 15 33 16N 100 0W
Douglas, *Alaska* 32 58 17N 134 24W
Douglas, *Ariz.* 19 31 21N 109 33W
Douglas, *Ga.* 12 31 31N 82 51W
Douglas, *Wyo.* 14 42 45N 105 24W
Douglas Park 24 41 51N 87 42W
Douglaston 23 40 46N 73 44W
Douglasville 12 33 45N 84 45W
Dove Creek 19 37 46N 108 54W
Dover, *Mass.* 25 42 14N 71 16W
Dover, *Del.* 10 39 10N 75 32W
Dover, *Ky.* 17 38 43N 83 52W
Dover, *N.H.* 9 43 12N 70 56W
Dover, *N.J.* 9 40 53N 74 34W
Dover, *Ohio* 8 40 32N 81 29W
Dover-Foxcroft 11 45 11N 69 13W
Dover Plains 9 41 43N 73 35W
Dowagiac 17 41 59N 86 6W
Dowling Park 12 30 15N 83 15W
Downers Grove 17 41 48N 88 1W
Downey, *Calif.* 31 33 56N 118 9W
Downey, *Idaho* 18 42 26N 112 7W
Downieville 20 39 34N 120 50W
Downing 16 40 29N 92 22W
Downsville 9 42 5N 74 50W
Doyle 20 40 2N 120 6W
Doylestown 9 40 21N 75 10W
Dracut 25 42 40N 71 17W
Drain 18 43 40N 123 19W
Drake 14 47 55N 100 23W
Dranesville 27 39 0N 77 20W
Drayton Plains 17 42 42N 83 23W
Dresher 26 40 9N 75 9W
Drexel 17 39 45N 84 18W
Drexel Hill 26 39 56N 75 18W
Drexel Inst. of Technology 26 39 57N 75 11W
Driftwood 8 41 20N 78 8W
Driggs 18 43 44N 111 6W
Druid Hill Park 27 39 19N 76 38W
Druid Lake 27 39 19N 76 38W
Drummond 18 46 40N 113 9W
Drummond I. 10 46 1N 83 39W
Drumright 15 35 59N 96 36W
Dryden 9 42 30N 76 18W
Du Bois 8 41 8N 78 46W
Du Quoin 16 38 1N 89 14W
Duanesburg 9 42 45N 74 11W
Duarte 31 34 8N 117 57W
Dublin, *Ga.* 12 32 32N 82 54W
Dublin, *Tex.* 15 32 5N 98 21W
Dubois, *Idaho* 18 44 10N 112 14W
Dubois, *Ind.* 17 38 27N 86 48W
Dubuque 16 42 30N 90 41W
Duchesne 18 40 10N 110 24W
Duck → 11 36 2N 87 52W
Duckwall, Mt. 20 37 58N 120 7W
Dudley 12 32 32N 83 5W
Duffryn Mawr 26 40 2N 75 27W
Dugger 17 39 4N 87 18W
Dulce 19 36 56N 107 0W
Duluth, *Ga.* 12 34 0N 84 9W
Duluth, *Minn.* 14 46 47N 92 6W
Dulworthtown 26 39 54N 75 33W
Dumas, *Ark.* 15 33 53N 91 29W
Dumas, *Tex.* 15 35 52N 101 58W
Dumbarton Pt. 30 37 29N 122 6W
Dumont 22 40 56N 73 59W
Duncan, *Ariz.* 19 32 43N 109 6W
Duncan, *Okla.* 15 34 30N 97 57W
Duncannon 8 40 23N 77 2W
Duncansville 8 40 25N 78 26W
Dundalk 27 39 17N 76 31W
Dundee, *Mich.* 17 41 57N 83 40W
Dundee, *N.Y.* 8 42 32N 76 59W
Dunedin 11 28 1N 82 47W
Dunellen 22 40 35N 74 26W
Dunkirk 8 42 29N 79 20W
Dunmore 9 41 25N 75 38W
Dunn 11 35 19N 78 37W
Dunn Loring 27 38 54N 77 13W
Dunning, *Ill.* 24 41 56N 87 48W
Dunning, *Nebr.* 14 41 50N 100 6W
Dunphy 18 40 42N 116 31W
Dunseith 14 48 50N 100 3W
Dunsmuir 18 41 13N 122 16W
Dupree 14 45 4N 101 35W
Dupuyer 18 48 13N 112 30W
Duquesne 29 40 22N 79 52W
Durand, *Ga.* 12 32 54N 84 51W
Durand, *Ill.* 16 42 26N 89 20W
Durand, *Mich.* 17 42 55N 83 59W
Durand, *Wis.* 14 44 38N 91 58W
Durango 19 37 16N 107 53W
Durant, *Iowa* 16 41 36N 90 54W
Durant, *Miss.* 15 33 4N 89 51W
Durant, *Okla.* 15 33 59N 96 25W
Durham, *Calif.* 20 39 39N 121 48W
Durham, *N.C.* 11 35 59N 78 54W
Durham, *N.H.* 9 43 8N 70 56W
Duryea 9 41 20N 75 45W
Dushore 9 41 31N 76 24W
Dutch Harbor 32 53 53N 166 32W
Dwight 17 41 5N 88 26W
Dyer 17 37 24N 86 13W
Dyersburg 15 36 3N 89 23W
Dyersville 16 42 29N 91 8W

E

Eads 14 38 29N 102 47W
Eagar 19 34 6N 109 17W
Eagle, *Alaska* 32 64 47N 141 12W
Eagle, *Colo.* 18 39 39N 106 50W
Eagle Butte 14 45 0N 101 10W
Eagle Cr. → 17 38 36N 85 4W
Eagle Grove 16 42 40N 93 54W
Eagle L., *Calif.* 18 40 39N 120 45W
Eagle L., *Maine* 11 46 20N 69 22W
Eagle Lake, *Maine* 11 47 3N 68 36W
Eagle Lake, *Tex.* 15 29 35N 96 20W
Eagle Mountain 21 33 49N 115 27W
Eagle Nest 19 36 33N 105 16W
Eagle Pass 15 28 43N 100 30W
Eagle Pk. 20 38 10N 119 25W
Eagle River, *Mich.* 10 47 24N 88 18W
Eagle River, *Wis.* 14 45 55N 89 15W
Eagle Rock 31 34 8N 118 12 E
Eagles Mere 9 41 25N 76 33W
Eagleville 16 40 28N 93 59W
Earle 15 35 16N 90 28W
Earlimart 21 35 53N 119 16W
Earlville 17 41 35N 88 55W
Early Branch 12 32 45N 80 55W
Earth 15 34 14N 102 24W
Easley 11 34 50N 82 36W
East Acton 25 42 28N 71 24W
East Arlington 27 38 51N 77 4W
East Atlantic Beach 23 40 35N 73 43W
East Aurora 8 42 46N 78 37W
East B., *N.Y.* 23 40 38N 73 32W
East B., *Fla.* 12 30 5N 85 32W
East Billerica 25 42 35N 71 13W
East Boston 25 42 22N 71 1W
East Brady 8 40 59N 79 36W
East Braintree 25 42 13N 70 58W
East Chicago 24 41 38N 87 26W
East Cleveland 29 41 32N 81 35W
East Detroit 28 42 27N 82 58W
East Dublin 12 32 32N 82 52W
East Dubuque 16 42 30N 90 39W
East Elmhurst 23 40 45N 73 52W
East Farmingdale 23 40 44N 73 25W
East Grand Forks 14 47 56N 97 1W
East Greenwich 9 41 40N 71 27W
East Half Hollow Hills 23 40 47N 73 19W
East Hanover 22 40 49N 74 21W
East Hartford 9 41 46N 72 39W
East Helena 18 46 35N 111 56W
East Hills 23 40 47N 73 37W
East Holliston 25 42 12N 71 25W
East Huntington 23 40 52N 73 24W
East Lansing 17 42 44N 84 29W
East Lexington 25 42 25N 71 12W
East Liverpool 8 40 37N 80 35W
East Los Angeles 31 34 1N 118 10W
East Meadow 23 40 42N 73 31W
East Moline 16 41 32N 90 26W
East Naples 13 26 8N 81 46W
East New York 23 40 40N 73 53W
East Newark 22 40 45N 74 10W
East Northport 23 40 52N 73 18W
East Norwich 23 40 50N 73 31W
East Orange 22 40 46N 74 11W
East Palatka 12 29 39N 81 36W
East Palestine 8 40 50N 80 33W
East Palo Alto 30 37 28N 122 8W
East Paterson 22 40 53N 74 8W
East Peoria 16 40 40N 89 34W
East Pines 27 38 57N 76 54W
East Point, *Mass.* 25 42 25N 70 54W
East Point, *Ga.* 12 33 41N 84 27W
East Potomac Park 27 38 52N 77 1W
East Providence 9 41 49N 71 23W
East Richmond 30 37 56N 122 19W
East Rochester 8 43 7N 77 29W
East Rockaway 23 40 38N 73 40W
East Rutherford 22 40 50N 74 5W
East St. Louis 16 38 37N 90 9W
East Stroudsburg 9 41 1N 75 11W
East Tawas 10 44 17N 83 29W
East Tohopekaliga Lake 13 28 18N 81 15W
East Troy 17 42 47N 88 24W
East Walker → 20 38 52N 119 10W
East Weymouth 25 42 13N 70 55W
East Williston 23 40 45N 73 37W
East Windsor 9 40 17N 74 34W
Eastchester 23 40 56N 73 49W
Eastchester B. 23 40 50N 73 47W
Easthampton 9 42 16N 72 40W
Eastlake 29 41 38N 81 28W
Eastland 15 32 24N 98 49W
Eastman, *Ga.* 12 32 12N 83 11W
Eastman, *Wis.* 16 43 10N 91 1W
Easton, *Md.* 10 38 47N 76 5W
Easton, *Pa.* 9 40 41N 75 13W
Easton, *Wash.* 20 47 14N 121 11W
Eastover 12 33 52N 80 41W
Eastpoint, *Md.* 27 39 17N 76 34W
Eastpoint, *Fla.* 12 29 44N 84 53W
Eastpointe 8 42 27N 82 56W
Eastport 11 44 56N 67 0W
Eastsound 20 48 42N 122 55W
Eaton, *Colo.* 14 40 32N 104 42W
Eaton, *Ohio* 17 39 45N 84 38W
Eaton Rapids 17 42 31N 84 39W
Eatons Neck Pt. 23 40 57N 73 24W
Eatonton 12 33 20N 83 23W
Eatontown 9 40 19N 74 4W
Eatonville 20 46 52N 122 16W
Eau Claire 14 44 49N 91 30W
Ebensburg 8 40 29N 78 44W
Echechonnee → 12 32 39N 83 36W
Echo 12 31 29N 85 28W
Echo B. 23 40 54N 73 45W
Echo Mt. 31 34 12N 118 8W
Eclectic 12 32 38N 86 2W
Econfina 12 30 22N 85 35W
Eddington 26 40 5N 74 55W
Eddystone 26 39 51N 75 20W
Eddyville 16 41 9N 92 38W
Eden, *N.C.* 11 36 29N 79 53W
Eden, *N.Y.* 8 42 39N 78 55W
Eden, *Tex.* 15 31 13N 99 51W
Edenton 11 36 4N 76 39W
Edgar 14 40 22N 97 58W
Edgartown 9 41 23N 70 31W
Edge Hill 26 40 7N 75 9W
Edgefield 12 33 47N 81 56W
Edgeley 14 46 22N 98 43W
Edgemar 30 37 39N 122 29W
Edgemere 27 39 14N 76 26W
Edgemont, *Pa.* 26 39 58N 75 26W
Edgemont, *S. Dak.* 14 43 18N 103 50W
Edgerton, *Ohio* 17 41 27N 84 45W
Edgerton, *Wis.* 16 42 50N 89 4W
Edgewater 13 28 59N 80 54W
Edgewater Park 26 40 3N 74 54W
Edgewood 17 38 55N 88 40W
Edina 16 40 10N 92 11W
Edinboro 8 41 52N 80 8W
Edinburg, *Ill.* 16 39 39N 89 23W
Edinburg, *Ind.* 17 39 21N 85 58W
Edinburg, *Tex.* 15 26 18N 98 10W
Edison, *N.J.* 22 40 31N 74 23W
Edison, *Ga.* 12 31 34N 84 44W
Edison, *Wash.* 20 48 33N 122 27W
Edison Park 24 42 1N 87 48W
Edisto → 12 32 29N 80 21W
Edisto Beach 12 32 29N 80 20W
Edisto I. 12 32 35N 80 20W
Edmeston 9 42 42N 75 15W
Edmond 15 35 39N 97 29W
Edmonds 20 47 49N 122 23W
Edmondston 27 38 56N 76 54W
Edna 15 28 59N 96 39W
Edwards, *Calif.* 21 34 55N 117 51W
Edwards, *N.Y.* 9 44 20N 75 15W
Edwards → 16 41 9N 90 59W
Edwards Air Force Base 21 34 50N 117 40W
Edwards Plateau 15 30 45N 101 20W
Edwardsburg 17 41 48N 86 6W
Edwardsport 17 38 49N 87 15W
Edwardsville, *Ill.* 16 38 49N 89 58W
Edwardsville, *Pa.* 9 41 15N 75 56W
Eek 32 60 14N 162 2W
Eel →, *Ind.* 17 39 7N 86 57W
Eel →, *Ind.* 17 40 45N 86 22W
Effingham, *Ill.* 17 39 7N 88 33W
Effingham, *S.C.* 12 34 5N 79 46W
Egan Range 18 39 35N 114 55W
Ehrenberg 21 33 36N 114 31W
Ehrhardt 12 33 6N 81 1W
Ekalaka 14 45 53N 104 33W
El Cajon 21 32 48N 116 58W
El Campo 15 29 12N 96 16W
El Centro 21 32 48N 115 34W
El Cerrito 30 37 54N 122 18W
El Dorado, *Ark.* 15 33 12N 92 40W
El Dorado, *Kans.* 15 37 49N 96 52W
El Granada 30 37 30N 122 27W
El Monte 31 34 3N 118 1W
El Paso, *Ill.* 16 40 44N 89 1W
El Paso, *Tex.* 19 31 45N 106 29W
El Paso Robles 20 35 38N 120 41W
El Portal 20 37 41N 119 47W
El Reno 15 35 32N 97 57W
El Rio 21 34 14N 119 10W
El Segundo 31 33 55N 118 24W
El Sereno 31 34 6N 118 10 E
El Sobrante 30 37 58N 122 17W
Elam 26 39 51N 75 32W
Elba 12 31 25N 86 4W
Elbe 20 46 45N 122 10W
Elberfeld 17 38 10N 87 27W
Elbert, Mt. 2 39 7N 106 27W
Elberton 12 34 7N 82 52W
Elburn 17 41 54N 88 28W
Eldon, *Mo.* 16 38 21N 92 35W
Eldon, *Wash.* 20 47 33N 123 3W
Eldora 16 42 22N 93 5W
Eldorado, *Ill.* 17 37 49N 88 26W
Eldorado, *Tex.* 15 30 52N 100 36W
Eldorado Springs 16 37 52N 94 1W
Eldorendo 12 31 3N 84 39W
Eldred 8 41 58N 78 23W
Eldridge 16 41 39N 90 35W
Eleele 32 21 54N 159 35W
Elephant Butte Reservoir 19 33 9N 107 11W
Elfin Cove 32 58 12N 136 22W
Elgin, *Ill.* 17 42 2N 88 17W
Elgin, *N. Dak.* 14 46 24N 101 51W
Elgin, *Oreg.* 18 45 34N 117 55W
Elgin, *S.C.* 12 34 10N 80 48W
Elgin, *Tex.* 15 30 21N 97 22W
Elim 32 64 37N 162 15W
Elizabeth, *N.J.* 22 40 39N 74 13W
Elizabeth, *Ill.* 16 42 19N 90 13W
Elizabeth City 11 36 18N 76 14W
Elizabethton 11 36 21N 82 13W
Elizabethtown, *Ky.* 10 37 42N 85 52W
Elizabethtown, *N.Y.* 9 44 13N 73 36W
Elizabethtown, *Pa.* 9 40 9N 76 36W
Elk → 11 34 46N 87 16W
Elk City 15 35 25N 99 25W
Elk Creek 20 39 36N 122 32W
Elk Grove 20 38 25N 121 22W
Elk River, *Idaho* 18 46 47N 116 11W
Elk River, *Minn.* 14 45 18N 93 35W
Elkader 16 42 51N 91 24W
Elkhart, *Ind.* 17 41 41N 85 58W
Elkhart, *Kans.* 15 37 0N 101 54W
Elkhart → 17 41 41N 85 58W
Elkhorn 17 42 40N 88 33W
Elkhorn → 14 41 8N 96 19W
Elkin 11 36 15N 80 51W
Elkins 10 38 55N 79 51W
Elkins Park 26 40 4N 75 8W
Elkland 8 41 59N 77 19W
Elko, *Ga.* 12 32 20N 83 42W
Elko, *Nev.* 18 40 50N 115 46W
Elkridge 27 39 13N 76 42W
Elkton 8 43 49N 83 11W
Ellaville 12 32 14N 84 19W
Ellen, Mt. 9 44 9N 72 56W
Ellenburg 9 44 54N 73 48W
Ellendale 14 46 0N 98 32W
Ellensburg 18 46 59N 120 34W
Ellenton 12 31 11N 83 35W
Ellenville 9 41 43N 74 24W
Ellettsville 17 39 14N 86 38W
Ellicott City 27 39 15N 76 49W
Ellicottville 8 42 17N 78 40W
Elliott 12 34 6N 80 10W
Elliott Key 13 25 27N 80 12W
Ellis 14 38 56N 99 34W
Ellis I. 22 40 41N 74 2W
Ellisville 15 31 36N 89 12W
Elloree 12 33 32N 80 34W
Ellsworth, *Kans.* 14 38 44N 98 14W
Ellsworth, *Maine* 11 44 33N 68 25W
Ellwood City 8 40 52N 80 17W
Elzey 13 29 19N 82 48W
Elma 20 47 0N 123 25W
Elmer 16 39 57N 92 39W
Elmhurst, *Ill.* 24 41 53N 87 55W
Elmhurst, *N.Y.* 23 40 44N 73 53W
Elmira 8 42 6N 76 48W
Elmira Heights 8 42 8N 76 50W
Elmodel 12 31 21N 84 29W
Elmont 23 40 42N 73 42W
Elmore, *Ala.* 12 32 32N 86 19W
Elmore, *Calif.* 21 33 7N 115 49W
Elmore, *Minn.* 17 41 29N 83 18W
Elmwood, *Md.* 27 39 20N 76 31W
Elmwood, *N.Y.* 23 40 51N 73 20W
Elmwood, *Ill.* 16 40 47N 89 58W
Elmwood Park, *Ill.* 24 41 55N 87 48W
Elmwood Park, *N.J.* 22 40 54N 74 7W
Elnora 17 38 53N 87 5W
Eloy 19 32 45N 111 33W
Elsie 20 45 52N 123 36W
Elsmere 26 39 44N 75 35W
Eltingville 22 40 32N 74 9W
Elwell, L. 18 48 22N 111 17W
Elwood, *Ill.* 17 41 24N 88 7W
Elwood, *Ind.* 17 40 17N 85 50W
Elwood, *Nebr.* 14 40 36N 99 52W
Ely, *Minn.* 14 47 55N 91 51W
Ely, *Nev.* 18 39 15N 114 54W
Elyria 8 41 22N 82 7W
Embarras → 17 38 39N 87 37W
Emerson, *N.J.* 22 40 57N 74 2W
Emerson, *Ga.* 12 34 8N 84 45W
Emeryville 30 37 49N 122 17W
Eminence 17 38 22N 85 11W
Emlenton 8 41 11N 79 43W
Emmalane 12 32 46N 82 0W
Emmaus 9 40 32N 75 30W
Emmetsburg 16 43 7N 94 41W
Emmett, *Idaho* 18 43 52N 116 30W
Emmett, *Mich.* 8 42 59N 82 46W
Empire 12 32 21N 83 18W
Empire State Building 22 40 44N 73 59W
Emporia, *Kans.* 14 38 25N 96 11W
Emporia, *Va.* 11 36 42N 77 32W
Emporium 8 41 31N 78 14W
Encampment 18 41 12N 106 47W
Encinitas 21 33 3N 117 17W
Encino, *Calif.* 31 34 9N 118 28W
Encino, *N. Mex.* 19 34 39N 105 28W
Encino Res. 31 34 8N 118 30W
Enderlin 14 46 38N 97 36W
Endicott 9 42 6N 76 4W
Endicott Mts. 32 68 0N 152 0W
Endwell 9 42 6N 76 2W
Enfield, *Pa.* 26 40 6N 75 11W
Enfield, *Conn.* 9 41 58N 72 36W
Enfield, *Ill.* 17 38 6N 88 20W
Enfield, *N.H.* 9 43 39N 72 9W
England 15 34 33N 91 58W
Englewood, *Ill.* 24 41 46N 87 38W
Englewood, *N.J.* 22 40 53N 73 58W
Englewood, *Colo.* 14 39 39N 104 59W
Englewood, *Fla.* 13 26 58N 82 21W
Englewood, *Ohio* 17 39 53N 84 18W
Englewood Cliffs 22 40 53N 73 59W
English 17 38 20N 86 28W
English → 16 41 29N 91 32W
Enid 15 36 24N 97 53W
Ennis, *Mont.* 18 45 21N 111 44W
Ennis, *Tex.* 15 32 20N 96 38W
Enosburg Falls 9 44 55N 72 48W
Ensley 13 30 31N 87 16W
Enterprise, *Ala.* 12 31 19N 85 51W
Enterprise, *Oreg.* 18 45 25N 117 17W
Enumclaw 20 47 12N 121 59W
Ephraim 18 39 22N 111 35W
Ephrata, *Pa.* 9 40 11N 76 11W
Ephrata, *Wash.* 18 47 19N 119 33W
Equality 17 37 44N 88 20W
Erdenheim 26 40 5N 75 13W
Erial 26 39 46N 75 0W
Eridu 12 30 18N 83 45W
Erie, *Mich.* 17 41 47N 83 31W

Glenwood

Erie, *Pa.* **8** 42 8N 80 5W
Erie, L. **2** 42 15N 81 0W
Erie Canal **8** 43 5N 78 43W
Erskine **14** 47 40N 96 0W
Erwin **11** 36 9N 82 25W
Escalante **19** 37 47N 111 36W
Escalante —► **19** 37 24N 110 57W
Escambia —► **11** 30 32N 87 11W
Escanaba **10** 45 45N 87 4W
Escondido **21** 33 7N 117 5W
Esom Hill **12** 33 57N 85 23W
Espanola, *Fla.* **13** 29 31N 81 19W
Espanola, *N. Mex.* **19** 35 59N 106 5W
Espenberg, C. **32** 66 33N 163 36W
Essex, *Md.* **27** 39 18N 76 28W
Essex, *Calif.* **21** 34 44N 115 15W
Essex, *Ill.* **17** 41 11N 88 11W
Essex, *N.Y.* **9** 44 19N 73 21W
Essex Falls **22** 40 49N 74 16W
Essex Junction **9** 44 29N 73 7W
Estancia **19** 34 46N 106 4W
Estero **13** 26 26N 81 49W
Estherville **14** 43 24N 94 50W
Estill **12** 32 45N 81 15W
Ethel **20** 46 32N 122 46W
Etowah **11** 35 20N 84 32W
Euclid **29** 41 34N 81 33W
Eudora **15** 33 7N 91 16W
Eufaula, *Ala.* **12** 31 54N 85 9W
Eufaula, *Okla.* **15** 35 17N 95 35W
Eufaula L. **15** 35 18N 95 21W
Eugene **18** 44 5N 123 4W
Eulonia **12** 31 32N 81 26W
Eunice, *La.* **15** 30 30N 92 25W
Eunice, *N. Mex.* **15** 32 26N 103 10W
Eureka, *Calif.* **18** 40 47N 124 9W
Eureka, *Ill.* **16** 40 43N 89 16W
Eureka, *Kans.* **15** 37 49N 96 17W
Eureka, *Mo.* **16** 38 30N 90 38W
Eureka, *Mont.* **18** 48 53N 115 3W
Eureka, *Nev.* **18** 39 31N 115 58W
Eureka, *S.C.* **12** 33 42N 81 46W
Eureka, *S. Dak.* **14** 45 46N 99 38W
Eustis **11** 28 51N 81 41W
Eustis, L. **13** 28 50N 81 44W
Eutawville **12** 33 24N 80 21W
Evans **14** 40 23N 104 41W
Evans City **8** 40 46N 80 4W
Evans Mills **9** 44 6N 75 48W
Evansdale **16** 42 30N 92 17W
Evanston, *Ill.* **24** 42 3N 87 40W
Evanston, *Wyo.* **18** 41 16N 110 58W
Evansville, *Ill.* **16** 38 5N 89 56W
Evansville, *Ind.* **17** 37 58N 87 35W
Evansville, *Wis.* **16** 42 47N 89 18W
Eveleth **14** 47 28N 92 32W
Everett, *Mass.* **25** 42 24N 71 3W
Everett, *Ga.* **12** 31 24N 81 38W
Everett, *Pa.* **8** 40 1N 78 23W
Everett, *Wash.* **20** 47 59N 122 12W
Everglades, The **11** 25 50N 81 0W
Everglades National Park **11** 25 30N 81 0W
Evergreen, *Ala.* **11** 31 26N 86 57W
Evergreen, *Mont.* **18** 48 9N 114 13W
Evergreen Park **24** 41 43N 87 42W
Evesboro **26** 39 54N 74 55W
Ewing, *Mo.* **16** 40 6N 91 43W
Ewing, *Nebr.* **14** 42 16N 98 21W
Excelsior Springs **16** 39 20N 94 13W
Exeter, *Calif.* **20** 36 18N 119 9W
Exeter, *N.H.* **9** 42 59N 70 57W
Exira **16** 41 35N 94 52W

F

Fabens **19** 31 30N 106 10W
Faceville **12** 30 45N 84 38W
Fagatogo **33** 14 17S 170 41W
Fair Haven **10** 43 36N 73 16W
Fair Lawn **22** 40 55N 74 7W
Fair Oaks **20** 38 39N 121 16W
Fairbanks, *Alaska* **32** 64 51N 147 43W
Fairbanks, *Fla.* **12** 29 44N 82 16W
Fairborn **17** 39 49N 84 2W
Fairburn **12** 33 34N 84 35W
Fairbury, *Ill.* **17** 40 45N 88 31W
Fairbury, *Nebr.* **14** 40 8N 97 11W
Fairfax, *Del.* **26** 39 47N 75 33W
Fairfax, *Ala.* **12** 32 48N 85 11W
Fairfax, *Ohio* **17** 39 5N 83 37W
Fairfax, *S.C.* **12** 32 59N 81 15W
Fairfax, *Vt.* **9** 44 40N 73 1W
Fairfax, *Va.* **27** 38 50N 77 19W
Fairfax Station **27** 38 48N 77 19W
Fairfield, *N.J.* **22** 40 53N 74 17W
Fairfield, *Ala.* **11** 33 29N 86 55W
Fairfield, *Calif.* **20** 38 15N 122 3W
Fairfield, *Conn.* **9** 41 9N 73 16W
Fairfield, *Idaho* **18** 43 21N 114 44W
Fairfield, *Ill.* **17** 38 23N 88 22W
Fairfield, *Iowa* **16** 40 56N 91 57W
Fairfield, *Ohio* **17** 39 21N 84 34W
Fairfield, *Tex.* **15** 31 44N 96 10W
Fairhaven B. **25** 42 25N 71 21W
Fairhaven Hill **25** 42 26N 71 21W
Fairhope **11** 30 31N 87 54W
Fairland **27** 39 4N 76 57W
Fairmead **20** 37 5N 120 10W
Fairmont, *Minn.* **14** 43 39N 94 28W
Fairmont, *W. Va.* **10** 39 29N 80 9W
Fairmont Terrace **30** 37 42N 122 7W
Fairmount, *Calif.* **21** 34 45N 118 26W
Fairmount, *N.Y.* **9** 43 5N 76 12W
Fairmount Heights **27** 38 54N 76 54W
Fairmount Park **26** 40 3N 75 13W
Fairplay **19** 39 15N 106 2W
Fairport **8** 43 6N 77 27W
Fairport Harbor **8** 41 45N 81 17W
Fairview, *N.J.* **22** 40 48N 73 59W
Fairview, *N.Y.* **23** 41 1N 73 46W
Fairview, *Mont.* **14** 47 51N 104 3W
Fairview, *Okla.* **15** 36 16N 98 29W
Fairview Park **29** 41 26N 81 52W
Fairweather, Mt. **32** 58 55N 137 32W
Faith **14** 45 2N 102 2W
Fajardo **32** 18 20N 65 39W
Falcon Reservoir **15** 26 34N 99 10W
Falconer **8** 42 7N 79 13W
Falfurrias **15** 27 14N 98 9W
Fall River **9** 41 43N 71 10W
Fallbrook **21** 33 23N 117 15W
Fallon, *Calif.* **31** 33 59N 117 54W
Fallon, *Nev.* **18** 39 28N 118 47W
Falls Church **27** 38 53N 77 12W
Falls City **14** 40 3N 95 36W
Falls Creek **8** 41 9N 78 48W
Falmouth, *Fla.* **12** 30 21N 83 8W
Falmouth, *Ky.* **17** 38 41N 84 20W
Falmouth, *Mass.* **9** 41 33N 70 37W
Famoso **21** 35 37N 119 12W
Fanwood **22** 40 37N 74 23W
Far Rockaway **23** 40 36N 73 45W
Farewell **32** 62 31N 153 54W
Fargo, *Ga.* **12** 30 41N 82 34W
Fargo, *N. Dak.* **14** 46 53N 96 48W
Faribault **14** 44 18N 93 16W
Farm Pond **25** 42 13N 71 20W
Farmer City **17** 40 15N 88 39W
Farmersburg **17** 39 15N 87 23W
Farmerville **15** 32 47N 92 24W
Farmingdale, *N.Y.* **23** 40 43N 73 27W
Farmingdale, *N.J.* **9** 40 12N 74 10W
Farmington, *Mich.* **28** 42 26N 83 22W
Farmington, *Calif.* **20** 37 55N 120 59W
Farmington, *Ga.* **12** 33 47N 83 26W
Farmington, *Ill.* **16** 40 42N 90 0W
Farmington, *Iowa* **16** 40 38N 91 44W
Farmington, *Maine* **11** 44 40N 70 9W
Farmington, *Mo.* **16** 37 47N 90 25W
Farmington, *N.H.* **9** 43 24N 71 4W
Farmington, *N. Mex.* **19** 36 44N 108 12W
Farmington, *Utah* **18** 41 0N 111 12W
Farmington —► **9** 41 51N 72 38W
Farmington Hills **28** 42 29N 83 23W
Farmland **17** 40 15N 85 5W
Farmville **10** 37 18N 78 24W
Farrar Pond **25** 42 24N 71 21W
Farrell **8** 41 13N 80 30W
Farson **18** 42 6N 109 27W
Farwell **15** 34 23N 103 2W
Faulkton **14** 45 2N 99 8W
Fawnskin **21** 34 16N 116 56W
Fayette, *Ala.* **11** 33 41N 87 50W
Fayette, *Iowa* **16** 42 51N 91 48W
Fayette, *Mo.* **16** 39 9N 92 41W
Fayette, *Ohio* **17** 41 40N 84 20W
Fayetteville, *Ark.* **15** 36 4N 94 10W
Fayetteville, *Ga.* **12** 33 27N 84 27W
Fayetteville, *N.C.* **11** 35 3N 78 53W
Fayetteville, *Tenn.* **11** 35 9N 86 34W
Fear, C. **11** 33 50N 77 58W
Feasterville **26** 40 9N 75 0W
Feather —► **18** 38 47N 121 36W
Feather Falls **20** 39 36N 121 16W
Federal Way **20** 47 18N 122 19W
Felda **13** 26 34N 81 26W
Felicity **17** 38 51N 84 6W
Fellowship **26** 39 56N 74 57W
Fellsmere **13** 27 46N 80 36W
Felton **20** 37 3N 122 4W
Feltonville **26** 40 1N 75 8W
Fennimore **16** 42 59N 90 39W
Fenton **17** 42 48N 83 42W
Fergus Falls **14** 46 17N 96 4W
Ferguson **16** 38 45N 90 18W
Fernandina Beach **12** 30 40N 81 27W
Ferndale, *Md.* **27** 39 11N 76 38W
Ferndale, *Mich.* **28** 42 27N 83 7W
Ferndale, *Wash.* **20** 48 51N 122 36W
Fernley **18** 39 36N 119 15W
Ferriday **15** 31 38N 91 33W
Ferron **19** 39 5N 111 8W
Ferry **23** 41 0N 73 52W
Ferrysburg **17** 43 5N 86 13W
Fertile **14** 47 32N 96 17W
Fessenden **14** 47 39N 99 38W
Festus **16** 38 13N 90 24W
Fields Corner **25** 42 18N 71 3W
Fillmore, *Calif.* **21** 34 24N 118 55W
Fillmore, *Utah* **19** 38 58N 112 20W
Findlay **17** 41 2N 83 39W
Finger Lakes **9** 42 40N 76 30W
Finley **14** 47 31N 97 50W
Firebaugh **20** 36 52N 120 27W
Fisheating Cr. —► **13** 26 57N 81 7W
Fishers I. **9** 41 15N 72 0W
Fishkill **9** 41 32N 73 53W
Fitchburg **9** 42 35N 71 48W
Fitzgerald **12** 31 43N 83 15W
Five Points **20** 36 26N 120 6W
Flagler Beach **13** 29 29N 81 8W
Flagstaff **19** 35 12N 111 39W
Flagstaff L. **11** 45 12N 70 18W
Flambeau —► **14** 45 18N 91 14W
Flaming Gorge Reservoir **18** 41 10N 109 25W
Flamingo **13** 25 8N 80 57W
Flanagan **17** 40 53N 88 52W
Flandreau **14** 44 3N 96 36W
Flanigan **20** 40 10N 119 53W
Flat —► **17** 42 56N 85 20W
Flat Rock, *Ill.* **17** 38 54N 87 40W
Flat Rock, *Mich.* **17** 42 6N 83 17W
Flatbush **22** 40 39N 73 56W
Flathead L. **18** 47 51N 114 8W
Flatrock —► **17** 39 12N 85 56W
Flattery, C. **2** 48 23N 124 29W
Flatwoods **10** 38 31N 82 43W
Fleetwood **9** 40 27N 75 49W
Flemingsburg **17** 38 25N 83 45W
Flemington **8** 41 7N 77 28W
Flint **17** 43 1N 83 41W
Flint —► **12** 30 57N 84 34W
Flint Pk. **31** 34 9N 118 11 E
Floodwood **14** 46 55N 92 55W
Flora, *Ill.* **10** 38 40N 88 29W
Flora, *Ind.* **17** 40 33N 86 31W
Florahome **12** 29 44N 81 54W
Floral City **13** 28 45N 82 17W
Floral Park **23** 40 43N 73 42W
Florala **11** 31 0N 86 20W
Florence, *Calif.* **31** 33 57N 118 13W
Florence, *N.J.* **26** 39 44N 74 55W
Florence, *Ala.* **11** 34 48N 87 41W
Florence, *Ariz.* **19** 33 2N 111 23W
Florence, *Colo.* **14** 38 23N 105 8W
Florence, *Oreg.* **18** 43 58N 124 7W
Florence, *S.C.* **11** 34 12N 79 46W
Floresville **15** 29 8N 98 10W
Florham Park **22** 40 46N 74 23W
Florida □ **2** 28 0N 82 0W
Florida, Straits of **2** 25 0N 80 0W
Florida City **13** 25 27N 80 29W
Florida Keys **13** 24 40N 81 0W
Florida Ridge **13** 27 38N 80 24W
Florissant **16** 38 48N 90 20W
Flourtown **26** 40 6N 75 13W
Flower Hill **23** 40 48N 73 40W
Floydada **15** 33 59N 101 20W
Flushing, *N.Y.* **23** 40 45N 73 49W
Flushing, *Mich.* **17** 43 4N 83 51W
Flushing Meadows Corona Park **23** 40 44N 73 50W
Folcroft **26** 39 53N 75 16W
Foley, *Ala.* **11** 30 24N 87 41W
Foley, *Fla.* **12** 30 4N 83 32W
Folkston **12** 30 50N 82 0W
Follansbee **8** 40 19N 80 35W
Folsom **26** 39 53N 75 19W
Folsom L. **20** 38 42N 121 9W
Fond du Lac **14** 43 47N 88 27W
Fonda, *Iowa* **16** 42 35N 94 51W
Fonda, *N.Y.* **9** 42 57N 74 22W
Fontana **21** 34 6N 117 26W
Fontenelle Reservoir **18** 42 1N 110 3W
Ford City, *Calif.* **21** 35 9N 119 27W
Ford City, *Pa.* **8** 40 46N 79 32W
Fordham Univ. **23** 40 51N 73 51W
Fords **22** 40 31N 74 19W
Fordyce **15** 33 49N 92 25W
Foremans Corner **27** 39 11N 76 33W
Forest **15** 32 22N 89 29W
Forest Acres **12** 34 1N 80 58W
Forest City, *Iowa* **14** 43 16N 93 39W
Forest City, *N.C.* **11** 35 20N 81 52W
Forest City, *Pa.* **9** 41 39N 75 28W
Forest Grove **20** 45 31N 123 7W
Forest Heights **27** 38 48N 77 0W
Forest Hills, *N.Y.* **23** 40 42N 73 51W
Forest Hills, *Pa.* **29** 40 25N 79 51W
Forest Park, *Ill.* **24** 41 51N 87 47W
Forest Park, *Ga.* **12** 33 37N 84 22W
Forest View **24** 41 48N 87 47W
Foresthill **20** 39 1N 120 49W
Foreston **12** 33 38N 80 4W
Forestville, *Calif.* **20** 38 28N 122 54W
Forestville, *N.Y.* **8** 42 28N 79 10W
Forestville, *Md.* **27** 38 50N 76 52W
Forks **20** 47 57N 124 23W
Forksville **9** 41 29N 76 35W
Forman **14** 46 7N 97 38W
Forrest City **15** 35 1N 90 47W
Forreston **16** 42 8N 89 35W
Forsyth, *Ga.* **12** 33 2N 83 56W
Forsyth, *Mont.* **18** 46 16N 106 41W
Fort Ann **9** 43 25N 73 30W
Fort Atkinson **17** 42 56N 88 50W
Fort Benton **18** 47 49N 110 40W
Fort Bragg **18** 39 26N 123 48W
Fort Bridger **18** 41 19N 110 23W
Fort Collins **14** 40 35N 105 5W
Fort Covington **9** 44 59N 74 29W
Fort Davis, *Ala.* **12** 32 15N 85 43W
Fort Davis, *Tex.* **15** 30 35N 103 54W
Fort Defiance **19** 35 45N 109 5W
Fort Dodge **14** 42 30N 94 11W
Fort Drum **13** 27 32N 80 48W
Fort du Pont Park **27** 38 52N 76 56W
Fort Edward **9** 43 16N 73 35W
Fort Fairfield **11** 46 46N 67 50W
Fort Foote Village **27** 38 46N 77 1W
Fort Gaines **12** 31 36N 85 3W
Fort Garland **19** 37 26N 105 26W
Fort Hancock **19** 31 18N 105 51W
Fort Howard **27** 39 12N 76 26W
Fort Irwin **21** 35 16N 116 34W
Fort Kent **11** 47 15N 68 36W
Fort Klamath **18** 42 42N 122 0W
Fort Knox **17** 37 54N 85 57W
Fort Laramie **14** 42 13N 104 31W
Fort Lauderdale **11** 26 7N 80 8W
Fort Lee **22** 40 50N 73 58W
Fort Leonard Wood **16** 37 46N 92 11W
Fort Lupton **14** 40 5N 104 49W
Fort McHenry Nat. Mon. **27** 35 15N 76 35W
Fort Madison **16** 40 38N 91 27W
Fort Meade **11** 27 45N 81 48W
Fort Mitchell **12** 32 20N 85 1W
Fort Morgan **14** 40 15N 103 48W
Fort Motte **12** 33 44N 80 42W
Fort Myers **11** 26 39N 81 52W
Fort Myers Beach **13** 26 26N 81 52W
Fort Myers Villas **13** 26 34N 81 52W
Fort Payne **11** 34 26N 85 43W
Fort Peck **18** 48 1N 106 27W
Fort Peck Dam **18** 48 0N 106 26W
Fort Peck L. **18** 48 0N 106 26W
Fort Pierce **11** 27 27N 80 20W
Fort Pierre **14** 44 21N 100 22W
Fort Plain **9** 42 56N 74 37W
Fort Recovery **17** 40 25N 84 47W
Fort Ross **20** 38 32N 123 13W
Fort Scott **15** 37 50N 94 42W
Fort Smith **15** 35 23N 94 25W
Fort Stockton **15** 30 53N 102 53W
Fort Sumner **15** 34 28N 104 15W
Fort Thomas **17** 39 5N 84 27W
Fort Thompson **14** 44 3N 99 26W
Fort Valley **12** 32 33N 83 53W
Fort Walton Beach **11** 30 25N 86 36W
Fort Washington **26** 40 8N 75 13W
Fort Wayne **17** 41 4N 85 9W
Fort White **12** 29 55N 82 43W
Fort Worth **15** 32 45N 97 18W
Fort Yates **14** 46 5N 100 38W
Fort Yukon **32** 66 34N 145 16W
Fortsonia **12** 34 1N 82 47W
Fortuna, *Calif.* **18** 40 36N 124 9W
Fortuna, *N. Dak.* **14** 48 55N 103 47W
Fossil **18** 45 0N 120 9W
Foster **17** 38 48N 84 13W
Foster City **30** 37 33N 122 15W
Fosters Pond **25** 42 36N 71 8W
Fostoria **17** 41 10N 83 25W
Foulweather, C. **6** 44 50N 124 5W
Fountain, *Colo.* **14** 38 41N 104 42W
Fountain, *Fla.* **12** 30 29N 85 25W
Fountain Springs **21** 35 54N 118 51W
Four Mountains, Is. of **32** 53 0N 170 0W
Fowl Meadow Res. **25** 42 13N 71 8W
Fowler, *Calif.* **20** 36 38N 119 41W
Fowler, *Colo.* **14** 38 8N 104 2W
Fowler, *Ind.* **17** 40 37N 87 19W
Fowler, *Mich.* **17** 43 0N 84 45W
Fowlerville **17** 42 40N 84 4W
Fowlstown **12** 30 48N 84 33W
Fox Chase **26** 40 4N 75 5W
Fox Is. **32** 52 30N 166 0W
Foxboro **9** 42 4N 71 16W
Foxhall **27** 39 4N 77 3W
Frackville **9** 40 47N 76 14W
Framingham **25** 42 18N 71 24W
Francesville **17** 40 59N 86 53W
Francis Case, L. **14** 43 4N 98 34W
Franconia **27** 38 47N 77 7W
Frankford, *Pa.* **26** 40 1N 75 5W
Frankford, *Mo.* **16** 39 29N 91 19W
Frankfort, *Ind.* **17** 40 17N 86 31W
Frankfort, *Kans.* **14** 39 42N 96 25W
Frankfort, *Ky.* **17** 38 12N 84 52W
Frankfort, *N.Y.* **9** 43 2N 75 4W
Frankfort, *Ohio* **17** 39 24N 83 11W
Franklin, *Ga.* **12** 33 17N 85 6W
Franklin, *Ill.* **16** 39 37N 90 3W
Franklin, *Ind.* **17** 39 29N 86 3W
Franklin, *Ky.* **11** 36 43N 86 35W
Franklin, *La.* **15** 29 48N 91 30W
Franklin, *Mass.* **9** 42 5N 71 24W
Franklin, *N.H.* **9** 43 27N 71 39W
Franklin, *Nebr.* **14** 40 6N 98 57W
Franklin, *Ohio* **17** 39 34N 84 18W
Franklin, *Pa.* **8** 41 24N 79 50W
Franklin, *Va.* **11** 36 41N 76 56W
Franklin, *W. Va.* **10** 38 39N 79 20W
Franklin D. Roosevelt L. **18** 48 18N 118 9W
Franklin L., *N.J.* **22** 40 59N 74 13W
Franklin L., *Nev.* **18** 40 25N 115 22W
Franklin Lakes **22** 40 59N 74 13W
Franklin Park, *Mass.* **25** 42 18N 71 5W
Franklin Park, *Ill.* **24** 41 55N 87 52W
Franklin Park, *Va.* **27** 38 55N 77 9W
Franklin Res. **31** 34 5N 118 24W
Franklin Roosevelt Park **26** 39 54N 75 10W
Franklin Square **23** 40 42N 73 40W
Franklinton **15** 30 51N 90 9W
Franklinville **8** 42 20N 78 27W
Franks Pk. **18** 43 58N 109 18W
Fraser **8** 42 32N 82 57W
Frederick, *Md.* **10** 39 25N 77 25W
Frederick, *Okla.* **15** 34 23N 99 1W
Frederick, *S. Dak.* **14** 45 50N 98 31W
Fredericksburg, *Pa.* **9** 40 27N 76 26W
Fredericksburg, *Tex.* **15** 30 16N 98 52W
Fredericksburg, *Va.* **10** 38 18N 77 28W
Fredericktown, *Mo.* **15** 37 34N 90 18W
Fredericktown, *Ohio* **8** 40 29N 82 33W
Fredonia, *Ariz.* **19** 36 57N 112 32W
Fredonia, *Kans.* **15** 37 32N 95 49W
Fredonia, *N.Y.* **8** 42 26N 79 20W
Freeburg **16** 38 19N 91 56W
Freehold **9** 40 16N 74 17W
Freel Peak **20** 38 52N 119 54W
Freeland **9** 41 1N 75 54W
Freeman, *Calif.* **21** 35 35N 117 53W
Freeman, *Mo.* **16** 38 37N 94 30W
Freeman, *S. Dak.* **14** 43 21N 97 26W
Freeport, *N.Y.* **23** 40 39N 73 35W
Freeport, *Fla.* **12** 30 30N 86 8W
Freeport, *Ill.* **16** 42 17N 89 36W
Freeport, *Ohio* **8** 40 12N 81 15W
Freeport, *Pa.* **8** 40 41N 79 41W
Freeport, *Tex.* **15** 28 57N 95 21W
Fremont, *Calif.* **20** 37 32N 121 57W
Fremont, *Ind.* **17** 41 44N 84 56W
Fremont, *Mich.* **10** 43 28N 85 57W
Fremont, *Nebr.* **14** 41 26N 96 30W
Fremont, *Ohio* **17** 41 21N 83 7W
Fremont —► **19** 38 24N 110 42W
French Camp **20** 37 53N 121 16W
French Creek —► **8** 41 24N 79 50W
French Lick **17** 38 33N 86 37W
Frenchburg **17** 37 57N 83 38W
Frenchman Cr. —►, *N. Amer.* **18** 48 31N 107 10W
Frenchman Cr. —►, *Nebr.* **14** 40 14N 100 50W
Fresh Meadows **23** 40 43N 73 47W
Fresh Pond **25** 42 22N 71 8W
Fresno **20** 36 44N 119 47W
Fresno Reservoir **18** 48 36N 109 57W
Frewsburg **8** 42 3N 79 10W
Friant **20** 36 59N 119 43W
Friday Harbor **20** 48 32N 123 1W
Friedens **8** 40 3N 78 59W
Friendship **8** 42 12N 78 8W
Frio —► **15** 28 26N 98 11W
Friona **15** 34 38N 102 43W
Fritch **15** 35 38N 101 36W
Front Range **6** 40 25N 105 45W
Front Royal **10** 38 55N 78 12W
Frostburg **10** 39 39N 78 56W
Frostproof **13** 27 45N 81 32W
Fruithurst **12** 33 44N 85 26W
Fruitland Park **13** 28 51N 81 54W
Fryeburg **9** 44 1N 70 59W
Fuller Park **31** 33 51N 117 56W
Fullerton, *Md.* **27** 39 22N 76 30W
Fullerton, *Calif.* **21** 33 53N 117 56W
Fullerton, *Nebr.* **14** 41 22N 97 58W
Fulton, *Ill.* **16** 41 52N 90 11W
Fulton, *Ind.* **17** 40 57N 86 16W
Fulton, *Mo.* **16** 38 52N 91 57W
Fulton, *N.Y.* **9** 43 19N 76 25W
Funston **12** 31 12N 83 52W
Furman **12** 32 41N 81 11W

G

Gabbettville **12** 32 57N 85 8W
Gabriels **9** 44 26N 74 12W
Gadsden, *Ala.* **12** 34 1N 86 1W
Gadsden, *S.C.* **12** 33 51N 80 46W
Gaffney **11** 35 5N 81 39W
Gage Park **24** 41 47N 87 42W
Gail **15** 32 46N 101 27W
Gaines **8** 41 46N 77 35W
Gainesville, *Fla.* **13** 29 40N 82 20W
Gainesville, *Ga.* **11** 34 18N 83 50W
Gainesville, *Mo.* **15** 36 36N 92 26W
Gainesville, *Tex.* **15** 33 38N 97 8W
Galax **11** 36 40N 80 56W
Galena, *Alaska* **32** 64 44N 156 56W
Galena, *Ill.* **16** 42 25N 90 26W
Galesburg, *Ill.* **16** 40 57N 90 22W
Galesburg, *Mich.* **17** 42 17N 85 26W
Galeton **8** 41 44N 77 39W
Galien **17** 41 48N 86 30W
Galion **8** 40 44N 82 47W
Galiuro Mts. **19** 32 30N 110 20W
Gallatin, *Mo.* **16** 39 55N 93 58W
Gallatin, *Tenn.* **11** 36 24N 86 27W
Gallipolis **10** 38 49N 82 12W
Galloo I. **9** 43 55N 76 25W
Gallup **19** 35 32N 108 45W
Galt, *Calif.* **20** 38 15N 121 18W
Galt, *Mo.* **16** 40 8N 93 23W
Galva **16** 41 10N 90 3W
Galveston, *Ind.* **17** 40 35N 86 11W
Galveston, *Tex.* **15** 29 18N 94 48W
Galveston B. **15** 29 36N 94 50W
Gambell **32** 63 47N 171 45W
Gambier **8** 40 22N 82 23W
Ganado **19** 35 43N 109 33W
Gannett Peak **18** 43 11N 109 39W
Garapan **33** 15 12N 145 53 E
Garberville **18** 40 6N 123 48W
Garden City, *Mich.* **28** 42 20N 83 20W
Garden City, *N.Y.* **23** 40 43N 73 37W
Garden City, *Ga.* **12** 32 6N 81 9W
Garden City, *Kans.* **15** 37 58N 100 53W
Garden City, *Mo.* **16** 38 34N 94 12W
Garden City, *Tex.* **15** 31 52N 101 29W
Garden Grove **21** 33 47N 117 55W
Gardena **31** 33 53N 118 18W
Gardi **12** 31 32N 81 48W
Gardiner, *Maine* **11** 44 14N 69 47W
Gardiner, *Mont.* **18** 45 2N 110 22W
Gardiners I. **9** 41 6N 72 6W
Gardner, *Fla.* **13** 27 21N 81 48W
Gardner, *Ill.* **17** 41 12N 88 17W
Gardner, *Mass.* **9** 42 34N 71 59W
Gardnerville **20** 38 56N 119 45W
Gareloi I. **32** 51 48N 178 48W
Garey **21** 34 53N 120 19W
Garfield, *N.J.* **22** 40 52N 74 7W
Garfield, *Wash.* **18** 47 1N 117 9W
Garfield Heights **29** 41 25N 81 37W
Garfield Park **24** 41 52N 87 42W
Garland, *Tex.* **15** 32 55N 96 38W
Garland, *Utah* **18** 41 47N 112 10W
Garner **16** 43 6N 93 36W
Garnett **14** 38 17N 95 14W
Garrett **17** 41 21N 85 8W
Garrison, *Md.* **27** 39 24N 76 45W
Garrison, *Ky.* **17** 38 36N 83 10W
Garrison, *Mont.* **18** 46 31N 112 49W
Garrison, *N. Dak.* **14** 47 40N 101 25W
Garrison Res. = Sakakawea, L. **14** 47 30N 101 25W
Garvanza **31** 34 6N 118 11 E
Garwood **22** 40 38N 74 18W
Gary **17** 41 36N 87 20W
Gas City **17** 40 29N 85 37W
Gasconade **16** 38 40N 91 34W
Gasconade —► **16** 38 41N 91 33W
Gasparilla I. **13** 26 46N 82 16W
Gaston **12** 33 49N 81 5W
Gastonia **11** 35 16N 81 11W
Gates **8** 43 9N 77 42W
Gatesville **15** 31 26N 97 45W
Gaviota **21** 34 29N 120 13W
Gay **12** 33 6N 84 35W
Gaylord **10** 45 2N 84 41W
Geist Res. **26** 39 57N 75 24W
Geistown **8** 40 18N 78 52W
Genesee, *Idaho* **18** 46 33N 116 56W
Genesee, *Pa.* **8** 41 59N 77 54W
Genesee —► **8** 43 16N 77 36W
Geneseo, *Ill.* **16** 41 27N 90 9W
Geneseo, *N.Y.* **8** 42 48N 77 49W
Geneva, *Ala.* **12** 31 2N 85 52W
Geneva, *Ga.* **12** 32 35N 84 33W
Geneva, *Ill.* **17** 41 53N 88 18W
Geneva, *Ind.* **17** 40 36N 84 58W
Geneva, *N.Y.* **8** 42 52N 76 59W
Geneva, *Nebr.* **14** 40 32N 97 36W
Geneva, *Ohio* **8** 41 48N 80 57W
Geneva, L. **17** 42 38N 88 30W
Genoa, *Ill.* **17** 42 6N 88 42W
Genoa, *N.Y.* **9** 42 40N 76 32W
Genoa, *Nebr.* **14** 41 27N 97 44W
Genoa, *Nev.* **20** 39 2N 119 50W
Genoa City **17** 42 30N 88 20W
George, L., *Fla.* **11** 29 17N 81 36W
George, L., *N.Y.* **9** 43 37N 73 33W
George West **15** 28 20N 98 7W
Georges I. **25** 42 19N 70 55W
Georgetown, *Calif.* **20** 38 54N 120 50W
Georgetown, *Colo.* **18** 39 42N 105 42W
Georgetown, *Fla.* **13** 29 23N 81 38W
Georgetown, *Ga.* **12** 31 53N 85 6W
Georgetown, *Ill.* **17** 39 59N 87 38W
Georgetown, *Ky.* **10** 38 13N 84 33W
Georgetown, *N.Y.* **9** 42 46N 75 44W
Georgetown, *Ohio* **17** 38 52N 83 54W
Georgetown, *S.C.* **11** 33 23N 79 17W
Georgetown, *Tex.* **15** 30 38N 97 41W
Georgetown, *D.C.* **27** 38 54N 77 3W
Georgetown Rowley State Forest **25** 42 41N 70 56W
Georgia □ **12** 32 50N 83 15W
Gerald **16** 38 24N 91 20W
Geraldine **18** 47 36N 110 16W
Gering **14** 41 50N 103 40W
Gerlach **18** 40 39N 119 21W
Germantown, *Md.* **27** 39 24N 76 28W
Germantown, *Pa.* **26** 40 2N 75 11W
Germantown, *Ohio* **17** 39 38N 84 22W
Germantown, *Tenn.* **15** 35 5N 89 49W
Gettysburg, *Pa.* **10** 39 50N 77 14W
Gettysburg, *S. Dak.* **14** 45 1N 99 57W
Geyser **18** 47 16N 110 30W
Geyserville **20** 38 42N 122 54W
Giant **30** 37 58N 122 20W
Giant Forest **20** 36 36N 118 43W
Gibbon **14** 40 45N 98 51W
Gibbsboro **26** 39 50N 74 57W
Gibbstown **26** 39 49N 75 17W
Gibson **12** 33 14N 82 36W
Gibson City **17** 40 28N 88 22W
Gibsonburg **17** 41 23N 83 19W
Gibsonton **13** 27 51N 82 23W
Gibsonville **20** 39 46N 120 54W
Giddings **15** 30 11N 96 56W
Gifford **13** 27 40N 80 25W
Gila —► **2** 32 43N 114 33W
Gila Bend **19** 32 57N 112 43W
Gila Bend Mts. **19** 33 10N 113 0W
Gilbert **12** 33 56N 81 24W
Gilead **9** 44 24N 70 59W
Gilgo Beach **23** 40 36N 73 24W
Gilgo I. **23** 40 37N 73 23W
Gillespie **16** 39 8N 89 49W
Gillette, *N.J.* **22** 40 40N 74 29W
Gillette, *Wyo.* **14** 44 18N 105 30W
Gilman **17** 40 46N 88 0W
Gilman City **16** 40 8N 93 53W
Gilmer **15** 32 44N 94 57W
Gilroy **20** 37 1N 121 34W
Girard, *Ga.* **12** 33 3N 81 43W
Girard, *Ill.* **16** 39 27N 89 47W
Girard, *Kans.* **15** 37 31N 94 51W
Girard, *Ohio* **8** 41 9N 80 42W
Girard, *Pa.* **8** 42 0N 80 19W
Girard, *Pa.* **8** 42 0N 80 19W
Glacier Hills **22** 40 51N 74 28W
Glacier National Park **18** 48 30N 113 18W
Glacier Peak **18** 48 7N 121 7W
Gladewater **15** 32 33N 94 56W
Gladstone, *Mich.* **10** 45 51N 87 1W
Gladstone, *Mo.* **16** 39 13N 94 35W
Gladwin **10** 43 59N 84 29W
Glamis **21** 32 55N 115 5W
Glasco, *Kans.* **14** 39 22N 97 50W
Glasco, *N.Y.* **9** 42 3N 73 57W
Glasgow, *Ky.* **10** 37 0N 85 55W
Glasgow, *Mo.* **16** 39 14N 92 51W
Glasgow, *Mont.* **18** 48 12N 106 38W
Glassmanor **27** 38 49N 77 0W
Glastonbury **9** 41 43N 72 37W
Glen **9** 44 7N 71 11W
Glen Canyon **19** 37 30N 110 40W
Glen Canyon Dam **19** 36 57N 111 29W
Glen Canyon National Recreation Area **19** 37 15N 111 0W
Glen Cove **23** 40 52N 73 38W
Glen Echo **27** 38 58N 77 8W
Glen Hd. **23** 40 49N 73 37W
Glen Lyon **9** 41 10N 76 5W
Glen Mills **26** 39 55N 75 29W
Glen Oaks **23** 40 45N 73 43W
Glen Riddle **26** 39 53N 75 26W
Glen Ridge **22** 40 48N 74 12W
Glen Rock **22** 40 57N 74 7W
Glen Ullin **14** 46 49N 101 50W
Glenardon **27** 38 56N 76 51W
Glencoe, *Ill.* **24** 42 7N 87 44W
Glencoe, *Ala.* **12** 33 57N 85 56W
Glencoe, *Minn.* **14** 44 46N 94 9W
Glendale, *Calif.* **31** 34 9N 118 15 E
Glendale, *Ariz.* **19** 33 32N 112 11W
Glendale, *Calif.* **21** 34 9N 118 15W
Glendale, *Fla.* **12** 30 52N 86 7W
Glendive **14** 47 7N 104 43W
Glendo **14** 42 30N 105 2W
Glendora **26** 39 50N 75 4W
Glenfield **9** 43 43N 75 24W
Glenmont, *Ohio* **8** 40 31N 82 6W
Glenmont, *Md.* **27** 39 3N 77 4W
Glenn **20** 39 31N 122 1W
Glenns Ferry **18** 42 57N 115 18W
Glennville **12** 31 56N 81 56W
Glenolden **26** 39 54N 75 17W
Glenrock **18** 42 52N 105 52W
Glens Falls **9** 43 19N 73 39W
Glenshaw **29** 40 32N 79 58W
Glenside **26** 40 6N 75 9W
Glenview **24** 42 3N 87 48W
Glenview Countryside **24** 42 3N 87 49W
Glenview Woods **24** 42 4N 87 46W
Glenville, *N.Y.* **23** 41 1N 73 41W
Glenville, *W. Va.* **10** 38 56N 80 50W
Glenwood, *Ala.* **12** 31 40N 86 10W

Glenwood

Glenwood, *Ark.* **15** 34 20N 93 33W
Glenwood, *Ga.* **12** 32 11N 82 40W
Glenwood, *Hawaii* **32** 19 29N 155 9W
Glenwood, *Iowa* **14** 41 3N 95 45W
Glenwood, *Minn.* **14** 45 39N 95 23W
Glenwood, *Wash.* **20** 46 1N 121 17W
Glenwood Landing **23** 40 48N 73 38W
Glenwood Springs **18** 39 33N 107 19W
Globe **19** 33 24N 110 47W
Gloucester **9** 42 37N 70 40W
Gloucester City **26** 39 53N 75 7W
Gloucester Point **10** 37 15N 76 29W
Gloversville **9** 43 3N 74 21W
Gobles **17** 42 22N 85 53W
Godfrey, *Ga.* **12** 33 27N 83 30W
Godfrey, *Ill.* **16** 38 58N 90 11W
Goeselville **24** 41 37N 87 46W
Goffstown **9** 43 1N 71 36W
Gogebic, L. **14** 46 30N 89 35W
Golconda **18** 40 58N 117 30W
Gold **8** 41 52N 77 50W
Gold Beach **18** 42 25N 124 25W
Gold Creek **32** 62 46N 149 41W
Gold Hill **18** 42 26N 123 3W
Golden **16** 40 7N 91 1W
Golden Gate **30** 37 48N 122 29W
Golden Gate Bridge **30** 37 49N 122 28W
Golden Gate National Recreation Area **30** 37 49N 122 31W
Golden Gate Park **30** 37 46N 122 28W
Goldendale **18** 45 49N 120 50W
Goldfield **19** 37 42N 117 14W
Goldsboro **11** 35 23N 77 59W
Goldsmith **15** 31 59N 102 37W
Goldthwaite **15** 31 27N 98 34W
Goleta **21** 34 27N 119 50W
Goliad **15** 28 40N 97 23W
Gonzales, *Calif.* **20** 36 30N 121 26W
Gonzales, *Tex.* **15** 29 30N 97 27W
Gooding **18** 42 56N 114 43W
Goodland **14** 39 21N 101 43W
Goodman Hill **25** 42 22N 71 23W
Goodsprings **21** 35 49N 115 27W
Goodwater **12** 33 4N 86 3W
Goose Creek **12** 32 59N 80 2W
Goose L. **18** 41 56N 120 26W
Gorda **20** 35 53N 121 26W
Gordon, *Ga.* **12** 32 54N 83 20W
Gordon, *Nebr.* **14** 42 48N 102 12W
Gorham **9** 44 23N 71 10W
Gorin **16** 40 22N 92 1W
Gorman **21** 34 47N 118 51W
Goshen, *Calif.* **20** 36 21N 119 25W
Goshen, *Ind.* **17** 41 35N 85 50W
Goshen, *N.Y.* **9** 41 24N 74 20W
Goshenville **26** 39 59N 75 32W
Gosport **17** 39 21N 86 40W
Gothenburg **14** 40 56N 100 10W
Gough **12** 33 6N 82 14W
Goulds **13** 25 33N 80 23W
Gouverneur **9** 44 20N 75 28W
Govan **12** 33 13N 81 11W
Governor's I. **22** 40 41N 74 1W
Gowanda **8** 42 28N 78 56W
Gowrie **16** 42 17N 94 17W
Grabill **17** 41 13N 84 57W
Graceville **12** 30 58N 85 31W
Gracewood **12** 33 22N 82 2W
Gracias a Dios, C. **2** 15 0N 83 10W
Grady, *Ala.* **12** 31 59N 86 3W
Grady, *N. Mex.* **15** 34 49N 103 19W
Gradyville **26** 39 56N 75 27W
Grafton, *Ill.* **16** 38 58N 90 26W
Grafton, *N. Dak.* **14** 48 25N 97 25W
Grafton, *W. Va.* **10** 39 21N 80 2W
Graham, *Ga.* **12** 31 50N 82 30W
Graham, *Tex.* **15** 33 6N 98 35W
Graham, Mt. **19** 32 42N 109 52W
Graham Memorial Park **27** 39 25N 76 29W
Grahamsville **9** 41 51N 74 33W
Grampian **8** 40 58N 78 37W
Granada **15** 38 4N 102 19W
Granada Hills **31** 34 16N 118 30W
Granbury **15** 32 27N 97 47W
Granby **18** 40 5N 105 56W
Grand →, *Mich.* **17** 43 4N 86 15W
Grand →, *Mo.* **16** 39 23N 93 7W
Grand →, *S. Dak.* **14** 45 40N 100 45W
Grand Blanc **17** 42 56N 83 38W
Grand Canyon **2** 36 3N 112 9W
Grand Canyon National Park **19** 36 15N 112 30W
Grand Coulee **18** 47 57N 119 0W
Grand Coulee Dam **18** 47 57N 118 59W
Grand Forks **14** 47 55N 97 3W
Grand Gorge **9** 42 21N 74 29W
Grand Haven **17** 43 4N 86 13W
Grand I., *Mich.* **10** 46 31N 86 40W
Grand I., *N.Y.* **8** 43 0N 78 58W
Grand Island **14** 40 55N 98 21W
Grand Isle, *La.* **15** 29 14N 90 0W
Grand Isle, *Vt.* **9** 44 43N 73 18W
Grand Junction, *Colo.* **19** 39 4N 108 33W
Grand Junction, *Iowa* **16** 42 2N 94 14W
Grand L., *La.* **15** 29 55N 92 47W
Grand L., *Ohio* **17** 40 32N 84 25W
Grand Lake **18** 40 15N 105 49W
Grand Ledge **17** 42 45N 84 45W
Grand Marais **10** 46 40N 85 59W
Grand Portage **14** 47 58N 89 41W
Grand Prairie **15** 32 47N 97 0W
Grand Rapids, *Mich.* **17** 42 58N 85 40W
Grand Rapids, *Minn.* **14** 47 14N 93 31W
Grand Ridge **12** 30 43N 85 1W
Grand River **16** 40 49N 93 58W
Grand Teton **18** 43 54N 111 50W
Grand Teton National Park **18** 43 50N 110 50W
Grande, Rio → **2** 25 58N 97 9W
Grandfalls **15** 31 20N 102 51W
Grandview, *Mo.* **16** 38 53N 94 32W
Grandview, *Wash.* **18** 46 15N 119 54W
Grandview Heights **17** 39 58N 83 2W
Granger **18** 41 35N 109 58W
Grangeville **18** 45 56N 116 7W
Granite **27** 39 20N 76 51W
Granite City **16** 38 42N 90 9W
Granite Falls **14** 44 49N 95 33W
Granite Mt. **21** 33 5N 116 28W
Granite Pk. **18** 45 10N 109 48W
Graniteville, *N.Y.* **22** 40 37N 74 10W
Graniteville, *S.C.* **12** 33 34N 81 49W
Graniteville, *Vt.* **9** 44 8N 72 29W
Grant, *Fla.* **13** 27 56N 80 32W
Grant, *Nebr.* **14** 40 53N 101 42W
Grant, Mt. **18** 38 34N 118 48W
Grant City **16** 40 29N 94 25W
Grant Park **24** 41 52N 87 37W
Grant Range **19** 38 30N 115 25W
Grants **19** 35 9N 107 52W
Grants Pass **18** 42 26N 123 19W
Grantsville **18** 40 36N 112 28W
Grantville **12** 33 14N 84 50W
Granville, *Ill.* **16** 41 16N 89 14W
Granville, *N. Dak.* **14** 48 16N 100 47W
Granville, *N.Y.* **9** 43 24N 73 16W
Granville, *Ohio* **8** 40 4N 82 31W
Grape I. **25** 42 16N 70 55W
Grass Hassock Channel **23** 40 36N 73 47W
Grass Range **18** 47 0N 109 0W
Grass Valley, *Calif.* **20** 39 13N 121 4W
Grass Valley, *Oreg.* **18** 45 22N 120 47W
Grassey B. **23** 40 37N 73 47W
Grassflat **8** 41 0N 78 6W
Grassy Sprain Res. **23** 40 58N 73 50W
Gratis **17** 39 38N 84 32W
Gratz **17** 38 28N 84 57W
Gravesend **22** 40 36N 73 56W
Gray **12** 33 1N 83 32W
Grayling **10** 44 40N 84 43W
Grays Harbor **18** 46 59N 124 1W
Grays L. **18** 43 4N 111 26W
Grays River **20** 46 21N 123 37W
Grayville **17** 38 16N 88 0W
Great Barrington **9** 42 12N 73 22W
Great Basin **2** 40 0N 117 0W
Great Basin Nat. Park **18** 38 55N 114 14W
Great Bend, *Kans.* **14** 38 22N 98 46W
Great Bend, *Pa.* **9** 41 58N 75 45W
Great Blue Hill **25** 42 12N 71 4W
Great Brewster I. **25** 42 19N 70 53W
Great Captain I. **23** 40 59N 73 37W
Great Falls, *Mont.* **18** 47 30N 111 17W
Great Falls, *Va.* **27** 38 59N 77 17W
Great Falls Park **27** 38 59N 77 14W
Great Kills **22** 40 32N 74 9W
Great Kills Harbour **22** 40 32N 74 8W
Great Lakes **2** 46 0N 84 0W
Great Miami → **10** 39 20N 84 40W
Great Neck **23** 40 48N 73 44W
Great Plains **2** 47 0N 105 0W
Great Pond **25** 42 11N 71 2W
Great Sacandaga Res. **9** 43 6N 74 16W
Great Salt L. **2** 41 15N 112 40W
Great Salt Lake Desert **18** 40 50N 113 30W
Great Salt Plains L. **15** 36 45N 98 8W
Great Sitkin I. **32** 52 3N 176 6W
Great Smoky Mts. Nat. Park **11** 35 40N 83 40W
Great South B. **23** 40 39N 73 19W
Greater Antilles **2** 17 40N 74 0W
Greater Pittsburgh International Airport **29** 40 29N 80 13W
Greco I. **30** 37 30N 122 10W
Greece **8** 43 13N 77 41W
Greeley, *Colo.* **14** 40 25N 104 42W
Greeley, *Nebr.* **14** 41 33N 98 32W
Greeleyville **12** 33 40N 79 59W
Green **18** 43 9N 123 22W
Green →, *Ky.* **10** 37 54N 87 30W
Green →, *Utah* **19** 38 11N 109 53W
Green B. **10** 45 0N 87 30W
Green Bay **10** 44 31N 88 0W
Green Brae **30** 37 57N 122 31W
Green Brook **22** 40 35N 74 26W
Green City **16** 40 16N 92 57W
Green Cove Springs **12** 29 59N 81 42W
Green Mts. **9** 43 45N 72 45W
Green Pond, *N.J.* **22** 41 1N 74 29W
Green Pond, *S.C.* **12** 32 44N 80 37W
Green River, *Utah* **19** 38 59N 110 10W
Green River, *Wyo.* **18** 41 32N 109 28W
Green Tree **29** 40 25N 80 4W
Green Valley **19** 31 52N 110 56W
Green Village **22** 40 44N 74 27W
Greenacres City **13** 26 38N 80 7W
Greenbank **20** 48 6N 122 34W
Greenbelt **27** 39 0N 76 52W
Greenbelt Park **27** 38 58N 76 53W
Greenbush, *Mich.* **8** 44 35N 83 19W
Greenbush, *Minn.* **14** 48 42N 96 11W
Greencastle **17** 39 38N 86 52W
Greene, *Iowa* **16** 42 54N 92 48W
Greene, *N.Y.* **9** 42 20N 75 46W
Greenfield, *Calif.* **20** 36 19N 121 15W
Greenfield, *Calif.* **21** 35 15N 119 0W
Greenfield, *Ill.* **16** 39 21N 90 12W
Greenfield, *Ind.* **17** 39 47N 85 46W
Greenfield, *Iowa* **16** 41 18N 94 28W
Greenfield, *Mass.* **9** 42 35N 72 36W
Greenfield, *Mo.* **15** 37 25N 93 51W
Greenfield, *Ohio* **17** 39 21N 83 23W
Greenfields Village **26** 39 49N 75 9W
Greenland ■ **2** 66 0N 45 0W
Greenlawn **23** 40 52N 73 22W
Greenpoint **22** 40 43N 73 57W
Greenport **9** 41 6N 72 22W
Greensboro, *Fla.* **12** 30 34N 84 45W
Greensboro, *Ga.* **12** 33 35N 83 11W
Greensboro, *N.C.* **11** 36 4N 79 48W
Greensboro, *Vt.* **9** 44 36N 72 18W
Greensburg, *Ind.* **17** 39 20N 85 29W
Greensburg, *Kans.* **15** 37 36N 99 18W
Greensburg, *Pa.* **8** 40 18N 79 33W
Greentown **17** 40 29N 85 58W
Greenup **17** 39 15N 88 10W
Greenvale **23** 40 48N 73 35W
Greenville, *Ala.* **11** 31 50N 86 38W
Greenville, *Calif.* **20** 40 8N 120 57W
Greenville, *Fla.* **12** 30 28N 83 38W
Greenville, *Ga.* **12** 33 2N 84 43W
Greenville, *Ill.* **16** 38 53N 89 25W
Greenville, *Ind.* **17** 38 22N 85 59W
Greenville, *Maine* **11** 45 28N 69 35W
Greenville, *Mich.* **17** 43 11N 85 15W
Greenville, *Miss.* **15** 33 24N 91 4W
Greenville, *Mo.* **15** 37 8N 90 27W
Greenville, *N.C.* **11** 35 37N 77 23W
Greenville, *N.H.* **9** 42 46N 71 49W
Greenville, *N.Y.* **9** 42 25N 74 1W
Greenville, *Ohio* **17** 40 6N 84 38W
Greenville, *Pa.* **8** 41 24N 80 23W
Greenville, *S.C.* **11** 34 51N 82 24W
Greenville, *Tenn.* **11** 36 13N 82 51W
Greenville, *Tex.* **15** 33 8N 96 7W
Greenville Chauncey **23** 40 59N 73 50W
Greenwich, *Conn.* **23** 41 1N 73 37W
Greenwich, *N.Y.* **9** 43 5N 73 30W
Greenwich, *Ohio* **8** 41 2N 82 31W
Greenwich Pt. **23** 41 0N 73 34W
Greenwich Village **22** 40 44N 73 59W
Greenwood, *Mass.* **25** 42 29N 71 2W
Greenwood, *Ark.* **15** 35 13N 94 16W
Greenwood, *Fla.* **12** 30 52N 85 10W
Greenwood, *Ind.* **17** 39 37N 86 7W
Greenwood, *Miss.* **15** 33 31N 90 11W
Greenwood, *S.C.* **11** 34 12N 82 10W
Greenwood L. **12** 34 11N 81 54W
Gregory **14** 43 14N 99 20W
Grenada **15** 33 47N 89 49W
Grenadier I. **9** 44 3N 76 22W
Gresham **20** 45 30N 122 26W
Gresston **12** 32 17N 83 15W
Gretna **12** 30 37N 84 40W
Greybull **18** 44 30N 108 3W
Gridley **20** 39 22N 121 42W
Griffin **12** 33 15N 84 16W
Griffin, L. **13** 28 52N 81 51W
Griffith Park **31** 34 7N 118 18 E
Grimes **20** 39 4N 121 54W
Grinnell **16** 41 45N 92 43W
Groesbeck **15** 30 48N 96 31W
Groom **15** 35 12N 101 6W
Grosse Pointe **28** 42 23N 82 54W
Groton, *Conn.* **9** 41 21N 72 5W
Groton, *N.Y.* **9** 42 36N 76 22W
Groton, *S. Dak.* **14** 45 27N 98 6W
Grovania **12** 32 22N 83 40W
Grove City, *Ohio* **17** 39 53N 83 6W
Grove City, *Pa.* **8** 41 10N 80 5W
Grove Hall **25** 42 18N 71 4W
Grove Hill **11** 31 42N 87 47W
Groveland, *Calif.* **20** 37 50N 120 14W
Groveland, *Fla.* **13** 28 34N 81 51W
Grover City **21** 35 7N 120 37W
Grover Hill **17** 41 1N 84 29W
Groves **15** 29 57N 93 54W
Groveton, *N.H.* **9** 44 36N 71 31W
Groveton, *Va.* **27** 38 46N 77 6W
Grovetown **12** 33 27N 82 12W
Grundy Center **16** 42 22N 92 47W
Gruver **15** 36 16N 101 24W
Grymes Hill **22** 40 36N 74 6W
Guadalupe **21** 34 59N 120 33W
Guadalupe → **15** 28 27N 96 47W
Guadalupe I. **2** 29 0N 118 50W
Guadalupe Mts. Nat. Park **15** 32 0N 104 30W
Guadalupe Peak **19** 31 50N 104 52W
Guam ■ **33** 13 27N 144 45 E
Guánica **32** 17 58N 66 55W
Guayama **32** 17 59N 66 7W
Guerneville **20** 38 30N 123 0W
Guernsey **14** 42 19N 104 45W
Guilford **9** 41 17N 72 41W
Guinda **20** 38 50N 122 12W
Gulf Breeze **13** 30 22N 87 9W
Gulf Hammock **13** 29 15N 82 43W
Gulf Islands National Seashore **13** 30 10N 87 10W
Gulfport, *Fla.* **13** 27 44N 82 43W
Gulfport, *Miss.* **15** 30 22N 89 6W
Gulkana **32** 62 16N 145 23W
Gullivan B. **13** 25 45N 81 40W
Gulph Mills **26** 40 4N 75 20W
Gunnison, *Colo.* **19** 38 33N 106 56W
Gunnison, *Utah* **18** 39 9N 111 49W
Gunnison → **19** 39 4N 108 35W
Guntersville **11** 34 21N 86 18W
Gurdon **15** 33 55N 93 9W
Gurnee **17** 42 22N 87 55W
Gurnet Point **9** 42 1N 70 34W
Gustavus **32** 58 25N 135 44W
Gustine **20** 37 16N 121 0W
Guthrie, *Okla.* **15** 35 53N 97 25W
Guthrie, *Tex.* **15** 33 37N 100 19W
Guthrie Center **16** 41 41N 94 30W
Guttenberg, *N.J.* **22** 40 48N 74 0W
Guttenberg, *Iowa* **16** 42 47N 91 6W
Guymon **15** 36 41N 101 29W
Guyton **12** 32 20N 81 24W
Gwinn **10** 46 19N 87 27W

H

Hacienda Heights **31** 33 59N 117 59W
Hackensack **22** 40 52N 74 4W
Hackettstown **9** 40 51N 74 50W
Haddock **12** 33 2N 83 26W
Haddon Heights **26** 39 53N 75 3W
Haddonfield **26** 39 53N 75 3W
Hagemeister I. **32** 58 39N 160 54W
Hagerman **15** 33 7N 104 20W
Hagerstown, *Ind.* **17** 39 55N 85 10W
Hagerstown, *Md.* **10** 39 39N 77 43W
Haggetts Pond **25** 42 39N 71 11W
Hahira **12** 30 59N 83 22W
Haight-Ashbury **30** 37 46N 122 26W
Hailey **18** 43 31N 114 19W
Haines, *Alaska* **32** 59 14N 135 26W
Haines, *Oreg.* **18** 44 55N 117 56W
Haines City **11** 28 7N 81 38W
Halawa **32** 21 9N 156 47W
Hale **16** 39 36N 93 20W
Haleakala Crater **32** 20 43N 156 16W
Haledon **22** 40 57N 74 11W
Halesite **23** 40 53N 73 24W
Halethorpe **27** 39 14N 76 41W
Haleyville **11** 34 14N 87 37W
Half Hollow Hills **23** 40 48N 73 21W
Half Moon B. **24** 37 27N 122 25W
Half Moon Bay Airport **30** 37 31N 122 30W
Half Moon Bay Beaches **24** 37 28N 122 28W
Halfmoon Landing **12** 31 42N 81 16W
Halifax **8** 40 25N 76 55W
Hallandale **13** 25 59N 80 8W
Hallettsville **15** 29 27N 96 57W
Hallock **14** 48 47N 96 57W
Hallstead **9** 41 58N 75 45W
Hamburg, *Ark.* **15** 33 14N 91 48W
Hamburg, *N.Y.* **8** 42 43N 78 50W
Hamburg, *Pa.* **9** 40 33N 75 59W
Hamden **9** 41 23N 72 54W
Hamilton, *Ala.* **11** 34 9N 87 59W
Hamilton, *Alaska* **32** 62 54N 163 53W
Hamilton, *Ga.* **12** 32 45N 84 53W
Hamilton, *Ill.* **16** 40 24N 91 21W
Hamilton, *Ind.* **17** 41 33N 84 56W
Hamilton, *Mo.* **16** 39 45N 94 0W
Hamilton, *Mont.* **18** 46 15N 114 10W
Hamilton, *N.Y.* **9** 42 50N 75 33W
Hamilton, *Ohio* **17** 39 24N 84 34W
Hamilton, *Tex.* **15** 31 42N 98 7W
Hamilton City **20** 39 45N 122 1W
Hamilton Mt. **9** 43 25N 74 22W
Hamlet **11** 34 53N 79 42W
Hamlin, *N.Y.* **8** 43 17N 77 55W
Hamlin, *Tex.* **15** 32 53N 100 8W
Hammel Arverne **23** 40 35N 73 48W
Hammond, *Ind.* **24** 41 36N 87 29W
Hammond, *Ill.* **17** 39 48N 88 36W
Hammond, *La.* **15** 30 30N 90 28W
Hammond, *N.Y.* **9** 44 27N 75 42W
Hammondsport **8** 42 25N 77 13W
Hammonton **10** 39 39N 74 48W
Hampton, *Ark.* **15** 33 32N 92 28W
Hampton, *Fla.* **12** 29 52N 82 8W
Hampton, *Ga.* **12** 33 23N 84 17W
Hampton, *Iowa* **16** 42 45N 93 13W
Hampton, *N.H.* **9** 42 57N 70 50W
Hampton, *S.C.* **12** 32 52N 81 7W
Hampton, *Va.* **10** 37 2N 76 21W
Hampton Bays **9** 40 53N 72 30W
Hampton Springs **12** 30 5N 83 40W
Hamtramck **28** 42 23N 83 4W
Hana **32** 20 45N 155 59W
Hanahan **12** 32 55N 80 0W
Hancock, *Mich.* **14** 47 8N 88 35W
Hancock, *N.Y.* **9** 41 57N 75 17W
Hanford **20** 36 20N 119 39W
Hankinson **14** 46 4N 96 54W
Hanksville **19** 38 22N 110 43W
Hanna **18** 41 52N 106 34W
Hannibal, *Mo.* **16** 39 42N 91 22W
Hannibal, *N.Y.* **9** 43 19N 76 35W
Hanover, *Ind.* **17** 38 43N 85 28W
Hanover, *N.H.* **9** 43 42N 72 17W
Hanover, *Ohio* **8** 40 4N 82 16W
Hanover, *Pa.* **10** 39 48N 76 59W
Hansen Flood Control Basin **31** 34 15N 118 23W
Hanson **12** 30 34N 83 21W
Hapeville **12** 33 40N 84 25W
Happy **15** 34 45N 101 52W
Happy Camp **18** 41 48N 123 23W
Haralson **12** 33 14N 84 34W
Harbor Beach **8** 43 51N 82 39W
Harbor Hills **23** 40 46N 73 44W
Hardeeville **12** 32 17N 81 5W
Hardin, *Ill.* **16** 39 10N 90 37W
Hardin, *Mont.* **18** 45 44N 107 37W
Harding **25** 42 12N 71 19W
Harding, L. **12** 32 40N 85 5W
Hardinsburg **17** 37 47N 86 28W
Hardwick, *Ga.* **12** 33 4N 83 14W
Hardwick, *Vt.* **9** 44 30N 72 22W
Harewood Park **27** 39 22N 76 21W
Harlan, *Iowa* **14** 41 39N 95 19W
Harlan, *Ky.* **11** 36 51N 83 19W
Harlem, *N.Y.* **22** 40 48N 73 56W
Harlem, *Ga.* **12** 33 25N 82 19W
Harlem, *Mont.* **18** 48 32N 108 47W
Harleyville **12** 33 13N 80 27W
Harlingen **15** 26 12N 97 42W
Harlowton **18** 46 26N 109 50W
Harmonville **26** 40 5N 75 18W
Harney, L. **13** 28 45N 81 3W
Harney Basin **18** 43 30N 119 0W
Harney L. **18** 43 14N 119 8W
Harney Peak **14** 43 52N 103 32W
Harold **13** 30 40N 86 53W
Harold Parker State Forest **25** 42 37N 71 4W
Harper, Mt. **32** 64 14N 143 51W
Harper Woods **28** 42 26N 82 56W
Harriman **11** 35 56N 84 33W
Harrington Park **22** 40 59N 73 59W
Harris, L. **13** 28 47N 81 49W
Harrisburg, *Ill.* **17** 37 44N 88 32W
Harrisburg, *Nebr.* **14** 41 33N 103 44W
Harrisburg, *Pa.* **8** 40 16N 76 53W
Harrison, *N.J.* **22** 40 44N 74 9W
Harrison, *N.Y.* **23** 40 57N 73 42W
Harrison, *Ark.* **15** 36 14N 93 7W
Harrison, *Ga.* **12** 32 50N 82 43W
Harrison, *Maine* **9** 44 7N 70 39W
Harrison, *Nebr.* **14** 42 41N 103 53W
Harrison Bay **32** 70 40N 151 0W
Harrisonburg **10** 38 27N 78 52W
Harrisonville, *Md.* **27** 39 22N 76 49W
Harrisonville, *Mo.* **16** 38 39N 94 21W
Harrisville, *Mich.* **8** 44 39N 83 17W
Harrisville, *N.Y.* **9** 44 9N 75 19W
Harrisville, *Pa.* **8** 41 8N 80 0W
Harrodsburg, *Ind.* **17** 39 1N 86 33W
Harrodsburg, *Ky.* **17** 37 46N 84 51W
Harry S. Truman Reservoir **16** 38 16N 93 24W
Hart **10** 43 42N 86 22W
Hart I., *Md.* **27** 39 14N 76 23W
Hart I., *N.Y.* **23** 40 51N 73 46W
Hartford, *N.J.* **26** 39 58N 74 53W
Hartford, *Ala.* **12** 31 6N 85 42W
Hartford, *Conn.* **9** 41 46N 72 41W
Hartford, *Ga.* **12** 32 17N 83 28W
Hartford, *Ky.* **10** 37 27N 86 55W
Hartford, *Mich.* **17** 42 13N 86 10W
Hartford, *S. Dak.* **14** 43 38N 96 57W
Hartford, *Wis.* **14** 43 19N 88 22W
Hartford City **17** 40 27N 85 22W
Hartland **17** 43 6N 88 21W
Hartsdale **23** 41 1N 73 48W
Hartselle **11** 34 27N 86 56W
Hartshorne **15** 34 51N 95 34W
Hartstown **8** 41 33N 80 23W
Hartsville **11** 34 23N 80 4W
Hartwell **11** 34 21N 82 56W
Harvard **17** 42 25N 88 37W
Harvard, Mt. **31** 34 12N 118 4W
Harvard Univ. **25** 42 23N 71 7W
Harvey, *Ill.* **24** 41 36N 87 39W
Harvey, *N. Dak.* **14** 47 47N 99 56W
Harwood Heights **24** 41 57N 87 46W
Hasbrouck Heights **22** 40 51N 74 6W
Haskell **15** 33 10N 99 44W
Hastings, *Fla.* **12** 29 43N 81 31W
Hastings, *Mich.* **17** 42 39N 85 17W
Hastings, *Minn.* **14** 44 44N 92 51W
Hastings, *Nebr.* **14** 40 35N 98 23W
Hastings-on-Hudson **23** 40 59N 73 51W
Hatch **19** 32 40N 107 9W
Hatchineha, L. **13** 28 2N 81 25W
Hatteras, C. **2** 35 14N 75 32W
Hattiesburg **15** 31 20N 89 17W
Haubstadt **17** 38 12N 87 34W
Havana, *Fla.* **12** 30 37N 84 25W
Havana, *Ill.* **16** 40 18N 90 4W
Havasu, L. **21** 34 18N 114 28W
Havelock **11** 34 53N 76 54W
Haverford **26** 40 0N 75 18W
Haverhill, *Fla.* **13** 26 42N 80 7W
Haverhill, *Mass.* **9** 42 47N 71 5W
Haverstraw **9** 41 12N 73 58W
Havertown **26** 39 58N 75 18W
Havre **18** 48 33N 109 41W
Haw → **11** 35 36N 79 3W
Hawaii □ **32** 19 30N 156 30W
Hawaii I. **32** 20 0N 155 0W
Hawaiian Is. **32** 20 30N 156 0W
Hawarden **14** 43 0N 96 29W
Hawesville **17** 37 54N 86 45W
Hawk Point **16** 38 58N 91 8W
Hawkinsville **12** 32 17N 83 28W
Hawley, *Minn.* **14** 46 53N 96 19W
Hawley, *Pa.* **9** 41 28N 75 11W
Haworth **22** 40 57N 73 59W
Hawthorne, *Calif.* **31** 33 54N 118 21W
Hawthorne, *N.J.* **22** 40 57N 74 8W
Hawthorne, *Fla.* **13** 29 36N 82 5W
Hawthorne, *Nev.* **18** 38 32N 118 38W
Hay Springs **14** 42 41N 102 41W
Hayden **18** 40 30N 107 16W
Hayes **14** 44 23N 101 1W
Hayford **24** 41 45N 87 42W
Haylow **12** 30 50N 82 54W
Hayneville **12** 32 23N 83 37W
Hays **14** 38 53N 99 20W
Haysville **17** 38 28N 86 55W
Hayward, *Calif.* **30** 37 40N 122 4W
Hayward, *Wis.* **14** 46 1N 91 29W
Hayward Fault **30** 37 46N 122 10W
Haywood Municipal Airport **30** 32 39N 122 9W
Hazard **10** 37 15N 83 12W
Hazel Park **28** 42 28N 83 5W
Hazelton **14** 46 29N 100 17W
Hazen **14** 47 18N 101 38W
Hazlehurst, *Ga.* **12** 31 52N 82 36W
Hazlehurst, *Miss.* **15** 31 52N 90 24W
Hazlet **9** 40 25N 74 12W
Hazleton, *Ind.* **17** 38 29N 87 33W
Hazleton, *Pa.* **9** 40 57N 75 59W
Headland **12** 31 21N 85 21W
Healdsburg **20** 38 37N 122 52W
Healdton **15** 34 14N 97 29W
Heard Pond **25** 42 20N 71 23W
Hearne **15** 30 53N 96 36W
Heart → **14** 46 46N 100 50W
Heart Pond **25** 42 33N 71 23W
Heavener **15** 34 53N 94 36W
Hebbronville **15** 27 18N 98 41W
Hebbville **27** 39 20N 76 45W
Heber **21** 32 44N 115 32W
Heber City **18** 40 31N 111 25W
Heber Springs **15** 35 30N 92 2W
Hebgen L. **18** 44 52N 111 20W
Hebron, *N. Dak.* **14** 46 54N 102 3W
Hebron, *Nebr.* **14** 40 10N 97 35W
Hecla **14** 45 53N 98 9W
Hedrick **16** 41 11N 92 19W
Heflin **12** 33 39N 85 35W
Hegewisch **24** 41 39N 87 32W
Helena, *Ark.* **15** 34 32N 90 36W
Helena, *Ga.* **12** 32 5N 82 55W
Helena, *Mont.* **18** 46 36N 112 2W
Helendale **21** 34 44N 117 19W
Hellertown **9** 40 35N 75 21W
Helper **18** 39 41N 110 51W
Hemet **21** 33 45N 116 58W
Hemingford **14** 42 19N 103 4W
Hempstead, *N.Y.* **23** 40 42N 73 37W
Hempstead, *Tex.* **15** 30 6N 96 5W
Hempstead Harbor **23** 40 50N 73 39W
Henderson, *Ga.* **12** 32 21N 83 47W
Henderson, *Ky.* **17** 37 50N 87 35W
Henderson, *N.C.* **11** 36 20N 78 25W
Henderson, *Nev.* **21** 36 2N 114 59W
Henderson, *Tenn.* **11** 35 26N 88 38W
Henderson, *Tex.* **15** 32 9N 94 48W
Hendersonville, *N.C.* **11** 35 19N 82 28W
Hendersonville, *S.C.* **12** 32 48N 80 43W
Hendersonville, *Tenn.* **11** 36 18N 86 37W
Henlopen, C. **10** 38 48N 75 6W
Hennepin **16** 41 15N 89 21W
Hennessey **15** 36 6N 97 54W
Henrietta **15** 33 49N 98 12W
Henry **16** 41 7N 89 22W
Henryetta **15** 35 27N 95 59W
Hephzibah **12** 33 19N 82 6W
Heppner **18** 45 21N 119 33W
Herbert I. **32** 52 45N 170 7W
Herculaneum **16** 38 16N 90 23W
Hereford **15** 34 49N 102 24W
Herington **14** 38 40N 96 57W
Herkimer **9** 43 0N 74 59W
Herlong **20** 40 8N 120 8W
Hermann **14** 38 42N 91 27W
Hermiston **18** 45 51N 119 17W
Hermitage **16** 37 56N 93 19W
Hermon **9** 44 28N 75 14W
Hermosa Beach **31** 33 51N 118 23W
Hernandez **20** 36 24N 120 46W
Hernando, *Fla.* **13** 28 54N 82 23W
Hernando, *Miss.* **15** 34 50N 90 0W
Herndon **8** 40 43N 76 51W
Hernwood Heights **27** 39 22N 76 49W
Herod **12** 31 42N 84 26W
Herreid **14** 45 50N 100 4W
Herricks **23** 40 45N 73 39W
Herrin **16** 37 48N 89 2W
Hershey **9** 40 17N 76 39W
Hesperia **21** 34 25N 117 18W
Hetch Hetchy Aqueduct **20** 37 29N 122 19W
Hettinger **14** 46 0N 102 42W
Heuvelton **9** 44 37N 75 25W
Hewitt **15** 31 27N 97 11W
Hewlett Neck **23** 40 37N 73 41W
Hi Vista **21** 34 45N 117 46W
Hialeah **11** 25 50N 80 17W
Hiawatha **14** 39 51N 95 32W
Hibbing **14** 47 25N 92 56W
Hibernia **22** 40 57N 74 29W
Hickman **15** 36 34N 89 11W
Hickory **11** 35 44N 81 21W
Hickory Hills **24** 41 43N 87 49W
Hicksville, *N.Y.* **23** 40 46N 73 30W
Hicksville, *Ohio* **17** 41 18N 84 46W
Hidalgo **17** 39 9N 88 9W
Higbee **16** 39 19N 92 31W
Higgins **15** 36 7N 100 2W
Higgins Corner **20** 39 2N 121 5W
Higginsville **16** 39 4N 93 43W
High Bridge **9** 40 40N 74 54W
High Point **11** 35 57N 80 0W
High Springs **12** 29 50N 82 36W
Highland, *Ill.* **16** 38 44N 89 41W
Highland, *Ind.* **17** 41 33N 87 28W
Highland, *Wis.* **16** 43 5N 90 22W
Highland City **13** 27 58N 81 53W
Highland Home **12** 31 57N 86 19W
Highland Mills **12** 33 17N 84 17W
Highland Park, *Calif.* **31** 34 7N 118 13 E
Highland Park, *Mich.* **28** 42 24N 83 6W
Highland Park, *N.J.* **22** 40 30N 74 25W
Highland Park, *Ill.* **17** 42 11N 87 48W
Highland View **12** 29 50N 85 19W
Highmore **14** 44 31N 99 27W
Highway Highlands **31** 34 14N 118 16W
Hiko **20** 37 32N 115 14W
Hiland Park **12** 30 12N 85 33W
Hilda **12** 33 16N 81 15W
Hill City, *Idaho* **18** 43 18N 115 3W
Hill City, *Kans.* **14** 39 22N 99 51W
Hill City, *S. Dak.* **14** 43 56N 103 35W
Hillcrest Center **21** 35 23N 118 57W
Hillcrest Heights **27** 38 49N 76 57W
Hillgrove District **31** 34 1N 117 58W
Hilliard **12** 30 41N 81 55W
Hillsboro, *Ga.* **12** 33 11N 83 38W
Hillsboro, *Ill.* **16** 39 9N 89 29W
Hillsboro, *Iowa* **16** 40 50N 91 42W
Hillsboro, *Kans.* **14** 38 21N 97 12W
Hillsboro, *Mo.* **16** 38 14N 90 34W
Hillsboro, *N. Dak.* **14** 47 26N 97 3W
Hillsboro, *N.H.* **9** 43 7N 71 54W
Hillsboro, *Ohio* **17** 39 12N 83 37W
Hillsboro, *Oreg.* **20** 45 31N 122 59W
Hillsboro, *Tex.* **15** 32 1N 97 8W
Hillsboro Canal **13** 26 30N 80 15W
Hillsborough **30** 37 32N 122 21W
Hillsdale, *N.J.* **22** 41 0N 74 1W
Hillsdale, *Calif.* **30** 37 32N 122 18W
Hillsdale, *Mich.* **17** 41 56N 84 38W
Hillsdale, *N.Y.* **9** 42 11N 73 30W
Hillsdale Manor **22** 41 1N 74 3W

Kingfisher

Hillside, *Ill.* 24 41 52N 87 55W
Hillside, *N.Y.* 23 40 42N 73 46W
Hillside Manor 23 40 44N 73 40W
Hilltonia 12 32 53N 81 40W
Hilltop 26 39 49N 75 4W
Hillwood 27 38 52N 77 9W
Hilo 32 19 44N 155 5W
Hilton 8 43 17N 77 48W
Hilton Head Island 12 32 13N 80 45W
Hinckley 14 46 1N 92 56W
Hines 12 29 45N 83 14W
Hinesville 12 31 51N 81 36W
Hingham, *Mass.* 25 42 14N 70 54W
Hingham, *Mont.* 18 48 33N 110 25W
Hingham B. 25 42 17N 70 56W
Hingham Harbor 25 42 15N 70 53W
Hinsdale, *Ill.* 24 41 47N 87 55W
Hinsdale, *N.H.* 9 42 47N 72 29W
Hinson 12 30 39N 84 25W
Hinton 10 37 40N 80 54W
Hispaniola 2 19 0N 71 0W
Hobart, *Ind.* 17 41 32N 87 15W
Hobart, *Okla.* 15 35 1N 99 6W
Hobbs 15 32 42N 103 8W
Hobe Sound 13 27 4N 80 8W
Hoboken, *N.J.* 22 40 44N 74 3W
Hoboken, *Ga.* 12 31 11N 82 8W
Hodgkins 24 41 46N 87 53W
Hoffman I. 22 40 34N 74 3W
Hogansville 12 33 10N 84 55W
Hoh → 20 47 45N 124 29W
Hohenwald 11 35 33N 87 33W
Hohokus 22 41 0N 74 5W
Hoisington 14 38 31N 98 47W
Holbrook 19 34 54N 110 10W
Holden, *Mo.* 16 38 43N 94 1W
Holden, *Utah* 18 39 6N 112 16W
Holdenville 15 35 5N 96 24W
Holder 13 28 58N 82 25W
Holdrege 14 40 26N 99 23W
Holgate 17 41 15N 84 8W
Holiday 13 28 13N 82 43W
Holland, *Mich.* 17 42 47N 86 7W
Holland, *N.Y.* 8 42 38N 78 32W
Hollandale 15 33 10N 90 51W
Holley, *Fla.* 13 30 27N 86 54W
Holley, *N.Y.* 8 43 14N 78 2W
Hollidaysburg 8 40 26N 78 24W
Hollis, *N.Y.* 23 40 42N 73 45W
Hollis, *Okla.* 15 34 41N 99 55W
Hollister, *Calif.* 20 36 51N 121 24W
Hollister, *Idaho* 18 42 21N 114 35W
Holly 17 42 48N 83 38W
Holly Hill, *Fla.* 11 29 16N 81 3W
Holly Hill, *S.C.* 12 33 19N 80 25W
Holly Oak 26 39 47N 75 27W
Holly Springs, *Ga.* 12 34 10N 84 30W
Holly Springs, *Miss.* 15 34 46N 89 27W
Hollydale 31 33 55N 118 10W
Hollywood 11 26 1N 80 9W
Hollywood Bowl 31 34 6N 118 21W
Hollywood-Burbank Airport 31 34 11N 118 21W
Holmen 14 43 58N 91 15W
Holmes 26 39 53N 75 18W
Holmes → 12 30 30N 85 50W
Holmes Acres 27 38 51N 77 13W
Holmes Beach 13 27 31N 82 43W
Holmesburg 26 40 2N 75 2W
Holopaw 13 28 8N 81 5W
Holt 13 30 43N 86 45W
Holton 14 39 28N 95 44W
Holtville 21 32 49N 115 23W
Holy Cross 32 62 12N 159 46W
Holyoke, *Colo.* 14 40 35N 102 18W
Holyoke, *Mass.* 9 42 12N 72 37W
Homedale 18 43 37N 116 56W
Homeland 12 30 51N 82 1W
Homer, *Alaska* 32 59 39N 151 33W
Homer, *Ill.* 17 40 4N 87 57W
Homer, *La.* 15 32 48N 93 4W
Homer, *Mich.* 17 42 9N 84 49W
Homer City 8 40 32N 79 10W
Homerville 12 31 2N 82 45W
Homestead, *Pa.* 29 40 24N 79 55W
Homestead, *Fla.* 11 25 28N 80 29W
Homestead Valley 30 37 53N 122 32W
Hometown 24 41 44N 87 42W
Homewood, *Calif.* 20 39 4N 120 8W
Homewood, *Ill.* 17 41 34N 87 40W
Homosassa Springs 13 28 48N 82 35W
Honcut 20 39 20N 121 32W
Hondo 15 29 21N 99 9W
Honduras, G. de 2 16 50N 87 0W
Honesdale 9 41 34N 75 16W
Honey L. 20 40 15N 120 19W
Honeyville 12 30 3N 85 11W
Honolulu 32 21 19N 157 52W
Hood, Mt. 18 45 23N 121 42W
Hood Pond 25 42 40N 70 57W
Hood River 18 45 43N 121 31W
Hoodsport 20 47 24N 123 9W
Hooker 15 36 52N 101 13W
Hoonah 32 58 7N 135 27W
Hooper Bay 32 61 32N 166 6W
Hoopeston 17 40 28N 87 40W
Hoover 11 33 20N 86 11W
Hoover Dam 21 36 1N 114 44W
Hooversville 8 40 9N 78 55W
Hop Bottom 9 41 42N 75 46W
Hope, *Ariz.* 21 33 43N 113 42W
Hope, *Ark.* 15 33 40N 93 36W
Hope, *Ind.* 17 39 18N 85 46W
Hope, Pt. 32 68 20N 166 50W
Hopedale 9 42 8N 71 33W
Hopelawn 22 40 31N 74 17W
Hopewell 10 37 18N 77 17W
Hopkins, *Mich.* 17 42 37N 85 46W
Hopkins, *Mo.* 16 40 33N 94 49W
Hopkins, *S.C.* 12 33 54N 80 53W
Hopkinsville 11 36 52N 87 29W
Hopland 20 38 58N 123 7W
Hoquiam 20 46 59N 123 53W
Horatio 12 34 1N 80 33W
Horn Pond 25 42 28N 71 9W
Hornbeck 15 31 20N 93 24W
Hornbrook 18 41 55N 122 33W
Hornell 8 42 20N 77 40W
Hornitos 20 37 30N 120 14W
Horse Cr. → 13 27 6N 81 58W
Horse Creek 14 41 57N 105 10W
Horseheads 8 42 10N 76 49W
Hortense 12 31 20N 81 57W
Horton 14 39 40N 95 32W
Hosford 12 30 23N 84 48W
Hot Creek Range 18 38 40N 116 20W
Hot Springs, *Ark.* 15 34 31N 93 3W
Hot Springs, *S. Dak.* 14 43 26N 103 29W
Hotchkiss 19 38 48N 107 43W
Houghs Neck 25 42 15N 70 57W
Houghton, *Mich.* 14 47 7N 88 34W
Houghton, *N.Y.* 8 42 25N 78 10W
Houghton L. 10 44 21N 84 44W
Houlton 11 46 8N 67 51W
Houma 15 29 36N 90 43W
Housatonic → 9 41 10N 73 7W
Houston, *Fla.* 12 30 15N 82 54W
Houston, *Mo.* 15 37 22N 91 58W
Houston, *Tex.* 15 29 46N 95 22W
Howard, *Ga.* 12 32 36N 84 23W
Howard, *Pa.* 8 41 1N 77 40W
Howard, *S. Dak.* 14 44 1N 97 32W
Howard Beach 23 40 39N 73 50W
Howe 18 43 48N 113 0W
Howell 17 42 36N 83 56W
Hualapai Peak 19 35 5N 113 54W
Huasna 21 35 6N 120 24W
Hubbard, *Iowa* 16 42 18N 93 18W
Hubbard, *Ohio* 8 41 9N 80 34W
Hubbard, *Tex.* 15 31 51N 96 48W
Hudson, *Fla.* 13 28 22N 82 42W
Hudson, *Mass.* 9 42 23N 71 34W
Hudson, *Mich.* 17 41 51N 84 21W
Hudson, *N.Y.* 9 42 15N 73 46W
Hudson, *Wis.* 14 44 58N 92 45W
Hudson, *Wyo.* 18 42 54N 108 35W
Hudson → 2 40 42N 74 2W
Hudson Falls 9 43 18N 73 35W
Hudsonville 17 42 52N 85 52W
Huger 12 33 6N 79 48W
Hughes 32 66 3N 154 15W
Hughesville 9 41 14N 76 44W
Hugo, *Colo.* 14 39 8N 103 28W
Hugo, *Okla.* 15 34 1N 95 31W
Hugoton 15 37 11N 101 21W
Huguenot 22 40 32N 74 13W
Huguenot Park 22 40 31N 74 12W
Hull, *Mass.* 25 42 18N 70 54W
Hull, *Fla.* 13 27 7N 81 56W
Hull, *Ill.* 16 39 43N 91 13W
Hulman Aqueduct 25 42 20N 71 23W
Hulmeville 26 40 8N 74 55W
Humacao 32 18 9N 65 50W
Humansville 16 37 48N 93 35W
Humboldt, *Iowa* 16 42 44N 94 13W
Humboldt, *Tenn.* 15 35 50N 88 55W
Humboldt → 18 39 59N 118 36W
Humboldt Park 24 41 54N 87 42W
Hume, *Calif.* 20 36 48N 118 54W
Hume, *Mo.* 16 38 6N 94 34W
Humeston 16 40 52N 93 30W
Humphreys, Mt. 20 37 17N 118 40W
Humphreys Peak 19 35 21N 111 41W
Humptulips 20 47 14N 123 57W
Hunter 9 42 13N 74 13W
Hunters Pt. 30 37 43N 122 21W
Hunters Valley 27 38 54N 77 17W
Huntingburg 17 38 18N 86 57W
Huntingdon 8 40 30N 78 1W
Huntington, *N.Y.* 23 40 51N 73 25W
Huntington, *Ind.* 17 40 53N 85 30W
Huntington, *Oreg.* 18 44 21N 117 16W
Huntington, *Utah* 18 39 20N 110 58W
Huntington, *W. Va.* 10 38 25N 82 27W
Huntington, *Va.* 27 38 47N 77 4W
Huntington B. 23 40 54N 73 24W
Huntington Bay 23 40 56N 73 26W
Huntington Beach 21 33 40N 118 5W
Huntington Park 31 33 58N 118 13W
Huntington Station 23 40 50N 73 23W
Huntington Woods 28 42 28N 83 10W
Huntley 17 42 10N 88 26W
Huntsville, *Ala.* 11 34 44N 86 35W
Huntsville, *Mo.* 16 39 26N 92 33W
Huntsville, *Tex.* 15 30 43N 95 33W
Hurffville 26 39 45N 75 6W
Hurley, *N. Mex.* 19 32 42N 108 8W
Hurley, *Wis.* 14 46 27N 90 11W
Huron, *Calif.* 20 36 12N 120 6W
Huron, *Ohio* 8 41 24N 82 33W
Huron, *S. Dak.* 14 44 22N 98 13W
Huron, L. 2 44 30N 82 40W
Hurricane 19 37 11N 113 17W
Hurstboro 12 32 15N 85 25W
Huslia 32 65 41N 156 24W
Hustontown 8 40 3N 78 2W
Hutchinson, *Kans.* 15 38 5N 97 56W
Hutchinson, *Minn.* 14 44 54N 94 22W
Hutsonville 17 39 7N 87 40W
Hyannis, *Mass.* 10 41 39N 70 17W
Hyannis, *Nebr.* 14 42 0N 101 46W
Hyattsville 27 38 57N 76 57W
Hydaburg 32 55 15N 132 50W
Hyde Park, *Mass.* 25 42 15N 71 7W
Hyde Park, *Ill.* 24 41 47N 87 35W
Hyde Park, *N.Y.* 9 41 47N 73 56W
Hyndman Peak 18 43 45N 114 8W
Hynes 31 33 52N 118 10W
Hyrum 18 41 38N 111 51W
Hysham 18 46 18N 107 14W

I

Iamonia L. 12 30 38N 84 14W
Iberia 16 38 5N 92 18W
Ida Grove 14 42 21N 95 28W
Idabel 15 33 54N 94 50W
Idaho □ 18 45 0N 115 0W
Idaho City 18 43 50N 115 50W
Idaho Falls 18 43 30N 112 2W
Idria 20 36 25N 120 41W
Ilchester 27 39 14N 76 46W
Iliamna L. 32 59 30N 155 0W
Ilio Pt. 32 21 13N 157 16W
Ilion 9 43 1N 75 2W
Illinois □ 16 40 15N 89 30W
Illinois → 16 38 58N 90 28W
Illiopolis 16 39 51N 89 15W
Ilwaco 20 46 19N 124 3W
Imlay 18 40 40N 118 9W
Imlay City 8 43 2N 83 5W
Immokalee 11 26 25N 81 25W
Imperial, *Calif.* 21 32 51N 115 34W
Imperial, *Nebr.* 14 40 31N 101 39W
Imperial Beach 21 32 35N 117 8W
Imperial Dam 21 32 55N 114 25W
Imperial Reservoir 21 32 53N 114 28W
Imperial Valley 21 33 0N 115 30W
Incline Village 18 39 10N 119 58W
Independence, *Calif.* 20 36 48N 118 12W
Independence, *Iowa* 16 42 28N 91 54W
Independence, *Kans.* 15 37 14N 95 42W
Independence, *Ky.* 17 38 57N 84 33W
Independence, *Mo.* 16 39 6N 94 25W
Independence Mts. 18 41 20N 116 0W
Index 20 47 50N 121 33W
Indialantic 13 28 6N 80 34W
Indian →, *Fla.* 11 27 59N 80 34W
Indian →, *Fla.* 13 27 10N 80 10W
Indian Harbour Beach 13 28 10N 80 35W
Indian Lake 9 43 47N 74 16W
Indian Rocks Beach 13 27 53N 82 51W
Indian Springs 21 36 35N 115 40W
Indiana 8 40 37N 79 9W
Indiana □ 17 40 0N 86 0W
Indiana Harbor 24 41 40N 87 26W
Indiana Harbor Canal 24 41 39N 87 26W
Indianapolis 17 39 46N 86 9W
Indianola, *Iowa* 16 41 22N 93 34W
Indianola, *Miss.* 15 33 27N 90 39W
Indiantown 13 27 1N 80 28W
Indio 21 33 43N 116 13W
Indrio 13 27 31N 80 21W
Industry 16 40 20N 90 36W
Inglewood 31 33 57N 118 19W
Inglis 13 29 2N 82 40W
Ingomar 18 46 35N 107 23W
Inkster 28 42 17N 83 16W
Inlet 9 43 45N 74 48W
Intercession City 13 28 16N 81 31W
Interlachen 13 29 37N 81 53W
Interlaken 9 42 37N 76 44W
International Falls 14 48 36N 93 25W
Inverness, *Md.* 27 39 15N 76 29W
Inverness, *Ala.* 12 32 1N 85 45W
Inverness, *Fla.* 11 28 50N 82 20W
Inwood 23 40 36N 73 45W
Inyo Mts. 20 36 40N 118 0W
Inyokern 21 35 39N 117 49W
Iola 15 37 55N 95 24W
Ione 20 38 21N 120 56W
Ionia 17 42 59N 85 4W
Iowa □ 14 42 18N 93 30W
Iowa → 16 41 10N 91 1W
Iowa City 16 41 40N 91 32W
Iowa Falls 16 42 31N 93 16W
Iowa Park 15 33 57N 98 40W
Ipswich, *Mass.* 25 42 41N 70 50W
Ipswich, *S. Dak.* 14 45 27N 99 2W
Iron City 12 31 1N 84 49W
Iron Mountain 10 45 49N 88 4W
Iron River 14 46 6N 88 39W
Irondequoit 8 43 13N 77 35W
Ironton, *Mo.* 15 37 36N 90 38W
Ironton, *Ohio* 10 38 32N 82 41W
Ironwood 14 46 27N 90 9W
Iroquois → 17 41 5N 87 49W
Irvine, *Calif.* 21 33 41N 117 46W
Irvine, *Ky.* 17 37 42N 83 58W
Irving 15 32 49N 96 56W
Irving Park 24 41 57N 87 42W
Irvington, *N.Y.* 23 41 2N 73 52W
Irvington, *Ky.* 17 37 53N 86 17W
Irvona 8 40 46N 78 33W
Irwindale 31 34 6N 117 54W
Irwinton 12 32 49N 83 10W
Irwinville 12 31 39N 83 23W
Isabel 14 45 24N 101 26W
Isabela 32 18 30N 67 2W
Iselin 22 40 34N 74 19W
Ishpeming 10 46 29N 87 40W
Isla Vista 21 34 25N 119 53W
Islamorada 13 24 56N 80 37W
Island Channel 23 40 35N 73 52W
Island Park 23 40 36N 73 38W
Island Pond 9 44 49N 71 53W
Isle of Hope 12 31 58N 81 5W
Isle Royale 14 48 0N 88 54W
Isle Royale National Park 14 48 0N 88 55W
Isleton 20 38 10N 121 37W
Islington 25 42 13N 71 13W
Istokpoga, L. 11 27 23N 81 17W
Ithaca 9 42 27N 76 30W
Ithan 26 40 1N 75 21W
Iuka 17 38 37N 88 47W
Ivanhoe, *Calif.* 20 36 23N 119 13W
Ivanhoe, *Minn.* 14 44 28N 96 15W

J

J. Paul Getty Museum 31 34 2N 118 33W
Jackman 11 45 35N 70 17W
Jacksboro 15 33 14N 98 15W
Jackson, *Ala.* 11 31 31N 87 53W
Jackson, *Calif.* 20 38 21N 120 46W
Jackson, *Ga.* 12 33 20N 83 57W
Jackson, *Ky.* 10 37 33N 83 23W
Jackson, *Mich.* 17 42 15N 84 24W
Jackson, *Minn.* 14 43 37N 95 1W
Jackson, *Miss.* 15 32 18N 90 12W
Jackson, *Mo.* 15 37 23N 89 40W
Jackson, *N.H.* 9 44 10N 71 11W
Jackson, *Ohio* 10 39 3N 82 39W
Jackson, *S.C.* 12 33 20N 81 47W
Jackson, *Tenn.* 11 35 37N 88 49W
Jackson, *Wyo.* 18 43 29N 110 46W
Jackson Center 17 40 27N 84 4W
Jackson Heights 23 40 44N 73 53W
Jackson L., *Fla.* 12 30 30N 84 17W
Jackson L., *Ga.* 12 33 19N 83 50W
Jackson L., *Wyo.* 18 43 52N 110 36W
Jackson Park 24 41 46N 87 34W
Jacksonville, *N.J.* 22 40 57N 74 18W
Jacksonville, *Ala.* 12 33 49N 85 46W
Jacksonville, *Ark.* 15 34 52N 92 7W
Jacksonville, *Calif.* 20 37 52N 120 24W
Jacksonville, *Fla.* 12 30 20N 81 39W
Jacksonville, *Ga.* 12 31 49N 82 59W
Jacksonville, *Ill.* 16 39 44N 90 14W
Jacksonville, *N.C.* 11 34 45N 77 26W
Jacksonville, *Tex.* 15 31 58N 95 17W
Jacksonville Beach 12 30 17N 81 24W
Jacob Lake 19 36 43N 112 13W
Jacumba 21 32 37N 116 11W
Jaffrey 9 42 49N 72 2W
Jakin 12 31 6N 84 59W
Jal 15 32 7N 103 12W
Jalama 21 34 29N 120 29W
Jaluit I. 33 6 0N 169 30 E
Jamaica, *N.Y.* 23 40 42N 73 48W
Jamaica, *Iowa* 16 41 51N 94 18W
Jamaica B. 23 40 36N 73 49W
Jamaica Plain 25 42 18N 71 6W
James 12 32 58N 83 29W
James →, *S. Dak.* 14 42 52N 97 18W
James →, *Va.* 10 36 56N 76 27W
James Island 12 32 45N 79 55W
Jamesport 16 39 58N 93 48W
Jamestown, *Ind.* 17 39 56N 86 38W
Jamestown, *Mo.* 16 38 48N 92 30W
Jamestown, *N. Dak.* 14 46 54N 98 42W
Jamestown, *N.Y.* 8 42 6N 79 14W
Jamestown, *Ohio* 17 39 39N 83 44W
Jamestown, *Pa.* 8 41 29N 80 27W
Jamestown, *S.C.* 12 33 17N 79 42W
Janesville 16 42 41N 89 1W
Jasonville 17 39 10N 87 12W
Jasper, *Ala.* 11 33 50N 87 17W
Jasper, *Fla.* 12 30 31N 82 57W
Jasper, *Ind.* 17 38 24N 86 56W
Jasper, *Tex.* 15 30 56N 94 1W
Jay 13 30 57N 87 9W
Jay Peak 9 44 55N 72 32W
Jayton 15 33 15N 100 34W
Jean 21 35 47N 115 20W
Jeanerette 15 29 55N 91 40W
Jeannette 8 40 20N 79 36W
Jefferson, *N.J.* 26 39 45N 75 12W
Jefferson, *Ga.* 12 34 7N 83 35W
Jefferson, *Iowa* 16 42 1N 94 23W
Jefferson, *Ohio* 8 41 44N 80 46W
Jefferson, *Tex.* 15 32 46N 94 21W
Jefferson, *Wis.* 17 43 0N 88 48W
Jefferson, Mt., *Nev.* 18 38 51N 117 0W
Jefferson, Mt., *Oreg.* 18 44 41N 121 48W
Jefferson City, *Mo.* 16 38 34N 92 10W
Jefferson City, *Tenn.* 11 36 7N 83 30W
Jefferson Park 24 41 58N 87 46W
Jeffersontown 17 38 12N 85 35W
Jeffersonville, *Pa.* 26 40 8N 75 23W
Jeffersonville, *Ga.* 12 32 41N 83 20W
Jeffersonville, *Ind.* 17 38 17N 85 44W
Jeffersonville, *Ohio* 17 39 39N 83 34W
Jeffrey City 18 42 30N 107 49W
Jekyll I. 12 31 4N 81 25W
Jena, *Fla.* 13 29 40N 83 22W
Jena, *La.* 15 31 41N 92 8W
Jenkins 10 37 10N 82 38W
Jenkintown 26 40 6N 75 8W
Jenner 20 38 27N 123 7W
Jennings, *Fla.* 12 30 36N 83 6W
Jennings, *La.* 15 30 13N 92 40W
Jennings, *Mo.* 16 38 43N 90 16W
Jensen Beach 13 27 15N 80 14W
Jericho 23 40 47N 73 32W
Jerico Springs 16 37 37N 94 1W
Jermyn 9 41 31N 75 31W
Jerome 18 42 44N 114 31W
Jersey 12 33 43N 83 47W
Jersey City 22 40 42N 74 4W
Jersey Shore 8 41 12N 77 15W
Jerseyville 16 39 7N 90 20W
Jerusalem 12 30 58N 81 50W
Jessup L. 13 28 43N 81 14W
Jesup, *Ga.* 12 31 36N 81 53W
Jesup, *Iowa* 16 42 29N 92 4W
Jetmore 15 38 4N 99 54W
Jewell 16 42 20N 93 39W
Jewett 8 40 22N 81 2W
Jewett City 9 41 36N 72 0W
Jim Thorpe 9 40 52N 75 44W
Joaquin Miller Park 30 37 48N 122 11W
Johannesburg 21 35 22N 117 38W
John Day 18 44 25N 118 57W
John Day → 18 45 44N 120 39W
John F. Kennedy Int. Airport 23 40 39N 73 45W
John F. Kennedy Nat. Hist. Site 25 42 20N 71 7W
John H. Kerr Reservoir 11 36 36N 78 18W
John Hancock Center 24 41 53N 87 37W
John Hopkins Univ. 27 39 19N 76 37W
John McLaren Park 30 37 43N 122 24W
Johnnie 21 36 25N 116 5W
Johns I. 12 32 40N 80 10W
Johns Island 12 32 47N 80 7W
Johnson, *Kans.* 15 37 34N 101 45W
Johnson, *Vt.* 9 44 38N 72 41W
Johnson City, *Ill.* 16 37 49N 88 56W
Johnson City, *N.Y.* 9 42 7N 75 58W
Johnson City, *Tenn.* 11 36 19N 82 21W
Johnson City, *Tex.* 15 30 17N 98 25W
Johnsonburg 8 41 29N 78 41W
Johnsondale 21 35 58N 118 32W
Johnston 12 33 50N 81 48W
Johnstown, *N.Y.* 9 43 0N 74 22W
Johnstown, *Ohio* 8 40 9N 82 41W
Johnstown, *Pa.* 8 40 20N 78 55W
Joliet 17 41 32N 88 5W
Jolon 20 35 58N 121 9W
Jones Beach State Park 23 40 35N 73 32W
Jones Inlet 23 40 34N 73 34W
Jonesboro, *Ark.* 15 35 50N 90 42W
Jonesboro, *Ga.* 12 33 31N 84 22W
Jonesboro, *La.* 15 32 15N 92 43W
Jonesburg 16 38 51N 91 18W
Jonestown 27 39 13N 76 48W
Jonesville, *Ind.* 17 39 5N 85 54W
Jonesville, *Mich.* 17 41 59N 84 40W
Joplin 15 37 6N 94 31W
Joppatowne 27 39 24N 76 20W
Jordan, *Mont.* 18 47 19N 106 55W
Jordan, *N.Y.* 9 43 4N 76 29W
Jordan Valley 18 42 59N 117 3W
Josephine Pk. 31 34 17N 118 7W
Joshua Tree 21 34 8N 116 19W
Joshua Tree National Park 21 33 55N 116 0W
Jourdanton 15 28 55N 98 33W
Judith → 18 47 44N 109 39W
Judith, Pt. 9 41 22N 71 29W
Judith Gap 18 46 41N 109 45W
Julesburg 14 40 59N 102 16W
Julian 21 33 4N 116 38W
Juliette, L. 12 33 2N 83 50W
Jumbo Pk. 21 36 12N 114 11W
Junction, *Tex.* 15 30 29N 99 46W
Junction, *Utah* 19 38 14N 112 13W
Junction City, *Ga.* 12 32 36N 84 28W
Junction City, *Kans.* 14 39 2N 96 50W
Junction City, *Oreg.* 18 44 13N 123 12W
Juneau 32 58 18N 134 25W
Juniata → 8 40 30N 77 40W
Juniper 12 32 32N 84 36W
Juno Beach 13 26 52N 80 3W
Juntura 18 43 45N 118 5W
Jupiter 13 26 57N 80 6W
Justice 24 41 44N 87 49W

K

Ka Lae 32 18 55N 155 41W
Kaala 32 21 31N 158 9W
Kabetogama 14 48 28N 92 59W
Kadoka 14 43 50N 101 31W
Kaena Pt. 32 21 35N 158 17W
Kagamil I. 32 53 0N 169 43W
Kahoka 16 40 25N 91 44W
Kahoolawe 32 20 33N 156 37W
Kahuku Pt. 32 21 43N 157 59W
Kahului 32 20 54N 156 28W
Kailua Kona 32 19 39N 155 59W
Kaiwi Channel 32 21 15N 157 30W
Kaiyuh Mts. 32 64 30N 158 0W
Kake 32 56 59N 133 57W
Kaktovik 32 70 8N 143 38W
Kalaallit Nunaat = Greenland ■ 2 66 0N 45 0W
Kalama 20 46 1N 122 51W
Kalamazoo 17 42 17N 85 35W
Kalamazoo → 17 42 40N 86 10W
Kalaupapa 32 21 12N 156 59W
Kalispell 18 48 12N 114 19W
Kalkaska 10 44 44N 85 11W
Kalona 16 41 29N 91 43W
Kamalino 32 21 50N 160 14W
Kamiah 18 46 14N 116 2W
Kampsville 16 39 18N 90 37W
Kanab 19 37 3N 112 32W
Kanab → 19 36 24N 112 38W
Kanaga I. 32 51 45N 177 22W
Kanakanak 32 59 0N 158 58W
Kanaskat 20 47 19N 121 54W
Kanawha → 10 38 50N 82 9W
Kane 8 41 40N 78 49W
Kaneohe 32 21 25N 157 48W
Kankakee 17 41 7N 87 52W
Kankakee → 17 41 23N 88 15W
Kannapolis 11 35 30N 80 37W
Kanowha 16 42 57N 93 47W
Kansas 17 39 33N 87 56W
Kansas □ 14 38 30N 99 0W
Kansas → 14 39 7N 94 37W
Kansas City, *Kans.* 16 39 7N 94 38W
Kansas City, *Mo.* 16 39 6N 94 35W
Kantishna 32 63 31N 151 5W
Kapaa 32 22 5N 159 19W
Kaplan 15 30 0N 92 17W
Kapowsin 20 46 59N 122 13W
Karlstad 14 48 35N 96 31W
Karnes City 15 28 53N 97 54W
Karthaus 8 41 8N 78 9W
Kaskaskia → 16 37 58N 89 57W
Kasson 14 44 2N 92 45W
Katahdin, Mt. 11 45 54N 68 56W
Katalla 32 60 12N 144 31W
Kathleen 13 28 7N 82 2W
Katmai National Park and Preserve 32 58 20N 155 0W
Kauai 32 22 3N 159 30W
Kauai Channel 32 21 45N 158 50W
Kaufman 15 32 35N 96 19W
Kaukauna 10 44 17N 88 17W
Kaunakakai 6 21 6N 157 1W
Kaupulehu 32 19 43N 155 53W
Kawaihae 32 20 3N 155 50W
Kawaihoa Pt. 32 21 47N 160 12W
Kawaikimi 32 22 5N 159 29W
Kayak I. 32 59 56N 144 23W
Kaycee 18 43 43N 106 38W
Kayenta 19 36 44N 110 15W
Kaysville 18 41 2N 111 56W
Keaau 32 19 37N 155 2W
Keanae 32 20 52N 156 9W
Kearney, *Mo.* 16 39 22N 94 22W
Kearney, *Nebr.* 14 40 42N 99 5W
Kearny, *N.J.* 22 40 45N 74 8W
Kearny, *Ariz.* 19 33 3N 110 55W
Kearsarge, Mt. 9 43 22N 71 50W
Keeler 20 36 29N 117 52W
Keene, *Calif.* 21 35 13N 118 33W
Keene, *N.H.* 9 42 56N 72 17W
Keene, *N.Y.* 9 44 16N 73 46W
Keeseville 9 44 29N 73 30W
Keithsburg 16 41 6N 90 56W
Keizer 18 44 57N 123 1W
Keller 12 31 50N 81 15W
Kelleys I. 8 41 36N 82 42W
Kellogg 18 47 32N 116 7W
Kelseyville 20 38 59N 122 50W
Kelso 20 46 9N 122 54W
Kemmerer 18 41 48N 110 32W
Kemp, L. 15 33 46N 99 9W
Kemp Mill 27 39 0N 77 1W
Kempton 17 40 17N 86 14W
Kenai 32 60 33N 151 16W
Kenai Mts. 32 60 0N 150 0W
Kenansville 13 27 53N 80 59W
Kendall 13 25 41N 80 19W
Kendall Green 25 42 22N 71 16W
Kendallville 17 41 27N 85 16W
Kendrick 13 29 15N 82 10W
Kenedy 15 28 49N 97 51W
Kenilworth, *Ill.* 24 42 5N 87 42W
Kenilworth, *N.J.* 22 40 40N 74 16W
Kenmare 14 48 41N 102 5W
Kennebago Lake 9 45 4N 70 40W
Kennebec 14 43 54N 99 52W
Kennebec → 11 43 45N 69 46W
Kennebunk 9 43 23N 70 33W
Kennedy Grove Regional Rec. Area 30 37 56N 122 14W
Kenner 15 29 59N 90 15W
Kennesaw 12 34 1N 84 37W
Kennett 15 36 14N 90 3W
Kennewick 18 46 12N 119 7W
Kenosha 17 42 35N 87 49W
Kensington, *N.Y.* 22 40 38N 73 57W
Kensington, *Pa.* 26 39 59N 75 6W
Kensington, *Calif.* 30 37 54N 122 17W
Kensington, *Md.* 27 39 1N 77 4W
Kent, *Ohio* 8 41 9N 81 22W
Kent, *Tex.* 15 31 4N 104 13W
Kent, *Wash.* 20 47 23N 122 14W
Kent Woodlands 30 37 56N 122 34W
Kentfield 30 37 57N 122 33W
Kentland, *Ind.* 17 40 46N 87 27W
Kentland, *Md.* 27 38 55N 76 53W
Kenton 17 40 39N 83 37W
Kentucky □ 10 37 0N 84 0W
Kentucky → 17 38 41N 85 11W
Kentucky L. 11 37 1N 88 16W
Kentwood 15 30 56N 90 31W
Kenwood, *Md.* 27 39 20N 76 30W
Kenwood, *Mass.* 25 42 40N 71 14W
Keokuk 16 40 24N 91 24W
Keosauqua 16 40 44N 91 58W
Keota 16 41 22N 91 57W
Kepuhi 32 21 10N 157 10W
Kerman 20 36 43N 120 4W
Kermit 15 31 52N 103 6W
Kern → 21 35 16N 119 18W
Kernville 21 35 45N 118 26W
Kerrville 15 30 3N 99 8W
Ketchikan 32 55 21N 131 39W
Ketchum 18 43 41N 114 22W
Kettering, *Ohio* 17 39 41N 84 10W
Kettering, *Md.* 27 38 53N 76 49W
Kettle Falls 18 48 37N 118 3W
Kettleman City 20 36 1N 119 58W
Keuka L. 8 42 30N 77 9W
Kewanee 16 41 14N 89 56W
Kewanna 17 41 1N 86 25W
Kewaunee 10 44 27N 87 31W
Keweenaw B. 10 47 0N 88 15W
Keweenaw Pen. 10 47 30N 88 0W
Keweenaw Pt. 10 47 25N 87 43W
Key Biscayne 13 25 42N 80 10W
Key Colony Beach 13 24 45N 80 57W
Key Largo 13 25 5N 80 27W
Key West 13 24 33N 81 48W
Keyesport 16 38 45N 89 17W
Keyser 10 39 26N 78 59W
Keysville 12 33 14N 82 14W
Keytesville 16 39 26N 92 56W
Kihei 6 20 47N 156 28W
Kijik 32 60 20N 154 20W
Kilauea 32 22 13N 159 25W
Kilauea Crater 32 19 25N 155 17W
Kilbuck Mts. 32 60 30N 160 0W
Kildare 12 32 32N 81 27W
Kilgore 15 32 23N 94 53W
Killdeer 14 47 26N 102 48W
Killeen 15 31 7N 97 44W
Kim 15 37 15N 103 21W
Kimball, *Nebr.* 14 41 14N 103 40W
Kimball, *S. Dak.* 14 43 45N 98 57W
Kimberly 18 42 32N 114 22W
Kimberton 26 40 7N 75 34W
Kinard 12 30 16N 85 15W
Kincaid 16 39 35N 89 25W
Kinchafoonee Cr. → 12 31 38N 84 10W
Kinde 8 43 56N 83 0W
King City, *Calif.* 20 36 13N 121 8W
King City, *Mo.* 16 40 3N 94 31W
King of Prussia 26 40 5N 75 23W
Kingfisher 15 35 52N 97 56W

Kingman

Kingman, Ariz. 21 35 12N 114 4W
Kingman, Ind. 17 39 58N 87 18W
Kingman, Kans. 15 37 39N 98 7W
Kings → 20 36 3N 119 50W
Kings Canyon National Park 20 36 50N 118 40W
Kings Mountain 11 35 15N 81 20W
Kings Mt. 30 37 27N 122 19W
Kings Park, N.Y. 9 40 53N 73 16W
Kings Park, Va. 27 38 48N 77 17W
King's Peak 18 40 46N 110 27W
King's Point 23 40 48N 73 45W
Kingsburg 20 36 31N 119 33W
Kingsbury 17 41 31N 86 42W
Kingsford 10 45 48N 88 4W
Kingsland 12 30 48N 81 41W
Kingsley 14 42 35N 95 58W
Kingsport 11 36 33N 82 33W
Kingston, Mo. 16 39 39N 94 2W
Kingston, N.H. 9 42 56N 71 3W
Kingston, N.Y. 9 41 56N 73 59W
Kingston, Pa. 9 41 16N 75 54W
Kingston, R.I. 9 41 29N 71 30W
Kingston Pk. 21 35 45N 115 54W
Kingstree 12 33 40N 79 50W
Kingsville 15 27 31N 97 52W
Kingwood 15 29 54N 95 18W
Kinmundy 17 38 46N 88 51W
Kinnelon 22 40 59N 74 23W
Kinsley 15 37 55N 99 25W
Kinsman 8 41 26N 80 35W
Kinston, Ala. 12 31 13N 86 10W
Kinston, N.C. 11 35 16N 77 35W
Kinzua 8 41 52N 78 58W
Kinzua Dam 8 41 53N 79 0W
Kiowa, Kans. 15 37 1N 98 29W
Kiowa, Okla. 15 34 43N 95 54W
Kipnuk 32 59 56N 164 3W
Kirkland 17 42 6N 88 51W
Kirklin 17 40 12N 86 22W
Kirksville 16 40 12N 92 35W
Kirkwood 16 38 35N 90 24W
Kirtland 19 36 44N 108 21W
Kishwaukee → 16 42 12N 89 8W
Kiska I. 32 51 59N 177 30 E
Kissimmee 11 28 18N 81 24W
Kissimmee → 11 27 9N 80 52W
Kissimmee, L. 13 27 55N 81 17W
Kit Carson 14 38 46N 102 48W
Kittanning 8 40 49N 79 31W
Kittatinny Mts. 9 41 0N 75 0W
Kittery 11 43 5N 70 45W
Kivalina 32 67 44N 164 33W
Klamath → 18 41 33N 124 5W
Klamath Falls 18 42 13N 121 46W
Klamath Mts. 18 41 20N 123 0W
Klickitat 18 45 49N 121 9W
Klickitat → 20 45 42N 121 17W
Kline 12 33 8N 81 21W
Knights Ferry 20 37 50N 120 40W
Knights Landing 20 38 48N 121 43W
Knightstown 17 39 48N 85 32W
Knowland State Arboretum and Park 30 37 45N 122 7W
Knox 17 41 18N 86 37W
Knoxville, Ga. 12 32 47N 83 59W
Knoxville, Iowa 16 41 19N 93 6W
Knoxville, Pa. 8 41 57N 77 27W
Knoxville, Tenn. 11 35 58N 83 55W
Kobuk 32 66 55N 156 52W
Kobuk → 32 66 55N 157 0W
Kodiak 32 57 47N 152 24W
Kodiak I. 32 57 30N 152 45W
Kokomo 17 40 29N 86 8W
Kooskia 18 46 9N 115 59W
Korona 13 29 25N 81 12W
Koror 33 7 20N 134 28 E
Kosciusko 15 33 4N 89 35W
Koshkonong L. 17 42 52N 88 58W
Kotzebue 32 66 53N 162 39W
Kotzebue Sound 32 66 20N 163 0W
Kountze 15 30 22N 94 19W
Kouts 17 41 19N 87 2W
Koyuk 32 64 56N 161 9W
Koyukuk → 32 64 55N 157 32W
Kremmling 18 40 4N 106 24W
Kresson 26 39 51N 74 54W
Kualakahi Chan 32 22 2N 159 53W
Kuiu I. 32 57 45N 134 10W
Kumukahi, C. 32 19 31N 154 49W
Kupreanof I. 32 56 50N 133 30W
Kuskokwim → 32 60 5N 162 25W
Kuskokwim B. 32 59 45N 162 25W
Kuskokwim Mts. 32 62 30N 156 0W
Kwethluk 32 60 49N 161 26W
Kwigillingok 32 59 51N 163 8W
Kwiguk 32 62 46N 164 30W
Kyburz 20 38 47N 120 18W

L

La Barge 18 42 16N 110 12W
La Belle, Fla. 11 26 46N 81 26W
La Belle, Mo. 16 40 7N 91 55W
La Crescent 14 43 50N 91 18W
La Crescenta 31 34 13N 118 14W
La Crosse, Fla. 12 29 51N 82 24W
La Crosse, Kans. 14 38 32N 99 18W
La Crosse, Wis. 14 43 48N 91 15W
La Fayette 11 34 42N 85 17W
La Follette 11 36 23N 84 7W
La Fontaine 17 40 40N 85 43W
La Grande 18 45 20N 118 5W
La Grange, Ill. 24 41 48N 87 53W
La Grange, Calif. 20 37 42N 120 27W
La Grange, Ga. 12 33 2N 85 2W
La Grange, Ky. 10 38 25N 85 23W
La Grange, Mo. 16 40 3N 91 35W
La Grange, Tex. 15 29 54N 96 52W
La Grange Highlands 24 41 46N 87 53W
La Grange Park 24 41 49N 87 51W
La Guardia Airport 23 40 46N 73 52W
La Habra 31 33 56N 117 57W
La Habre Heights 31 33 59N 117 56W
La Harpe 16 40 35N 90 58W
La Junta 15 37 59N 103 33W
La Mesa 21 32 46N 117 3W
La Moille 16 41 32N 89 17W
La Moine → 16 39 59N 90 31W
La Monte 16 38 46N 93 26W
La Moure 14 46 21N 98 18W
La Pine 18 43 40N 121 30W
La Plata 16 40 2N 92 29W
La Porte, Ind. 17 41 36N 86 43W
La Porte, Tex. 15 29 39N 95 1W
La Porte City 16 42 19N 92 12W
La Puente 31 34 1N 117 54W
La Push 20 47 55N 124 38W
La Rue 17 40 35N 83 23W
La Salle 16 41 20N 89 6W
La Selva Beach 20 36 56N 121 51W
Laau Pt. 32 21 6N 157 19W
Labrador Sea 2 57 0N 54 0W
Lacey 20 47 7N 122 49W
Lackawanna 8 42 50N 78 50W
Lackawaxen 9 41 29N 74 59W
Lacon 16 41 2N 89 24W
Lacona, Iowa 16 41 12N 93 23W
Lacona, N.Y. 9 43 39N 76 10W
Laconia 9 43 32N 71 28W
Lacoochee 13 28 28N 82 11W
Ladd 16 41 23N 89 13W
Laddonia 16 39 15N 91 39W
Ladson 12 32 59N 80 6W
Lady Lake 13 28 55N 81 55W
Ladysmith 14 45 28N 91 12W
Lafayette, Calif. 30 37 52N 122 6W
Lafayette, Ala. 12 32 54N 85 24W
Lafayette, Colo. 14 39 58N 105 12W
Lafayette, Ind. 17 40 25N 86 54W
Lafayette, La. 15 30 14N 92 1W
Lafayette, Tenn. 11 36 31N 86 2W
Lafayette Hill 26 40 5N 75 15W
Lafayette Res. 30 37 52N 122 8W
Lagrange 17 41 39N 85 25W
Laguna 19 35 2N 107 25W
Laguna Beach 21 33 33N 117 47W
Lahaina 32 20 53N 156 41W
Lake Alfred 13 28 6N 81 44W
Lake Alpine 20 38 29N 120 0W
Lake Andes 14 43 9N 98 32W
Lake Arthur 15 30 5N 92 41W
Lake Avenue Woods 24 42 4N 87 53W
Lake Bird 12 30 14N 83 37W
Lake Butler 12 30 1N 82 21W
Lake Charles 15 30 14N 93 13W
Lake City, Colo. 19 38 2N 107 19W
Lake City, Fla. 12 30 11N 82 38W
Lake City, Iowa 16 42 16N 94 44W
Lake City, Mich. 10 44 20N 85 13W
Lake City, Minn. 14 44 27N 92 16W
Lake City, Pa. 8 42 1N 80 21W
Lake City, S.C. 12 33 52N 79 45W
Lake Clarke Shores 13 26 39N 80 5W
Lake Elsinore 21 33 38N 117 20W
Lake Forest 17 42 15N 87 50W
Lake Geneva 17 42 36N 88 26W
Lake George 9 43 26N 73 43W
Lake Harbor 13 26 42N 80 48W
Lake Havasu City 21 34 27N 114 22W
Lake Helen 13 28 59N 81 14W
Lake Hiawatha 22 40 52N 74 23W
Lake Hughes 21 34 41N 118 26W
Lake Isabella 21 35 38N 118 28W
Lake Jackson 15 29 3N 95 27W
Lake Junction 18 44 35N 110 28W
Lake Mead National Recreation Area 21 36 15N 114 30W
Lake Michigan Beach 17 42 13N 86 25W
Lake Mills, Iowa 14 43 25N 93 32W
Lake Mills, Wis. 17 43 5N 88 55W
Lake Monroe 13 28 50N 81 19W
Lake Odessa 17 42 47N 85 8W
Lake Orion 17 42 47N 83 14W
Lake Park, Fla. 13 26 48N 80 3W
Lake Park, Ga. 12 30 41N 83 11W
Lake Placid, Fla. 13 27 18N 81 22W
Lake Placid, N.Y. 9 44 17N 73 59W
Lake Pleasant 9 43 28N 74 25W
Lake Providence 15 32 48N 91 10W
Lake Villa 17 42 25N 88 5W
Lake Village 15 33 20N 91 17W
Lake Wales 11 27 54N 81 35W
Lake Worth 11 26 37N 80 3W
Lakehurst 9 40 1N 74 19W
Lakeland, Fla. 11 28 3N 81 57W
Lakeland, Ga. 12 31 2N 83 4W
Lakeport, Calif. 20 39 3N 122 55W
Lakeport, Mich. 8 43 7N 82 30W
Lakeside, Ariz. 19 34 9N 109 58W
Lakeside, Calif. 21 32 52N 116 55W
Lakeside, Nebr. 14 42 3N 102 26W
Lakeside, Ohio 8 41 32N 82 46W
Lakeview, Ill. 24 41 56N 87 38W
Lakeview, Oreg. 18 42 11N 120 21W
Lakeville 14 44 39N 93 14W
Lakewood, Colo. 14 39 44N 105 5W
Lakewood, N.J. 9 40 6N 74 13W
Lakewood, N.Y. 8 42 6N 79 19W
Lakewood, Ohio 8 41 29N 81 48W
Lakewood, Wash. 20 47 11N 122 32W
Lakin 15 37 57N 101 15W
Lakota 14 48 2N 98 21W
Lamar, Colo. 14 38 5N 102 37W
Lamar, Mo. 15 37 30N 94 16W
Lame Deer 18 45 37N 106 40W
Lamesa 15 32 44N 101 58W
Lamoille → 9 44 38N 73 13W
Lamoni 16 40 37N 93 56W
Lamont, Calif. 21 35 15N 118 55W
Lamont, Fla. 12 30 23N 83 49W
Lamont, Iowa 16 42 35N 91 40W
Lamont, Wyo. 18 42 13N 107 29W
Lampasas 15 31 4N 98 11W
Lamy 19 35 29N 105 53W
Lanai 32 20 50N 156 55W
Lanai City 32 20 50N 156 55W
Lanark Village 12 29 53N 84 36W
Lancaster, Calif. 21 34 42N 118 8W
Lancaster, Ky. 10 37 37N 84 35W
Lancaster, Mo. 16 40 31N 92 32W
Lancaster, N.H. 9 44 29N 71 34W
Lancaster, N.Y. 8 42 54N 78 40W
Lancaster, Ohio 10 39 43N 82 36W
Lancaster, Pa. 9 40 2N 76 19W
Lancaster, S.C. 11 34 43N 80 46W
Lancaster, Wis. 16 42 51N 90 43W
Lander 18 42 50N 108 44W
Landisburg 8 40 21N 77 19W
Landover Hills 27 38 56N 76 54W
Lane 12 33 32N 79 53W
Lanesboro 9 41 57N 75 34W
Lanett 12 32 52N 85 12W
Langdon 14 48 45N 98 22W
Langley 27 38 57N 77 10W
Langley Park 27 38 59N 76 58W
Langtry 15 29 49N 101 34W
Lanham 27 38 59N 76 51W
Lansdale 9 40 14N 75 17W
Lansdowne, Md. 27 39 14N 76 38W
Lansdowne, Pa. 26 39 56N 75 16W
L'Anse, Mich. 10 46 42N 88 25W
L'Anse, Mich. 14 46 45N 88 27W
Lansford 9 40 50N 75 53W
Lansing 17 42 44N 84 33W
Lantana 13 26 35N 80 3W
Laona 10 45 34N 88 40W
Lapeer 17 43 3N 83 19W
Laporte 9 41 25N 76 30W
Laramie 14 41 19N 105 35W
Laramie → 18 42 13N 104 33W
Laramie Mts. 14 42 0N 105 30W
Larchmont 23 40 55N 73 44W
Laredo 15 27 30N 99 30W
Largo 11 27 55N 82 47W
Largo Key 13 25 15N 80 18W
Larimore 14 47 54N 97 38W
Larkspur 30 37 55N 122 31W
Larned 14 38 11N 99 6W
Larose 15 29 34N 90 23W
Las Animas 14 38 4N 103 13W
Las Cruces 19 32 19N 106 47W
Las Lomas 31 34 8N 117 59W
Las Trampas Regional Park 30 37 49N 122 3W
Las Trampas Ridge 30 37 50N 122 3W
Las Vegas, N. Mex. 19 35 36N 105 13W
Las Vegas, Nev. 21 36 10N 115 9W
Lassen Pk. 18 40 29N 121 31W
Lassen Volcanic National Park 18 40 30N 121 20W
Lastchance Cr. → 20 40 2N 121 15W
Lathrop 16 39 33N 94 20W
Lathrop Wells 21 36 39N 116 24W
Laton 20 36 26N 119 41W
Latrobe 8 40 19N 79 23W
Lattingtown 23 40 52N 73 36W
Laughlin 19 35 8N 114 35W
Laurel, Fla. 13 27 8N 82 27W
Laurel, Ind. 17 39 31N 85 11W
Laurel, Miss. 15 31 41N 89 8W
Laurel, Mont. 18 45 40N 108 46W
Laurel Bay 12 32 27N 80 47W
Laurel Hollow 23 40 51N 73 28W
Laurel Springs 26 39 49N 75 0W
Laurelton 23 40 40N 73 45W
Laurence Hanscom Field 25 42 28N 71 16W
Laurens 11 34 30N 82 1W
Laurinburg 11 34 47N 79 28W
Laurium 10 47 14N 88 27W
Lawndale, Ill. 24 41 50N 87 42W
Lawndale, Calif. 31 33 52N 118 22W
Lawndale, Pa. 26 40 3N 75 5W
Lawnside 26 39 51N 75 1W
Lawrence, Mass. 25 42 43N 71 7W
Lawrence, N.Y. 23 40 36N 73 43W
Lawrence, Ind. 17 39 50N 86 2W
Lawrence, Kans. 14 38 58N 95 14W
Lawrence Park 26 39 57N 75 20W
Lawrenceburg, Ind. 17 39 6N 84 52W
Lawrenceburg, Ky. 17 38 2N 84 54W
Lawrenceburg, Tenn. 11 35 14N 87 20W
Lawrenceville, Ga. 12 33 57N 83 59W
Lawrenceville, Ill. 17 38 44N 87 41W
Lawrenceville, Pa. 8 41 59N 77 8W
Laws 20 37 24N 118 20W
Lawson 16 39 26N 94 12W
Lawtey 12 30 3N 82 5W
Lawton, Mich. 17 42 10N 85 50W
Lawton, Okla. 15 34 37N 98 25W
Layton, Fla. 13 24 50N 80 47W
Layton, Utah 18 41 4N 111 58W
Laytonville 18 39 41N 123 29W
Le Claire 16 41 36N 90 21W
Le Mars 14 42 47N 96 10W
Le Roy 17 40 21N 88 46W
Le Sueur 14 44 28N 93 55W
Lead 14 44 21N 103 46W
Leadville 19 39 15N 106 18W
Leaf → 15 30 59N 88 44W
Leakin Park 27 39 18N 76 41W
Leamington 18 39 32N 112 17W
Leary 12 31 29N 84 31W
Leavenworth, Ind. 17 38 12N 86 21W
Leavenworth, Kans. 14 39 19N 94 55W
Leavenworth, Wash. 18 47 36N 120 40W
Leawood 16 38 57N 94 37W
Lebam 20 46 34N 123 33W
Lebanon, Ill. 16 38 36N 89 49W
Lebanon, Ind. 17 40 3N 86 28W
Lebanon, Kans. 14 39 49N 98 33W
Lebanon, Ky. 10 37 34N 85 15W
Lebanon, Mo. 16 37 41N 92 40W
Lebanon, N.H. 9 43 39N 72 15W
Lebanon, Ohio 17 39 26N 84 13W
Lebanon, Oreg. 18 44 32N 122 55W
Lebanon, Pa. 9 40 20N 76 26W
Lebanon, Tenn. 11 36 12N 86 18W
Lebanon Junction 17 37 50N 85 44W
Lebec 21 34 50N 118 52W
Lecontes Mills 8 41 5N 78 17W
Lee, Fla. 12 30 25N 83 18W
Lee, Mass. 9 42 19N 73 15W
Lee Vining 20 37 58N 119 7W
Leech L. 14 47 10N 94 24W
Leechburg 8 40 37N 79 36W
Leeds 11 33 33N 86 33W
Leeper 8 41 22N 79 18W
Lee's Summit 16 38 55N 94 23W
Leesburg, Fla. 11 28 49N 81 53W
Leesburg, Ga. 12 31 44N 84 10W
Leesburg, Ohio 17 39 21N 83 33W
Leesville 15 31 9N 93 16W
Leetonia 8 40 53N 80 45W
Lehigh Acres 13 26 36N 81 39W
Lehighton 9 40 50N 75 43W
Lehua I. 32 22 1N 160 6W
Leisure City 13 25 31N 80 26W
Leisure World 30 37 51N 122 4W
Leland, Mich. 10 45 1N 85 45W
Leland, Miss. 15 33 24N 90 54W
Lemhi Ra. 18 44 30N 113 30W
Lemmon 14 45 57N 102 10W
Lemon Grove 21 32 45N 117 2W
Lemoore 20 36 18N 119 46W
Lenni 26 39 53N 75 27W
Lennox, Calif. 31 33 56N 118 20W
Lennox, S. Dak. 14 43 21N 96 53W
Lenoir 11 35 55N 81 32W
Lenoir City 11 35 48N 84 16W
Lenox, Ga. 12 31 16N 83 28W
Lenox, Iowa 16 40 53N 94 34W
Lenox, Mass. 9 42 22N 73 17W
Lenwood 21 34 53N 117 7W
Leola 14 45 43N 98 56W
Leominster 9 42 32N 71 46W
Leon 16 40 44N 93 45W
Leon → 15 31 14N 97 28W
Leonardtown 10 38 17N 76 38W
Leonia, N.J. 22 40 51N 73 59W
Leonia, Fla. 12 30 55N 86 1W
Leopard 26 40 1N 75 26W
Leoti 14 38 29N 101 21W
Leslie, Ga. 12 31 57N 84 5W
Leslie, Mich. 17 42 27N 84 26W
Lester 20 47 12N 121 29W
Leucadia 21 33 4N 117 18W
Levelland 15 33 35N 102 23W
Levittown, N.Y. 23 40 43N 73 31W
Levittown, Pa. 9 40 9N 74 51W
Lewes 10 38 46N 75 9W
Lewis → 20 45 51N 122 48W
Lewis Range 18 48 5N 113 5W
Lewis Run 8 41 52N 78 39W
Lewisburg, Ohio 17 39 51N 84 33W
Lewisburg, Pa. 8 40 58N 76 54W
Lewisburg, Tenn. 11 35 27N 86 48W
Lewisburg, W. Va. 10 37 48N 80 27W
Lewisdale 27 38 58N 76 59W
Lewisport 17 37 56N 86 54W
Lewiston, Idaho 18 46 25N 117 1W
Lewiston, Maine 11 44 6N 70 13W
Lewiston, N.Y. 8 43 11N 79 3W
Lewistown, Ill. 16 40 24N 90 9W
Lewistown, Mont. 18 47 4N 109 26W
Lewistown, Pa. 8 40 36N 77 34W
Lexington, Mass. 25 42 25N 71 12W
Lexington, Ga. 12 33 52N 83 7W
Lexington, Ill. 17 40 39N 88 47W
Lexington, Ky. 17 38 3N 84 30W
Lexington, Mich. 8 43 16N 82 32W
Lexington, Mo. 16 39 11N 93 52W
Lexington, N.C. 11 35 49N 80 15W
Lexington, N.Y. 9 42 15N 74 22W
Lexington, Nebr. 14 40 47N 99 45W
Lexington, Ohio 8 40 41N 82 35W
Lexington, S.C. 12 33 59N 81 11W
Lexington, Tenn. 11 35 39N 88 24W
Lexington, Va. 10 37 47N 79 27W
Lexington Park 10 38 16N 76 27W
Libby 18 48 23N 115 33W
Liberal 15 37 3N 100 55W
Liberty, Ind. 17 39 38N 84 56W
Liberty, Mo. 16 39 15N 94 25W
Liberty, N.Y. 9 41 48N 74 45W
Liberty, Pa. 8 41 34N 77 6W
Liberty, Tex. 15 30 3N 94 48W
Liberty Center 17 41 27N 84 1W
Liberty I. 22 40 41N 74 2W
Liberty Plain 25 42 11N 70 52W
Liberty Res. 27 39 23N 76 52W
Libertyville 17 42 18N 87 57W
Library of Congress 27 38 53N 77 0W
Licking → 17 39 6N 84 30W
Lido Beach 23 40 35N 73 37W
Lighthouse Point 13 26 15N 80 7W
Lighthouse Pt. 12 29 54N 84 21W
Ligonier 8 40 15N 79 14W
Lihue 32 21 59N 159 23W
Lima, Pa. 26 39 55N 75 26W
Lima, Mont. 18 44 38N 112 36W
Lima, Ohio 17 40 44N 84 6W
Limerick 9 43 41N 70 48W
Limestone 8 42 2N 78 38W
Limon 14 39 16N 103 41W
Linbigh 27 39 21N 76 31W
Lincoln, Mass. 25 42 25N 71 18W
Lincoln, Calif. 20 38 54N 121 17W
Lincoln, Ill. 16 40 9N 89 22W
Lincoln, Kans. 14 39 3N 98 9W
Lincoln, Maine 11 45 22N 68 30W
Lincoln, N.H. 9 44 3N 71 40W
Lincoln, N. Mex. 19 33 30N 105 23W
Lincoln, Nebr. 14 40 49N 96 41W
Lincoln Center 22 40 46N 73 59W
Lincoln City 18 44 57N 124 1W
Lincoln Heights 31 34 4N 118 12 E
Lincoln Memorial 27 38 53N 77 3W
Lincoln Park, Ill. 24 41 57N 87 38W
Lincoln Park, Mich. 28 42 14N 83 9W
Lincoln Park, N.J. 22 40 56N 74 18W
Lincoln Park, Calif. 30 37 47N 122 30W
Lincoln Park, Ga. 12 32 52N 84 20W
Lincolnton, Ga. 12 33 48N 82 29W
Lincolnton, N.C. 11 35 29N 81 16W
Lincolnwood 24 42 1N 87 43W
Lind 18 46 58N 118 37W
Linda 20 39 8N 121 34W
Lindale 12 34 11N 85 11W
Linden, N.J. 22 40 38N 74 14W
Linden, Ala. 11 32 18N 87 48W
Linden, Calif. 20 38 1N 121 5W
Linden, Ind. 17 40 11N 86 54W
Linden, Mich. 17 42 49N 83 47W
Linden, Tex. 15 33 1N 94 22W
Lindenhurst 23 40 40N 73 22W
Lindenwold 26 39 49N 74 59W
Lindsay, Calif. 20 36 12N 119 5W
Lindsay, Okla. 15 34 50N 97 38W
Lindsborg 14 38 35N 97 40W
Linesville 8 41 39N 80 26W
Lineville, Ala. 12 33 19N 85 45W
Lineville, Iowa 16 40 35N 93 32W
Lingle 14 42 8N 104 21W
Linn 16 38 29N 91 51W
Linneus 16 39 53N 93 11W
Linthicum Heights 27 39 12N 76 47W
Linton, Ind. 17 39 2N 87 10W
Linton, N. Dak. 14 46 16N 100 14W
Linwood, Pa. 26 39 49N 75 25W
Linwood, Ala. 12 31 56N 85 52W
Lipscomb 15 36 14N 100 16W
Lisbon, N. Dak. 14 46 27N 97 41W
Lisbon, N.H. 9 44 13N 71 55W
Lisbon, Ohio 8 40 46N 80 46W
Lisbon Falls 11 44 0N 70 4W
Lisburne, C. 32 68 53N 166 13W
Litchfield, Calif. 20 40 24N 120 23W
Litchfield, Conn. 9 41 45N 73 11W
Litchfield, Ill. 16 39 11N 89 39W
Litchfield, Minn. 14 45 8N 94 32W
Lititz 9 40 9N 76 18W
Little Belt Mts. 18 46 40N 110 45W
Little Blue → 14 39 42N 96 41W
Little Colorado → 19 36 12N 111 48W
Little Falls, N.J. 22 40 52N 74 14W
Little Falls, Minn. 14 45 59N 94 22W
Little Falls, N.Y. 9 43 3N 74 51W
Little Ferry 22 40 50N 74 2W
Little Fork → 14 48 31N 93 35W
Little Haw Cr. → 13 29 23N 81 24W
Little Humboldt → 18 41 1N 117 43W
Little Lake 21 35 56N 117 55W
Little Missouri → 14 47 36N 102 25W
Little Neck 23 40 46N 73 43W
Little Red → 15 35 11N 91 27W
Little Rock 15 34 45N 92 17W
Little Sable Pt. 10 43 38N 86 33W
Little Sioux → 14 41 48N 96 4W
Little Snake → 18 40 27N 108 26W
Little Tallapoosa → 12 33 18N 85 34W
Little Valley 8 42 15N 78 48W
Little Wabash → 17 37 55N 88 5W
Little White → 14 43 40N 100 40W
Little York 16 41 1N 90 45W
Littlefield 15 33 55N 102 20W
Littleton 9 44 18N 71 46W
Live Oak, Calif. 20 39 17N 121 40W
Live Oak, Fla. 12 30 18N 82 59W
Livermore 20 37 41N 121 47W
Livermore, Mt. 15 30 38N 104 11W
Livermore Falls 11 44 29N 70 11W
Liverpool 9 43 6N 76 13W
Livingston, Ala. 11 32 35N 88 11W
Livingston, Calif. 20 37 23N 120 43W
Livingston, Mont. 18 45 40N 110 34W
Livingston, S.C. 11 33 32N 80 53W
Livingston, Tenn. 11 36 23N 85 19W
Livingston, Tex. 15 30 43N 94 56W
Livingston, Wis. 16 42 54N 90 26W
Livingston, L. 15 30 50N 95 10W
Livingston Manor 9 41 54N 74 50W
Livingstone 22 40 47N 74 19W
Livonia, Mich. 28 42 24N 83 22W
Livonia, N.Y. 8 42 49N 77 40W
Lizella 12 32 48N 83 49W
Llano 15 30 45N 98 41W
Llano → 15 30 39N 98 26W
Llano Estacado 15 33 30N 103 0W
Lloyd Harbor 23 40 54N 73 26W
Lloyd Pt. 23 40 56N 73 29W
Loa 19 38 24N 111 39W
Lobos, Pt. 30 37 46N 122 30W
Loch Raven Village 27 39 23N 76 34W
Lochearn 27 39 20N 76 43W
Lochloose L. 13 29 30N 82 7W
Lock Haven 8 41 8N 77 28W
Lockeford 20 38 10N 121 9W
Lockhart 15 29 53N 97 40W
Lockney 15 34 7N 101 27W
Lockport, Ill. 17 41 35N 88 3W
Lockport, N.Y. 8 43 10N 78 42W
Locust Cr. → 16 39 40N 93 17W
Locust Grove, N.Y. 23 40 48N 73 29W
Locust Grove, Ga. 12 33 21N 84 7W
Locust Manor 23 40 41N 73 45W
Locust Valley 23 40 52N 73 36W
Lodge Grass 18 45 19N 107 22W
Lodgepole Cr. → 14 41 20N 104 30W
Lodi, N.J. 22 40 52N 74 5W
Lodi, Calif. 20 38 8N 121 16W
Lodi, Ohio 8 41 2N 82 1W
Logan, Pa. 26 40 2N 75 8W
Logan, Iowa 14 41 39N 95 47W
Logan, Ohio 10 39 32N 82 25W
Logan, Utah 18 41 44N 111 50W
Logan, W. Va. 10 37 51N 81 59W
Logan Int. Airport 25 42 22N 71 0W
Logan Martin Reservoir 12 33 26N 86 20W
Logan Square 24 41 55N 87 42W
Logandale 21 36 36N 114 29W
Logansport, Ind. 17 40 45N 86 22W
Logansport, La. 15 31 58N 94 0W
Loganville 12 33 50N 83 54W
Lohrville 16 42 17N 94 33W
Lola, Mt. 20 39 26N 120 22W
Lolo 18 46 45N 114 5W
Loma 18 47 56N 110 30W
Loma Linda 21 34 3N 117 16W
Lombard 17 41 53N 88 1W
Lompoc 21 34 38N 120 28W
London, Ky. 10 37 8N 84 5W
London, Ohio 17 39 53N 83 27W
London Mills 16 40 43N 90 11W
Lone Pine 20 36 36N 118 4W
Long B. 11 33 35N 78 45W
Long Beach, N.Y. 23 40 35N 73 39W
Long Beach, Calif. 21 33 47N 118 11W
Long Beach, Wash. 20 46 21N 124 3W
Long Branch 9 40 18N 74 0W
Long Creek 18 44 43N 119 6W
Long I., Mass. 25 42 19N 70 59W
Long I., N.Y. 23 40 45N 73 30W
Long Island City 22 40 45N 73 56W
Long Island Sd. 9 41 10N 73 0W
Long Lake 9 43 58N 74 25W
Long Pond 25 42 41N 71 22W
Long Prairie → 14 46 20N 94 36W
Longboat Key 13 27 23N 82 39W
Longjohn Slough 24 41 42N 87 52W
Longmeadow 9 42 3N 72 34W
Longmont 14 40 10N 105 6W
Longview, Tex. 15 32 30N 94 44W
Longview, Wash. 20 46 8N 122 57W
Longwood 13 28 42N 81 21W
Lonoke 15 34 47N 91 54W
Loogootee 17 38 41N 86 55W
Lookout, C. 11 34 35N 76 32W
Lopez 8 41 27N 76 20W
Lorain 8 41 28N 82 11W
Loraine 16 40 9N 91 13W
Lordsburg 19 32 21N 108 43W
Loreley 27 39 23N 76 24W
Lorimor 16 41 8N 94 3W
Los Alamos, Calif. 21 34 44N 120 17W
Los Alamos, N. Mex. 19 35 53N 106 19W
Los Altos 20 37 23N 122 7W
Los Angeles 21 34 4N 118 15W
Los Angeles Aqueduct 21 35 22N 118 5W
Los Angeles Int. Airport 31 33 56N 118 23W
Los Banos 20 37 4N 120 51W
Los Gatos 20 37 14N 121 59W
Los Lunas 19 34 48N 106 44W
Los Nietos 31 33 57N 118 4W
Los Olivos 21 34 40N 120 7W
Loudonville 8 40 38N 82 14W
Loughman 13 28 14N 81 34W
Louisa 10 38 7N 82 36W
Louisburg 16 38 37N 94 41W
Louisiana 16 39 27N 91 3W
Louisiana □ 15 30 50N 92 0W
Louisville, Ala. 12 31 47N 85 33W
Louisville, Ga. 12 33 0N 82 25W
Louisville, Ky. 17 38 15N 85 46W
Louisville, Miss. 15 33 7N 89 3W
Louisville, Ohio 8 40 50N 81 16W
Loup City 14 41 17N 98 58W
Louvale 12 32 10N 84 50W
Loveland, Colo. 14 40 24N 105 5W
Loveland, Ohio 17 39 16N 84 16W
Lovell 18 44 50N 108 24W
Lovelock 18 40 11N 118 28W
Loves Park 16 42 19N 89 3W
Lovett 12 32 38N 82 46W
Lovilia 16 41 8N 92 55W
Loving 15 32 17N 104 6W
Lovington, Ill. 17 39 43N 88 38W
Lovington, N. Mex. 15 32 57N 103 21W
Lowden 16 41 52N 90 56W
Lowe, Mt. 31 34 13N 118 5W
Lowe Pond 25 42 41N 71 0W
Lowell, Mass. 25 42 38N 71 16W
Lowell, Fla. 13 29 20N 82 12W
Lowell, Ind. 17 41 18N 87 25W
Lowell Dracut State Forest 25 42 39N 71 22W
Lowellville 8 41 2N 80 32W
Lower Alkali L. 18 41 16N 120 2W
Lower Crystal Springs Res. 30 37 31N 122 21W
Lower Lake 20 38 55N 122 37W
Lower Montville 22 40 53N 74 21W
Lower New York B. 22 40 32N 74 5W
Lower Red L. 14 47 58N 95 0W
Lower Van Norman L. 31 34 17N 118 28W
Lowery City 16 38 8N 93 44W
Lowville 9 43 47N 75 29W
Loyalton 20 39 41N 120 14W
Lubbock 15 33 35N 101 51W
Lucedale 11 30 56N 88 35W
Lucerne 20 39 6N 122 48W
Lucerne Valley 21 34 27N 116 57W
Lucia 20 36 2N 121 33W
Luckey 17 41 27N 83 29W
Ludington 10 43 57N 86 27W
Ludlow, Calif. 21 34 43N 116 10W
Ludlow, Pa. 8 41 43N 78 56W
Ludlow, Vt. 9 43 24N 72 42W
Ludowici 12 31 43N 81 45W
Lufkin 15 31 21N 94 44W
Lukens, Mt. 31 34 16N 118 12W
Luling 15 29 41N 97 39W
Lulu 12 30 7N 82 29W
Luma 33 14 15 S 169 32W
Lumber City 12 31 56N 82 41W
Lumberton 11 34 37N 79 0W
Lumpkin 12 32 3N 84 48W
Luning 18 38 30N 118 11W
Luray, S.C. 12 32 49N 81 14W
Luray, Va. 10 38 40N 78 28W
Lusk 14 42 46N 104 27W
Luthersville 12 33 13N 84 45W
Lutherville-Timonium 27 39 25N 76 36W
Lutz 13 28 9N 82 28W
Luverne, Ala. 12 31 43N 86 16W
Luverne, Minn. 14 43 39N 96 13W
Lykens 9 40 34N 76 42W
Lyman 18 41 20N 110 18W
Lynbrook 23 40 38N 73 41W

Monmouth

Lynchburg, Ohio 17 39 15N 83 48W
Lynchburg, S.C. 12 34 3N 80 4W
Lynchburg, Va. 10 37 25N 79 9W
Lynden 20 48 57N 122 27W
Lyndhurst 22 40 49N 74 7W
Lyndonville, N.Y. 8 43 20N 78 23W
Lyndonville, Vt. 9 44 31N 72 1W
Lynn, Mass. 25 42 28N 70 57W
Lynn, Ind. 17 40 3N 84 56W
Lynn Harbor 25 42 26N 70 56W
Lynn Haven 12 30 15N 85 39W
Lynne 13 29 12N 81 55W
Lynnfield 25 42 32N 71 2W
Lynnwood 20 47 49N 122 19W
Lynwood 31 33 55N 118 11W
Lyons, Ill. 24 41 48N 87 49W
Lyons, Ga. 12 32 12N 82 19W
Lyons, Kans. 14 38 21N 98 12W
Lyons, N.Y. 8 43 5N 77 0W
Lyons Falls 9 43 37N 75 22W
Lyonsville 22 40 57N 74 26W

M

Mableton 12 33 49N 84 35W
McAlester 15 34 56N 95 46W
McAllen 15 26 12N 98 14W
McAlpin 12 30 8N 82 57W
McCall 18 44 55N 116 6W
McCamey 15 31 8N 102 14W
McCammon 18 42 39N 112 12W
McCarthy 32 61 26N 142 56W
McCleary 20 47 3N 123 16W
Macclenny 12 30 17N 82 7W
McCloud 18 41 15N 122 8W
McClure 8 40 42N 77 19W
McClure, L. 20 37 35N 120 16W
McClusky 14 47 29N 100 27W
McComb 15 31 15N 90 27W
McConaughy, L. 14 41 14N 101 40W
McCook, Ill. 24 41 47N 87 49W
McCook, Nebr. 14 40 12N 100 38W
McCormick 12 33 55N 82 17W
McCullough Mt. 21 35 35N 115 13W
McDavid 13 30 52N 87 19W
McDermitt 18 41 59N 117 43W
McDonald 8 40 22N 80 14W
McDonough 12 33 27N 84 9W
Macedonia 8 41 19N 81 31W
McFarland 21 35 41N 119 14W
McGehee 15 33 38N 91 24W
McGill 18 39 23N 114 47W
McGraw 9 42 36N 76 8W
McGregor 16 43 1N 91 11W
McHenry 17 42 21N 88 16W
Machias, Maine 11 44 43N 67 28W
Machias, N.Y. 8 42 25N 78 30W
McIntosh 14 45 55N 101 21W
Mackay 18 43 55N 113 37W
McKees Rocks 29 40 28N 80 3W
McKeesport 29 40 21N 79 51W
McKenna 20 46 56N 122 33W
McKenzie 11 36 8N 88 31W
McKenzie —▸ 18 44 7N 123 6W
Mackinaw 16 40 32N 89 21W
Mackinaw —▸ 16 40 33N 89 44W
Mackinaw City 10 45 47N 84 44W
McKinley, Mt. 32 63 4N 151 0W
McKinney 15 33 12N 96 37W
McKinnon 12 31 25N 81 56W
McKittrick 21 35 18N 119 37W
McLaughlin 14 45 49N 100 49W
McLean, Ill. 16 40 19N 89 10W
McLean, Tex. 15 35 14N 100 36W
Mclean, Va. 27 38 56N 77 10W
McLeansboro 17 38 6N 88 32W
McLoughlin, Mt. 18 42 27N 122 19W
McMechen 8 39 57N 80 44W
McMinnville, Oreg. 18 45 13N 123 12W
McMinnville, Tenn. 11 35 41N 85 46W
McMurray 20 48 19N 122 14W
Macomb 16 40 27N 90 40W
Macon, Ga. 12 32 51N 83 38W
Macon, Ill. 16 39 43N 89 0W
Macon, Miss. 11 33 7N 88 34W
Macon, Mo. 16 39 44N 92 28W
Macoupin Cr. —▸ 16 39 11N 90 38W
McPherson 14 38 22N 97 40W
McPherson Pk. 21 34 53N 119 53W
McRae 12 32 4N 82 54W
Madeira 17 39 11N 84 22W
Madeira Beach 13 27 48N 82 48W
Madera, Calif. 20 36 57N 120 3W
Madera, Pa. 8 40 49N 78 26W
Madill 15 34 6N 96 46W
Madison, N.J. 22 40 45N 74 24W
Madison, Calif. 20 38 41N 121 59W
Madison, Fla. 12 30 28N 83 25W
Madison, Ga. 12 33 36N 83 28W
Madison, Ind. 17 38 44N 85 23W
Madison, Mo. 16 39 28N 92 13W
Madison, Nebr. 14 41 50N 97 27W
Madison, Ohio 8 41 46N 81 3W
Madison, S. Dak. 14 44 0N 97 7W
Madison, Wis. 16 43 4N 89 24W
Madison —▸ 18 45 56N 111 31W
Madison Heights, Mich. 28 42 29N 83 6W
Madison Heights, Va. 10 37 25N 79 8W
Madisonville, Ky. 10 37 20N 87 30W
Madisonville, Tex. 15 30 57N 95 55W
Madras 18 44 38N 121 8W
Madre, Laguna 15 27 0N 97 30W
Madrid, Ala. 12 31 2N 85 24W
Madrid, Iowa 16 41 53N 93 49W
Madrid, N.Y. 9 44 45N 75 8W
Magdalena 19 34 7N 107 15W
Magee 15 31 52N 89 44W
Magnolia, N.J. 26 39 51N 75 1W
Magnolia, Ark. 15 33 16N 93 14W
Magnolia, Miss. 15 31 9N 90 28W
Mahaffey 8 40 53N 78 44W
Mahanoy City 9 40 49N 76 9W
Mahnomen 14 47 19N 95 58W
Mahomet 17 40 12N 88 24W
Mahopac 9 41 22N 73 45W
Mahukona 32 20 11N 155 52W
Maine □ 11 45 20N 69 0W
Makapuu Hd. 32 21 19N 157 39W
Makena 32 20 39N 156 27W
Malabar 13 28 0N 80 34W
Malad City 18 42 12N 112 15W
Malden, Mass. 25 42 26N 71 3W
Malden, Mo. 15 36 34N 89 57W
Malheur —▸ 18 44 4N 116 59W
Malheur L. 18 43 20N 118 48W
Malibu 21 34 2N 118 41W
Mallard 16 42 56N 94 41W
Malone, Fla. 12 30 57N 85 10W
Malone, N.Y. 9 44 51N 74 18W
Malta, Idaho 18 42 18N 113 22W
Malta, Mont. 18 48 21N 107 52W
Malvern, Pa. 26 40 2N 75 31W
Malvern, Ark. 15 34 22N 92 49W
Malverne 23 40 40N 73 40W
Mamaroneck 23 40 56N 73 41W
Mamaroneck Harbour 23 40 56N 73 42W
Mammoth 19 32 43N 110 39W
Mammoth Cave National Park 10 37 8N 86 13W
Mana 32 22 2N 159 47W
Manasquan 9 40 8N 74 3W
Manassa 19 37 11N 105 56W
Manati 32 18 26N 66 29W
Manayunk 26 40 1N 75 12W
Manchester, Calif. 20 38 58N 123 41W
Manchester, Conn. 9 41 47N 72 31W
Manchester, Ga. 12 32 51N 84 37W
Manchester, Iowa 16 42 29N 91 27W
Manchester, Ky. 10 37 9N 83 46W
Manchester, Mich. 17 42 9N 84 2W
Manchester, N.H. 9 42 59N 71 28W
Manchester, N.Y. 8 42 56N 77 16W
Manchester, Pa. 9 40 4N 76 43W
Manchester, Tenn. 11 35 29N 86 5W
Manchester, Vt. 9 43 10N 73 5W
Mandan 14 46 50N 100 54W
Mangonia Park 13 26 45N 80 4W
Mangum 15 34 53N 99 30W
Manhasset 23 40 47N 73 40W
Manhasset B. 23 40 49N 73 43W
Manhasset Hills 23 40 45N 73 39W
Manhattan, N.Y. 22 40 48N 73 57W
Manhattan, Kans. 14 39 11N 96 35W
Manhattan Beach 31 33 53N 118 24W
Manhatten, N.Y. 22 40 34N 73 56W
Manhatten, Ill. 17 41 26N 87 59W
Manila 18 40 59N 109 43W
Manistee 10 44 15N 86 19W
Manistee —▸ 10 44 15N 86 21W
Manistique 10 45 57N 86 15W
Manito 16 40 26N 89 47W
Manitou Beach 17 41 58N 84 19W
Manitou Is. 10 45 8N 86 0W
Manitou Springs 14 38 52N 104 55W
Manitowoc 10 44 5N 87 40W
Mankato, Kans. 14 39 47N 98 13W
Mankato, Minn. 14 44 10N 94 0W
Manning, Oreg. 20 45 45N 123 13W
Manning, S.C. 12 33 42N 80 13W
Manning State Park 25 42 34N 71 20W
Manoa 26 39 58N 75 18W
Manorhaven 23 40 50N 73 41W
Mansfield, Ga. 12 33 31N 83 44W
Mansfield, La. 15 32 2N 93 43W
Mansfield, Mass. 9 42 2N 71 13W
Mansfield, Ohio 8 40 45N 82 31W
Mansfield, Pa. 8 41 48N 77 5W
Mansfield, Mt. 9 44 33N 72 49W
Manson 16 42 32N 94 32W
Manteca 20 37 48N 121 13W
Manteno 17 41 15N 87 50W
Manteo 11 35 55N 75 40W
Manti 18 39 16N 111 38W
Manton 10 44 25N 85 24W
Mantua 26 39 47N 75 10W
Manua Is. 33 14 13S 169 35W
Many 15 31 34N 93 29W
Manzano Mts. 19 34 40N 106 20W
Maple —▸ 17 42 59N 84 57W
Maple Heights 29 41 25N 81 33W
Maple L. 24 41 43N 87 53W
Maple Shade 26 39 57N 75 0W
Maple Valley 20 47 25N 122 3W
Mapleton 18 44 2N 123 52W
Maplewood 22 40 43N 74 16W
Maquoketa 16 42 4N 90 40W
Marana 19 32 27N 111 13W
Marathon, Fla. 13 24 43N 81 5W
Marathon, Iowa 16 42 52N 94 59W
Marathon, N.Y. 9 42 26N 76 2W
Marathon, N.Y. 9 42 27N 76 2W
Marathon, Tex. 15 30 12N 103 15W
Marble Falls 15 30 35N 98 16W
Marblehead 25 42 29N 70 51W
Marceline 16 39 43N 92 57W
Marcella 22 40 59N 74 29W
Marco 13 25 58N 81 44W
Marcus Hook 26 39 49N 75 25W
Marcy, Mt. 9 44 7N 73 56W
Marengo 16 41 48N 92 4W
Marfa 15 30 19N 104 1W
Margate 13 26 15N 80 12W
Marian, L. 13 27 53N 81 6W
Mariana Trench 33 13 0N 145 0 E
Marianna, Ark. 15 34 46N 90 46W
Marianna, Fla. 12 30 46N 85 14W
Marias —▸ 18 47 56N 110 30W
Maricopa, Ariz. 19 33 4N 112 3W
Maricopa, Calif. 21 35 4N 119 24W
Marienville 8 41 28N 79 8W
Marietta, Ga. 12 33 57N 84 33W
Marietta, Ohio 10 39 25N 81 27W
Marin City 30 37 52N 122 30W
Marin Headlands State Park 30 37 50N 122 28W
Marin Is. 30 37 57N 122 27W
Marin Pen. 30 37 50N 122 30W
Marina 20 36 41N 121 48W
Marine City 8 42 43N 82 30W
Marine World 30 37 32N 122 16W
Marineland 12 29 40N 81 13W
Mariners Harbour 22 40 38N 74 10W
Marinette 10 45 6N 87 38W
Marion, Ala. 11 32 38N 87 19W
Marion, Ill. 16 37 44N 88 56W
Marion, Ind. 17 40 32N 85 40W
Marion, Iowa 16 42 2N 91 36W
Marion, Kans. 14 38 21N 97 1W
Marion, N.C. 11 35 41N 82 1W
Marion, Ohio 17 40 35N 83 8W
Marion, S.C. 11 34 11N 79 24W
Marion, Va. 11 36 50N 81 31W
Marion, L. 12 33 28N 80 10W
Mariposa 20 37 29N 119 58W
Marked Tree 15 35 32N 90 25W
Markham, Ill. 24 41 35N 87 40W
Markham, Pa. 26 39 53N 75 30W
Markham, Mt. 31 34 14N 118 6W
Markleeville 20 38 42N 119 47W
Marksville 15 31 8N 92 4W
Marlboro, Mass. 9 42 19N 71 33W
Marlboro, N.Y. 9 41 36N 73 59W
Marlin 15 31 18N 96 54W
Marlow, Ga. 12 32 16N 81 23W
Marlow, Okla. 15 34 39N 97 58W
Marlton 26 39 53N 74 55W
Marple 26 39 56N 75 20W
Marquesas Keys 13 24 35N 82 10W
Marquette 10 46 33N 87 24W
Marquette Park 24 41 46N 87 42W
Marrero 15 29 54N 90 6W
Mars Hill 11 46 31N 67 52W
Marseilles 17 41 20N 88 43W
Marsh I. 15 29 34N 91 53W
Marshall, Ark. 15 35 55N 92 38W
Marshall, Ill. 17 39 23N 87 42W
Marshall, Mich. 17 42 16N 84 58W
Marshall, Minn. 14 44 25N 95 45W
Marshall, Mo. 16 39 7N 93 12W
Marshall, Tex. 15 32 33N 94 23W
Marshall Is. ■ 33 9 0N 171 0 E
Marshalltown 16 42 3N 92 55W
Marshallville 12 32 27N 83 56W
Marshfield, Mo. 15 37 15N 92 54W
Marshfield, Vt. 9 44 20N 72 20W
Marshfield, Wis. 14 44 40N 90 10W
Mart 15 31 33N 96 50W
Martensdale 16 41 23N 93 45W
Martha's Vineyard 9 41 25N 70 38W
Martin, S. Dak. 14 43 11N 101 44W
Martin, Tenn. 15 36 21N 88 51W
Martin L. 12 32 41N 85 55W
Martin State Nat. Airport 27 39 19N 76 24W
Martinez, Calif. 20 38 1N 122 8W
Martinez, Ga. 11 33 31N 82 4W
Martins Ferry 8 40 6N 80 44W
Martins Pond 25 42 35N 71 7W
Martinsburg, Pa. 8 40 19N 78 20W
Martinsburg, W. Va. 10 39 27N 77 58W
Martinsville, Ill. 17 39 20N 87 53W
Martinsville, Ind. 17 39 26N 86 25W
Martinsville, Va. 11 36 41N 79 52W
Maryland □ 10 39 0N 76 30W
Maryland, Univ. of 27 38 58N 76 56W
Marysville, Calif. 20 39 9N 121 35W
Marysville, Kans. 14 39 51N 96 39W
Marysville, Mich. 8 42 54N 82 29W
Marysville, Ohio 17 40 14N 83 22W
Marysville, Wash. 20 48 3N 122 11W
Maryville, Mo. 16 40 21N 94 52W
Maryville, Tenn. 11 35 46N 83 58W
Masaryktown 13 28 27N 82 27W
Mascoutah 16 38 29N 89 48W
Mascuppic L. 25 42 40N 71 23W
Mason, Mich. 17 42 35N 84 27W
Mason, Nev. 20 38 56N 119 8W
Mason, Ohio 17 39 22N 84 19W
Mason, Tex. 15 30 45N 99 14W
Mason City, Ill. 16 40 12N 89 42W
Mason City, Iowa 16 43 9N 93 12W
Maspeth 22 40 43N 73 55W
Massachusetts □ 9 42 30N 72 0W
Massachusetts B. 9 42 20N 70 50W
Massachusett's Inst. of Tech. 25 42 22N 71 6W
Massapequa 23 40 40N 73 28W
Massena 9 44 56N 74 54W
Massillon 8 40 48N 81 32W
Mastic 9 40 47N 72 54W
Matagorda B. 15 28 40N 96 0W
Matagorda I. 15 28 15N 96 30W
Mathis 15 28 6N 97 50W
Matinecock 23 40 51N 73 36W
Mattapan 25 42 16N 71 6W
Matteson 17 41 30N 87 42W
Matthews 17 40 23N 85 30W
Mattituck 9 40 59N 72 32W
Mattoon 10 39 29N 88 23W
Maui 32 20 48N 156 20W
Maumee 17 41 34N 83 39W
Maumee —▸ 17 41 42N 83 28W
Mauna Kea 32 19 50N 155 28W
Mauna Loa 32 19 30N 155 35W
Maupin 18 45 11N 121 5W
Maurepas, L. 15 30 15N 90 30W
Mauston 14 43 48N 90 5W
Max 14 47 49N 101 18W
Maxeys 12 33 45N 83 11W
Maxwell 20 39 17N 122 11W
May, C. 10 38 56N 74 58W
Mayagüez 32 18 12N 67 9W
Maybell 18 40 31N 108 5W
Mayer 19 34 24N 112 14W
Mayesville 12 34 0N 80 12W
Mayfair 26 40 2N 75 3W
Mayfield, Ga. 12 33 21N 82 48W
Mayfield, Ky. 11 36 44N 88 38W
Mayfield, N.Y. 9 43 6N 74 16W
Mayfield Heights 29 41 31N 81 28W
Mayhill 19 32 53N 105 29W
Maynard, Mass. 9 42 26N 71 27W
Maynard, Wash. 20 47 59N 122 55W
Mayo 12 30 3N 83 10W
Maysville, Ky. 17 38 39N 83 46W
Maysville, Mo. 16 39 53N 94 22W
Mayville, N. Dak. 14 47 30N 97 20W
Mayville, N.Y. 8 42 15N 79 30W
Maywood, Ill. 24 41 52N 87 51W
Maywood, Calif. 31 33 59N 118 12W
Maywood, N.J. 22 40 53N 74 3W
Mazomanie 16 43 11N 89 48W
Mazon 17 41 14N 88 25W
McGrath 32 62 58N 155 40W
Mead, L. 21 36 1N 114 44W
Meade 15 37 17N 100 20W
Meade River = Atkasuk 32 70 30N 157 20W
Meadow I. 23 40 36N 73 32W
Meadow L. 23 40 44N 73 50W
Meadow Valley Wash —▸ 21 36 40N 114 34W
Meadowood 27 39 4N 77 0W
Meadville, Mo. 16 39 47N 93 18W
Meadville, Pa. 8 41 39N 80 9W
Meansville 12 33 3N 84 18W
Meares, C. 18 45 37N 124 0W
Mecca 21 33 34N 116 5W
Mechanicsburg 8 40 13N 77 1W
Mechanicsville 16 41 54N 91 16W
Mechanicville 9 42 54N 73 41W
Medart 12 30 5N 84 23W
Medaryville 17 41 5N 86 55W
Medfield 25 42 11N 71 18W
Medford, Mass. 25 42 25N 71 7W
Medford, Oreg. 18 42 19N 122 52W
Medford, Wis. 14 45 9N 90 20W
Media 26 39 55N 75 23W
Mediapolis 16 41 0N 91 10W
Medicine Bow 18 41 54N 106 12W
Medicine Bow Pk. 18 41 21N 106 19W
Medicine Bow Ra. 18 41 10N 106 25W
Medicine Lake 14 48 30N 104 30W
Medicine Lodge 15 37 17N 98 35W
Medina, N. Dak. 14 46 54N 99 18W
Medina, N.Y. 8 43 13N 78 23W
Medina, Ohio 8 41 8N 81 52W
Medina —▸ 15 29 16N 98 29W
Medina L. 15 29 32N 98 56W
Medora 17 38 49N 86 10W
Meeker 18 40 2N 107 55W
Meeteetse 18 44 9N 108 52W
Mehlville 14 38 30N 90 19W
Meigs 12 31 4N 84 6W
Mekoryok 32 60 20N 166 20W
Melbourne, Fla. 11 28 5N 80 37W
Melbourne, Iowa 16 41 57N 93 6W
Melcher 16 41 14N 93 15W
Mellen 14 46 20N 90 40W
Mellette 14 45 9N 98 30W
Melrose, Mass. 25 42 27N 71 2W
Melrose, N.Y. 22 40 49N 73 55W
Melrose, Iowa 16 40 59N 93 3W
Melrose, Minn. 14 45 40N 94 49W
Melrose, N. Mex. 15 34 26N 103 38W
Melrose Park 24 41 53N 87 50W
Melstone 18 46 36N 107 52W
Melville 23 40 47N 73 24W
Memphis, Fla. 13 27 32N 82 34W
Memphis, Mich. 8 42 54N 82 46W
Memphis, Mo. 16 40 28N 92 10W
Memphis, Tenn. 15 35 8N 90 3W
Memphis, Tex. 15 34 44N 100 33W
Memphremagog, L. 9 45 0N 72 12W
Mena 15 34 35N 94 15W
Menard 15 30 55N 99 47W
Mendenhall, C. 32 59 45N 166 10W
Mendocino 18 39 19N 123 48W
Mendocino, C. 2 40 26N 124 25W
Mendon 17 42 0N 85 27W
Mendota, Calif. 20 36 45N 120 23W
Mendota, Ill. 16 41 33N 89 7W
Menlo Park 30 37 27N 122 11W
Menlo Park Terrace 22 40 34N 74 18W
Menominee 10 45 6N 87 37W
Menominee —▸ 10 45 6N 87 36W
Menomonee Falls 17 43 11N 88 7W
Menomonie 14 44 53N 91 55W
Mentone 17 41 10N 86 2W
Mentor 8 41 40N 81 21W
Mequon 17 43 14N 87 59W
Meramec —▸ 16 38 24N 90 21W
Merced 20 37 18N 120 29W
Merced —▸ 20 37 21N 120 59W
Merced, L. 30 37 43N 122 29W
Merced Pk. 20 37 36N 119 24W
Mercedes 15 26 9N 97 55W
Mercer, Mo. 16 40 31N 93 32W
Mercer, Pa. 8 41 14N 80 15W
Mercer Island 20 47 35N 122 15W
Merchantville 26 39 56N 75 3W
Mercury 21 36 40N 115 58W
Meredith, L. 15 35 43N 101 33W
Meredosia 16 39 50N 90 34W
Meriden, N.J. 22 40 56N 74 27W
Meriden, Conn. 9 41 32N 72 48W
Meridian, Calif. 20 39 9N 121 55W
Meridian, Ga. 12 31 27N 81 23W
Meridian, Idaho 18 43 37N 116 24W
Meridian, Miss. 11 32 22N 88 42W
Merion Station 26 39 59N 75 15W
Merkel 15 32 28N 100 1W
Merrick 23 40 39N 73 32W
Merrill, Oreg. 18 42 1N 121 36W
Merrill, Wis. 14 45 11N 89 41W
Merrillville, Ga. 12 30 57N 83 53W
Merrillville, Ind. 17 41 29N 87 20W
Merrimack —▸ 9 42 49N 70 49W
Merriman 14 42 55N 101 42W
Merrionette Park 24 41 41N 87 40W
Merritt, L. 30 37 48N 122 15W
Merritt Island 13 28 21N 80 42W
Merryville 15 30 45N 93 33W
Mershon 12 31 28N 82 15W
Mertzon 15 31 16N 100 49W
Mesa 19 33 25N 111 50W
Mesa Verde National Park 19 37 11N 108 29W
Meshoppen 9 41 36N 76 3W
Mesilla 19 32 16N 106 48W
Mesopotamia 8 41 27N 80 57W
Mesquite 19 36 47N 114 6W
Meta 16 38 19N 92 10W
Metairie 15 29 58N 90 10W
Metaline Falls 18 48 52N 117 22W
Metamora 16 40 47N 89 22W
Metcalf 12 30 43N 83 59W
Methuen 25 42 42N 71 12W
Metlakatla 32 55 8N 131 35W
Metropolis 15 37 9N 88 44W
Metropolitan Opera 22 40 46N 73 59W
Metter 12 32 24N 82 3W
Metuchen 22 40 32N 74 21W
Mexia 15 31 41N 96 29W
Mexican Water 19 36 57N 109 32W
Mexico, Maine 9 44 34N 70 33W
Mexico, Mo. 16 39 10N 91 53W
Mexico, N.Y. 9 43 28N 76 18W
Mexico, G. of 2 25 0N 90 0W
Mexico B. 9 43 35N 76 20W
Mexico Beach 12 29 57N 85 25W
Miami, Fla. 11 25 47N 80 11W
Miami, Okla. 15 36 53N 94 53W
Miami, Tex. 15 35 42N 100 38W
Miami Beach 11 25 47N 80 8W
Miami Canal 13 26 30N 80 45W
Miami Shores 13 25 52N 80 12W
Miami Springs 13 25 49N 80 17W
Miamisburg 17 39 38N 84 17W
Micanopy 13 29 30N 82 17W
Miccasukee, L. 12 30 33N 83 53W
Micco 13 27 53N 80 30W
Miccosukee 12 30 36N 84 3W
Michelson, Mt. 32 69 20N 144 20W
Michigan □ 10 44 0N 85 0W
Michigan, L. 2 44 0N 87 0W
Michigan Center 17 42 14N 84 20W
Michigan City 17 41 43N 86 54W
Mickleton 26 39 47N 75 14W
Micronesia, Federated States of ■ 33 11 0N 160 0 E
Middle —▸ 16 41 26N 93 30W
Middle Alkali L. 18 41 27N 120 5W
Middle B. 23 40 36N 73 36W
Middle Bass I. 8 41 41N 82 49W
Middle Brewster I. 25 42 20N 70 51W
Middle Fork Feather —▸ 20 38 33N 121 30W
Middle Loup —▸ 14 41 17N 98 24W
Middle Raccoon —▸ 16 41 35N 93 35W
Middle River 27 39 20N 76 26W
Middle Village 23 40 43N 73 52W
Middleboro 9 41 54N 70 55W
Middleborough 27 39 18N 76 26W
Middleburg, Fla. 12 30 4N 81 52W
Middleburg, N.Y. 9 42 36N 74 20W
Middleburg, Pa. 8 40 47N 77 3W
Middlebury, Ind. 17 41 41N 85 42W
Middlebury, Vt. 9 44 1N 73 10W
Middleport, N.Y. 8 43 13N 78 29W
Middleport, Ohio 10 39 0N 82 3W
Middlesboro 11 36 36N 83 43W
Middlesex, N.J. 22 40 34N 74 30W
Middlesex, N.Y. 8 42 42N 77 16W
Middlesex Fells Reservation 25 42 27N 71 6W
Middlesex Res. 22 40 37N 74 19W
Middleton, Mass. 25 42 35N 71 0W
Middleton, Wis. 16 43 6N 89 30W
Middleton I. 32 59 26N 146 20W
Middleton Pond 25 42 35N 71 1W
Middletown, Calif. 20 38 45N 122 37W
Middletown, Conn. 9 41 34N 72 39W
Middletown, N.Y. 9 41 27N 74 25W
Middletown, Ohio 17 39 31N 84 24W
Middletown, Pa. 9 40 12N 76 44W
Middleville, N.Y. 23 40 54N 73 19W
Middleville, Mich. 17 42 43N 85 28W
Midland, Calif. 21 33 52N 114 48W
Midland, Mich. 10 43 37N 84 14W
Midland, Pa. 8 40 39N 80 27W
Midland, Tex. 15 32 0N 102 3W
Midland Beach 22 40 34N 74 6W
Midland Park 22 40 59N 74 8W
Midlothian, Ill. 24 41 37N 87 43W
Midlothian, Tex. 15 32 30N 97 0W
Midville 12 32 49N 82 14W
Midway, Ala. 12 32 5N 85 31W
Midway, Fla. 12 30 30N 84 27W
Midway Wells 21 32 41N 115 7W
Midwest 18 43 25N 106 16W
Midwest City 15 35 27N 97 24W
Mifflintown 8 40 34N 77 24W
Milaca 14 45 45N 93 39W
Milan, Ga. 12 32 1N 83 4W
Milan, Ill. 16 41 27N 90 34W
Milan, Mich. 17 42 5N 83 41W
Milan, Mo. 16 40 12N 93 7W
Milan, Tenn. 11 35 55N 88 46W
Milbank 14 45 13N 96 38W
Milburn 22 40 43N 74 19W
Miles City 14 46 25N 105 51W
Milford, Md. 27 39 21N 76 43W
Milford, Calif. 20 40 10N 120 22W
Milford, Conn. 9 41 14N 73 3W
Milford, Del. 10 38 55N 75 26W
Milford, Ga. 12 31 23N 84 33W
Milford, Ill. 17 40 38N 87 42W
Milford, Mass. 9 42 8N 71 31W
Milford, Mich. 17 42 35N 83 36W
Milford, N.H. 9 42 50N 71 39W
Milford, Pa. 9 41 19N 74 48W
Milford, Utah 19 38 24N 113 1W
Milk —▸ 18 48 4N 106 19W
Mill Neck 23 40 53N 73 33W
Mill Shoals 17 38 15N 88 21W
Mill Valley 30 37 54N 122 32W
Millbrae 30 37 35N 122 22W
Millbrook 9 41 47N 73 42W
Mille Lacs L. 14 46 15N 93 39W
Milledgeville, Ga. 12 33 5N 83 14W
Milledgeville, Ill. 16 41 58N 89 46W
Millen 12 32 48N 81 57W
Miller 14 44 31N 98 59W
Miller I. 27 39 15N 76 21W
Miller Meadow 24 41 51N 87 49W
Millersburg, Ind. 17 41 32N 85 42W
Millersburg, Ohio 8 40 33N 81 55W
Millersburg, Pa. 8 40 32N 76 58W
Millerton 9 41 57N 73 31W
Millerton L. 20 37 1N 119 41W
Millheim 8 40 54N 77 29W
Milligan 13 30 45N 86 38W
Millington 15 35 20N 89 53W
Millinocket 11 45 39N 68 43W
Millis 25 42 10N 71 21W
Mills College 30 37 46N 122 10W
Millsboro 8 40 0N 80 0W
Milltown 26 39 57N 75 32W
Millvale 29 40 28N 79 59W
Millville, N.J. 10 39 24N 75 2W
Millville, Pa. 9 41 7N 76 32W
Millwood, Ga. 12 31 16N 82 40W
Millwood, Md. 27 38 52N 76 52W
Millwood L. 15 33 42N 93 58W
Milo 11 45 15N 68 59W
Milolii 32 19 11N 155 55W
Milroy 17 39 30N 85 28W
Milton, Mass. 25 42 14N 71 2W
Milton, Calif. 20 38 3N 120 51W
Milton, Fla. 11 30 38N 87 3W
Milton, Iowa 16 40 41N 92 10W
Milton, Pa. 8 41 1N 76 51W
Milton, Vt. 9 44 38N 73 7W
Milton, Wis. 17 42 47N 88 56W
Milton-Freewater 18 45 56N 118 23W
Milton Village 25 42 15N 71 4W
Milwaukee 17 43 2N 87 55W
Milwaukie 20 45 27N 122 38W
Mims 13 28 40N 80 51W
Minden, La. 15 32 37N 93 17W
Minden, Nev. 20 38 57N 119 46W
Mineola, N.Y. 23 40 44N 73 38W
Mineola, Tex. 15 32 40N 95 29W
Mineral King 20 36 27N 118 36W
Mineral Point 16 42 52N 90 11W
Mineral Wells 15 32 48N 98 7W
Minersville 9 40 41N 76 16W
Minerva 8 40 44N 81 6W
Minetto 9 43 24N 76 28W
Mingo Junction 8 40 19N 80 37W
Minidoka 18 42 45N 113 29W
Minier 16 40 26N 89 19W
Minneapolis, Kans. 14 39 8N 97 42W
Minneapolis, Minn. 14 44 59N 93 16W
Minnesota □ 14 46 0N 94 15W
Minnesota —▸ 14 44 54N 93 9W
Minnewaukan 14 48 4N 99 15W
Minonk 16 40 54N 89 2W
Minooka 17 41 27N 88 16W
Minot 14 48 14N 101 18W
Minster 17 40 24N 84 23W
Minto 32 64 53N 149 11W
Minturn 18 39 35N 106 26W
Minute Man Nat. Hist. Park 25 42 25N 71 16W
Miramar, Calif. 30 37 29N 122 27W
Miramar, Fla. 13 25 59N 80 15W
Mishawaka 17 41 40N 86 11W
Mishawum L. 25 42 30N 71 8W
Mission, Calif. 30 37 44N 122 25W
Mission, S. Dak. 14 43 18N 100 39W
Mission, Tex. 15 26 13N 98 20W
Mission Viejo 21 33 36N 117 40W
Mississinewa Res. 17 40 46N 86 3W
Mississippi □ 15 33 0N 90 0W
Mississippi —▸ 2 29 9N 89 15W
Mississippi River Delta 2 29 10N 89 15W
Mississippi Sd. 15 30 20N 89 0W
Missoula 18 46 52N 114 1W
Missouri □ 14 38 25N 92 30W
Missouri —▸ 2 38 49N 90 7W
Missouri City 15 29 37N 95 32W
Missouri Valley 14 41 34N 95 53W
Mist 20 45 59N 123 15W
Mitchell, Ga. 12 33 13N 82 42W
Mitchell, Ind. 17 38 44N 86 28W
Mitchell, Nebr. 14 41 57N 103 49W
Mitchell, Oreg. 18 44 34N 120 9W
Mitchell, S. Dak. 14 43 43N 98 2W
Mitchell, Mt. 11 35 46N 82 16W
Moab 19 38 35N 109 33W
Moapa 21 36 40N 114 37W
Moberly 16 39 25N 92 26W
Mobile 11 30 41N 88 3W
Mobile B. 11 30 30N 88 0W
Mobridge 14 45 32N 100 26W
Mocanaqua 9 41 9N 76 8W
Moclips 20 47 14N 124 13W
Modena 19 37 48N 113 56W
Modesto 20 37 39N 121 0W
Modoc, Ga. 12 32 37N 82 19W
Modoc, S.C. 12 33 44N 82 13W
Mogollon Rim 19 34 10N 110 50W
Mohall 14 48 46N 101 31W
Mohave, L. 21 35 12N 114 34W
Mohawk —▸ 9 42 47N 73 41W
Mohican, C. 32 60 12N 167 25W
Mohicanville Reservoir 8 40 45N 82 0W
Mojave 21 35 3N 118 10W
Mojave Desert 21 35 0N 116 30W
Mokane 16 38 41N 91 53W
Mokelumne —▸ 20 38 13N 121 28W
Mokelumne Hill 20 38 18N 120 43W
Molena 12 33 1N 84 30W
Moline 16 41 30N 90 31W
Molino 13 30 43N 87 20W
Molokai 32 21 8N 157 0W
Momence 17 41 10N 87 40W
Monaca 8 40 41N 80 17W
Monadnock, Mt. 9 42 52N 72 7W
Monahans 15 31 36N 102 54W
Moncks Corner 12 33 12N 80 1W
Monessen 8 40 9N 79 54W
Monett 15 36 55N 93 55W
Moniac 12 30 31N 82 14W
Monmouth, Ill. 16 40 55N 90 39W

Monmouth

Monmouth, *Oreg.* **18** 44 51N 123 14W
Mono L. **20** 38 1N 119 1W
Monolith **21** 35 7N 118 22W
Monon **17** 40 52N 86 53W
Monona, *Iowa* **16** 43 3N 91 23W
Monona, *Wis.* **16** 43 4N 89 20W
Monongahela **8** 40 12N 79 56W
Monroe, *Ga.* **12** 33 47N 83 43W
Monroe, *Iowa* **16** 41 31N 93 6W
Monroe, *La.* **15** 32 30N 92 7W
Monroe, *Mich.* **17** 41 55N 83 24W
Monroe, *N.C.* **11** 34 59N 80 33W
Monroe, *N.Y.* **9** 41 20N 74 11W
Monroe, *Ohio* **17** 39 27N 84 22W
Monroe, *Utah* **19** 38 38N 112 7W
Monroe, *Wash.* **20** 47 51N 121 58W
Monroe, *Wis.* **16** 42 36N 89 38W
Monroe, L. **13** 28 50N 81 19W
Monroe City **16** 39 39N 91 44W
Monroe Res. **17** 39 1N 86 31W
Monroeton **9** 41 43N 76 29W
Monroeville, *Pa.* **29** 40 26N 79 46W
Monroeville, *Ala.* **11** 31 31N 87 20W
Monroeville, *Ind.* **17** 40 59N 84 52W
Monrovia **31** 34 9N 118 1W
Montague I. **32** 60 0N 147 30W
Montalvo **21** 34 15N 119 12W
Montana □ **18** 47 0N 110 0W
Montara **30** 37 32N 122 30W
Montara, Pt. **30** 37 32N 122 31W
Montara Mt. **30** 37 32N 122 27W
Montauk **9** 41 3N 71 57W
Montauk Pt. **9** 41 4N 71 52W
Montchanin **26** 39 47N 75 35W
Montclair **22** 40 49N 74 12W
Monte Rio **20** 38 28N 123 0W
Monte Vista **19** 37 35N 106 9W
Montebello **31** 34 1N 118 8W
Montecito **21** 34 26N 119 40W
Montello **14** 43 48N 89 20W
Monterey, *Calif.* **20** 36 37N 121 55W
Monterey, *Ind.* **17** 41 11N 86 30W
Monterey B. **20** 36 45N 122 0W
Monterey Park **31** 34 3N 118 7W
Montesano **20** 46 59N 123 36W
Montevideo **14** 44 57N 95 43W
Montezuma, *Ga.* **12** 32 18N 84 2W
Montezuma, *Ind.* **17** 39 48N 87 22W
Montezuma, *Iowa* **16** 41 35N 92 32W
Montgomery, *Ala.* **12** 32 23N 86 19W
Montgomery, *Ga.* **12** 31 57N 81 7W
Montgomery, *Ill.* **17** 41 44N 88 21W
Montgomery, *Pa.* **8** 41 10N 76 53W
Montgomery, *W. Va.* **10** 38 11N 81 19W
Montgomery City **16** 38 59N 91 30W
Monticello, *Ark.* **15** 33 38N 91 47W
Monticello, *Fla.* **12** 30 33N 83 52W
Monticello, *Ga.* **12** 33 18N 83 40W
Monticello, *Ill.* **17** 40 1N 88 34W
Monticello, *Ind.* **17** 40 45N 86 46W
Monticello, *Iowa* **16** 42 15N 91 12W
Monticello, *Ky.* **11** 36 50N 84 51W
Monticello, *Minn.* **14** 45 18N 93 48W
Monticello, *Miss.* **15** 31 33N 90 7W
Monticello, *Mo.* **16** 40 7N 91 43W
Monticello, *N.Y.* **9** 41 39N 74 42W
Monticello, *Utah* **19** 37 52N 109 21W
Montour Falls **8** 42 21N 76 51W
Montoursville **8** 41 15N 76 55W
Montpelier, *Idaho* **18** 42 19N 111 18W
Montpelier, *Ind.* **17** 40 33N 85 17W
Montpelier, *Ohio* **17** 41 35N 84 37W
Montpelier, *Vt.* **9** 44 16N 72 35W
Montpelier, *Md.* **27** 39 3N 76 50W
Montrose, *Calif.* **31** 34 12N 118 12W
Montrose, *Colo.* **19** 38 29N 107 53W
Montrose, *Pa.* **9** 41 50N 75 53W
Montrose, *Md.* **27** 39 2N 77 7W
Montrose, L. **16** 38 18N 93 50W
Montvale **22** 41 2N 74 1W
Montville **22** 40 55N 74 23W
Mooers **9** 44 58N 73 35W
Moonachie **22** 40 50N 74 2W
Moorcroft **14** 44 16N 104 57W
Moore Haven **13** 26 50N 81 6W
Moorefield **10** 39 5N 78 59W
Moores Res. **9** 44 45N 71 50W
Moorestown **26** 39 58N 74 56W
Mooresville **17** 39 37N 86 22W
Moorhead **14** 46 53N 96 45W
Moorpark **21** 34 17N 118 53W
Moose → **9** 43 38N 75 24W
Moose Lake **14** 46 27N 92 46W
Moosehead L. **11** 45 38N 69 40W
Mooselookmeguntic L. **11** 44 55N 70 49W
Moosilauke, Mt. **9** 44 3N 71 40W
Moosup **9** 41 43N 71 53W
Mora, *Ga.* **12** 31 25N 82 57W
Mora, *Minn.* **14** 45 53N 93 18W
Mora, *N. Mex.* **19** 35 58N 105 20W
Mora → **15** 35 35N 104 25W
Moraga **30** 37 49N 122 7W
Moran, *Kans.* **15** 37 55N 95 10W
Moran, *Wyo.* **18** 43 53N 110 37W
Moravia, *Iowa* **16** 40 53N 92 49W
Moravia, *N.Y.* **9** 42 43N 76 25W
Moreau → **14** 45 18N 100 43W
Morehead **17** 38 11N 83 26W
Morehead City **11** 34 43N 76 43W
Moreland **12** 33 17N 84 46W
Morenci **17** 41 43N 84 13W
Moreno Valley **21** 33 56N 117 15W
Morgan, *Ga.* **12** 31 32N 84 36W
Morgan, *Utah* **18** 41 2N 111 41W
Morgan City **15** 29 42N 91 12W
Morgan Hill **20** 37 8N 121 39W
Morgan Park **24** 41 41N 87 38W
Morganfield **10** 37 41N 87 55W
Morganton **11** 35 45N 81 41W
Morgantown, *Ind.* **17** 39 22N 86 16W
Morgantown, *W. Va.* **10** 39 38N 79 57W
Moriarty **19** 34 59N 106 3W
Morningside **27** 38 49N 76 53W
Morocco **17** 40 57N 87 27W
Morongo Valley **21** 34 3N 116 37W
Moroni **18** 39 32N 111 35W
Morrilton **15** 35 9N 92 44W
Morris, *Ga.* **12** 31 48N 84 57W
Morris, *Ill.* **17** 41 22N 88 26W
Morris, *Minn.* **14** 45 35N 95 55W
Morris, *N.Y.* **9** 42 33N 75 15W
Morris, *Pa.* **8** 41 35N 77 17W
Morris Plains **22** 40 49N 74 29W
Morrison **16** 41 49N 89 58W
Morrisonville **16** 39 25N 89 27W
Morristown, *N.J.* **22** 40 47N 74 28W
Morristown, *Ariz.* **19** 33 51N 112 37W
Morristown, *Ind.* **17** 39 40N 85 42W
Morristown, *N.Y.* **9** 44 35N 75 39W
Morristown, *Tenn.* **11** 36 13N 83 18W
Morrisville, *N.Y.* **9** 42 53N 75 35W
Morrisville, *Pa.* **9** 40 13N 74 47W
Morrisville, *Vt.* **9** 44 34N 72 36W
Morro Bay **20** 35 22N 120 51W
Morses Pond **25** 42 17N 71 19W
Morton, *Pa.* **26** 39 54N 75 20W
Morton, *Ill.* **16** 40 37N 89 28W
Morton, *Tex.* **15** 33 44N 102 46W
Morton, *Wash.* **20** 46 34N 122 17W
Morton Grove **24** 42 2N 87 46W
Morven **12** 30 57N 83 30W
Moscow, *Idaho* **18** 46 44N 117 0W
Moscow, *Pa.* **9** 41 20N 75 31W
Moses Lake **18** 47 8N 119 17W
Mosquero **15** 35 47N 103 58W
Mosquito Creek L. **8** 41 18N 80 46W
Moss Beach **30** 37 31N 122 30W
Mossy Head **13** 30 45N 86 19W
Mott **14** 46 23N 102 20W
Moulton **16** 40 41N 92 41W
Moultrie **12** 31 11N 83 47W
Moultrie, L. **12** 33 20N 80 5W
Mound City, *Mo.* **14** 40 7N 95 14W
Mound City, *S. Dak.* **14** 45 44N 100 4W
Moundsville **8** 39 55N 80 44W
Mount Airy, *Pa.* **26** 40 3N 75 10W
Mount Airy, *N.C.* **11** 36 31N 80 37W
Mount Ayr **16** 40 43N 94 14W
Mount Carmel, *Ill.* **17** 38 25N 87 46W
Mount Carmel, *Pa.* **9** 40 47N 76 24W
Mount Carroll **16** 42 6N 89 59W
Mount Charleston **21** 36 16N 115 37W
Mount Clemens **28** 42 35N 82 53W
Mount Desert I. **11** 44 21N 68 20W
Mount Dora **11** 28 48N 81 38W
Mount Eden **17** 38 3N 85 9W
Mount Edgecumbe **32** 57 3N 135 21W
Mount Ephraim **26** 39 52N 75 5W
Mount Greenwood **24** 41 42N 87 42W
Mount Holly **9** 39 59N 74 47W
Mount Holly Springs **8** 40 7N 77 12W
Mount Hood Memorial Park **25** 42 26N 71 1W
Mount Horeb **16** 43 1N 89 44W
Mount Jewett **8** 41 44N 78 39W
Mount Kisco **9** 41 12N 73 44W
Mount Laguna **21** 32 52N 116 25W
Mount Lebanon **29** 40 22N 80 2W
Mount Morris **8** 42 44N 77 52W
Mount Olive **16** 39 4N 89 44W
Mount Oliver **29** 40 24N 79 59W
Mount Olivet **17** 38 32N 84 2W
Mount Orab **17** 39 2N 83 55W
Mount Penn **9** 40 20N 75 54W
Mount Pleasant, *Iowa* **16** 40 58N 91 33W
Mount Pleasant, *Mich.* **10** 43 36N 84 46W
Mount Pleasant, *Pa.* **8** 40 9N 79 33W
Mount Pleasant, *S.C.* **12** 32 47N 79 52W
Mount Pleasant, *Tenn.* **11** 35 32N 87 12W
Mount Pleasant, *Tex.* **15** 33 9N 94 58W
Mount Pleasant, *Utah* **18** 39 33N 111 27W
Mount Pleasant Park **27** 39 22N 76 34W
Mount Pocono **9** 41 7N 75 22W
Mount Prospect **24** 42 3N 87 54W
Mount Pulaski **16** 40 1N 89 17W
Mount Rainier Nat. Park **20** 46 55N 121 50W
Mount Royal **26** 39 48N 75 12W
Mount Shasta **18** 41 19N 122 19W
Mount Signal **21** 32 39N 115 37W
Mount Sterling, *Ill.* **16** 39 59N 90 45W
Mount Sterling, *Ky.* **17** 38 4N 83 56W
Mount Sterling, *Ohio* **17** 39 43N 83 16W
Mount Tamalpais State Park **30** 37 53N 122 34W
Mount Union **8** 40 23N 77 53W
Mount Upton **9** 42 26N 75 23W
Mount Vernon, *N.Y.* **23** 40 54N 73 49W
Mount Vernon, *Ga.* **12** 32 11N 82 36W
Mount Vernon, *Ill.* **10** 38 19N 88 55W
Mount Vernon, *Ind.* **17** 37 56N 87 54W
Mount Vernon, *Ind.* **17** 38 17N 88 57W
Mount Vernon, *Iowa* **16** 41 55N 91 23W
Mount Vernon, *Ohio* **8** 40 23N 82 29W
Mount Vernon, *Wash.* **20** 48 25N 122 20W
Mount Washington **17** 38 3N 85 33W
Mount Wilson Observatory **31** 34 13N 118 4W
Mount Zion **17** 39 46N 88 53W
Mountain Center **21** 33 42N 116 44W
Mountain City, *Nev.* **18** 41 50N 115 58W
Mountain City, *Tenn.* **11** 36 29N 81 48W
Mountain Dale **9** 41 41N 74 32W
Mountain Grove **15** 37 8N 92 16W
Mountain Home, *Ark.* **15** 36 20N 92 23W
Mountain Home, *Idaho* **18** 43 8N 115 41W
Mountain Iron **14** 47 32N 92 37W
Mountain Lakes **22** 40 54N 74 27W
Mountain Pass **21** 35 29N 115 35W
Mountain Spring Ls. **22** 41 2N 74 21W
Mountain View, *N.J.* **22** 40 55N 74 15W
Mountain View, *Ark.* **15** 35 52N 92 7W
Mountain View, *Calif.* **20** 37 23N 122 5W
Mountain Village **32** 62 5N 163 43W
Mountainair **19** 34 31N 106 15W
Mountainside **22** 40 40N 74 21W
Mountlake Terrace **20** 47 47N 122 19W
Moweaqua **16** 39 38N 89 1W
Muckalee Cr. → **12** 31 38N 84 9W
Muddy Cr. → **19** 38 24N 110 42W
Muir Beach **30** 37 51N 122 34W
Muirkirk **27** 39 3N 76 53W
Mukwonago **17** 42 52N 88 20W
Mulberry **13** 27 54N 81 59W
Mulberry Grove **16** 38 56N 89 16W
Muldraugh **17** 37 56N 85 59W
Mule Creek Junction **14** 43 19N 104 8W
Muleshoe **15** 34 13N 102 43W
Mulford Gardens **30** 37 42N 122 10W
Mullen **14** 42 3N 101 1W
Mullens **10** 37 35N 81 23W
Mullica Hill **26** 39 44N 75 13W
Mullins **11** 34 12N 79 15W
Mulvane **15** 37 29N 97 15W
Muncie **17** 40 12N 85 23W
Munday **15** 33 27N 99 38W
Munhall **29** 40 24N 79 54W
Munising **10** 46 25N 86 40W
Munsey Park **23** 40 47N 73 40W
Munson **13** 30 52N 86 52W
Murdo **14** 43 53N 100 43W
Murfreesboro, *N.C.* **11** 36 27N 77 6W
Murfreesboro, *Tenn.* **11** 35 51N 86 24W
Murphy **18** 43 13N 116 33W
Murphys **20** 38 8N 120 28W
Murphysboro **16** 37 46N 89 20W
Murray, *Iowa* **16** 41 3N 93 57W
Murray, *Ky.* **11** 36 37N 88 19W
Murray, *Utah* **18** 40 40N 111 53W
Murray, L. **12** 34 3N 81 13W
Murrayville **16** 39 35N 90 15W
Murrieta **21** 33 33N 117 13W
Murrysville **29** 40 25N 79 41W
Muscatine **16** 41 25N 91 3W
Muscoda **16** 43 11N 90 27W
Musella **12** 32 48N 84 2W
Muskegon **17** 43 14N 86 16W
Muskegon → **10** 43 14N 86 21W
Muskegon Heights **17** 43 12N 86 16W
Muskogee **15** 35 45N 95 22W
Musselshell → **18** 47 21N 107 57W
Muttontown **23** 40 49N 73 32W
Myakka → **13** 26 56N 82 11W
Myerstown **9** 40 22N 76 19W
Myrtle Beach **11** 33 42N 78 53W
Myrtle Creek **18** 43 1N 123 17W
Myrtle Grove **13** 30 23N 87 17W
Myrtle Point **18** 43 4N 124 8W
Mystic, *Conn.* **9** 41 21N 71 58W
Mystic, *Iowa* **16** 40 47N 92 57W
Mystic Lakes **25** 42 26N 71 8W

N

Naalehu **32** 19 4N 155 35W
Nabesna **32** 62 22N 143 0W
Naches **18** 46 44N 120 42W
Naches → **20** 46 38N 120 31W
Nacimiento L. **20** 35 46N 120 53W
Nacogdoches **15** 31 36N 94 39W
Nahant **25** 42 25N 70 54W
Nahant B. **25** 42 26N 70 54W
Nahant Harbor **25** 42 25N 70 55W
Nahunta **12** 31 12N 81 59W
Nakalele Pt. **32** 21 2N 156 35W
Naknek **32** 58 44N 157 1W
Nampa **18** 43 34N 116 34W
Nanticoke **9** 41 12N 76 0W
Nantucket I. **2** 41 16N 70 5W
Nantucket Beach **25** 42 16N 70 52W
Nanty Glo **8** 40 28N 78 50W
Napa **20** 38 18N 122 17W
Napa → **20** 38 10N 122 19W
Napamute **32** 61 30N 158 45W
Napanoch **9** 41 44N 74 22W
Naperville **17** 41 46N 88 9W
Naples **11** 26 8N 81 48W
Naples Park **13** 26 17N 81 46W
Napoleon, *N. Dak.* **14** 46 30N 99 46W
Napoleon, *Ohio* **17** 41 23N 84 8W
Nappanee **17** 41 27N 86 0W
Nara Visa **15** 35 37N 103 6W
Narberth **26** 40 0N 75 16W
Nares Str. **2** 80 0N 70 0W
Naselle **20** 46 22N 123 49W
Nashua, *Iowa* **16** 42 57N 92 32W
Nashua, *Mont.* **18** 48 8N 106 22W
Nashua, *N.H.* **9** 42 45N 71 28W
Nashville, *Ark.* **15** 33 57N 93 51W
Nashville, *Ga.* **12** 31 12N 83 15W
Nashville, *Ill.* **16** 38 21N 89 23W
Nashville, *Ind.* **17** 39 12N 86 15W
Nashville, *Mich.* **17** 42 36N 85 5W
Nashville, *Tenn.* **11** 36 10N 86 47W
Nassau **9** 42 31N 73 37W
Nassau Shore **23** 40 39N 73 26W
Natchez **15** 31 34N 91 24W
Natchitoches **15** 31 46N 93 5W
Natick **25** 42 16N 71 19W
National Arboretum **27** 38 54N 76 59W
National City **21** 32 41N 117 6W
Natrona Heights **8** 40 37N 79 44W
Natural Bridge **9** 44 5N 75 30W
Naugatuck **9** 41 30N 73 3W
Naushon I. **9** 41 29N 70 45W
Nauvoo **16** 40 33N 91 23W
Navajo Reservoir **19** 36 48N 107 36W
Navarre, *Fla.* **13** 30 24N 86 52W
Navarre, *Ohio* **8** 40 43N 81 31W
Navarro → **20** 39 11N 123 45W
Navasota **15** 30 23N 96 5W
Nazareth **9** 40 44N 75 19W
Neah Bay **20** 48 22N 124 37W
Near Is. **32** 52 30N 174 0 E
Nebraska □ **14** 41 30N 99 30W
Nebraska City **14** 40 41N 95 52W
Necedah **14** 44 2N 90 4W
Neches → **15** 29 58N 93 51W
Needham **25** 42 16N 71 13W
Needham Heights **25** 42 17N 71 14W
Needles **21** 34 51N 114 37W
Needmore **12** 30 41N 82 43W
Neely Henry L. **12** 33 55N 86 2W
Neenah **10** 44 11N 88 28W
Neeses **12** 33 33N 81 7W
Negaunee **10** 46 30N 87 36W
Nehalem → **20** 45 40N 123 56W
Neillsville **14** 44 34N 90 36W
Neilton **18** 47 25N 123 53W
Neligh **14** 42 8N 98 2W
Nelson, *Ariz.* **19** 35 31N 113 19W
Nelson, *Nev.* **21** 35 42N 114 50W
Nelson I. **32** 60 40N 164 40W
Nenana **32** 64 34N 149 5W
Neodesha **15** 37 25N 95 41W
Neoga **17** 39 19N 88 27W
Neosho **15** 36 52N 94 22W
Neosho → **15** 36 48N 95 18W
Nephi **18** 39 43N 111 50W
Neptune **9** 40 13N 74 2W
Nescopeck **9** 41 3N 76 12W
Ness City **14** 38 27N 99 54W
Neuse → **11** 35 6N 76 29W
Nevada, *Iowa* **16** 42 1N 93 27W
Nevada, *Mo.* **16** 37 51N 94 22W
Nevada □ **18** 39 0N 117 0W
Nevada, Sierra **2** 39 0N 120 30W
Nevada City **20** 39 16N 121 1W
Neville Island **29** 40 30N 80 6W
New →, *Fla.* **12** 29 50N 84 40W
New →, *W. Va.* **10** 38 10N 81 12W
New Albany, *Ind.* **17** 38 18N 85 49W
New Albany, *Miss.* **15** 34 29N 89 0W
New Albany, *Pa.* **9** 41 36N 76 27W
New Athens **16** 38 19N 89 53W
New Baltimore **8** 42 41N 82 44W
New Bedford **9** 41 38N 70 56W
New Berlin, *Ill.* **16** 39 44N 89 55W
New Berlin, *N.Y.* **9** 42 37N 75 20W
New Berlin, *Pa.* **8** 40 50N 76 57W
New Berlin, *Wis.* **17** 42 59N 88 6W
New Bern **11** 35 7N 77 3W
New Bethlehem **8** 41 0N 79 20W
New Bloomfield **8** 40 25N 77 11W
New Boston **15** 33 28N 94 25W
New Braunfels **15** 29 42N 98 8W
New Brighton, *N.Y.* **22** 40 38N 74 5W
New Brighton, *Pa.* **8** 40 42N 80 19W
New Britain **9** 41 40N 72 47W
New Brockton **12** 31 23N 85 56W
New Brunswick **22** 40 30N 74 29W
New Buffalo **17** 41 47N 86 45W
New Canton **16** 39 37N 91 8W
New Carlisle, *Ind.* **17** 41 45N 86 32W
New Carlisle, *Ohio* **17** 39 56N 84 2W
New Carrollton **27** 38 58N 76 52W
New Cassell **23** 40 45N 73 32W
New Castle, *Ind.* **17** 39 55N 85 22W
New Castle, *Ky.* **17** 38 26N 85 10W
New Castle, *Pa.* **8** 41 0N 80 21W
New City **9** 41 9N 73 59W
New Concord **8** 39 59N 81 54W
New Cumberland **8** 40 30N 80 36W
New Cuyama **21** 34 57N 119 38W
New Don Pedro Reservoir **20** 37 43N 120 24W
New Dorp **22** 40 34N 74 7W
New Dorp Beach **22** 40 33N 74 6W
New Ellenton **12** 33 28N 81 41W
New England **14** 46 32N 102 52W
New Franklin **16** 39 1N 92 44W
New Glarus **16** 42 49N 89 38W
New Hampshire □ **9** 44 0N 71 30W
New Hampton **16** 43 3N 92 19W
New Harmony **17** 38 8N 87 56W
New Hartford **9** 43 4N 75 18W
New Haven, *Conn.* **9** 41 18N 72 55W
New Haven, *Ill.* **17** 37 55N 88 8W
New Haven, *Ind.* **17** 41 4N 85 1W
New Haven, *Mich.* **8** 42 44N 82 48W
New Haven, *Mo.* **16** 38 37N 91 13W
New Holland **9** 40 6N 76 5W
New Hyde Park **23** 40 43N 73 39W
New Iberia **15** 30 1N 91 49W
New Jersey □ **10** 40 0N 74 30W
New Kensington **29** 40 34N 79 46W
New Lexington **10** 39 43N 82 13W
New London, *Conn.* **9** 41 22N 72 6W
New London, *Iowa* **16** 40 55N 91 24W
New London, *Mo.* **16** 39 35N 91 24W
New London, *Ohio* **8** 41 5N 82 24W
New London, *Wis.* **14** 44 23N 88 45W
New Madison **17** 39 58N 84 43W
New Madrid **15** 36 36N 89 32W
New Martinsville **10** 39 39N 80 52W
New Meadows **18** 44 58N 116 18W
New Melones L. **20** 37 57N 120 31W
New Miami **17** 39 26N 84 32W
New Milford, *N.J.* **22** 40 56N 74 0W
New Milford, *Conn.* **9** 41 35N 73 25W
New Milford, *Pa.* **9** 41 52N 75 44W
New Orleans **15** 29 58N 90 4W
New Palestine **17** 39 45N 85 52W
New Paris **17** 39 51N 84 48W
New Pekin **17** 38 31N 86 2W
New Philadelphia **8** 40 30N 81 27W
New Plymouth **18** 43 58N 116 49W
New Port Richey **13** 28 16N 82 43W
New Providence **22** 40 42N 74 23W
New Richmond, *Ohio* **17** 38 57N 84 17W
New Richmond, *Wis.* **14** 45 7N 92 32W
New Roads **15** 30 42N 91 26W
New Rochelle **23** 40 55N 73 45W
New Rockford **14** 47 41N 99 8W
New Salem **14** 46 51N 101 25W
New Sharon **16** 41 28N 92 39W
New Smyrna Beach **11** 29 1N 80 56W
New Springville **22** 40 35N 74 9W
New Town **14** 47 59N 102 30W
New Ulm **14** 44 19N 94 28W
New Utrecht **22** 40 36N 73 59W
New Vernon **22** 40 44N 74 30W
New Vienna **17** 39 19N 83 42W
New Virginia **16** 41 11N 93 44W
New York **9** 40 45N 74 0W
New York □ **9** 43 0N 75 0W
New York Aquarium **22** 40 33N 73 59W
New York Botanical Gdns. **23** 40 51N 73 51W
New York Mts. **19** 35 0N 115 20W
New York Univ. **22** 40 43N 73 59W
New Zion **12** 33 51N 80 2W
Newark, *N.J.* **22** 40 43N 74 10W
Newark, *Calif.* **30** 37 32N 122 2W
Newark, *Del.* **10** 39 41N 75 46W
Newark, *N.Y.* **8** 43 3N 77 6W
Newark, *Ohio* **8** 40 3N 82 24W
Newark B. **22** 40 41N 74 8W
Newark Int. Airport **22** 40 41N 74 10W
Newark Valley **9** 42 14N 76 11W
Newberg, *Mo.* **16** 37 55N 91 54W
Newberg, *Oreg.* **18** 45 18N 122 58W
Newberry, *Fla.* **12** 29 39N 82 37W
Newberry, *Mich.* **10** 46 21N 85 30W
Newberry, *S.C.* **11** 34 17N 81 37W
Newberry Springs **21** 34 50N 116 41W
Newburgh, *Ind.* **17** 37 57N 87 24W
Newburgh, *N.Y.* **9** 41 30N 74 1W
Newbury, *N.H.* **9** 43 19N 72 3W
Newbury, *Vt.* **9** 44 5N 72 4W
Newburyport **11** 42 49N 70 53W
Newcastle, *Calif.* **20** 38 53N 121 8W
Newcastle, *Wyo.* **14** 43 50N 104 11W
Newcomb **9** 43 58N 74 10W
Newcomerstown **8** 40 16N 81 36W
Newell **14** 44 43N 103 25W
Newenham, C. **32** 58 39N 162 11W
Newfane **8** 43 17N 78 43W
Newfield **9** 42 18N 76 33W
Newfound L. **9** 43 40N 71 47W
Newfoundland, *N. Amer.* **2** 49 0N 55 0W
Newfoundland, *N.J.* **22** 41 2N 74 25W
Newfoundland, *Pa.* **9** 41 18N 75 19W
Newhalen **32** 59 43N 154 54W
Newhall **21** 34 23N 118 32W
Newington **12** 32 35N 81 30W
Newkirk **15** 36 53N 97 3W
Newman, *Calif.* **20** 37 19N 121 1W
Newman, *Ill.* **17** 39 48N 87 59W
Newmans L. **13** 29 40N 82 12W
Newmarket, *N.H.* **9** 43 4N 70 56W
Newmarket, *N.H.* **9** 43 5N 70 56W
Newnan **12** 33 23N 84 48W
Newport, *Ark.* **15** 35 37N 91 16W
Newport, *Ind.* **17** 39 53N 87 25W
Newport, *Ky.* **17** 39 5N 84 30W
Newport, *N.H.* **9** 43 22N 72 10W
Newport, *N.Y.* **9** 43 11N 75 1W
Newport, *Oreg.* **18** 44 39N 124 3W
Newport, *Pa.* **8** 40 29N 77 8W
Newport, *R.I.* **9** 41 29N 71 19W
Newport, *Tenn.* **11** 35 58N 83 11W
Newport, *Vt.* **9** 44 56N 72 13W
Newport, *Wash.* **18** 48 11N 117 3W
Newport Beach **21** 33 37N 117 56W
Newport News **10** 36 59N 76 25W
Newportville **26** 40 7N 74 53W
Newton, *Mass.* **25** 42 19N 71 13W
Newton, *Ga.* **12** 31 19N 84 20W
Newton, *Ill.* **17** 38 59N 88 10W
Newton, *Iowa* **16** 41 42N 93 3W
Newton, *Kans.* **15** 38 3N 97 21W
Newton, *Miss.* **15** 32 19N 89 10W
Newton, *N.C.* **11** 35 40N 81 13W
Newton, *N.J.* **9** 41 3N 74 45W
Newton, *Tex.* **15** 30 51N 93 46W
Newton Falls **8** 41 11N 80 59W
Newton Highlands **25** 42 19N 71 13W
Newtonville **25** 42 20N 71 11W
Newtown **16** 40 22N 93 20W
Newtown Square **26** 39 59N 75 24W
Newville **8** 40 10N 77 24W
Nezperce **18** 46 14N 116 14W
Niagara Falls **2** 43 5N 79 4W
Niangua → **16** 38 0N 92 48W
Niantic **9** 41 20N 72 11W
Nicaragua, L. de **2** 12 0N 85 30W
Niceville **11** 30 31N 86 30W
Nicholasville **17** 37 53N 84 34W
Nicholls **12** 31 31N 82 38W
Nichols **9** 42 1N 76 22W
Nicholson, *Ga.* **12** 34 7N 83 26W
Nicholson, *Pa.* **9** 41 37N 75 47W
Nicholville **9** 44 41N 74 39W
Niihau **32** 21 54N 160 9W
Nikolski **32** 52 56N 168 52W
Niland **21** 33 14N 115 31W
Niles, *Ill.* **24** 42 1N 87 48W
Niles, *Mich.* **10** 41 50N 86 15W
Niles, *Ohio* **8** 41 11N 80 46W
Ninety Six **12** 34 11N 82 1W
Niobrara **14** 42 45N 98 2W
Niobrara → **14** 42 46N 98 3W
Nipomo **21** 35 3N 120 29W
Nipton **21** 35 28N 115 16W
Nisqually → **20** 47 6N 122 42W
Nixon **15** 29 16N 97 46W
Noatak **32** 67 34N 162 58W
Noatak → **32** 68 0N 161 0W
Noble **17** 38 42N 88 14W
Noblesville **17** 40 3N 86 1W
Nocatee **13** 27 10N 81 53W
Nocona **15** 33 47N 97 44W
Nogales **19** 31 20N 110 56W
Nokomis, *Fla.* **13** 27 7N 82 27W
Nokomis, *Ill.* **16** 39 18N 89 18W
Noma **12** 30 59N 85 37W
Nome **32** 64 30N 165 25W
Nonopapa **32** 21 50N 160 15W
Noorvik **32** 66 50N 161 3W
Nora Springs **16** 43 9N 93 1W
Norborne **16** 39 18N 93 40W
Norco **21** 33 56N 117 33W
Norcross **12** 33 56N 84 13W
Norfolk, *Nebr.* **14** 42 2N 97 25W
Norfolk, *Va.* **10** 36 51N 76 17W
Norfork L. **15** 36 15N 92 14W
Normal **16** 40 31N 88 59W
Norman **15** 35 13N 97 26W
Norman Park **12** 31 16N 83 41W
Normandy Heights **27** 39 17N 76 48W
Norridge **24** 41 57N 87 49W
Norris City **17** 37 59N 88 20W
Norristown, *Pa.* **26** 40 7N 75 20W
Norristown, *Ga.* **12** 32 30N 82 30W
North **12** 33 37N 81 6W
North Acton **25** 42 30N 71 23W
North Adams **9** 42 42N 73 7W
North Amityville **23** 40 41N 73 25W
North Andover **25** 42 41N 71 7W
North Arlington **22** 40 47N 74 7W
North Atlanta **12** 33 52N 84 21W
North Augusta **12** 33 30N 81 59W
North Babylon **23** 40 43N 73 19W
North Baltimore **17** 41 11N 83 41W
North Bass I. **8** 41 43N 82 49W
North Bellmore **23** 40 40N 73 32W
North Bend, *Oreg.* **18** 43 24N 124 14W
North Bend, *Pa.* **8** 41 20N 77 42W
North Bend, *Wash.* **20** 47 30N 121 47W
North Bennington **9** 42 56N 73 15W
North Bergen **22** 40 48N 74 0W
North Berwick **9** 43 18N 70 44W
North Beverly **25** 42 34N 70 51W
North Billerica **25** 42 35N 71 16W
North Braddock **29** 40 25N 79 51W
North Brighton **25** 42 21N 71 8W
North Caldwell **22** 40 52N 74 15W
North Cambridge **25** 42 23N 71 7W
North Canadian → **15** 35 16N 95 31W
North Canton **8** 40 53N 81 24W
North Carolina □ **11** 35 30N 80 0W
North Cascades National Park **18** 48 45N 121 10W
North Charleston **12** 32 53N 79 58W
North Chelmsford **25** 42 38N 71 23W
North Chicago **17** 42 19N 87 51W
North Cohasset **25** 42 15N 70 50W
North College Hill **17** 39 13N 84 33W
North Creek **9** 43 41N 73 59W
North Dakota □ **14** 47 30N 100 15W
North Druid Hills **12** 33 49N 84 19W
North East **8** 42 13N 79 50W
North English **16** 41 31N 92 5W
North Fabius → **16** 39 54N 91 30W
North Fair Oaks **30** 37 28N 122 11W
North Fork **20** 37 14N 119 21W
North Fork, Salt → **16** 39 26N 91 53W
North Fork American → **20** 38 57N 120 59W
North Fork Edisto → **12** 33 16N 80 54W
North Fork Feather → **20** 38 33N 121 30W
North Fork Grand → **14** 45 47N 102 16W
North Fork Red → **15** 34 24N 99 14W
North Fort Myers **13** 26 41N 81 53W
North Hackensack **22** 40 54N 74 2W
North Haledon **22** 40 58N 74 11W
North Highlands **20** 38 40N 121 23W
North Hills **23** 40 46N 73 40W
North Hollywood **31** 34 9N 118 22W

Philadelphia Int. Airport

North Judson 17 41 13N 86 46W
North Kingsville 8 41 54N 80 42W
North Las Vegas 21 36 12N 115 7W
North Lexington 25 42 27N 71 14W
North Liberty 17 41 32N 86 26W
North Lindenhurst 23 40 42N 73 22W
North Little Rock 15 34 45N 92 16W
North Long Beach 31 33 53N 118 10W
North Loup → 14 41 17N 98 24W
North Manchester 17 41 0N 85 46W
North Massapequa 23 40 42N 73 27W
North Merrick 23 40 41N 73 33W
North Miami 13 25 54N 80 11W
North Miami Beach 13 25 56N 80 10W
North Myrtle Beach 11 33 48N 78 42W
North Naples 13 26 12N 81 48W
North New Hyde Park 23 40 44N 73 42W
North New River Canal 13 26 30N 80 30W
North Olmsted 29 41 24N 81 55W
North Palisade 20 37 6N 118 31W
North Pelham 23 40 54N 73 46W
North Plainfield 22 40 37N 74 27W
North Platte 14 41 8N 100 46W
North Platte → 14 41 7N 100 42W
North Point 27 39 16N 76 29W
North Powder 18 45 2N 117 55W
North Pt. 8 45 2N 83 16W
North Randolph 25 42 11N 71 5W
North Reading 25 42 34N 71 5W
North Res. 25 42 27N 71 6W
North Richmond 30 37 57N 122 22W
North Riverside 24 41 50N 87 48W
North Saugus 25 42 29N 71 0W
North Springfield 27 38 48N 77 11W
North Sudbury 25 42 24N 71 24W
North Syracuse 9 43 8N 76 7W
North Tewksbury 25 42 38N 71 14W
North Tonawanda 8 43 2N 78 53W
North Troy 9 45 0N 72 24W
North Truchas Pk. 19 36 0N 105 30W
North Valley Stream 23 40 41N 73 42W
North Vernon 17 39 0N 85 38W
North Wantagh 23 40 41N 73 30W
North Webster 17 41 25N 85 48W
North Weymouth 25 42 14N 70 56W
North Wildwood 10 39 0N 74 48W
North Wilmington 25 42 34N 71 9W
North Woburn 25 42 30N 71 10W
Northampton, Mass. 9 42 19N 72 38W
Northampton, Pa. 9 40 41N 75 30W
Northbridge 9 42 9N 71 39W
Northbrook 24 42 7N 87 50W
Northeastern Univ. 25 42 20N 71 4W
Northern Marianas ■ 33 17 0N 145 0 E
Northfield, Ill. 24 42 5N 87 45W
Northfield, Minn. 14 44 27N 93 9W
Northfield, Vt. 9 44 9N 72 40W
Northlake 24 41 54N 87 53W
Northome 14 47 52N 94 17W
Northport, N.Y. 23 40 54N 73 20W
Northport, Ala. 11 33 14N 87 35W
Northport, Wash. 18 48 55N 117 48W
Northport B. 23 40 54N 73 22W
Northridge 31 34 14N 118 30W
Northvale 22 41 0N 73 59W
Northville 9 43 13N 74 11W
Northway 32 62 58N 141 56W
Northwestern Univ. 24 42 3N 87 40W
Northwood, Iowa 14 43 27N 93 13W
Northwood, N. Dak. 14 47 44N 97 34W
Norton 14 39 50N 99 53W
Norton B. 32 64 45N 161 15W
Norton Sd. 32 63 50N 164 0W
Norton Shores 17 43 8N 86 15W
Norumbega Res. 25 42 19N 71 17W
Norwalk, Calif. 31 33 53N 118 4W
Norwalk, Conn. 9 41 7N 73 22W
Norwalk, Iowa 14 41 29N 93 41W
Norwalk, Ohio 8 41 15N 82 37W
Norway, Maine 11 44 13N 70 32W
Norway, Mich. 10 45 47N 87 55W
Norway, S.C. 12 33 27N 81 7W
Norwich, Conn. 9 41 31N 72 5W
Norwich, N.Y. 9 42 32N 75 32W
Norwood, Mass. 25 42 11N 71 13W
Norwood, N.J. 22 40 59N 73 57W
Norwood, Pa. 26 39 53N 75 17W
Norwood, N.Y. 9 44 45N 75 0W
Norwood, Ohio 17 39 10N 84 27W
Norwood Memorial Airport 25 42 11N 71 9W
Norwood Park 24 41 59N 87 48W
Notasulga 12 32 34N 85 41W
Nottingham 26 40 7N 74 58W
Nottoway → 10 36 33N 76 55W
Novato 20 38 6N 122 35W
Novelty 16 40 1N 92 12W
Novinger 16 40 14N 92 43W
Nowata 15 36 42N 95 38W
Noxen 9 41 25N 76 4W
Noxon 18 48 0N 115 43W
Nueces → 15 27 51N 97 30W
Nulato 32 64 43N 158 6W
Nunda 8 42 35N 77 56W
Nunivak I. 32 60 10N 166 30W
Nutley 22 40 49N 74 9W
Nutting L. 25 42 32N 71 16W
Nyack 9 41 5N 73 55W
Nyssa 18 43 53N 117 0W

O

Oacoma 14 43 48N 99 24W
Oahe, L. 14 44 27N 100 24W
Oahe Dam 14 44 27N 100 24W
Oahu 32 21 28N 157 58W
Oak Beach 23 40 38N 73 19W
Oak Creek 17 42 52N 87 55W
Oak Forest 24 41 36N 87 44W
Oak Harbor 20 48 18N 122 39W
Oak Hill, Fla. 13 28 52N 80 51W
Oak Hill, W. Va. 10 37 59N 81 9W
Oak Hill Park 25 42 17N 71 11W
Oak Lane 26 40 3N 75 8W
Oak Lawn 24 41 42N 87 45W
Oak Park, Ill. 24 41 52N 87 47W
Oak Park, Mich. 28 42 27N 83 11W
Oak Park, Ga. 12 32 22N 82 19W
Oak Ridge, N.J. 22 41 2N 74 28W
Oak Ridge, Tenn. 11 36 1N 84 16W
Oak Valley 26 39 48N 75 9W
Oak View, Calif. 21 34 24N 119 18W
Oak View, Md. 27 39 1N 76 58W
Oakdale, Calif. 20 37 46N 120 51W
Oakdale, La. 15 30 49N 92 40W
Oakes 14 46 8N 98 6W
Oakesdale 18 47 8N 117 15W
Oakfield, Ga. 12 31 47N 83 58W
Oakfield, N.Y. 8 43 4N 78 16W
Oakford 16 40 6N 89 58W
Oakhurst 20 37 19N 119 40W
Oakland, N.J. 22 41 1N 74 13W
Oakland, Calif. 30 37 48N 122 18W
Oakland, Ill. 17 39 39N 88 2W
Oakland, Md. 27 38 52N 76 54W
Oakland City 17 38 20N 87 21W
Oakland Coliseum 30 37 44N 122 11W
Oakland Gardens 23 40 45N 73 46W
Oakland Int. Airport 30 37 43N 122 12W
Oakland Mills 27 39 13N 76 49W
Oakland Naval Air Station 30 37 47N 122 19W
Oakland Park 13 26 10N 80 8W
Oakland Pontiac Airport 28 42 40N 83 24W
Oaklawn 27 38 46N 76 56W
Oakley, Idaho 18 42 15N 113 53W
Oakley, Kans. 14 39 8N 100 51W
Oakmont 29 40 31N 79 50W
Oakridge 18 43 45N 122 28W
Oaks 26 40 8N 75 26W
Oaktown 17 38 52N 87 27W
Oakville 20 46 51N 123 14W
Oakwood, N.Y. 22 40 34N 74 7W
Oakwood, Ohio 17 41 6N 84 23W
Oakwood Beach 22 40 33N 74 7W
Oasis, Calif. 21 33 28N 116 6W
Oasis, Nev. 20 37 29N 117 55W
Oatman 21 35 1N 114 19W
Oberlin, Kans. 14 39 49N 100 32W
Oberlin, La. 15 30 37N 92 46W
Oberlin, Ohio 8 41 18N 82 13W
Oblong 17 39 0N 87 55W
O'Brien 12 30 2N 82 57W
Ocala 11 29 11N 82 8W
Ocanomowoc 14 43 7N 88 30W
Ocean City, Md. 10 38 20N 75 5W
Ocean City, N.J. 10 39 17N 74 35W
Ocean City, Wash. 20 47 4N 124 10W
Ocean Park 20 46 30N 124 3W
Oceano 21 35 6N 120 37W
Oceanport 9 40 19N 74 3W
Oceanside, N.Y. 23 40 38N 73 37W
Oceanside, Calif. 21 33 12N 117 23W
Ochlocknee 12 30 58N 84 3W
Ochlockonee → 12 29 59N 84 26W
Ochopee 13 25 54N 81 18W
Ocilla 12 31 36N 83 15W
Ocmulgee → 12 31 58N 82 33W
Ocoee 13 28 34N 81 33W
Oconee → 12 31 58N 82 33W
Oconee, L. 12 33 28N 83 15W
Oconee National Forest 12 33 15N 83 45W
Oconomowoc 17 43 7N 88 30W
Oconto 10 44 53N 87 52W
Oconto Falls 10 44 52N 88 9W
Odell 17 41 0N 88 31W
Odessa, Mo. 16 39 0N 93 57W
Odessa, Tex. 15 31 52N 102 23W
Odessa, Wash. 18 47 20N 118 41W
O'Donnell 15 32 58N 101 50W
Odum 12 31 40N 82 2W
Oella 27 39 16N 76 46W
Oelrichs 14 43 11N 103 14W
Oelwein 14 42 41N 91 55W
O'Fallon 16 38 49N 90 42W
Ofu 33 14 11S 169 41W
Ogallala 14 41 8N 101 43W
Ogden, Pa. 26 39 49N 75 27W
Ogden, Iowa 16 42 2N 94 2W
Ogden, Utah 18 41 13N 111 58W
Ogdensburg 9 44 42N 75 30W
Ogeechee → 12 31 50N 81 3W
Ogilby 21 32 49N 114 50W
Oglesby 16 41 18N 89 4W
Oglethorpe 12 32 18N 84 4W
O'Hare, L. 24 41 57N 87 53W
Ohatchee 12 33 47N 86 0W
Ohio □ 8 40 15N 82 45W
Ohio → 2 36 59N 89 8W
Ohio City 17 40 46N 84 37W
Oil City 8 41 26N 79 42W
Oildale 21 35 25N 119 1W
Ojai 21 34 27N 119 15W
Okanogan 18 48 22N 119 35W
Okanogan → 18 48 6N 119 44W
Okawville 16 38 26N 89 33W
Okeechobee 11 27 15N 80 50W
Okeechobee, L. 11 27 0N 80 50W
Okefenokee Swamp 12 30 40N 82 20W
Oklahoma □ 15 35 20N 97 30W
Oklahoma City 15 35 30N 97 30W
Oklawaha → 13 29 28N 81 41W
Oklawaha, L. 13 29 30N 81 45W
Okmulgee 15 35 37N 95 58W
Okolona, Ky. 17 38 8N 85 41W
Okolona, Miss. 15 34 0N 88 45W
Ola 15 35 2N 93 13W
Olancha 21 36 17N 118 1W
Olancha Pk. 21 36 15N 118 7W
Olanta 12 33 56N 79 56W
Olar 12 33 11N 81 11W
Olathe 14 38 53N 94 49W
Olcott 8 43 20N 78 42W
Old Baldy Pk. = San Antonio, Mt. 21 34 17N 117 38W
Old Brookville 23 40 49N 73 35W
Old Dale 21 34 8N 115 47W
Old Forge, N.Y. 9 43 43N 74 58W
Old Forge, Pa. 9 41 22N 75 45W
Old Forge Village 22 40 48N 74 29W
Old Harbor, Mass. 25 42 19N 71 1W
Old Harbor, Alaska 32 57 12N 153 18W
Old Road B. 27 39 12N 76 27W
Old Speck Mt. 9 44 34N 70 57W
Old Tappan 22 41 0N 73 59W
Old Town, Ill. 24 41 54N 87 37W
Old Town, Fla. 13 29 36N 82 59W
Old Town, Maine 11 44 56N 68 39W
Old Washington 8 40 2N 81 27W
Old Westbury 23 40 46N 73 35W
Oldsmar 13 28 2N 82 40W
Olean 8 42 5N 78 26W
Olema 20 38 3N 122 47W
Olin 16 42 0N 91 9W
Olive Hill 17 38 18N 83 13W
Olivehurst 20 39 6N 121 34W
Oliver 12 32 31N 81 32W
Olney, Pa. 26 40 2N 75 8W
Olney, Ill. 17 38 44N 88 5W
Olney, Tex. 15 33 22N 98 45W
Olosega 33 14 11S 169 38W
Olton 15 34 11N 102 8W
Olustee 12 30 12N 82 26W
Olympia 20 47 3N 122 53W
Olympic Mts. 20 47 55N 123 45W
Olympic Nat. Park 20 47 48N 123 30W
Olympus, Mt. 20 47 48N 123 43W
Olyphant 9 41 27N 75 36W
Omaha 14 41 17N 95 58W
Omak 18 48 25N 119 31W
Omega 12 31 21N 83 36W
Ona 13 27 29N 81 55W
Onaga 14 39 29N 96 10W
Onalaska 14 43 53N 91 14W
Onancock 10 37 43N 75 45W
Onarga 17 40 43N 88 1W
Onawa 14 42 2N 96 6W
Oneco 13 27 25N 82 31W
Oneida, Ill. 16 41 4N 90 13W
Oneida, N.Y. 9 43 6N 75 39W
Oneida L. 9 43 12N 75 54W
O'Neill 14 42 27N 98 39W
Oneonta 9 42 27N 75 4W
Onida 14 44 42N 100 4W
Onslow B. 11 34 20N 77 15W
Ontario, Calif. 21 34 4N 117 39W
Ontario, Oreg. 18 44 2N 116 58W
Ontario, L. 2 43 20N 78 0W
Ontonagon 14 46 52N 89 19W
Onyx 21 35 41N 118 14W
Ookala 32 20 1N 155 17W
Opelika 12 32 39N 85 23W
Opelousas 15 30 32N 92 5W
Opheim 18 48 51N 106 24W
Ophir 32 63 10N 156 31W
Opp 12 31 17N 86 16W
Opportunity 18 47 39N 117 15W
Oquawka 16 40 56N 90 57W
Oracle 19 32 37N 110 46W
Oradell 22 40 57N 74 2W
Oradell Res. 22 40 58N 74 0W
Orange, N.J. 22 40 46N 74 15W
Orange, Calif. 21 33 47N 117 51W
Orange, Mass. 9 42 35N 72 19W
Orange, Tex. 15 30 6N 93 44W
Orange, Va. 10 38 15N 78 7W
Orange City 13 28 57N 81 18W
Orange Cove 20 36 38N 119 19W
Orange Grove 15 27 58N 97 56W
Orange L. 13 29 25N 82 13W
Orange Park 12 30 10N 81 42W
Orangeburg 12 33 30N 80 52W
Orangeville 16 42 28N 89 39W
Orbisonia 8 40 15N 77 54W
Orcas I. 20 48 42N 122 56W
Orchard City 19 38 50N 107 58W
Orcutt 21 34 52N 120 27W
Ord 14 41 36N 98 56W
Orderville 19 37 17N 112 38W
Ordway 14 38 13N 103 46W
Oregon, Ill. 16 42 1N 89 20W
Oregon, Ohio 17 41 38N 83 25W
Oregon, Wis. 16 42 56N 89 23W
Oregon □ 18 44 0N 121 0W
Oregon City 20 45 21N 122 36W
Orem 18 40 19N 111 42W
Orient 16 41 12N 94 25W
Orient Heights 25 42 23N 70 59W
Orinda 30 37 52N 122 10W
Orinda Village 30 37 53N 122 12W
Orion, Ala. 12 31 58N 86 0W
Orion, Ill. 16 41 21N 90 23W
Oriskany 9 43 10N 75 20W
Orland, Calif. 20 39 45N 122 12W
Orland, Ind. 17 41 47N 85 12W
Orland L. 24 41 38N 87 52W
Orland Park 24 41 37N 87 52W
Orlando 11 28 33N 81 23W
Orleans 9 44 49N 72 12W
Ormond Beach 11 29 17N 81 3W
Ormond by the Sea 13 29 21N 81 4W
Oro Grande 21 34 36N 117 20W
Oro Valley 19 32 26N 110 58W
Orofino 18 46 29N 116 15W
Orono 11 44 53N 68 40W
Oroville, Calif. 20 39 31N 121 33W
Oroville, Wash. 18 48 56N 119 26W
Oroville, L. 20 39 33N 121 29W
Orrick 16 39 13N 94 3W
Orrville 8 40 50N 81 46W
Orting 20 47 6N 122 12W
Ortonville 14 45 19N 96 27W
Orwell, N.Y. 9 43 35N 75 50W
Orwell, Ohio 8 41 32N 80 52W
Orwigsburg 9 40 38N 76 6W
Osage 14 43 17N 92 49W
Osage → 16 38 35N 91 57W
Osage City 14 38 38N 95 50W
Osawatomie 14 38 31N 94 57W
Osborne 14 39 26N 98 42W
Osceola, Ark. 15 35 42N 89 58W
Osceola, Iowa 16 41 2N 93 46W
Osceola, Mo. 16 38 3N 93 42W
Osceola National Forest 12 30 20N 82 30W
Oscoda 8 44 26N 83 20W
Osgood 17 39 8N 85 18W
Oshkosh, Nebr. 14 41 24N 102 21W
Oshkosh, Wis. 14 44 1N 88 33W
Osierfield 12 31 40N 83 7W
Oskaloosa 16 41 18N 92 39W
Osprey 13 27 12N 82 29W
Ossabaw I. 12 31 50N 81 5W
Ossabaw Sd. 12 31 50N 81 6W
Ossining 9 41 10N 73 55W
Ossipee 9 43 41N 71 7W
Osterburg 8 40 16N 78 31W
Oswegatchie → 9 44 42N 75 30W
Oswego 9 43 27N 76 31W
Oswego → 9 43 27N 76 30W
Othello 18 46 50N 119 10W
Otsego 17 42 27N 85 42W
Ottawa, Ill. 17 41 21N 88 51W
Ottawa, Kans. 14 38 37N 95 16W
Ottawa, Ohio 17 41 1N 84 3W
Otter Cr. → 9 44 13N 73 17W
Otter Creek 13 29 19N 82 46W
Otterbein 17 40 29N 87 6W
Otterville 16 38 42N 93 0W
Ottoville 17 40 57N 84 22W
Ottumwa 16 41 1N 92 25W
Ouachita → 15 31 38N 91 49W
Ouachita, L. 15 34 34N 93 12W
Ouachita Mts. 15 34 40N 94 25W
Ouray 19 38 1N 107 40W
Outer Brewster I. 25 42 20N 70 52W
Outer Mission 30 37 43N 122 26W
Overland 16 38 41N 90 22W
Overland Park 14 38 55N 94 50W
Overlea 27 39 21N 76 32W
Overton 21 36 33N 114 27W
Ovid, Mich. 17 43 1N 84 22W
Ovid, N.Y. 9 42 41N 76 49W
Oviedo 13 28 40N 81 13W
Owasco L. 9 42 50N 76 31W
Owatonna 14 44 5N 93 14W
Owego 9 42 6N 76 16W
Owens → 20 36 32N 117 59W
Owens L. 21 36 26N 117 57W
Owensboro 17 37 46N 87 7W
Owensville, Ind. 17 38 16N 87 41W
Owensville, Mo. 16 38 21N 91 30W
Owenton 17 38 32N 84 50W
Owings Mills 27 39 25N 76 47W
Owingsville 17 38 9N 83 46W
Owosso 17 43 0N 84 10W
Owyhee 18 41 57N 116 6W
Owyhee → 18 43 49N 117 2W
Owyhee, L. 18 43 38N 117 14W
Oxford, Ala. 12 33 36N 85 51W
Oxford, Iowa 16 41 43N 91 47W
Oxford, Mass. 9 42 7N 71 52W
Oxford, Mich. 17 42 49N 83 16W
Oxford, Miss. 15 34 22N 89 31W
Oxford, N.C. 11 36 19N 78 35W
Oxford, N.Y. 9 42 27N 75 36W
Oxford, Ohio 17 39 31N 84 45W
Oxnard 21 34 12N 119 11W
Oxon Hill 27 38 48N 76 59W
Oyster B. 23 40 52N 73 31W
Oyster Bay 9 40 52N 73 32W
Oyster Bay Cove 23 40 51N 73 29W
Oyster Bay Harbour 23 40 53N 73 32W
Ozark, Ala. 12 31 28N 85 39W
Ozark, Ark. 15 35 29N 93 50W
Ozark, Mo. 15 37 1N 93 12W
Ozark Plateau 2 37 20N 91 40W
Ozarks, L. of the 16 38 12N 92 38W
Ozette L. 20 48 6N 124 38W
Ozona 15 30 43N 101 12W
Ozone Park 23 40 40N 73 50W

P

Paauilo 32 20 2N 155 22W
Pace 13 30 36N 87 10W
Pacific 16 38 29N 90 45W
Pacific Grove 20 36 38N 121 56W
Pacific Manor 30 37 38N 122 27W
Pacific Palisades 31 34 2N 118 32W
Pacifica 30 37 37N 122 29W
Packanack L. 22 40 56N 74 15W
Packwood 20 46 36N 121 40W
Padre I. 15 27 10N 97 25W
Paducah, Ky. 10 37 5N 88 37W
Paducah, Tex. 15 34 1N 100 18W
Page 19 36 57N 111 27W
Pago Pago 33 14 16S 170 43W
Pagosa Springs 19 37 16N 107 1W
Pahala 32 19 12N 155 29W
Pahoa 32 19 30N 154 57W
Pahokee 11 26 50N 80 40W
Pahrump 21 36 12N 115 59W
Pahute Mesa 20 37 20N 116 45W
Paia 32 20 54N 156 22W
Paicines 20 36 44N 121 17W
Pailolo Channel 32 21 0N 156 40W
Painesville 8 41 43N 81 15W
Painted Desert 19 36 0N 111 0W
Paintsville 10 37 49N 82 48W
Paisley 18 42 42N 120 32W
Pala 21 33 22N 117 5W
Palacios 15 28 42N 96 13W
Palatine 17 42 7N 88 3W
Palatka 12 29 39N 81 38W
Palau ■ 33 7 30N 134 30 E
Palermo 18 39 26N 121 33W
Palestine 15 31 46N 95 38W
Palisades 22 41 1N 73 54W
Palisades Park 22 40 50N 74 1W
Palisades Reservoir 18 43 20N 111 12W
Palm Bay 11 28 2N 80 35W
Palm Beach 11 26 43N 80 2W
Palm Coast 11 29 32N 81 10W
Palm Desert 21 33 43N 116 22W
Palm Harbor 13 28 5N 82 47W
Palm Springs 21 33 50N 116 33W
Palmdale, Calif. 21 34 35N 118 7W
Palmdale, Fla. 13 26 57N 81 19W
Palmer 32 61 36N 149 7W
Palmer Lake 14 39 7N 104 55W
Palmer Park 27 38 55N 76 52W
Palmerton 9 40 48N 75 37W
Palmetto, Fla. 11 27 31N 82 34W
Palmetto, Ga. 12 33 31N 84 40W
Palmyra, N.J. 26 40 0N 75 1W
Palmyra, Ill. 16 39 26N 90 0W
Palmyra, Mo. 16 39 48N 91 32W
Palmyra, N.Y. 8 43 5N 77 18W
Palmyra, Pa. 9 40 18N 76 36W
Palmyra, Wis. 17 42 52N 88 36W
Palo Alto 30 37 27N 122 9W
Palo Verde 21 33 26N 114 44W
Palomar Park 30 37 29N 122 16W
Palos Heights 24 41 39N 87 47W
Palos Hills 24 41 42N 87 49W
Palos Hills Forest 24 41 40N 87 52W
Palos Park 24 41 40N 87 50W
Palos Verdes 31 33 48N 118 23W
Palos Verdes, Pt. 21 33 43N 118 26W
Pamlico → 11 35 20N 76 28W
Pamlico Sd. 11 35 20N 76 0W
Pampa 15 35 32N 100 58W
Pana 16 39 23N 89 5W
Panaca 19 37 47N 114 23W
Panacea 12 30 2N 84 23W
Panamá, G. de 2 8 4N 79 20W
Panama City 12 30 10N 85 40W
Panama City Beach 12 30 11N 85 48W
Panamint Range 21 36 20N 117 20W
Panamint Springs 21 36 20N 117 28W
Panguitch 19 37 50N 112 26W
Panhandle 15 35 21N 101 23W
Panora 16 41 42N 94 22W
Panorama City 31 34 13N 118 26W
Paola 14 38 35N 94 53W
Paoli, Pa. 26 40 2N 75 28W
Paoli, Ind. 17 38 33N 86 28W
Paonia 19 38 52N 107 36W
Papaikou 32 19 47N 155 6W
Paradise, Calif. 20 39 46N 121 37W
Paradise, Nev. 21 36 9N 115 10W
Paradise Cay 30 37 54N 122 28W
Paradise Valley 18 41 30N 117 32W
Paragould 15 36 3N 90 29W
Paramount 31 33 53N 118 11W
Paramus 22 40 56N 74 2W
Paris, Idaho 18 42 14N 111 24W
Paris, Ill. 17 39 36N 87 42W
Paris, Ky. 17 38 13N 84 15W
Paris, Mo. 16 39 29N 92 0W
Paris, Tenn. 11 36 18N 88 19W
Paris, Tex. 15 33 40N 95 33W
Parish 9 43 25N 76 8W
Parishville 9 44 38N 74 49W
Park 20 48 45N 122 18W
Park City 15 37 48N 97 20W
Park Falls 14 45 56N 90 27W
Park Forest 17 41 29N 87 40W
Park Hills 15 37 53N 90 28W
Park Range 18 40 0N 106 30W
Park Rapids 14 46 55N 95 4W
Park Ridge, Ill. 24 42 0N 87 50W
Park Ridge, N.J. 22 41 2N 74 2W
Park River 14 48 24N 97 45W
Parkchester 23 40 49N 73 50W
Parker, Ariz. 21 34 9N 114 17W
Parker, Pa. 8 41 5N 79 41W
Parker Dam 21 34 18N 114 8W
Parkersburg, Iowa 16 42 35N 92 47W
Parkersburg, W. Va. 10 39 16N 81 34W
Parkfield 20 35 54N 120 26W
Parkland 20 47 9N 122 26W
Parklawn 27 38 50N 77 7W
Parkside 30 37 44N 122 29W
Parkston 14 43 24N 97 59W
Parksville 12 33 47N 82 13W
Parkville, Md. 27 39 23N 76 34W
Parkville, N.Y. 22 40 38N 73 57W
Parma, Ohio 29 41 24N 81 43W
Parma, Idaho 18 43 47N 116 57W
Parma Heights 29 41 23N 81 45W
Parowan 19 37 51N 112 50W
Parris I. 12 32 20N 80 41W
Parrish 13 27 35N 82 26W
Parrott 12 31 54N 84 31W
Parsippany 22 40 51N 74 26W
Parsons 15 37 20N 95 16W
Pasadena, Calif. 31 34 9N 118 8W
Pasadena, Tex. 15 29 43N 95 13W
Pascagoula 15 30 21N 88 33W
Pascagoula → 15 30 23N 88 37W
Pasco 18 46 14N 119 6W
Pascoag 9 41 57N 71 42W
Paso Robles 19 35 38N 120 41W
Passaic 22 40 51N 74 9W
Patagonia 19 31 33N 110 45W
Patapsco Valley State Park 27 39 18N 76 47W
Patchogue 9 40 46N 73 1W
Pateros 18 48 3N 119 54W
Paterson 22 40 54N 74 9W
Pathfinder Reservoir 18 42 28N 106 51W
Patten 11 46 0N 68 38W
Patterson, Calif. 20 37 28N 121 8W
Patterson, Ga. 12 31 23N 82 8W
Patterson, La. 15 29 42N 91 18W
Patterson, Mt. 20 38 29N 119 20W
Patterson Park 27 39 17N 76 34W
Patton 8 40 38N 78 39W
Pattonsburg 16 40 3N 94 8W
Paul Smiths 9 44 26N 74 15W
Paulding 17 41 8N 84 35W
Pauls Valley 15 34 44N 97 13W
Paulsboro 26 39 49N 75 14W
Pauma Valley 21 33 16N 116 58W
Pavilion 8 42 52N 78 1W
Pavlof Is. 32 55 30N 161 30W
Pavo 12 30 58N 83 45W
Paw Paw 17 42 13N 85 53W
Pawhuska 15 36 40N 96 20W
Pawling 9 41 34N 73 36W
Pawnee, Ill. 16 39 36N 89 35W
Pawnee, Okla. 15 36 20N 96 48W
Pawnee City 14 40 7N 96 9W
Pawpaw 16 41 41N 88 59W
Pawtucket 9 41 53N 71 23W
Paxton, Ill. 17 40 27N 88 6W
Paxton, Nebr. 14 41 7N 101 21W
Payette 18 44 5N 116 56W
Payne 17 41 5N 84 44W
Paynesville 14 45 23N 94 43W
Payson 19 34 14N 111 20W
Pe Ell 20 46 34N 123 18W
Pea → 12 31 1N 85 51W
Peabody 25 42 32N 70 57W
Peabody Inst. 27 39 17N 76 37W
Peace → 13 26 56N 82 6W
Peach Springs 19 35 32N 113 25W
Peachtree City 12 33 25N 84 35W
Peale, Mt. 19 38 26N 109 14W
Pearblossom 21 34 30N 117 55W
Pearl 16 39 28N 90 38W
Pearl → 15 30 11N 89 32W
Pearl City, Hawaii 32 21 24N 157 59W
Pearl City, Ill. 16 42 16N 89 50W
Pearl Harbor 32 21 21N 157 57W
Pearl River 9 41 4N 74 2W
Pearsall 15 28 54N 99 6W
Pearson 12 31 18N 82 51W
Pease → 15 34 12N 99 2W
Pebble Beach 20 36 34N 121 57W
Pecatonica 16 42 19N 89 22W
Pecatonica → 16 42 26N 89 12W
Pecos 15 31 26N 103 30W
Pecos → 15 29 42N 101 22W
Peddocks I. 25 42 17N 70 56W
Pedricktown 26 39 45N 75 24W
Pedro Valley 30 37 35N 122 29W
Pee Dee → 11 33 22N 79 16W
Peebles 17 38 57N 83 24W
Peekskill 9 41 17N 73 55W
Pekin 16 40 35N 89 40W
Pelham, N.Y. 23 40 54N 73 46W
Pelham, Ga. 12 31 8N 84 9W
Pelham B. Park 23 40 52N 73 48W
Pelham Manor 23 40 53N 73 46W
Pelican 32 57 58N 136 14W
Pelion 12 33 46N 81 15W
Pell City 12 33 35N 86 17W
Pella 16 41 25N 92 55W
Pembina 14 48 58N 97 15W
Pembroke 12 32 8N 81 37W
Pembroke Pines 13 26 5N 80 14W
Pend Oreille → 18 49 4N 117 37W
Pend Oreille, L. 18 48 10N 116 21W
Pendleton, Ind. 17 40 0N 85 45W
Pendleton, Oreg. 18 45 40N 118 47W
Penfield 8 41 13N 78 35W
Penn Hills 29 40 27N 79 50W
Penn Square 26 40 8N 75 19W
Penn Wynne 26 39 59N 75 16W
Penn Yan 8 42 40N 77 3W
Penndel 26 40 9N 74 54W
Pennington 20 39 15N 121 47W
Penns Grove 26 39 44N 75 27W
Pennsauken 26 39 57N 75 5W
Pennsburg 9 40 23N 75 29W
Pennsylvania □ 10 40 45N 77 30W
Pennsylvania, Univ. of 26 39 51N 75 11W
Pennville 17 40 30N 85 9W
Penobscot → 11 44 30N 68 48W
Penobscot B. 11 44 35N 68 50W
Pensacola 11 30 25N 87 13W
Peoria, Ariz. 19 33 35N 112 14W
Peoria, Ill. 16 40 42N 89 36W
Peoria Heights 16 40 45N 89 35W
Peotone 17 41 20N 87 48W
Pepacton Reservoir 9 42 5N 74 58W
Pequannock 22 40 57N 74 17W
Percy 16 38 5N 89 41W
Perham 14 46 36N 95 34W
Perkasie 9 40 22N 75 18W
Perrine 13 25 36N 80 21W
Perris 21 33 47N 117 14W
Perry, Fla. 12 30 7N 83 35W
Perry, Ga. 12 32 28N 83 44W
Perry, Iowa 16 41 51N 94 6W
Perry, Mich. 17 42 50N 84 13W
Perry, Mo. 16 39 26N 91 40W
Perry, Okla. 15 36 17N 97 14W
Perry, S.C. 12 33 38N 81 19W
Perry Hall 27 39 24N 76 28W
Perrysburg 17 41 34N 83 38W
Perrysville 29 40 32N 80 1W
Perryton 15 36 24N 100 48W
Perryville, Alaska 32 55 55N 159 9W
Perryville, Mo. 16 37 43N 89 52W
Perth Amboy 22 40 30N 74 16W
Peru, Ill. 16 41 20N 89 8W
Peru, Ind. 17 40 45N 86 4W
Peru, N.Y. 9 44 35N 73 32W
Peshtigo 10 45 4N 87 46W
Petaluma 20 38 14N 122 39W
Peterborough 9 42 53N 71 57W
Peters Pond 25 42 43N 71 15W
Petersburg, Alaska 32 56 48N 132 58W
Petersburg, Ill. 16 40 1N 89 51W
Petersburg, Ind. 17 38 30N 87 17W
Petersburg, Pa. 8 40 34N 78 3W
Petersburg, Va. 10 37 14N 77 24W
Petersburg, W. Va. 10 39 1N 79 5W
Petoskey 10 45 22N 84 57W
Petrey 12 31 51N 86 13W
Petrified Forest National Park 19 35 0N 109 30W
Pharr 15 26 12N 98 11W
Phelps 8 42 58N 77 3W
Phenix City 11 32 28N 85 0W
Philadelphia, Pa. 26 39 57N 75 11W
Philadelphia, Miss. 15 32 46N 89 7W
Philadelphia, N.Y. 9 44 9N 75 43W
Philadelphia Airport 26 40 4N 75 0W
Philadelphia Int. Airport 26 39 52N 75 16W

Philip

Philip **14** 44 2N 101 40W
Philip Smith Mts. **32** 68 0N 146 0W
Philippi **10** 39 9N 80 3W
Philipsburg, *Mont.* **18** 46 20N 113 18W
Philipsburg, *Pa.* **8** 40 54N 78 13W
Phillips **14** 45 42N 90 24W
Phillipsburg, *Ga.* **12** 31 25N 83 30W
Phillipsburg, *Kans.* **14** 39 45N 99 19W
Phillipsburg, *N.J.* **9** 40 42N 75 12W
Philmont **9** 42 15N 73 39W
Philomath, *Ga.* **12** 33 44N 82 59W
Philomath, *Oreg.* **18** 44 32N 123 22W
Phoenicia **9** 42 5N 74 14W
Phoenix, *Ill.* **24** 41 36N 87 37W
Phoenix, *Ariz.* **19** 33 27N 112 4W
Phoenix, *N.Y.* **9** 43 14N 76 18W
Phoenixville **26** 40 7N 75 31W
Picayune **15** 30 32N 89 41W
Pickwick L. **11** 35 4N 88 15W
Pico Rivera **31** 33 59N 118 5W
Piedmont, *Calif.* **30** 37 49N 122 14W
Piedmont, *Ala.* **12** 33 55N 85 37W
Piedmont, *S.C.* **7** 34 0N 81 30W
Piercefield **9** 44 13N 74 35W
Pierpont **8** 41 45N 80 34W
Pierre **14** 44 22N 100 21W
Pierson **13** 29 14N 81 28W
Piggott **15** 36 23N 90 11W
Pike Road **12** 32 17N 86 6W
Pikes Peak **14** 38 50N 105 3W
Pikesville **27** 39 22N 76 42W
Pikeville **12** 37 29N 82 31W
Pilarcitos L. **30** 37 33N 122 25W
Pilgrim Corner **26** 39 57N 75 19W
Pillar Pt. **24** 37 29N 122 30W
Pilot Grove **16** 38 53N 92 55W
Pilot Point **15** 33 24N 96 58W
Pilot Rock **18** 45 29N 118 50W
Pima **19** 32 54N 109 50W
Pimmit Hills **27** 38 54N 77 12W
Pinckard **12** 31 19N 85 33W
Pinckneyville **16** 38 5N 89 23W
Pine Bluff **15** 34 13N 92 1W
Pine Bluffs **14** 41 11N 104 4W
Pine Brook **22** 40 51N 74 18W
Pine City **14** 45 50N 92 59W
Pine Cr. → **8** 41 10N 77 16W
Pine Flat Res. **20** 36 50N 119 20W
Pine Grove **9** 40 33N 76 23W
Pine Hill, *N.J.* **26** 39 47N 74 59W
Pine Hill, *Fla.* **13** 28 32N 81 28W
Pine Is. **13** 26 36N 82 7W
Pine Level **12** 32 4N 86 4W
Pine Mountain **12** 32 52N 84 51W
Pine Orchard **27** 39 16N 76 52W
Pine Ridge **14** 43 2N 102 33W
Pine River **14** 46 43N 94 24W
Pine Valley **21** 32 50N 116 32W
Pinecrest **20** 38 12N 120 1W
Pinedale, *Calif.* **20** 36 50N 119 48W
Pinedale, *Wyo.* **18** 42 52N 109 52W
Pinehurst, *Mass.* **25** 42 31N 71 12W
Pinehurst, *Ga.* **12** 32 12N 83 46W
Pinellas Park **13** 27 50N 82 43W
Pines Lake **22** 40 59N 74 15W
Pinetop **19** 34 8N 109 56W
Pinetta **12** 30 36N 83 21W
Pineview **12** 32 7N 83 30W
Pineville, *La.* **15** 31 19N 92 26W
Pineville, *S.C.* **12** 33 26N 80 1W
Pinewood **12** 33 44N 80 27W
Pinnacles **20** 36 33N 121 19W
Pinon Hills **21** 34 26N 117 39W
Pinos, Mt. **21** 34 49N 119 8W
Pinos Pt. **19** 36 38N 121 57W
Pioche **19** 37 56N 114 27W
Pipestone **14** 44 0N 96 19W
Piqua **17** 40 9N 84 15W
Piru **21** 34 25N 118 48W
Piscataway **22** 40 34N 74 27W
Pismo Beach **21** 35 9N 120 38W
Pit → **18** 40 47N 122 6W
Pitman **26** 39 44N 75 7W
Pittsburg, *Calif.* **20** 38 2N 121 53W
Pittsburg, *Kans.* **15** 37 25N 94 42W
Pittsburg, *Tex.* **15** 33 0N 94 59W
Pittsburgh **8** 40 26N 80 1W
Pittsfield, *Ill.* **16** 39 36N 90 49W
Pittsfield, *Maine* **11** 44 47N 69 23W
Pittsfield, *Mass.* **9** 42 27N 73 15W
Pittsfield, *N.H.* **9** 43 18N 71 20W
Pittston **9** 41 19N 75 47W
Pittsview **12** 32 11N 85 10W
Pixley **20** 35 58N 119 18W
Placerville **20** 38 44N 120 48W
Placid, L. **13** 27 15N 81 22W
Plainedge **23** 40 43N 73 27W
Plainfield, *N.J.* **22** 40 36N 74 23W
Plainfield, *Ill.* **17** 41 37N 88 12W
Plainfield, *Ohio* **8** 40 13N 81 43W
Plainfield, *Vt.* **9** 44 17N 72 26W
Plains, *Ga.* **12** 32 2N 84 24W
Plains, *Mont.* **18** 47 28N 114 53W
Plains, *Tex.* **15** 33 11N 102 50W
Plainview, *N.Y.* **23** 40 46N 73 27W
Plainview, *Nebr.* **14** 42 21N 97 47W
Plainview, *Tex.* **15** 34 11N 101 43W
Plainwell **10** 42 27N 85 38W
Plaistow **9** 42 50N 71 6W
Planada **20** 37 16N 120 19W
Plandome **23** 40 48N 73 42W
Plandome Heights **23** 40 48N 73 42W
Plano **15** 33 1N 96 42W
Plant City **11** 28 1N 82 7W
Plantation **13** 26 8N 80 15W
Plaquemine **15** 30 17N 91 14W
Plaster City **21** 32 47N 115 51W
Platinum **32** 59 1N 161 49W
Platte **14** 43 23N 98 51W
Platte →, *Mo.* **16** 39 16N 94 50W
Platte →, *Nebr.* **2** 41 4N 95 53W
Platte City **16** 39 22N 94 47W
Platteville **16** 42 44N 90 29W
Plattsburg **16** 39 34N 94 27W
Plattsburgh **9** 44 42N 73 28W
Plattsmouth **14** 41 1N 95 53W
Pleasant Hill, *Calif.* **30** 37 56N 122 4W
Pleasant Hill, *Ill.* **16** 39 27N 90 52W
Pleasant Hill, *Mo.* **16** 38 47N 94 16W
Pleasant Hills **29** 40 20N 79 58W
Pleasant Mount **9** 41 44N 75 26W
Pleasanton, *Calif.* **20** 37 39N 121 52W
Pleasanton, *Tex.* **15** 28 58N 98 29W
Pleasantville, *Iowa* **16** 41 23N 93 18W
Pleasantville, *N.J.* **10** 39 24N 74 32W
Pleasantville, *Pa.* **8** 41 35N 79 34W
Pleasure Ridge Park **17** 38 9N 85 50W
Plentywood **14** 48 47N 104 34W
Plum **8** 40 29N 79 47W
Plum I. **9** 41 11N 72 12W
Plumas **20** 39 45N 120 4W
Plummer **18** 47 20N 116 53W
Plumsock **26** 39 58N 75 28W
Plymouth, *Calif.* **20** 38 29N 120 51W
Plymouth, *Ill.* **16** 40 18N 90 58W
Plymouth, *Ind.* **17** 41 21N 86 19W
Plymouth, *Mass.* **9** 41 57N 70 40W
Plymouth, *N.C.* **11** 35 52N 76 43W
Plymouth, *N.H.* **9** 43 46N 71 41W
Plymouth, *Pa.* **9** 41 14N 75 57W
Plymouth, *Wis.* **10** 43 45N 87 59W
Plymouth Meeting **26** 40 6N 75 16W
Pocahontas, *Ark.* **15** 36 16N 90 58W
Pocahontas, *Ill.* **16** 38 50N 89 33W
Pocahontas, *Iowa* **16** 42 44N 94 40W
Pocatello **18** 42 52N 112 27W
Pocomoke City **10** 38 5N 75 34W
Pohnpei **33** 6 55N 158 10 E
Point Arena **20** 38 55N 123 41W
Point Baker **32** 56 21N 133 37W
Point Breeze **26** 39 54N 75 13W
Point Hope **32** 68 21N 166 47W
Point Lay **32** 69 46N 163 3W
Point Lookout **23** 40 35N 73 34W
Point Pleasant, *N.J.* **9** 40 5N 74 4W
Point Pleasant, *W. Va.* **10** 38 51N 82 8W
Point View Res. **22** 40 58N 74 14W
Pojoaque **19** 35 54N 106 1W
Polacca **19** 35 50N 110 23W
Polk **8** 41 22N 79 56W
Polo, *Ill.* **16** 41 59N 89 35W
Polo, *Mo.* **16** 39 33N 94 3W
Polson **18** 47 41N 114 9W
Pomeroy, *Ohio* **10** 39 2N 82 2W
Pomeroy, *Wash.* **18** 46 28N 117 36W
Pomme de Terre L. **16** 37 54N 93 19W
Pomona **21** 34 4N 117 45W
Pomona Park **13** 29 30N 81 36W
Pompano Beach **11** 26 14N 80 8W
Pompeys Pillar **18** 45 59N 107 57W
Pompton Lakes **22** 41 0N 74 15W
Pompton Plains **22** 40 58N 74 18W
Ponca **14** 42 34N 96 43W
Ponca City **15** 36 42N 97 5W
Ponce **32** 18 1N 66 37W
Ponce de Leon **12** 30 44N 85 56W
Ponce de Leon B. **13** 25 15N 81 10W
Ponchatoula **15** 30 26N 90 26W
Pond **21** 35 43N 119 20W
Ponkapog **25** 42 11N 71 4W
Ponkapog Pond **25** 42 11N 71 5W
Pontchartrain L. **15** 30 5N 90 5W
Ponte Vedra Beach **13** 30 15N 81 23W
Pontiac, *Mich.* **28** 42 38N 83 17W
Pontiac, *Ill.* **17** 40 53N 88 38W
Pooler **12** 32 7N 81 15W
Poorman **32** 64 5N 155 48W
Poplar **14** 48 7N 105 12W
Poplar Bluff **15** 36 46N 90 24W
Poplarville **15** 30 51N 89 32W
Porcupine → **32** 66 34N 145 19W
Port Alexander **32** 56 15N 134 38W
Port Allegany **8** 41 48N 78 17W
Port Allen **15** 30 27N 91 12W
Port Angeles **20** 48 7N 123 27W
Port Aransas **15** 27 50N 97 4W
Port Arthur **15** 29 54N 93 56W
Port Austin **8** 44 3N 83 1W
Port Charlotte **13** 26 59N 82 6W
Port Chester **23** 41 0N 73 40W
Port Chester Harbour **23** 40 58N 73 38W
Port Clinton **17** 41 31N 82 56W
Port Ewen **9** 41 54N 73 59W
Port Gamble **20** 47 51N 122 35W
Port Gibson **15** 31 58N 90 59W
Port Heiden **32** 56 55N 158 41W
Port Henry **9** 44 3N 73 28W
Port Hope **8** 43 57N 82 43W
Port Hueneme **21** 34 7N 119 12W
Port Huron **8** 42 58N 82 26W
Port Jefferson **9** 40 57N 73 3W
Port Jervis **9** 41 22N 74 41W
Port Kennedy **26** 40 6N 75 25W
Port Lavaca **15** 28 37N 96 38W
Port Leyden **9** 43 35N 75 21W
Port Matilda **8** 40 48N 78 3W
Port Mayaca **13** 26 59N 80 36W
Port Neches **15** 30 0N 93 59W
Port Newark **22** 40 41N 74 9W
Port Orange **13** 29 9N 80 59W
Port Orchard **20** 47 32N 122 38W
Port Orford **18** 42 45N 124 30W
Port Reading **22** 40 34N 74 13W
Port Richmond **22** 40 38N 74 7W
Port Royal Sd. **12** 32 15N 80 40W
Port St. Joe **12** 29 49N 85 18W
Port St. Lucie **11** 27 20N 80 20W
Port Salerno **13** 27 9N 80 12W
Port Sanilac **8** 43 26N 82 33W
Port Sulphur **15** 29 29N 89 42W
Port Townsend **20** 48 7N 122 45W
Port Washington, *N.Y.* **23** 40 49N 73 42W
Port Washington, *Wis.* **10** 43 23N 87 53W
Port Washington North **23** 40 50N 73 41W
Port Wentworth **12** 32 9N 81 10W
Portadale **12** 30 34N 83 54W
Portage, *Mich.* **17** 42 12N 85 35W
Portage, *Pa.* **8** 40 23N 78 41W
Portage, *Wis.* **14** 43 33N 89 28W
Portage → **17** 41 31N 83 5W
Portage Park **24** 41 56N 87 45W
Portageville **15** 36 26N 89 42W
Portal **12** 32 33N 81 56W
Portales **15** 34 11N 103 20W
Porter **17** 41 36N 87 4W
Porterville **20** 36 4N 119 1W
Porthill **18** 48 59N 116 30W
Portland, *Conn.* **9** 41 34N 72 38W
Portland, *Fla.* **12** 30 31N 86 12W
Portland, *Ind.* **17** 40 26N 84 59W
Portland, *Maine* **11** 43 39N 70 16W
Portland, *Mich.* **17** 42 52N 84 54W
Portland, *Oreg.* **20** 45 32N 122 37W
Portland, *Pa.* **9** 40 55N 75 6W
Portland, *Tex.* **15** 27 53N 97 20W
Portola **20** 39 49N 120 28W
Portrero **30** 37 46N 122 25W
Portsmouth, *N.H.* **11** 43 5N 70 45W
Portsmouth, *Ohio* **10** 38 44N 82 57W
Portsmouth, *R.I.* **9** 41 36N 71 15W
Portsmouth, *Va.* **10** 36 50N 76 18W
Portville **8** 42 3N 78 20W
Posen **24** 41 38N 87 41W
Poseyville **17** 38 10N 87 47W
Possum Kingdom L. **15** 32 52N 98 26W
Post **15** 33 12N 101 23W
Post Falls **18** 47 43N 116 57W
Poston **21** 34 0N 114 24W
Postville **16** 43 5N 91 34W
Potawatomi Woods **24** 42 8N 87 53W
Poteau **15** 35 3N 94 37W
Poteet **15** 29 2N 98 35W
Potomac **27** 38 59N 77 13W
Potomac → **10** 38 0N 76 23W
Potosi **16** 37 56N 90 47W
Potosi Mt. **21** 35 57N 115 29W
Potrero Pt. **30** 37 45N 122 22W
Potsdam **9** 44 40N 74 59W
Pottersville **9** 43 43N 73 50W
Potterville **12** 32 31N 84 7W
Pottstown **9** 40 15N 75 39W
Pottsville **9** 40 41N 76 12W
Poughkeepsie **9** 41 42N 73 56W
Poulan **12** 31 31N 83 47W
Poulsbo **20** 47 44N 122 39W
Poultney **9** 43 31N 73 14W
Poway **21** 32 58N 117 2W
Powder → **14** 46 45N 105 26W
Powder River **18** 43 2N 106 59W
Powder Springs **12** 33 52N 84 41W
Powderhorn L. **24** 41 38N 87 31W
Powell **18** 44 45N 108 46W
Powell, L. **19** 36 57N 111 29W
Powelton **12** 33 26N 82 52W
Powers **10** 45 41N 87 32W
Pozo **21** 35 20N 120 24W
Prairie City **18** 44 28N 118 43W
Prairie Dog Town Fork → **15** 34 30N 99 23W
Prairie du Chien **16** 43 3N 91 9W
Prairie du Rocher **16** 38 5N 90 6W
Pratt **15** 37 39N 98 44W
Prattville **11** 32 28N 86 29W
Preakness **22** 40 56N 74 12W
Premont **15** 27 22N 98 7W
Prentice **14** 45 33N 90 17W
Prescott, *Ariz.* **19** 34 33N 112 28W
Prescott, *Ark.* **15** 33 48N 93 23W
Prescott Valley **19** 34 40N 112 18W
Presho **14** 43 54N 100 3W
Presidio **15** 29 34N 104 22W
Presque I. **8** 42 9N 80 6W
Presque Isle **11** 46 41N 68 1W
Preston, *Ga.* **12** 32 4N 84 32W
Preston, *Idaho* **18** 42 6N 111 53W
Preston, *Iowa* **16** 42 3N 90 24W
Preston, *Minn.* **14** 43 40N 92 5W
Prestonburg **10** 37 39N 82 46W
Price **18** 39 36N 110 49W
Prichard **11** 30 44N 88 5W
Priest L. **18** 48 35N 116 52W
Priest River **18** 48 10N 116 54W
Priest Valley **20** 36 10N 120 39W
Prince of Wales, C. **32** 65 36N 168 5W
Prince of Wales I. **32** 55 47N 132 50W
Prince William Sd. **32** 60 40N 147 0W
Princes B. **22** 40 30N 74 12W
Princeton, *Calif.* **20** 39 24N 122 1W
Princeton, *Ill.* **16** 41 23N 89 28W
Princeton, *Ind.* **17** 38 21N 87 34W
Princeton, *Ky.* **10** 37 7N 87 53W
Princeton, *Mo.* **16** 40 24N 93 35W
Princeton, *N.J.* **9** 40 21N 74 39W
Princeton, *W. Va.* **10** 37 22N 81 6W
Princeville **16** 40 56N 89 46W
Prineville **18** 44 18N 120 51W
Proctor **9** 43 40N 73 2W
Prophetstown **16** 41 40N 89 56W
Prospect **9** 43 18N 75 9W
Prospect Heights **24** 42 5N 87 55W
Prospect Hill Park **25** 42 23N 71 13W
Prospect Park, *N.J.* **22** 40 55N 74 10W
Prospect Park, *Pa.* **26** 39 53N 75 18W
Prospect Pt. **23** 40 52N 73 42W
Prosser **18** 46 12N 119 46W
Providence, *Md.* **27** 39 25N 76 34W
Providence, *Ky.* **10** 37 24N 87 46W
Providence, *R.I.* **9** 41 49N 71 24W
Providence Mts. **21** 35 10N 115 15W
Provo **18** 40 14N 111 39W
Prudhoe Bay **32** 70 18N 148 22W
Pryor **15** 36 19N 95 19W
Pueblo **14** 38 16N 104 37W
Puente Hills **31** 33 59N 117 56W
Puerco → **19** 34 22N 107 50W
Puerto Rico ■ **32** 18 15N 66 45W
Puget Sound **18** 47 50N 122 30W
Pukoo **32** 21 4N 156 48W
Pulaski, *N.Y.* **9** 43 34N 76 8W
Pulaski, *Tenn.* **11** 35 12N 87 2W
Pulaski, *Va.* **10** 37 3N 80 47W
Pulga **20** 39 48N 121 29W
Pullman **18** 46 44N 117 10W
Pumphrey **27** 39 13N 76 39W
Punta Gorda **11** 26 56N 82 3W
Punta Rassa **13** 26 26N 81 59W
Punxsatawney **8** 40 57N 78 59W
Purcell **15** 35 1N 97 22W
Purchase **23** 41 2N 73 43W
Purvis **15** 31 9N 89 25W
Putnam **9** 41 55N 71 55W
Putnamville Res. **25** 42 36N 70 56W
Putney **12** 31 29N 84 8W
Putty Hill **27** 39 22N 76 30W
Puyallup **20** 47 12N 122 18W
Pymatuning Reservoir **8** 41 30N 80 28W
Pyote **15** 31 32N 103 8W
Pyramid L. **18** 40 1N 119 35W
Pyramid Pk. **21** 36 25N 116 37W

Q

Quabbin Reservoir **9** 42 20N 72 20W
Quakertown **9** 40 26N 75 21W
Quanah **15** 34 18N 99 44W
Quannapowitt, L. **25** 42 30N 71 4W
Quartzsite **21** 33 40N 114 13W
Queen City **16** 40 25N 92 34W
Queens Village **23** 40 43N 73 44W
Queensland **12** 31 46N 83 14W
Queets **20** 47 32N 124 20W
Quemado, *N. Mex.* **19** 34 20N 108 30W
Quemado, *Tex.* **15** 28 58N 100 35W
Questa **19** 36 42N 105 36W
Quilcene **20** 47 49N 122 53W
Quinault → **20** 47 21N 124 18W
Quincy, *Mass.* **25** 42 14N 71 0W
Quincy, *Calif.* **20** 39 56N 120 57W
Quincy, *Fla.* **12** 30 35N 84 34W
Quincy, *Ill.* **14** 39 56N 91 23W
Quincy, *Wash.* **18** 47 22N 119 56W
Quincy B. **25** 42 16N 70 59W
Quinhagak **32** 59 45N 161 54W
Quitman **12** 30 47N 83 34W

R

Raccoon → **16** 41 35N 93 37W
Raccoon Cr. → **17** 39 47N 87 23W
Raccoon Str. **30** 37 52N 122 26W
Racine **17** 42 41N 87 51W
Rackerby **20** 39 26N 121 22W
Radcliff **17** 37 51N 85 57W
Radford **10** 37 8N 80 34W
Radnor **26** 40 2N 75 21W
Ragland **12** 33 45N 86 9W
Rahway **22** 40 36N 74 17W
Raiford **12** 30 4N 82 14W
Rail Tree Hill **25** 42 32N 71 22W
Rainbow City **12** 33 57N 86 5W
Rainbow Lakes **22** 40 53N 74 27W
Rainier **20** 46 53N 122 41W
Rainier, Mt., *Wash.* **2** 46 52N 121 46W
Rainier, Mt., *Md.* **27** 38 56N 76 57W
Raleigh, *Fla.* **13** 29 25N 82 32W
Raleigh, *N.C.* **11** 35 47N 78 39W
Ralls **15** 33 41N 101 24W
Ralston **8** 41 30N 76 57W
Ramblewood **26** 39 55N 74 56W
Ramer **12** 32 3N 86 13W
Ramona **21** 33 2N 116 52W
Rampart **32** 65 30N 150 10W
Ramsey, *Ill.* **16** 39 8N 89 7W
Ramsey, *N.J.* **9** 41 4N 74 9W
Ranchester **18** 44 54N 107 10W
Rancho Cucamonga **21** 34 10N 117 30W
Randallstown **27** 39 21N 76 46W
Randle **20** 46 32N 121 57W
Randolph, *Mass.* **25** 42 10N 71 3W
Randolph, *N.Y.* **8** 42 10N 78 59W
Randolph, *Utah* **18** 41 40N 111 11W
Randolph, *Vt.* **9** 43 55N 72 40W
Randolph Hills **27** 39 3N 77 6W
Randsburg **21** 35 22N 117 39W
Rangeley **9** 44 58N 70 39W
Rangeley L. **9** 44 55N 70 43W
Rangely **18** 40 5N 108 48W
Ranger **15** 32 28N 98 41W
Rankin, *Ill.* **17** 40 28N 87 54W
Rankin, *Tex.* **15** 31 13N 101 56W
Ransom **17** 41 9N 88 39W
Rantoul **17** 40 19N 88 9W
Rapid City **14** 44 5N 103 14W
Rapid River **10** 45 55N 86 58W
Raquette → **9** 45 0N 74 42W
Raquette Lake **9** 43 49N 74 40W
Raritan B. **22** 40 29N 74 12W
Rat Islands **32** 52 0N 178 0 E
Rathbun Res. **16** 40 49N 92 53W
Raton **15** 36 54N 104 24W
Ravalli **18** 47 17N 114 11W
Ravena **9** 42 28N 73 49W
Ravenel **12** 32 46N 80 15W
Ravenna, *Ky.* **17** 37 42N 83 55W
Ravenna, *Nebr.* **14** 41 1N 98 55W
Ravenna, *Ohio* **8** 41 9N 81 15W
Ravenswood **10** 38 57N 81 46W
Ravenswood Pt. **30** 37 30N 122 8W
Ravenwood **16** 40 22N 94 41W
Rawlins **18** 41 47N 107 14W
Ray **14** 48 21N 103 10W
Ray City **12** 31 5N 83 11W
Ray Mts. **32** 66 0N 152 0W
Rayle **12** 33 48N 82 54W
Raymond, *Calif.* **20** 37 13N 119 54W
Raymond, *Ga.* **12** 33 20N 84 43W
Raymond, *Ill.* **16** 39 19N 89 34W
Raymond, *N.H.* **9** 43 2N 71 11W
Raymond, *Wash.* **20** 46 41N 123 44W
Raymondville **15** 26 29N 97 47W
Raytown **16** 39 1N 94 28W
Rayville **15** 32 29N 91 46W
Reading, *Mass.* **25** 42 31N 71 5W
Reading, *Mich.* **17** 41 50N 84 45W
Reading, *Ohio* **17** 39 13N 84 26W
Reading, *Pa.* **9** 40 20N 75 56W
Reading Highlands **25** 42 31N 71 5W
Red →, *La.* **2** 31 1N 91 45W
Red →, *N. Dak.* **14** 49 0N 97 15W
Red Bank **9** 40 21N 74 5W
Red Bank Battle Mon. **26** 39 52N 75 11W
Red Bluff **18** 40 11N 122 15W
Red Bluff L. **15** 31 54N 103 55W
Red Bud **16** 38 13N 89 59W
Red Cloud **14** 40 5N 98 32W
Red Creek **9** 43 14N 76 45W
Red Head **12** 30 29N 85 51W
Red Hook **9** 41 55N 73 53W
Red Lake Falls **14** 47 53N 96 16W
Red Lodge **18** 45 11N 109 15W
Red Mountain **21** 35 37N 117 38W
Red Oak **14** 41 1N 95 14W
Red Rock **30** 37 55N 122 25W
Red Rock, L. **16** 41 22N 92 59W
Red Slate Mt. **20** 37 31N 118 52W
Red Wing **14** 44 34N 92 31W
Redbay **12** 30 35N 85 57W
Reddick **13** 29 22N 82 12W
Redding **18** 40 35N 122 24W
Redfield **14** 44 53N 98 31W
Redford **9** 44 38N 73 48W
Redford Township **28** 42 23N 83 17W
Redkey **17** 40 21N 85 9W
Redlands **21** 34 4N 117 11W
Redmond, *Oreg.* **18** 44 17N 121 11W
Redmond, *Wash.* **20** 47 41N 122 7W
Redondo Beach **21** 33 50N 118 23W
Redwood **9** 44 18N 75 48W
Redwood City **30** 37 29N 122 14W
Redwood Falls **14** 44 32N 95 7W
Redwood National Park **18** 41 40N 124 5W
Redwood Pt. **30** 37 32N 122 11W
Redwood Regional Park **30** 37 48N 122 8W
Reed City **10** 43 53N 85 31W
Reedley **20** 36 36N 119 27W
Reedsburg **14** 43 32N 90 0W
Reedsport **18** 43 42N 124 6W
Reedsville **8** 40 39N 77 35W
Reese → **18** 40 48N 117 4W
Reeves Hill **25** 42 20N 71 20W
Refugio **15** 28 18N 97 17W
Register **12** 32 22N 81 53W
Rego Park **23** 40 43N 73 51W
Reidsville, *Ga.* **12** 32 6N 82 7W
Reidsville, *N.C.* **11** 36 21N 79 40W
Reinbeck **16** 42 19N 92 36W
Rembert **12** 34 6N 80 32W
Remington **17** 40 46N 87 9W
Rend Lake **16** 38 2N 88 58W
Renfroe **12** 32 14N 84 43W
Reno **20** 39 31N 119 48W
Renovo **8** 41 20N 77 45W
Rensselaer, *Ind.* **17** 40 57N 87 9W
Rensselaer, *N.Y.* **9** 42 38N 73 45W
Renton **20** 47 29N 122 12W
Rentz **12** 32 25N 82 59W
Repaupo **26** 39 48N 75 18W
Republic, *Mo.* **15** 37 7N 93 29W
Republic, *Wash.* **18** 48 39N 118 44W
Republican → **14** 39 4N 96 48W
Reseda **31** 34 12N 118 31W
Reserve **19** 33 43N 108 45W
Reservoir Pond **25** 42 10N 71 7W
Reston **27** 38 57N 77 20W
Revere **25** 42 25N 71 0W
Revillagigedo, Is. de **2** 18 40N 112 0W
Rex **32** 64 10N 149 20W
Rexburg **18** 43 49N 111 47W
Reyes, Pt. **20** 38 0N 123 0W
Reynolds, *Ga.* **12** 32 33N 84 6W
Reynolds, *Ill.* **16** 41 20N 90 40W
Reynolds Channel **23** 40 35N 73 41W
Reynoldsville, *Ga.* **12** 30 51N 84 47W
Reynoldsville, *Pa.* **8** 41 5N 78 58W
Rheem Valley **30** 37 50N 122 8W
Rhine **12** 31 59N 83 12W
Rhinebeck **9** 41 56N 73 55W
Rhinelander **14** 45 38N 89 25W
Rhode Island □ **9** 41 40N 71 30W
Rice **21** 34 5N 114 51W
Rice Lake **14** 45 30N 91 44W
Riceboro **12** 31 44N 81 26W
Richardson B. **30** 37 52N 122 29W
Richardson Lakes **10** 44 46N 70 58W
Richardson Springs **20** 39 51N 121 46W
Richey **14** 47 39N 105 4W
Richfield **19** 38 46N 112 5W
Richfield Springs **9** 42 51N 74 59W
Richford **9** 45 0N 72 40W
Richland, *Ga.* **12** 32 5N 84 40W
Richland, *Iowa* **16** 41 13N 92 0W
Richland, *Mo.* **16** 37 51N 92 26W
Richland, *Wash.* **18** 46 17N 119 18W
Richland Center **14** 43 21N 90 23W
Richlands **10** 37 6N 81 48W
Richmond, *Calif.* **30** 37 46N 122 27W
Richmond, *Calif.* **30** 37 56N 122 21W
Richmond, *Ind.* **17** 39 50N 84 53W
Richmond, *Ky.* **17** 37 45N 84 18W
Richmond, *Mich.* **8** 42 49N 82 45W
Richmond, *Mo.* **14** 39 17N 93 58W
Richmond, *Tex.* **15** 29 35N 95 46W
Richmond, *Utah* **18** 41 56N 111 48W
Richmond, *Va.* **10** 37 33N 77 27W
Richmond, *Vt.* **9** 44 24N 72 59W
Richmond, Pt. **30** 37 54N 122 23W
Richmond Heights **13** 25 38N 80 23W
Richmond Hill, *N.Y.* **23** 40 41N 73 51W
Richmond Hill, *Ga.* **12** 31 56N 81 18W
Richmond Inner Harbour **30** 37 54N 122 20W
Richmond Valley **22** 40 31N 74 13W
Richwood, *Ohio* **17** 40 26N 83 18W
Richwood, *W. Va.* **10** 38 14N 80 32W
Rickers I. **23** 40 47N 73 53W
Riddlesburg **8** 40 9N 78 15W
Riderwood **27** 39 24N 76 37W
Ridge Farm **17** 39 54N 87 39W
Ridge Spring **12** 33 51N 81 40W
Ridgecrest **21** 35 38N 117 40W
Ridgefield, *N.J.* **22** 40 49N 74 0W
Ridgefield, *Conn.* **9** 41 17N 73 30W
Ridgefield, *Wash.* **20** 45 49N 122 45W
Ridgefield Park **22** 40 52N 74 1W
Ridgeland **12** 32 29N 80 59W
Ridgeville, *Ind.* **17** 40 18N 85 2W
Ridgeville, *S.C.* **12** 33 6N 80 19W
Ridgewood, *N.Y.* **23** 40 42N 73 53W
Ridgewood, *N.J.* **9** 40 59N 74 7W
Ridgway, *Ill.* **17** 37 48N 88 16W
Ridgway, *Pa.* **8** 41 25N 78 44W
Ridley Creek State Park **26** 39 57N 75 26W
Ridley Park **26** 39 52N 75 19W
Riffe L. **20** 46 32N 122 26W
Rifle **18** 39 32N 107 47W
Rigby **18** 43 40N 111 55W
Riggins **18** 45 25N 116 19W
Riley **18** 43 32N 119 28W
Rimersburg **8** 41 3N 79 30W
Rimrock **20** 46 38N 121 10W
Rincon **12** 32 18N 81 14W
Ringwood **9** 41 7N 74 15W
Rio Grande = Grande, Rio → **2** 25 58N 97 9W
Rio Grande City **15** 26 23N 98 49W
Rio Rancho **19** 35 14N 106 38W
Rio Vista **20** 38 10N 121 42W
Ripley, *Calif.* **21** 33 32N 114 39W
Ripley, *N.Y.* **8** 42 16N 79 43W
Ripley, *Ohio* **17** 38 45N 83 51W
Ripley, *Tenn.* **15** 35 45N 89 32W
Ripley, *W. Va.* **10** 38 49N 81 43W
Ripon, *Calif.* **20** 37 44N 121 7W
Ripon, *Wis.* **10** 43 51N 88 50W
Rippling Ridge **27** 39 11N 76 37W
Rising Sun **17** 38 57N 84 51W
Rison **15** 33 58N 92 11W
Rita Blanca Cr. → **15** 35 40N 102 29W
Ritchie **27** 38 52N 76 51W
Ritter, Mt. **20** 37 41N 119 12W
Rittman **8** 40 58N 81 47W
Ritzville **18** 47 8N 118 23W
River Edge **22** 40 56N 74 1W
River Forest **24** 41 53N 87 49W
River Grove **24** 41 55N 87 50W
River Pines **25** 42 33N 71 17W
River Rouge **28** 42 16N 83 8W
River Vale **22** 40 59N 74 1W
Riverbank **20** 37 44N 120 56W
Riverdale, *Ill.* **24** 41 38N 87 37W
Riverdale, *N.J.* **22** 40 59N 74 17W
Riverdale, *Calif.* **20** 36 26N 119 52W
Riverdale, *Ga.* **12** 33 34N 84 25W
Riverdale, *Md.* **27** 38 57N 76 54W
Riverhead **9** 40 55N 72 40W
Riverside, *Mass.* **25** 42 32N 71 18W
Riverside, *Ill.* **24** 41 49N 87 49W
Riverside, *N.Y.* **23** 40 54N 73 54W
Riverside, *Conn.* **23** 41 1N 73 34W
Riverside, *N.J.* **26** 40 2N 74 57W
Riverside, *Calif.* **21** 33 59N 117 22W
Riverton, *N.J.* **26** 40 0N 75 0W
Riverton, *Ill.* **16** 39 51N 89 33W
Riverton, *Wyo.* **18** 43 2N 108 23W
Riverton Heights **20** 47 28N 122 17W
Riverview, *Mich.* **28** 42 10N 83 11W
Riverview, *Fla.* **13** 27 52N 82 20W
Riviera **21** 35 4N 114 35W
Riviera Beach **13** 26 47N 80 3W
Roachdale **17** 39 51N 86 48W
Roan Plateau **18** 39 20N 109 20W
Roanoke, *Ala.* **12** 33 9N 85 22W
Roanoke, *Ind.* **17** 40 58N 85 22W
Roanoke, *Va.* **10** 37 16N 79 56W
Roanoke → **11** 35 57N 76 42W
Roanoke I. **11** 35 55N 75 40W
Roanoke Rapids **11** 36 28N 77 40W
Robbins **24** 41 38N 87 42W
Robert E. Lee Memorial Park **27** 39 23N 76 40 E
Robert Lee **15** 31 54N 100 29W
Roberta **12** 32 43N 84 1W
Roberts **17** 40 37N 88 11W
Robertsdale, *Ind.* **24** 41 40N 87 30W
Robertsdale, *Pa.* **8** 40 11N 78 6W
Robesonia **9** 40 21N 76 8W
Robinson **17** 39 0N 87 44W
Robstown **15** 27 47N 97 40W
Rochelle, *Ga.* **12** 31 57N 83 27W
Rochelle, *Ill.* **16** 41 56N 89 4W
Rochelle Park **22** 40 54N 74 4W
Rochester, *Ind.* **17** 41 4N 86 13W
Rochester, *Minn.* **14** 44 1N 92 28W
Rochester, *N.H.* **9** 43 18N 70 59W
Rochester, *N.Y.* **8** 43 10N 77 37W
Rochester Hills **17** 42 41N 83 8W
Rock Creek **8** 41 40N 80 52W
Rock Creek Park **27** 38 56N 77 2W
Rock Falls **16** 41 47N 89 41W
Rock Hill **11** 34 56N 81 1W
Rock Island **16** 41 30N 90 34W
Rock Rapids **14** 43 26N 96 10W
Rock Springs, *Mont.* **18** 46 49N 106 15W
Rock Springs, *Wyo.* **18** 41 35N 109 14W
Rock Valley **14** 43 12N 96 18W
Rockaway **22** 40 53N 73 56W
Rockaway Beach **30** 37 36N 122 29W
Rockaway Islet **23** 40 34N 73 53W
Rockaway Neck **22** 40 51N 74 21W

Sharpsburg

Rockaway Point **23** 40 33N 73 54W
Rockdale, *Md.* **27** 39 21N 76 46W
Rockdale, *Tex.* **15** 30 39N 97 0W
Rockdale, *Wash.* **20** 47 22N 121 28W
Rockford, *Ala.* **12** 32 53N 86 13W
Rockford, *Ill.* **16** 42 16N 89 6W
Rockford, *Iowa* **16** 43 3N 92 57W
Rockford, *Mich.* **17** 43 7N 85 34W
Rockford, *Ohio* **17** 40 41N 84 39W
Rockingham **11** 34 57N 79 46W
Rocklake **14** 48 47N 99 15W
Rockland, *Del.* **26** 39 47N 75 34W
Rockland, *Idaho* **18** 42 34N 112 53W
Rockland, *Maine* **11** 44 6N 69 7W
Rockland, *Mich.* **14** 46 44N 89 11W
Rockledge **13** 28 20N 80 43W
Rocklege **26** 40 4N 75 5W
Rockleigh **22** 41 0N 73 55W
Rocklin **20** 38 48N 121 14W
Rockport, *Ind.* **17** 37 53N 87 3W
Rockport, *Mass.* **9** 42 39N 70 37W
Rockport, *Mo.* **14** 40 25N 95 31W
Rockport, *Tex.* **15** 28 2N 97 3W
Rocksprings **15** 30 1N 100 13W
Rockville, *Conn.* **9** 41 52N 72 28W
Rockville, *Ind.* **17** 39 46N 87 14W
Rockville, *Md.* **27** 39 4N 77 10W
Rockville Centre **23** 40 39N 73 38W
Rockwall **15** 32 56N 96 28W
Rockwell City **16** 42 24N 94 38W
Rockwood, *Maine* **11** 45 41N 69 45W
Rockwood, *Tenn.* **11** 35 52N 84 41W
Rocky Comfort Cr. → **12** 32 59N 82 25W
Rocky Ford, *Colo.* **14** 38 3N 103 43W
Rocky Ford, *Ga.* **12** 32 40N 81 50W
Rocky Fork Lake **17** 39 12N 83 23W
Rocky Hill **26** 39 58N 75 32W
Rocky Mount **11** 35 57N 77 48W
Rocky Mountain National Park **18** 40 25N 105 45W
Rocky Mts. **2** 49 0N 115 0W
Rocky Ridge **30** 37 47N 122 2W
Rocky River **29** 41 28N 81 50W
Rodeo Cove **30** 37 49N 122 32W
Rodgers Forge **27** 39 22N 76 37W
Roebling **9** 40 7N 74 47W
Rogers **15** 36 20N 94 7W
Rogers City **10** 45 25N 83 49W
Rogers Park **24** 42 0N 87 40W
Rogue → **18** 42 26N 124 26W
Rohnert Park **20** 38 16N 122 40W
Rojo, Cabo **32** 17 56N 67 12W
Roland Lake **27** 39 23N 76 38W
Roland Park **27** 39 20N 76 39W
Rolfe **16** 42 49N 94 31W
Rolla **16** 37 57N 91 46W
Rolling Fork → **17** 37 55N 85 50W
Roma **15** 26 25N 99 1W
Romain C. **11** 33 0N 79 22W
Romano C. **13** 25 51N 81 41W
Romanzof C. **32** 61 49N 166 6W
Rome, *Ga.* **11** 34 15N 85 10W
Rome, *N.Y.* **9** 43 13N 75 27W
Rome, *Pa.* **9** 41 51N 76 21W
Romney **10** 39 21N 78 45W
Romulus **28** 42 13N 83 23W
Ronan **18** 47 32N 114 6W
Roodhouse **16** 39 29N 90 24W
Roof Butte **19** 36 28N 109 5W
Roopville **12** 33 27N 85 8W
Roosevelt, *N.Y.* **23** 40 40N 73 35W
Roosevelt, *Utah* **18** 40 18N 109 59W
Rosalia **18** 47 14N 117 22W
Rosamond **21** 34 52N 118 10W
Roscoe, *Miss.* **16** 37 58N 93 48W
Roscoe, *N.Y.* **9** 41 56N 74 55W
Rose Hill **27** 38 47N 77 6W
Rose Tree **26** 39 56N 75 23W
Roseau **14** 48 51N 95 46W
Rosebank **22** 40 36N 74 4W
Rosebud, *S. Dak.* **14** 43 14N 100 51W
Rosebud, *Tex.* **15** 31 4N 96 59W
Roseburg **18** 43 13N 123 20W
Rosedale, *Md.* **27** 39 19N 76 31W
Rosedale, *N.Y.* **23** 40 39N 73 43W
Rosedale, *Miss.* **15** 33 51N 91 2W
Roseland, *Ill.* **24** 41 42N 87 37W
Roseland, *N.J.* **22** 40 49N 74 17W
Roseland, *Calif.* **20** 38 25N 122 43W
Roselle **22** 40 39N 74 15W
Roselle Park **22** 40 39N 74 16W
Rosemead **31** 34 4N 118 4W
Rosemont, *Ill.* **24** 41 59N 87 52W
Rosemont, *Pa.* **26** 40 1N 75 19W
Rosenberg **15** 29 34N 95 49W
Rosendale **16** 40 4N 94 51W
Roseville, *Mich.* **28** 42 30N 82 57W
Roseville, *Calif.* **20** 38 45N 121 17W
Roseville, *Ill.* **16** 40 44N 90 40W
Rosier **12** 32 59N 82 15W
Roslindale **25** 42 17N 71 7W
Roslyn, *N.Y.* **23** 40 47N 73 38W
Roslyn, *Pa.* **26** 40 7N 75 8W
Roslyn Estates **23** 40 47N 73 40W
Roslyn Harbour **23** 40 48N 73 38W
Ross **30** 37 57N 122 33W
Ross L. **18** 48 44N 121 4W
Rossford **17** 41 36N 83 34W
Rosslyn **27** 38 53N 77 4W
Rossville, *Md.* **27** 39 20N 76 28W
Rossville, *N.Y.* **22** 40 32N 74 12W
Rossville, *Ind.* **17** 40 25N 86 36W
Roswell, *Ga.* **12** 34 2N 84 22W
Roswell, *N. Mex.* **15** 33 24N 104 32W
Rotan **15** 32 51N 100 28W
Rotterdam **9** 42 48N 74 1W
Round Mountain **18** 38 43N 117 4W
Round Oak **12** 33 7N 83 37W
Round Rock **15** 30 31N 97 41W
Roundup **18** 46 27N 108 33W
Rouses Point **9** 44 59N 73 22W
Rouseville **8** 41 28N 79 42W
Rowesville **12** 33 22N 80 50W
Rowland **31** 34 0N 117 55W
Rowley **25** 42 43N 70 52W
Roxboro **11** 36 24N 78 59W
Roxborough **26** 40 1N 75 13W
Roxbury, *Mass.* **25** 42 19N 71 5W
Roxbury, *N.Y.* **23** 40 33N 73 53W
Roxbury, *Pa.* **8** 40 6N 77 39W
Roy, *Fla.* **13** 29 37N 81 29W
Roy, *Mont.* **18** 47 20N 108 58W
Roy, *N. Mex.* **15** 35 57N 104 12W
Roy, *Utah* **18** 41 10N 112 2W
Royal Center **17** 40 52N 86 30W
Royal Oak **28** 42 30N 83 9W
Rubicon → **20** 38 53N 121 4W
Rubio Woods **24** 41 38N 87 45W
Ruby **32** 64 45N 155 30W
Ruby L. **18** 40 10N 115 28W
Ruby Mts. **18** 40 30N 115 20W
Rudyard **10** 46 14N 84 36W
Rufflin **12** 33 0N 80 49W
Rugby **14** 48 22N 100 0W
Ruidoso **19** 33 20N 105 41W
Rumford **11** 44 33N 70 33W
Rumson **9** 40 23N 74 0W
Runnemede **26** 39 50N 75 4W
Rupert **18** 42 37N 113 41W
Rushmore, Mt. **14** 43 53N 103 28W
Rushville, *Ill.* **16** 40 7N 90 34W
Rushville, *Ind.* **17** 39 37N 85 27W
Rushville, *Nebr.* **14** 42 43N 102 28W
Ruskin **13** 27 43N 82 26W
Russell, *Fla.* **12** 30 3N 81 45W
Russell, *Kans.* **14** 38 54N 98 52W
Russell, *N.Y.* **9** 44 27N 75 9W
Russell, *Pa.* **8** 41 56N 79 8W
Russellville, *Ala.* **11** 34 30N 87 44W
Russellville, *Ark.* **15** 35 17N 93 8W
Russellville, *Ky.* **11** 36 51N 86 53W
Russian → **20** 38 27N 123 8W
Russian Mission **32** 61 47N 161 19W
Russiaville **17** 40 25N 86 16W
Ruston **15** 32 32N 92 38W
Ruth **8** 43 42N 82 45W
Rutherford, *N.J.* **22** 40 49N 74 6W
Rutherford, *Calif.* **20** 38 26N 122 24W
Rutland **9** 43 37N 72 58W
Rutledge **12** 33 38N 83 37W
Ruxton **27** 39 23N 76 38W
Ryderwood **20** 46 23N 123 3W
Rye **23** 40 58N 73 40W
Rye Patch Reservoir **18** 40 28N 118 19W
Ryegate **18** 46 18N 109 15W

S

Sabattis **9** 44 6N 74 40W
Sabina **17** 39 29N 83 38W
Sabinal **15** 29 19N 99 28W
Sabine → **15** 29 59N 93 47W
Sabine L. **15** 29 53N 93 51W
Sabine Pass **15** 29 44N 93 54W
Sabinsville **8** 41 52N 77 31W
Sable, C. **13** 25 9N 81 8W
Sabula **16** 42 4N 90 10W
Sac City **16** 42 25N 95 0W
Sackets Harbor **9** 43 57N 76 7W
Saco, *Maine* **11** 43 30N 70 27W
Saco, *Mont.* **18** 48 28N 107 21W
Sacramento **20** 38 35N 121 29W
Sacramento → **2** 38 3N 121 56W
Sacramento Mts. **19** 32 30N 105 30W
Sacramento Valley **20** 39 30N 122 0W
Saddle Brook **22** 40 53N 74 5W
Saddle Mt. **20** 45 58N 123 41W
Saddle River **22** 41 1N 74 6W
Saddle Rock **23** 40 47N 73 45W
Sadieville **17** 38 23N 84 32W
Saegertown **8** 41 43N 80 9W
Safford **19** 32 50N 109 43W
Sag Bridge **24** 41 41N 87 55W
Sag Harbor **9** 41 0N 72 18W
Sagamore **8** 40 46N 79 14W
Sagamore Neck **23** 40 53N 73 29W
Saganashkee Slough **24** 41 41N 87 53W
Saginaw **10** 43 26N 83 56W
Saginaw → **10** 43 39N 83 51W
Saginaw B. **10** 43 50N 83 40W
Saguache **19** 38 5N 106 8W
Saguaro Nat. Park **19** 32 12N 110 38W
Sahuarita **19** 31 57N 110 58W
St. Albans, *N.Y.* **23** 40 42N 73 44W
St. Albans, *Vt.* **9** 44 49N 73 5W
St. Albans, *W. Va.* **10** 38 23N 81 50W
St. Andrew Sd. **12** 31 0N 81 25W
St. Andrews **12** 32 47N 80 0W
St. Anne **17** 41 1N 87 43W
St. Anthony **18** 43 58N 111 41W
St. Augustine **12** 29 54N 81 19W
St. Augustine Beach **12** 29 51N 81 16W
St. Catherines I. **12** 31 40N 81 10W
St. Charles, *Ill.* **17** 41 54N 88 19W
St. Charles, *Mo.* **16** 38 47N 90 29W
St. Charles, *Va.* **10** 36 48N 83 4W
St. Clair, *Ga.* **12** 33 9N 82 13W
St. Clair, *Mich.* **8** 42 50N 82 30W
St. Clair, *Mo.* **16** 38 21N 90 59W
St. Clair, *Pa.* **9** 40 43N 76 12W
St. Clair → **8** 42 38N 82 31W
St. Clair, L. **8** 42 27N 82 39W
St. Clair Shores **28** 42 29N 82 54W
St. Clairsville **8** 40 5N 80 54W
St. Cloud, *Fla.* **11** 28 15N 81 17W
St. Cloud, *Minn.* **14** 45 34N 94 10W
St. Croix **32** 17 45N 64 45W
St. Croix → **14** 44 45N 92 48W
St. Croix Falls **14** 45 24N 92 38W
St. David **16** 40 30N 90 3W
St. Davids **26** 40 2N 75 23W
St. Elias, Mt. **32** 60 18N 140 56W
St. Elmo **17** 39 2N 88 51W
St. Francis **14** 39 47N 101 48W
St. Francis → **15** 34 38N 90 36W
St. Francisville, *Ill.* **17** 38 36N 87 39W
St. Francisville, *La.* **15** 30 47N 91 23W
St. George, *Ga.* **12** 30 31N 82 2W
St. George, *S.C.* **12** 33 11N 80 35W
St. George, *Utah* **19** 37 6N 113 35W
St. George, C. **13** 29 40N 85 5W
St. George I. **13** 29 35N 84 55W
St. Helena **18** 38 30N 122 28W
St. Helena, Mt. **20** 38 40N 122 36W
St. Helena Sd. **12** 32 15N 80 25W
St. Helens **20** 45 52N 122 48W
St. Helens, Mt. **20** 46 12N 122 12W
St. Ignace **10** 45 52N 84 44W
St. Ignatius **18** 47 19N 114 6W
St. James, *Minn.* **14** 43 59N 94 38W
St. James, *Mo.* **16** 38 0N 91 37W
St. James City **13** 26 29N 82 5W
St. Joe **17** 41 19N 84 54W
St. John **15** 38 0N 98 46W
St. John → **11** 45 12N 66 5W
St. John I. **32** 18 20N 64 42W
St. Johns, *Ariz.* **19** 34 30N 109 22W
St. Johns, *Mich.* **17** 43 0N 84 33W
St. Johns → **12** 30 24N 81 24W
St. Johnsbury **9** 44 25N 72 1W
St. Johnsville **9** 43 0N 74 43W
St. Joseph, *Ill.* **17** 40 7N 88 2W
St. Joseph, *La.* **15** 31 55N 91 14W
St. Joseph, *Mich.* **17** 42 6N 86 29W
St. Joseph, *Mo.* **16** 39 46N 94 50W
St. Joseph → **17** 42 7N 86 29W
St. Joseph Pt. **12** 29 52N 85 24W
St. Lawrence I. **32** 63 30N 170 30W
St. Louis **16** 38 37N 90 12W
St. Louis → **14** 47 15N 92 45W
St. Lucie **13** 27 29N 80 20W
St. Lucie Canal **13** 27 10N 80 18W
St. Maries **18** 47 19N 116 35W
St. Marks **12** 30 9N 84 12W
St. Marks → **12** 30 8N 84 12W
St. Marys, *Ga.* **12** 30 44N 81 33W
St. Marys, *Mo.* **16** 37 53N 89 57W
St. Marys, *Pa.* **8** 41 26N 78 34W
St. Marys → **12** 30 43N 81 27W
St. Matthews, *Ky.* **17** 38 15N 85 39W
St. Matthews, *S.C.* **12** 33 40N 80 46W
St. Meinrad **17** 38 10N 86 49W
St. Michael **32** 63 29N 162 2W
St. Paris **17** 40 8N 83 58W
St. Paul, *Ind.* **17** 39 26N 85 38W
St. Paul, *Minn.* **14** 44 57N 93 6W
St. Paul, *Nebr.* **14** 41 13N 98 27W
St. Peter **14** 44 20N 93 57W
St. Petersburg **11** 27 46N 82 39W
St. Petersburg Beach **13** 27 45N 82 45W
St. Regis **18** 47 18N 115 6W
St. Simons I. **12** 31 12N 81 15W
St. Simons Island **11** 31 9N 81 22W
St. Stephen **12** 33 24N 79 55W
St. Thomas I. **32** 18 20N 64 55W
Ste. Genevieve **16** 37 59N 90 2W
Saipan **33** 15 12N 145 45 E
Sakakawea, L. **14** 47 30N 101 25W
Salamanca **8** 42 10N 78 43W
Salamonie L. **17** 40 46N 85 37W
Sale City **12** 31 16N 84 1W
Salem, *Mass.* **25** 42 30N 70 54W
Salem, *Ala.* **12** 32 36N 85 14W
Salem, *Fla.* **12** 29 53N 83 25W
Salem, *Ill.* **16** 38 38N 88 57W
Salem, *Ind.* **17** 38 36N 86 6W
Salem, *Mo.* **15** 37 39N 91 32W
Salem, *N.H.* **9** 42 45N 71 12W
Salem, *N.J.* **10** 39 34N 75 28W
Salem, *N.Y.* **9** 43 10N 73 20W
Salem, *Ohio* **8** 40 54N 80 52W
Salem, *Oreg.* **18** 44 56N 123 2W
Salem, *S. Dak.* **14** 43 44N 97 23W
Salem, *Va.* **10** 37 18N 80 3W
Salem Harbor **25** 42 30N 70 52W
Salem Maritime Nat. Hist. Site **25** 42 31N 70 52W
Salida **6** 38 32N 106 0W
Salina, *Kans.* **14** 38 50N 97 37W
Salina, *Utah* **19** 38 58N 111 51W
Salinas **20** 36 40N 121 39W
Salinas → **20** 36 45N 121 48W
Saline →, *Ark.* **15** 33 10N 92 8W
Saline →, *Kans.* **14** 38 52N 97 30W
Salisbury, *Md.* **10** 38 22N 75 36W
Salisbury, *Mo.* **16** 39 25N 92 48W
Salisbury, *N.C.* **11** 35 40N 80 29W
Salkehatchie → **12** 32 37N 80 53W
Salley **12** 33 34N 81 18W
Sallisaw **15** 35 28N 94 47W
Salmon **18** 45 11N 113 54W
Salmon → **18** 45 51N 116 47W
Salmon River Mts. **18** 45 0N 114 30W
Salome **21** 33 47N 113 37W
Salt →, *Ariz.* **19** 33 23N 112 19W
Salt →, *Mo.* **16** 39 28N 91 4W
Salt Lake City **18** 40 45N 111 53W
Salt Springs **13** 29 21N 81 44W
Salters **12** 33 36N 79 51W
Salton City **21** 33 29N 115 51W
Salton Sea **21** 33 15N 115 45W
Saltsburg **8** 40 29N 79 27W
Saluda **12** 34 0N 81 46W
Saluda → **11** 34 1N 81 4W
Salvador, L. **15** 29 43N 90 15W
Salvisa **17** 37 54N 84 51W
Sam Rayburn Reservoir **15** 31 4N 94 5W
Samoset **13** 27 28N 82 33W
Samson **12** 31 7N 86 3W
San Andreas **20** 38 12N 120 41W
San Andreas Fault **30** 37 27N 122 18W
San Andreas L. **30** 37 35N 122 25W
San Andres Mts. **19** 33 0N 106 30W
San Angelo **15** 31 28N 100 26W
San Anselmo **20** 37 59N 122 34W
San Antonio, *N. Mex.* **19** 33 55N 106 52W
San Antonio, *Tex.* **15** 29 25N 98 30W
San Antonio → **15** 28 30N 96 54W
San Antonio, Mt. **21** 34 17N 117 38W
San Ardo **20** 36 1N 120 54W
San Augustine **15** 31 30N 94 7W
San Benito **15** 26 8N 97 38W
San Benito → **20** 36 53N 121 34W
San Benito Mt. **20** 36 22N 120 37W
San Bernardino **21** 34 7N 117 19W
San Bernardino Mts. **21** 34 10N 116 45W
San Blas, C. **12** 29 40N 85 21W
San Bruno **30** 37 36N 122 24W
San Bruno, Pt. **30** 37 39N 122 22W
San Bruno Mt. **30** 37 41N 122 26W
San Carlos, *Calif.* **30** 37 30N 122 16W
San Carlos, *Ariz.* **19** 33 21N 110 27W
San Carlos L. **19** 33 11N 110 32W
San Clemente **21** 33 26N 117 37W
San Clemente I. **21** 32 53N 118 29W
San Diego, *Calif.* **21** 32 43N 117 9W
San Diego, *Tex.* **15** 27 46N 98 14W
San Felipe → **21** 33 12N 115 49W
San Fernando **31** 34 17N 118 26W
San Fernando Airport **31** 34 17N 118 25W
San Fernando Valley **31** 34 12N 118 31W
San Francisco **20** 37 47N 122 25W
San Francisco → **19** 32 59N 109 22W
San Francisco, Univ. of **30** 37 47N 122 27W
San Francisco B. **30** 37 39N 122 14W
San Francisco Int. Airport **30** 37 37N 122 22W
San Francisco State Univ. **30** 37 43N 122 28W
San Gabriel **31** 34 5N 118 5W
San Gabriel Mts. **21** 34 20N 118 0W
San Gabriel Pk. **31** 34 14N 118 5W
San Germán **32** 18 5N 67 3W
San Gorgonio Mt. **21** 34 7N 116 51W
San Gregorio **20** 37 20N 122 23W
San Jacinto **21** 33 47N 116 57W
San Joaquin **20** 36 36N 120 11W
San Joaquin → **2** 38 4N 121 51W
San Joaquin Valley **20** 37 20N 121 0W
San Jon **15** 35 6N 103 20W
San Jose, *Calif.* **20** 37 20N 121 53W
San Jose, *Ill.* **16** 40 18N 89 36W
San Jose → **19** 34 25N 106 45W
San Juan, *Dom. Rep.* **32** 18 49N 71 12W
San Juan, *Puerto Rico* **32** 18 28N 66 7W
San Juan → **19** 37 16N 110 26W
San Juan, C. **32** 18 23N 65 37W
San Juan Bautista **20** 36 51N 121 32W
San Juan Capistrano **21** 33 30N 117 40W
San Juan Cr. → **20** 35 40N 120 22W
San Juan I. **20** 48 32N 123 5W
San Juan Mts. **19** 37 30N 107 0W
San Leandro **30** 37 43N 122 9W
San Leandro B. **30** 37 45N 122 13W
San Lorenzo **30** 37 41N 122 6W
San Lucas **20** 36 8N 121 1W
San Luis, *Ariz.* **19** 32 29N 114 47W
San Luis, *Colo.* **19** 37 12N 105 25W
San Luis Obispo **21** 35 17N 120 40W
San Luis Reservoir **20** 37 4N 121 5W
San Manuel **19** 32 36N 110 38W
San Marcos, *Calif.* **21** 33 9N 117 10W
San Marcos, *Tex.* **15** 29 53N 97 56W
San Marino **31** 34 7N 118 5W
San Mateo **30** 37 33N 122 19W
San Miguel **20** 35 45N 120 42W
San Miguel I. **21** 34 2N 120 23W
San Nicolas I. **21** 33 15N 119 30W
San Onofre **21** 33 22N 117 34W
San Pablo **30** 37 57N 122 20W
San Pablo, Pt. **30** 37 57N 122 25W
San Pablo Res. **30** 37 55N 122 14W
San Pablo Ridge **30** 37 55N 122 15W
San Pablo Str. **30** 37 58N 122 25W
San Pedro → **19** 32 59N 110 47W
San Pedro, Pt. **30** 37 35N 122 31W
San Pedro Channel **21** 33 30N 118 25W
San Quentin **30** 37 56N 122 27W
San Rafael, *Calif.* **30** 37 58N 122 30W
San Rafael, *N. Mex.* **19** 35 7N 107 53W
San Rafael B. **30** 37 57N 122 28W
San Rafael Hills **31** 34 10N 118 12W
San Rafael Mt. **21** 34 41N 119 52W
San Rafael Mts. **21** 34 40N 119 50W
San Saba **15** 31 12N 98 43W
San Simeon **20** 35 39N 121 11W
San Simon **19** 32 16N 109 14W
Sanak I. **32** 54 25N 162 40W
Sand Cr. → **17** 39 3N 85 51W
Sand Hills **14** 42 10N 101 30W
Sand Point **32** 55 20N 160 30W
Sand Springs **15** 36 9N 96 7W
Sanders, *Ariz.* **19** 35 13N 109 20W
Sanders, *Ky.* **17** 38 40N 84 56W
Sanderson, *Fla.* **12** 30 15N 82 16W
Sanderson, *Tex.* **15** 30 9N 102 24W
Sandersville **12** 32 59N 82 48W
Sandoval **16** 38 37N 89 7W
Sandpoint **18** 48 17N 116 33W
Sands Point **23** 40 50N 73 43W
Sandusky, *Mich.* **8** 43 25N 82 50W
Sandusky, *Ohio* **8** 41 27N 82 42W
Sandusky → **17** 41 27N 83 0W
Sandwich **17** 41 39N 88 37W
Sandy, *Oreg.* **20** 45 24N 122 16W
Sandy, *Pa.* **8** 41 6N 78 46W
Sandy, *Utah* **18** 40 35N 111 50W
Sandy Cr. → **18** 41 51N 109 47W
Sandy Pond **25** 42 26N 71 18W
Sandy Springs **12** 33 56N 84 23W
Sandy Valley **21** 35 49N 115 36W
Sanford, *Fla.* **11** 28 48N 81 16W
Sanford, *Maine* **11** 43 27N 70 47W
Sanford, *N.C.* **11** 35 29N 79 10W
Sangamon → **16** 40 7N 90 20W
Sanger **20** 36 42N 119 33W
Sangre de Cristo Mts. **19** 37 30N 105 20W
Sanibel **11** 26 26N 82 1W
Sanibel I. **13** 26 26N 82 6W
Santa Ana **21** 33 46N 117 52W
Santa Barbara **21** 34 25N 119 42W
Santa Barbara Channel **21** 34 15N 120 0W
Santa Barbara I. **21** 33 29N 119 2W
Santa Catalina, Gulf of **21** 33 10N 117 50W
Santa Catalina I. **21** 33 23N 118 25W
Santa Clara, *Calif.* **20** 37 21N 121 57W
Santa Clara, *Utah* **19** 37 8N 113 39W
Santa Clarita **21** 34 24N 118 30W
Santa Cruz **20** 36 58N 122 1W
Santa Cruz I. **21** 34 1N 119 43W
Santa Fe **19** 35 41N 105 57W
Santa Fe, L. **12** 29 45N 82 5W
Santa Fe Flood Control Basin **31** 34 7N 117 57W
Santa Fe Springs **31** 33 56N 118 3W
Santa Lucia Range **20** 36 0N 121 20W
Santa Margarita **20** 35 23N 120 37W
Santa Margarita → **21** 33 13N 117 23W
Santa Maria **21** 34 57N 120 26W
Santa Monica **31** 34 1N 118 29W
Santa Monica B. **31** 33 58N 118 30W
Santa Monica Mt. **31** 34 6N 118 29W
Santa Paula **21** 34 21N 119 4W
Santa Rita **19** 32 48N 108 4W
Santa Rosa, *Calif.* **20** 38 26N 122 43W
Santa Rosa, *N. Mex.* **15** 34 57N 104 41W
Santa Rosa Beach **12** 30 22N 86 14W
Santa Rosa I. **21** 33 58N 120 6W
Santa Rosa Range **18** 41 45N 117 40W
Santa Ynez → **21** 35 41N 120 36W
Santa Ynez Mts. **21** 34 30N 120 0W
Santa Ysabel **21** 33 7N 116 40W
Santaquin **18** 39 59N 111 47W
Santee **21** 32 50N 116 58W
Santee → **11** 33 7N 79 17W
Santo Domingo Pueblo **19** 35 31N 106 22W
Sapelo I. **12** 31 25N 81 12W
Sapelo Island **12** 31 23N 81 17W
Sapelo Sound **12** 31 30N 81 10W
Sappho **20** 48 4N 124 16W
Sapulpa **15** 35 59N 96 5W
Saranac **17** 42 56N 85 13W
Saranac L. **9** 44 20N 74 10W
Saranac Lake **9** 44 20N 74 8W
Saranap **30** 37 52N 122 4W
Sarasota **11** 27 20N 82 32W
Saratoga, *Calif.* **20** 37 16N 122 2W
Saratoga, *Wyo.* **18** 41 27N 106 49W
Saratoga Springs **9** 43 5N 73 47W
Sardinia **17** 39 0N 83 49W
Sardis **12** 32 58N 81 46W
Sargasso Sea **2** 27 0N 72 0W
Sargent **12** 33 26N 84 52W
Sarichef C. **32** 54 38N 164 59W
Sarita **15** 27 13N 97 47W
Sasser **12** 31 43N 84 21W
Satellite Beach **13** 28 10N 80 36W
Satilla → **12** 30 59N 81 29W
Saugatuck **17** 42 40N 86 12W
Saugerties **9** 42 5N 73 57W
Saugus, *Mass.* **25** 42 28N 71 0W
Saugus, *Calif.* **21** 34 25N 118 32W
Sauk Centre **14** 45 44N 94 57W
Sauk City **16** 43 17N 89 43W
Sauk Rapids **14** 45 35N 94 10W
Sault Ste. Marie **10** 46 30N 84 21W
Saunemin **17** 40 54N 88 24W
Sausalito **30** 37 51N 122 28W
Savage **14** 47 27N 104 21W
Savanna **16** 42 5N 90 8W
Savannah, *Ga.* **12** 32 5N 81 6W
Savannah, *Mo.* **16** 39 56N 94 50W
Savannah, *Tenn.* **11** 35 14N 88 15W
Savannah → **12** 32 2N 80 53W
Savannah Beach **12** 32 1N 80 51W
Savona **8** 42 17N 77 13W
Sawatch Range **19** 38 30N 106 30W
Sawtooth Range **18** 44 3N 114 58W
Sawyer Ridge **30** 37 34N 122 24W
Saxonville **25** 42 19N 71 24W
Saxton **8** 40 13N 78 15W
Saylorville L. **16** 41 48N 93 46W
Sayre, *Okla.* **15** 35 18N 99 38W
Sayre, *Pa.* **9** 41 59N 76 32W
Sayreville **9** 40 28N 74 22W
Scammon Bay **32** 61 51N 165 35W
Scappoose **20** 45 45N 122 53W
Scarsdale **23** 40 58N 73 47W
Schaghticoke **9** 42 54N 73 35W
Schaumburg **17** 42 2N 88 5W
Schell City **16** 38 1N 94 7W
Schell Creek Ra. **18** 39 15N 114 30W
Schellsburg **8** 40 3N 78 39W
Schenectady **9** 42 49N 73 57W
Schenevus **9** 42 33N 74 50W
Schiller Park **24** 41 56N 87 52W
Schiller Woods **24** 41 57N 87 51W
Schneider **17** 41 13N 87 28W
Schoharie **9** 42 40N 74 19W
Schoharie → **9** 42 57N 74 18W
Scholls **20** 45 24N 122 56W
Schoolcraft **17** 42 7N 85 38W
Schroon Lake **9** 43 50N 73 46W
Schurz **18** 38 57N 118 49W
Schuyler **14** 41 27N 97 4W
Schuylerville **9** 43 6N 73 35W
Schuylkill → **9** 39 53N 75 12W
Schuylkill Haven **9** 40 37N 76 11W
Scioto → **10** 38 44N 83 1W
Scituate **9** 42 12N 70 44W
Scobey **14** 48 47N 105 25W
Scotch Plains **22** 40 39N 74 22W
Scotia, *Calif.* **18** 40 29N 124 6W
Scotia, *N.Y.* **9** 42 50N 73 58W
Scotia, *S.C.* **12** 32 41N 81 15W
Scott City **14** 38 29N 100 54W
Scottdale **8** 40 6N 79 35W
Scottsbluff **14** 41 52N 103 40W
Scottsboro **11** 34 40N 86 2W
Scottsburg **17** 38 41N 85 47W
Scottsdale **19** 33 29N 111 56W
Scottsville, *Ky.* **11** 36 45N 86 11W
Scottsville, *N.Y.* **8** 43 2N 77 47W
Scottville **10** 43 58N 86 17W
Scranton, *Iowa* **16** 42 1N 94 33W
Scranton, *Pa.* **9** 41 25N 75 40W
Screven **12** 31 29N 82 1W
Sea Cliff **23** 40 50N 73 38W
Seabrook **27** 38 58N 76 49W
Seacliff **30** 37 47N 122 28W
Seaford **10** 38 39N 75 37W
Seagate **22** 40 34N 74 0W
Seagraves **15** 32 57N 102 34W
Seal Slough **30** 37 34N 122 17W
Seale **12** 32 18N 85 10W
Sealy **15** 29 47N 96 9W
Seaman **17** 38 57N 83 34W
Searchlight **21** 35 28N 114 55W
Searcy **15** 35 15N 91 44W
Searles L. **21** 35 44N 117 21W
Sears Tower **24** 41 52N 87 38W
Seaside, *Calif.* **20** 36 37N 121 50W
Seaside, *Oreg.* **20** 46 0N 123 56W
Seat Pleasant **27** 38 53N 76 53W
Seattle **20** 47 36N 122 20W
Seavey Hill **25** 42 42N 71 23W
Sebago L. **9** 43 52N 70 34W
Sebago Lake **9** 43 51N 70 34W
Sebastian **13** 27 49N 80 28W
Sebastopol **20** 38 24N 122 49W
Sebewaing **10** 43 44N 83 27W
Sebring, *Fla.* **11** 27 30N 81 27W
Sebring, *Ohio* **8** 40 55N 81 2W
Secaucus **22** 40 47N 74 3W
Security-Widefield **14** 38 45N 104 45W
Sedalia **16** 38 42N 93 14W
Sedan **15** 37 8N 96 11W
Sedgefield **22** 40 51N 74 26W
Sedona **19** 34 52N 111 46W
Sedro Woolley **20** 48 30N 122 14W
Segovia = Coco → **2** 15 0N 83 8W
Seguam I. **32** 52 19N 172 30W
Seguam Pass **32** 52 0N 172 30W
Seguin **15** 29 34N 97 58W
Segula I. **32** 52 0N 177 50 E
Seiling **15** 36 9N 98 56W
Selah **18** 46 39N 120 32W
Selawik **32** 66 36N 160 0W
Selby **14** 45 31N 100 2W
Selden **14** 39 33N 100 34W
Seldovia **32** 59 26N 151 43W
Seligman **19** 35 20N 112 53W
Selinsgrove **8** 40 48N 76 52W
Sells **19** 31 55N 111 53W
Selma, *Ala.* **11** 32 25N 87 1W
Selma, *Calif.* **20** 36 34N 119 37W
Selma, *N.C.* **11** 35 32N 78 17W
Selmer **11** 35 10N 88 36W
Seminoe Reservoir **18** 42 9N 106 55W
Seminole, *Fla.* **13** 27 50N 82 47W
Seminole, *Okla.* **15** 35 14N 96 41W
Seminole, *Tex.* **15** 32 43N 102 39W
Seminole, L. **12** 30 43N 84 52W
Seminole Draw → **15** 32 27N 102 20W
Semisopochnoi I. **32** 51 55N 179 36 E
Senatobia **15** 34 37N 89 58W
Seneca **11** 34 41N 82 57W
Seneca Falls **9** 42 55N 76 48W
Seneca L. **8** 42 40N 76 54W
Senecaville L. **8** 39 55N 81 25W
Senoia **12** 33 18N 84 33W
Sentinel **19** 32 52N 113 13W
Sepulveda **31** 34 13N 118 27W
Sepulveda Flood Control Basin **31** 34 10N 118 28W
Sequim **20** 48 5N 123 6W
Sequoia National Park **20** 36 30N 118 30W
Serramonte **30** 37 39N 122 28W
Sesser **16** 38 5N 89 1W
Settlement Pt. **11** 26 40N 79 0W
Seven Corners **27** 38 53N 77 9W
Sevier **19** 38 39N 112 11W
Sevier → **19** 39 4N 113 6W
Sevier Desert **18** 39 40N 112 45W
Sevier L. **18** 38 54N 113 9W
Seville, *Fla.* **13** 29 19N 81 30W
Seville, *Ga.* **12** 31 58N 83 36W
Seward, *Alaska* **32** 60 7N 149 27W
Seward, *Nebr.* **14** 40 55N 97 6W
Seward, *Pa.* **8** 40 25N 79 1W
Seward Peninsula **32** 65 30N 166 0W
Sewaren **22** 40 33N 74 15W
Sewell **26** 39 46N 75 8W
Sewickley **8** 40 32N 80 12W
Seymour, *Conn.* **9** 41 24N 73 4W
Seymour, *Ind.* **17** 38 58N 85 53W
Seymour, *Iowa* **16** 40 45N 93 7W
Seymour, *Tex.* **15** 33 35N 99 16W
Shabbona Woods **24** 41 36N 87 33W
Shady Dale **12** 33 24N 83 36W
Shady Grove **12** 30 17N 83 38W
Shady Oak **27** 39 1N 77 17W
Shadyside **8** 39 58N 80 45W
Shafer, L. **17** 40 46N 86 46W
Shafter **21** 35 30N 119 16W
Shaker Heights **29** 41 28N 81 33W
Shaktolik **32** 64 30N 161 15W
Shalimar **13** 30 27N 86 36W
Shamokin **9** 40 47N 76 34W
Shamrock **15** 35 13N 100 15W
Shandon **20** 35 39N 120 23W
Shannontown **12** 33 53N 80 21W
Sharon, *Mass.* **9** 42 7N 71 11W
Sharon, *Pa.* **8** 41 14N 80 31W
Sharon, *Wis.* **17** 42 30N 88 44W
Sharon Hill **26** 39 54N 75 16W
Sharon Springs, *Kans.* **14** 38 54N 101 45W
Sharon Springs, *N.Y.* **9** 42 48N 74 37W
Sharp Park **30** 37 38N 122 29W
Sharpes **13** 28 26N 80 46W
Sharpsburg **29** 40 29N 79 56W

Sharpsville

Sharpsville 8 41 15N 80 29W
Shasta, Mt. 2 41 25N 122 12W
Shasta L. 18 40 43N 122 25W
Shaver L. 20 37 9N 119 18W
Shawangunk Mts. 9 41 35N 74 30W
Shawano 10 44 47N 88 36W
Shawnee, Ga. 12 32 29N 81 25W
Shawnee, Kans. 16 39 1N 94 43W
Shawnee, Okla. 15 35 20N 96 55W
Shawsheen Village 25 42 40N 71 7W
Shea Stadium 23 40 45N 73 50W
Sheboygan 10 43 46N 87 45W
Sheepshead B. 22 40 35N 73 55W
Sheffield, Ala. 11 34 46N 87 41W
Sheffield, Ill. 16 41 21N 89 44W
Sheffield, Iowa 16 42 54N 93 13W
Sheffield, Mass. 9 42 5N 73 21W
Sheffield, Pa. 8 41 42N 79 3W
Shelbina 16 39 47N 92 2W
Shelburn 17 39 11N 87 24W
Shelburne 9 44 23N 73 14W
Shelburne Falls 9 42 36N 72 45W
Shelby, Mich. 10 43 37N 86 22W
Shelby, Miss. 15 33 57N 90 46W
Shelby, Mont. 18 48 30N 111 51W
Shelby, N.C. 11 35 17N 81 32W
Shelby, Ohio 8 40 53N 82 40W
Shelbyville, Ill. 17 39 24N 88 48W
Shelbyville, Ind. 17 39 31N 85 47W
Shelbyville, Ky. 17 38 13N 85 14W
Shelbyville, Mo. 16 39 48N 92 2W
Shelbyville, Tenn. 11 35 29N 86 28W
Shelbyville, L. 17 39 26N 88 46W
Sheldon, Iowa 14 43 11N 95 51W
Sheldon, Mo. 16 37 40N 94 18W
Sheldon, S.C. 12 32 36N 80 48W
Sheldon Point 32 62 32N 164 52W
Shelikof Strait 32 57 30N 155 0W
Shellman 12 31 46N 84 37W
Shellman Bluff 12 31 35N 81 19W
Shellsburg 16 42 6N 91 52W
Shelter Cove 30 37 35N 122 30W
Shelter I 9 41 5N 72 21W
Shelton, Conn. 9 41 19N 73 5W
Shelton, Wash. 20 47 13N 123 6W
Shenandoah, Iowa 14 40 46N 95 22W
Shenandoah, Pa. 9 40 49N 76 12W
Shenandoah, Va. 10 38 29N 78 37W
Shenandoah → 10 39 19N 77 44W
Shenandoah National Park 10 38 35N 78 22W
Shepherdsville 17 37 59N 85 43W
Sherborn 25 42 14N 71 22W
Sherburne 9 42 41N 75 30W
Sheridan, Ark. 15 34 19N 92 24W
Sheridan, Ill. 17 41 32N 88 41W
Sheridan, Ind. 17 40 8N 86 13W
Sheridan, Mo. 16 40 31N 94 37W
Sheridan, Wyo. 18 44 48N 106 58W
Sherman 15 33 40N 96 35W
Sherman Oaks 31 34 8N 118 29W
Sherwood 17 41 17N 84 33W
Sherwood Forest 30 37 57N 122 16W
Sheyenne → 14 47 2N 96 50W
Shickshinny 9 41 9N 76 9W
Shillington 9 40 18N 75 58W
Shiloh 12 32 49N 84 42W
Shinglehouse 8 41 58N 78 12W
Shingler 12 31 35N 83 47W
Shipley 27 39 12N 76 39W
Shippan Pt. 23 41 1N 73 31W
Shippensburg 8 40 3N 77 31W
Shippenville 8 41 15N 79 28W
Shiprock 19 36 47N 108 41W
Shirley 17 39 53N 85 35W
Shishmaref 32 66 15N 166 4W
Shively 17 38 12N 85 49W
Shoal Cr. → 16 39 44N 93 32W
Shoals 17 38 40N 86 47W
Short Hills 22 40 44N 74 21W
Shorter 12 32 24N 85 57W
Shorterville 12 31 34N 85 6W
Shoshone, Calif. 21 35 58N 116 16W
Shoshone, Idaho 18 42 56N 114 25W
Shoshone L. 18 44 22N 110 43W
Shoshone Mts. 18 39 20N 117 25W
Shoshoni 18 43 14N 108 7W
Show Low 19 34 15N 110 2W
Shreveport 15 32 31N 93 45W
Shullsburg 16 42 35N 90 13W
Shumagin Is. 32 55 7N 160 30W
Shungnak 32 66 52N 157 9W
Shuyak I. 32 58 31N 152 30W
Sibley, Ill. 17 40 35N 88 23W
Sibley, Iowa 14 43 24N 95 45W
Sidell 17 39 55N 87 49W
Sidney, Mont. 14 47 43N 104 9W
Sidney, N.Y. 9 42 19N 75 24W
Sidney, Nebr. 14 41 8N 102 59W
Sidney, Ohio 17 40 17N 84 9W
Sidney Lanier L. 12 34 10N 84 4W
Sierra Blanca 19 31 11N 105 22W
Sierra Blanca Peak 19 33 23N 105 49W
Sierra City 20 39 34N 120 38W
Sierra Madre 31 34 9N 118 3W
Sierra Nevada 20 37 30N 119 0W
Sierra Vista 19 31 33N 110 18W
Sierraville 20 39 36N 120 22W
Signal 21 34 30N 113 38W
Signal Pk. 21 33 20N 114 2W
Sigourney 16 41 20N 92 12W
Sigsbee 12 31 16N 83 52W
Sikeston 15 36 53N 89 35W
Siler City 11 35 44N 79 28W
Siloam 12 33 32N 83 5W
Siloam Springs 15 36 11N 94 32W
Silsbee 15 30 21N 94 11W
Silver City 19 32 46N 108 17W
Silver Cr. → 18 43 16N 119 13W
Silver Creek 8 42 33N 79 10W
Silver Grove 17 39 2N 84 24W
Silver Hill, Mass. 25 42 24N 71 18W
Silver Hill, Md. 27 38 49N 76 57W
Silver L., Mass. 25 42 33N 71 9W
Silver L., Calif. 20 38 39N 120 6W
Silver Lake, Calif. 21 35 21N 116 7W
Silver Lake, Ind. 17 41 4N 85 53W
Silver Lake, Oreg. 18 43 8N 121 3W
Silver Lake, Wis. 17 42 33N 88 13W
Silver Mt. 31 34 12N 117 55W
Silver Spring 27 38 59N 77 2W
Silver Springs 13 29 13N 82 3W
Silverton, Colo. 19 37 49N 107 40W
Silverton, Tex. 15 34 28N 101 19W
Silvies → 18 43 34N 119 2W
Simi Valley 21 34 16N 118 47W
Simmler 21 35 21N 119 59W
Simsbury 9 41 53N 72 48W
Sinclair 18 41 47N 107 7W
Sinclair, L. 12 33 8N 83 12W
Sinclairville 8 42 16N 79 16W
Singac 22 40 53N 74 14W
Sinton 15 28 2N 97 31W
Sioux City 14 42 30N 96 24W
Sioux Falls 14 43 33N 96 44W
Siren 14 45 47N 92 24W
Sirmans 12 30 21N 83 39W
Sirretta Pk. 21 35 56N 118 19W
Sisseton 14 45 40N 97 3W
Sisters 18 44 18N 121 33W
Sitka 32 57 3N 135 20W
Skagit → 20 48 23N 122 22W
Skagway 32 59 28N 135 19W
Skaneateles 9 42 57N 76 26W
Skaneateles L. 9 42 51N 76 22W
Skillet → 17 38 5N 88 5W
Skokie 24 42 2N 87 43W
Skokie Lagoons 24 42 7N 87 46W
Skowhegan 11 44 46N 69 43W
Skunk → 16 40 42N 91 7W
Skykomish 18 47 42N 121 22W
Slater 16 39 13N 93 4W
Slatington 9 40 45N 75 37W
Slaton 15 33 26N 101 39W
Sleepy Eye 14 44 18N 94 43W
Slide Mt. 9 42 0N 74 25W
Slidell 15 30 17N 89 47W
Sligo 8 41 6N 79 29W
Slippery Rock 8 41 3N 80 3W
Sloan 21 35 57N 115 13W
Sloansville 9 42 45N 74 22W
Slocomb 12 31 7N 85 36W
Slone Canyon Res. 31 34 6N 118 27W
Sloop Channel 23 40 36N 73 31W
Sloughhouse 20 38 26N 121 12W
Smalleytown 22 40 39N 74 28W
Smarr 12 32 59N 83 53W
Smartville 20 39 13N 121 18W
Smethport 8 41 49N 78 27W
Smith Center 14 39 47N 98 47W
Smith Forest Preserve 24 41 59N 87 45W
Smith Mills 22 41 0N 74 23W
Smithfield, N.C. 11 35 31N 78 21W
Smithfield, Utah 18 41 50N 111 50W
Smiths 12 32 32N 85 6W
Smithville, Ga. 12 31 54N 84 15W
Smithville, Mo. 16 39 23N 94 35W
Smithville, Tex. 15 30 1N 97 10W
Smoaks 12 33 5N 80 49W
Smoke Rise 22 41 0N 74 24W
Smoky Hill → 14 39 4N 96 48W
Smoky Hills 14 39 15N 99 30W
Smyrna, Del. 10 39 18N 75 36W
Smyrna, Ga. 12 33 53N 84 31W
Snake → 2 46 12N 119 2W
Snake Range 18 39 0N 114 20W
Snake River Plain 18 42 50N 114 0W
Snelling, Calif. 20 37 31N 120 26W
Snelling, S.C. 12 33 15N 81 27W
Snohomish 20 47 55N 122 6W
Snow Hill 10 38 11N 75 24W
Snow Mt., Calif. 20 39 23N 122 45W
Snow Mt., Maine 9 45 18N 70 48W
Snow Shoe 8 41 2N 77 57W
Snowdoun 12 32 15N 86 18W
Snowflake 19 34 30N 110 5W
Snowshoe Pk. 18 48 13N 115 41W
Snowville 18 41 58N 112 43W
Snowy Mt. 9 43 42N 74 23W
Snyder, Okla. 15 34 40N 98 57W
Snyder, Tex. 15 32 44N 100 55W
Socastee 11 33 41N 79 1W
Social Circle 12 33 39N 83 43W
Society Hill 12 34 31N 79 51W
Socorro, N. Mex. 19 34 4N 106 54W
Socorro, Tex. 19 31 39N 106 18W
Soda L. 19 35 10N 116 4W
Soda Springs 18 42 39N 111 36W
Soddy-Daisy 15 35 17N 85 10W
Sodus 8 43 14N 77 4W
Soledad 20 36 26N 121 20W
Solomon, N. Fork → 14 39 29N 98 26W
Solomon, S. Fork → 14 39 25N 99 12W
Solon Springs 14 46 22N 91 49W
Solvang 21 34 36N 120 8W
Solvay 9 43 3N 76 13W
Somerdale 23 39 50N 75 1W
Somers 18 48 5N 114 13W
Somerset, Ky. 10 37 5N 84 36W
Somerset, Mass. 9 41 47N 71 8W
Somerset, Pa. 8 40 1N 79 5W
Somerset, Md. 27 38 57N 77 5W
Somersworth 9 43 16N 70 52W
Somerton, Pa. 26 40 7N 75 1W
Somerton, Ariz. 19 32 36N 114 43W
Somerville, Mass. 25 42 22N 71 5W
Somerville, N.J. 9 40 35N 74 38W
Sonoma 20 38 18N 122 28W
Sonora, Calif. 20 37 59N 120 23W
Sonora, Tex. 15 30 34N 100 39W
Sonoran Desert 21 33 40N 114 15W
Sopchoppy 12 30 4N 84 29W
Soperton 12 32 23N 82 35W
Sorento 16 39 1N 89 35W
Souderton 9 40 19N 75 19W
Soundview 23 40 49N 73 53W
South Baldy 19 33 59N 107 11W
South Basin 30 37 42N 122 22W
South Bass I. 8 41 40N 82 49W
South Bay 13 26 40N 80 43W
South Beach 22 40 35N 74 4W
South Beloit 16 42 29N 89 2W
South Bend, Ind. 17 41 41N 86 15W
South Bend, Wash. 20 46 40N 123 48W
South Boston, Mass. 25 42 20N 71 2W
South Boston, Va. 11 36 42N 78 54W
South Braintree 25 42 11N 70 59W
South Brooklyn 22 40 41N 73 59W
South C. = Ka Lae 32 18 55N 155 41W
South Cape 32 18 58N 155 24 E
South Carolina □ 11 34 0N 81 0W
South Charleston 10 38 22N 81 44W
South Chelmsford 25 42 34N 71 22W
South Chicago 24 41 44N 87 32W
South Congaree 12 33 53N 81 9W
South Dakota □ 14 44 15N 100 0W
South Daytona 13 29 10N 81 0W
South Deerfield 9 42 29N 72 37W
South Deering 24 41 42N 87 33W
South Euclid 29 41 31N 81 32W
South Floral Park 23 40 42N 73 41W
South Fork American → 20 38 45N 121 5W
South Fork Edisto → 12 33 16N 80 54W
South Fork Feather → 20 39 17N 121 36W
South Fork Grand → 14 45 43N 102 17W
South Fork Republican → 14 40 3N 101 31W
South Gate 31 33 56N 118 12W
South Grand → 16 38 17N 93 25W
South Hackensack 22 40 51N 74 2W
South Hadley 9 42 16N 72 35W
South Hamilton 25 42 36N 70 52W
South Haven 17 42 24N 86 16W
South Hempstead 23 40 40N 73 37W
South Hingham 25 42 12N 70 53W
South Holland 24 41 36N 87 35W
South Huntington 23 40 49N 73 23W
South Lake Tahoe 20 38 57N 119 59W
South Lawn 27 38 47N 77 0W
South Lawrence 25 42 41N 71 9W
South Lincoln 25 42 24N 71 19W
South Loup → 14 41 4N 98 39W
South Lynnfield 25 42 30N 70 59W
South Lyon 17 42 28N 83 39W
South Miami 13 25 42N 80 18W
South Milwaukee 17 42 55N 87 52W
South Newport 12 31 38N 81 24W
South of Market 30 37 46N 122 24W
South Orange 22 40 45N 74 14W
South Oyster B. 23 40 38N 73 27W
South Ozone Park 23 40 41N 73 49W
South Paris 9 44 14N 70 31W
South Pasadena 31 34 7N 118 8W
South Peabody 25 42 30N 70 57W
South Pekin 16 40 30N 89 39W
South Pittsburg 11 35 1N 85 42W
South Plainfield 22 40 35N 74 24W
South Platte → 14 41 7N 100 42W
South Ponte Vedra Beach 12 30 3N 81 20W
South Portland 11 43 38N 70 15W
South Pt. 8 44 52N 83 19W
South Quincy 25 42 13N 71 0W
South Res. 25 42 26N 71 6W
South River 9 40 27N 74 23W
South San Francisco 30 37 38N 122 26W
South San Gabriel 31 34 3N 118 6W
South Shore 24 41 45N 87 34W
South Sioux City 14 42 28N 96 24W
South Sudbury 25 42 21N 71 24W
South Valley Stream 23 40 38N 73 43W
South Venice 13 27 3N 82 25W
South Wayne 16 42 34N 89 53W
South Westbury 23 40 44N 73 34W
South Weymouth 25 42 10N 70 56W
South Whitley 17 41 5N 85 38W
South Williamsport 8 41 13N 77 0W
Southampton 9 40 53N 72 23W
Southaven 15 34 59N 90 2W
Southbridge 9 42 5N 72 2W
Southeast C. 32 62 56N 169 39W
Southern Pines 11 35 11N 79 24W
Southfield 28 42 28N 83 15W
Southgate 28 42 11N 83 12W
Southington 9 41 36N 72 53W
Southold 9 41 4N 72 26W
Southport, Fla. 11 30 17N 85 38W
Southport, N.Y. 8 42 3N 76 49W
Spangler 8 40 39N 78 48W
Spanish Fork 18 40 7N 111 39W
Sparkill 22 41 1N 73 55W
Sparks, Ga. 12 31 11N 83 26W
Sparks, Nev. 20 39 32N 119 45W
Sparr 13 29 20N 82 7W
Sparrows Point 27 39 13N 76 29W
Sparta, Ga. 12 33 17N 82 58W
Sparta, Ill. 16 38 8N 89 42W
Sparta, Mich. 17 43 10N 85 42W
Sparta, N.J. 9 41 2N 74 38W
Sparta, Wis. 14 43 56N 90 49W
Spartanburg 11 34 56N 81 57W
Spartansburg 8 41 49N 79 41W
Spearfish 14 44 30N 103 52W
Spearman 15 36 12N 101 12W
Spectacle I. 25 42 19N 70 59W
Speculator 9 43 30N 74 25W
Speedway 17 39 47N 86 15W
Spenard 32 61 11N 149 55W
Spencer, Idaho 18 44 22N 112 11W
Spencer, Ind. 17 39 17N 86 46W
Spencer, Iowa 14 43 9N 95 9W
Spencer, N.Y. 9 42 13N 76 30W
Spencer, Nebr. 14 42 53N 98 42W
Spencerville 17 40 43N 84 21W
Spickard 16 40 14N 93 36W
Spirit Lake 20 46 15N 122 9W
Splitrock Res. 22 40 58N 74 26W
Spofford 15 29 10N 100 25W
Spokane 18 47 40N 117 24W
Spoon → 16 40 19N 90 4W
Spooner 14 45 50N 91 53W
Spot Pond 25 42 26N 71 4W
Sprague 18 47 18N 117 59W
Spray 18 44 50N 119 48W
Spring City 9 40 11N 75 33W
Spring Cr. → 12 30 54N 84 45W
Spring Creek 18 40 45N 115 38W
Spring Garden 20 39 52N 120 47W
Spring Green 16 43 11N 90 4W
Spring Hill, Ala. 12 31 42N 85 58W
Spring Hill, Fla. 13 28 27N 82 41W
Spring Mts. 19 36 0N 115 45W
Spring Pond 25 42 29N 70 56W
Spring Valley, Calif. 21 32 45N 117 5W
Spring Valley, Ill. 16 41 20N 89 12W
Springboro 8 41 48N 80 22W
Springdale 15 36 11N 94 8W
Springer 15 36 22N 104 36W
Springerville 19 34 8N 109 17W
Springfield, N.J. 22 40 42N 74 18W
Springfield, Pa. 26 39 56N 75 19W
Springfield, Colo. 15 37 24N 102 37W
Springfield, Fla. 12 30 10N 85 37W
Springfield, Ga. 12 32 22N 81 18W
Springfield, Ill. 16 39 48N 89 39W
Springfield, Ky. 17 37 41N 85 13W
Springfield, Mass. 9 42 6N 72 35W
Springfield, Mo. 15 37 13N 93 17W
Springfield, Ohio 17 39 55N 83 49W
Springfield, Oreg. 18 44 3N 123 1W
Springfield, S.C. 12 33 30N 81 17W
Springfield, Tenn. 11 36 31N 86 53W
Springfield, Vt. 9 43 18N 72 29W
Springfield, Va. 27 38 46N 77 10W
Springfield, L. 16 39 46N 89 36W
Springhill 15 33 0N 93 28W
Springvale, Ga. 12 31 50N 84 53W
Springvale, Maine 9 43 28N 70 48W
Springville, Calif. 20 36 8N 118 49W
Springville, N.Y. 8 42 31N 78 40W
Springville, Utah 18 40 10N 111 37W
Springwater 8 42 38N 77 35W
Spruce-Creek 8 40 36N 78 9W
Spruce Mt. 9 44 12N 72 19W
Spur 15 33 28N 100 52W
Spurgeon 17 38 14N 87 15W
Squam L. 9 43 45N 71 32W
Squantum 25 42 17N 71 0W
Stafford 15 37 58N 98 36W
Stafford, L. 13 29 20N 82 29W
Stafford Springs 9 41 57N 72 18W
Stamford, Conn. 9 41 3N 73 32W
Stamford, N.Y. 9 42 25N 74 38W
Stamford, Tex. 15 32 57N 99 48W
Stamford Harbor 23 41 0N 73 34W
Stamping Ground 17 38 16N 84 41W
Stamps 15 33 22N 93 30W
Standish 10 43 59N 83 57W
Stanford 18 47 9N 110 13W
Stanford Univ. 30 37 26N 122 10W
Stanhope 16 42 17N 93 48W
Stanislaus → 20 37 40N 121 14W
Stanley, Idaho 18 44 13N 114 56W
Stanley, N. Dak. 14 48 19N 102 23W
Stanley, N.Y. 8 42 48N 77 6W
Stanton 15 32 8N 101 48W
Stanwood 20 48 15N 122 23W
Staples 14 46 21N 94 48W
Stapleton 22 40 36N 74 5W
Star Lake 9 44 10N 75 2W
Starke 12 29 57N 82 7W
Stars Mill 12 33 19N 84 31W
State Center 16 42 1N 93 10W
State College 8 40 48N 77 52W
Stateline 20 38 57N 119 56W
Staten 22 40 34N 74 7W
Staten I. 9 40 35N 74 9W
Staten Island Zoo 22 40 38N 74 6W
Statenville 12 30 42N 83 2W
Statesboro 12 32 27N 81 47W
Statesville 11 35 47N 80 53W
Statham 12 33 58N 83 35W
Stauffer 21 34 45N 119 3W
Staunton, Ill. 16 39 1N 89 47W
Staunton, Va. 10 38 9N 79 4W
Stayton 18 44 48N 122 48W
Steamboat Springs 18 40 29N 106 50W
Steele, Ala. 12 33 56N 86 12W
Steele, N. Dak. 14 46 51N 99 55W
Steelton 8 40 14N 76 50W
Steelville 16 37 58N 91 22W
Steens Mt. 18 42 35N 118 40W
Steilacoom 20 47 10N 122 36W
Steinberger Slough 30 37 32N 122 13W
Steinhatchee 12 29 40N 83 23W
Stephenville 15 32 13N 98 12W
Sterling, Colo. 14 40 37N 103 13W
Sterling, Ga. 12 31 16N 81 34W
Sterling, Ill. 16 41 48N 89 42W
Sterling, Kans. 14 38 13N 98 12W
Sterling City 15 31 51N 101 0W
Sterling Heights 28 42 35N 83 3W
Sterling Park 30 37 41N 122 27W
Sterling Run 8 41 25N 78 12W
Steubenville 8 40 22N 80 37W
Stevens Point 14 44 31N 89 34W
Stevens Pottery 12 32 57N 83 17W
Stevens Village 32 66 1N 149 6W
Stevenson, Md. 27 39 24N 76 42W
Stevenson, Wash. 20 45 42N 121 53W
Stevensville 18 46 30N 114 5W
Steward 16 41 51N 89 1W
Stewardson 17 39 16N 88 38W
Stewart, Ga. 12 33 25N 83 52W
Stewart, Nev. 20 39 5N 119 46W
Stewart Manor 23 40 43N 73 40W
Stewarts Point 20 38 39N 123 24W
Stewartsville 16 39 45N 94 30W
Stewartville 14 43 51N 92 29W
Stickney 24 41 49N 87 46W
Stigler 15 35 15N 95 8W
Stillmore 12 32 27N 82 13W
Stillwater, Minn. 14 45 3N 92 49W
Stillwater, N.Y. 9 42 55N 73 41W
Stillwater, Okla. 15 36 7N 97 4W
Stillwater Range 18 39 50N 118 5W
Stillwater Reservoir 9 43 54N 75 3W
Stillwell 12 32 23N 81 15W
Stilwell 15 35 49N 94 38W
Stock Island 13 24 32N 81 34W
Stockbridge, Ga. 12 33 33N 84 14W
Stockbridge, Mich. 17 42 27N 84 11W
Stockton, Calif. 20 37 58N 121 17W
Stockton, Ill. 16 42 21N 90 1W
Stockton, Kans. 14 39 26N 99 16W
Stockton, Mo. 16 37 42N 93 48W
Stockton Plateau 15 30 30N 102 30W
Stone Mountain 12 33 49N 84 10W
Stone Park 24 41 53N 87 52W
Stoneboro 8 41 20N 80 7W
Stoneham 25 42 29N 71 5W
Stonehurst 31 34 15N 118 21W
Stonington 16 39 44N 89 12W
Stony Brook Res. 25 42 15N 71 8W
Stony Point 9 41 14N 73 59W
Stony Pt. 9 43 50N 76 18W
Stony River 32 61 47N 156 35W
Stonyford 20 39 23N 122 33W
Storm Lake 14 42 39N 95 13W
Storrs 9 41 49N 72 15W
Story City 16 42 11N 93 36W
Stoughton 16 42 55N 89 13W
Stovall 12 32 58N 84 51W
Stove Pipe Wells Village 21 36 35N 117 11W
Stow 8 41 10N 81 27W
Stow L. 30 37 46N 122 28W
Stratford, N.J. 26 39 49N 75 0W
Stratford, Calif. 20 36 11N 119 49W
Stratford, Conn. 9 41 12N 73 8W
Stratford, Tex. 15 36 20N 102 4W
Strathmore 20 36 9N 119 4W
Strattanville 8 41 12N 79 19W
Stratton 9 45 8N 70 26W
Stratton Mt. 9 43 4N 72 55W
Strawberry → 18 40 10N 110 24W
Strawberry Hill 25 42 14N 71 15W
Strawberry Pk. 31 34 16N 118 7W
Strawberry Point 16 42 41N 91 32W
Strawberry Pt. 30 37 53N 122 30W
Streator 17 41 8N 88 50W
Streetsboro 8 41 14N 81 21W
Stromsburg 14 41 7N 97 36W
Stronghurst 16 40 45N 90 55W
Strongsville 8 41 19N 81 50W
Stroudsburg 9 40 59N 75 12W
Struthers 8 41 4N 80 39W
Stryker 18 48 41N 114 46W
Stuart, Fla. 11 27 12N 80 15W
Stuart, Iowa 16 41 30N 94 19W
Stuart, Nebr. 14 42 36N 99 8W
Stuart I. 32 63 55N 164 50W
Studio City 31 34 8N 118 24W
Sturgeon Bay 10 44 50N 87 23W
Sturgis, Mich. 17 41 48N 85 25W
Sturgis, S. Dak. 14 44 25N 103 31W
Stuttgart 15 34 30N 91 33W
Stuyvesant 9 42 23N 73 45W
Success, L. 23 40 45N 73 42W
Sudan 15 34 4N 102 32W
Sudbury 25 42 22N 71 24W
Suffolk 10 36 44N 76 35W
Sugar →, Ill. 16 42 26N 89 12W
Sugar →, Ind. 17 39 50N 87 23W
Sugar Cr. → 16 40 9N 89 38W
Sugar Hill 12 34 6N 84 2W
Sugargrove 8 41 59N 79 21W
Sugartown 26 39 59N 75 30W
Suisun City 20 38 15N 122 2W
Suitland 27 38 50N 76 55W
Sullivan, Ill. 17 39 36N 88 37W
Sullivan, Ind. 17 39 6N 87 24W
Sullivan, Mo. 16 38 13N 91 10W
Sully 16 41 34N 92 50W
Sulphur, La. 15 30 14N 93 23W
Sulphur, Okla. 15 34 31N 96 58W
Sulphur Springs 15 33 8N 95 36W
Sultan 20 47 52N 121 49W
Sumatra 12 30 1N 84 59W
Summer L. 18 42 50N 120 45W
Summerland Key 13 24 40N 81 27W
Summersville 10 38 17N 80 51W
Summerton 12 33 36N 80 20W
Summertown 12 32 45N 82 16W
Summerville, Ga. 11 34 29N 85 21W
Summerville, S.C. 12 33 1N 80 11W
Summit, Ill. 24 41 47N 87 47W
Summit, N.J. 22 40 43N 74 22W
Summit, Alaska 32 63 20N 149 7W
Summit Peak 19 37 21N 106 42W
Sumner, Ill. 17 38 42N 87 53W
Sumner, Iowa 16 42 51N 92 6W
Sumner, Wash. 20 47 12N 122 14W
Sumter 12 33 55N 80 21W
Sun City, Ariz. 19 33 36N 112 17W
Sun City, Calif. 21 33 42N 117 11W
Sun City Center 13 27 43N 82 18W
Sun Lakes 19 33 10N 111 52W
Sun Prairie 16 43 11N 89 13W
Sun Valley, Calif. 31 34 13N 118 21W
Sun Valley, Idaho 18 43 42N 114 21W
Sunburst 18 48 53N 111 55W
Sunbury 9 40 52N 76 48W
Suncook 9 43 8N 71 27W
Sundance 14 44 24N 104 23W
Sunland 31 34 15N 118 18W
Sunland Park 19 31 50N 106 40W
Sunnyside 18 46 20N 120 0W
Sunnyvale 20 37 23N 122 2W
Sunset 30 37 44N 122 29W
Sunshine Acres 31 33 56N 117 59W
Suntaug L. 25 42 31N 71 0W
Supai 19 36 15N 112 41W
Superior, Ariz. 19 33 18N 111 6W
Superior, Mont. 18 47 12N 114 53W
Superior, Nebr. 14 40 1N 98 4W
Superior, Wis. 14 46 44N 92 6W
Superior, L. 2 47 0N 87 0W
Sur, Pt. 20 36 18N 121 54W
Surf 21 34 41N 120 36W
Surfside 13 25 53N 80 8W
Surrency 12 31 44N 82 12W
Susanville 18 40 25N 120 39W
Susquehanna 9 41 57N 75 36W
Susquehanna → 9 39 33N 76 5W
Sussex 9 41 13N 74 37W
Sutherland 14 41 10N 101 8W
Sutherlin 18 43 23N 123 19W
Sutter 20 39 10N 121 45W
Sutter Creek 20 38 24N 120 48W
Sutton, Nebr. 14 40 36N 97 52W
Sutton, W. Va. 10 38 40N 80 43W
Sutwik I. 32 56 34N 157 12W
Suwanee 12 34 3N 84 4W
Suwannee 13 29 20N 83 9W
Suwannee → 11 29 17N 83 10W
Suwannee Sd. 13 29 20N 83 15W
Swainsboro 12 32 36N 82 20W
Swampscott 25 42 28N 70 53W
Swan Peak 18 47 43N 113 38W
Swan Ra. 18 48 0N 113 45W
Swansea 12 33 44N 81 6W
Swarthmore 26 39 54N 75 22W
Swedesboro 26 39 45N 75 17W
Swedesburg 26 40 5N 75 19W
Sweet Home 18 44 24N 122 44W
Sweet Springs 16 38 58N 93 25W
Sweetgrass 18 48 59N 111 58W
Sweetwater, Nev. 20 38 27N 119 9W
Sweetwater, Tenn. 11 35 36N 84 28W
Sweetwater, Tex. 15 32 28N 100 25W
Sweetwater → 18 42 31N 107 2W
Swinburne I. 22 40 33N 74 3W
Swissvale 29 40 25N 79 52W
Swords 12 33 33N 83 18W
Swoyerville 9 41 18N 75 53W
Sycamore, Ga. 12 31 40N 83 38W
Sycamore, S.C. 12 33 2N 81 13W
Sycamore Mills 26 39 57N 75 25W
Sykesville 8 41 3N 78 50W
Sylacauga 12 33 10N 86 15W
Sylvan Beach 9 43 12N 75 44W
Sylvania, Ga. 12 32 45N 81 38W
Sylvania, Ohio 17 41 43N 83 42W
Sylvester 12 31 32N 83 50W
Syosset 23 40 49N 73 30W
Syracuse, Ind. 17 41 26N 85 45W
Syracuse, Kans. 15 37 59N 101 45W
Syracuse, N.Y. 9 43 3N 76 9W
Syracuse, Nebr. 14 40 39N 96 11W

T

Taberg 9 43 18N 75 37W
Table Grove 16 40 20N 90 27W
Table Rock L. 15 36 36N 93 19W
Tabor 22 40 52N 74 28W
Tacoma 20 47 14N 122 26W
Tacony 26 40 1N 75 2W
Taft, Calif. 21 35 8N 119 28W
Taft, Fla. 13 28 26N 81 22W
Tahlequah 15 35 55N 94 58W
Tahoe, L. 20 39 6N 120 2W
Tahoe City 20 39 10N 120 9W
Tahoka 15 33 10N 101 48W
Taholah 20 47 21N 124 17W
Takoma Park 27 38 58N 77 0W
Talbotton 12 32 41N 84 32W
Talihina 15 34 45N 95 3W
Talkeetna 32 62 20N 150 6W
Talkeetna Mts. 32 62 20N 149 0W
Talladega 12 33 26N 86 6W
Tallahassee 12 30 27N 84 17W
Tallapoosa 12 33 45N 85 17W
Tallapoosa → 12 32 30N 86 16W
Tallassee 12 32 32N 85 54W
Talleyville 26 39 48N 75 32W
Tallmadge 8 41 6N 81 27W
Tallulah 15 32 25N 91 11W
Talmapais Valley 30 37 52N 122 32W
Talquin, L. 12 30 23N 84 39W
Tama 16 41 58N 92 35W
Tamaqua 9 40 48N 75 58W
Tamarac 13 26 12N 80 10W
Tamaroa 16 38 8N 89 14W
Tamiami Canal 13 25 50N 81 0W
Tampa 11 27 57N 82 27W
Tampa B. 11 27 50N 82 30W
Tampico 16 41 38N 89 47W
Tampier Slough 24 41 39N 87 54W
Tanana 32 65 10N 152 4W
Tanana → 32 65 10N 151 58W
Tanforan Park 30 37 37N 122 24W
Tannersville 9 41 3N 75 18W
Taos 19 36 24N 105 35W
Tappan 22 41 1N 73 57W
Tappan, L. 22 41 1N 73 59W
Tarboro, Ga. 12 31 1N 81 48W
Tarboro, N.C. 11 35 54N 77 32W
Target Rock 23 40 55N 73 26W
Tarpon Springs 11 28 9N 82 45W
Tarrytown, Ga. 12 32 19N 82 34W
Tarrytown, N.Y. 9 41 4N 73 52W
Tarzana 31 34 10N 118 32W
Tatum 15 33 16N 103 19W
Tatum Cr. → 12 30 43N 82 32W
Tau 33 14 15S 169 30W
Taunton 9 41 54N 71 6W
Tavares 13 28 48N 81 44W
Tavernier 13 25 1N 80 31W
Tawas City 10 44 16N 83 31W
Taylor, Mich. 28 42 13N 83 15W
Taylor, Alaska 32 65 40N 164 50W
Taylor, Fla. 12 30 26N 82 18W
Taylor, Nebr. 14 41 46N 99 23W
Taylor, Pa. 9 41 23N 75 43W
Taylor, Tex. 15 30 34N 97 25W

Watertown

Taylor, Mt. **19** 35 14N 107 37W
Taylorsville **17** 38 2N 85 21W
Taylortown **22** 40 56N 74 23W
Taylorville **16** 39 33N 89 18W
Teague **15** 31 38N 96 17W
Teaneck **22** 40 52N 74 1W
Techny **24** 42 6N 87 48W
Tecopa **21** 35 51N 116 13W
Tecumseh, *Mich.* **17** 42 0N 83 57W
Tecumseh, *Okla.* **15** 35 15N 96 56W
Tehachapi **21** 35 8N 118 27W
Tehachapi Mts. **21** 35 0N 118 30W
Tejon Pass **21** 34 49N 118 53W
Tekamah **14** 41 47N 96 13W
Tekoa **18** 47 14N 117 4W
Telescope Pk. **21** 36 10N 117 5W
Tell City **17** 37 57N 86 46W
Teller **32** 65 16N 166 22W
Telluride **19** 37 56N 107 49W
Telogia **12** 30 21N 84 49W
Temblor Range **21** 35 20N 119 50W
Temecula **21** 33 30N 117 9W
Temescal, L. **30** 37 50N 122 13W
Tempe **19** 33 25N 111 56W
Tempiute **20** 37 39N 115 38W
Temple **15** 31 6N 97 21W
Temple City **31** 34 6N 118 3W
Temple Hills Park **27** 38 48N 76 56W
Temple Terrace **13** 28 2N 82 23W
Templeton **20** 35 33N 120 42W
Ten Thousand Is. **13** 25 55N 81 45W
Tenafly **22** 40 54N 73 58W
Tenaha **15** 31 57N 94 15W
Tenino **20** 46 51N 122 51W
Tennessee □ **11** 36 0N 86 30W
Tennessee → **2** 37 4N 88 34W
Tennille **12** 32 56N 82 48W
Tennyson **17** 38 5N 87 7W
Terra Bella **21** 35 58N 119 3W
Terre Haute **17** 39 28N 87 25W
Terrebonne B. **15** 29 5N 90 35W
Terrell **15** 32 44N 96 17W
Terry **14** 46 47N 105 19W
Terryville **9** 41 41N 73 3W
Tetlin **32** 63 8N 142 31W
Tetlin Junction **32** 63 29N 142 55W
Teton → **18** 47 56N 110 31W
Tewksbury **25** 42 37N 71 12W
Texarkana, *Ark.* **15** 33 26N 94 2W
Texarkana, *Tex.* **15** 33 26N 94 3W
Texas □ **15** 31 40N 98 30W
Texas City **15** 29 24N 94 54W
Texline **15** 36 23N 103 2W
Texoma, L. **15** 33 50N 96 34W
Thalmann **12** 31 18N 81 41W
Thames → **9** 41 18N 72 5W
Thatcher, *Ariz.* **19** 32 51N 109 46W
Thatcher, *Colo.* **15** 37 33N 104 7W
Thayer **15** 36 31N 91 33W
The Dalles **18** 45 36N 121 10W
The Glen **27** 39 2N 77 12W
The Loop **24** 41 52N 87 37W
The Narrows **22** 40 37N 74 3W
The White House **27** 38 53N 77 1W
The Woodlands **15** 30 9N 95 27W
Thedford **14** 41 59N 100 35W
Theodore **11** 30 33N 88 10W
Theodore Roosevelt National Memorial Park **14** 47 0N 103 25W
Theodore Roosevelt Res. **19** 33 46N 111 0W
Theresa **9** 44 13N 75 48W
Theressa **12** 29 50N 82 4W
Thermopolis **18** 43 39N 108 13W
Thibodaux **15** 29 48N 90 49W
Thief River Falls **14** 48 7N 96 10W
Thomas **15** 35 45N 98 45W
Thomas Hill Reservoir **16** 39 34N 92 39W
Thomaston, *N.Y.* **23** 40 47N 73 43W
Thomaston, *Ga.* **12** 32 53N 84 20W
Thomasville, *Ala.* **11** 31 55N 87 44W
Thomasville, *Ga.* **12** 30 50N 83 59W
Thomasville, *N.C.* **11** 35 53N 80 5W
Thompson **9** 41 52N 75 31W
Thompson → **14** 39 46N 93 37W
Thompson Falls **18** 47 36N 115 21W
Thompson I. **25** 42 19N 70 59W
Thompson Pk. **18** 41 0N 123 0W
Thompson Springs **19** 38 58N 109 43W
Thompsontown **8** 40 33N 77 14W
Thomson, *Ga.* **11** 33 28N 82 30W
Thomson, *Ga.* **12** 33 28N 82 30W
Thomson, *Ill.* **16** 41 58N 90 6W
Thornton, *Pa.* **26** 39 54N 75 31W
Thornton, *Iowa* **16** 42 57N 93 23W
Thorntown **17** 40 8N 86 36W
Thorofare **26** 39 50N 75 11W
Thousand Oaks **21** 34 10N 118 50W
Three Forks **18** 45 54N 111 33W
Three Oaks **17** 41 48N 86 36W
Three Rivers, *Calif.* **20** 36 26N 118 54W
Three Rivers, *Mich.* **17** 41 57N 85 38W
Three Rivers, *Tex.* **15** 28 28N 98 11W
Three Sisters **18** 44 4N 121 51W
Throgs Neck **23** 40 48N 73 49W
Thunder B. **8** 45 0N 83 20W
Thunderbolt **12** 32 3N 81 4W
Tiburon **30** 37 52N 122 27W
Tiburon Pen. **30** 37 53N 122 28W
Tice **13** 26 40N 81 49W
Ticonderoga **9** 43 51N 73 26W
Tidioute **8** 41 41N 79 24W
Tierra Amarilla **19** 36 42N 106 33W
Tiffin **17** 41 7N 83 11W
Tiffin → **17** 41 20N 84 24W
Tifton **12** 31 27N 83 31W
Tigalda I. **32** 54 6N 165 5W
Tignall **12** 33 52N 82 44W
Tilden **14** 42 3N 97 50W
Tillamook **18** 45 27N 123 51W
Tillman **12** 32 28N 81 6W
Tilton **9** 43 27N 71 36W
Tiltonsville **8** 40 10N 80 41W
Timber Lake **14** 45 26N 101 5W
Timber Mt. **20** 37 6N 116 28W
Timmonsville **12** 34 8N 79 57W
Tin Mt. **20** 36 50N 117 10W
Tinian **33** 15 0N 145 38 E
Tinley Creek Woods **24** 41 38N 87 48W
Tinley Park **24** 41 35N 87 46W
Tioga, *N. Dak.* **14** 48 23N 102 56W
Tioga, *Pa.* **8** 41 55N 77 8W
Tionesta **8** 41 30N 79 28W
Tipp City **17** 39 58N 84 11W
Tippecanoe → **17** 40 30N 86 45W
Tipton, *Calif.* **20** 36 4N 119 19W
Tipton, *Ind.* **17** 40 17N 86 2W
Tipton, *Iowa* **16** 41 46N 91 8W
Tipton, *Mo.* **16** 38 39N 92 47W
Tipton Mt. **21** 35 32N 114 12W
Tiptonville **15** 36 23N 89 29W
Tishomingo **15** 34 14N 96 41W
Titusville, *Fla.* **11** 28 37N 80 49W
Titusville, *Pa.* **8** 41 38N 79 41W
Tobay Beach **23** 40 36N 73 26W
Tobin **20** 39 55N 121 19W
Tobyhanna **9** 41 11N 75 25W
Toccoa **11** 34 35N 83 19W
Todt Hill **22** 40 36N 74 6W
Tohopekaliga L. **13** 28 12N 81 24W
Toiyabe Range **18** 39 30N 117 0W
Tokeland **20** 46 42N 123 59W
Tolageak **32** 70 2N 162 50W
Toledo, *Ill.* **17** 39 16N 88 15W
Toledo, *Iowa* **16** 42 0N 92 35W
Toledo, *Ohio* **17** 41 39N 83 33W
Toledo, *Oreg.* **18** 44 37N 123 56W
Toledo, *Wash.* **18** 46 26N 122 51W
Toledo Bend Reservoir **15** 31 11N 93 34W
Tollhouse **20** 37 1N 119 24W
Tolono **17** 39 59N 88 16W
Tomah **14** 43 59N 90 30W
Tomahawk **14** 45 28N 89 44W
Tomales **20** 38 15N 122 53W
Tomales B. **20** 38 15N 123 58W
Tombigbee → **11** 31 8N 87 57W
Tombstone **19** 31 43N 110 4W
Toms Place **20** 37 34N 118 41W
Toms River **9** 39 58N 74 12W
Tonasket **18** 48 42N 119 26W
Tonawanda **8** 43 1N 78 53W
Tongue → **14** 46 25N 105 52W
Tonica **16** 41 13N 89 4W
Tonkawa **15** 36 41N 97 18W
Tonopah **19** 38 4N 117 14W
Tooele **18** 40 32N 112 18W
Toomsboro **12** 32 50N 83 5W
Topaz **20** 38 41N 119 30W
Topeka **14** 39 3N 95 40W
Topock **21** 34 46N 114 29W
Toppenish **18** 46 23N 120 19W
Topsfield **25** 42 38N 70 57W
Toro Pk. **21** 33 34N 116 24W
Toronto **8** 40 28N 80 36W
Torrance **21** 33 50N 118 19W
Torresdale **26** 40 3N 74 59W
Torrey **19** 38 18N 111 25W
Torrington, *Conn.* **9** 41 48N 73 7W
Torrington, *Wyo.* **14** 42 4N 104 11W
Tortola **32** 18 19N 64 45W
Totowa **22** 40 54N 74 13W
Tottenville **22** 40 30N 74 14W
Toulon **16** 41 6N 89 52W
Towaco **22** 40 55N 74 18W
Towanda, *Ill.* **17** 40 36N 88 53W
Towanda, *Pa.* **9** 41 46N 76 27W
Tower **14** 47 48N 92 17W
Town Farm Hill **25** 42 40N 71 3W
Towner **14** 48 21N 100 25W
Townley **22** 40 41N 74 14W
Towns **12** 32 0N 82 45W
Townsend, *Ga.* **12** 31 33N 81 31W
Townsend, *Mont.* **18** 46 19N 111 31W
Towson **27** 39 24N 76 36W
Tracy, *Calif.* **20** 37 44N 121 26W
Tracy, *Minn.* **14** 44 14N 95 37W
Traer **16** 42 12N 92 28W
Trapper Pk. **18** 45 54N 114 18W
Traverse City **10** 44 46N 85 38W
Travilah **27** 39 4N 77 15W
Travilah Regional Park **27** 39 4N 77 17W
Travis **22** 40 35N 74 11W
Travis, L. **15** 30 24N 97 55W
Treasure I. **30** 37 49N 122 22W
Treasure Island **13** 27 46N 82 46W
Tremont **23** 40 50N 73 52W
Tremonton **18** 41 43N 112 10W
Trenton, *Fla.* **13** 29 37N 82 49W
Trenton, *Mich.* **17** 42 8N 83 11W
Trenton, *Mo.* **16** 40 5N 93 37W
Trenton, *N.J.* **9** 40 14N 74 46W
Trenton, *Nebr.* **14** 40 11N 101 1W
Trenton, *S.C.* **12** 33 45N 81 51W
Tres Pinos **20** 36 48N 121 19W
Trevose **26** 40 8N 74 59W
Tribly **13** 28 28N 82 12W
Tribune **14** 38 28N 101 45W
Trinidad, *Colo.* **15** 37 10N 104 31W
Trinidad, *Md.* **27** 38 54N 76 59W
Trinity **15** 30 57N 95 22W
Trinity →, *Calif.* **18** 41 11N 123 42W
Trinity →, *Tex.* **15** 29 45N 94 43W
Trinity Range **18** 40 15N 118 45W
Trinway **8** 40 9N 82 1W
Tripoli **16** 42 49N 92 16W
Trona **21** 35 46N 117 23W
Tropic **19** 37 37N 112 5W
Trout Lake **20** 46 0N 121 32W
Trout Run **8** 41 23N 77 3W
Troy, *Mich.* **28** 42 35N 83 9W
Troy, *Ala.* **12** 31 48N 85 58W
Troy, *Ill.* **16** 38 44N 89 54W
Troy, *Ind.* **17** 37 59N 86 55W
Troy, *Kans.* **14** 39 47N 95 5W
Troy, *Mo.* **16** 38 59N 90 59W
Troy, *Mont.* **18** 48 28N 115 53W
Troy, *N.Y.* **9** 42 44N 73 41W
Troy, *Ohio* **17** 40 2N 84 12W
Troy, *Pa.* **9** 41 47N 76 47W
Troy, *S.C.* **12** 33 59N 82 17W
Troy Hills **22** 40 50N 74 23W
Truchas Peak **15** 35 58N 105 39W
Truckee **20** 39 20N 120 11W
Trujillo **15** 35 32N 104 42W
Truk **33** 7 25N 151 46 E
Trumann **15** 35 41N 90 31W
Trumansburg **9** 42 33N 76 40W
Trumbull, Mt. **19** 36 25N 113 8W
Truth or Consequences **19** 33 8N 107 15W
Truxton **9** 42 45N 76 2W
Tryonville **8** 41 42N 79 48W
Tsala Apopka L. **13** 28 53N 82 19W
Tuba City **19** 36 8N 111 14W
Tuckahoe **23** 40 56N 73 49W
Tucker **12** 33 51N 84 13W
Tucson **19** 32 13N 110 58W
Tucumcari **15** 35 10N 103 44W
Tugidak I. **32** 56 30N 154 40W
Tujunga **31** 34 15N 118 16W
Tulare **20** 36 13N 119 21W
Tulare Lake Bed **20** 36 0N 119 48W
Tularosa **19** 33 5N 106 1W
Tulia **15** 34 32N 101 46W
Tullahoma **11** 35 22N 86 13W
Tully **9** 42 48N 76 7W
Tulsa **15** 36 10N 95 55W
Tumwater **20** 47 1N 122 54W
Tunica **15** 34 41N 90 23W
Tunkhannock **9** 41 32N 75 57W
Tuntutuliak **32** 60 22N 162 38W
Tuolumne **20** 37 58N 120 15W
Tuolumne → **20** 37 36N 121 13W
Tupelo **11** 34 16N 88 43W
Tupman **21** 35 18N 119 21W
Tupper Lake **9** 44 14N 74 28W
Turbeville **12** 33 54N 80 1W
Turkey → **16** 42 43N 91 2W
Turlock **20** 37 30N 120 51W
Turner, *Md.* **27** 39 14N 76 31W
Turner, *Mont.* **18** 48 51N 108 24W
Turner Hill **25** 42 40N 70 53W
Turners Falls **9** 42 36N 72 33W
Turnersville **26** 39 46N 75 3W
Turtle Creek **29** 40 24N 79 49W
Turtle Lake **14** 47 31N 100 53W
Tuscaloosa **11** 33 12N 87 34W
Tuscarawas → **8** 40 24N 81 25W
Tuscarora Mt. **8** 40 55N 77 55W
Tuscola, *Ill.* **17** 39 48N 88 17W
Tuscola, *Tex.* **15** 32 12N 99 48W
Tuscumbia, *Ala.* **11** 34 44N 87 42W
Tuscumbia, *Mo.* **16** 38 14N 92 28W
Tuskegee **12** 32 25N 85 42W
Tustin **21** 33 44N 117 49W
Tuttle Creek L. **14** 39 22N 96 40W
Tutuila **33** 14 19S 170 50W
Twain **20** 40 1N 121 3W
Twain Harte **20** 38 2N 120 14W
Twentynine Palms **21** 34 8N 116 3W
Twin Bridges **18** 45 33N 112 20W
Twin City **12** 32 35N 82 10W
Twin Falls **18** 42 34N 114 28W
Twin Lakes **12** 30 43N 83 13W
Twin Oaks **26** 39 50N 75 25W
Twin Valley **14** 47 16N 96 16W
Twinsburg **8** 41 18N 81 26W
Twitchell Reservoir **21** 34 59N 120 19W
Two Harbors **14** 47 2N 91 40W
Two Rivers **10** 44 9N 87 34W
Ty Ty **12** 31 28N 83 39W
Tyler, *Minn.* **14** 44 18N 96 8W
Tyler, *Tex.* **15** 32 21N 95 18W
Tyndall **14** 43 0N 97 50W
Tyrone **8** 40 40N 78 14W

U

U.S.A. = United States of America ■ **6** 37 0N 96 0W
Uhrichsville **8** 40 24N 81 21W
Uinta Mts. **18** 40 45N 110 30W
Ukiah **20** 39 9N 123 13W
Ulak I. **32** 51 22N 178 57W
Ulysses **15** 37 35N 101 22W
Umatilla **18** 45 55N 119 21W
Umbagog L. **9** 44 46N 71 3W
Umiat **32** 69 22N 152 8W
Uminak I. **32** 53 20N 168 20W
Umnak I. **32** 53 15N 168 20W
Umpqua → **18** 43 40N 124 12W
Unadilla, *Ga.* **12** 32 16N 83 44W
Unadilla, *N.Y.* **9** 42 20N 75 19W
Unalaska **32** 53 53N 166 32W
Uncompahgre Peak **19** 38 4N 107 28W
Uncompahgre Plateau **19** 38 20N 108 15W
Unimak I. **32** 54 45N 164 0W
Unimak Pass **32** 54 15N 164 30W
Union, *N.J.* **22** 40 42N 74 16W
Union, *Miss.* **15** 32 34N 89 7W
Union, *Mo.* **16** 38 27N 91 0W
Union, *S.C.* **11** 34 43N 81 37W
Union City, *N.J.* **22** 40 45N 74 2W
Union City, *Calif.* **30** 37 36N 122 2W
Union City, *Ga.* **12** 33 35N 84 33W
Union City, *Pa.* **8** 41 54N 79 51W
Union City, *Tenn.* **15** 36 26N 89 3W
Union Gap **18** 46 33N 120 28W
Union Grove **17** 42 41N 88 3W
Union Park **13** 28 34N 81 17W
Union Point **12** 33 37N 83 4W
Union Port **23** 40 48N 73 51W
Union Springs **12** 32 9N 85 43W
Union Star **16** 39 59N 94 36W
Uniondale **23** 40 42N 73 35W
Uniontown, *Ky.* **17** 37 47N 87 56W
Uniontown, *Pa.* **10** 39 54N 79 44W
Unionville, *Ga.* **12** 31 26N 83 30W
Unionville, *Mo.* **16** 40 29N 93 1W
United Nations H.Q. **22** 40 45N 73 59W
United States of America ■ **6** 37 0N 96 0W
Universal City **31** 34 8N 118 21W
University City **16** 38 40N 90 20W
University Gardens **23** 40 46N 73 42W
University Heights, *Ohio* **29** 41 29N 81 31W
University Heights, *Calif.* **30** 37 26N 122 13W
University Park, *N. Mex.* **19** 32 17N 106 45W
University Park, *Md.* **27** 38 58N 76 56W
Upatoie → **12** 32 22N 84 58W
Upolu Pt. **32** 20 16N 155 52W
Upper Alkali L. **18** 41 47N 120 8W
Upper Arlington **17** 40 0N 83 4W
Upper Brookville **23** 40 50N 73 35W
Upper Crystal Springs Res. **24** 37 28N 122 20W
Upper Darby **26** 39 57N 75 16W
Upper Klamath L. **18** 42 25N 121 55W
Upper Lake **20** 39 10N 122 54W
Upper New York B. **22** 40 39N 74 3W
Upper Red L. **14** 48 8N 94 45W
Upper St. Clair **29** 40 21N 80 3W
Upper San Leandro Res. **30** 37 46N 122 6W
Upper Sandusky **17** 40 50N 83 17W
Upton **14** 44 6N 104 38W
Uptons Hill **25** 42 33N 71 0W
Uptown **24** 41 58N 87 40W
Urbana, *Ill.* **17** 40 7N 88 12W
Urbana, *Mo.* **16** 37 51N 93 10W
Urbana, *Ohio* **17** 40 7N 83 45W
Urbandale **16** 41 38N 93 43W
Usher **13** 29 24N 82 49W
Utah □ **18** 39 20N 111 30W
Utah L. **18** 40 10N 111 58W
Ute Creek → **15** 35 21N 103 50W
Utica, *N.Y.* **9** 43 6N 75 14W
Utica, *Ohio* **8** 40 14N 82 27W
Uvalda **12** 32 2N 82 31W
Uvalde **15** 29 13N 99 47W

V

Vacaville **20** 38 21N 121 59W
Vail **6** 39 40N 106 20W
Valdez **32** 61 7N 146 16W
Valdosta **12** 30 50N 83 17W
Vale, *Oreg.* **18** 43 59N 117 15W
Vale, *Va.* **27** 38 55N 77 20W
Valencia **19** 34 48N 106 43W
Valentine **15** 30 35N 104 30W
Valier **18** 48 18N 112 16W
Vallejo **20** 38 7N 122 14W
Vallemar **30** 37 36N 122 28W
Valley Center **21** 33 13N 117 2W
Valley City **14** 46 55N 98 0W
Valley Falls, *Oreg.* **18** 42 29N 120 17W
Valley Falls, *R.I.* **9** 41 54N 71 24W
Valley Forge **26** 40 5N 75 27W
Valley Forge Hist. State Park **26** 40 5N 75 27W
Valley Mede **27** 39 16N 76 50W
Valley Park **16** 38 33N 90 29W
Valley Springs **20** 38 12N 120 50W
Valley Station **17** 38 6N 85 52W
Valley Stream **23** 40 40N 73 43W
Valley View **9** 40 39N 76 33W
Valley Wells **21** 35 27N 115 46W
Valmeyer **16** 38 18N 90 19W
Valparaiso, *Fla.* **13** 30 29N 86 30W
Valparaiso, *Ind.* **17** 41 28N 87 4W
Van Alstyne **15** 33 25N 96 35W
Van Buren, *Ark.* **15** 35 26N 94 21W
Van Buren, *Maine* **11** 47 10N 67 58W
Van Buren, *Mo.* **15** 37 0N 91 1W
Van Horn **15** 31 3N 104 50W
Van Horne **16** 42 1N 92 4W
Van Nuys **31** 34 11N 118 27W
Van Nuys Airport **31** 34 12N 118 29W
Van Wert **17** 40 52N 84 35W
Vance **12** 33 26N 80 25W
Vanceburg **17** 38 36N 83 19W
Vancouver **20** 45 38N 122 40W
Vandalia, *Ill.* **16** 38 58N 89 6W
Vandalia, *Mo.* **16** 39 19N 91 29W
Vandalia, *Ohio* **17** 39 54N 84 12W
Vandenburg **21** 34 35N 120 33W
Vandergrift **8** 40 36N 79 34W
Varna **16** 41 2N 89 14W
Varnville **12** 32 51N 81 5W
Varysburg **8** 42 46N 78 19W
Vassar **10** 43 22N 83 35W
Vaucluse **12** 33 37N 81 49W
Vaughn, *Mont.* **18** 47 33N 111 33W
Vaughn, *N. Mex.* **19** 34 36N 105 13W
Vega **15** 35 15N 102 26W
Vega Baja **32** 18 27N 66 23W
Velva **14** 48 4N 100 56W
Venetie **32** 67 1N 146 25W
Venice, *Calif.* **31** 33 59N 118 27W
Venice, *Fla.* **13** 27 6N 82 27W
Ventucopa **21** 34 50N 119 29W
Ventura **21** 34 17N 119 18W
Venus **13** 27 4N 81 22W
Verde → **6** 33 33N 111 40W
Verdery **12** 34 7N 82 15W
Verdi **20** 39 31N 119 59W
Verdugo Mt. **31** 34 12N 118 17W
Vergennes **9** 44 10N 73 15W
Vermilion **8** 41 25N 82 22W
Vermilion →, *Ill.* **16** 41 19N 89 4W
Vermilion →, *Ind.* **17** 39 57N 87 27W
Vermilion, B. **15** 29 45N 91 55W
Vermilion L. **14** 47 53N 92 26W
Vermillion **14** 42 47N 96 56W
Vermont **16** 40 18N 90 26W
Vermont □ **9** 44 0N 73 0W
Verna **13** 27 23N 82 16W
Vernal **18** 40 27N 109 32W
Vernalis **20** 37 36N 121 17W
Vernon, *Ill.* **16** 38 48N 89 5W
Vernon, *Ind.* **17** 38 59N 85 36W
Vernon, *Tex.* **15** 34 9N 99 17W
Vernonia **20** 45 52N 123 11W
Vero Beach **11** 27 38N 80 24W
Verona, *N.J.* **22** 40 49N 74 15W
Verona, *Wis.* **16** 42 59N 89 32W
Versailles, *Ill.* **16** 39 53N 90 39W
Versailles, *Ind.* **17** 39 4N 85 15W
Versailles, *Ky.* **17** 38 3N 84 44W
Versailles, *Mo.* **16** 38 26N 92 51W
Versailles, *Ohio* **17** 40 13N 84 29W
Vesta **12** 33 58N 82 56W
Vets Stadium **26** 39 54N 75 10W
Vevay **17** 38 45N 85 4W
Vicksburg, *Ariz.* **21** 33 45N 113 45W
Vicksburg, *Mich.* **17** 42 7N 85 32W
Vicksburg, *Miss.* **15** 32 21N 90 53W
Victor **8** 42 58N 77 24W
Victoria, *Ill.* **16** 41 2N 90 6W
Victoria, *Kans.* **14** 38 52N 99 9W
Victoria, *Tex.* **15** 28 48N 97 0W
Victorville **21** 34 32N 117 18W
Vidal **21** 34 7N 114 31W
Vidal Junction **21** 34 11N 114 34W
Vidalia **12** 32 13N 82 25W
Vidette **12** 33 2N 82 15W
Vienna, *Ga.* **12** 32 6N 83 47W
Vienna, *Ill.* **15** 37 25N 88 54W
Vienna, *Mo.* **16** 38 11N 91 57W
Vienna, *Va.* **27** 38 54N 77 16W
Vieques, Isla de **32** 18 8N 65 25W
Villa Grove **17** 39 52N 88 10W
Villa Rica **12** 33 44N 84 55W
Village Green **26** 39 52N 75 26W
Villanova **26** 40 1N 75 20W
Villanueva **19** 35 16N 105 22W
Ville Platte **15** 30 41N 92 17W
Villisca **16** 40 56N 94 59W
Vincennes **17** 38 41N 87 32W
Vincent **21** 34 33N 118 11W
Vine Grove **17** 37 49N 85 59W
Vineland **10** 39 29N 75 2W
Vinita **15** 36 39N 95 9W
Vinton, *Calif.* **20** 39 48N 120 10W
Vinton, *Iowa* **16** 42 10N 92 1W
Vinton, *La.* **15** 30 11N 93 35W
Viola **16** 41 12N 90 35W
Virden **16** 39 30N 89 46W
Virgin → **19** 36 28N 114 21W
Virgin Gorda **32** 18 30N 64 26W
Virgin Is. (British) ■ **32** 18 30N 64 30W
Virginia, *Ill.* **16** 39 57N 90 13W
Virginia, *Minn.* **14** 47 31N 92 32W
Virginia □ **10** 37 30N 78 45W
Virginia Beach **10** 36 51N 75 59W
Virginia City, *Mont.* **18** 45 18N 111 56W
Virginia City, *Nev.* **20** 39 19N 119 39W
Viroqua **14** 43 34N 90 53W
Visalia **20** 36 20N 119 18W
Visitacion Valley **30** 37 42N 122 23W
Vista **21** 33 12N 117 14W
Vivian **15** 32 53N 93 59W
Volborg **14** 45 51N 105 41W

W

Waban, L. **25** 42 17N 71 18W
Wabash **17** 40 48N 85 49W
Wabash → **10** 37 48N 88 2W
Wabasso **13** 27 45N 80 26W
Waccasassa B. **13** 29 10N 82 50W
Wacissa **12** 30 22N 83 59W
Waco **15** 31 33N 97 9W
Waddington **9** 44 52N 75 12W
Wadena **14** 46 26N 95 8W
Wadley, *Ala.* **12** 33 7N 85 34W
Wadley, *Ga.* **12** 32 52N 82 24W
Wadsworth, *Nev.* **18** 39 38N 119 17W
Wadsworth, *Ohio* **8** 41 2N 81 44W
Wagener **12** 33 39N 81 22W
Wagner **14** 43 5N 98 18W
Wagon Mound **15** 36 1N 104 42W
Wagoner **15** 35 58N 95 22W
Wahiawa **32** 21 30N 158 2W
Wahoo **14** 41 13N 96 37W
Wahpeton **14** 46 16N 96 36W
Wailuku **32** 20 53N 156 30W
Wainiha **32** 22 9N 159 34W
Wainwright **32** 70 38N 160 2W
Waipahu **32** 21 23N 158 1W
Waitsburg **18** 46 16N 118 9W
Wakarusa **17** 41 32N 86 1W
Wake Forest **11** 35 59N 78 30W
Wake I. **33** 19 18N 166 36 E
WaKeeney **14** 39 1N 99 53W
Wakefield, *Mass.* **25** 42 30N 71 5W
Wakefield, *Mich.* **14** 46 29N 89 56W
Wakulla **12** 30 14N 84 14W
Wakulla Beach **12** 30 6N 84 16W
Walcott **18** 41 46N 106 51W
Walden, *Colo.* **18** 40 44N 106 17W
Walden, *N.Y.* **9** 41 34N 74 11W
Waldo **12** 29 48N 82 10W
Waldport **18** 44 26N 124 4W
Waldron **15** 34 54N 94 5W
Waldwick **22** 41 1N 74 5W
Wales **32** 65 37N 168 5W
Walker, *Minn.* **14** 47 6N 94 35W
Walker, *Mo.* **16** 37 54N 94 14W
Walker L. **18** 38 42N 118 43W
Walkerton **17** 41 28N 86 29W
Wall **14** 44 0N 102 8W
Wall Street **22** 40 42N 74 0W
Walla Walla **18** 46 4N 118 20W
Wallace, *Idaho* **18** 47 28N 115 56W
Wallace, *N.C.* **11** 34 44N 77 59W
Wallenpaupack, L. **9** 41 25N 75 15W
Wallingford **9** 41 27N 72 50W
Wallington **22** 40 50N 74 8W
Wallowa **18** 45 34N 117 32W
Wallowa Mts. **18** 45 20N 117 30W
Wallula **18** 46 5N 118 54W
Walnut **16** 41 33N 89 36W
Walnut Creek **30** 37 53N 122 3W
Walnut Grove **12** 34 4N 86 18W
Walnut Heights **30** 37 52N 122 2W
Walnut Hill **13** 30 53N 87 30W
Walnut Ridge **15** 36 4N 90 57W
Walpole **9** 42 9N 71 15W
Walsenburg **15** 37 38N 104 47W
Walsh **15** 37 23N 102 17W
Walt Whitman Br. **26** 39 54N 75 9W
Walter F. George Reservoir **12** 31 38N 85 4W
Walterboro **12** 32 55N 80 40W
Walters **15** 34 22N 98 19W
Waltham **25** 42 23N 71 14W
Waltman **18** 43 4N 107 12W
Walton, *Ky.* **17** 38 52N 84 37W
Walton, *N.Y.* **9** 42 10N 75 8W
Waltonville **16** 38 13N 89 2W
Wamego **14** 39 12N 96 18W
Wamsutter **18** 41 40N 107 58W
Wanaque **22** 41 1N 74 17W
Wantagh Seaford **23** 40 39N 73 28W
Wapakoneta **17** 40 34N 84 12W
Wapato **18** 46 27N 120 25W
Wapello **16** 41 11N 91 11W
Wappingers Falls **9** 41 36N 73 55W
Wapsipinicon → **16** 41 44N 90 19W
Ward **26** 39 52N 75 30W
Ward Mt. **20** 37 12N 118 54W
Ware **9** 42 16N 72 14W
Wareham **9** 41 46N 70 43W
Waresboro **12** 31 15N 82 29W
Warm Springs, *Ga.* **12** 32 53N 84 41W
Warm Springs, *Nev.* **19** 38 10N 116 20W
Warminster **9** 40 12N 75 6W
Warner Mts. **18** 41 40N 120 15W
Warner Robins **12** 32 37N 83 36W
Warren, *Mich.* **28** 42 31N 83 0W
Warren, *Ark.* **15** 33 37N 92 4W
Warren, *Ill.* **16** 42 29N 90 0W
Warren, *Minn.* **14** 48 12N 96 46W
Warren, *Ohio* **8** 41 14N 80 49W
Warren, *Pa.* **8** 41 51N 79 9W
Warren Hill **25** 42 35N 71 21W
Warrensburg, *Ill.* **16** 39 56N 89 4W
Warrensburg, *Mo.* **14** 38 46N 93 44W
Warrensburg, *N.Y.* **9** 43 29N 73 46W
Warrenton, *Ga.* **12** 33 24N 82 40W
Warrenton, *Mo.* **16** 38 49N 91 9W
Warrenton, *Oreg.* **20** 46 10N 123 56W
Warrenville **12** 33 32N 81 48W
Warrington **11** 30 23N 87 17W
Warroad **14** 48 54N 95 19W
Warsaw, *Ill.* **16** 40 22N 91 26W
Warsaw, *Ind.* **17** 41 14N 85 51W
Warsaw, *Ky.* **17** 38 47N 84 54W
Warsaw, *Mo.* **16** 38 15N 93 23W
Warsaw, *N.Y.* **8** 42 45N 78 8W
Warsaw, *Ohio* **8** 40 20N 82 0W
Warthen **12** 33 6N 82 48W
Warwick, *Ga.* **12** 31 50N 83 57W
Warwick, *N.Y.* **9** 41 16N 74 22W
Warwick, *R.I.* **9** 41 42N 71 28W
Wasatch Ra. **2** 40 30N 111 15W
Wasco, *Calif.* **21** 35 36N 119 20W
Wasco, *Oreg.* **18** 45 36N 120 42W
Waseca **14** 44 5N 93 30W
Washburn, *Ill.* **16** 40 55N 89 17W
Washburn, *N. Dak.* **14** 47 17N 101 2W
Washburn, *Wis.* **14** 46 40N 90 54W
Washington, *D.C.* **10** 38 54N 77 2W
Washington, *Ga.* **12** 33 44N 82 44W
Washington, *Ind.* **17** 38 40N 87 10W
Washington, *Iowa* **16** 41 18N 91 42W
Washington, *Mo.* **16** 38 33N 91 1W
Washington, *N.C.* **11** 35 33N 77 3W
Washington, *N.J.* **9** 40 46N 74 59W
Washington, *Pa.* **8** 40 10N 80 15W
Washington, *Utah* **19** 37 8N 113 31W
Washington □ **18** 47 30N 120 30W
Washington, Mt. **2** 44 16N 71 18W
Washington Court House **17** 39 32N 83 26W
Washington Heights **22** 40 51N 73 56W
Washington I. **10** 45 23N 86 54W
Washington Memorial Museum **26** 40 5N 75 26W
Washington Nat. Airport **27** 38 51N 77 2W
Washington Park **24** 41 47N 87 36W
Washington Square **26** 40 9N 75 19W
Washington Township **22** 41 0N 74 3W
Washougal **20** 45 35N 122 21W
Wassaw I. **12** 31 53N 80 58W
Wassaw Sd. **12** 31 55N 80 55W
Watching Mts. **22** 40 43N 74 20W
Watchung **22** 40 38N 74 29W
Water Valley **15** 34 10N 89 38W
Waterbury, *Conn.* **9** 41 33N 73 3W
Waterbury, *Vt.* **9** 44 20N 72 46W
Wateree → **12** 33 45N 80 37W
Waterford, *Calif.* **20** 37 38N 120 46W
Waterford, *Pa.* **8** 41 57N 79 59W
Waterford, *Wis.* **17** 42 46N 88 13W
Waterloo, *Ill.* **16** 38 20N 90 9W
Waterloo, *Ind.* **17** 41 26N 85 1W
Waterloo, *Iowa* **16** 42 30N 92 21W
Waterloo, *N.Y.* **8** 42 54N 76 52W
Waterloo, *Wis.* **16** 43 11N 88 59W
Waterman **17** 41 46N 88 47W
Waterman Mt. **31** 34 14N 117 56W
Watersmeet **14** 46 16N 89 11W
Waterton Lakes Nat. Park **18** 48 45N 115 0W
Watertown, *Mass.* **25** 42 22N 71 10W
Watertown, *Conn.* **9** 41 36N 73 7W
Watertown, *Fla.* **12** 30 11N 82 36W
Watertown, *N.Y.* **9** 43 59N 75 55W

X

Y

Z

The WORLD IN FOCUS

Planet Earth

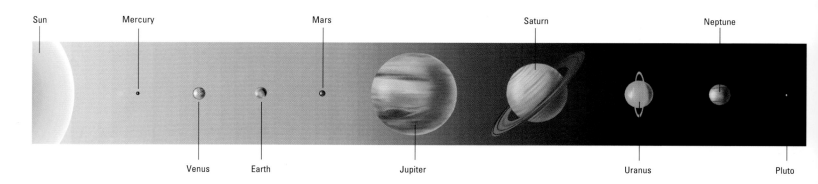

Sun Mercury Mars Saturn Neptune

Venus Earth Jupiter Uranus Pluto

The Solar System

A minute part of one of the billions of galaxies (collections of stars) that comprises the Universe, the Solar System lies some 27,000 light-years from the center of our own galaxy, the "Milky Way." Thought to be over 4,700 million years old, it consists of a central sun with nine planets and their moons revolving around it, attracted by its gravitational pull. The planets orbit the Sun in the same direction – counter-clockwise when viewed from the Northern Heavens – and almost in the same plane. Their orbital paths, however, vary enormously.

The Sun's diameter is 109 times that of Earth, and the temperature at its core – caused by continuous thermonuclear fusions of hydrogen into helium – is estimated to be 27 million degrees Fahrenheit. It is the Solar System's only source of light and heat.

Profile of the Planets

	Mean distance from Sun (million miles)	Mass (Earth = 1)	Period of orbit (Earth years)	Period of rotation (Earth days)	Equatorial diameter (miles)	Number of known satellites
Mercury	36.4	0.055	0.24 years	58.67	3,031	0
Venus	66.9	0.815	0.62 years	243.00	7,521	0
Earth	93.0	1.0	1.00 years	1.00	7,926	1
Mars	141.2	0.107	1.88 years	1.03	4,217	2
Jupiter	483.4	317.8	11.86 years	0.41	88,730	16
Saturn	886.8	95.2	29.46 years	0.43	74,500	20
Uranus	1,784.8	14.5	84.01 years	0.75	31,763	15
Neptune	2,797.8	17.1	164.80 years	0.80	30,775	8
Pluto	3,662.5	0.002	248.50 years	6.39	1,450	1

All planetary orbits are elliptical in form, but only Pluto and Mercury follow paths that deviate noticeably from a circular one. Near perihelion – its closest approach to the Sun – Pluto actually passes inside the orbit of Neptune, an event that last occurred in 1983. Pluto did not regain its station as outermost planet until February 1999.

The Seasons

Seasons occur because the Earth's axis is tilted at a constant angle of 23½°. When the northern hemisphere is tilted to a maximum extent toward the Sun, on 21 June, the Sun is overhead at the Tropic of Cancer (latitude 23½° North). This is midsummer, or the summer solstice, in the northern hemisphere.

On 22 or 23 September, the Sun is overhead at the Equator, and day and night are of equal length throughout the world. This is the autumn equinox in the northern hemisphere. On 21 or 22 December, the Sun is overhead at the Tropic of Capricorn (23½° South), the winter solstice in the northern hemisphere. The overhead Sun then tracks north until, on 21 March, it is overhead at the Equator. This is the spring (vernal) equinox in the northern hemisphere.

In the southern hemisphere, the seasons are the reverse of those in the north.

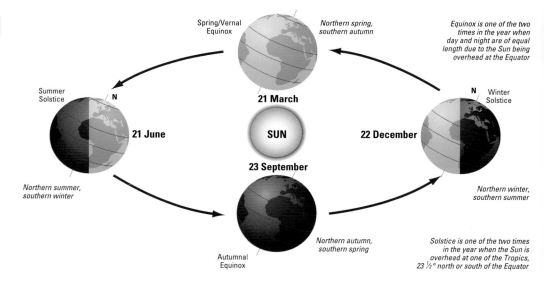

Equinox is one of the two times in the year when day and night are of equal length due to the Sun being overhead at the Equator

Solstice is one of the two times in the year when the Sun is overhead at one of the Tropics, 23 ½° north or south of the Equator

Day and Night

The Sun appears to rise in the east, reach its highest point at noon, and then set in the west, to be followed by night. In reality, it is not the Sun that is moving but the Earth rotating from west to east. The moment when the Sun's upper limb first appears above the horizon is termed sunrise; the moment when the Sun's upper limb disappears below the horizon is sunset.

At the summer solstice in the northern hemisphere (21 June), the Arctic has total daylight and the Antarctic total darkness. The opposite occurs at the winter solstice (21 or 22 December). At the Equator, the length of day and night are almost equal all year.

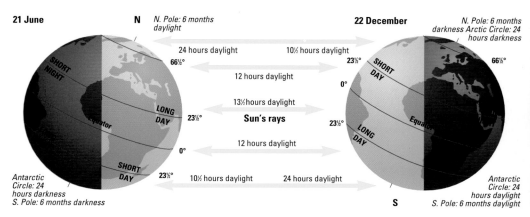

2

Time

Year: The time taken by the Earth to revolve around the Sun, or 365.24 days.

Leap Year: A calendar year of 366 days, 29 February being the additional day. It offsets the difference between the calendar and the solar year.

Month: The approximate time taken by the Moon to revolve around the Earth. The 12 months of the year in fact vary from 28 (29 in a Leap Year) to 31 days.

Week: An artificial period of 7 days, not based on astronomical time.

Day: The time taken by the Earth to complete one rotation on its axis.

Hour: 24 hours make one day. Usually the day is divided into hours AM (ante meridiem or before noon) and PM (post meridiem or after noon), although most timetables now use the 24-hour system, from midnight to midnight.

Sunrise

Sunset

The Moon

The Moon rotates more slowly than the Earth, making one complete turn on its axis in just over 27 days. Since this corresponds to its period of revolution around the Earth, the Moon always presents the same

Phases of the Moon

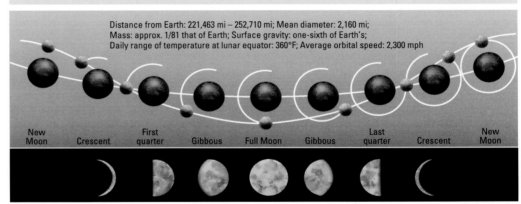

Distance from Earth: 221,463 mi – 252,710 mi; Mean diameter: 2,160 mi; Mass: approx. 1/81 that of Earth; Surface gravity: one-sixth of Earth's; Daily range of temperature at lunar equator: 360°F; Average orbital speed: 2,300 mph

New Moon — Crescent — First quarter — Gibbous — Full Moon — Gibbous — Last quarter — Crescent — New Moon

hemisphere or face to us, and we never see "the dark side." The interval between one full Moon and the next (and between new Moons) is about 29½ days – a lunar month. The apparent changes in the shape of the Moon are caused by its changing position in relation to the Earth; like the planets, it produces no light of its own and shines only by reflecting the rays of the Sun.

Eclipses

When the Moon passes between the Sun and the Earth it causes a partial eclipse of the Sun (1) if the Earth passes through the Moon's outer shadow (P), or a total eclipse (2) if the inner cone shadow crosses the Earth's surface. In a lunar eclipse, the Earth's shadow crosses the Moon and, again, provides either a partial or total eclipse.

Eclipses of the Sun and the Moon do not occur every month because of the 5° difference between the plane of the Moon's orbit and the plane in which the Earth moves. In the 1990s only 14 lunar eclipses are possible, for example, seven partial and seven total; each is visible only from certain, and variable, parts of the world. The same period witnesses 13 solar eclipses – six partial (or annular) and seven total.

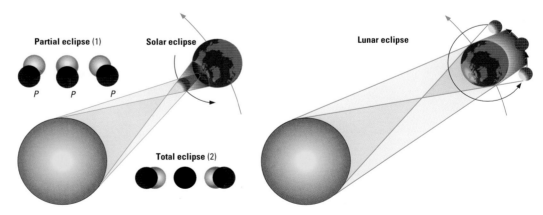

Partial eclipse (1)

Solar eclipse

Lunar eclipse

Total eclipse (2)

Tides

The daily rise and fall of the ocean's tides are the result of the gravitational pull of the Moon and that of the Sun, though the effect of the latter is only 46.6% as strong as that of the Moon. This effect is greatest on the hemisphere facing the Moon and causes a tidal "bulge." When the Sun, Earth and Moon are in line, tide-raising forces are at a maximum and Spring tides occur: high tide reaches the highest values, and low tide falls to low levels. When lunar and solar forces are least coincidental with the Sun and Moon at an angle (near the Moon's first and third quarters), Neap tides occur, which have a small tidal range.

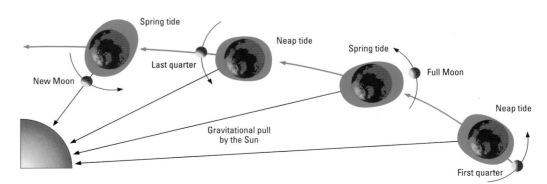

Restless Earth

The Earth's Structure

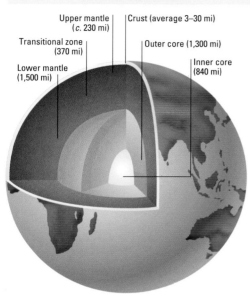

Upper mantle (c. 230 mi)
Crust (average 3–30 mi)
Transitional zone (370 mi)
Outer core (1,300 mi)
Lower mantle (1,500 mi)
Inner core (840 mi)

Continental Drift

About 200 million years ago the original Pangaea land mass began to split into two continental groups, which further separated over time to produce the present-day configuration.

180 million years ago

135 million years ago

Trench
Rift
New ocean floor
Zones of slippage

Present day

Notable Earthquakes Since 1900

Year	Location	Richter Scale	Deaths
1906	San Francisco, USA	8.3	503
1906	Valparaiso, Chile	8.6	22,000
1908	Messina, Italy	7.5	83,000
1915	Avezzano, Italy	7.5	30,000
1920	Gansu (Kansu), China	8.6	180,000
1923	Yokohama, Japan	8.3	143,000
1927	Nan Shan, China	8.3	200,000
1932	Gansu (Kansu), China	7.6	70,000
1933	Sanriku, Japan	8.9	2,990
1934	Bihar, India/Nepal	8.4	10,700
1935	Quetta, India (now Pakistan)	7.5	60,000
1939	Chillan, Chile	8.3	28,000
1939	Erzincan, Turkey	7.9	30,000
1960	Agadir, Morocco	5.8	12,000
1962	Khorasan, Iran	7.1	12,230
1968	N.E. Iran	7.4	12,000
1970	N. Peru	7.7	66,794
1972	Managua, Nicaragua	6.2	5,000
1974	N. Pakistan	6.3	5,200
1976	Guatemala	7.5	22,778
1976	Tangshan, China	8.2	255,000
1978	Tabas, Iran	7.7	25,000
1980	El Asnam, Algeria	7.3	20,000
1980	S. Italy	7.2	4,800
1985	Mexico City, Mexico	8.1	4,200
1988	N.W. Armenia	6.8	55,000
1990	N. Iran	7.7	36,000
1993	Maharashtra, India	6.4	30,000
1994	Los Angeles, USA	6.6	51
1995	Kobe, Japan	7.2	5,000
1995	Sakhalin Is., Russia	7.5	2,000
1997	N.E. Iran	7.1	2,500
1998	Takhar, Afghanistan	6.1	4,200
1998	Rostaq, Afghanistan	7.0	5,000

The highest magnitude recorded on the Richter scale is 8.9 in Japan on 2 March 1933 which killed 2,990 people.

Earthquakes

Earthquake magnitude is usually rated according to either the Richter or the Modified Mercalli scale, both devised by seismologists in the 1930s. The Richter scale measures absolute earthquake power with mathematical precision: each step upward represents a tenfold increase in shockwave amplitude. Theoretically, there is no upper limit, but the largest earthquakes measured have been rated at between 8.8 and 8.9. The 12–point Mercalli scale, based on observed effects, is often more meaningful, ranging from I (earthquakes noticed only by seismographs) to XII (total destruction); intermediate points include V (people awakened at night; unstable objects overturned), VII (collapse of ordinary buildings; chimneys and monuments fall) and IX (conspicuous cracks in ground; serious damage to reservoirs).

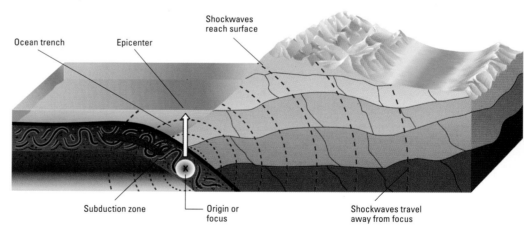

Ocean trench
Epicenter
Shockwaves reach surface
Subduction zone
Origin or focus
Shockwaves travel away from focus

Structure and Earthquakes

Mobile land areas
Submarine zones of mobile land areas
Stable land platforms
Submarine extensions of stable land platforms
Mid-oceanic volcanic ridges
Oceanic platforms

1976 ○ Principal earthquakes and dates

Earthquakes are a series of rapid vibrations originating from the slipping or faulting of parts of the Earth's crust when stresses within build up to breaking point. They usually happen at depths varying from 5 to 20 miles. Severe earthquakes cause extensive damage when they take place in populated areas, destroying structures and severing communications. Most initial loss of life occurs due to secondary causes such as falling masonry, fires and flooding.

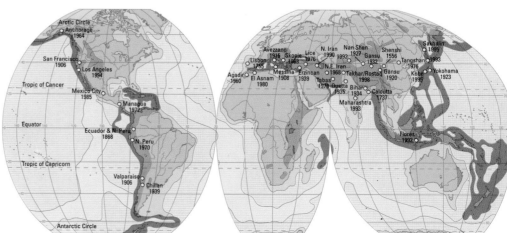

Projection: Interrupted Mollweide

Plate Tectonics

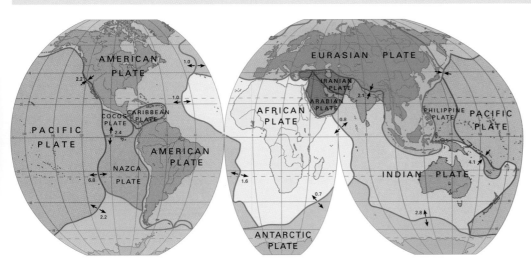

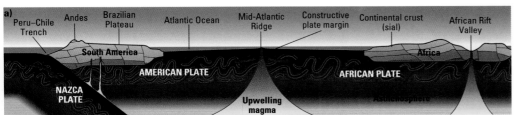

a) Peru–Chile Trench | Andes | Brazilian Plateau | Atlantic Ocean | Mid-Atlantic Ridge | Constructive plate margin | Continental crust (sial) | African Rift Valley

South America   Africa

AMERICAN PLATE   AFRICAN PLATE

NAZCA PLATE

Upwelling magma   Asthenosphere

The drifting of the continents is a feature that is unique to Planet Earth. The complementary, almost jigsaw-puzzle fit of the coastlines on each side of the Atlantic Ocean inspired Alfred Wegener's theory of continental drift in 1915. The theory suggested that the ancient super-continent, which Wegener named Pangaea, incorporated all of the Earth's land masses and gradually split up to form today's continents.

The original debate about continental drift was a prelude to a more radical idea: plate tectonics. The basic theory is that the Earth's crust is made up of a series of rigid plates which float on a soft layer of the mantle and are moved about by continental convection currents within the Earth's interior. These plates diverge and converge along margins marked by seismic activity. Plates diverge from mid-ocean ridges where molten lava pushes upward and forces the plates apart at rates of up to 1.6 in [40 mm] a year.

The three diagrams, left, give some examples of plate boundaries from around the world. Diagram (a) shows sea-floor spreading at the Mid-Atlantic Ridge as the American and African plates slowly diverge. The same thing is happening in (b) where sea-floor spreading at the Mid-Indian Ocean Ridge is forcing the Indian plate to collide into the Eurasian plate. In (c) oceanic crust (sima) is being subducted beneath lighter continental crust (sial).

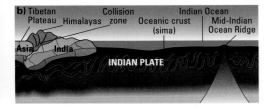

b) Tibetan Plateau | Collision zone | Indian Ocean | Oceanic crust (sima) | Mid-Indian Ocean Ridge

Himalayas

Asia   India

INDIAN PLATE

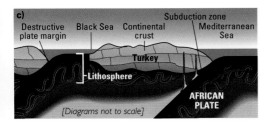

c) Destructive plate margin | Black Sea | Continental crust | Subduction zone | Mediterranean Sea

Turkey

Lithosphere

AFRICAN PLATE

[Diagrams not to scale]

Volcanoes

Volcanoes occur when hot liquefied rock beneath the Earth's crust is pushed up by pressure to the surface as molten lava. Some volcanoes erupt in an explosive way, throwing out rocks and ash, whilst others are effusive and lava flows out of the vent. There are volcanoes which are both, such as Mount Fuji. An accumulation of lava and cinders creates cones of variable size and shape. As a result of many eruptions over centuries, Mount Etna in Sicily has a circumference of more than 75 miles [120 km].

Climatologists believe that volcanic ash, if ejected high into the atmosphere, can influence temperature and weather for several years afterward. The 1991 eruption of Mount Pinatubo in the Philippines ejected more than 20 million tons of dust and ash 20 miles [32 km] into the atmosphere and is believed to have accelerated ozone depletion over a large part of the globe.

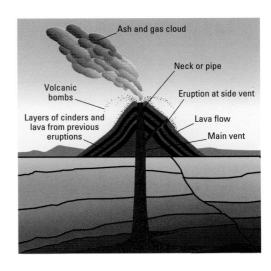

Ash and gas cloud

Neck or pipe

Volcanic bombs

Eruption at side vent

Layers of cinders and lava from previous eruptions

Lava flow

Main vent

Distribution of Volcanoes

Volcanoes today may be the subject of considerable scientific study but they remain both dramatic and unpredictable: in 1991 Mount Pinatubo, 62 miles [100 km] north of the Philippines capital Manila, suddenly burst into life after lying dormant for more than six centuries. Most of the world's active volcanoes occur in a belt around the Pacific Ocean, on the edge of the Pacific plate, called the "ring of fire." Indonesia has the greatest concentration with 90 volcanoes, 12 of which are active. The most famous, Krakatoa, erupted in 1883 with such force that the resulting tidal wave killed 36,000 people and tremors were felt as far away as Australia.

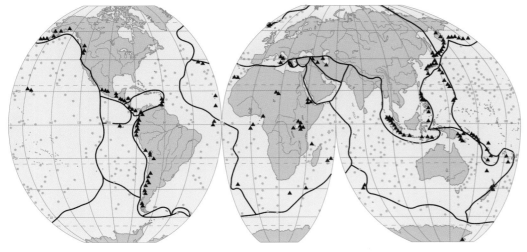

•   Submarine volcanoes

▲   Land volcanoes active since 1700

—   Boundaries of tectonic plates

Landforms

The Rock Cycle

James Hutton first proposed the rock cycle in the late 1700s after he observed the slow but steady effects of erosion.

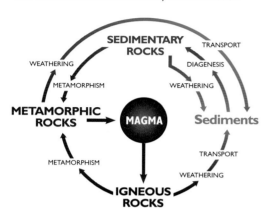

Above and below the surface of the oceans, the features of the Earth's crust are constantly changing. The phenomenal forces generated by convection currents in the molten core of our planet carry the vast segments or "plates" of the crust across the globe in an endless cycle of creation and destruction. A continent may travel little more than 1 in [25 mm] per year, yet in the vast span of geological time this process throws up giant mountain ranges and creates new land.

Destruction of the landscape, however, begins as soon as it is formed. Wind, water, ice and sea, the main agents of erosion, mount a constant assault that even the most resistant rocks cannot withstand. Mountain peaks may dwindle by as little as a fraction of an inch each year, but if they are not uplifted by further movements of the crust they will eventually be reduced to rubble and transported away.

Water is the most powerful agent of erosion – it has been estimated that 100 billion tons of sediment are washed into the oceans every year. Three Asian rivers account for 20% of this total, the Huang He, in China, and the Brahmaputra and Ganges in Bangladesh.

Rivers and glaciers, like the sea itself, generate much of their effect through abrasion – pounding the land with the debris they carry with them. But as well as destroying they also create new landforms, many of them spectacular: vast deltas like those of the Mississippi and the Nile, or the deep fjords cut by glaciers in British Columbia, Norway and New Zealand.

Geologists once considered that landscapes evolved from "young," newly uplifted mountainous areas, through a "mature" hilly stage, to an "old age" stage when the land was reduced to an almost flat plain, or peneplain. This theory, called the "cycle of erosion," fell into disuse when it became evident that so many factors, including the effects of plate tectonics and climatic change, constantly interrupt the cycle, which takes no account of the highly complex interactions that shape the surface of our planet.

Mountain Building

Mountains are formed when pressures on the Earth's crust caused by continental drift become so intense that the surface buckles or cracks. This happens where oceanic crust is subducted by continental crust or, more dramatically, where two tectonic plates collide: the Rockies, Andes, Alps, Urals and Himalayas resulted from such impacts. These are all known as fold mountains because they were formed by the compression of the rocks, forcing the surface to bend and fold like a crumpled rug. The Himalayas are formed from the folded former sediments of the Tethys Sea which was trapped in the collision zone between the Indian and Eurasian plates.

The other main mountain-building process occurs when the crust fractures to create faults, allowing rock to be forced upward in large blocks; or when the pressure of magma within the crust forces the surface to bulge into a dome, or erupts to form a volcano. Large mountain ranges may reveal a combination of those features; the Alps, for example, have been compressed so violently that the folds are fragmented by numerous faults and intrusions of molten igneous rock.

Over millions of years, even the greatest mountain ranges can be reduced by the agents of erosion (most notably rivers) to a low rugged landscape known as a peneplain.

Types of faults: Faults occur where the crust is being stretched or compressed so violently that the rock strata break in a horizontal or vertical movement. They are classified by the direction in which the blocks of rock have moved. A normal fault results when a vertical movement causes the surface to break apart; compression causes a reverse fault. Horizontal movement causes shearing, known as a strike-slip fault. When the rock breaks in two places, the central block may be pushed up in a horst fault, or sink (creating a rift valley) in a graben fault.

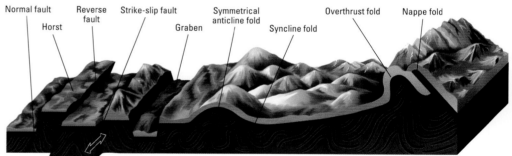

Types of fold: Folds occur when rock strata are squeezed and compressed. They are common therefore at destructive plate margins and where plates have collided, forcing the rocks to buckle into mountain ranges. Geographers give different names to the degrees of fold that result from continuing pressure on the rock. A simple fold may be symmetric, with even slopes on either side, but as the pressure builds up, one slope becomes steeper and the fold becomes asymmetric. Later, the ridge or "anticline" at the top of the fold may slide over the lower ground or "syncline" to form a recumbent fold. Eventually, the rock strata may break under the pressure to form an overthrust and finally a nappe fold.

Continental Glaciation

Ice sheets were at their greatest extent about 200,000 years ago. The maximum advance of the last Ice Age was about 18,000 years ago, when ice covered virtually all of Canada and reached as far south as the Bristol Channel in Britain.

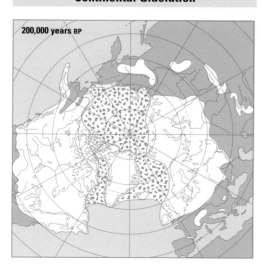

200,000 years BP

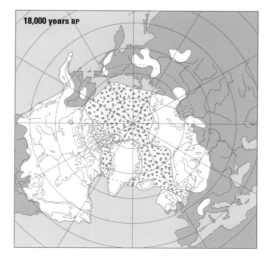

18,000 years BP

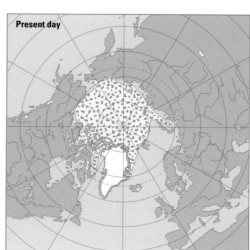

Present day

Natural Landforms

A stylized diagram to show a selection of landforms found in the mid-latitudes.

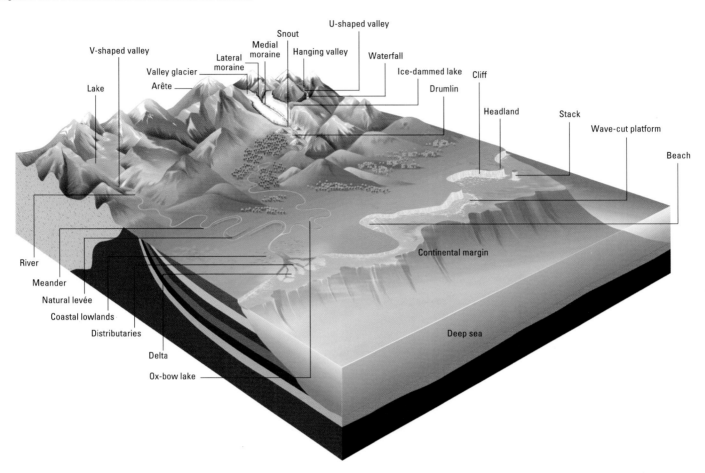

Labels: V-shaped valley, Valley glacier, Arête, Lake, Lateral moraine, Medial moraine, Snout, Hanging valley, U-shaped valley, Waterfall, Ice-dammed lake, Drumlin, Cliff, Headland, Stack, Wave-cut platform, Beach, River, Meander, Natural levée, Coastal lowlands, Distributaries, Delta, Ox-bow lake, Continental margin, Deep sea

Desert Landscapes

The popular image that deserts are all huge expanses of sand is wrong. Despite harsh conditions, deserts contain some of the most varied and interesting landscapes in the world. They are also one of the most extensive environments – the hot and cold deserts together cover almost 40% of the Earth's surface.

The three types of hot desert are known by their Arabic names: sand desert, called *erg*, covers only about one-fifth of the world's desert; the rest is divided between *hammada* (areas of bare rock) and *reg* (broad plains covered by loose gravel or pebbles).

In areas of *erg*, such as the Namib Desert, the shape of the dunes reflects the character of local winds. Where winds are constant in direction, crescent-shaped *barchan* dunes form. In areas of bare rock, wind-blown sand is a major agent of erosion. The erosion is mainly confined to within 6.5 ft [2 m] of the surface, producing characteristic, mushroom-shaped rocks.

Erg

Hammada

Reg

Surface Processes

Catastrophic changes to natural landforms are periodically caused by such phenomena as avalanches, landslides and volcanic eruptions, but most of the processes that shape the Earth's surface operate extremely slowly in human terms. One estimate, based on a study in the United States, suggested that 3 ft [1 m] of land was removed from the entire surface of the country, on average, every 29,500 years. However, the time scale varies from 1,300 years to 154,200 years depending on the terrain and climate.

In hot, dry climates, mechanical weathering, a result of rapid temperature changes, causes the outer layers of rock to peel away, while in cold mountainous regions, boulders are prised apart when water freezes in cracks in rocks. Chemical weathering, at its greatest in warm, humid regions, is responsible for hollowing out limestone caves and decomposing granites.

The erosion of soil and rock is greatest on sloping land and the steeper the slope, the greater the tendency for mass wasting – the movement of soil and rock downhill under the influence of gravity. The mechanisms of mass wasting (ranging from very slow to very rapid) vary with the type of material, but the presence of water as a lubricant is usually an important factor.

Running water is the world's leading agent of erosion and transportation. The energy of a river depends on several factors, including its velocity and volume, and its erosive power is at its peak when it is in full flood. Sea waves also exert tremendous erosive power during storms when they hurl pebbles against the shore, undercutting cliffs and hollowing out caves.

Glacier ice forms in mountain hollows and spills out to form valley glaciers, which transport rocks shattered by frost action. As glaciers move, rocks embedded into the ice erode steep-sided, U-shaped valleys. Evidence of glaciation in mountain regions includes cirques, knife-edged ridges, or arêtes, and pyramidal peaks.

Oceans

The Great Oceans

Relative sizes of the world's oceans

- Pacific
- Atlantic
- Indian
- Arctic

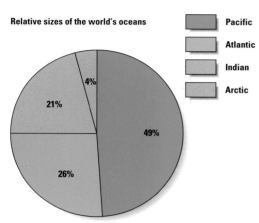

4%

21%

49%

26%

In a strict geographical sense there are only three true oceans – the Atlantic, Indian and Pacific. The legendary "Seven Seas" would require these to be divided at the Equator and the addition of the Arctic Ocean – which accounts for less than 4% of the total sea area. The International Hydrographic Bureau does not recognize the Antarctic Ocean (even less the "Southern Ocean") as a separate entity.

The Earth is a watery planet: more than 70% of its surface – over 140,000,000 sq miles [360,000,000 sq km] – is covered by the oceans and seas. The mighty Pacific alone accounts for nearly 36% of the total, and 49% of the sea area. Gravity holds in around 320 million cu. miles [1,400 million cu. km] of water, of which over 97% is saline.

The vast underwater world starts in the shallows of the seaside and plunges to depths of more than 36,000 ft [11,000 m]. The continental shelf, part of the land mass, drops gently to around 650 ft [200 m]; here the seabed falls away suddenly at an angle of 3° to 6° – the continental slope. The third stage, called the continental rise, is more gradual with gradients varying from 1 in 100 to 1 in 700. At an average depth of 16,500 ft [5,000 m] there begins the aptly-named abyssal plain – massive submarine depths where sunlight fails to penetrate and few creatures can survive.

From these plains rise volcanoes which, taken from base to top, rival and even surpass the tallest continental mountains in height. Mount Kea, on Hawaii, reaches a total of 33,400 ft [10,203 m], some 4,500 ft [1,355 m] more than Mount Everest, though scarcely 40% is visible above sea level.

In addition, there are underwater mountain chains up to 600 miles [1,000 km] across, whose peaks sometimes appear above sea level as islands such as Iceland and Tristan da Cunha.

The Ocean Depths

Average and maximum depths of the world's great oceans, in feet

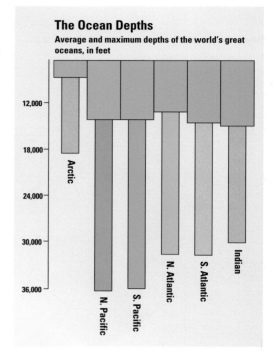

12,000

18,000

24,000

30,000

36,000

Arctic

N. Pacific

S. Pacific

N. Atlantic

S. Atlantic

Indian

Ocean Currents

January temperatures and ocean currents

ACTUAL SURFACE TEMPERATURE

°F
- 86
- 68
- 50
- 32
- 14
- – 4
- – 22
- – 40

OCEAN CURRENTS

Cold	Warm	Speed (knots)
		Less than 0.5
		0.5 – 1.0
		Over 1.0

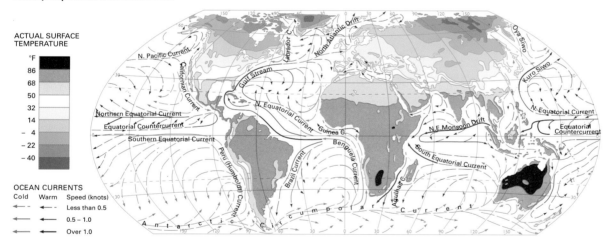

July temperatures and ocean currents

ACTUAL SURFACE TEMPERATURE

°F
- 86
- 68
- 50
- 32
- 14

OCEAN CURRENTS

Cold	Warm	Speed (knots)
		Less than 0.5
		0.5 – 1.0
		Over 1.0

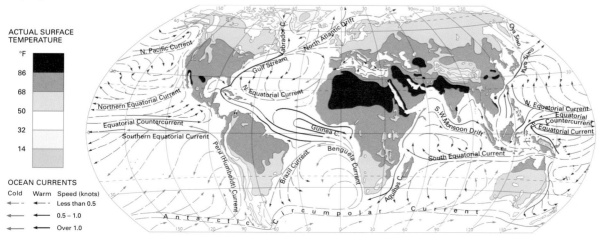

Moving immense quantities of energy as well as billions of tons of water every hour, the ocean currents are a vital part of the great heat engine that drives the Earth's climate. They themselves are produced by a twofold mechanism. At the surface, winds push huge masses of water before them; in the deep ocean, below an abrupt temperature gradient that separates the churning surface waters from the still depths, density variations cause slow vertical movements.

The pattern of circulation of the great surface currents is determined by the displacement known as the Coriolis effect. As the Earth turns beneath a moving object – whether it is a tennis ball or a vast mass of water – it appears to be deflected to one side. The deflection is most obvious near the Equator, where the Earth's surface is spinning eastward at 1,050 mph [1,700 km/h]; currents moving poleward are curved clockwise in the northern hemisphere and counterclockwise in the southern.

The result is a system of spinning circles known as gyres. The Coriolis effect piles up water on the left of each gyre, creating a narrow, fast-moving stream that is matched by a slower, broader returning current on the right. North and south of the Equator, the fastest currents are located in the west and in the east respectively. In each case, warm water moves from the Equator and cold water returns to it. Cold currents often bring an upwelling of nutrients with them, supporting the world's most economically important fisheries.

Depending on the prevailing winds, some currents on or near the Equator may reverse their direction in the course of the year – a seasonal variation on which Asian monsoon rains depend, and whose occasional failure can bring disaster to millions.

World Fishing Areas

Main commercial fishing areas (numbered FAO regions)

Catch by top marine fishing areas, thousand tons (1992)

1.	Pacific, NW	[61]	26,667	29.3%
2.	Pacific, SE	[87]	15,317	16.8%
3.	Atlantic, NE	[27]	12,202	13.4%
4.	Pacific, WC	[71]	8,496	9.3%
5.	Indian, W	[51]	4,129	4.5%
6.	Indian, E	[57]	3,595	4.0%
7.	Atlantic, EC	[34]	3,591	3.9%
8.	Pacific, NE	[67]	3,470	3.8%

Principal fishing areas

Leading fishing nations

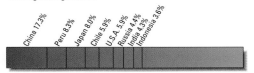

China 17.3% Peru 8.3% Japan 8.0% Chile 5.9% U.S.A. 5.9% Russia 4.4% India 4.3% Indonesia 3.6%

World total (1993): 111,762,080 tons
(Marine catch 83.1% Inland catch 16.9%)

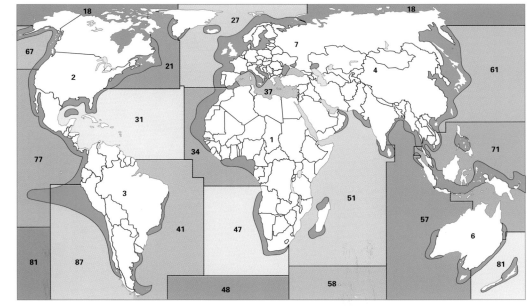

Marine Pollution

Sources of marine oil pollution (latest available year)

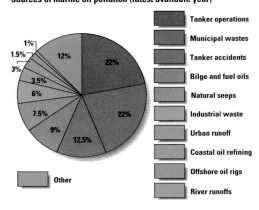

- Tanker operations
- Municipal wastes
- Tanker accidents
- Bilge and fuel oils
- Natural seeps
- Industrial waste
- Urban runoff
- Coastal oil refining
- Offshore oil rigs
- River runoffs
- Other

Oil Spills

Major oil spills from tankers and combined carriers

Year	Vessel	Location	Spill (barrels)**	Cause
1979	Atlantic Empress	West Indies	1,890,000	collision
1983	Castillo De Bellver	South Africa	1,760,000	fire
1978	Amoco Cadiz	France	1,628,000	grounding
1991	Haven	Italy	1,029,000	explosion
1988	Odyssey	Canada	1,000,000	fire
1967	Torrey Canyon	UK	909,000	grounding
1972	Sea Star	Gulf of Oman	902,250	collision
1977	Hawaiian Patriot	Hawaiian Is.	742,500	fire
1979	Independenta	Turkey	696,350	collision
1993	Braer	UK	625,000	grounding
1996	Sea Empress	UK	515,000	grounding

Other sources of major oil spills

1983	Nowruz oilfield	The Gulf	4,250,000[†]	war
1979	Ixtoc 1 oilwell	Gulf of Mexico	4,200,000[†]	blow out
1991	Kuwait	The Gulf	2,500,000[†]	war

** 1 barrel = 0.15 tons/159 lit./35 Imperial gal./42 US gal. [†] estimated

River Pollution

Sources of river pollution, USA (latest available year)

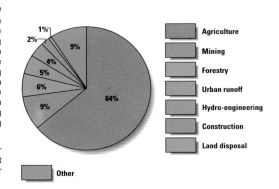

- Agriculture
- Mining
- Forestry
- Urban runoff
- Hydro-engineering
- Construction
- Land disposal
- Other

Water Pollution

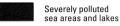
Severely polluted
sea areas and lakes

Polluted sea
areas and lakes

Areas of frequent oil pollution
by shipping

Major oil tanker spills

Major oil rig blow outs

Offshore dumpsites for industrial
and municipal waste

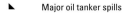
Severely polluted
rivers and estuaries

The most notorious tanker spillage of the
1980s occurred when the *Exxon Valdez* ran
aground in Prince William Sound, Alaska,
in 1989, spilling 267,000 barrels of crude oil
close to shore in a sensitive ecological area.
This rates as the world's 28th worst spill in
terms of volume.

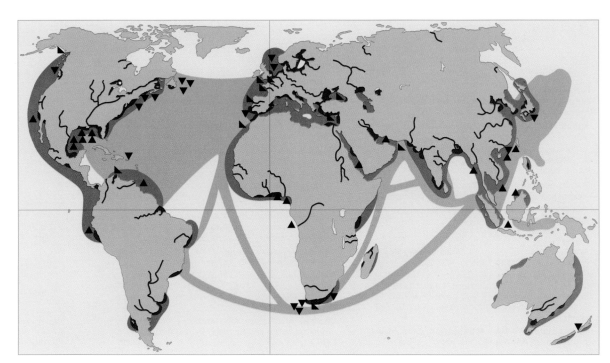

Climate

Climatic Regions

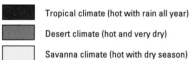

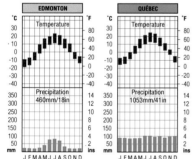

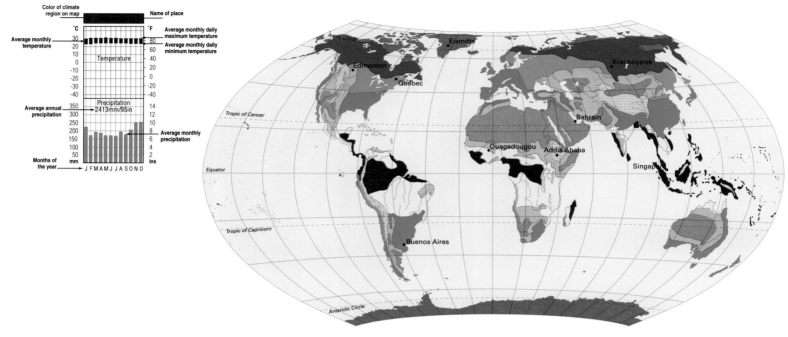

Tropical climate (hot with rain all year)

Desert climate (hot and very dry)

Savanna climate (hot with dry season)

Steppe climate (warm and dry)

Mild climate (warm and wet)

Continental climate (wet with cold winter)

Subarctic climate (very cold winter)

Polar climate (very cold and dry)

Mountainous climate (altitude affects climate)

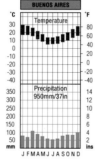

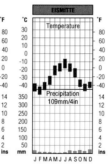

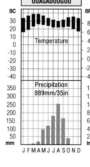

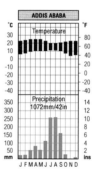

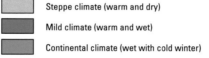

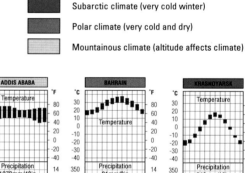

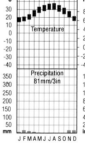

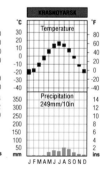

Climate Records

Temperature

Highest recorded shade temperature: Al Aziziyah, Libya, 136.4°F [58°C], 13 September 1922.

Highest mean annual temperature: Dallol, Ethiopia, 94°F [34.4°C], 1960–66.

Longest heatwave: Marble Bar, W. Australia, 162 days over 100°F [38°C], 23 October 1923 to 7 April 1924.

Lowest recorded temperature (outside poles): Verkhoyansk, Siberia, –90°F [–68°C], 6 February 1933.

Lowest mean annual temperature: Plateau Station, Antarctica, –72.0°F [–56.6°C]

Pressure

Longest drought: Calama, N. Chile, no recorded rainfall in 400 years to 1971.

Wettest place (12 months): Cherrapunji, Meghalaya, N. E. India, 1,040 in [26,470 mm], August 1860 to August 1861. Cherrapunji also holds the record for the most rainfall in one month: 115 in [2,930 mm], July 1861.

Wettest place (average): Mawsynram, India, mean annual rainfall 467.4 in [11,873 mm].

Wettest place (24 hours): Cilaos, Réunion, Indian Ocean, 73.6 in [1,870 mm], 15–16 March 1952.

Heaviest hailstones: Gopalganj, Bangladesh, up to 2.25 lb [1.02 kg], 14 April 1986 (killed 92 people).

Heaviest snowfall (continuous): Bessans, Savoie, France, 68 in [1,730 mm] in 19 hours, 5–6 April 1969.

Heaviest snowfall (season/year): Paradise Ranger Station, Mt Rainier, Washington, USA, 1,224.5 in [31,102 mm], 19 February 1971 to 18 February 1972.

Pressure and winds

Highest barometric pressure: Agata, Siberia (at 862 ft [262 m] altitude), 1,083.8 mb, 31 December 1968.

Lowest barometric pressure: Typhoon Tip, Guam, Pacific Ocean, 870 mb, 12 October 1979.

Highest recorded wind speed: Mt Washington, New Hampshire, USA, 231 mph [371 km/h], 12 April 1934. This is three times as strong as hurricane force on the Beaufort Scale.

Windiest place: Commonwealth Bay, Antarctica, where gales frequently reach over 200 mph [320 km/h].

Climate

Climate is weather in the long term: the seasonal pattern of hot and cold, wet and dry, averaged over time (usually 30 years). At the simplest level, it is caused by the uneven heating of the Earth. Surplus heat at the Equator passes toward the poles, leveling out the energy differential. Its passage is marked by a ceaseless churning of the atmosphere and the oceans, further agitated by the Earth's diurnal spin and the motion it imparts to moving air and water. The heat's means of transport – by winds and ocean currents, by the continual evaporation and recondensation of water molecules – is the weather itself. There are four basic types of climate, each of which can be further subdivided: tropical, desert (dry), temperate and polar.

Composition of Dry Air

Nitrogen	78.09%	Sulfur dioxide	trace
Oxygen	20.95%	Nitrogen oxide	trace
Argon	0.93%	Methane	trace
Water vapor	0.2–4.0%	Dust	trace
Carbon dioxide	0.03%	Helium	trace
Ozone	0.00006%	Neon	trace

10

El Niño

In a normal year, southeasterly trade winds drive surface waters westward off the coast of South America, drawing cold, nutrient-rich water up from below. In an El Niño year (which occurs every 2–7 years), warm water from the west Pacific suppresses up-welling in the east, depriving the region of nutrients. The water is warmed by as much as 12°F [7°C], disturbing the tropical atmospheric circulation. During an intense El Niño, the southeast trade winds change direction and become equatorial westerlies, resulting in climatic extremes in many regions of the world, such as drought in parts of Australia and India, and heavy rainfall in southeastern USA. An intense El Niño occurred in 1997–8, with resultant freak weather conditions across the entire Pacific region.

Normal year

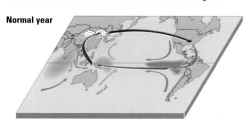

El Niño event

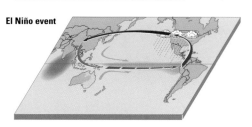

Beaufort Wind Scale

Named after the 19th-century British naval officer who devised it, the Beaufort Scale assesses wind speed according to its effects. It was originally designed as an aid for sailors, but has since been adapted for use on the land.

Scale	Wind speed km/h	mph	Effect
0	0–1	0–1	**Calm** Smoke rises vertically
1	1–5	1–3	**Light air** Wind direction shown only by smoke drift
2	6–11	4–7	**Light breeze** Wind felt on face; leaves rustle; vanes moved by wind
3	12–19	8–12	**Gentle breeze** Leaves and small twigs in constant motion; wind extends small flag
4	20–28	13–18	**Moderate** Raises dust and loose paper; small branches move
5	29–38	19–24	**Fresh** Small trees in leaf sway; wavelets on inland waters
6	39–49	25–31	**Strong** Large branches move; difficult to use umbrellas
7	50–61	32–38	**Near gale** Whole trees in motion; difficult to walk against wind
8	62–74	39–46	**Gale** Twigs break from trees; walking very difficult
9	75–88	47–54	**Strong gale** Slight structural damage
10	89–102	55–63	**Storm** Trees uprooted; serious structural damage
11	103–117	64–72	**Violent storm** Widespread damage
12	118+	73+	**Hurricane**

Conversions

°C = (°F − 32) × 5/9; °F = (°C × 9/5) + 32; 0°C = 32°F
1 in = 25.4 mm; 1 mm = 0.0394 in; 100 mm = 3.94 in

Temperature

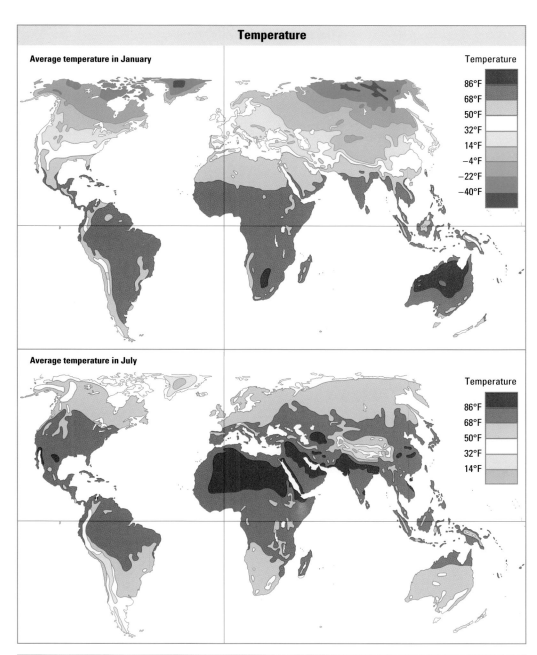

Average temperature in January

Temperature
86°F
68°F
50°F
32°F
14°F
−4°F
−22°F
−40°F

Average temperature in July

Temperature
86°F
68°F
50°F
32°F
14°F

Precipitation

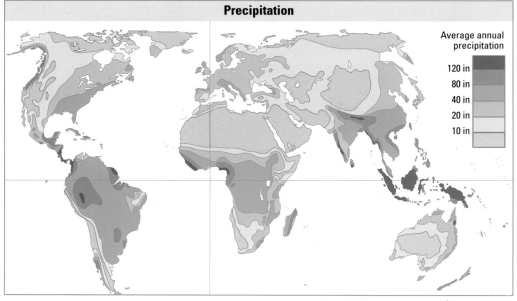

Average annual precipitation
120 in
80 in
40 in
20 in
10 in

Water and Vegetation

The Hydrological Cycle

The world's water balance is regulated by the constant recycling of water between the oceans, atmosphere and land. The movement of water between these three reservoirs is known as the hydrological cycle. The oceans play a vital role in the hydrological cycle: 74% of the total precipitation falls over the oceans and 84% of the total evaporation comes from the oceans.

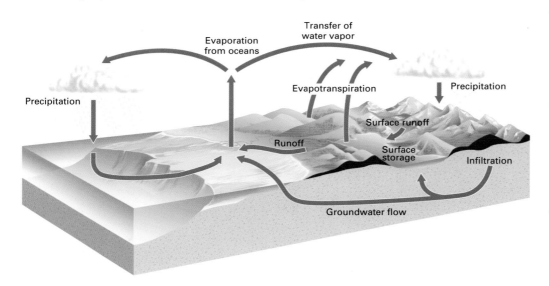

Water Distribution

The distribution of planetary water, by percentage. Oceans and ice caps together account for more than 99% of the total; the breakdown of the remainder is estimated.

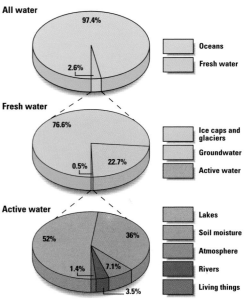

All water
- 97.4% Oceans
- 2.6% Fresh water

Fresh water
- 76.6% Ice caps and glaciers
- 22.7% Groundwater
- 0.5% Active water

Active water
- 52% Lakes
- 36% Soil moisture
- 7.1% Atmosphere
- 1.4% Rivers
- 3.5% Living things

Water Utilization

| | Domestic | Industrial | Agriculture |

The percentage breakdown of water usage by sector, selected countries (1996)

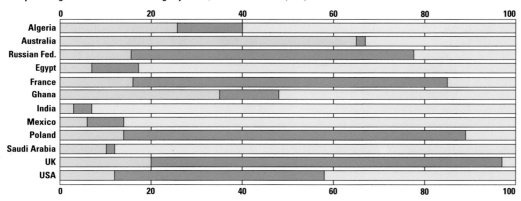

Algeria, Australia, Russian Fed., Egypt, France, Ghana, India, Mexico, Poland, Saudi Arabia, UK, USA

Water Usage

Almost all the world's water is 3,000 million years old, and all of it cycles endlessly through the hydrosphere, though at different rates. Water vapor circulates over days, even hours, deep ocean water circulates over millennia, and ice-cap water remains solid for millions of years.

Fresh water is essential to all terrestrial life. Humans cannot survive more than a few days without it, and even the hardiest desert plants and animals could not exist without some water. Agriculture requires huge quantities of fresh water: without large-scale irrigation most of the world's people would starve. In the USA, agriculture uses 42% and industry 45% of all water withdrawals.

The United States is one of the heaviest users of water in the world. According to the latest figures the average American uses 380 liters a day and the average household uses 415,000 liters a year. This is two to four times more than in Western Europe.

Water Supply

Percentage of total population with access to safe drinking water (1995)

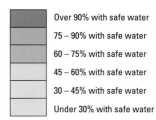

- Over 90% with safe water
- 75 – 90% with safe water
- 60 – 75% with safe water
- 45 – 60% with safe water
- 30 – 45% with safe water
- Under 30% with safe water

- Under 80 liters per person per day domestic water consumption
- Over 320 liters per person per day domestic water consumption

NB: 80 liters of water a day is considered necessary for a reasonable quality of life.

Least well-provided countries

Paraguay	8%	Central Afr. Rep	18%
Afghanistan	10%	Bhutan	21%
Cambodia	13%	Congo (D. Rep.)	25%

Natural Vegetation

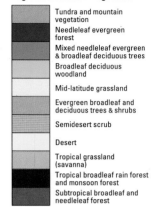

Regional variation in vegetation

- Tundra and mountain vegetation
- Needleleaf evergreen forest
- Mixed needleleaf evergreen & broadleaf deciduous trees
- Broadleaf deciduous woodland
- Mid-latitude grassland
- Evergreen broadleaf and deciduous trees & shrubs
- Semidesert scrub
- Desert
- Tropical grassland (savanna)
- Tropical broadleaf rain forest and monsoon forest
- Subtropical broadleaf and needleleaf forest

The map shows the natural "climax vegetation" of regions, as dictated by climate and topography. In most cases, however, agricultural activity has drastically altered the vegetation pattern. Western Europe, for example, lost most of its broadleaf forest many centuries ago, while irrigation has turned some natural semidesert into productive land.

Land Use by Continent

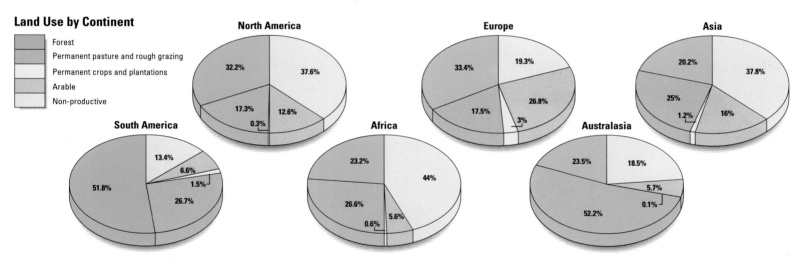

- Forest
- Permanent pasture and rough grazing
- Permanent crops and plantations
- Arable
- Non-productive

North America
- 32.2%
- 37.6%
- 17.3%
- 12.6%
- 0.3%

Europe
- 19.3%
- 33.4%
- 26.8%
- 17.5%
- 3%

Asia
- 20.2%
- 37.8%
- 25%
- 16%
- 1.2%

South America
- 13.4%
- 6.6%
- 1.5%
- 51.8%
- 26.7%

Africa
- 23.2%
- 44%
- 26.6%
- 5.6%
- 0.6%

Australasia
- 23.5%
- 18.5%
- 5.7%
- 0.1%
- 52.2%

Forestry: Production

	Forest and woodland (million hectares)	Annual production (1996, million cubic meters)	
		Fuelwood and charcoal	Industrial roundwood*
World	*3,987.9*	*1,864.8*	*1,489.5*
S. America	829.3	193.0	129.9
N. & C. America	709.8	155.4	600.4
Africa	684.6	519.9	67.9
Asia	131.8	905.2	280.2
Europe	157.3	82.4	369.7
Australasia	157.2	8.7	41.5

Paper and Board

Top producers (1996)**		Top exporters (1996)**	
USA	85,173	Canada	13,393
China	30,253	USA	9,113
Japan	30,014	Finland	8,529
Canada	18,414	Sweden	7,483
Germany	14,733	Germany	6,319

* roundwood is timber as it is felled
** in thousand tons

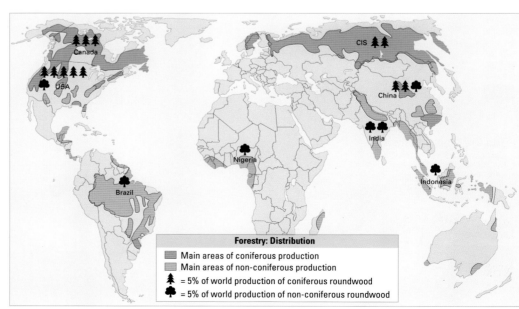

Forestry: Distribution

- Main areas of coniferous production
- Main areas of non-coniferous production
- 🌲 = 5% of world production of coniferous roundwood
- 🌳 = 5% of world production of non-coniferous roundwood

Environment

Humans have always had a dramatic effect on their environment, at least since the development of agriculture almost 10,000 years ago. Generally, the Earth has accepted human interference without obvious ill effects: the complex systems that regulate the global environment have been able to absorb substantial damage while maintaining a stable and comfortable home for the planet's trillions of lifeforms. But advancing human technology and the rapidly-expanding populations it supports are now threatening to overwhelm the Earth's ability to compensate.

Industrial wastes, acid rainfall, desertification and large-scale deforestation all combine to create environmental change at a rate far faster than the great slow cycles of planetary evolution can accommodate. As a result of overcultivation, overgrazing and overcutting of groundcover for firewood, desertification is affecting as much as 60% of the world's croplands. In addition, with fire and chainsaws, humans are destroying more forest in a day than their ancestors could have done in a century, upsetting the balance between plant and animal, carbon dioxide and oxygen, on which all life ultimately depends.

The fossil fuels that power industrial civilization have pumped enough carbon dioxide and other so-called greenhouse gases into the atmosphere to make climatic change a near-certainty. As a result of the combination of these factors, the Earth's average temperature has risen by approximately 1°F [0.5°C] since the beginning of the 20th century, and it is still rising.

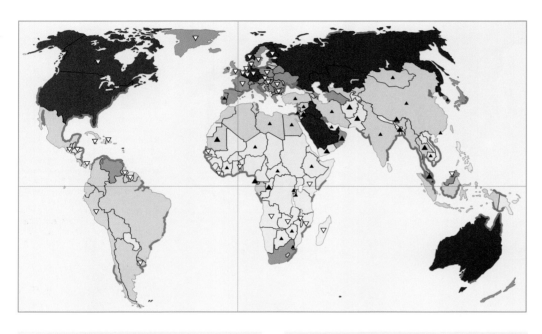

Global Warming

Carbon dioxide emissions in tons per person per year (1995)

■	Over 10 tons of CO$_2$
▨	5 – 10 tons of CO$_2$
▨	1 – 5 tons of CO$_2$
□	Under 1 ton of CO$_2$

Changes in CO$_2$ emissions 1980–90

▲	Over 100% increase in emissions
▴	50–100% increase in emissions
▽	Reduction in emissions
—	Coastal areas in danger of flooding from rising sea levels caused by global warming

High atmospheric concentrations of heat-absorbing gases, especially carbon dioxide, appear to be causing a steady rise in average temperatures worldwide – up to 3°F [1.5°C] by the year 2020, according to some estimates. Global warming is likely to bring with it a rise in sea levels that may flood some of the Earth's most densely populated coastal areas.

Greenhouse Power

Relative contributions to the Greenhouse Effect by the major heat-absorbing gases in the atmosphere.

The chart combines greenhouse potency and volume. Carbon dioxide has a greenhouse potential of only 1, but its concentration of 350 parts per million makes it predominate. CFC 12, with 25,000 times the absorption capacity of CO$_2$, is present only as 0.00044 ppm.

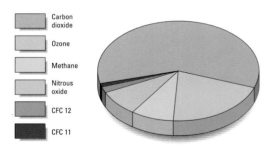

- Carbon dioxide
- Ozone
- Methane
- Nitrous oxide
- CFC 12
- CFC 11

Ozone Layer

The ozone "hole" over the northern hemisphere on 12 March 1995.

The colors represent Dobson Units (DU). The ozone "hole" is seen as the dark blue and purple patch in the center, where ozone values are around 120 DU or lower. Normal levels are around 280 DU. The ozone "hole" over Antarctica is much larger.

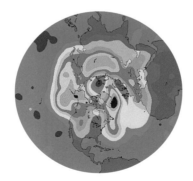

Carbon Dioxide

Carbon dioxide released in millions of tons (1992)

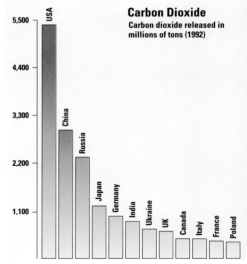

USA, China, Russia, Japan, Germany, India, Ukraine, UK, Canada, Italy, France, Poland

The Greenhouse Effect

Carbon dioxide is increased by burning fossil fuels and cutting forests

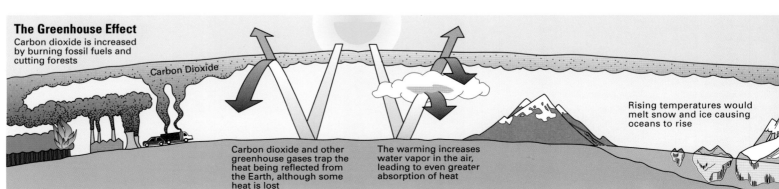

Carbon Dioxide

Carbon dioxide and other greenhouse gases trap the heat being reflected from the Earth, although some heat is lost

The warming increases water vapor in the air, leading to even greater absorption of heat

Rising temperatures would melt snow and ice causing oceans to rise

- Existing deserts
- Areas with a high risk of desertification
- Areas with a moderate risk of desertification
- Former areas of rain forest
- Existing rainforest

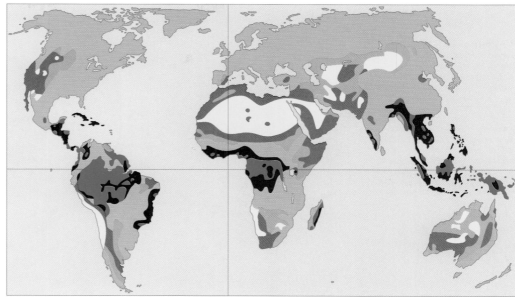

Forest Clearance

Thousands of hectares of forest cleared annually, tropical countries surveyed 1981–85 and 1987–90. Loss as a percentage of remaining stocks is shown in figures on each column.

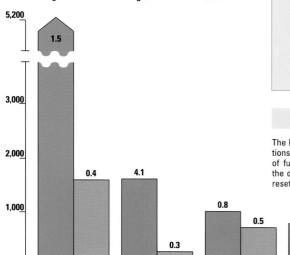

Deforestation

The Earth's remaining forests are under attack from three directions: expanding agriculture, logging, and growing consumption of fuelwood, often in combination. Sometimes deforestation is the direct result of government policy, as in the efforts made to resettle the urban poor in some parts of Brazil; just as often, it comes about despite state attempts at conservation. Loggers, licensed or unlicensed, blaze a trail into virgin forest, often destroying twice as many trees as they harvest. Landless farmers follow, burning away most of what remains to plant their crops, completing the destruction.

Ozone Depletion

The ozone layer, 15–18 miles [25–30 km] above sea level, acts as a barrier to most of the Sun's harmful ultra-violet radiation, protecting us from the ionizing radiation that can cause skin cancer and cataracts. In recent years, however, two holes in the ozone layer have been observed during winter: one over the Arctic and the other, the size of the USA, over Antarctica. By 1996, ozone had been reduced to around a half of its 1970 amount. The ozone (O_3) is broken down by chlorine released into the atmosphere as CFCs (chlorofluorocarbons) – chemicals used in refrigerators, packaging and aerosols.

Air Pollution

Sulfur dioxide is the main pollutant associated with industrial cities. According to the World Health Organization, at least 600 million people live in urban areas where sulfur dioxide concentrations regularly reach damaging levels. One of the world's most dangerously polluted urban areas is Mexico City, due to a combination of its enclosed valley location, 3 million cars and 60,000 factories. In May 1998, this lethal cocktail was added to by nearby forest fires and the resultant air pollution led to over 20% of the population (3 million people) complaining of respiratory problems.

Acid Rain

Killing trees, poisoning lakes and rivers and eating away buildings, acid rain is mostly produced by sulfur dioxide emissions from industry and volcanic eruptions. By the mid 1990s, acid rain had sterilized 4,000 or more of Sweden's lakes and left 45% of Switzerland's alpine conifers dead or dying, while the monuments of Greece were dissolving in Athens' smog. Prevailing wind patterns mean that the acids often fall many hundreds of miles from where the original pollutants were discharged. In parts of Europe acid deposition has slightly decreased, following reductions in emissions, but not by enough.

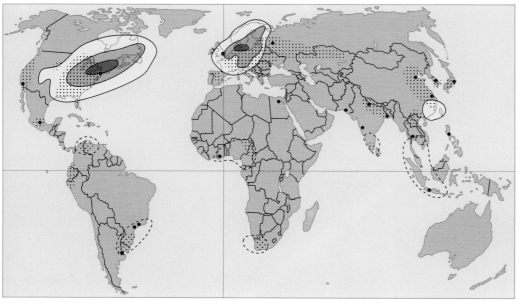

World Pollution

Acid rain and sources of acidic emissions (latest available year)

Acid rain is caused by high levels of sulfur and nitrogen in the atmosphere. They combine with water vapor and oxygen to form acids (H_2SO_4 and HNO_3) which fall as precipitation.

- Regions where sulfur and nitrogen oxides are released in high concentrations, mainly from fossil fuel combustion
- Major cities with high levels of air pollution (including nitrogen and sulfur emissions)

Areas of heavy acid deposition

pH numbers indicate acidity, decreasing from a neutral 7. Normal rain, slightly acid from dissolved carbon dioxide, never exceeds a pH of 5.6.

- pH less than 4.0 (most acidic)
- pH 4.0 to 4.5
- pH 4.5 to 5.0
- Areas where acid rain is a potential problem

Population

Demographic Profiles

Developed nations such as the UK have populations evenly spread across the age groups and, usually, a growing proportion of elderly people. The great majority of the people in developing nations, however, are in the younger age groups, about to enter their most fertile years. In time, these population profiles should resemble the world profile (even Kenya has made recent progress with reducing its birth rate), but the transition will come about only after a few more generations of rapid population growth.

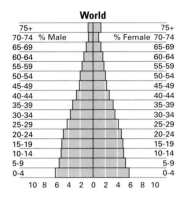

World

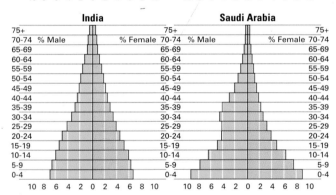

UK

Kenya

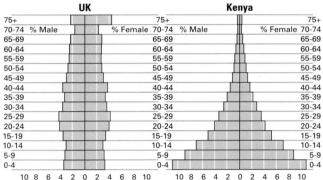

India

Saudi Arabia

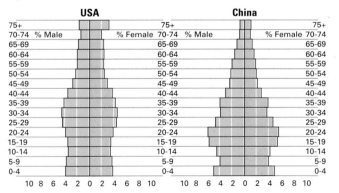

USA

China

Most Populous Nations [in millions (1998 estimates)]

1.	China	1,237	9. Bangladesh	125	17. Iran	64
2.	India	984	10. Nigeria	111	18. Thailand	60
3.	USA	270	11. Mexico	99	19. France	59
4.	Indonesia	213	12. Germany	82	20. UK	59
5.	Brazil	170	13. Philippines	78	21. Ethiopia	58
6.	Russia	147	14. Vietnam	76	22. Italy	57
7.	Pakistan	135	15. Egypt	66	23. Ukraine	50
8.	Japan	126	16. Turkey	65	24. Congo (=Zaïre)	49

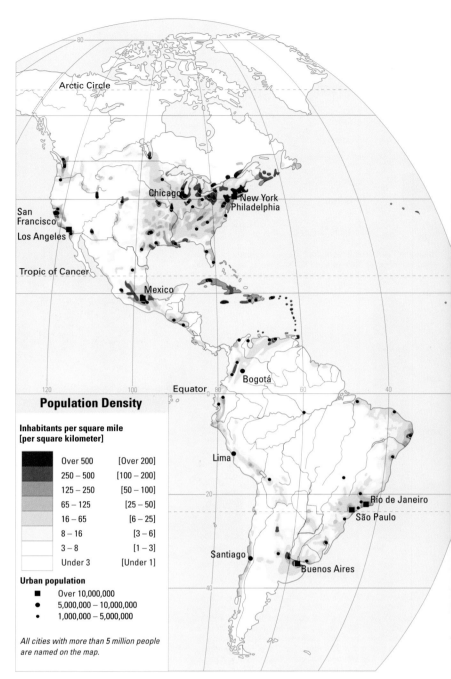

Population Density

Inhabitants per square mile [per square kilometer]

Over 500	[Over 200]
250 – 500	[100 – 200]
125 – 250	[50 – 100]
65 – 125	[25 – 50]
16 – 65	[6 – 25]
8 – 16	[3 – 6]
3 – 8	[1 – 3]
Under 3	[Under 1]

Urban population

- ■ Over 10,000,000
- ● 5,000,000 – 10,000,000
- • 1,000,000 – 5,000,000

All cities with more than 5 million people are named on the map.

Continental Comparisons

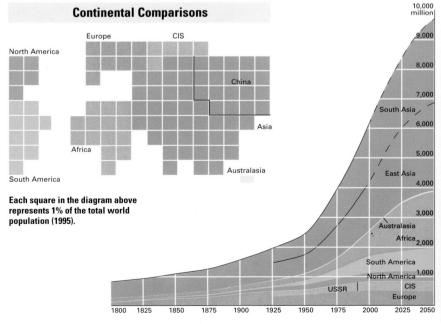

Each square in the diagram above represents 1% of the total world population (1995).

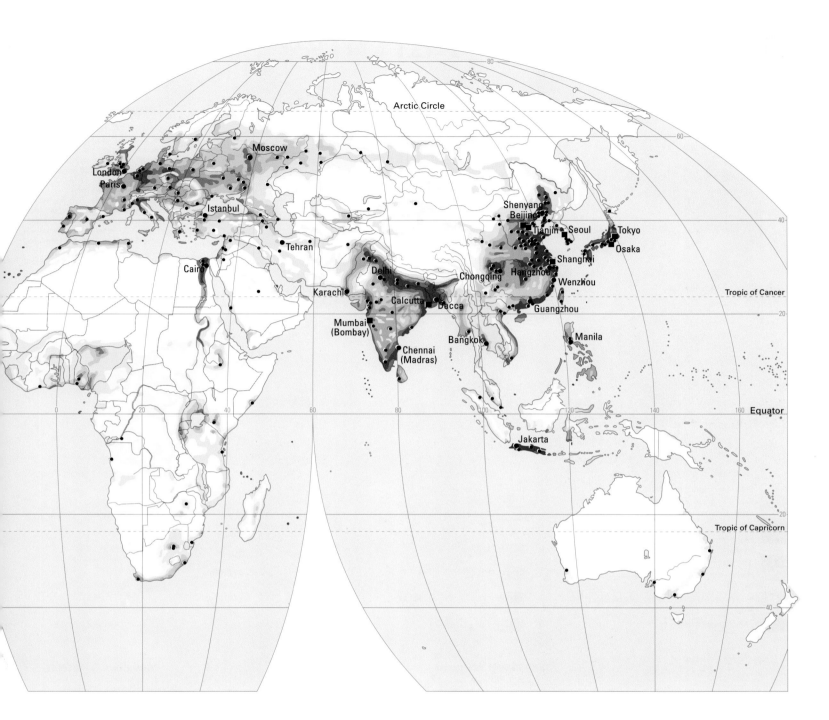

Moscow

London
Paris

Istanbul

Tehran

Cairo

Karachi

Delhi

Mumbai
(Bombay)

Calcutta

Dacca

Chennai
(Madras)

Bangkok

Shenyang

Beijing

Tianjin

Seoul

Tokyo

Osaka

Shanghai

Hangzhou

Chongqing

Wenzhou

Guangzhou

Manila

Jakarta

Arctic Circle

Tropic of Cancer

Equator

Tropic of Capricorn

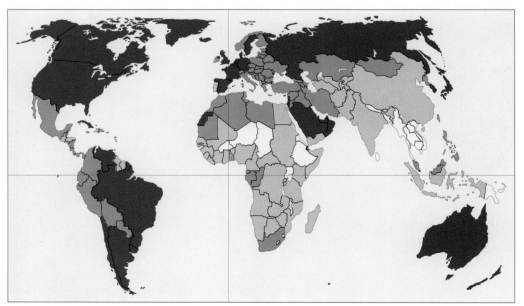

Urban Population

Percentage of total population living in towns and cities (1997)

Over 75%

50 – 75%

25 – 50%

10 – 25%

Under 10%

Most urbanized		Least urbanized	
Singapore	100%	Rwanda	6%
Belgium	97%	Bhutan	8%
Israel	91%	Burundi	8%
Uruguay	91%	Nepal	11%
Netherlands	89%	Swaziland	12%
[UK 89%]			

The Human Family

Predominant Languages

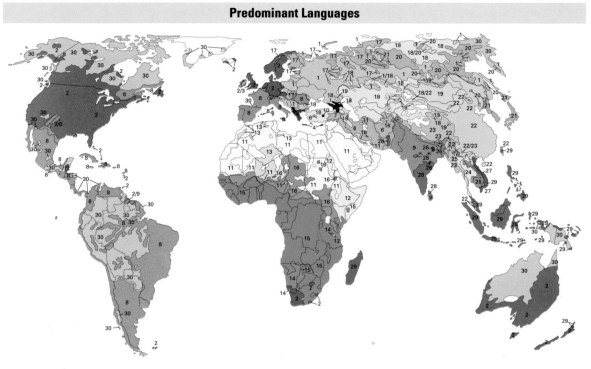

Languages of the World

Language can be classified by ancestry and structure. For example, the Romance and Germanic groups are both derived from an Indo-European language believed to have been spoken 5,000 years ago.

Mother tongues (in millions)
Chinese 1,069 (Mandarin 864), English 443, Hindi 352, Spanish 341, Russian 293, Arabic 197, Bengali 184, Portuguese 173, Malay-Indonesian 142, Japanese 125, French 121, German 118, Urdu 92, Punjabi 84, Korean 71.

Official languages (% of total population)
English 27%, Chinese 19%, Hindi 13.5%, Spanish 5.4%, Russian 5.2%, French 4.2%, Arabic 3.3%, Portuguese 3%, Malay 3%, Bengali 2.9%, Japanese 2.3%.

INDO-EUROPEAN FAMILY

1. Balto-Slavic group (incl. Russian, Ukrainian)
2. Germanic group (incl. English, German)
3. Celtic group
4. Greek
5. Albanian
6. Iranian group
7. Armenian
8. Romance group (incl. Spanish, Portuguese, French, Italian)
9. Indo-Aryan group (incl. Hindi, Bengali, Urdu, Punjabi, Marathi)

 CAUCASIAN FAMILY

AFRO-ASIATIC FAMILY

11. Semitic group (incl. Arabic)
12. Kushitic group
13. Berber group

14. KHOISAN FAMILY

15. NIGER-CONGO FAMILY

16. NILO-SAHARAN FAMILY

17. URALIC FAMILY

ALTAIC FAMILY

18. Turkic group
19. Mongolian group
20. Tungus-Manchu group
21. Japanese and Korean

SINO-TIBETAN FAMILY

22. Sinitic (Chinese) languages
23. Tibetic-Burmic languages

24. TAI FAMILY

AUSTRO-ASIATIC FAMILY

25. Mon-Khmer group
26. Munda group
27. Vietnamese

28. DRAVIDIAN FAMILY (incl. Telugu, Tamil)

29. AUSTRONESIAN FAMILY (incl. Malay-Indonesian)

30. OTHER LANGUAGES

Predominant Religions

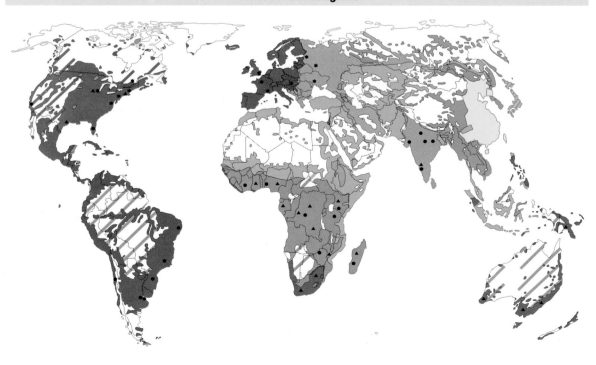

Religious Adherents

Religious adherents in millions:

Christian	1,669	Hindu	663
Roman Catholic	*952*	Buddhist	312
Protestant	*337*	Chinese Folk	172
Orthodox	*162*	Tribal	92
Anglican	*70*	Jewish	18
Other Christian	*148*	Sikhs	17
Muslim	966		
Sunni	*841*		
Shia	*125*		

- Roman Catholicism
- Orthodox and other Eastern Churches
- Protestantism
- Sunni Islam
- Shia Islam
- Buddhism
- Hinduism
- Confucianism
- Judaism
- Shintoism
- Tribal Religions

United Nations

Created in 1945 to promote peace and cooperation and based in New York, the United Nations is the world's largest international organization, with 185 members and an annual budget of US $2.6 billion (1996–97). Each member of the General Assembly has one vote, while the permanent members of the 15-nation Security Council – USA, Russia, China, UK and France – hold a veto. The Secretariat is the UN's principal administrative arm. The 54 members of the Economic and Social Council are responsible for economic, social, cultural, educational, health and related matters. The UN has 16 specialized agencies – based in Canada, France, Switzerland and Italy, as well as the USA – which help members in fields such as education (UNESCO), agriculture (FAO), medicine (WHO) and finance (IFC). By the end of 1994, all the original 11 trust territories of the Trusteeship Council had become independent.

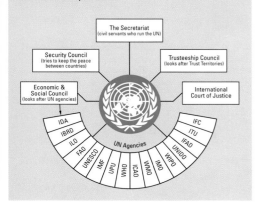

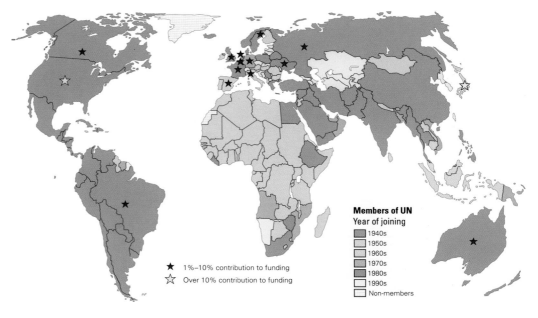

Members of UN
Year of joining
- 1940s
- 1950s
- 1960s
- 1970s
- 1980s
- 1990s
- Non-members

★ 1%–10% contribution to funding
☆ Over 10% contribution to funding

MEMBERSHIP OF THE UN In 1945 there were 51 members; by December 1994 membership had increased to 185 following the admission of Palau. There are 7 independent states which are not members of the UN – Kiribati, Nauru, Switzerland, Taiwan, Tonga, Tuvalu and the Vatican City. All the successor states of the former USSR had joined by the end of 1992. The official languages of the UN are Chinese, English, French, Russian, Spanish and Arabic.

FUNDING The UN budget for 1996–97 was US $2.6 billion. Contributions are assessed by the members' ability to pay, with the maximum 25% of the total, the minimum 0.01%. Contributions for 1996 were: USA 25.0%, Japan 15.4%, Germany 9.0%, France 6.4%, UK 5.3%, Italy 5.2%, Russia 4.5%, Canada 3.1%, Spain 2.4%, Brazil 1.6%, Netherlands 1.6%, Australia 1.5%, Sweden 1.2%, Ukraine 1.1%, Belgium 1.0%.

International Organizations

EU European Union (evolved from the European Community in 1993). The 15 members – Austria, Belgium, Denmark, Finland, France, Germany, Greece, Ireland, Italy, Luxembourg, Netherlands, Portugal, Spain, Sweden and the UK – aim to integrate economies, coordinate social developments and bring about political union. These members of what is now the world's biggest market share agricultural and industrial policies and tariffs on trade. The original body, the European Coal and Steel Community (ECSC), was created in 1951 following the signing of the Treaty of Paris.

EFTA European Free Trade Association (formed in 1960). Portugal left the original "Seven" in 1989 to join what was then the EC, followed by Austria, Finland and Sweden in 1995. Only 4 members remain: Norway, Iceland, Switzerland and Liechtenstein.

ACP African-Caribbean-Pacific (formed in 1963). Members have economic ties with the EU.

NATO North Atlantic Treaty Organization (formed in 1949). It continues after 1991 despite the winding up of the Warsaw Pact. The Czech Republic, Hungary and Poland were the latest members to join in 1999.

OAS Organization of American States (formed in 1948). It aims to promote social and economic cooperation between developed countries of North America and developing nations of Latin America.

ASEAN Association of Southeast Asian Nations (formed in 1967). Burma and Laos joined in 1997.

OAU Organization of African Unity (formed in 1963). Its 53 members represent over 94% of Africa's population. Arabic, French, Portuguese and English are recognized as working languages.

LAIA Latin American Integration Association (1980). Its aim is to promote freer regional trade.

OECD Organization for Economic Cooperation and Development (formed in 1961). It comprises the 29 major Western free-market economies. Poland, Hungary and South Korea joined in 1996. "G8" is its "inner group" comprising Canada, France, Germany, Italy, Japan, Russia, the UK and the USA.

COMMONWEALTH The Commonwealth of Nations evolved from the British Empire; it comprises 16 Queen's realms, 32 republics and 5 indigenous monarchies, giving a total of 53.

OPEC Organization of Petroleum Exporting Countries (formed in 1960). It controls about three-quarters of the world's oil supply. Gabon left the organization in 1996.

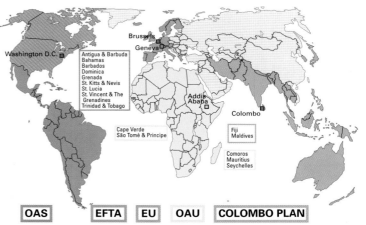

OAS **EFTA** **EU** **OAU** **COLOMBO PLAN**

ARAB LEAGUE (formed in 1945). The League's aim is to promote economic, social, political and military cooperation. There are 21 member nations.

COLOMBO PLAN (formed in 1951). Its 26 members aim to promote economic and social development in Asia and the Pacific.

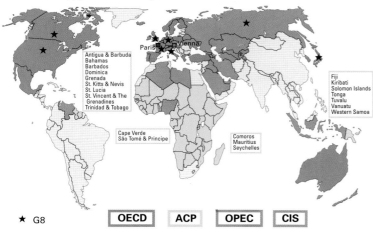

★ G8

OECD **ACP** **OPEC** **CIS**

NATO **LAIA** **ARAB LEAGUE** **COMMONWEALTH** **ASEAN**

Wealth

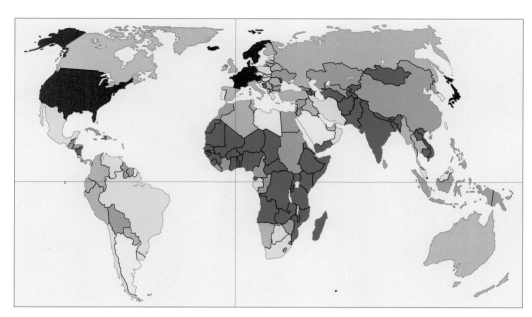

Gross National Product per capita: the value of total production divided by the population (1997)

■	Over 400% of world average
	200 – 400% of world average
	100 – 200% of world average

[World average wealth per person US $6,316]

	50 – 100% of world average
	25 – 50% of world average
	10 – 25% of world average
	Under 10% of world average

GNP per capita growth rate (%), selected countries, 1985–94

Thailand	8.2	Brazil	–0.4
Chile	6.9	Zimbabwe	–0.6
Japan	3.2	USA	–1.3
Germany	1.9	UK	–1.4
Australia	1.2	Armenia	–12.9

Wealth Creation

The Gross National Product (GNP) of the world's largest economies, US $ million (1997)

1.	USA	7,690,100	23.	Turkey	199,500
2.	Japan	4,772,300	24.	Denmark	171,400
3.	Germany	2,319,300	25.	Thailand	169,600
4.	France	1,526,400	26.	Hong Kong	164,400
5.	UK	1,220,200	27.	Norway	158,900
6.	Italy	1,155,400	28.	Poland	138,900
7.	China	1,055,400	29.	South Africa	130,200
8.	Brazil	773,400	30.	Saudi Arabia	128,900
9.	Canada	583,900	31.	Greece	126,200
10.	Spain	570,100	32.	Finland	123,800
11.	South Korea	485,200	33.	Portugal	103,900
12.	Russia	403,500	34.	Singapore	101,800
13.	Netherlands	402,700	35.	Malaysia	98,200
14.	Australia	380,000	36.	Philippines	89,300
15.	India	373,900	37.	Israel	87,600
16.	Mexico	348,600	38.	Colombia	86,800
17.	Switzerland	313,500	39.	Venezuela	78,700
18.	Argentina	305,700	40.	Chile	73,300
19.	Belgium	268,400	41.	Egypt	71,200
20.	Sweden	232,000	42.	Pakistan	67,200
21.	Austria	225,900	43.	Ireland	66,400
22.	Indonesia	221,900	44.	Peru	60,800

The Wealth Gap

The world's richest and poorest countries, by Gross National Product per capita in US $ (1997)

1.	Luxembourg	45,360	1.	Mozambique	90
2.	Switzerland	44,220	2.	Ethiopia	110
3.	Japan	37,850	3.	Congo (D. Rep.)	110
4.	Norway	36,090	4.	Burundi	180
5.	Liechtenstein	33,000	5.	Sierra Leone	200
6.	Singapore	32,940	6.	Niger	200
7.	Denmark	32,500	7.	Rwanda	210
8.	Bermuda	31,870	8.	Tanzania	210
9.	USA	28,740	9.	Nepal	210
10.	Germany	28,260	10.	Malawi	220
11.	Austria	27,980	11.	Chad	240
12.	Iceland	26,580	12.	Madagascar	250
13.	Belgium	26,420	13.	Mali	260
14.	Sweden	26,220	14.	Yemen	270
15.	France	26,050	15.	Cambodia	300
16.	Netherlands	25,820	16.	Bosnia-Herzegovina	300
17.	Monaco	25,000	17.	Gambia, The	320
18.	Hong Kong	22,990	18.	Haiti	330
19.	Finland	20,580	19.	Kenya	330
20.	UK	18,700	20.	Angola	340

GNP per capita is calculated by dividing a country's Gross National Product by its total population.

Continental Shares

Shares of population and of wealth (GNP) by continent

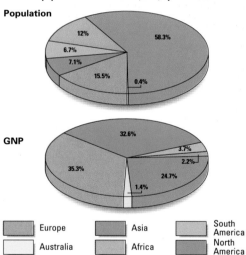

Population

GNP

Europe	Asia	South America	
Australia	Africa	North America	

Inflation

Average annual rate of inflation (1990–96)

	Over 50%
	20 – 50%
	7.5 – 20%
	1 – 7.5%
	Negative inflation
	No data available

Highest average inflation		**Lowest average inflation**	
Congo (D. Rep.)	2747%	Oman	–3.0%
Georgia	2279%	Bahrain	–0.5%
Angola	1103%	Brunei	–0.0%
Turkmenistan	1074%	Saudi Araba	1.0%
Armenia	897%	Japan	1.0%

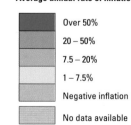

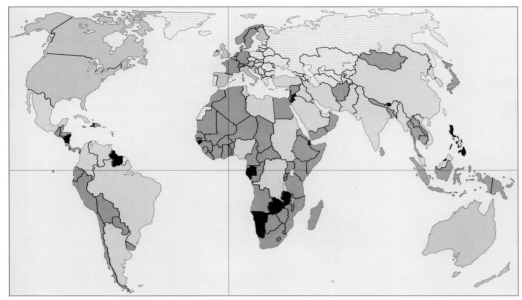

Aid provided or received, divided by the total population, in US $ (1995)

- Over $100 per person
- $10 – $100 per person
- $0 – $10 per person
- No aid given or received   } Providers
- $0 – $10 per person
- $10 – $100 per person   } Receivers
- Over $100 per person

Top 5 providers per capita (1994)		Top 5 receivers per capita (1994)	
France	$279	São Tomé & P.	$378
Denmark	$260	Cape Verde	$314
Norway	$247	Djibouti	$235
Sweden	$201	Surinam	$198
Germany	$166	Mauritania	$153

Debt and Aid

International debtors and the aid they receive (1996)

Although aid grants make a vital contribution to many of the world's poorer countries, they are usually dwarfed by the burden of debt that the developing economies are expected to repay. In 1992, they had to pay US $160,000 million in debt service charges alone – more than two and a half times the amount of Official Development Assistance (ODA) the developing countries were receiving, and US $60,000 million more than total private flows of aid in the same year. In 1990, the debts of Mozambique, one of the world's poorest countries, were estimated to be 75 times its entire earnings from exports.

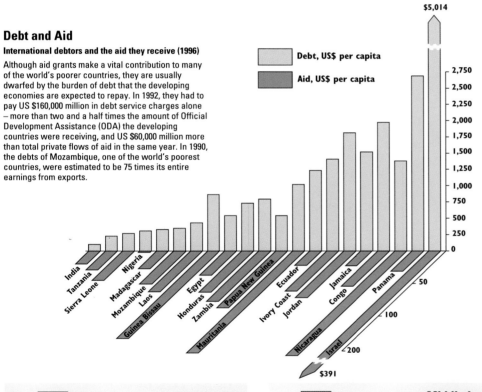

- Debt, US$ per capita
- Aid, US$ per capita

Distribution of Spending

Percentage share of household spending, selected countries

- Food
- Clothing
- Energy & Housing
- Medicine & Education
- Transport
- Other

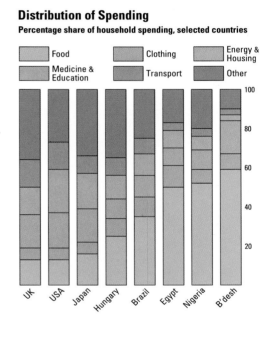

UK, USA, Japan, Hungary, Brazil, Egypt, Nigeria, B'desh

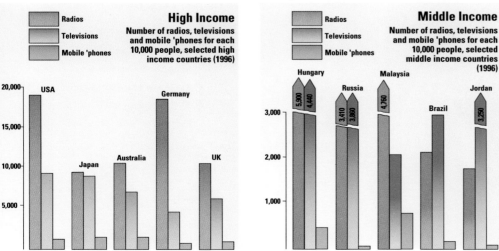

High Income
Number of radios, televisions and mobile 'phones for each 10,000 people, selected high income countries (1996)

- Radios
- Televisions
- Mobile 'phones

USA, Japan, Australia, Germany, UK

Middle Income
Number of radios, televisions and mobile 'phones for each 10,000 people, selected middle income countries (1996)

- Radios
- Televisions
- Mobile 'phones

Hungary (5,900 / 4,440), Russia (3,410 / 3,860), Malaysia (4,760), Brazil, Jordan (3,250)

Low Income
Number of radios, televisions and mobile 'phones for each 10,000 people, selected low income countries (1996)

- Radios
- Televisions
- Mobile 'phones

Albania (1,730 / 1,790), Nigeria (1,700), China (1,780 / 1,610), India, Laos (1,340)

Quality of Life

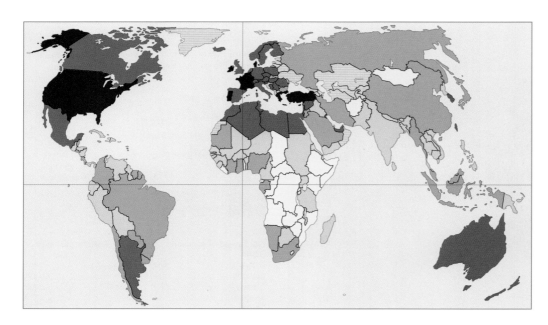

Daily Food Consumption

Average daily food intake in calories per person (1995)

- Over 3,500 calories per person
- 3,000 – 3,500 calories per person
- 2,500 – 3,000 calories per person
- 2,000 – 2,500 calories per person
- Under 2,000 calories per person
- No available data

Top 5 countries

Cyprus	3,708 cal.
Denmark	3,704 cal.
Portugal	3,639 cal.
Ireland	3,638 cal.
USA	3,603 cal.

Bottom 5 countries

Congo (D.Rep.)	1,879 cal.
Djibouti	1,831 cal.
Togo	1,754 cal.
Burundi	1,749 cal.
Mozambique	1,678 cal.

[UK 3,149 calories]

Hospital Capacity

Hospital beds available for each 1,000 people (1996)

Highest capacity		Lowest capacity	
Switzerland	20.8	Benin	0.2
Japan	16.2	Nepal	0.2
Tajikistan	16.0	Afghanistan	0.3
Norway	13.5	Bangladesh	0.3
Belarus	12.4	Ethiopia	0.3
Kazakstan	12.2	Mali	0.4
Moldova	12.2	Burkina Faso	0.5
Ukraine	12.2	Niger	0.5
Latvia	11.9	Guinea	0.6
Russia	11.8	India	0.6

[UK 4.9] [USA 4.2]

Although the ratio of people to hospital beds gives a good approximation of a country's health provision, it is not an absolute indicator. Raw numbers may mask inefficiency and other weaknesses: the high availability of beds in Kazakstan, for example, has not prevented infant mortality rates over three times as high as in the United Kingdom and the United States.

Life Expectancy

Years of life expectancy at birth, selected countries (1997)

The chart shows combined data for both sexes. On average, women live longer than men worldwide, even in developing countries with high maternal mortality rates. Overall, life expectancy is steadily rising, though the difference between rich and poor nations remains dramatic.

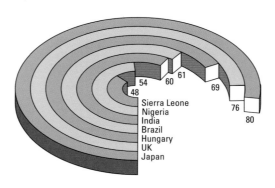

Causes of Death

Causes of death for selected countries by % (1992–94)

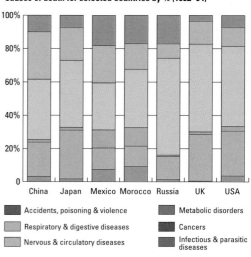

China Japan Mexico Morocco Russia UK USA

- Accidents, poisoning & violence
- Respiratory & digestive diseases
- Nervous & circulatory diseases
- Metabolic disorders
- Cancers
- Infectious & parasitic diseases

Child Mortality

Number of babies who will die under the age of one, per 1,000 births (average 1990–95)

- Over 150 deaths per 1,000 births
- 100 – 150 deaths per 1,000 births
- 50 – 100 deaths per 1,000 births
- 20 – 50 deaths per 1,000 births
- 10 – 20 deaths per 1,000 births
- Under 10 deaths per 1,000 births

Highest child mortality

Afghanistan	162
Mali	159
Sierra Leone	143
Guinea-Bissau	140
Malawi	138

Lowest child mortality

Hong Kong	6
Denmark	6
Japan	5
Iceland	5
Finland	5

[UK 8 deaths]

Percentage of the total population unable to read or write (latest available year)

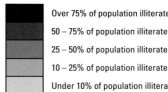

■	Over 75% of population illiterate
■	50 – 75% of population illiterate
■	25 – 50% of population illiterate
■	10 – 25% of population illiterate
■	Under 10% of population illiterate

Educational expenditure per person (latest available year)

Top 5 countries		Bottom 5 countries	
Sweden	$997	Chad	$2
Qatar	$989	Bangladesh	$3
Canada	$983	Ethiopia	$3
Norway	$971	Nepal	$4
Switzerland	$796	Somalia	$4

Fertility and Education

Fertility rates compared with female education, selected countries (1992–95)

■ Percentage of females aged 12–17 in secondary education

■ Fertility rate: average number of children borne per woman

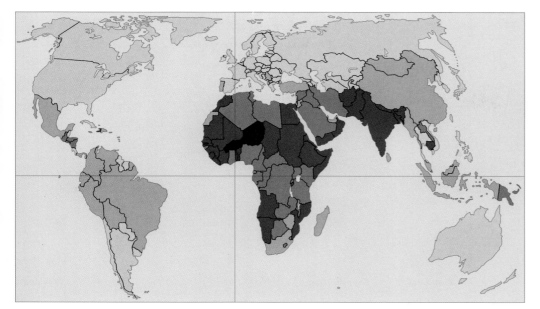

Living Standards

At first sight, most international contrasts in living standards are swamped by differences in wealth. The rich not only have more money, they have more of everything, including years of life. Those with only a little money are obliged to spend most of it on food and clothing, the basic maintenance costs of their existence; air travel and tourism are unlikely to feature on their expenditure lists. However, poverty and wealth are both relative: slum dwellers living on social security payments in an affluent industrial country have far more resources at their disposal than an average African peasant, but feel their own poverty nonetheless. A middle-class Indian lawyer cannot command a fraction of the earnings of a counterpart living in New York, London or Rome; nevertheless, he rightly sees himself as prosperous.

The rich not only live longer, on average, than the poor, they also die from different causes. Infectious and parasitic diseases, all but eliminated in the developed world, remain a scourge in the developing nations. On the other hand, more than two-thirds of the populations of OECD nations eventually succumb to cancer or circulatory disease.

Women in the Work Force

Women in paid employment as a percentage of the total work force (latest available year)

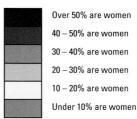

■	Over 50% are women
■	40 – 50% are women
■	30 – 40% are women
■	20 – 30% are women
□	10 – 20% are women
■	Under 10% are women

Most women in the work force		Fewest women in the work force	
Cambodia	56%	Saudi Arabia	4%
Kazakstan	54%	Oman	6%
Burundi	53%	Afghanistañ	8%
Mozambique	53%	Algeria	9%
Turkmenistan	52%	Libya	9%

[USA 45] [UK 44]

Energy

Production

[Each square represents 1% of world energy production]

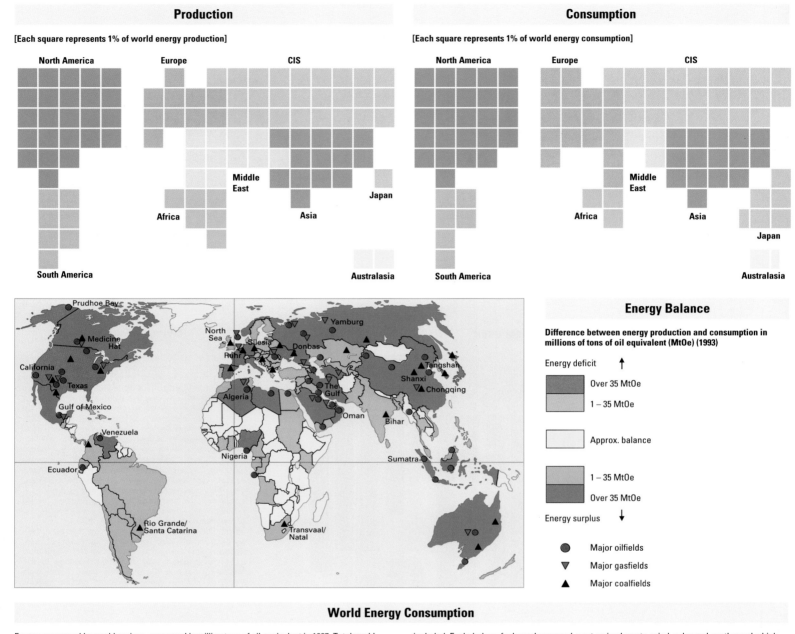

North America

Europe

CIS

Middle East

Africa

Asia

Japan

South America

Australasia

Consumption

[Each square represents 1% of world energy consumption]

North America

Europe

CIS

Middle East

Africa

Asia

Japan

South America

Australasia

Energy Balance

Difference between energy production and consumption in millions of tons of oil equivalent (MtOe) (1993)

Energy deficit ↑

- Over 35 MtOe
- 1 – 35 MtOe

- Approx. balance

- 1 – 35 MtOe
- Over 35 MtOe

Energy surplus ↓

- ● Major oilfields
- ▽ Major gasfields
- ▲ Major coalfields

World Energy Consumption

Energy consumed by world regions, measured in million tons of oil equivalent in 1997. Total world consumption was 8,509 MtOe. Only energy from oil, gas, coal, nuclear and hydroelectric sources are included. Excluded are fuels such as wood, peat, animal waste, wind, solar and geothermal which, though important in some countries, are unreliably documented in terms of consumption statistics.

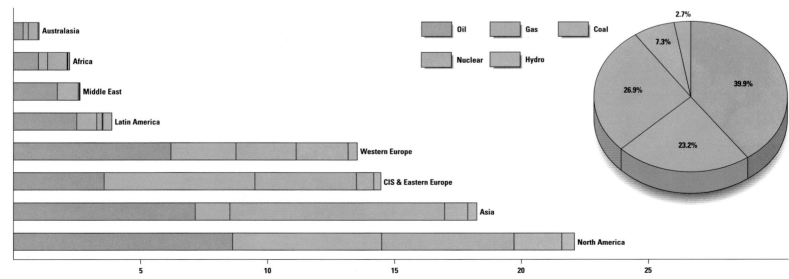

Oil   Gas   Coal

Nuclear   Hydro

2.7%
7.3%
39.9%
26.9%
23.2%

Australasia
Africa
Middle East
Latin America
Western Europe
CIS & Eastern Europe
Asia
North America

5   10   15   20   25

CARTOGRAPHY BY PHILIP'S. COPYRIGHT GEORGE PHILIP LTD

Energy

Energy is used to keep us warm or cool, fuel our industries and our transport systems, and even feed us; high-intensity agriculture, with its use of fertilizers, pesticides and machinery, is heavily energy-dependent. Although we live in a high-energy society, there are vast discrepancies between rich and poor; for example, a North American consumes 13 times as much energy as a Chinese person. But even developing nations have more power at their disposal than was imaginable a century ago.

The distribution of energy supplies, most importantly fossil fuels (coal, oil and natural gas), is very uneven. In addition, the diagrams and map opposite show that the largest producers of energy are not necessarily the largest consumers. The movement of energy supplies around the world is therefore an important component of international trade. In 1995, total world movements in oil amounted to 1,815 million tons.

As the finite reserves of fossil fuels are depleted, renewable energy sources, such as solar, hydro-thermal, wind, tidal and biomass, will become increasingly important around the world.

Nuclear Power

Percentage of electricity generated by nuclear power stations, leading nations (1995)

1.	Lithuania............85%	11.	Spain...............33%
2.	France................77%	12.	Finland.............30%
3.	Belgium............56%	13.	Germany.........29%
4.	Slovak Rep. 49%	14.	Japan...............29%
5.	Sweden..............48%	15.	UK....................27%
6.	Bulgaria............41%	16.	Ukraine...........27%
7.	Hungary............41%	17.	Czech Rep. 22%
8.	Switzerland.........39%	18.	Canada.............19%
9.	Slovenia............38%	19.	USA..................18%
10.	South Korea........33%	20.	Russia 12%

Although the 1980s were a bad time for the nuclear power industry (major projects ran over budget, and fears of long-term environmental damage were heavily reinforced by the 1986 disaster at Chernobyl), the industry picked up in the early 1990s. However, whilst the number of reactors is still increasing, orders for new plants have shrunk. This is partly due to the increasingly difficult task of disposing of nuclear waste.

Hydroelectricity

Percentage of electricity generated by hydroelectric power stations, leading nations (1995)

1.	Paraguay...........99.9%	11.	Rwanda.............97.6%
2.	Congo (Zaïre)....99.7%	12.	Malawi..............97.6%
3.	Bhutan..............99.6%	13.	Cameroon.........96.9%
4.	Zambia..............99.5%	14.	Nepal................96.7%
5.	Norway.............99.4%	15.	Laos.................95.3%
6.	Ghana...............99.3%	16.	Albania.............95.2%
7.	Congo...............99.3%	17.	Iceland.............94.0%
8.	Uganda.............99.1%	17.	Brazil 92.2%
9.	Burundi.............98.3%	19.	Honduras.........87.6%
10.	Uruguay...........98.0%	20.	Tanzania...........87.1%

Countries heavily reliant on hydroelectricity are usually small and non-industrial: a high proportion of hydroelectric power more often reflects a modest energy budget than vast hydroelectric resources. The USA, for instance, produces only 9% of power requirements from hydroelectricity; yet that 9% amounts to more than three times the hydropower generated by all of Africa.

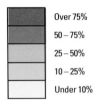

Fuel Exports

Fuels as a percentage of total value of exports (1990–94)

- Over 75%
- 50 – 75%
- 25 – 50%
- 10 – 25%
- Under 10%

Conversion Rates

1 barrel = 0.15 tons or 159 liters or 35 Imperial gallons or 42 US gallons

1 ton = 6.67 barrels or 1,075 liters or 233 Imperial gallons or 280 US gallons

1 ton oil = 1.5 tons hard coal or 3.0 tones lignite or 12,000 kWh

1 Imperial gallon = 1.201 US gallons or 4.546 liters or 277.4 cubic inches

Measurements
For historical reasons, oil is traded in "barrels." The weight and volume equivalents (shown right) are all based on average-density "Arabian light" crude oil.

The energy equivalents given for a ton of oil are also somewhat imprecise: oil and coal of different qualities will have varying energy contents, a fact usually reflected in their price on world markets.

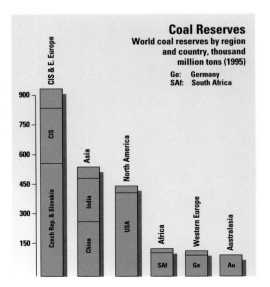

Coal Reserves
World coal reserves by region and country, thousand million tons (1995)
Ge: Germany
SAf: South Africa

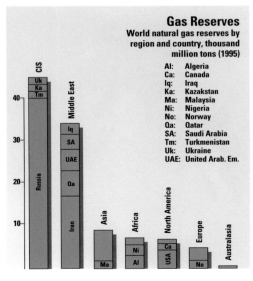

Gas Reserves
World natural gas reserves by region and country, thousand million tons (1995)
Al: Algeria
Ca: Canada
Iq: Iraq
Ka: Kazakstan
Ma: Malaysia
Ni: Nigeria
No: Norway
Qa: Qatar
SA: Saudi Arabia
Tm: Turkmenistan
Uk: Ukraine
UAE: United Arab. Em.

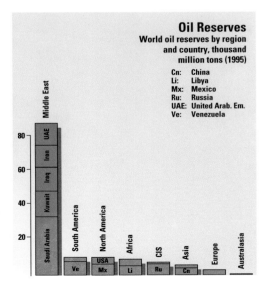

Oil Reserves
World oil reserves by region and country, thousand million tons (1995)
Cn: China
Li: Libya
Mx: Mexico
Ru: Russia
UAE: United Arab. Em.
Ve: Venezuela

Production

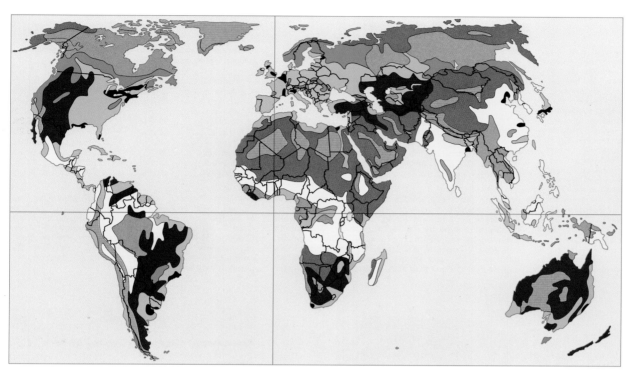

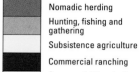

Agriculture

Predominant type of farming or land use.

Nomadic herding

Hunting, fishing and gathering

Subsistence agriculture

Commercial ranching

Commercial livestock and grain farming

Urban areas

Forestry

Unproductive land

The development of agriculture has transformed human existence more than any other. The whole business of farming is constantly developing: due mainly to the new varieties of rice and wheat, world grain production has increased by over 70% since 1965. New machinery and modern agricultural techniques enable relatively few farmers to produce enough food for the world's 6 billion or so people.

Staple Crops

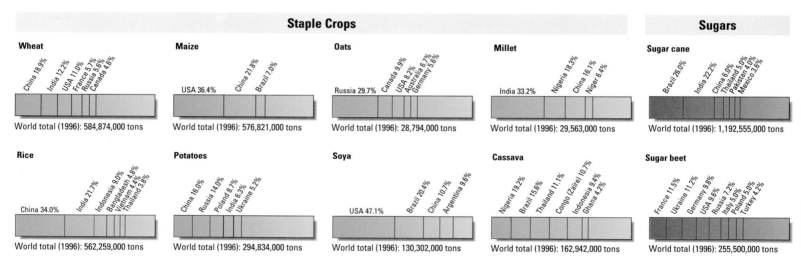

Wheat
China 18.9%
India 12.2%
USA 11.0%
France 5.7%
Russia 5.6%
Canada 4.6%
World total (1996): 584,874,000 tons

Maize
USA 36.4%
China 21.8%
Brazil 7.0%
World total (1996): 576,821,000 tons

Oats
Russia 29.7%
Canada 9.9%
USA 8.2%
Australia 6.7%
Germany 5.6%
World total (1996): 28,794,000 tons

Millet
India 33.2%
Nigeria 18.3%
China 16.1%
Niger 6.4%
World total (1996): 29,563,000 tons

Rice
China 34.0%
India 21.7%
Indonesia 9.0%
Bangladesh 4.8%
Vietnam 4.4%
Thailand 3.8%
World total (1996): 562,259,000 tons

Potatoes
China 16.0%
Russia 14.0%
Poland 8.7%
India 6.3%
Ukraine 5.2%
World total (1996): 294,834,000 tons

Soya
USA 47.1%
Brazil 20.4%
China 10.7%
Argentina 9.6%
World total (1996): 130,302,000 tons

Cassava
Nigeria 19.2%
Brazil 15.6%
Thailand 11.1%
Congo (Zaire) 10.7%
Indonesia 9.4%
Ghana 4.2%
World total (1996): 162,942,000 tons

Sugars

Sugar cane
Brazil 26.0%
India 22.2%
China 6.0%
Thailand 5.0%
Pakistan 4.0%
Mexico 3.6%
World total (1996): 1,192,555,000 tons

Sugar beet
France 11.5%
Ukraine 11.2%
Germany 9.8%
USA 9.6%
Russia 7.2%
Italy 5.0%
Poland 5.0%
Turkey 4.2%
World total (1996): 255,500,000 tons

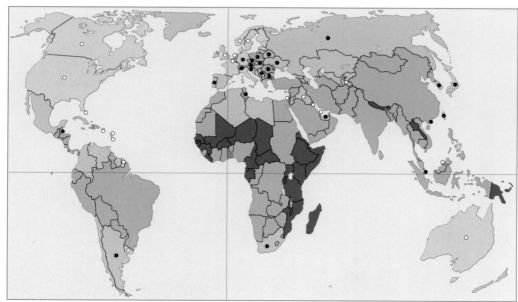

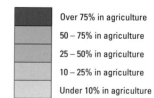

Balance of Employment

Percentage of total work force employed in agriculture, including forestry and fishing (1990–92)

Over 75% in agriculture

50 – 75% in agriculture

25 – 50% in agriculture

10 – 25% in agriculture

Under 10% in agriculture

Employment in industry and services

● Over a third of total work force employed in manufacturing

○ Over two-thirds of total work force employed in service industries (work in offices, shops, tourism, transport, construction and government)

Mineral Production

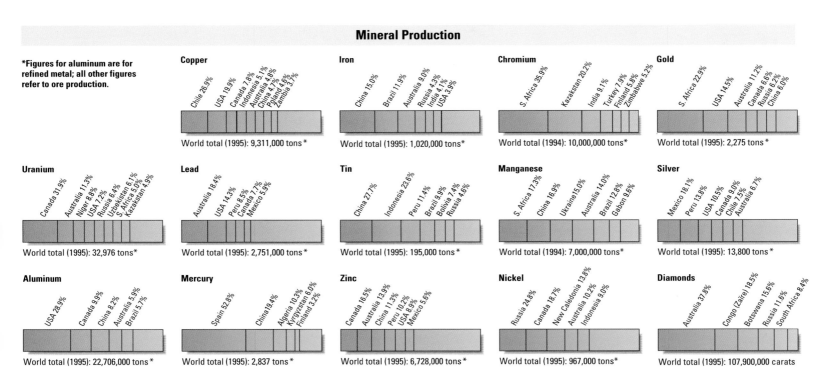

*Figures for aluminum are for refined metal; all other figures refer to ore production.

Copper
Chile 26.9% | USA 19.9% | Canada 7.8% | Indonesia 5.1% | Australia 4.8% | China 4.7% | Poland 4.6% | Zambia 3.7%
World total (1995): 9,311,000 tons*

Iron
China 15.0% | Brazil 11.9% | Australia 9.0% | Russia 4.3% | India 4.1% | USA 3.9%
World total (1995): 1,020,000 tons*

Chromium
S. Africa 35.9% | Kazakstan 20.2% | India 9.1% | Turkey 7.9% | Finland 5.8% | Zimbabwe 5.2%
World total (1994): 10,000,000 tons*

Gold
S. Africa 22.9% | USA 14.5% | Australia 11.2% | Canada 6.6% | Russia 6.2% | China 6.0%
World total (1995): 2,275 tons*

Uranium
Canada 31.9% | Australia 11.3% | Niger 8.8% | USA 7.2% | Russia 6.4% | Uzbekistan 6.1% | S. Africa 5.0% | Kazakstan 4.9%
World total (1995): 32,976 tons*

Lead
Australia 18.4% | USA 14.3% | Peru 8.5% | Canada 7.7% | Mexico 5.9%
World total (1995): 2,751,000 tons*

Tin
China 27.7% | Indonesia 23.6% | Peru 11.4% | Brazil 9.9% | Bolivia 7.4% | Russia 4.6%
World total (1995): 195,000 tons*

Manganese
S. Africa 17.3% | China 16.9% | Ukraine 15.0% | Australia 14.0% | Brazil 12.6% | Gabon 9.6%
World total (1994): 7,000,000 tons*

Silver
Mexico 18.1% | Peru 13.8% | USA 10.5% | Canada 9.0% | Chile 7.5% | Australia 6.7%
World total (1995): 13,800 tons*

Aluminum
USA 28.9% | Canada 9.9% | China 8.2% | Australia 5.9% | Brazil 5.7%
World total (1995): 22,706,000 tons*

Mercury
Spain 52.8% | China 19.4% | Algeria 10.3% | Kyrgyzstan 6.0% | Finland 3.2%
World total (1995): 2,837 tons*

Zinc
Canada 16.5% | Australia 13.9% | China 11.3% | Peru 10.2% | USA 9.8% | Mexico 5.6%
World total (1995): 6,728,000 tons*

Nickel
Russia 24.8% | Canada 18.7% | New Caledonia 13.8% | Australia 10.2% | Indonesia 9.0%
World total (1995): 967,000 tons*

Diamonds
Australia 37.8% | Congo (Zaire) 18.5% | Botswana 15.6% | Russia 11.6% | South Africa 8.4%
World total (1995): 107,900,000 carats

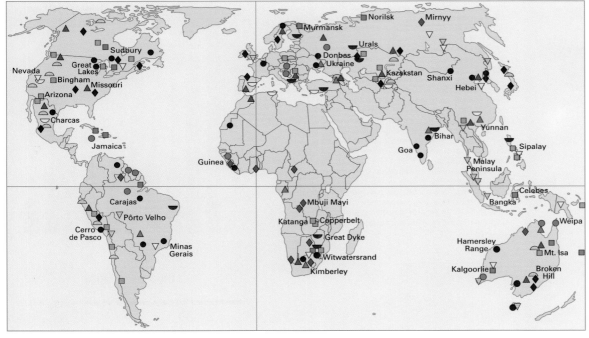

Mineral Distribution

The map shows the richest sources of the most important minerals. Major mineral locations are named.

Light metals
● Bauxite

Base metals
■ Copper
▲ Lead
▽ Mercury
▽ Tin
◆ Zinc

Iron and ferro-alloys
● Iron
◥ Chrome
▲ Manganese
■ Nickel

Precious metals
▽ Gold
◠ Silver

Precious stones
◆ Diamonds

The map does not show undersea deposits, most of which are considered inaccessible.

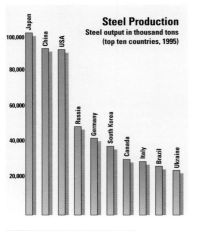

Steel Production
Steel output in thousand tons (top ten countries, 1995)

(Japan, China, USA, Russia, Germany, South Korea, Canada, Italy, Brazil, Ukraine)

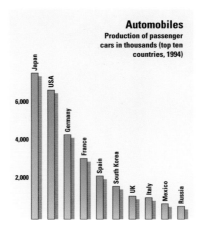

Ship Building
Merchant vessels launched by the top ten countries, in thousand gross registered tons (1996)

(Japan, South Korea, Germany, Taiwan, China, Italy, Spain, Poland, France, Finland)

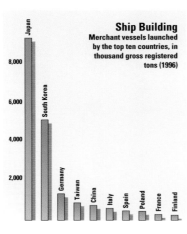

Automobiles
Production of passenger cars in thousands (top ten countries, 1994)

(Japan, USA, Germany, France, Spain, South Korea, UK, Italy, Mexico, Russia)

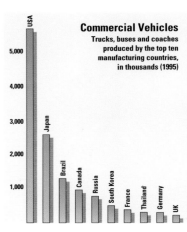

Commercial Vehicles
Trucks, buses and coaches produced by the top ten manufacturing countries, in thousands (1995)

(USA, Japan, Brazil, Canada, Russia, South Korea, France, Thailand, Germany, UK)

Trade

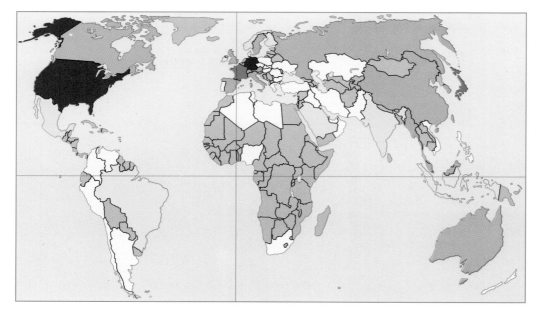

Over 10% of world trade

5 – 10% of world trade

1 – 5% of world trade

0.5 – 1% of world trade

0.1 – 0.5% of world trade

Under 0.1% of world trade

International trade is dominated by a handful of powerful maritime nations. The members of "G8," the inner circle of OECD (see page 19), and the top seven countries listed in the diagram below, account for more than half the total. The majority of nations – including all but four in Africa – contribute less than one quarter of 1% to the worldwide total of exports; the EU countries account for 40%, the Pacific Rim nations over 35%.

The Main Trading Nations

The imports and exports of the top ten trading nations as a percentage of world trade (1994). Each country's trade in manufactured goods is shown in dark blue.

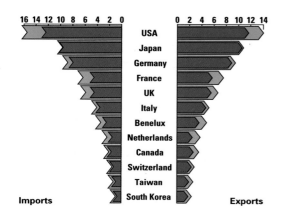

16 14 12 10 8 6 4 2 0   0 2 4 6 8 10 12 14

USA
Japan
Germany
France
UK
Italy
Benelux
Netherlands
Canada
Switzerland
Taiwan
South Korea

Imports   **Exports**

Patterns of Trade

Thriving international trade is the outward sign of a healthy world economy, the obvious indicator that some countries have goods to sell and others the means to buy them. Global exports expanded to an estimated US $3.92 trillion in 1994, an increase due partly to economic recovery in industrial nations but also to export-led growth strategies in many developing nations and lowered regional trade barriers. International trade remains dominated, however, by the rich, industrialized countries of the Organization for Economic Development: between them, OECD members account for almost 75% of world imports and exports in most years. However, continued rapid economic growth in some developing countries is altering global trade patterns. The "tiger economies" of Southeast Asia are particularly vibrant, averaging more than 8% growth between 1992 and 1994. The size of the largest trading economies means that imports and exports usually represent only a small percentage of their total wealth. In export-concious Japan, for example, trade in goods and services amounts to less than 18% of GDP. In poorer countries, trade – often in a single commodity – may amount to 50% of GDP.

Traded Products

Top ten manufactures traded, by value in billions of US $ (latest available year)

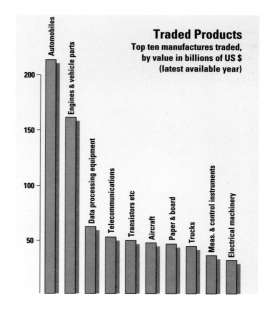

Balance of Trade

Value of exports in proportion to the value of imports (1995)

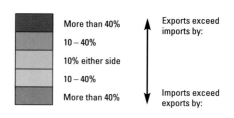

More than 40%

10 – 40%

10% either side

10 – 40%

More than 40%

Exports exceed imports by:

Imports exceed exports by:

The total world trade balance should amount to zero, since exports must equal imports on a global scale. In practice, at least $100 billion in exports go unrecorded, leaving the world with an apparent deficit and many countries in a better position than public accounting reveals. However, a favorable trade balance is not necessarily a sign of prosperity: many poorer countries must maintain a high surplus in order to service debts, and do so by restricting imports below the levels needed to sustain successful economies.

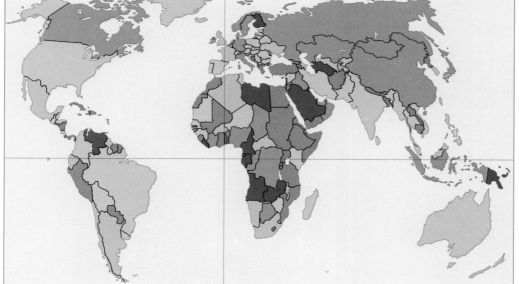

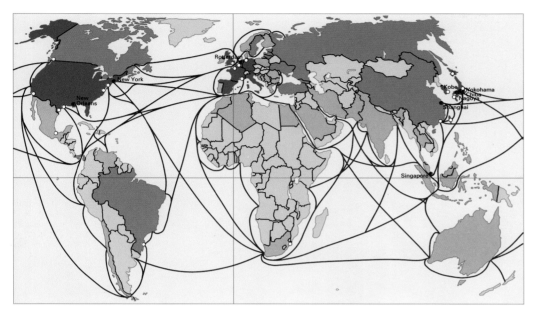

Seaborne Freight

Freight unloaded in millions of tonnes (latest available year)

- Over 100
- 50 – 100
- 10 – 50
- 5 – 10
- Under 5
- Landlocked countries

Major seaports

- ● Over 100 million tonnes per year
- ○ 50–100 million tonnes per year
- ── Major shipping routes

Cargoes

Type of seaborne freight

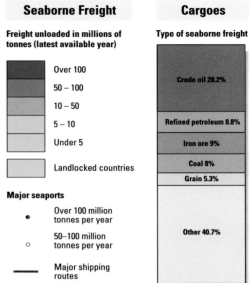

- Crude oil 28.2%
- Refined petroleum 8.8%
- Iron ore 9%
- Coal 8%
- Grain 5.3%
- Other 40.7%

Merchant Fleets

Merchant fleets in thousand gross tonnage (1996). A large number of vessels are registered in Liberia and Panama but they are not part of the national fleet.

Hong Kong, Denmark, Taiwan, Italy, Turkey, India, Germany, South Korea, Philippines, USA, Russia, China, Japan, Singapore, Norway, Cyprus, Greece, Bahamas, Liberia, Panama

20,000   40,000   60,000   80,000   100,000

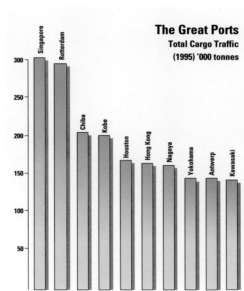

The Great Ports

Total Cargo Traffic

(1995) '000 tonnes

Singapore, Rotterdam, Chiba, Kobe, Houston, Hong Kong, Nagoya, Yokohama, Antwerp, Kawasaki

50   100   150   200   250   300

World Shipping

World merchant fleet by type of vessel and deadweight tonnage (latest available year)

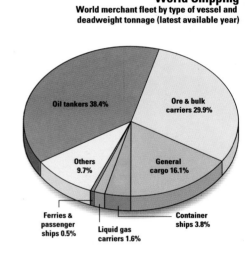

- Oil tankers 38.4%
- Ore & bulk carriers 29.9%
- Others 9.7%
- General cargo 16.1%
- Ferries & passenger ships 0.5%
- Liquid gas carriers 1.6%
- Container ships 3.8%

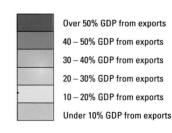

Dependence on Trade

Value of exports as a percentage of Gross Domestic Product (1997)

- Over 50% GDP from exports
- 40 – 50% GDP from exports
- 30 – 40% GDP from exports
- 20 – 30% GDP from exports
- 10 – 20% GDP from exports
- Under 10% GDP from exports

- ○ Most dependent on industrial exports (over 75% of total exports)
- ◐ Most dependent on fuel exports (over 75% of total exports)
- ◌ Most dependent on mineral and metal exports (over 75% of total exports)

Travel and Tourism

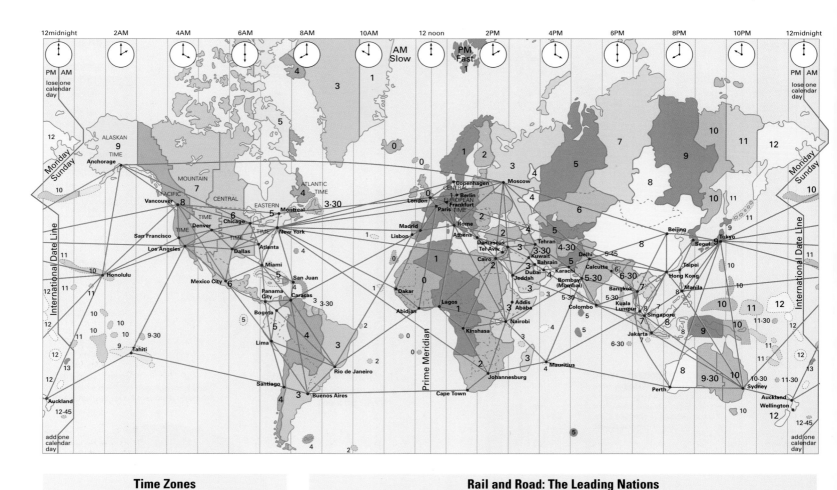

Time zone map labels (clock times across top): 12 midnight, 2AM, 4AM, 6AM, 8AM, 10AM, 12 noon, 2PM, 4PM, 6PM, 8PM, 10PM, 12 midnight

Time Zones

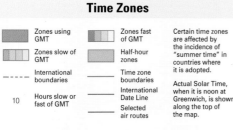

Zones using GMT
Zones slow of GMT
International boundaries
10 Hours slow or fast of GMT

Zones fast of GMT
Half-hour zones
Time zone boundaries
International Date Line
Selected air routes

Certain time zones are affected by the incidence of "summer time" in countries where it is adopted.

Actual Solar Time, when it is noon at Greenwich, is shown along the top of the map.

The world is divided into 24 time zones, each centered on meridians at 15° intervals, which is the longitudinal distance the sun travels every hour. The meridian running through Greenwich, London, passes through the middle of the first zone.

Rail and Road: The Leading Nations

Total rail network ('000 miles) (1995)	Passenger miles per head per year	Total road network ('000 miles)	Vehicle miles per head per year	Number of vehicles per mile of roads
1. USA 146.5	Japan 1,253	USA 3,898.6	USA 7,766	Hong Kong 176
2. Russia 54.3	Belarus...............1,167	India 1,839.7	Luxembourg 4,961	Taiwan 131
3. India 40.0	Russia.................1,134	Brazil 1,133.0	Kuwait 4,503	Singapore 94
4. China 34.0	Switzerland 1,099	Japan 702.3	France 4,435	Kuwait 87
5. Germany 25.0	Ukraine.................904	China 646.5	Sweden 4,341	Brunei 60
6. Australia............22.2	Austria 725	Russia 549.0	Germany 4,227	Italy 57
7. Argentina 21.3	France 628	Canada 527.5	Denmark 4,200	Israel 54
8. France 19.8	Netherlands 617	France 504.0	Austria 4,048	Thailand 45
9. Mexico...............16.5	Latvia 570	Australia 503.2	Netherlands 3,716	Ukraine.................45
10. South Africa.......16.3	Denmark 549	Germany 395.1	UK 3,563	UK 42
11. Poland................15.5	Slovak Rep. 535	Romania............286.8	Canada 3,411	Netherlands 41
12. Ukraine...............14.0	Romania 528	Turkey 241.0	Italy 3,013	Germany 39

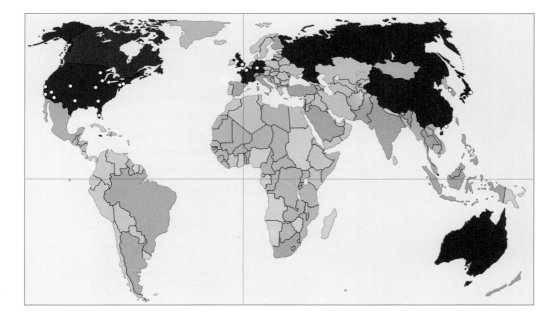

Air Travel

Passenger miles (the number of passengers – international and domestic – multiplied by the distance flown by each passenger from the airport of origin) (1996)

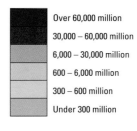

- Over 60,000 million
- 30,000 – 60,000 million
- 6,000 – 30,000 million
- 600 – 6,000 million
- 300 – 600 million
- Under 300 million

○ Major airports (handling over 25 million passengers in 1995)

World's busiest airports (total passengers)		World's busiest airports (international passengers)	
1. Chicago	(O'Hare)	1. London	(Heathrow)
2. Atlanta	(Hatsfield)	2. London	(Gatwick)
3. Dallas	(Dallas/Ft Worth)	3. Frankfurt	(International)
4. Los Angeles	(Intern'l)	4. New York	(Kennedy)
5. London	(Heathrow)	5. Paris	(De Gaulle)

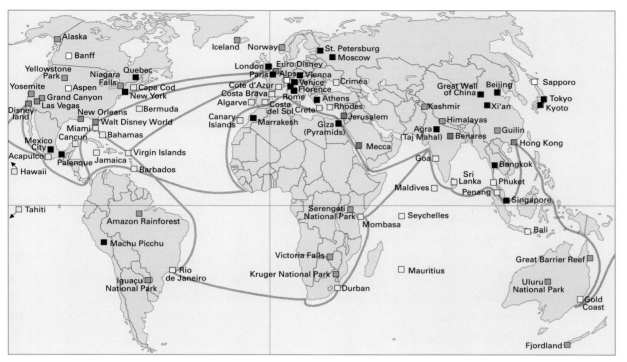

Destinations

- ■ Cultural and historical centers
- ☐ Coastal resorts
- ☐ Ski resorts
- Centers of entertainment
- Places of pilgrimage
- Places of great natural beauty
- — Popular holiday cruise routes

Visitors to the USA

Overseas travelers to the USA, thousands (1997 estimates)

1.	Canada	13,900
2.	Mexico	12,370
3.	Japan	4,640
4.	UK	3,350
5.	Germany	1,990
6.	France	1,030
7.	Taiwan	885
8.	Venezuela	860
9.	South Korea	800
10.	Brazil	785

In 1996, the USA earned the most from tourism, with receipts of more than US $75 billion.

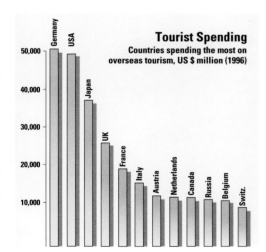

Tourist Spending

Countries spending the most on overseas tourism, US $ million (1996)

Importance of Tourism

		Arrivals from abroad (1996)	% of world total (1996)
1.	France	66,800,000	10.2%
2.	USA	49,038,000	7.5%
3.	Spain	43,403,000	6.6%
4.	Italy	34,087,000	5.2%
5.	UK	25,960,000	3.9%
6.	China	23,770,000	3.6%
7.	Poland	19,514,000	3.0%
8.	Mexico	18,667,000	2.9%
9.	Canada	17,610,000	2.7%
10.	Czech Republic	17,400,000	2.7%
11.	Hungary	17,248,000	2.6%
12.	Austria	16,642,000	2.5%

In 1996, there was a 4.6% rise, to 593 million, in the total number of people traveling abroad. Small economies in attractive areas are often completely dominated by tourism: in some West Indian islands, for example, tourist spending provides over 90% of total income.

Tourist Earning

Countries receiving the most from overseas tourism, US $ million (1996)

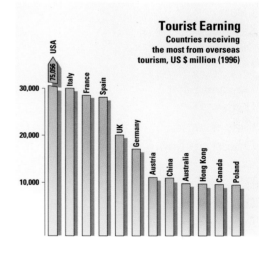

Tourism

Tourism receipts as a percentage of Gross National Product (1994)

- Over 10% of GNP from tourism
- 5 – 10% of GNP from tourism
- 2.5 – 5% of GNP from tourism
- 1 – 2.5% of GNP from tourism
- 0.5 – 1% of GNP from tourism
- Under 0.5% of GNP from tourism

Countries spending the most on promoting tourism, millions of US $ (1996)		Fastest growing tourist destinations, % change in receipts (1994–5)	
Australia	88	South Korea	49%
Spain	79	Czech Republic	27%
UK	79	India	21%
France	73	Russia	19%
Singapore	54	Philippines	18%

The World In Focus: Index

WORLD MAPS

SETTLEMENTS

■ PARIS   ▪ Berne   ◉ Livorno   ◎ Brugge   ◎ Algeciras   ○ Frejus   ○ Oberammergau   ○ Thira

Settlement symbols and type styles vary according to the scale of each map and indicate the importance
of towns on the map rather than specific population figures

∴   Ruins or Archæological Sites   Wells in Desert

ADMINISTRATION

——— International Boundaries

- - - - · International Boundaries
(Undefined or Disputed)

············· Internal Boundaries

National Parks

Country Names
NICARAGUA

Administrative
Area Names

KENT

CALABRIA

International boundaries show the *de facto* situation where there are rival claims to territory

COMMUNICATIONS

——— Principal Roads

——— Other Roads

┤- - -├ Road Tunnels

⤳ Passes

✈ Airfields

——— Principal Railways

- - - Railways
Under Construction

——— Other Railways

┤- - -├ Railway Tunnels

⊥⊥⊥⊥⊥ Principal Canals

PHYSICAL FEATURES

~~~ Perennial Streams

- - - Intermittent Streams

⬭ Perennial Lakes

⬭ Intermittent Lakes

🝆 Swamps and Marshes

Permanent Ice
and Glaciers

▲ 8848   Elevations in metres

▼ 8500   Sea Depths in metres

1134   Height of Lake Surface
Above Sea Level in metres

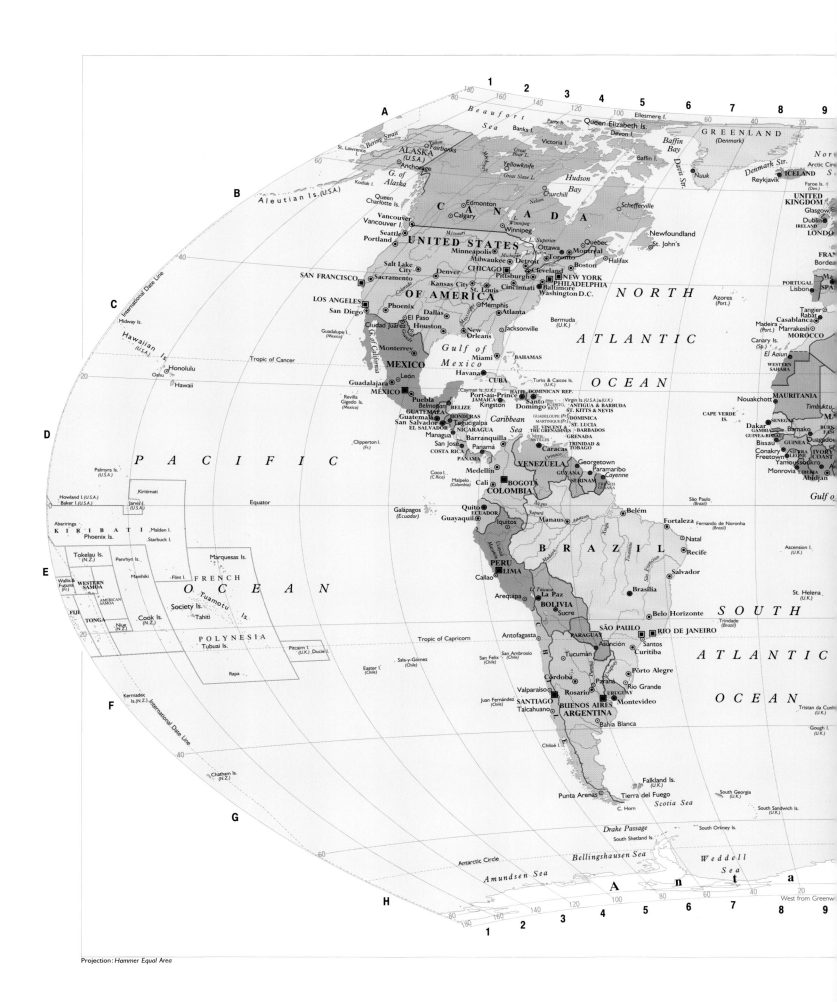

Projection: Hammer Equal Area

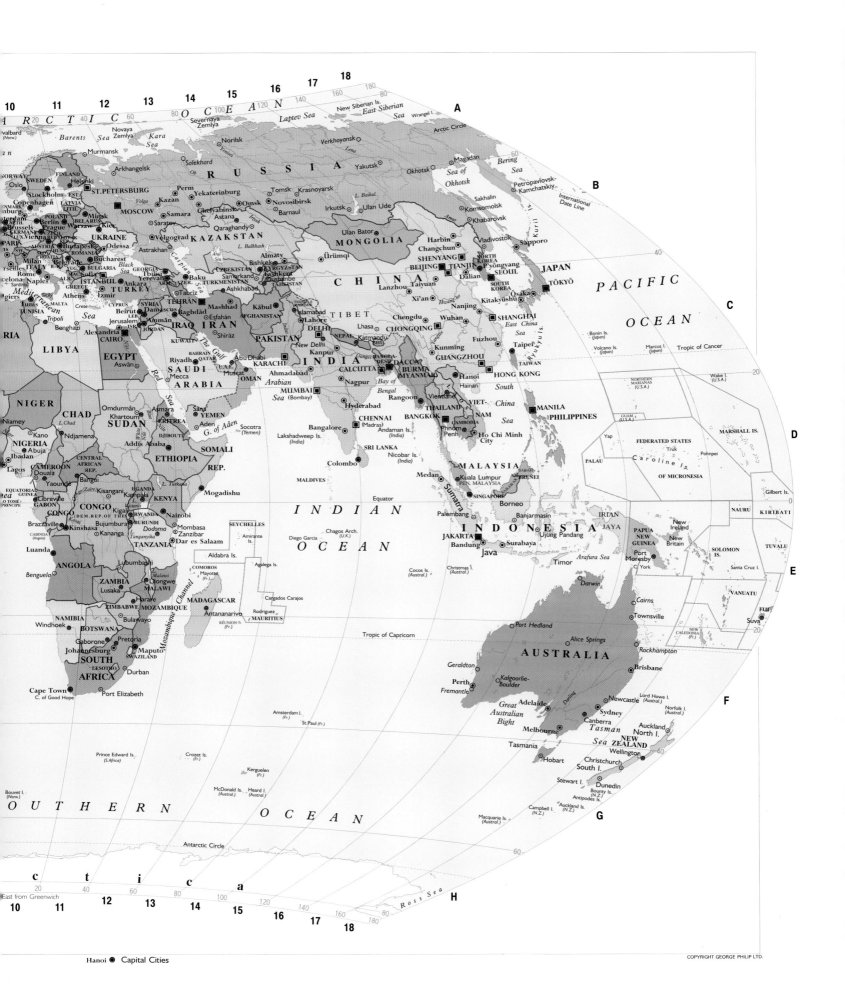

A R C T I C   O C E A N

Svalbard *(Norw.)*

Barents Sea   Novaya Zemlya   *Kara Sea*

Severnaya Zemlya   *Laptev Sea*   New Siberian Is.   *East Siberian Sea*   Wrangel I.   **A**

Murmansk   Arkhangelsk   Salekhard   Norilsk   *Ob*   *Yenisey*   Verkhoyansk   *Lena*   Arctic Circle

R U S S I A   Yakutsk   Okhotsk   *Sea of Okhotsk*   Magadan   *Bering Sea*   **B**

NORWAY   Oslo   SWEDEN   FINLAND   Helsinki   ST.PETERSBURG   Perm   Yekaterinburg   Tomsk   Krasnoyarsk   L. Baikal   Petropavlovsk-Kamchatskiy

Stockholm   EST.   MOSCOW   Kazan   *Volga*   Chelyabinsk   Omsk   Novosibirsk   Irkutsk   Ulan Ude   Sakhalin   Komsomolsk   International Date Line

DENMARK   LAT.   Minsk   Samara   Astana   Barnaul   Khabarovsk   *Amur*   *Kuril*

Hamburg   POLAND   LITH.   BELARUS   Saratov   Qaraghandy   Ulan Bator   Harbin   Vladivostok   Sapporo

Brussels   Berlin   Warsaw   Kiev   UKRAINE   Volgograd   KAZAKSTAN   MONGOLIA   Changchun   **C**

Prague   GERMANY   CZECH   SLOVAK.   Odessa   Astrakhan   *L. Balkhash*   Ürümqi   SHENYANG   NORTH KOREA   P'yongyang   JAPAN

PARIS   Vienna   AUSTRIA   HUNGARY   ROMANIA   *Aral Sea*   Almaty   BEIJING   TIANJIN   Dalian   SEOUL   TŌKYŌ   PACIFIC

SWITZ.   CROATIA   Budapest   Belgrade   Bucharest   *Black Sea*   GEORGIA   Bishkek   KYRGYZSTAN   Lanzhou   Taiyuan   SOUTH KOREA   Osaka   Kitakyushu

Milan   YUG.   BULGARIA   Tbilisi   Baku   UZBEKISTAN   Tashkent   CHINA   Xi'an   *Huang He*   OCEAN

Rome   ITALY   ALB.   MAC.   Sofia   ARM.   AZER.   Yerevan   Samarkand   TAJIKISTAN   Chengdu   Wuhan   SHANGHAI   *East China Sea*

Marseilles   Naples   GREECE   ISTANBUL   Ankara   TURKMENISTAN   Ashkhabad   Kābul   Dushanbe   CHONGQING   *Ryukyu Is.*

Barcelona   Sardinia   Athens   Izmir   TURKEY   Tabriz   Mashhad   AFGHANISTAN   T I B E T   Lhasa   Kunming   Fuzhou   Taipei   Bonin Is. *(Japan)*   Volcano Is. *(Japan)*   Marcus I. *(Japan)*   Tropic of Cancer

Sicily   Crete   CYPRUS   SYRIA   Beirut   Damascus   TEHRĀN   Esfahān   Islamabad   Lahore   DELHI   GUANGZHOU   TAIWAN

Tunis   TUNISIA   MALTA   Jerusalem   LEB.   ISR.   Baghdād   IRAQ   IRAN   PAKISTAN   New Delhi   NEPAL   Katmandu   BHU.   HONG KONG   Hainan

Algiers   Tripoli   Benghazi   Alexandria   JORDAN   Shirāz   KUWAIT   *The Gulf*   Kanpur   BANGLA-DESH   DACCA   BURMA   *South China Sea*   **C**

ALGERIA   CAIRO   BAHRAIN   QATAR   Abu Dhabi   *Indus*   INDIA   CALCUTTA   MYANMAR   Hanoi   Vientiane   Volcano

LIBYA   EGYPT   Riyadh   U.A.E.   Muscat   KARACHI   Ahmadabad   Nagpur   Rangoon   THAILAND   BANGKOK   VIET-NAM

SAUDI   Mecca   OMAN   *Arabian Sea*   *Bay of Bengal*   CAMBODIA   Phnom Penh

NIGER   Aswān   ARABIA   *Red Sea*   MUMBAI (Bombay)   Hyderabad   CHENNAI (Madras)   Andaman Is. *(India)*   Ho Chi Minh City   MANILA   PHILIPPINES   NORTHERN MARIANAS *(U.S.A.)*   Wake I. *(U.S.A.)*   **D**

CHAD   Omdurmân   Khartoum   Asmara   San'ā   YEMEN   Bangalore   Lakshadweep Is. *(India)*   Nicobar Is. *(India)*

Niamey   NIGERIA   Kano   Ndjamena   SUDAN   ERITREA   Aden   *G. of Aden*   Socotra *(Yemen)*   SRI LANKA   MALAYSIA   SABAH   Yap   FEDERATED STATES   MARSHALL IS.

Abuja   Addis Ababa   DJIBOUTI   SOMALI REP.   Colombo   MALDIVES   Medan   Kuala Lumpur   BRUNEI   PALAU   Truk   Pohnpei   *Caroline Is.*

Ibadan   Lagos   CENTRAL AFRICAN REP.   ETHIOPIA   PEN. MALAYSIA   OF MICRONESIA   Gilbert Is.

CAMEROON   Douala   Bangui   *L. Turkana*   SINGAPORE   Borneo   NAURU   KIRIBATI

EQUATORIAL GUINEA   SÃO TOMÉ & PRÍNCIPE   Yaounde   UGANDA   Kisangani   Kampala   KENYA   Equator   Palembang   Banjarmasin   IRIAN   **D**

GABON   Libreville   CONGO   DEM. REP. OF THE   Kigali   RWANDA   Nairobi   Sumatra   I N D O N E S I A   JAYA   PAPUA NEW GUINEA   New Ireland

Brazzaville   Kinshasa   *Congo/Zaïre*   BURUNDI   Bujumbura   Dodoma   Mombasa   *Victoria*   JAKARTA   Ujung Pandang   New Britain   SOLOMON IS.   TUVALU

CABINDA *(Angola)*   Kananga   Zanzibar   *Tanganyika*   Dar es Salaam   SEYCHELLES   Amirante Is.   Chagos Arch. *(U.K.)*   Bandung   Surabaya   Java   Timor   *Arafura Sea*   Port Moresby   Santa Cruz I.   **E**

Luanda   TANZANIA   Aldabra Is.   Diego Garcia   C. York   VANUATU

Benguela   ANGOLA   Lubumbashi   COMOROS   Mayotte *(Fr.)*   Agalega Is. *(Maur.)*   I N D I A N   O C E A N   Cocos Is. *(Austral.)*   Christmas I. *(Austral.)*   FIJI   Suva

ZAMBIA   Lilongwe   *Malawi*   MALAWI   Cargados Carajos   Darwin   NEW CALEDONIA *(Fr.)*

Lusaka   Harare   MOZAMBIQUE   MADAGASCAR   Antananarivo   Rodriguez I. *(Fr.)*   Cairns   Townsville

NAMIBIA   ZIMBABWE   Bulawayo   *Mozambique Channel*   RÉUNION *(Fr.)*   MAURITIUS   Port Hedland   Alice Springs   Rockhampton   Tropic of Capricorn   **F**

Windhoek   BOTSWANA   Gaborone   Pretoria   Maputo   SWAZILAND   Geraldton   A U S T R A L I A   Brisbane

Johannesburg   SOUTH   LESOTHO   Durban   AFRICA   Perth   Kalgoorlie-Boulder   Adelaide   Newcastle   Lord Howe I. *(Austral.)*   Norfolk I. *(Austral.)*

Cape Town   C. of Good Hope   Port Elizabeth   Amsterdam I. *(Fr.)*   St.Paul *(Fr.)*   Fremantle   *Great Australian Bight*   *Darling*   Sydney   Auckland   North I.

Prince Edward Is. *(S.Africa)*   Crozet Is. *(Fr.)*   Kerguelen *(Fr.)*   Canberra   Melbourne   *Tasman Sea*   Wellington   NEW ZEALAND

Bouvet I. *(Norw.)*   McDonald I. *(Austral.)*   Heard I. *(Austral.)*   Tasmania   Hobart   Christchurch   South I.

S O U T H E R N   O C E A N   Stewart I.   Dunedin   Antipodes Is. *(N.Z.)*   Bounty Is. *(N.Z.)*   **G**

Antarctic Circle   Macquarie Is. *(Austral.)*   Campbell I. *(N.Z.)*   Auckland I. *(N.Z.)*

A n t a r c t i c a   *Ross Sea*   **H**

Hanoi ● Capital Cities

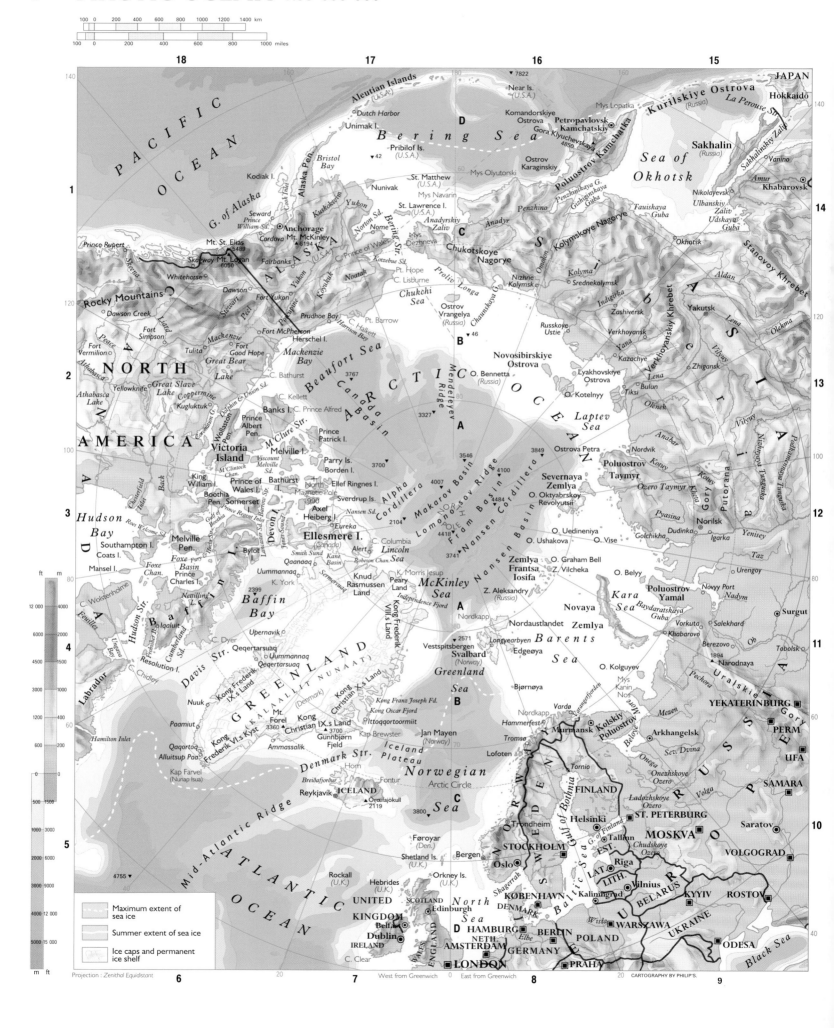

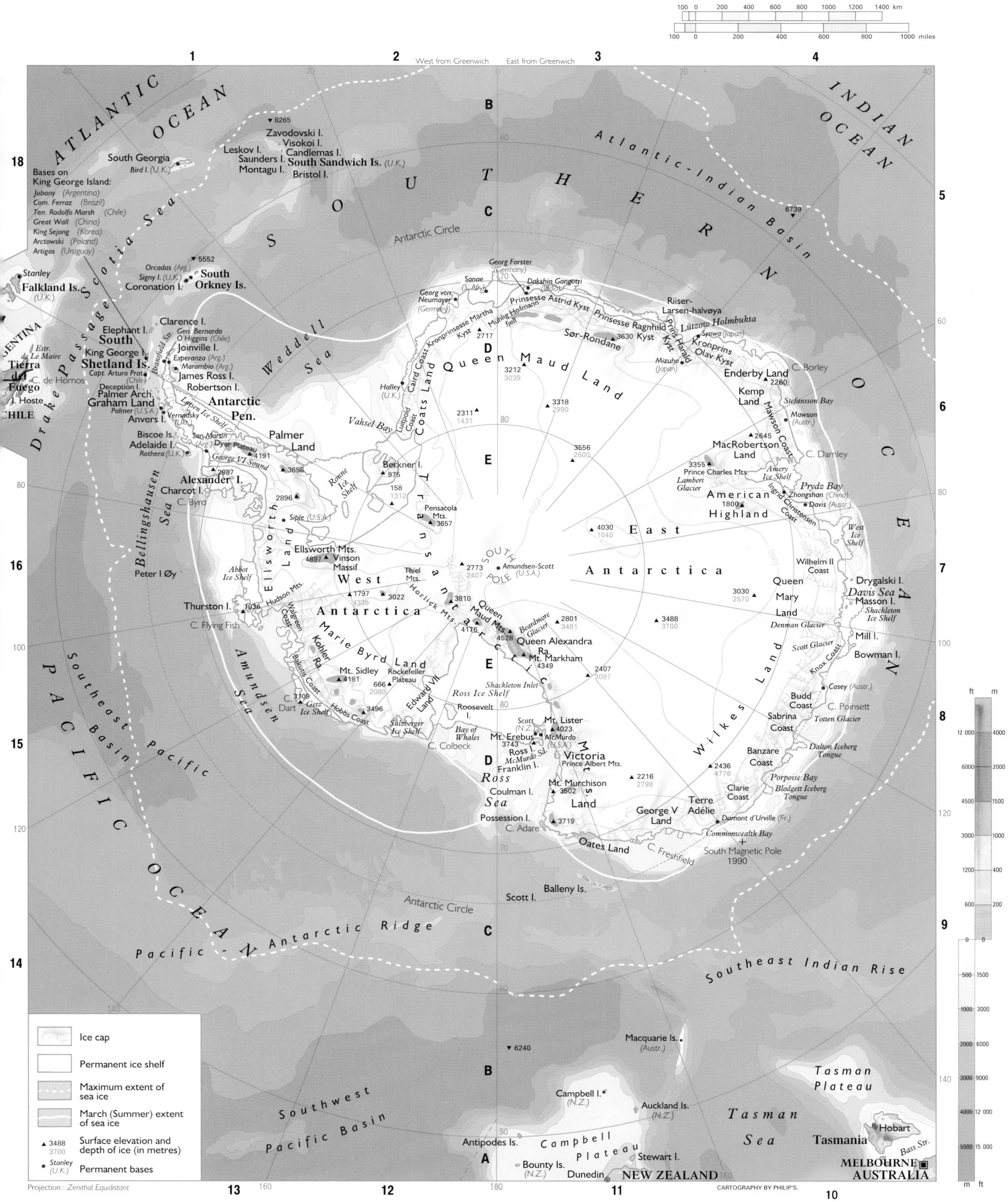

100 0 200 400 600 800 1000 1200 1400 km
100 0 200 400 600 800 1000 miles

ATLANTIC OCEAN

West from Greenwich | East from Greenwich

INDIAN OCEAN

SOUTHERN OCEAN

▼8265

Zavodovski I.
Visokoi I.
Leskov I. Candlemas I.
Saunders I. South Sandwich Is. (U.K.)
Montagu I. Bristol I.

South Georgia
Bird I. (U.K.)

Bases on
King George Island:
Jubany (Argentina)
Com. Ferraz (Brazil)
Ten. Rodolfo Marsh (Chile)
Great Wall (China)
King Sejong (Korea)
Arctowski (Poland)
Artigas (Uruguay)

Antarctic Circle

Scotia Sea

▼5552

Orcadas (Arg.)
Signy I. (U.K.) South
Coronation I. Orkney Is.

Stanley
Falkland Is.
(U.K.)

Atlantic-Indian Basin

6739

Georg Forster
(Germany)
Sanae Dakshin Gangotri (India)
(S. Afr.)
Georg von Prinsesse Astrid Kyst
Neumayer Prinsesse Martha Prinsesse Ragnhild Kyst
(Germany) Kyst Mühlig-Holmfjell Riiser-
Kronprinsesse Martha 2717 Sør-Rondane 3630 Kyst Larsen-halvøya
Kronprins Syowa (Japan)
Georg Queen Maud Land 3212 Olav Kyst Lützow-Holmbukta
3039 Prins Harald Kyst
Halley 3318 Mizuho Enderby Land C. Borley
(U.K.) 2990 (Japan)

GENTINA

Estr.
de Le Maire
C. de Hornos
Tierra
del
Fuego
I. Hoste
CHILE

Elephant I.
Gen. Bernardo
O'Higgins (Chile)
King George I. Esperanza (Arg.)
South Marambio (Arg.)
Shetland Is. Capt. Arturo Prat (Chile)
Deception I. (Chile)
Palmer Arch. James Ross I.
Graham Land Robertson I.
Palmer (U.S.A.) Antarctic
Vernadsky Pen.
Anvers I. (U.K.)
San Martin Palmer
Biscoe Is. (Arg.) Land
Adelaide I. Dyer Plateau
Rothera (U.K.)

Weddell Sea

Larsen Ice Shelf

Vahsel Bay

Coats Land
Caird Coast

Kronprinsesse Martha

Kemp
Land

2311 Mawson (Austr.)
1431 Stefansson Bay
MacRobertson
Land 2645
3556 C. Darnley
2600 3355 Prince Charles Mts.
Amery Lambert
Ice Shelf Glacier Prydz Bay
American Zhongshan (China)
Highland Davis (Austr.)
1800 Ingrid Christensen Coast
1040 East West
Antarctica Ice Shelf

Alexander I.
Charcot I.
C. Byrd
2987
2896
Siple (U.S.A.)
Pensacola
Mts.
3657
Ellsworth Mts.
4897 Vinson
Massif

Berkner I.
975
158
1312

Ronne
Ice
Shelf

Filchner Ice Shelf

3658

South Pole
Amundsen-Scott
(U.S.A.)
2773
2407

Thiel
Mts.
3810

Queen Mary
Land
3030
2570
Wilhelm II
Coast
Drygalski I.
Davis Sea
Masson I.
Shackleton
Ice Shelf
Mill I.
Bowman I.

Bellingshausen Sea

Peter I Øy

Thurston I.
1797
4335
3022
1036
C. Flying Fish

West
Antarctica
Hudson Mts.
Ellsworth Land
4176

Kohler Ra.
Marie Byrd Land

Horlick Mts.
Queen
Maud Mts.
4528
Beardmore
Glacier
2801
3491
Queen Alexandra
Ra.
Mt. Markham
4349

Scott Glacier
Knox Coast
Casey (Austr.)
Budd
Coast C. Poinsett
Sabrina Totten Glacier
Coast

Transantarctic Mts.

Amundsen Sea

Mt. Sidley
4181
Rockefeller
Plateau
666
2080
Dart
3108
Getz
Ice Shelf
Hobbs Coast
3496
Edward VII
Land
Roosevelt I.
Bay of
Whales
Salzberger
Ice Shelf
C. Colbeck

Shackleton Inlet
2407
3087
Ross Ice Shelf

80

Budd
Coast
Banzare
Coast
2436
4776
Clarie
Coast
Terre
Adélie
George V
Land
Porpoise Bay
Blodgett Iceberg
Tongue
Dalton Iceberg
Tongue
Commonwealth Bay
South Magnetic
Pole
1990

Wilkes Land

Southeast
Pacific
Basin

PACIFIC OCEAN

Scott
Ross
(N.Z.)
Mt. Lister
4023
Mt. Erebus
3743 McMurdo
(U.S.A.)
McMurdo Sd.
Franklin I.
Victoria
Prince Albert Mts.
Mt. Murchison
3502
Coulman I.
Possession I.
C. Adare
Ross
Sea
3719
Oates Land
C. Freshfield
Dumont d'Urville (Fr.)

Pacific-Antarctic Ridge

Antarctic Circle

Scott I.

Balleny Is.

Southeast Indian Rise

▼6240

Macquarie Is.
(Austr.)

Tasman
Plateau

Southwest
Pacific Basin

Campbell I.
(N.Z.)
Auckland Is.
(N.Z.)
Tasman
Sea
Tasmania
Hobart

Antipodes Is.
(N.Z.)
Campbell
Plateau
Stewart I.
Bounty Is.
(N.Z.) Dunedin NEW ZEALAND

MELBOURNE
AUSTRALIA

CARTOGRAPHY BY PHILIP'S.

ft m
12 000 4000
6000 2000
4500 1500
3000 1000
1200 400
600 200
0 0
500 1500
1000 3000
2000 6000
3000 9000
4000 12 000
5000 15 000
m ft

Legend:
- Ice cap
- Permanent ice shelf
- Maximum extent of sea ice
- March (Summer) extent of sea ice
- ▲3488 / 3700 Surface elevation and depth of ice (in metres)
- • Stanley (U.K.) Permanent bases

Projection: Zenithal Equidistant

The Antarctic Treaty was signed in Washington in 1959 so that scientific and technical research could continue unhampered by international politics.

All territorial claims covering land areas south of latitude 60°S have been suspended. Those claims were:

Norwegian claim 45°E – 20°W
Australian claims 45°E – 136°E
142°E – 160°E

French claim 136°E – 142°E
New Zealand claim 160°E – 150°W
Chilean claim 90°W – 53°W

British claim 80°W – 20°W
Argentine claim 74°W – 53°W

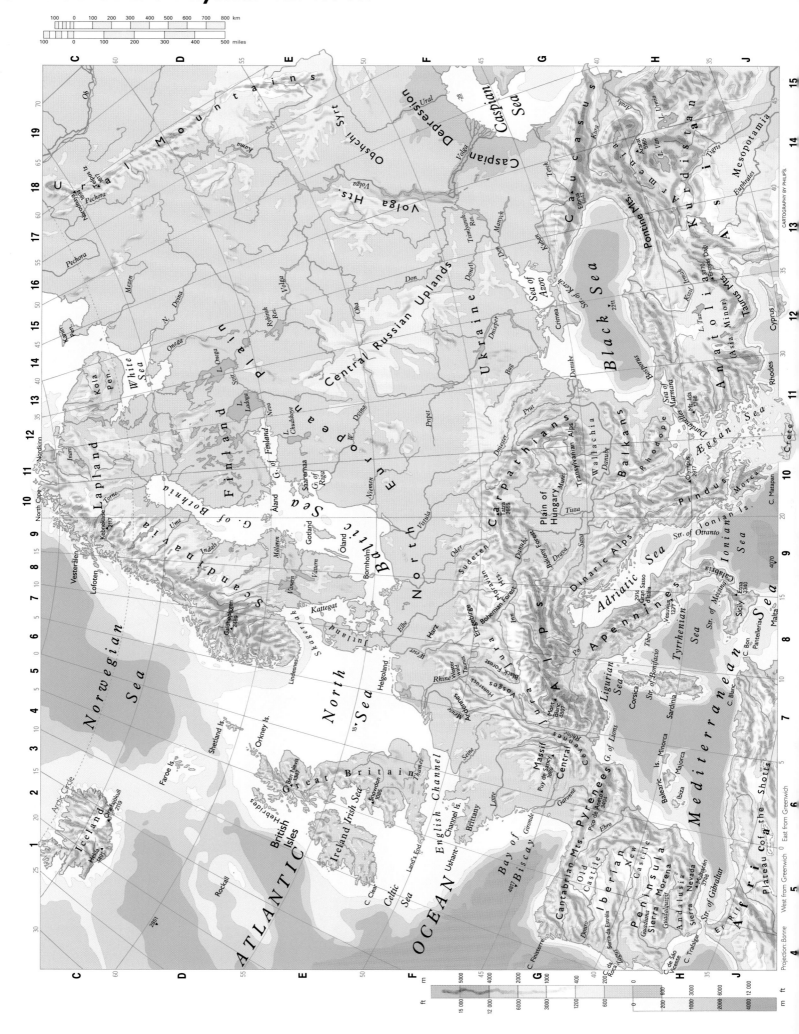

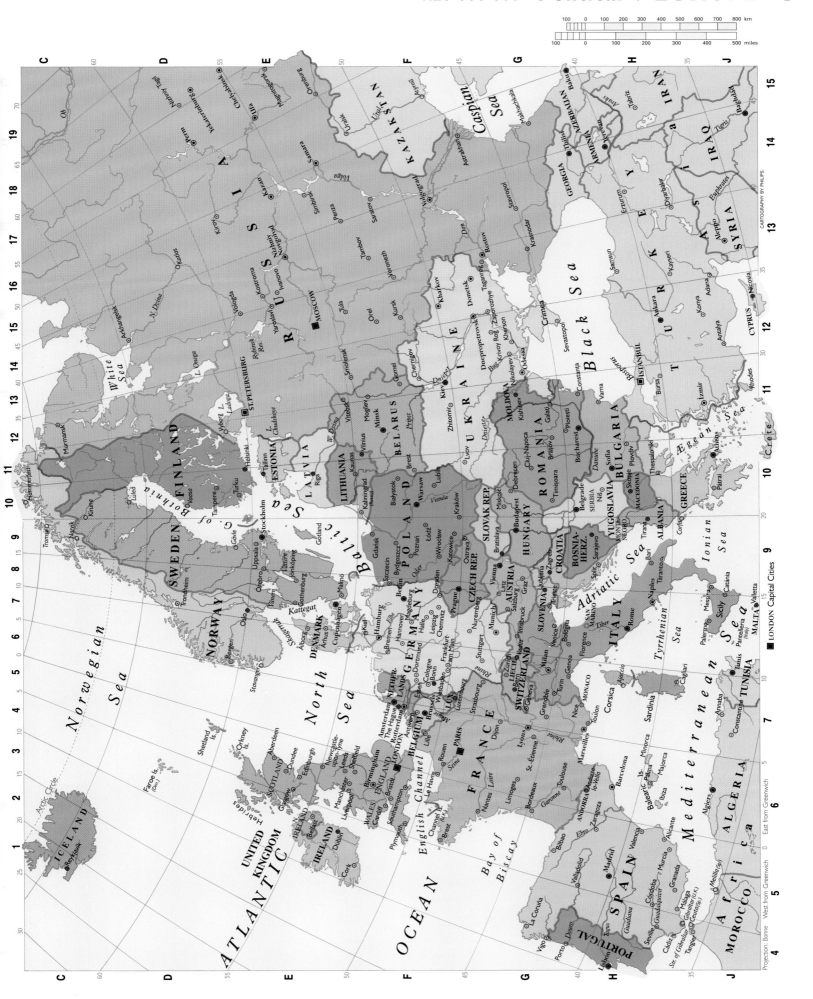

100 0 100 200 300 400 500 600 700 800 km
100 0 100 200 300 400 500 miles

CARTOGRAPHY BY PHILIPS

■ LONDON Capital Cities

Projection: Bonne   West from Greenwich   0   East from Greenwich

SCANDINAVIA 1:5 000 000

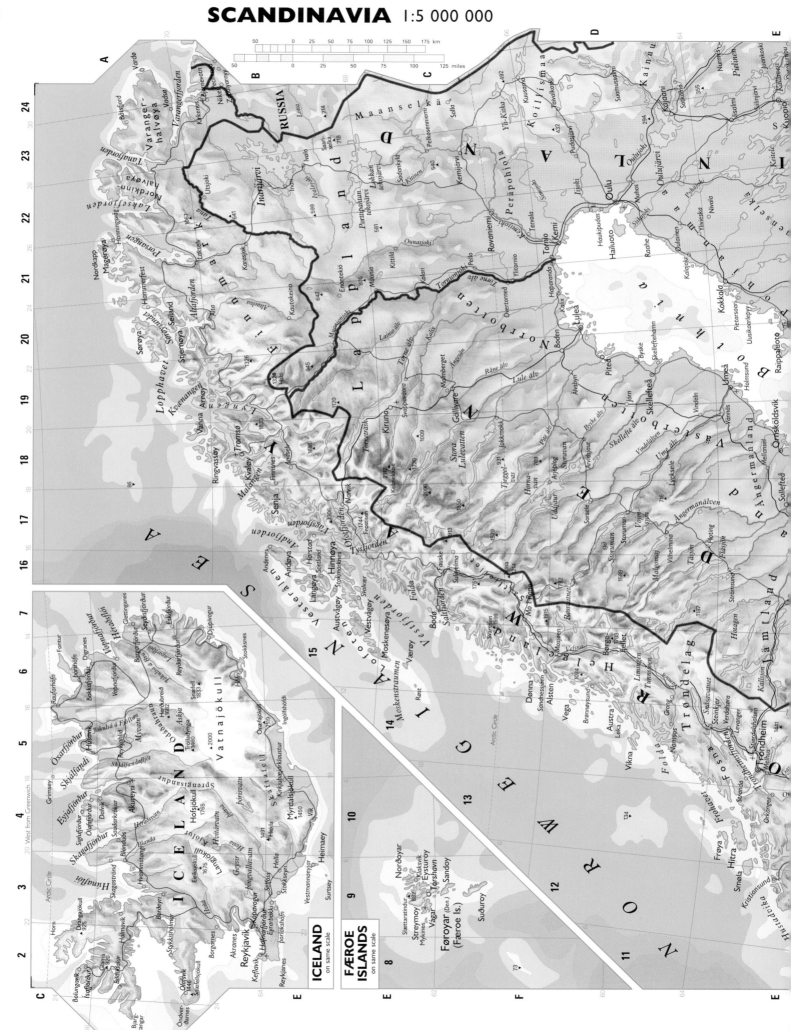

ICELAND
on same scale

FÆROE
ISLANDS
on same scale

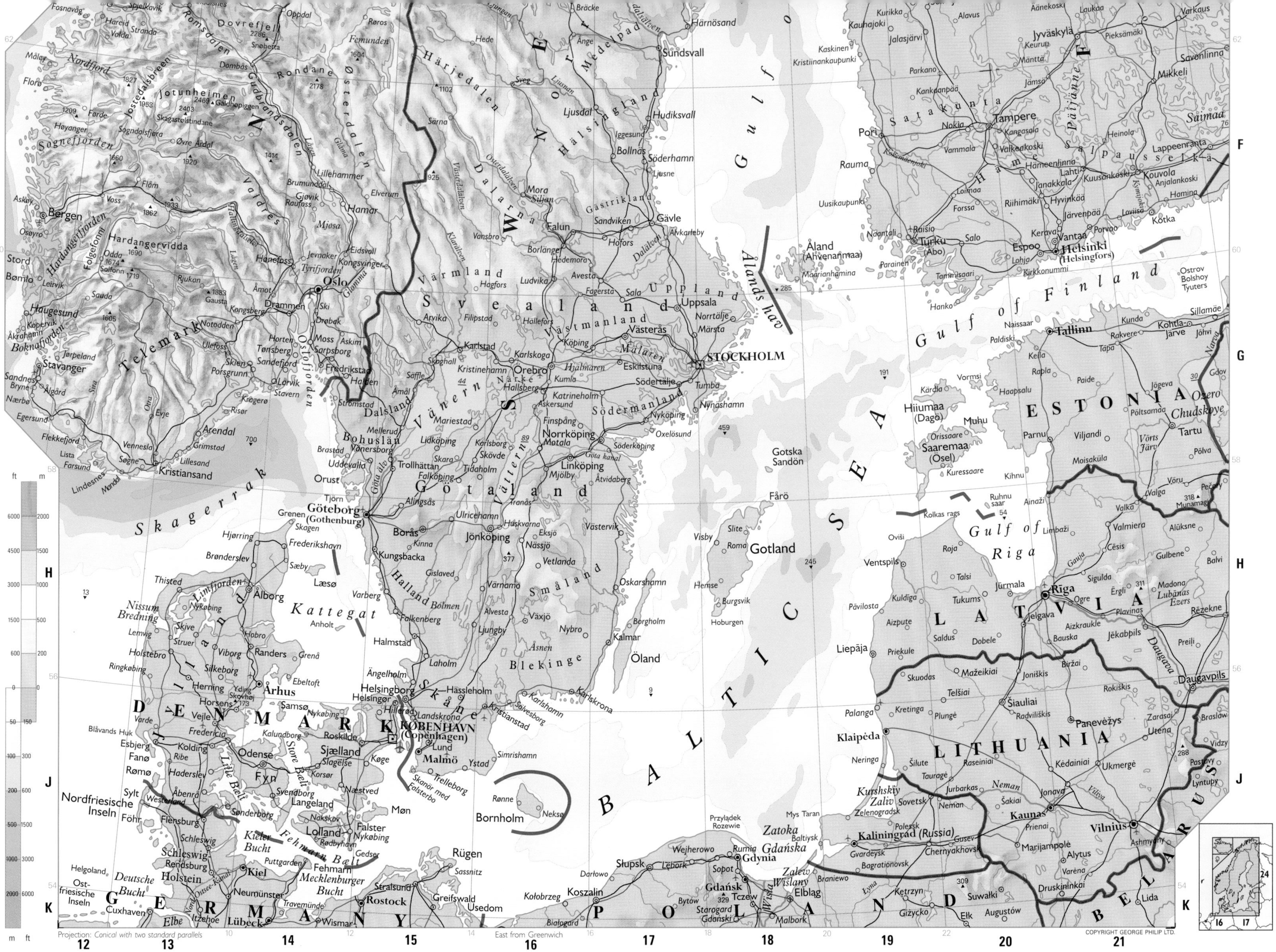

BALTIC SEA

FINLAND

ESTONIA

LATVIA

LITHUANIA

RUSSIA

POLAND

GERMANY

DENMARK

SWEDEN

NORWAY

Gulf of Finland

Gulf of Riga

Gulf of Bothnia

Ålands hav

Kattegat

Skagerrak

Gotland

Öland

Bornholm

Rügen

Usedom

Åland (Ahvenanmaa)

Hiiumaa (Dagö)

Saaremaa (Ösel)

Muhu

Helsinki (Helsingfors)

Tallinn

Tartu

Riga

Daugavpils

Vilnius

Kaunas

Klaipéda

Kaliningrad (Russia)

Gdańsk (Danzig)

Gdynia

Szczecin

Stockholm

Uppsala

Göteborg (Gothenburg)

Malmö

København (Copenhagen)

Oslo

Bergen

Stavanger

Kristiansand

Tampere

Turku (Åbo)

Pori

Visby

Kalmar

Karlskrona

Kiel

Lübeck

Rostock

Århus

Ålborg

Odense

København

Daugava

Neman

Elbe

East from Greenwich

Projection: Conical with two standard parallels

COPYRIGHT GEORGE PHILIP LTD

ft   m
6000 2000
4500 1500
3000 1000
1500   500
 600   200
 300   150
 150   50
   0   0
      200   600
     2000 6000

F   G   H   J   K

12 13 14 15 16 17 18 19 20 21

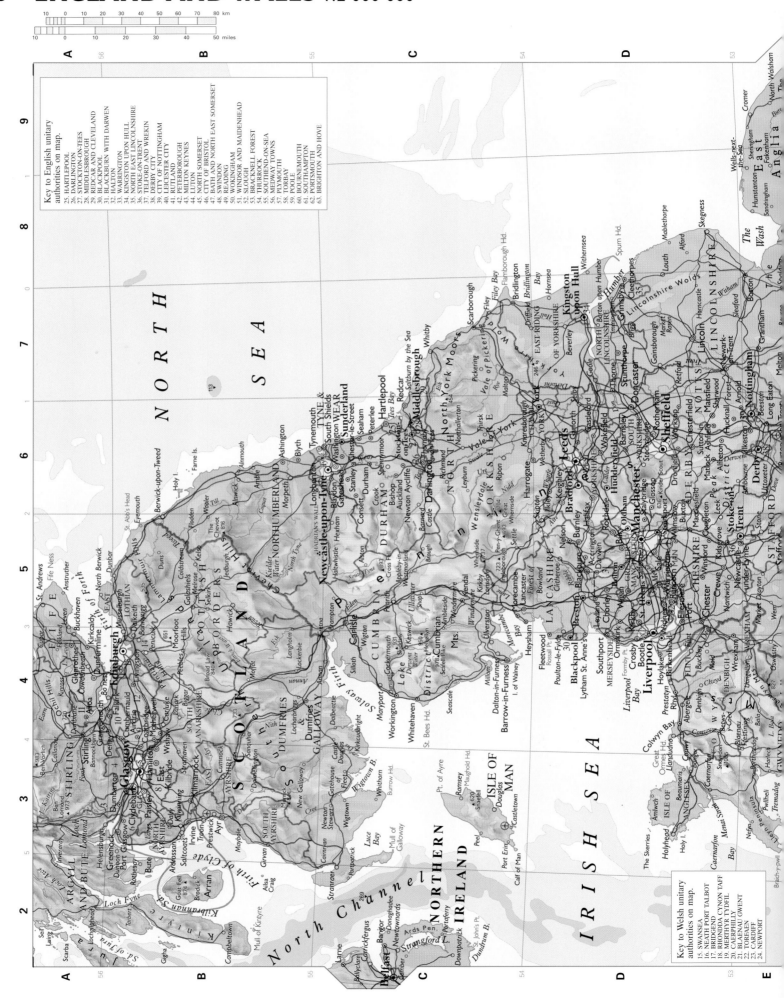

ENGLAND

WALES

FRANCE

NORMANDIE

ENGLISH CHANNEL

Bristol Channel

Cardigan Bay

Lyme Bay

Strait of Dover

Baie de la Seine

Baie de la Somme

LONDON

BIRMINGHAM

Bristol

Cardiff

Plymouth

Southampton

Portsmouth

Bournemouth

Brighton

Le Havre

Rouen

Caen

Cherbourg

Dieppe

Boulogne-sur-Mer

Calais

CHANNEL ISLANDS (U.K.)

Guernsey

Jersey

Alderney

Sark

Herm

ISLE OF WIGHT

CORNWALL

DEVON

DORSET

SOMERSET

WILTSHIRE

HANTS

SUSSEX

SURREY

KENT

ESSEX

SUFFOLK

SEINE-MARITIME

CALVADOS

MANCHE

SHROPSHIRE

HEREFORD

GLOUCS.

BERKSHIRE

OXFORD

BUCKS.

BEDFORD

NORTHAMPTON

CAMBRIDGE

WARWICK

WORCESTER

POWYS

CEREDIGION

PEMBROKESHIRE

CARMARTHENSHIRE

GLAMORGAN

Isles of Scilly
On same scale

Isles of Scilly

St. Mary's

Tresco

Projection: Lambert's Conformal Conic

East from Greenwich

West from Greenwich

m / ft

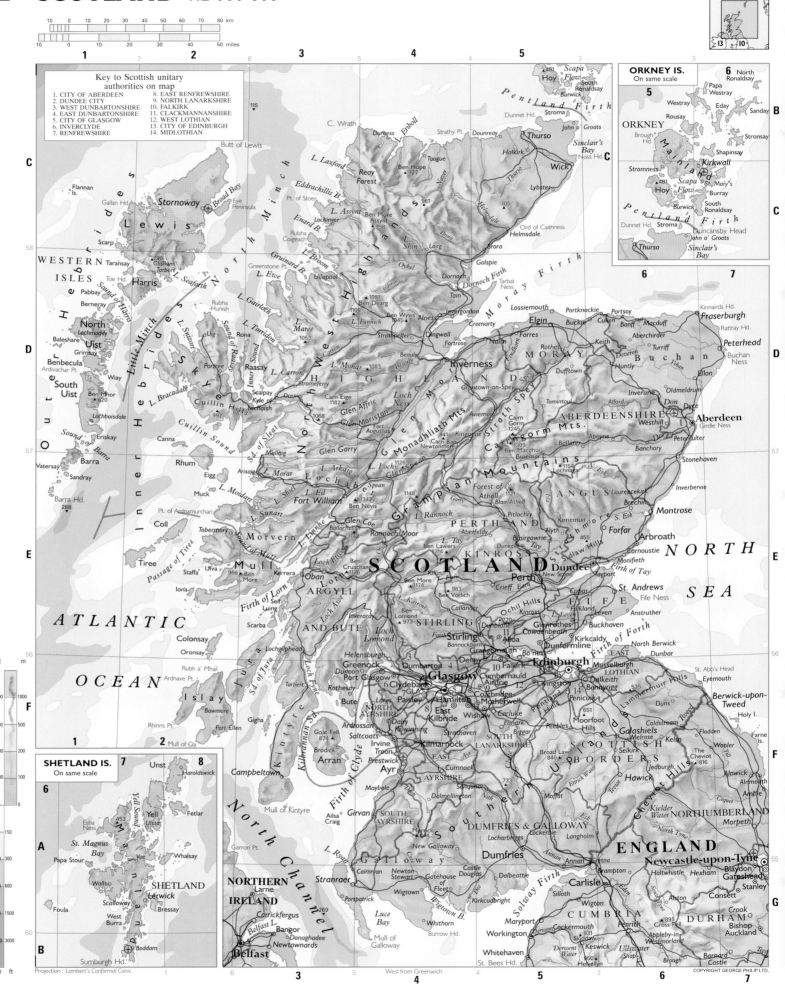

Key to Scottish unitary
authorities on map

1. CITY OF ABERDEEN   8. EAST RENFREWSHIRE
2. DUNDEE CITY   9. NORTH LANARKSHIRE
3. WEST DUNBARTONSHIRE   10. FALKIRK
4. EAST DUNBARTONSHIRE   11. CLACKMANNANSHIRE
5. CITY OF GLASGOW   12. WEST LOTHIAN
6. INVERCLYDE   13. CITY OF EDINBURGH
7. RENFREWSHIRE   14. MIDLOTHIAN

ORKNEY IS.
On same scale

ORKNEY

SHETLAND IS.
On same scale

SHETLAND

Projection : Lambert's Conformal Conic

West from Greenwich

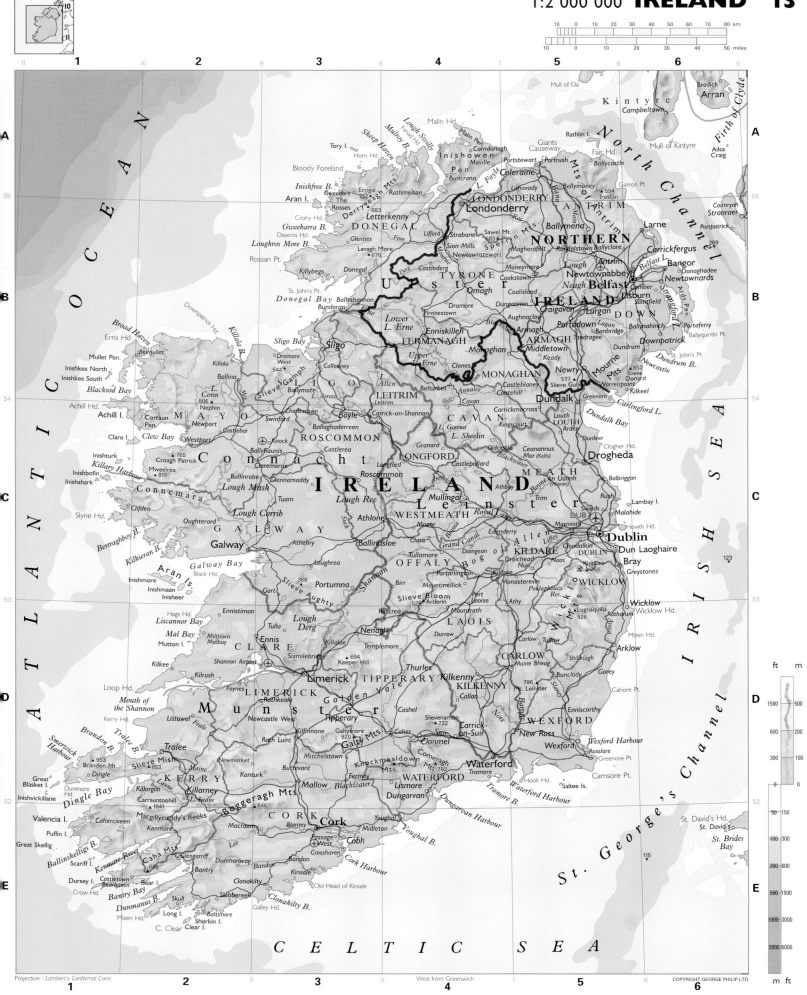

10 0 10 20 30 40 50 60 70 80 km
10 0 10 20 30 40 50 miles

A

OCEAN

Mull of Oa
Kintyre
Brodick
Arran
Campbeltown
Firth of Clyde
Mull of Kintyre
Ailsa Craig

Tory I.
Sheep Haven
Lough Swilly
Malin Hd.
Malin Pen.
Cardonagh
Inishowen
Pen.
Maville
Giants Causeway
Portstewart
Portrush
Rathlin I.
Ballycastle
Fair Hd.
Garron Pt.

Horn Hd.
Bloody Foreland
Inishfree B.
Gweedore
Errigal
752
The Rosses
683
Derryveagh Mts.
Crohy Hd.
Letterkenny
Gweebarra B.
DONEGAL
Dawros Hd.
676
Lavagh More
Glenties
Loughros More B.
Rossan Pt.
Killybegs
Donegal

Rathmelton
LONDONDERRY
Londonderry
Lifford
Strabane
Sion Mills
Newtownstewart
Sawel Mt.
683
Spering Mts.
Limavady
ANTRIM
Ballymoney
554
Trostan
Ballymena
Coleraine
NORTHERN
Magherafelt
Moneymore
Cookstown
Coalisland
Dungannon
IRELAND
Randalstown Ballyclare
Antrim
Lough Neagh
Lurgan
Craigavon
Portadown
Armagh
Banbridge
Larne
Carrickfergus
269
Cairnryan
Stranraer
Portpatrick
Belfast L.
Belfast
Newtownabbey
Lisburn
Saintfield
DOWN
Bangor
Donaghadee
Newtownards
Comber
Ards Pen.
Strangford L.
Portaferry
Ballynahinch
Ballyquintin Pt.
Downpatrick

TYRONE
Omagh
Dromore
Irvinestown
Enniskillen
FERMANAGH
Lower L. Erne
Upper Erne
Clones
Monaghan
MONAGHAN
577
Castleblaney
Aughnacloy
Middletown
Keady
Newry
Slieve Gullion
Warrenpoint
Mourne Mts.
852
Slieve Donard
Newcastle
Dundrum B.
Greenore
Kilkeel
Carlingford L.

St. John's Pt.
Donegal Bay
Ballyshannon
Ballintra
Bundoran
Belleek
Lough Melvin
Garrison
Manorhamilton
Kiltyclogher
Belcoo
Swanlinbar
Belturbet
Annalee
Cootehill
Carrickmacross
Kingscourt
Ardee
LOUTH
Louth
Dundalk
Dundalk Bay
Dunleer
Clogher Hd.

Broad Haven
Erris Hd.
Mullet Pen.
Belmullet
Inishkea North
Inishkea South
Blacksod Bay
Achill Hd.
Achill I.
Clare I.
Clew Bay
Inishturk
Killary Harbour
Inishbofin
Inishshark

Sligo Bay
Sligo
Slieve Gamph
Ballina
Killala
Killala B.
Dromore West
544
Colloney
L. Arrow
L. Gill
SLIGO
LEITRIM
Leitrim
L. Allen
Drumshanbo
Ballymote
Charlestown
Swinford
Boyle
Carrick-on-Shannon
Ballaghaderreen
ROSCOMMON
Castlerea
Ballyhaunis
Knock
Claremorris
Castlebar
Newport
Westport
Corraun Pen.
L. Conn
806
Nephin
MAYO
Croagh Patrick
765
Mweelrea
819
Ballinrobe
Lough Mask

CAVAN
L. Gowna
L. Sheelin
Granard
Cavan
Oldcastle
Ceanannus Mor (Kells)
Blackwater
MEATH
Kingscourt
Castlepollard
LONGFORD
Longford
Edgeworthstown
Ballymahon
Athboy
Trim
Navan
An Uaimh
Boyne
Drogheda
Balbriggan
Dunleer

Connacht
Connemara
Clifden
Slyne Hd.
Bertraghboy B.
Lough Corrib
Oughterard
GALWAY
Galway
Galway Bay
Kilkieran B.
Aran Is.
Inishmore
Inishmaan
Inisheer
Black Hd.
368
Slieve Aughty
Gort
Loughrea
Athenry
Tuam
Glennamaddy
Roscommon
Ballinasloe
Athlone
Lough Ree
Moate
WESTMEATH
Mullingar
Royal Canal
Clara
Tullamore
OFFALY
Portarlington
Edenderry
Bog of Allen
Daingean
Philipstown
KILDARE
Kildare
Droichead Nua
Naas
Clane
Maynooth
Rush
Lambay I.
Swords
Malahide
Howth Hd.
DUBLIN
Dublin
Dun Laoghaire
Bray
Greystones
123

IRELAND
Leinster
Grand Canal
Liffey
Clondalkin
Monasterevin
Portlaoise
Stradbally
Athy
Carlow
CARLOW
Muine Bheag
Tullow
Bunclody
Wicklow
Wicklow Hd.
Rathdrum
Lugnaquilla
926
Wicklow Mts.
Arklow
Shillelagh
Gorey
Enniscorthy
WEXFORD
New Ross
Wexford
Wexford Harbour
Rosslare
Greenore Pt.
Carnsore Pt.

Ennistimon
Hags Hd.
Liscannor Bay
Mal Bay
Mutton I.
Milltown Malbay
Kilkee
Kilrush
Loop Hd.
Mouth of the Shannon
Kerry Hd.
Shannon Airport
Sixmilebridge
Ennis
CLARE
Tulla
Lough Derg
Killaloe
Portumna
Birr
Roscrea
Nenagh
Templemore
694
Keeper Hill
Shannon
Slieve Bloom
526
Arderin
Mountmellick
Port Laoise
LAOIS
Mountrath
Durrow
Abbeyleix
Thurles
Kilkenny
KILKENNY
Callan
Mountain
796
Mt. Leinster
Graiguenamanagh
Barrow
Nore

Limerick
LIMERICK
Rathkeale
Foynes
Listowel
Newcastle West
Feale
Abbeyfeale
Kilmallock
Rath Luirc
Kilfinnane
TIPPERARY
Tipperary
Golden Vale
Cashel
Caher
Galty Mts.
920
Galtymore
Mitchelstown
Slievenamon
722
Carrick-on-Suir
Clonmel
Comeragh Mts.
792
Waterford
Suir
WEXFORD
New Ross
Munster
Tralee B.
Brandon B.
Smerwick Harbour
Brandon Hd.
953
Brandon Mt.
Dingle
Slieve Mish
853
KERRY
Tralee
Maine
Newmarket
Kanturk
Buttevant
Fermoy
Mallow
Blackwater
Lismore
WATERFORD
Dungarvan
Dungarvan Harbour
Tramore
Tramore B.
Waterford Harbour
Hook Hd.
Saltee Is.

Great Blasket I.
Inishvickillane
Dunmore Hd.
Dingle Bay
Valencia I.
Puffin I.
Great Skellig
Ballinskelligs B.
Scariff I.
Dursey I.
Crow Hd.
Cahersiveen
Killorglin
Laune
Killarney
L. Leane
Carrauntoohil
1041
Macgillycuddy's Reeks
Kenmare
Kenmare River
Caha Mts.
686
Glengarriff
Castletown Bearhaven
Bear I.
Bantry
Bantry Bay
Dunmanus B.
Long I.
Skull
Mizen Hd.
Baltimore
Sherkin I.
Clear I.
C. Clear
CORK
646
Boggeragh Mts.
Macroom
Lee
Blarney
Cork
Cork
Midleton
Cobh
Passage West
Crosshaven
Cork Harbour
Kinsale
Bandon
Clonakilty
Clonakilty B.
Galley Hd.
Old Head of Kinsale
Youghal
Youghal B.
Dunmanway
Skibbereen

ATLANTIC
115

North Channel
IRISH SEA
St. George's Channel
St. David's Hd.
St. David's
St. Brides Bay
CELTIC SEA

ft m
1500 500
600 200
300 100
0 0
50 150
100 300
200 600
1000 3000
2000 6000
m ft

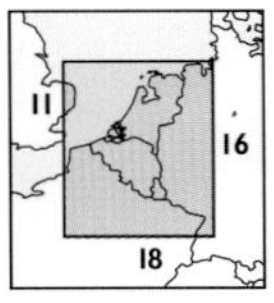

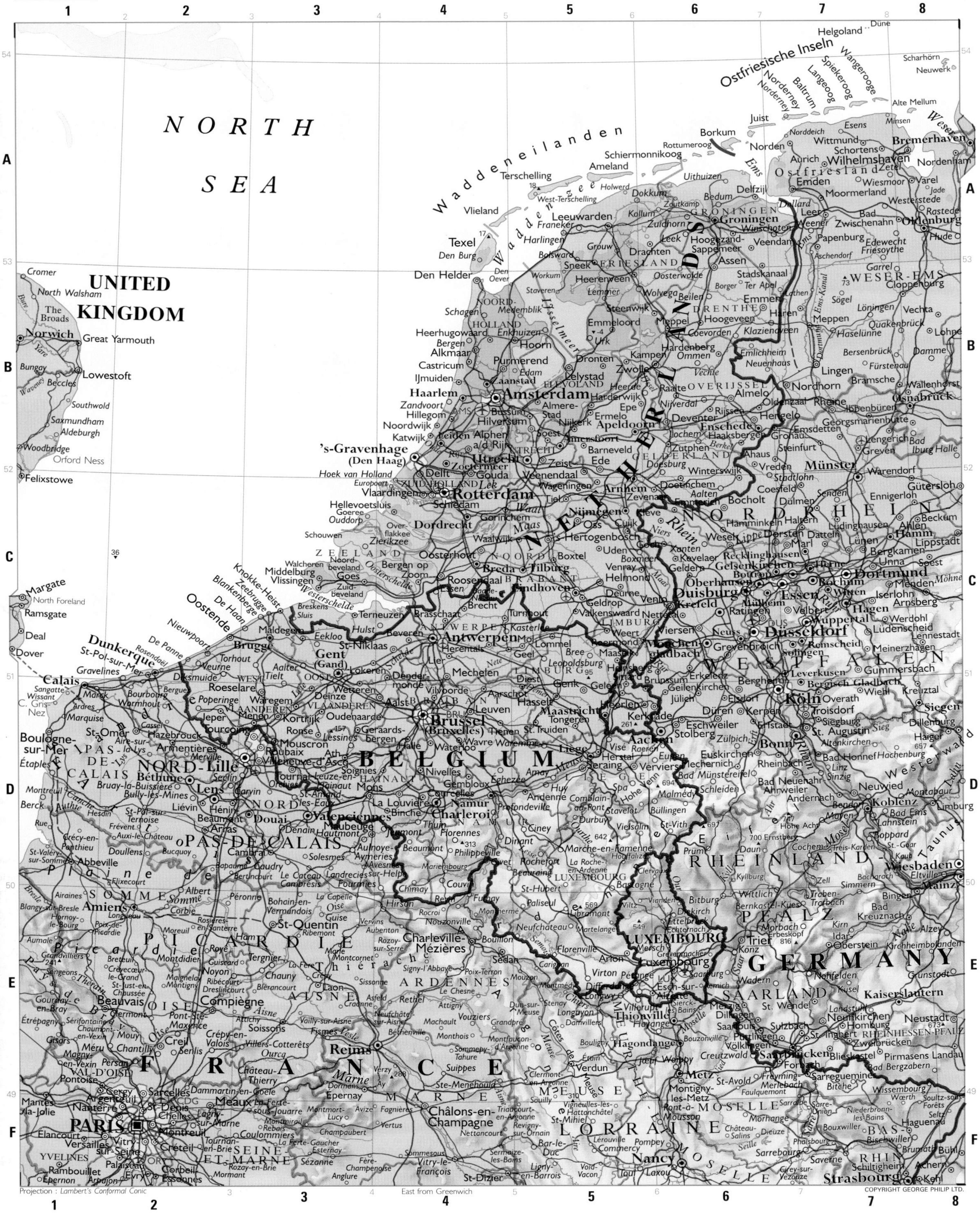

10 0 10 20 30 40 50 60 70 80 90 km
10 0 10 20 30 40 50 60 miles

NORTH SEA

UNITED KINGDOM

NETHERLANDS

BELGIUM

LUXEMBOURG

GERMANY

FRANCE

Cromer · North Walsham · The Broads · Norwich · Great Yarmouth · Bungay · Beccles · Lowestoft · Southwold · Saxmundham · Aldeburgh · Woodbridge · Orford Ness · Felixstowe · Margate · North Foreland · Ramsgate · Deal · Dover · Calais · Sangatte · Wissant · C. Gris Nez · Marquise · Boulogne-sur-Mer · Étaples · Berck · Montreuil

Waddeneilanden · Terschelling · Vlieland · Texel · Den Burg · Den Helder · Schagen · Harlingen · Franeker · Leeuwarden · Dokkum · Schiermonnikoog · Ameland · Groningen · Winschoten · Assen · Emmen · Meppel · Hoogeveen · Zwolle · Almelo · Enschede · Hengelo · Deventer · Apeldoorn · Amersfoort · Amsterdam · Haarlem · Zaanstad · Hilversum · Utrecht · 's-Gravenhage (Den Haag) · Hoek van Holland · Delft · Rotterdam · Schiedam · Vlaardingen · Dordrecht · Gorinchem · Arnhem · Nijmegen · Ede · Wageningen · 's-Hertogenbosch · Tilburg · Breda · Eindhoven · Helmond · Venlo · Roermond · Weert · Maastricht · Middelburg · Vlissingen · Goes · Bergen op Zoom · Roosendaal · Terneuzen · Brugge · Oostende · Gent (Gand) · Antwerpen · Mechelen · Brussel (Bruxelles) · Leuven · Hasselt · Genk · Tongeren · Kortrijk · Roeselare · Ieper · Lille · Namur · Charleroi · Mons · La Louvière · Dinant · Bastogne · Luxembourg

Bremerhaven · Bremen · Wilhelmshaven · Emden · Oldenburg · Münster · Osnabrück · Dortmund · Essen · Bochum · Duisburg · Düsseldorf · Köln · Bonn · Aachen · Koblenz · Wiesbaden · Mainz · Wuppertal · Hagen · Siegen · Saarbrücken · Kaiserslautern · Trier

Paris · Amiens · Beauvais · Compiègne · Reims · Épernay · Châlons-en-Champagne · Charleville-Mézières · Sedan · Verdun · Metz · Thionville · Nancy · St-Quentin · Cambrai · Douai · Lens · Arras · Valenciennes · Maubeugé · Strasbourg

ARDENNES · SOMME · PICARDIE · PAS-DE-CALAIS · NORD · LORRAINE · SAARLAND · RHEINLAND-PFALZ · NORDRHEIN-WESTFALEN · PFALZ

Projection: Lambert's Conformal Conic   East from Greenwich   COPYRIGHT GEORGE PHILIP LTD.

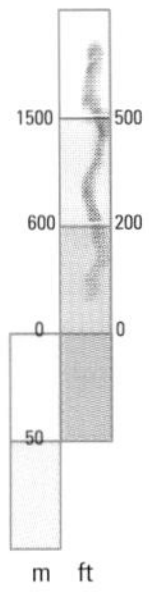

Underlined towns give their name to the administrative area in which they stand.

NORTH

SEA

DENMARK

BALTIC SEA

UNITED
KINGDOM

NETHERLANDS

AMSTERDAM

ROTTERDAM

HAMBURG

BERLIN

G E R M A N Y

BELGIUM

BRUSSEL
(Bruxelles)

LUXEMBOURG

PRAHA
(Prague)

C Z E C H

F R A N C E

PARIS

SWITZERLAND

A U S T R I A

MÜNCHEN
(Munich)

MILANO

I T A L Y

SLOVENIA

TORINO
(Turin)

MARSEILLE

ADRIATIC
SEA

MONACO

Golfo di
Génova

Projection: Conical with two standard parallels

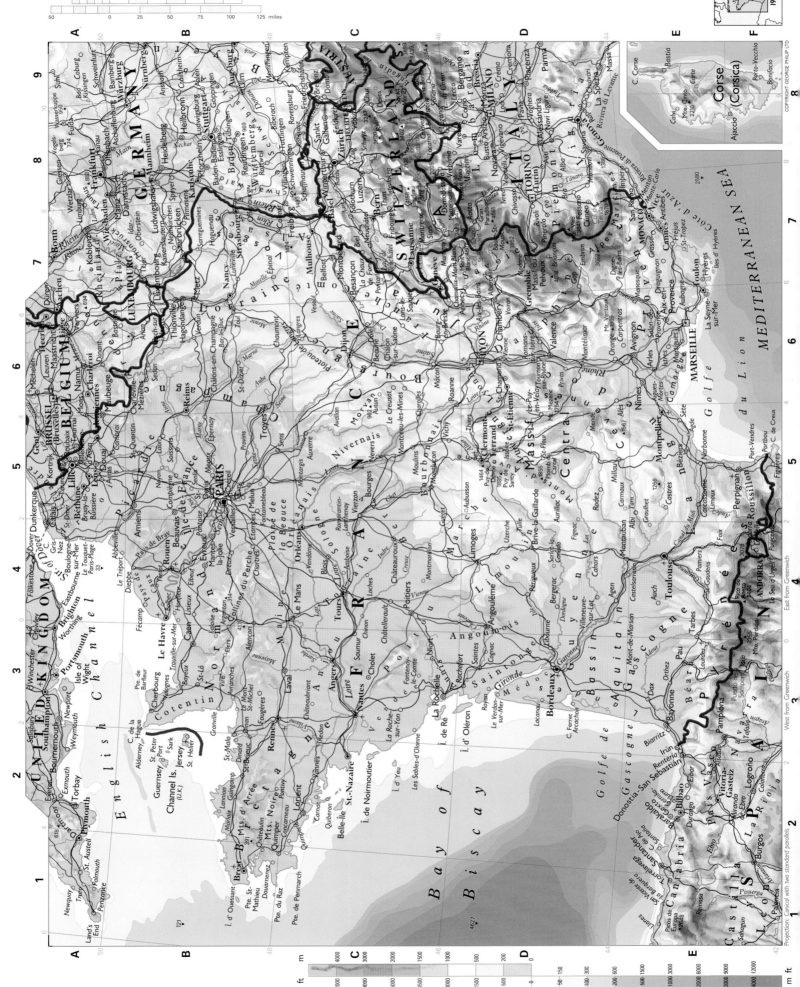

Corse (Corsica)

MEDITERRANEAN SEA

Bay of Biscay

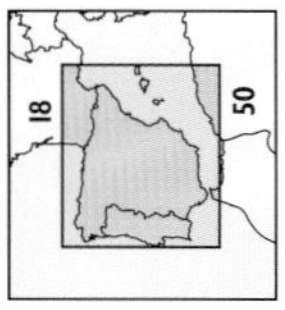

50 0 25 50 75 100 125 150 175 km
50 0 25 50 75 100 125 miles

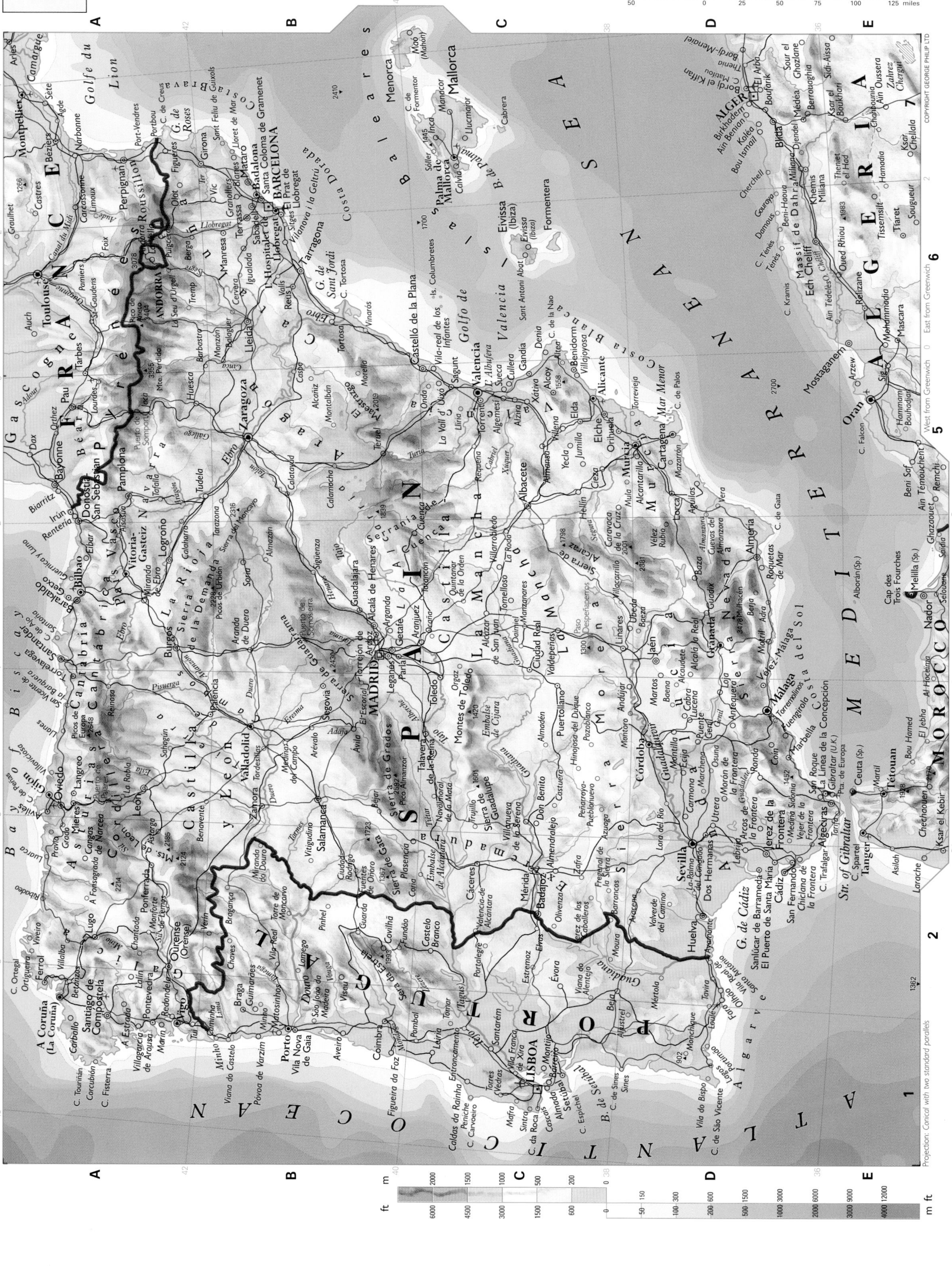

COPYRIGHT GEORGE PHILIP LTD

F R A N C E

P y r é n é e s

ANDORRA

S P A I N

P O R T U G A L

MADRID

LISBOA

BARCELONA

Zaragoza

Valencia

Sevilla

Málaga

Porto

A L G E R I A

M O R O C C O

M E D I T E R R A N E A N   S E A

Islas Baleares

Menorca

Mallorca

Eivissa (Ibiza)

Formentera

B a y   o f   B i s c a y

A T L A N T I C   O C E A N

Golfe du Lion

Costa Brava

Costa Dorada

Costa Blanca

Costa del Sol

Projection: Conical with two standard parallels

West from Greenwich East from Greenwich

Projection: Conical with two standard parallels

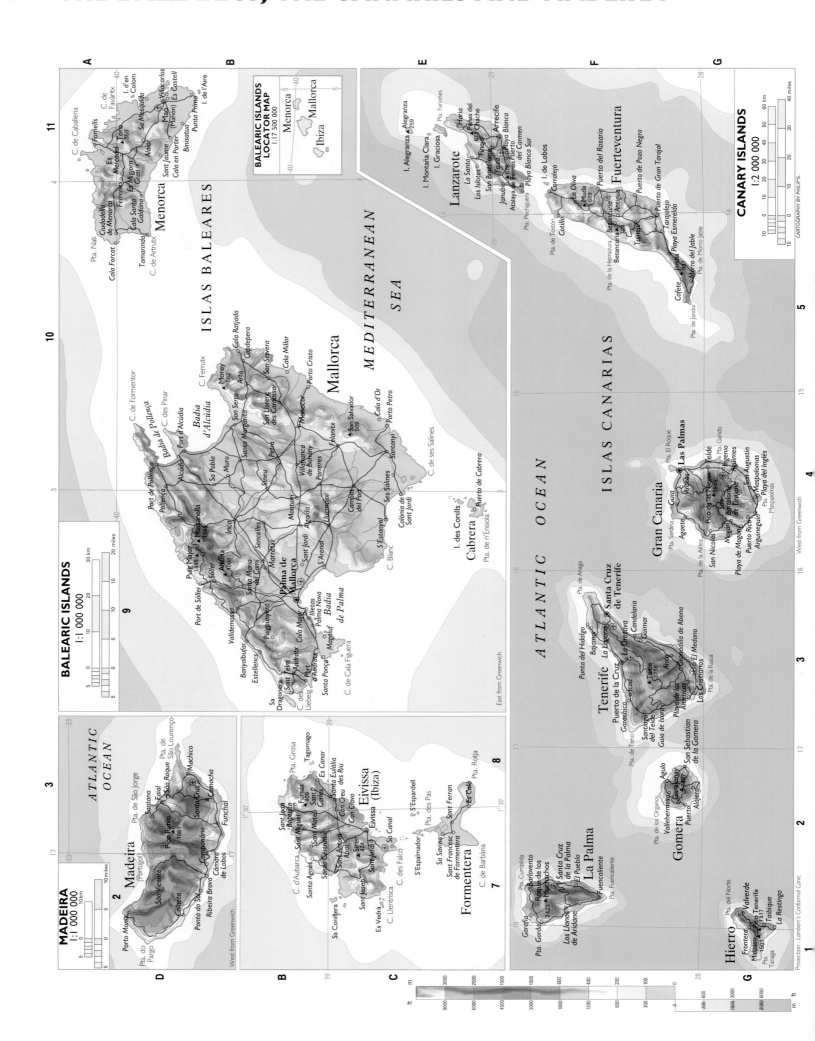

BALEARIC ISLANDS LOCATOR MAP
1:17 500 000

Menorca

Mallorca

Ibiza

Menorca

Pta. Nati
C. de Caballeria
Ciudadella de Menorca
Ferreries
Es Mercadal
Cala Santa Galdana
Tamarindo
C. d'Artrutx
Fornells
Sa Mesquida
Maó (Mahón)
Alaior
Es Migjorn Gran
Sant Jaume
Cala en Porter
Binisafua
I. d'en Colom
Villacarlos
Es Castell
Punta Prima
I. de l'Aire
Toro 358

ISLAS BALEARES

MEDITERRANEAN SEA

C. de Formentor
C. de Pollença
C. des Pinar
Badia de Pollença
Port de Pollença
Pollença
Alcúdia
Port d'Alcúdia
Badia d'Alcúdia
Sa Pobla
Muro
Santa Margarita
Can Picafort
Morey 562
Artà
Capdepera
Cala Ratjada
Cala Mesquida
San Serra
San Llorenç des Cardassar
Son Servera
Cala Millor
Porto Cristo
Cala d'Or
Porto Petro
C. Ferrutx
Mallorca
Inca
Binissalem
Santa Maria del Camí
Sineu
Petra
Sencelles
Vilafranca de Bonany
Manacor
Felanitx
San Salvador 509
Santanyí
Puig Major 1445
Sóller
Port de Sóller
Valldemossa
Banyalbufar
Estellencs
Puigpunyent
Santa Ponça
Andratx
Port d'Andratx
C. de Cala Figuera
Sa Dragonera
Sant Telm
C. des Llebeig
Palma de Mallorca
Marratxí
Alaró 1068
Bunyola
Algaida
Montuïri
Porreres
Llucmajor
Campos del Port
Ses Salines
C. de ses Salines
Colònia de Sant Jordi
S'Estanyol
S'Arenal
Magaluf
Illetas
Palma Nova
Cala Major
Badia de Palma
Sant Jordi
C. Blanc
Colònia de Sant Jordi
I. des Conills
Cabrera
Puerto de Cabrera
Pta. de n'Ensiola

BALEARIC ISLANDS
1:1 000 000

ATLANTIC OCEAN

Porto Moniz
Pta. do Pargo
Ponta do Sol
Ribeira Brava
Câmara de Lobos
Funchal
São Vicente
Santana
Faial
São Roque
Santa Cruz
Machico
Caniçal
Camacha
Pico Ruivo 1861
Curral das Freiras
Campanário
Pta. de São Lourenço
Pta. de São Jorge

MADEIRA
1:1 000 000
Madeira (Portugal)

West from Greenwich

ATLANTIC OCEAN

Pta. Grossa
Tagomago
Sant Joan Baptista
Santa Eulàlia del Riu
Portinatx
Sant Miquel de Balansat
Sant Mateu
Sant Carles
Es Canar
Santa Agnès
Sant Antoni de Portmany
Sant Rafel
Sant Josep
Eivissa (Ibiza)
Can Creuc des Riu
Sant Jordi 424
Ses Salines
Es Cubells
C. d'Aubarca
Es Vedrà
C. Llentrisca
C. des Falcó
Sa Conillera
Eivissa (Ibiza)

S'Espalmador
S'Espardell
Sant Francesc de Formentera
Sant Ferran
Es Caló
Pta. Rotja
Sa Savina
Sa Sorina
C. de Barbària

Formentera

East from Greenwich

MEDITERRANEAN SEA

I. Alegranza
Alegranza 259
I. Montaña Clara
I. Graciosa
La Graciosa
Pta. Fariones
Haria
Palmas del Chache
Arrecife
Lanzarote
La Santa
Los Islotes
San Bartolomé
Tinajo
Yaiga
Teguise
Puerto del Carmen
Playa Blanca
Atalaya de Femés
Janubio
Pta. Pechiguera
I. de Lobos
Corralejo
Pta. de Tostón
Cotillo
La Oliva
Puerto del Rosario
Muda 659
Betancuria
Betancuría 724
Tuineje
Antigua
Puerto de Pozo Negro
Tarajalejo
Puerto de Gran Tarajal
Playa Esmeralda
Cofete
Pta. de Jandía
Jandía Playa Esmerelda
Morro del Jable
Pta. de Morro Jable
Fuerteventura

ATLANTIC OCEAN

ISLAS CANARIAS

Pta. El Roque
Las Palmas
Gáldar
Guía
Arucas
Pico de las Nieves 1949
Telde
Agaete
San Nicolás
Pta. de la Aldea
Pta. Sardina
Mogán
Puerto Rico
Arguineguín
Playa del Inglés
Maspalomas
Pta. Maspalomas
Ingenio
Agüimes
San Agustín
San Bartolomé de Tirajana
Gran Canaria

Pta. de Anaga
Santa Cruz de Tenerife
La Laguna
La Orotava
Candelaria
Güímar
Punta del Hidalgo
Bajamar
Puerto de la Cruz
Icod
Garachico
Santiago del Teide
Guía de Isora
Teide 3718
Arico
Granadilla de Abona
El Médano
Playa de las Américas
Los Cristianos
Pta. de la Rasca
Pta. de Teno
Tenerife

Pta. de los Organos
Vallehermoso
Agulo
Hermigua
San Sebastián de la Gomera
Alojera
Chipude
Playa de Santiago
Gomera

Pta. Cumplida
Barlovento
Santa Cruz de la Palma
Roque de los Machachos 2423
Los Llanos de Aridane
El Pueblo
Fuencaliente
Garafía
Pta. Gorda
Sa Coxilera
La Palma

Pta. del Norte
Valverde
Frontera
Malpaso 1501
Pico de Tenerife 1717
Taibique
La Restinga
Pta. Tanaja
Pta. Orchilla
Hierro

West from Greenwich

CANARY ISLANDS
1:2 000 000

CARTOGRAPHY BY PHILIP'S

Projection: Lambert's Conformal Conic

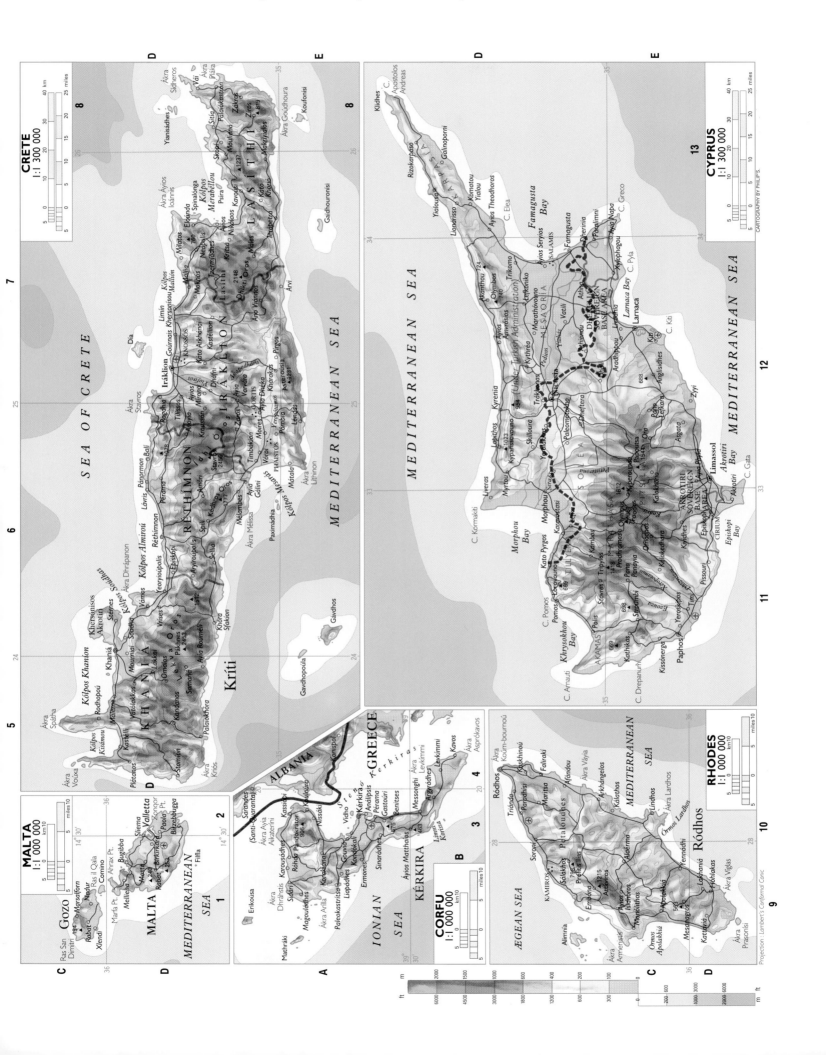

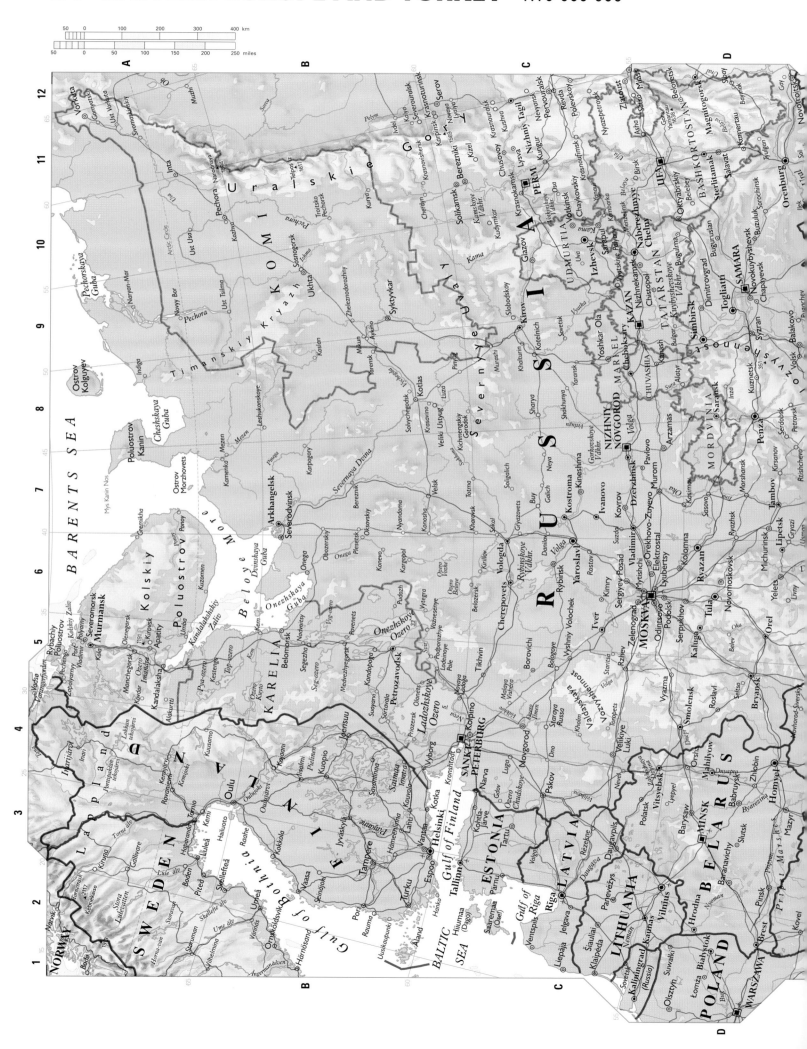

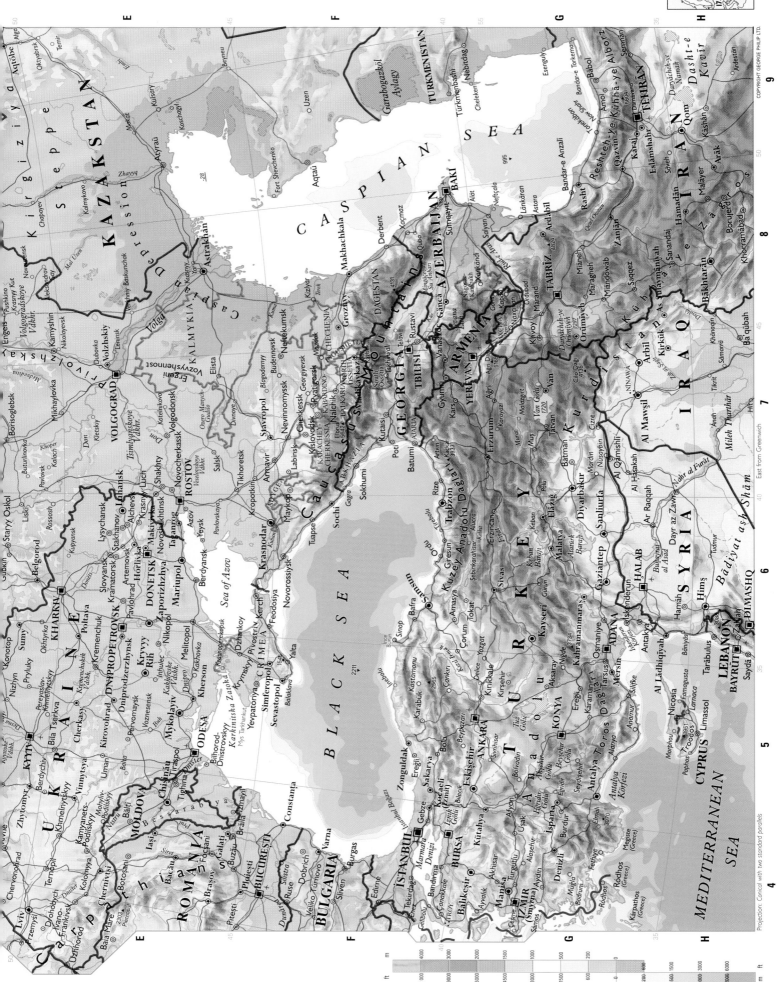

RUSSIA
1 Adygea
2 Karachey-Cherkessia
3 Kabardino-Balkaria
4 North Ossetia
5 Ingushetia
6 Chechenia
7 Dagestan
8 Mordvinia
9 Chuvashia
10 Mari El
11 Tatarstan
12 Udmurtia
13 Khakassia
AZERBAIJAN
14 Naxçivan
GEORGIA   UKRAINE
15 Ajaria   17 Crimea
16 Abkhazia

Projection: Conical Orthomorphic with two standard parallels

East from Greenwich

A B C D E F

9 10 11 12 13 14 15 16 17 18 19

OCEAN

Laptev Sea

East Siberian Sea

Mys Dezhneva (East C.)

Ostrov Shmidta

Mys Arkticheskiy

Ostrov Komsomolets

Ostrov Pioner

Ostrov Oktyabrskoy Revolyutsii

▲965

Severnaya Zemlya

Proliv Vilkitskogo

Mys Chelyuskin

Ostrova Delonga

Ostrov Genriyetty

Ostrov Zhanetty

Ostrova Zhokhova

Ostrov Bennetta

Ostrov Faddeyevskiy

Ostrov Maly Lyakhovskiy

Ostrov Bolshoy Lyakhovskiy

Novosibirskiye Ostrova

Ostrov Belkovskiy

Ostrov Kotelny

Ostrov Novaya Sibir

Ostrov Stolbovoy

Lyakhovskiye

Proliv Dmitriya Lapteva

Mys Buorkhaya

3800

Ostrova Medvezhi

Ostrov Vrangelya

Ostrov Ayon

Ueleń

St. Lawrence I. (U.S.A.)

Providenya

Anadyrskiy Zaliv

Beringovskiy

Chukchi Sea

Bering Sea

Chukotskoye Nagorye

Mys Shmidta

Ambarchik

Uelen

Vankarem

Egvekinot

Anadyr

1843

Perek

Ust Chaun

Bilibino

1853

Chersky

Pevek

Nizhne Kolymsk

Srednekolymsk

Bolshoy Anyuy

1752

Yerepol

Markovo

Penzhino

2652

Koryakskoye Nagorye

Tilichiki

Kavacha

Chokurdakh

Indigirka

Kolyma

Khonuu

Zyryanka

Pobeda ▲3147

Ust-Nera

Omolon

Paren

Gizhiga

Evensk

Nayakhan

Penzhinskaya Guba

Gora

Ossora

Ostrov Karaginskiy

Khandyga

Susuman

Yagodnoye

Orotukan

Atka

Magadan

Palatka

Ust-Omchug

Ust-Maya

2959

Ayan

Okhotsk

Okhotskiy Perevoz

Ulya

Nelkan

4574 Gora Klyuchevskaya

Ust-Kamchatsk

3621

Poluostrov Kamchatka

Kirovskiy

Nikolskoye

Komandorskiye Ostrova

 Chen 2682

Taskan

Omsukchan

Tit-Ary

Ust Olenek

Tiksi

Ust Kuyga

Kazachye

Druzhina

Kyusyur

Bulun

Deputatskiy

Batagay

Verkhoyansk

2389

Zhigansk

Vilyuysk

Verkhnevilyuysk

Namtsy

Yakutsk

Maya

Aldan

Tommot

Aim

Chogda

Uchur

Maya

2246

Khrebet Dzhugdzur

Ayan

Okha

Sea of Okhotsk

1780

Ust Khayryuzovo

Tigil

Palana

Zaliv Shelikhova

Pobeda

Zaliv

Ust-Bolsheretsk

Petropavlovsk-Kamchatskiy

3456

Ostrov Paramushir

Ostrov Onekotan

Kurilskiye Ostrova

RUSSIA

S A K H A

Verkhoyanskiy Khrebet

Khrebet Cherskogo

Gory Putorana 1701

Norilsk

Yessey

Kotuy

962

Arctic Circle

Olenek

Zhilinda

Kystatyam

Sangar

Batamay

Borogontsy

Lena

Ytyk Kyuyel

Pokrovsk

Amga

Ust-Mil

Nyurba

Sinsk

Olekminsk

Lensk

Vilyuy

Mirnyy

Suntar

Chernyshevskiy

Yukta

Yerbogachen

Vanavara

Mutoray

Kuyumba

Tura

Nizhnyaya Tunguska

Podkamennaya Tunguska

Severo-Yeniseyskiy

1104

Yeniseysk

Boguchany

Angara

Kansk

Ilanskiy

Tayshet

Bratsk

Nizhneudinsk

Tulun

Zima

Krasnoyarsk

Artemovsk

Vostochnyy Sayan

Cheremkhovo

Usolye Sibirskoye

Angarsk

1620

Irkutsk

Munku-Sardyk 3491

Toora-Khem

Kyzyl

Turan

Samogaltay

Uvs Nuur

Tannu Ola

Hyargas Nuur

Döröö Nuur

Uliastay

Altay

4266

Hami

Gaxun Nur

MONGOLIA

Hangayn Nuruu

2800

Ulaanbaatar

Lun

Tsetserleg

Ondörhaan

Choybalsan

Tamsagbulag

Saynshand

Erenhot

Dalandzadgad

3957

Gobi

Baotou

Hohhot

Zhangjiakou

BEIJING

Chengde

Yingkou

Chifeng

Linxi

1949

Xilinhot

Tao'an

Songhua

Baicheng

CHANGCHUN

Siping

SHENYANG

ANSHAN

FUSHUN

Tonghua

2744

JILIN

Yanji

Dong bei

Mudanjiang

HARBIN

QIQIHAR

Da Hinggan Ling

Hailar

Manzhouli

Hulun Nur

Ergun

Ang'angxi

Nen Jiang

Nenjiang

Heihe

Hegang

Jiamusi

Songhua

Boli

Mudanjiang

Suifenhe

Dalnerechensk

Arsenyev

Ussuriysk

Artem

Vladivostok

Nakhodka

Kraskino

Chŏngjin

Wŏnsan

Kansŏng

SOUL

INCH'ŏN

SOUTH KOREA

TAEJON

TAEGU

PUSAN

PYONGYANG

Namp'o

NORTH KOREA

Dandong

DALIAN

Yichun

Khrebet Sikhote Alin

Dalnegorsk

Terney

Amgu

Rudnaya Pristan

Svobodnyy

Belogorsk

Zavitinsk

Shimanovsk

Blagoveshchensk

Skovorodino

Zeya

2640

Chegdomyn

Norsk

Bureya

2078

Obluchye

Birobidzhan

Khabarovsk

Nikolayevsk-na-Amure

Bikin

Lesozavodsk

Amur

Komsomolsk

Amgun

Ulya

Chumikan

Tugur

Sakhalinskiy Zaliv

Ostrov Bolshoy Shantar

Aleksandrovsk-Sakhalinskiy

Sakhalin

Poronaysk

Uglegorsk

Kholmsk

Korsakov

Yuzhno-Sakhalinsk

Dolinsk

Vanino

Sovetskaya Gavan

Zaliv

1558 Gora Lopatina

Ostrov Iturup

Ostrov Kunashir

Wakkanai

Hokkaido

Rumoi

Otaru

SAPPORO

Abashiri

Kushiro

Obihiro

2290

Hakodate

Aomori

Hachinohe

Akita

Honshū

Niigata

Kanazawa

2744

3776 Fuji-San

JAPAN

Kanazawa

OSAKA

Sea of Japan

Nagornyy

Neryungri

Tynda

Stanovoy Khrebet

Chulman

Nagornyy

Aldan

Yablonovyy Khrebet

Stanovoy Khrebet

Chita

Shilka

Nerchinsk

Sretensk

Bukachacha

Mogocha

2840

Bagdarin

2999 Chara

Bodaybo

Mama

Korshunovo

Ust-Kut

Zheleznogorsk-Ilimskiy

Magistralnyy

Ust-Ilimsk

Makarovo

Kirensk

Kondratyevo

Kalakan

Karalon

Ust-Nyukzha

Dzhalinda

Mogocha

Skovorodino

Ushumun

Magdagachi

Poyarkovo

Gulian

1054

Argun

Zabaykalsk

Borzya

Olovyannaya

Aginskoye

Khilok

Petrovsk-Zabaykalskiy

Ulan Ude

458

Barguzin

Baykal

Kyakhta

Gusinoozersk

Zakamensk

Darhan

Sühbaatar

Hentiyn Nuruu

Öndörhaan

Hatgal

Hövsgöl Nuur

Mörön

O L A

1146

Poluostrov Taymyr

Gory Byrranga

Nordvik

Khatanga

Ust Olenek

Novorybnoye

Volochanka

Kheta

Saskylakh

Anabar

Olenek

Olenyok

Pyasina

Ostrov Bolshoy Begichev

Khankala

10 11 12 13 14

80 90 100 110 120 130

60 50 40

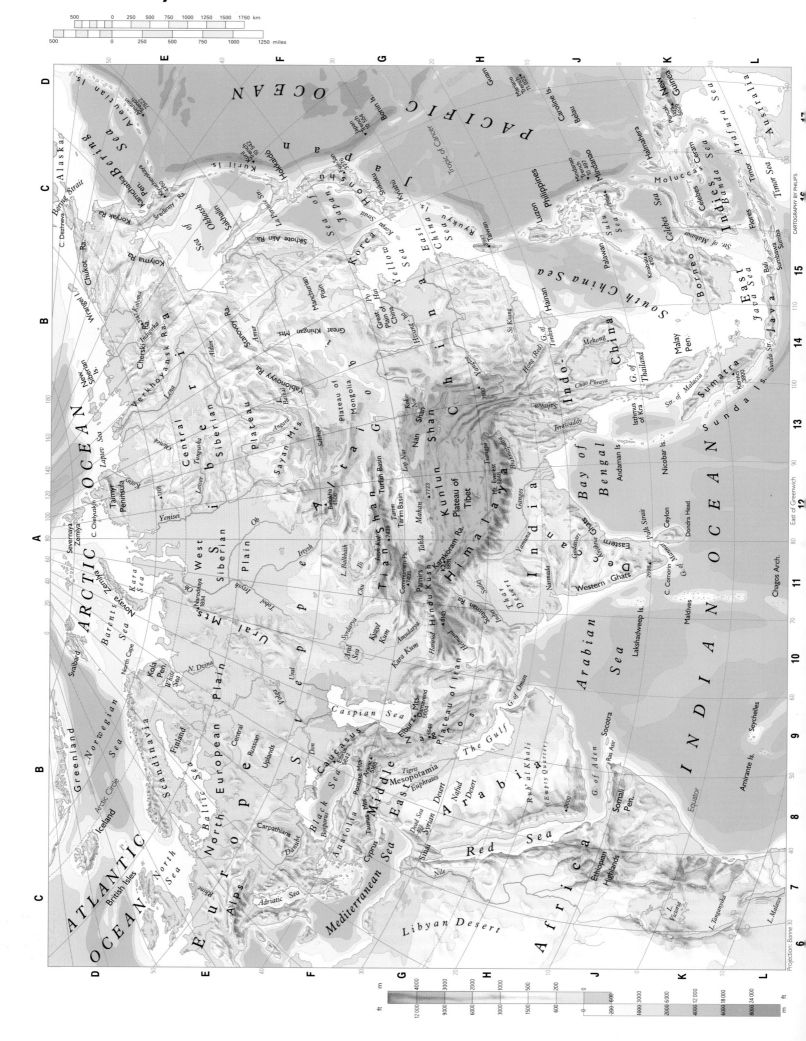

CARTOGRAPHY BY PHILIPS

Projection: Bonne 30

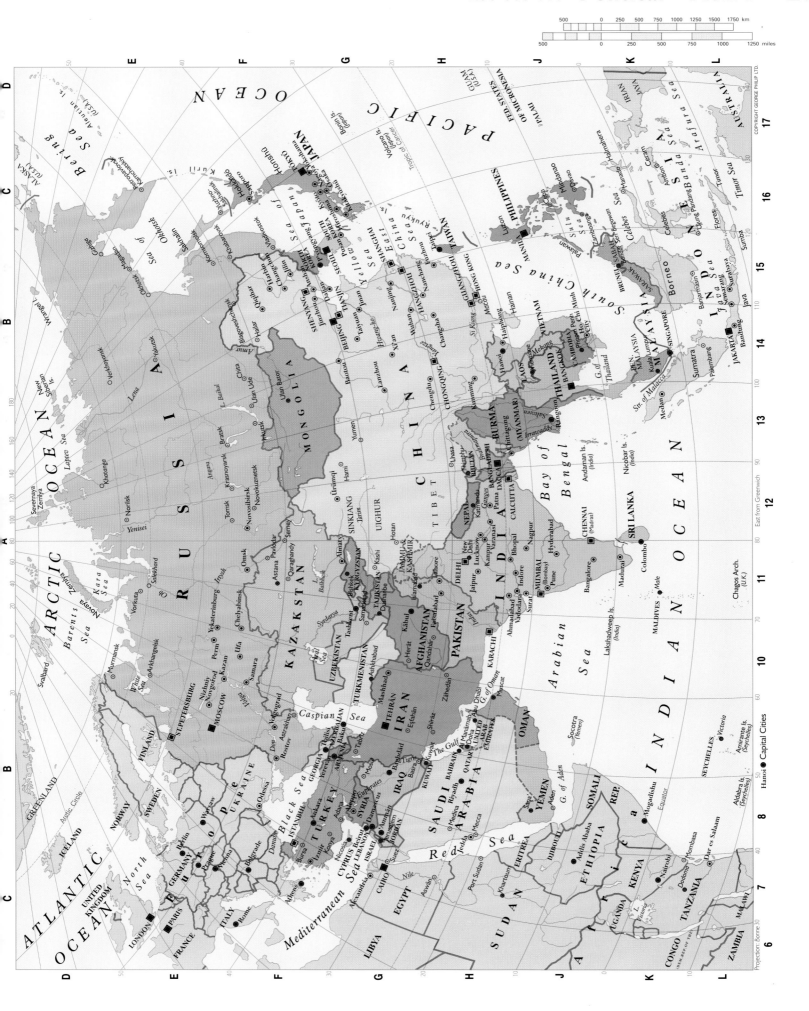

JAPAN 1:5 000 000

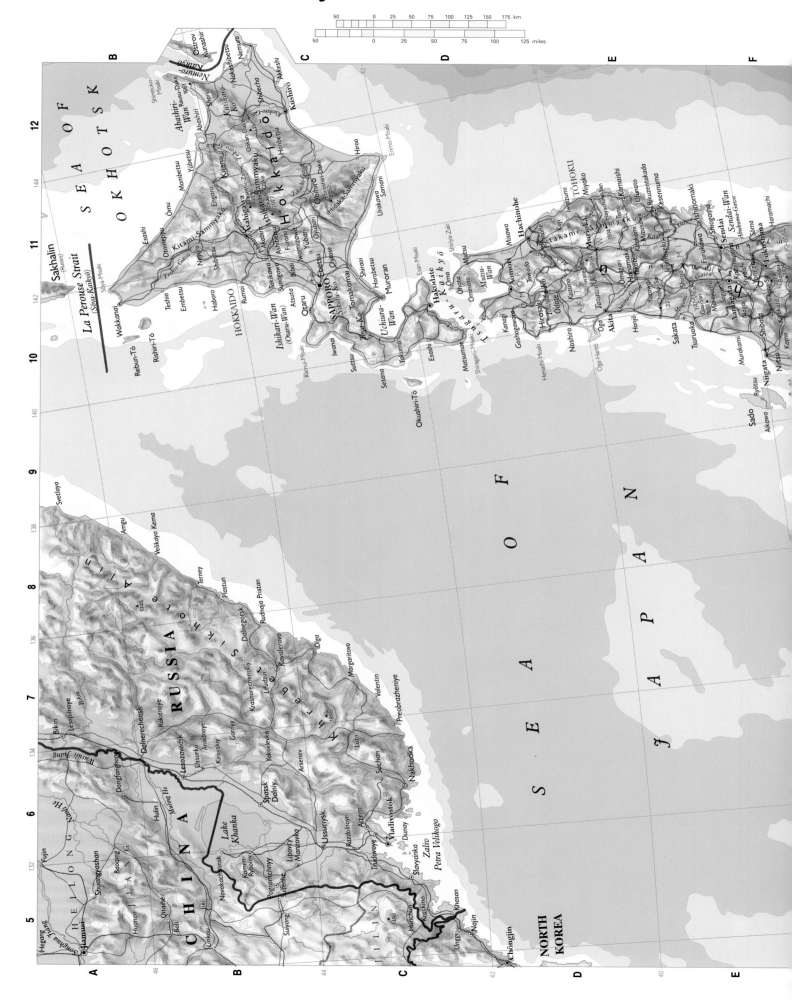

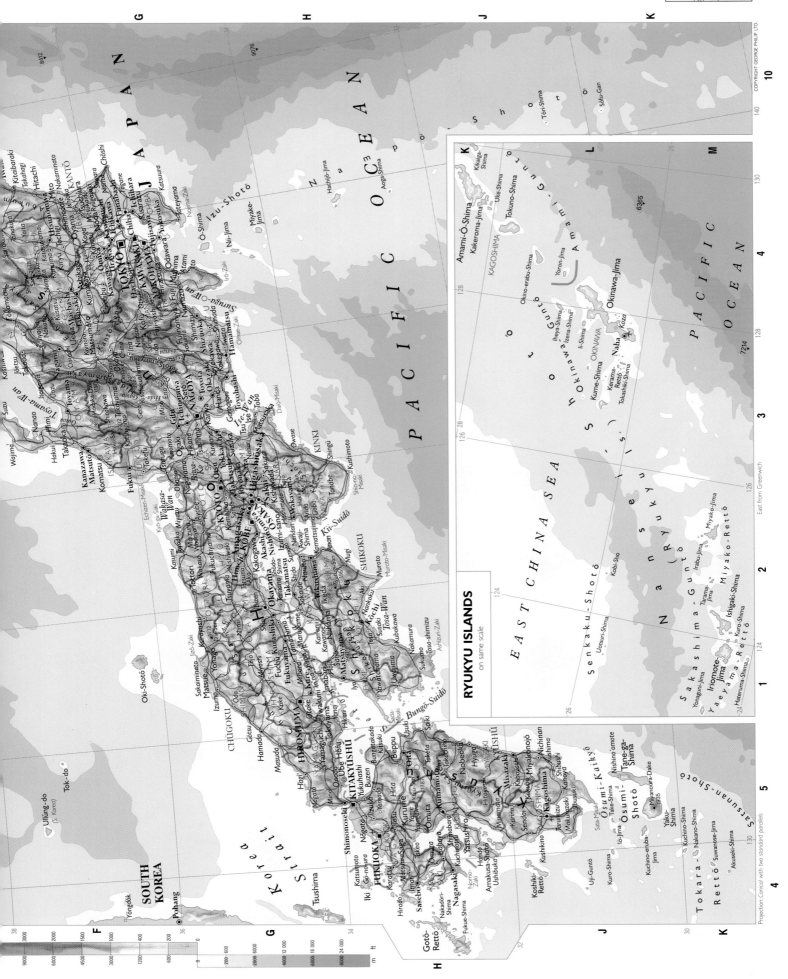

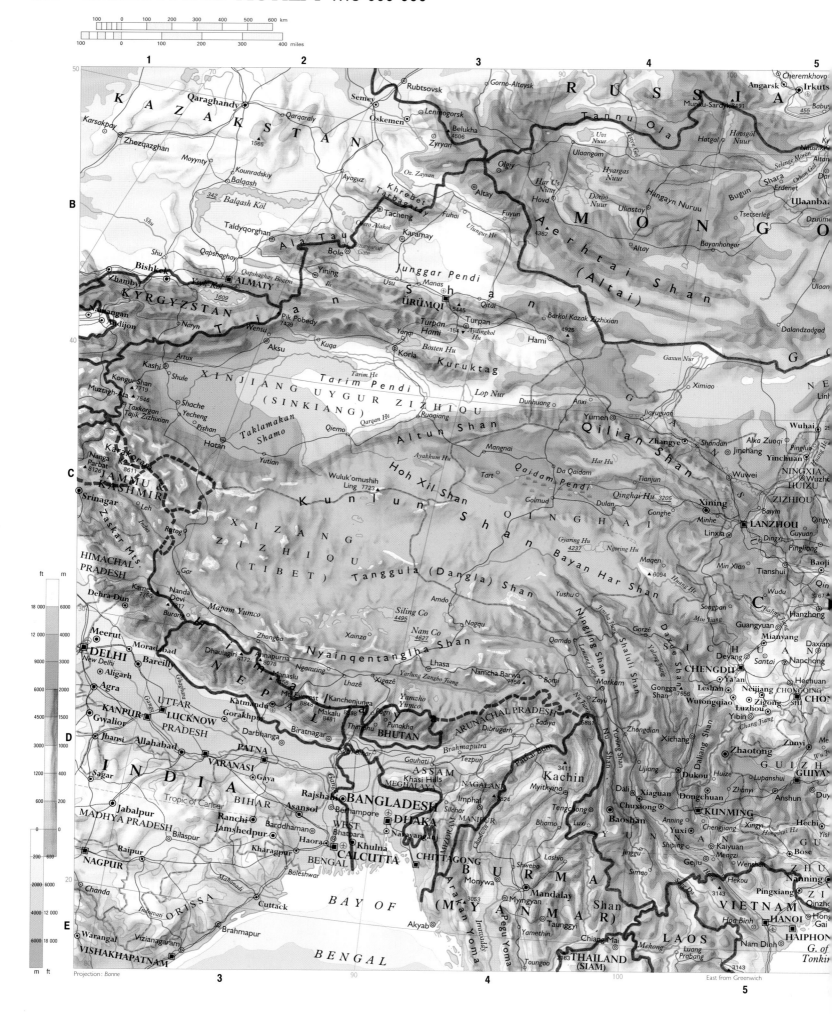

SEA OF

JAPAN

EAST CHINA

SEA

PACIFIC

OCEAN

SOUTH CHINA

SEA

YELLOW

SEA

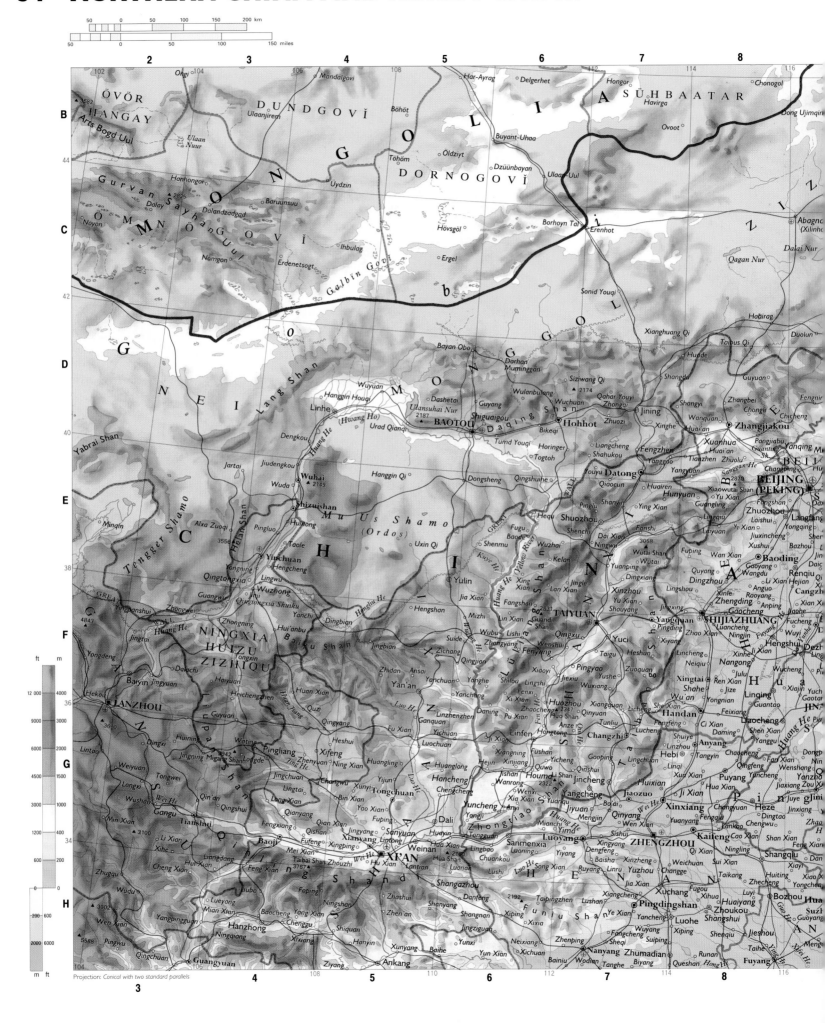

50 0 50 100 150 200 km
50 0 50 100 150 miles

ft m
12 000 4000
9000 3000
6000 2000
4500 1500
3000 1000
1200 400
600 200
0 0
200 600
2000 6000
m ft

Projection: Conical with two standard parallels

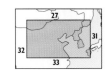

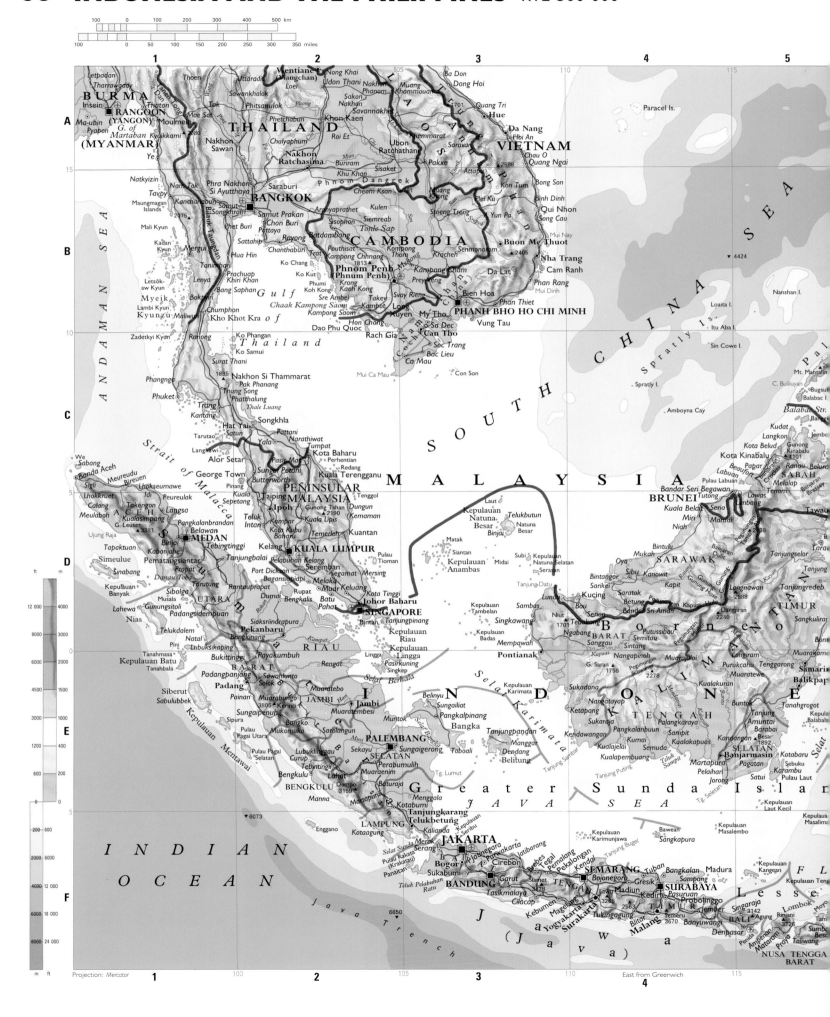

Projection: Mercator

East from Greenwich

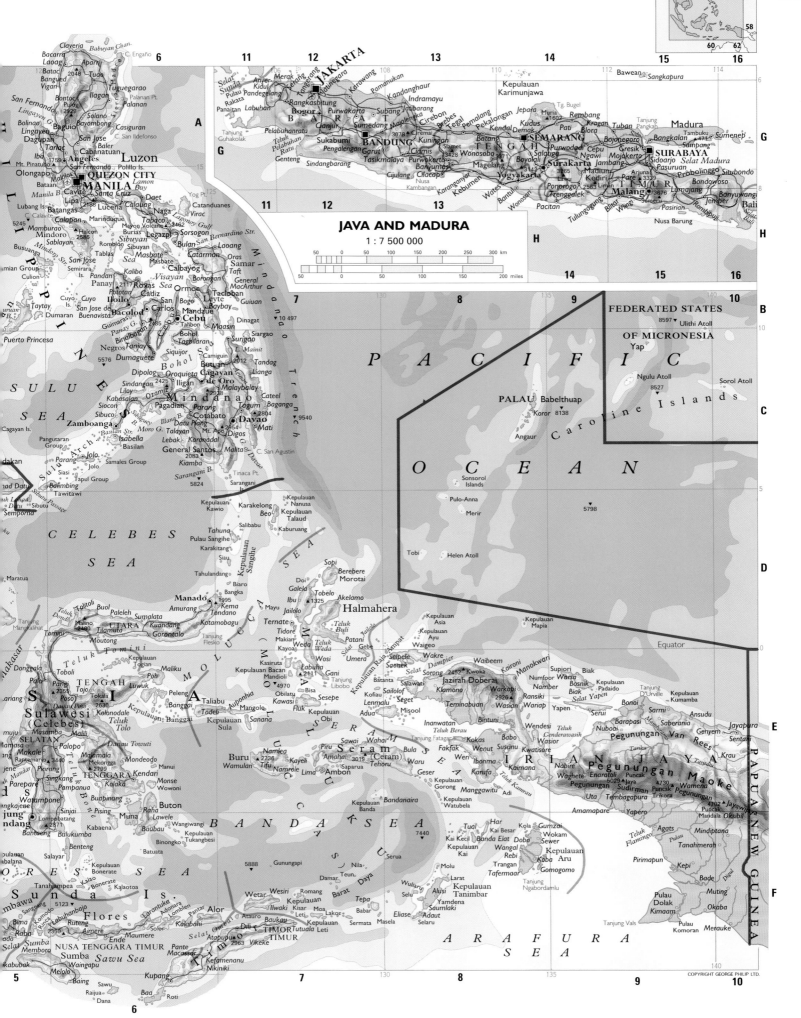

JAVA AND MADURA
1 : 7 500 000

50   0   50   100   150   200   250   300 km
50   0   50   100   150   200 miles

FEDERATED STATES
OF MICRONESIA

PACIFIC

OCEAN

Caroline Islands

PALAU Babelthuap

CELEBES
SEA

MOLUCCA
SEA

Halmahera

SULU
SEA

Mindanao

SULAWESI
(Celebes)

SERAM SEA

BANDA SEA

IRIAN JAYA

Pegunungan Maoke

FLORES SEA

NUSA TENGGARA TIMUR

TIMOR
TIMUR

Sawu Sea

ARAFURA
SEA

PAPUA NEW GUINEA

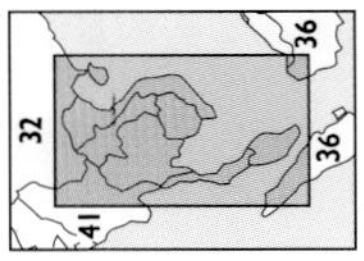

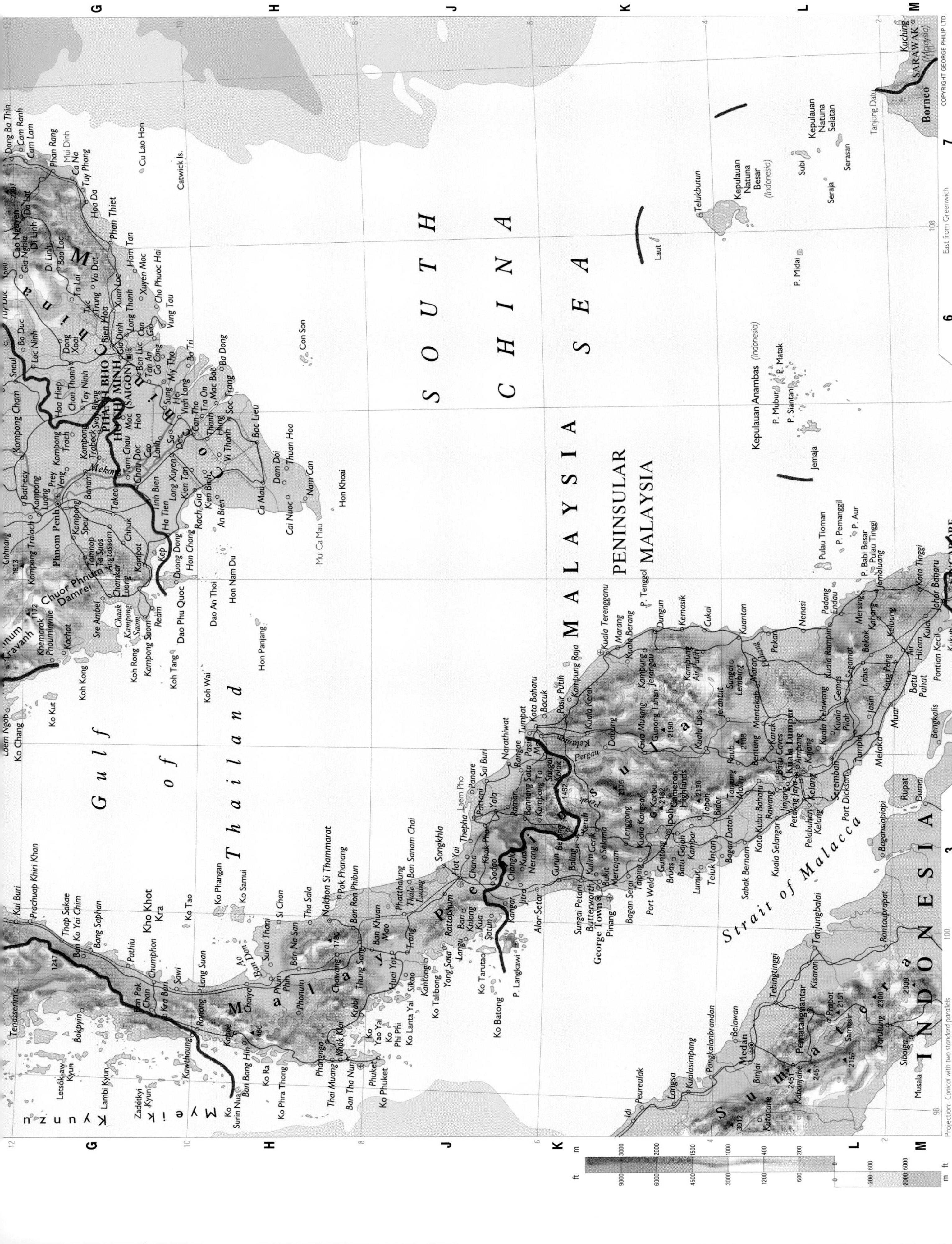

S O U T H   C H I N A   S E A

Gulf of Thailand

Gulf of Thailand

MALAYSIA

PENINSULAR MALAYSIA

Strait of Malacca

INDONESIA

Thailand

Borneo

SARAWAK (Malaysia)

Kuching

Kepulauan Natuna Selatan (Indonesia)

Kepulauan Natuna Besar

Subi
Seraja
Serasan

Telukbutun

Kepulauan Anambas (Indonesia)

P. Mubur
P. Siantan
P. Matak
Jemaja

Laut

P. Midai

SINGAPORE
Singapore
Batam
Bintan
Tanjungpinang

PHAT BHO
HO CHI MINH (SAIGON)
Phnom Penh

Mekong

Kompong Cham
Kompong Thom
Kompong Speu

Chuor Phnum Damrei

Krâvanh

Phan Rang
Phan Thiet
Phan Tan
Ham Moc
Vo Dat
Vung Tau

Con Son

Ca Mau
Mui Ca Mau

Kota Baharu
Tumpat
Pasir
Kota Baharu
Pasir Putih
Kampung Raja
Kuala Terengganu
Marang
Kuala Berang
Dungun
Kemasik
Cukai
Kuantan
Pekan
Nenasi
Endau
Mersing

Kuala Tahan
Gunong Tahan
2190

Cameron Highlands
2182
Ipoh
Kuala Kangsar
Taiping
George Town
Pinang
Butterworth
Bagan Serai
Port Weld

Kuala Lumpur
Kelang
Port Dickson
Melaka
Muar
Batu Pahat
Pontian Kecil
Johor Baharu

Medan
Binjai
Tebingtinggi
Pematangsiantar
Kisaran
Tanjungbalai

S u m a t e r a

Bagansiapiapi
Dumai

Strait of Malacca

Ko Samui
Ko Phangan
Surat Thani
Nakhon Si Thammarat
Phatthalung
Songkhla
Hat Yai
Pattani
Yala
Narathiwat

Phuket
Ko Phuket
Krabi
Trang
Satun
P. Langkawi
Ko Tarutao

Prachuap Khiri Khan
Chumphon

COPYRIGHT GEORGE PHILIP LTD.

East from Greenwich

Projection: Conical with two standard parallels

ft
9000
6000
4500
3000
1500
1000
600
200

m

m
3000
2000
1500
900
600
300
120
60

ft

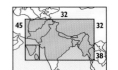

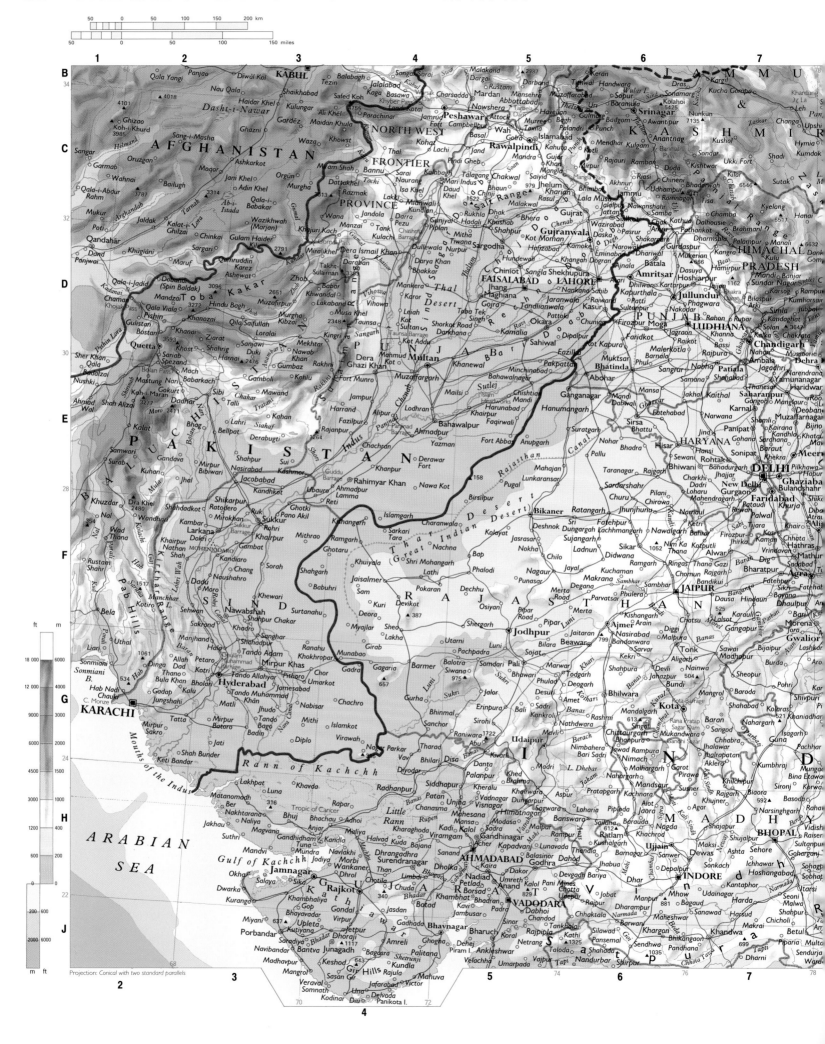

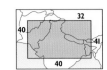

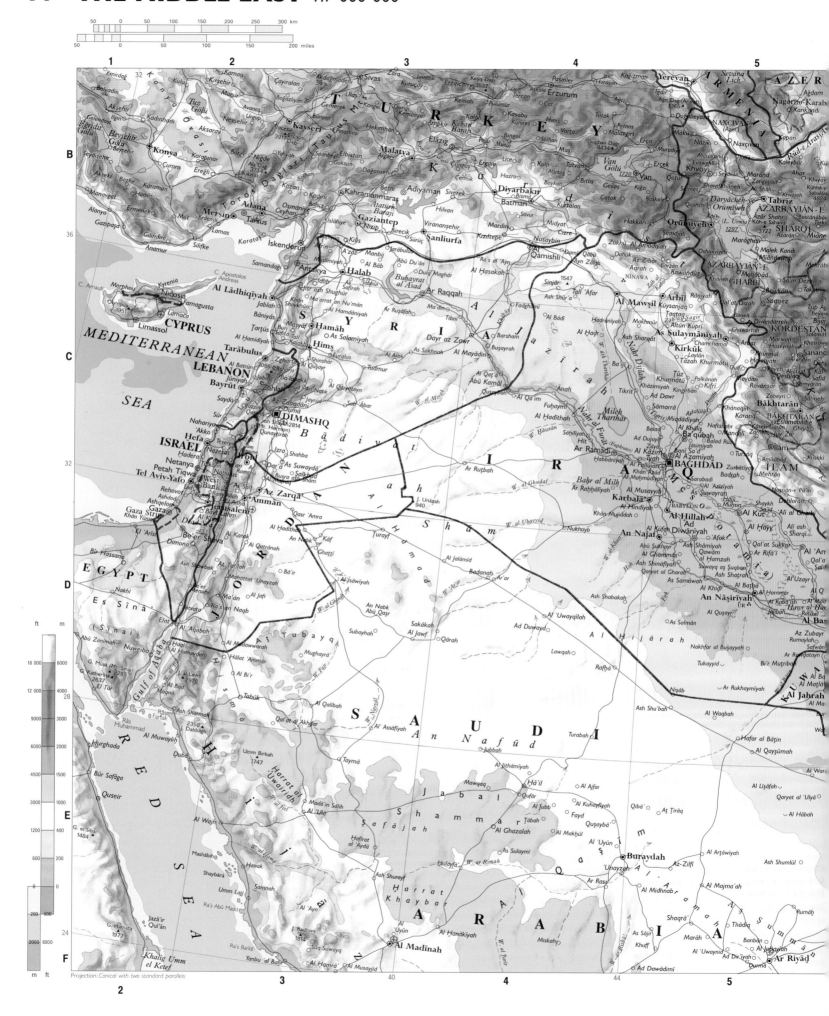

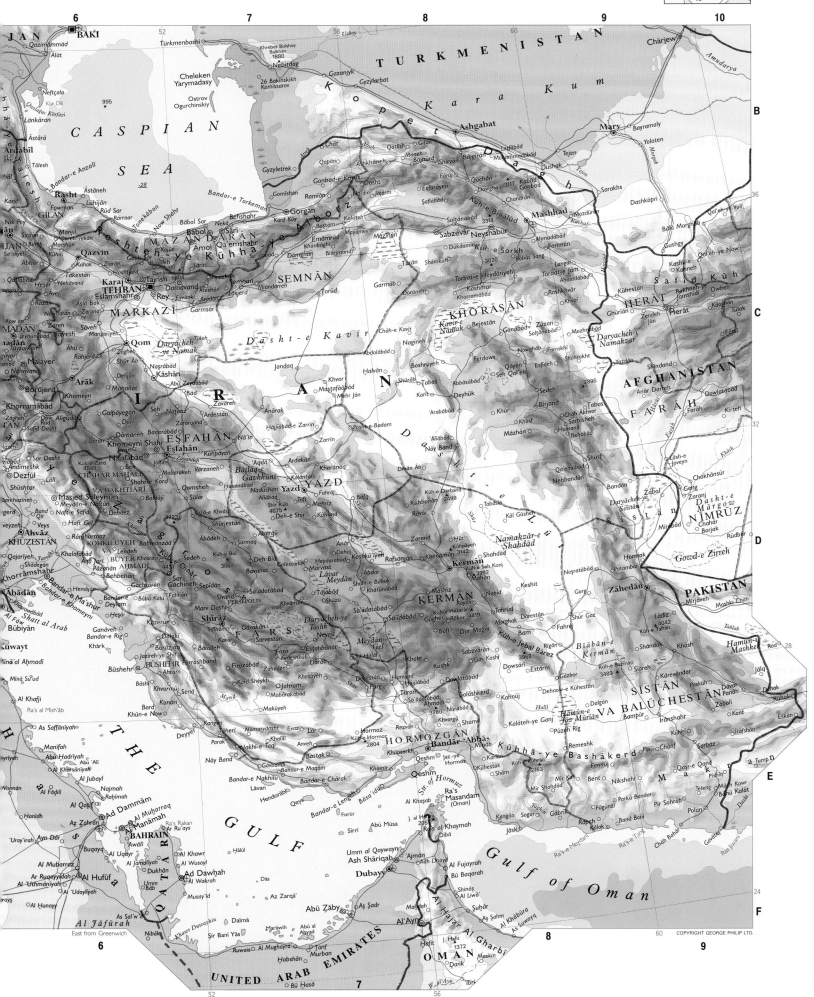

CASPIAN SEA

TURKMENISTAN

Kopet Dagh

Kara Kum

Ashgabat · Mary

BAKI

Lānkārān

Ardabil

Rasht

GILĀN

Qazvin

TEHRĀN

Karaj

MARKAZI

MĀZANDARĀN

Reshteh-ye Kūhhā-ye Alborz

SEMNĀN

Gorgan

Sabzevār · Neyshābūr · Mashhad

Kuh-e Binālūd

KHORĀSĀN

Qom

Dasht-e Kavīr

Kāshān

Arāk

Esfahān

ESFAHĀN

YAZD

Yazd

Dasht-e Lūt

HERĀT

Herāt

AFGHANISTAN

FARĀH

Ahvāz

KHUZESTĀN

CHAHĀR MAHĀLL VA BAKHTIĀRĪ

KOHKĪLŪYEH VA BŪYER AHMADĪ

Zāgros

FĀRS

Shīrāz

PERSEPOLIS

KERMĀN

Kermān

NĪMRŪZ

Zāhedān

PAKISTAN

SĪSTĀN VA BALŪCHESTĀN

HORMOZGĀN

Bandar-e 'Abbās

Qeshm

Str. of Hormuz

Kūhhā-ye Bashākerd

Makran

BAHRAIN

Manāmah

QATAR

Ad Dawḥah

THE GULF

Dubayy

UNITED ARAB EMIRATES

Abū Ẓaby

Al 'Ayn

OMAN

Gulf of Oman

East from Greenwich

COPYRIGHT GEORGE PHILIP LTD.

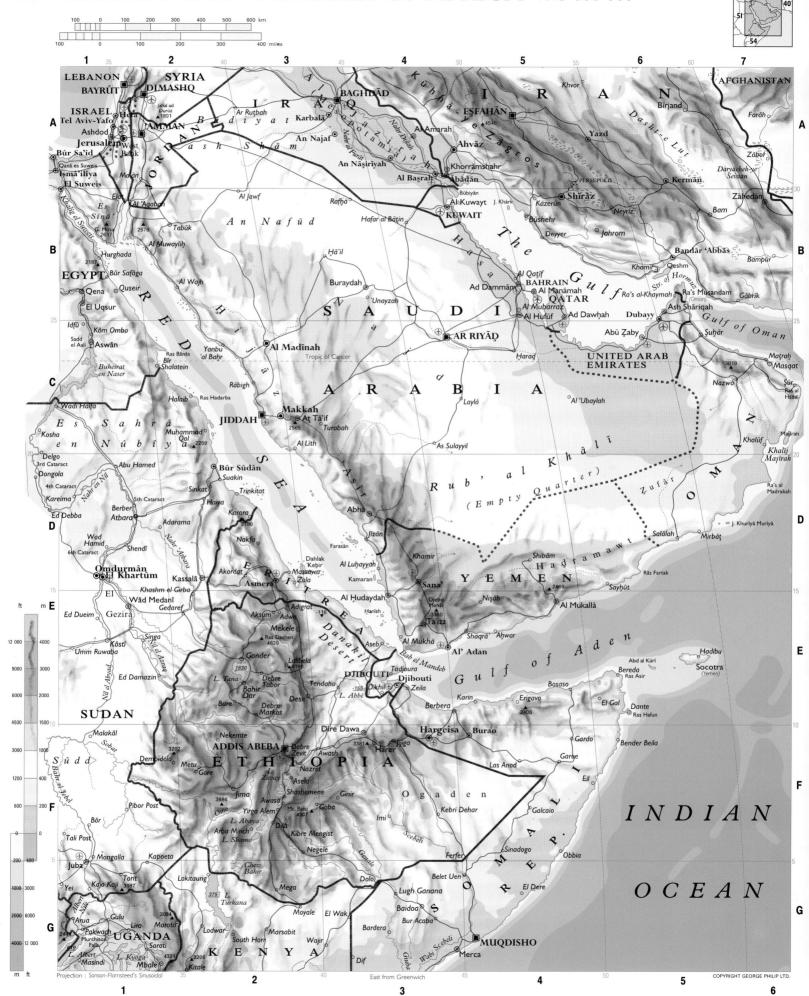

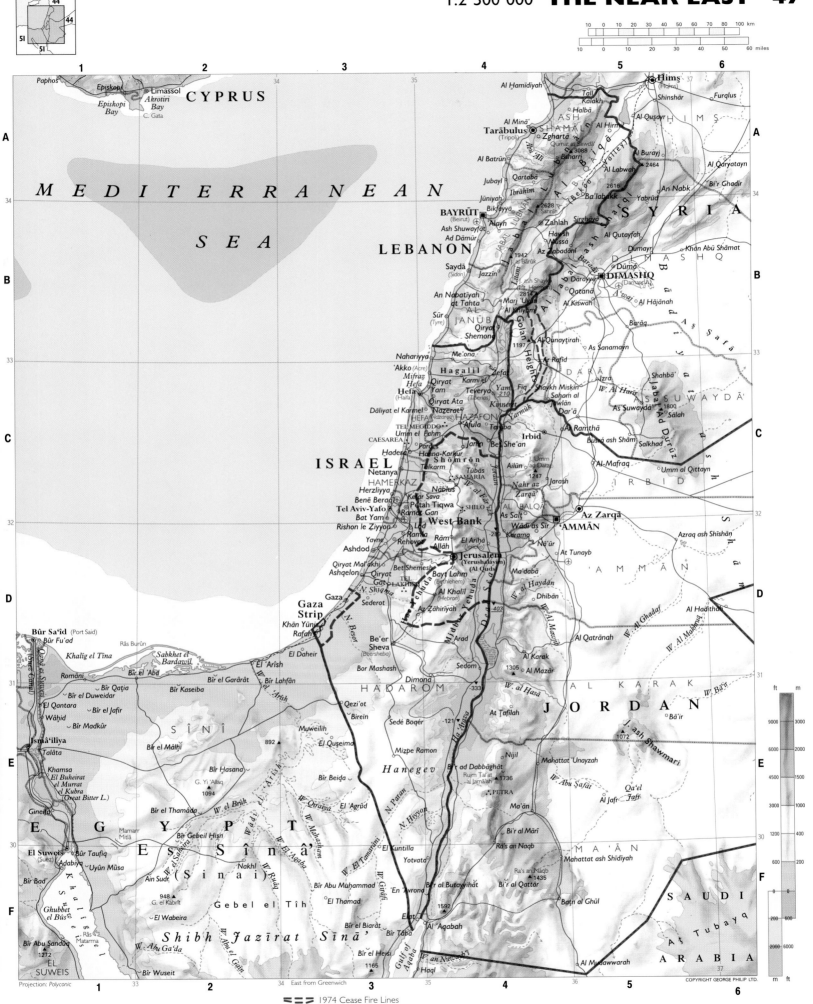

=== 1974 Cease Fire Lines

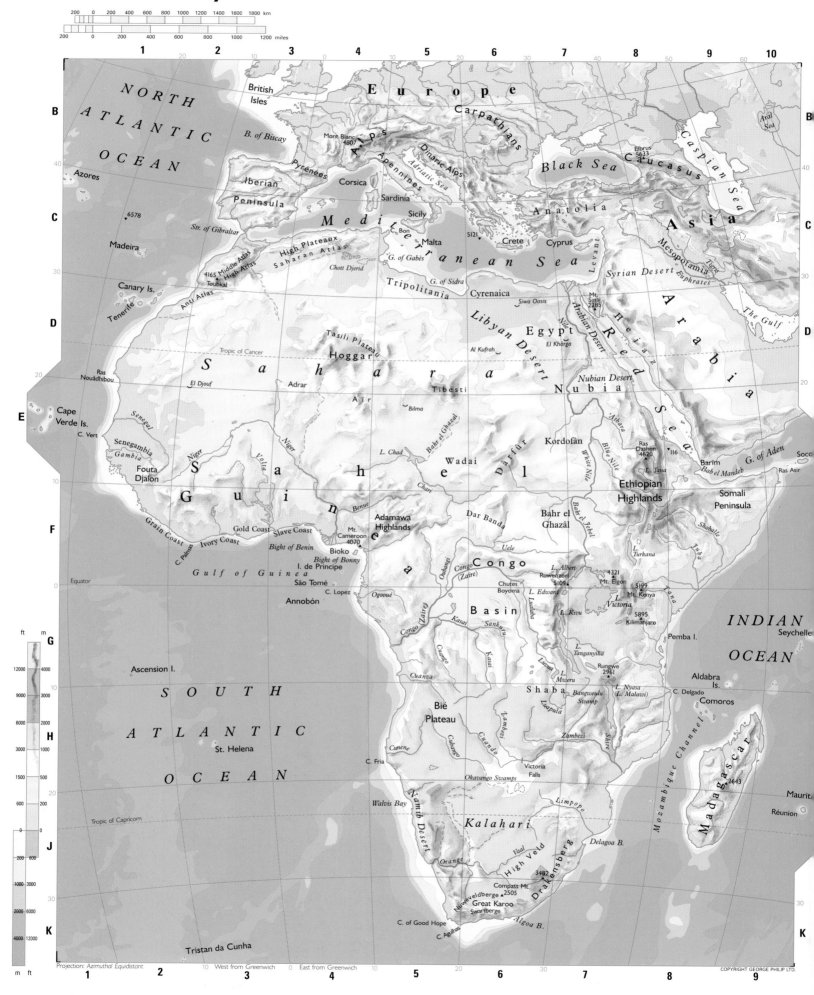

200 0 200 400 600 800 1000 1200 1400 1600 1800 km
200 0 200 400 600 800 1000 1200 miles

1 **2** **3** **4** **5** **6** **7** **8** **9** **10**

NORTH
ATLANTIC
OCEAN

B. of Biscay

British Isles

Europe

Carpathians

Alps
Mont Blanc
4807

Pyrénées
Corsica
Apennines
Dinaric Alps
Adriatic Sea

Black Sea
Caucasus
Elbrus
5633

Caspian Sea

Aral Sea

Azores

6578

Madeira

Iberian
Peninsula

Str. of Gibraltar

Sardinia

Sicily
C. Bon
Malta
5121
Crete

Anatolia

Cyprus

Asia

Mesopotamia
Tigris
Euphrates

Canary Is.

Tenerife

High Plateaux
Middle Atlas
4165
High Atlas
Toubkal
Anti Atlas

Saharan Atlas
Chott Djerid

Mediterranean Sea
G. of Gabès
G. of Sidra

Tripolitania
Cyrenaica
Siwa Oasis

Libyan Desert
Egypt
El Khârga

Mt. Sinai
2285

Levant
Syrian Desert

Hejaz
Arabian Desert

Arabia

The Gulf

Tropic of Cancer

Ras
Nouâdhibou

El Djouf

Sahara

Tasili Plateau
Hoggar

Adrar

Aïr

Tibesti
Bilma

Al Kufrah

Nubia
Nubian Desert

Red Sea

Cape
Verde Is.

C. Vert

Senegambia
Gambia

Senegal

Niger

Volta

Niger

S
u
d
a
n

L. Chad

Bahr el Ghazal

Wadai
Chari

Darfur

Kordofân

White Nile
Blue Nile

Ras
Dashen
4620

116

Athara

Barim
Bab el Mandeb

G. of Aden
Soco

Ras Asir

Fouta
Djalon

Grain Coast

C. Palmas
Ivory Coast

Gold Coast
Slave Coast

Bight of Benin

Guinea

Benue

Mt.
Cameroon
4070

Bioko
Bight of Bonny
I. de Principe
São Tomé

Adamawa
Highlands

Dar Banda

Uele

Bahr el
Ghazâl

Sahel

Ethiopian
Highlands

Somali
Peninsula

Shaballe

L.
Turkana

Juba

Equator

Gulf of Guinea

C. Lopez

Annobón

Ogooué

Congo (Zaïre)

Oubangi

Congo
(Zaïre)

Congo
Basin

Chutes
Boyoma

L. Albert
Ruwenzori
5109

L. Edward

L. Kivu

L. Victoria

Mt. Elgon
5199
Mt. Kenya
5895

4321

Kilimanjaro

Tana

INDIAN
OCEAN

Seychelle

Ascension I.

SOUTH

ATLANTIC

OCEAN

St. Helena

Congo (Zaïre)

Kasai

Cuango

Kasai

Sankuru

Cuanza

Lualaba

Luvua

L.
Tanganyika

L.
Mweru

Rungwe
2961

Pemba I.

Aldabra
Is.

Comoros

Bié
Plateau

Shaba

Bangweulu
Swamp

Luapula

L. Nyasa
(L. Malawi)

Shire

C. Delgado

ft   m

12000   4000

9000   3000

6000   2000

3000   1000

1500   500

600   200

0   0

200   600

1000   3000

2000   6000

4000   12000

m   ft

C. Fria

Walvis Bay

Cunene

Cubango

Cuando

Zambezi

Zambezi

Victoria
Falls

Okavango Swamps

Limpopo

Mozambique Channel

Madagascar
2643

Maurit

Réunion

Tropic of Capricorn

Namib Desert

Kalahari

Orange

Vaal

High Veld

Delagoa B.

Drakensberg

3482
Compass Mt.
2505

Nieuweldberge
Swartberge

Great Karoo

Algoa B.

C. of Good Hope

C. Agulhas

Tristan da Cunha

Projection: Azimuthal Equidistant

West from Greenwich   East from Greenwich

COPYRIGHT GEORGE PHILIP LTD.

200 0 200 400 600 800 1000 1200 1400 1600 1800 km
200 0 200 400 600 800 1000 1200 miles

Projection: Azimuthal Equidistant

West from Greenwich   0   East from Greenwich

● Dakar   Capital Cities

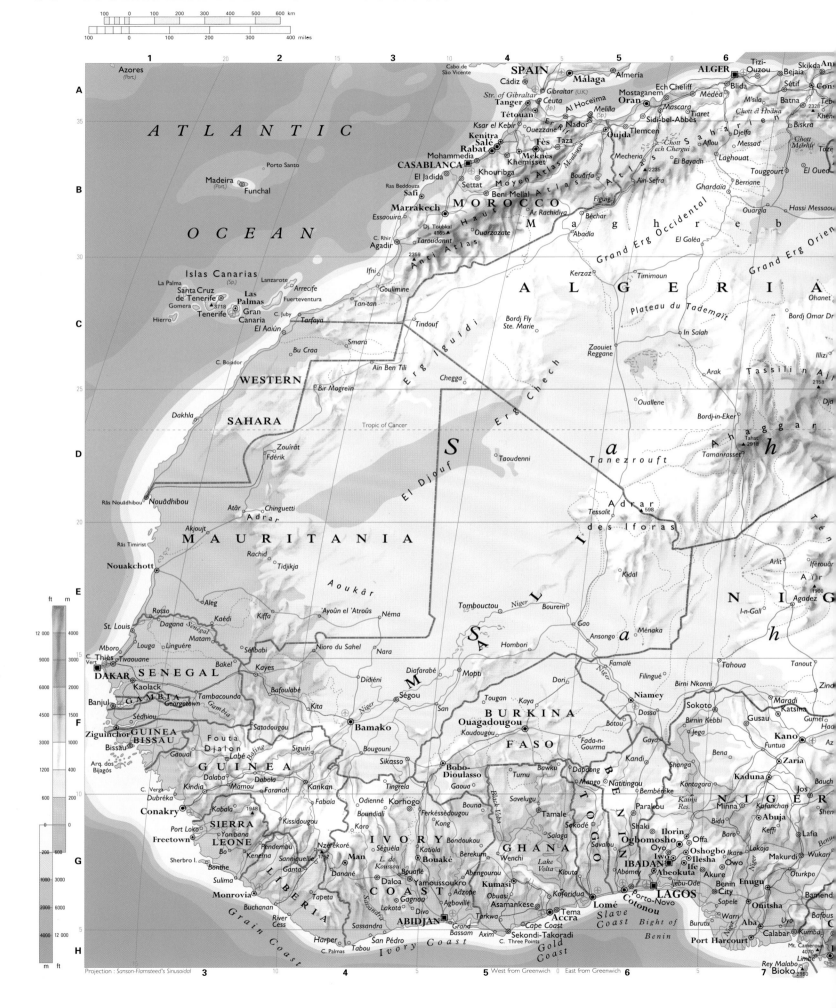

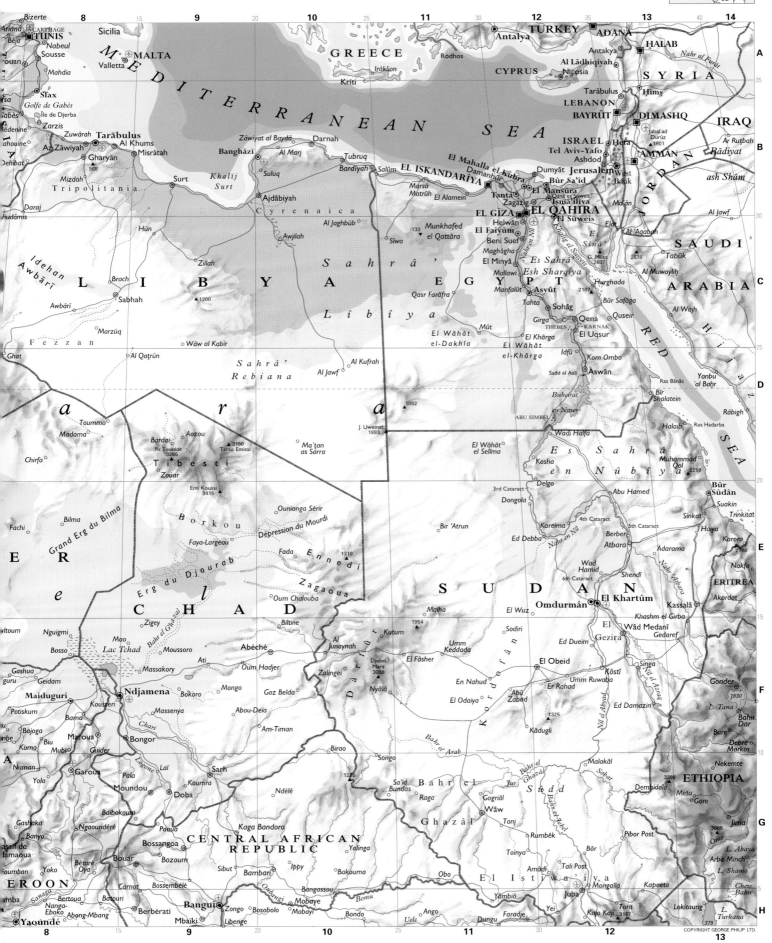

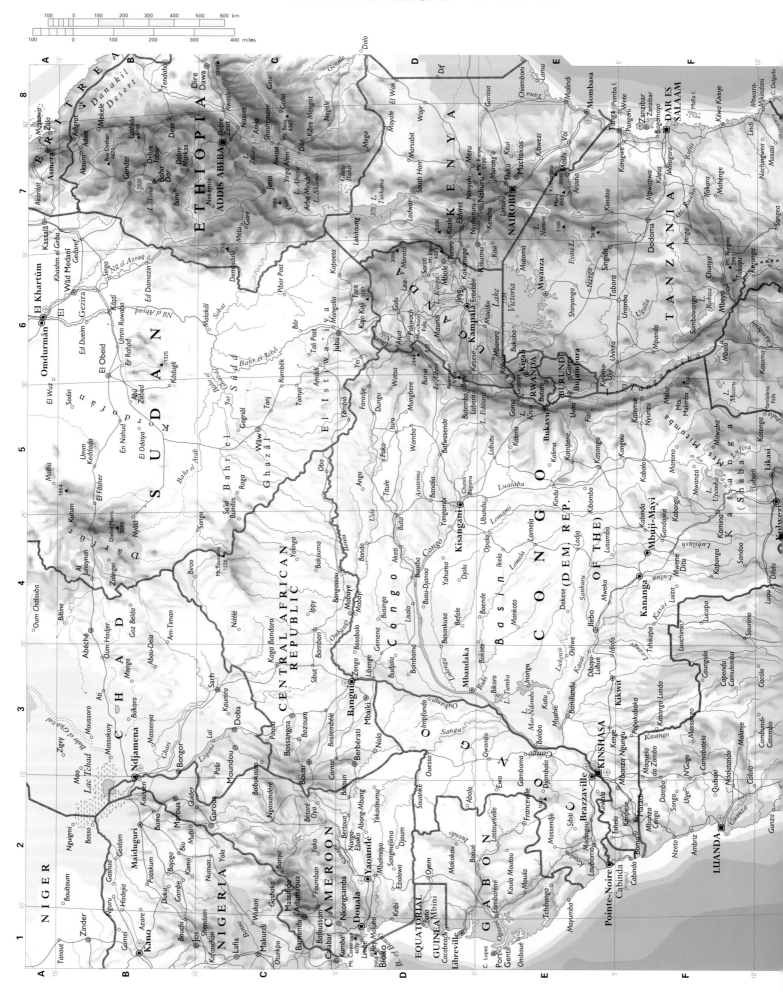

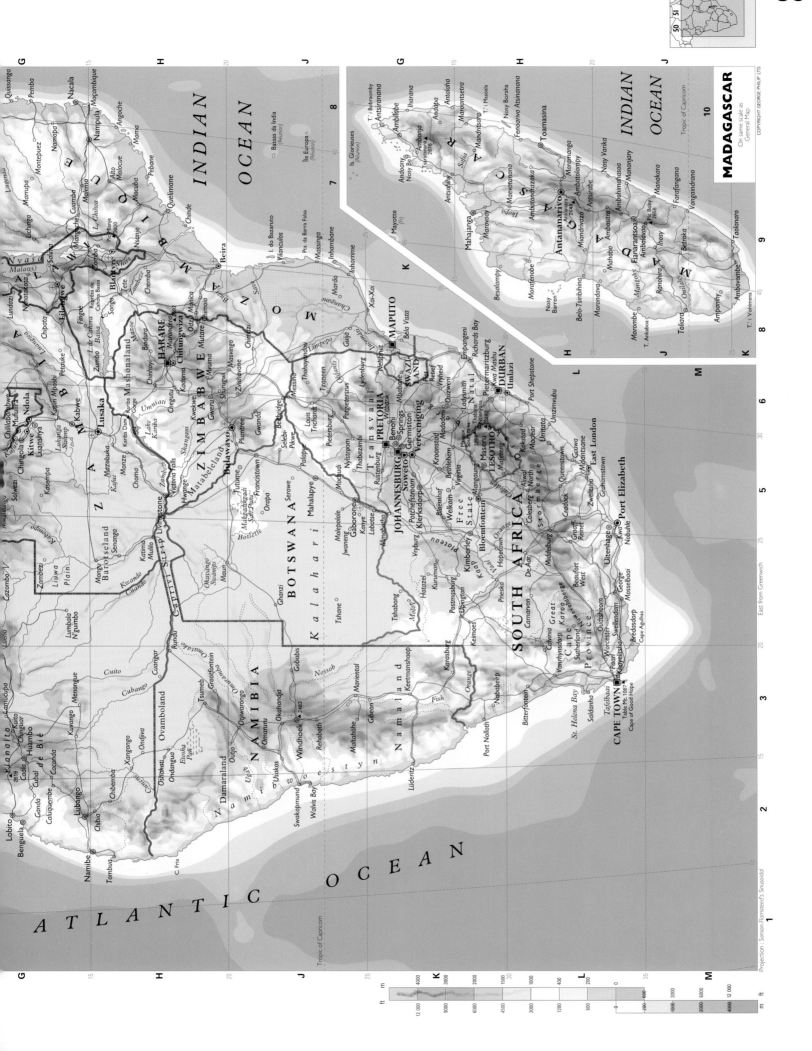

MADAGASCAR
On same scale as
General Map

COPYRIGHT GEORGE PHILIP LTD.

INDIAN OCEAN

ATLANTIC OCEAN

Projection : Sanson-Flamsteed's Sinusoidal

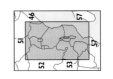

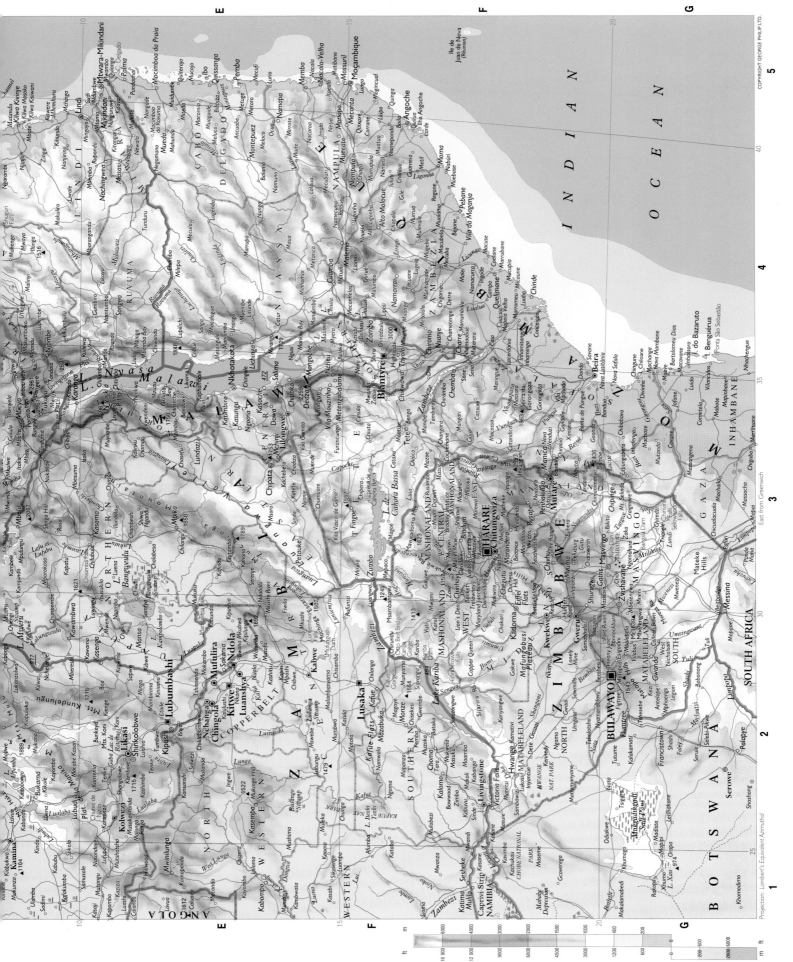

INDIAN OCEAN

I N D I A N

O C E A N

L. Nyasa

Malawi

MALAWI

ZAMBIA

MOZAMBIQUE

ZIMBABWE

BOTSWANA

SOUTH AFRICA

ANGOLA

NAMIBIA

HARARE

BULAWAYO

Lusaka

Lubumbashi

Beira

Projection: Lambert's Equivalent Azimuthal

East from Greenwich

m   ft

m   ft

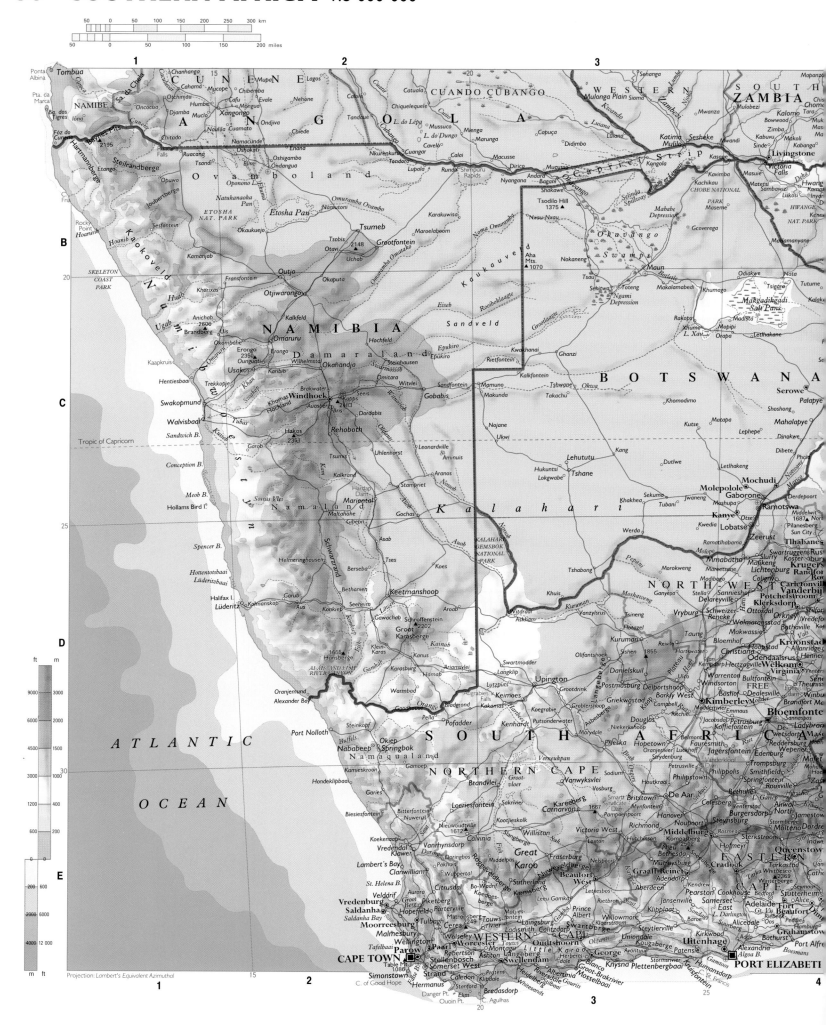

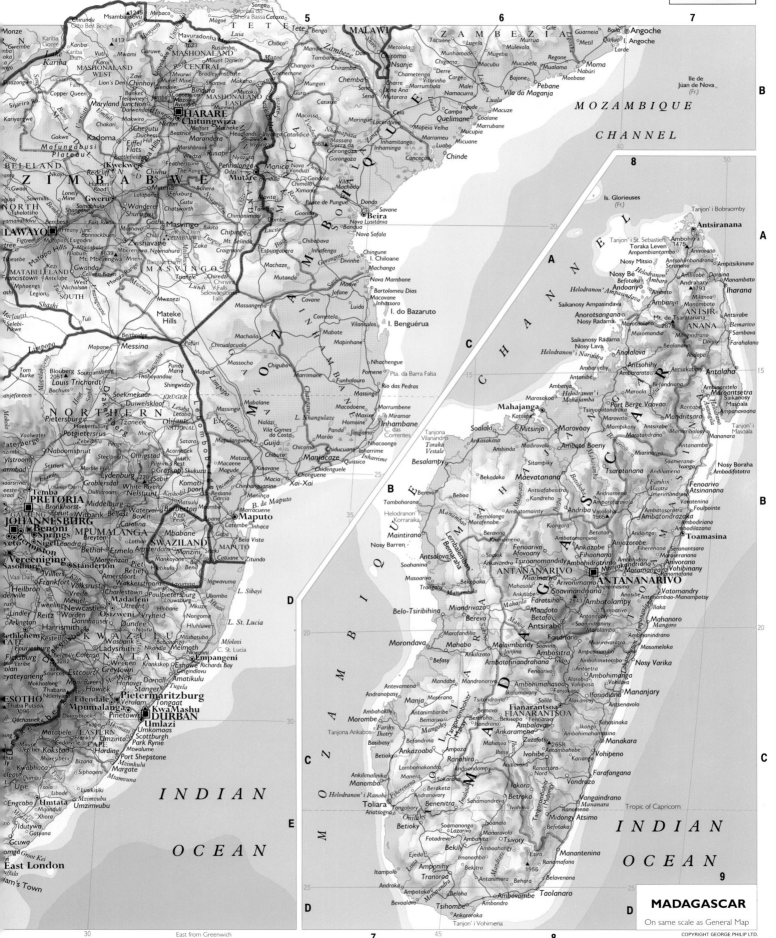

MOZAMBIQUE CHANNEL

INDIAN OCEAN

MADAGASCAR
On same scale as General Map

East from Greenwich

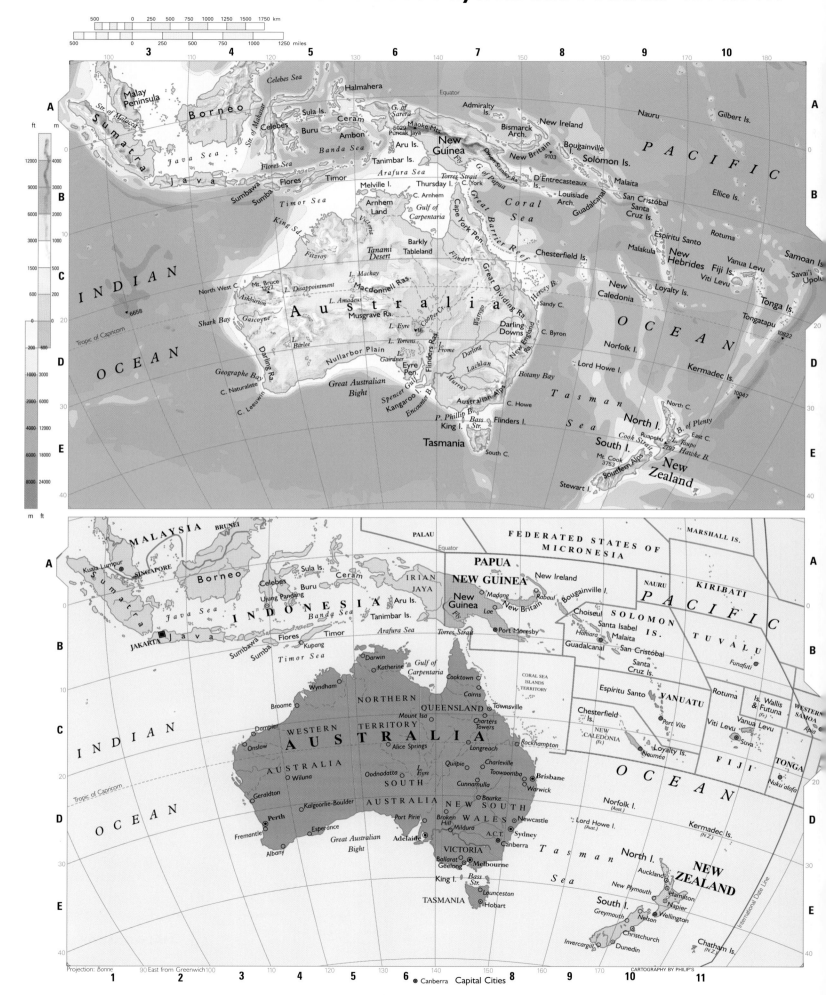

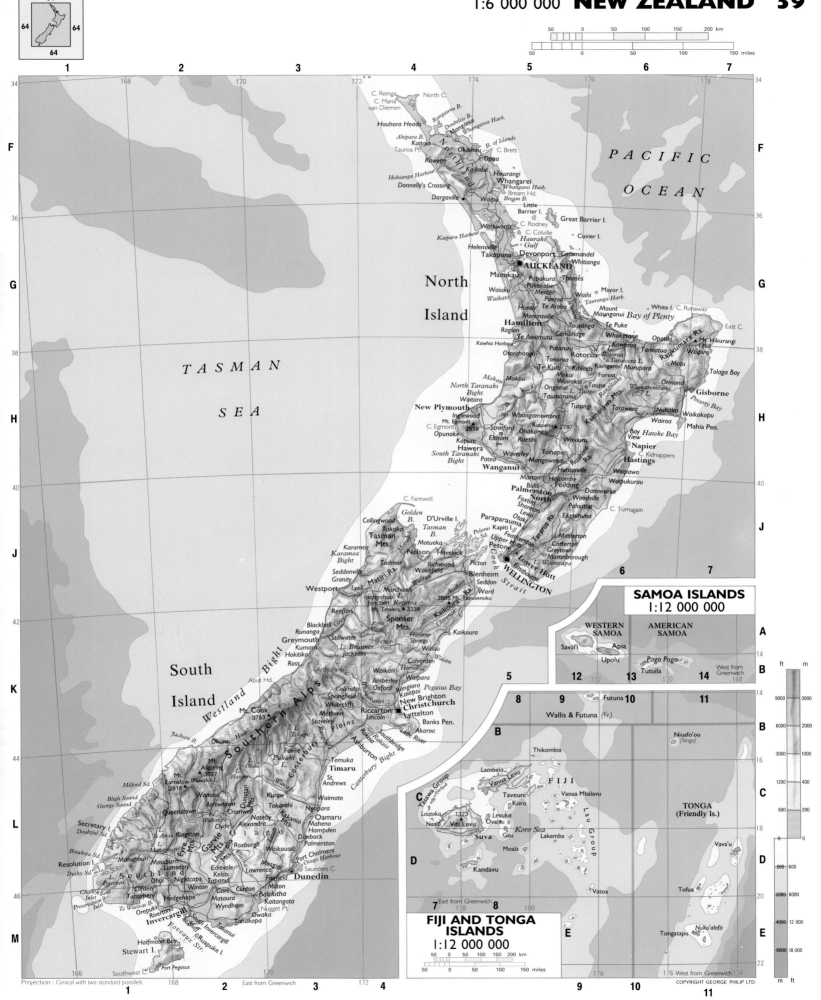

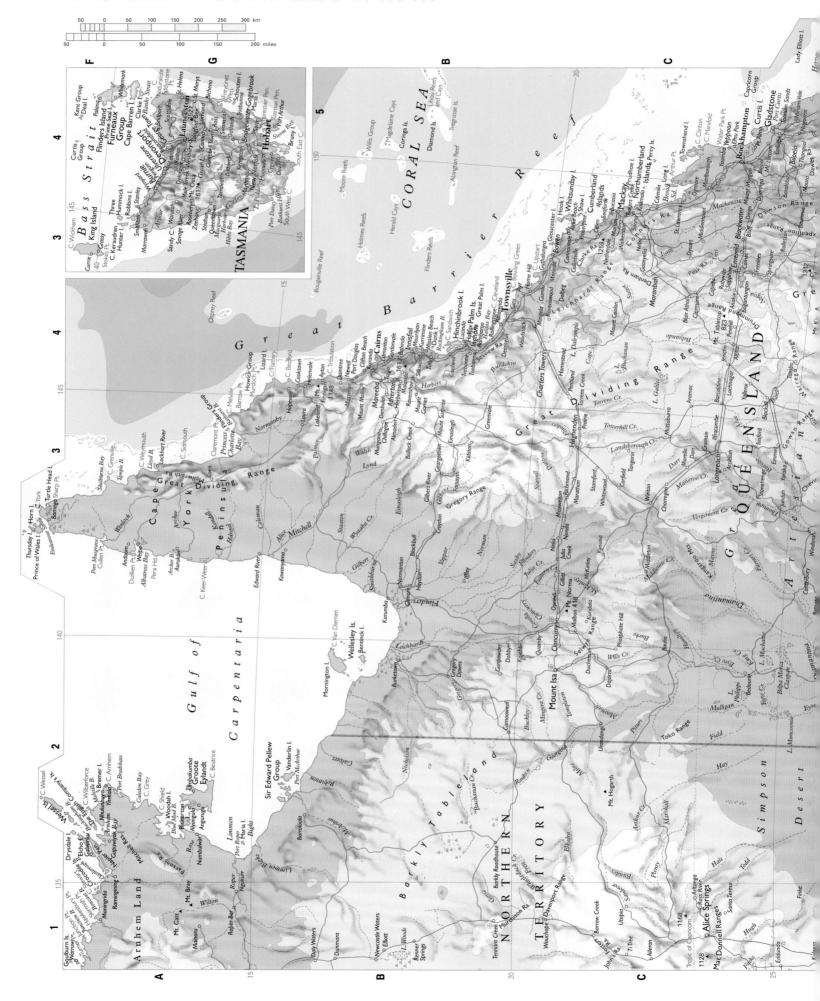

7 8 9 10

6

1 2 3 4 5

B MOSKVA
Volga
Yekaterinburg
RUSSIA
Tomsk
Novosibirsk
Irkutsk
O₂ Baykal
Chita
Lena
Amur
Sea of Okhotsk
Okhotsk
Poluostrov Kamchatka
Komandorskiye Ostrova (Russia)
Near Is. (U.S.A.)
Ber Sea
Andreano (U.S.A.)

Astana (Aqmola)
Semey
Ulaanbaatar
Blagoveshchensk
Khabarovsk
Sakhalin
Petropavlovsk-Kamchatskiy
7822
Aleutia

KAZAKSTAN
Aral Sea
Balqash Köl
Altaj
MONGOLIA
La Perouse Str.
Kurilskiye Ostrova (Russia)
Kuril Trench
Aleutian Trench

Almaty
Ürümqi
Changchun
SHENYANG
Harbin
Vladivostok
Sapporo
Hakodate
10,542

Toshkent
KYRGYZSTAN
BEIJING
TIANJIN
Taiyuan
NORTH KOREA
SOUL
Sea of Japan
Sendai

TAJIKISTAN
CHINA
Lanzhou
Xi'an
Dalian
SOUTH KOREA
Nagoya
Kyōto
TOKYO
Fuji-San 3776
Emperor Seamount Chain

AFGHANISTAN
Kabul
Srinagar
Kunlun Shan
XIZANG
Qingdao
Kitakyūshū
Osaka
JAPAN
Yokohama
10,554

PAKISTAN
Lhasa
Himalaya
Nanjing
Wuhan
Shikoku
Kyūshū
Japan Trench
Midway Is. (U.S.A.)

Lahore
DELHI
Everest
Chang J
CHONGQING
HANGZHOU
SHANGHAI
East China Sea
Ogasawara Gunto (Japan)
Lisianski I. (U.S.A.)

Kanpur
Ganga
NEPAL
Brahmaputra
Changsha
Kunming
Fuzhou
Taipei
Ryūkyu-rettō (Japan)
Minami-Tori-Shima (Japan)

Hyderabad
BANGLADESH
DHAKA
CALCUTTA
GUANGZHOU
HONG KONG
Macau
TAIWAN
Kazan-Rettō (Japan)
Wake I. (U.S.A.)
Necker Ridge
P

INDIA
BURMA
Mandalay
LAOS
Hanoi
Hainan
South Honshu Ridge
Marcus Ridge
A

Bay of Bengal
Rangoon
THAILAND
VIETNAM
C. Engano
Luzon
NORTHERN MARIANAS (U.S.A.)
Saipan
MARSHALL IS.
Bikini Atoll

CHENNAI (Madras)
BANGKOK
CAMBODIA
Paracel Is.
MANILA
GUAM (U.S.A.) 11,022
Mariana Trench
Enewetak Atoll

SRI LANKA
Andaman Is. (India)
Phnom Penh
Phanh Bho Ho Chi Minh
Mindoro
PHILIPPINES
Samar
Yap
Caroline Is.
Micronesia
Jaluit I.
Dalap-Uliga-Darrit

Colombo
Nicobar Is. (India)
G. of Thailand
South China Sea
Palawan
10,497
Truk
Pohnpei
Palikir
FEDERATED STATES OF MICRONESIA
Butaritari

MALAYSIA
Sulu Sea
Mindanao
Mindanao Trench
Koror
PALAU
Tarawa
Gilbert Is.
Howland I. (U)
Baker I. (U)

Kuala Lumpur
PEN. MALAYSIA
BRUNEI
SABAH
Celebes Sea
4101
Maluku
Melanesia
NAURU
Banaba
Phoenix Is.
Abariringa
Enderbury

SINGAPORE
SARAWAK
Borneo
Sulawesi
Halmahera
Seram
PAPUA NEW GUINEA
NAURU
KI

Sumatera
INDONESIA
Buru
Puncak Jaya 5029
IRIAN JAYA
Admiralty Is.
Bismarck Arch.
New Ireland
SOLOMON IS.
Fongafale
TUVALU
Tokelau (N.Z.)

Palembang
Ujung Pandang
Banda Sea
New Guinea
Lae
Rabaul
Bougainville
Honiara
Guadalcanal
Rotuma
Is. Wallis & Futuna (Fr.)
WESTER SAMOA

JAKARTA
Surabaya
Jawa
Flores Sea
7440
Seram
New Britain
Port Moresby
Santa Cruz I. 9165
Espiritu Santo
Vanua Levu
Apia

Java Sea
Bali
Sumbawa
Sumba
Flores
Timor
Arafura Sea
Torres Strait
C. York
VANUATU
Is. Chesterfield
Port Vila
Viti Levu
FIJI
Suva
Nuku'alofa

INDIAN
Cocos Is. (Austral.)
Java Trench
Christmas I. (Austral.)
Sunda Islands
C. Arnhem
Darwin
Gulf of Carpentaria
Coral Sea
NEW CALEDONIA (Fr.)
Nouméa
7570
Is. Loyauté
TONGA

OCEAN
Broome
Cairns
Townsville
AUSTRALIA
Great Dividing Ra.
Rockhampton
Norfolk I. (Austral.)
10,822
Tonga Trench

North West C.
Mount Isa
Alice Springs
Brisbane
Darling
Kermadec Is. (N.Z.)

Geraldton
L. Eyre
Murray
Lord Howe I. (Austral.)
Kermadec Trench 10,047

Perth
Great Australian Bight
Albany
Adelaide
Canberra
Sydney
Mt. Kosciuszko 2237
Tasman Sea
NEW ZEALAND
Auckland

Melbourne
Bass Str.
Tasmania
Hobart
Mt. Cook 3753
Cook Strait
Wellington
Christchurch
Chatham (N.Z.)

Nouvelle Amsterdam (Fr.)
I. St. Paul (Fr.)
Mid-Indian Ridge
Dunedin
Bounty Is. (N.Z.)

Is. Crozet (Fr.)
Kerguelen (Fr.)
Invercargill
Antipodes Is. (N.Z.)

Auckland Is. (N.Z.)
Campbell I. (N.Z.)
Macquarie Is. (Austral.)

Heard I. (Austral.)

Projection: Mollweide's Homolographic
East from Greenwich

ft m
12 000 4000
9000 3000
6000 2000
3000 1000
1500 500
600 200
0 0
200 600
1000 3000
2000 6000
4000 12 000
6000 18 000
8000 24 000
m ft

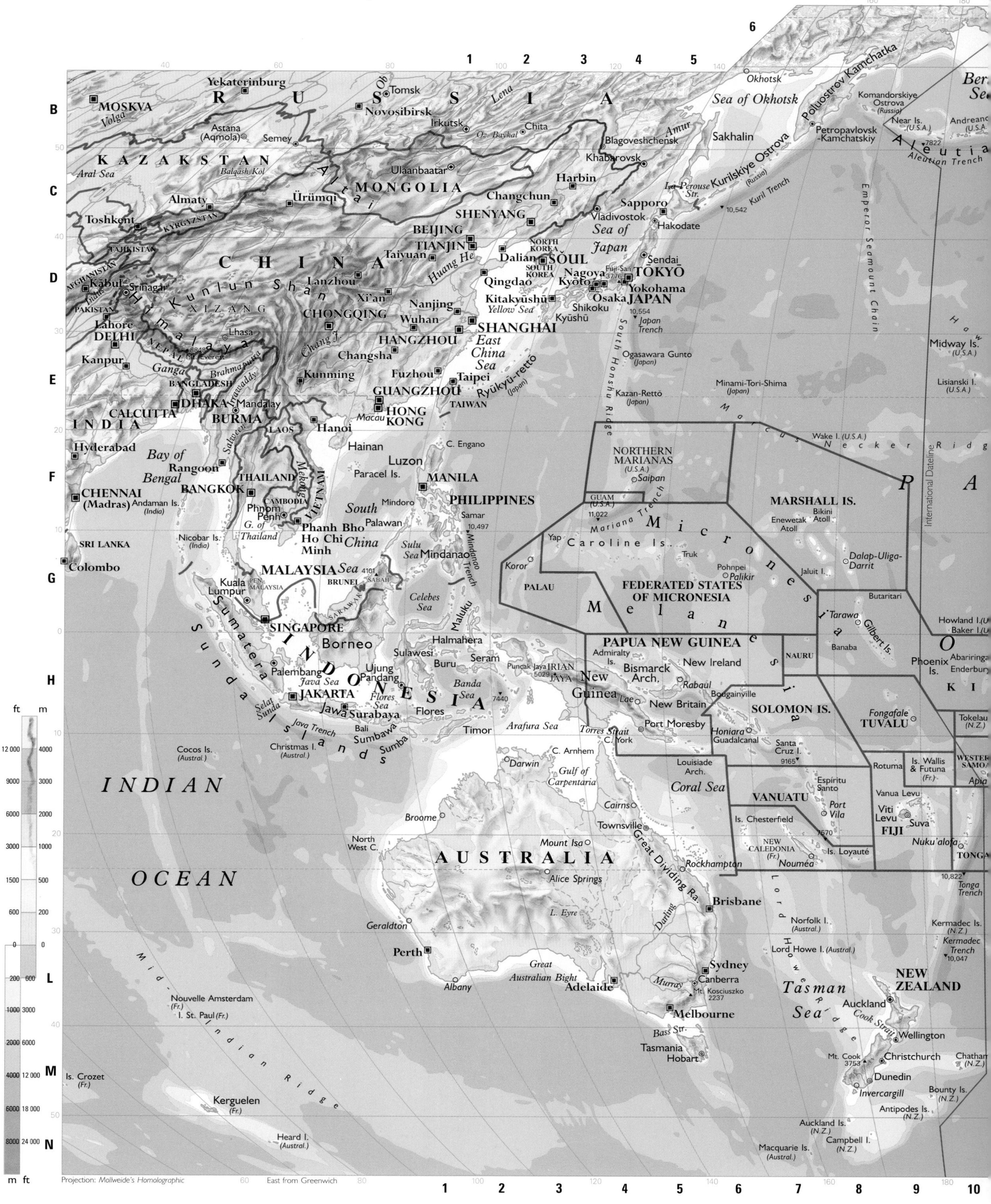

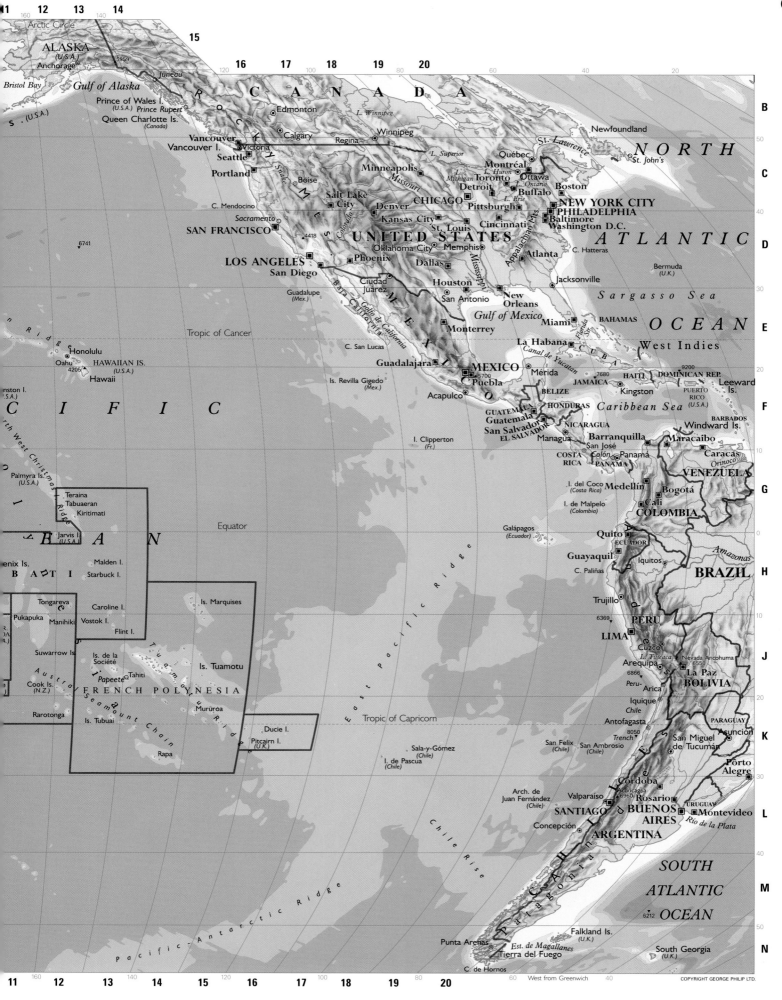

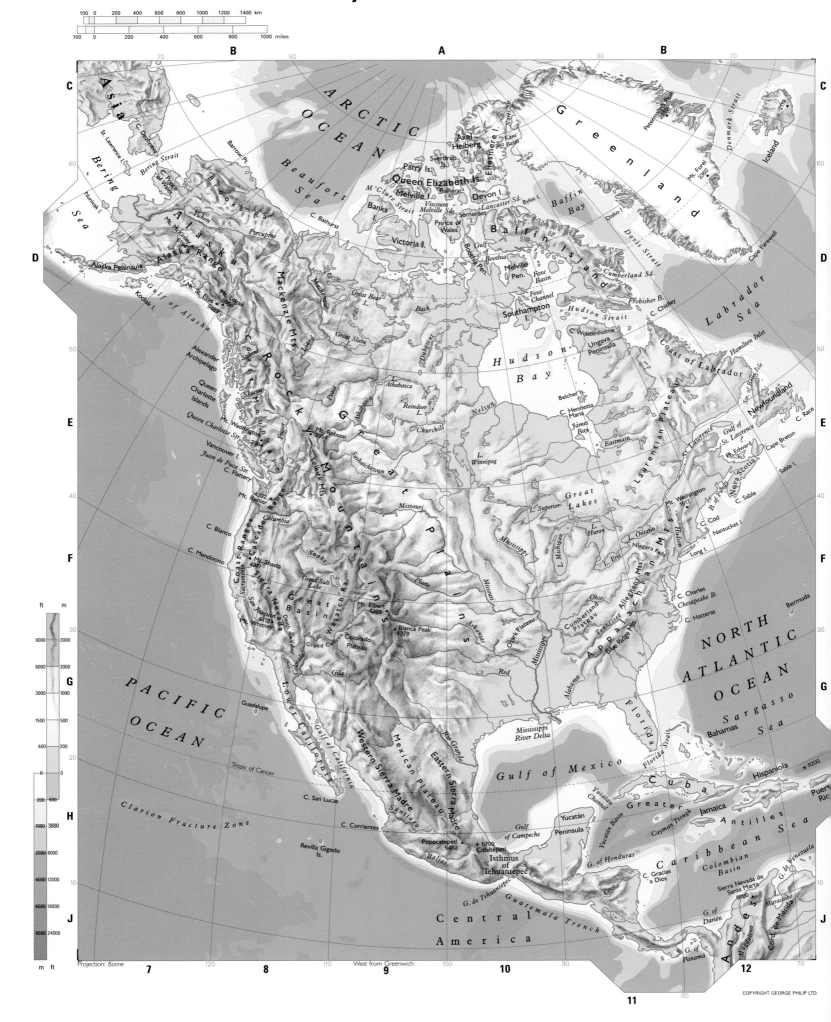

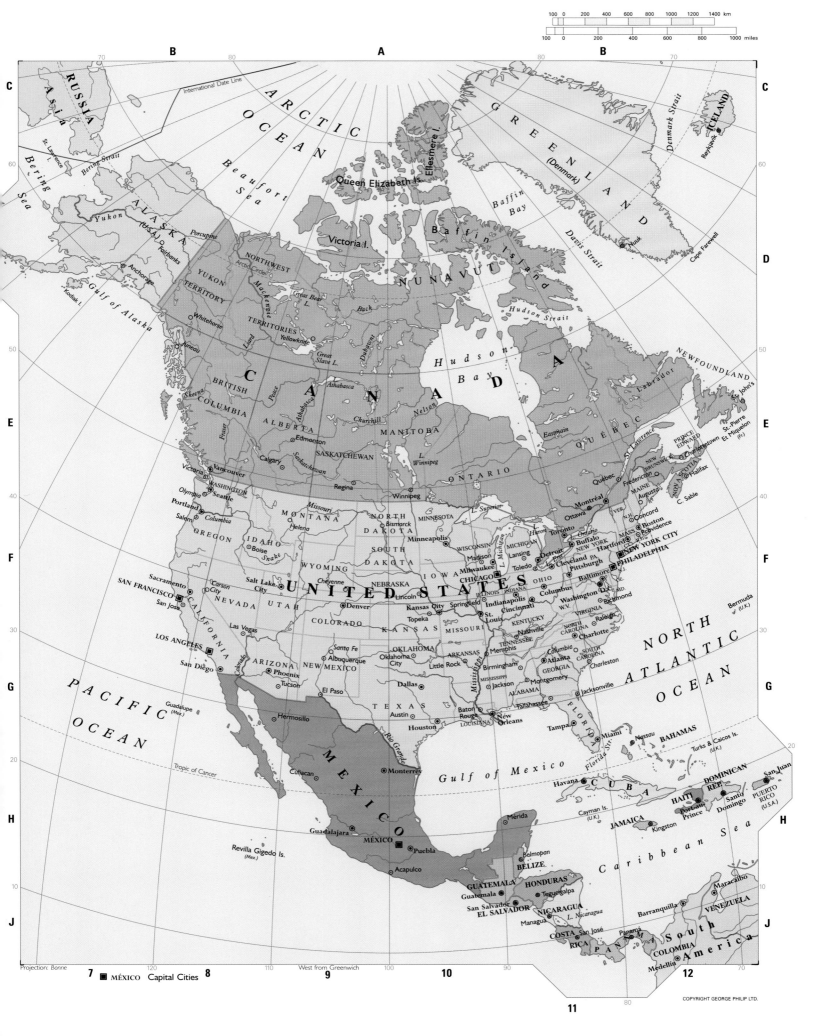

100 0 200 400 600 800 1000 1200 1400 km
100 0 200 400 600 800 1000 miles

C **RUSSIA** *Asia*

ARCTIC
OCEAN

St. Lawrence

Bering Strait

Bering
Sea

*Beaufort
Sea*

Queen Elizabeth Is.

Ellesmere I.

GREENLAND
(Denmark)

Denmark Strait

ICELAND

Reykjavik

60

*Baffin
Bay*

C

Yukon

ALASKA
(U.S.A.)

Porcupine

Fairbanks

Baffin Island

Davis Strait

Nuuk

Cape Farewell

D

Anchorage

NORTHWEST

Arctic Circle

YUKON
TERRITORY

Mackenzie

*Great Bear
L.*

Bach

NUNAVUT

Hudson Strait

Kodiak I.

Gulf of Alaska

Whitehorse

Juneau

TERRITORIES

Yellowknife

Liard

*Great
Slave L.*

Dubawnt

*Hudson
Bay*

NEWFOUNDLAND

50

Skeena

Fraser

BRITISH
COLUMBIA

C A N A D A

Peace

Athabasca

L.
Athabasca

Churchill

Nelson

Labrador

Eastmain

50

E

Victoria

Vancouver

ALBERTA

Edmonton

Calgary

SASKATCHEWAN

Saskatchewan

Regina

MANITOBA

L.
Winnipeg

ONTARIO

QUÉBEC

St. Lawrence

**PRINCE
EDWARD
I.**

St-Pierre
Et Miquelon
(Fr.)

St. John's

E

40

Olympia

Seattle

WASHINGTON

Portland

Salem

Columbia

OREGON

MONTANA

Helena

Missouri

Winnipeg

**NORTH
DAKOTA**

Bismarck

MINNESOTA

L. Superior

Quebec

Ottawa

Montréal

MAINE
Augusta

Fredericton

**NEW
BRUNSWICK**

**NOVA
SCOTIA**

Halifax

Charlottetown

C. Sable

40

F

Sacramento

San Francisco

San Jose

CALIFORNIA

IDAHO

Boise

Snake

WYOMING

**SOUTH
DAKOTA**

NEBRASKA

Minneapolis

IOWA

WISCONSIN

Madison

Milwaukee

MICHIGAN

Lansing

CHICAGO

ILLINOIS

INDIANA

Indianapolis

L. Michigan

L. Huron

Detroit

Toledo

Cleveland

OHIO

PA.

Pittsburgh

Columbus

Toronto

L. Ontario

L. Erie

Buffalo

**NEW
YORK**

Hartford

MASS.

Boston

Providence

Concord

N.H.

VER.

Albany

NEW YORK CITY

PHILADELPHIA

F

30

Carson
City

Salt Lake
City

Cheyenne

Denver

COLORADO

NEVADA

UTAH

Las Vegas

Lincoln

Kansas City

Topeka

KANSAS

MISSOURI

Springfield

St.
Louis

Cincinnati

KENTUCKY

Nashville

TENNESSEE

Memphis

W.VA.

VIRGINIA

Richmond

Washington D.C.

Baltimore

MD.

Raleigh

**NORTH
CAROLINA**

Charlotte

Bermuda
(U.K.)

30

Los Angeles

San Diego

Colorado

ARIZONA

Phoenix

Tucson

Santa Fe

Albuquerque

NEW MEXICO

OKLAHOMA

Oklahoma
City

ARKANSAS

Little Rock

Mississippi

Birmingham

MISSISSIPPI

ALABAMA

Montgomery

GEORGIA

Atlanta

Columbia

**SOUTH
CAROLINA**

Charleston

**NORTH
ATLANTIC**

G

PACIFIC

Guadalupe
(Mex.)

El Paso

Dallas

TEXAS

Austin

Houston

LOUISIANA

Baton
Rouge

New
Orleans

Jackson

Jacksonville

Tallahassee

FLORIDA

Tampa

OCEAN

G

Tropic of Cancer

OCEAN

Hermosillo

Rio Grande

Monterrey

Gulf of Mexico

Florida Str.

Miami

Nassau

BAHAMAS

Turks & Caicos Is.
(U.K.)

20

Culiacan

M E X I C O

Havana

CUBA

HAITI

**DOMINICAN
REP.**

San Juan

**PUERTO
RICO**
(U.S.A.)

20

H

Revilla Gigedo Is.
(Mex.)

Guadalajara

MÉXICO

Puebla

Acapulco

Mérida

Cayman Is.
(U.K.)

JAMAICA

Kingston

Port-au-
Prince

Santo
Domingo

Caribbean Sea

H

Belmopan

BELIZE

GUATEMALA

Guatemala

HONDURAS

Tegucigalpa

Maracaibo

VENEZUELA

10

San Salvador

EL SALVADOR

NICARAGUA

Managua

L. Nicaragua

Barranquilla

10

J

**COSTA
RICA**

San José

PANAMA

Panama

COLOMBIA

Medellin

*South
America*

J

Projection: *Bonne*

West from Greenwich

COPYRIGHT GEORGE PHILIP LTD.

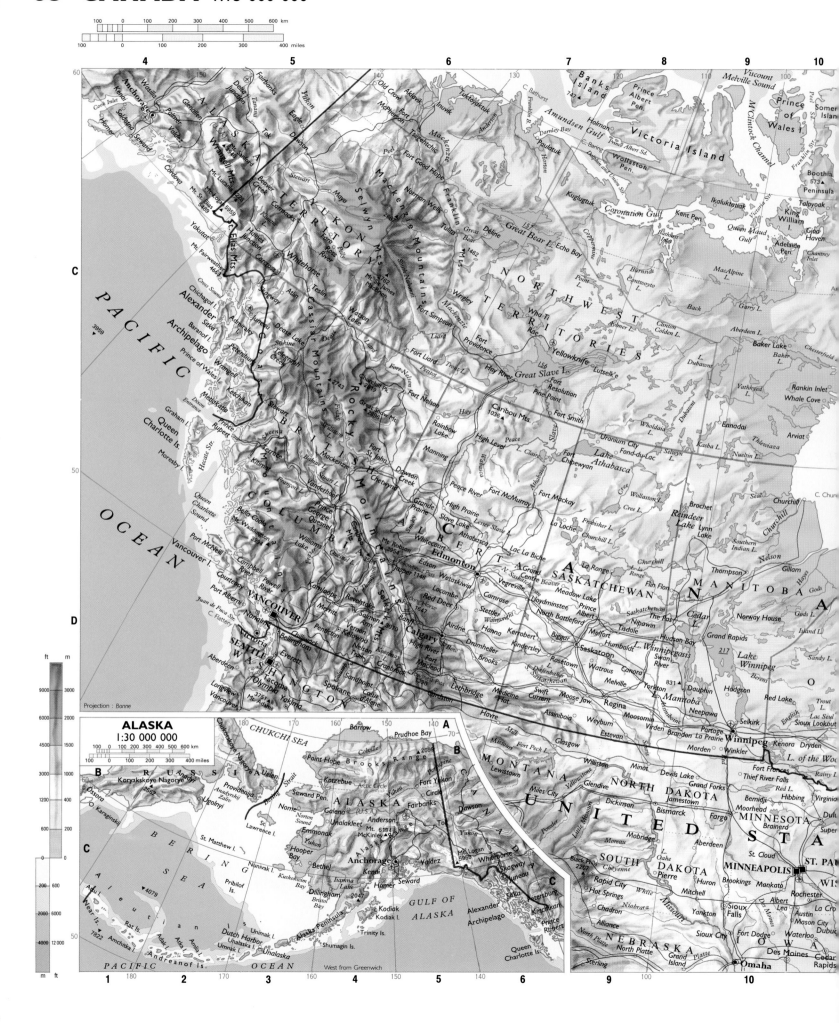

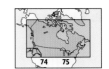

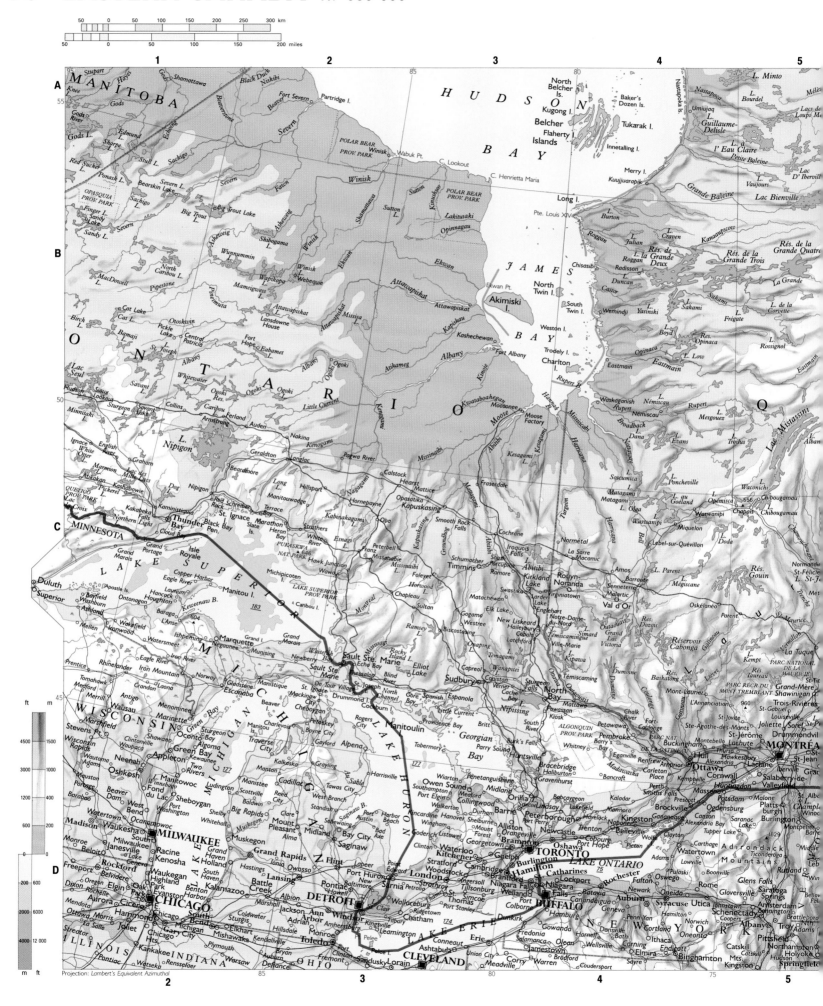

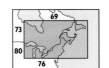

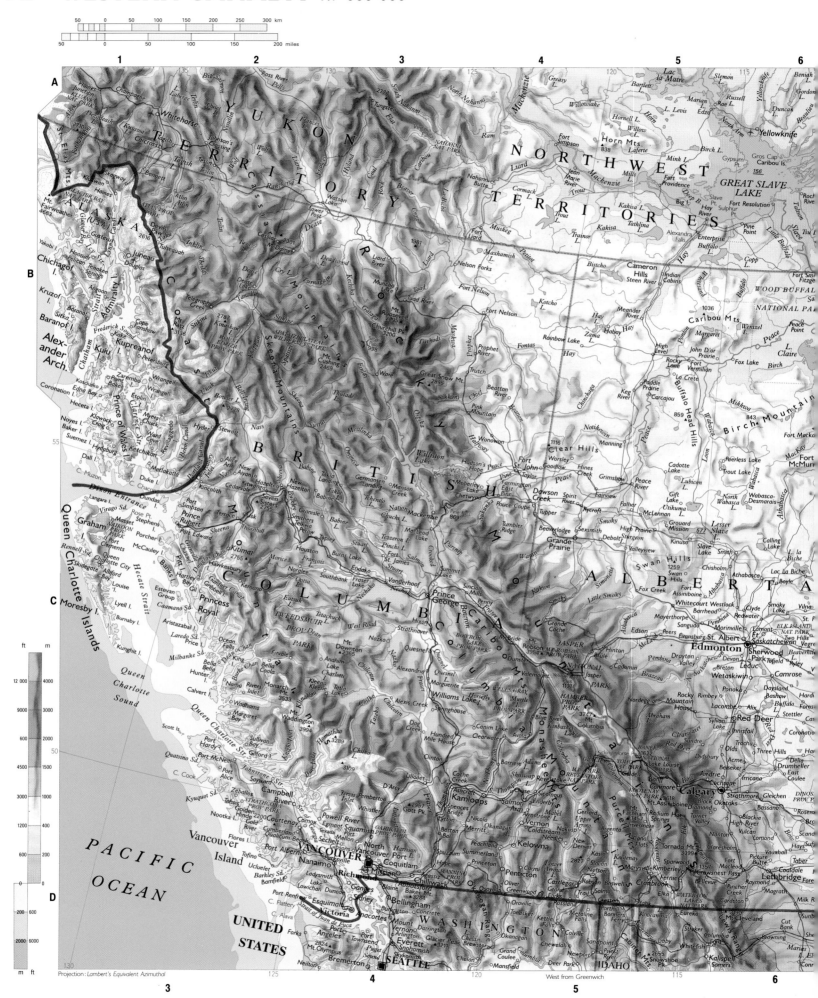

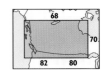

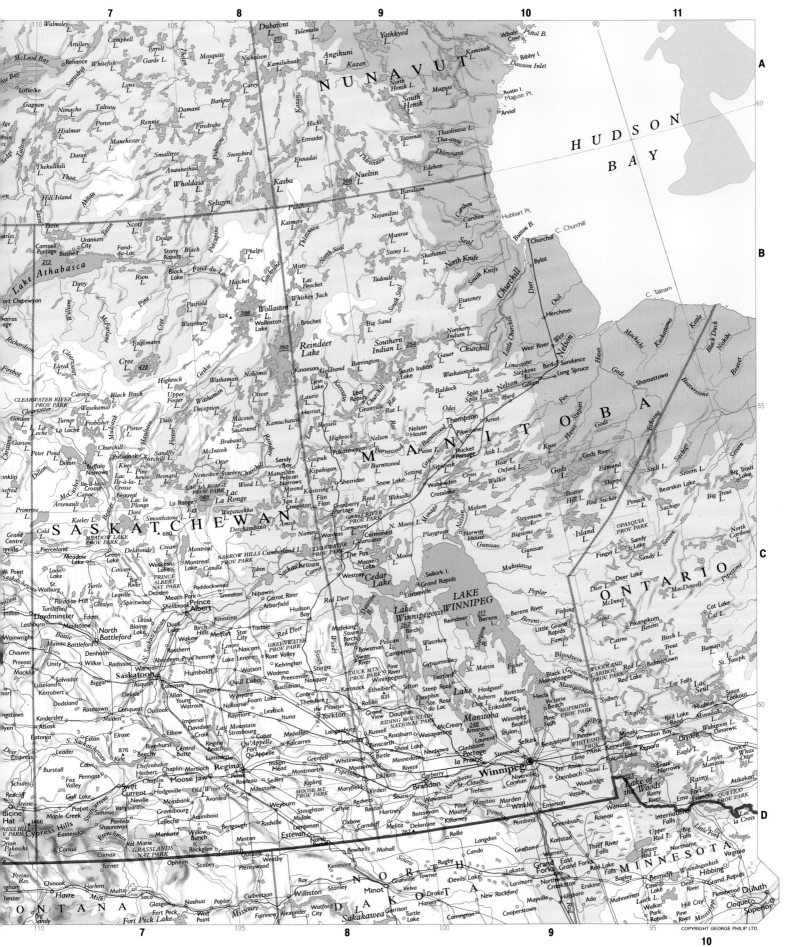

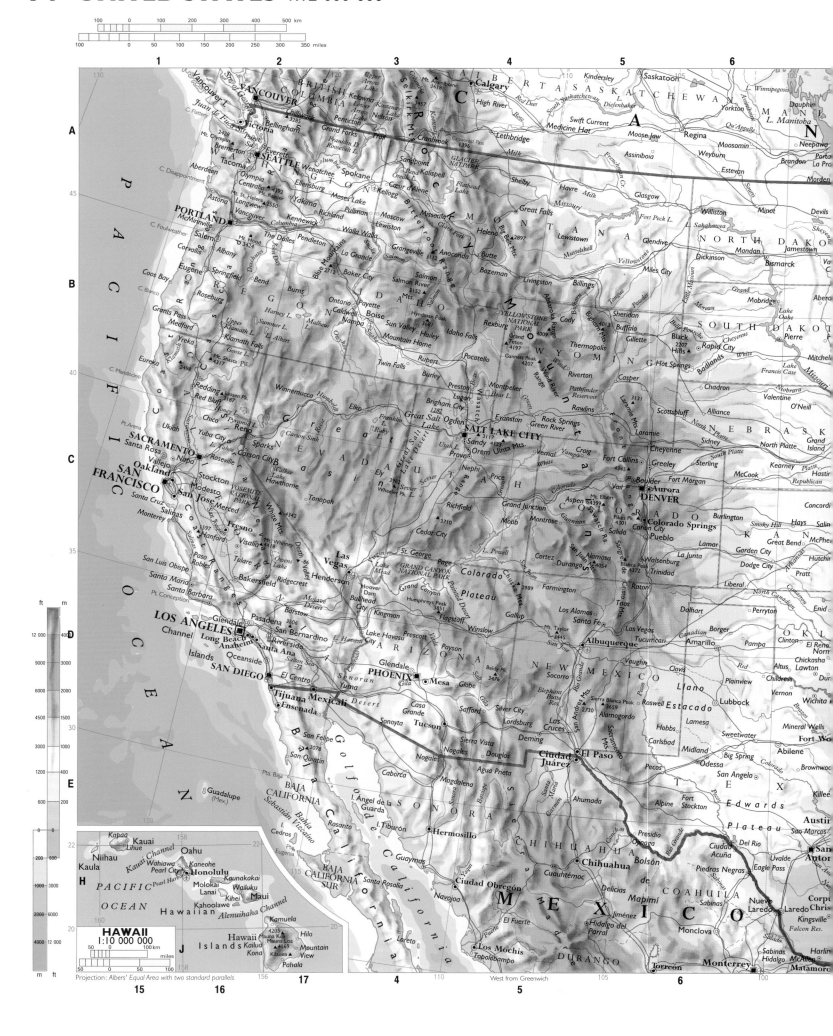

Projection: Albers' Equal Area with two standard parallels

West from Greenwich

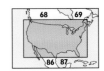

COPYRIGHT GEORGE PHILIP LTD.

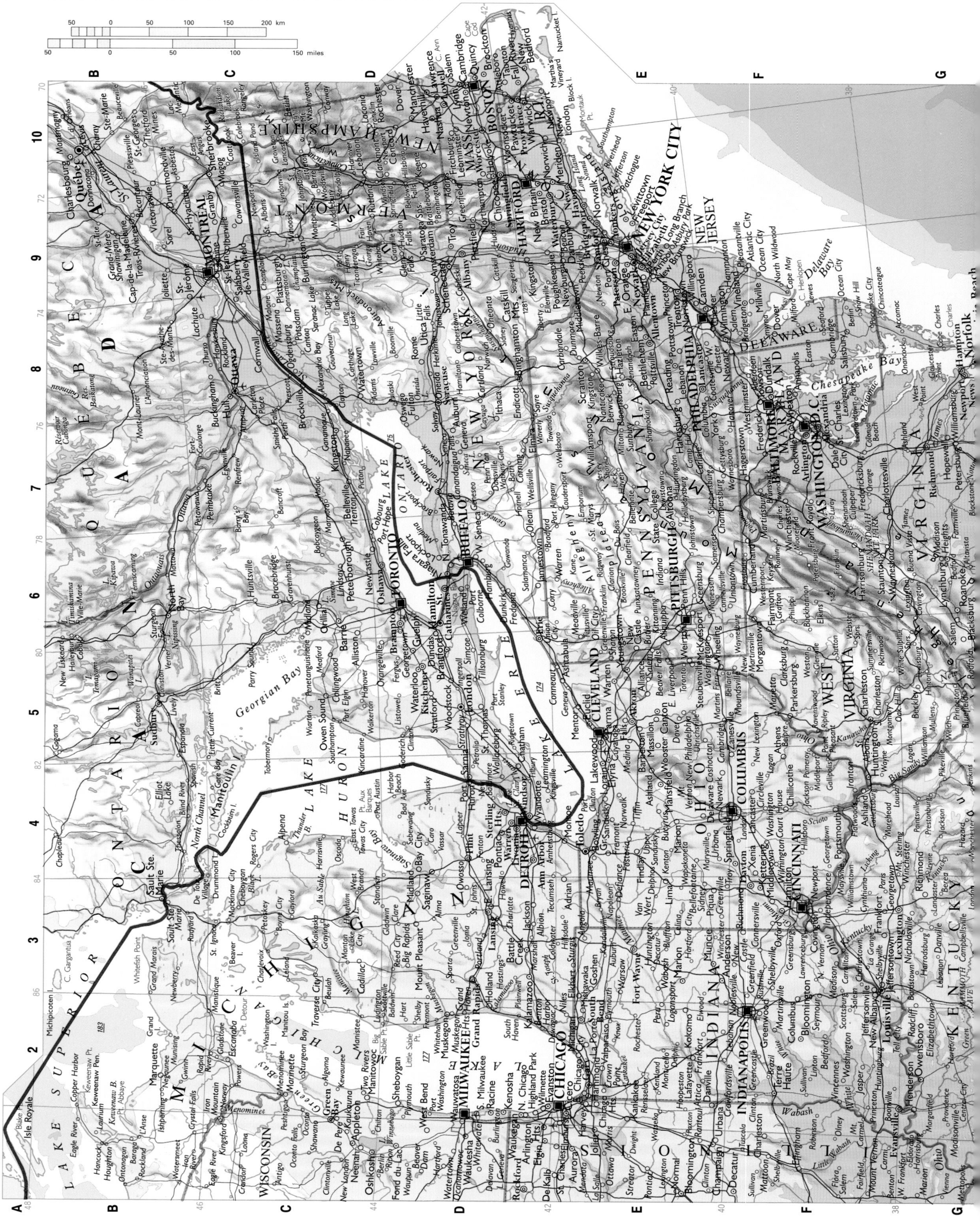

50 0 50 100 150 200 km
50 0 50 100 150 miles

LAKE SUPERIOR

QUEBEC

ONTARIO

NEW HAMPSHIRE

VERMONT

MICHIGAN

WISCONSIN

NEW YORK

MASS.

R.I.

CONN.

NEW JERSEY

PENNSYLVANIA

DELAWARE

MARYLAND

WEST VIRGINIA

VIRGINIA

OHIO

INDIANA

KENTUCKY

ILLINOIS

Georgian Bay

LAKE HURON

LAKE ERIE

LAKE ONTARIO

LAKE MICHIGAN

Chesapeake Bay

Delaware Bay

Montréal, Québec, Ottawa, Toronto, Hamilton, Buffalo, Detroit, Cleveland, Pittsburgh, Chicago, Milwaukee, Indianapolis, Cincinnati, Columbus, Boston, Hartford, New York City, Philadelphia, Baltimore, Washington D.C.

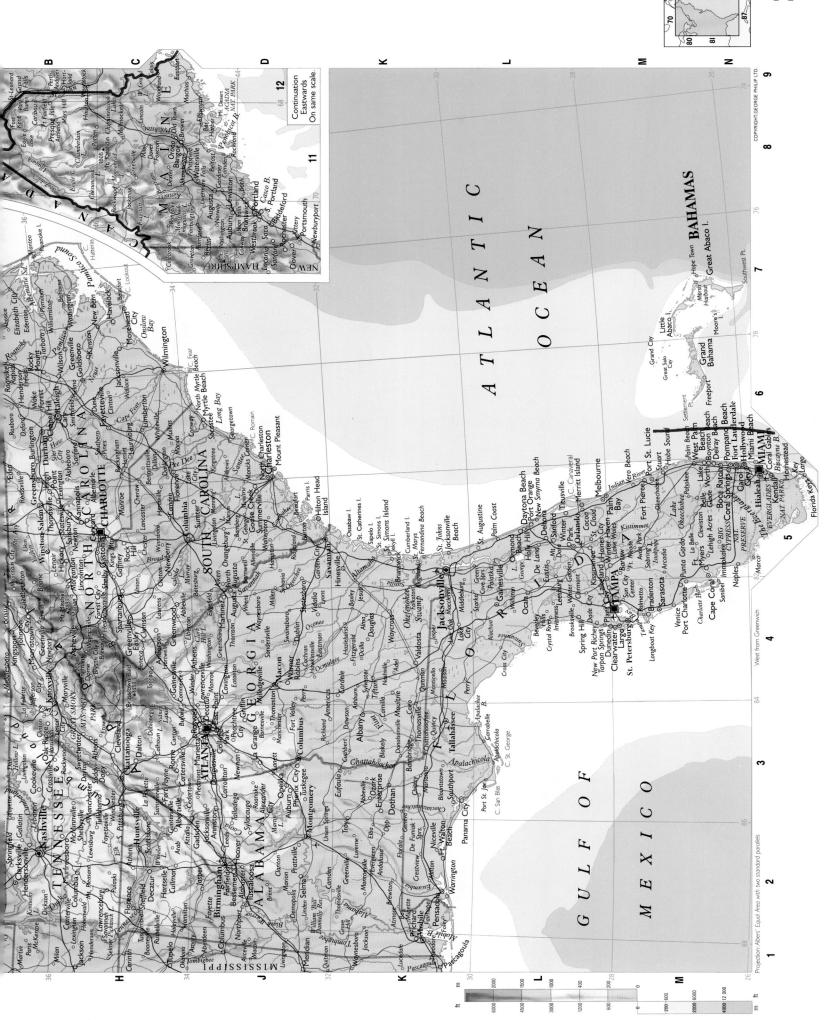

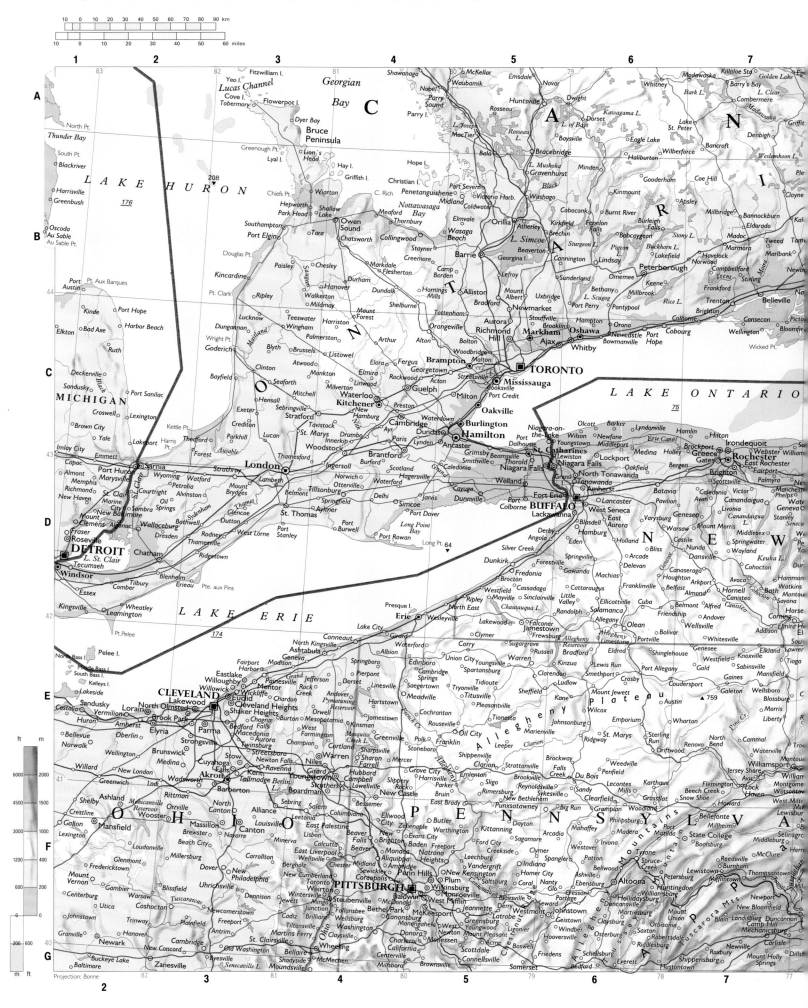

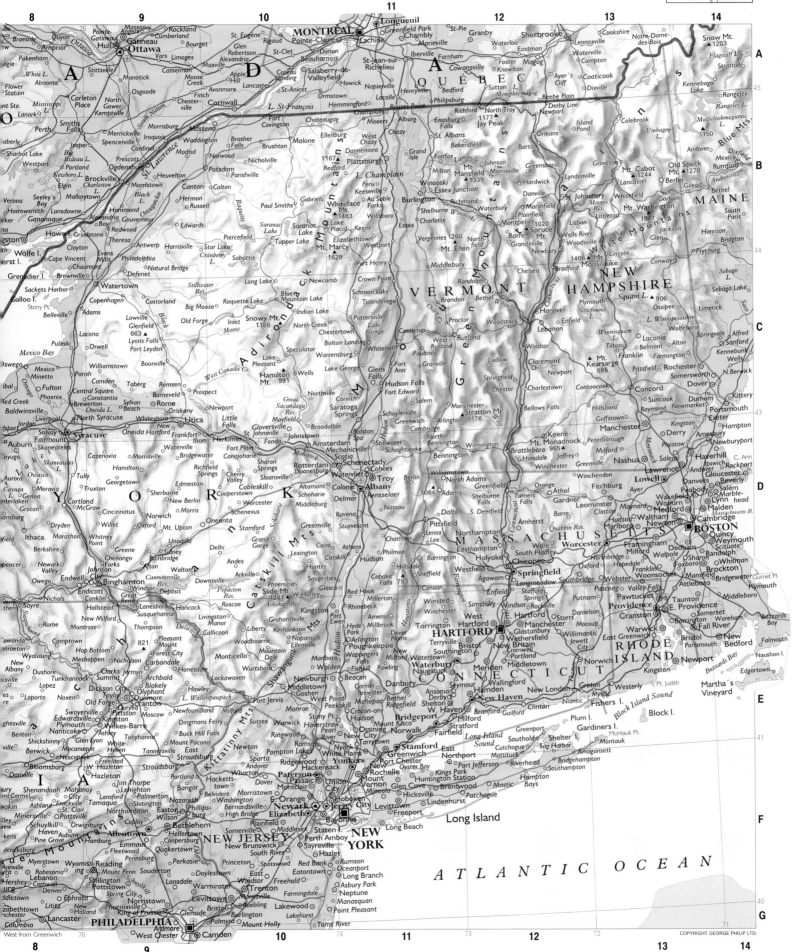

COPYRIGHT GEORGE PHILIP LTD.

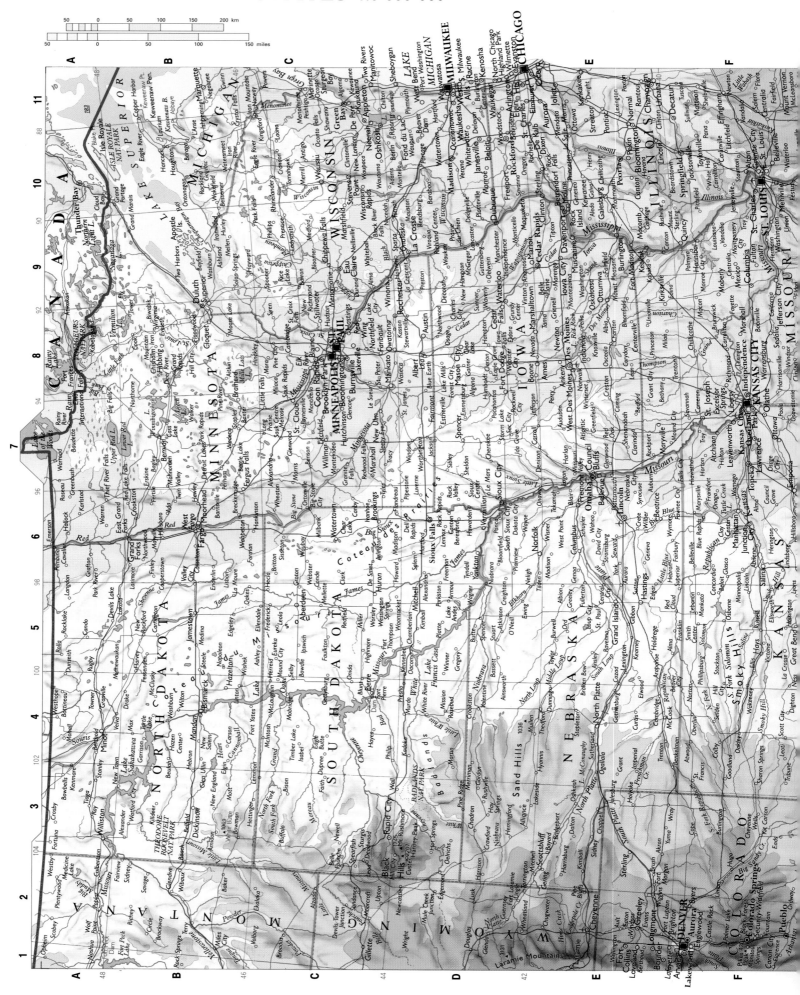

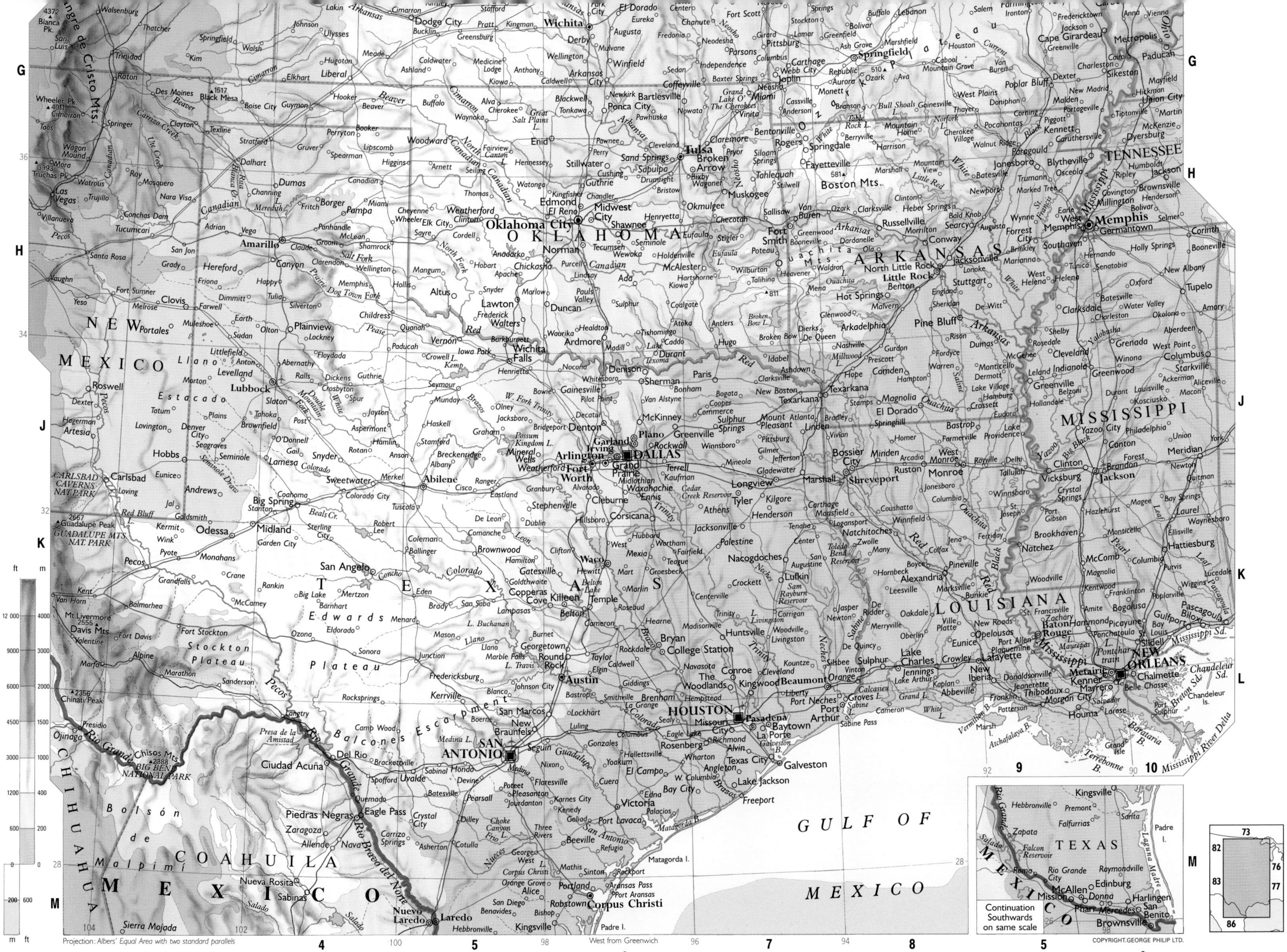

TENNESSEE

MISSISSIPPI

ARKANSAS

LOUISIANA

OKLAHOMA

TEXAS

NEW MEXICO

COAHUILA

CHIHUAHUA

MEXICO

GULF OF MEXICO

Laguna Madre

Rio Grande

Rio Bravo del Norte

Edwards Plateau

Stockton Plateau

Llano Estacado

Balcones Escarpment

Sangre de Cristo Mts.

Boston Mts.

Ouachita Mts.

Guadalupe Mts.

Davis Mts.

Chisos Mts.

BIG BEND NATIONAL PARK

CARLSBAD CAVERNS NAT. PARK

GUADALUPE MTS. NAT. PARK

Mississippi River Delta

Continuation Southwards on same scale

Projection: Albers' Equal Area with two standard parallels

COPYRIGHT.GEORGE PHILIP LTD.

West from Greenwich

DALLAS Fort Worth Arlington Grand Prairie Garland Irving Plano

HOUSTON Pasadena Baytown Galveston

SAN ANTONIO Austin San Marcos New Braunfels Seguin

Corpus Christi

NEW ORLEANS Metairie Kenner Chalmette

Memphis West Memphis Germantown

Tulsa Broken Arrow Oklahoma City Norman Edmond Midwest City Shawnee

Wichita

Little Rock North Little Rock

Shreveport Bossier City

Baton Rouge

Jackson

Amarillo Lubbock Odessa Midland El Paso

Laredo Nuevo Laredo

Eagle Pass Piedras Negras

Del Rio Ciudad Acuña

Brownsville Matamoros Harlingen McAllen Edinburg

ft m 12 000 9000 6000 4500 3000 1500 600 200 0

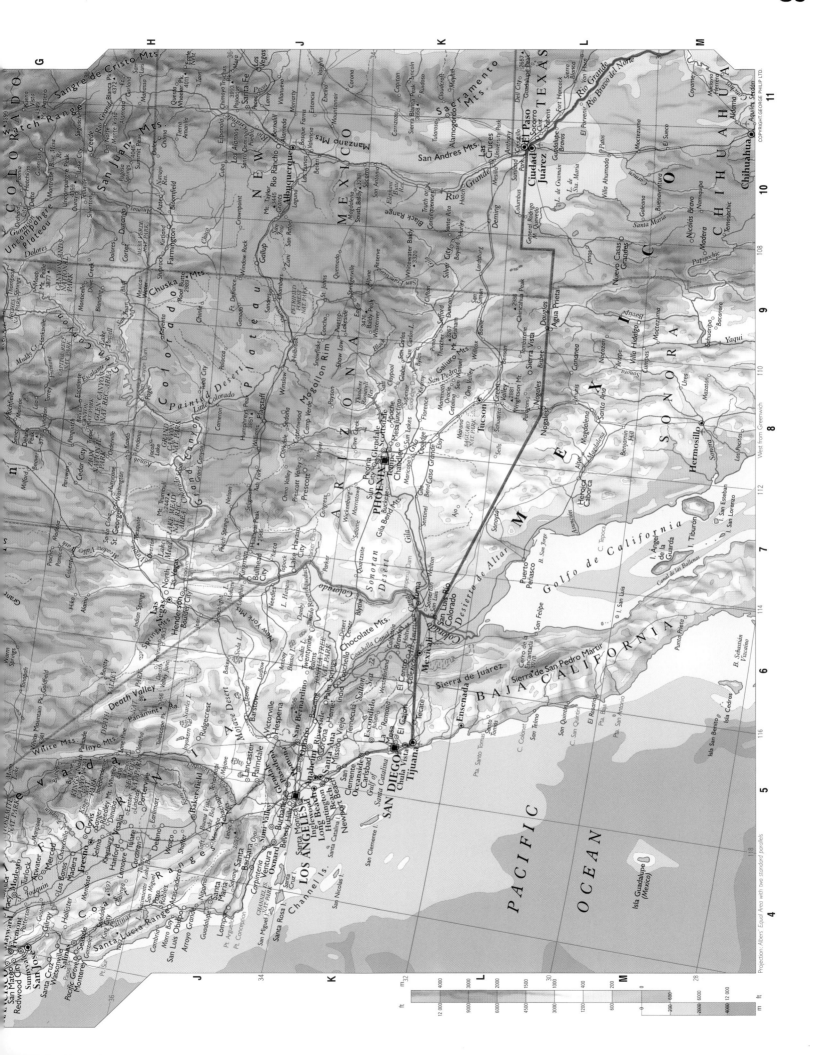

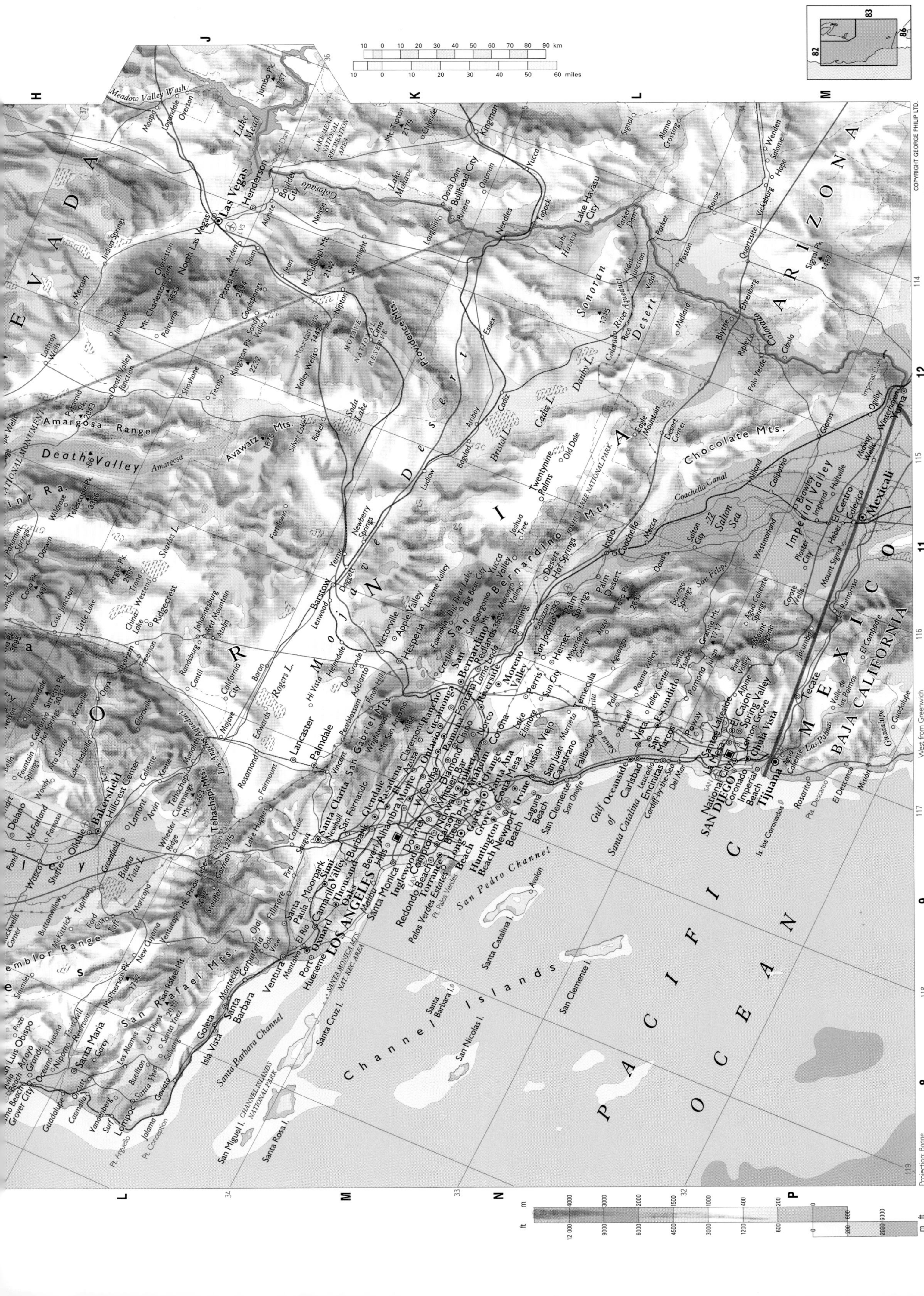

COPYRIGHT GEORGE PHILIP LTD.

Scale
10 0 10 20 30 40 50 60 70 80 90 km
10 0 10 20 30 40 50 60 miles

13

14

12

11

10

9

8

West from Greenwich

114 115 116 117 118 119

34 33 32

H J K L M

N E V A D A

A R I Z O N A

M O J A V E   D E S E R T

S O N O R A N   D E S E R T

C A L I F O R N I A

B A J A   C A L I F O R N I A

M E X I C O

P A C I F I C   O C E A N

Channel Islands

Places and features:
Meadow Valley Wash
Lake Mead
LAKE MEAD NATIONAL RECREATION AREA
Las Vegas
North Las Vegas
Henderson
Boulder City
Overton
Moapa
Nelson
Searchlight
Mt. Charleston 3633
Pahrump
Indian Springs
Goodsprings
Jean
Nipton
McCullough Mt. 2132
Potosi Mt. 2594
Mountain Pass 1443
Amargosa Range
Death Valley
DEATH VALLEY NATIONAL MONUMENT
Telescope Pk. 3366
Furnace Creek
Shoshone
Tecopa
Baker
Soda Lake
Silver L.
Avawatz Mts. 1816
Cadiz L.
Bristol L.
Danby L.
Providence Mts.
Essex
Amboy
Cadiz
Bagdad
Ludlow
Newberry Springs
Daggett
Barstow
Yermo
Fort Irwin
Soda Lake
Mt. Tipton 2179
Chloride
Kingman
Yucca
Hackberry
Davis Dam
Bullhead City
Riviera
Oatman
Topock
Needles
Lake Havasu City
Lake Havasu
Parker Dam
Parker
Poston
Bouse
Quartzsite
Vicksburg
Salome
Hope
Aguila
Signal Pk. 1482
Ehrenberg
Blythe
Ripley
Cibola
Palo Verde
Midland
Desert Center
Chocolate Mts.
Coachella Canal
Eagle Mountain
Chuckwalla Mts.
JOSHUA TREE NATIONAL PARK
Twentynine Palms
Joshua Tree
Yucca Valley
Morongo Valley
Desert Hot Springs
Palm Springs
Palm Desert
Indio
Coachella
Mecca
Salton Sea
Salton City
Brawley
Westmorland
Calipatria
Niland
El Centro
Imperial
Heber
Calexico
Mexicali
Holtville
Yuma
Winterhaven
Ogilby
Midway Wells
Coyote Wells
Ocotillo
Plaster City
Borrego Springs
ANZA-BORREGO DESERT STATE PARK
San Felipe
Warner Springs
Julian
Ramona
Escondido
San Marcos
Vista
Fallbrook
Temecula
Murrieta
Hemet
San Jacinto 3293
Banning
Beaumont
San Bernardino
Redlands
Loma Linda
Moreno Valley
Riverside
Perris
Sun City
Lake Elsinore
Corona
Ontario
Cucamonga
Rancho
Claremont
Pomona
Fontana
Rialto
Colton
Crestline
Big Bear Lake
Big Bear City
San Gorgonio Mt. 3505
Victorville
Hesperia
Apple Valley
Lucerne Valley
Adelanto
Hodge
Helendale
Oro Grande
Phelan
Wrightwood
San Gabriel Mts.
Mt. San Antonio
Hi Vista
California City
Rogers L.
Boron
Mojave
Rosamond
Edwards
Lancaster
Palmdale
Vincent
Lake Hughes
Gorman
Frazier Park
Castaic
Santa Clarita
Newhall
San Fernando
Burbank
Glendale
Pasadena
Alhambra
Monterey Park
Whittier
Downey
Norwalk
Bellflower
Compton
Inglewood
LOS ANGELES
Santa Monica
Beverly Hills
Culver City
Torrance
Redondo Beach
Palos Verdes
Pt. Palos Verdes
Long Beach
San Pedro
Huntington Beach
Newport Beach
Costa Mesa
Santa Ana
Garden Grove
Anaheim
Fullerton
Orange
Tustin
Irvine
Laguna Beach
San Juan Capistrano
San Clemente
San Onofre
Oceanside
Carlsbad
Encinitas
Leucadia
Cardiff-by-the-Sea
Del Mar
La Jolla
SAN DIEGO
National City
Coronado
Chula Vista
Imperial Beach
Tijuana
Rosarito
Tecate
El Cajon
La Mesa
Lemon Grove
Spring Valley
Santee
Lakeside
Poway
Alpine
Valley Center
Pauma Valley
Pala
Gulf of Santa Catalina
Santa Catalina I.
Avalon
San Clemente I.
San Nicolas I.
San Pedro Channel
Ventura
Oxnard
Port Hueneme
Point Mugu
Camarillo
Thousand Oaks
Moorpark
Simi Valley
Fillmore
Santa Paula
Ojai
Santa Barbara
Goleta
Isla Vista
Carpinteria
Montecito
Santa Barbara Channel
San Miguel I.
Santa Rosa I.
Santa Cruz I.
Santa Barbara I.
CHANNEL ISLANDS NATIONAL PARK
Pt. Conception
Pt. Arguello
Lompoc
Vandenberg
Surf
Guadalupe
Santa Maria
Santa Ynez
Solvang
Buellton
Los Alamos
Los Olivos
San Luis Obispo
Arroyo Grande
Grover City
Oceano
Nipomo
Bakersfield
Delano
McFarland
Wasco
Shafter
Oildale
Lamont
Arvin
Taft
Maricopa
Tehachapi 1215
Tehachapi Mts.
Tejon Pass
Mt. Pinos 2693
San Emigdio Mts.
San Rafael Mts.
Sierra Madre
Frazier Mt. 2493
Temblor Range

Projection: Bonne

Elevation scale (m / ft):
m 4000 3000 2000 1500 1000 400 200 0
ft 12 000 9000 6000 4500 3000 1500 600 0
m 200 600 2000 6000 ft

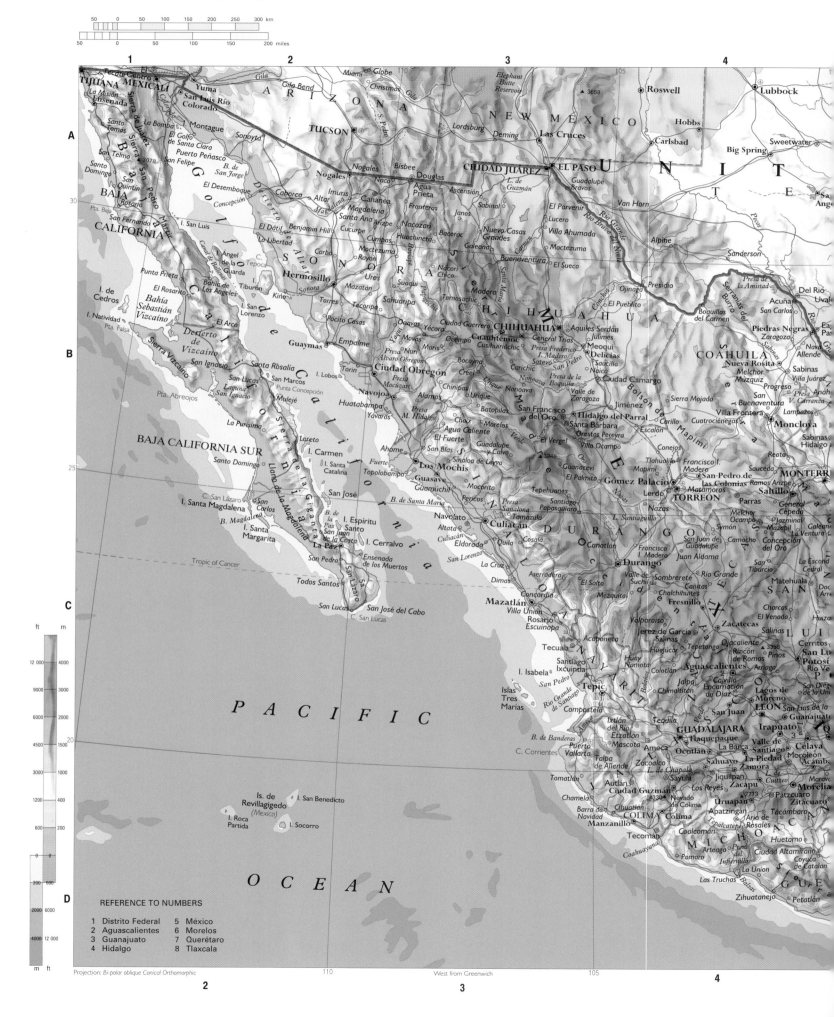

REFERENCE TO NUMBERS

1 Distrito Federal
2 Aguascalientes
3 Guanajuato
4 Hidalgo
5 México
6 Morelos
7 Querétaro
8 Tlaxcala

Projection: Bi-polar oblique Conical Orthomorphic

West from Greenwich

Wichita
Falls
Denison
Sherman
Paris
Camden
Greenville
ARKANSAS
Tuscaloosa
Opelika
McRae
Denton
Greenville
Texarkana
El Dorado
MISSISSIPPI
Columbus
Cordele
FORT WORTH
DALLAS
Longview
Marshall
Monroe
Tallulah
Vicksburg
Meridian
Selma
ALABAMA
Phenix City
Montgomery
Americus
Tifton
GEORGIA
Abilene
Ranger
Cleburne
Tyler
Corsicana
Shreveport
Jackson
Laurel
Troy
Albany
Waycross
Brownwood
Waco
Palestine
Nacogdoches
Natchez
Hattiesburg
Flomaton
Dothan
Valdosta
Hillsboro
Lufkin
Alexandria
McComb
Tallahassee
Lake
City
Temple
Huntsville
Bryan
Baton
Rouge
Bogalusa
Biloxi
MOBILE
Pensacola
Panama City
FLORIDA
Austin
HOUSTON
Beaumont
Lafayette
NEW
ORLEANS
Gulfport
Apalachee
Bay

SAN
ANTONIO
Port
Arthur
Galveston
Clearwater

GULF   OF

Corpus Christi

Laredo
Kingsville
MEXICO
Nuevo Laredo
Zapata
Reynosa
Matamoros
Tropic of Cancer
CUBA

Golfo
de
Campeche

Mérida   YUCATÁN
Cancún

Campeche
QUINTANA
ROO

Ciudad del
Carmen
CAMPECHE
BELIZE
BÉLIZE

MÉXICO
PUEBLA
Veracruz
TABASCO
Villahermosa
GUATEMALA

OAXACA
CHIAPAS
HONDURAS

Golfo de   GUATEMALA
Tehuantepec

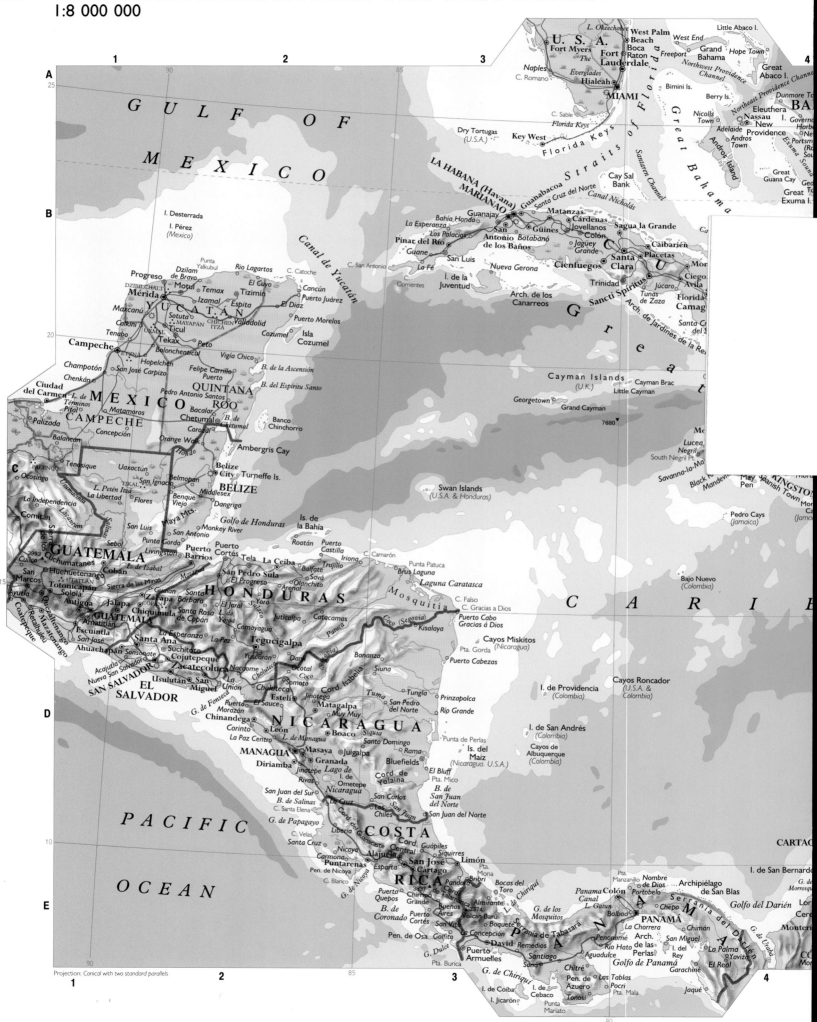

Projection: Conical with two standard parallels

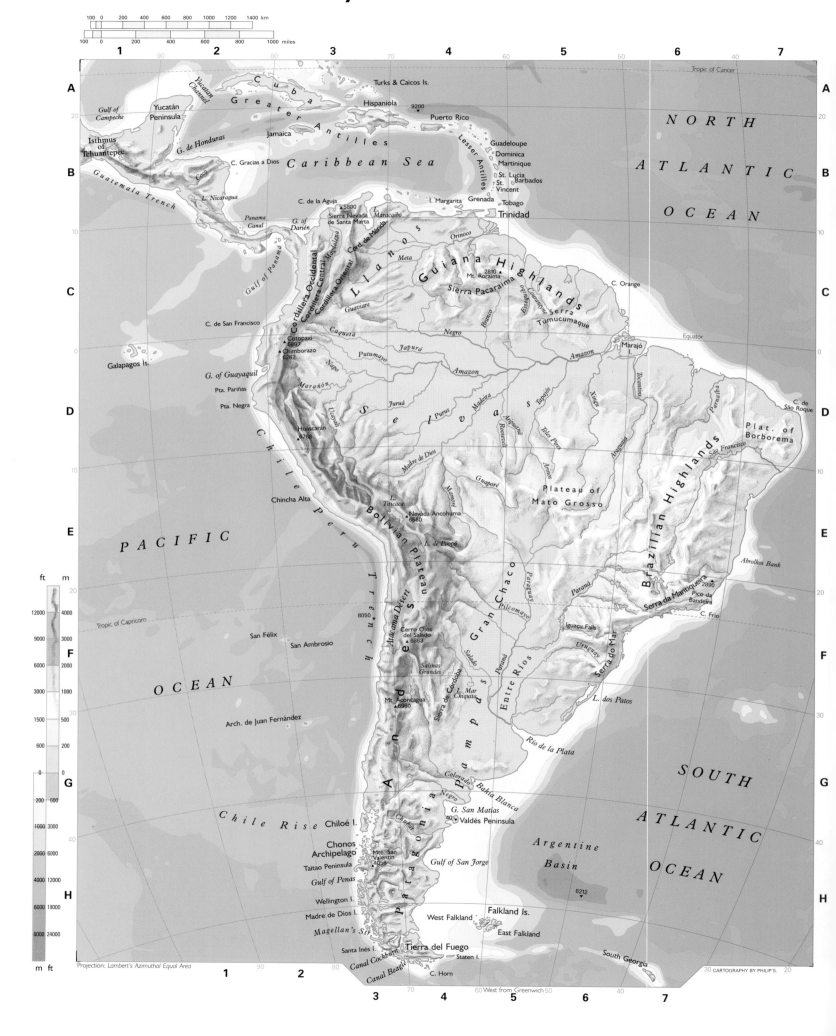

Projection: Lambert's Azimuthal Equal Area

CARTOGRAPHY BY PHILIP'S

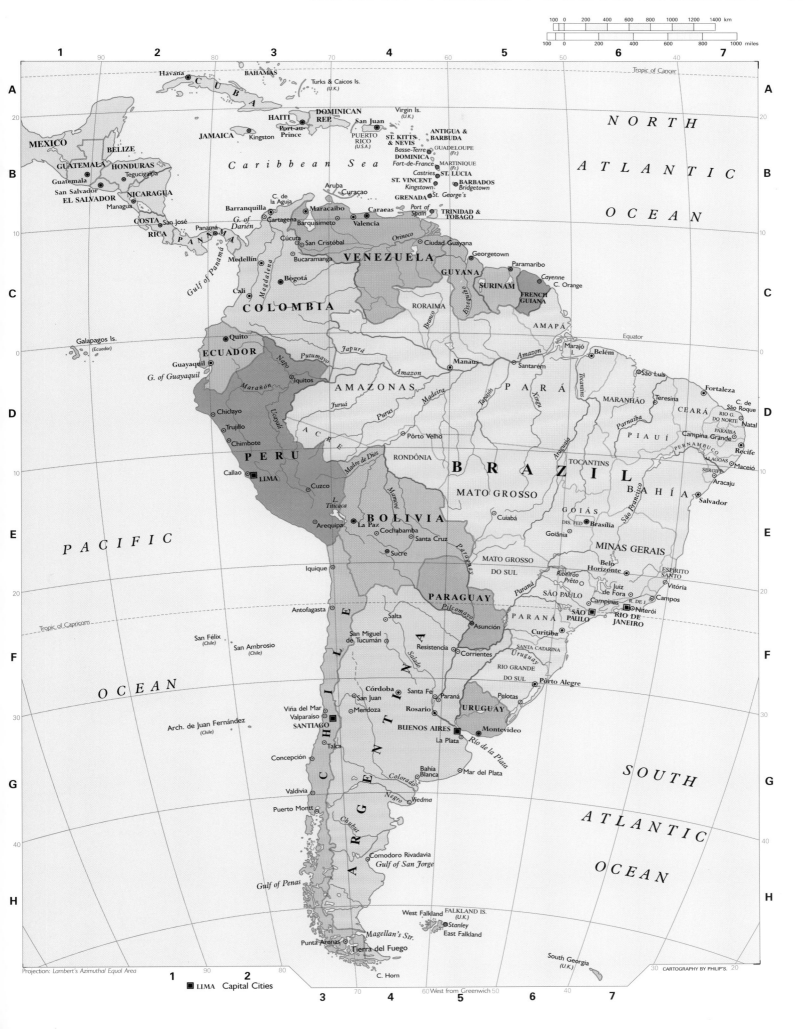

Projection: Lambert's Azimuthal Equal Area

1

◼ LIMA Capital Cities

CARTOGRAPHY BY PHILIP'S.

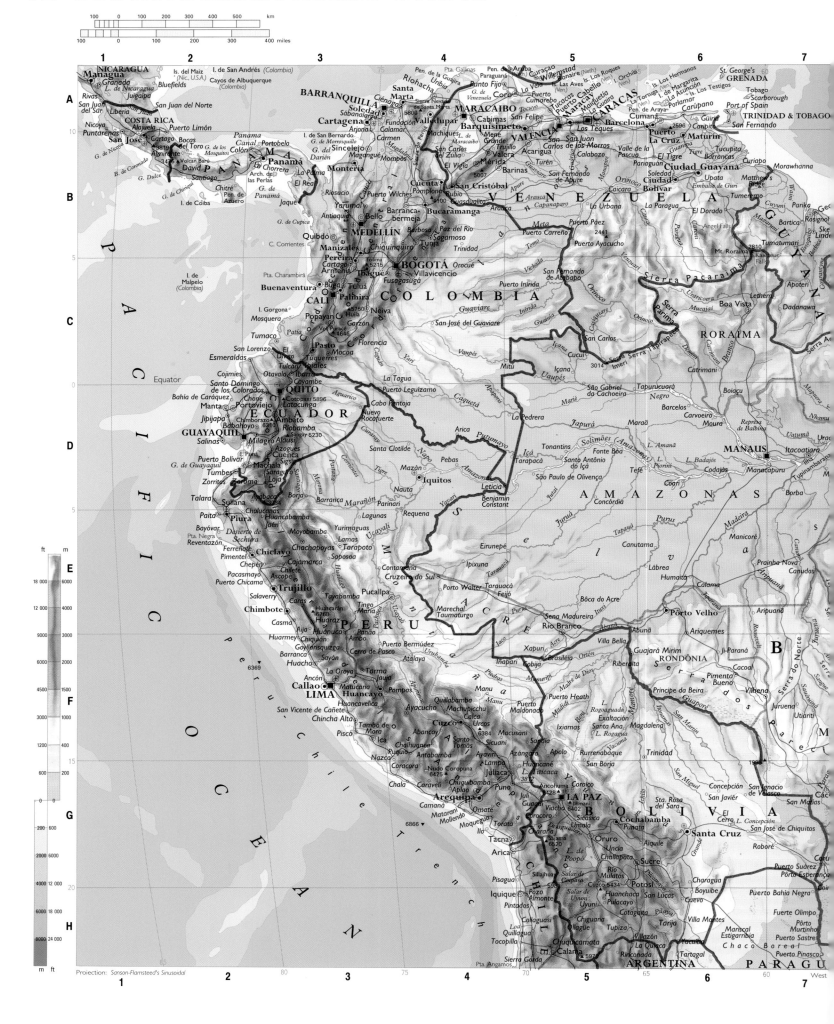

A

ATLANTIC

B

OCEAN

C

Equator

São Paulo
(Braz.)

Fernando de Noronha
(Braz.)

Rocas

D

RINAM
FRENCH
GUIANA

AMAPÁ

P A R Á

B R A Z I L

MARANHÃO

CEARÁ

RIO GRANDE
DO NORTE

PIAUÍ

PARAÍBA

PERNAMBUCO

ALAGOAS

SERGIPE

TOCANTINS

B A H I A

O GROSSO
Planalto do

Mato Grosso

MATO GROSSO
DO SUL

GOIÁS

DIST.
FED.
BRASÍLIA

MINAS GERAIS

SÃO
PAULO

E

F

G

H

Paramaribo
Nieuw Amsterdam
Moengo
Albina
St-Laurent
Iracoubo
Sinnamary
Kourou
Cayenne

Camopi
Oiapoque
C. Orange
St. Georges

Amapá
I. de Maracá

Serra do
Navio

Macapá
Mazagão
Afuá
I. Caviana
I. Mexiana
C. Maguarinho
Chaves
I. de Soure
Curuçá Salinópolis
Bragança

Óbidos
Monte
Alegre
Prainha
Almeirim
Gurupá
Pôrto de Móz
Breves
Marajó
BELÉM
Castanhal
Abaetetuba
Cametá

Santarém
Altamira
Aveiro
Brasília Legal
Itaituba

Viseu
Vigia
Curuçá
Turiaçu
Gururupu
B. de São Marcos
São Luís
Alcântara
Barreirinhas
Tutóia

Rosário
Pinheiro
Parnaíba
Luís Correia
Camocim
Granja
Itapipoca
Caucaia
FORTALEZA
Cascavel
Aracati

Maracanaú
Baturité
Russas
Areia Branca
Macau
Ceará Mirim
Natal

Sobral
Ipu
Quixadá
Crateús
Senador Pompeu
Mossoró
Caraúbas
Currais
Novos

Teresina
Amarante
Valença
do Piauí
Iguatu
Cedro
Cajàzeiras
Sousa
Patos
Caicó

Floriano
Oeiras
Picos
Juàzeiro
do Norte
Crato
Ouricuri

Uruçuí
São João
do Piauí
Chapada do Araripe
Salgueiro
Pesqueira
Garanhuns
Campina
Grande
João Pessoa
Olinda
RECIFE
Jaboatão

Santa
Filomena
São Francisco
Petrolina
Juàzeiro
Nova Casa
Nova
Petrolândia
Palmeira
dos
Índios
Arapiraca
Maceió

Caracol
Novo Remanso
Paulistana
Paulo
Afonso
Propriá
Penedo

Palmas
Pôrto Nacional
Barra
Senhor do
Bonfim
Capela
Aracaju

Xique-Xique
Jacobina
Queimadas
Serrinha
São Cristóvão
Estância

Gurupi
Mundo
Novo
Feira de
Santana
Alagoinhas

Peixe
Taguatinga
Barreiras
Itaberaba
Cachoeira
Santo Amaro

Paranã
Ibotirama
Bom Jesus
da Lapa Serra
do Sincorá
Valença
SALVADOR

Campos Belos
São Domingos
Santa Maria
da Vitória
Caetité
Brumado
Jequié

Posse
Carinhanha
Ubaitaba
Itabuna
Ilhéus

Niquelândia
Aruanã
Januária
São Francisco
Janaúba
Vitória da
Conquista
Canavieiras

Formosa
Montes
Claros
Pedra Azul
Belmonte
Pôrto Seguro

Luziânia
Salinas
Jequitinhonha
Itamaraju

Anápolis
Goiânia
Araçuaí
Teófilo Otoni
Nanuque
Prado
Caravelas

Vianópolis
Patos
de Minas
Diamantina
Governador
Valadares
Mucuri

Morrinhos
Paracatu
Pirapora
Ipatinga
Conceição da Barra
São Mateus

Catalão
Araguari
Uberlândia
Curvelo
Caratinga
Colatina
Linhares

Uberaba
Araxá
Sete Lagoas
Sabará
Ponte Nova
Cariacica
Vitória
Vila Velha

BELO HORIZONTE
Ouro
Prêto
Cachoeiro de Itapemirim

Trindade
(Braz.)

Ribeirão Prêto
Divinópolis
Barbacena
Juiz de Fora
Campos

Poços de
Caldas
São João
del Rei
Nova Friburgo

Campinas
Volta Redonda
Petrópolis
Niterói
Cabo Frio
RIO DE JANEIRO

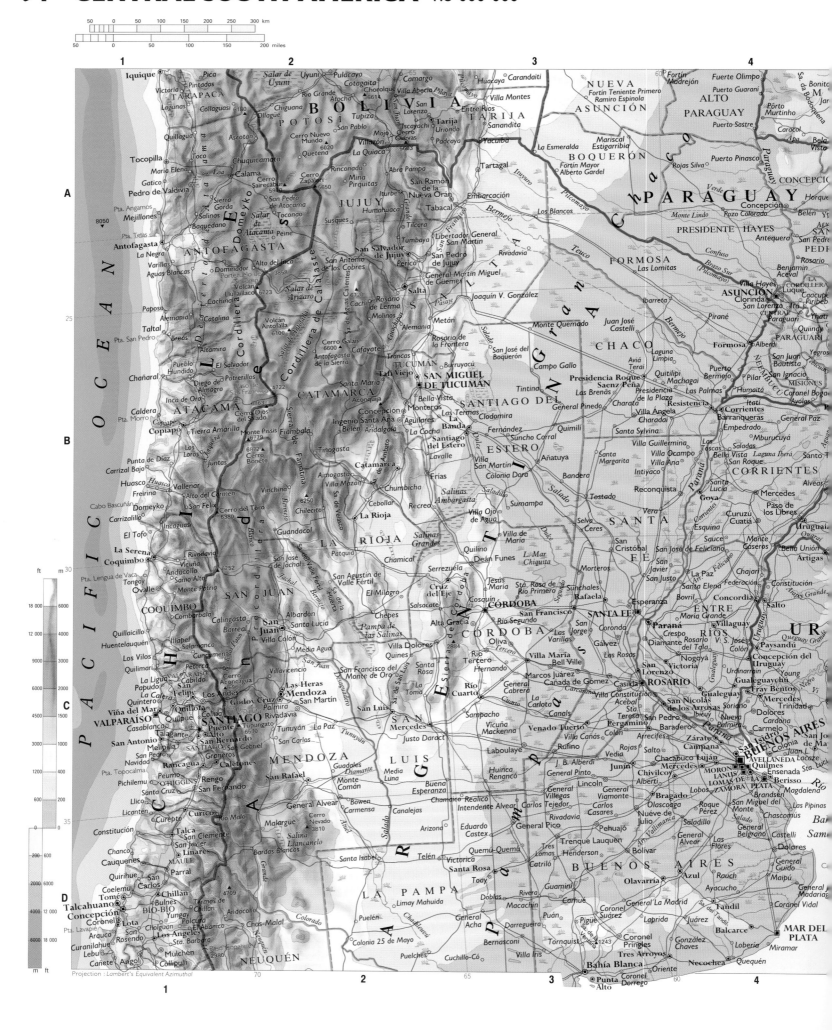

Projection : Lambert's Equivalent Azimuthal

5   6   7

BELO HORIZONTE
Nova Lima
Itabirito

VITÓRIA
Itaquari
Vila Velha
Guarapari

MATO GROSSO
DO SUL

Três Lagoas
Andradina
Mirassol
São José
Olímpia
Passos
Oliveira
Conselheiro
Congonhas
Ouro
Prêto
Ponte Nova
Castelo
Cachoeiro
de Itapemirim

Sidrolândia
Nioaque

Xavantina
Mirandópolis
Araçatuba
Catanduva
Bebedouro
Batatais
São Sebastião
do Paraiso
Campo Belo
Lafaiete
São João
del Rei
Ubá
Carangola
Muriaé

Maracaju
Nova Alvorada
do Sul
Panorama
Biriguí
Taquaritinga
Ribeirão
Prêto
Guaxupé
Três
Pontas
Barbacena
Cataguases
Alegre

Dourados
Presidente
Epitácio
Adamantina
Lins
Renápolis
Novo
Horizonte
Mocóca
Casa
Branca
Alfenas
Varginha
Santos
Dumont
Leopoldina
Cambuci
Guarus

Lopes
Laguna
Presidente
Prudente
Tupã
Pirajuí
Jaboticabal
Poços de
Caldas
Juiz de Fora
Três
Rios
CAMPOS
Cabo de
São Tomé

Ponta Porã
Martinópolis
Marília
Garça
Bariri
São
Carlos
Araraquara
da Boa Vista
Pinhal
Ouro Fino
Volta
Redonda
Barra do Pirai
Paraíba do Sul
RIO DE JANEIRO

Pedro Juan Caballero
Dourados
Rancharia
Paraguaçu
Paulista
Bauru
Jaú
Rio Claro
Americana
Guaratinguetá
Barra
Petrópolis
Nova Friburgo
Macaé

Ivinhema
Rosana
Assis
Piracicaba
Limeira
Bragança
Barra Mansa
NOVA IGUAÇU
DUQUE DE CAXIAS

Paranaví
Santa Cruz
do Rio Pardo
CAMPINAS
Itu
Mogí Mirim
Paulista
São José dos
Jacarei
Angra dos
Reis
SÃO GONÇALO
NITERÓI
RIO DE JANEIRO

Ponta Pora
Naviraí
Centenário do Sul
PARANÁ
Botucatu
Jundiaí
Sorocaba
SÃO PAULO
Moji das Cruzes
Cabo Frio

Cianorte
Londrina
Cambará
Ourinhos
Avaré
Tatuí
SANTO ANDRÉ
Tropic of Capricorn

Umuarama
Maringá
Apucarana
Jacarèzinho
Itapetininga
São Bernardo
do Campo
Santos
Lª de Araruama

Cruzeiro
do Oeste
Rolândia
Joaquim
Távora
Itaporanga
Itapeva
São Vicente
Guarujá

Goio-Erê
Mandaguari
Ibaiti
Itararé
Apiaí
Itanhaém
Ilha de São Sebastião
Pta. de Boi

Guaira
Porto Mendes
Campo
Mourão
Cândido de Abreu
Tibagi
Jaguariaíva
Juquiá
Ilha Comprida

BRAZIL
Cascavel
Sª das Araras
Piratanga
Castro
Apiaí
Registro
Iguape

Medianeira
Guarapuava
Prudentópolis
Palmeira
CURITIBA
Ilha do Cardoso

Foz do Iguaçu
Laranjeiras
do Sul
Ponta
Grossa
Irati
Antonina
Paranaguá

Ciudad
del Este
Cat. del
Iguaçu
Guaratuba

PARANÁ
Francisco
Beltrão
União da
Vitória
São Mateus
do Sul
Matinhos
Joinville

Eldorado
Bernardo
de Irigoyen
Pato Branco
Rio Negro
Mafra
São Francisco do Sul

MISIONES
Palmas
Pôrto União
Espigão
Cleveland
São Miguel
do Oeste
Xanxerê
Caçador
Itajaí
Blumenau

Corpus
Chapecó
Joaçaba
SANTA
Santa Cecília
Brusque

Encarnación
Oberá
Concordia
Frederico
Westphalen
CATARINA
Curitibanos
Rio do Sul
São José

Leandro N. Alem
Santa Rosa
Palmeira
das Missões
Campos
Novos
São
Ilha de Santa Catarina
Florianópolis

San Javier
Ijuí
Carazinho
Passo
Fundo
Lajes

Apóstoles
São Luís
Gonzaga
Cruz Alta
Vacaria
Joaquim

Santo Angelo
Guaporé
São
Joaquim
Laguna

Santiago
RIO GRANDE
Bento Gonçalves
Tubarão
Cabo Santa Marta Grande

São Borja
Caxias do Sul
Criciúma

ATLANTIC

Santa Maria
Santa Cruz
do Sul
Nôvo Hamburgo
Torres
Araranguá

Alegrete
Montenegro
Taquara

Cachoeira do Sul
Canoas
São
Leopoldo
Osorio

Rio Pardo
Viamão
PÔRTO ALEGRE

DO SUL
São
Gabriel
Caçapava
do Sul
Encantadas
Tapes

Santana do
Livramento
Dom Pedrito
Camaquã
Camaquã

Rivera
Santana
Bagé
Sa. do Canguçu
São Lourenço
do Sul
Mostardas

Pinheiro
Machado
Canguçu

acuarembó
Pelotas
Lagoa dos Patos

UAY
Melo
Jaguarão
Rio Grande

Rio Branco
São José do Norte

Fraile
Muerto
Vergara
Lagoa Mangueira

San Gregorio
Treinta y Tres
Santa Vitória do Palmar

Blanquillo
Cerro
Chato
Lascano
Chuy

José Batlle
y Ordóñez
Aigua
Castillos

Tala
Minas
Rocha

San Carlos

MONTEVIDEO
Maldonado

OCEAN

Plata

5304

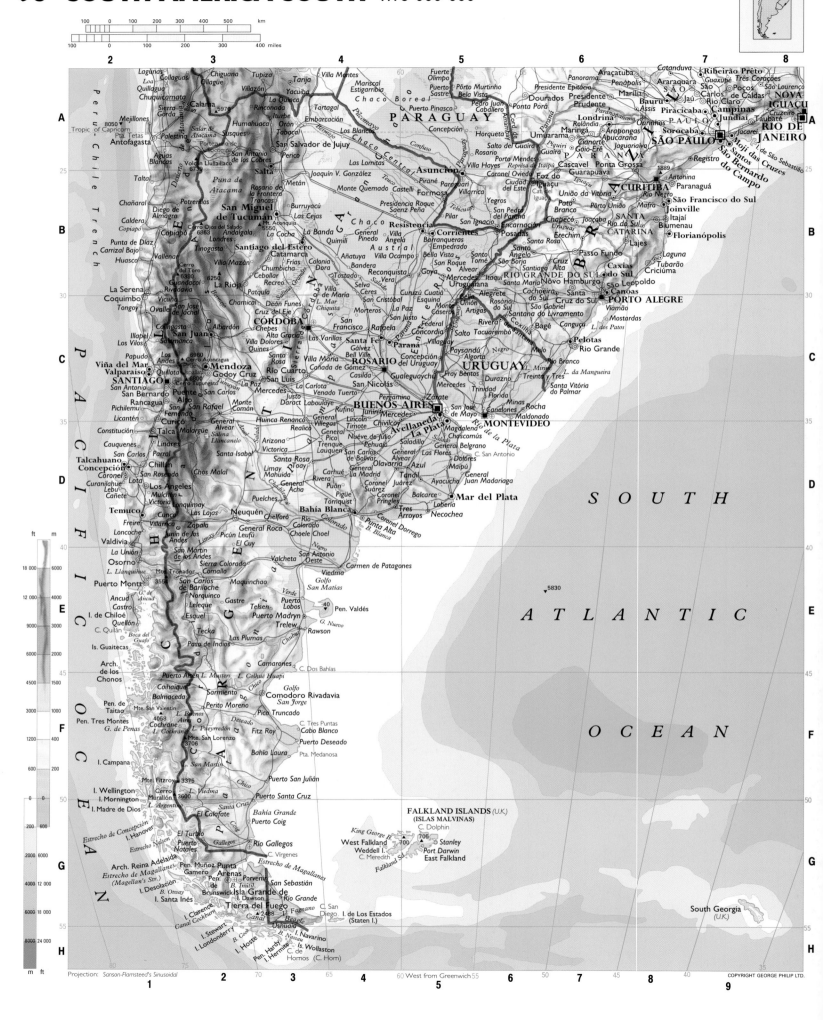

INDEX

The index contains the names of all the principal places and features shown on the World Maps. Each name is followed by an additional entry in italics giving the country or region within which it is located. The alphabetical order of names composed of two or more words is governed primarily by the first word and then by the second. This is an example of the rule:

Mīr Kūh, *Iran*	**45 E8**	26 22N	58 55 E
Mīr Shahdād, *Iran*	**45 E8**	26 15N	58 29 E
Mira, *Italy*	**20 B5**	45 26N	12 8 E
Mira por vos Cay, *Bahamas* .	**89 B5**	22 9N	74 30W
Miraj, *India*	**40 L9**	16 50N	74 45 E

Physical features composed of a proper name (Erie) and a description (Lake) are positioned alphabetically by the proper name. The description is positioned after the proper name and is usually abbreviated:

Erie, L., *N. Amer.*	**78 D4**	42 15N	81 0W

Where a description forms part of a settlement or administrative name however, it is always written in full and put in its true alphabetic position:

Mount Morris, *U.S.A.*	**78 D7**	42 44N	77 52W

Names beginning with M' and Mc are indexed as if they were spelled Mac. Names beginning St. are alphabetised under Saint, but Sankt, Sint, Sant', Santa and San are all spelt in full and are alphabetised accordingly. If the same place name occurs two or more times in the index and all are in the same country, each is followed by the name of the administrative subdivision in which it is located. The names are placed in the alphabetical order of the subdivisions. For example:

Jackson, *Ky., U.S.A.*	**76 G4**	37 33N	83 23W
Jackson, *Mich., U.S.A.*	**76 D3**	42 15N	84 24W
Jackson, *Minn., U.S.A.*	**80 D7**	43 37N	95 1W

The number in bold type which follows each name in the index refers to the number of the map page where that feature or place will be found. This is usually the largest scale at which the place or feature appears.

The letter and figure which are in bold type immediately after the page number give the grid square on the map page, within which the feature is situated. The letter represents the latitude and the figure the longitude.

In some cases the feature itself may fall within the specified square, while the name is outside. This is usually the case only with features which are larger than a grid square.

For a more precise location the geographical coordinates which follow the letter/figure references give the latitude and the longitude of each place. The first set of figures represent the latitude which is the distance north or south of the Equator measured as an angle at the centre of the earth. The Equator is latitude 0°, the North Pole is 90°N, and the South Pole 90°S.

The second set of figures represent the longitude, which is the distance East or West of the prime meridian, which runs through Greenwich, England. Longitude is also measured as an angle at the centre of the earth and is given East or West of the prime meridian, from 0° to 180° in either direction.

The unit of measurement for latitude and longitude is the degree, which is subdivided into 60 minutes. Each index entry states the position of a place in degrees and minutes, a space being left between the degrees and the minutes.

The latitude is followed by N(orth) or S(outh) and the longitude by E(ast) or W(est).

Rivers are indexed to their mouths or confluences, and carry the symbol → after their names. A solid square ■ follows the name of a country, while an open square □ refers to a first order administrative area.

Abbreviations used in the index

A.C.T. – Australian Capital Territory
Afghan. – Afghanistan
Ala. – Alabama
Alta. – Alberta
Amer. – America(n)
Arch. – Archipelago
Ariz. – Arizona
Ark. – Arkansas
Atl. Oc. – Atlantic Ocean
B. – Baie, Bahía, Bay, Bucht, Bugt
B.C. – British Columbia
Bangla. – Bangladesh
Barr. – Barrage
Bos.-H. – Bosnia-Herzegovina
C. – Cabo, Cap, Cape, Coast
C.A.R. – Central African Republic
C. Prov. – Cape Province
Calif. – California
Cent. – Central
Chan. – Channel
Colo. – Colorado
Conn. – Connecticut
Cord. – Cordillera
Cr. – Creek
Czech. – Czech Republic
D.C. – District of Columbia
Del. – Delaware
Dep. – Dependency
Des. – Desert
Dist. – District
Dj. – Djebel
Domin. – Dominica
Dom. Rep. – Dominican Republic
E. – East

E. Salv. – El Salvador
Eq. Guin. – Equatorial Guinea
Fla. – Florida
Falk. Is. – Falkland Is.
G. – Golfe, Golfo, Gulf, Guba, Gebel
Ga. – Georgia
Gt. – Great, Greater
Guinea-Biss. – Guinea-Bissau
H.K. – Hong Kong
H.P. – Himachal Pradesh
Hants. – Hampshire
Harb. – Harbor, Harbour
Hd. – Head
Hts. – Heights
I.(s). – Île, Ilha, Insel, Isla, Island, Isle
Ill. – Illinois
Ind. – Indiana
Ind. Oc. – Indian Ocean
Ivory C. – Ivory Coast
J. – Jabal, Jebel, Jazira
Junc. – Junction
K. – Kap, Kapp
Kans. – Kansas
Kep. – Kepulauan
Ky. – Kentucky
L. – Lac, Lacul, Lago, Lagoa, Lake, Limni, Loch, Lough
La. – Louisiana
Liech. – Liechtenstein
Lux. – Luxembourg
Mad. P. – Madhya Pradesh
Madag. – Madagascar
Man. – Manitoba
Mass. – Massachusetts

Md. – Maryland
Me. – Maine
Medit. S. – Mediterranean Sea
Mich. – Michigan
Minn. – Minnesota
Miss. – Mississippi
Mo. – Missouri
Mont. – Montana
Mozam. – Mozambique
Mt.(e) – Mont, Monte, Monti, Montaña, Mountain
N. – Nord, Norte, North, Northern, Nouveau
N.B. – New Brunswick
N.C. – North Carolina
N. Cal. – New Caledonia
N. Dak. – North Dakota
N.H. – New Hampshire
N.I. – North Island
N.J. – New Jersey
N. Mex. – New Mexico
N.S. – Nova Scotia
N.S.W. – New South Wales
N.W.T. – North West Territory
N.Y. – New York
N.Z. – New Zealand
Nebr. – Nebraska
Neths. – Netherlands
Nev. – Nevada
Nfld. – Newfoundland
Nic. – Nicaragua
O. – Oued, Ouadi
Occ. – Occidentale
Okla. – Oklahoma
Ont. – Ontario
Or. – Orientale

Oreg. – Oregon
Os. – Ostrov
Oz. – Ozero
P. – Pass, Passo, Pasul, Pulau
P.E.I. – Prince Edward Island
Pa. – Pennsylvania
Pac. Oc. – Pacific Ocean
Papua N.G. – Papua New Guinea
Pass. – Passage
Pen. – Peninsula, Péninsule
Phil. – Philippines
Pk. – Park, Peak
Plat. – Plateau
Prov. – Province, Provincial
Pt. – Point
Pta. – Ponta, Punta
Pte. – Pointe
Qué. – Québec
Queens. – Queensland
R. – Rio, River
R.I. – Rhode Island
Ra.(s). – Range(s)
Raj. – Rajasthan
Reg. – Region
Rep. – Republic
Res. – Reserve, Reservoir
S. – San, South, Sea
Si. Arabia – Saudi Arabia
S.C. – South Carolina
S. Dak. – South Dakota
S.I. – South Island
S. Leone – Sierra Leone
Sa. – Serra, Sierra
Sask. – Saskatchewan
Scot. – Scotland
Sd. – Sound

Sev. – Severnaya
Sib. – Siberia
Sprs. – Springs
St. – Saint
Sta. – Santa, Station
Ste. – Sainte
Sto. – Santo
Str. – Strait, Stretto
Switz. – Switzerland
Tas. – Tasmania
Tenn. – Tennessee
Tex. – Texas
Tg. – Tanjung
Trin. & Tob. – Trinidad & Tobago
U.A.E. – United Arab Emirates
U.K. – United Kingdom
U.S.A. – United States of America
Ut. P. – Uttar Pradesh
Va. – Virginia
Vdkhr. – Vodokhranilishche
Vf. – Vírful
Vic. – Victoria
Vol. – Volcano
Vt. – Vermont
W. – Wadi, West
W. Va. – West Virginia
Wash. – Washington
Wis. – Wisconsin
Wlkp. – Wielkopolski
Wyo. – Wyoming
Yorks. – Yorkshire
Yug. – Yugoslavia

A Coruña

A

A Coruña, *Spain* **19 A1** 43 20N 8 25W
A Estrada, *Spain* **19 A1** 42 43N 8 27W
A Fonsagrada, *Spain* **19 A2** 43 8N 7 4W
Aachen, *Germany* **16 C4** 50 45N 6 6 E
Aalborg = Ålborg, *Denmark* **9 H13** 57 2N 9 54 E
Aalen, *Germany* **16 D6** 48 51N 10 6 E
Aalst, *Belgium* **15 D4** 50 56N 4 2 E
Aalten, *Neths.* **15 C6** 51 56N 6 35 E
Aalter, *Belgium* **15 C3** 51 5N 3 28 E
Äänekoski, *Finland* **9 E21** 62 36N 25 44 E
Aarau, *Switz.* **18 C8** 47 23N 8 4 E
Aare →, *Switz.* **18 C8** 47 33N 8 14 E
Aarhus = Århus, *Denmark* **9 H14** 56 8N 10 11 E
Aarschot, *Belgium* **15 D4** 50 59N 4 49 E
Aba, *Dem. Rep. of the Congo* **54 B3** 3 58N 30 17 E
Aba, *Nigeria* **50 G7** 5 10N 7 19 E
Ābādān, *Iran* **45 D6** 30 22N 48 20 E
Ābādeh, *Iran* **45 D7** 31 8N 52 40 E
Abadla, *Algeria* **50 B5** 31 2N 2 45W
Abaetetuba, *Brazil* **93 D9** 1 40S 48 50W
Abagnar Qi, *China* **34 C9** 43 52N 116 2 E
Abai, *Paraguay* **95 B4** 25 58S 55 54W
Abakan, *Russia* **27 D10** 53 40N 91 10 E
Abancay, *Peru* **92 F4** 13 35S 72 55W
Abariringa, *Kiribati* **64 H10** 2 50S 171 40W
Abarqū, *Iran* **45 D7** 31 10N 53 20 E
Abashiri, *Japan* **30 C12** 44 0N 144 15 E
Abashiri-Wan, *Japan* **30 C12** 44 0N 144 30 E
Abay, *Kazakstan* **26 E8** 49 38N 72 53 E
Abaya, L., *Ethiopia* **46 F2** 6 30N 37 50 E
Abaza, *Russia* **26 D10** 52 39N 90 6 E
'Abbāsābād, *Iran* **45 C8** 33 34N 58 23 E
Abbay = Nîl el Azraq →, *Sudan* **51 E12** 15 38N 32 31 E
Abbaye, Pt., *U.S.A.* **76 B1** 46 58N 88 8W
Abbé, L., *Ethiopia* **46 E3** 11 8N 41 47 E
Abbeville, *France* **18 A4** 50 6N 1 49 E
Abbeville, *Ala., U.S.A.* **77 K3** 31 34N 85 15W
Abbeville, *La., U.S.A.* **81 L8** 29 58N 92 8W
Abbeville, *S.C., U.S.A.* **77 H4** 34 11N 82 23W
Abbot Ice Shelf, *Antarctica* **5 D16** 73 0S 92 0W
Abbottabad, *Pakistan* **42 B5** 34 10N 73 15 E
Abd al Kūrī, *Ind. Oc.* **46 E5** 12 5N 52 20 E
Ābdar, *Iran* **45 D7** 30 16N 55 19 E
'Abdolābād, *Iran* **45 C8** 34 12N 56 30 E
Abdulpur, *Bangla.* **43 G13** 24 15N 88 59 E
Abéché, *Chad* **51 F10** 13 50N 20 35 E
Abengourou, *Ivory C.* **50 G5** 6 42N 3 27W
Åbenrå, *Denmark* **9 J13** 55 3N 9 25 E
Abeokuta, *Nigeria* **50 G6** 7 3N 3 19 E
Aber, *Uganda* **54 B3** 2 12N 32 25 E
Aberaeron, *U.K.* **11 E3** 52 15N 4 15W
Aberayron = Aberaeron, *U.K.* **11 E3** 52 15N 4 15W
Aberchirder, *U.K.* **12 D6** 57 34N 2 37W
Abercorn = Mbala, *Zambia* **55 D3** 8 46S 31 24 E
Abercorn, *Australia* **63 D5** 25 12S 151 5 E
Aberdare, *U.K.* **11 F4** 51 43N 3 27W
Aberdare Ra., *Kenya* **54 C4** 0 15S 36 50 E
Aberdeen, *Australia* **63 E5** 32 9S 150 56 E
Aberdeen, *Canada* **73 C7** 52 20N 106 8W
Aberdeen, *S. Africa* **56 E3** 32 28S 24 2 E
Aberdeen, *U.K.* **12 D6** 57 9N 2 5W
Aberdeen, *Ala., U.S.A.* **77 J1** 33 49N 88 33W
Aberdeen, *Idaho, U.S.A.* **82 E7** 42 57N 112 50W
Aberdeen, *Md., U.S.A.* **76 F7** 39 31N 76 10W
Aberdeen, *S. Dak., U.S.A.* **80 C5** 45 28N 98 29W
Aberdeen, *Wash., U.S.A.* **84 D3** 46 59N 123 50W
Aberdeen, City of □, *U.K.* **12 D6** 57 10N 2 10W
Aberdeenshire □, *U.K.* **12 D6** 57 17N 2 36W
Aberdovey = Aberdyfi, *U.K.* **11 E3** 52 33N 4 3W
Aberdyfi, *U.K.* **11 E3** 52 33N 4 3W
Aberfeldy, *U.K.* **12 E5** 56 37N 3 51W
Abergavenny, *U.K.* **11 F4** 51 49N 3 1W
Abergele, *U.K.* **10 D4** 53 17N 3 35W
Abernathy, *U.S.A.* **81 J4** 33 50N 101 51W
Abert, L., *U.S.A.* **82 E3** 42 38N 120 14W
Aberystwyth, *U.K.* **11 E3** 52 25N 4 5W
Abhā, *Si. Arabia* **46 D3** 18 0N 42 34 E
Abhar, *Iran* **45 B6** 36 9N 49 13 E
Abhayapuri, *India* **43 F14** 26 24N 90 38 E
Abidjan, *Ivory C.* **50 G5** 5 26N 3 58W
Abilene, *Kans., U.S.A.* **80 F6** 38 55N 97 13W
Abilene, *Tex., U.S.A.* **81 J5** 32 28N 99 43W
Abingdon, *U.K.* **11 F6** 51 40N 1 17W
Abingdon, *U.S.A.* **77 G5** 36 43N 81 59W
Abington Reef, *Australia* **62 B4** 18 0S 149 35 E
Abitau →, *Canada* **73 B7** 59 53N 109 3W
Abitibi →, *Canada* **70 B3** 51 3N 80 55W
Abitibi, L., *Canada* **70 C4** 48 40N 79 40W
Abkhaz Republic = Abkhazia □, *Georgia* **25 F7** 43 12N 41 5 E
Abkhazia □, *Georgia* **25 F7** 43 12N 41 5 E
Abminga, *Australia* **63 D1** 26 8S 134 51 E
Åbo = Turku, *Finland* **9 F20** 60 30N 22 19 E
Abohar, *India* **42 D6** 30 10N 74 10 E
Abolo, *Congo* **52 D2** 0 8N 14 16 E
Abomey, *Benin* **50 G6** 7 10N 2 5 E
Abong-Mbang, *Cameroon* **52 D2** 4 0N 13 8 E
Abou-Deïa, *Chad* **51 F9** 11 20N 19 20 E
Aboyne, *U.K.* **12 D6** 57 4N 2 47W
Abra Pampa, *Argentina* **94 A2** 22 43S 65 42W
Abraham L., *Canada* **72 C5** 52 15N 116 35W
Abreojos, Pta., *Mexico* **86 B2** 26 50N 113 40W
Abrud, *Romania* **17 E12** 46 19N 23 5 E
Absaroka Range, *U.S.A.* **82 D9** 44 45N 109 50W
Abu, *India* **42 G5** 24 41N 72 50 E
Abu al Abyad, *U.A.E.* **45 E7** 24 11N 53 50 E
Abū al Khaşīb, *Iraq* **45 D6** 30 25N 48 0 E
Abū 'Alī, *Si. Arabia* **45 E6** 27 20N 49 27 E
Abū 'Alī →, *Lebanon* **47 A4** 34 25N 35 50 E
Abu Dhabi = Abū Ẓāby, *U.A.E.* **45 E7** 24 28N 54 22 E
Abū Du'ān, *Syria* **44 B3** 36 25N 38 15 E
Abu el Gairi, W. →, *Egypt* **47 F2** 29 35N 33 30 E
Abu Ga'da, W. →, *Egypt* **47 F1** 29 15N 32 53 E
Abū Ḩadrīyah, *Si. Arabia* **45 E6** 27 20N 48 58 E
Abu Hamed, *Sudan* **51 E12** 19 32N 33 13 E
Abū Kamāl, *Syria* **44 C4** 34 30N 41 0 E
Abū Madd, Ra's, *Si. Arabia* **44 E3** 24 50N 37 7 E
Abū Mūsā, *U.A.E.* **45 E7** 25 52N 55 3 E
Abu Şafāt, W. →, *Jordan* **47 E5** 30 24N 36 7 E
Abu Simbel, *Egypt* **51 D12** 22 18N 31 40 E
Abū Şukhayr, *Iraq* **44 D5** 31 54N 44 30 E
Abû Zabad, *Sudan* **51 F11** 12 25N 29 10 E
Abū Ẓāby, *U.A.E.* **45 E7** 24 28N 54 22 E
Abū Zeydābād, *Iran* **45 C6** 33 54N 51 45 E
Abuja, *Nigeria* **50 G7** 9 16N 7 2 E
Abukuma-Gawa →, *Japan* **30 E10** 38 6N 140 52 E
Abukuma-Sammyaku, *Japan* **30 F10** 37 30N 140 45 E
Abunã, *Brazil* **92 E5** 9 40S 65 20W
Abunã →, *Brazil* **92 E5** 9 41S 65 20W
Aburo, *Dem. Rep. of the Congo* **54 B3** 2 4N 30 53 E
Abut Hd., *N.Z.* **59 K3** 43 7S 170 15 E
Acadia National Park, *U.S.A.* **77 C11** 44 20N 68 13W
Açailândia, *Brazil* **93 D9** 4 57S 47 0W
Acajutla, *El Salv.* **88 D2** 13 36N 89 50W
Acámbaro, *Mexico* **86 D4** 20 0N 100 40W
Acaponeta, *Mexico* **86 C3** 22 30N 105 20W
Acapulco, *Mexico* **87 D5** 16 51N 99 56W
Acarai, Serra, *Brazil* **92 C7** 1 50N 57 50W
Acarigua, *Venezuela* **92 B5** 9 33N 69 12W
Acatlán, *Mexico* **87 D5** 18 10N 98 3W
Acayucan, *Mexico* **87 D6** 17 59N 94 58W
Accomac, *U.S.A.* **76 G8** 37 43N 75 40W
Accra, *Ghana* **50 G5** 5 35N 0 6W
Accrington, *U.K.* **10 D5** 53 45N 2 22W
Acebal, *Argentina* **94 C3** 33 20S 60 50W
Aceh □, *Indonesia* **36 D1** 4 15N 97 30 E
Achalpur, *India* **40 J10** 21 22N 77 32 E
Acheng, *China* **35 B14** 45 30N 126 58 E
Acher, *India* **42 H5** 23 10N 72 32 E
Achill Hd., *Ireland* **13 C1** 53 58N 10 15W
Achill I., *Ireland* **13 C1** 53 58N 10 1W
Achinsk, *Russia* **27 D10** 56 20N 90 20 E
Acireale, *Italy* **20 F6** 37 37N 15 10 E
Ackerman, *U.S.A.* **81 J10** 33 19N 89 11W
Acklins I., *Bahamas* **89 B5** 22 30N 74 0W
Acme, *Canada* **72 C6** 51 33N 113 30W
Acme, *U.S.A.* **78 F5** 40 8N 79 26W
Aconcagua, Cerro, *Argentina* **94 C2** 32 39S 70 0W
Aconquija, Mt., *Argentina* **94 B2** 27 0S 66 0W
Açores, Is. dos = Azores, *Atl. Oc.* **50 A1** 38 44N 29 0W
Acraman, L., *Australia* **63 E2** 32 2S 135 23 E
Acre = 'Akko, *Israel* **47 C4** 32 55N 35 4 E
Acre □, *Brazil* **92 E4** 9 1S 71 0W
Acre →, *Brazil* **92 E5** 8 45S 67 22W
Acton, *Canada* **78 C4** 43 38N 80 3W
Acuña, *Mexico* **86 B4** 29 18N 100 55W
Ad Dammām, *Si. Arabia* **45 E6** 26 20N 50 5 E
Ad Dāmūr, *Lebanon* **47 B4** 33 44N 35 27 E
Ad Dawādimī, *Si. Arabia* **44 E5** 24 35N 44 15 E
Ad Dawḩah, *Qatar* **45 E6** 25 15N 51 35 E
Ad Dawr, *Iraq* **44 C4** 34 27N 43 47 E
Ad Dir'īyah, *Si. Arabia* **44 E5** 24 44N 46 35 E
Ad Dīwānīyah, *Iraq* **44 D5** 32 0N 45 0 E
Ad Dujayl, *Iraq* **44 C5** 33 51N 44 14 E
Ad Duwayd, *Si. Arabia* **44 D4** 30 15N 42 17 E
Ada, *Minn., U.S.A.* **80 B6** 47 18N 96 31W
Ada, *Okla., U.S.A.* **81 H6** 34 46N 96 41W
Adabiya, *Egypt* **47 F1** 29 53N 32 28 E
Adair, C., *Canada* **69 A12** 71 31N 71 24W
Adaja →, *Spain* **19 B3** 41 32N 4 52W
Adak I., *U.S.A.* **68 C2** 51 45N 176 45W
Adamaoua, Massif de l', *Cameroon* **52 C2** 7 20N 12 20 E
Adamawa Highlands = Adamaoua, Massif de l', *Cameroon* **52 C2** 7 20N 12 20 E
Adamello, Mte., *Italy* **18 C9** 46 9N 10 30 E
Adaminaby, *Australia* **63 F4** 36 0S 148 45 E
Adams, *Mass., U.S.A.* **79 D11** 42 38N 73 7W
Adams, *N.Y., U.S.A.* **79 C8** 43 49N 76 1W
Adams, *Wis., U.S.A.* **80 D10** 43 57N 89 49W
Adam's Bridge, *Sri Lanka* **40 Q11** 9 15N 79 40 E
Adams L., *Canada* **72 C5** 51 10N 119 40W
Adams Mt., *U.S.A.* **84 D5** 46 12N 121 30W
Adam's Peak, *Sri Lanka* **40 R12** 6 48N 80 30 E
Adana, *Turkey* **25 G6** 37 0N 35 16 E
Adapazarı = Sakarya, *Turkey* **25 F5** 40 48N 30 25 E
Adarama, *Sudan* **51 E12** 17 10N 34 52 E
Adare, C., *Antarctica* **5 D11** 71 0S 171 0 E
Adaut, *Indonesia* **37 F8** 8 8S 131 7 E
Adavale, *Australia* **63 D3** 25 52S 144 32 E
Adda →, *Italy* **18 D8** 45 8N 9 53 E
Addis Ababa = Addis Abeba, *Ethiopia* **46 F2** 9 2N 38 42 E
Addis Abeba, *Ethiopia* **46 F2** 9 2N 38 42 E
Addison, *U.S.A.* **78 D7** 42 1N 77 14W
Addo, *S. Africa* **56 E4** 33 32S 25 45 E
Ādeh, *Iran* **44 B5** 37 42N 45 11 E
Adel, *U.S.A.* **77 K4** 31 8N 83 25W
Adelaide, *Australia* **63 E2** 34 52S 138 30 E
Adelaide, *Bahamas* **88 A4** 25 4N 77 31W
Adelaide, *S. Africa* **56 E4** 32 42S 26 20 E
Adelaide I., *Antarctica* **5 C17** 67 15S 68 30W
Adelaide Pen., *Canada* **68 B10** 68 15N 97 30W
Adelaide River, *Australia* **60 B5** 13 15S 131 7 E
Adelanto, *U.S.A.* **85 L9** 34 35N 117 22W
Adele I., *Australia* **60 C3** 15 32S 123 9 E
Adélie, Terre, *Antarctica* **5 C10** 68 0S 140 0 E
Adélie Land = Adélie, Terre, *Antarctica* **5 C10** 68 0S 140 0 E
Aden = Al 'Adan, *Yemen* **46 E4** 12 45N 45 0 E
Aden, G. of, *Asia* **46 E4** 12 30N 47 30 E
Adendorp, *S. Africa* **56 E3** 32 15S 24 30 E
Adh Dhayd, *U.A.E.* **45 E7** 25 17N 55 53 E
Adhoi, *India* **42 H4** 23 26N 70 32 E
Adi, *Indonesia* **37 E8** 4 15S 133 30 E
Adieu, C., *Australia* **61 F5** 32 0S 132 10 E
Adieu Pt., *Australia* **60 C3** 15 14S 124 35 E
Adige →, *Italy* **20 B5** 45 9N 12 20 E
Adigrat, *Ethiopia* **46 E2** 14 20N 39 26 E
Adilabad, *India* **40 K11** 19 33N 78 20 E
Adin Khel, *Afghan.* **40 C6** 32 45N 68 5 E
Adirondack Mts., *U.S.A.* **79 C10** 44 0N 74 0W
Adjumani, *Uganda* **54 B3** 3 20N 31 50 E
Adlavik Is., *Canada* **71 A8** 55 2N 57 45W
Admiralty G., *Australia* **60 B4** 14 20S 125 55 E
Admiralty I., *U.S.A.* **72 B2** 57 30N 134 30W
Admiralty Is., *Papua N. G.* **64 H6** 2 0S 147 0 E
Adonara, *Indonesia* **37 F6** 8 15S 123 5 E
Adoni, *India* **40 M10** 15 33N 77 18 E
Adour →, *France* **18 E3** 43 32N 1 32W
Adra, *India* **43 H12** 23 30N 86 42 E
Adra, *Spain* **19 D4** 36 43N 3 3W
Adrano, *Italy* **20 F6** 37 40N 14 50 E
Adrar, *Algeria* **48 D4** 27 51N 0 11 E
Adrar, *Mauritania* **50 D3** 20 30N 7 30 E
Adrian, *Mich., U.S.A.* **76 E3** 41 54N 84 2W
Adrian, *Tex., U.S.A.* **81 H3** 35 16N 102 40W
Adriatic Sea, *Medit. S.* **20 C6** 43 0N 16 0 E
Adua, *Indonesia* **37 E7** 1 45S 129 50 E
Adwa, *Ethiopia* **46 E2** 14 15N 38 52 E
Adygea □, *Russia* **25 F7** 45 0N 40 0 E
Adzhar Republic = Ajaria □, *Georgia* **25 F7** 41 30N 42 0 E
Adzopé, *Ivory C.* **50 G5** 6 7N 3 49W
Ægean Sea, *Medit. S.* **21 E11** 38 30N 25 0 E
Aerhtai Shan, *Mongolia* **32 B4** 46 40N 92 45 E
'Afak, *Iraq* **44 C5** 32 4N 45 15 E
Afándou, *Greece* **23 C10** 36 18N 28 12 E
Afghanistan ■, *Asia* **40 C4** 33 0N 65 0 E
Aflou, *Algeria* **50 B6** 34 7N 2 3 E
Africa **48 E6** 10 0N 20 0 E
'Afrīn, *Syria* **44 B3** 36 32N 36 50 E
Afton, *N.Y., U.S.A.* **79 D9** 42 14N 75 32W
Afton, *Wyo., U.S.A.* **82 E8** 42 44N 110 56W
Afuá, *Brazil* **93 D8** 0 15S 50 20W
'Afula, *Israel* **47 C4** 32 37N 35 17 E
Afyon, *Turkey* **25 G5** 38 45N 30 33 E
Afyonkarahisar = Afyon, *Turkey* **25 G5** 38 45N 30 33 E
Agadès = Agadez, *Niger* **50 E7** 16 58N 7 59 E
Agadez, *Niger* **50 E7** 16 58N 7 59 E
Agadir, *Morocco* **50 B4** 30 28N 9 55W
Agaete, *Canary Is.* **22 F4** 28 6N 15 43W
Agar, *India* **42 H7** 23 40N 76 2 E
Agartala, *India* **41 H17** 23 50N 91 23 E
Agassiz, *Canada* **72 D4** 49 14N 121 46W
Agats, *Indonesia* **37 F9** 5 33S 138 0 E
Agawam, *U.S.A.* **79 D12** 42 5N 72 37W
Agboville, *Ivory C.* **50 G5** 5 55N 4 15W
Ağdam, *Azerbaijan* **44 B5** 40 0N 46 58 E
Agde, *France* **18 E5** 43 19N 3 28 E
Agen, *France* **18 D4** 44 12N 0 38 E
Āgh Kand, *Iran* **45 B6** 37 15N 48 4 E
Aginskoye, *Russia* **27 D12** 51 6N 114 32 E
Agnew, *Australia* **61 E3** 28 1S 120 31 E
Agori, *India* **43 G10** 24 33N 82 57 E
Agra, *India* **42 F7** 27 17N 77 58 E
Ağrı, *Turkey* **25 G7** 39 44N 43 3 E
Agri →, *Italy* **20 D7** 40 13N 16 44 E
Ağrı Dağı, *Turkey* **25 G7** 39 50N 44 15 E
Ağrı Karakose = Ağrı, *Turkey* **25 G7** 39 44N 43 3 E
Agrigento, *Italy* **20 F5** 37 19N 13 34 E
Agrinion, *Greece* **21 E9** 38 37N 21 27 E
Agua Caliente, *Baja Calif., Mexico* **85 N10** 32 29N 116 59W
Agua Caliente, *Sinaloa, Mexico* **86 B3** 26 30N 108 20W
Agua Caliente Springs, *U.S.A.* **85 N10** 32 56N 116 19W
Água Clara, *Brazil* **93 H8** 20 25S 52 45W
Agua Hechicero, *Mexico* **85 N10** 32 26N 116 14W
Agua Prieta, *Mexico* **86 A3** 31 20N 109 32W
Aguadilla, *Puerto Rico* **89 C6** 18 26N 67 10W
Aguadulce, *Panama* **88 E3** 8 15N 80 32W
Aguanga, *U.S.A.* **85 M10** 33 27N 116 51W
Aguanish, *Canada* **71 B7** 50 14N 62 2W
Aguanus →, *Canada* **71 B7** 50 13N 62 5W
Aguapey →, *Argentina* **94 B4** 29 7S 56 36W
Aguaray Guazú →, *Paraguay* **94 A4** 24 47S 57 19W
Aguarico →, *Ecuador* **92 D3** 0 59S 75 11W
Aguas Blancas, *Chile* **94 A2** 24 15S 69 55W
Aguas Calientes, Sierra de, *Argentina* **94 B2** 25 26S 66 40W
Aguascalientes, *Mexico* **86 C4** 21 53N 102 12W
Aguascalientes □, *Mexico* **86 C4** 22 0N 102 20W
Aguilares, *Argentina* **94 B2** 27 26S 65 35W
Aguilas, *Spain* **19 D5** 37 23N 1 35W
Agüimes, *Canary Is.* **22 G4** 27 58N 15 27W
Aguja, C. de la, *Colombia* **90 B3** 11 18N 74 12W
Agulhas, C., *S. Africa* **56 E3** 34 52S 20 0 E
Agulo, *Canary Is.* **22 F2** 28 11N 17 12W
Agung, *Indonesia* **36 F5** 8 20S 115 28 E
Agur, *Uganda* **54 B3** 2 28N 32 55 E
Agusan →, *Phil.* **37 C7** 9 0N 125 30 E
Aha Mts., *Botswana* **56 B3** 19 45S 21 0 E
Ahaggar, *Algeria* **50 D7** 23 0N 6 30 E
Ahar, *Iran* **44 B5** 38 35N 47 0 E
Ahipara B., *N.Z.* **59 F4** 35 5S 173 5 E
Ahiri, *India* **40 K12** 19 30N 80 0 E
Ahmad Wal, *Pakistan* **42 E1** 29 18N 65 58 E
Ahmadabad, *India* **42 H5** 23 0N 72 40 E
Aḩmadābād, *Khorāsān, Iran* **45 C9** 35 3N 60 50 E
Aḩmadābād, *Khorāsān, Iran* **45 C8** 35 49N 59 42 E
Aḩmadī, *Iran* **45 E8** 27 56N 56 42 E
Ahmadnagar, *India* **40 K9** 19 7N 74 46 E
Ahmadpur, *Pakistan* **42 E4** 29 12N 71 10 E
Ahmadpur Lamma, *Pakistan* **42 E4** 28 19N 70 3 E
Ahmedabad = Ahmadabad, *India* **42 H5** 23 0N 72 40 E
Ahmednagar = Ahmadnagar, *India* **40 K9** 19 7N 74 46 E
Ahome, *Mexico* **86 B3** 25 55N 109 11W
Ahoskie, *U.S.A.* **77 G7** 36 17N 76 59W
Ahram, *Iran* **45 D6** 28 52N 51 16 E
Ahrax Pt., *Malta* **23 D1** 35 59N 14 22 E
Āhū, *Iran* **45 C6** 34 33N 50 2 E
Ahuachapán, *El Salv.* **88 D2** 13 54N 89 52W
Ahvāz, *Iran* **45 D6** 31 20N 48 40 E
Ahvenanmaa = Åland, *Finland* **9 F19** 60 15N 20 0 E
Aḩwar, *Yemen* **46 E4** 13 30N 46 40 E
Ai →, *India* **43 F14** 26 26N 90 44 E
Aichi □, *Japan* **31 G8** 35 0N 137 15 E
Aigua, *Uruguay* **95 C5** 34 13S 54 46W
Aigues-Mortes, *France* **18 E6** 43 35N 4 12 E
Aihui, *China* **33 A7** 50 10N 127 30 E
Aija, *Peru* **92 E3** 9 50S 77 45W
Aikawa, *Japan* **30 E9** 38 2N 138 15 E
Aiken, *U.S.A.* **77 J5** 33 34N 81 43W
Aileron, *Australia* **62 C1** 22 39S 133 20 E
Aillik, *Canada* **71 A8** 55 11N 59 18W
Ailsa Craig, *U.K.* **12 F3** 55 15N 5 6W
'Ailūn, *Jordan* **47 C4** 32 18N 35 47 E
Aim, *Russia* **27 D14** 59 0N 133 55 E
Aimere, *Indonesia* **37 F6** 8 45S 121 3 E
Aimogasta, *Argentina* **94 B2** 28 33S 66 50W
Aïn Ben Tili, *Mauritania* **50 C4** 25 59N 9 27W
Aïn-Sefra, *Algeria* **50 B5** 32 47N 0 37W
'Ain Sudr, *Egypt* **47 F2** 29 50N 33 6 E
Ainaži, *Latvia* **9 H21** 57 50N 24 24 E
Ainsworth, *U.S.A.* **80 D5** 42 33N 99 52W
Aiquile, *Bolivia* **92 G5** 18 10S 65 10W
Aïr, *Niger* **50 E7** 18 30N 8 0 E
Air Force I., *Canada* **69 B12** 67 58N 74 5W
Air Hitam, *Malaysia* **39 M4** 1 55N 103 11 E
Airdrie, *Canada* **72 C6** 51 18N 114 2W
Airdrie, *U.K.* **12 F5** 55 52N 3 57W
Aire →, *U.K.* **10 D7** 53 43N 0 55W
Aire, I. de l', *Spain* **22 B11** 39 48N 4 16 E
Airlie Beach, *Australia* **62 C4** 20 16S 148 43 E
Aisne →, *France* **18 B5** 49 26N 2 50 E
Ait, *India* **43 G8** 25 54N 79 14 E
Aitkin, *U.S.A.* **80 B8** 46 32N 93 42W
Aiud, *Romania* **17 E12** 46 19N 23 44 E
Aix-en-Provence, *France* **18 E6** 43 32N 5 27 E
Aix-la-Chapelle = Aachen, *Germany* **16 C4** 50 45N 6 6 E
Aix-les-Bains, *France* **18 D6** 45 41N 5 53 E
Aíyion, *Greece* **21 E10** 38 15N 22 5 E
Aizawl, *India* **41 H18** 23 40N 92 44 E
Aizkraukle, *Latvia* **9 H21** 56 36N 25 11 E
Aizpute, *Latvia* **9 H19** 56 43N 21 40 E
Aizuwakamatsu, *Japan* **30 F9** 37 30N 139 56 E
Ajaccio, *France* **18 F8** 41 55N 8 40 E
Ajaigarh, *India* **43 G9** 24 52N 80 16 E
Ajalpan, *Mexico* **87 D5** 18 22N 97 15W
Ajanta Ra., *India* **40 J9** 20 28N 75 50 E
Ajari Rep. = Ajaria □, *Georgia* **25 F7** 41 30N 42 0 E
Ajaria □, *Georgia* **25 F7** 41 30N 42 0 E
Ajax, *Canada* **78 C5** 43 50N 79 1W
Ajdâbiyah, *Libya* **51 B10** 30 54N 20 4 E
Ajka, *Hungary* **17 E9** 47 4N 17 31 E
'Ajmān, *U.A.E.* **45 E7** 25 25N 55 30 E
Ajmer, *India* **42 F6** 26 28N 74 37 E
Ajnala, *India* **42 D6** 31 50N 74 48 E
Ajo, *U.S.A.* **83 K7** 32 22N 112 52W
Ajo, C. de, *Spain* **19 A4** 43 31N 3 35W
Akabira, *Japan* **30 C11** 43 33N 142 5 E
Akamas □, *Cyprus* **23 D11** 35 3N 32 18 E
Akanthou, *Cyprus* **23 D12** 35 22N 33 45 E
Akaroa, *N.Z.* **59 K4** 43 49S 172 59 E
Akashi, *Japan* **31 G7** 34 45N 134 58 E
Akbarpur, *Bihar, India* **43 G10** 24 39N 83 58 E
Akbarpur, *Ut. P., India* **43 F10** 26 25N 82 32 E
Akelamo, *Indonesia* **37 D7** 1 35N 129 40 E
Aketi, *Dem. Rep. of the Congo* **52 D4** 2 38N 23 47 E
Akharnai, *Greece* **21 E10** 38 5N 23 44 E
Akhelóös →, *Greece* **21 E9** 38 19N 21 7 E
Akhisar, *Turkey* **21 E12** 38 56N 27 48 E
Akhnur, *India* **43 C6** 32 52N 74 45 E
Akhtyrka = Okhtyrka, *Ukraine* **25 D5** 50 25N 35 0 E
Aki, *Japan* **31 H6** 33 30N 133 54 E
Akimiski I., *Canada* **70 B3** 52 50N 81 30W
Akita, *Japan* **30 E10** 39 45N 140 7 E
Akita □, *Japan* **30 E10** 39 40N 140 30 E
Akjoujt, *Mauritania* **50 E3** 19 45N 14 15W
Akkeshi, *Japan* **30 C12** 43 2N 144 51 E
'Akko, *Israel* **47 C4** 32 55N 35 4 E
Aklavik, *Canada* **68 B6** 68 12N 135 0W
Aklera, *India* **42 G7** 24 26N 76 32 E
Akmolinsk = Astana, *Kazakstan* **26 D8** 51 10N 71 30 E
Akō, *Japan* **31 G7** 34 45N 134 24 E
Akola, *India* **40 J10** 20 42N 77 2 E
Akordat, *Eritrea* **46 D2** 15 30N 37 40 E
Akpatok I., *Canada* **69 B13** 60 25N 68 8W
Åkrahamn, *Norway* **9 G11** 59 15N 5 10 E
Akranes, *Iceland* **8 D2** 64 19N 22 5W
Akron, *Colo., U.S.A.* **80 E3** 40 10N 103 13W
Akron, *Ohio, U.S.A.* **78 E3** 41 5N 81 31W
Akrotiri, *Cyprus* **23 E11** 34 36N 32 57 E
Akrotiri Bay, *Cyprus* **23 E12** 34 35N 33 10 E
Aksai Chin, *India* **43 B8** 35 15N 79 55 E
Aksaray, *Turkey* **25 G5** 38 25N 34 2 E
Aksay, *Kazakstan* **25 D9** 51 11N 53 0 E
Akşehir, *Turkey* **44 B1** 38 18N 31 30 E
Akşehir Gölü, *Turkey* **25 G5** 38 30N 31 25 E
Aksu, *China* **32 B3** 41 5N 80 10 E
Aksum, *Ethiopia* **46 E2** 14 5N 38 40 E
Aktogay, *Kazakstan* **26 E8** 46 57N 79 40 E
Aktsyabrski, *Belarus* **17 B15** 52 38N 28 53 E
Aktyubinsk = Aqtöbe, *Kazakstan* **25 D10** 50 17N 57 10 E
Akure, *Nigeria* **50 G7** 7 15N 5 5 E
Akureyri, *Iceland* **8 D4** 65 40N 18 6W
Akuseki-Shima, *Japan* **31 K4** 29 27N 129 37 E
Akyab = Sittwe, *Burma* **41 J18** 20 18N 92 45 E
Al 'Adan, *Yemen* **46 E4** 12 45N 45 0 E
Al Aḩsā = Hasa □, *Si. Arabia* **45 E6** 25 50N 49 0 E
Al Ajfar, *Si. Arabia* **44 E4** 27 26N 43 0 E
Al Amādīyah, *Iraq* **44 B4** 37 5N 43 30 E
Al 'Amārah, *Iraq* **44 D5** 31 55N 47 15 E
Al 'Aqabah, *Jordan* **47 F4** 29 31N 35 0 E
Al Arak, *Syria* **44 C3** 34 38N 38 35 E
Al 'Aramah, *Si. Arabia* **44 E5** 25 30N 46 0 E
Al Arţāwīyah, *Si. Arabia* **44 E5** 26 31N 45 20 E
Al 'Āşimah = 'Ammān □, *Jordan* **47 D5** 31 40N 36 30 E
Al 'Assāfīyah, *Si. Arabia* **44 D3** 28 17N 38 59 E
Al 'Ayn, *Oman* **45 E7** 24 15N 55 45 E
Al 'Ayn, *Si. Arabia* **44 E3** 25 4N 38 6 E
Al 'Azamīyah, *Iraq* **44 C5** 33 22N 44 22 E
Al 'Azīzīyah, *Iraq* **44 C5** 32 54N 45 4 E
Al Bāb, *Syria* **44 B3** 36 23N 37 29 E
Al Bad', *Si. Arabia* **44 D2** 28 28N 35 1 E
Al Bādī, *Iraq* **44 C4** 35 56N 41 32 E
Al Baḩrah, *Kuwait* **44 D5** 29 40N 47 52 E
Al Baḩral Mayyit = Dead Sea, *Asia* **47 D4** 31 30N 35 30 E
Al Balqā' □, *Jordan* **47 C4** 32 5N 35 45 E
Al Bārūk, J., *Lebanon* **47 B4** 33 39N 35 40 E
Al Başrah, *Iraq* **44 D5** 30 30N 47 50 E
Al Baţḩā, *Iraq* **44 D5** 31 6N 45 53 E
Al Batrūn, *Lebanon* **47 A4** 34 15N 35 40 E
Al Baydā, *Libya* **51 B10** 32 50N 21 44 E
Al Biqā, *Lebanon* **47 A5** 34 10N 36 10 E
Al Bi'r, *Si. Arabia* **44 D3** 28 51N 36 16 E
Al Burayj, *Syria* **47 A5** 34 15N 36 46 E
Al Faḑilī, *Si. Arabia* **45 E6** 26 58N 49 10 E

Amadeus, L.

Al Fallūjah, Iraq 44 C4 33 20N 43 55 E
Al Fāw, Iraq 45 D6 30 0N 48 30 E
Al Fujayrah, U.A.E. 45 E8 25 7N 56 18 E
Al Ghadaf, W. →, Jordan 47 D5 31 26N 36 43 E
Al Ghammās, Iraq 44 D5 31 45N 44 37 E
Al Ghazālah, Si. Arabia 44 E4 26 48N 41 19 E
Al Hābah, Si. Arabia 44 E5 27 10N 47 0 E
Al Ḥadīthah, Iraq 44 C4 34 0N 41 13 E
Al Ḥadīthah, Si. Arabia 47 D6 31 28N 37 8 E
Al Ḥaḍr, Iraq 44 C4 35 35N 42 44 E
Al Ḥājānah, Syria 47 B5 33 20N 36 33 E
Al Hajar al Gharbi, Oman 45 E8 24 10N 56 15 E
Al Hāmad, Si. Arabia 44 D3 31 30N 39 30 E
Al Hamdāniyah, Syria 44 C3 35 25N 36 50 E
Al Ḥamīdīyah, Syria 47 A4 34 42N 35 57 E
Al Ḥammār, Iraq 44 D5 30 57N 46 51 E
Al Ḥamrā', Si. Arabia 44 E3 24 2N 38 55 E
Al Ḥanākīyah, Si. Arabia 44 E4 24 51N 40 31 E
Al Ḥarīr, W. →, Syria 47 C4 32 44N 35 59 E
Al Ḥasā, W. →, Jordan 47 D4 31 4N 35 29 E
Al Ḥasakah, Syria 44 B4 36 35N 40 45 E
Al Ḥaydān, W. →, Jordan 47 D4 31 29N 35 34 E
Al Ḥayy, Iraq 44 C5 32 5N 46 5 E
Al Ḥijarah, Asia 44 D4 30 0N 44 0 E
Al Ḥillah, Iraq 44 C5 32 30N 44 25 E
Al Hindīyah, Iraq 44 C5 32 30N 44 10 E
Al Hirmil, Lebanon 47 A5 34 26N 36 24 E
Al Hoceïma, Morocco 50 A5 35 8N 3 58W
Al Ḥudaydah, Yemen 46 E3 14 50N 43 0 E
Al Hufūf, Si. Arabia 45 E6 25 25N 49 45 E
Al Ḥumayḍah, Si. Arabia 44 D2 29 14N 34 56 E
Al Ḥunayy, Si. Arabia 45 E6 25 58N 48 45 E
Al 'Isāwīyah, Si. Arabia 44 D3 30 43N 37 59 E
Al Jafr, Jordan 47 E5 30 18N 36 14 E
Al Jāfūrah, Si. Arabia 45 E7 25 0N 50 15 E
Al Jaghbūb, Libya 51 C10 29 42N 24 38 E
Al Jahrah, Kuwait 44 D5 29 25N 47 40 E
Al Jalāmīd, Si. Arabia 44 D3 31 20N 40 6 E
Al Jamalīyah, Qatar 45 E6 25 37N 51 5 E
Al Janūb □, Lebanon 47 B4 33 20N 35 20 E
Al Jawf, Libya 51 D10 24 10N 23 24 E
Al Jawf, Si. Arabia 44 D3 29 55N 39 40 E
Al Jazirah, Iraq 44 C5 33 30N 44 0 E
Al Jithāmīyah, Si. Arabia 44 E4 27 41N 41 43 E
Al Jubayl, Si. Arabia 45 E6 27 0N 49 50 E
Al Jubaylah, Si. Arabia 45 E5 24 55N 46 25 E
Al Jubb, Si. Arabia 44 E4 27 11N 42 17 E
Al Junaynah, Sudan 51 F10 13 27N 22 45 E
Al Kabā'ish, Iraq 44 D5 30 58N 47 0 E
Al Karak, Jordan 47 D4 31 11N 35 42 E
Al Karak □, Jordan 47 E5 31 0N 36 0 E
Al Kāẓim Tyah, Iraq 44 C5 33 22N 44 12 E
Al Khābūra, Oman 45 F8 23 57N 57 5 E
Al Khafji, Si. Arabia 45 E6 28 24N 48 29 E
Al Khalīl, West Bank 47 D4 31 32N 35 6 E
Al Khāliş, Iraq 44 C5 33 49N 44 32 E
Al Kharsānīyah, Si. Arabia 45 E6 27 13N 49 18 E
Al Khaşab, Oman 45 E8 26 14N 56 15 E
Al Khawr, Qatar 45 E6 25 41N 51 30 E
Al Khiḍr, Iraq 44 D5 31 12N 45 33 E
Al Khiyām, Lebanon 47 B4 33 20N 35 36 E
Al Khums, Libya 51 B8 32 40N 14 17 E
Al Kiswah, Syria 47 B5 33 23N 36 14 E
Al Kūfah, Iraq 44 C5 32 2N 44 24 E
Al Kufrah, Libya 51 D10 24 17N 23 15 E
Al Kuhayfiyah, Si. Arabia 44 E4 27 12N 43 3 E
Al Kūt, Iraq 44 C5 32 30N 46 0 E
Al Kuwayt, Kuwait 44 D5 29 30N 48 0 E
Al Labwah, Lebanon 47 A5 34 11N 36 20 E
Al Lādhiqīyah, Syria 44 C2 35 30N 35 45 E
Al Līth, Si. Arabia 46 C3 20 9N 40 15 E
Al Liwā', Oman 45 E8 24 31N 56 36 E
Al Luḥayyah, Yemen 46 D3 15 45N 42 40 E
Al Madīnah, Iraq 44 D5 30 57N 47 16 E
Al Madīnah, Si. Arabia 46 C2 24 35N 39 52 E
Al Mafraq, Jordan 47 C5 32 17N 36 14 E
Al Maḥmūdīyah, Iraq 44 C5 33 3N 44 21 E
Al Majma'ah, Si. Arabia 44 E5 25 57N 45 22 E
Al Makhruq, W. →, Jordan 47 D6 31 28N 37 0 E
Al Makḥūl, Si. Arabia 44 E4 26 37N 42 39 E
Al Manāmah, Bahrain 45 E6 26 10N 50 30 E
Al Maqwa', Kuwait 44 D5 29 10N 47 59 E
Al Marj, Libya 51 B10 32 25N 20 30 E
Al Maṭlā, Kuwait 44 D5 29 24N 47 40 E
Al Mawjib, W. →, Jordan 47 D4 31 28N 35 36 E
Al Mawşil, Iraq 44 B4 36 15N 43 5 E
Al Mayādin, Syria 44 C4 35 1N 40 27 E
Al Mazār, Jordan 47 D4 31 4N 35 41 E
Al Midhnab, Si. Arabia 44 E5 25 50N 44 18 E
Al Minā', Lebanon 47 A4 34 24N 35 49 E
Al Miqdādīyah, Iraq 44 C5 34 0N 45 0 E
Al Mubarraz, Si. Arabia 45 E6 25 30N 49 40 E
Al Mudawwarah, Jordan 47 F5 29 19N 36 0 E
Al Mughayrā', U.A.E. 45 E7 24 5N 53 32 E
Al Muḥarraq, Bahrain 45 E6 26 15N 50 40 E
Al Mukallā, Yemen 46 E4 14 33N 49 2 E
Al Mukhā, Yemen 46 E3 13 18N 43 15 E
Al Musayjīd, Si. Arabia 44 E3 24 5N 39 5 E
Al Musayyib, Iraq 44 C5 32 49N 44 20 E
Al Muwayliḥ, Si. Arabia 44 E2 27 40N 35 30 E
Al Qā'im, Iraq 44 C4 34 21N 41 7 E
Al Qalībah, Si. Arabia 44 D3 28 24N 37 42 E
Al Qāmishli, Syria 44 B4 37 10N 41 10 E
Al Qaryatayn, Syria 47 A6 34 12N 37 13 E
Al Qaşīm, Si. Arabia 44 E4 26 0N 43 0 E
Al Qaṭ'ā, Syria 44 C4 34 40N 40 48 E
Al Qaṭīf, Si. Arabia 45 E6 26 35N 50 0 E
Al Qatrānah, Jordan 47 D5 31 12N 36 6 E
Al Qaṭrūn, Libya 51 D9 24 56N 15 3 E
Al Qayşūmah, Si. Arabia 44 D5 28 20N 46 7 E
Al Quds = Jerusalem, Israel 47 D4 31 47N 35 10 E
Al Qunayṭirah, Syria 47 C4 32 55N 35 45 E
Al Qurnah, Iraq 44 D5 31 1N 47 25 E
Al Quşayr, Iraq 44 D5 30 39N 45 50 E
Al Quşayr, Syria 47 A5 34 31N 36 34 E
Al Qutayfah, Syria 47 B5 33 44N 36 36 E
Al 'Ubaylah, Si. Arabia 46 C5 21 59N 50 57 E
Al 'Uḍaylīyah, Si. Arabia 45 E6 25 8N 49 18 E
Al 'Ulā, Si. Arabia 44 E3 26 35N 38 0 E
Al 'Uqayr, Si. Arabia 45 E6 25 40N 50 15 E
Al 'Uthmānīyah, Si. Arabia 45 E6 25 5N 49 22 E
Al 'Uwaynid, Si. Arabia 44 E5 24 50N 46 0 E
Al 'Uwayqīlah, Si. Arabia 44 D4 30 30N 42 10 E
Al 'Uyūn, Ḥijāz, Si. Arabia 44 E3 24 33N 39 35 E
Al 'Uyūn, Najd, Si. Arabia 44 E4 26 30N 43 50 E
Al 'Uzayr, Iraq 44 D5 31 19N 47 25 E
Al Wajh, Si. Arabia 44 E3 26 10N 36 30 E
Al Wakrah, Qatar 45 E6 25 10N 51 40 E
Al Wannān, Si. Arabia 45 E6 26 55N 48 24 E
Al Waqbah, Si. Arabia 44 D5 28 48N 45 33 E
Al Wari'āh, Si. Arabia 44 E5 27 51N 47 25 E
Al Wusayl, Qatar 45 E6 25 29N 51 29 E
Ala Dağ, Turkey 44 B2 37 44N 35 9 E
Ala Tau Shankou =
Dzungarian Gates,
Kazakstan 32 B3 45 0N 82 0 E
Alabama □, U.S.A. 77 J2 33 0N 87 0W
Alabama →, U.S.A. 77 K2 31 8N 87 57W
Alabaster, U.S.A. 77 J2 33 15N 86 49W
Alaçam Dağları, Turkey 21 E13 39 18N 28 49 E
Alachua, U.S.A. 77 L4 29 47N 82 30W
Alaérma, Greece 23 C9 36 9N 27 57 E
Alagoa Grande, Brazil 93 E11 7 3S 35 35W
Alagoas □, Brazil 93 E11 9 0S 36 0W
Alagoinhas, Brazil 93 F11 12 7S 38 20W
Alaior, Spain 22 B11 39 57N 4 8 E
Alajero, Canary Is. 22 F2 28 3N 17 13W
Alajuela, Costa Rica 88 D3 10 2N 84 8W
Alakamisy, Madag. 57 C8 21 19S 47 14 E
Alaknanda →, India 43 D8 30 8N 78 36 E
Alakurtti, Russia 24 A5 67 0N 30 30 E
Alamarvdasht, Iran 45 E7 27 37N 52 59 E
Alameda, Calif., U.S.A. 84 H4 37 46N 122 15W
Alameda, N. Mex., U.S.A. 83 J10 35 11N 106 37W
Alamo, U.S.A. 85 J11 37 22N 115 10W
Alamo Crossing, U.S.A. 85 L13 34 16N 113 33W
Alamogordo, U.S.A. 83 K11 32 54N 105 57W
Alamos, Mexico 86 B3 27 0N 109 0W
Alamosa, U.S.A. 83 H11 37 28N 105 52W
Åland, Finland 9 F19 60 15N 20 0 E
Ålands hav, Sweden 9 F18 60 0N 19 30 E
Alandur, India 40 N12 13 0N 80 15 E
Alania = North Ossetia □,
Russia 25 F7 43 30N 44 30 E
Alanya, Turkey 25 G5 36 38N 32 0 E
Alaotra, Farihin', Madag. 57 B8 17 30S 48 30 E
Alapayevsk, Russia 26 D7 57 52N 61 42 E
Alaşehir, Turkey 21 E13 38 23N 28 30 E
Alaska □, U.S.A. 68 B5 64 0N 154 0W
Alaska, G. of, Pac. Oc. 68 C5 58 0N 145 0W
Alaska Peninsula, U.S.A. 68 C4 56 0N 159 0W
Alaska Range, U.S.A. 68 B4 62 50N 151 0W
Älät, Azerbaijan 25 G8 39 58N 49 25 E
Alatyr, Russia 24 D8 54 55N 46 35 E
Alausi, Ecuador 92 D3 2 0S 78 50W
Alava, C., U.S.A. 82 B1 48 10N 124 44W
Alavus, Finland 9 E20 62 35N 23 36 E
Alawoona, Australia 63 E3 34 45S 140 30 E
'Alayh, Lebanon 47 B4 33 46N 35 33 E
Alba, Italy 18 D8 44 42N 8 2 E
Alba-Iulia, Romania 17 E12 46 8N 23 39 E
Albacete, Spain 19 C5 39 0N 1 50W
Albacutya, L., Australia 63 F3 35 45S 141 58 E
Albanel, L., Canada 70 B5 50 55N 73 12W
Albania ■, Europe 21 D9 41 0N 20 0 E
Albany, Australia 61 G2 35 1S 117 58 E
Albany, Ga., U.S.A. 77 K3 31 35N 84 10W
Albany, N.Y., U.S.A. 79 D11 42 39N 73 45W
Albany, Oreg., U.S.A. 82 D2 44 38N 123 6W
Albany, Tex., U.S.A. 81 J5 32 44N 99 18W
Albany →, Canada 70 B3 52 17N 81 31W
Albardón, Argentina 94 C2 31 20S 68 30W
Albatross B., Australia 62 A3 12 45S 141 30 E
Albemarle, U.S.A. 77 H5 35 21N 80 11W
Albemarle Sd., U.S.A. 77 H7 36 5N 76 0W
Alberche →, Spain 19 C3 39 58N 4 46W
Alberdi, Paraguay 94 B4 26 14S 58 20W
Albert, L., Australia 63 F2 35 30S 139 10 E
Albert Edward Ra., Australia 60 C4 18 17S 127 57 E
Albert L., Africa 54 B3 1 30N 31 0 E
Albert Lea, U.S.A. 80 D8 43 39N 93 22W
Albert Nile →, Uganda 54 B3 3 36N 32 2 E
Albert Town, Bahamas 89 B5 22 37N 74 33W
Alberta □, Canada 72 C6 54 40N 115 0W
Alberti, Argentina 94 D3 35 1S 60 16W
Albertinia, S. Africa 56 E3 34 11S 21 34 E
Alberton, Canada 71 C7 46 50N 64 0W
Albertville = Kalemie,
Dem. Rep. of the Congo 54 D2 5 55S 29 9 E
Albertville, France 18 D7 45 40N 6 22 E
Albertville, U.S.A. 77 H2 34 16N 86 13W
Albi, France 18 E5 43 56N 2 9 E
Albia, U.S.A. 80 E8 41 2N 92 48W
Albina, Surinam 93 B8 5 37N 54 15W
Albina, Ponta, Angola 56 B1 15 52S 11 44 E
Albion, Mich., U.S.A. 76 D3 42 15N 84 45W
Albion, Nebr., U.S.A. 80 E6 41 42N 98 0W
Albion, Pa., U.S.A. 78 E4 41 53N 80 22W
Alborán, Medit. S. 19 E4 35 57N 3 0W
Ålborg, Denmark 9 H13 57 2N 9 54 E
Alborz, Reshteh-ye Kūhhā-
ye, Iran 45 C7 36 0N 52 0 E
Albuquerque, U.S.A. 83 J10 35 5N 106 39W
Albuquerque, Cayos de,
Caribbean 88 D3 12 10N 81 50W
Alburg, U.S.A. 79 B11 44 59N 73 18W
Albury-Wodonga, Australia 63 F4 36 3S 146 56 E
Alcalá de Henares, Spain 19 B4 40 28N 3 22W
Alcalá la Real, Spain 19 D4 37 27N 3 57W
Álcamo, Italy 20 F5 37 59N 12 55 E
Alcaníz, Spain 19 B5 41 2N 0 8W
Alcântara, Brazil 93 D10 2 20S 44 30W
Alcántara, Embalse de,
Spain 19 C2 39 44N 6 50W
Alcantarilla, Spain 19 D5 37 59N 1 12W
Alcaraz, Sierra de, Spain 19 C4 38 40N 2 20W
Alcaudete, Spain 19 D3 37 35N 4 5W
Alcázar de San Juan, Spain 19 C4 39 24N 3 12W
Alchevsk, Ukraine 25 E6 48 30N 38 45 E
Alcira = Alzira, Spain 19 C5 39 9N 0 30W
Alcova, U.S.A. 82 E10 42 34N 106 43W
Alcoy, Spain 19 C5 38 43N 0 30W
Alcúdia, Spain 22 B10 39 51N 3 7 E
Alcúdia, B. d', Spain 22 B10 39 47N 3 15 E
Aldabra Is., Seychelles 49 G8 9 22S 46 28 E
Aldama, Mexico 87 C5 23 0N 98 4W
Aldan, Russia 27 D13 58 40N 125 30 E
Aldan →, Russia 27 C13 63 28N 129 35 E
Aldea, Pta. de la, Canary Is. 22 G4 28 0N 15 50W
Aldeburgh, U.K. 11 E9 52 10N 1 37 E
Alder Pk., U.S.A. 84 K5 35 53N 121 22W
Alderney, U.K. 11 H5 49 42N 2 11W
Aldershot, U.K. 11 F7 51 15N 0 44W
Aledo, U.S.A. 80 E9 41 12N 90 45W
Aleg, Mauritania 50 E3 17 3N 13 55W
Alegranza, Canary Is. 22 E6 29 23N 13 32W
Alegranza, I., Canary Is. 22 E6 29 23N 13 32W
Alegre, Brazil 95 A7 20 50S 41 30W
Alegrete, Brazil 95 B4 29 40S 56 0W
Aleisk, Russia 26 D9 52 40N 83 0 E
Aleksandriya =
Oleksandriya, Ukraine 17 C14 50 37N 26 19 E
Aleksandrov Gay, Russia 25 D8 50 9N 48 34 E
Aleksandrovsk-Sakhalinskiy,
Russia 27 D15 50 50N 142 20 E
Além Paraíba, Brazil 95 A7 21 52S 42 41W
Alemania, Argentina 94 B2 25 40S 65 30W
Alemania, Chile 94 B2 25 10S 69 55W
Alençon, France 18 B4 48 27N 0 4 E
Alenquer, Brazil 93 D8 1 56S 54 46W
Alenuihaha Channel, U.S.A. 74 H17 20 30N 156 0W
Aleppo = Ḥalab, Syria 44 B3 36 10N 37 15 E
Alès, France 18 D6 44 9N 4 5 E
Alessándria, Italy 18 D8 44 54N 8 37 E
Ålesund, Norway 9 E12 62 28N 6 12 E
Aleutian Is., Pac. Oc. 68 C2 52 0N 175 0W
Aleutian Trench, Pac. Oc. 64 C10 48 0N 180 0 E
Alexander, U.S.A. 80 B3 47 51N 103 39W
Alexander, Mt., Australia 61 E3 28 58S 120 16 E
Alexander Arch., U.S.A. 68 C6 56 0N 136 0W
Alexander Bay, S. Africa 56 D2 28 40S 16 30 E
Alexander City, U.S.A. 77 J3 32 56N 85 58W
Alexander I., Antarctica 5 C17 69 0S 70 0W
Alexandra, Australia 63 F4 37 8S 145 40 E
Alexandra, N.Z. 59 L2 45 14S 169 25 E
Alexandra Falls, Canada 72 A5 60 29N 116 18W
Alexandria = El Iskandarîya,
Egypt 51 B11 31 13N 29 58 E
Alexandria, B.C., Canada 72 C4 52 35N 122 27W
Alexandria, Ont., Canada 79 A10 45 19N 74 38W
Alexandria, Romania 17 G13 43 57N 25 24 E
Alexandria, S. Africa 56 E4 33 38S 26 28 E
Alexandria, U.K. 12 F4 55 59N 4 35W
Alexandria, La., U.S.A. 81 K8 31 18N 92 27W
Alexandria, Minn., U.S.A. 80 C7 45 53N 95 22W
Alexandria, S. Dak., U.S.A. 80 D6 43 39N 97 47W
Alexandria, Va., U.S.A. 76 F7 38 48N 77 3W
Alexandria Bay, U.S.A. 79 B9 44 20N 75 55W
Alexandrina, L., Australia 63 F2 35 25S 139 10 E
Alexandroúpolis, Greece 21 D11 40 50N 25 54 E
Alexis →, Canada 71 B8 52 33N 56 8W
Alexis Creek, Canada 72 C4 52 10N 123 20W
Alfabia, Spain 22 B9 39 44N 2 44 E
Alfenas, Brazil 95 A6 21 20S 46 10W
Alford, Aberds., U.K. 12 D6 57 14N 2 41W
Alford, Lincs., U.K. 10 D8 53 15N 0 10 E
Alfred, Maine, U.S.A. 79 C14 43 29N 70 43W
Alfred, N.Y., U.S.A. 78 D7 42 16N 77 48W
Alfreton, U.K. 10 D6 53 6N 1 24W
Alga, Kazakstan 25 E10 49 53N 57 20 E
Algaida, Spain 22 B9 39 33N 2 53 E
Ålgård, Norway 9 G11 58 46N 5 53 E
Algarve, Portugal 19 D1 36 58N 8 20W
Algeciras, Spain 19 D3 36 9N 5 28W
Algemesí, Spain 19 C5 39 11N 0 27W
Alger, Algeria 50 A6 36 42N 3 8 E
Algeria ■, Africa 50 C6 28 30N 2 0 E
Alghero, Italy 20 D3 40 33N 8 19 E
Algiers = Alger, Algeria 50 A6 36 42N 3 8 E
Algoa B., S. Africa 56 E4 33 50S 25 45 E
Algoma, U.S.A. 76 C2 44 36N 87 26W
Algona, U.S.A. 80 D7 43 4N 94 14W
Algonac, U.S.A. 78 D2 42 37N 82 32W
Algonquin Prov. Park,
Canada 70 C4 45 50N 78 30W
Algorta, Uruguay 96 C5 32 25S 57 23W
Alhambra, U.S.A. 85 L8 34 8N 118 6W
Alhucemas = Al Hoceïma,
Morocco 50 A5 35 8N 3 58W
'Alī al Gharbī, Iraq 44 C5 32 30N 46 45 E
'Alī ash Sharqī, Iraq 44 C5 32 7N 46 44 E
'Alī Khēl, Afghan. 42 C3 33 57N 69 43 E
Alī Shāh, Iran 44 B5 38 9N 45 50 E
'Alīābād, Khorāsān, Iran 45 C8 32 30N 57 30 E
'Alīābād, Kordestān, Iran 44 C5 35 4N 46 58 E
'Alīābād, Yazd, Iran 45 D7 31 41N 53 49 E
Aliağa, Turkey 21 E12 38 47N 26 59 E
Aliákmon →, Greece 21 D10 40 30N 22 36 E
Alicante, Spain 19 C5 38 23N 0 30W
Alice, S. Africa 56 E4 32 48S 26 55 E
Alice, U.S.A. 81 M5 27 45N 98 5W
Alice →, Queens.,
Australia 62 C3 24 2S 144 50 E
Alice →, Queens.,
Australia 62 B3 15 35S 142 20 E
Alice Arm, Canada 72 B3 55 29N 129 31W
Alice Springs, Australia 62 C1 23 40S 133 50 E
Alicedale, S. Africa 56 E4 33 15S 26 4 E
Aliceville, U.S.A. 77 J1 33 8N 88 9W
Aliganj, India 43 F8 27 30N 79 10 E
Aligarh, Raj., India 42 G7 25 55N 76 15 E
Aligarh, Ut. P., India 42 F8 27 55N 78 10 E
Alīgūdarz, Iran 45 C6 33 25N 49 45 E
Alimnía, Greece 23 C9 36 16N 27 43 E
Alingsås, Sweden 9 H15 57 56N 12 31 E
Alipur, Pakistan 42 E4 29 25N 70 55 E
Alipur Duar, India 41 F16 26 30N 89 35 E
Aliquippa, U.S.A. 78 F4 40 37N 80 15W
Alitus = Alytus, Lithuania 9 J21 54 24N 24 3 E
Aliwal North, S. Africa 56 E4 30 45S 26 45 E
Alix, Canada 72 C6 52 24N 113 11W
Aljustrel, Portugal 19 D1 37 55N 8 10W
Alkmaar, Neths. 15 B4 52 37N 4 45 E
All American Canal, U.S.A. 83 K6 32 45N 115 15W
Allagash →, U.S.A. 77 B11 47 5N 69 3W
Allah Dad, Pakistan 42 G2 25 38N 67 34 E
Allahabad, India 43 G9 25 25N 81 58 E
Allan, Canada 73 C7 51 53N 106 4W
Allanmyo, Burma 41 K19 19 30N 95 17 E
Allanridge, S. Africa 56 D4 27 45S 26 40 E
Allegany, U.S.A. 78 D6 42 6N 78 30W
Allegheny →, U.S.A. 78 F5 40 27N 80 1W
Allegheny Mts., U.S.A. 76 G6 38 15N 80 10W
Allegheny Reservoir, U.S.A. 78 E6 41 50N 79 0W
Allen, Bog of, Ireland 13 C5 53 15N 7 0W
Allen, L., Ireland 13 B3 54 8N 8 4W
Allendale, U.S.A. 77 J5 33 1N 81 18W
Allende, Mexico 86 B4 28 20N 100 50W
Allentown, U.S.A. 79 F9 40 37N 75 29W
Alleppey, India 40 Q10 9 30N 76 28 E
Aller →, Germany 16 B5 52 56N 9 12 E
Alliance, Nebr., U.S.A. 80 D3 42 6N 102 52W
Alliance, Ohio, U.S.A. 78 F3 40 55N 81 6W
Allier →, France 18 C5 46 57N 3 4 E
Alliford Bay, Canada 72 C2 53 12N 131 58W
Alliston, Canada 78 B5 44 9N 79 52W
Alloa, U.K. 12 E5 56 7N 3 47W
Allora, Australia 63 D5 28 2S 152 0 E
Alluitsup Paa = Sydprøven,
Greenland 4 C5 60 30N 45 35W
Alma, Canada 71 C5 48 35N 71 40W
Alma, Ga., U.S.A. 77 K4 31 33N 82 28W
Alma, Kans., U.S.A. 80 F6 39 1N 96 17W
Alma, Mich., U.S.A. 76 D3 43 23N 84 39W
Alma, Nebr., U.S.A. 80 E5 40 6N 99 22W
Alma Ata = Almaty,
Kazakstan 26 E8 43 15N 76 57 E
Almada, Portugal 19 C1 38 40N 9 9W
Almaden, Australia 62 B3 17 22S 144 40 E
Almadén, Spain 19 C3 38 49N 4 52W
Almanor, L., U.S.A. 82 F3 40 14N 121 9W
Almansa, Spain 19 C5 38 51N 1 5W
Almanzor, Pico, Spain 19 B3 40 15N 5 18W
Almanzora →, Spain 19 D5 37 14N 1 46W
Almaty, Kazakstan 26 E8 43 15N 76 57 E
Almazán, Spain 19 B4 41 30N 2 30W
Almeirim, Brazil 93 D8 1 30S 52 34W
Almelo, Neths. 15 B6 52 22N 6 42 E
Almendralejo, Spain 19 C2 38 41N 6 26W
Almere-Stad, Neths. 15 B5 52 20N 5 15 E
Almería, Spain 19 D4 36 52N 2 27W
Almirante, Panama 88 E3 9 10N 82 30W
Almiroú, Kólpos, Greece 23 D6 35 23N 24 20 E
Almond, U.S.A. 78 D7 42 19N 77 44W
Almont, U.S.A. 78 D1 42 55N 83 3W
Almonte, Canada 79 A8 45 14N 76 12W
Almora, India 43 E8 29 38N 79 40 E
Alness, U.K. 12 D4 57 41N 4 16W
Alnmouth, U.K. 10 B6 55 24N 1 37W
Alnwick, U.K. 10 B6 55 24N 1 42W
Aloi, Uganda 54 B3 2 16N 33 10 E
Alon, Burma 41 H19 22 12N 95 5 E
Alor, Indonesia 37 F6 8 15S 124 30 E
Alor Setar, Malaysia 39 J3 6 7N 100 22 E
Alot, India 42 H6 23 56N 75 40 E
Aloysius, Mt., Australia 61 E4 26 0S 128 38 E
Alpaugh, U.S.A. 84 K7 35 53N 119 29W
Alpena, U.S.A. 76 C4 45 4N 83 27W
Alpha, Australia 62 C4 23 39S 146 37 E
Alphen aan den Rijn, Neths. 15 B4 52 7N 4 40 E
Alpine, Ariz., U.S.A. 83 K9 33 51N 109 9W
Alpine, Calif., U.S.A. 85 N10 32 50N 116 46W
Alpine, Tex., U.S.A. 81 K3 30 22N 103 40W
Alps, Europe 18 C8 46 30N 9 30 E
Alsace, France 18 B7 48 15N 7 25 E
Alsask, Canada 73 C7 51 21N 109 59W
Alsasua, Spain 19 A4 42 54N 2 10W
Alsek →, U.S.A. 72 B1 59 10N 138 12W
Alsten, Norway 8 D15 65 58N 12 40 E
Alston, U.K. 10 C5 54 49N 2 25W
Alta, Norway 8 B20 69 57N 23 10 E
Alta Gracia, Argentina 94 C3 31 40S 64 30W
Alta Sierra, U.S.A. 85 K8 35 42N 118 33W
Altaelva →, Norway 8 B20 69 54N 23 17 E
Altafjorden, Norway 8 A20 70 5N 23 5 E
Altai = Aerhtai Shan,
Mongolia 32 B4 46 40N 92 45 E
Altamaha →, U.S.A. 77 K5 31 20N 81 20W
Altamira, Brazil 93 D8 3 12S 52 10W
Altamira, Chile 94 B2 25 47S 69 51W
Altamira, Mexico 87 C5 22 24N 97 55W
Altamont, U.S.A. 79 D10 42 43N 74 3W
Altamura, Italy 20 D7 40 49N 16 33 E
Altanbulag, Mongolia 32 A5 50 16N 106 30 E
Altar, Mexico 86 A2 30 40N 111 50W
Altar, Desierto de, Mexico 86 B2 30 10N 112 0W
Altata, Mexico 86 C3 24 30N 108 0W
Altavista, U.S.A. 76 G6 37 6N 79 17W
Altay, China 32 B3 47 48N 88 10 E
Altea, Spain 19 C5 38 38N 0 2W
Altiplano = Bolivian Plateau,
S. Amer. 90 E4 20 0S 67 30W
Alto Araguaia, Brazil 93 G8 17 15S 53 20W
Alto Cuchumatanes =
Cuchumatanes, Sierra de
los, Guatemala 88 C1 15 35N 91 25W
Alto del Carmen, Chile 94 B1 28 46S 70 30W
Alto del Inca, Chile 94 A2 24 10S 68 10W
Alto Ligonha, Mozam. 55 F4 15 30S 38 11 E
Alto Molocue, Mozam. 55 F4 15 50S 37 35 E
Alto Paraguay □, Paraguay 94 A4 21 0S 58 30W
Alto Paraná □, Paraguay 95 B5 25 30S 54 50W
Alton, Canada 78 C4 43 54N 80 5W
Alton, U.K. 11 F7 51 9N 0 59W
Alton, Ill., U.S.A. 80 F9 38 53N 90 11W
Alton, N.H., U.S.A. 79 C13 43 27N 71 13W
Altoona, U.S.A. 78 F6 40 31N 78 24W
Altūn Kūprī, Iraq 44 C5 35 45N 44 9 E
Altun Shan, China 32 C3 38 30N 88 0 E
Alturas, U.S.A. 82 F3 41 29N 120 32W
Altus, U.S.A. 81 H5 34 38N 99 20W
Alucra, Turkey 25 F6 40 22N 38 47 E
Alūksne, Latvia 9 H22 57 24N 27 3 E
Alunite, U.S.A. 85 K12 35 59N 114 55W
Alusi, Indonesia 37 F8 7 35S 131 40 E
Alva, U.S.A. 81 G5 36 48N 98 40W
Alvarado, Mexico 87 D5 18 40N 95 50W
Alvarado, U.S.A. 81 J6 32 24N 97 13W
Alvaro Obregón, Presa,
Mexico 86 B3 27 55N 109 52W
Alvear, Argentina 94 B4 29 5S 56 30W
Alvesta, Sweden 9 H16 56 54N 14 35 E
Alvin, U.S.A. 81 L7 29 26N 95 15W
Alvinston, Canada 78 D3 42 49N 81 52W
Älvkarleby, Sweden 9 F17 60 34N 17 26 E
Alvord Desert, U.S.A. 82 E4 42 30N 118 25W
Älvsbyn, Sweden 8 D19 65 40N 21 0 E
Alwar, India 42 F7 27 38N 76 34 E
Alxa Zuoqi, China 34 E3 38 50N 105 40 E
Alyangula, Australia 62 A2 13 55S 136 30 E
Alyata = Älät, Azerbaijan 25 G8 39 58N 49 25 E
Alyth, U.K. 12 E5 56 38N 3 13W
Alytus, Lithuania 9 J21 54 24N 24 3 E
Alzada, U.S.A. 80 C2 45 2N 104 25W
Alzira, Spain 19 C5 39 9N 0 30W
Am-Timan, Chad 51 F10 11 0N 20 10 E
Amadeus, L., Australia 61 D5 24 54S 131 0 E

Bardstown

Bahir Dar, *Ethiopia* **46 E2** 11 37N 37 10 E
Bahmanzād, *Iran* **45 D6** 31 15N 51 47 E
Bahr el Ghazâl □, *Sudan* **51 G11** 7 0N 28 0 E
Bahraich, *India* **43 F9** 27 38N 81 37 E
Bahrain ■, *Asia* **45 E6** 26 0N 50 35 E
Bahror, *India* **42 F7** 27 51N 76 20 E
Bāhū Kalāt, *Iran* **45 E9** 25 43N 61 25 E
Bai Bung, Mui = Ca Mau, Mui, *Vietnam* **39 H5** 8 38N 104 44 E
Bai Duc, *Vietnam* **38 C5** 18 3N 105 49 E
Bai Thuong, *Vietnam* **38 C5** 19 54N 105 23 E
Baia Mare, *Romania* **17 E12** 47 40N 23 35 E
Baião, *Brazil* **93 D9** 2 40S 49 40W
Baïbokoum, *Chad* **51 G9** 7 46N 15 43 E
Baicheng, *China* **35 B12** 45 38N 122 42 E
Baidoa, *Somali Rep.* **46 G3** 3 8N 43 30 E
Baie Comeau, *Canada* **71 C6** 49 12N 68 10W
Baie-St-Paul, *Canada* **71 C5** 47 28N 70 32W
Baie Trinité, *Canada* **71 C6** 49 25N 67 20W
Baie Verte, *Canada* **71 C8** 49 55N 56 12W
Baihar, *India* **43 H9** 22 6N 80 33 E
Baihe, *China* **34 H6** 32 50N 110 5 E
Ba'ījī, *Iraq* **44 C4** 35 0N 43 30 E
Baijnath, *India* **43 E8** 29 55N 79 37 E
Baikal, L. = Baykal, Oz., *Russia* **27 D11** 53 0N 108 0 E
Baikunthpur, *India* **43 H10** 23 15N 82 33 E
Baile Atha Cliath = Dublin, *Ireland* **13 C5** 53 21N 6 15W
Băileşti, *Romania* **17 F12** 44 1N 23 20 E
Bainbridge, *Ga., U.S.A.* **77 K3** 30 55N 84 35W
Bainbridge, *N.Y., U.S.A.* **79 D9** 42 18N 75 29W
Baing, *Indonesia* **37 F6** 10 14S 120 34 E
Bainiu, *China* **34 H7** 32 50N 112 15 E
Bā'ir, *Jordan* **47 E5** 30 45N 36 55 E
Bairin Youqi, *China* **35 C10** 43 30N 118 35 E
Bairin Zuoqi, *China* **35 C10** 43 58N 119 15 E
Bairnsdale, *Australia* **63 F4** 37 48S 147 36 E
Baisha, *China* **34 G7** 34 20N 112 32 E
Baitadi, *Nepal* **43 E9** 29 35N 80 25 E
Baiyin, *China* **34 F3** 36 45N 104 14 E
Baiyu Shan, *China* **34 F4** 37 15N 107 30 E
Baj Baj, *India* **43 H13** 22 30N 88 5 E
Baja, *Hungary* **17 E10** 46 12N 18 59 E
Baja, Pta., *Mexico* **86 B1** 29 50N 116 0W
Baja California, *Mexico* **86 A1** 31 10N 115 12W
Baja California □, *Mexico* **86 B2** 30 0N 115 0W
Baja California Sur □, *Mexico* **86 B2** 25 50N 111 50W
Bajag, *India* **43 H9** 22 40N 81 21 E
Bajamar, *Canary Is.* **22 F3** 28 33N 16 20W
Bajana, *India* **42 H4** 23 7N 71 49 E
Bājgīrān, *Iran* **45 B8** 37 36N 58 24 E
Bajimba, Mt., *Australia* **63 D5** 29 17S 152 6 E
Bajo Nuevo, *Caribbean* **88 C4** 15 40N 78 50W
Bajoga, *Nigeria* **51 F8** 10 57N 11 20 E
Bajool, *Australia* **62 C5** 23 40S 150 35 E
Bakel, *Senegal* **50 F3** 14 56N 12 20W
Baker, *Calif., U.S.A.* **85 K10** 35 16N 116 4W
Baker, *Mont., U.S.A.* **80 B2** 46 22N 104 17W
Baker, L., *Canada* **68 B10** 64 0N 96 0W
Baker City, *U.S.A.* **82 D5** 44 47N 117 50W
Baker I., *Pac. Oc.* **64 G10** 0 10N 176 35W
Baker I., *U.S.A.* **72 B2** 55 20N 133 40W
Baker L., *Australia* **61 E4** 26 54S 126 5 E
Baker Lake, *Canada* **68 B10** 64 20N 96 3W
Baker Mt., *U.S.A.* **82 B3** 48 50N 121 49W
Bakers Creek, *Australia* **62 C4** 21 13S 149 7 E
Baker's Dozen Is., *Canada* **70 A4** 56 45N 78 45W
Bakersfield, *Calif., U.S.A.* **85 K8** 35 23N 119 1W
Bakersfield, *Vt., U.S.A.* **79 B12** 44 45N 72 48W
Bākhtarān, *Iran* **44 C5** 34 23N 47 0 E
Bākhtarān □, *Iran* **44 C5** 34 0N 46 30 E
Bakı, *Azerbaijan* **25 F8** 40 29N 49 56 E
Bakkafjörður, *Iceland* **8 C6** 66 2N 14 48W
Bakony, *Hungary* **17 E9** 47 10N 17 30 E
Bakony Forest = Bakony, *Hungary* **17 E9** 47 10N 17 30 E
Bakouma, *C.A.R.* **52 C4** 5 40N 22 56 E
Bakswaho, *India* **43 G8** 24 15N 79 18 E
Baku = Bakı, *Azerbaijan* **25 F8** 40 29N 49 56 E
Bakutis Coast, *Antarctica* **5 D15** 74 0S 120 0W
Baky = Bakı, *Azerbaijan* **25 F8** 40 29N 49 56 E
Bala, *Canada* **78 A5** 45 1N 79 37W
Bala, *U.K.* **10 E4** 52 54N 3 36W
Bala, L., *U.K.* **10 E4** 52 53N 3 37W
Balabac I., *Phil.* **36 C5** 8 0N 117 0 E
Balabac Str., *E. Indies* **36 C5** 7 53N 117 5 E
Balabagh, *Afghan.* **42 B4** 34 25N 70 12 E
Ba'labakk, *Lebanon* **47 B5** 34 0N 36 10 E
Balabalangan, Kepulauan, *Indonesia* **36 E5** 2 20S 117 30 E
Balad, *Iraq* **44 C5** 34 1N 44 9 E
Balad Rūz, *Iraq* **44 C5** 33 42N 45 5 E
Bālādeh, *Fārs, Iran* **45 D6** 29 17N 51 56 E
Bālādeh, *Māzandaran, Iran* **45 B6** 36 12N 51 48 E
Balaghat, *India* **40 J12** 21 49N 80 12 E
Balaghat Ra., *India* **40 K10** 18 50N 76 30 E
Balaguer, *Spain* **19 B6** 41 50N 0 50 E
Balaklava, *Ukraine* **25 F5** 44 30N 33 30 E
Balakovo, *Russia* **24 D8** 52 4N 47 55 E
Balamau, *India* **43 F9** 27 10N 80 21 E
Balancán, *Mexico* **87 D6** 17 48N 91 32W
Balashov, *Russia* **25 D7** 51 30N 43 10 E
Balasinor, *India* **42 H5** 22 57N 73 23 E
Balasore = Baleshwar, *India* **41 J15** 21 35N 87 3 E
Balaton, *Hungary* **17 E9** 46 50N 17 40 E
Balbina, Reprêsa de, *Brazil* **92 D7** 2 0S 59 30W
Balboa, *Panama* **88 E4** 8 57N 79 34W
Balbriggan, *Ireland* **13 C5** 53 37N 6 11W
Balcarce, *Argentina* **94 D4** 38 0S 58 10W
Balcarres, *Canada* **73 C8** 50 50N 103 35W
Balchik, *Bulgaria* **21 C13** 43 28N 28 11 E
Balclutha, *N.Z.* **59 M2** 46 15S 169 45 E
Balcones Escarpment, *U.S.A.* **81 L5** 29 30N 99 15W
Bald Hd., *Australia* **61 G2** 35 6S 118 1 E
Bald I., *Australia* **61 F2** 34 57S 118 27 E
Bald Knob, *U.S.A.* **81 H9** 35 19N 91 34W
Baldock L., *Canada* **73 B9** 56 33N 97 57W
Baldwin, *Mich., U.S.A.* **76 D3** 43 54N 85 51W
Baldwin, *Pa., U.S.A.* **78 F5** 40 23N 79 59W
Baldwinsville, *U.S.A.* **79 C8** 43 10N 76 20W
Baldy Mt., *U.S.A.* **82 B9** 48 9N 109 39W
Baldy Peak, *U.S.A.* **83 K9** 33 54N 109 34W
Baleares, Is., *Spain* **22 B10** 39 30N 3 0 E
Balearic Is. = Baleares, Is., *Spain* **22 B10** 39 30N 3 0 E
Baleine = Whale →, *Canada* **71 A6** 58 15N 67 40W
Baler, *Phil.* **37 A6** 15 46N 121 34 E
Baleshare, *U.K.* **12 D1** 57 31N 7 22W
Baleshwar, *India* **41 J15** 21 35N 87 3 E
Balfate, *Honduras* **88 C2** 15 48N 86 25W
Balí, *Greece* **23 D6** 35 25N 24 47 E
Bali, *India* **42 G5** 25 11N 73 17 E
Bali □, *Indonesia* **36 F5** 8 20S 115 0 E
Bali, Selat, *Indonesia* **37 H16** 8 18S 114 25 E
Baliapal, *India* **43 J12** 21 40N 87 17 E
Balikeşir, *Turkey* **21 E12** 39 39N 27 53 E
Balikpapan, *Indonesia* **36 E5** 1 10S 116 55 E
Balimbing, *Phil.* **37 C5** 5 5N 119 58 E
Baling, *Malaysia* **39 K3** 5 41N 100 55 E
Balipara, *India* **41 F18** 26 50N 92 45 E
Balkan Mts. = Stara Planina, *Bulgaria* **21 C10** 43 15N 23 0 E
Balkhash = Balqash, *Kazakstan* **26 E8** 46 50N 74 50 E
Balkhash, Ozero = Balqash Köl, *Kazakstan* **26 E8** 46 0N 74 50 E
Balla, *Bangla.* **41 G17** 24 10N 91 35 E
Ballachulish, *U.K.* **12 E3** 56 41N 5 8W
Balladonia, *Australia* **61 F3** 32 27S 123 51 E
Ballaghaderreen, *Ireland* **13 C3** 53 55N 8 34W
Ballarat, *Australia* **63 F3** 37 33S 143 50 E
Ballard, L., *Australia* **61 E3** 29 20S 120 40 E
Ballater, *U.K.* **12 D5** 57 3N 3 3W
Ballenas, Canal de, *Mexico* **86 B2** 29 10N 113 45W
Balleny Is., *Antarctica* **5 C11** 66 30S 163 0 E
Ballia, *India* **43 G11** 25 46N 84 12 E
Ballina, *Australia* **63 D5** 28 50S 153 31 E
Ballina, *Ireland* **13 B2** 54 7N 9 9W
Ballinasloe, *Ireland* **13 C3** 53 20N 8 13W
Ballinger, *U.S.A.* **81 K5** 31 45N 99 57W
Ballinrobe, *Ireland* **13 C2** 53 38N 9 13W
Ballinskelligs B., *Ireland* **13 E1** 51 48N 10 13W
Ballston Spa, *U.S.A.* **79 D11** 43 0N 73 51W
Ballycastle, *U.K.* **13 A5** 55 12N 6 15W
Ballyclare, *U.K.* **13 B5** 54 46N 6 0W
Ballyhaunis, *Ireland* **13 C3** 53 46N 8 46W
Ballymena, *U.K.* **13 B5** 54 52N 6 17W
Ballymoney, *U.K.* **13 A5** 55 5N 6 31W
Ballymote, *Ireland* **13 B3** 54 5N 8 31W
Ballynahinch, *U.K.* **13 B6** 54 24N 5 54W
Ballyquintin Pt., *U.K.* **13 B6** 54 20N 5 30W
Ballyshannon, *Ireland* **13 B3** 54 30N 8 11W
Balmaceda, *Chile* **96 F2** 46 0S 71 50W
Balmertown, *Canada* **73 C10** 51 4N 93 41W
Balmoral, *Australia* **63 F3** 37 15S 141 48 E
Balmorhea, *U.S.A.* **81 K3** 30 59N 103 45W
Balonne →, *Australia* **63 D4** 28 47S 147 56 E
Balotra, *India* **42 G5** 25 50N 72 14 E
Balqash, *Kazakstan* **26 E8** 46 50N 74 50 E
Balqash Köl, *Kazakstan* **26 E8** 46 0N 74 50 E
Balrampur, *India* **43 F10** 27 30N 82 20 E
Balranald, *Australia* **63 E3** 34 38S 143 33 E
Balsas, *Mexico* **87 D5** 18 0N 99 40W
Balsas →, *Brazil* **93 E9** 7 15S 44 35W
Balsas →, *Mexico* **86 D4** 17 55N 102 10W
Balston Spa, *U.S.A.* **79 D11** 43 0N 73 52W
Balta, *Ukraine* **17 D15** 48 2N 29 45 E
Bălţi, *Moldova* **17 E14** 47 48N 27 58 E
Baltic Sea, *Europe* **9 H18** 57 0N 19 0 E
Baltimore, *Ireland* **13 E2** 51 29N 9 22W
Baltimore, *Md., U.S.A.* **76 F7** 39 17N 76 37W
Baltimore, *Ohio, U.S.A.* **78 G2** 39 51N 82 36W
Baltit, *Pakistan* **43 A6** 36 15N 74 40 E
Baltiysk, *Russia* **9 J18** 54 41N 19 58 E
Baluchistan □, *Pakistan* **40 F4** 27 30N 65 0 E
Balurghat, *India* **43 G13** 25 15N 88 44 E
Balvi, *Latvia* **9 H22** 57 8N 27 15 E
Balya, *Turkey* **21 E12** 39 44N 27 35 E
Bam, *Iran* **45 D8** 29 7N 58 14 E
Bama, *Nigeria* **51 F8** 11 33N 13 41 E
Bamaga, *Australia* **62 A3** 10 50S 142 25 E
Bamaji L., *Canada* **70 B1** 51 9N 91 25W
Bamako, *Mali* **50 F4** 12 34N 7 55W
Bambari, *C.A.R.* **52 C4** 5 40N 20 35 E
Bambaroo, *Australia* **62 B4** 18 50S 146 10 E
Bamberg, *Germany* **16 D6** 49 54N 10 54 E
Bamberg, *U.S.A.* **77 J5** 33 18N 81 2W
Bambili, *Dem. Rep. of the Congo* **54 B2** 3 40N 26 0 E
Bamenda, *Cameroon* **52 C1** 5 57N 10 11 E
Bamfield, *Canada* **72 D3** 48 45N 125 10W
Bāmīān □, *Afghan.* **40 B5** 35 0N 67 0 E
Bamiancheng, *China* **35 C13** 43 15N 124 2 E
Bampūr, *Iran* **45 E9** 27 15N 60 21 E
Ban Ban, *Laos* **38 C4** 19 31N 103 30 E
Ban Bang Hin, *Thailand* **39 H2** 9 32N 98 35 E
Ban Chiang Klang, *Thailand* **38 C3** 19 25N 100 55 E
Ban Chik, *Laos* **38 D4** 17 15N 102 22 E
Ban Choho, *Thailand* **38 E4** 15 2N 102 9 E
Ban Dan Lan Hoi, *Thailand* **38 D2** 17 0N 99 35 E
Ban Don = Surat Thani, *Thailand* **39 H2** 9 6N 99 20 E
Ban Don, *Vietnam* **38 F6** 12 53N 107 48 E
Ban Don, Ao →, *Thailand* **39 H2** 9 20N 99 25 E
Ban Dong, *Thailand* **38 C3** 19 30N 100 59 E
Ban Hong, *Thailand* **38 C2** 18 18N 98 50 E
Ban Kaeng, *Thailand* **38 D3** 17 29N 100 7 E
Ban Kantang, *Thailand* **39 J2** 7 25N 99 31 E
Ban Keun, *Laos* **38 C4** 18 22N 102 35 E
Ban Khai, *Thailand* **38 F3** 12 46N 101 18 E
Ban Kheun, *Laos* **38 B3** 20 13N 101 7 E
Ban Khlong Kua, *Thailand* **39 J3** 6 57N 100 8 E
Ban Khuan Mao, *Thailand* **39 J2** 7 50N 99 37 E
Ban Ko Yai Chim, *Thailand* **39 G2** 11 17N 99 26 E
Ban Kok, *Thailand* **38 D4** 16 40N 103 40 E
Ban Laem, *Thailand* **38 F2** 13 13N 99 59 E
Ban Lao Ngam, *Laos* **38 E6** 15 28N 106 10 E
Ban Le Kathe, *Thailand* **38 E2** 15 49N 98 53 E
Ban Mae Chedi, *Thailand* **38 C2** 19 11N 99 31 E
Ban Mae Laeng, *Thailand* **38 B2** 20 1N 99 17 E
Ban Mae Sariang, *Thailand* **38 C1** 18 10N 97 56 E
Ban Mê Thuôt = Buon Ma Thuot, *Vietnam* **38 F7** 12 40N 108 3 E
Ban Mi, *Thailand* **38 E3** 15 3N 100 32 E
Ban Muong Mo, *Laos* **38 C4** 19 4N 103 58 E
Ban Na Mo, *Laos* **38 D5** 17 7N 105 40 E
Ban Na San, *Thailand* **39 H2** 8 53N 99 52 E
Ban Na Tong, *Laos* **38 B3** 20 56N 101 47 E
Ban Nam Bac, *Laos* **38 B4** 20 38N 102 20 E
Ban Nam Ma, *Laos* **38 A3** 22 2N 101 37 E
Ban Ngang, *Laos* **38 E6** 15 59N 106 11 E
Ban Nong Bok, *Laos* **38 D5** 17 5N 104 48 E
Ban Nong Boua, *Laos* **38 E6** 15 40N 106 33 E
Ban Nong Pling, *Thailand* **38 E3** 15 40N 100 10 E
Ban Pak Chan, *Thailand* **39 G2** 10 32N 98 51 E
Ban Phai, *Thailand* **38 D4** 16 4N 102 44 E
Ban Pong, *Thailand* **38 F2** 13 50N 99 55 E
Ban Ron Phibun, *Thailand* **39 H2** 8 9N 99 51 E
Ban Sanam Chai, *Thailand* **39 J3** 7 33N 100 25 E
Ban Sangkha, *Thailand* **38 E4** 14 37N 103 52 E
Ban Tak, *Thailand* **38 D2** 17 2N 99 4 E
Ban Tako, *Thailand* **38 E4** 14 5N 102 40 E
Ban Tha Dua, *Thailand* **38 D2** 17 59N 98 39 E
Ban Tha Li, *Thailand* **38 D3** 17 37N 101 25 E
Ban Tha Nun, *Thailand* **39 H2** 8 12N 98 18 E
Ban Thahine, *Laos* **38 E5** 14 12N 105 33 E
Ban Xien Kok, *Laos* **38 B3** 20 54N 100 39 E
Ban Yen Nhan, *Vietnam* **38 B6** 20 57N 106 2 E
Banaba, *Kiribati* **64 H8** 0 45S 169 50 E
Banalia, *Dem. Rep. of the Congo* **54 B2** 1 32N 25 5 E
Banam, *Cambodia* **39 G5** 11 20N 105 17 E
Bananal, I. do, *Brazil* **93 F8** 11 30S 50 30W
Banaras = Varanasi, *India* **43 G10** 25 22N 83 0 E
Banas →, *Gujarat, India* **42 H4** 23 45N 71 25 E
Banas →, *Mad. P., India* **43 G9** 24 15N 81 30 E
Bânâs, Ras, *Egypt* **51 D13** 23 57N 35 59 E
Banbān, *Si. Arabia* **44 E5** 25 1N 46 35 E
Banbridge, *U.K.* **13 B5** 54 22N 6 16W
Banbury, *U.K.* **11 E6** 52 4N 1 20W
Banchory, *U.K.* **12 D6** 57 3N 2 29W
Bancroft, *Canada* **78 A7** 45 3N 77 51W
Band Bonī, *Iran* **45 E8** 25 30N 59 33 E
Band Qīr, *Iran* **45 D6** 31 39N 48 53 E
Banda, *India* **43 G9** 25 30N 80 26 E
Banda, *Mad. P., India* **43 G8** 24 3N 78 57 E
Banda, Kepulauan, *Indonesia* **37 E7** 4 37S 129 50 E
Banda Aceh, *Indonesia* **36 C1** 5 35N 95 20 E
Banda Banda, Mt., *Australia* **63 E5** 31 10S 152 28 E
Banda Elat, *Indonesia* **37 F8** 5 40S 133 5 E
Banda Is. = Banda, Kepulauan, *Indonesia* **37 E7** 4 37S 129 50 E
Banda Sea, *Indonesia* **37 F7** 6 0S 130 0 E
Bandai-San, *Japan* **30 F10** 37 36N 140 4 E
Bandān, *Iran* **45 D9** 31 23N 60 44 E
Bandanaira, *Indonesia* **37 E7** 4 32S 129 54 E
Bandanwara, *India* **42 F6** 26 9N 74 38 E
Bandar = Machilipatnam, *India* **41 L12** 16 12N 81 8 E
Bandār 'Abbās, *Iran* **45 E8** 27 15N 56 15 E
Bandar-e Anzalī, *Iran* **45 B6** 37 30N 49 30 E
Bandar-e Bushehr = Būshehr, *Iran* **45 D6** 28 55N 50 55 E
Bandar-e Chārak, *Iran* **45 E7** 26 45N 54 20 E
Bandar-e Deylam, *Iran* **45 D6** 30 5N 50 10 E
Bandar-e Khomeynı, *Iran* **45 D6** 30 30N 49 5 E
Bandar-e Lengeh, *Iran* **45 E7** 26 35N 54 58 E
Bandar-e Maqām, *Iran* **45 E7** 26 56N 53 29 E
Bandar-e Ma'shur, *Iran* **45 D6** 30 35N 49 10 E
Bandar-e Nakhīlū, *Iran* **45 E7** 26 58N 53 30 E
Bandar-e Rīg, *Iran* **45 D6** 29 29N 50 38 E
Bandar-e Torkeman, *Iran* **45 B7** 37 0N 54 10 E
Bandar Maharani = Muar, *Malaysia* **39 L4** 2 3N 102 34 E
Bandar Penggaram = Batu Pahat, *Malaysia* **39 M4** 1 50N 102 56 E
Bandar Seri Begawan, *Brunei* **36 D5** 4 52N 115 0 E
Bandar Sri Aman, *Malaysia* **36 D4** 1 15N 111 32 E
Bandawe, *Malawi* **55 E3** 11 58S 34 5 E
Bandeira, Pico da, *Brazil* **95 A7** 20 26S 41 47W
Bandera, *Argentina* **94 B3** 28 55S 62 20W
Banderas, B. de, *Mexico* **86 C3** 20 40N 105 30W
Bandhogarh, *India* **43 H9** 23 40N 81 2 E
Bandi →, *India* **42 F6** 26 12N 75 47 E
Bandikui, *India* **42 F7** 27 3N 76 34 E
Bandırma, *Turkey* **21 D13** 40 20N 28 0 E
Bandon, *Ireland* **13 E3** 51 44N 8 44W
Bandon →, *Ireland* **13 E3** 51 43N 8 37W
Bandula, *Mozam.* **55 F3** 19 0S 33 7 E
Bandundu, *Dem. Rep. of the Congo* **52 E3** 3 15S 17 22 E
Bandung, *Indonesia* **37 G12** 6 54S 107 36 E
Bāneh, *Iran* **44 C5** 35 59N 45 53 E
Banes, *Cuba* **89 B4** 21 0N 75 42W
Banff, *Canada* **72 C5** 51 10N 115 34W
Banff, *U.K.* **12 D6** 57 40N 2 33W
Banff Nat. Park, *Canada* **72 C5** 51 30N 116 15W
Bang Fai →, *Laos* **38 D5** 16 57N 104 45 E
Bang Hieng →, *Laos* **38 D5** 16 10N 105 10 E
Bang Krathum, *Thailand* **38 D3** 16 34N 100 18 E
Bang Lamung, *Thailand* **38 F3** 13 3N 100 56 E
Bang Mun Nak, *Thailand* **38 D3** 16 2N 100 23 E
Bang Pa In, *Thailand* **38 E3** 14 14N 100 35 E
Bang Rakam, *Thailand* **38 D3** 16 45N 100 7 E
Bang Saphan, *Thailand* **39 G2** 11 14N 99 28 E
Bangaduni I., *India* **43 J13** 21 34N 88 52 E
Bangala Dam, *Zimbabwe* **55 G3** 21 7S 31 25 E
Bangalore, *India* **40 N10** 12 59N 77 40 E
Banganga →, *India* **42 F6** 27 6N 77 25 E
Bangaon, *India* **43 H13** 23 0N 88 47 E
Bangassou, *C.A.R.* **52 D4** 4 55N 23 7 E
Banggai, *Indonesia* **37 E6** 1 34S 123 30 E
Banggai, Kepulauan, *Indonesia* **37 E6** 1 40S 123 30 E
Banggai Arch. = Banggai, Kepulauan, *Indonesia* **37 E6** 1 40S 123 30 E
Banggi, *Malaysia* **36 C5** 7 17N 117 12 E
Banghāzī, *Libya* **51 B10** 32 11N 20 3 E
Bangka, *Sulawesi, Indonesia* **37 D7** 1 50N 125 5 E
Bangka, *Sumatera, Indonesia* **36 E3** 2 0S 105 50 E
Bangka, Selat, *Indonesia* **36 E3** 2 30S 105 30 E
Bangkalan, *Indonesia* **37 G15** 7 2S 112 46 E
Bangkinang, *Indonesia* **36 D2** 0 18N 101 5 E
Bangko, *Indonesia* **36 E2** 2 5S 102 9 E
Bangkok, *Thailand* **38 F3** 13 45N 100 35 E
Bangladesh ■, *Asia* **41 H17** 24 0N 90 0 E
Bangong Co, *India* **43 B8** 35 50N 79 20 E
Bangor, *Down, U.K.* **13 B6** 54 40N 5 40W
Bangor, *Gwynedd, U.K.* **10 D3** 53 14N 4 8W
Bangor, *Maine, U.S.A.* **69 D13** 44 48N 68 46W
Bangor, *Pa., U.S.A.* **79 F9** 40 52N 75 13W
Bangued, *Phil.* **37 A6** 17 40N 120 37 E
Bangui, *C.A.R.* **52 D3** 4 23N 18 35 E
Banguru, *Dem. Rep. of the Congo* **54 B2** 0 30N 27 10 E
Bangweulu, L., *Zambia* **55 E3** 11 0S 30 0 E
Bangweulu Swamp, *Zambia* **55 E3** 11 20S 30 15 E
Bani, *Dom. Rep.* **89 C5** 18 16N 70 22W
Banī Sa'd, *Iraq* **44 C5** 33 34N 44 32 E
Banihal Pass, *India* **43 C6** 33 30N 75 12 E
Bāniyās, *Syria* **44 C3** 35 10N 36 0 E
Banja Luka, *Bos.-H.* **20 B7** 44 49N 17 11 E
Banjar, *India* **42 D7** 31 38N 77 21 E
Banjar →, *India* **43 H9** 22 36N 80 22 E
Banjarmasin, *Indonesia* **36 E4** 3 20S 114 35 E
Banjul, *Gambia* **50 F2** 13 28N 16 40W
Banka, *India* **43 G12** 24 53N 86 55 E
Banket, *Zimbabwe* **55 F3** 17 27S 30 19 E
Bankipore, *India* **41 G14** 25 35N 85 10 E
Banks I., *B.C., Canada* **72 C3** 53 20N 130 0W
Banks I., *N.W.T., Canada* **68 A7** 73 15N 121 30W
Banks Pen., *N.Z.* **59 K4** 43 45S 173 15 E
Banks Str., *Australia* **62 G4** 40 40S 148 10 E
Bankura, *India* **43 H12** 23 11N 87 18 E
Banmankhi, *India* **43 G12** 25 53N 87 11 E
Bann →, *Arm., U.K.* **13 B5** 54 30N 6 31W
Bann →, *L'derry., U.K.* **13 A5** 55 8N 6 41W
Bannang Sata, *Thailand* **39 J3** 6 16N 101 16 E
Banning, *U.S.A.* **85 M10** 33 56N 116 53W
Banningville = Bandundu, *Dem. Rep. of the Congo* **52 E3** 3 15S 17 22 E
Bannockburn, *Canada* **78 B7** 44 39N 77 33W
Bannockburn, *U.K.* **12 E5** 56 5N 3 55W
Bannockburn, *Zimbabwe* **55 G2** 20 17S 29 48 E
Bannu, *Pakistan* **40 C7** 33 0N 70 18 E
Bano, *India* **43 H11** 22 40N 84 55 E
Bansgaon, *India* **43 F10** 26 33N 83 21 E
Banská Bystrica, *Slovak Rep.* **17 D10** 48 46N 19 14 E
Banswara, *India* **42 H6** 23 32N 74 24 E
Bantaeng, *Indonesia* **37 F5** 5 32S 119 56 E
Bantry, *Ireland* **13 E2** 51 41N 9 27W
Bantry B., *Ireland* **13 E2** 51 37N 9 44W
Bantul, *Indonesia* **37 G14** 7 55S 110 19 E
Bantva, *India* **42 J4** 21 29N 70 12 E
Banu, *Afghan.* **40 B6** 35 35N 69 5 E
Banyak, Kepulauan, *Indonesia* **36 D1** 2 10N 97 10 E
Banyalbufar, *Spain* **22 B9** 39 42N 2 31 E
Banyo, *Cameroon* **52 C2** 6 52N 11 45 E
Banyumas, *Indonesia* **37 G13** 7 32S 109 18 E
Banyuwangi, *Indonesia* **37 H16** 8 13S 114 21 E
Banzare Coast, *Antarctica* **5 C9** 68 0S 125 0 E
Banzyville = Mobayi, *Dem. Rep. of the Congo* **52 D4** 4 15N 21 8 E
Bao Lac, *Vietnam* **38 A5** 22 57N 105 40 E
Bao Loc, *Vietnam* **39 G6** 11 32N 107 48 E
Baocheng, *China* **34 H4** 33 12N 106 56 E
Baode, *China* **34 E6** 39 1N 111 5 E
Baodi, *China* **35 E9** 39 38N 117 20 E
Baoding, *China* **34 E8** 38 50N 115 28 E
Baoji, *China* **34 G4** 34 20N 107 5 E
Baoshan, *China* **32 D4** 25 10N 99 5 E
Baotou, *China* **34 D6** 40 32N 110 2 E
Baoying, *China* **35 H10** 33 17N 119 20 E
Bap, *India* **42 F5** 27 23N 72 18 E
Bapatla, *India* **41 M12** 15 55N 80 30 E
Bāqerābād, *Iran* **45 C6** 33 2N 51 58 E
Ba'qūbah, *Iraq* **44 C5** 33 45N 44 50 E
Baquedano, *Chile* **94 A2** 23 20S 69 52W
Bar, *Montenegro, Yug.* **21 C8** 42 8N 19 6 E
Bar, *Ukraine* **17 D14** 49 4N 27 40 E
Bar Bigha, *India* **43 G11** 25 21N 85 47 E
Bar Harbor, *U.S.A.* **77 C11** 44 23N 68 13W
Bar-le-Duc, *France* **18 B6** 48 47N 5 10 E
Bara, *India* **43 G9** 25 16N 81 43 E
Bara Banki, *India* **43 F9** 26 55N 81 12 E
Barabai, *Indonesia* **36 E5** 2 32S 115 34 E
Baraboo, *U.S.A.* **80 D10** 43 28N 89 45W
Baracoa, *Cuba* **89 B5** 20 20N 74 30W
Baradā →, *Syria* **47 B5** 33 33N 36 34 E
Baradero, *Argentina* **94 C4** 33 52S 59 29W
Baradine, *Australia* **63 E4** 30 56S 149 4 E
Baraga, *U.S.A.* **80 B10** 46 47N 88 30W
Barah →, *India* **42 F6** 27 42N 77 5 E
Barahona, *Dom. Rep.* **89 C5** 18 13N 71 7W
Barail Range, *India* **41 G18** 25 15N 93 20 E
Barakaldo, *Spain* **19 A4** 43 18N 2 59W
Barakar →, *India* **43 G12** 24 7N 86 14 E
Barakhola, *India* **41 G18** 25 0N 92 45 E
Barakot, *India* **43 J11** 21 33N 84 59 E
Barakpur, *India* **43 H13** 22 44N 88 30 E
Baralaba, *Australia* **62 C4** 24 13S 149 50 E
Baralzon L., *Canada* **73 B9** 60 0N 98 3W
Baramula, *India* **43 B6** 34 15N 74 20 E
Baran, *India* **42 G7** 25 9N 76 40 E
Baran →, *Pakistan* **42 G3** 25 13N 68 17 E
Baranavichy, *Belarus* **17 B14** 53 10N 26 0 E
Baranof, *U.S.A.* **72 B2** 57 5N 134 50W
Baranof I., *U.S.A.* **68 C6** 57 0N 135 0W
Barapasi, *Indonesia* **37 E9** 2 15S 137 5 E
Barasat, *India* **43 H13** 22 46N 88 31 E
Barat Daya, Kepulauan, *Indonesia* **37 F7** 7 30S 128 0 E
Barataria B., *U.S.A.* **81 L10** 29 20N 89 55W
Barauda, *India* **42 H6** 23 33N 75 15 E
Baraut, *India* **42 E7** 29 13N 77 7 E
Barbacena, *Brazil* **95 A7** 21 15S 43 56W
Barbados ■, *W. Indies* **89 D8** 13 10N 59 30W
Barbària, C. de, *Spain* **22 C7** 38 39N 1 24 E
Barbastro, *Spain* **19 A6** 42 2N 0 5 E
Barberton, *S. Africa* **57 D5** 25 42S 31 2 E
Barberton, *U.S.A.* **78 E3** 41 0N 81 39W
Barbosa, *Colombia* **92 B4** 5 57N 73 37W
Barbourville, *U.S.A.* **77 G4** 36 52N 83 53W
Barbuda, *W. Indies* **89 C7** 17 30N 61 40W
Barcaldine, *Australia* **62 C4** 23 43S 145 6 E
Barcellona Pozzo di Gotto, *Italy* **20 E6** 38 9N 15 13 E
Barcelona, *Spain* **19 B7** 41 21N 2 10 E
Barcelona, *Venezuela* **92 A6** 10 10N 64 40W
Barcelos, *Brazil* **92 D6** 1 0S 63 0W
Barcoo →, *Australia* **62 D3** 25 30S 142 50 E
Bardaï, *Chad* **51 D9** 21 25N 17 0 E
Bardas Blancas, *Argentina* **94 D2** 35 49S 69 45W
Barddhaman, *India* **43 H12** 23 14N 87 39 E
Bardejov, *Slovak Rep.* **17 D11** 49 18N 21 15 E
Bardera, *Somali Rep.* **46 G3** 2 20N 42 27 E
Bardīyah, *Libya* **51 B10** 31 45N 25 5 E
Bardsey I., *U.K.* **10 E3** 52 45N 4 47W
Bardstown, *U.S.A.* **76 G3** 37 49N 85 28W

Big Timber

Belfast, *Maine, U.S.A.* **77 C11** 44 26N 69 1W
Belfast, *N.Y., U.S.A.* **78 D6** 42 21N 78 7W
Belfast L., *U.K.* **13 B6** 54 40N 5 50W
Belfield, *U.S.A.* **80 B3** 46 53N 103 12W
Belfort, *France* **18 C7** 47 38N 6 50 E
Belfry, *U.S.A.* **82 D9** 45 9N 109 1W
Belgaum, *India* **40 M9** 15 55N 74 35 E
Belgium ■, *Europe* **15 D4** 50 30N 5 0 E
Belgorod, *Russia* **25 D6** 50 35N 36 35 E
Belgorod-Dnestrovskiy = Bilhorod-Dnistrovskyy, *Ukraine* **25 E5** 46 11N 30 23 E
Belgrade = Beograd, *Serbia, Yug.* **21 B9** 44 50N 20 37 E
Belgrade, *U.S.A.* **82 D8** 45 47N 111 11W
Belhaven, *U.S.A.* **77 H7** 35 33N 76 37W
Beli Drim →, *Europe* **21 C9** 42 6N 20 25 E
Belinyu, *Indonesia* **36 E3** 1 35S 105 50 E
Beliton Is. = Belitung, *Indonesia* **36 E3** 3 10S 107 50 E
Belitung, *Indonesia* **36 E3** 3 10S 107 50 E
Belize ■, *Cent. Amer.* **87 D7** 17 0N 88 30W
Belize City, *Belize* **87 D7** 17 25N 88 0W
Belkovskiy, Ostrov, *Russia* **27 B14** 75 32N 135 44 E
Bell →, *Canada* **70 C4** 49 48N 77 38W
Bell I., *Canada* **71 B8** 50 46N 55 35W
Bell-Irving →, *Canada* **72 B3** 56 12N 129 5W
Bell Peninsula, *Canada* **69 B11** 63 50N 82 0W
Bell Ville, *Argentina* **94 C3** 32 40S 62 40W
Bella Bella, *Canada* **72 C3** 52 10N 128 10W
Bella Coola, *Canada* **72 C3** 52 25N 126 40W
Bella Unión, *Uruguay* **94 C4** 30 15S 57 40W
Bella Vista, *Corrientes, Argentina* **94 B4** 28 33S 59 0W
Bella Vista, *Tucuman, Argentina* **94 B2** 27 10S 65 25W
Bellaire, *U.S.A.* **78 F4** 40 1N 80 45W
Bellary, *India* **40 M10** 15 10N 76 56 E
Bellata, *Australia* **63 D4** 29 53S 149 46 E
Belle-Chasse, *U.S.A.* **81 L10** 29 51N 89 59W
Belle Fourche, *U.S.A.* **80 C3** 44 40N 103 51W
Belle Fourche →, *U.S.A.* **80 C3** 44 26N 102 18W
Belle Glade, *U.S.A.* **77 M5** 26 41N 80 40W
Belle-Île, *France* **18 C2** 47 20N 3 10W
Belle Isle, *Canada* **71 B8** 51 57N 55 25W
Belle Isle, Str. of, *Canada* **71 B8** 51 30N 56 30W
Belle Plaine, *U.S.A.* **80 E8** 41 54N 92 17W
Bellefontaine, *U.S.A.* **76 E4** 40 22N 83 46W
Bellefonte, *U.S.A.* **78 F7** 40 55N 77 47W
Belleoram, *Canada* **71 C8** 47 31N 55 25W
Belleville, *Canada* **78 B7** 44 10N 77 23W
Belleville, *Ill., U.S.A.* **80 F10** 38 31N 89 59W
Belleville, *Kans., U.S.A.* **80 F6** 39 50N 97 38W
Belleville, *N.Y., U.S.A.* **79 C8** 43 46N 76 10W
Bellevue, *Canada* **72 D6** 49 35N 114 22W
Bellevue, *Idaho, U.S.A.* **82 E6** 43 28N 114 16W
Bellevue, *Nebr., U.S.A.* **80 E7** 41 8N 95 53W
Bellevue, *Ohio, U.S.A.* **78 E2** 41 17N 82 51W
Bellevue, *Wash., U.S.A.* **84 C4** 47 37N 122 12W
Bellin = Kangirsuk, *Canada* **69 C13** 60 0N 70 0W
Bellingen, *Australia* **63 E5** 30 25S 152 50 E
Bellingham, *U.S.A.* **68 D7** 48 46N 122 29W
Bellingshausen Sea, *Antarctica* **5 C17** 66 0S 80 0W
Bellinzona, *Switz.* **18 C8** 46 11N 9 1 E
Bello, *Colombia* **92 B3** 6 20N 75 33W
Bellows Falls, *U.S.A.* **79 C12** 43 8N 72 27W
Bellpat, *Pakistan* **42 E3** 29 0N 68 5 E
Belluno, *Italy* **20 A5** 46 9N 12 13 E
Bellwood, *U.S.A.* **78 F6** 40 36N 78 20W
Belmont, *Canada* **78 D3** 42 53N 81 5W
Belmont, *S. Africa* **56 D3** 29 28S 24 22 E
Belmont, *U.S.A.* **78 D6** 42 14N 78 2W
Belmonte, *Brazil* **93 G11** 16 0S 39 0W
Belmopan, *Belize* **87 D7** 17 18N 88 30W
Belmullet, *Ireland* **13 B2** 54 14N 9 58W
Belo Horizonte, *Brazil* **93 G10** 19 55S 43 56W
Belo-sur-Mer, *Madag.* **57 C7** 20 42S 44 0 E
Belo-Tsiribihina, *Madag.* **57 B7** 19 40S 44 30 E
Belogorsk, *Russia* **27 D13** 51 0N 128 20 E
Beloha, *Madag.* **57 D8** 25 10S 45 3 E
Beloit, *Kans., U.S.A.* **80 F5** 39 28N 98 6W
Beloit, *Wis., U.S.A.* **80 D10** 42 31N 89 2W
Belokorovichi, *Ukraine* **17 C15** 51 7N 28 2 E
Belomorsk, *Russia* **24 B5** 64 35N 34 54 E
Belonia, *India* **41 H17** 23 15N 91 30 E
Beloretsk, *Russia* **24 D10** 53 58N 58 24 E
Belorussia = Belarus ■, *Europe* **17 B14** 53 30N 27 0 E
Belovo, *Russia* **26 D9** 54 30N 86 0 E
Beloye, Ozero, *Russia* **24 B6** 60 10N 37 35 E
Beloye More, *Russia* **24 A6** 66 30N 38 0 E
Belozersk, *Russia* **24 B6** 60 1N 37 45 E
Belpre, *U.S.A.* **76 F5** 39 17N 81 34W
Belrain, *India* **43 E9** 28 23N 80 55 E
Belt, *U.S.A.* **82 C8** 47 23N 110 55W
Beltana, *Australia* **63 E2** 30 48S 138 25 E
Belterra, *Brazil* **93 D8** 2 45S 55 0W
Belton, *U.S.A.* **81 K6** 31 3N 97 28W
Belton L., *U.S.A.* **81 K6** 31 8N 97 32W
Beltsy = Bălţi, *Moldova* **17 E14** 47 48N 27 58 E
Belturbet, *Ireland* **13 B4** 54 6N 7 26W
Belukha, *Russia* **26 E9** 49 50N 86 50 E
Beluran, *Malaysia* **36 C5** 5 48N 117 35 E
Belvidere, *Ill., U.S.A.* **80 D10** 42 15N 88 50W
Belvidere, *N.J., U.S.A.* **79 F9** 40 50N 75 5W
Belyando →, *Australia* **62 C4** 21 38S 146 50 E
Belyy, Ostrov, *Russia* **26 B8** 73 30N 71 0 E
Belyy Yar, *Russia* **26 D9** 58 26N 84 39 E
Belzoni, *U.S.A.* **81 J9** 33 11N 90 29W
Bemaraha, Lembalemban' i, *Madag.* **57 B7** 18 40S 44 45 E
Bemarivo, *Madag.* **57 C7** 21 45S 44 45 E
Bemarivo →, *Madag.* **57 B8** 15 27S 47 40 E
Bemavo, *Madag.* **57 C8** 21 33S 45 25 E
Bembéréke, *Benin* **50 F6** 10 11N 2 43 E
Bembesi, *Zimbabwe* **55 G2** 20 0S 28 58 E
Bembesi →, *Zimbabwe* **55 F2** 18 57S 27 47 E
Bemetara, *India* **43 J9** 21 42N 81 32 E
Bemidji, *U.S.A.* **80 B7** 47 28N 94 53W
Ben, *Iran* **45 C6** 32 32N 50 45 E
Ben Cruachan, *U.K.* **12 E3** 56 26N 5 8W
Ben Dearg, *U.K.* **12 D4** 57 47N 4 56W
Ben Hope, *U.K.* **12 C4** 58 25N 4 36W
Ben Lawers, *U.K.* **12 E4** 56 32N 4 14W
Ben Lomond, *N.S.W., Australia* **63 E5** 30 1S 151 43 E
Ben Lomond, *Tas., Australia* **62 G4** 41 38S 147 42 E
Ben Lomond, *U.K.* **12 E4** 56 11N 4 38W
Ben Luc, *Vietnam* **39 G6** 10 39N 106 29 E
Ben Macdhui, *U.K.* **12 D5** 57 4N 3 40W
Ben Mhor, *U.K.* **12 D1** 57 15N 7 18W
Ben More, *Arg. & Bute, U.K.* **12 E2** 56 26N 6 1W
Ben More, *Stirl., U.K.* **12 E4** 56 23N 4 32W
Ben More Assynt, *U.K.* **12 C4** 58 8N 4 52W
Ben Nevis, *U.K.* **12 E3** 56 48N 5 1W
Ben Quang, *Vietnam* **38 D6** 17 3N 106 55 E
Ben Vorlich, *U.K.* **12 E4** 56 21N 4 14W
Ben Wyvis, *U.K.* **12 D4** 57 40N 4 35W
Bena, *Nigeria* **50 F7** 11 20N 5 50 E
Benalla, *Australia* **63 F4** 36 30S 146 0 E
Benares = Varanasi, *India* **43 G10** 25 22N 83 0 E
Benavente, *Spain* **19 A3** 42 2N 5 43W
Benavides, *U.S.A.* **81 M5** 27 36N 98 25W
Benbecula, *U.K.* **12 D1** 57 26N 7 21W
Benbonyathe, *Australia* **63 E2** 30 25S 139 11 E
Bend, *U.S.A.* **82 D3** 44 4N 121 19W
Bendemeer, *Australia* **63 E5** 30 53S 151 8 E
Bender Beila, *Somali Rep.* **46 F5** 9 30N 50 48 E
Bendery = Tighina, *Moldova* **17 E15** 46 50N 29 30 E
Bendigo, *Australia* **63 F3** 36 40S 144 15 E
Benē Beraq, *Israel* **47 C3** 32 6N 34 51 E
Benenitra, *Madag.* **57 C8** 23 27S 45 5 E
Benevento, *Italy* **20 D6** 41 8N 14 45 E
Benga, *Mozam.* **55 F3** 16 11S 33 40 E
Bengal, Bay of, *Ind. Oc.* **41 M17** 15 0N 90 0 E
Bengbu, *China* **35 H9** 32 58N 117 20 E
Benghazi = Banghāzī, *Libya* **51 B10** 32 11N 20 3 E
Bengkalis, *Indonesia* **36 D2** 1 30N 102 10 E
Bengkulu, *Indonesia* **36 E2** 3 50S 102 12 E
Bengkulu □, *Indonesia* **36 E2** 3 48S 102 16 E
Bengough, *Canada* **73 D7** 49 25N 105 10W
Benguela, *Angola* **53 G2** 12 37S 13 25 E
Benguérua, I., *Mozam.* **57 C6** 21 58S 35 28 E
Beni, *Dem. Rep. of the Congo* **54 B2** 0 30N 29 27 E
Beni →, *Bolivia* **92 F5** 10 23S 65 24W
Beni Mellal, *Morocco* **50 B4** 32 21N 6 21W
Beni Suef, *Egypt* **51 C12** 29 5N 31 6 E
Beniah L., *Canada* **72 A6** 63 23N 112 17W
Benicia, *U.S.A.* **84 G4** 38 3N 122 9W
Benidorm, *Spain* **19 C5** 38 33N 0 9W
Benin ■, *Africa* **50 G6** 10 0N 2 0 E
Benin, Bight of, *W. Afr.* **50 H6** 5 0N 3 0 E
Benin City, *Nigeria* **50 G7** 6 20N 5 31 E
Benitses, *Greece* **23 A3** 39 32N 19 55 E
Benjamin Aceval, *Paraguay* **94 A4** 24 58S 57 34W
Benjamin Constant, *Brazil* **92 D4** 4 40S 70 15W
Benjamin Hill, *Mexico* **86 A2** 30 10N 111 10W
Benkelman, *U.S.A.* **80 E4** 40 3N 101 32W
Bennett, *Canada* **72 B2** 59 56N 134 53W
Bennett, L., *Australia* **60 D5** 22 50S 131 2 E
Bennetta, Ostrov, *Russia* **27 B15** 76 21N 148 56 E
Bennettsville, *U.S.A.* **77 H6** 34 37N 79 41W
Bennington, *N.H., U.S.A.* **79 D11** 43 0N 71 55W
Bennington, *Vt., U.S.A.* **79 D11** 42 53N 73 12W
Benoni, *S. Africa* **57 D4** 26 11S 28 18 E
Benque Viejo, *Belize* **87 D7** 17 5N 89 8W
Benson, *Ariz., U.S.A.* **83 L8** 31 58N 110 18W
Benson, *Minn., U.S.A.* **80 C7** 45 19N 95 36W
Bent, *Iran* **45 E8** 26 20N 59 31 E
Benteng, *Indonesia* **37 F6** 6 10S 120 30 E
Bentinck I., *Australia* **62 B2** 17 3S 139 35 E
Bento Gonçalves, *Brazil* **95 B5** 29 10S 51 31W
Benton, *Ark., U.S.A.* **81 H8** 34 34N 92 35W
Benton, *Calif., U.S.A.* **84 H8** 37 48N 118 32W
Benton, *Ill., U.S.A.* **80 G10** 38 0N 88 55W
Benton, *Pa., U.S.A.* **79 E8** 41 12N 76 23W
Benton Harbor, *U.S.A.* **76 D2** 42 6N 86 27W
Bentonville, *U.S.A.* **81 G7** 36 22N 94 13W
Bentung, *Malaysia* **39 L3** 3 31N 101 55 E
Benue →, *Nigeria* **50 G7** 7 48N 6 46 E
Benxi, *China* **35 D12** 41 20N 123 48 E
Beo, *Indonesia* **37 D7** 4 25N 126 50 E
Beograd, *Serbia, Yug.* **21 B9** 44 50N 20 37 E
Beppu, *Japan* **31 H5** 33 15N 131 30 E
Beqaa Valley = Al Biqā, *Lebanon* **47 A5** 34 10N 36 10 E
Ber Mota, *India* **42 H3** 23 27N 68 34 E
Berach →, *India* **42 G6** 25 15N 75 2 E
Berati, *Albania* **21 D8** 40 43N 19 59 E
Berau, Teluk, *Indonesia* **37 E8** 2 30S 132 30 E
Berber, *Sudan* **51 E12** 18 0N 34 0 E
Berbera, *Somali Rep.* **46 E4** 10 30N 45 2 E
Berbérati, *C.A.R.* **52 D3** 4 15N 15 40 E
Berbice →, *Guyana* **92 B7** 6 20N 57 32W
Berdichev = Berdychiv, *Ukraine* **17 D15** 49 57N 28 30 E
Berdsk, *Russia* **26 D9** 54 47N 83 2 E
Berdyansk, *Ukraine* **25 E6** 46 45N 36 50 E
Berdychiv, *Ukraine* **17 D15** 49 57N 28 30 E
Berea, *U.S.A.* **76 G3** 37 34N 84 17W
Berebere, *Indonesia* **37 D7** 2 25N 128 45 E
Bereda, *Somali Rep.* **46 E5** 11 45N 51 0 E
Berehove, *Ukraine* **17 D12** 48 15N 22 35 E
Berekum, *Ghana* **50 G5** 7 29N 2 34W
Berens →, *Canada* **73 C9** 52 25N 97 2W
Berens I., *Canada* **73 C9** 52 18N 97 18W
Berens River, *Canada* **73 C9** 52 25N 97 0W
Beresford, *U.S.A.* **80 D6** 43 5N 96 47W
Berestechko, *Ukraine* **17 C13** 50 22N 25 5 E
Berevo, *Mahajanga, Madag.* **57 B7** 17 14S 44 17 E
Berevo, *Toliara, Madag.* **57 B7** 19 44S 44 58 E
Bereza, *Belarus* **17 B13** 52 31N 24 51 E
Berezhany, *Ukraine* **17 D13** 49 26N 24 58 E
Berezina = Byarezina →, *Belarus* **17 B16** 52 33N 30 14 E
Bereznik, *Russia* **24 B7** 62 51N 42 40 E
Berezniki, *Russia* **24 C10** 59 24N 56 46 E
Berezovo, *Russia* **26 C7** 64 0N 65 0 E
Berga, *Spain* **19 A6** 42 6N 1 48 E
Bergama, *Turkey* **21 E12** 39 8N 27 11 E
Bérgamo, *Italy* **18 D8** 45 41N 9 43 E
Bergen, *Neths.* **15 B4** 52 40N 4 43 E
Bergen, *Norway* **9 F11** 60 20N 5 20 E
Bergen, *U.S.A.* **78 C7** 43 5N 77 57W
Bergen op Zoom, *Neths.* **15 C4** 51 28N 4 18 E
Bergerac, *France* **18 D4** 44 51N 0 30 E
Bergholz, *U.S.A.* **78 F4** 40 31N 80 53W
Bergisch Gladbach, *Germany* **15 D7** 50 59N 7 8 E
Bergville, *S. Africa* **57 D4** 28 52S 29 18 E
Berhala, Selat, *Indonesia* **36 E2** 1 0S 104 15 E
Berhampore = Baharampur, *India* **43 G13** 24 2N 88 27 E
Berhampur = Brahmapur, *India* **41 K14** 19 15N 84 54 E
Bering Sea, *Pac. Oc.* **68 C1** 58 0N 171 0 E
Bering Strait, *Pac. Oc.* **68 B3** 65 30N 169 0W
Beringovskiy, *Russia* **27 C18** 63 3N 179 19 E
Berisso, *Argentina* **94 C4** 34 56S 57 50W
Berja, *Spain* **19 D4** 36 50N 2 56W
Berkeley, *U.S.A.* **84 H4** 37 52N 122 16W
Berkner I., *Antarctica* **5 D18** 79 30S 50 0W
Berkshire, *U.S.A.* **79 D8** 42 19N 76 11W
Berkshire Downs, *U.K.* **11 F6** 51 33N 1 29W
Berlin, *Germany* **16 B7** 52 30N 13 25 E
Berlin, *Md., U.S.A.* **76 F8** 38 20N 75 13W
Berlin, *N.H., U.S.A.* **79 B13** 44 28N 71 11W
Berlin, *N.Y., U.S.A.* **79 D11** 42 42N 73 23W
Berlin, *Wis., U.S.A.* **76 D1** 43 58N 88 57W
Berlin L., *U.S.A.* **78 E4** 41 3N 81 0W
Bermejo →, *Formosa, Argentina* **94 B4** 26 51S 58 23W
Bermejo →, *San Juan, Argentina* **94 C2** 32 30S 67 30W
Bermen, L., *Canada* **71 B6** 53 35N 68 55W
Bermuda ■, *Atl. Oc.* **66 F13** 32 45N 65 0W
Bern, *Switz.* **18 C7** 46 57N 7 28 E
Bernalillo, *U.S.A.* **83 J10** 35 18N 106 33W
Bernardo de Irigoyen, *Argentina* **95 B5** 26 15S 53 40W
Bernardo O'Higgins □, *Chile* **94 C1** 34 15S 70 45W
Bernardsville, *U.S.A.* **79 F10** 40 43N 74 34W
Bernasconi, *Argentina* **94 D3** 37 55S 63 44W
Bernburg, *Germany* **16 C6** 51 47N 11 44 E
Berne = Bern, *Switz.* **18 C7** 46 57N 7 28 E
Berneray, *U.K.* **12 D1** 57 43N 7 11W
Bernier I., *Australia* **61 D1** 24 50S 113 12 E
Bernina, Piz, *Switz.* **18 C8** 46 20N 9 54 E
Beroroha, *Madag.* **57 C8** 21 40S 45 10 E
Beroun, *Czech Rep.* **16 D8** 49 57N 14 5 E
Berri, *Australia* **63 E3** 34 14S 140 35 E
Berriane, *Algeria* **50 B6** 32 50N 3 46 E
Berrigan, *Australia* **63 F4** 35 38S 145 49 E
Berry, *Australia* **63 E5** 34 46S 150 43 E
Berry, *France* **18 C5** 46 50N 2 0 E
Berry Is., *Bahamas* **88 A4** 25 40N 77 50W
Berryessa L., *U.S.A.* **84 G4** 38 31N 122 6W
Berryville, *U.S.A.* **81 G8** 36 22N 93 34W
Bershad, *Ukraine* **17 D15** 48 22N 29 31 E
Berthold, *U.S.A.* **80 A4** 48 19N 101 44W
Berthoud, *U.S.A.* **80 E2** 40 19N 105 5W
Bertoua, *Cameroon* **52 D2** 4 30N 13 45 E
Bertraghboy B., *Ireland* **13 C2** 53 22N 9 54W
Berwick, *U.S.A.* **79 E8** 41 3N 76 14W
Berwick-upon-Tweed, *U.K.* **10 B6** 55 46N 2 0W
Berwyn Mts., *U.K.* **10 E4** 52 54N 3 26W
Besal, *Pakistan* **43 B5** 35 4N 73 56 E
Besalampy, *Madag.* **57 B7** 16 43S 44 29 E
Besançon, *France* **18 C7** 47 15N 6 2 E
Besar, *Indonesia* **36 E5** 2 40S 116 0 E
Besnard L., *Canada* **73 B7** 55 25N 106 0W
Besni, *Turkey* **44 B3** 37 41N 37 52 E
Besor, N. →, *Egypt* **47 D3** 31 28N 34 22 E
Bessarabiya, *Moldova* **17 E15** 47 0N 28 10 E
Bessarabka = Basarabeasca, *Moldova* **17 E15** 46 21N 28 58 E
Bessemer, *Ala., U.S.A.* **77 J2** 33 24N 86 58W
Bessemer, *Mich., U.S.A.* **80 B9** 46 29N 90 3W
Bessemer, *Pa., U.S.A.* **78 F4** 40 59N 80 30W
Beswick, *Australia* **60 B5** 14 34S 132 53 E
Bet She'an, *Israel* **47 C4** 32 30N 35 30 E
Bet Shemesh, *Israel* **47 D4** 31 44N 35 0 E
Betafo, *Madag.* **57 B8** 19 50S 46 51 E
Betancuria, *Canary Is.* **22 F5** 28 25N 14 3W
Betanzos, *Spain* **19 A1** 43 15N 8 12W
Bétaré Oya, *Cameroon* **52 C2** 5 40N 14 5 E
Bethal, *S. Africa* **57 D4** 26 27S 29 28 E
Bethanien, *Namibia* **56 D2** 26 31S 17 8 E
Bethany, *Canada* **78 B6** 44 11N 78 34W
Bethany, *U.S.A.* **80 E7** 40 16N 94 2W
Bethel, *Alaska, U.S.A.* **68 B3** 60 48N 161 45W
Bethel, *Conn., U.S.A.* **79 E11** 41 22N 73 25W
Bethel, *Maine, U.S.A.* **79 B14** 44 25N 70 47W
Bethel, *Vt., U.S.A.* **79 C12** 43 50N 72 38W
Bethel Park, *U.S.A.* **78 F4** 40 20N 80 1W
Bethlehem = Bayt Lahm, *West Bank* **47 D4** 31 43N 35 12 E
Bethlehem, *S. Africa* **57 D4** 28 14S 28 18 E
Bethlehem, *U.S.A.* **79 F9** 40 37N 75 23W
Bethulie, *S. Africa* **56 E4** 30 30S 25 59 E
Béthune, *France* **18 A5** 50 30N 2 38 E
Betioky, *Madag.* **57 C7** 23 48S 44 20 E
Betong, *Thailand* **39 K3** 5 45N 101 5 E
Betoota, *Australia* **62 D3** 25 45S 140 42 E
Betroka, *Madag.* **57 C8** 23 16S 46 0 E
Betsiamites, *Canada* **71 C6** 48 56N 68 40W
Betsiamites →, *Canada* **71 C6** 48 56N 68 38W
Betsiboka →, *Madag.* **57 B8** 16 3S 46 36 E
Bettendorf, *U.S.A.* **80 E9** 41 32N 90 30W
Bettiah, *India* **43 F11** 26 48N 84 33 E
Betul, *India* **40 J10** 21 58N 77 59 E
Betung, *Malaysia* **36 D4** 1 24N 111 31 E
Betws-y-Coed, *U.K.* **10 D4** 53 5N 3 48W
Beulah, *Mich., U.S.A.* **76 C2** 44 38N 86 6W
Beulah, *N. Dak., U.S.A.* **80 B4** 47 16N 101 47W
Beveren, *Belgium* **15 C4** 51 12N 4 16 E
Beverley, *Australia* **61 F2** 32 9S 116 56 E
Beverley, *U.K.* **10 D7** 53 51N 0 26W
Beverley Hills, *U.S.A.* **77 L4** 28 56N 82 28W
Beverly, *U.S.A.* **79 D14** 42 33N 70 53W
Beverly Hills, *U.S.A.* **85 L8** 34 4N 118 25W
Bewas →, *India* **43 H8** 23 59N 79 21 E
Bexhill, *U.K.* **11 G8** 50 51N 0 29 E
Beyānlū, *Iran* **44 C5** 36 0N 47 51 E
Beyneu, *Kazakstan* **25 E10** 45 18N 55 9 E
Beypazarı, *Turkey* **25 F5** 40 10N 31 56 E
Beyşehir Gölü, *Turkey* **25 G5** 37 41N 31 33 E
Béziers, *France* **18 E5** 43 20N 3 12 E
Bezwada = Vijayawada, *India* **41 L12** 16 31N 80 39 E
Bhabua, *India* **43 G10** 25 3N 83 37 E
Bhachau, *India* **40 H7** 23 20N 70 16 E
Bhadar →, *Gujarat, India* **42 H5** 22 17N 72 20 E
Bhadar →, *Gujarat, India* **42 J3** 21 27N 69 47 E
Bhadarwah, *India* **43 C6** 32 58N 75 46 E
Bhadohi, *India* **43 G10** 25 25N 82 34 E
Bhadra, *India* **42 E6** 29 8N 75 14 E
Bhadrakh, *India* **41 J15** 21 10N 86 30 E
Bhadran, *India* **42 H5** 22 19N 72 6 E
Bhadravati, *India* **40 N9** 13 49N 75 40 E
Bhag, *Pakistan* **42 E2** 29 2N 67 49 E
Bhagalpur, *India* **43 G12** 25 10N 87 0 E
Bhagirathi →, *Ut. P., India* **43 D8** 30 8N 78 35 E
Bhagirathi →, *W. Bengal, India* **43 H13** 23 25N 88 23 E
Bhakkar, *Pakistan* **42 D4** 31 40N 71 5 E
Bhakra Dam, *India* **42 D7** 31 30N 76 45 E
Bhamo, *Burma* **41 G20** 24 15N 97 15 E
Bhandara, *India* **40 J11** 21 5N 79 42 E
Bhanpura, *India* **42 G6** 24 31N 75 44 E
Bhanrer Ra., *India* **43 H8** 23 40N 79 45 E
Bhaptiahi, *India* **43 F12** 26 19N 86 44 E
Bharat = India ■, *Asia* **40 K11** 20 0N 78 0 E
Bharatpur, *Mad. P., India* **43 H9** 23 44N 81 46 E
Bharatpur, *Raj., India* **42 F7** 27 15N 77 30 E
Bharno, *India* **43 H11** 23 14N 84 53 E
Bhatinda, *India* **42 D6** 30 15N 74 57 E
Bhatpara, *India* **43 H13** 22 50N 88 25 E
Bhattu, *India* **42 E6** 29 36N 75 19 E
Bhaun, *Pakistan* **42 C5** 32 55N 72 40 E
Bhaunagar = Bhavnagar, *India* **40 J8** 21 45N 72 10 E
Bhavnagar, *India* **40 J8** 21 45N 72 10 E
Bhawanipatna, *India* **41 K12** 19 55N 80 10 E
Bhawari, *India* **42 G5** 25 42N 73 4 E
Bhayavadar, *India* **42 J4** 21 51N 70 15 E
Bhera, *Pakistan* **42 C5** 32 29N 72 57 E
Bhikangaon, *India* **42 J6** 21 52N 75 57 E
Bhilsa = Vidisha, *India* **42 H7** 23 28N 77 53 E
Bhilwara, *India* **42 G6** 25 25N 74 38 E
Bhima →, *India* **40 L10** 16 25N 77 17 E
Bhimavaram, *India* **41 L12** 16 30N 81 30 E
Bhimbar, *Pakistan* **43 C6** 32 59N 74 3 E
Bhind, *India* **43 F8** 26 30N 78 46 E
Bhinga, *India* **43 F9** 27 43N 81 56 E
Bhinmal, *India* **42 G5** 25 0N 72 15 E
Bhiwandi, *India* **40 K8** 19 20N 73 0 E
Bhiwani, *India* **42 E7** 28 50N 76 9 E
Bhogava →, *India* **42 H5** 22 26N 72 20 E
Bhola, *Bangla.* **41 H17** 22 45N 90 35 E
Bholari, *Pakistan* **42 G3** 25 19N 68 13 E
Bhopal, *India* **42 H7** 23 20N 77 30 E
Bhubaneshwar, *India* **41 J14** 20 15N 85 50 E
Bhuj, *India* **42 H3** 23 15N 69 49 E
Bhusaval, *India* **40 J9** 21 3N 75 46 E
Bhutan ■, *Asia* **41 F17** 27 25N 90 30 E
Biafra, B. of = Bonny, Bight of, *Africa* **52 D1** 3 30N 9 20 E
Biak, *Indonesia* **37 E9** 1 10S 136 6 E
Biała Podlaska, *Poland* **17 B12** 52 4N 23 6 E
Białogard, *Poland* **16 A8** 54 2N 15 58 E
Białystok, *Poland* **17 B12** 53 10N 23 10 E
Biaora, *India* **42 H7** 23 56N 76 56 E
Bīārjmand, *Iran* **45 B7** 36 6N 55 53 E
Biaro, *Indonesia* **37 D7** 2 5N 125 26 E
Biarritz, *France* **18 E3** 43 29N 1 33W
Bibai, *Japan* **30 C10** 43 19N 141 52 E
Bibby I., *Canada* **73 A10** 61 55N 93 0W
Biberach, *Germany* **16 D5** 48 5N 9 47 E
Bibungwa, *Dem. Rep. of the Congo* **54 C2** 2 40S 28 15 E
Bic, *Canada* **71 C6** 48 20N 68 41W
Bicester, *U.K.* **11 F6** 51 54N 1 9W
Bicheno, *Australia* **62 G4** 41 52S 148 18 E
Bichia, *India* **43 H9** 22 27N 80 42 E
Bickerton I., *Australia* **62 A2** 13 45S 136 10 E
Bida, *Nigeria* **50 G7** 9 3N 5 58 E
Bidar, *India* **40 L10** 17 55N 77 35 E
Biddeford, *U.S.A.* **77 D10** 43 30N 70 28W
Bideford, *U.K.* **11 F3** 51 1N 4 13W
Bideford Bay, *U.K.* **11 F3** 51 5N 4 20W
Bidhuna, *India* **43 F8** 26 49N 79 31 E
Bidor, *Malaysia* **39 K3** 4 6N 101 15 E
Bié, Planalto de, *Angola* **53 G3** 12 0S 16 0 E
Bieber, *U.S.A.* **82 F3** 41 7N 121 8W
Biel, *Switz.* **18 C7** 47 8N 7 14 E
Bielefeld, *Germany* **16 B5** 52 1N 8 33 E
Biella, *Italy* **18 D8** 45 34N 8 3 E
Bielsk Podlaski, *Poland* **17 B12** 52 47N 23 12 E
Bielsko-Biała, *Poland* **17 D10** 49 50N 19 2 E
Bien Hoa, *Vietnam* **39 G6** 10 57N 106 49 E
Bienne = Biel, *Switz.* **18 C7** 47 8N 7 14 E
Bienville, L., *Canada* **70 A5** 55 5N 72 40W
Biesiesfontein, *S. Africa* **56 E2** 30 57S 17 58 E
Big →, *Canada* **71 B8** 54 50N 58 55W
Big B., *Canada* **71 A7** 55 43N 60 35W
Big Bear City, *U.S.A.* **85 L10** 34 16N 116 51W
Big Bear Lake, *U.S.A.* **85 L10** 34 15N 116 56W
Big Belt Mts., *U.S.A.* **82 C8** 46 30N 111 25W
Big Bend, *Swaziland* **57 D5** 26 50S 31 58 E
Big Bend National Park, *U.S.A.* **81 L3** 29 20N 103 5W
Big Black →, *U.S.A.* **81 K9** 32 3N 91 4W
Big Blue →, *U.S.A.* **80 F6** 39 35N 96 34W
Big Creek, *U.S.A.* **84 H7** 37 11N 119 14W
Big Cypress National Preserve, *U.S.A.* **77 M5** 26 0N 81 10W
Big Cypress Swamp, *U.S.A.* **77 M5** 26 12N 81 10W
Big Falls, *U.S.A.* **80 A8** 48 12N 93 48W
Big Fork →, *U.S.A.* **80 A8** 48 31N 93 43W
Big Horn Mts. = Bighorn Mts., *U.S.A.* **82 D10** 44 30N 107 30W
Big I., *Canada* **72 A5** 61 7N 116 45W
Big Lake, *U.S.A.* **81 K4** 31 12N 101 28W
Big Moose, *U.S.A.* **79 C10** 43 49N 74 58W
Big Muddy Cr. →, *U.S.A.* **80 A2** 48 8N 104 36W
Big Pine, *U.S.A.* **84 H8** 37 10N 118 17W
Big Piney, *U.S.A.* **82 E8** 42 32N 110 7W
Big Rapids, *U.S.A.* **76 D3** 43 42N 85 29W
Big Rideau L., *Canada* **79 B8** 44 40N 76 15W
Big River, *Canada* **73 C7** 53 50N 107 0W
Big Run, *U.S.A.* **78 F6** 40 57N 78 55W
Big Sable Pt., *U.S.A.* **76 C2** 44 3N 86 1W
Big Salmon →, *Canada* **72 A2** 61 52N 134 55W
Big Sand L., *Canada* **73 B9** 57 45N 99 45W
Big Sandy, *U.S.A.* **82 B8** 48 11N 110 7W
Big Sandy →, *U.S.A.* **76 F4** 38 25N 82 36W
Big Sandy Cr. →, *U.S.A.* **80 F3** 38 7N 102 29W
Big Sioux →, *U.S.A.* **80 D6** 42 29N 96 27W
Big Spring, *U.S.A.* **81 J4** 32 15N 101 28W
Big Stone City, *U.S.A.* **80 C6** 45 18N 96 28W
Big Stone Gap, *U.S.A.* **77 G4** 36 52N 82 47W
Big Stone L., *U.S.A.* **80 C6** 45 30N 96 35W
Big Sur, *U.S.A.* **84 J5** 36 15N 121 48W
Big Timber, *U.S.A.* **82 D9** 45 50N 109 57W

Big Trout L.

Big Trout L., *Canada* **70 B2** 53 40N 90 0W
Big Trout Lake, *Canada* . . . **70 B2** 53 45N 90 0W
Biğa, *Turkey* . . . . **21 D12** 40 13N 27 14 E
Bigadiç, *Turkey* . . . . **21 E13** 39 22N 28 7 E
Biggar, *Canada* **73 C7** 52 4N 108 0W
Biggar, *U.K.* **12 F5** 55 38N 3 32W
Bigge I., *Australia* . . . . **60 B4** 14 35S 125 10 E
Biggenden, *Australia* . . . . . **63 D5** 25 31S 152 4 E
Biggleswade, *U.K.* **11 E7** 52 5N 0 14W
Biggs, *U.S.A.* **84 F5** 39 25N 121 43W
Bighorn, *U.S.A.* **82 C10** 46 10N 107 27W
Bighorn →, *U.S.A.* **82 C10** 46 10N 107 28W
Bighorn L., *U.S.A.* **82 D9** 44 55N 108 15W
Bighorn Mts., *U.S.A.* **82 D10** 44 30N 107 30W
Bigstone L., *Canada* **73 C9** 53 42N 95 44W
Bigwa, *Tanzania* . . . . **54 D4** 7 10S 39 10 E
Bihać, *Bos.-H.* . . . . **16 F8** 44 49N 15 57 E
Bihar, *India* . . . . **43 G11** 25 5N 85 40 E
Bihar □, *India* . . . . **43 G12** 25 0N 86 0 E
Biharamulo, *Tanzania* . . . . . **54 C3** 2 25S 31 25 E
Bihariganj, *India* . . . . **43 G12** 25 44N 86 59 E
Bihor, Munţii, *Romania* . . . **17 E12** 46 29N 22 47 E
Bijagós, Arquipélago dos,
Guinea-Biss. **50 F2** 11 15N 16 10W
Bijaipur, *India* . . . . **42 F7** 26 2N 77 20 E
Bijapur, *Karnataka, India* . . **40 L9** 16 50N 75 55 E
Bijapur, *Mad. P., India* . . . **41 K12** 18 50N 80 50 E
Bījār, *Iran* . . . . **44 C5** 35 52N 47 35 E
Bijawar, *India* . . . . **43 G8** 24 38N 79 30 E
Bijeljina, *Bos.-H.* . . . . **21 B8** 44 46N 19 14 E
Bijnor, *India* . . . . **42 E8** 29 27N 78 11 E
Bikaner, *India* . . . . **42 E5** 28 2N 73 18 E
Bikapur, *India* . . . . **43 F10** 26 30N 82 7 E
Bikeqi, *China* . . . . **34 D6** 40 43N 111 20 E
Bikfayyā, *Lebanon* . . . . **47 B4** 33 55N 35 41 E
Bikin, *Russia* . . . . **27 E14** 46 50N 134 20 E
Bikin →, *Russia* . . . . **30 A7** 46 51N 134 2 E
Bikini Atoll, *Marshall Is.* . . . **64 F8** 12 0N 167 30 E
Bikoro,
Dem. Rep. of the Congo . **52 E3** 0 48S 18 15 E
Bila Tserkva, *Ukraine* . . . . . **17 D16** 49 45N 30 10 E
Bilara, *India* . . . . **42 F5** 26 14N 73 53 E
Bilaspur, *Mad. P., India* . . . **43 H10** 22 2N 82 15 E
Bilaspur, *Punjab, India* . . . **42 D7** 31 19N 76 50 E
Bilauk Taungdan, *Thailand* **38 F2** 13 0N 99 0 E
Bilbao, *Spain* **19 A4** 43 16N 2 56W
Bilbo = Bilbao, *Spain* **19 A4** 43 16N 2 56W
Bíldudalur, *Iceland* **8 D2** 65 41N 23 36W
Bílé Karpaty, *Europe* . . . . . . **17 D9** 49 5N 18 0 E
Bilecik, *Turkey* . . . . **25 F5** 40 5N 30 5 E
Bilgram, *India* . . . . **43 F9** 27 11N 80 2 E
Bilhaur, *India* . . . . **43 F9** 26 51N 80 5 E
Bilhorod-Dnistrovskyy,
Ukraine . . . . **25 E5** 46 11N 30 23 E
Bilibino, *Russia* . . . . **27 C17** 68 3N 166 20 E
Bilibiza, *Mozam.* . . . . **55 E5** 12 30S 40 20 E
Billabalong Roadhouse,
Australia . . . . **61 E2** 27 25S 115 49 E
Billiluna, *Australia* . . . . **60 C4** 19 37S 127 41 E
Billings, *U.S.A.* **82 D9** 45 47N 108 30W
Billiton Is. = Belitung,
Indonesia . . . . **36 E3** 3 10S 107 50 E
Bilma, *Niger* . . . . **51 E8** 18 50N 13 30 E
Biloela, *Australia* . . . . **62 C5** 24 24S 150 31 E
Biloxi, *U.S.A.* **81 K10** 30 24N 88 53W
Bilpa Morea Claypan,
Australia . . . . **62 D3** 25 0S 140 0 E
Biltine, *Chad* . . . . **51 F10** 14 40N 20 50 E
Bima, *Indonesia* . . . . **37 F5** 8 22S 118 49 E
Bimini Is., *Bahamas* **88 A4** 25 42N 79 25W
Bin Xian, *Heilongjiang,
China* . . . . **35 B14** 45 42N 127 32 E
Bin Xian, *Shaanxi, China* . . **34 G5** 35 2N 108 4 E
Bina-Etawah, *India* . . . . **42 G8** 24 13N 78 14 E
Bināb, *Iran* . . . . **45 B6** 36 35N 48 41 E
Binalbagan, *Phil.* . . . . **37 B6** 10 12N 122 50 E
Binalong, *Australia* . . . . **63 E4** 34 40S 148 39 E
Bīnālūd, Kūh-e, *Iran* . . . . . . **45 B8** 36 30N 58 30 E
Binatang = Bintangor,
Malaysia . . . . **36 D4** 2 10N 111 40 E
Binche, *Belgium* . . . . **15 D4** 50 26N 4 10 E
Bindki, *India* . . . . **43 F9** 26 2N 80 36 E
Bindura, *Zimbabwe* . . . . **55 F3** 17 18S 31 18 E
Bingara, *Australia* . . . . **63 D5** 29 52S 150 36 E
Bingham, *U.S.A.* **77 C11** 45 3N 69 53W
Binghamton, *U.S.A.* **79 D9** 42 6N 75 55W
Bingöl, *Turkey* . . . . **44 B4** 38 53N 40 29 E
Binh Dinh = An Nhon,
Vietnam . . . . **38 F7** 13 55N 109 7 E
Binh Khe, *Vietnam* . . . . **38 F7** 13 57N 108 51 E
Binh Son, *Vietnam* . . . . **38 E7** 15 20N 108 40 E
Binhai, *China* . . . . **35 G10** 34 2N 119 49 E
Binisatua, *Spain* . . . . **22 B11** 39 50N 4 11 E
Binjai, *Indonesia* . . . . **36 D1** 3 20N 98 30 E
Binnaway, *Australia* . . . . **63 E4** 31 28S 149 24 E
Binongko, *Indonesia* . . . . . . **37 F6** 5 55S 123 55 E
Binscarth, *Canada* **73 C8** 50 37N 101 17W
Bintan, *Indonesia* . . . . **36 D2** 1 0N 104 0 E
Bintangor, *Malaysia* . . . . . . **36 D4** 2 10N 111 40 E
Bintulu, *Malaysia* . . . . **36 D4** 3 10N 113 0 E
Bintuni, *Indonesia* . . . . **37 E8** 2 7S 133 32 E
Binzert = Bizerte, *Tunisia* . . **51 A7** 37 15N 9 50 E
Binzhou, *China* . . . . **35 F10** 37 20N 118 2 E
Bío Bío □, *Chile* **94 D1** 37 35S 72 0W
Bioko, *Eq. Guin.* . . . . **52 D1** 3 30N 8 40 E
Bir, *India* . . . . **40 K9** 19 0N 75 54 E
Bîr Abu Muḥammad, *Egypt* **47 F3** 29 44N 34 14 E
Bi'r ad Dabbāghāt, *Jordan* . **47 E4** 30 26N 35 32 E
Bi'r al Butayyihāt, *Jordan* . **47 F4** 29 47N 35 20 E
Bi'r al Mārī, *Jordan* . . . . . . **47 E4** 30 4N 35 33 E
Bi'r al Qattār, *Jordan* . . . . . **47 F4** 29 47N 35 32 E
Bir 'Atrun, *Sudan* . . . . **51 E11** 18 15N 26 40 E
Bîr Beiḍa, *Egypt* . . . . **47 E3** 30 25N 34 29 E
Bîr el 'Abd, *Egypt* . . . . **47 D2** 31 2N 33 0 E
Bîr el Biarât, *Egypt* . . . . **47 F3** 29 30N 34 43 E
Bîr el Duweidar, *Egypt* . . . . **47 E1** 30 56N 32 32 E
Bîr el Garârât, *Egypt* . . . . . **47 D2** 31 3N 33 34 E
Bîr el Heisi, *Egypt* . . . . **47 F3** 29 22N 34 36 E
Bîr el Jafir, *Egypt* . . . . **47 E1** 30 50N 32 41 E
Bîr el Mâlḥi, *Egypt* . . . . **47 E2** 30 38N 33 19 E
Bîr el Thamâda, *Egypt* . . . . **47 E2** 30 12N 33 27 E
Bîr Gebeil Ḥiṣn, *Egypt* . . . . **47 E2** 30 2N 33 18 E
Bi'r Ghadīr, *Syria* . . . . **47 A6** 34 6N 37 3 E
Bîr Ḥasana, *Egypt* . . . . **47 E2** 30 29N 33 46 E
Bîr Kaseiba, *Egypt* . . . . **47 E2** 31 0N 33 17 E
Bîr Lahfân, *Egypt* . . . . **47 E2** 31 0N 33 51 E
Bîr Madkûr, *Egypt* . . . . **47 E1** 30 44N 32 33 E
Bir Mogreïn, *Mauritania* . . . **50 C3** 25 10N 11 25W
Bi'r Muṭribah, *Kuwait* . . . . . **44 D5** 29 54N 47 17 E
Bîr Qaṭia, *Egypt* . . . . **47 E1** 30 58N 32 45 E
Bîr Shalatein, *Egypt* . . . . . . **51 D13** 23 5N 35 25 E
Biratnagar, *Nepal* . . . . **43 F12** 26 27N 87 17 E
Birawa,
Dem. Rep. of the Congo . **54 C2** 2 20S 28 48 E
Birch →, *Canada* **72 B6** 58 28N 112 17W
Birch Hills, *Canada* **73 C7** 52 59N 105 25W
Birch I., *Canada* **73 C9** 52 26N 99 54W
Birch L., *N.W.T., Canada* . . **72 A5** 62 4N 116 33W
Birch L., *Ont., Canada* **70 B1** 51 23N 92 18W
Birch Mts., *Canada* **72 B6** 57 30N 113 10W
Birch River, *Canada* **73 C8** 52 24N 101 6W
Birchip, *Australia* . . . . **63 F3** 35 56S 142 55 E
Bird, *Canada* **73 B10** 56 30N 94 13W
Bird I. = Las Aves, Is.,
W. Indies **89 C7** 15 45N 63 55W
Birdsville, *Australia* . . . . **62 D2** 25 51S 139 20 E
Birdum Cr., *Australia* . . . . . **60 C5** 15 14S 133 0 E
Birecik, *Turkey* . . . . **44 B3** 37 2N 38 0 E
Birein, *Israel* . . . . **47 E3** 30 50N 34 28 E
Bireuen, *Indonesia* . . . . **36 C1** 5 14N 96 39 E
Birigui, *Brazil* **95 A5** 21 18S 50 16W
Birjand, *Iran* . . . . **45 C8** 32 53N 59 13 E
Birkenhead, *U.K.* **10 D4** 53 23N 3 2W
Bîrlad = Bârlad, *Romania* . **17 E14** 46 15N 27 38 E
Birmingham, *U.K.* **11 E6** 52 29N 1 52W
Birmingham, *U.S.A.* **77 J2** 33 31N 86 48W
Birmitrapur, *India* . . . . **41 H14** 22 24N 84 46 E
Birni Nkonni, *Niger* . . . . **50 F7** 13 55N 5 15 E
Birnin Kebbi, *Nigeria* . . . . . **50 F6** 12 32N 4 12 E
Birobidzhan, *Russia* . . . . . . **27 E14** 48 50N 132 50 E
Birr, *Ireland* **13 C4** 53 6N 7 54W
Birrie →, *Australia* . . . . . . **63 D4** 29 43S 146 37 E
Birsilpur, *India* . . . . **42 E5** 28 11N 72 15 E
Birsk, *Russia* . . . . **24 C10** 55 25N 55 30 E
Birtle, *Canada* **73 C8** 50 30N 101 5W
Birur, *India* . . . . **40 N9** 13 30N 75 55 E
Biržai, *Lithuania* . . . . **9 H21** 56 11N 24 45 E
Birzebbugga, *Malta* . . . . **23 D2** 35 49N 14 32 E
Bisa, *Indonesia* . . . . **37 E7** 1 15S 127 28 E
Bisalpur, *India* . . . . **43 E8** 28 14N 79 48 E
Bisbee, *U.S.A.* **83 L9** 31 27N 109 55W
Biscay, B. of, *Atl. Oc.* **18 D1** 45 0N 2 0W
Biscayne B., *U.S.A.* **77 N5** 25 40N 80 12W
Biscoe Bay, *Antarctica* **5 D13** 77 0S 152 0W
Biscoe Is., *Antarctica* **5 C17** 66 0S 67 0W
Biscostasing, *Canada* **70 C3** 47 18N 82 9W
Bishkek, *Kyrgyzstan* . . . . . . **26 E8** 42 54N 74 46 E
Bishnupur, *India* . . . . **43 H12** 23 8N 87 20 E
Bisho, *S. Africa* . . . . **57 E4** 32 50S 27 23 E
Bishop, *Calif., U.S.A.* **84 H8** 37 22N 118 24W
Bishop, *Tex., U.S.A.* **81 M6** 27 35N 97 48W
Bishop Auckland, *U.K.* **10 C6** 54 39N 1 40W
Bishop's Falls, *Canada* **71 C8** 49 2N 55 30W
Bishop's Stortford, *U.K.* . . . **11 F8** 51 52N 0 10 E
Bisina, L., *Uganda* . . . . **54 B3** 1 38N 33 56 E
Biskra, *Algeria* . . . . **50 B7** 34 50N 5 44 E
Bismarck, *U.S.A.* **80 B4** 46 48N 100 47W
Bismarck Arch., *Papua N. G.* **64 H7** 2 30S 150 0 E
Biso, *Uganda* . . . . **54 B3** 1 44N 31 26 E
Bison, *U.S.A.* **80 C3** 45 31N 102 28W
Bīsotūn, *Iran* . . . . **44 C5** 34 23N 47 26 E
Bissagos = Bijagós,
Arquipélago dos,
Guinea-Biss. **50 F2** 11 15N 16 10W
Bissau, *Guinea-Biss.* **50 F2** 11 45N 15 45W
Bistcho L., *Canada* **72 B5** 59 45N 118 50W
Bistriţa, *Romania* . . . . **17 E13** 47 9N 24 35 E
Bistriţa →, *Romania* . . . . . **17 E14** 46 30N 26 57 E
Biswan, *India* . . . . **43 F9** 27 29N 81 2 E
Bitola, *Macedonia* . . . . **21 D9** 41 1N 21 20 E
Bitolj = Bitola, *Macedonia* . **21 D9** 41 1N 21 20 E
Bitter Creek, *U.S.A.* **82 F9** 41 33N 108 33W
Bitterfontein, *S. Africa* . . . . **56 E2** 31 1S 18 32 E
Bitterroot →, *U.S.A.* **82 C6** 46 52N 114 7W
Bitterroot Range, *U.S.A.* . . . **82 D6** 46 0N 114 20W
Bitterwater, *U.S.A.* **84 J6** 36 23N 121 0W
Biu, *Nigeria* . . . . **51 F8** 10 40N 12 3 E
Biwa-Ko, *Japan* . . . . **31 G8** 35 15N 136 10 E
Biwabik, *U.S.A.* **80 B8** 47 32N 92 21W
Bixby, *U.S.A.* **81 H7** 35 57N 95 53W
Biyang, *China* . . . . **34 H7** 32 38N 113 21 E
Biysk, *Russia* . . . . **26 D9** 52 40N 85 0 E
Bizana, *S. Africa* . . . . **57 E4** 30 50S 29 52 E
Bizen, *Japan* . . . . **31 G7** 34 43N 134 8 E
Bizerte, *Tunisia* . . . . **51 A7** 37 15N 9 50 E
Bjargtangar, *Iceland* **8 D1** 65 30N 24 30W
Bjelovar, *Croatia* . . . . **20 B7** 45 56N 16 49 E
Bjørnevatn, *Norway* . . . . **8 B23** 69 40N 30 0 E
Bjørnøya, *Arctic* . . . . **4 B8** 74 30N 19 0 E
Black →, *Canada* **78 B5** 44 42N 79 19W
Black →, *Ariz., U.S.A.* **83 K8** 33 44N 110 13W
Black →, *Ark., U.S.A.* **81 H9** 35 38N 91 20W
Black →, *Mich., U.S.A.* . . . **78 D2** 42 59N 82 27W
Black →, *N.Y., U.S.A.* **79 C8** 43 59N 76 4W
Black →, *Wis., U.S.A.* **80 D9** 43 57N 91 22W
Black Bay Pen., *Canada* **70 C2** 48 38N 88 21W
Black Birch L., *Canada* **73 B7** 56 53N 107 45W
Black Diamond, *Canada* **72 C6** 50 45N 114 14W
Black Duck →, *Canada* . . . **70 A2** 56 51N 89 2W
Black Forest =
Schwarzwald, *Germany* . **16 D5** 48 30N 8 20 E
Black Forest, *U.S.A.* **80 F2** 39 0N 104 43W
Black Hd., *Ireland* **13 C2** 53 9N 9 16W
Black Hills, *U.S.A.* **80 D3** 44 0N 103 45W
Black I., *Canada* **73 C9** 51 12N 96 30W
Black L., *Canada* **73 B7** 59 12N 105 15W
Black L., *Mich., U.S.A.* **76 C3** 45 28N 84 16W
Black L., *N.Y., U.S.A.* **79 B9** 44 31N 75 36W
Black Lake, *Canada* **73 B7** 59 11N 105 20W
Black Mesa, *U.S.A.* **81 G3** 36 58N 102 58W
Black Mt. = Mynydd Du,
U.K. **11 F4** 51 52N 3 50W
Black Mts., *U.K.* **11 F4** 51 55N 3 7W
Black Range, *U.S.A.* **83 K10** 33 15N 107 50W
Black River, *Jamaica* **88 C4** 18 0N 77 50W
Black River Falls, *U.S.A.* . . . **80 C9** 44 18N 90 51W
Black Sea, *Eurasia* . . . . **25 F6** 43 30N 35 0 E
Black Tickle, *Canada* **71 B8** 53 28N 55 45W
Black Volta →, *Africa* **50 G5** 8 41N 1 33W
Black Warrior →, *U.S.A.* . . **77 J2** 32 32N 87 51W
Blackall, *Australia* . . . . **62 C4** 24 25S 145 45 E
Blackball, *N.Z.* . . . . **59 K3** 42 22S 171 26 E
Blackbull, *Australia* . . . . **62 B3** 17 55S 141 45 E
Blackburn, *U.K.* **10 D5** 53 45N 2 29W
Blackburn with Darwen □,
U.K. **10 D5** 53 45N 2 29W
Blackfoot, *U.S.A.* **82 E7** 43 11N 112 21W
Blackfoot →, *U.S.A.* **82 C7** 46 52N 113 53W
Blackfoot River Reservoir,
U.S.A. **82 E8** 43 0N 111 43W
Blackie, *Canada* **72 C6** 50 36N 113 37W
Blackpool, *U.K.* **10 D4** 53 49N 3 3W
Blackpool □, *U.K.* **10 D4** 53 49N 3 3W
Blackriver, *U.S.A.* **78 B1** 44 46N 83 17W
Blacks Harbour, *Canada* . . . **71 C6** 45 3N 66 49W
Blacksburg, *U.S.A.* **76 G5** 37 14N 80 25W
Blacksod B., *Ireland* **13 B1** 54 6N 10 0W
Blackstone, *U.S.A.* **76 G7** 37 4N 78 0W
Blackstone Ra., *Australia* . . **61 E4** 26 0S 128 30 E
Blackwater, *Australia* . . . . . **62 C4** 23 35S 148 53 E
Blackwater →, *Meath,
Ireland* **13 C4** 53 39N 6 41W
Blackwater →, *Waterford,
Ireland* **13 D4** 52 4N 7 52W
Blackwater →, *U.K.* **13 B5** 54 31N 6 35W
Blackwell, *U.S.A.* **81 G6** 36 48N 97 17W
Blackwells Corner, *U.S.A.* . . **85 K7** 35 37N 119 47W
Blaenau Ffestiniog, *U.K.* . . . **10 E4** 53 0N 3 56W
Blaenau Gwent □, *U.K.* . . . **11 F4** 51 48N 3 12W
Blagodarnoye =
Blagodarnyy, *Russia* . . . . **25 E7** 45 7N 43 37 E
Blagodarnyy, *Russia* . . . . . . **25 E7** 45 7N 43 37 E
Blagoevgrad, *Bulgaria* . . . . . **21 C10** 42 2N 23 5 E
Blagoveshchensk, *Russia* . . . **27 D13** 50 20N 127 30 E
Blain, *U.S.A.* **78 F7** 40 20N 77 31W
Blaine, *Minn., U.S.A.* **80 C8** 45 10N 93 13W
Blaine, *Wash., U.S.A.* **84 B4** 48 59N 122 45W
Blaine Lake, *Canada* **73 C7** 52 51N 106 52W
Blair, *U.S.A.* **80 E6** 41 33N 96 8W
Blair Athol, *Australia* . . . . . . **62 C4** 22 42S 147 31 E
Blair Atholl, *U.K.* **12 E5** 56 46N 3 50W
Blairgowrie, *U.K.* **12 E5** 56 35N 3 21W
Blairsden, *U.S.A.* **84 F6** 39 47N 120 37W
Blairsville, *U.S.A.* **78 F5** 40 26N 79 16W
Blake Pt., *U.S.A.* **80 A10** 48 11N 88 25W
Blakely, *Ga., U.S.A.* **77 K3** 31 23N 84 56W
Blakely, *Pa., U.S.A.* **79 E9** 41 28N 75 37W
Blanc, C., *Spain* . . . . **22 B9** 39 21N 2 51 E
Blanc, Mont, *Alps* . . . . **18 D7** 45 48N 6 50 E
Blanc-Sablon, *Canada* **71 B8** 51 24N 57 12W
Blanca, B., *Argentina* **96 D4** 39 10S 61 30W
Blanca Peak, *U.S.A.* **83 H11** 37 35N 105 29W
Blanche, C., *Australia* . . . . . **63 E1** 33 1S 134 9 E
Blanche, L., *S. Austral.,
Australia* . . . . **63 D2** 29 15S 139 40 E
Blanche, L., *W. Austral.,
Australia* . . . . **60 D3** 22 25S 123 17 E
Blanco, *S. Africa* . . . . **56 E3** 33 55S 22 23 E
Blanco, *U.S.A.* **81 K5** 30 6N 98 25W
Blanco →, *Argentina* **94 C2** 30 20S 68 42W
Blanco, C., *Costa Rica* **88 E2** 9 34N 85 8W
Blanco, C., *U.S.A.* **82 E1** 42 51N 124 34W
Blanda →, *Iceland* **8 D3** 65 37N 20 9W
Blandford Forum, *U.K.* **11 G5** 50 51N 2 9W
Blanding, *U.S.A.* **83 H9** 37 37N 109 29W
Blanes, *Spain* . . . . **19 B7** 41 40N 2 48 E
Blankenberge, *Belgium* . . . . **15 C3** 51 20N 3 9 E
Blanquilla, I., *Venezuela* . . . **89 D7** 11 51N 64 37W
Blanquillo, *Uruguay* **95 C4** 32 53S 55 37W
Blantyre, *Malawi* . . . . **55 F4** 15 45S 35 0 E
Blarney, *Ireland* **13 E3** 51 56N 8 33W
Blasdell, *U.S.A.* **78 D6** 42 48N 78 50W
Blåvands Huk, *Denmark* . . . **9 J13** 55 33N 8 4 E
Blaydon, *U.K.* **10 C6** 54 58N 1 42W
Blayney, *Australia* . . . . **63 E4** 33 32S 149 14 E
Blaze, Pt., *Australia* . . . . **60 B5** 12 56S 130 11 E
Blekinge, *Sweden* . . . . **9 H16** 56 25N 15 20 E
Blenheim, *Canada* **78 D3** 42 20N 82 0W
Blenheim, *N.Z.* . . . . **59 J4** 41 38S 173 57 E
Bletchley, *U.K.* **11 F7** 51 59N 0 44W
Blida, *Algeria* . . . . **50 A6** 36 30N 2 49 E
Bligh Sound, *N.Z.* . . . . **59 L1** 44 47S 167 32 E
Blind River, *Canada* **70 C3** 46 10N 82 58W
Bliss, *Idaho, U.S.A.* **82 E6** 42 56N 114 57W
Bliss, *N.Y., U.S.A.* **78 D6** 42 34N 78 15W
Blissfield, *U.S.A.* **78 F3** 40 24N 81 58W
Blitar, *Indonesia* . . . . **37 H15** 8 5S 112 11 E
Block I., *U.S.A.* **79 E13** 41 11N 71 35W
Block Island Sd., *U.S.A.* . . . **79 E13** 41 15N 71 40W
Blodgett Iceberg Tongue,
Antarctica . . . . **5 C9** 66 8S 130 35 E
Bloemfontein, *S. Africa* . . . . **56 D4** 29 6S 26 7 E
Bloemhof, *S. Africa* . . . . **56 D4** 27 38S 25 32 E
Blois, *France* . . . . **18 C4** 47 35N 1 20 E
Blönduós, *Iceland* **8 D3** 65 40N 20 12W
Bloodvein →, *Canada* **73 C9** 51 47N 96 43W
Bloody Foreland, *Ireland* . . . **13 A3** 55 10N 8 17W
Bloomer, *U.S.A.* **80 C9** 45 6N 91 29W
Bloomfield, *Canada* **78 C7** 43 59N 77 14W
Bloomfield, *Iowa, U.S.A.* . . . **80 E8** 40 45N 92 25W
Bloomfield, *N. Mex., U.S.A.* **83 H10** 36 43N 107 59W
Bloomfield, *Nebr., U.S.A.* . . **80 D6** 42 36N 97 39W
Bloomington, *Ill., U.S.A.* . . . **80 E10** 40 28N 89 0W
Bloomington, *Ind., U.S.A.* . . **76 F2** 39 10N 86 32W
Bloomington, *Minn., U.S.A.* **80 C8** 44 50N 93 17W
Bloomsburg, *U.S.A.* **79 F8** 41 0N 76 27W
Blora, *Indonesia* . . . . **37 G14** 6 57S 111 25 E
Blossburg, *U.S.A.* **78 E7** 41 41N 77 4W
Blouberg, *S. Africa* . . . . **57 C4** 23 8S 28 59 E
Blountstown, *U.S.A.* **77 K3** 30 27N 85 3W
Blue Earth, *U.S.A.* **80 D8** 43 38N 94 6W
Blue Mesa Reservoir, *U.S.A.* **83 G10** 38 28N 107 20W
Blue Mountain Lake, *U.S.A.* **79 C10** 43 52N 74 30W
Blue Mts., *Maine, U.S.A.* . . **79 B14** 44 50N 70 35W
Blue Mts., *Oreg., U.S.A.* . . . **82 D4** 45 15N 119 0W
Blue Mts., *Pa., U.S.A.* **79 F8** 40 30N 76 30W
Blue Mud B., *Australia* . . . . **62 A2** 13 30S 136 0 E
Blue Nile = Nîl el
Azraq →, *Sudan* . . . . . . **51 E12** 15 38N 32 31 E
Blue Rapids, *U.S.A.* **80 F6** 39 41N 96 39W
Blue Ridge Mts., *U.S.A.* . . . **77 G5** 36 30N 80 15W
Blue River, *Canada* **72 C5** 52 6N 119 18W
Bluefield, *U.S.A.* **76 G5** 37 15N 81 17W
Bluefields, *Nic.* **88 D3** 12 20N 83 50W
Bluff, *Australia* . . . . **62 C4** 23 35S 149 4 E
Bluff, *N.Z.* . . . . **59 M2** 46 37S 168 20 E
Bluff, *U.S.A.* **83 H9** 37 17N 109 33W
Bluff Knoll, *Australia* . . . . . . **61 F2** 34 24S 118 15 E
Bluff Pt., *Australia* . . . . **61 E1** 27 50S 114 5 E
Bluffton, *U.S.A.* **76 E3** 40 44N 85 11W
Blumenau, *Brazil* **95 B6** 27 0S 49 0W
Blunt, *U.S.A.* **80 C5** 44 31N 99 59W
Bly, *U.S.A.* **82 E3** 42 24N 121 3W
Blyth, *Canada* **78 C3** 43 44N 81 26W
Blyth, *U.K.* **10 B6** 55 8N 1 31W
Blythe, *U.S.A.* **85 M12** 33 37N 114 36W
Blytheville, *U.S.A.* **81 H10** 35 56N 89 55W
Bo, *S. Leone* **50 G3** 7 55N 11 50W
Bo Duc, *Vietnam* . . . . **39 G6** 11 58N 106 50 E
Bo Hai, *China* . . . . **35 E10** 39 0N 119 0 E
Bo Xian = Bozhou, *China* . . **34 H8** 33 55N 115 41 E
Boa Vista, *Brazil* **92 C6** 2 48N 60 30W
Boaco, *Nic.* **88 D2** 12 29N 85 35W
Bo'ai, *China* . . . . **34 G7** 35 10N 113 3 E
Boalsburg, *U.S.A.* **78 F7** 40 46N 77 47W
Boardman, *U.S.A.* **78 E4** 41 2N 80 40W
Bobadah, *Australia* . . . . **63 E4** 32 19S 146 41 E
Bobbili, *India* . . . . **41 K13** 18 35N 83 30 E
Bobcaygeon, *Canada* **78 B6** 44 33N 78 33W
Bobo-Dioulasso,
Burkina Faso **50 F5** 11 8N 4 13W
Bóbr →, *Poland* . . . . **16 B8** 52 4N 15 4 E
Bobraomby, Tanjon' i,
Madag. . . . . **57 A8** 12 40S 49 10 E
Bobruysk = Babruysk,
Belarus . . . . **17 B15** 53 10N 29 15 E
Boby, Pic, *Madag.* . . . . **53 J9** 22 12S 46 55 E
Bôca do Acre, *Brazil* **92 E5** 8 50S 67 27W
Boca Raton, *U.S.A.* **77 M5** 26 21N 80 5W
Bocas del Toro, *Panama* . . . **88 E3** 9 15N 82 20W
Bochnia, *Poland* . . . . **17 D11** 49 58N 20 27 E
Bochum, *Germany* . . . . **16 C4** 51 28N 7 13 E
Bocoyna, *Mexico* **86 B3** 27 52N 107 35W
Bodaybo, *Russia* . . . . **27 D12** 57 50N 114 0 E
Boddam, *U.K.* **12 B7** 59 56N 1 17W
Boddington, *Australia* . . . . . **61 F2** 32 50S 116 30 E
Bodega Bay, *U.S.A.* **84 G3** 38 20N 123 3W
Boden, *Sweden* . . . . **8 D19** 65 50N 21 42 E
Bodensee, *Europe* . . . . **18 C8** 47 35N 9 25 E
Bodhan, *India* . . . . **40 K10** 18 40N 77 44 E
Bodmin, *U.K.* **11 G3** 50 28N 4 43W
Bodmin Moor, *U.K.* **11 G3** 50 33N 4 36W
Bodø, *Norway* . . . . **8 C16** 67 17N 14 24 E
Bodrog →, *Hungary* . . . . . . **17 D11** 48 11N 21 22 E
Bodrum, *Turkey* . . . . **21 F12** 37 3N 27 30 E
Boende,
Dem. Rep. of the Congo . **52 E4** 0 24S 21 12 E
Boerne, *U.S.A.* **81 L5** 29 47N 98 44W
Bogalusa, *U.S.A.* **81 K10** 30 47N 89 52W
Bogan →, *Australia* . . . . **63 D4** 29 59S 146 17 E
Bogan Gate, *Australia* . . . . . **63 E4** 33 7S 147 49 E
Bogantungan, *Australia* . . . . **62 C4** 23 41S 147 17 E
Bogata, *U.S.A.* **81 J7** 33 28N 95 13W
Boggabilla, *Australia* . . . . . . **63 D5** 28 36S 150 24 E
Boggabri, *Australia* . . . . **63 E5** 30 45S 150 5 E
Boggeragh Mts., *Ireland* . . . **13 D3** 52 2N 8 55W
Boglan = Solhan, *Turkey* . . **44 B4** 38 57N 41 3 E
Bognor Regis, *U.K.* **11 G7** 50 47N 0 40W
Bogo, *Phil.* . . . . **37 B6** 11 3N 124 0 E
Bogong, Mt., *Australia* . . . . . **63 F4** 36 47S 147 17 E
Bogor, *Indonesia* . . . . **37 G12** 6 36S 106 48 E
Bogotá, *Colombia* **92 C4** 4 34N 74 0W
Bogotol, *Russia* . . . . **26 D9** 56 15N 89 50 E
Bogra, *Bangla.* . . . . **41 G16** 24 51N 89 22 E
Boguchany, *Russia* . . . . **27 D10** 58 40N 97 30 E
Bohemian Forest =
Böhmerwald, *Germany* . . **16 D7** 49 8N 13 14 E
Böhmerwald, *Germany* . . . . **16 D7** 49 8N 13 14 E
Bohol, *Phil.* . . . . **37 C6** 9 50N 124 10 E
Bohol Sea, *Phil.* . . . . **37 C6** 9 0N 124 0 E
Bohuslän, *Sweden* . . . . **9 G14** 58 25N 12 0 E
Boi, Pta. de, *Brazil* **95 A6** 23 55S 45 15W
Boiaçu, *Brazil* **92 D6** 0 27S 61 46W
Boileau, C., *Australia* . . . . . . **60 C3** 17 40S 122 7 E
Boise, *U.S.A.* **82 E5** 43 37N 116 13W
Boise City, *U.S.A.* **81 G3** 36 44N 102 31W
Boissevain, *Canada* **73 D8** 49 15N 100 5W
Bojador C., *W. Sahara* **50 C3** 26 0N 14 30W
Bojana →, *Albania* . . . . **21 D8** 41 52N 19 22 E
Bojnūrd, *Iran* . . . . **45 B8** 37 30N 57 20 E
Bojonegoro, *Indonesia* . . . . **37 G14** 7 11S 111 54 E
Bokaro, *India* . . . . **43 H11** 23 46N 85 55 E
Bokhara →, *Australia* . . . . . **63 D4** 29 55S 146 42 E
Boknafjorden, *Norway* . . . . . **9 G11** 59 14N 5 40 E
Bokoro, *Chad* . . . . **51 F9** 12 25N 17 14 E
Bokote,
Dem. Rep. of the Congo . **52 E4** 0 12S 21 8 E
Bokpyin, *Burma* . . . . **39 G2** 11 18N 98 42 E
Bolan →, *Pakistan* . . . . **42 E2** 28 38N 67 42 E
Bolan Pass, *Pakistan* . . . . . . **40 E5** 29 50N 67 20 E
Bolaños →, *Mexico* **86 C4** 21 14N 104 8W
Bolbec, *France* . . . . **18 B4** 49 30N 0 30 E
Boldājī, *Iran* . . . . **45 D6** 31 56N 51 3 E
Bole, *China* . . . . **32 B3** 45 11N 81 37 E
Bolekhiv, *Ukraine* . . . . **17 D12** 49 0N 23 57 E
Bolesławiec, *Poland* . . . . **16 C8** 51 17N 15 37 E
Bolgrad = Bolhrad, *Ukraine* **17 F15** 45 40N 28 32 E
Bolhrad, *Ukraine* . . . . **17 F15** 45 40N 28 32 E
Bolívar, *Argentina* **94 D3** 36 15S 60 53W
Bolivar, *Mo., U.S.A.* **81 G8** 37 37N 93 25W
Bolivar, *N.Y., U.S.A.* **78 D6** 42 4N 78 10W
Bolivar, *Tenn., U.S.A.* **81 H10** 35 12N 89 0W
Bolivia ■, *S. Amer.* **92 G6** 17 6S 64 0W
Bolivian Plateau, *S. Amer.* . **90 E4** 20 0S 67 30W
Bollnäs, *Sweden* . . . . **9 F17** 61 21N 16 24 E
Bollon, *Australia* . . . . **63 D4** 28 2S 147 29 E
Bolmen, *Sweden* . . . . **9 H15** 56 55N 13 40 E
Bolobo,
Dem. Rep. of the Congo . **52 E3** 2 6S 16 20 E
Bologna, *Italy* . . . . **20 B4** 44 29N 11 20 E
Bologoye, *Russia* . . . . **24 C5** 57 55N 34 5 E
Bolonchenticul, *Mexico* **87 D7** 20 0N 89 49W
Boloven, Cao Nguyen, *Laos* **38 E6** 15 10N 106 30 E
Bolpur, *India* . . . . **43 H12** 23 40N 87 45 E
Bolsena, L. di, *Italy* . . . . **20 C4** 42 36N 11 56 E
Bolshevik, Ostrov, *Russia* . . **27 B11** 78 30N 102 0 E
Bolshoi Kavkas = Caucasus
Mountains, *Eurasia* . . . . . **25 F7** 42 50N 44 0 E
Bolshoy Anyuy →, *Russia* **27 C17** 68 30N 160 49 E
Bolshoy Begichev, Ostrov,
Russia . . . . **27 B12** 74 20N 112 30 E
Bolshoy Lyakhovskiy,
Ostrov, *Russia* . . . . **27 B15** 73 35N 142 0 E
Bolshoy Tyuters, Ostrov,
Russia . . . . **9 G22** 59 51N 27 13 E
Bolsward, *Neths.* . . . . **15 A5** 53 3N 5 32 E
Bolt Head, *U.K.* **11 G4** 50 12N 3 48W
Bolton, *Canada* **78 C5** 43 54N 79 45W

Broad Arrow

Broad Arrow, Australia .... 61 F3 30 23S 121 15 E
Broad B., U.K. 12 C2 58 14N 6 18W
Broad Haven, Ireland 13 B2 54 20N 9 55W
Broad Law, U.K. 12 F5 55 30N 3 21W
Broad Sd., Australia ...... 62 C4 22 0S 149 45 E
Broadalbin, U.S.A. 79 C10 43 4N 74 12W
Broadback →, Canada ... 70 B4 51 21N 78 52W
Broadford, Australia ...... 63 F4 37 14S 145 4 E
Broadhurst Ra., Australia .. 60 D3 22 30S 122 30 E
Broads, The, U.K. .... 10 E9 52 45N 1 30 E
Broadus, U.S.A. 80 C2 45 27N 105 25W
Brochet, Canada 73 B8 57 53N 101 40W
Brochet, L., Canada 73 B8 58 36N 101 35W
Brocken, Germany .... 16 C6 51 47N 10 37 E
Brockport, U.S.A. 78 C7 43 13N 77 56W
Brockton, U.S.A. 79 D13 42 5N 71 1W
Brockville, Canada 79 B9 44 35N 75 41W
Brockway, Mont., U.S.A. .. 80 B2 47 18N 105 45W
Brockway, Pa., U.S.A. 78 E6 41 15N 78 47W
Brocton, U.S.A. 78 D5 42 23N 79 26W
Brodeur Pen., Canada 69 A11 72 30N 88 10W
Brodhead, Mt., U.S.A. 78 E7 41 39N 77 47W
Brodick, U.K. 12 F3 55 35N 5 9W
Brodnica, Poland .... 17 B10 53 15N 19 25 E
Brody, Ukraine .... 17 C13 50 5N 25 10 E
Brogan, U.S.A. 82 D5 44 15N 117 31W
Broken Arrow, U.S.A. 81 G7 36 3N 95 48W
Broken Bow, Nebr., U.S.A. . 80 E5 41 24N 99 38W
Broken Bow, Okla., U.S.A. . 81 H7 34 2N 94 44W
Broken Bow Lake, U.S.A. .. 81 H7 34 9N 94 40W
Broken Hill = Kabwe, Zambia .... 55 E2 14 30S 28 29 E
Broken Hill, Australia ..... 63 E3 31 58S 141 29 E
Bromley, U.K. .... 11 F8 51 24N 0 2 E
Bromsgrove, U.K. 11 E5 52 21N 2 2W
Brønderslev, Denmark .... 9 H13 57 16N 9 57 E
Bronkhorstspruit, S. Africa . 57 D4 25 46S 28 45 E
Brønnøysund, Norway .... 8 D15 65 28N 12 14 E
Brook Park, U.S.A. 78 E4 41 24N 81 51W
Brookhaven, U.S.A. 81 K9 31 35N 90 26W
Brookings, Oreg., U.S.A. .. 82 E1 42 3N 124 17W
Brookings, S. Dak., U.S.A. . 80 C6 44 19N 96 48W
Brooklin, Canada 78 C6 43 55N 78 55W
Brooklyn Park, U.S.A. 80 C8 45 6N 93 23W
Brooks, Canada 72 C6 50 35N 111 55W
Brooks Range, U.S.A. 68 B5 68 0N 152 0W
Brooksville, U.S.A. 77 L4 28 33N 82 23W
Brookton, Australia .... 61 F2 32 22S 117 0 E
Brookville, U.S.A. 78 E5 41 10N 79 5W
Broom, L., U.K. 12 D3 57 55N 5 15W
Broome, Australia .... 60 C3 18 0S 122 15 E
Brora, U.K. 12 C5 58 0N 3 52W
Brora →, U.K. 12 C5 58 0N 3 51W
Brosna →, Ireland 13 C4 53 14N 7 58W
Brothers, U.S.A. 82 E3 43 49N 120 36W
Brough, U.K. 10 C5 54 32N 2 18W
Brough Hd., U.K. 12 B5 59 8N 3 20W
Broughton Island = Qikiqtarjuaq, Canada 69 B13 67 33N 63 0W
Brown, L., Australia ...... 61 F2 31 5S 118 15 E
Brown, Pt., Australia ...... 63 E1 32 32S 133 50 E
Brown City, U.S.A. 78 C2 43 13N 82 59W
Brown Willy, U.K. 11 G3 50 35N 4 37W
Brownfield, U.S.A. 81 J3 33 11N 102 17W
Browning, U.S.A. 82 B7 48 34N 113 1W
Brownsville, Oreg., U.S.A. . 82 D2 44 24N 122 59W
Brownsville, Pa., U.S.A. ... 78 F5 40 1N 79 53W
Brownsville, Tenn., U.S.A. . 81 H10 35 36N 89 16W
Brownsville, Tex., U.S.A. .. 81 N6 25 54N 97 30W
Brownville, U.S.A. 79 C9 44 0N 75 59W
Brownwood, U.S.A. 81 K5 31 43N 98 59W
Browse I., Australia ...... 60 B3 14 7S 123 33 E
Bruas, Malaysia .... 39 K3 4 30N 100 47 E
Bruay-la-Buissière, France . 18 A5 50 29N 2 33 E
Bruce, Mt., Australia ...... 60 D2 22 37S 118 8 E
Bruce Pen., Canada 78 B3 45 0N 81 30W
Bruce Rock, Australia ..... 61 F2 31 52S 118 8 E
Bruck an der Leitha, Austria 17 D9 48 1N 16 47 E
Bruck an der Mur, Austria . 16 E8 47 24N 15 16 E
Brue →, U.K. 11 F5 51 13N 2 59W
Bruges = Brugge, Belgium 15 C3 51 13N 3 13 E
Brugge, Belgium .... 15 C3 51 13N 3 13 E
Bruin, U.S.A. 78 E5 41 3N 79 43W
Brûlé, Canada 72 C5 53 15N 117 58W
Brumado, Brazil 93 F10 14 14S 41 40W
Brumunddal, Norway ..... 9 F14 60 53N 10 56 E
Bruneau, U.S.A. 82 E6 42 53N 115 48W
Bruneau →, U.S.A. 82 E6 42 56N 115 57W
Brunei = Bandar Seri Begawan, Brunei .... 36 D5 4 52N 115 0 E
Brunei ■, Asia .... 36 D5 4 50N 115 0 E
Brunner, L., N.Z. .... 59 K3 42 37S 171 27 E
Brunssum, Neths. .... 15 D5 50 57N 5 59 E
Brunswick = Braunschweig, Germany .... 16 B6 52 15N 10 31 E
Brunswick, Ga., U.S.A. 77 K5 31 10N 81 30W
Brunswick, Maine, U.S.A. .. 77 D11 43 55N 69 58W
Brunswick, Md., U.S.A. 76 F7 39 19N 77 38W
Brunswick, Mo., U.S.A. 80 F8 39 26N 93 8W
Brunswick, Ohio, U.S.A. ... 78 E3 41 14N 81 51W
Brunswick, Pen. de, Chile .. 96 G2 53 30S 71 30W
Brunswick B., Australia ... 60 C3 15 15S 124 50 E
Brunswick Junction, Australia .... 61 F2 33 15S 115 50 E
Bruny I., Australia .... 62 G4 43 20S 147 15 E
Brus Laguna, Honduras ... 88 C3 15 47N 84 35W
Brush, U.S.A. 80 E3 40 15N 103 37W
Brushton, U.S.A. 79 B10 44 50N 74 31W
Brusque, Brazil 95 B6 27 5S 49 0W
Brussel, Belgium .... 15 D4 50 51N 4 21 E
Brussels = Brussel, Belgium 15 D4 50 51N 4 21 E
Brussels, Canada 78 C3 43 44N 81 15W
Bruthen, Australia .... 63 F4 37 42S 147 50 E
Bruxelles = Brussel, Belgium .... 15 D4 50 51N 4 21 E
Bryan, Ohio, U.S.A. 76 E3 41 28N 84 33W
Bryan, Tex., U.S.A. 81 K6 30 40N 96 22W
Bryan, Mt., Australia ...... 63 E2 33 30S 139 0 E
Bryansk, Russia .... 24 D5 53 13N 34 25 E
Bryce Canyon National Park, U.S.A. 83 H7 37 30N 112 10W
Bryne, Norway .... 9 G11 58 44N 5 38 E
Bryson City, U.S.A. 77 H4 35 26N 83 27W
Bsharri, Lebanon .... 47 A5 34 15N 36 0 E
Bū Baqarah, U.A.E. .... 45 E8 25 35N 56 25 E
Bu Craa, W. Sahara 50 C3 26 45N 12 50W
Bū Ḥasā, U.A.E. .... 45 F7 23 30N 53 20 E
Bua Yai, Thailand .... 38 E4 15 33N 102 26 E
Buapinang, Indonesia ..... 37 E6 4 40S 121 30 E
Bubanza, Burundi .... 54 C2 3 6S 29 23 E
Būbiyān, Kuwait .... 45 D6 29 45N 48 15 E
Bucaramanga, Colombia .. 92 B4 7 0N 73 0W
Bucasia, Australia .... 62 C4 21 2S 149 10 E
Buccaneer Arch., Australia . 60 C3 16 7S 123 20 E
Buchach, Ukraine .... 17 D13 49 5N 25 25 E
Buchan, U.K. 12 D6 57 32N 2 21W
Buchan Ness, U.K. 12 D7 57 29N 1 46W
Buchanan, Canada 73 C8 51 40N 102 45W
Buchanan, Liberia 50 G3 5 57N 10 2W
Buchanan, L., Queens., Australia .... 62 C4 21 35S 145 52 E
Buchanan, L., W. Austral., Australia .... 61 E3 25 33S 123 2 E
Buchanan, L., U.S.A. 81 K5 30 45N 98 25W
Buchanan Cr. →, Australia 62 B2 19 13S 136 33 E
Buchans, Canada 71 C8 48 50N 56 52W
Bucharest = Bucureşti, Romania .... 17 F14 44 27N 26 10 E
Buchon, Pt., U.S.A. 84 K6 35 15N 120 54W
Buck Hill Falls, U.S.A. 79 E9 41 11N 75 16W
Buckeye, U.S.A. 83 K7 33 22N 112 35W
Buckeye Lake, U.S.A. 78 G2 39 55N 82 29W
Buckhannon, U.S.A. 76 F5 39 0N 80 8W
Buckhaven, U.K. 12 E5 56 11N 3 3W
Buckhorn L., Canada 78 B6 44 29N 78 23W
Buckie, U.K. 12 D6 57 41N 2 58W
Buckingham, Canada 70 C4 45 37N 75 24W
Buckingham, U.K. 11 F7 51 59N 0 57W
Buckingham B., Australia .. 62 A2 12 10S 135 40 E
Buckinghamshire □, U.K. .. 11 F7 51 53N 0 55W
Buckle Hd., Australia ..... 60 B4 14 26S 127 52 E
Buckleboo, Australia ...... 63 E2 32 54S 136 12 E
Buckley, U.K. 10 D4 53 10N 3 5W
Buckley →, Australia ..... 62 C2 20 10S 138 49 E
Bucklin, U.S.A. 81 G5 37 33N 99 38W
Bucks L., U.S.A. 84 F5 39 54N 121 12W
Bouctouche, Canada 71 C7 46 30N 64 45W
Bucureşti, Romania ...... 17 F14 44 27N 26 10 E
Bucyrus, U.S.A. 76 E4 40 48N 82 59W
Budalin, Burma .... 41 H19 22 20N 95 10 E
Budapest, Hungary ...... 17 E10 47 29N 19 5 E
Budaun, India .... 43 E8 28 5N 79 10 E
Budd Coast, Antarctica ... 5 C8 68 0S 112 0 E
Bude, U.K. 11 G3 50 49N 4 34W
Budennovsk, Russia ...... 25 F7 44 50N 44 10 E
Budge Budge = Baj Baj, India .... 43 H13 22 30N 88 5 E
Budgewoi, Australia ...... 63 E5 33 13S 151 34 E
Budjala, Dem. Rep. of the Congo . 52 D3 2 50N 19 40 E
Buellton, U.S.A. 85 L6 34 37N 120 12W
Buena Esperanza, Argentina 94 C2 34 45S 65 15W
Buena Park, U.S.A. 85 M9 33 52N 117 59W
Buena Vista, Colo., U.S.A. . 83 G10 38 51N 106 8W
Buena Vista, Va., U.S.A. ... 76 G6 37 44N 79 21W
Buena Vista Lake Bed, U.S.A. 85 K7 35 12N 119 18W
Buenaventura, Colombia .. 92 C3 3 53N 77 4W
Buenaventura, Mexico 86 B3 29 50N 107 30W
Buenos Aires, Argentina .. 94 C4 34 30S 58 20W
Buenos Aires, Costa Rica .. 88 E3 9 10N 83 20W
Buenos Aires □, Argentina 94 D4 36 30S 60 0W
Buenos Aires, L., Chile 96 F2 46 35S 72 30W
Buffalo, Mo., U.S.A. 81 G8 37 39N 93 6W
Buffalo, N.Y., U.S.A. 78 D6 42 53N 78 53W
Buffalo, Okla., U.S.A. 81 G5 36 50N 99 38W
Buffalo, S. Dak., U.S.A. ... 80 C3 45 35N 103 33W
Buffalo, Wyo., U.S.A. 82 D10 44 21N 106 42W
Buffalo →, Canada 72 A5 60 5N 115 5W
Buffalo Head Hills, Canada 72 B5 57 25N 115 55W
Buffalo L., Canada 72 A5 60 12N 115 25W
Buffalo L., Alta., Canada ... 72 C6 52 27N 112 54W
Buffalo Narrows, Canada .. 73 B7 55 51N 108 29W
Buffels →, S. Africa ...... 56 D2 29 36S 17 3 E
Buford, U.S.A. 77 H4 34 10N 84 0W
Bug = Buh →, Ukraine .... 25 E5 46 59N 31 58 E
Bug →, Poland .... 17 B11 52 31N 21 5 E
Buga, Colombia 92 C3 4 0N 76 15W
Buganda, Uganda .... 54 C3 0 0 31 30 E
Buganga, Uganda .... 54 C3 0 3S 32 0 E
Bugel, Tanjung, Indonesia . 37 G14 6 26S 111 3 E
Bugibba, Malta .... 23 D1 35 57N 14 25 E
Bugsuk, Phil. .... 36 C5 8 15N 117 15 E
Bugulma, Russia .... 24 D9 54 33N 52 48 E
Bugun Shara, Mongolia ... 32 B5 49 0N 104 0 E
Buguruslan, Russia ...... 24 D9 53 39N 52 26 E
Buh →, Ukraine .... 25 E5 46 59N 31 58 E
Buhl, U.S.A. 82 E6 42 36N 114 46W
Builth Wells, U.K. 11 E4 52 9N 3 25W
Buir Nur, Mongolia .... 33 B6 47 50N 117 42 E
Bujumbura, Burundi ...... 54 C2 3 16S 29 18 E
Bukachacha, Russia ...... 27 D12 52 55N 116 50 E
Bukama, Dem. Rep. of the Congo . 55 D2 9 10S 25 50 E
Bukavu, Dem. Rep. of the Congo . 54 C2 2 20S 28 52 E
Bukene, Tanzania .... 54 C3 4 15S 32 48 E
Bukhara = Bukhoro, Uzbekistan .... 26 F7 39 48N 64 25 E
Bukhoro, Uzbekistan ...... 26 F7 39 48N 64 25 E
Bukima, Tanzania .... 54 C3 1 50S 33 25 E
Bukit Mertajam, Malaysia .. 39 K3 5 22N 100 28 E
Bukittinggi, Indonesia ..... 36 E2 0 20S 100 20 E
Bukoba, Tanzania .... 54 C3 1 20S 31 49 E
Bukuya, Uganda .... 54 B3 0 40N 31 52 E
Būl, Kuh-e, Iran .... 45 D7 30 48N 52 45 E
Bula, Indonesia .... 37 E8 3 6S 130 30 E
Bulahdelah, Australia ..... 63 E5 32 23S 152 13 E
Bulan, Phil. .... 37 B6 12 40N 123 52 E
Bulandshahr, India .... 42 E7 28 28N 77 51 E
Bulawayo, Zimbabwe ...... 55 G2 20 7S 28 32 E
Buldan, Turkey .... 21 E13 38 2N 28 50 E
Bulgar, Russia .... 24 D8 54 57N 49 4 E
Bulgaria ■, Europe .... 21 C11 42 35N 25 30 E
Buli, Teluk, Indonesia ..... 37 D7 1 5N 128 25 E
Buliluyan, C., Phil. .... 36 C5 8 20N 117 15 E
Bulkley →, Canada 72 B3 55 15N 127 40W
Bull Shoals L., U.S.A. 81 G8 36 22N 92 35W
Bullhead City, U.S.A. 85 K12 35 8N 114 32W
Büllingen, Belgium .... 15 D6 50 25N 6 16 E
Bullock Creek, Australia ... 62 B3 17 43S 144 31 E
Bulloo →, Australia ...... 63 D3 28 43S 142 30 E
Bulloo L., Australia ...... 63 D3 28 43S 142 25 E
Bulls, N.Z. .... 59 J5 40 10S 175 24 E
Bulnes, Chile 94 D1 36 42S 72 19W
Bulsar = Valsad, India .... 40 J8 20 40N 72 58 E
Bultfontein, S. Africa ..... 56 D4 28 18S 26 10 E
Bulukumba, Indonesia .... 37 F6 5 33S 120 11 E
Bulun, Russia .... 27 B13 70 37N 127 30 E
Bumba, Dem. Rep. of the Congo . 52 D4 2 13N 22 30 E
Bumbiri I., Tanzania ...... 54 C3 1 40S 31 55 E
Bumhpa Bum, Burma ..... 41 F20 26 51N 97 14 E
Bumi →, Zimbabwe ...... 55 F2 17 0S 28 20 E
Buna, Kenya .... 54 B4 2 58N 39 30 E
Bunazi, Tanzania .... 54 C3 1 3S 31 23 E
Bunbury, Australia .... 61 F2 33 20S 115 35 E
Bunclody, Ireland 13 D5 52 39N 6 40W
Buncrana, Ireland 13 A4 55 8N 7 27W
Bundaberg, Australia ..... 63 C5 24 54S 152 22 E
Bundey →, Australia ..... 62 C2 21 46S 135 37 E
Bundi, India .... 42 G6 25 30N 75 35 E
Bundoran, Ireland 13 B3 54 28N 8 16W
Bung Kan, Thailand ...... 38 C4 18 23N 103 37 E
Bungatakada, Japan ...... 31 H5 33 35N 131 25 E
Bungay, U.K. .... 11 E9 52 27N 1 28 E
Bungil Cr. →, Australia ... 63 D4 27 5S 149 5 E
Bungo-Suidō, Japan ...... 31 H6 33 0N 132 15 E
Bungoma, Kenya .... 54 B3 0 34N 34 34 E
Bungu, Tanzania .... 54 D4 7 35S 39 0 E
Bunia, Dem. Rep. of the Congo . 54 B3 1 35N 30 20 E
Bunji, Pakistan .... 43 B6 35 45N 74 40 E
Bunkie, U.S.A. 81 K8 30 57N 92 11W
Buntok, Indonesia .... 36 E4 1 40S 114 58 E
Bunyu, Indonesia .... 36 D5 3 35N 117 50 E
Buol, Indonesia .... 37 D6 1 15N 121 32 E
Buon Brieng, Vietnam ..... 38 F7 13 9N 108 12 E
Buon Ma Thuot, Vietnam ... 38 F7 12 40N 108 3 E
Buong Long, Cambodia .... 38 F6 13 44N 106 59 E
Buorkhaya, Mys, Russia ... 27 B14 71 50N 132 40 E
Buqayq, Si. Arabia .... 45 E6 26 0N 49 45 E
Bur Acaba, Somali Rep. ... 46 G3 3 12N 44 20 E
Bûr Safâga, Egypt .... 44 E2 26 43N 33 57 E
Bûr Sa'îd, Egypt .... 51 B12 31 16N 32 18 E
Bûr Sûdân, Sudan .... 51 E13 19 32N 37 9 E
Bura, Kenya .... 54 C4 1 4S 39 58 E
Burakin, Australia .... 61 F2 30 31S 117 10 E
Burao, Somali Rep. .... 46 F4 9 32N 45 32 E
Burāq, Syria .... 47 B5 33 11N 36 29 E
Buraydah, Si. Arabia ...... 44 E5 26 20N 44 8 E
Burbank, U.S.A. 85 L8 34 11N 118 19W
Burda, India .... 42 G6 25 50N 77 35 E
Burdekin →, Australia .... 62 B4 19 38S 147 25 E
Burdur, Turkey .... 25 G5 37 45N 30 17 E
Burdwan = Barddhaman, India .... 43 H12 23 14N 87 39 E
Bure, Ethiopia .... 46 E2 10 40N 37 4 E
Bure →, U.K. .... 10 E9 52 38N 1 43 E
Bureya →, Russia .... 27 E13 49 27N 129 30 E
Burford, Canada 78 C4 43 7N 80 27W
Burgas, Bulgaria .... 21 C12 42 33N 27 29 E
Burgeo, Canada 71 C8 47 37N 57 38W
Burgersdorp, S. Africa .... 56 E4 31 0S 26 20 E
Burges, Mt., Australia ..... 61 F3 30 50S 121 5 E
Burgos, Spain 19 A4 42 21N 3 41W
Burgsvik, Sweden .... 9 H18 57 3N 18 19 E
Burgundy = Bourgogne, France .... 18 C6 47 0N 4 50 E
Burhaniye, Turkey .... 21 E12 39 30N 26 58 E
Burhanpur, India .... 40 J10 21 18N 76 14 E
Burhi Gandak →, India ... 43 G12 25 20N 86 37 E
Burhner →, India .... 43 H9 22 43N 80 31 E
Burias, Phil. .... 37 B6 12 55N 123 5 E
Burica, Pta., Costa Rica ... 88 E3 8 3N 82 51W
Burien, U.S.A. 84 C4 47 28N 122 21W
Burigi, L., Tanzania ...... 54 C3 2 2S 31 22 E
Burin, Canada 71 C8 47 1N 55 14W
Buriram, Thailand .... 38 E4 15 0N 103 0 E
Burj Sāfitā, Syria .... 44 C3 34 48N 36 7 E
Burkburnett, U.S.A. 81 H5 34 6N 98 34W
Burke →, Australia ...... 62 C2 23 12S 139 33 E
Burke Chan., Canada 72 C3 52 10N 127 30W
Burketown, Australia ..... 62 B2 17 45S 139 33 E
Burkina Faso ■, Africa ... 50 F5 12 0N 1 0W
Burk's Falls, Canada 70 C4 45 37N 79 24W
Burleigh Falls, Canada 78 B6 44 33N 78 12W
Burley, U.S.A. 82 E7 42 32N 113 48W
Burlingame, U.S.A. 84 H4 37 35N 122 21W
Burlington, Canada 78 C5 43 18N 79 45W
Burlington, Colo., U.S.A. .. 80 F3 39 18N 102 16W
Burlington, Iowa, U.S.A. ... 80 E9 40 49N 91 14W
Burlington, Kans., U.S.A. .. 80 F7 38 12N 95 45W
Burlington, N.C., U.S.A. ... 77 G6 36 6N 79 26W
Burlington, N.J., U.S.A. ... 79 F10 40 4N 74 51W
Burlington, Vt., U.S.A. 79 B11 44 29N 73 12W
Burlington, Wash., U.S.A. . 84 B4 48 28N 122 20W
Burlington, Wis., U.S.A. ... 76 D1 42 41N 88 17W
Burlyu-Tyube, Kazakstan .. 26 E8 46 30N 79 10 E
Burma ■, Asia .... 41 J20 21 0N 96 30 E
Burnaby I., Canada 72 C2 52 25N 131 19W
Burnet, U.S.A. 81 K5 30 45N 98 14W
Burney, U.S.A. 82 F3 40 53N 121 40W
Burnham, U.S.A. 78 F7 40 38N 77 34W
Burnham-on-Sea, U.K. 11 F5 51 14N 3 0W
Burnie, Australia .... 62 G4 41 4S 145 56 E
Burnley, U.K. 10 D5 53 47N 2 14W
Burns, U.S.A. 82 E4 43 35N 119 3W
Burns Lake, Canada 72 C3 54 20N 125 45W
Burnside →, Canada 68 B9 66 51N 108 4W
Burnside, L., Australia .... 61 E3 25 22S 123 0 E
Burnsville, U.S.A. 80 C8 44 47N 93 17W
Burnt L., Canada 71 B7 53 35N 64 4W
Burnt River, Canada 78 B6 44 41N 78 42W
Burntwood →, Canada 73 B9 56 8N 96 34W
Burntwood L., Canada 73 B8 55 22N 100 26W
Burqān, Kuwait .... 44 D5 29 0N 47 57 E
Burra, Australia .... 63 E2 33 40S 138 55 E
Burray, U.K. 12 C6 58 51N 2 54W
Burren Junction, Australia . 63 E4 30 7S 148 59 E
Burrinjuck Res., Australia . 63 F4 35 0S 148 36 E
Burro, Serranías del, Mexico 86 B4 29 0N 102 0W
Burrow Hd., U.K. 12 G4 54 41N 4 24W
Burruyacú, Argentina 94 B3 26 30S 64 40W
Burry Port, U.K. 11 F3 51 41N 4 15W
Bursa, Turkey .... 21 D13 40 15N 29 5 E
Burstall, Canada 73 C7 50 39N 109 54W
Burton, Ohio, U.S.A. 78 E3 41 28N 81 8W
Burton, S.C., U.S.A. 77 J5 32 25N 80 45W
Burton, L., Canada 70 B4 54 45N 78 20W
Burton upon Trent, U.K. ... 10 E6 52 48N 1 38W
Buru, Indonesia .... 37 E7 3 30S 126 30 E
Burûn, Râs, Egypt .... 47 D2 31 14N 33 7 E
Burundi ■, Africa .... 54 C3 3 15S 30 0 E
Bururi, Burundi .... 54 C2 3 57S 29 37 E
Burutu, Nigeria .... 50 G7 5 20N 5 29 E
Burwell, U.S.A. 80 E5 41 47N 99 8W
Burwick, U.K. 12 C5 58 45N 2 58W
Bury, U.K. 10 D5 53 35N 2 17W
Bury St. Edmunds, U.K. ... 11 E8 52 15N 0 43 E
Buryatia □, Russia ...... 27 D12 53 0N 110 0 E
Busango Swamp, Zambia . 55 E2 14 15S 25 45 E
Buşayrah, Syria .... 44 C4 35 9N 40 26 E
Būshehr, Iran .... 45 D6 28 55N 50 55 E
Būshehr □, Iran .... 45 D6 28 20N 51 45 E
Bushell, Canada 73 B7 59 31N 108 45W
Bushenyi, Uganda .... 54 C3 0 35S 30 10 E
Bushire = Būshehr, Iran ... 45 D6 28 55N 50 55 E
Businga, Dem. Rep. of the Congo . 52 D4 3 16N 20 59 E
Buşra ash Shām, Syria .... 47 C5 32 30N 36 25 E
Busselton, Australia ..... 61 F2 33 42S 115 15 E
Bussum, Neths. .... 15 B5 52 16N 5 10 E
Busto Arsizio, Italy .... 18 D8 45 37N 8 51 E
Busu-Djanoa, Dem. Rep. of the Congo . 52 D4 1 43N 21 23 E
Busuanga, Phil. .... 37 B6 12 10N 120 0 E
Buta, Dem. Rep. of the Congo . 54 B1 2 50N 24 53 E
Butare, Rwanda .... 54 C2 2 31S 29 52 E
Butaritari, Kiribati .... 64 G9 3 30N 174 0 E
Bute, U.K. 12 F3 55 48N 5 2W
Bute Inlet, Canada 72 C4 50 40N 124 53W
Butemba, Uganda .... 54 B3 1 9N 31 37 E
Butembo, Dem. Rep. of the Congo . 54 B2 0 9N 29 18 E
Butha Qi, China .... 33 B7 48 0N 122 32 E
Butiaba, Uganda .... 54 B3 1 50N 31 20 E
Butler, Mo., U.S.A. 80 F7 38 16N 94 20W
Butler, Pa., U.S.A. 78 F5 40 52N 79 54W
Buton, Indonesia .... 37 F6 5 0S 122 45 E
Butte, Mont., U.S.A. 82 C7 46 0N 112 32W
Butte, Nebr., U.S.A. 80 D5 42 58N 98 51W
Butte Creek →, U.S.A. ... 84 F5 39 12N 121 56W
Butterworth = Gcuwa, S. Africa .... 57 E4 32 20S 28 11 E
Butterworth, Malaysia .... 39 K3 5 24N 100 23 E
Buttevant, Ireland 13 D3 52 14N 8 40W
Buttfield, Mt., Australia ... 61 D4 24 45S 128 9 E
Button B., Canada 73 B10 58 45N 94 23W
Buttonwillow, U.S.A. 85 K7 35 24N 119 28W
Butty Hd., Australia ...... 61 F3 33 54S 121 39 E
Butuan, Phil. .... 37 C7 8 57N 125 33 E
Butung = Buton, Indonesia 37 F6 5 0S 122 45 E
Buturlinovka, Russia ..... 25 D7 50 50N 40 35 E
Buxa Duar, India .... 43 F13 27 45N 89 35 E
Buxar, India .... 43 G10 25 34N 83 58 E
Buxtehude, Germany ..... 16 B5 53 28N 9 39 E
Buxton, U.K. 10 D6 53 16N 1 54W
Buy, Russia .... 24 C7 58 28N 41 28 E
Büyük Menderes →, Turkey .... 21 F12 37 28N 27 11 E
Büyükçekmece, Turkey .... 21 D13 41 2N 28 35 E
Buzău, Romania .... 17 F14 45 10N 26 50 E
Buzău →, Romania ...... 17 F14 45 26N 27 44 E
Buzen, Japan .... 31 H5 33 35N 131 5 E
Buzi →, Mozam. .... 55 F3 19 50S 34 43 E
Buzuluk, Russia .... 24 D9 52 48N 52 12 E
Buzzards B., U.S.A. 79 E14 41 45N 70 37W
Buzzards Bay, U.S.A. 79 E14 41 44N 70 37W
Bwana Mkubwe, Dem. Rep. of the Congo . 55 E2 13 8S 28 38 E
Byarezina →, Belarus .... 17 B16 52 33N 30 14 E
Bydgoszcz, Poland ...... 17 B9 53 10N 18 0 E
Byelarus = Belarus ■, Europe .... 17 B14 53 30N 27 0 E
Byelorussia = Belarus ■, Europe .... 17 B14 53 30N 27 0 E
Byers, U.S.A. 80 F2 39 43N 104 14W
Byesville, U.S.A. 78 G3 39 58N 81 32W
Byford, Australia .... 61 F2 32 15S 116 0 E
Bykhaw, Belarus .... 17 B16 53 31N 30 14 E
Bykhov = Bykhaw, Belarus 17 B16 53 31N 30 14 E
Bylas, U.S.A. 83 K8 33 8N 110 7W
Bylot, Canada 73 B10 58 25N 94 8W
Bylot I., Canada 69 A12 73 13N 78 34W
Byrd, C., Antarctica 5 C17 69 38S 76 7W
Byrock, Australia .... 63 E4 30 40S 146 27 E
Byron Bay, Australia ...... 63 D5 28 43S 153 37 E
Byrranga, Gory, Russia ... 27 B11 75 0N 100 0 E
Byrranga Mts. = Byrranga, Gory, Russia .... 27 B11 75 0N 100 0 E
Byske, Sweden .... 8 D19 64 57N 21 11 E
Byske älv →, Sweden .... 8 D19 64 57N 21 13 E
Bytom, Poland .... 17 C10 50 25N 18 54 E
Bytów, Poland .... 17 A9 54 10N 17 30 E
Byumba, Rwanda .... 54 C3 1 35S 30 4 E

C

Ca →, Vietnam .... 38 C5 18 45N 105 45 E
Ca Mau, Vietnam .... 39 H5 9 7N 105 8 E
Ca Mau, Mui, Vietnam .... 39 H5 8 38N 104 44 E
Ca Na, Vietnam .... 39 G7 11 20N 108 54 E
Caacupé, Paraguay 94 B4 25 23S 57 5W
Caála, Angola .... 53 G3 12 46S 15 30 E
Caamano Sd., Canada 72 C3 52 55N 129 25W
Caazapá, Paraguay 94 B4 26 8S 56 19W
Caazapá □, Paraguay 95 B4 26 10S 56 0W
Cabanatuan, Phil. .... 37 A6 15 30N 120 58 E
Cabano, Canada 71 C6 47 40N 68 56W
Cabazon, U.S.A. 85 M10 33 55N 116 47W
Cabedelo, Brazil 93 E12 7 0S 34 50W
Cabildo, Chile 94 C1 32 30S 71 5W
Cabimas, Venezuela 92 A4 10 23N 71 25W
Cabinda, Angola .... 52 F2 5 33S 12 11 E
Cabinda □, Angola ...... 52 F2 5 0S 12 30 E
Cabinet Mts., U.S.A. 82 C6 48 0N 115 30W
Cabo Blanco, Argentina ... 96 F3 47 15S 65 47W
Cabo Frio, Brazil 95 A7 22 51S 42 3W
Cabo Pantoja, Peru 92 D3 1 0S 75 10W
Cabonga, Réservoir, Canada 70 C4 47 20N 76 40W
Cabool, U.S.A. 81 G8 37 7N 92 6W
Caboolture, Australia ..... 63 D5 27 5S 152 58 E

Corrientes

114

Desolación, I.

Dalton, *Mass., U.S.A.* **79 D11** 42 28N 73 11W
Dalton, *Nebr., U.S.A.* **80 E3** 41 25N 102 58W
Dalton Iceberg Tongue, *Antarctica* ..... **5 C9** 66 15S 121 30 E
Dalton-in-Furness, *U.K.* **10 C4** 54 10N 3 11W
Dalvík, *Iceland* **8 D4** 65 58N 18 32W
Dalwallinu, *Australia* ..... **61 F2** 30 17S 116 40 E
Daly →, *Australia* ..... **60 B5** 13 35S 130 19 E
Daly City, *U.S.A.* **84 H4** 37 42N 122 28W
Daly L., *Canada* **73 B7** 56 32N 105 39W
Daly River, *Australia* ..... **60 B5** 13 46S 130 42 E
Daly Waters, *Australia* ..... **62 B1** 16 15S 133 24 E
Dam Doi, *Vietnam* ..... **39 H5** 8 50N 105 12 E
Dam Ha, *Vietnam* ..... **38 B6** 21 21N 107 36 E
Daman, *India* ..... **40 J8** 20 25N 72 57 E
Dāmaneh, *Iran* ..... **45 C6** 33 1N 50 29 E
Damanhûr, *Egypt* ..... **51 B12** 31 0N 30 30 E
Damant L., *Canada* **73 A7** 61 45N 105 5W
Damanzhuang, *China* ..... **34 E9** 38 5N 116 35 E
Damar, *Indonesia* ..... **37 F7** 7 7S 128 40 E
Damaraland, *Namibia* ..... **56 C2** 20 0S 15 0 E
Damascus = Dimashq, *Syria* **47 B5** 33 30N 36 18 E
Damāvand, *Iran* ..... **45 C7** 35 47N 52 0 E
Damāvand, Qolleh-ye, *Iran* **45 C7** 35 56N 52 10 E
Damba, *Angola* ..... **52 F3** 6 44S 15 20 E
Dâmboviţa →, *Romania* . **17 F14** 44 12N 26 26 E
Dame Marie, *Haiti* **89 C5** 18 36N 74 26W
Dāmghān, *Iran* ..... **45 B7** 36 10N 54 17 E
Damiel, *Spain* **19 C4** 39 4N 3 37W
Damietta = Dumyât, *Egypt* **51 B12** 31 24N 31 48 E
Daming, *China* ..... **34 F8** 36 15N 115 6 E
Damīr Qābū, *Syria* ..... **44 B4** 36 58N 41 51 E
Dammam = Ad Dammām, *Si. Arabia* ..... **45 E6** 26 20N 50 5 E
Damodar →, *India* ..... **43 H12** 23 17N 87 35 E
Damoh, *India* ..... **43 H8** 23 50N 79 28 E
Dampier, *Australia* ..... **60 D2** 20 41S 116 42 E
Dampier, Selat, *Indonesia* . **37 E8** 0 40S 131 0 E
Dampier Arch., *Australia* .. **60 D2** 20 38S 116 32 E
Damrei, Chuor Phnum, *Cambodia* ..... **39 G4** 11 30N 103 0 E
Dan Xian, *China* ..... **38 C7** 19 31N 109 33 E
Dana, *Indonesia* ..... **37 F6** 11 0S 122 52 E
Dana, L., *Canada* **70 B4** 50 53N 77 20W
Dana, Mt., *U.S.A.* **84 H7** 37 54N 119 12W
Danakil Depression, *Ethiopia* **46 E3** 12 45N 41 0 E
Danané, *Ivory C.* **50 G4** 7 16N 8 9W
Danau Poso, *Indonesia* ..... **37 E6** 1 52S 120 35 E
Danbury, *U.S.A.* **79 E11** 41 24N 73 28W
Danby L., *U.S.A.* **83 J6** 34 13N 115 5W
Dand, *Afghan.* ..... **42 D1** 31 28N 65 32 E
Dandeldhura, *Nepal* ..... **43 E9** 29 20N 80 35 E
Dandeli, *India* ..... **40 M9** 15 5N 74 30 E
Dandenong, *Australia* ..... **63 F4** 38 0S 145 15 E
Dandong, *China* ..... **35 D13** 40 10N 124 20 E
Danfeng, *China* ..... **34 H6** 33 45N 110 25 E
Danger Is. = Pukapuka, *Cook Is.* **65 J11** 10 53S 165 49W
Danger Pt., *S. Africa* ..... **56 E2** 34 40S 19 17 E
Dangla Shan = Tanggula Shan, *China* ..... **32 C4** 32 40N 92 10 E
Dangrek, Phnom, *Thailand* **38 E5** 14 15N 105 0 E
Dangriga, *Belize* **87 D7** 17 0N 88 13W
Dangshan, *China* ..... **34 G9** 34 27N 116 22 E
Daniel, *U.S.A.* **82 E8** 42 52N 110 4W
Daniel's Harbour, *Canada* . **71 B8** 50 13N 57 35W
Danielskuil, *S. Africa* ..... **56 D3** 28 11S 23 33 E
Danielson, *U.S.A.* **79 E13** 41 48N 71 53W
Danilov, *Russia* ..... **24 C7** 58 16N 40 13 E
Daning, *China* ..... **34 F6** 36 28N 110 45 E
Danissa, *Kenya* ..... **54 B5** 3 15N 40 58 E
Dank, *Oman* ..... **45 F8** 23 33N 56 16 E
Dankhar Gompa, *India* ..... **40 C11** 32 10N 78 10 E
Danlí, *Honduras* **88 D2** 14 4N 86 35W
Dannemora, *U.S.A.* **79 B11** 44 43N 73 44W
Dannevirke, *N.Z.* ..... **59 J6** 40 12S 176 8 E
Dannhauser, *S. Africa* ..... **57 D5** 28 0S 30 3 E
Dansville, *U.S.A.* **78 D7** 42 34N 77 42W
Danta, *India* ..... **42 G5** 24 11N 72 46 E
Dantan, *India* ..... **43 J12** 21 57N 87 20 E
Dante, *Somali Rep.* ..... **46 E5** 10 25N 51 16 E
Danube = Dunărea →, *Europe* ..... **17 F15** 45 20N 29 40 E
Danvers, *U.S.A.* **79 D14** 42 34N 70 56W
Danville, *Ill., U.S.A.* **76 E2** 40 8N 87 37W
Danville, *Ky., U.S.A.* **76 G3** 37 39N 84 46W
Danville, *Pa., U.S.A.* **79 F8** 40 58N 76 37W
Danville, *Va., U.S.A.* **77 G6** 36 36N 79 23W
Danville, *Vt., U.S.A.* **79 B12** 44 25N 72 9W
Danzig = Gdańsk, *Poland* . **17 A10** 54 22N 18 40 E
Dapaong, *Togo* ..... **50 F6** 10 55N 0 16 E
Daqing Shan, *China* ..... **34 D6** 40 40N 111 0 E
Dar Banda, *Africa* ..... **48 F6** 8 0N 23 0 E
Dar el Beida = Casablanca, *Morocco* **50 B4** 33 36N 7 36W
Dar es Salaam, *Tanzania* .. **54 D4** 6 50S 39 12 E
Dar Mazār, *Iran* ..... **45 D8** 29 14N 57 20 E
Dar'ā, *Syria* ..... **47 C5** 32 36N 36 7 E
Dar'ā □, *Syria* ..... **47 C5** 32 55N 36 10 E
Dārāb, *Iran* ..... **45 D7** 28 50N 54 30 E
Daraban, *Pakistan* ..... **42 D4** 31 44N 70 20 E
Daraj, *Libya* ..... **51 B8** 30 10N 10 28 E
Dārān, *Iran* ..... **45 C6** 32 59N 50 24 E
Dārayyā, *Syria* ..... **47 B5** 33 28N 36 15 E
Darband, *Pakistan* ..... **42 B5** 34 20N 72 50 E
Darband, Kūh-e, *Iran* ..... **45 D8** 31 34N 57 8 E
Darbhanga, *India* ..... **43 F11** 26 15N 85 55 E
D'Arcy, *Canada* **72 C4** 50 27N 122 35W
Dardanelle, *Ark., U.S.A.* **81 H8** 35 13N 93 9W
Dardanelle, *Calif., U.S.A.* .. **84 G7** 38 20N 119 50W
Dardanelles = Çanakkale Boğazı, *Turkey* ..... **21 D12** 40 17N 26 32 E
Dārestān, *Iran* ..... **45 D8** 29 9N 58 42 E
Dârfûr, *Sudan* ..... **51 F10** 13 40N 24 0 E
Dargai, *Pakistan* ..... **42 B4** 34 25N 71 55 E
Dargan Ata, *Uzbekistan* ..... **26 E7** 40 29N 62 10 E
Dargaville, *N.Z.* ..... **59 F4** 35 57S 173 52 E
Darhan, *Mongolia* ..... **32 B5** 49 37N 106 21 E
Darhan Muminggan Lianheqi, *China* ..... **34 D6** 41 40N 110 28 E
Darıca, *Turkey* ..... **21 D13** 40 45N 29 23 E
Darién, G. del, *Colombia* .. **92 B3** 9 0N 77 0W
Dariganga = Ovoot, *Mongolia* ..... **34 B7** 45 21N 113 45 E
Darjeeling = Darjiling, *India* **43 F13** 27 3N 88 18 E
Darjiling, *India* ..... **43 F13** 27 3N 88 18 E
Darkan, *Australia* ..... **61 F2** 33 20S 116 43 E
Darkhana, *Pakistan* ..... **42 D5** 30 39N 72 11 E
Darkhazīneh, *Iran* ..... **45 D6** 31 54N 48 39 E
Darkot Pass, *Pakistan* ..... **43 A5** 36 45N 73 26 E
Darling →, *Australia* ..... **63 E3** 34 4S 141 54 E
Darling Downs, *Australia* .. **63 D5** 27 30S 150 30 E
Darling Ra., *Australia* ..... **61 F2** 32 30S 116 0 E
Darlington, *U.K.* **10 C6** 54 32N 1 33W
Darlington, *U.S.A.* **77 H6** 34 18N 79 52W
Darlington □, *U.K.* **10 C6** 54 32N 1 33W
Darlington, L., *S. Africa* ..... **56 E4** 33 10S 25 9 E
Darlington Point, *Australia* . **63 E4** 34 37S 146 1 E
Darlot, L., *Australia* ..... **61 E3** 27 48S 121 35 E
Darłowo, *Poland* ..... **16 A9** 54 25N 16 25 E
Darmstadt, *Germany* ..... **16 D5** 49 51N 8 39 E
Darnah, *Libya* ..... **51 B10** 32 45N 22 45 E
Darnall, *S. Africa* ..... **57 D5** 29 23S 31 18 E
Darnley, C., *Antarctica* ..... **5 C6** 68 0S 69 0 E
Darnley B., *Canada* **68 B7** 69 30N 123 30W
Darr →, *Australia* ..... **62 C3** 23 39S 143 50 E
Darra Pezu, *Pakistan* ..... **42 C4** 32 19N 70 44 E
Darrequeira, *Argentina* **94 D3** 37 42S 63 10W
Darrington, *U.S.A.* **82 B3** 48 15N 121 36W
Dart →, *U.K.* **11 G4** 50 24N 3 39W
Dart, C., *Antarctica* **5 D14** 73 6S 126 20W
Dartford, *U.K.* ..... **11 F8** 51 26N 0 13 E
Dartmoor, *U.K.* **11 G4** 50 38N 3 57W
Dartmouth, *Canada* **71 D7** 44 40N 63 30W
Dartmouth, *U.K.* **11 G4** 50 21N 3 36W
Dartmouth, L., *Australia* ..... **63 D4** 26 4S 145 18 E
Dartuch, C. = Artrutx, C. de, *Spain* ..... **22 B10** 39 55N 3 49 E
Darvaza, *Turkmenistan* ..... **26 E6** 40 11N 58 24 E
Darvel, Teluk = Lahad Datu, Teluk, *Malaysia* ..... **37 D5** 4 50N 118 20 E
Darwen, *U.K.* **10 D5** 53 42N 2 29W
Darwha, *India* ..... **40 J10** 20 15N 77 45 E
Darwin, *Australia* ..... **60 B5** 12 25S 130 51 E
Darwin, *U.S.A.* **85 J9** 36 15N 117 35W
Darya Khan, *Pakistan* ..... **42 D4** 31 48N 71 6 E
Daryoi Amu = Amudarya →, *Uzbekistan* ..... **26 E6** 43 58N 59 34 E
Dās, *U.A.E.* ..... **45 E7** 25 20N 53 30 E
Dashetai, *China* ..... **34 D5** 41 0N 109 5 E
Dashhowuz, *Turkmenistan* . **26 E6** 41 49N 59 58 E
Dashköpri, *Turkmenistan* .. **45 B9** 36 16N 62 8 E
Dasht, *Iran* ..... **45 B8** 37 17N 56 7 E
Dasht →, *Pakistan* ..... **40 G2** 25 10N 61 40 E
Dasht-e Mārgow, *Afghan.* . **40 D3** 30 40N 62 30 E
Dasht-i-Nawar, *Afghan.* ..... **42 C3** 33 52N 68 0 E
Daska, *Pakistan* ..... **42 C6** 32 20N 74 20 E
Dasuya, *India* ..... **42 D6** 31 49N 75 38 E
Datça, *Turkey* ..... **21 F12** 36 46N 27 40 E
Datia, *India* ..... **43 G8** 25 39N 78 27 E
Datong, *China* ..... **34 D7** 40 6N 113 18 E
Dattakhel, *Pakistan* ..... **42 C3** 32 54N 69 46 E
Datu, Tanjung, *Indonesia* .. **36 D3** 2 5N 109 39 E
Datu Piang, *Phil.* ..... **37 C6** 7 2N 124 30 E
Daud Khel, *Pakistan* ..... **42 C4** 32 53N 71 34 E
Daudnagar, *India* ..... **43 G11** 25 2N 84 24 E
Daugava →, *Latvia* ..... **9 H21** 57 4N 24 3 E
Daugavpils, *Latvia* ..... **9 J22** 55 53N 26 32 E
Daulpur, *India* ..... **42 F7** 26 45N 77 59 E
Dauphin, *Canada* **73 C8** 51 9N 100 5W
Dauphin, *U.S.A.* **78 F8** 40 22N 76 56W
Dauphin L., *Canada* **73 C9** 51 20N 99 45W
Dauphiné, *France* ..... **18 D6** 45 15N 5 25 E
Dausa, *India* ..... **42 F7** 26 52N 76 20 E
Davangere, *India* ..... **40 M9** 14 25N 75 55 E
Davao, *Phil.* ..... **37 C7** 7 0N 125 40 E
Davao, G. of, *Phil.* ..... **37 C7** 6 30N 125 48 E
Dāvar Panāh, *Iran* ..... **45 E9** 27 25N 62 15 E
Davenport, *Calif., U.S.A.* .. **84 H4** 37 1N 122 12W
Davenport, *Iowa, U.S.A.* .. **80 E9** 41 32N 90 35W
Davenport, *Wash., U.S.A.* . **82 C4** 47 39N 118 9W
Davenport Ra., *Australia* .. **62 C1** 20 28S 134 0 E
Daventry, *U.K.* **11 E6** 52 16N 1 10W
David, *Panama* **88 E3** 8 30N 82 30W
David City, *U.S.A.* **80 E6** 41 15N 97 8W
David Gorodok = Davyd Haradok, *Belarus* ..... **17 B14** 52 4N 27 8 E
Davidson, *Canada* **73 C7** 51 16N 105 59W
Davis, *U.S.A.* **84 G5** 38 33N 121 44W
Davis Dam, *U.S.A.* **85 K12** 35 11N 114 34W
Davis Inlet, *Canada* **71 A7** 55 50N 60 59W
Davis Mts., *U.S.A.* **81 K2** 30 50N 103 55W
Davis Sea, *Antarctica* ..... **5 C7** 66 0S 92 0 E
Davis Str., *N. Amer.* **69 B14** 65 0N 58 0W
Davos, *Switz.* ..... **18 C8** 46 48N 9 49 E
Davy L., *Canada* **73 B7** 58 53N 108 18W
Davyd Haradok, *Belarus* ..... **17 B14** 52 4N 27 8 E
Dawei, *Burma* ..... **38 E2** 14 2N 98 12 E
Dawes Ra., *Australia* ..... **62 C5** 24 40S 150 40 E
Dawlish, *U.K.* **11 G4** 50 35N 3 28W
Dawros Hd., *Ireland* **13 B3** 54 50N 8 33W
Dawson, *Canada* **68 B6** 64 10N 139 30W
Dawson, *U.S.A.* **77 K3** 31 46N 84 27W
Dawson, I., *Chile* **96 G2** 53 50S 70 50W
Dawson B., *Canada* **73 C8** 52 53N 100 49W
Dawson Creek, *Canada* **72 B4** 55 45N 120 15W
Dawson Inlet, *Canada* **73 A10** 61 50N 93 25W
Dawson Ra., *Australia* ..... **62 C4** 24 30S 149 48 E
Dax, *France* **18 E3** 43 44N 1 3W
Daxian, *China* ..... **32 C5** 31 15N 107 23 E
Daxindian, *China* ..... **35 F11** 37 30N 120 50 E
Daxinggou, *China* ..... **35 C15** 43 25N 129 40 E
Daxue Shan, *China* ..... **32 C5** 30 30N 101 30 E
Daylesford, *Australia* ..... **63 F3** 37 21S 144 9 E
Dayr az Zawr, *Syria* ..... **44 C4** 35 20N 40 5 E
Daysland, *Canada* **72 C6** 52 50N 112 20W
Dayton, *Nev., U.S.A.* **84 F7** 39 14N 119 36W
Dayton, *Ohio, U.S.A.* **76 F3** 39 45N 84 12W
Dayton, *Pa., U.S.A.* **78 F5** 40 53N 79 15W
Dayton, *Tenn., U.S.A.* **77 H3** 35 30N 85 1W
Dayton, *Wash., U.S.A.* **82 C4** 46 19N 117 59W
Dayton, *Wyo., U.S.A.* **82 D10** 44 53N 107 16W
Daytona Beach, *U.S.A.* **77 L5** 29 13N 81 1W
Dayville, *U.S.A.* **82 D4** 44 28N 119 32W
De Aar, *S. Africa* ..... **56 E3** 30 39S 24 0 E
De Funiak Springs, *U.S.A.* . **77 K2** 30 43N 86 7W
De Grey →, *Australia* ..... **60 D2** 20 12S 119 13 E
De Haan, *Belgium* ..... **15 C3** 51 16N 3 2 E
De Kalb, *U.S.A.* **80 E10** 41 56N 88 46W
De Land, *U.S.A.* **77 L5** 29 2N 81 18W
De Leon, *U.S.A.* **81 J5** 32 7N 98 32W
De Panne, *Belgium* ..... **15 C2** 51 6N 2 34 E
De Pere, *U.S.A.* **76 C1** 44 27N 88 4W
De Queen, *U.S.A.* **81 H7** 34 2N 94 21W
De Quincy, *U.S.A.* **81 K8** 30 27N 93 26W
De Ridder, *U.S.A.* **81 K8** 30 51N 93 17W
De Smet, *U.S.A.* **80 C6** 44 23N 97 33W
De Soto, *U.S.A.* **80 F9** 38 8N 90 34W
De Tour Village, *U.S.A.* **76 C4** 46 0N 83 56W
De Witt, *U.S.A.* **81 H9** 34 18N 91 20W
Dead Sea, *Asia* ..... **47 D4** 31 30N 35 30 E
Deadwood, *U.S.A.* **80 C3** 44 23N 103 44W
Deadwood L., *Canada* **72 B3** 59 10N 128 30W
Deal, *U.K.* ..... **11 F9** 51 13N 1 25 E
Deal I., *Australia* ..... **62 F4** 39 30S 147 20 E
Dealesville, *S. Africa* ..... **56 D4** 28 41S 25 44 E
Dean →, *Canada* **72 C3** 52 49N 126 58W
Dean, Forest of, *U.K.* **11 F5** 51 45N 2 33W
Dean Chan., *Canada* **72 C3** 52 30N 127 15W
Deán Funes, *Argentina* **94 C3** 30 20S 64 20W
Dease →, *Canada* **72 B3** 59 56N 128 32W
Dease L., *Canada* **72 B2** 58 40N 130 5W
Dease Lake, *Canada* **72 B2** 58 25N 130 6W
Death Valley, *U.S.A.* **85 J10** 36 15N 116 50W
Death Valley Junction, *U.S.A.* **85 J10** 36 20N 116 25W
Death Valley National Park, *U.S.A.* **85 J10** 36 45N 117 15W
Debar, *Macedonia* ..... **21 D9** 41 31N 20 30 E
Debden, *Canada* **73 C7** 53 30N 106 50W
Dębica, *Poland* ..... **17 C11** 50 2N 21 25 E
Debolt, *Canada* **72 B5** 55 12N 118 1W
Deborah East, L., *Australia* **61 F2** 30 45S 119 0 E
Deborah West, L., *Australia* **61 F2** 30 45S 118 50 E
Debre Markos, *Ethiopia* ..... **46 E2** 10 20N 37 40 E
Debre Tabor, *Ethiopia* ..... **46 E2** 11 50N 38 26 E
Debre Zeyit, *Ethiopia* ..... **46 F2** 11 48N 38 30 E
Debrecen, *Hungary* ..... **17 E11** 47 33N 21 42 E
Decatur, *Ala., U.S.A.* **77 H2** 34 36N 86 59W
Decatur, *Ga., U.S.A.* **77 J3** 33 47N 84 18W
Decatur, *Ill., U.S.A.* **80 F10** 39 51N 88 57W
Decatur, *Ind., U.S.A.* **76 E3** 40 50N 84 56W
Decatur, *Tex., U.S.A.* **81 J6** 33 14N 97 35W
Deccan, *India* ..... **40 L11** 18 0N 79 0 E
Deception Bay, *Australia* ..... **63 D5** 27 10S 153 5 E
Deception L., *Canada* **73 B8** 56 33N 104 13W
Dechhu, *India* ..... **42 F5** 26 46N 72 20 E
Děčín, *Czech Rep.* ..... **16 C8** 50 47N 14 12 E
Deckerville, *U.S.A.* **78 C2** 43 32N 82 44W
Decorah, *U.S.A.* **80 D9** 43 18N 91 48W
Dedéagach = Alexandroúpolis, *Greece* **21 D11** 40 50N 25 54 E
Dedham, *U.S.A.* **79 D13** 42 15N 71 10W
Dedza, *Malawi* ..... **55 E3** 14 20S 34 20 E
Dee →, *Aberds., U.K.* **12 D6** 57 9N 2 5W
Dee →, *Dumf. & Gall., U.K.* **12 G4** 54 51N 4 3W
Dee →, *Wales, U.K.* **10 D4** 53 22N 3 17W
Deep B., *Canada* **72 A5** 61 15N 116 35W
Deepwater, *Australia* ..... **63 D5** 29 25S 151 51 E
Deer →, *Canada* **73 B10** 58 23N 94 13W
Deer L., *Canada* **73 C10** 52 40N 94 20W
Deer Lake, *Nfld., Canada* **71 C8** 49 11N 57 27W
Deer Lake, *Ont., Canada* **73 C10** 52 36N 94 20W
Deer Lodge, *U.S.A.* **82 C7** 46 24N 112 44W
Deer Park, *U.S.A.* **82 C5** 47 57N 117 28W
Deer River, *U.S.A.* **80 B8** 47 20N 93 48W
Deeragun, *Australia* ..... **62 B4** 19 16S 146 33 E
Deerdepoort, *S. Africa* ..... **56 C4** 24 37S 26 27 E
Deferiet, *U.S.A.* **79 B9** 44 2N 75 41W
Defiance, *U.S.A.* **76 E3** 41 17N 84 22W
Degana, *India* ..... **42 F6** 26 50N 74 20 E
Dégelis, *Canada* **71 C6** 47 30N 68 35W
Deggendorf, *Germany* ..... **16 D7** 48 50N 12 57 E
Degh →, *Pakistan* ..... **42 D5** 31 3N 73 21 E
Deh Bīd, *Iran* ..... **45 D7** 30 39N 53 11 E
Deh-e Shīr, *Iran* ..... **45 D7** 31 29N 53 45 E
Dehaj, *Iran* ..... **45 D7** 30 42N 54 53 E
Dehak, *Iran* ..... **45 E9** 27 11N 62 37 E
Dehdez, *Iran* ..... **45 D6** 31 43N 50 17 E
Dehej, *India* ..... **42 J5** 21 44N 72 40 E
Dehestān, *Iran* ..... **45 D7** 28 30N 55 35 E
Dehgolān, *Iran* ..... **44 C5** 35 17N 47 25 E
Dehi Titan, *Afghan.* ..... **40 C3** 33 45N 63 50 E
Dehibat, *Tunisia* ..... **51 B8** 32 0N 10 47 E
Dehlorān, *Iran* ..... **44 C5** 32 41N 47 16 E
Dehnow-e Kūhestān, *Iran* ..... **45 E8** 27 58N 58 32 E
Dehra Dun, *India* ..... **42 D8** 30 20N 78 4 E
Dehri, *India* ..... **43 G11** 24 50N 84 15 E
Dehui, *China* ..... **35 B13** 44 30N 125 40 E
Deinze, *Belgium* ..... **15 D3** 50 59N 3 32 E
Dej, *Romania* ..... **17 E12** 47 10N 23 52 E
Dekese, *Dem. Rep. of the Congo* . **52 E4** 3 24S 21 24 E
Del Mar, *U.S.A.* **85 N9** 32 58N 117 16W
Del Norte, *U.S.A.* **83 H10** 37 41N 106 21W
Del Rio, *U.S.A.* **81 L4** 29 22N 100 54W
Delambre I., *Australia* ..... **60 D2** 20 26S 117 5 E
Delano, *U.S.A.* **85 K7** 35 46N 119 15W
Delano Peak, *U.S.A.* **83 G7** 38 22N 112 22W
Delareyville, *S. Africa* ..... **56 D4** 26 41S 25 26 E
Delaronde L., *Canada* **73 C7** 54 3N 107 3W
Delavan, *U.S.A.* **80 D10** 42 38N 88 39W
Delaware, *U.S.A.* **76 E4** 40 18N 83 4W
Delaware □, *U.S.A.* **76 F8** 39 0N 75 20W
Delaware →, *U.S.A.* **79 G9** 39 15N 75 20W
Delaware B., *U.S.A.* **76 F8** 39 0N 75 10W
Delay →, *Canada* **71 A5** 56 56N 71 28W
Delegate, *Australia* ..... **63 F4** 37 4S 148 56 E
Delevan, *U.S.A.* **78 D6** 42 29N 78 29W
Delft, *Neths.* ..... **15 B4** 52 1N 4 22 E
Delfzijl, *Neths.* ..... **15 A6** 53 20N 6 55 E
Delgado, C., *Mozam.* ..... **55 E5** 10 45S 40 40 E
Delgerhet, *Mongolia* ..... **34 B6** 45 50N 110 30 E
Delgo, *Sudan* ..... **51 D12** 20 6N 30 40 E
Delhi, *Canada* **78 D4** 42 51N 80 30W
Delhi, *India* ..... **42 E7** 28 38N 77 17 E
Delhi, *La., U.S.A.* **81 J9** 32 28N 91 30W
Delhi, *N.Y., U.S.A.* **79 D10** 42 17N 74 55W
Delia, *Canada* **72 C6** 51 38N 112 23W
Delice, *Turkey* ..... **25 G5** 39 54N 34 2 E
Delicias, *Mexico* **86 B3** 28 10N 105 30W
Delījān, *Iran* ..... **45 C6** 33 59N 50 40 E
Déline, *Canada* **68 B7** 65 10N 123 30W
Delisle, *Canada* **73 C7** 51 55N 107 8W
Dell City, *U.S.A.* **83 L11** 31 56N 105 12W
Dell Rapids, *U.S.A.* **80 D6** 43 50N 96 43W
Delmar, *U.S.A.* **79 D11** 42 37N 73 47W
Delmenhorst, *Germany* ..... **16 B5** 53 3N 8 37 E
Delong, Ostrova, *Russia* ..... **27 B15** 76 40N 149 20 E
Deloraine, *Australia* ..... **62 G4** 41 30S 146 40 E
Deloraine, *Canada* **73 D8** 49 15N 100 29W
Delphi, *U.S.A.* **76 E2** 40 36N 86 41W
Delphos, *U.S.A.* **76 E3** 40 51N 84 21W
Delportshoop, *S. Africa* ..... **56 D3** 28 22S 24 20 E
Delray Beach, *U.S.A.* **77 M5** 26 28N 80 4W
Delta, *Colo., U.S.A.* **83 G9** 38 44N 108 4W
Delta, *Utah, U.S.A.* **82 G7** 39 21N 112 35W
Delta Junction, *U.S.A.* **68 B5** 64 2N 145 44W
Deltona, *U.S.A.* **77 L5** 28 54N 81 16W
Delungra, *Australia* ..... **63 D5** 29 39S 150 51 E
Delvada, *India* ..... **42 J4** 20 46N 71 2 E
Delvinë, *Albania* ..... **21 E9** 39 59N 20 6 E
Demak, *Indonesia* ..... **37 G14** 6 53S 110 38 E
Demanda, Sierra de la, *Spain* **19 A4** 42 15N 3 0W
Demavand = Damāvand, *Iran* ..... **45 C7** 35 47N 52 0 E
Dembia, *Dem. Rep. of the Congo* . **54 B2** 3 33N 25 48 E
Dembidolo, *Ethiopia* ..... **46 F1** 8 34N 34 50 E
Demchok, *India* ..... **43 C8** 32 42N 79 29 E
Demer →, *Belgium* ..... **15 D4** 50 57N 4 42 E
Deming, *N. Mex., U.S.A.* .. **83 K10** 32 16N 107 46W
Deming, *Wash., U.S.A.* **84 B4** 48 50N 122 13W
Demini →, *Brazil* **92 D6** 0 46S 62 56W
Demirci, *Turkey* ..... **21 E13** 39 2N 28 38 E
Demirköy, *Turkey* ..... **21 D12** 41 49N 27 45 E
Demopolis, *U.S.A.* **77 J2** 32 31N 87 50W
Dempo, *Indonesia* ..... **36 E2** 4 2S 103 15 E
Den Burg, *Neths.* ..... **15 A4** 53 3N 4 47 E
Den Chai, *Thailand* ..... **38 D3** 17 59N 100 4 E
Den Haag = 's-Gravenhage, *Neths.* ..... **15 B4** 52 7N 4 17 E
Den Helder, *Neths.* ..... **15 B4** 52 57N 4 45 E
Den Oever, *Neths.* ..... **15 B5** 52 56N 5 2 E
Denair, *U.S.A.* **84 H6** 37 32N 120 48W
Denau, *Uzbekistan* ..... **26 F7** 38 16N 67 54 E
Denbigh, *Canada* **78 A7** 45 8N 77 15W
Denbigh, *U.K.* **10 D4** 53 12N 3 25W
Denbighshire □, *U.K.* **10 D4** 53 8N 3 22W
Dendang, *Indonesia* ..... **36 E3** 3 7S 107 56 E
Dendermonde, *Belgium* ..... **15 C4** 51 2N 4 5 E
Dengfeng, *China* ..... **34 G7** 34 25N 113 2 E
Dengkou, *China* ..... **34 D4** 40 18N 106 55 E
Denham, *Australia* ..... **61 E1** 25 56S 113 31 E
Denham Ra., *Australia* ..... **62 C4** 21 55S 147 46 E
Denham Sd., *Australia* ..... **61 E1** 25 45S 113 15 E
Denholm, *Canada* **73 C7** 52 39N 108 1W
Denia, *Spain* ..... **19 C6** 38 49N 0 8 E
Denial B., *Australia* ..... **63 E1** 32 14S 133 32 E
Deniliquin, *Australia* ..... **63 F3** 35 30S 144 58 E
Denison, *Iowa, U.S.A.* **80 E7** 42 1N 95 21W
Denison, *Tex., U.S.A.* **81 J6** 33 45N 96 33W
Denison Plains, *Australia* .. **60 C4** 18 35S 128 0 E
Denizli, *Turkey* ..... **25 G4** 37 42N 29 2 E
Denman Glacier, *Antarctica* **5 C7** 66 45S 99 25 E
Denmark, *Australia* ..... **61 F2** 34 59S 117 25 E
Denmark ■, *Europe* ..... **9 J13** 55 45N 10 0 E
Denmark Str., *Atl. Oc.* **4 C6** 66 0N 30 0W
Dennison, *U.S.A.* **78 F3** 40 24N 81 19W
Denny, *U.K.* **12 E5** 56 1N 3 55W
Denpasar, *Indonesia* ..... **36 F5** 8 45S 115 14 E
Denton, *Mont., U.S.A.* **82 C9** 47 19N 109 57W
Denton, *Tex., U.S.A.* **81 J6** 33 13N 97 8W
D'Entrecasteaux, Pt., *Australia* ..... **61 F2** 34 50S 115 57 E
Denver, *Colo., U.S.A.* **80 F2** 39 44N 104 59W
Denver, *Pa., U.S.A.* **79 F8** 40 14N 76 8W
Denver City, *U.S.A.* **81 J3** 32 58N 102 50W
Deoband, *India* ..... **42 E7** 29 42N 77 43 E
Deogarh, *India* ..... **42 G5** 25 32N 73 54 E
Deoghar, *India* ..... **43 G12** 24 30N 86 42 E
Deolali, *India* ..... **40 K8** 19 58N 73 50 E
Deoli = Devli, *India* ..... **42 G6** 25 50N 75 20 E
Deora, *India* ..... **42 F4** 26 22N 70 55 E
Deori, *India* ..... **43 H8** 23 24N 79 1 E
Deoria, *India* ..... **43 F10** 26 31N 83 48 E
Deosai Mts., *Pakistan* ..... **43 B6** 35 40N 75 0 E
Deosri, *India* ..... **43 F14** 26 46N 90 29 E
Depalpur, *India* ..... **42 H6** 22 51N 75 33 E
Deping, *China* ..... **35 F9** 37 25N 116 58 E
Deposit, *U.S.A.* **79 D9** 42 4N 75 25W
Depuch I., *Australia* ..... **60 D2** 20 37S 117 44 E
Deputatskiy, *Russia* ..... **27 C14** 69 18N 139 54 E
Dera Ghazi Khan, *Pakistan* . **42 D4** 30 5N 70 43 E
Dera Ismail Khan, *Pakistan* **42 D4** 31 50N 70 50 E
Derabugti, *Pakistan* ..... **42 E3** 29 2N 69 9 E
Derawar Fort, *Pakistan* ..... **42 E4** 28 46N 71 20 E
Derbent, *Russia* ..... **25 F8** 42 5N 48 15 E
Derby, *Australia* ..... **60 C3** 17 18S 123 38 E
Derby, *U.K.* **10 E6** 52 56N 1 28W
Derby, *Conn., U.S.A.* **79 E11** 41 19N 73 5W
Derby, *Kans., U.S.A.* **81 G6** 37 33N 97 16W
Derby, *N.Y., U.S.A.* **78 D6** 42 41N 78 58W
Derby City □, *U.K.* **10 E6** 52 56N 1 28W
Derby Line, *U.S.A.* **79 B12** 45 0N 72 6W
Derbyshire □, *U.K.* **10 D6** 53 11N 1 38W
Derg →, *U.K.* **13 B4** 54 44N 7 26W
Derg, L., *Ireland* **13 D3** 53 0N 8 20W
Dergaon, *India* ..... **41 F19** 26 45N 94 0 E
Dermott, *U.S.A.* **81 J9** 33 32N 91 26W
Derry = Londonderry, *U.K.* **13 B4** 55 0N 7 20W
Derry = Londonderry □, *U.K.* **13 B4** 55 0N 7 20W
Derry, *N.H., U.S.A.* **79 D13** 42 53N 71 19W
Derry, *Pa., U.S.A.* **78 F5** 40 20N 79 18W
Derryveagh Mts., *Ireland* **13 B3** 54 56N 8 11W
Derwent →, *Cumb., U.K.* **10 C4** 54 39N 3 33W
Derwent →, *Derby, U.K.* **10 E6** 52 57N 1 28W
Derwent →, *N. Yorks., U.K.* **10 D7** 53 45N 0 58W
Derwent Water, *U.K.* **10 C4** 54 35N 3 9W
Des Moines, *Iowa, U.S.A.* .. **80 E8** 41 35N 93 37W
Des Moines, *N. Mex., U.S.A.* **81 G3** 36 46N 103 50W
Des Moines →, *U.S.A.* **80 E9** 40 23N 91 25W
Desaguadero →, *Argentina* **94 C2** 34 30S 66 46W
Desaguadero →, *Bolivia* **92 G5** 16 35S 69 5W
Descanso, Pta., *Mexico* **85 N9** 32 21N 117 3W
Deschaillons, *Canada* **71 C5** 46 32N 72 7W
Deschambault L., *Canada* . **73 C8** 54 50N 103 30W
Deschutes →, *U.S.A.* **82 D3** 45 38N 120 55W
Dese, *Ethiopia* ..... **46 E2** 11 5N 39 40 E
Deseado →, *Argentina* **96 F3** 47 45S 65 54W
Desert Center, *U.S.A.* **85 M11** 33 43N 115 24W
Desert Hot Springs, *U.S.A.* **85 M10** 33 58N 116 30W
Deshnok, *India* ..... **42 F5** 27 48N 73 21 E
Desna →, *Ukraine* ..... **17 C16** 50 33N 30 32 E
Desolación, I., *Chile* **96 G2** 53 0S 74 0W

Eddystone Pt.

Dowerin, Australia 61 F2 31 12S 117 2 E
Dowgha'i, Iran 45 B8 36 54N 58 32 E
Dowlatābād, Iran 45 D8 28 20N 56 40 E
Down □, U.K. 13 B5 54 23N 6 2W
Downey, Calif., U.S.A. 85 M8 33 56N 118 7W
Downey, Idaho, U.S.A. 82 E7 42 26N 112 7W
Downham Market, U.K. 11 E8 52 37N 0 23 E
Downieville, U.S.A. 84 F6 39 34N 120 50W
Downpatrick, U.K. 13 B6 54 20N 5 43W
Downpatrick Hd., Ireland 13 B2 54 20N 9 21W
Downsville, U.S.A. 79 D10 42 5N 74 50W
Downton, Mt., Canada 72 C4 52 42N 124 52W
Dowsārī, Iran 45 D8 28 25N 57 59 E
Doyle, U.S.A. 84 E6 40 2N 120 6W
Doylestown, U.S.A. 79 F9 40 21N 75 10W
Dozois, Rés., Canada 70 C4 47 30N 77 5W
Dra Khel, Pakistan 42 F2 27 58N 66 45 E
Drachten, Neths. 15 A6 53 7N 6 5 E
Drăgăşani, Romania 17 F13 44 39N 24 17 E
Dragichyn, Belarus 17 B13 52 15N 25 8 E
Dragoman, Prokhod, Bulgaria 21 C10 42 58N 22 53 E
Draguignan, France 18 E7 43 32N 6 27 E
Drain, U.S.A. 82 E2 43 40N 123 19W
Drake, U.S.A. 80 B4 47 55N 100 23W
Drake Passage, S. Ocean 5 B17 58 0S 68 0W
Drakensberg, S. Africa 57 E4 31 0S 28 0 E
Dráma, Greece 21 D11 41 9N 24 10 E
Drammen, Norway 9 G14 59 42N 10 12 E
Drangajökull, Iceland 8 C2 66 9N 22 15W
Dras, India 43 B6 34 25N 75 48 E
Drau = Drava →, Croatia 21 B8 45 33N 18 55 E
Drava →, Croatia 21 B8 45 33N 18 55 E
Drayton Valley, Canada 72 C6 53 12N 114 58W
Drenthe □, Neths. 15 B6 52 52N 6 40 E
Drepanum, C., Cyprus 23 E11 34 54N 32 19 E
Dresden, Canada 78 D2 42 35N 82 11W
Dresden, Germany 16 C7 51 3N 13 44 E
Dreux, France 18 B4 48 44N 1 23 E
Driffield, U.K. 10 C7 54 0N 0 26W
Driftwood, U.S.A. 78 E6 41 20N 78 8W
Driggs, U.S.A. 82 E8 43 44N 111 6W
Drina →, Bos.-H. 21 B8 44 53N 19 21 E
Drini →, Albania 21 C8 42 1N 19 38 E
Drøbak, Norway 9 G14 59 39N 10 39 E
Drochia, Moldova 17 D14 48 2N 27 48 E
Drogheda, Ireland 13 C5 53 43N 6 22W
Drogichin = Dragichyn, Belarus 17 B13 52 15N 25 8 E
Drogobych = Drohobych, Ukraine 17 D12 49 20N 23 30 E
Drohobych, Ukraine 17 D12 49 20N 23 30 E
Droichead Atha = Drogheda, Ireland 13 C5 53 43N 6 22W
Droichead Nua, Ireland 13 C5 53 11N 6 48W
Droitwich, U.K. 11 E5 52 16N 2 8W
Dromedary, C., Australia 63 F5 36 17S 150 10 E
Dromore, U.K. 13 B4 54 31N 7 28W
Dromore West, Ireland 13 B3 54 15N 8 52W
Dronfield, U.K. 10 D6 53 19N 1 27W
Dronten, Neths. 15 B5 52 32N 5 43 E
Drumbo, Canada 78 C4 43 16N 80 35W
Drumheller, Canada 72 C6 51 25N 112 40W
Drummond, U.S.A. 82 C7 46 40N 113 9W
Drummond I., U.S.A. 76 C4 46 1N 83 39W
Drummond Pt., Australia 63 E2 34 9S 135 16 E
Drummond Ra., Australia 62 C4 23 45S 147 10 E
Drummondville, Canada 70 C5 45 55N 72 25W
Drumright, U.S.A. 81 H6 35 59N 96 36W
Druskininkai, Lithuania 9 J20 54 3N 23 58 E
Drut →, Belarus 17 B16 53 8N 30 5 E
Druzhina, Russia 27 C15 68 14N 145 18 E
Dry Tortugas, U.S.A. 88 B3 24 38N 82 55W
Dryden, Canada 73 D10 49 47N 92 50W
Dryden, U.S.A. 79 D8 42 30N 76 18W
Drygalski I., Antarctica 5 C7 66 0S 92 0 E
Drysdale →, Australia 60 B4 13 59S 126 51 E
Drysdale I., Australia 62 A2 11 41S 136 0 E
Du Bois, U.S.A. 78 E6 41 8N 78 46W
Du Gué →, Canada 70 A5 57 21N 70 45W
Du Quoin, U.S.A. 80 G10 38 1N 89 14W
Duanesburg, U.S.A. 79 D10 42 45N 74 11W
Duaringa, Australia 62 C4 23 42S 149 42 E
Dubā, Si. Arabia 44 E2 27 10N 35 40 E
Dubai = Dubayy, U.A.E. 45 E7 25 18N 55 20 E
Dubăsari, Moldova 17 E15 47 15N 29 10 E
Dubăsari Vdkhr., Moldova 17 E15 47 30N 29 0 E
Dubawnt →, Canada 73 A8 64 33N 100 6W
Dubawnt, L., Canada 73 A8 63 4N 101 42W
Dubayy, U.A.E. 45 E7 25 18N 55 20 E
Dubbo, Australia 63 E4 32 11S 148 35 E
Dubele, Dem. Rep. of the Congo 54 B2 2 56N 29 35 E
Dublin, Ireland 13 C5 53 21N 6 15W
Dublin, Ga., U.S.A. 77 J4 32 32N 82 54W
Dublin, Tex., U.S.A. 81 J5 32 5N 98 21W
Dublin □, Ireland 13 C5 53 24N 6 20W
Dubno, Ukraine 17 C13 50 25N 25 45 E
Dubois, U.S.A. 82 D7 44 10N 112 14W
Dubossary = Dubăsari, Moldova 17 E15 47 15N 29 10 E
Dubossary Vdkhr. = Dubăsari Vdkhr., Moldova 17 E15 47 30N 29 0 E
Dubovka, Russia 25 E7 49 5N 44 50 E
Dubrajpur, India 43 H12 23 48N 87 25 E
Dubréka, Guinea 50 G3 9 46N 13 31W
Dubrovitsa = Dubrovytsya, Ukraine 17 C14 51 31N 26 35 E
Dubrovnik, Croatia 21 C8 42 39N 18 6 E
Dubrovytsya, Ukraine 17 C14 51 31N 26 35 E
Dubuque, U.S.A. 80 D9 42 30N 90 41W
Duchesne, U.S.A. 82 F8 40 10N 110 24W
Duchess, Australia 62 C2 21 20S 139 50 E
Ducie I., Pac. Oc. 65 K15 24 40S 124 48W
Duck →, U.S.A. 77 G2 36 2N 87 52W
Duck Cr. →, Australia 60 D2 22 37S 116 53 E
Duck Lake, Canada 73 C7 52 50N 106 16W
Duck Mountain Prov. Park, Canada 73 C8 51 45N 101 0W
Duckwall, Mt., U.S.A. 84 H6 37 58N 120 7W
Dudhi, India 41 G13 24 15N 83 10 E
Dudinka, Russia 27 C9 69 30N 86 13 E
Dudley, U.K. 11 E5 52 31N 2 5W
Dudwa, India 43 E9 28 30N 80 41 E
Duero = Douro →, Europe 19 B1 41 8N 8 40W
Dufftown, U.K. 12 D5 57 27N 3 8W
Dugi Otok, Croatia 16 G8 44 0N 15 3 E
Duifken Pt., Australia 62 A3 12 33S 141 38 E
Duisburg, Germany 16 C4 51 26N 6 45 E
Duiwelskloof, S. Africa 57 C5 23 42S 30 10 E
Dūkdamīn, Iran 45 C8 35 59N 57 43 E
Dukelský Průsmyk, Slovak Rep. 17 D11 49 25N 21 42 E
Dukhān, Qatar 45 E6 25 25N 50 50 E
Duki, Pakistan 40 D6 30 14N 68 25 E
Duku, Nigeria 51 F8 10 43N 10 43 E
Dulce, U.S.A. 83 H10 36 56N 107 0W
Dulce →, Argentina 94 C3 30 32S 62 33W
Dulce, G., Costa Rica 88 E3 8 40N 83 20W
Dulf, Iraq 44 C5 35 7N 45 51 E
Dulit, Banjaran, Malaysia 36 D4 3 15N 114 30 E
Duliu, China 34 E9 39 2N 116 55 E
Dullewala, Pakistan 42 D4 31 50N 71 25 E
Dulq Maghār, Syria 44 B3 36 22N 38 39 E
Duluth, U.S.A. 80 B8 46 47N 92 6W
Dum Dum, India 43 H13 22 39N 88 33 E
Dum Duma, India 41 F19 27 40N 95 40 E
Dūmā, Syria 47 B5 33 34N 36 24 E
Dumaguete, Phil. 37 C6 9 17N 123 15 E
Dumai, Indonesia 36 D2 1 35N 101 28 E
Dumaran, Phil. 37 B5 10 33N 119 50 E
Dumas, Ark., U.S.A. 81 J9 33 53N 91 29W
Dumas, Tex., U.S.A. 81 H4 35 52N 101 58W
Ḑumayr, Syria 47 B5 33 39N 36 42 E
Dumbarton, U.K. 12 F4 55 57N 4 33W
Dumbleyung, Australia 61 F2 33 17S 117 42 E
Dumfries, U.K. 12 F5 55 4N 3 37W
Dumfries & Galloway □, U.K. 12 F5 55 9N 3 58W
Dumka, India 43 G12 24 12N 87 15 E
Dumoine →, Canada 70 C4 46 13N 77 51W
Dumoine, L., Canada 70 C4 46 55N 77 55W
Dumraon, India 43 G11 25 33N 84 8 E
Dumyât, Egypt 51 B12 31 24N 31 48 E
Dún Dealgan = Dundalk, Ireland 13 B5 54 1N 6 24W
Dun Laoghaire, Ireland 13 C5 53 17N 6 8W
Duna = Dunărea →, Europe 17 F15 45 20N 29 40 E
Dunagiri, India 43 D8 30 31N 79 52 E
Dunaj = Dunărea →, Europe 17 F15 45 20N 29 40 E
Dunakeszi, Hungary 17 E10 47 37N 19 8 E
Dunărea →, Europe 17 F15 45 20N 29 40 E
Dunaújváros, Hungary 17 E10 46 58N 18 57 E
Dunav = Dunărea →, Europe 17 F15 45 20N 29 40 E
Dunay, Russia 30 C6 42 52N 132 22 E
Dunback, N.Z. 59 L3 45 23S 170 36 E
Dunbar, U.K. 12 E6 56 0N 2 31W
Dunblane, U.K. 12 E5 56 11N 3 58W
Duncan, Canada 72 D4 48 45N 123 40W
Duncan, Ariz., U.S.A. 83 K9 32 43N 109 6W
Duncan, Okla., U.S.A. 81 H6 34 30N 97 57W
Duncan, L., Canada 70 B4 53 29N 77 58W
Duncan L., Canada 72 A6 62 51N 113 58W
Duncan Town, Bahamas 88 B4 22 15N 75 45W
Duncannon, U.S.A. 78 F7 40 23N 77 2W
Duncansby Head, U.K. 12 C5 58 38N 3 1W
Duncansville, U.S.A. 78 F6 40 25N 78 26W
Dundalk, Canada 78 B4 44 10N 80 24W
Dundalk, Ireland 13 B5 54 1N 6 24W
Dundalk, U.S.A. 76 F7 39 16N 76 32W
Dundalk Bay, Ireland 13 C5 53 55N 6 15W
Dundas, Canada 78 C5 43 17N 79 59W
Dundas, L., Australia 61 F3 32 35S 121 50 E
Dundas I., Canada 72 C2 54 30N 130 50W
Dundas Str., Australia 60 B5 11 15S 131 35 E
Dundee, S. Africa 57 D5 28 11S 30 15 E
Dundee, U.K. 12 E6 56 28N 2 59W
Dundee, U.S.A. 78 D8 42 32N 76 59W
Dundee City □, U.K. 12 E6 56 30N 2 58W
Dundgovĭ □, Mongolia 34 B4 45 10N 106 0 E
Dundrum, U.K. 13 B6 54 16N 5 52W
Dundrum B., U.K. 13 B6 54 13N 5 47W
Dunedin, N.Z. 59 L3 45 50S 170 33 E
Dunedin, U.S.A. 77 L4 28 1N 82 47W
Dunedoo, Australia 63 E4 32 0S 149 25 E
Dunfermline, U.K. 12 E5 56 5N 3 27W
Dungannon, Canada 78 C3 43 51N 81 36W
Dungannon, U.K. 13 B5 54 31N 6 46W
Dungarpur, India 42 H5 23 52N 73 45 E
Dungarvan, Ireland 13 D4 52 5N 7 37W
Dungarvan Harbour, Ireland 13 D4 52 4N 7 35W
Dungeness, U.K. 11 G8 50 54N 0 59 E
Dungo, L. do, Angola 56 B2 17 15S 19 0 E
Dungog, Australia 63 E5 32 22S 151 46 E
Dungu, Dem. Rep. of the Congo 54 B2 3 40N 28 32 E
Dungun, Malaysia 39 K4 4 45N 103 25 E
Dunhua, China 35 C15 43 20N 128 14 E
Dunhuang, China 32 B4 40 8N 94 36 E
Dunk I., Australia 62 B4 17 59S 146 29 E
Dunkeld, Australia 63 E4 33 25S 149 29 E
Dunkeld, U.K. 12 E5 56 34N 3 35W
Dunkerque, France 18 A5 51 2N 2 20 E
Dunkery Beacon, U.K. 11 F4 51 9N 3 36W
Dunkirk = Dunkerque, France 18 A5 51 2N 2 20 E
Dunkirk, U.S.A. 78 D5 42 29N 79 20W
Dúnleary = Dun Laoghaire, Ireland 13 C5 53 17N 6 8W
Dunleer, Ireland 13 C5 53 50N 6 24W
Dunmanus B., Ireland 13 E2 51 31N 9 50W
Dunmanway, Ireland 13 E2 51 43N 9 6W
Dunmara, Australia 62 B1 16 42S 133 25 E
Dunmore, U.S.A. 79 E9 41 25N 75 38W
Dunmore Hd., Ireland 13 D1 52 10N 10 35W
Dunmore Town, Bahamas 88 A4 25 30N 76 39W
Dunn, U.S.A. 77 H6 35 19N 78 37W
Dunnet Hd., U.K. 12 C5 58 40N 3 21W
Dunning, U.S.A. 80 E4 41 50N 100 6W
Dunnville, Canada 78 D5 42 54N 79 36W
Dunolly, Australia 63 F3 36 51S 143 44 E
Dunoon, U.K. 12 F4 55 57N 4 56W
Dunphy, U.S.A. 82 F5 40 42N 116 31W
Duns, U.K. 12 F6 55 47N 2 20W
Dunseith, U.S.A. 80 A4 48 50N 100 3W
Dunsmuir, U.S.A. 82 F2 41 13N 122 16W
Dunstable, U.K. 11 F7 51 53N 0 32W
Dunstan Mts., N.Z. 59 L2 44 53S 169 35 E
Dunster, Canada 72 C5 53 8N 119 50W
Dunvegan L., Canada 73 A7 60 8N 107 10W
Duolun, China 34 C9 42 12N 116 28 E
Duong Dong, Vietnam 39 G4 10 13N 103 58 E
Dupree, U.S.A. 80 C4 45 4N 101 35W
Dupuyer, U.S.A. 82 B7 48 13N 112 30W
Duque de Caxias, Brazil 95 A7 22 45S 43 19W
Durack →, Australia 60 C4 15 33S 127 52 E
Durack Ra., Australia 60 C4 16 50S 127 40 E
Durance →, France 18 E6 43 55N 4 45 E
Durand, U.S.A. 80 C9 44 38N 91 58W
Durango, Mexico 86 C4 24 3N 104 39W
Durango, U.S.A. 83 H10 37 16N 107 53W
Durango □, Mexico 86 C4 25 0N 105 0W
Durant, Miss., U.S.A. 81 J10 33 4N 89 51W
Durant, Okla., U.S.A. 81 J6 33 59N 96 25W
Durazno, Uruguay 94 C4 33 25S 56 31W
Durazzo = Durrësi, Albania 21 D8 41 19N 19 28 E
Durban, S. Africa 57 D5 29 49S 31 1 E
Durbuy, Belgium 15 D5 50 21N 5 28 E
Düren, Germany 16 C4 50 48N 6 29 E
Durg, India 41 J12 21 15N 81 22 E
Durgapur, India 43 H12 23 30N 87 20 E
Durham, Canada 78 B4 44 10N 80 49W
Durham, U.K. 10 C6 54 47N 1 34W
Durham, Calif., U.S.A. 84 F5 39 39N 121 48W
Durham, N.C., U.S.A. 77 H6 35 59N 78 54W
Durham, N.H., U.S.A. 79 C14 43 8N 70 56W
Durham □, U.K. 10 C6 54 42N 1 45W
Ḑurmā, Si. Arabia 44 E5 24 37N 46 8 E
Durmitor, Montenegro, Yug. 21 C8 43 10N 19 0 E
Durness, U.K. 12 C4 58 34N 4 45W
Durrësi, Albania 21 D8 41 19N 19 28 E
Durrow, Ireland 13 D4 52 51N 7 24W
Dursey I., Ireland 13 E1 51 36N 10 12W
Dursunbey, Turkey 21 E13 39 35N 28 37 E
Duru, Dem. Rep. of the Congo 54 B2 4 14N 28 50 E
Durūz, Jabal ad, Jordan 47 C5 32 35N 36 40 E
D'Urville, Tanjung, Indonesia 37 E9 1 28S 137 54 E
D'Urville I., N.Z. 59 J4 40 50S 173 55 E
Duryea, U.S.A. 79 E9 41 20N 75 45W
Dushak, Turkmenistan 26 F7 37 13N 60 1 E
Dushanbe, Tajikistan 26 F7 38 33N 68 48 E
Dushore, U.S.A. 79 E8 41 31N 76 24W
Dusky Sd., N.Z. 59 L1 45 47S 166 30 E
Dussejour, C., Australia 60 B4 14 45S 128 13 E
Düsseldorf, Germany 16 C4 51 14N 6 47 E
Dutch Harbor, U.S.A. 68 C3 53 53N 166 32W
Dutlwe, Botswana 56 C3 23 58S 23 46 E
Dutton, Canada 78 D3 42 39N 81 30W
Dutton →, Australia 62 C3 20 44S 143 10 E
Duwayhin, Khawr, U.A.E. 45 E6 24 20N 51 25 E
Duyun, China 32 D5 26 18N 107 29 E
Duzdab = Zāhedān, Iran 45 D9 29 30N 60 50 E
Dvina, Severnaya →, Russia 24 B7 64 32N 40 30 E
Dvinsk = Daugavpils, Latvia 9 J22 55 53N 26 32 E
Dvinskaya Guba, Russia 24 B6 65 0N 39 0 E
Dwarka, India 42 H3 22 18N 69 8 E
Dwellingup, Australia 61 F2 32 43S 116 4 E
Dwight, Canada 78 A5 45 20N 79 1W
Dwight, U.S.A. 76 E1 41 5N 88 26W
Dyatlovo = Dzyatlava, Belarus 17 B13 53 28N 25 28 E
Dyce, U.K. 12 D6 57 13N 2 12W
Dyer, C., Canada 69 B13 66 40N 61 0W
Dyer Bay, Canada 78 A3 45 10N 81 20W
Dyer Plateau, Antarctica 5 D17 70 45S 65 30W
Dyersburg, U.S.A. 81 G10 36 3N 89 23W
Dyfi →, U.K. 11 E3 52 32N 4 3W
Dymer, Ukraine 17 C16 50 47N 30 18 E
Dysart, Australia 62 C4 22 32S 148 23 E
Dzamin Üüd = Borhoyn Tal, Mongolia 34 C6 43 50N 111 58 E
Dzerzhinsk, Russia 24 C7 56 14N 43 30 E
Dzhalinda, Russia 27 D13 53 26N 124 0 E
Dzhambul = Zhambyl, Kazakstan 26 E8 42 54N 71 22 E
Dzhankoy, Ukraine 25 E5 45 40N 34 20 E
Dzhezkazgan = Zhezqazghan, Kazakstan 26 E7 47 44N 67 40 E
Dzhizak = Jizzakh, Uzbekistan 26 E7 40 6N 67 50 E
Dzhugdzur, Khrebet, Russia 27 D14 57 30N 138 0 E
Dzhungarskiye Vorota = Dzungarian Gates, Kazakstan 32 B3 45 0N 82 0 E
Działdowo, Poland 17 B11 53 15N 20 15 E
Dzibilchaltun, Mexico 87 C7 21 5N 89 36W
Dzierżoniów, Poland 17 C9 50 45N 16 39 E
Dzilam de Bravo, Mexico 87 C7 21 24N 88 53W
Dzungaria = Junggar Pendi, China 32 B3 44 30N 86 0 E
Dzungarian Gates, Kazakstan 32 B3 45 0N 82 0 E
Dzuumod, Mongolia 32 B5 47 45N 106 58 E
Dzyarzhynsk, Belarus 17 B14 53 40N 27 1 E
Dzyatlava, Belarus 17 B13 53 28N 25 28 E

E

Eabamet L., Canada 70 B2 51 30N 87 46W
Eads, U.S.A. 80 F3 38 29N 102 47W
Eagar, U.S.A. 83 J9 34 6N 109 17W
Eagle, Alaska, U.S.A. 68 B5 64 47N 141 12W
Eagle, Colo., U.S.A. 82 G10 39 39N 106 50W
Eagle →, Canada 71 B8 53 36N 57 26W
Eagle Butte, U.S.A. 80 C4 45 0N 101 10W
Eagle Grove, U.S.A. 80 D8 42 40N 93 54W
Eagle L., Canada 73 D10 49 42N 93 13W
Eagle L., Calif., U.S.A. 82 F3 40 39N 120 45W
Eagle L., Maine, U.S.A. 77 B11 46 20N 69 22W
Eagle Lake, Canada 78 A6 45 8N 78 29W
Eagle Lake, Maine, U.S.A. 77 B11 47 3N 68 36W
Eagle Lake, Tex., U.S.A. 81 L6 29 35N 96 20W
Eagle Mountain, U.S.A. 85 M11 33 49N 115 27W
Eagle Nest, U.S.A. 83 H11 36 33N 105 16W
Eagle Pass, U.S.A. 81 L4 28 43N 100 30W
Eagle Pk., U.S.A. 84 G7 38 10N 119 25W
Eagle Pt., Australia 60 C3 16 11S 124 23 E
Eagle River, Mich., U.S.A. 76 B1 47 24N 88 18W
Eagle River, Wis., U.S.A. 80 C10 45 55N 89 15W
Eaglehawk, Australia 63 F3 36 44S 144 15 E
Eagles Mere, U.S.A. 79 E8 41 25N 76 33W
Ealing, U.K. 11 F7 51 31N 0 20W
Ear Falls, Canada 73 C10 50 38N 93 13W
Earle, U.S.A. 81 H9 35 16N 90 28W
Earlimart, U.S.A. 85 K7 35 53N 119 16W
Earn →, U.K. 12 E5 56 21N 3 18W
Earn, L., U.K. 12 E4 56 23N 4 13W
Earnslaw, Mt., N.Z. 59 L2 44 32S 168 27 E
Earth, U.S.A. 81 H3 34 14N 102 24W
Easley, U.S.A. 77 H4 34 50N 82 36W
East Anglia, U.K. 10 E9 52 30N 1 0 E
East Angus, Canada 71 C5 45 30N 71 40W
East Aurora, U.S.A. 78 D6 42 46N 78 37W
East Ayrshire □, U.K. 12 F4 55 26N 4 11W
East Bengal, Bangla. 41 H17 24 0N 90 0 E
East Beskids = Vychodné Beskydy, Europe 17 D11 49 20N 22 0 E
East Brady, U.S.A. 78 F5 40 59N 79 36W
East C., N.Z. 59 G7 37 42S 178 35 E
East Chicago, U.S.A. 76 E2 41 38N 87 27W
East China Sea, Asia 33 D7 30 0N 126 0 E
East Coulee, Canada 72 C6 51 23N 112 27W
East Dereham, U.K. 11 E8 52 41N 0 57 E
East Dunbartonshire □, U.K. 12 F4 55 57N 4 13W
East Falkland, Falk. Is. 96 G5 51 30S 58 30W
East Grand Forks, U.S.A. 80 B6 47 56N 97 1W
East Greenwich, U.S.A. 79 E13 41 40N 71 27W
East Grinstead, U.K. 11 F8 51 7N 0 0 E
East Hartford, U.S.A. 79 E12 41 46N 72 39W
East Helena, U.S.A. 82 C8 46 35N 111 56W
East Indies, Asia 28 K15 0 0 120 0 E
East Kilbride, U.K. 12 F4 55 47N 4 11W
East Lansing, U.S.A. 76 D3 42 44N 84 29W
East Liverpool, U.S.A. 78 F4 40 37N 80 35W
East London, S. Africa 57 E4 33 0S 27 55 E
East Lothian □, U.K. 12 F6 55 58N 2 44W
East Main = Eastmain, Canada 70 B4 52 10N 78 30W
East Northport, U.S.A. 79 F11 40 53N 73 20W
East Orange, U.S.A. 79 F10 40 46N 74 13W
East Pacific Ridge, Pac. Oc. 65 J17 15 0S 110 0W
East Palestine, U.S.A. 78 F4 40 50N 80 33W
East Pine, Canada 72 B4 55 48N 120 12W
East Point, U.S.A. 77 J3 33 41N 84 27W
East Providence, U.S.A. 79 E13 41 49N 71 23W
East Pt., Canada 71 C7 46 27N 61 58W
East Renfrewshire □, U.K. 12 F4 55 46N 4 21W
East Retford = Retford, U.K. 10 D7 53 19N 0 56W
East Riding of Yorkshire □, U.K. 10 D7 53 55N 0 30W
East Rochester, U.S.A. 78 C7 43 7N 77 29W
East St. Louis, U.S.A. 80 F9 38 37N 90 9W
East Schelde = Oosterschelde →, Neths. 15 C4 51 33N 4 0 E
East Siberian Sea, Russia 27 B17 73 0N 160 0 E
East Stroudsburg, U.S.A. 79 E9 41 1N 75 11W
East Sussex □, U.K. 11 G8 50 56N 0 19 E
East Tawas, U.S.A. 76 C4 44 17N 83 29W
East Timor = Timor Timur □, Indonesia 37 F7 9 0S 125 0 E
East Toorale, Australia 63 E4 30 27S 145 28 E
East Walker →, U.S.A. 84 G7 38 52N 119 10W
East Windsor, U.S.A. 79 F10 40 17N 74 34W
Eastbourne, N.Z. 59 J5 41 19S 174 55 E
Eastbourne, U.K. 11 G8 50 46N 0 18 E
Eastend, Canada 73 D7 49 32N 108 50W
Easter I. = Pascua, I. de, Pac. Oc. 65 K17 27 0S 109 0W
Eastern □, Kenya 54 C4 0 0 38 30 E
Eastern □, Uganda 54 B3 1 50N 33 45 E
Eastern Cape □, S. Africa 56 E4 32 0S 26 0 E
Eastern Cr. →, Australia 62 C3 20 40S 141 35 E
Eastern Ghats, India 40 N11 14 0N 78 50 E
Eastern Group = Lau Group, Fiji 59 C9 17 0S 178 30W
Eastern Group, Australia 61 F3 33 30S 124 30 E
Eastern Transvaal = Mpumalanga □, S. Africa 57 B5 26 0S 30 0 E
Easterville, Canada 73 C9 53 8N 99 49W
Easthampton, U.S.A. 79 D12 42 16N 72 40W
Eastlake, U.S.A. 78 E3 41 40N 81 26W
Eastland, U.S.A. 81 J5 32 24N 98 49W
Eastleigh, U.K. 11 G6 50 58N 1 21W
Eastmain, Canada 70 B4 52 10N 78 30W
Eastmain →, Canada 70 B4 52 27N 78 26W
Eastman, Canada 79 A12 45 18N 72 19W
Eastman, U.S.A. 77 J4 32 12N 83 11W
Easton, Md., U.S.A. 76 F7 38 47N 76 5W
Easton, Pa., U.S.A. 79 F9 40 41N 75 13W
Easton, Wash., U.S.A. 84 C5 47 14N 121 11W
Eastpointe, U.S.A. 78 D2 42 27N 82 56W
Eastport, U.S.A. 77 C12 44 56N 67 0W
Eastsound, U.S.A. 84 B4 48 42N 122 55W
Eaton, U.S.A. 80 E2 40 32N 104 42W
Eatonia, Canada 73 C7 51 13N 109 25W
Eatonton, U.S.A. 77 J4 33 20N 83 23W
Eatontown, U.S.A. 79 F10 40 19N 74 4W
Eatonville, U.S.A. 84 D4 46 52N 122 16W
Eau Claire, U.S.A. 80 C9 44 49N 91 30W
Eau Claire, L. à l', Canada 70 A5 56 10N 74 25W
Ebbw Vale, U.K. 11 F4 51 46N 3 12W
Ebeltoft, Denmark 9 H14 56 12N 10 41 E
Ebensburg, U.S.A. 78 F6 40 29N 78 44W
Eberswalde-Finow, Germany 16 B7 52 50N 13 49 E
Ebetsu, Japan 30 C10 43 7N 141 34 E
Ebolowa, Cameroon 52 D2 2 55N 11 10 E
Ebro →, Spain 19 B6 40 43N 0 54 E
Eceabat, Turkey 21 D12 40 11N 26 21 E
Ech Cheliff, Algeria 50 A6 36 10N 1 20 E
Echigo-Sammyaku, Japan 31 F9 36 50N 139 50 E
Echizen-Misaki, Japan 31 G7 35 59N 135 57 E
Echo Bay, N.W.T., Canada 68 B8 66 5N 117 55W
Echo Bay, Ont., Canada 70 C3 46 29N 84 4W
Echoing →, Canada 70 B1 55 51N 92 5W
Echternach, Lux. 15 E6 49 49N 6 25 E
Echuca, Australia 63 F3 36 10S 144 20 E
Ecija, Spain 19 D3 37 30N 5 10W
Eclipse Is., Australia 60 B4 13 54S 126 19 E
Eclipse Sd., Canada 69 A11 72 38N 79 0W
Ecuador ■, S. Amer. 92 D3 2 0S 78 0W
Ed Damazin, Sudan 51 F12 11 46N 34 21 E
Ed Debba, Sudan 51 E12 18 0N 30 51 E
Ed Dueim, Sudan 51 F12 14 0N 32 10 E
Edam, Canada 73 C7 53 11N 108 46W
Edam, Neths. 15 B5 52 31N 5 3 E
Eday, U.K. 12 B6 59 11N 2 47W
Eddrachillis B., U.K. 12 C3 58 17N 5 14W
Eddystone Pt., Australia 62 G4 40 59S 148 20 E

Felipe Carrillo Puerto

Felipe Carrillo Puerto, Mexico **87 D7** 19 38N 88 3W
Felixstowe, U.K. **11 F9** 51 58N 1 23 E
Felton, U.S.A. **84 H4** 37 3N 122 4W
Femer Bælt = Fehmarn Bælt, Europe **9 J14** 54 35N 11 20 E
Femunden, Norway **9 E14** 62 10N 11 53 E
Fen He →, China **34 G6** 35 36N 110 42 E
Fenelon Falls, Canada **78 B6** 44 32N 78 45W
Feng Xian, Jiangsu, China **34 G9** 34 43N 116 35 E
Feng Xian, Shaanxi, China **34 H4** 33 54N 106 40 E
Fengcheng, China **35 D13** 40 28N 124 5 E
Fengfeng, China **34 F8** 36 28N 114 8 E
Fengjie, China **33 C5** 31 5N 109 36 E
Fengning, China **34 D9** 41 10N 116 33 E
Fengqiu, China **34 G8** 35 2N 114 25 E
Fengrun, China **35 E10** 39 48N 118 8 E
Fengtai, China **34 E9** 39 50N 116 18 E
Fengxiang, China **34 G4** 34 29N 107 25 E
Fengyang, China **35 H9** 32 51N 117 29 E
Fengzhen, China **34 D7** 40 25N 113 2 E
Fenoarivo Afovoany, Madag. **57 B8** 18 26S 46 34 E
Fenoarivo Atsinanana, Madag. **57 B8** 17 22S 49 25 E
Fens, The, U.K. **10 E7** 52 38N 0 2W
Fenton, U.S.A. **76 D4** 42 48N 83 42W
Fenxi, China **34 F6** 36 40N 111 31 E
Fenyang, China **34 F6** 37 18N 111 48 E
Feodosiya, Ukraine **25 E6** 45 2N 35 16 E
Ferdows, Iran **45 C8** 33 58N 58 2 E
Ferfer, Somali Rep. **46 F4** 5 4N 45 9 E
Fergana = Farghona, Uzbekistan **26 E8** 40 23N 71 19 E
Fergus, Canada **78 C4** 43 43N 80 24W
Fergus Falls, U.S.A. **80 B6** 46 17N 96 4W
Ferkéssédougou, Ivory C. **50 G4** 9 35N 5 6W
Ferland, Canada **70 B2** 50 19N 88 27W
Fermanagh □, U.K. **13 B4** 54 21N 7 40W
Fermo, Italy **20 C5** 43 9N 13 43 E
Fermont, Canada **71 B6** 52 47N 67 5W
Fermont, Qué., Canada **69 C13** 50 28N 67 29W
Fermoy, Ireland **13 D3** 52 9N 8 16W
Fernández, Argentina **94 B3** 27 55S 63 50W
Fernandina Beach, U.S.A. **77 K5** 30 40N 81 27W
Fernando de Noronha, Brazil **93 D12** 4 0S 33 10W
Fernando Póo = Bioko, Eq. Guin. **52 D1** 3 30N 8 40 E
Ferndale, U.S.A. **84 B4** 48 51N 122 36W
Fernie, Canada **72 D5** 49 30N 115 5W
Fernlees, Australia **62 C4** 23 51S 148 7 E
Fernley, U.S.A. **82 G4** 39 36N 119 15W
Ferozepore = Firozpur, India **42 D6** 30 55N 74 40 E
Ferrara, Italy **20 B4** 44 50N 11 35 E
Ferreñafe, Peru **92 E3** 6 42S 79 50W
Ferrerías, Spain **22 B11** 39 59N 4 1 E
Ferret, C., France **18 D3** 44 38N 1 15W
Ferriday, U.S.A. **81 K9** 31 38N 91 33W
Ferrol, Spain **19 A1** 43 29N 8 15W
Ferron, U.S.A. **83 G8** 39 5N 111 8W
Ferrutx, C., Spain **22 B10** 39 47N 3 21 E
Ferryland, Canada **71 C9** 47 2N 52 53W
Fertile, U.S.A. **80 B6** 47 32N 96 17W
Fès, Morocco **50 B5** 34 0N 5 0W
Fessenden, U.S.A. **80 B5** 47 39N 99 38W
Festus, U.S.A. **80 F9** 38 13N 90 24W
Feteşti, Romania **17 F14** 44 22N 27 51 E
Fethiye, Turkey **25 G4** 36 36N 29 6 E
Fetlar, U.K. **12 A8** 60 36N 0 52W
Feuilles →, Canada **69 C12** 58 47N 70 4W
Fez = Fès, Morocco **50 B5** 34 0N 5 0W
Fezzan, Libya **51 C8** 27 0N 13 0 E
Fiambalá, Argentina **94 B2** 27 45S 67 37W
Fianarantsoa, Madag. **57 C8** 21 26S 47 5 E
Fianarantsoa □, Madag. **57 B8** 19 30S 47 0 E
Ficksburg, S. Africa **57 D4** 28 51S 27 53 E
Field →, Australia **62 C2** 23 48S 138 0 E
Field I., Australia **60 B5** 12 5S 132 23 E
Fieri, Albania **21 D8** 40 43N 19 33 E
Fife □, U.K. **12 E5** 56 16N 3 1W
Fife Ness, U.K. **12 E6** 56 17N 2 35W
Fifth Cataract, Sudan **51 E12** 18 23N 33 47 E
Figeac, France **18 D5** 44 37N 2 2 E
Figtree, Zimbabwe **55 G2** 20 22S 28 20 E
Figueira da Foz, Portugal **19 B1** 40 7N 8 54W
Figueres, Spain **19 A7** 42 18N 2 58 E
Figuig, Morocco **50 B5** 32 5N 1 11W
Fihaonana, Madag. **57 B8** 18 36S 47 12 E
Fiherenana, Madag. **57 B8** 18 29S 48 24 E
Fiherenana →, Madag. **57 C7** 23 19S 43 37 E
Fiji ■, Pac. Oc. **59 C8** 17 20S 179 0 E
Filey, U.K. **10 C7** 54 12N 0 18W
Filey B., U.K. **10 C7** 54 12N 0 15W
Filfla, Malta **23 D1** 35 47N 14 24 E
Filiatrá, Greece **21 F9** 37 9N 21 35 E
Filingué, Niger **50 F6** 14 21N 3 22 E
Filipstad, Sweden **9 G16** 59 43N 14 9 E
Fillmore, Calif., U.S.A. **85 L8** 34 24N 118 55W
Fillmore, Utah, U.S.A. **83 G7** 38 58N 112 20W
Finch, Canada **79 A9** 45 11N 75 7W
Findhorn →, U.K. **12 D5** 57 38N 3 38W
Findlay, U.S.A. **76 E4** 41 2N 83 39W
Finger L., Canada **70 B1** 53 33N 93 30W
Finger Lakes, U.S.A. **79 D8** 42 40N 76 30W
Fingoè, Mozam. **55 E3** 14 55S 31 50 E
Finisterre, C. = Fisterra, C., Spain **19 A1** 42 50N 9 19W
Finke, Australia **62 D1** 25 34S 134 35 E
Finland ■, Europe **8 E22** 63 0N 27 0 E
Finland, G. of, Europe **9 G21** 60 0N 26 0 E
Finlay →, Canada **72 B3** 57 0N 125 10W
Finley, Australia **63 F4** 35 38S 145 35 E
Finley, U.S.A. **80 B6** 47 31N 97 50W
Finn →, Ireland **13 B4** 54 51N 7 28W
Finnigan, Mt., Australia **62 B4** 15 49S 145 17 E
Finniss, C., Australia **63 E1** 33 8S 134 51 E
Finnmark, Norway **8 B20** 69 37N 23 57 E
Finnsnes, Norway **8 B18** 69 14N 18 0 E
Finspång, Sweden **9 G16** 58 43N 15 47 E
Fiora →, Italy **20 C4** 42 20N 11 34 E
Fiq, Syria **47 C4** 32 46N 35 41 E
Firat = Furāt, Nahr al →, Asia **44 D5** 31 0N 47 25 E
Firebag →, Canada **73 B6** 57 45N 111 21W
Firebaugh, U.S.A. **84 J6** 36 52N 120 27W
Firedrake L., Canada **73 A8** 61 25N 104 30W
Firenze, Italy **20 C4** 43 46N 11 15 E
Firk →, Iraq **44 D5** 30 59N 44 34 E
Firozabad, India **43 F8** 27 10N 78 25 E
Firozpur, India **42 D6** 30 55N 74 40 E
Firozpur-Jhirka, India **42 F7** 27 48N 76 57 E
Fīrūzābād, Iran **45 D7** 28 52N 52 35 E
Fīrūzkūh, Iran **45 C7** 35 50N 52 50 E
Firvale, Canada **72 C3** 52 27N 126 13W
Fish →, Namibia **56 D2** 28 7S 17 10 E
Fish →, S. Africa **56 E3** 31 30S 20 16 E
Fisher, Australia **61 F5** 30 30S 131 0 E
Fisher B., Canada **73 C9** 51 35N 97 13W
Fishers I., U.S.A. **79 E13** 41 15N 72 0W
Fishguard, U.K. **11 E3** 52 0N 4 58W
Fishing L., Canada **73 C9** 52 10N 95 24W
Fishkill, U.S.A. **79 E11** 41 32N 73 53W
Fisterra, C., Spain **19 A1** 42 50N 9 19W
Fitchburg, U.S.A. **79 D13** 42 35N 71 48W
Fitz Roy, Argentina **96 F3** 47 0S 67 0W
Fitzgerald, Canada **72 B6** 59 51N 111 36W
Fitzgerald, U.S.A. **77 K4** 31 43N 83 15W
Fitzmaurice →, Australia **60 B5** 14 45S 130 5 E
Fitzroy →, Queens., Australia **62 C5** 23 32S 150 52 E
Fitzroy →, W. Austral., Australia **60 C3** 17 31S 123 35 E
Fitzroy, Mte., Argentina **96 F2** 49 17S 73 5W
Fitzroy Crossing, Australia **60 C4** 18 9S 125 38 E
Fitzwilliam I., Canada **78 A3** 45 30N 81 45W
Fiume = Rijeka, Croatia **16 F8** 45 20N 14 21 E
Five Points, U.S.A. **84 J6** 36 26N 120 6W
Fizi, Dem. Rep. of the Congo **54 C2** 4 17S 28 55 E
Flagstaff, U.S.A. **83 J8** 35 12N 111 39W
Flagstaff L., Maine, U.S.A. **77 C10** 45 12N 70 19W
Flagstaff L., Maine, U.S.A. **79 A14** 45 12N 70 18W
Flaherty I., Canada **70 A4** 56 15N 79 15W
Flåm, Norway **9 F12** 60 50N 7 7 E
Flambeau →, U.S.A. **80 C9** 45 18N 91 14W
Flamborough Hd., U.K. **10 C7** 54 7N 0 5W
Flaming Gorge Reservoir, U.S.A. **82 F9** 41 10N 109 25W
Flamingo, Teluk, Indonesia **37 F9** 5 30S 138 0 E
Flanders = Flandre, Europe **18 A5** 50 50N 2 30 E
Flandre, Europe **18 A5** 50 50N 2 30 E
Flandre Occidentale = West-Vlaanderen □, Belgium **15 D2** 51 0N 3 0 E
Flandre Orientale = Oost-Vlaanderen □, Belgium **15 C3** 51 5N 3 50 E
Flandreau, U.S.A. **80 C6** 44 3N 96 36W
Flanigan, U.S.A. **84 E7** 40 10N 119 53W
Flannan Is., U.K. **12 C1** 58 9N 7 52W
Flåsjön, Sweden **8 D16** 64 5N 15 40 E
Flat →, Canada **72 A3** 61 33N 125 18W
Flathead L., U.S.A. **82 C7** 47 51N 114 8W
Flattery, C., Australia **62 A4** 14 58S 145 21 E
Flattery, C., U.S.A. **84 B2** 48 23N 124 29W
Flatwoods, U.S.A. **76 F4** 38 31N 82 43W
Fleetwood, U.K. **10 D4** 53 55N 3 1W
Fleetwood, U.S.A. **79 F9** 40 27N 75 49W
Flekkefjord, Norway **9 G12** 58 18N 6 39 E
Flemington, U.S.A. **78 E7** 41 7N 77 28W
Flensburg, Germany **16 A5** 54 47N 9 27 E
Flers, France **18 B3** 48 47N 0 33W
Flesherton, Canada **78 B4** 44 16N 80 33W
Flesko, Tanjung, Indonesia **37 D6** 0 29N 124 30 E
Fleurieu Pen., Australia **63 F2** 35 40S 138 5 E
Flevoland □, Neths. **15 B5** 52 30N 5 30 E
Flin Flon, Canada **73 C8** 54 46N 101 53W
Flinders →, Australia **62 B3** 17 36S 140 36 E
Flinders B., Australia **61 F2** 34 19S 115 19 E
Flinders Group, Australia **62 A3** 14 11S 144 15 E
Flinders I., S. Austral., Australia **63 E1** 33 44S 134 41 E
Flinders I., Tas., Australia **62 G4** 40 0S 148 0 E
Flinders Ranges, Australia **63 E2** 31 30S 138 30 E
Flinders Reefs, Australia **62 B4** 17 37S 148 31 E
Flint, U.K. **10 D4** 53 15N 3 8W
Flint, U.S.A. **76 D4** 43 1N 83 41W
Flint →, U.S.A. **77 K3** 30 57N 84 34W
Flint I., Kiribati **65 J12** 11 26S 151 48W
Flintshire □, U.K. **10 D4** 53 17N 3 17W
Flodden, U.K. **10 B5** 55 37N 2 8W
Floodwood, U.S.A. **80 B8** 46 55N 92 55W
Flora, U.S.A. **76 F1** 38 40N 88 29W
Florala, U.S.A. **77 K2** 31 0N 86 20W
Florence = Firenze, Italy **20 C4** 43 46N 11 15 E
Florence, Ala., U.S.A. **77 H2** 34 48N 87 41W
Florence, Ariz., U.S.A. **83 K8** 33 2N 111 23W
Florence, Colo., U.S.A. **80 F2** 38 23N 105 8W
Florence, Oreg., U.S.A. **82 E1** 43 58N 124 7W
Florence, S.C., U.S.A. **77 H6** 34 12N 79 46W
Florence, L., Australia **63 D2** 28 53S 138 9 E
Florencia, Colombia **92** 1 36N 75 36W
Florennes, Belgium **15 D4** 50 15N 4 35 E
Florenville, Belgium **15 E5** 49 40N 5 19 E
Flores, Guatemala **88 C2** 16 59N 89 50W
Flores, Indonesia **37 F6** 8 35S 121 0 E
Flores I., Canada **72 D3** 49 20N 126 10W
Flores Sea, Indonesia **37 F6** 6 30S 120 0 E
Floreşti, Moldova **17 E15** 47 53N 28 17 E
Floresville, U.S.A. **81 L5** 29 8N 98 10W
Floriano, Brazil **93 E10** 6 50S 43 0W
Florianópolis, Brazil **95 B6** 27 30S 48 30W
Florida, Cuba **88 B4** 21 32N 78 14W
Florida, Uruguay **95 C4** 34 7S 56 10W
Florida □, U.S.A. **77 L5** 28 0N 82 0W
Florida, Straits of, U.S.A. **88 B4** 25 0N 80 0W
Florida B., U.S.A. **88 B3** 25 0N 80 45W
Florida Keys, U.S.A. **77 N5** 24 40N 81 0W
Flórina, Greece **21 D9** 40 48N 21 26 E
Florø, Norway **9 F11** 61 35N 5 1 E
Flower Station, Canada **79 A8** 45 10N 76 41W
Flowerpot I., Canada **78 A3** 45 18N 81 38W
Floydada, U.S.A. **81 J4** 33 59N 101 20W
Fluk, Indonesia **37 E7** 1 42S 127 44 E
Flushing = Vlissingen, Neths. **15 C3** 51 26N 3 34 E
Flying Fish, C., Antarctica **5 D15** 72 6S 102 29W
Foam Lake, Canada **73 C8** 51 40N 103 32W
Foça, Turkey **21 E12** 38 39N 26 46 E
Focşani, Romania **17 F14** 45 41N 27 15 E
Fóggia, Italy **20 D6** 41 27N 15 34 E
Fogo, Canada **71 C9** 49 43N 54 17W
Fogo I., Canada **71 C9** 49 40N 54 5W
Föhr, Germany **16 A5** 54 43N 8 30 E
Foix, France **18 E4** 42 58N 1 38 E
Folda, Nord-Trøndelag, Norway **8 D14** 64 32N 10 30 E
Folda, Nordland, Norway **8 C16** 67 38N 14 50 E
Foley, U.S.A. **77 K2** 30 24N 87 41W
Foleyet, Canada **70 C3** 48 15N 82 25W
Folgefonni, Norway **9 F12** 60 3N 6 23 E
Foligno, Italy **20 C5** 42 57N 12 42 E
Folkestone, U.K. **11 F9** 51 5N 1 12 E
Folkston, U.S.A. **77 K5** 30 50N 82 0W
Follansbee, U.S.A. **78 F4** 40 19N 80 35W
Folsom L., U.S.A. **84 G5** 38 42N 121 9W
Fond-du-Lac, Canada **73 B7** 59 19N 107 12W
Fond du Lac, U.S.A. **80 D10** 43 47N 88 27W
Fond-du-Lac →, Canada **73 B7** 59 17N 106 0W
Fonda, U.S.A. **79 D10** 42 57N 74 22W
Fondi, Italy **20 D5** 41 21N 13 25 E
Fongafale, Tuvalu **64 H9** 8 31S 179 13 E
Fonsagrada = A Fonsagrada, Spain **19 A2** 43 8N 7 4W
Fonseca, G. de, Cent. Amer. **88 D2** 13 10N 87 40W
Fontainebleau, France **18 B5** 48 24N 2 40 E
Fontana, U.S.A. **85 L9** 34 6N 117 26W
Fontas →, Canada **72 B4** 58 14N 121 48W
Fonte Boa, Brazil **92 D5** 2 33S 66 0W
Fontenay-le-Comte, France **18 C3** 46 28N 0 48W
Fontenelle Reservoir, U.S.A. **82 E8** 42 1N 110 3W
Fontur, Iceland **8 C6** 66 23N 14 32W
Foochow = Fuzhou, China **33 D6** 26 5N 119 16 E
Foping, China **34 H5** 33 41N 108 0 E
Forbes, Australia **63 E4** 33 22S 148 0 E
Forbesganj, India **43 F12** 26 17N 87 18 E
Ford City, Calif., U.S.A. **85 K7** 35 9N 119 27W
Ford City, Pa., U.S.A. **78 F5** 40 46N 79 32W
Førde, Norway **9 F11** 61 27N 5 53 E
Ford's Bridge, Australia **63 D4** 29 41S 145 29 E
Fordyce, U.S.A. **81 J8** 33 49N 92 25W
Forel, Mt., Greenland **4 C6** 66 52N 36 55W
Foremost, Canada **72 D6** 49 26N 111 34W
Forest, Canada **78 C3** 43 6N 82 0W
Forest, U.S.A. **81 J10** 32 22N 89 29W
Forest City, Iowa, U.S.A. **80 D8** 43 16N 93 39W
Forest City, N.C., U.S.A. **77 H5** 35 20N 81 52W
Forest City, Pa., U.S.A. **79 E9** 41 39N 75 28W
Forest Grove, U.S.A. **84 E3** 45 31N 123 7W
Forestburg, Canada **72 C6** 52 35N 112 1W
Foresthill, U.S.A. **84 F6** 39 1N 120 49W
Forestier Pen., Australia **62 G4** 43 0S 148 0 E
Forestville, Canada **71 C6** 48 48N 69 2W
Forestville, Calif., U.S.A. **84 G4** 38 28N 122 54W
Forestville, N.Y., U.S.A. **78 D5** 42 28N 79 10W
Forfar, U.K. **12 E6** 56 39N 2 53W
Forks, U.S.A. **84 C2** 47 57N 124 23W
Forksville, U.S.A. **79 E8** 41 29N 76 35W
Forli, Italy **20 B5** 44 13N 12 3 E
Forman, U.S.A. **80 B6** 46 7N 97 38W
Formby Pt., U.K. **10 D4** 53 33N 3 6W
Formentera, Spain **22 C7** 38 43N 1 27 E
Formentor, C. de, Spain **22 B10** 39 58N 3 13 E
Former Yugoslav Republic of Macedonia ■, Europe **21 D9** 41 53N 21 40 E
Fórmia, Italy **20 D5** 41 15N 13 37 E
Formosa = Taiwan ■, Asia **33 D7** 23 30N 121 0 E
Formosa, Argentina **94 B4** 26 15S 58 10W
Formosa, Brazil **93 G9** 15 32S 47 20W
Formosa □, Argentina **94 B4** 25 0S 60 0W
Formosa, Serra, Brazil **93 F8** 12 0S 55 0W
Formosa Bay, Kenya **54 C5** 2 40S 40 20 E
Fornells, Spain **22 A11** 40 3N 4 7 E
Føroyar, Atl. Oc. **8 F9** 62 0N 7 0W
Forres, U.K. **12 D5** 57 37N 3 37W
Forrest, Australia **61 F4** 30 51S 128 6 E
Forrest, Mt., Australia **61 D4** 24 48S 127 45 E
Forrest City, U.S.A. **81 H9** 35 1N 90 47W
Forsayth, Australia **62 B3** 18 33S 143 34 E
Forssa, Finland **9 F20** 60 49N 23 38 E
Forst, Germany **16 C8** 51 45N 14 37 E
Forsyth, U.S.A. **82 C10** 46 16N 106 41W
Fort Abbas, Pakistan **42 E5** 29 12N 72 52 E
Fort Albany, Canada **70 B3** 52 15N 81 35W
Fort Ann, U.S.A. **79 C11** 43 25N 73 30W
Fort Assiniboine, Canada **72 C6** 54 20N 114 45W
Fort Augustus, U.K. **12 D4** 57 9N 4 42W
Fort Beaufort, S. Africa **56 E4** 32 46S 26 40 E
Fort Benton, U.S.A. **82 C8** 47 49N 110 40W
Fort Bragg, U.S.A. **82 G2** 39 26N 123 48W
Fort Bridger, U.S.A. **82 F8** 41 19N 110 23W
Fort Chipewyan, Canada **73 B6** 58 42N 111 8W
Fort Collins, U.S.A. **80 E2** 40 35N 105 5W
Fort-Coulonge, Canada **70 C4** 45 50N 76 45W
Fort Covington, U.S.A. **79 B10** 44 59N 74 29W
Fort Davis, U.S.A. **81 K3** 30 35N 103 54W
Fort-de-France, Martinique **89 D7** 14 36N 61 2W
Fort Defiance, U.S.A. **83 J9** 35 45N 109 5W
Fort Dodge, U.S.A. **80 D7** 42 30N 94 11W
Fort Edward, U.S.A. **79 C11** 43 16N 73 35W
Fort Erie, Canada **78 D6** 42 54N 78 56W
Fort Fairfield, U.S.A. **77 B12** 46 46N 67 50W
Fort Frances, Canada **73 D10** 48 36N 93 24W
Fort Garland, U.S.A. **83 H11** 37 26N 105 26W
Fort George = Chisasibi, Canada **70 B4** 53 50N 79 0W
Fort Good-Hope, Canada **68 B7** 66 14N 128 40W
Fort Hancock, U.S.A. **83 L11** 31 18N 105 51W
Fort Hertz = Putao, Burma **41 F20** 27 28N 97 30 E
Fort Hope, Canada **70 B2** 51 30N 88 0W
Fort Irwin, U.S.A. **85 K10** 35 16N 116 34W
Fort Jameson = Chipata, Zambia **55 E3** 13 38S 32 28 E
Fort Kent, U.S.A. **77 B11** 47 15N 68 36W
Fort Klamath, U.S.A. **82 E3** 42 42N 122 0W
Fort-Lamy = Ndjamena, Chad **51 F8** 12 10N 14 59 E
Fort Laramie, U.S.A. **80 D2** 42 13N 104 31W
Fort Lauderdale, U.S.A. **77 M5** 26 7N 80 8W
Fort Liard, Canada **72 A4** 60 14N 123 30W
Fort Liberté, Haiti **89 C5** 19 42N 71 51W
Fort Lupton, U.S.A. **80 E2** 40 5N 104 49W
Fort Mackay, Canada **72 B6** 57 12N 111 41W
Fort Macleod, Canada **72 D6** 49 45N 113 30W
Fort McMurray, Canada **72 B6** 56 44N 111 7W
Fort McPherson, Canada **68 B6** 67 30N 134 55W
Fort Madison, U.S.A. **80 E9** 40 38N 91 27W
Fort Meade, U.S.A. **77 M5** 27 45N 81 48W
Fort Morgan, U.S.A. **80 E3** 40 15N 103 48W
Fort Munro, Pakistan **42 E3** 29 54N 69 58 E
Fort Myers, U.S.A. **77 M5** 26 39N 81 52W
Fort Nelson, Canada **72 B4** 58 50N 122 44W
Fort Nelson →, Canada **72 B4** 59 32N 124 0W
Fort Norman = Tulita, Canada **68 B7** 64 57N 125 30W
Fort Payne, U.S.A. **77 H3** 34 26N 85 43W
Fort Peck, U.S.A. **82 B10** 48 1N 106 27W
Fort Peck Dam, U.S.A. **82 C10** 48 0N 106 26W
Fort Peck L., U.S.A. **82 C10** 48 0N 106 26W
Fort Pierce, U.S.A. **77 M5** 27 27N 80 20W
Fort Pierre, U.S.A. **80 C4** 44 21N 100 22W
Fort Plain, U.S.A. **79 D10** 42 56N 74 37W
Fort Portal, Uganda **54 B3** 0 40N 30 20 E
Fort Providence, Canada **72 A5** 61 3N 117 40W
Fort Qu'Appelle, Canada **73 C8** 50 45N 103 50W
Fort Resolution, Canada **72 A6** 61 10N 113 40W
Fort Rixon, Zimbabwe **55 G2** 20 2S 29 17 E
Fort Rosebery = Mansa, Zambia **55 E2** 11 13S 28 55 E
Fort Ross, U.S.A. **84 G3** 38 32N 123 13W
Fort Rousset = Owando, Congo **52 E3** 0 29S 15 55 E
Fort Rupert = Waskaganish, Canada **70 B4** 51 30N 78 40W
Fort St. James, Canada **72 C4** 54 30N 124 10W
Fort St. John, Canada **72 B4** 56 15N 120 50W
Fort Sandeman = Zhob, Pakistan **42 D3** 31 20N 69 31 E
Fort Saskatchewan, Canada **72 C6** 53 40N 113 15W
Fort Scott, U.S.A. **81 G7** 37 50N 94 42W
Fort Severn, Canada **70 A2** 56 0N 87 40W
Fort Shevchenko, Kazakstan **25 F9** 44 35N 50 23 E
Fort Simpson, Canada **72 A4** 61 45N 121 15W
Fort Smith, Canada **72 B6** 60 0N 111 51W
Fort Smith, U.S.A. **81 H7** 35 23N 94 25W
Fort Stockton, U.S.A. **81 K3** 30 53N 102 53W
Fort Sumner, U.S.A. **81 H2** 34 28N 104 15W
Fort Thompson, U.S.A. **80 C5** 44 3N 99 26W
Fort Trinquet = Bir Mogreïn, Mauritania **50 C3** 25 10N 11 25W
Fort Valley, U.S.A. **77 J4** 32 33N 83 53W
Fort Vermilion, Canada **72 B5** 58 24N 116 0W
Fort Walton Beach, U.S.A. **77 K2** 30 25N 86 36W
Fort Wayne, U.S.A. **76 E3** 41 4N 85 9W
Fort William, U.K. **12 E3** 56 49N 5 7W
Fort Worth, U.S.A. **81 J6** 32 45N 97 18W
Fort Yates, U.S.A. **80 B4** 46 5N 100 38W
Fort Yukon, U.S.A. **68 B5** 66 34N 145 16W
Fortaleza, Brazil **93 D11** 3 45S 38 35W
Forteau, Canada **71 B8** 51 28N 56 58W
Fortescue →, Australia **60 D2** 21 0S 116 4 E
Forth →, U.K. **12 E5** 56 9N 3 50W
Forth, Firth of, U.K. **12 E6** 56 5N 2 55W
Fortrose, U.K. **12 D4** 57 35N 4 9W
Fortuna, Calif., U.S.A. **82 F1** 40 36N 124 9W
Fortuna, N. Dak., U.S.A. **80 A3** 48 55N 103 47W
Fortune, Canada **71 C8** 47 4N 55 50W
Fortune B., Canada **71 C8** 47 30N 55 22W
Forūr, Iran **45 E7** 26 17N 54 32 E
Foshan, China **33 D6** 23 4N 113 5 E
Fosna, Norway **8 E14** 63 50N 10 20 E
Fosnavåg, Norway **9 E11** 62 22N 5 38 E
Fossano, Italy **18 D7** 44 33N 7 43 E
Fossil, U.S.A. **82 D3** 45 0N 120 9W
Foster, Australia **63 F4** 38 40S 146 15 E
Foster, Canada **79 A12** 45 17N 72 30W
Foster →, Canada **73 B7** 55 47N 105 49W
Fosters Ra., Australia **62 C1** 21 35S 133 48 E
Fostoria, U.S.A. **76 E4** 41 10N 83 25W
Fougères, France **18 B3** 48 21N 1 14W
Foul Pt., Sri Lanka **40 Q12** 8 35N 81 18 E
Foula, U.K. **12 A6** 60 10N 2 5W
Foulness I., U.K. **11 F8** 51 36N 0 55 E
Foulpointe, Madag. **57 B8** 17 41S 49 31 E
Foulweather, C., U.S.A. **74 B2** 44 50N 124 5W
Foumban, Cameroon **52 C2** 5 45N 10 50 E
Fountain, U.S.A. **80 F2** 38 41N 104 42W
Fountain Springs, U.S.A. **85 K8** 35 54N 118 51W
Fouriesburg, S. Africa **56 D4** 28 38S 28 14 E
Foúrnoi, Greece **21 F12** 37 36N 26 32 E
Fourth Cataract, Sudan **51 E12** 18 47N 32 3 E
Fouta Djalon, Guinea **50 F3** 11 20N 12 10W
Foux, Cap-à-, Haiti **89 C5** 19 43N 73 27W
Foveaux Str., N.Z. **59 M2** 46 42S 168 10 E
Fowey, U.K. **11 G3** 50 20N 4 39W
Fowler, Calif., U.S.A. **84 J7** 36 38N 119 41W
Fowler, Colo., U.S.A. **80 F3** 38 8N 104 2W
Fowlers B., Australia **61 F5** 31 59S 132 34 E
Fowman, Iran **45 B6** 37 13N 49 19 E
Fox →, Canada **73 B10** 56 3N 93 18W
Fox Creek, Canada **72 C5** 54 24N 116 48W
Fox Lake, Canada **72 B6** 58 28N 114 31W
Fox Valley, Canada **73 C7** 50 30N 109 25W
Foxboro, U.S.A. **79 D13** 42 4N 71 16W
Foxe Basin, Canada **69 B12** 66 0N 77 0W
Foxe Chan., Canada **69 B12** 65 0N 80 0W
Foxe Pen., Canada **69 B12** 65 0N 76 0W
Foxton, N.Z. **59 J5** 40 29S 175 18 E
Foyle, Lough, U.K. **13 A4** 55 7N 7 4W
Foynes, Ireland **13 D2** 52 37N 9 7W
Fóz do Cunene, Angola **56 B1** 17 15S 11 48 E
Foz do Iguaçu, Brazil **95 B5** 25 30S 54 30W
Frackville, U.S.A. **79 F8** 40 47N 76 14W
Fraile Muerto, Uruguay **95 C5** 32 31S 54 32W
Framingham, U.S.A. **79 D13** 42 17N 71 25W
Franca, Brazil **93 H9** 20 33S 47 30W
Francavilla Fontana, Italy **21 D7** 40 32N 17 35 E
France ■, Europe **18 C5** 47 0N 3 0 E
Frances, Australia **63 F3** 36 41S 140 55 E
Frances →, Canada **72 A3** 60 16N 129 10W
Frances L., Canada **72 A3** 61 23N 129 30W
Franceville, Gabon **52 E2** 1 40S 13 32 E
Franche-Comté, France **18 C6** 46 50N 5 55 E
Francis Case, L., U.S.A. **80 D5** 43 4N 98 34W
Francisco Beltrão, Brazil **95 B5** 26 5S 53 4W
Francisco I. Madero, Coahuila, Mexico **86 B4** 25 48N 103 18W
Francisco I. Madero, Durango, Mexico **86 C4** 24 32N 104 22W
Francistown, Botswana **57 C4** 21 7S 27 33 E
François, Canada **71 C8** 47 35N 56 45W
François L., Canada **72 C3** 54 0N 125 30W
Franeker, Neths. **15 A5** 53 12N 5 33 E
Frankford, Canada **78 B7** 44 12N 77 36W
Frankfort, S. Africa **57 D4** 27 17S 28 30 E
Frankfort, Ind., U.S.A. **76 E2** 40 17N 86 31W
Frankfort, Kans., U.S.A. **80 F6** 39 42N 96 25W
Frankfort, Ky., U.S.A. **76 F3** 38 12N 84 52W
Frankfort, N.Y., U.S.A. **79 C9** 43 2N 75 4W

Gatton

Frankfurt, Brandenburg, Germany 16 B8 52 20N 14 32 E
Frankfurt, Hessen, Germany 16 C5 50 7N 8 41 E
Fränkische Alb, Germany 16 D6 49 10N 11 23 E
Frankland ➤, Australia 61 G2 35 0S 116 48 E
Franklin, Ky., U.S.A. 77 G2 36 43N 86 35W
Franklin, La., U.S.A. 81 L9 29 48N 91 30W
Franklin, Mass., U.S.A. 79 D13 42 5N 71 24W
Franklin, N.H., U.S.A. 79 C13 43 27N 71 39W
Franklin, Nebr., U.S.A. 80 E5 40 6N 98 57W
Franklin, Pa., U.S.A. 78 E5 41 24N 79 50W
Franklin, Va., U.S.A. 77 G7 36 41N 76 56W
Franklin, W. Va., U.S.A. 76 F6 38 39N 79 20W
Franklin B., Canada 68 B7 69 45N 126 0W
Franklin D. Roosevelt L., U.S.A. 82 B4 48 18N 118 9W
Franklin I., Antarctica 5 D11 76 10S 168 30 E
Franklin L., U.S.A. 82 F6 40 25N 115 22W
Franklin Mts., Canada 68 B7 65 0N 125 0W
Franklin Str., Canada 68 A10 72 0N 96 0W
Franklinton, U.S.A. 81 K9 30 51N 90 9W
Franklinville, U.S.A. 78 D6 42 20N 78 27W
Franks Pk., U.S.A. 82 E9 43 58N 109 18W
Frankston, Australia 63 F4 38 8S 145 8 E
Frantsa Iosifa, Zemlya, Russia 26 A6 82 0N 55 0 E
Franz, Canada 70 C3 48 25N 84 30W
Franz Josef Land = Frantsa Iosifa, Zemlya, Russia 26 A6 82 0N 55 0 E
Fraser, U.S.A. 78 D2 42 32N 82 57W
Fraser ➤, B.C., Canada 72 D4 49 7N 123 11W
Fraser ➤, Nfld., Canada 71 A7 56 39N 62 10W
Fraser, Mt., Australia 61 E2 25 35S 118 20 E
Fraser I., Australia 63 D5 25 15S 153 10 E
Fraser Lake, Canada 72 C4 54 0N 124 50W
Fraserburg, S. Africa 56 E3 31 55S 21 30 E
Fraserburgh, U.K. 12 D6 57 42N 2 1W
Fraserdale, Canada 70 C3 49 55N 81 37W
Fray Bentos, Uruguay 94 C4 33 10S 58 15W
Fredericia, Denmark 9 J13 55 34N 9 45 E
Frederick, Md., U.S.A. 76 F7 39 25N 77 25W
Frederick, Okla., U.S.A. 81 H5 34 23N 99 1W
Frederick, S. Dak., U.S.A. 80 C5 45 50N 98 31W
Fredericksburg, Pa., U.S.A. 79 F8 40 27N 76 26W
Fredericksburg, Tex., U.S.A. 81 K5 30 16N 98 52W
Fredericksburg, Va., U.S.A. 76 F7 38 18N 77 28W
Fredericktown, Mo., U.S.A. 81 G9 37 34N 90 18W
Fredericktown, Ohio, U.S.A. 78 F2 40 29N 82 33W
Frederico I. Madero, Presa, Mexico 86 B3 28 7N 105 40W
Frederico Westphalen, Brazil 95 B5 27 22S 53 24W
Fredericton, Canada 71 C6 45 57N 66 40W
Fredericton Junction, Canada 71 C6 45 41N 66 40W
Frederikshåb, Greenland 4 C5 62 0N 49 43W
Frederikshavn, Denmark 9 H14 57 28N 10 31 E
Frederiksted, Virgin Is. 89 C7 17 43N 64 53W
Fredonia, Ariz., U.S.A. 83 H7 36 57N 112 32W
Fredonia, Kans., U.S.A. 81 G7 37 32N 95 49W
Fredonia, N.Y., U.S.A. 78 D5 42 26N 79 20W
Fredrikstad, Norway 9 G14 59 13N 10 57 E
Free State □, S. Africa 56 D4 28 30S 27 0 E
Freehold, U.S.A. 79 F10 40 16N 74 17W
Freel Peak, U.S.A. 84 G7 38 52N 119 54W
Freeland, U.S.A. 79 E9 41 1N 75 54W
Freels, C., Canada 71 C9 49 15N 53 30W
Freeman, Calif., U.S.A. 85 K9 35 35N 117 53W
Freeman, S. Dak., U.S.A. 80 D6 43 21N 97 26W
Freeport, Bahamas 88 A4 26 30N 78 47W
Freeport, Ill., U.S.A. 80 D10 42 17N 89 36W
Freeport, N.Y., U.S.A. 79 F11 40 39N 73 35W
Freeport, Ohio, U.S.A. 78 F3 40 12N 81 15W
Freeport, Pa., U.S.A. 78 F5 40 41N 79 41W
Freeport, Tex., U.S.A. 81 L7 28 57N 95 21W
Freetown, S. Leone 50 G3 8 30N 13 17W
Frégate, L., Canada 70 B5 53 15N 74 45W
Fregenal de la Sierra, Spain 19 C2 38 10N 6 39W
Freibourg = Fribourg, Switz. 18 C7 46 49N 7 9 E
Freiburg, Germany 16 E4 47 59N 7 51 E
Freire, Chile 96 D2 38 54S 72 38W
Freirina, Chile 94 B1 28 30S 71 10W
Freising, Germany 16 D6 48 24N 11 45 E
Freistadt, Austria 16 D8 48 30N 14 30 E
Fréjus, France 18 E7 43 25N 6 44 E
Fremantle, Australia 61 F2 32 7S 115 47 E
Fremont, Calif., U.S.A. 84 H4 37 32N 121 57W
Fremont, Mich., U.S.A. 76 D3 43 28N 85 57W
Fremont, Nebr., U.S.A. 80 E6 41 26N 96 30W
Fremont, Ohio, U.S.A. 76 E4 41 21N 83 7W
Fremont ➤, U.S.A. 83 G8 38 24N 110 42W
French Camp, U.S.A. 84 H5 37 53N 121 16W
French Creek ➤, U.S.A. 78 E5 41 24N 79 50W
French Guiana ■, S. Amer. 93 C8 4 0N 53 0W
French Pass, N.Z. 59 J4 40 55S 173 55 E
French Polynesia ■, Pac. Oc. 65 K13 20 0S 145 0W
Frenchman Cr. ➤, N. Amer. 82 B10 48 31N 107 10W
Frenchman Cr. ➤, U.S.A. 80 E4 40 14N 100 50W
Fresco ➤, Brazil 93 E8 7 15S 51 30W
Freshfield, C., Antarctica 5 C10 68 25S 151 10 E
Fresnillo, Mexico 86 C4 23 10N 103 0W
Fresno, U.S.A. 84 J7 36 44N 119 47W
Fresno Reservoir, U.S.A. 82 B9 48 36N 109 57W
Frew ➤, Australia 62 C2 20 0S 135 38 E
Frewsburg, U.S.A. 78 D5 42 3N 79 10W
Freycinet Pen., Australia 62 G4 42 10S 148 25 E
Fria, C., Namibia 56 B1 18 0S 12 0 E
Friant, U.S.A. 84 J7 36 59N 119 43W
Frías, Argentina 94 B2 28 40S 65 5W
Fribourg, Switz. 18 C7 46 49N 7 9 E
Friday Harbor, U.S.A. 84 B3 48 32N 123 1W
Friedens, U.S.A. 78 F6 40 3N 78 59W
Friedrichshafen, Germany 16 E5 47 39N 9 30 E
Friendly Is. = Tonga ■, Pac. Oc. 59 D11 19 50S 174 30W
Friendship, U.S.A. 78 D6 42 12N 78 8W
Friesland □, Neths. 15 A5 53 5N 5 50 E
Frio ➤, U.S.A. 81 L5 28 26N 98 11W
Frio, C., Brazil 90 F6 22 50S 41 50W
Friona, U.S.A. 81 H3 34 38N 102 43W
Fritch, U.S.A. 81 H4 35 38N 101 36W
Frobisher B., Canada 69 B13 62 30N 66 0W
Frobisher Bay = Iqaluit, Canada 69 B13 63 44N 68 31W
Frobisher L., Canada 73 B7 56 20N 108 15W
Frohavet, Norway 8 E13 64 0N 9 30 E
Frome, U.K. 11 F5 51 14N 2 19W
Frome ➤, U.K. 11 G5 50 41N 2 6W
Frome, L., Australia 63 E2 30 45S 139 45 E
Front Range, U.S.A. 74 C5 40 25N 105 45W
Front Royal, U.S.A. 76 F6 38 55N 78 12W
Frontera, Canary Is. 22 G2 27 47N 17 59W
Frontera, Mexico 87 D6 18 30N 92 40W
Fronteras, Mexico 86 A3 30 56N 109 31W
Frosinone, Italy 20 D5 41 38N 13 19 E
Frostburg, U.S.A. 76 F6 39 39N 78 56W
Frostisen, Norway 8 B17 68 14N 17 10 E
Frøya, Norway 8 E13 63 43N 8 40 E
Frunze = Bishkek, Kyrgyzstan 26 E8 42 54N 74 46 E
Frutal, Brazil 93 H9 20 0S 49 0W
Frýdek-Místek, Czech Rep. 17 D10 49 40N 18 20 E
Fryeburg, U.S.A. 79 B14 44 1N 70 59W
Fu Xian = Wafangdian, China 35 E11 39 38N 121 58 E
Fu Xian, China 34 G5 36 0N 109 20 E
Fucheng, China 34 F9 37 50N 116 10 E
Fuchou = Fuzhou, China 33 D6 26 5N 119 16 E
Fuchū, Japan 31 G6 34 34N 133 14 E
Fuencaliente, Canary Is. 22 F2 28 28N 17 50W
Fuencaliente, Pta., Canary Is. 22 F2 28 27N 17 51W
Fuengirola, Spain 19 D3 36 32N 4 41W
Fuentes de Oñoro, Spain 19 B2 40 33N 6 52W
Fuerte ➤, Mexico 86 B3 25 50N 109 25W
Fuerte Olimpo, Paraguay 94 A4 21 0S 57 51W
Fuerteventura, Canary Is. 22 F6 28 30N 14 0W
Fufeng, China 34 G5 34 22N 108 0 E
Fugou, China 34 G8 34 3N 114 25 E
Fugu, China 34 E6 39 2N 111 3 E
Fuhai, China 32 B3 47 2N 87 25 E
Fuḩaymī, Iraq 44 C4 34 16N 42 10 E
Fuji, Japan 31 G9 35 9N 138 39 E
Fuji-San, Japan 31 G9 35 22N 138 44 E
Fuji-yoshida, Japan 31 G9 35 30N 138 46 E
Fujian □, China 33 D6 26 0N 118 0 E
Fujinomiya, Japan 31 G9 35 10N 138 40 E
Fujisawa, Japan 31 G9 35 22N 139 29 E
Fujiyama, Mt. = Fuji-San, Japan 31 G9 35 22N 138 44 E
Fukien = Fujian □, China 33 D6 26 0N 118 0 E
Fukuchiyama, Japan 31 G7 35 19N 135 9 E
Fukue-Shima, Japan 31 H4 32 40N 128 45 E
Fukui, Japan 31 F8 36 5N 136 10 E
Fukui □, Japan 31 G8 36 0N 136 12 E
Fukuoka, Japan 31 H5 33 39N 130 21 E
Fukuoka □, Japan 31 H5 33 30N 131 0 E
Fukushima, Japan 30 F10 37 44N 140 28 E
Fukushima □, Japan 30 F10 37 30N 140 15 E
Fukuyama, Japan 31 G6 34 35N 133 20 E
Fulda, Germany 16 C5 50 32N 9 40 E
Fulda ➤, Germany 16 C5 51 25N 9 39 E
Fulford Harbour, Canada 84 B3 48 47N 123 27W
Fullerton, Calif., U.S.A. 85 M9 33 53N 117 56W
Fullerton, Nebr., U.S.A. 80 E6 41 22N 97 58W
Fulongquan, China 35 B13 44 20N 124 42 E
Fulton, Mo., U.S.A. 80 F9 38 52N 91 57W
Fulton, N.Y., U.S.A. 79 C8 43 19N 76 25W
Funabashi, Japan 31 G10 35 45N 140 0 E
Funchal, Madeira 22 D3 32 38N 16 54W
Fundación, Colombia 92 A4 10 31N 74 11W
Fundão, Portugal 19 B2 40 8N 7 30W
Fundy, B. of, Canada 71 D6 45 0N 66 0W
Funing, Hebei, China 35 E10 39 53N 119 12 E
Funing, Jiangsu, China 35 H10 33 45N 119 50 E
Funiu Shan, China 34 H7 33 30N 112 20 E
Funtua, Nigeria 50 F7 11 30N 7 18 E
Fuping, Hebei, China 34 E8 38 48N 114 12 E
Fuping, Shaanxi, China 34 G5 34 42N 109 10 E
Furano, Japan 30 C11 43 21N 142 23 E
Furāt, Nahr al ➤, Asia 44 D5 31 0N 47 25 E
Fürg, Iran 45 D7 28 18N 55 13 E
Furnás, Spain 22 B8 39 3N 1 32 E
Furnas, Represa de, Brazil 95 A6 20 50S 45 30W
Furneaux Group, Australia 62 G4 40 10S 147 50 E
Furqlus, Syria 47 A6 34 36N 37 8 E
Fürstenwalde, Germany 16 B8 52 22N 14 3 E
Fürth, Germany 16 D6 49 28N 10 59 E
Furukawa, Japan 30 E10 38 34N 140 58 E
Fury and Hecla Str., Canada 69 B11 69 56N 84 0W
Fusagasuga, Colombia 92 C4 4 21N 74 22W
Fushan, Shandong, China 35 F11 37 30N 121 15 E
Fushan, Shanxi, China 34 G6 35 58N 111 51 E
Fushun, China 35 D12 41 50N 123 56 E
Fusong, China 35 C14 42 20N 127 15 E
Futuna, Wall. & F. Is. 59 B8 14 25S 178 20 E
Fuxin, China 35 C11 42 5N 121 48 E
Fuyang, China 34 H8 33 0N 115 48 E
Fuyang He ➤, China 34 E9 38 12N 117 0 E
Fuyu, China 35 B13 45 12N 124 43 E
Fuzhou, China 33 D6 26 5N 119 16 E
Fylde, U.K. 10 D5 53 50N 2 58W
Fyn, Denmark 9 J14 55 20N 10 30 E
Fyne, L., U.K. 12 F3 55 59N 5 23W

G

Gabela, Angola 52 G2 11 0S 14 24 E
Gabès, Tunisia 51 B8 33 53N 10 2 E
Gabès, G. de, Tunisia 51 B8 34 0N 10 30 E
Gabon ■, Africa 52 E2 0 10S 10 0 E
Gaborone, Botswana 56 C4 24 45S 25 57 E
Gabriels, U.S.A. 79 B10 44 26N 74 12W
Gābrīk, Iran 45 E8 25 44N 58 28 E
Gabrovo, Bulgaria 21 C11 42 52N 25 19 E
Gāch Sār, Iran 45 B6 36 7N 51 19 E
Gachsārān, Iran 45 D6 30 15N 50 45 E
Gadag, India 40 M9 15 30N 75 45 E
Gadap, Pakistan 42 G2 25 5N 67 28 E
Gadarwara, India 43 H8 22 50N 78 50 E
Gadhada, India 42 J4 22 0N 71 35 E
Gadra, Pakistan 42 G4 25 40N 70 38 E
Gadsden, U.S.A. 77 H3 34 1N 86 1W
Gadwal, India 40 L10 16 10N 77 50 E
Gaffney, U.S.A. 77 H5 35 5N 81 39W
Gafsa, Tunisia 50 B7 34 24N 8 43 E
Gagaria, India 42 G4 25 43N 70 46 E
Gagnoa, Ivory C. 50 G4 6 56N 5 16W
Gagnon, Canada 71 B6 51 50N 68 5W
Gagnon, L., Canada 73 A6 62 3N 110 27W
Gahini, Rwanda 54 C3 1 50S 30 30 E
Gahmar, India 43 G10 25 27N 83 49 E
Gai Xian = Gaizhou, China 35 D12 40 22N 122 20 E
Gaïdhouronísi, Greece 23 E7 34 53N 25 41 E
Gail, U.S.A. 81 J4 32 46N 101 27W
Gaillimh = Galway, Ireland 13 C2 53 17N 9 3W
Gaines, U.S.A. 78 E7 41 46N 77 35W
Gainesville, Fla., U.S.A. 77 L4 29 40N 82 20W
Gainesville, Ga., U.S.A. 77 H4 34 18N 83 50W
Gainesville, Mo., U.S.A. 81 G8 36 36N 92 26W
Gainesville, Tex., U.S.A. 81 J6 33 38N 97 8W
Gainsborough, U.K. 10 D7 53 24N 0 46W
Gairdner, L., Australia 63 E2 31 30S 136 0 E
Gairloch, L., U.K. 12 D3 57 43N 5 45W
Gaizhou, China 35 D12 40 22N 122 20 E
Gaj ➤, Pakistan 42 F2 26 26N 67 21 E
Gakuch, Pakistan 43 A5 36 7N 73 45 E
Galán, Cerro, Argentina 94 B2 25 55S 66 52W
Galana ➤, Kenya 54 C5 3 9S 40 8 E
Galápagos, Pac. Oc. 90 D1 0 0 91 0W
Galashiels, U.K. 12 F6 55 37N 2 49W
Galaţi, Romania 17 F15 45 27N 28 2 E
Galatina, Italy 21 D8 40 10N 18 10 E
Galax, U.S.A. 77 G5 36 40N 80 56W
Galcaio, Somali Rep. 46 F4 6 30N 47 30 E
Galdhøpiggen, Norway 9 F12 61 38N 8 18 E
Galeana, Mexico 86 C4 24 50N 100 4W
Galeana, Nuevo León, Mexico 86 A3 24 50N 100 4W
Galela, Indonesia 37 D7 1 50N 127 49 E
Galena, U.S.A. 68 B4 64 44N 156 56W
Galera Point, Trin. & Tob. 89 D7 10 8N 61 0W
Galesburg, U.S.A. 80 E9 40 57N 90 22W
Galeton, U.S.A. 78 E7 41 44N 77 39W
Galich, Russia 24 C7 58 22N 42 24 E
Galicia □, Spain 19 A2 42 43N 7 45W
Galilee = Hagalil, Israel 47 C4 32 53N 35 18 E
Galilee, L., Australia 62 C4 22 20S 145 50 E
Galilee, Sea of = Yam Kinneret, Israel 47 C4 32 45N 35 35 E
Galinoporni, Cyprus 23 D13 35 31N 34 18 E
Galion, U.S.A. 78 F2 40 44N 82 47W
Galiuro Mts., U.S.A. 83 K8 32 30N 110 20W
Galiwinku, Australia 62 A2 12 2S 135 34 E
Gallan Hd., U.K. 12 C1 58 15N 7 2W
Gallatin, U.S.A. 77 G2 36 24N 86 27W
Galle, Sri Lanka 40 R12 6 5N 80 10 E
Gállego ➤, Spain 19 B5 41 39N 0 51W
Gallegos ➤, Argentina 96 G3 51 35S 69 0W
Galley Hd., Ireland 13 E3 51 32N 8 55W
Gallinas, Pta., Colombia 92 A4 12 28N 71 40W
Gallipoli = Gelibolu, Turkey 21 D12 40 28N 26 43 E
Gallípoli, Italy 21 D8 40 3N 17 58 E
Gallipolis, U.S.A. 76 F4 38 49N 82 12W
Gällivare, Sweden 8 C19 67 9N 20 40 E
Galloo I., U.S.A. 79 C8 43 55N 76 25W
Galloway, U.K. 12 F4 55 1N 4 29W
Galloway, Mull of, U.K. 12 G4 54 39N 4 52W
Gallup, U.S.A. 83 J9 35 32N 108 45W
Galoya, Sri Lanka 40 Q12 8 10N 80 55 E
Galt, U.S.A. 84 G5 38 15N 121 18W
Galty Mts., Ireland 13 D3 52 22N 8 10W
Galtymore, Ireland 13 D3 52 21N 8 11W
Galva, U.S.A. 80 E9 41 10N 90 3W
Galveston, U.S.A. 81 L7 29 18N 94 48W
Galveston B., U.S.A. 81 L7 29 36N 94 50W
Gálvez, Argentina 94 C3 32 0S 61 14W
Galway, Ireland 13 C2 53 17N 9 3W
Galway □, Ireland 13 C2 53 22N 9 1W
Galway B., Ireland 13 C2 53 13N 9 10W
Gam ➤, Vietnam 38 B5 21 55N 105 12 E
Gamagori, Japan 31 G8 34 50N 137 14 E
Gambat, Pakistan 42 F3 27 17N 68 26 E
Gambhir ➤, India 42 F6 26 58N 77 27 E
Gambia ■, W. Afr. 50 F2 13 25N 16 0W
Gambia ➤, W. Afr. 50 F2 13 28N 16 34W
Gambier, U.S.A. 78 F2 40 22N 82 23W
Gambier, C., Australia 60 B5 11 56S 130 57 E
Gambier Is., Australia 63 F2 35 3S 136 30 E
Gambo, Canada 71 C9 48 47N 54 13W
Gamboli, Pakistan 42 E3 29 53N 68 24 E
Gamboma, Congo 52 E3 1 55S 15 52 E
Gamlakarleby = Kokkola, Finland 8 E20 63 50N 23 8 E
Gammon ➤, Canada 73 C9 51 24N 95 44W
Gan Jiang ➤, China 33 D6 29 15N 116 0 E
Ganado, U.S.A. 83 J9 35 43N 109 33W
Gananoque, Canada 79 B8 44 20N 76 10W
Ganāveh, Iran 45 D6 29 35N 50 35 E
Gäncä, Azerbaijan 25 F8 40 45N 46 20 E
Gancheng, China 38 C7 18 51N 108 37 E
Gand = Gent, Belgium 15 C3 51 2N 3 42 E
Ganda, Angola 53 G2 13 3S 14 35 E
Gandajika, Dem. Rep. of the Congo 52 F4 6 45S 23 57 E
Gandak ➤, India 43 G11 25 39N 85 13 E
Gandava, Pakistan 42 E2 28 32N 67 32 E
Gander, Canada 71 C9 48 58N 54 35W
Gander L., Canada 71 C9 48 58N 54 35W
Ganderowe Falls, Zimbabwe 55 F2 17 20S 29 10 E
Gandhi Sagar, India 42 G6 24 40N 75 40 E
Gandhinagar, India 42 H5 23 15N 72 45 E
Gandía, Spain 19 C5 38 58N 0 9W
Gando, Pta., Canary Is. 22 G4 27 55N 15 22W
Ganedidalem = Gani, Indonesia 37 E7 0 48S 128 14 E
Ganga ➤, India 43 H14 23 20N 90 30 E
Ganga Sagar, India 43 J13 21 38N 88 5 E
Gangan ➤, India 43 E8 28 38N 78 58 E
Ganganagar, India 42 E5 29 56N 73 56 E
Gangapur, India 42 F7 26 32N 76 49 E
Gangaw, Burma 41 H19 22 5N 94 5 E
Gangdisê Shan, China 41 D12 31 20N 81 0 E
Ganges = Ganga ➤, India 43 H14 23 20N 90 30 E
Ganges, Canada 72 D4 48 51N 123 31W
Ganges, Mouths of the, India 43 J14 21 30N 90 0 E
Gangoh, India 42 E7 29 46N 77 18 E
Gangroti, India 43 D8 30 50N 79 10 E
Gangtok, India 41 F16 27 20N 88 37 E
Gangu, China 34 G3 34 40N 105 15 E
Gangyao, China 35 B14 44 12N 126 37 E
Gani, Indonesia 37 E7 0 48S 128 14 E
Ganj, India 43 F8 27 45N 78 57 E
Gannett Peak, U.S.A. 82 E9 43 11N 109 39W
Ganquan, China 34 F5 36 20N 109 20 E
Gansu □, China 34 G3 36 0N 104 0 E
Ganta, Liberia 50 G4 7 15N 8 59W
Gantheaume, C., Australia 63 F2 36 4S 137 32 E
Gantheaume B., Australia 61 E1 27 40S 114 10 E
Gantsevichi = Hantsavichy, Belarus 17 B14 52 49N 26 30 E
Ganyem = Genyem, Indonesia 37 E10 2 46S 140 12 E
Ganyu, China 35 G10 34 50N 119 8 E
Ganzhou, China 33 D6 25 51N 114 56 E
Gao, Mali 50 E5 16 15N 0 5W
Gaomi, China 35 F10 36 20N 119 42 E
Gaoping, China 34 G7 35 45N 112 55 E
Gaotang, China 34 F9 36 50N 116 15 E
Gaoua, Burkina Faso 50 F5 10 20N 3 8W
Gaoual, Guinea 50 F3 11 45N 13 25W
Gaoxiong = Kaohsiung, Taiwan 33 D7 22 35N 120 16 E
Gaoyang, China 34 E8 38 40N 115 45 E
Gaoyou Hu, China 35 H10 32 45N 119 20 E
Gaoyuan, China 35 F9 37 8N 117 58 E
Gap, France 18 D7 44 33N 6 5 E
Gapat ➤, India 43 G10 24 30N 82 28 E
Gapuwiyak, Australia 62 A2 12 25S 135 43 E
Gar, China 32 C2 32 10N 79 58 E
Garabogazköl Aylagy, Turkmenistan 25 F9 41 0N 53 30 E
Garachico, Canary Is. 22 F3 28 22N 16 46W
Garachiné, Panama 88 E4 8 0N 78 12W
Garafia, Canary Is. 22 F2 28 48N 17 57W
Garah, Australia 63 D4 29 5S 149 38 E
Garajonay, Canary Is. 22 F2 28 7N 17 14W
Garanhuns, Brazil 93 E11 8 50S 36 30W
Garautha, India 43 G8 25 34N 79 18 E
Garba Tula, Kenya 54 B4 0 30N 38 32 E
Garberville, U.S.A. 82 F2 40 6N 123 48W
Garbiyang, India 43 D9 30 8N 80 54 E
Garda, L. di, Italy 20 B4 45 40N 10 41 E
Garde L., Canada 73 A7 62 50N 106 13W
Garden City, Ga., U.S.A. 77 J5 32 6N 81 9W
Garden City, Kans., U.S.A. 81 G4 37 58N 100 53W
Garden City, Tex., U.S.A. 81 K4 31 52N 101 29W
Garden Grove, U.S.A. 85 M9 33 47N 117 55W
Gardēz, Afghan. 42 C3 33 37N 69 9 E
Gardiner, Maine, U.S.A. 77 C11 44 14N 69 47W
Gardiner, Mont., U.S.A. 82 D8 45 2N 110 22W
Gardiners I., U.S.A. 79 E12 41 6N 72 6W
Gardner, U.S.A. 79 D13 42 34N 71 59W
Gardner Canal, Canada 72 C3 53 27N 128 8W
Gardnerville, U.S.A. 84 G7 38 56N 119 45W
Gardo, Somali Rep. 46 F4 9 30N 49 6 E
Garey, U.S.A. 85 L6 34 53N 120 19W
Garfield, U.S.A. 82 C5 47 1N 117 9W
Garforth, U.K. 10 D6 53 47N 1 24W
Gargano, Mte., Italy 20 D6 41 43N 15 43 E
Garibaldi Prov. Park, Canada 72 D4 49 50N 122 40W
Garies, S. Africa 56 E2 30 32S 17 59 E
Garigliano ➤, Italy 20 D5 41 13N 13 45 E
Garissa, Kenya 54 C4 0 25S 39 40 E
Garland, Tex., U.S.A. 81 J6 32 55N 96 38W
Garland, Utah, U.S.A. 82 F7 41 47N 112 10W
Garm, Tajikistan 26 F8 39 0N 70 20 E
Garmāb, Iran 45 C8 35 25N 56 45 E
Garmisch-Partenkirchen, Germany 16 E6 47 30N 11 6 E
Garmsār, Iran 45 C7 35 20N 52 25 E
Garner, U.S.A. 80 D8 43 6N 93 36W
Garnett, U.S.A. 80 F7 38 17N 95 14W
Garo Hills, India 43 G14 25 30N 90 30 E
Garoe, Somali Rep. 46 F4 8 25N 48 33 E
Garonne ➤, France 18 D3 45 2N 0 36W
Garot, India 42 G6 24 19N 75 41 E
Garoua, Cameroon 51 G8 9 19N 13 21 E
Garrauli, India 43 G8 25 5N 79 22 E
Garrison, Mont., U.S.A. 82 C7 46 31N 112 49W
Garrison, N. Dak., U.S.A. 80 B4 47 40N 101 25W
Garrison Res. = Sakakawea, L., U.S.A. 80 B4 47 30N 101 25W
Garron Pt., U.K. 13 A6 55 3N 5 59W
Garry ➤, U.K. 12 E5 56 44N 3 47W
Garry, L., Canada 68 B9 65 58N 100 18W
Garsen, Kenya 54 C5 2 20S 40 5 E
Garson L., Canada 73 B6 56 19N 110 2W
Garu, India 43 H11 23 40N 84 14 E
Garub, Namibia 56 D2 26 37S 16 0 E
Garut, Indonesia 37 G12 7 14S 107 53 E
Garvie Mts., N.Z. 59 L2 45 30S 168 50 E
Garwa = Garoua, Cameroon 51 G8 9 19N 13 21 E
Garwa, India 43 G10 24 11N 83 47 E
Gary, U.S.A. 76 E2 41 36N 87 20W
Garzê, China 32 C5 31 38N 100 1 E
Garzón, Colombia 92 C3 2 10N 75 40W
Gas-San, Japan 30 E10 38 32N 140 1 E
Gasan Kuli = Esenguly, Turkmenistan 26 F6 37 37N 53 59 E
Gascogne, France 18 E4 43 45N 0 20 E
Gascogne, G. de, Europe 18 D2 44 0N 2 0W
Gascony = Gascogne, France 18 E4 43 45N 0 20 E
Gascoyne ➤, Australia 61 D1 24 52S 113 37 E
Gascoyne Junction, Australia 61 E2 25 2S 115 17 E
Gashaka, Nigeria 51 G8 7 20N 11 29 E
Gasherbrum, Pakistan 43 B7 35 40N 76 40 E
Gashua, Nigeria 51 F8 12 54N 11 0 E
Gaspé, Canada 71 C7 48 52N 64 30W
Gaspé, C. de, Canada 71 C7 48 48N 64 7W
Gaspé, Pén. de, Canada 71 C6 48 45N 65 40W
Gaspésie, Parc de Conservation de la, Canada 71 C6 48 55N 65 50W
Gasteiz = Vitoria-Gasteiz, Spain 19 A4 42 50N 2 41W
Gastonia, U.S.A. 77 H5 35 16N 81 11W
Gastre, Argentina 96 E3 42 20S 69 15W
Gata, C., Cyprus 23 E12 34 34N 33 2 E
Gata, C. de, Spain 19 D4 36 41N 2 13W
Gata, Sierra de, Spain 19 B2 40 20N 6 45W
Gataga ➤, Canada 72 B3 58 35N 126 59W
Gatehouse of Fleet, U.K. 12 G4 54 53N 4 12W
Gates, U.S.A. 78 C7 43 9N 77 42W
Gateshead, U.K. 10 C6 54 57N 1 35W
Gatesville, U.S.A. 81 K6 31 26N 97 45W
Gaths, Zimbabwe 55 G3 20 2S 30 32 E
Gatico, Chile 94 A1 22 29S 70 20W
Gatineau, Canada 79 A9 45 29N 75 38W
Gatineau ➤, Canada 70 C4 45 27N 75 42W
Gatineau, Parc Nat. de la, Canada 70 C4 45 40N 76 0W
Gatton, Australia 63 D5 27 32S 152 17 E

Gatun, L.

Gatun, L., *Panama* **88 E4** 9 7N 79 56W
Gatyana, *S. Africa* **57 E4** 32 16S 28 31 E
Gau, *Fiji* **59 D8** 18 2S 179 18 E
Gauer L., *Canada* **73 B9** 57 0N 97 50W
Gauhati, *India* **41 F17** 26 10N 91 45 E
Gauja →, *Latvia* **9 H21** 57 10N 24 16 E
Gaula →, *Norway* **8 E14** 63 21N 10 14 E
Gauri Phanta, *India* **43 E9** 28 41N 80 36 E
Gausta, *Norway* **9 G13** 59 48N 8 40 E
Gauteng □, *S. Africa* **57 D4** 26 0S 28 0 E
Gāv Koshī, *Iran* **45 D8** 28 38N 57 12 E
Gāvakān, *Iran* **45 D7** 29 37N 53 10 E
Gavāter, *Iran* **45 E9** 25 10N 61 31 E
Gāvbandī, *Iran* **45 E7** 27 12N 53 4 E
Gavdhopoúla, *Greece* **23 E6** 34 56N 24 0 E
Gávdhos, *Greece* **23 E6** 34 50N 24 5 E
Gaviota, *U.S.A.* **85 L6** 34 29N 120 13W
Gāvkhūnī, Bāṭlāq-e, *Iran* **45 C7** 32 6N 52 52 E
Gävle, *Sweden* **9 F17** 60 40N 17 9 E
Gawachab, *Namibia* **56 D2** 27 4S 17 55 E
Gawilgarh Hills, *India* **40 J10** 21 15N 76 45 E
Gawler, *Australia* **63 E2** 34 30S 138 42 E
Gaxun Nur, *China* **32 B5** 42 22N 100 30 E
Gay, *Russia* **24 D10** 51 27N 58 27 E
Gaya, *India* **43 G11** 24 47N 85 4 E
Gaya, *Niger* **50 F6** 11 52N 3 28 E
Gaylord, *U.S.A.* **76 C3** 45 2N 84 41W
Gayndah, *Australia* **63 D5** 25 35S 151 32 E
Gaysin = Haysyn, *Ukraine* **17 D15** 48 57N 29 25 E
Gayvoron = Hayvoron, *Ukraine* **17 D15** 48 22N 29 52 E
Gaza, *Gaza Strip* **47 D3** 31 30N 34 28 E
Gaza □, *Mozam.* **57 C5** 23 10S 32 45 E
Gaza Strip □, *Asia* **47 D3** 31 29N 34 25 E
Gazanjyk, *Turkmenistan* **45 B7** 39 16N 55 32 E
Gāzbor, *Iran* **45 D8** 28 5N 58 51 E
Gazi, *Dem. Rep. of the Congo* **54 B1** 1 3N 24 30 E
Gaziantep, *Turkey* **25 G6** 37 6N 37 23 E
Gcuwa, *S. Africa* **57 E4** 32 20S 28 11 E
Gdańsk, *Poland* **17 A10** 54 22N 18 40 E
Gdańska, Zatoka, *Poland* **17 A10** 54 30N 19 20 E
Gdov, *Russia* **9 G22** 58 48N 27 55 E
Gdynia, *Poland* **17 A10** 54 35N 18 33 E
Gebe, *Indonesia* **37 D7** 0 5N 129 25 E
Gebze, *Turkey* **21 D13** 40 47N 29 25 E
Gedaref, *Sudan* **51 F13** 14 2N 35 28 E
Gediz →, *Turkey* **21 E12** 38 35N 26 48 E
Gedser, *Denmark* **9 J14** 54 35N 11 55 E
Geegully Cr. →, *Australia* **60 C3** 18 32S 123 41 E
Geel, *Belgium* **15 C4** 51 10N 4 59 E
Geelong, *Australia* **63 F3** 38 10S 144 22 E
Geelvink B. = Cenderwasih, Teluk, *Indonesia* **37 E9** 3 0S 135 20 E
Geelvink Chan., *Australia* **61 E1** 28 30S 114 0 E
Geesthacht, *Germany* **16 B6** 53 26N 10 22 E
Geidam, *Nigeria* **51 F8** 12 57N 11 57 E
Geikie →, *Canada* **73 B8** 57 45N 103 52W
Geistown, *U.S.A.* **78 F6** 40 18N 78 52W
Geita, *Tanzania* **54 C3** 2 48S 32 12 E
Gejiu, *China* **32 D5** 23 20N 103 10 E
Gel, Meydān-e, *Iran* **45 D7** 29 4N 54 50 E
Gela, *Italy* **20 F6** 37 4N 14 15 E
Gelderland □, *Neths.* **15 B6** 52 5N 6 10 E
Geldrop, *Neths.* **15 C5** 51 25N 5 32 E
Geleen, *Neths.* **15 D5** 50 57N 5 49 E
Gelibolu, *Turkey* **21 D12** 40 28N 26 43 E
Gelsenkirchen, *Germany* **16 C4** 51 32N 7 6 E
Gemas, *Malaysia* **39 L4** 2 37N 102 36 E
Gembloux, *Belgium* **15 D4** 50 34N 4 43 E
Gemena, *Dem. Rep. of the Congo* **52 D3** 3 13N 19 48 E
Gemerek, *Turkey* **44 B3** 39 15N 36 10 E
Gemlik, *Turkey* **21 D13** 40 26N 29 9 E
Genale, *Ethiopia* **46 F2** 6 0N 39 30 E
General Acha, *Argentina* **94 D3** 37 20S 64 38W
General Alvear, *Buenos Aires, Argentina* **94 D4** 36 0S 60 0W
General Alvear, *Mendoza, Argentina* **94 D2** 35 0S 67 40W
General Artigas, *Paraguay* **94 B4** 26 52S 56 16W
General Belgrano, *Argentina* **94 D4** 36 35S 58 47W
General Cabrera, *Argentina* **94 C3** 32 53S 63 52W
General Cepeda, *Mexico* **86 B4** 25 23N 101 27W
General Guido, *Argentina* **94 D4** 36 40S 57 50W
General Juan Madariaga, *Argentina* **94 D4** 37 0S 57 0W
General La Madrid, *Argentina* **94 D3** 37 17S 61 20W
General MacArthur, *Phil.* **37 B7** 11 18N 125 28 E
General Martin Miguel de Güemes, *Argentina* **94 A3** 24 50S 65 0W
General Paz, *Argentina* **94 B4** 27 45S 57 36W
General Pico, *Argentina* **94 D3** 35 45S 63 50W
General Pinedo, *Argentina* **94 B3** 27 15S 61 20W
General Pinto, *Argentina* **94 C3** 34 45S 61 50W
General Roca, *Argentina* **96 D3** 39 2S 67 35W
General Santos, *Phil.* **37 C7** 6 5N 125 14 E
General Trevino, *Mexico* **87 B5** 26 14N 99 29W
General Trías, *Mexico* **86 B3** 28 21N 106 22W
General Viamonte, *Argentina* **94 D3** 35 1S 61 3W
General Villegas, *Argentina* **94 D3** 35 5S 63 0W
Genesee, *Idaho, U.S.A.* **82 C5** 46 33N 116 56W
Genesee, *Pa., U.S.A.* **78 E7** 41 59N 77 54W
Genesee →, *U.S.A.* **78 C7** 43 16N 77 36W
Geneseo, *Ill., U.S.A.* **80 E9** 41 27N 90 9W
Geneseo, *N.Y., U.S.A.* **78 D7** 42 48N 77 49W
Geneva = Genève, *Switz.* **18 C7** 46 12N 6 9 E
Geneva, *Ala., U.S.A.* **77 K3** 31 2N 85 52W
Geneva, *N.Y., U.S.A.* **78 D8** 42 52N 76 59W
Geneva, *Nebr., U.S.A.* **80 E6** 40 32N 97 36W
Geneva, *Ohio, U.S.A.* **78 E4** 41 48N 80 57W
Geneva, L. = Léman, L., *Europe* **18 C7** 46 26N 6 30 E
Geneva, L., *U.S.A.* **76 D1** 42 38N 88 30W
Genève, *Switz.* **18 C7** 46 12N 6 9 E
Genil →, *Spain* **19 D3** 37 42N 5 19W
Genk, *Belgium* **15 D5** 50 58N 5 32 E
Gennargentu, Mti. del, *Italy* **20 D3** 40 1N 9 19 E
Genoa = Génova, *Italy* **18 D8** 44 25N 8 57 E
Genoa, *Australia* **63 F4** 37 29S 149 35 E
Genoa, *N.Y., U.S.A.* **79 D8** 42 40N 76 32W
Genoa, *Nebr., U.S.A.* **80 E6** 41 27N 97 44W
Genoa, *Nev., U.S.A.* **84 F7** 39 2N 119 50W
Génova, *Italy* **18 D8** 44 25N 8 57 E
Génova, G. di, *Italy* **20 C3** 44 0N 9 0 E
Genriyetty, Ostrov, *Russia* **27 B16** 77 6N 156 30 E
Gent, *Belgium* **15 C3** 51 2N 3 42 E
Genteng, *Indonesia* **37 G12** 7 22S 106 24 E
Genyem, *Indonesia* **37 E10** 2 46S 140 12 E
Geographe B., *Australia* **61 F2** 33 30S 115 15 E
Geographe Chan., *Australia* **61 D1** 24 30S 113 0 E
Georga, Zemlya, *Russia* **26 A5** 80 30N 49 0 E
George, *S. Africa* **56 E3** 33 58S 22 29 E
George →, *Canada* **71 A6** 58 49N 66 10W
George, L., *N.S.W., Australia* **63 F4** 35 10S 149 25 E
George, L., *S. Austral., Australia* **63 F3** 37 25S 140 0 E
George, L., *W. Austral., Australia* **60 D3** 22 45S 123 40 E
George, L., *Uganda* **54 B3** 0 5N 30 10 E
George, L., *Fla., U.S.A.* **77 L5** 29 17N 81 36W
George, L., *N.Y., U.S.A.* **79 C11** 43 37N 73 33W
George Gill Ra., *Australia* **60 D5** 24 22S 131 45 E
George River = Kangiqsualujjuaq, *Canada* **69 C13** 58 30N 65 59W
George Sound, *N.Z.* **59 L1** 44 52S 167 25 E
George Town, *Australia* **62 G4** 41 6S 146 49 E
George Town, *Bahamas* **88 B4** 23 33N 75 47W
George Town, *Malaysia* **39 K3** 5 25N 100 15 E
George V Land, *Antarctica* **5 C10** 69 0S 148 0 E
George VI Sound, *Antarctica* **5 D17** 71 0S 68 0W
George West, *U.S.A.* **81 L5** 28 20N 98 7W
Georgetown, *Australia* **62 B3** 18 17S 143 33 E
Georgetown, *Ont., Canada* **78 C5** 43 40N 79 56W
Georgetown, *P.E.I., Canada* **71 C7** 46 13N 62 24W
Georgetown, *Cayman Is.* **88 C3** 19 20N 81 24W
Georgetown, *Gambia* **50 F3** 13 30N 14 47W
Georgetown, *Guyana* **92 B7** 6 50N 58 12W
Georgetown, *Calif., U.S.A.* **84 G6** 38 54N 120 50W
Georgetown, *Colo., U.S.A.* **82 G11** 39 42N 105 42W
Georgetown, *Ky., U.S.A.* **76 F3** 38 13N 84 33W
Georgetown, *N.Y., U.S.A.* **79 D9** 42 46N 75 44W
Georgetown, *Ohio, U.S.A.* **76 F4** 38 52N 83 54W
Georgetown, *S.C., U.S.A.* **77 J6** 33 23N 79 17W
Georgetown, *Tex., U.S.A.* **81 K6** 30 38N 97 41W
Georgia □, *U.S.A.* **77 K5** 32 50N 83 15W
Georgia ■, *Asia* **25 F7** 42 0N 43 0 E
Georgia, Str. of, *Canada* **72 D4** 49 25N 124 0W
Georgian B., *Canada* **78 A4** 45 15N 81 0W
Georgina →, *Australia* **62 C2** 23 30S 139 47 E
Georgina I., *Canada* **78 B5** 44 22N 79 17W
Georgiu-Dezh = Liski, *Russia* **25 D6** 51 3N 39 30 E
Georgiyevsk, *Russia* **25 F7** 44 12N 43 28 E
Gera, *Germany* **16 C7** 50 53N 12 4 E
Geraardsbergen, *Belgium* **15 D3** 50 45N 3 53 E
Geral, Serra, *Brazil* **95 B6** 26 25S 50 0W
Geral de Goiás, Serra, *Brazil* **93 F9** 12 0S 46 0W
Geraldine, *U.S.A.* **82 C8** 47 36N 110 16W
Geraldton, *Australia* **61 E1** 28 48S 114 32 E
Geraldton, *Canada* **70 C2** 49 44N 86 59W
Gereshk, *Afghan.* **40 D4** 31 47N 64 35 E
Gerik, *Malaysia* **39 K3** 5 50N 101 15 E
Gering, *U.S.A.* **80 E3** 41 50N 103 40W
Gerlach, *U.S.A.* **82 F4** 40 39N 119 21W
Germansen Landing, *Canada* **72 B4** 55 43N 124 40W
Germantown, *U.S.A.* **81 M10** 35 5N 89 49W
Germany ■, *Europe* **16 C6** 51 0N 10 0 E
Germī, *Iran* **45 B6** 39 1N 48 3 E
Germiston, *S. Africa* **57 D4** 26 15S 28 10 E
Gernika-Lumo, *Spain* **19 A4** 43 19N 2 40W
Gero, *Japan* **31 G8** 35 48N 137 14 E
Gerona = Girona, *Spain* **19 B7** 41 58N 2 46 E
Gerrard, *Canada* **72 C5** 50 30N 117 17W
Geser, *Indonesia* **37 E8** 3 50S 130 54 E
Getafe, *Spain* **19 B4** 40 18N 3 44W
Gettysburg, *Pa., U.S.A.* **76 F7** 39 50N 77 14W
Gettysburg, *S. Dak., U.S.A.* **80 C5** 45 1N 99 57W
Getxo, *Spain* **19 A4** 43 21N 2 59W
Getz Ice Shelf, *Antarctica* **5 D14** 75 0S 130 0W
Geyser, *U.S.A.* **82 C8** 47 16N 110 30W
Geyserville, *U.S.A.* **84 G4** 38 42N 122 54W
Ghaggar →, *India* **42 E6** 29 30N 74 53 E
Ghaghara →, *India* **43 G11** 25 45N 84 40 E
Ghaghat →, *Bangla.* **43 G13** 25 19N 89 38 E
Ghagra, *India* **43 H11** 23 17N 84 33 E
Ghagra →, *India* **43 F9** 27 29N 81 9 E
Ghana ■, *W. Afr.* **50 G5** 8 0N 1 0W
Ghansor, *India* **43 H9** 22 39N 80 1 E
Ghanzi, *Botswana* **56 C3** 21 50S 21 34 E
Ghanzi □, *Botswana* **56 C3** 21 50S 21 45 E
Ghardaïa, *Algeria* **50 B6** 32 20N 3 37 E
Gharyān, *Libya* **51 B8** 32 10N 13 0 E
Ghat, *Libya* **51 D8** 24 59N 10 11 E
Ghatal, *India* **43 H12** 22 40N 87 46 E
Ghatampur, *India* **43 F9** 26 8N 80 13 E
Ghatsila, *India* **43 H12** 22 36N 86 29 E
Ghaṭṭī, *Si. Arabia* **44 D3** 31 16N 37 31 E
Ghawdex = Gozo, *Malta* **23 C1** 36 3N 14 13 E
Ghazal, Bahr el →, *Chad* **51 F9** 13 0N 15 47 E
Ghazâl, Bahr el →, *Sudan* **51 G12** 9 31N 30 25 E
Ghaziabad, *India* **42 E7** 28 42N 77 26 E
Ghazipur, *India* **43 G10** 25 38N 83 35 E
Ghaznī, *Afghan.* **42 C3** 33 30N 68 28 E
Ghaznī □, *Afghan.* **40 C6** 32 10N 68 20 E
Ghent = Gent, *Belgium* **15 C3** 51 2N 3 42 E
Ghīnah, Wādī al, *Si. Arabia* **44 D3** 30 27N 38 14 E
Ghizao, *Afghan.* **42 C1** 33 20N 65 44 E
Ghizar →, *Pakistan* **43 A5** 36 15N 73 43 E
Ghotaru, *India* **42 F4** 27 20N 70 1 E
Ghotki, *Pakistan* **42 E3** 28 5N 69 21 E
Ghowr □, *Afghan.* **40 C4** 34 0N 64 20 E
Ghudaf, W. al →, *Iraq* **44 C4** 32 56N 43 30 E
Ghudāmis, *Libya* **51 B7** 30 11N 9 29 E
Ghughri, *India* **43 H9** 22 39N 80 41 E
Ghugus, *India* **40 K11** 19 58N 79 12 E
Ghulam Mohammad Barrage, *Pakistan* **42 G3** 25 30N 68 20 E
Ghūrīān, *Afghan.* **40 B2** 34 17N 61 25 E
Gia Dinh, *Vietnam* **39 G6** 10 49N 106 42 E
Gia Lai = Plei Ku, *Vietnam* **38 F7** 13 57N 108 0 E
Gia Nghia, *Vietnam* **39 G6** 11 58N 107 42 E
Gia Ngoc, *Vietnam* **38 E7** 14 50N 108 58 E
Gia Vuc, *Vietnam* **38 E7** 14 42N 108 34 E
Giant Forest, *U.S.A.* **84 J8** 36 36N 118 43W
Giants Causeway, *U.K.* **13 A5** 55 16N 6 29W
Giarabub = Al Jaghbūb, *Libya* **51 C10** 29 42N 24 38 E
Giarre, *Italy* **20 F6** 37 43N 15 11 E
Gibara, *Cuba* **88 B4** 21 9N 76 11W
Gibb River, *Australia* **60 C4** 16 26S 126 26 E
Gibbon, *U.S.A.* **80 E5** 40 45N 98 51W
Gibeon, *Namibia* **53 K3** 25 7S 17 40 E
Gibraltar ■, *Europe* **19 D3** 36 7N 5 22W
Gibraltar, Str. of, *Medit. S.* **19 E3** 35 55N 5 40W
Gibson Desert, *Australia* **60 D4** 24 0S 126 0 E
Gibsons, *Canada* **72 D4** 49 24N 123 32W
Gibsonville, *U.S.A.* **84 F6** 39 46N 120 54W
Giddings, *U.S.A.* **81 K6** 30 11N 96 56W
Giessen, *Germany* **16 C5** 50 34N 8 41 E
Gīfān, *Iran* **45 B8** 37 54N 57 28 E
Gift Lake, *Canada* **72 B5** 55 53N 115 49W
Gifu, *Japan* **31 G8** 35 30N 136 45 E
Gifu □, *Japan* **31 G8** 35 40N 137 0 E
Giganta, Sa. de la, *Mexico* **86 B2** 25 30N 111 30W
Gigha, *U.K.* **12 F3** 55 42N 5 44W
Gíglio, *Italy* **20 C4** 42 20N 10 52 E
Gijón, *Spain* **19 A3** 43 32N 5 42W
Gil I., *Canada* **72 C3** 53 12N 129 15W
Gila →, *U.S.A.* **83 K6** 32 43N 114 33W
Gila Bend, *U.S.A.* **83 K7** 32 57N 112 43W
Gila Bend Mts., *U.S.A.* **83 K7** 33 10N 113 0W
Gīlān □, *Iran* **45 B6** 37 0N 50 0 E
Gilbert →, *Australia* **62 B3** 16 35S 141 15 E
Gilbert Is., *Kiribati* **64 G9** 1 0N 172 0 E
Gilbert River, *Australia* **62 B3** 18 9S 142 52 E
Gilead, *U.S.A.* **79 B14** 44 24N 70 59W
Gilford I., *Canada* **72 C3** 50 40N 126 30W
Gilgandra, *Australia* **63 E4** 31 43S 148 39 E
Gilgil, *Kenya* **54 C4** 0 30S 36 20 E
Gilgit, *India* **43 B6** 35 50N 74 15 E
Gilgit →, *Pakistan* **43 B6** 35 44N 74 37 E
Gilgunnia, *Australia* **63 E4** 32 26S 146 2 E
Gillam, *Canada* **73 B10** 56 20N 94 40W
Gillen, L., *Australia* **61 E3** 26 11S 124 38 E
Gilles, L., *Australia* **63 E2** 32 50S 136 45 E
Gillette, *U.S.A.* **80 C2** 44 18N 105 30W
Gilliat, *Australia* **62 C3** 20 40S 141 28 E
Gillingham, *U.K.* **11 F8** 51 23N 0 33 E
Gilmer, *U.S.A.* **81 J7** 32 44N 94 57W
Gilmore, L., *Australia* **61 F3** 32 29S 121 37 E
Gilroy, *U.S.A.* **84 H5** 37 1N 121 34W
Gimli, *Canada* **73 C9** 50 40N 97 0W
Gin Gin, *Australia* **63 D5** 25 0S 151 58 E
Gingin, *Australia* **61 F2** 31 22S 115 54 E
Ginir, *Ethiopia* **46 F3** 7 6N 40 40 E
Gióna, Óros, *Greece* **21 E10** 38 38N 22 14 E
Gippsland, *Australia* **63 F4** 37 52S 147 0 E
Gir Hills, *India* **42 J4** 21 0N 71 0 E
Girab, *India* **42 F4** 26 2N 70 38 E
Girâfi, W. →, *Egypt* **47 F3** 29 58N 34 39 E
Girard, *Kans., U.S.A.* **81 G7** 37 31N 94 51W
Girard, *Ohio, U.S.A.* **78 E4** 41 9N 80 42W
Girard, *Pa., U.S.A.* **78 D4** 42 0N 80 19W
Girard, *Pa., U.S.A.* **78 E4** 42 0N 80 19W
Girdle Ness, *U.K.* **12 D6** 57 9N 2 3W
Giresun, *Turkey* **25 F6** 40 55N 38 30 E
Girga, *Egypt* **51 C12** 26 17N 31 55 E
Giri →, *India* **42 D7** 30 28N 77 41 E
Giridih, *India* **43 G12** 24 10N 86 21 E
Girne = Kyrenia, *Cyprus* **23 D12** 35 20N 33 20 E
Girona, *Spain* **19 B7** 41 58N 2 46 E
Gironde →, *France* **18 D3** 45 32N 1 7W
Giru, *Australia* **62 B4** 19 30S 147 5 E
Girvan, *U.K.* **12 F4** 55 14N 4 51W
Gisborne, *N.Z.* **59 H7** 38 39S 178 5 E
Gisenyi, *Rwanda* **54 C2** 1 41S 29 15 E
Gislaved, *Sweden* **9 H15** 57 19N 13 32 E
Gitega, *Burundi* **54 C2** 3 26S 29 56 E
Giuba →, *Somali Rep.* **46 G3** 1 30N 42 35 E
Giurgiu, *Romania* **17 G13** 43 52N 25 57 E
Giza = El Gîza, *Egypt* **51 C12** 30 0N 31 10 E
Gizhiga, *Russia* **27 C17** 62 3N 160 30 E
Gizhiginskaya Guba, *Russia* **27 C16** 61 0N 158 0 E
Giżycko, *Poland* **17 A11** 54 2N 21 48 E
Gjirokastra, *Albania* **21 D9** 40 7N 20 10 E
Gjoa Haven, *Canada* **68 B10** 68 20N 96 8W
Gjøvik, *Norway* **9 F14** 60 47N 10 43 E
Glace Bay, *Canada* **71 C8** 46 11N 59 58W
Glacier Bay National Park and Preserve, *U.S.A.* **72 B1** 58 45N 136 30W
Glacier National Park, *Canada* **72 C5** 51 15N 117 30W
Glacier National Park, *U.S.A.* **82 B7** 48 30N 113 18W
Glacier Peak, *U.S.A.* **82 B3** 48 7N 121 7W
Gladewater, *U.S.A.* **81 J7** 32 33N 94 56W
Gladstone, *Queens., Australia* **62 C5** 23 52S 151 16 E
Gladstone, *S. Austral., Australia* **63 E2** 33 15S 138 22 E
Gladstone, *Canada* **73 C9** 50 13N 98 57W
Gladstone, *U.S.A.* **76 C2** 45 51N 87 1W
Gladwin, *U.S.A.* **76 D3** 43 59N 84 29W
Glåma = Glomma →, *Norway* **9 G14** 59 12N 10 57 E
Gláma, *Iceland* **8 D2** 65 48N 23 0W
Glamis, *U.S.A.* **85 N11** 32 55N 115 5W
Glasco, *Kans., U.S.A.* **80 F6** 39 22N 97 50W
Glasco, *N.Y., U.S.A.* **79 D11** 42 3N 73 57W
Glasgow, *U.K.* **12 F4** 55 51N 4 15W
Glasgow, *Ky., U.S.A.* **76 G3** 37 0N 85 55W
Glasgow, *Mont., U.S.A.* **82 B10** 48 12N 106 38W
Glaslyn, *Canada* **73 C7** 53 22N 108 21W
Glastonbury, *U.K.* **11 F5** 51 9N 2 43W
Glastonbury, *U.S.A.* **79 E12** 41 43N 72 37W
Glazov, *Russia* **24 C9** 58 9N 52 40 E
Gleichen, *Canada* **72 C6** 50 52N 113 3W
Gleiwitz = Gliwice, *Poland* **17 C10** 50 22N 18 41 E
Glen, *U.S.A.* **79 B13** 44 7N 71 11W
Glen Affric, *U.K.* **12 D3** 57 17N 5 1W
Glen Canyon, *U.S.A.* **83 H8** 37 30N 110 40W
Glen Canyon Dam, *U.S.A.* **83 H8** 36 57N 111 29W
Glen Canyon National Recreation Area, *U.S.A.* **83 H8** 37 15N 111 0W
Glen Coe, *U.K.* **12 E3** 56 40N 5 0W
Glen Cove, *U.S.A.* **79 F11** 40 52N 73 38W
Glen Garry, *U.K.* **12 D3** 57 3N 5 7W
Glen Innes, *Australia* **63 D5** 29 44S 151 44 E
Glen Lyon, *U.S.A.* **79 E8** 41 10N 76 5W
Glen Mor, *U.K.* **12 D4** 57 9N 4 37W
Glen Moriston, *U.K.* **12 D4** 57 11N 4 52W
Glen Robertson, *Canada* **79 A10** 45 22N 74 30W
Glen Spean, *U.K.* **12 E4** 56 53N 4 40W
Glen Ullin, *U.S.A.* **80 B4** 46 49N 101 50W
Glencoe, *Canada* **78 D3** 42 45N 81 43W
Glencoe, *S. Africa* **57 D5** 28 11S 30 11 E
Glencoe, *U.S.A.* **80 C7** 44 46N 94 9W
Glendale, *Ariz., U.S.A.* **83 K7** 33 32N 112 11W
Glendale, *Calif., U.S.A.* **85 L8** 34 9N 118 15W
Glendale, *Zimbabwe* **55 F3** 17 22S 31 5 E
Glendive, *U.S.A.* **80 B2** 47 7N 104 43W
Glendo, *U.S.A.* **80 D2** 42 30N 105 2W
Glenelg →, *Australia* **63 F3** 38 4S 140 59 E
Glenfield, *U.S.A.* **79 C9** 43 43N 75 24W
Glengarriff, *Ireland* **13 E2** 51 45N 9 34W
Glenmont, *U.S.A.* **78 F2** 40 31N 82 6W
Glenmorgan, *Australia* **63 D4** 27 14S 149 42 E
Glenn, *U.S.A.* **84 F4** 39 31N 122 1W
Glennallen, *U.S.A.* **68 B5** 62 0N 145 50W
Glennamaddy, *Ireland* **13 C3** 53 37N 8 33W
Glenns Ferry, *U.S.A.* **82 E6** 42 57N 115 18W
Glenore, *Australia* **62 B3** 17 50S 141 12 E
Glenreagh, *Australia* **63 E5** 30 2S 153 1 E
Glenrock, *U.S.A.* **82 E11** 42 52N 105 52W
Glenrothes, *U.K.* **12 E5** 56 12N 3 10W
Glens Falls, *U.S.A.* **79 C11** 43 19N 73 39W
Glenside, *U.S.A.* **79 F9** 40 6N 75 9W
Glenties, *Ireland* **13 B3** 54 49N 8 16W
Glenville, *U.S.A.* **76 F5** 38 56N 80 50W
Glenwood, *Canada* **71 C9** 49 0N 54 58W
Glenwood, *Ark., U.S.A.* **81 H8** 34 20N 93 33W
Glenwood, *Hawaii, U.S.A.* **74 J17** 19 29N 155 9W
Glenwood, *Iowa, U.S.A.* **80 E7** 41 3N 95 45W
Glenwood, *Minn., U.S.A.* **80 C7** 45 39N 95 23W
Glenwood, *Wash., U.S.A.* **84 D5** 46 1N 121 17W
Glenwood Springs, *U.S.A.* **82 G10** 39 33N 107 19W
Glettinganes, *Iceland* **8 D7** 65 30N 13 37W
Gliwice, *Poland* **17 C10** 50 22N 18 41 E
Globe, *U.S.A.* **83 K8** 33 24N 110 47W
Głogów, *Poland* **16 C9** 51 37N 16 5 E
Glomma →, *Norway* **9 G14** 59 12N 10 57 E
Glorieuses, Is., *Ind. Oc.* **57 A8** 11 30S 47 20 E
Glossop, *U.K.* **10 D6** 53 27N 1 56W
Gloucester, *Australia* **63 E5** 32 0S 151 59 E
Gloucester, *U.K.* **11 F5** 51 53N 2 15W
Gloucester, *U.S.A.* **79 D14** 42 37N 70 40W
Gloucester I., *Australia* **62 C4** 20 0S 148 30 E
Gloucester Point, *U.S.A.* **76 G7** 37 15N 76 29W
Gloucestershire □, *U.K.* **11 F5** 51 46N 2 15W
Gloversville, *U.S.A.* **79 C10** 43 3N 74 21W
Glovertown, *Canada* **71 C9** 48 40N 54 3W
Glusk, *Belarus* **17 B15** 52 53N 28 41 E
Gmünd, *Austria* **16 D8** 48 45N 15 0 E
Gmunden, *Austria* **16 E7** 47 55N 13 48 E
Gniezno, *Poland* **17 B9** 52 30N 17 35 E
Gnowangerup, *Australia* **61 F2** 33 58S 117 59 E
Go Cong, *Vietnam* **39 G6** 10 22N 106 40 E
Gō-no-ura, *Japan* **31 H4** 33 44N 129 40 E
Goa, *India* **40 M8** 15 33N 73 59 E
Goa □, *India* **40 M8** 15 33N 73 59 E
Goalen Hd., *Australia* **63 F5** 36 33S 150 4 E
Goalpara, *India* **41 F17** 26 10N 90 40 E
Goaltor, *India* **43 H12** 22 43N 87 10 E
Goalundo Ghat, *Bangla.* **43 H13** 23 50N 89 47 E
Goat Fell, *U.K.* **12 F3** 55 38N 5 11W
Goba, *Ethiopia* **46 F2** 7 1N 39 59 E
Goba, *Mozam.* **57 D5** 26 15S 32 13 E
Gobabis, *Namibia* **56 C2** 22 30S 19 0 E
Gobi, *Asia* **34 C6** 44 0N 110 0 E
Gobō, *Japan* **31 H7** 33 53N 135 10 E
Gochas, *Namibia* **56 C2** 24 59S 18 55 E
Godavari →, *India* **41 L13** 16 25N 82 18 E
Godavari Pt., *India* **41 L13** 17 0N 82 20 E
Godbout, *Canada* **71 C6** 49 20N 67 38W
Godda, *India* **43 G12** 24 50N 87 13 E
Goderich, *Canada* **78 C3** 43 45N 81 41W
Godfrey Ra., *Australia* **61 D2** 24 0S 117 0 E
Godhavn, *Greenland* **4 C5** 69 15N 53 38W
Godhra, *India* **42 H5** 22 49N 73 40 E
Godoy Cruz, *Argentina* **94 C2** 32 56S 68 52W
Gods →, *Canada* **70 A1** 56 22N 92 51W
Gods L., *Canada* **70 B1** 54 40N 94 15W
Gods River, *Canada* **73 C10** 54 50N 94 5W
Godthåb = Nuuk, *Greenland* **69 B14** 64 10N 51 35W
Godwin Austen = K2, *Pakistan* **43 B7** 35 58N 76 32 E
Goeie Hoop, Kaap die = Good Hope, C. of, *S. Africa* **56 E2** 34 24S 18 30 E
Goéland, L. au, *Canada* **70 C4** 49 50N 76 48W
Goeree, *Neths.* **15 C3** 51 50N 4 0 E
Goes, *Neths.* **15 C3** 51 30N 3 55 E
Goffstown, *U.S.A.* **79 C13** 43 1N 71 36W
Gogama, *Canada* **70 C3** 47 35N 81 43W
Gogebic, L., *U.S.A.* **80 B10** 46 30N 89 35W
Gogra = Ghaghara →, *India* **43 G11** 25 45N 84 40 E
Gogriâl, *Sudan* **51 G11** 8 30N 28 8 E
Gohana, *India* **42 E7** 29 8N 76 42 E
Goharganj, *India* **42 H7** 23 1N 77 41 E
Goi →, *India* **42 H6** 22 4N 74 46 E
Goiânia, *Brazil* **93 G9** 16 43S 49 20W
Goiás, *Brazil* **93 G8** 15 55S 50 10W
Goiás □, *Brazil* **93 F9** 12 10S 48 0W
Goio-Ere, *Brazil* **95 A5** 24 12S 53 1W
Gojō, *Japan* **31 G7** 34 21N 135 42 E
Gojra, *Pakistan* **42 D5** 31 10N 72 40 E
Gökçeada, *Turkey* **21 D11** 40 10N 25 50 E
Gökova Körfezi, *Turkey* **21 F12** 36 55N 27 50 E
Gokteik, *Burma* **41 H20** 22 26N 97 0 E
Gokurt, *Pakistan* **42 E2** 29 40N 67 26 E
Gol Gol, *Australia* **63 E3** 34 12S 142 14 E
Gola, *India* **43 E9** 28 3N 80 32 E
Golakganj, *India* **43 F13** 26 8N 89 52 E
Golan Heights = Hagolan, *Syria* **47 C4** 33 0N 35 45 E
Golāshkerd, *Iran* **45 E8** 27 59N 57 16 E
Golchikha, *Russia* **4 B12** 71 45N 83 30 E
Golconda, *U.S.A.* **82 F5** 40 58N 117 30W
Gold, *U.S.A.* **78 E7** 41 52N 77 50W
Gold Beach, *U.S.A.* **82 E1** 42 25N 124 25W
Gold Coast, *W. Afr.* **50 H5** 4 0N 1 40W
Gold Hill, *U.S.A.* **82 E2** 42 26N 123 3W
Gold River, *Canada* **72 D3** 49 46N 126 3W
Golden, *Canada* **72 C5** 51 20N 116 59W
Golden B., *N.Z.* **59 J4** 40 40S 172 50 E
Golden Gate, *U.S.A.* **82 H2** 37 54N 122 30W
Golden Hinde, *Canada* **72 D3** 49 40N 125 44W
Golden Lake, *Canada* **78 A7** 45 34N 77 21W
Golden Vale, *Ireland* **13 D3** 52 33N 8 17W
Goldendale, *U.S.A.* **82 D3** 45 49N 120 50W
Goldfield, *U.S.A.* **83 H5** 37 42N 117 14W
Goldsand L., *Canada* **73 B8** 57 2N 101 8W
Goldsboro, *U.S.A.* **77 H7** 35 23N 77 59W
Goldsmith, *U.S.A.* **81 K3** 31 59N 102 37W

Grenadines

Goldsworthy, *Australia* 60 D2 20 21S 119 30 E
Goldthwaite, *U.S.A.* 81 K5 31 27N 98 34W
Goleniów, *Poland* 16 B8 53 35N 14 50 E
Golestānak, *Iran* 45 D7 30 36N 54 14 E
Goleta, *U.S.A.* 85 L7 34 27N 119 50W
Golfito, *Costa Rica* 88 E3 8 41N 83 5W
Golfo Aranci, *Italy* 20 D3 40 59N 9 38 E
Goliad, *U.S.A.* 81 L6 28 40N 97 23W
Golpāyegān, *Iran* 45 C6 33 27N 50 18 E
Golra, *Pakistan* 42 C5 33 37N 72 56 E
Golspie, *U.K.* 12 D5 57 58N 3 59W
Goma, *Dem. Rep. of the Congo* 54 C2 1 37S 29 10 E
Gomal Pass, *Pakistan* 42 D3 31 56N 69 20 E
Gomati →, *India* 43 G10 25 32N 83 11 E
Gombari, *Dem. Rep. of the Congo* 54 B2 2 45N 29 3 E
Gombe, *Nigeria* 51 F8 10 19N 11 2 E
Gombe →, *Tanzania* 54 C3 4 38S 31 40 E
Gomel = Homyel, *Belarus* 17 B16 52 28N 31 0 E
Gomera, *Canary Is.* 22 F2 28 7N 17 14W
Gómez Palacio, *Mexico* 86 B4 25 40N 104 0W
Gomīshān, *Iran* 45 B7 37 4N 54 6 E
Gomogomo, *Indonesia* 37 F8 6 39S 134 43 E
Gomoh, *India* 41 H15 23 52N 86 10 E
Gompa = Ganta, *Liberia* 50 G4 7 15N 8 59W
Gonābād, *Iran* 45 C8 34 15N 58 45 E
Gonaïves, *Haiti* 89 C5 19 20N 72 42W
Gonâve, G. de la, *Haiti* 89 C5 19 29N 72 42W
Gonâve, I. de la, *Haiti* 89 C5 18 45N 73 0W
Gonbad-e Kāvūs, *Iran* 45 B7 37 20N 55 25 E
Gonda, *India* 43 F9 27 9N 81 58 E
Gondal, *India* 42 J4 21 58N 70 52 E
Gonder, *Ethiopia* 46 E2 12 39N 37 30 E
Gondia, *India* 40 J12 21 23N 80 10 E
Gondola, *Mozam.* 55 F3 19 10S 33 37 E
Gönen, *Turkey* 21 D12 40 6N 27 39 E
Gonghe, *China* 32 C5 36 18N 100 32 E
Gongolgon, *Australia* 63 E4 30 21S 146 54 E
Gongzhuling, *China* 35 C13 43 30N 124 40 E
Gonzales, *Calif., U.S.A.* 84 J5 36 30N 121 26W
Gonzales, *Tex., U.S.A.* 81 L6 29 30N 97 27W
González Chaves, *Argentina* 94 D3 38 2S 60 5W
Good Hope, C. of, *S. Africa* 56 E2 34 24S 18 30 E
Gooderham, *Canada* 78 B6 44 54N 78 21W
Gooding, *U.S.A.* 82 E6 42 56N 114 43W
Goodland, *U.S.A.* 80 F4 39 21N 101 43W
Goodlow, *Canada* 72 B4 56 20N 120 8W
Goodooga, *Australia* 63 D4 29 3S 147 28 E
Goodsprings, *U.S.A.* 85 K11 35 49N 115 27W
Goole, *U.K.* 10 D7 53 42N 0 53W
Goolgowi, *Australia* 63 E4 33 58S 145 41 E
Goolwa, *Australia* 63 F2 35 30S 138 47 E
Goomalling, *Australia* 61 F2 31 15S 116 49 E
Goomeri, *Australia* 63 D5 26 12S 152 6 E
Goonda, *Mozam.* 55 F3 19 48S 33 57 E
Goondiwindi, *Australia* 63 D5 28 30S 150 21 E
Goongarrie, L., *Australia* 61 F3 30 3S 121 9 E
Goonyella, *Australia* 62 C4 21 47S 147 58 E
Goose →, *Canada* 71 B7 53 20N 60 35W
Goose Creek, *U.S.A.* 77 J5 32 59N 80 2W
Goose L., *U.S.A.* 82 F3 41 56N 120 26W
Gop, *India* 40 H6 22 5N 69 50 E
Gopalganj, *India* 43 F11 26 28N 84 30 E
Göppingen, *Germany* 16 D5 48 42N 9 39 E
Gorakhpur, *India* 43 F10 26 47N 83 23 E
Goražde, *Bos.-H.* 21 C8 43 38N 18 58 E
Gorda, *U.S.A.* 84 K5 35 53N 121 26W
Gorda, Pta., *Canary Is.* 22 F2 28 45N 18 0W
Gorda, Pta., *Nic.* 88 D3 14 20N 83 10W
Gordan B., *Australia* 60 B5 11 35S 130 10 E
Gordon, *U.S.A.* 80 D3 42 48N 102 12W
Gordon →, *Australia* 62 G4 42 27S 145 30 E
Gordon L., *Alta., Canada* 73 B6 56 30N 110 25W
Gordon L., *N.W.T., Canada* 72 A6 63 5N 113 11W
Gordonvale, *Australia* 62 B4 17 5S 145 50 E
Gore, *Ethiopia* 46 F2 8 12N 35 32 E
Gore, *N.Z.* 59 M2 46 5S 168 58 E
Gore Bay, *Canada* 70 C3 45 57N 82 28W
Gorey, *Ireland* 13 D5 52 41N 6 18W
Gorg, *Iran* 45 D8 29 29N 59 43 E
Gorgān, *Iran* 45 B7 36 50N 54 29 E
Gorgona, I., *Colombia* 92 C3 3 0N 78 10W
Gorham, *U.S.A.* 79 B13 44 23N 71 10W
Goriganga →, *India* 43 E9 29 45N 80 23 E
Gorinchem, *Neths.* 15 C4 51 50N 4 59 E
Goris, *Armenia* 25 G8 39 31N 46 22 E
Gorízia, *Italy* 20 B5 45 56N 13 37 E
Gorki = Nizhniy Novgorod, *Russia* 24 C7 56 20N 44 0 E
Gorkiy = Nizhniy Novgorod, *Russia* 24 C7 56 20N 44 0 E
Gorkovskoye Vdkhr., *Russia* 24 C7 57 2N 43 4 E
Görlitz, *Germany* 16 C8 51 9N 14 58 E
Gorlovka = Horlivka, *Ukraine* 25 E6 48 19N 38 5 E
Gorman, *U.S.A.* 85 L8 34 47N 118 51W
Gorna Dzhumayo = Blagoevgrad, *Bulgaria* 21 C10 42 2N 23 5 E
Gorna Oryakhovitsa, *Bulgaria* 21 C11 43 7N 25 40 E
Gorno-Altay □, *Russia* 26 D9 51 0N 86 0 E
Gorno-Altaysk, *Russia* 26 D9 51 50N 86 5 E
Gornyatski, *Russia* 24 A11 67 32N 64 3 E
Gornyy, *Russia* 30 B6 44 57N 133 59 E
Gorodenka = Horodenka, *Ukraine* 17 D13 48 41N 25 29 E
Gorodok = Horodok, *Ukraine* 17 D12 49 46N 23 32 E
Gorokhov = Horokhiv, *Ukraine* 17 C13 50 30N 24 45 E
Goromonzi, *Zimbabwe* 55 F3 17 52S 31 22 E
Gorong, Kepulauan, *Indonesia* 37 E8 3 59S 131 25 E
Gorongose →, *Mozam.* 57 C5 20 30S 34 40 E
Gorongoza, *Mozam.* 55 F3 18 44S 34 2 E
Gorongoza, Sa. da, *Mozam.* 55 F3 18 27S 34 2 E
Gorontalo, *Indonesia* 37 D6 0 35N 123 5 E
Gort, *Ireland* 13 C3 53 3N 8 49W
Gortis, *Greece* 23 D6 35 4N 24 58 E
Gorzów Wielkopolski, *Poland* 16 B8 52 43N 15 15 E
Gosford, *Australia* 63 E5 33 23S 151 18 E
Goshen, *Calif., U.S.A.* 84 J7 36 21N 119 25W
Goshen, *Ind., U.S.A.* 76 E3 41 35N 85 50W
Goshen, *N.Y., U.S.A.* 79 E10 41 24N 74 20W
Goshogawara, *Japan* 30 D10 40 48N 140 27 E
Goslar, *Germany* 16 C6 51 54N 10 25 E
Gospič, *Croatia* 16 F8 44 35N 15 23 E
Gosport, *U.K.* 11 G6 50 48N 1 9W
Gosse →, *Australia* 62 B1 19 32S 134 37 E
Göta älv →, *Sweden* 9 H14 57 42N 11 54 E
Göta kanal, *Sweden* 9 G16 58 30N 15 58 E
Götaland, *Sweden* 9 G15 57 30N 14 30 E
Göteborg, *Sweden* 9 H14 57 43N 11 59 E
Gotha, *Germany* 16 C6 50 56N 10 42 E
Gothenburg = Göteborg, *Sweden* 9 H14 57 43N 11 59 E
Gothenburg, *U.S.A.* 80 E4 40 56N 100 10W
Gotland, *Sweden* 9 H18 57 30N 18 33 E
Gotō-Rettō, *Japan* 31 H4 32 55N 129 5 E
Gotska Sandön, *Sweden* 9 G18 58 24N 19 15 E
Gōtsu, *Japan* 31 G6 35 0N 132 14 E
Gott Pk., *Canada* 72 C4 50 18N 122 16W
Göttingen, *Germany* 16 C5 51 31N 9 55 E
Gottwaldov = Zlín, *Czech Rep.* 17 D9 49 14N 17 40 E
Goubangzi, *China* 35 D11 41 20N 121 52 E
Gouda, *Neths.* 15 B4 52 1N 4 42 E
Goúdhoura, Ákra, *Greece* 23 E8 34 59N 26 6 E
Gough I., *Atl. Oc.* 2 G9 40 10S 9 45W
Gouin, Rés., *Canada* 70 C5 48 35N 74 40W
Goulburn, *Australia* 63 E4 34 44S 149 44 E
Goulburn Is., *Australia* 62 A1 11 40S 133 20 E
Goulimine, *Morocco* 50 C3 28 56N 10 0W
Gourits →, *S. Africa* 56 E3 34 21S 21 52 E
Goúrnais, *Greece* 23 D7 35 19N 25 16 E
Gouverneur, *U.S.A.* 79 B9 44 20N 75 28W
Gouviá, *Greece* 23 A3 39 39N 19 50 E
Governador Valadares, *Brazil* 93 G10 18 15S 41 57W
Governor's Harbour, *Bahamas* 88 A4 25 10N 76 14W
Govindgarh, *India* 43 G9 24 23N 81 18 E
Gowan Ra., *Australia* 62 D4 25 0S 145 0 E
Gowanda, *U.S.A.* 78 D6 42 28N 78 56W
Gowd-e Zirreh, *Afghan.* 40 E3 29 45N 62 0 E
Gower, *U.K.* 11 F3 51 35N 4 10W
Gowna, L., *Ireland* 13 C4 53 51N 7 34W
Goya, *Argentina* 94 B4 29 10S 59 10W
Goyder Lagoon, *Australia* 63 D2 27 3S 138 58 E
Goyllarisquisga, *Peru* 92 F3 10 31S 76 24W
Goz Beïda, *Chad* 51 F10 12 10N 21 20 E
Gozo, *Malta* 23 C1 36 3N 14 13 E
Graaff-Reinet, *S. Africa* 56 E3 32 13S 24 32 E
Gračac, *Croatia* 16 F8 44 18N 15 57 E
Gracias a Dios, C., *Honduras* 88 D3 15 0N 83 10W
Graciosa, I., *Canary Is.* 22 E6 29 15N 13 32W
Grado, *Spain* 19 A2 43 23N 6 4W
Grady, *U.S.A.* 81 H3 34 49N 103 19W
Grafham Water, *U.K.* 11 E7 52 19N 0 18W
Grafton, *Australia* 63 D5 29 38S 152 58 E
Grafton, *N. Dak., U.S.A.* 80 A6 48 25N 97 25W
Grafton, *W. Va., U.S.A.* 76 F5 39 21N 80 2W
Graham, *Canada* 70 C1 49 20N 90 30W
Graham, *U.S.A.* 81 J5 33 6N 98 35W
Graham, Mt., *U.S.A.* 83 K9 32 42N 109 52W
Graham Bell, Ostrov = Greem-Bell, Ostrov, *Russia* 26 A7 81 0N 62 0 E
Graham I., *B.C., Canada* 72 C2 53 40N 132 30W
Graham I., *N.W.T., Canada* 68 C6 77 25N 90 30W
Graham Land, *Antarctica* 5 C17 65 0S 64 0W
Grahamstown, *S. Africa* 56 E4 33 19S 26 31 E
Grahamsville, *U.S.A.* 79 E10 41 51N 74 33W
Grain Coast, *W. Afr.* 50 H3 4 20N 10 0W
Grajaú, *Brazil* 93 E9 5 50S 46 4W
Grajaú →, *Brazil* 93 D10 3 41S 44 48W
Grampian, *U.S.A.* 78 F6 40 58N 78 37W
Grampian Highlands = Grampian Mts., *U.K.* 12 E5 56 50N 4 0W
Grampian Mts., *U.K.* 12 E5 56 50N 4 0W
Grampians, The, *Australia* 63 F3 37 0S 142 20 E
Gran Canaria, *Canary Is.* 22 G4 27 55N 15 35W
Gran Chaco, *S. Amer.* 94 B3 25 0S 61 0W
Gran Paradiso, *Italy* 18 D7 45 33N 7 17 E
Gran Sasso d'Itália, *Italy* 20 C5 42 27N 13 42 E
Granada, *Nic.* 88 D2 11 58N 86 0W
Granada, *Spain* 19 D4 37 10N 3 35W
Granada, *U.S.A.* 81 F3 38 4N 102 19W
Granadilla de Abona, *Canary Is.* 22 F3 28 7N 16 33W
Granard, *Ireland* 13 C4 53 47N 7 30W
Granbury, *U.S.A.* 81 J6 32 27N 97 47W
Granby, *Canada* 79 A12 45 25N 72 45W
Granby, *U.S.A.* 82 F11 40 5N 105 56W
Grand →, *Canada* 78 D5 42 51N 79 34W
Grand →, *Mo., U.S.A.* 80 F8 39 23N 93 7W
Grand →, *S. Dak., U.S.A.* 80 C4 45 40N 100 45W
Grand Bahama, *Bahamas* 88 A4 26 40N 78 30W
Grand Bank, *Canada* 71 C8 47 6N 55 48W
Grand Bassam, *Ivory C.* 50 G5 5 10N 3 49W
Grand-Bourg, *Guadeloupe* 89 C7 15 53N 61 19W
Grand Canal = Yun Ho →, *China* 35 E9 39 10N 117 10 E
Grand Canyon, *U.S.A.* 83 H7 36 3N 112 9W
Grand Canyon National Park, *U.S.A.* 83 H7 36 15N 112 30W
Grand Cayman, *Cayman Is.* 88 C3 19 20N 81 20W
Grand Centre, *Canada* 73 C6 54 25N 110 13W
Grand Coulee, *U.S.A.* 82 C4 47 57N 119 0W
Grand Coulee Dam, *U.S.A.* 82 C4 47 57N 118 59W
Grand Erg du Bilma, *Niger* 51 E8 18 30N 14 0 E
Grand Erg Occidental, *Algeria* 50 B6 30 20N 1 0 E
Grand Erg Oriental, *Algeria* 50 B7 30 0N 6 30 E
Grand Falls, *Canada* 71 C6 47 3N 67 44W
Grand Falls-Windsor, *Canada* 71 C8 48 56N 55 40W
Grand Forks, *Canada* 72 D5 49 0N 118 30W
Grand Forks, *U.S.A.* 80 B6 47 55N 97 3W
Grand Gorge, *U.S.A.* 79 D10 42 21N 74 29W
Grand Haven, *U.S.A.* 76 D2 43 4N 86 13W
Grand I., *Mich., U.S.A.* 76 B2 46 31N 86 40W
Grand I., *N.Y., U.S.A.* 78 D6 43 0N 78 58W
Grand Island, *U.S.A.* 80 E5 40 55N 98 21W
Grand Isle, *La., U.S.A.* 81 L9 29 14N 90 0W
Grand Isle, *Vt., U.S.A.* 79 B11 44 43N 73 18W
Grand Junction, *U.S.A.* 83 G9 39 4N 108 33W
Grand L., *N.B., Canada* 71 C6 45 57N 66 7W
Grand L., *Nfld., Canada* 71 C8 49 0N 57 30W
Grand L., *Nfld., Canada* 71 B7 53 40N 60 30W
Grand L., *U.S.A.* 81 L8 29 55N 92 47W
Grand Lake, *U.S.A.* 82 F11 40 15N 105 49W
Grand Manan I., *Canada* 71 D6 44 45N 66 52W
Grand Marais, *Canada* 80 B9 47 45N 90 25W
Grand Marais, *U.S.A.* 76 B3 46 40N 85 59W
Grand-Mère, *Canada* 70 C5 46 36N 72 40W
Grand Prairie, *U.S.A.* 81 J6 32 47N 97 0W
Grand Rapids, *Canada* 73 C9 53 12N 99 19W
Grand Rapids, *Mich., U.S.A.* 76 D2 42 58N 85 40W
Grand Rapids, *Minn., U.S.A.* 80 B8 47 14N 93 31W
Grand St-Bernard, Col du, *Europe* 18 D7 45 50N 7 10 E
Grand Teton, *U.S.A.* 82 E8 43 54N 111 50W
Grand Teton National Park, *U.S.A.* 82 D8 43 50N 110 50W
Grand Union Canal, *U.K.* 11 E7 52 7N 0 53W
Grand View, *Canada* 73 C8 51 10N 100 42W
Grande →, *Jujuy, Argentina* 94 A2 24 20S 65 2W
Grande →, *Mendoza, Argentina* 94 D2 36 52S 69 45W
Grande →, *Bolivia* 92 G6 15 51S 64 39W
Grande →, *Bahia, Brazil* 93 F10 11 30S 44 30W
Grande →, *Minas Gerais, Brazil* 93 H8 20 6S 51 4W
Grande, B., *Argentina* 96 G3 50 30S 68 20W
Grande, Rio →, *U.S.A.* 81 N6 25 58N 97 9W
Grande Baleine, R. de la →, *Canada* 70 A4 55 16N 77 47W
Grande Cache, *Canada* 72 C5 53 53N 119 8W
Grande-Entrée, *Canada* 71 C7 47 30N 61 40W
Grande Prairie, *Canada* 72 B5 55 10N 118 50W
Grande-Rivière, *Canada* 71 C7 48 26N 64 30W
Grande-Vallée, *Canada* 71 C6 49 14N 65 8W
Grandfalls, *U.S.A.* 81 K3 31 20N 102 51W
Grandview, *U.S.A.* 82 C4 46 15N 119 54W
Graneros, *Chile* 94 C1 34 5S 70 45W
Grangemouth, *U.K.* 12 E5 56 1N 3 42W
Granger, *U.S.A.* 82 F9 41 35N 109 58W
Grangeville, *U.S.A.* 82 D5 45 56N 116 7W
Granisle, *Canada* 72 C3 54 53N 126 13W
Granite City, *U.S.A.* 80 F9 38 42N 90 9W
Granite Falls, *U.S.A.* 80 C7 44 49N 95 33W
Granite L., *Canada* 71 C8 48 8N 57 5W
Granite Mt., *U.S.A.* 85 M10 33 5N 116 28W
Granite Pk., *U.S.A.* 82 D9 45 10N 109 48W
Graniteville, *U.S.A.* 79 B12 44 8N 72 29W
Granity, *N.Z.* 59 J3 41 39S 171 51 E
Granja, *Brazil* 93 D10 3 7S 40 50W
Granollers, *Spain* 19 B7 41 39N 2 18 E
Grant, *U.S.A.* 80 E4 40 53N 101 42W
Grant, Mt., *U.S.A.* 82 G4 38 34N 118 48W
Grant City, *U.S.A.* 80 E7 40 29N 94 25W
Grant I., *Australia* 60 B5 11 10S 132 52 E
Grant Range, *U.S.A.* 83 G6 38 30N 115 25W
Grantham, *U.K.* 10 E7 52 55N 0 38W
Grantown-on-Spey, *U.K.* 12 D5 57 20N 3 36W
Grants, *U.S.A.* 83 J10 35 9N 107 52W
Grants Pass, *U.S.A.* 82 E2 42 26N 123 19W
Grantsville, *U.S.A.* 82 F7 40 36N 112 28W
Granville, *France* 18 B3 48 50N 1 35W
Granville, *N. Dak., U.S.A.* 80 A4 48 16N 100 47W
Granville, *N.Y., U.S.A.* 79 C11 43 24N 73 16W
Granville, *Ohio, U.S.A.* 78 F2 40 4N 82 31W
Granville L., *Canada* 73 B8 56 18N 100 30W
Graskop, *S. Africa* 57 C5 24 56S 30 49 E
Grass →, *Canada* 73 B9 56 3N 96 33W
Grass Range, *U.S.A.* 82 C9 47 0N 109 0W
Grass River Prov. Park, *Canada* 73 C8 54 40N 100 50W
Grass Valley, *Calif., U.S.A.* 84 F6 39 13N 121 4W
Grass Valley, *Oreg., U.S.A.* 82 D3 45 22N 120 47W
Grasse, *France* 18 E7 43 38N 6 56 E
Grassflat, *U.S.A.* 78 F6 41 0N 78 6W
Grasslands Nat. Park, *Canada* 73 D7 49 11N 107 38W
Grassy, *Australia* 62 G3 40 3S 144 5 E
Graulhet, *France* 18 E4 43 45N 1 59 E
Gravelbourg, *Canada* 73 D7 49 50N 106 35W
's-Gravenhage, *Neths.* 15 B4 52 7N 4 17 E
Gravenhurst, *Canada* 78 B5 44 52N 79 20W
Gravesend, *Australia* 63 D5 29 35S 150 20 E
Gravesend, *U.K.* 11 F8 51 26N 0 22 E
Gravois, Pointe-à-, *Haiti* 89 C5 18 15N 73 56W
Grayling, *U.S.A.* 76 C3 44 40N 84 43W
Grays Harbor, *U.S.A.* 82 C1 46 59N 124 1W
Grays L., *U.S.A.* 82 E8 43 4N 111 26W
Grays River, *U.S.A.* 84 D3 46 21N 123 37W
Graz, *Austria* 16 E8 47 4N 15 27 E
Greasy L., *Canada* 72 A4 62 55N 122 12W
Great Abaco I., *Bahamas* 88 A4 26 25N 77 10W
Great Artesian Basin, *Australia* 62 C3 23 0S 144 0 E
Great Australian Bight, *Australia* 61 F5 33 30S 130 0 E
Great Bahama Bank, *Bahamas* 88 B4 23 15N 78 0W
Great Barrier I., *N.Z.* 59 G5 36 11S 175 25 E
Great Barrier Reef, *Australia* 62 B4 18 0S 146 50 E
Great Barrington, *U.S.A.* 79 D11 42 12N 73 22W
Great Basin, *U.S.A.* 82 G5 40 0N 117 0W
Great Basin Nat. Park, *U.S.A.* 82 G6 38 55N 114 14W
Great Bear →, *Canada* 68 B7 65 0N 124 0W
Great Bear L., *Canada* 68 B8 65 30N 120 0W
Great Belt = Store Bælt, *Denmark* 9 J14 55 20N 11 0 E
Great Bend, *Kans., U.S.A.* 80 F5 38 22N 98 46W
Great Bend, *Pa., U.S.A.* 79 E9 41 58N 75 45W
Great Blasket I., *Ireland* 13 D1 52 6N 10 32W
Great Britain, *Europe* 6 E5 54 0N 2 15W
Great Codroy, *Canada* 71 C8 47 51N 59 16W
Great Dividing Ra., *Australia* 62 C4 23 0S 146 0 E
Great Driffield = Driffield, *U.K.* 10 C7 54 0N 0 26W
Great Exuma I., *Bahamas* 88 B4 23 30N 75 50W
Great Falls, *U.S.A.* 82 C8 47 30N 111 17W
Great Fish = Groot Vis →, *S. Africa* 56 E4 33 28S 27 5 E
Great Guana Cay, *Bahamas* 88 B4 24 0N 76 20W
Great Inagua I., *Bahamas* 89 B5 21 0N 73 20W
Great Indian Desert = Thar Desert, *India* 42 F5 28 0N 72 0 E
Great Karoo, *S. Africa* 56 E3 31 55S 21 0 E
Great Lake, *Australia* 62 G4 41 50S 146 40 E
Great Lakes, *N. Amer.* 66 E11 46 0N 84 0W
Great Malvern, *U.K.* 11 E5 52 7N 2 18W
Great Miami →, *U.S.A.* 76 F3 39 20N 84 40W
Great Ormes Head, *U.K.* 10 D4 53 20N 3 52W
Great Ouse →, *U.K.* 10 E8 52 48N 0 21 E
Great Palm I., *Australia* 62 B4 18 45S 146 40 E
Great Plains, *N. Amer.* 74 A6 47 0N 105 0W
Great Ruaha →, *Tanzania* 54 D4 7 56S 37 52 E
Great Sacandaga Res., *U.S.A.* 79 C10 43 6N 74 16W
Great Saint Bernard Pass = Grand St-Bernard, Col du, *Europe* 18 D7 45 50N 7 10 E
Great Salt L., *U.S.A.* 82 F7 41 15N 112 40W
Great Salt Lake Desert, *U.S.A.* 82 F7 40 50N 113 30W
Great Salt Plains L., *U.S.A.* 81 G5 36 45N 98 8W
Great Sandy Desert, *Australia* 60 D3 21 0S 124 0 E
Great Sangi = Sangihe, Pulau, *Indonesia* 37 D7 3 45N 125 30 E
Great Skellig, *Ireland* 13 E1 51 47N 10 33W
Great Slave L., *Canada* 72 A5 61 23N 115 38W
Great Smoky Mts. Nat. Park, *U.S.A.* 77 H4 35 40N 83 40W
Great Snow Mt., *Canada* 72 B4 57 26N 124 0W
Great Stour = Stour →, *U.K.* 11 F9 51 18N 1 22 E
Great Victoria Desert, *Australia* 61 E4 29 30S 126 30 E
Great Wall, *China* 34 E5 38 30N 109 30 E
Great Whernside, *U.K.* 10 C6 54 10N 1 58W
Great Yarmouth, *U.K.* 11 E9 52 37N 1 44 E
Greater Antilles, *W. Indies* 89 C5 17 40N 74 0W
Greater London □, *U.K.* 11 F7 51 31N 0 6W
Greater Manchester □, *U.K.* 10 D5 53 30N 2 15W
Greater Sunda Is., *Indonesia* 36 F4 7 0S 112 0 E
Greco, C., *Cyprus* 23 E13 34 57N 34 5 E
Gredos, Sierra de, *Spain* 19 B3 40 20N 5 0W
Greece, *U.S.A.* 78 C7 43 13N 77 41W
Greece ■, *Europe* 21 E9 40 0N 23 0 E
Greeley, *Colo., U.S.A.* 80 E2 40 25N 104 42W
Greeley, *Nebr., U.S.A.* 80 E5 41 33N 98 32W
Greem-Bell, Ostrov, *Russia* 26 A7 81 0N 62 0 E
Green, *U.S.A.* 82 E2 43 9N 123 22W
Green →, *Ky., U.S.A.* 76 G2 37 54N 87 30W
Green →, *Utah, U.S.A.* 83 G9 38 11N 109 53W
Green B., *U.S.A.* 76 C2 45 0N 87 30W
Green Bay, *U.S.A.* 76 C2 44 31N 88 0W
Green C., *Australia* 63 F5 37 13S 150 1 E
Green Cove Springs, *U.S.A.* 77 L5 29 59N 81 42W
Green Lake, *Canada* 73 C7 54 17N 107 47W
Green Mts., *U.S.A.* 79 C12 43 45N 72 45W
Green River, *Utah, U.S.A.* 83 G8 38 59N 110 10W
Green River, *Wyo., U.S.A.* 82 F9 41 32N 109 28W
Green Valley, *U.S.A.* 83 L8 31 52N 110 56W
Greenbank, *U.S.A.* 84 B4 48 6N 122 34W
Greenbush, *Mich., U.S.A.* 78 B1 44 35N 83 19W
Greenbush, *Minn., U.S.A.* 80 A6 48 42N 96 11W
Greencastle, *U.S.A.* 76 F2 39 38N 86 52W
Greene, *U.S.A.* 79 D9 42 20N 75 46W
Greenfield, *Calif., U.S.A.* 84 J5 36 19N 121 15W
Greenfield, *Calif., U.S.A.* 85 K8 35 15N 119 0W
Greenfield, *Ind., U.S.A.* 76 F3 39 47N 85 46W
Greenfield, *Iowa, U.S.A.* 80 E7 41 18N 94 28W
Greenfield, *Mass., U.S.A.* 79 D12 42 35N 72 36W
Greenfield, *Mo., U.S.A.* 81 G8 37 25N 93 51W
Greenfield Park, *Canada* 79 A11 45 29N 73 29W
Greenland ■, *N. Amer.* 4 C5 66 0N 45 0W
Greenland Sea, *Arctic* 4 B7 73 0N 10 0W
Greenock, *U.K.* 12 F4 55 57N 4 46W
Greenore, *Ireland* 13 B5 54 2N 6 8W
Greenore Pt., *Ireland* 13 D5 52 14N 6 19W
Greenough, *Australia* 61 E1 28 58S 114 43 E
Greenough →, *Australia* 61 E1 28 51S 114 38 E
Greenough Pt., *Canada* 78 B3 44 58N 81 26W
Greenport, *U.S.A.* 79 E12 41 6N 72 22W
Greensboro, *Ga., U.S.A.* 77 J4 33 35N 83 11W
Greensboro, *N.C., U.S.A.* 77 G6 36 4N 79 48W
Greensboro, *Vt., U.S.A.* 79 B12 44 36N 72 18W
Greensburg, *Ind., U.S.A.* 76 F3 39 20N 85 29W
Greensburg, *Kans., U.S.A.* 81 G5 37 36N 99 18W
Greensburg, *Pa., U.S.A.* 78 F5 40 18N 79 33W
Greenstone Pt., *U.K.* 12 D3 57 55N 5 37W
Greenvale, *Australia* 62 B4 18 59S 145 7 E
Greenville, *Ala., U.S.A.* 77 K2 31 50N 86 38W
Greenville, *Calif., U.S.A.* 84 E6 40 8N 120 57W
Greenville, *Maine, U.S.A.* 77 C11 45 28N 69 35W
Greenville, *Mich., U.S.A.* 76 D3 43 11N 85 15W
Greenville, *Miss., U.S.A.* 81 J9 33 24N 91 4W
Greenville, *Mo., U.S.A.* 81 G9 37 8N 90 27W
Greenville, *N.C., U.S.A.* 77 H7 35 37N 77 23W
Greenville, *N.H., U.S.A.* 79 D13 42 46N 71 49W
Greenville, *N.Y., U.S.A.* 79 D10 42 25N 74 1W
Greenville, *Ohio, U.S.A.* 76 E3 40 6N 84 38W
Greenville, *Pa., U.S.A.* 78 E4 41 24N 80 23W
Greenville, *S.C., U.S.A.* 77 H4 34 51N 82 24W
Greenville, *Tenn., U.S.A.* 77 G4 36 13N 82 51W
Greenville, *Tex., U.S.A.* 81 J6 33 8N 96 7W
Greenwater Lake Prov. Park, *Canada* 73 C8 52 32N 103 30W
Greenwich, *U.K.* 11 F8 51 29N 0 1 E
Greenwich, *Conn., U.S.A.* 79 E11 41 2N 73 38W
Greenwich, *N.Y., U.S.A.* 79 C11 43 5N 73 30W
Greenwich, *Ohio, U.S.A.* 78 E2 41 2N 82 31W
Greenwood, *Canada* 72 D5 49 10N 118 40W
Greenwood, *Ark., U.S.A.* 81 H7 35 13N 94 16W
Greenwood, *Ind., U.S.A.* 76 F2 39 37N 86 7W
Greenwood, *Miss., U.S.A.* 81 J9 33 31N 90 11W
Greenwood, *S.C., U.S.A.* 77 H4 34 12N 82 10W
Greenwood, Mt., *Australia* 60 B5 13 48S 130 4 E
Gregory, *U.S.A.* 80 D5 43 14N 99 20W
Gregory →, *Australia* 62 B2 17 53S 139 17 E
Gregory, L., *S. Austral., Australia* 63 D2 28 55S 139 0 E
Gregory, L., *W. Austral., Australia* 61 E2 25 38S 119 58 E
Gregory Downs, *Australia* 62 B2 18 35S 138 45 E
Gregory L., *Australia* 60 D4 20 0S 127 40 E
Gregory Ra., *Queens., Australia* 62 B3 19 30S 143 40 E
Gregory Ra., *W. Austral., Australia* 60 D3 21 20S 121 12 E
Greifswald, *Germany* 16 A7 54 5N 13 23 E
Greiz, *Germany* 16 C7 50 39N 12 10 E
Gremikha, *Russia* 24 A6 67 59N 39 47 E
Grenå, *Denmark* 9 H14 56 25N 10 53 E
Grenada, *U.S.A.* 81 J10 33 47N 89 49W
Grenada ■, *W. Indies* 89 D7 12 10N 61 40W
Grenadier I., *U.S.A.* 79 B8 44 3N 76 22W
Grenadines, *W. Indies* 89 D7 12 40N 61 20W

Henryville

Hamadān □, Iran 45 C6 35 0N 49 0 E
Hamāh, Syria 44 C3 35 5N 36 40 E
Hamamatsu, Japan 31 G8 34 45N 137 45 E
Hamar, Norway 9 F14 60 48N 11 7 E
Hamâta, Gebel, Egypt 44 E2 24 17N 35 0 E
Hambantota, Sri Lanka 40 R12 6 10N 81 10 E
Hamber Prov. Park, Canada 72 C5 52 20N 118 0W
Hamburg, Germany 16 B5 53 33N 9 59 E
Hamburg, Ark., U.S.A. 81 J9 33 14N 91 48W
Hamburg, N.Y., U.S.A. 78 D6 42 43N 78 50W
Hamburg, Pa., U.S.A. 79 F9 40 33N 75 59W
Ḩamḑ, W. al →, Si. Arabia 44 E3 24 55N 36 20 E
Hamden, U.S.A. 79 E12 41 23N 72 54W
Häme, Finland 9 F20 61 38N 25 10 E
Hämeenlinna, Finland 9 F21 61 0N 24 28 E
Hamelin Pool, Australia 61 E1 26 22S 114 20 E
Hameln, Germany 16 B5 52 6N 9 21 E
Hamerkaz □, Israel 47 C3 32 15N 34 55 E
Hamersley Ra., Australia 60 D2 22 0S 117 45 E
Hamhung, N. Korea 35 E14 39 54N 127 30 E
Hami, China 32 B4 42 55N 93 25 E
Hamilton, Australia 63 F3 37 45S 142 2 E
Hamilton, Canada 78 C5 43 15N 79 50W
Hamilton, N.Z. 59 G5 37 47S 175 19 E
Hamilton, U.K. 12 F4 55 46N 4 2W
Hamilton, Ala., U.S.A. 77 H1 34 9N 87 59W
Hamilton, Mont., U.S.A. 82 C6 46 15N 114 10W
Hamilton, N.Y., U.S.A. 79 D9 42 50N 75 33W
Hamilton, Ohio, U.S.A. 76 F3 39 24N 84 34W
Hamilton, Tex., U.S.A. 81 K5 31 42N 98 7W
Hamilton →, Australia 62 C2 23 30S 139 47 E
Hamilton City, U.S.A. 84 F4 39 45N 122 1W
Hamilton Inlet, Canada 71 B8 54 0N 57 30W
Hamilton Mt., U.S.A. 79 C10 43 25N 74 22W
Hamina, Finland 9 F22 60 34N 27 12 E
Hamirpur, H.P., India 42 D7 31 41N 76 31 E
Hamirpur, Ut. P., India 43 G9 25 57N 80 9 E
Hamlet, U.S.A. 77 H6 34 53N 79 42W
Hamley Bridge, Australia 63 E2 34 17S 138 35 E
Hamlin = Hameln, Germany 16 B5 52 6N 9 21 E
Hamlin, N.Y., U.S.A. 78 C7 43 17N 77 55W
Hamlin, Tex., U.S.A. 81 J4 32 53N 100 8W
Hamm, Germany 16 C4 51 40N 7 50 E
Ḩammār, Hawr al, Iraq 44 D5 30 50N 47 10 E
Hammerfest, Norway 8 A20 70 39N 23 41 E
Hammond, Ind., U.S.A. 76 E2 41 38N 87 30W
Hammond, La., U.S.A. 81 K9 30 30N 90 28W
Hammond, N.Y., U.S.A. 79 B9 44 27N 75 42W
Hammondsport, U.S.A. 78 D7 42 25N 77 13W
Hammonton, U.S.A. 76 F8 39 39N 74 48W
Hampden, N.Z. 59 L3 45 18S 170 50 E
Hampshire □, U.K. 11 F6 51 7N 1 23W
Hampshire Downs, U.K. 11 F6 51 15N 1 10W
Hampton, N.B., Canada 71 C6 45 32N 65 51W
Hampton, Ont., Canada 78 C6 43 58N 78 45W
Hampton, Ark., U.S.A. 81 J8 33 32N 92 28W
Hampton, Iowa, U.S.A. 80 D8 42 45N 93 13W
Hampton, N.H., U.S.A. 79 D14 42 57N 70 50W
Hampton, S.C., U.S.A. 77 J5 32 52N 81 7W
Hampton, Va., U.S.A. 76 G7 37 2N 76 21W
Hampton Bays, U.S.A. 79 F12 40 53N 72 30W
Hampton Tableland, Australia 61 F4 32 0S 127 0 E
Hamyang, S. Korea 35 G14 35 32N 127 42 E
Han Pijesak, Bos.-H. 21 B8 44 5N 18 57 E
Hana, U.S.A. 74 H17 20 45N 155 59W
Hanak, Si. Arabia 44 E3 25 32N 37 0 E
Hanamaki, Japan 30 E10 39 23N 141 7 E
Hanang, Tanzania 54 C4 4 30S 35 25 E
Hanau, Germany 16 C5 50 7N 8 56 E
Hanbogd = Ihbulag, Mongolia 34 C4 43 11N 107 10 E
Hancheng, China 34 G6 35 31N 110 25 E
Hancock, Mich., U.S.A. 80 B10 47 8N 88 35W
Hancock, N.Y., U.S.A. 79 E9 41 57N 75 17W
Handa, Japan 31 G8 34 53N 136 55 E
Handan, China 34 F8 36 35N 114 28 E
Handeni, Tanzania 54 D4 5 25S 38 2 E
Handwara, India 43 B6 34 21N 74 20 E
Hanegev, Israel 47 E4 30 50N 35 0 E
Hanford, U.S.A. 84 J7 36 20N 119 39W
Hang Chat, Thailand 38 C2 18 20N 99 21 E
Hang Dong, Thailand 38 C2 18 41N 98 55 E
Hangang →, S. Korea 35 F14 37 50N 126 30 E
Hangayn Nuruu, Mongolia 32 B4 47 30N 99 0 E
Hangchou = Hangzhou, China 33 C7 30 18N 120 11 E
Hanggin Houqi, China 34 D4 40 58N 107 4 E
Hanggin Qi, China 34 E5 39 52N 108 50 E
Hangu, China 35 E9 39 18N 117 53 E
Hangzhou, China 33 C7 30 18N 120 11 E
Hangzhou Wan, China 33 C7 30 15N 120 45 E
Hanhongor, Mongolia 34 C3 43 55N 104 28 E
Ḩanīdh, Si. Arabia 45 E6 26 35N 48 38 E
Ḩanīsh, Yemen 46 E3 13 45N 42 46 E
Hankinson, U.S.A. 80 B6 46 4N 96 54W
Hanko, Finland 9 G20 59 50N 22 57 E
Hanksville, U.S.A. 83 G8 38 22N 110 43W
Hanle, India 43 C8 32 42N 79 4 E
Hanmer Springs, N.Z. 59 K4 42 32S 172 50 E
Hann →, Australia 60 C4 17 26S 126 17 E
Hann, Mt., Australia 60 C4 15 45S 126 0 E
Hanna, Canada 72 C6 51 40N 111 54W
Hanna, U.S.A. 82 F10 41 52N 106 34W
Hannah B., Canada 70 B4 51 40N 80 0W
Hannibal, Mo., U.S.A. 80 F9 39 42N 91 22W
Hannibal, N.Y., U.S.A. 79 C8 43 19N 76 35W
Hannover, Germany 16 B5 52 22N 9 46 E
Hanoi, Vietnam 32 D5 21 5N 105 55 E
Hanover = Hannover, Germany 16 B5 52 22N 9 46 E
Hanover, Canada 78 B3 44 9N 81 2W
Hanover, S. Africa 56 E3 31 4S 24 29 E
Hanover, N.H., U.S.A. 79 C12 43 42N 72 17W
Hanover, Ohio, U.S.A. 78 F2 40 4N 82 16W
Hanover, Pa., U.S.A. 76 F7 39 48N 76 59W
Hanover, I., Chile 96 G2 51 0S 74 50W
Hansdiha, India 43 G12 24 36N 87 5 E
Hansi, India 42 E6 29 10N 75 57 E
Hanson, L., Australia 63 E2 31 0S 136 15 E
Hantsavichy, Belarus 17 B14 52 49N 26 30 E
Hanumangarh, India 42 E6 29 35N 74 19 E
Hanzhong, China 34 H4 33 10N 107 1 E
Hanzhuang, China 35 G9 34 33N 117 23 E
Haora, India 43 H13 22 37N 88 20 E
Haparanda, Sweden 8 D21 65 52N 24 8 E
Happy, U.S.A. 81 H4 34 45N 101 52W
Happy Camp, U.S.A. 82 F2 41 48N 123 23W
Happy Valley-Goose Bay, Canada 71 B7 53 15N 60 20W
Hapsu, N. Korea 35 D15 41 13N 128 51 E
Hapur, India 42 E7 28 45N 77 45 E
Ḩaql, Si. Arabia 47 F3 29 10N 34 58 E
Har, Indonesia 37 F8 5 16S 133 14 E
Har-Ayrag, Mongolia 34 B5 45 47N 109 16 E
Har Hu, China 32 C4 38 20N 97 38 E
Har Us Nuur, Mongolia 32 B4 48 0N 92 0 E
Har Yehuda, Israel 47 D3 31 35N 34 57 E
Ḩaraḑ, Si. Arabia 46 C4 24 22N 49 0 E
Haranomachi, Japan 30 F10 37 38N 140 58 E
Harare, Zimbabwe 55 F3 17 43S 31 2 E
Harbin, China 35 B14 45 48N 126 40 E
Harbor Beach, U.S.A. 78 C2 43 51N 82 39W
Harbour Breton, Canada 71 C8 47 29N 55 50W
Harbour Deep, Canada 71 B8 50 25N 56 32W
Harda, India 42 H7 22 27N 77 5 E
Hardangerfjorden, Norway 9 F12 60 5N 6 0 E
Hardangervidda, Norway 9 F12 60 7N 7 20 E
Hardap Dam, Namibia 56 C2 24 32S 17 50 E
Hardenberg, Neths. 15 B6 52 34N 6 37 E
Harderwijk, Neths. 15 B5 52 21N 5 38 E
Hardey →, Australia 60 D2 22 45S 116 8 E
Hardin, U.S.A. 82 D10 45 44N 107 37W
Harding, S. Africa 57 E4 30 35S 29 55 E
Harding Ra., Australia 60 C3 16 17S 124 55 E
Hardisty, Canada 72 C6 52 40N 111 18W
Hardoi, India 43 F9 27 26N 80 6 E
Hardwar = Haridwar, India 42 E8 29 58N 78 9 E
Hardwick, U.S.A. 79 B12 44 30N 72 22W
Hardy, Pen., Chile 96 H3 55 30S 68 20W
Hare B., Canada 71 B8 51 15N 55 45W
Hareid, Norway 9 E12 62 22N 6 1 E
Harer, Ethiopia 46 F3 9 20N 42 8 E
Hargeisa, Somali Rep. 46 F3 9 30N 44 2 E
Hari →, Indonesia 36 E2 1 16S 104 5 E
Haria, Canary Is. 22 E6 29 8N 13 32W
Haridwar, India 42 E8 29 58N 78 9 E
Harim, Jabal al, Oman 45 E8 25 58N 56 14 E
Haringhata →, Bangla. 41 J16 22 0N 89 58 E
Harīrūd →, Asia 40 A2 37 24N 60 38 E
Härjedalen, Sweden 9 E15 62 22N 13 5 E
Harlan, Iowa, U.S.A. 80 E7 41 39N 95 19W
Harlan, Ky., U.S.A. 77 G4 36 51N 83 19W
Harlech, U.K. 10 E3 52 52N 4 6W
Harlem, U.S.A. 82 B9 48 32N 108 47W
Harlingen, Neths. 15 A5 53 11N 5 25 E
Harlingen, U.S.A. 81 M6 26 12N 97 42W
Harlow, U.K. 11 F8 51 46N 0 8 E
Harlowton, U.S.A. 82 C9 46 26N 109 50W
Harnai, Pakistan 42 D2 30 6N 67 56 E
Harney Basin, U.S.A. 82 E4 43 30N 119 0W
Harney L., U.S.A. 82 E4 43 14N 119 8W
Harney Peak, U.S.A. 80 D3 43 52N 103 32W
Härnösand, Sweden 9 E17 62 38N 17 55 E
Haroldswick, U.K. 12 A8 60 48N 0 50W
Harp L., Canada 71 A7 55 5N 61 50W
Harper, Liberia 50 H4 4 25N 7 43W
Harrai, India 43 H8 22 37N 79 13 E
Harrand, Pakistan 42 E4 29 28N 70 3 E
Harricana →, Canada 70 B4 50 56N 79 32W
Harriman, U.S.A. 77 H3 35 56N 84 33W
Harrington Harbour, Canada 71 B8 50 31N 59 30W
Harris, U.K. 12 D2 57 50N 6 55W
Harris, Sd. of, U.K. 12 D1 57 44N 7 6W
Harris L., Australia 63 E2 31 10S 135 10 E
Harris Pt., Canada 78 C2 43 6N 82 9W
Harrisburg, Ill., U.S.A. 81 G10 37 44N 88 32W
Harrisburg, Nebr., U.S.A. 80 E3 41 33N 103 44W
Harrisburg, Pa., U.S.A. 78 F8 40 16N 76 53W
Harrismith, S. Africa 57 D4 28 15S 29 8 E
Harrison, Ark., U.S.A. 81 G8 36 14N 93 7W
Harrison, Maine, U.S.A. 79 B14 44 7N 70 39W
Harrison, Nebr., U.S.A. 80 D3 42 41N 103 53W
Harrison, C., Canada 71 B8 54 55N 57 55W
Harrison L., Canada 72 D4 49 33N 121 50W
Harrisonburg, U.S.A. 76 F6 38 27N 78 52W
Harrisonville, U.S.A. 80 F7 38 39N 94 21W
Harriston, Canada 78 C4 43 57N 80 53W
Harrisville, Mich., U.S.A. 78 B1 44 39N 83 17W
Harrisville, N.Y., U.S.A. 79 B9 44 9N 75 19W
Harrisville, Pa., U.S.A. 78 E5 41 8N 80 0W
Harrodsburg, U.S.A. 76 G3 37 46N 84 51W
Harrogate, U.K. 10 C6 54 0N 1 33W
Harrow, U.K. 11 F7 51 35N 0 21W
Harrowsmith, Canada 79 B8 44 24N 76 40W
Harry S. Truman Reservoir, U.S.A. 80 F7 38 16N 93 24W
Harsin, Iran 44 C5 34 18N 47 33 E
Harstad, Norway 8 B17 68 48N 16 30 E
Harsud, India 42 H7 22 6N 76 44 E
Hart, U.S.A. 76 D2 43 42N 86 22W
Hart, L., Australia 63 E2 31 10S 136 25 E
Hartbees →, S. Africa 56 D3 28 45S 20 32 E
Hartford, Conn., U.S.A. 79 E12 41 46N 72 41W
Hartford, Ky., U.S.A. 76 G2 37 27N 86 55W
Hartford, S. Dak., U.S.A. 80 D6 43 38N 96 57W
Hartford, Wis., U.S.A. 80 D10 43 19N 88 22W
Hartford City, U.S.A. 76 E3 40 27N 85 22W
Hartland, Canada 71 C6 46 20N 67 32W
Hartland Pt., U.K. 11 F3 51 1N 4 32W
Hartlepool, U.K. 10 C6 54 42N 1 13W
Hartlepool □, U.K. 10 C6 54 42N 1 17W
Hartley Bay, Canada 72 C3 53 25N 129 15W
Hartmannberge, Namibia 56 B1 17 0S 13 0 E
Hartney, Canada 73 D8 49 30N 100 35W
Harts →, S. Africa 56 D3 28 24S 24 17 E
Hartselle, U.S.A. 77 H2 34 27N 86 56W
Hartshorne, U.S.A. 81 H7 34 51N 95 34W
Hartstown, U.S.A. 78 E4 41 33N 80 23W
Hartsville, U.S.A. 77 H5 34 23N 80 4W
Hartwell, U.S.A. 77 H4 34 21N 82 56W
Harunabad, Pakistan 42 E5 29 35N 73 8 E
Harvand, Iran 45 D7 28 25N 55 43 E
Harvey, Australia 61 F2 33 5S 115 54 E
Harvey, Ill., U.S.A. 76 E2 41 36N 87 50W
Harvey, N. Dak., U.S.A. 80 B5 47 47N 99 56W
Harwich, U.K. 11 F9 51 56N 1 17 E
Haryana □, India 42 E7 29 0N 76 10 E
Haryn →, Belarus 17 B14 52 7N 27 17 E
Harz, Germany 16 C6 51 38N 10 44 E
Hasa □, Si. Arabia 45 E6 25 50N 49 0 E
Ḩasanābād, Iran 45 C7 32 8N 52 44 E
Hasdo →, India 43 J10 21 44N 82 44 E
Hashimoto, Japan 31 G7 34 19N 135 37 E
Hashtjerd, Iran 45 C6 35 52N 50 40 E
Haskell, U.S.A. 81 J5 33 10N 99 44W
Haslemere, U.K. 11 F7 51 5N 0 43W
Hasselt, Belgium 15 D5 50 56N 5 21 E
Hassi Messaoud, Algeria 50 B7 31 51N 6 1 E
Hässleholm, Sweden 9 H15 56 10N 13 46 E
Hastings, N.Z. 59 H6 39 39S 176 52 E
Hastings, U.K. 11 G8 50 51N 0 35 E
Hastings, Mich., U.S.A. 76 D3 42 39N 85 17W
Hastings, Minn., U.S.A. 80 C8 44 44N 92 51W
Hastings, Nebr., U.S.A. 80 E5 40 35N 98 23W
Hastings Ra., Australia 63 E5 31 15S 152 14 E
Hat Yai, Thailand 39 J3 7 1N 100 27 E
Hatanbulag = Ergel, Mongolia 34 C5 43 8N 109 5 E
Hatay = Antalya, Turkey 25 G5 36 52N 30 45 E
Hatch, U.S.A. 83 K10 32 40N 107 9W
Hatchet L., Canada 73 B8 58 36N 103 40W
Hateruma-Shima, Japan 31 M1 24 3N 123 47 E
Hatfield P.O., Australia 63 E3 33 54S 143 49 E
Hatgal, Mongolia 32 A5 50 26N 100 9 E
Hathras, India 42 F8 27 36N 78 6 E
Hatia, Bangla. 41 H17 22 30N 91 5 E
Hato Mayor, Dom. Rep. 89 C6 18 46N 69 15W
Hatta, India 43 G8 24 7N 79 36 E
Hattah, Australia 63 E3 34 48S 142 17 E
Hatteras, C., U.S.A. 77 H8 35 14N 75 32W
Hattiesburg, U.S.A. 81 K10 31 20N 89 17W
Hatvan, Hungary 17 E10 47 40N 19 45 E
Hau Bon = Cheo Reo, Vietnam 36 B3 13 25N 108 28 E
Hau Duc, Vietnam 38 E7 15 20N 108 13 E
Haugesund, Norway 9 G11 59 23N 5 13 E
Haukipudas, Finland 8 D21 65 12N 25 20 E
Haultain →, Canada 73 B7 55 51N 106 46W
Hauraki G., N.Z. 59 G5 36 35S 175 5 E
Haut Atlas, Morocco 50 B4 32 30N 5 0W
Haut-Zaïre = Orientale □, Dem. Rep. of the Congo 54 B2 2 20N 26 0 E
Hautes Fagnes = Hohe Venn, Belgium 15 D6 50 30N 6 5 E
Hauts Plateaux, Algeria 48 C4 35 0N 1 0 E
Havana = La Habana, Cuba 88 B3 23 8N 82 22W
Havana, U.S.A. 80 E9 40 18N 90 4W
Havant, U.K. 11 G7 50 51N 0 58W
Havasu, L., U.S.A. 85 L12 34 18N 114 28W
Havel →, Germany 16 B7 52 50N 12 3 E
Havelian, Pakistan 42 B5 34 2N 73 10 E
Havelock, Canada 78 B7 44 26N 77 53W
Havelock, N.Z. 59 J4 41 17S 173 48 E
Havelock, U.S.A. 77 H7 34 53N 76 54W
Haverfordwest, U.K. 11 F3 51 48N 4 58W
Haverhill, U.S.A. 79 D13 42 47N 71 5W
Haverstraw, U.S.A. 79 E11 41 12N 73 58W
Havirga, Mongolia 34 B7 45 41N 113 5 E
Havířov, Czech. 17 D10 49 46N 18 20 E
Havlíčkův Brod, Czech Rep. 16 D8 49 36N 15 33 E
Havre, U.S.A. 82 B9 48 33N 109 41W
Havre-Aubert, Canada 71 C7 47 12N 61 56W
Havre-St.-Pierre, Canada 71 B7 50 18N 63 33W
Haw →, U.S.A. 77 H6 35 36N 79 3W
Hawaii □, U.S.A. 74 H16 19 30N 156 30W
Hawaii I., Pac. Oc. 74 J17 20 0N 155 0W
Hawaiian Is., Pac. Oc. 74 H17 20 30N 156 0W
Hawaiian Ridge, Pac. Oc. 65 E11 24 0N 165 0W
Hawarden, U.S.A. 80 D6 43 0N 96 29W
Hawea, L., N.Z. 59 L2 44 28S 169 19 E
Hawera, N.Z. 59 H5 39 35S 174 19 E
Hawick, U.K. 12 F6 55 26N 2 47W
Hawk Junction, Canada 70 C3 48 5N 84 38W
Hawke B., N.Z. 59 H6 39 25S 177 20 E
Hawker, Australia 63 E2 31 59S 138 22 E
Hawkesbury, Canada 70 C5 45 37N 74 37W
Hawkesbury I., Canada 72 C3 53 37N 129 3W
Hawkesbury Pt., Australia 62 A1 11 55S 134 5 E
Hawkinsville, U.S.A. 77 J4 32 17N 83 28W
Hawley, Minn., U.S.A. 80 B6 46 53N 96 19W
Hawley, Pa., U.S.A. 79 E9 41 28N 75 11W
Ḩawrān, W. →, Iraq 44 C4 33 58N 42 34 E
Hawsh Müssá, Lebanon 47 B4 33 45N 35 55 E
Hawthorne, U.S.A. 82 G4 38 32N 118 38W
Hay, Australia 63 E3 34 30S 144 51 E
Hay →, Australia 62 C2 24 50S 138 0 E
Hay →, Canada 72 A5 60 50N 116 26W
Hay, C., Australia 60 B4 14 5S 129 29 E
Hay I., Canada 78 B4 44 53N 80 58W
Hay L., Canada 72 B5 58 50N 118 50W
Hay-on-Wye, U.K. 11 E4 52 5N 3 8W
Hay River, Canada 72 A5 60 51N 115 44W
Hay Springs, U.S.A. 80 D3 42 41N 102 41W
Haya = Tehoru, Indonesia 37 E7 3 19S 129 37 E
Hayachine-San, Japan 30 E10 39 34N 141 29 E
Hayden, U.S.A. 82 F10 40 30N 107 16W
Haydon, Australia 62 B3 18 0S 141 30 E
Hayes, U.S.A. 80 C4 44 23N 101 1W
Hayes →, Canada 70 A1 57 3N 92 12W
Hayes Creek, Australia 60 B5 13 43S 131 22 E
Hayle, U.K. 11 G2 50 11N 5 26W
Hayling I., U.K. 11 G7 50 48N 0 59W
Hayrabolu, Turkey 21 D12 41 12N 27 5 E
Hays, Canada 72 C6 50 6N 111 48W
Hays, U.S.A. 80 F5 38 53N 99 20W
Haysyn, Ukraine 17 D15 48 57N 29 25 E
Hayvoron, Ukraine 17 D15 48 22N 29 52 E
Hayward, Calif., U.S.A. 84 H4 37 40N 122 5W
Hayward, Wis., U.S.A. 80 B9 46 1N 91 29W
Haywards Heath, U.K. 11 G7 51 0N 0 5W
Hazafon □, Israel 47 C4 32 40N 35 20 E
Hazārān, Kūh-e, Iran 45 D8 29 35N 57 20 E
Hazard, U.S.A. 76 G4 37 15N 83 12W
Hazaribag, India 43 H11 23 58N 85 26 E
Hazaribag Road, India 43 G11 24 12N 85 57 E
Hazelton, Canada 72 B3 55 20N 127 42W
Hazelton, U.S.A. 80 B4 46 29N 100 17W
Hazen, U.S.A. 80 B4 47 18N 101 38W
Hazlehurst, Ga., U.S.A. 77 K4 31 52N 82 36W
Hazlehurst, Miss., U.S.A. 81 K9 31 52N 90 24W
Hazlet, U.S.A. 79 F10 40 25N 74 12W
Hazleton, U.S.A. 79 F9 40 57N 75 59W
Hazlett, L., Australia 60 D4 21 30S 128 48 E
Hazro, Turkey 44 B4 38 15N 40 47 E
Head of Bight, Australia 61 F5 31 30S 131 25 E
Headlands, Zimbabwe 55 F3 18 15S 32 2 E
Healdsburg, U.S.A. 84 G4 38 37N 122 52W
Healdton, U.S.A. 81 H6 34 14N 97 29W
Healesville, Australia 63 F4 37 35S 145 30 E
Heard I., Ind. Oc. 3 G13 53 0S 74 0 E
Hearne, U.S.A. 81 K6 30 53N 96 36W
Hearst, Canada 70 C3 49 40N 83 41W
Heart →, U.S.A. 80 B4 46 46N 100 50W
Heart's Content, Canada 71 C9 47 54N 53 27W
Heath Pt., Canada 71 C7 49 8N 61 40W
Heavener, U.S.A. 81 H7 34 53N 94 36W
Hebbronville, U.S.A. 81 M5 27 18N 98 41W
Hebei □, China 34 E9 39 0N 116 0 E
Hebel, Australia 63 D4 28 58S 147 47 E
Heber, U.S.A. 85 N11 32 44N 115 32W
Heber City, U.S.A. 82 F8 40 31N 111 25W
Heber Springs, U.S.A. 81 H9 35 30N 92 2W
Hebert, Canada 73 C7 50 30N 107 10W
Hebgen L., U.S.A. 82 D8 44 52N 111 20W
Hebi, China 34 G8 35 57N 114 7 E
Hebrides, U.K. 6 D4 57 30N 7 0W
Hebron = Al Khalīl, West Bank 47 D4 31 32N 35 6 E
Hebron, Canada 69 C13 58 5N 62 30W
Hebron, N. Dak., U.S.A. 80 B3 46 54N 102 3W
Hebron, Nebr., U.S.A. 80 E6 40 10N 97 35W
Hecate Str., Canada 72 C2 53 10N 130 30W
Heceta I., U.S.A. 72 B2 55 46N 133 40W
Hechi, China 32 D5 24 40N 108 2 E
Hechuan, China 32 C5 30 2N 106 12 E
Hecla, U.S.A. 80 C5 45 53N 98 9W
Hecla I., Canada 73 C9 51 10N 96 43W
Hede, Sweden 9 E15 62 23N 13 30 E
Hedemora, Sweden 9 F16 60 18N 15 58 E
Heerde, Neths. 15 B6 52 24N 6 2 E
Heerenveen, Neths. 15 B5 52 57N 5 55 E
Heerhugowaard, Neths. 15 B4 52 40N 4 51 E
Heerlen, Neths. 18 A6 50 55N 5 58 E
Ḩefa, Israel 47 C4 32 46N 35 0 E
Ḩefa □, Israel 47 C4 32 40N 35 0 E
Hefei, China 33 C6 31 52N 117 18 E
Hegang, China 33 B8 47 20N 130 19 E
Heichengzhen, China 34 F4 36 24N 106 3 E
Heidelberg, Germany 16 D5 49 24N 8 42 E
Heidelberg, S. Africa 56 E3 34 6S 20 59 E
Heilbron, S. Africa 57 D4 27 16S 27 59 E
Heilbronn, Germany 16 D5 49 9N 9 13 E
Heilongjiang □, China 33 B7 48 0N 126 0 E
Heilunkiang = Heilongjiang □, China 33 B7 48 0N 126 0 E
Heimaey, Iceland 8 E3 63 26N 20 17W
Heinola, Finland 9 F22 61 13N 26 2 E
Heinze Is., Burma 41 M20 14 25N 97 45 E
Heishan, China 35 D12 41 40N 122 5 E
Heishui, China 35 C10 42 8N 119 30 E
Hejaz = Ḩijāz □, Si. Arabia 46 C3 24 0N 40 0 E
Hejian, China 34 E9 38 25N 116 5 E
Hejin, China 34 G6 35 35N 110 42 E
Hekımhan, Turkey 44 B3 38 50N 37 55 E
Hekla, Iceland 8 E4 63 56N 19 35W
Hekou, China 32 D5 22 30N 103 59 E
Helan Shan, China 34 E3 38 30N 105 55 E
Helen Atoll, Pac. Oc. 37 D8 2 40N 132 0 E
Helena, Ark., U.S.A. 81 H9 34 32N 90 36W
Helena, Mont., U.S.A. 82 C7 46 36N 112 2W
Helendale, U.S.A. 85 L9 34 44N 117 19W
Helensburgh, U.K. 12 E4 56 1N 4 43W
Helensville, N.Z. 59 G5 36 41S 174 29 E
Helenvale, Australia 62 B4 15 43S 145 14 E
Helgeland, Norway 8 C15 66 7N 13 29 E
Helgoland, Germany 16 A4 54 10N 7 53 E
Heligoland = Helgoland, Germany 16 A4 54 10N 7 53 E
Heligoland B. = Deutsche Bucht, Germany 16 A5 54 15N 8 0 E
Hella, Iceland 8 E3 63 50N 20 24W
Hellertown, U.S.A. 79 F9 40 35N 75 21W
Hellespont = Çanakkale Boğazı, Turkey 21 D12 40 17N 26 32 E
Hellevoetsluis, Neths. 15 C4 51 50N 4 8 E
Hellín, Spain 19 C5 38 31N 1 40W
Helmand □, Afghan. 40 D4 31 20N 64 0 E
Helmand →, Afghan. 40 D2 31 12N 61 34 E
Helmond, Neths. 15 C5 51 29N 5 41 E
Helmsdale, U.K. 12 C5 58 7N 3 39W
Helmsdale →, U.K. 12 C5 58 7N 3 40W
Helong, China 35 C15 42 40N 129 0 E
Helper, U.S.A. 82 G8 39 41N 110 51W
Helsingborg, Sweden 9 H15 56 3N 12 42 E
Helsingfors = Helsinki, Finland 9 F21 60 15N 25 3 E
Helsingør, Denmark 9 H15 56 2N 12 35 E
Helsinki, Finland 9 F21 60 15N 25 3 E
Helston, U.K. 11 G2 50 6N 5 17W
Helvellyn, U.K. 10 C4 54 32N 3 1W
Helwân, Egypt 51 C12 29 50N 31 20 E
Hemel Hempstead, U.K. 11 F7 51 44N 0 28W
Hemet, U.S.A. 85 M10 33 45N 116 58W
Hemingford, U.S.A. 80 D3 42 19N 103 4W
Hemmingford, Canada 79 A11 45 3N 73 35W
Hempstead, U.S.A. 81 K6 30 6N 96 5W
Hemse, Sweden 9 H18 57 15N 18 22 E
Henan □, China 34 H8 34 0N 114 0 E
Henares →, Spain 19 B4 40 24N 3 30W
Henashi-Misaki, Japan 30 D9 40 37N 139 51 E
Henderson, Argentina 94 D3 36 18S 61 43W
Henderson, Ky., U.S.A. 76 G2 37 50N 87 35W
Henderson, N.C., U.S.A. 77 G6 36 20N 78 25W
Henderson, Nev., U.S.A. 85 J12 36 2N 114 59W
Henderson, Tenn., U.S.A. 77 H1 35 26N 88 38W
Henderson, Tex., U.S.A. 81 J7 32 9N 94 48W
Hendersonville, N.C., U.S.A. 77 H4 35 19N 82 28W
Hendersonville, Tenn., U.S.A. 77 G2 36 18N 86 37W
Hendījān, Iran 45 D6 30 14N 49 43 E
Hendorābī, Iran 45 E7 26 40N 53 37 E
Hengcheng, China 34 E4 38 18N 106 28 E
Hengdaohezi, China 35 B15 44 52N 129 0 E
Hengelo, Neths. 15 B6 52 16N 6 48 E
Hengshan, China 34 F5 37 58N 109 5 E
Hengshui, China 34 F8 37 41N 115 40 E
Hengyang, China 33 D6 26 52N 112 33 E
Henlopen, C., U.S.A. 76 F8 38 48N 75 6W
Hennenman, S. Africa 56 D4 27 59S 27 1 E
Hennessey, U.S.A. 81 G6 36 6N 97 54W
Henrietta, U.S.A. 81 J5 33 49N 98 12W
Henrietta, Ostrov = Genriyetty, Ostrov, Russia 27 B16 77 6N 156 30 E
Henrietta Maria, C., Canada 70 A3 55 9N 82 20W
Henry, U.S.A. 80 E10 41 7N 89 22W
Henryetta, U.S.A. 81 H7 35 27N 95 59W
Henryville, Canada 79 A11 45 8N 73 11W

Hensall

Hensall, *Canada* **78 C3** 43 26N 81 30W
Hentiyn Nuruu, *Mongolia* **33 B5** 48 30N 108 30 E
Henty, *Australia* **63 F4** 35 30S 147 0 E
Henzada, *Burma* **41 L19** 17 38N 95 26 E
Heppner, *U.S.A.* **82 D4** 45 21N 119 33W
Hepworth, *Canada* **78 B3** 44 37N 81 9W
Hequ, *China* **34 E6** 39 20N 111 15 E
Héraðsflói, *Iceland* **8 D6** 65 42N 14 12W
Héraðsvötn →, *Iceland* **8 D4** 65 45N 19 25W
Herald Cays, *Australia* **62 B4** 16 58S 149 9 E
Herät, *Afghan.* **40 B3** 34 20N 62 7 E
Herät □, *Afghan.* **40 B3** 35 0N 62 0 E
Herbert →, *Australia* **62 B4** 18 31S 146 17 E
Herberton, *Australia* **62 B4** 17 20S 145 25 E
Herceg-Novi, *Montenegro, Yug.* **21 C8** 42 30N 18 33 E
Herchmer, *Canada* **73 B10** 57 22N 94 10W
Herðubreið, *Iceland* **8 D5** 65 11N 16 21W
Hereford, *U.K.* **11 E5** 52 4N 2 43W
Hereford, *U.S.A.* **81 H3** 34 49N 102 24W
Herefordshire □, *U.K.* **11 E5** 52 8N 2 40W
Herentals, *Belgium* **15 C4** 51 12N 4 51 E
Herford, *Germany* **16 B5** 52 7N 8 39 E
Herington, *U.S.A.* **80 F6** 38 40N 96 57W
Herkimer, *U.S.A.* **79 D10** 43 0N 74 59W
Herlong, *U.S.A.* **84 E6** 40 8N 120 8W
Herm, *U.K.* **11 H5** 49 30N 2 28W
Hermann, *U.S.A.* **80 F9** 38 42N 91 27W
Hermannsburg, *Australia* **60 D5** 23 57S 132 45 E
Hermanus, *S. Africa* **56 E2** 34 27S 19 12 E
Hermidale, *Australia* **63 E4** 31 30S 146 42 E
Hermiston, *U.S.A.* **82 D4** 45 51N 119 17W
Hermitage, *N.Z.* **59 K3** 43 44S 170 5 E
Hermite, I., *Chile* **96 H3** 55 50S 68 0W
Hermon, *U.S.A.* **79 B9** 44 28N 75 14W
Hermon, Mt. = Shaykh, J. ash, *Lebanon* **47 B4** 33 25N 35 50 E
Hermosillo, *Mexico* **86 B2** 29 10N 111 0W
Hernád →, *Hungary* **17 D11** 47 56N 21 8 E
Hernandarias, *Paraguay* **95 B5** 25 20S 54 40W
Hernandez, *U.S.A.* **84 J6** 36 24N 120 46W
Hernando, *Argentina* **94 C3** 32 28S 63 40W
Hernando, *U.S.A.* **81 H10** 34 50N 90 0W
Herndon, *U.S.A.* **78 F8** 40 43N 76 51W
Herne, *Germany* **15 C7** 51 32N 7 14 E
Herne Bay, *U.K.* **11 F9** 51 21N 1 8 E
Herning, *Denmark* **9 H13** 56 8N 8 58 E
Heroica = Caborca, *Mexico* **86 A2** 30 40N 112 10W
Heroica Nogales = Nogales, *Mexico* **86 A2** 31 20N 110 56W
Heron Bay, *Canada* **70 C2** 48 40N 86 25W
Herradura, Pta. de la, *Canary Is.* **22 F5** 28 26N 14 8W
Herreid, *U.S.A.* **80 C4** 45 50N 100 4W
Herrin, *U.S.A.* **81 G10** 37 48N 89 2W
Herriot, *Canada* **73 B8** 56 22N 101 16W
Hershey, *U.S.A.* **79 F8** 40 17N 76 39W
Hersonissos, *Greece* **23 D7** 35 18N 25 22 E
Herstal, *Belgium* **15 D5** 50 40N 5 38 E
Hertford, *U.K.* **11 F7** 51 48N 0 4W
Hertfordshire □, *U.K.* **11 F7** 51 51N 0 5W
's-Hertogenbosch, *Neths.* **15 C5** 51 42N 5 17 E
Hertzogville, *S. Africa* **56 D4** 28 9S 25 30 E
Hervey B., *Australia* **62 C5** 25 0S 152 52 E
Herzliyya, *Israel* **47 C3** 32 10N 34 50 E
Ḥeşār, *Fārs, Iran* **45 D6** 29 52N 50 16 E
Ḥeşār, *Markazī, Iran* **45 C6** 35 50N 49 12 E
Heshui, *China* **34 G5** 35 48N 108 0 E
Heshun, *China* **34 F7** 37 22N 113 32 E
Hesperia, *U.S.A.* **85 L9** 34 25N 117 18W
Hesse = Hessen □, *Germany* **16 C5** 50 30N 9 0 E
Hessen □, *Germany* **16 C5** 50 30N 9 0 E
Hetch Hetchy Aqueduct, *U.S.A.* **84 H5** 37 29N 122 19W
Hettinger, *U.S.A.* **80 C3** 46 0N 102 42W
Heuvelton, *U.S.A.* **79 B9** 44 37N 75 25W
Hewitt, *U.S.A.* **81 K6** 31 27N 97 11W
Hexham, *U.K.* **10 C5** 54 58N 2 4W
Hexigten Qi, *China* **35 C9** 43 18N 117 30 E
Heydarābād, *Iran* **45 D7** 30 33N 55 38 E
Heysham, *U.K.* **10 C5** 54 3N 2 53W
Heywood, *Australia* **63 F3** 38 8S 141 37 E
Heze, *China* **34 G8** 35 14N 115 20 E
Hi Vista, *U.S.A.* **85 L9** 34 45N 117 46W
Hialeah, *U.S.A.* **77 N5** 25 50N 80 17W
Hiawatha, *U.S.A.* **80 F7** 39 51N 95 32W
Hibbing, *U.S.A.* **80 B8** 47 25N 92 56W
Hibbs B., *Australia* **62 G4** 42 35S 145 15 E
Hibernia Reef, *Australia* **60 B3** 12 0S 123 23 E
Hickman, *U.S.A.* **81 G10** 36 34N 89 11W
Hickory, *U.S.A.* **77 H5** 35 44N 81 21W
Hicks, Pt., *Australia* **63 F4** 37 49S 149 17 E
Hicks L., *Canada* **73 A9** 61 25N 100 0W
Hicksville, *U.S.A.* **79 F11** 40 46N 73 32W
Hida-Gawa →, *Japan* **31 G8** 35 26N 137 3 E
Hida-Sammyaku, *Japan* **31 F8** 36 30N 137 40 E
Hidaka-Sammyaku, *Japan* **30 C11** 42 35N 142 45 E
Hidalgo, *Mexico* **87 C5** 24 15N 99 26W
Hidalgo □, *Mexico* **87 C5** 20 30N 99 10W
Hidalgo, Presa M., *Mexico* **86 B3** 26 30N 108 35W
Hidalgo, Pta. del, *Canary Is.* **22 F3** 28 33N 16 19W
Hidalgo del Parral, *Mexico* **86 B3** 26 58N 105 40W
Hierro, *Canary Is.* **22 G1** 27 44N 18 0W
Higashiajima-San, *Japan* **30 F10** 37 40N 140 10 E
Higashiōsaka, *Japan* **31 G7** 34 40N 135 37 E
Higgins, *U.S.A.* **81 G4** 36 7N 100 2W
Higgins Corner, *U.S.A.* **84 F5** 39 2N 121 5W
High Atlas = Haut Atlas, *Morocco* **50 B4** 32 30N 5 0W
High Bridge, *U.S.A.* **79 F10** 40 40N 74 54W
High Level, *Canada* **72 B5** 58 31N 117 8W
High Point, *U.S.A.* **77 H6** 35 57N 80 0W
High Prairie, *Canada* **72 B5** 55 30N 116 30W
High River, *Canada* **72 C6** 50 30N 113 50W
High Tatra = Tatry, *Slovak Rep.* **17 D11** 49 20N 20 0 E
High Veld, *Africa* **48 J6** 27 0S 27 0 E
High Wycombe, *U.K.* **11 F7** 51 37N 0 45W
Highland □, *U.K.* **12 D4** 57 17N 4 21W
Highland Park, *U.S.A.* **76 D2** 42 11N 87 48W
Highmore, *U.S.A.* **80 C5** 44 31N 99 27W
Highrock L., *Canada* **73 B8** 55 45N 100 30W
Highrock L., *Sask., Canada* **73 B7** 57 5N 105 32W
Higüey, *Dom. Rep.* **89 C6** 18 37N 68 42W
Hiiumaa, *Estonia* **9 G20** 58 50N 22 45 E
Ḥijāz □, *Si. Arabia* **46 C3** 24 0N 40 0 E
Hijo = Tagum, *Phil.* **37 C7** 7 33N 125 53 E
Hikari, *Japan* **31 H5** 33 58N 131 58 E
Hiko, *U.S.A.* **84 H11** 37 32N 115 14W
Hikone, *Japan* **31 G8** 35 15N 136 10 E
Hikurangi, *N.Z.* **59 F5** 35 36S 174 17 E
Hikurangi, Mt., *N.Z.* **59 H6** 38 21S 176 52 E
Hildesheim, *Germany* **16 B5** 52 9N 9 56 E
Hill →, *Australia* **61 F2** 30 23S 115 3 E
Hill City, *Idaho, U.S.A.* **82 E6** 43 18N 115 3W
Hill City, *Kans., U.S.A.* **80 F5** 39 22N 99 51W
Hill City, *S. Dak., U.S.A.* **80 D3** 43 56N 103 35W
Hill Island L., *Canada* **73 A7** 60 30N 109 50W
Hillcrest Center, *U.S.A.* **85 K8** 35 23N 118 57W
Hillegom, *Neths.* **15 B4** 52 18N 4 35 E
Hillerød, *Denmark* **9 J15** 55 56N 12 19 E
Hillsboro, *Kans., U.S.A.* **80 F6** 38 21N 97 12W
Hillsboro, *N. Dak., U.S.A.* **80 B6** 47 26N 97 3W
Hillsboro, *N.H., U.S.A.* **79 C13** 43 7N 71 54W
Hillsboro, *Ohio, U.S.A.* **76 F4** 39 12N 83 37W
Hillsboro, *Oreg., U.S.A.* **84 E4** 45 31N 122 59W
Hillsboro, *Tex., U.S.A.* **81 J6** 32 1N 97 8W
Hillsborough, *Grenada* **89 D7** 12 28N 61 28W
Hillsdale, *Mich., U.S.A.* **76 E3** 41 56N 84 38W
Hillsdale, *N.Y., U.S.A.* **79 D11** 42 11N 73 30W
Hillsport, *Canada* **70 C2** 49 27N 85 34W
Hillston, *Australia* **63 E4** 33 30S 145 31 E
Hilo, *U.S.A.* **74 J17** 19 44N 155 5W
Hilton, *U.S.A.* **78 C7** 43 17N 77 48W
Hilton Head Island, *U.S.A.* **77 J5** 32 13N 80 45W
Hilversum, *Neths.* **15 B5** 52 14N 5 10 E
Himachal Pradesh □, *India* **42 D7** 31 30N 77 0 E
Himalaya, *Asia* **43 E11** 29 0N 84 0 E
Himatnagar, *India* **40 H8** 23 37N 72 57 E
Himeji, *Japan* **31 G7** 34 50N 134 40 E
Himi, *Japan* **31 F8** 36 50N 136 55 E
Ḥimş, *Syria* **47 A5** 34 40N 36 45 E
Ḥimş □, *Syria* **47 A6** 34 30N 37 0 E
Hinche, *Haiti* **89 C5** 19 9N 72 1W
Hinchinbrook I., *Australia* **62 B4** 18 20S 146 15 E
Hinckley, *U.K.* **11 E6** 52 33N 1 22W
Hinckley, *U.S.A.* **80 B8** 46 1N 92 56W
Hindaun, *India* **42 F7** 26 44N 77 5 E
Hindmarsh, L., *Australia* **63 F3** 36 5S 141 55 E
Hindu Bagh, *Pakistan* **42 D2** 30 56N 67 50 E
Hindu Kush, *Asia* **40 B7** 36 0N 71 0 E
Hindubagh, *Pakistan* **40 D5** 30 56N 67 57 E
Hindupur, *India* **40 N10** 13 49N 77 32 E
Hines Creek, *Canada* **72 B5** 56 20N 118 40W
Hinesville, *U.S.A.* **77 K5** 31 51N 81 36W
Hinganghat, *India* **40 J11** 20 30N 78 52 E
Hingham, *U.S.A.* **82 B8** 48 33N 110 25W
Hingir, *India* **43 J10** 21 57N 83 41 E
Hingoli, *India* **40 K10** 19 41N 77 15 E
Hinna = Imi, *Ethiopia* **46 F3** 6 28N 42 10 E
Hinnøya, *Norway* **8 B16** 68 35N 15 50 E
Hinojosa del Duque, *Spain* **19 C3** 38 30N 5 9W
Hinsdale, *U.S.A.* **79 D12** 42 47N 72 29W
Hinton, *Canada* **72 C5** 53 26N 117 34W
Hinton, *U.S.A.* **76 G5** 37 40N 80 54W
Hirado, *Japan* **31 H4** 33 22N 129 33 E
Hirakud Dam, *India* **41 J13** 21 32N 83 45 E
Hiran →, *India* **43 H8** 23 6N 79 21 E
Hirapur, *India* **43 G8** 24 22N 79 13 E
Hiratsuka, *Japan* **31 G9** 35 19N 139 21 E
Hiroo, *Japan* **30 C11** 42 17N 143 19 E
Hirosaki, *Japan* **30 D10** 40 34N 140 28 E
Hiroshima, *Japan* **31 G6** 34 24N 132 30 E
Hiroshima □, *Japan* **31 G6** 34 50N 133 0 E
Hisar, *India* **42 E6** 29 12N 75 45 E
Hisb →, *Iraq* **44 D5** 31 45N 44 17 E
Ḥismá, *Si. Arabia* **44 D3** 28 30N 36 0 E
Hispaniola, *W. Indies* **89 C5** 19 0N 71 0W
Hīt, *Iraq* **44 C4** 33 38N 42 49 E
Hita, *Japan* **31 H5** 33 20N 130 58 E
Hitachi, *Japan* **31 F10** 36 36N 140 39 E
Hitchin, *U.K.* **11 F7** 51 58N 0 16W
Hitoyoshi, *Japan* **31 H5** 32 13N 130 45 E
Hitra, *Norway* **8 E13** 63 30N 8 45 E
Hixon, *Canada* **72 C4** 53 25N 122 35W
Ḥiyyon, N. →, *Israel* **47 E4** 30 25N 35 10 E
Hjalmar L., *Canada* **73 A7** 61 33N 109 25W
Hjälmaren, *Sweden* **9 G16** 59 18N 15 40 E
Hjørring, *Denmark* **9 H13** 57 29N 9 59 E
Hluhluwe, *S. Africa* **57 D5** 28 1S 32 15 E
Hlyboka, *Ukraine* **17 D13** 48 5N 25 56 E
Ho Chi Minh City = Phanh Bho Ho Chi Minh, *Vietnam* **39 G6** 10 58N 106 40 E
Ho Thuong, *Vietnam* **38 C5** 19 32N 105 48 E
Hoa Da, *Vietnam* **39 G7** 11 16N 108 40 E
Hoa Hiep, *Vietnam* **39 G5** 11 34N 105 51 E
Hoai Nhon, *Vietnam* **38 E7** 14 28N 109 1 E
Hoang Lien Son, *Vietnam* **38 A4** 22 0N 104 0 E
Hoare B., *Canada* **69 B13** 65 17N 62 30W
Hobart, *Australia* **62 G4** 42 50S 147 21 E
Hobart, *U.S.A.* **81 H5** 35 1N 99 6W
Hobbs, *U.S.A.* **81 J3** 32 42N 103 8W
Hobbs Coast, *Antarctica* **5 D14** 74 50S 131 0W
Hobe Sound, *U.S.A.* **77 M5** 27 4N 80 8W
Hoboken, *U.S.A.* **79 F10** 40 45N 74 4W
Hobro, *Denmark* **9 H13** 56 39N 9 46 E
Hoburgen, *Sweden* **9 H18** 56 55N 18 7 E
Hodaka-Dake, *Japan* **31 F8** 36 17N 137 39 E
Hodgeville, *Canada* **73 C7** 50 7N 106 58W
Hodgson, *Canada* **73 C9** 51 13N 97 36W
Hódmezővásárhely, *Hungary* **17 E11** 46 28N 20 22 E
Hodna, Chott el, *Algeria* **50 A6** 35 26N 4 43 E
Hodonín, *Czech Rep.* **17 D9** 48 50N 17 10 E
Hoeamdong, *N. Korea* **35 C16** 42 30N 130 16 E
Hoek van Holland, *Neths.* **15 C4** 52 0N 4 7 E
Hoengsŏng, *S. Korea* **35 F14** 37 29N 127 59 E
Hoeryong, *N. Korea* **35 C15** 42 30N 129 45 E
Hoeyang, *N. Korea* **35 E14** 38 43N 127 36 E
Hof, *Germany* **16 C6** 50 19N 11 55 E
Hofmeyr, *S. Africa* **56 E4** 31 39S 25 50 E
Höfn, *Iceland* **8 D6** 64 15N 15 13W
Hofors, *Sweden* **9 F17** 60 31N 16 15 E
Hofsjökull, *Iceland* **8 D4** 64 49N 18 48W
Hōfu, *Japan* **31 G5** 34 3N 131 34 E
Hogan Group, *Australia* **63 F4** 39 13S 147 1 E
Hogarth, Mt., *Australia* **62 C2** 21 48S 136 58 E
Hoggar = Ahaggar, *Algeria* **50 D7** 23 0N 6 30 E
Hogsty Reef, *Bahamas* **89 B5** 21 41N 73 48W
Hoh →, *U.S.A.* **84 C2** 47 45N 124 29W
Hohe Venn, *Belgium* **15 D6** 50 30N 6 5 E
Hohenwald, *U.S.A.* **77 H2** 35 33N 87 33W
Hohhot, *China* **34 D6** 40 52N 111 40 E
Hóhlakas, *Greece* **23 D9** 35 57N 27 53 E
Hoi An, *Vietnam* **38 E7** 15 30N 108 19 E
Hoisington, *U.S.A.* **80 F5** 38 31N 98 47W
Hōjō, *Japan* **31 H6** 33 58N 132 46 E
Hokianga Harbour, *N.Z.* **59 F4** 35 31S 173 22 E
Hokitika, *N.Z.* **59 K3** 42 42S 171 0 E
Hokkaidō □, *Japan* **30 C11** 43 30N 143 0 E
Holbrook, *Australia* **63 F4** 35 42S 147 18 E
Holbrook, *U.S.A.* **83 J8** 34 54N 110 10W
Holden, *U.S.A.* **82 G7** 39 6N 112 16W
Holdenville, *U.S.A.* **81 H6** 35 5N 96 24W
Holdrege, *U.S.A.* **80 E5** 40 26N 99 23W
Holguín, *Cuba* **88 B4** 20 50N 76 20W
Hollams Bird I., *Namibia* **56 C1** 24 40S 14 30 E
Holland, *Mich., U.S.A.* **76 D2** 42 47N 86 7W
Holland, *N.Y., U.S.A.* **78 D6** 42 38N 78 32W
Hollandale, *U.S.A.* **81 J9** 33 10N 90 51W
Hollandia = Jayapura, *Indonesia* **37 E10** 2 28S 140 38 E
Holley, *U.S.A.* **78 C6** 43 14N 78 2W
Hollidaysburg, *U.S.A.* **78 F6** 40 26N 78 24W
Hollis, *U.S.A.* **81 H5** 34 41N 99 55W
Hollister, *Calif., U.S.A.* **84 J5** 36 51N 121 24W
Hollister, *Idaho, U.S.A.* **82 E6** 42 21N 114 35W
Holly Hill, *U.S.A.* **77 L5** 29 16N 81 3W
Holly Springs, *U.S.A.* **81 H10** 34 46N 89 27W
Hollywood, *Calif., U.S.A.* **74 D3** 34 7N 118 25W
Hollywood, *Fla., U.S.A.* **77 N5** 26 1N 80 9W
Holman, *Canada* **68 A8** 70 42N 117 41W
Holman, *N.W.T., Canada* **68 A8** 70 44N 117 44W
Hólmavík, *Iceland* **8 D3** 65 42N 21 40W
Holmen, *U.S.A.* **80 D9** 43 58N 91 15W
Holmes Reefs, *Australia* **62 B4** 16 27S 148 0 E
Holmsund, *Sweden* **8 E19** 63 41N 20 20 E
Holroyd →, *Australia* **62 A3** 14 10S 141 36 E
Holstebro, *Denmark* **9 H13** 56 22N 8 37 E
Holsworthy, *U.K.* **11 G3** 50 48N 4 22W
Holton, *Canada* **71 B8** 54 31N 57 12W
Holton, *U.S.A.* **80 F7** 39 28N 95 44W
Holtville, *U.S.A.* **85 N11** 32 49N 115 23W
Holwerd, *Neths.* **15 A5** 53 22N 5 54 E
Holy I., *Angl., U.K.* **10 D3** 53 17N 4 37W
Holy I., *Northumb., U.K.* **10 B6** 55 40N 1 47W
Holyhead, *U.K.* **10 D3** 53 18N 4 38W
Holyoke, *Colo., U.S.A.* **80 E3** 40 35N 102 18W
Holyoke, *Mass., U.S.A.* **79 D12** 42 12N 72 37W
Holyrood, *Canada* **71 C9** 47 27N 53 8W
Homa Bay, *Kenya* **54 C3** 0 36S 34 30 E
Homalin, *Burma* **41 G19** 24 55N 95 0 E
Homand, *Iran* **45 C8** 32 28N 59 37 E
Homathko →, *Canada* **72 C4** 51 0N 124 56W
Hombori, *Mali* **50 E5** 15 20N 1 38W
Home B., *Canada* **69 B13** 68 40N 67 10W
Home Hill, *Australia* **62 B4** 19 43S 147 25 E
Homedale, *U.S.A.* **82 E5** 43 37N 116 56W
Homer, *Alaska, U.S.A.* **68 C4** 59 39N 151 33W
Homer, *La., U.S.A.* **81 J8** 32 48N 93 4W
Homer City, *U.S.A.* **78 F5** 40 32N 79 10W
Homestead, *Australia* **62 C4** 20 20S 145 40 E
Homestead, *U.S.A.* **77 N5** 25 28N 80 29W
Homewood, *U.S.A.* **84 F6** 39 4N 120 8W
Homoine, *Mozam.* **57 C6** 23 55S 35 8 E
Homs = Ḥimş, *Syria* **47 A5** 34 40N 36 45 E
Homyel, *Belarus* **17 B16** 52 28N 31 0 E
Hon Chong, *Vietnam* **39 G5** 10 25N 104 30 E
Hon Me, *Vietnam* **38 C5** 19 23N 105 56 E
Honan = Henan □, *China* **34 H8** 34 0N 114 0 E
Honbetsu, *Japan* **30 C11** 43 7N 143 37 E
Honcut, *U.S.A.* **84 F5** 39 20N 121 32W
Hondeklipbaai, *S. Africa* **56 E2** 30 19S 17 17 E
Hondo, *Japan* **31 H5** 32 27N 130 12 E
Hondo, *U.S.A.* **81 L5** 29 21N 99 9W
Hondo →, *Belize* **87 D7** 18 25N 88 21W
Honduras ■, *Cent. Amer.* **88 D2** 14 40N 86 30W
Honduras, G. de, *Caribbean* **88 C2** 16 50N 87 0W
Hønefoss, *Norway* **9 F14** 60 10N 10 18 E
Honesdale, *U.S.A.* **79 E9** 41 34N 75 16W
Honey L., *U.S.A.* **84 E6** 40 15N 120 19W
Honfleur, *France* **18 B4** 49 25N 0 13 E
Hong →, *Vietnam* **32 D5** 22 0N 104 0 E
Hong He →, *China* **34 H8** 32 25N 115 35 E
Hong Kong □, *China* **33 D6** 22 11N 114 14 E
Hongch'ŏn, *S. Korea* **35 F14** 37 44N 127 53 E
Hongjiang, *China* **33 D5** 27 7N 109 59 E
Hongliu He →, *China* **34 F5** 38 0N 109 50 E
Hongor, *Mongolia* **34 B7** 45 45N 112 50 E
Hongsa, *Laos* **38 C3** 19 43N 101 20 E
Hongshui He →, *China* **33 D5** 23 48N 109 30 E
Hongsŏng, *S. Korea* **35 F14** 36 37N 126 38 E
Hongtong, *China* **34 F6** 36 16N 111 40 E
Honguedo, Détroit d', *Canada* **71 C7** 49 15N 64 0W
Hongwon, *N. Korea* **35 E14** 40 0N 127 56 E
Hongze Hu, *China* **35 H10** 33 15N 118 35 E
Honiara, *Solomon Is.* **64 H7** 9 27S 159 57 E
Honiton, *U.K.* **11 G4** 50 47N 3 11W
Honjō, *Japan* **30 E10** 39 23N 140 3 E
Honningsvåg, *Norway* **8 A21** 70 59N 25 59 E
Honolulu, *U.S.A.* **74 H16** 21 19N 157 52W
Honshū, *Japan* **31 G9** 36 0N 138 0 E
Hood, Mt., *U.S.A.* **82 D3** 45 23N 121 42W
Hood, Pt., *Australia* **61 F2** 34 23S 119 34 E
Hood River, *U.S.A.* **82 D3** 45 43N 121 31W
Hoodsport, *U.S.A.* **84 C3** 47 24N 123 9W
Hoogeveen, *Neths.* **15 B6** 52 44N 6 28 E
Hoogezand-Sappemeer, *Neths.* **15 A6** 53 9N 6 45 E
Hooghly = Hugli →, *India* **43 J13** 21 56N 88 4 E
Hooghly-Chinsura = Chunchura, *India* **43 H13** 22 53N 88 27 E
Hook Hd., *Ireland* **13 D5** 52 7N 6 56W
Hook I., *Australia* **62 C4** 20 4S 149 0 E
Hook of Holland = Hoek van Holland, *Neths.* **15 C4** 52 0N 4 7 E
Hooker, *U.S.A.* **81 G4** 36 52N 101 13W
Hooker Creek, *Australia* **60 C5** 18 23S 130 38 E
Hoonah, *U.S.A.* **72 B1** 58 7N 135 27W
Hooper Bay, *U.S.A.* **68 B3** 61 32N 166 6W
Hoopeston, *U.S.A.* **76 E2** 40 28N 87 40W
Hoopstad, *S. Africa* **56 D4** 27 50S 25 55 E
Hoorn, *Neths.* **15 B5** 52 38N 5 4 E
Hoover, *U.S.A.* **77 J2** 33 20N 86 11W
Hoover Dam, *U.S.A.* **85 K12** 36 1N 114 44W
Hooversville, *U.S.A.* **78 F6** 40 9N 78 55W
Hop Bottom, *U.S.A.* **79 E9** 41 42N 75 46W
Hope, *Canada* **72 D4** 49 25N 121 25W
Hope, *Ariz., U.S.A.* **85 M13** 33 43N 113 42W
Hope, *Ark., U.S.A.* **81 J8** 33 40N 93 36W
Hope, L., *S. Austral., Australia* **63 D2** 28 24S 139 18 E
Hope, L., *W. Austral., Australia* **61 F3** 32 35S 120 15 E
Hope I., *Canada* **78 B4** 44 55N 80 11W
Hope Town, *Bahamas* **88 A4** 26 35N 76 57W
Hopedale, *Canada* **71 A7** 55 28N 60 13W
Hopedale, *U.S.A.* **79 D13** 42 8N 71 33W
Hopefield, *S. Africa* **56 E2** 33 3S 18 22 E
Hopei = Hebei □, *China* **34 E9** 39 0N 116 0 E
Hopelchén, *Mexico* **87 D7** 19 46N 89 50W
Hopetoun, *Vic., Australia* **63 F3** 35 42S 142 22 E
Hopetoun, *W. Austral., Australia* **61 F3** 33 57S 120 7 E
Hopetown, *S. Africa* **56 D3** 29 34S 24 3 E
Hopevale, *Australia* **62 B4** 15 16S 145 20 E
Hopewell, *U.S.A.* **76 G7** 37 18N 77 17W
Hopkins, L., *Australia* **60 D4** 24 15S 128 35 E
Hopkinsville, *U.S.A.* **77 G2** 36 52N 87 29W
Hopland, *U.S.A.* **84 G3** 38 58N 123 7W
Hoquiam, *U.S.A.* **84 D3** 46 59N 123 53W
Horden Hills, *Australia* **60 D5** 20 15S 130 0 E
Horinger, *China* **34 D6** 40 28N 111 48 E
Horlick Mts., *Antarctica* **5 E15** 84 0S 102 0W
Horlivka, *Ukraine* **25 E6** 48 19N 38 5 E
Hormak, *Iran* **45 D9** 29 58N 60 51 E
Hormoz, *Iran* **45 E7** 27 35N 55 0 E
Hormoz, Jaz.-ye, *Iran* **45 E8** 27 8N 56 28 E
Hormozgān □, *Iran* **45 E8** 27 30N 56 0 E
Hormuz, Kūh-e, *Iran* **45 E7** 27 27N 55 10 E
Hormuz, Str. of, *The Gulf* **45 E8** 26 30N 56 30 E
Horn, *Austria* **16 D8** 48 39N 15 40 E
Horn, *Iceland* **8 C2** 66 28N 22 28W
Horn →, *Canada* **72 A5** 61 30N 118 1W
Horn, Cape = Hornos, C. de, *Chile* **96 H3** 55 50S 67 30W
Horn Head, *Ireland* **13 A3** 55 14N 8 0W
Horn I., *Australia* **62 A3** 10 37S 142 17 E
Horn Mts., *Canada* **72 A5** 62 15N 119 15W
Hornavan, *Sweden* **8 C17** 66 15N 17 30 E
Hornbeck, *U.S.A.* **81 K8** 31 20N 93 24W
Hornbrook, *U.S.A.* **82 F2** 41 55N 122 33W
Horncastle, *U.K.* **10 D7** 53 13N 0 7W
Hornell, *U.S.A.* **78 D7** 42 20N 77 40W
Hornell L., *Canada* **72 A5** 62 20N 119 25W
Hornepayne, *Canada* **70 C3** 49 14N 84 48W
Hornings Mills, *Canada* **78 B4** 44 9N 80 12W
Hornitos, *U.S.A.* **84 H6** 37 30N 120 14W
Hornos, C. de, *Chile* **96 H3** 55 50S 67 30W
Hornsea, *U.K.* **10 D7** 53 55N 0 11W
Horobetsu, *Japan* **30 C10** 42 24N 141 6 E
Horodenka, *Ukraine* **17 D13** 48 41N 25 29 E
Horodok, *Khmelnytskyy, Ukraine* **17 D14** 49 10N 26 34 E
Horodok, *Lviv, Ukraine* **17 D12** 49 46N 23 32 E
Horokhiv, *Ukraine* **17 C13** 50 30N 24 45 E
Horqin Youyi Qianqi, *China* **35 A12** 46 5N 122 3 E
Horqueta, *Paraguay* **94 A4** 23 15S 56 55W
Horse Creek, *U.S.A.* **80 E3** 41 57N 105 10W
Horse Is., *Canada* **71 B8** 50 15N 55 50W
Horsefly L., *Canada* **72 C4** 52 25N 121 0W
Horseheads, *U.S.A.* **78 D8** 42 10N 76 49W
Horsens, *Denmark* **9 J13** 55 52N 9 51 E
Horsham, *Australia* **63 F3** 36 44S 142 13 E
Horsham, *U.K.* **11 F7** 51 4N 0 20W
Horten, *Norway* **9 G14** 59 25N 10 32 E
Horton, *U.S.A.* **80 F7** 39 40N 95 32W
Horton →, *Canada* **68 B7** 69 56N 126 52W
Horwood L., *Canada* **70 C3** 48 5N 82 20W
Hose, Gunung-Gunung, *Malaysia* **36 D4** 2 5N 114 6 E
Ḥoseynābād, *Khuzestān, Iran* **45 C6** 32 45N 48 20 E
Ḥoseynābād, *Kordestān, Iran* **44 C5** 35 33N 47 8 E
Hoshangabad, *India* **42 H7** 22 45N 77 45 E
Hoshiarpur, *India* **42 D6** 31 30N 75 58 E
Hospet, *India* **40 M10** 15 15N 76 20 E
Hoste, I., *Chile* **96 H3** 55 0S 69 0W
Hot, *Thailand* **38 C2** 18 8N 98 29 E
Hot Creek Range, *U.S.A.* **82 G6** 38 40N 116 20W
Hot Springs, *Ark., U.S.A.* **81 H8** 34 31N 93 3W
Hot Springs, *S. Dak., U.S.A.* **80 D3** 43 26N 103 29W
Hotagen, *Sweden* **8 E16** 63 50N 14 30 E
Hotan, *China* **32 C2** 37 25N 79 55 E
Hotazel, *S. Africa* **56 D3** 27 17S 22 58 E
Hotchkiss, *U.S.A.* **83 G10** 38 48N 107 43W
Hotham, C., *Australia* **60 B5** 12 2S 131 18 E
Hoting, *Sweden* **8 D17** 64 8N 16 15 E
Hotte, Massif de la, *Haiti* **89 C5** 18 30N 73 45W
Hottentotsbaai, *Namibia* **56 D1** 26 8S 14 59 E
Houffalize, *Belgium* **15 D5** 50 8N 5 48 E
Houghton, *Mich., U.S.A.* **80 B10** 47 7N 88 34W
Houghton, *N.Y., U.S.A.* **78 D6** 42 25N 78 10W
Houghton L., *U.S.A.* **76 C3** 44 21N 84 44W
Houhora Heads, *N.Z.* **59 F4** 34 49S 173 9 E
Houlton, *U.S.A.* **77 B12** 46 8N 67 51W
Houma, *U.S.A.* **81 L9** 29 36N 90 43W
Housatonic →, *U.S.A.* **79 E11** 41 10N 73 7W
Houston, *Canada* **72 C3** 54 25N 126 39W
Houston, *Mo., U.S.A.* **81 G9** 37 22N 91 58W
Houston, *Tex., U.S.A.* **81 L7** 29 46N 95 22W
Houtman Abrolhos, *Australia* **61 E1** 28 43S 113 48 E
Hovd, *Mongolia* **32 B4** 48 2N 91 37 E
Hove, *U.K.* **11 G7** 50 50N 0 10W
Hoveyzeh, *Iran* **45 D6** 31 27N 48 4 E
Hövsgöl, *Mongolia* **34 C5** 43 37N 109 39 E
Hövsgöl Nuur, *Mongolia* **32 A5** 51 0N 100 30 E
Howard, *Australia* **63 D5** 25 16S 152 32 E
Howard, *Pa., U.S.A.* **78 F7** 41 1N 77 40W
Howard, *S. Dak., U.S.A.* **80 C6** 44 1N 97 32W
Howe, *U.S.A.* **82 E7** 43 48N 113 0W
Howe, C., *Australia* **63 F5** 37 30S 150 0 E
Howe I., *Canada* **79 B8** 44 16N 76 17W
Howell, *U.S.A.* **76 D4** 42 36N 83 56W
Howick, *Canada* **79 A11** 45 11N 73 51W
Howick, *S. Africa* **57 D5** 29 28S 30 14 E
Howick Group, *Australia* **62 A4** 14 20S 145 30 E
Howitt, L., *Australia* **63 D2** 27 40S 138 40 E
Howland I., *Pac. Oc.* **64 G10** 0 48N 176 38W
Howrah = Haora, *India* **43 H13** 22 37N 88 20 E
Howth Hd., *Ireland* **13 C5** 53 22N 6 3W
Höxter, *Germany* **16 C5** 51 46N 9 22 E
Hoy, *U.K.* **12 C5** 58 50N 3 15W
Høyanger, *Norway* **9 F12** 61 13N 6 4 E

Indore

Indore, *India* **42 H6** 22 42N 75 53 E
Indramayu, *Indonesia* **37 G13** 6 20S 108 19 E
Indravati →, *India* **41 K12** 19 20N 80 20 E
Indre →, *France* **18 C4** 47 16N 0 11 E
Indulkana, *Australia* **63 D1** 26 58S 133 5 E
Indus →, *Pakistan* **42 G2** 24 20N 67 47 E
Indus, Mouth of the, *Pakistan* **42 H3** 24 0N 68 0 E
İnebolu, *Turkey* **25 F5** 41 55N 33 40 E
Infiernillo, Presa del, *Mexico* **86 D4** 18 9N 102 0W
Ingenio, *Canary Is.* **22 G4** 27 55N 15 26W
Ingenio Santa Ana, *Argentina* **94 B2** 27 25S 65 40W
Ingersoll, *Canada* **78 C4** 43 4N 80 55W
Ingham, *Australia* **62 B4** 18 43S 146 10 E
Ingleborough, *U.K.* **10 C5** 54 10N 2 22W
Inglewood, *Queens., Australia* **63 D5** 28 25S 151 2 E
Inglewood, *Vic., Australia* **63 F3** 36 29S 143 53 E
Inglewood, *N.Z.* **59 H5** 39 9S 174 14 E
Inglewood, *U.S.A.* **85 M8** 33 58N 118 21W
Ingólfshöfði, *Iceland* **8 E5** 63 48N 16 39W
Ingolstadt, *Germany* **16 D6** 48 46N 11 26 E
Ingomar, *U.S.A.* **82 C10** 46 35N 107 23W
Ingonish, *Canada* **71 C7** 46 42N 60 18W
Ingraj Bazar, *India* **43 G13** 24 58N 88 10 E
Ingrid Christensen Coast, *Antarctica* **5 C6** 69 30S 76 0 E
Ingulec = Inhulec, *Ukraine* **25 E5** 47 42N 33 14 E
Ingushetia □, *Russia* **25 E8** 43 20N 44 50 E
Ingwavuma, *S. Africa* **57 D5** 27 9S 31 59 E
Inhaca, I., *Mozam.* **57 D5** 26 1S 32 57 E
Inhafenga, *Mozam.* **57 C5** 20 36S 33 53 E
Inhambane, *Mozam.* **57 C6** 23 54S 35 30 E
Inhambane □, *Mozam.* **57 C5** 22 30S 34 20 E
Inhaminga, *Mozam.* **55 F4** 18 26S 35 0 E
Inharrime, *Mozam.* **57 C6** 24 30S 35 0 E
Inharrime →, *Mozam.* **57 C6** 24 30S 35 0 E
Inhulec, *Ukraine* **25 E5** 47 42N 33 14 E
Ining = Yining, *China* **26 E9** 43 58N 81 10 E
Inírida →, *Colombia* **92 C5** 3 55N 67 52W
Inishbofin, *Ireland* **13 C1** 53 37N 10 13W
Inisheer, *Ireland* **13 C2** 53 3N 9 32W
Inishfree B., *Ireland* **13 A3** 55 4N 8 23W
Inishkea North, *Ireland* **13 B1** 54 9N 10 11W
Inishkea South, *Ireland* **13 B1** 54 7N 10 12W
Inishmaan, *Ireland* **13 C2** 53 5N 9 35W
Inishmore, *Ireland* **13 C2** 53 8N 9 45W
Inishowen Pen., *Ireland* **13 A4** 55 14N 7 15W
Inishshark, *Ireland* **13 C1** 53 37N 10 16W
Inishturk, *Ireland* **13 C1** 53 42N 10 7W
Inishvickillane, *Ireland* **13 D1** 52 3N 10 37W
Injune, *Australia* **63 D4** 25 53S 148 32 E
Inklin →, *Canada* **72 B2** 58 50N 133 10W
Inle L., *Burma* **41 J20** 20 30N 96 58 E
Inlet, *U.S.A.* **79 C10** 43 45N 74 48W
Inn →, *Austria* **16 D7** 48 35N 13 28 E
Innamincka, *Australia* **63 D3** 27 44S 140 46 E
Inner Hebrides, *U.K.* **12 E2** 57 0N 6 30W
Inner Mongolia = Nei Monggol Zizhiqu □, *China* **34 D7** 42 0N 112 0 E
Inner Sound, *U.K.* **12 D3** 57 30N 5 55W
Innerkip, *Canada* **78 C4** 43 13N 80 42W
Innetalling I., *Canada* **70 A4** 56 0N 79 0W
Innisfail, *Australia* **62 B4** 17 33S 146 5 E
Innisfail, *Canada* **72 C6** 52 0N 113 57W
In'no-shima, *Japan* **31 G6** 34 19N 133 10 E
Innsbruck, *Austria* **16 E6** 47 16N 11 23 E
Inny →, *Ireland* **13 C4** 53 30N 7 50W
Inongo, *Dem. Rep. of the Congo* **52 E3** 1 55S 18 30 E
Inoucdjouac = Inukjuak, *Canada* **69 C12** 58 25N 78 15W
Inowrocław, *Poland* **17 B10** 52 50N 18 12 E
Inpundong, *N. Korea* **35 D14** 41 25N 126 34 E
Inscription, C., *Australia* **61 E1** 25 29S 112 59 E
Insein, *Burma* **41 L20** 16 50N 96 5 E
Inta, *Russia* **24 A11** 66 5N 60 8 E
Intendente Alvear, *Argentina* **94 D3** 35 12S 63 32W
Interlaken, *Switz.* **18 C7** 46 41N 7 50 E
Interlaken, *U.S.A.* **79 D8** 42 37N 76 44W
International Falls, *U.S.A.* **80 A8** 48 36N 93 25W
Intiyaco, *Argentina* **94 B3** 28 43S 60 5W
Inukjuak, *Canada* **69 C12** 58 25N 78 15W
Inútil, B., *Chile* **96 G2** 53 30S 70 15W
Inuvik, *Canada* **68 B6** 68 16N 133 40W
Inveraray, *U.K.* **12 E3** 56 14N 5 5W
Inverbervie, *U.K.* **12 E6** 56 51N 2 17W
Invercargill, *N.Z.* **59 M2** 46 24S 168 24 E
Inverclyde □, *U.K.* **12 F4** 55 55N 4 49W
Inverell, *Australia* **63 D5** 29 45S 151 8 E
Invergordon, *U.K.* **12 D4** 57 41N 4 10W
Inverloch, *Australia* **63 F4** 38 38S 145 45 E
Invermere, *Canada* **72 C5** 50 30N 116 2W
Inverness, *Canada* **71 C7** 46 15N 61 19W
Inverness, *U.K.* **12 D4** 57 29N 4 13W
Inverness, *U.S.A.* **77 L4** 28 50N 82 20W
Inverurie, *U.K.* **12 D6** 57 17N 2 23W
Investigator Group, *Australia* **63 E1** 34 45S 134 20 E
Investigator Str., *Australia* **63 F2** 35 30S 137 0 E
Inya, *Russia* **26 D9** 50 28N 86 37 E
Inyanga, *Zimbabwe* **55 F3** 18 12S 32 40 E
Inyangani, *Zimbabwe* **55 F3** 18 5S 32 50 E
Inyantue, *Zimbabwe* **55 F2** 18 30S 26 40 E
Inyo Mts., *U.S.A.* **84 J9** 36 40N 118 0W
Inyokern, *U.S.A.* **85 K9** 35 39N 117 49W
Inza, *Russia* **24 D8** 53 55N 46 25 E
Iō-Jima, *Japan* **31 J5** 30 48N 130 18 E
Ioánnina, *Greece* **21 E9** 39 42N 20 47 E
Iola, *U.S.A.* **81 G7** 37 55N 95 24W
Iona, *U.K.* **12 E2** 56 20N 6 25W
Ione, *U.S.A.* **84 G6** 38 21N 120 56W
Ionia, *U.S.A.* **76 D3** 42 59N 85 4W
Ionian Is. = Iónioi Nísoi, *Greece* **21 E9** 38 40N 20 0 E
Ionian Sea, *Medit. S.* **21 E7** 37 30N 17 30 E
Iónioi Nísoi, *Greece* **21 E9** 38 40N 20 0 E
Íos, *Greece* **21 F11** 36 41N 25 20 E
Iowa □, *U.S.A.* **80 D8** 42 18N 93 30W
Iowa →, *U.S.A.* **80 E9** 41 10N 91 1W
Iowa City, *U.S.A.* **80 E9** 41 40N 91 32W
Iowa Falls, *U.S.A.* **80 D8** 42 31N 93 16W
Iowa Park, *U.S.A.* **81 J5** 33 57N 98 40W
Ipala, *Tanzania* **54 C3** 4 30S 32 52 E
Ipameri, *Brazil* **93 G9** 17 44S 48 9W
Ipatinga, *Brazil* **93 G10** 19 32S 42 30W
Ipiales, *Colombia* **92 C3** 0 50N 77 37W
Ipin = Yibin, *China* **32 D5** 28 45N 104 32 E
Ipixuna, *Brazil* **92 E4** 7 0S 71 40W
Ipoh, *Malaysia* **39 K3** 4 35N 101 5 E
Ippy, *C.A.R.* **52 C4** 6 5N 21 7 E
İpsala, *Turkey* **21 D12** 40 55N 26 23 E
Ipswich, *Australia* **63 D5** 27 35S 152 40 E
Ipswich, *U.K.* **11 E9** 52 4N 1 10 E
Ipswich, *Mass., U.S.A.* **79 D14** 42 41N 70 50W
Ipswich, *S. Dak., U.S.A.* **80 C5** 45 27N 99 2W
Ipu, *Brazil* **93 D10** 4 23S 40 44W
Iqaluit, *Canada* **69 B13** 63 44N 68 31W
Iquique, *Chile* **92 H4** 20 19S 70 5W
Iquitos, *Peru* **92 D4** 3 45S 73 10W
Irabu-Jima, *Japan* **31 M2** 24 50N 125 10 E
Iracoubo, *Fr. Guiana* **93 B8** 5 30N 53 10W
Īrafshān, *Iran* **45 E9** 26 42N 61 56 E
Iráklion, *Greece* **23 D7** 35 20N 25 12 E
Iráklion □, *Greece* **23 D7** 35 10N 25 10 E
Irala, *Paraguay* **95 B5** 25 55S 54 35W
Iran ■, *Asia* **45 C7** 33 0N 53 0 E
Iran, Gunung-Gunung, *Malaysia* **36 D4** 2 20N 114 50 E
Iran, Plateau of, *Asia* **28 F9** 32 0N 55 0 E
Iran Ra. = Iran, Gunung-Gunung, *Malaysia* **36 D4** 2 20N 114 50 E
Īrānshahr, *Iran* **45 E9** 27 15N 60 40 E
Irapuato, *Mexico* **86 C4** 20 40N 101 30W
Iraq ■, *Asia* **44 C5** 33 0N 44 0 E
Irati, *Brazil* **95 B5** 25 25S 50 38W
Irbid, *Jordan* **47 C4** 32 35N 35 48 E
Irbid □, *Jordan* **47 C5** 32 15N 36 35 E
Ireland ■, *Europe* **13 C4** 53 50N 7 52W
Irhyangdong, *N. Korea* **35 D15** 41 15N 129 30 E
Iri, *S. Korea* **35 G14** 35 59N 127 0 E
Irian Jaya □, *Indonesia* **37 E9** 4 0S 137 0 E
Iringa, *Tanzania* **54 D4** 7 48S 35 43 E
Iringa □, *Tanzania* **54 D4** 7 48S 35 43 E
Iriomote-Jima, *Japan* **31 M1** 24 19N 123 48 E
Iriona, *Honduras* **88 C2** 15 57N 85 11W
Iriri →, *Brazil* **93 D8** 3 52S 52 37W
Irish Republic ■, *Europe* **13 C3** 53 0N 8 0W
Irish Sea, *U.K.* **10 D3** 53 38N 4 48W
Irkutsk, *Russia* **27 D11** 52 18N 104 20 E
Irma, *Canada* **73 C6** 52 55N 111 14W
Irō-Zaki, *Japan* **31 G9** 34 36N 138 51 E
Iron Baron, *Australia* **63 E2** 32 58S 137 11 E
Iron Gate = Portile de Fier, *Europe* **17 F12** 44 44N 22 30 E
Iron Knob, *Australia* **63 E2** 32 46S 137 8 E
Iron Mountain, *U.S.A.* **76 C1** 45 49N 88 4W
Iron River, *U.S.A.* **80 B10** 46 6N 88 39W
Irondequoit, *U.S.A.* **78 C7** 43 13N 77 35W
Ironstone Kopje, *Botswana* **56 D3** 25 17S 24 5 E
Ironton, *Mo., U.S.A.* **81 G9** 37 36N 90 38W
Ironton, *Ohio, U.S.A.* **76 F4** 38 32N 82 41W
Ironwood, *U.S.A.* **80 B9** 46 27N 90 9W
Iroquois, *Canada* **79 B9** 44 51N 75 19W
Iroquois Falls, *Canada* **70 C3** 48 46N 80 41W
Irpin, *Ukraine* **17 C16** 50 30N 30 15 E
Irrara Cr. →, *Australia* **63 D4** 29 35S 145 31 E
Irrawaddy □, *Burma* **41 L19** 17 0N 95 0 E
Irrawaddy →, *Burma* **41 M19** 15 50N 95 6 E
Irricana, *Canada* **72 C6** 51 19N 113 37W
Irtysh →, *Russia* **26 C7** 61 4N 68 52 E
Irumu, *Dem. Rep. of the Congo* **54 B2** 1 32N 29 53 E
Irún, *Spain* **19 A5** 43 20N 1 52W
Irunea = Pamplona, *Spain* **19 A5** 42 48N 1 38W
Irvine, *Canada* **73 D6** 49 57N 110 16W
Irvine, *U.K.* **12 F4** 55 37N 4 41W
Irvine, *Calif., U.S.A.* **85 M9** 33 41N 117 46W
Irvine, *Ky., U.S.A.* **76 G4** 37 42N 83 58W
Irvinestown, *U.K.* **13 B4** 54 28N 7 39W
Irving, *U.S.A.* **81 J6** 32 49N 96 56W
Irvona, *U.S.A.* **78 F6** 40 46N 78 33W
Irwin →, *Australia* **61 E1** 29 15S 114 54 E
Irymple, *Australia* **63 E3** 34 14S 142 8 E
Isa Khel, *Pakistan* **42 C4** 32 41N 71 17 E
Isaac →, *Australia* **62 C4** 22 55S 149 20 E
Isabel, *U.S.A.* **80 C4** 45 24N 101 26W
Isabela, I., *Mexico* **86 C3** 21 51N 105 55W
Isabelia, Cord., *Nic.* **88 D2** 13 30N 85 25W
Isabella, *Phil.* **37 C6** 6 40N 122 10 E
Isabella Ra., *Australia* **60 D3** 21 0S 121 4 E
Ísafjarðardjúp, *Iceland* **8 C2** 66 10N 23 0W
Ísafjörður, *Iceland* **8 C2** 66 5N 23 9W
Isagarh, *India* **42 G7** 24 48N 77 51 E
Isahaya, *Japan* **31 H5** 32 52N 130 2 E
Isaka, *Tanzania* **54 C3** 3 56S 32 59 E
Isan →, *India* **43 F9** 26 51N 80 7 E
Isana = Içana →, *Brazil* **92 C5** 0 26N 67 19W
Isar →, *Germany* **16 D7** 48 48N 12 57 E
Íschia, *Italy* **20 D5** 40 44N 13 57 E
Isdell →, *Australia* **60 C3** 16 27S 124 51 E
Ise, *Japan* **31 G8** 34 25N 136 45 E
Ise-Wan, *Japan* **31 G8** 34 43N 136 43 E
Iseramagazi, *Tanzania* **54 C3** 4 37S 32 10 E
Isère →, *France* **18 D6** 44 59N 4 51 E
Isérnia, *Italy* **20 D6** 41 36N 14 14 E
Isfahan = Eşfahān, *Iran* **45 C6** 32 39N 51 43 E
Ishigaki-Shima, *Japan* **31 M2** 24 20N 124 10 E
Ishikari-Gawa →, *Japan* **30 C10** 43 15N 141 23 E
Ishikari-Sammyaku, *Japan* **30 C11** 43 30N 143 0 E
Ishikari-Wan, *Japan* **30 C10** 43 25N 141 1 E
Ishikawa □, *Japan* **31 F8** 36 30N 136 30 E
Ishim, *Russia* **26 D7** 56 10N 69 30 E
Ishim →, *Russia* **26 D8** 57 45N 71 10 E
Ishinomaki, *Japan* **30 E10** 38 32N 141 20 E
Ishioka, *Japan* **31 F10** 36 11N 140 16 E
Ishkuman, *Pakistan* **43 A5** 36 30N 73 50 E
Ishpeming, *U.S.A.* **76 B2** 46 29N 87 40W
Isil Kul, *Russia* **26 D8** 54 55N 71 16 E
Isiolo, *Kenya* **54 B4** 0 24N 37 33 E
Isiro, *Dem. Rep. of the Congo* **54 B2** 2 53N 27 40 E
Isisford, *Australia* **62 C3** 24 15S 144 21 E
İskenderun, *Turkey* **25 G6** 36 32N 36 10 E
İskenderun Körfezi, *Turkey* **25 G6** 36 40N 35 50 E
Iskŭr →, *Bulgaria* **21 C11** 43 45N 24 25 E
Iskut →, *Canada* **72 B2** 56 45N 131 49W
Isla →, *U.K.* **12 E5** 56 32N 3 20W
Isla Vista, *U.S.A.* **85 L7** 34 25N 119 53W
Islam Headworks, *Pakistan* **42 E5** 29 49N 72 33 E
Islamabad, *Pakistan* **42 C5** 33 40N 73 10 E
Islamgarh, *Pakistan* **42 F4** 27 51N 70 48 E
Islamkot, *Pakistan* **42 G4** 24 42N 70 13 E
Islampur, *India* **43 G11** 25 9N 85 12 E
Island L., *Canada* **73 C10** 53 47N 94 25W
Island Lagoon, *Australia* **63 E2** 31 30S 136 40 E
Island Pond, *U.S.A.* **79 B13** 44 49N 71 53W
Islands, B. of, *Canada* **71 C8** 49 11N 58 15W
Islay, *U.K.* **12 F2** 55 46N 6 10W
Isle →, *France* **18 D3** 44 55N 0 15W
Isle aux Morts, *Canada* **71 C8** 47 35N 59 0W
Isle of Wight □, *U.K.* **11 G6** 50 41N 1 17W
Isle Royale, *U.S.A.* **80 B10** 48 0N 88 54W
Isle Royale National Park, *U.S.A.* **80 B10** 48 0N 88 55W
Isleton, *U.S.A.* **84 G5** 38 10N 121 37W
Ismail = Izmayil, *Ukraine* **17 F15** 45 22N 28 46 E
Ismâ'ilîya, *Egypt* **51 B12** 30 37N 32 18 E
Isogstalo, *India* **43 B8** 34 15N 78 46 E
Isparta, *Turkey* **25 G5** 37 47N 30 30 E
Íspica, *Italy* **20 F6** 36 47N 14 55 E
Israel ■, *Asia* **47 D3** 32 0N 34 50 E
Issoire, *France* **18 D5** 45 32N 3 15 E
Issyk-Kul = Ysyk-Köl, *Kyrgyzstan* **28 E11** 42 26N 76 12 E
Issyk-Kul, Ozero = Ysyk-Köl, Ozero, *Kyrgyzstan* **26 E8** 42 25N 77 15 E
İstanbul, *Turkey* **21 D13** 41 0N 29 0 E
İstanbul Boğazı, *Turkey* **21 D13** 41 10N 29 10 E
Istiaía, *Greece* **21 E10** 38 57N 23 9 E
Istokpoga, L., *U.S.A.* **77 M5** 27 23N 81 17W
Istra, *Croatia* **16 F7** 45 10N 14 0 E
Istres, *France* **18 E6** 43 31N 4 59 E
Istria = Istra, *Croatia* **16 F7** 45 10N 14 0 E
Itá, *Paraguay* **94 B4** 25 29S 57 21W
Itaberaba, *Brazil* **93 F10** 12 32S 40 18W
Itabira, *Brazil* **93 G10** 19 37S 43 13W
Itabirito, *Brazil* **95 A7** 20 15S 43 48W
Itabuna, *Brazil* **93 F11** 14 48S 39 16W
Itacaunas →, *Brazil* **93 E9** 5 21S 49 8W
Itacoatiara, *Brazil* **92 D7** 3 8S 58 25W
Itaipú, Représa de, *Brazil* **95 B5** 25 30S 54 30W
Itaituba, *Brazil* **93 D7** 4 10S 55 50W
Itajaí, *Brazil* **95 B6** 27 50S 48 39W
Itajubá, *Brazil* **95 A6** 22 24S 45 30W
Itaka, *Tanzania* **55 D3** 8 50S 32 49 E
Italy ■, *Europe* **20 C5** 42 0N 13 0 E
Itamaraju, *Brazil* **93 G11** 17 5S 39 31W
Itampolo, *Madag.* **57 C7** 24 41S 43 57 E
Itapecuru-Mirim, *Brazil* **93 D10** 3 24S 44 20W
Itaperuna, *Brazil* **95 A7** 21 10S 41 54W
Itapetininga, *Brazil* **95 A6** 23 36S 48 7W
Itapeva, *Brazil* **95 A6** 23 59S 48 59W
Itapicuru →, *Bahia, Brazil* **93 F11** 11 47S 37 32W
Itapicuru →, *Maranhão, Brazil* **93 D10** 2 52S 44 12W
Itapipoca, *Brazil* **93 D11** 3 30S 39 35W
Itapuá □, *Paraguay* **95 B4** 26 40S 55 40W
Itaquari, *Brazil* **95 A7** 20 20S 40 25W
Itaquí, *Brazil* **94 B4** 29 8S 56 30W
Itararé, *Brazil* **95 A6** 24 6S 49 23W
Itarsi, *India* **42 H7** 22 36N 77 51 E
Itatí, *Argentina* **94 B4** 27 16S 58 15W
Itchen →, *U.K.* **11 G6** 50 55N 1 22W
Itezhi Tezhi, L., *Zambia* **55 F2** 15 30S 25 30 E
Ithaca = Itháki, *Greece* **21 E9** 38 25N 20 40 E
Ithaca, *U.S.A.* **79 D8** 42 27N 76 30W
Itháki, *Greece* **21 E9** 38 25N 20 40 E
Itiquira →, *Brazil* **93 G7** 17 18S 56 44W
Ito, *Japan* **31 G9** 34 58N 139 5 E
Ito Aba I., *S. China Sea* **36 B4** 10 23N 114 21 E
Itoigawa, *Japan* **31 F8** 37 2N 137 51 E
Itonamas →, *Bolivia* **92 F6** 12 28S 64 24W
Ittoqqortoormiit = Scoresbysund, *Greenland* **4 B6** 70 20N 23 0W
Itu, *Brazil* **95 A6** 23 17S 47 15W
Ituiutaba, *Brazil* **93 G9** 19 0S 49 25W
Itumbiara, *Brazil* **93 G9** 18 20S 49 10W
Ituna, *Canada* **73 C8** 51 10N 103 24W
Itunge Port, *Tanzania* **55 D3** 9 40S 33 55 E
Iturbe, *Argentina* **94 A2** 23 0S 65 25W
Ituri →, *Dem. Rep. of the Congo* **54 B2** 1 40N 27 1 E
Iturup, Ostrov, *Russia* **27 E15** 45 0N 148 0 E
Ituxi →, *Brazil* **92 E6** 7 18S 64 51W
Ituyuro →, *Argentina* **94 A3** 22 40S 63 50W
Itzehoe, *Germany* **16 B5** 53 55N 9 31 E
Ivaí →, *Brazil* **95 A5** 23 18S 53 42W
Ivalo, *Finland* **8 B22** 68 38N 27 35 E
Ivalojoki →, *Finland* **8 B22** 68 40N 27 40 E
Ivanava, *Belarus* **17 B13** 52 7N 25 29 E
Ivanhoe, *Australia* **63 E3** 32 56S 144 20 E
Ivanhoe, *Calif., U.S.A.* **84 J7** 36 23N 119 13W
Ivanhoe, *Minn., U.S.A.* **80 C6** 44 28N 96 15W
Ivano-Frankivsk, *Ukraine* **17 D13** 48 40N 24 40 E
Ivano-Frankovsk = Ivano-Frankivsk, *Ukraine* **17 D13** 48 40N 24 40 E
Ivanovo = Ivanava, *Belarus* **17 B13** 52 7N 25 29 E
Ivanovo, *Russia* **24 C7** 57 5N 41 0 E
Ivato, *Madag.* **57 C8** 20 37S 47 10 E
Ivatsevichy, *Belarus* **17 B13** 52 43N 25 21 E
Ivdel, *Russia* **24 B11** 60 42N 60 24 E
Ivindo →, *Gabon* **52 D2** 0 9S 12 9 E
Ivinheima →, *Brazil* **95 A5** 23 14S 53 42W
Ivinhema, *Brazil* **95 A5** 22 10S 53 37W
Ivohibe, *Madag.* **57 C8** 22 31S 46 57 E
Ivory Coast, *Africa* **50 H4** 5 0N 5 0W
Ivory Coast ■, *Africa* **50 G4** 7 30N 5 0W
Ivrea, *Italy* **18 D7** 45 28N 7 52 E
Ivujivik, *Canada* **69 B12** 62 24N 77 55W
Ivybridge, *U.K.* **11 G4** 50 23N 3 56W
Iwaizumi, *Japan* **30 E10** 39 50N 141 45 E
Iwaki, *Japan* **31 F10** 37 3N 140 55 E
Iwakuni, *Japan* **31 G6** 34 15N 132 8 E
Iwamizawa, *Japan* **30 C10** 43 12N 141 46 E
Iwanai, *Japan* **30 C10** 42 58N 140 30 E
Iwata, *Japan* **31 G8** 34 42N 137 51 E
Iwate □, *Japan* **30 E10** 39 30N 141 30 E
Iwate-San, *Japan* **30 E10** 39 51N 141 0 E
Iwo, *Nigeria* **50 G6** 7 39N 4 9 E
Ixiamas, *Bolivia* **92 F5** 13 50S 68 5W
Ixopo, *S. Africa* **57 E5** 30 11S 30 5 E
Ixtepec, *Mexico* **87 D5** 16 32N 95 10W
Ixtlán del Río, *Mexico* **86 C4** 21 5N 104 21W
Iyo, *Japan* **31 H6** 33 45N 132 45 E
Izabal, L. de, *Guatemala* **88 C2** 15 30N 89 10W
Izamal, *Mexico* **87 C7** 20 56N 89 1W
Izena-Shima, *Japan* **31 L3** 26 56N 127 56 E
Izhevsk, *Russia* **24 C9** 56 51N 53 14 E
Izhma →, *Russia* **24 A9** 65 19N 52 54 E
Izmayil, *Ukraine* **17 F15** 45 22N 28 46 E
İzmir, *Turkey* **21 E12** 38 25N 27 8 E
İzmit = Kocaeli, *Turkey* **25 F4** 40 45N 29 50 E
İznik Gölü, *Turkey* **21 D13** 40 27N 29 30 E
Izra, *Syria* **47 C5** 32 51N 36 15 E
Izu-Shotō, *Japan* **31 G10** 34 30N 140 0 E
Izúcar de Matamoros, *Mexico* **87 D5** 18 36N 98 28W
Izumi-sano, *Japan* **31 G7** 34 23N 135 18 E
Izumo, *Japan* **31 G6** 35 20N 132 46 E
Izyaslav, *Ukraine* **17 C14** 50 5N 26 50 E

J

Jabalpur, *India* **43 H8** 23 9N 79 58 E
Jabbūl, *Syria* **44 B3** 36 4N 37 30 E
Jabiru, *Australia* **60 B5** 12 40S 132 53 E
Jablah, *Syria* **44 C3** 35 20N 36 0 E
Jablonec nad Nisou, *Czech Rep.* **16 C8** 50 43N 15 10 E
Jaboatão, *Brazil* **93 E11** 8 7S 35 1W
Jaboticabal, *Brazil* **95 A6** 21 15S 48 17W
Jaca, *Spain* **19 A5** 42 35N 0 33W
Jacareí, *Brazil* **95 A6** 23 20S 46 0W
Jacarèzinho, *Brazil* **95 A6** 23 5S 49 58W
Jackman, *U.S.A.* **77 C10** 45 35N 70 17W
Jacksboro, *U.S.A.* **81 J5** 33 14N 98 15W
Jackson, *Ala., U.S.A.* **77 K2** 31 31N 87 53W
Jackson, *Calif., U.S.A.* **84 G6** 38 21N 120 46W
Jackson, *Ky., U.S.A.* **76 G4** 37 33N 83 23W
Jackson, *Mich., U.S.A.* **76 D3** 42 15N 84 24W
Jackson, *Minn., U.S.A.* **80 D7** 43 37N 95 1W
Jackson, *Miss., U.S.A.* **81 J9** 32 18N 90 12W
Jackson, *Mo., U.S.A.* **81 G10** 37 23N 89 40W
Jackson, *N.H., U.S.A.* **79 B13** 44 10N 71 11W
Jackson, *Ohio, U.S.A.* **76 F4** 39 3N 82 39W
Jackson, *Tenn., U.S.A.* **77 H1** 35 37N 88 49W
Jackson, *Wyo., U.S.A.* **82 E8** 43 29N 110 46W
Jackson B., *N.Z.* **59 K2** 43 58S 168 42 E
Jackson L., *U.S.A.* **82 E8** 43 52N 110 36W
Jacksons, *N.Z.* **59 K3** 42 46S 171 32 E
Jackson's Arm, *Canada* **71 C8** 49 52N 56 47W
Jacksonville, *Ala., U.S.A.* **77 J3** 33 49N 85 46W
Jacksonville, *Ark., U.S.A.* **81 H8** 34 52N 92 7W
Jacksonville, *Calif., U.S.A.* **84 H6** 37 52N 120 24W
Jacksonville, *Fla., U.S.A.* **77 K5** 30 20N 81 39W
Jacksonville, *Ill., U.S.A.* **80 F9** 39 44N 90 14W
Jacksonville, *N.C., U.S.A.* **77 H7** 34 45N 77 26W
Jacksonville, *Tex., U.S.A.* **81 K7** 31 58N 95 17W
Jacksonville Beach, *U.S.A.* **77 K5** 30 17N 81 24W
Jacmel, *Haiti* **89 C5** 18 14N 72 32W
Jacob Lake, *U.S.A.* **83 H7** 36 43N 112 13W
Jacobabad, *Pakistan* **42 E3** 28 20N 68 29 E
Jacobina, *Brazil* **93 F10** 11 11S 40 30W
Jacques Cartier, Dét. de, *Canada* **71 C7** 50 0N 63 30W
Jacques-Cartier, Mt., *Canada* **71 C6** 48 57N 66 0W
Jacques Cartier, Parc Prov., *Canada* **71 C5** 47 15N 71 33W
Jacuí →, *Brazil* **95 C5** 30 2S 51 15W
Jacumba, *U.S.A.* **85 N10** 32 37N 116 11W
Jacundá →, *Brazil* **93 D8** 1 57S 50 26W
Jadotville = Likasi, *Dem. Rep. of the Congo* **55 E2** 10 55S 26 48 E
Jaén, *Peru* **92 E3** 5 25S 78 40W
Jaén, *Spain* **19 D4** 37 44N 3 43W
Jafarabad, *India* **42 J4** 20 52N 71 22 E
Jaffa = Tel Aviv-Yafo, *Israel* **47 C3** 32 4N 34 48 E
Jaffa, C., *Australia* **63 F2** 36 58S 139 40 E
Jaffna, *Sri Lanka* **40 Q12** 9 45N 80 2 E
Jaffrey, *U.S.A.* **79 D12** 42 49N 72 2W
Jagadhri, *India* **42 D7** 30 10N 77 20 E
Jagadishpur, *India* **43 G11** 25 30N 84 21 E
Jagdalpur, *India* **41 K13** 19 3N 82 0 E
Jagersfontein, *S. Africa* **56 D4** 29 44S 25 27 E
Jaghīn →, *Iran* **45 E8** 27 17N 57 13 E
Jagodina, *Serbia, Yug.* **21 C9** 44 5N 21 15 E
Jagraon, *India* **40 D9** 30 50N 75 25 E
Jagtial, *India* **40 K11** 18 50N 79 0 E
Jaguariaíva, *Brazil* **95 A6** 24 10S 49 50W
Jaguaribe →, *Brazil* **93 D11** 4 25S 37 45W
Jagüey Grande, *Cuba* **88 B3** 22 35N 81 7W
Jahanabad, *India* **43 G11** 25 13N 84 59 E
Jahazpur, *India* **42 G6** 25 37N 75 17 E
Jahrom, *Iran* **45 D7** 28 30N 53 31 E
Jaijon, *India* **42 D7** 31 21N 76 9 E
Jailolo, *Indonesia* **37 D7** 1 5N 127 30 E
Jailolo, Selat, *Indonesia* **37 D7** 0 5N 129 5 E
Jaipur, *India* **42 F6** 27 0N 75 50 E
Jais, *India* **43 F9** 26 15N 81 32 E
Jaisalmer, *India* **42 F4** 26 55N 70 54 E
Jaisinghnagar, *India* **43 H8** 23 38N 78 34 E
Jaitaran, *India* **42 F5** 26 12N 73 56 E
Jaithari, *India* **43 H8** 23 14N 78 37 E
Jājarm, *Iran* **45 B8** 36 58N 56 27 E
Jakam →, *India* **42 H6** 23 54N 74 13 E
Jakarta, *Indonesia* **37 G12** 6 9S 106 49 E
Jakhal, *India* **42 E6** 29 48N 75 50 E
Jakhau, *India* **42 H3** 23 13N 68 43 E
Jakobstad = Pietarsaari, *Finland* **8 E20** 63 40N 22 43 E
Jal, *U.S.A.* **81 J3** 32 7N 103 12W
Jalalabad, *Afghan.* **42 B4** 34 30N 70 29 E
Jalalabad, *India* **43 F8** 27 41N 79 42 E
Jalalpur Jattan, *Pakistan* **42 C6** 32 38N 74 11 E
Jalama, *U.S.A.* **85 L6** 34 29N 120 29W
Jalapa, *Guatemala* **88 D2** 14 39N 89 59W
Jalapa Enríquez, *Mexico* **87 D5** 19 32N 96 55W
Jalasjärvi, *Finland* **9 E20** 62 29N 22 47 E
Jalaun, *India* **43 F8** 26 8N 79 25 E
Jaldhaka →, *Bangla.* **43 F13** 26 16N 89 16 E
Jalesar, *India* **42 F8** 27 29N 78 19 E
Jaleswar, *Nepal* **43 F11** 26 38N 85 48 E
Jalgaon, *Maharashtra, India* **40 J10** 21 2N 76 31 E
Jalgaon, *Maharashtra, India* **40 J9** 21 0N 75 42 E
Jalībah, *Iraq* **44 D5** 30 35N 46 32 E
Jalisco □, *Mexico* **86 D4** 20 0N 104 0W
Jalkot, *Pakistan* **43 B5** 35 14N 73 24 E
Jalna, *India* **40 K9** 19 48N 75 38 E
Jalón →, *Spain* **19 B5** 41 47N 1 4W
Jalor, *India* **42 G5** 25 21N 72 37 E
Jalpa, *Mexico* **86 C4** 21 38N 102 58W
Jalpaiguri, *India* **41 F16** 26 32N 88 46 E
Jaluit I., *Marshall Is.* **64 G8** 6 0N 169 30 E

Juruena

Jalūlā, Iraq 44 C5 34 16N 45 10 E
Jamaica ■, W. Indies 88 C4 18 10N 77 30W
Jamalpur, Bangla. 41 G16 24 52N 89 56 E
Jamalpur, India 43 G12 25 18N 86 28 E
Jamalpurganj, India 43 H13 23 2N 87 59 E
Jamanxim →, Brazil 93 D7 4 43S 56 18W
Jambi, Indonesia 36 E2 1 38S 103 30 E
Jambi □, Indonesia 36 E2 1 30S 102 30 E
Jambusar, India 42 H5 22 3N 72 51 E
James →, S. Dak., U.S.A. 80 D6 42 52N 97 18W
James →, Va., U.S.A. 76 G7 36 56N 76 27W
James B., Canada 70 B3 54 0N 80 0W
James Ranges, Australia 60 D5 24 10S 132 30 E
James Ross I., Antarctica 5 C18 63 58S 57 50W
Jamesabad, Pakistan 42 G3 25 17N 69 15 E
Jamestown, Australia 63 E2 33 10S 138 32 E
Jamestown, S. Africa 56 E4 31 6S 26 45 E
Jamestown, N. Dak., U.S.A. 80 B5 46 54N 98 42W
Jamestown, N.Y., U.S.A. 78 D5 42 6N 79 14W
Jamestown, Pa., U.S.A. 78 E4 41 29N 80 27W
Jamīlābād, Iran 45 C6 34 24N 48 28 E
Jamiltepec, Mexico 87 D5 16 17N 97 49W
Jamira →, India 43 J13 21 35N 88 28 E
Jamkhandi, India 40 L9 16 30N 75 15 E
Jammu, India 42 C6 32 43N 74 54 E
Jammu & Kashmir □, India 43 B7 34 25N 77 0 E
Jamnagar, India 42 H4 22 30N 70 6 E
Jamni →, India 43 G8 25 13N 78 35 E
Jampur, Pakistan 42 E4 29 39N 70 40 E
Jamrud, Pakistan 42 C4 33 59N 71 24 E
Jämsä, Finland 9 F21 61 53N 25 10 E
Jamshedpur, India 43 H12 22 44N 86 12 E
Jamtara, India 43 H12 23 59N 86 49 E
Jämtland, Sweden 8 E15 63 31N 14 0 E
Jan L., Canada 73 C8 54 56N 102 55W
Jan Mayen, Arctic 4 B7 71 0N 9 0W
Janakkala, Finland 9 F21 60 54N 24 36 E
Janaúba, Brazil 93 G10 15 48S 43 19W
Jand, Pakistan 42 C5 33 30N 72 6 E
Jandaq, Iran 45 C7 34 3N 54 22 E
Jandia, Canary Is. 22 F5 28 6N 14 21W
Jandia, Pta. de, Canary Is. 22 F5 28 3N 14 31W
Jandola, Pakistan 42 C4 32 20N 70 9 E
Jandowae, Australia 63 D5 26 45S 151 7 E
Janesville, U.S.A. 80 D10 42 41N 89 1W
Janghai, India 43 G10 25 33N 82 19 E
Janīn, West Bank 47 C4 32 28N 35 18 E
Janjgir, India 43 J10 22 1N 82 34 E
Janos, Mexico 86 A3 30 45N 108 10W
Januária, Brazil 93 G10 15 25S 44 25W
Janubio, Canary Is. 22 F6 28 56N 13 50W
Jaora, India 42 H6 23 40N 75 10 E
Japan ■, Asia 31 G8 36 0N 136 0 E
Japan, Sea of, Asia 30 E7 40 0N 135 0 E
Japan Trench, Pac. Oc. 28 F18 32 0N 142 0 E
Japen = Yapen, Indonesia 37 E9 1 50S 136 0 E
Japla, India 43 G11 24 33N 84 1 E
Japurá →, Brazil 92 D5 3 8S 65 46W
Jaquarão, Brazil 95 C5 32 34S 53 23W
Jaqué, Panama 88 E4 7 27N 78 8W
Jarābulus, Syria 44 B3 36 49N 38 1 E
Jarama →, Spain 19 B4 40 24N 3 32W
Jaranwala, Pakistan 42 D5 31 15N 73 26 E
Jarash, Jordan 47 C4 32 17N 35 54 E
Jardim, Brazil 94 A4 21 28S 56 2W
Jardines de la Reina, Arch. de los, Cuba 88 B4 20 50N 78 50W
Jargalang, China 35 C12 43 5N 122 55 E
Jargalant = Hovd, Mongolia 32 B4 48 2N 91 37 E
Jari →, Brazil 93 D8 1 9S 51 54W
Jarīr, W. al →, Si. Arabia 44 E4 25 38N 42 30 E
Jarosław, Poland 17 C12 50 2N 22 42 E
Jarrahdale, Australia 61 F2 32 24S 116 5 E
Jarrahi →, Iran 45 D6 30 49N 48 48 E
Jarres, Plaine des, Laos 38 C4 19 27N 103 10 E
Jartai, China 34 E3 39 45N 105 48 E
Jarud Qi, China 35 B11 44 28N 120 50 E
Järvenpää, Finland 9 F21 60 29N 25 5 E
Jarvis, Canada 78 D4 42 53N 80 6W
Jarvis I., Pac. Oc. 65 H12 0 15S 159 55W
Jarwa, India 43 F10 27 38N 82 30 E
Jasdan, India 42 H4 22 2N 71 12 E
Jashpurnagar, India 43 H11 22 54N 84 9 E
Jasidih, India 43 G12 24 31N 86 39 E
Jāsimīyah, Iraq 44 C5 33 45N 44 41 E
Jasin, Malaysia 39 L4 2 20N 102 26 E
Jāsk, Iran 45 E8 25 38N 57 45 E
Jasło, Poland 17 D11 49 45N 21 30 E
Jaso, India 43 G9 24 30N 80 29 E
Jasper, Alta., Canada 72 C5 52 55N 118 5W
Jasper, Ont., Canada 79 B9 44 52N 75 57W
Jasper, Ala., U.S.A. 77 J2 33 50N 87 17W
Jasper, Fla., U.S.A. 77 K4 30 31N 82 57W
Jasper, Ind., U.S.A. 76 F2 38 24N 86 56W
Jasper, Tex., U.S.A. 81 K8 30 56N 94 1W
Jasper Nat. Park, Canada 72 C5 52 50N 118 8W
Jasrasar, India 42 F5 27 43N 73 49 E
Jászberény, Hungary 17 E10 47 30N 19 55 E
Jataí, Brazil 93 G8 17 58S 51 48W
Jati, Pakistan 42 G3 24 20N 68 19 E
Jatibarang, Indonesia 37 G13 6 28S 108 18 E
Jatinegara, Indonesia 37 G12 6 13S 106 52 E
Játiva = Xátiva, Spain 19 C5 38 59N 0 32W
Jaú, Brazil 95 A6 22 10S 48 30W
Jauja, Peru 92 F3 11 45S 75 15W
Jaunpur, India 43 G10 25 46N 82 44 E
Java = Jawa, Indonesia 37 G14 7 0S 110 0 E
Java Barat □, Indonesia 37 G12 7 0S 107 0 E
Java Sea, Indonesia 36 E3 4 35S 107 15 E
Java Tengah □, Indonesia 37 G14 7 0S 110 0 E
Java Timur □, Indonesia 37 G15 8 0S 113 0 E
Java Trench, Ind. Oc. 36 F3 9 0S 105 0 E
Javhlant = Uliastay, Mongolia 32 B4 47 56N 97 28 E
Jawa, Indonesia 37 G14 7 0S 110 0 E
Jawad, India 42 G6 24 36N 74 51 E
Jay Peak, U.S.A. 79 B12 44 55N 72 32W
Jaya, Puncak, Indonesia 37 E9 3 57S 137 17 E
Jayanti, India 41 F16 26 45N 89 40 E
Jayapura, Indonesia 37 E10 2 28S 140 38 E
Jayawijaya, Pegunungan, Indonesia 37 F9 5 0S 139 0 E
Jaynagar, India 41 F15 26 43N 86 9 E
Jayrūd, Syria 44 C3 33 49N 36 44 E
Jayton, U.S.A. 81 J4 33 15N 100 34W
Jāz Mūrīān, Hāmūn-e, Iran 45 E8 27 20N 58 55 E
Jazīreh-ye Shīf, Iran 45 D6 29 4N 50 54 E
Jazminal, Mexico 86 C4 24 56N 101 25W
Jazzīn, Lebanon 47 B4 33 31N 35 35 E
Jean, U.S.A. 85 K11 35 47N 115 20W
Jean Marie River, Canada 72 A4 61 32N 120 38W
Jean Rabel, Haiti 89 C5 19 50N 73 5W
Jeanerette, U.S.A. 81 L9 29 55N 91 40W
Jeanette, Ostrov = Zhannetty, Ostrov, Russia 27 B16 76 43N 158 0 E
Jeannette, U.S.A. 78 F5 40 20N 79 36W
Jebāl Bārez, Kūh-e, Iran 45 D8 28 30N 58 20 E
Jebel, Bahr el →, Sudan 51 G12 9 30N 30 25 E
Jedburgh, U.K. 12 F6 55 29N 2 33W
Jedda = Jiddah, Si. Arabia 46 C2 21 29N 39 10 E
Jeddore L., Canada 71 C8 48 3N 55 55W
Jędrzejów, Poland 17 C11 50 35N 20 15 E
Jefferson, Iowa, U.S.A. 80 D7 42 1N 94 23W
Jefferson, Ohio, U.S.A. 78 E4 41 44N 80 46W
Jefferson, Tex., U.S.A. 81 J7 32 46N 94 21W
Jefferson, Mt., Nev., U.S.A. 82 G5 38 51N 117 0W
Jefferson, Mt., Oreg., U.S.A. 82 D3 44 41N 121 48W
Jefferson City, Mo., U.S.A. 80 F8 38 34N 92 10W
Jefferson City, Tenn., U.S.A. 77 G4 36 7N 83 30W
Jeffersontown, U.S.A. 76 F3 38 12N 85 35W
Jeffersonville, U.S.A. 76 F3 38 17N 85 44W
Jeffrey City, U.S.A. 82 E10 42 30N 107 49W
Jega, Nigeria 50 F6 12 15N 4 23 E
Jēkabpils, Latvia 9 H21 56 29N 25 57 E
Jekyll I., U.S.A. 77 K5 31 4N 81 25W
Jelenia Góra, Poland 16 C8 50 50N 15 45 E
Jelgava, Latvia 9 H20 56 41N 23 49 E
Jemaja, Indonesia 39 L5 3 5N 105 45 E
Jemaluang, Malaysia 39 L4 2 16N 103 52 E
Jember, Indonesia 37 H15 8 11S 113 41 E
Jembongan, Malaysia 36 C5 6 45N 117 20 E
Jena, Germany 16 C6 50 54N 11 35 E
Jena, U.S.A. 81 K8 31 41N 92 8W
Jenkins, U.S.A. 76 G4 37 10N 82 38W
Jenner, U.S.A. 84 G3 38 27N 123 7W
Jennings, U.S.A. 81 K8 30 13N 92 40W
Jepara, Indonesia 37 G14 7 40S 109 14 E
Jeparit, Australia 63 F3 36 8S 142 1 E
Jequié, Brazil 93 F10 13 51S 40 5W
Jequitinhonha, Brazil 93 G10 16 30S 41 0W
Jequitinhonha →, Brazil 93 G11 15 51S 38 53W
Jerantut, Malaysia 39 L4 3 56N 102 22 E
Jérémie, Haiti 89 C5 18 40N 74 10W
Jerez, Punta, Mexico 87 C5 22 58N 97 40W
Jerez de García Salinas, Mexico 86 C4 22 39N 103 0W
Jerez de la Frontera, Spain 19 D2 36 41N 6 7W
Jerez de los Caballeros, Spain 19 C2 38 20N 6 45W
Jericho = El Arīḥā, West Bank 47 D4 31 52N 35 27 E
Jericho, Australia 62 C4 23 38S 146 6 E
Jerilderie, Australia 63 F4 35 20S 145 41 E
Jermyn, U.S.A. 79 E9 41 31N 75 31W
Jerome, U.S.A. 82 E6 42 44N 114 31W
Jerramungup, Australia 61 F2 33 55S 118 55 E
Jersey, U.K. 11 H5 49 11N 2 7W
Jersey City, U.S.A. 79 F10 40 44N 74 4W
Jersey Shore, U.S.A. 78 E7 41 12N 77 15W
Jerseyville, U.S.A. 80 F9 39 7N 90 20W
Jerusalem, Israel 47 D4 31 47N 35 10 E
Jervis B., Australia 63 F5 35 8S 150 46 E
Jervis Inlet, Canada 72 C4 50 0N 123 57W
Jesselton = Kota Kinabalu, Malaysia 36 C5 6 0N 116 4 E
Jessore, Bangla. 41 H16 23 10N 89 10 E
Jesup, U.S.A. 77 K5 31 36N 81 53W
Jesús Carranza, Mexico 87 D5 17 28N 95 1W
Jesús María, Argentina 94 C3 30 59S 64 5W
Jetmore, U.S.A. 81 F5 38 4N 99 54W
Jetpur, India 42 J4 21 45N 70 10 E
Jevnaker, Norway 9 F14 60 15N 10 26 E
Jewett, U.S.A. 78 F3 40 22N 81 2W
Jewett City, U.S.A. 79 E13 41 36N 72 0W
Jeyhūnābād, Iran 45 C6 34 58N 48 59 E
Jeypore, India 41 K13 18 50N 82 38 E
Jha Jha, India 43 G12 24 46N 86 22 E
Jhabua, India 42 H6 22 46N 74 36 E
Jhajjar, India 42 E7 28 37N 76 42 E
Jhal, Pakistan 42 E2 28 17N 67 27 E
Jhal Jhao, Pakistan 40 F4 26 20N 65 35 E
Jhalawar, India 42 G7 24 40N 76 10 E
Jhalida, India 43 H11 23 22N 85 58 E
Jhalrapatan, India 42 G7 24 33N 76 10 E
Jhang Maghiana, Pakistan 42 D5 31 15N 72 22 E
Jhansi, India 43 G8 25 30N 78 36 E
Jhargram, India 43 H12 22 27N 86 59 E
Jharia, India 43 H12 23 45N 86 26 E
Jharsuguda, India 41 J14 21 56N 84 5 E
Jhelum, Pakistan 42 C5 33 0N 73 45 E
Jhelum →, Pakistan 42 D5 31 20N 72 10 E
Jhilmilli, India 43 H10 23 24N 82 51 E
Jhudo, Pakistan 42 G3 24 58N 69 18 E
Jhunjhunu, India 42 E6 28 10N 75 30 E
Ji-Paraná, Brazil 92 F6 10 52S 62 57W
Ji Xian, Hebei, China 34 F8 37 35N 115 30 E
Ji Xian, Henan, China 34 G8 35 22N 114 5 E
Ji Xian, Shanxi, China 34 F6 36 7N 110 40 E
Jia Xian, Henan, China 34 H7 33 59N 113 12 E
Jia Xian, Shaanxi, China 34 E6 38 12N 110 28 E
Jiamusi, China 33 B8 46 40N 130 26 E
Ji'an, Jiangxi, China 33 D6 27 6N 114 59 E
Ji'an, Jilin, China 35 D14 41 5N 126 10 E
Jianchang, China 35 D11 40 55N 120 35 E
Jianchangying, China 35 D10 40 10N 118 50 E
Jiangcheng, China 32 D5 22 36N 101 52 E
Jiangmen, China 33 D6 22 32N 113 0 E
Jiangsu □, China 35 H11 33 0N 120 0 E
Jiangxi □, China 33 D6 27 30N 116 0 E
Jiao Xian = Jiaozhou, China 35 F11 36 18N 120 1 E
Jiaohe, Hebei, China 34 E9 38 2N 116 20 E
Jiaohe, Jilin, China 35 C14 43 40N 127 22 E
Jiaozhou, China 35 F11 36 18N 120 1 E
Jiaozhou Wan, China 35 F11 36 5N 120 10 E
Jiaozuo, China 34 G7 35 16N 113 12 E
Jiawang, China 35 G9 34 28N 117 26 E
Jiaxiang, China 34 G9 35 25N 116 20 E
Jiaxing, China 33 C7 30 49N 120 45 E
Jiayi = Chiai, Taiwan 33 D7 23 29N 120 25 E
Jibuti = Djibouti ■, Africa 46 E3 12 0N 43 0 E
Jicarón, I., Panama 88 E3 7 10N 81 50W
Jiddah, Si. Arabia 46 C2 21 29N 39 10 E
Jido, India 41 E19 29 2N 94 58 E
Jieshou, China 34 H8 33 18N 115 22 E
Jiexiu, China 34 F6 37 2N 111 55 E
Jiggalong, Australia 60 D3 23 21S 120 47 E
Jigni, India 43 G8 25 45N 79 25 E
Jihlava, Czech Rep. 16 D8 49 28N 15 35 E
Jihlava →, Czech Rep. 17 D9 48 55N 16 36 E
Jijiga, Ethiopia 46 F3 9 20N 42 50 E
Jilin, China 35 C14 43 44N 126 30 E
Jilin □, China 35 C14 44 0N 127 0 E
Jilong = Chilung, Taiwan 33 D7 25 3N 121 45 E
Jim Thorpe, U.S.A. 79 F9 40 52N 75 44W
Jima, Ethiopia 46 F2 7 40N 36 47 E
Jiménez, Mexico 86 B4 27 10N 104 54W
Jimo, China 35 F11 36 23N 120 30 E
Jin Xian = Jinzhou, China 34 E8 38 2N 115 2 E
Jin Xian, China 35 E11 38 55N 121 42 E
Jinan, China 34 F9 36 38N 117 1 E
Jincheng, China 34 G7 35 29N 112 50 E
Jind, India 42 E7 29 19N 76 22 E
Jindabyne, Australia 63 F4 36 25S 148 35 E
Jindřichův Hradec, Czech Rep. 16 D8 49 10N 15 2 E
Jing He →, China 34 G5 34 27N 109 4 E
Jingbian, China 34 F5 37 20N 108 30 E
Jingchuan, China 34 G4 35 20N 107 20 E
Jingdezhen, China 33 D6 29 20N 117 11 E
Jinggu, China 32 D5 23 35N 100 41 E
Jinghai, China 34 E9 38 55N 116 55 E
Jingle, China 34 E6 38 20N 111 55 E
Jingning, China 34 G3 35 30N 105 43 E
Jingpo Hu, China 35 C15 43 55N 128 55 E
Jingtai, China 34 F3 37 10N 104 6 E
Jingxing, China 34 E8 38 2N 114 8 E
Jingyang, China 34 G5 34 30N 108 50 E
Jingyu, China 35 C14 42 25N 126 45 E
Jingyuan, China 34 F3 36 30N 104 40 E
Jingziguan, China 34 H6 33 15N 111 0 E
Jinhua, China 33 D6 29 8N 119 38 E
Jining, Nei Mongol Zizhiqu, China 34 D7 41 5N 113 0 E
Jining, Shandong, China 34 G9 35 22N 116 34 E
Jinja, Uganda 54 B3 0 25N 33 12 E
Jinjang, Malaysia 39 L3 3 13N 101 39 E
Jinji, China 34 F4 37 58N 106 8 E
Jinnah Barrage, Pakistan 40 C7 32 58N 71 33 E
Jinotega, Nic. 88 D2 13 6N 85 59W
Jinotepe, Nic. 88 D2 11 50N 86 10W
Jinsha Jiang →, China 32 D5 28 50N 104 36 E
Jinxi, China 35 D11 40 52N 120 50 E
Jinxiang, China 34 G9 35 5N 116 22 E
Jinzhou, Hebei, China 34 E8 38 2N 115 2 E
Jinzhou, Liaoning, China 35 D11 41 5N 121 3 E
Jiparaná →, Brazil 92 E6 8 3S 62 52W
Jipijapa, Ecuador 92 D2 1 0S 80 40W
Jiquilpan, Mexico 86 D4 19 57N 102 42W
Jishan, China 34 G6 35 34N 110 58 E
Jisr ash Shughūr, Syria 44 C3 35 49N 36 18 E
Jitarning, Australia 61 F2 32 48S 117 57 E
Jitra, Malaysia 39 J3 6 16N 100 25 E
Jiu →, Romania 17 F12 43 47N 23 48 E
Jiudengkou, China 34 E4 39 56N 106 40 E
Jiujiang, China 33 D6 29 42N 115 58 E
Jiutai, China 35 B13 44 10N 125 50 E
Jiuxiangcheng, China 34 H8 33 12N 114 50 E
Jiuxincheng, China 34 E8 39 17N 115 59 E
Jixi, China 35 B16 45 20N 130 50 E
Jiyang, China 35 F9 37 0N 117 12 E
Jiyuan, China 34 G7 35 7N 112 57 E
Jīzān, Si. Arabia 46 D3 17 0N 42 20 E
Jize, China 34 F8 36 54N 114 56 E
Jīzl, Wādī al, Si. Arabia 44 E3 25 39N 38 25 E
Jizō-Zaki, Japan 31 G6 35 34N 133 20 E
Jizzakh, Uzbekistan 26 E7 40 6N 67 50 E
Joaçaba, Brazil 95 B5 27 5S 51 31W
João Pessoa, Brazil 93 E12 7 10S 34 52W
Joaquín V. González, Argentina 94 B3 25 10S 64 0W
Jobat, India 42 H6 22 25N 74 34 E
Jodhpur, India 42 F5 26 23N 73 8 E
Jodiya, India 42 H4 22 42N 70 18 E
Joensuu, Finland 24 B4 62 37N 29 49 E
Jōetsu, Japan 31 F9 37 12N 138 10 E
Jofane, Mozam. 57 C5 21 15S 34 18 E
Jogbani, India 43 F12 26 25N 87 15 E
Jõgeva, Estonia 9 G22 58 45N 26 24 E
Jogjakarta = Yogyakarta, Indonesia 37 G14 7 49S 110 22 E
Johannesburg, S. Africa 57 D4 26 10S 28 2 E
Johannesburg, U.S.A. 85 K9 35 22N 117 38W
Johilla →, India 43 H9 23 37N 81 14 E
John Day, U.S.A. 82 D4 44 25N 118 57W
John Day →, U.S.A. 82 D3 45 44N 120 39W
John D'Or Prairie, Canada 72 B5 58 30N 115 8W
John H. Kerr Reservoir, U.S.A. 77 G6 36 36N 78 18W
John o' Groats, U.K. 12 C5 58 38N 3 4W
Johnnie, U.S.A. 85 J10 36 25N 116 5W
John's Ra., Australia 62 C1 21 55S 133 23 E
Johnson, Kans., U.S.A. 81 G4 37 34N 101 45W
Johnson, Vt., U.S.A. 79 B12 44 38N 72 41W
Johnson City, N.Y., U.S.A. 79 D9 42 7N 75 58W
Johnson City, Tenn., U.S.A. 77 G4 36 19N 82 21W
Johnson City, Tex., U.S.A. 81 K5 30 17N 98 25W
Johnsonburg, U.S.A. 78 E6 41 29N 78 41W
Johnsondale, U.S.A. 85 K8 35 58N 118 32W
Johnson's Crossing, Canada 72 A2 60 29N 133 18W
Johnston, L., Australia 61 F3 32 25S 120 30 E
Johnston Falls = Mambilima Falls, Zambia 55 E2 10 31S 28 45 E
Johnston I., Pac. Oc. 65 F11 17 10N 169 8W
Johnstone Str., Canada 72 C3 50 28N 126 0W
Johnstown, N.Y., U.S.A. 79 C10 43 0N 74 22W
Johnstown, Ohio, U.S.A. 78 F2 40 9N 82 41W
Johnstown, Pa., U.S.A. 78 F6 40 20N 78 55W
Johor Baharu, Malaysia 39 M4 1 28N 103 46 E
Jõhvi, Estonia 9 G22 59 22N 27 27 E
Joinville, Brazil 95 B6 26 15S 48 55W
Joinville I., Antarctica 5 C18 65 0S 55 30W
Jojutla, Mexico 87 D5 18 37N 99 11W
Jokkmokk, Sweden 8 C18 66 35N 19 50 E
Jökulsá á Bru →, Iceland 8 D6 65 40N 14 16W
Jökulsá á Fjöllum →, Iceland 8 C5 66 10N 16 30W
Jolfā, Āzarbājān-e Sharqī, Iran 44 B5 38 57N 45 38 E
Jolfā, Eşfahan, Iran 45 C6 32 58N 51 37 E
Joliet, U.S.A. 76 E1 41 32N 88 5W
Joliette, Canada 70 C5 46 3N 73 24W
Jolo, Phil. 37 C6 6 0N 121 0 E
Jolon, U.S.A. 84 K5 35 58N 121 9W
Jombang, Indonesia 37 G15 7 33S 112 14 E
Jonava, Lithuania 9 J21 55 8N 24 12 E
Jones Sound, Canada 4 B3 76 0N 85 0W
Jonesboro, Ark., U.S.A. 81 H9 35 50N 90 42W
Jonesboro, La., U.S.A. 81 J8 32 15N 92 43W
Joniškis, Lithuania 9 H20 56 13N 23 35 E
Jönköping, Sweden 9 H16 57 45N 14 8 E
Jonquière, Canada 71 C5 48 27N 71 14W
Joplin, U.S.A. 81 G7 37 6N 94 31W
Jora, India 42 F6 26 20N 77 49 E
Jordan, Mont., U.S.A. 82 C10 47 19N 106 55W
Jordan, N.Y., U.S.A. 79 C8 43 4N 76 29W
Jordan ■, Asia 47 E5 31 0N 36 0 E
Jordan →, Asia 47 D4 31 48N 35 32 E
Jordan Valley, U.S.A. 82 E5 42 59N 117 3W
Jorhat, India 41 F19 26 45N 94 12 E
Jörn, Sweden 8 D19 65 4N 20 1 E
Jorong, Indonesia 36 E4 3 58S 114 56 E
Jørpeland, Norway 9 G11 59 3N 6 1 E
Jorquera →, Chile 94 B2 28 3S 69 58W
Jos, Nigeria 50 G7 9 53N 8 51 E
José Batlle y Ordóñez, Uruguay 95 C4 33 20S 55 10W
Joseph, L., Nfld., Canada 71 B6 52 45N 65 18W
Joseph, L., Ont., Canada 78 A5 45 10N 79 44W
Joseph Bonaparte G., Australia 60 B4 14 35S 128 50 E
Joshinath, India 43 D8 30 34N 79 34 E
Joshua Tree, U.S.A. 85 L10 34 8N 116 19W
Joshua Tree National Park, U.S.A. 85 M10 33 55N 116 0W
Jostedalsbreen, Norway 9 F12 61 40N 6 59 E
Jotunheimen, Norway 9 F13 61 35N 8 25 E
Jourdanton, U.S.A. 81 L5 28 55N 98 33W
Jovellanos, Cuba 88 B3 22 40N 81 10W
Ju Xian, China 35 F10 36 35N 118 20 E
Juan Aldama, Mexico 86 C4 24 20N 103 23W
Juan Bautista Alberdi, Argentina 94 C3 34 26S 61 48W
Juan de Fuca Str., Canada 84 B3 48 15N 124 0W
Juan de Nova, Ind. Oc. 57 B7 17 3S 43 45 E
Juan Fernández, Arch. de, Pac. Oc. 90 G2 33 50S 80 0W
Juan José Castelli, Argentina 94 B3 25 27S 60 57W
Juan L. Lacaze, Uruguay 94 C4 34 26S 57 25W
Juankoski, Finland 8 E23 63 3N 28 19 E
Juárez, Argentina 94 D4 37 40S 59 43W
Juárez, Mexico 85 N11 32 20N 115 57W
Juárez, Sierra de, Mexico 86 A1 32 0N 116 0W
Juàzeiro, Brazil 93 E10 9 30S 40 30W
Juàzeiro do Norte, Brazil 93 E11 7 10S 39 18W
Juba, Sudan 51 H12 4 50N 31 35 E
Jubayl, Lebanon 47 A4 34 5N 35 39 E
Jubbah, Si. Arabia 44 D4 28 2N 40 56 E
Jubbal, India 42 D7 31 5N 77 40 E
Jubbulpore = Jabalpur, India 43 H8 23 9N 79 58 E
Jubilee L., Australia 61 E4 29 0S 126 50 E
Juby, C., Morocco 50 C3 28 0N 12 59W
Júcar = Xúquer →, Spain 19 C5 39 5N 0 10W
Júcaro, Cuba 88 B4 21 37N 78 51W
Juchitán, Mexico 87 D5 16 27N 95 5W
Judaea = Har Yehuda, Israel 47 D3 31 35N 34 57 E
Judith →, U.S.A. 82 C9 47 44N 109 39W
Judith, Pt., U.S.A. 79 E13 41 22N 71 29W
Judith Gap, U.S.A. 82 C9 46 41N 109 45W
Jugoslavia = Yugoslavia ■, Europe 21 B9 43 20N 20 0 E
Juigalpa, Nic. 88 D2 12 6N 85 26W
Juiz de Fora, Brazil 95 A7 21 43S 43 19W
Jujuy □, Argentina 94 A2 23 20S 65 40W
Julesburg, U.S.A. 80 E3 40 59N 102 16W
Juli, Peru 92 G5 16 10S 69 25W
Julia Cr. →, Australia 62 C3 20 0S 141 11 E
Julia Creek, Australia 62 C3 20 39S 141 44 E
Juliaca, Peru 92 G4 15 25S 70 10W
Julian, U.S.A. 85 M10 33 4N 116 38W
Julian L., Canada 70 B4 54 25N 77 57W
Julianatop, Surinam 93 C7 3 40N 56 30W
Julianehåb, Greenland 4 C5 60 43N 46 0W
Julimes, Mexico 86 B3 28 25N 105 27W
Jullundur, India 42 D6 31 20N 75 40 E
Julu, China 34 F8 37 15N 115 2 E
Jumbo, Zimbabwe 55 F3 17 30S 30 58 E
Jumbo Pk., U.S.A. 85 J12 36 12N 114 11W
Jumentos Cays, Bahamas 88 B4 23 0N 75 40W
Jumilla, Spain 19 C5 38 28N 1 19W
Jumla, Nepal 43 E10 29 15N 82 13 E
Jumna = Yamuna →, India 43 G9 25 30N 81 53 E
Junagadh, India 42 J4 21 30N 70 30 E
Junction, Tex., U.S.A. 81 K5 30 29N 99 46W
Junction, Utah, U.S.A. 83 G7 38 14N 112 13W
Junction B., Australia 62 A1 11 52S 133 55 E
Junction City, Kans., U.S.A. 80 F6 39 2N 96 50W
Junction City, Oreg., U.S.A. 82 D2 44 13N 123 12W
Junction Pt., Australia 62 A1 11 45S 133 50 E
Jundah, Australia 62 C3 24 46S 143 2 E
Jundiaí, Brazil 95 A6 24 30S 47 0W
Juneau, U.S.A. 72 B2 58 18N 134 25W
Junee, Australia 63 E4 34 53S 147 35 E
Jungfrau, Switz. 18 C7 46 32N 7 58 E
Junggar Pendi, China 32 B3 44 30N 86 0 E
Jungshahi, Pakistan 42 G2 24 52N 67 44 E
Juniata →, U.S.A. 78 F7 40 30N 77 40W
Junín, Argentina 94 C3 34 33S 60 57W
Junín de los Andes, Argentina 96 D2 39 45S 71 0W
Jūniyah, Lebanon 47 B4 33 59N 35 38 E
Juntas, Chile 94 B2 28 24S 69 58W
Juntura, U.S.A. 82 E4 43 45N 118 5W
Jur, Nahr el →, Sudan 51 G11 8 45N 29 15 E
Jura = Jura, Mts. du, Europe 18 C7 46 40N 6 5 E
Jura = Schwäbische Alb, Germany 16 D5 48 20N 9 30 E
Jura, U.K. 12 F3 56 0N 5 50W
Jura, Mts. du, Europe 18 C7 46 40N 6 5 E
Jura, Sd. of, U.K. 12 F3 55 57N 5 45W
Jurbarkas, Lithuania 9 J20 55 4N 22 46 E
Jurien, Australia 61 F2 30 18S 115 2 E
Jūrmala, Latvia 9 H20 56 58N 23 34 E
Juruá →, Brazil 92 D5 2 37S 65 44W
Juruena, Brazil 92 F7 13 0S 58 10W

Juruena

131

133

Laporte

Kyustendil, *Bulgaria* **21 C10** 42 16N 22 41 E
Kyusyur, *Russia* **27 B13** 70 19N 127 30 E
Kyyiv, *Ukraine* **17 C16** 50 30N 30 28 E
Kyyivske Vdskh., *Ukraine* **17 C16** 51 0N 30 25 E
Kyzyl, *Russia* **27 D10** 51 50N 94 30 E
Kyzyl Kum, *Uzbekistan* **26 E7** 42 30N 65 0 E
Kyzyl-Kyya, *Kyrgyzstan* **26 E8** 40 16N 72 8 E
Kzyl-Orda = Qyzylorda, *Kazakstan* **26 E7** 44 48N 65 28 E

L

La Alcarria, *Spain* **19 B4** 40 31N 2 45W
La Asunción, *Venezuela* **92 A6** 11 2N 63 53W
La Baie, *Canada* **71 C5** 48 19N 70 53W
La Banda, *Argentina* **94 B3** 27 45S 64 10W
La Barca, *Mexico* **86 C4** 20 20N 102 40W
La Barge, *U.S.A.* **82 E8** 42 16N 110 12W
La Belle, *U.S.A.* **77 M5** 26 46N 81 26W
La Biche →, *Canada* **72 B4** 59 57N 123 50W
La Biche, L., *Canada* **72 C6** 54 50N 112 5W
La Bomba, *Mexico* **86 A1** 31 53N 115 2W
La Calera, *Chile* **94 C1** 32 50S 71 10W
La Canal = Sa Canal, *Spain* **22 C7** 38 51N 1 23 E
La Carlota, *Argentina* **94 C3** 33 30S 63 20W
La Ceiba, *Honduras* **88 C2** 15 40N 86 50W
La Chaux-de-Fonds, *Switz.* **18 C7** 47 7N 6 50 E
La Chorrera, *Panama* **88 E4** 8 53N 79 47W
La Cocha, *Argentina* **94 B2** 27 50S 65 40W
La Concepción, *Panama* **88 E3** 8 31N 82 37W
La Concordia, *Mexico* **87 D6** 16 8N 92 38W
La Coruña = A Coruña, *Spain* **19 A1** 43 20N 8 25W
La Crescent, *U.S.A.* **80 D9** 43 50N 91 18W
La Crete, *Canada* **72 B5** 58 11N 116 24W
La Crosse, *Kans., U.S.A.* **80 F5** 38 32N 99 18W
La Crosse, *Wis., U.S.A.* **80 D9** 43 48N 91 15W
La Cruz, *Costa Rica* **88 D2** 11 4N 85 39W
La Cruz, *Mexico* **86 C3** 23 55N 106 54W
La Désirade, *Guadeloupe* **89 C7** 16 18N 61 3W
La Escondida, *Mexico* **86 C5** 24 6N 99 55W
La Esmeralda, *Paraguay* **94 A3** 22 16S 62 33W
La Esperanza, *Cuba* **88 B3** 22 46N 83 44W
La Esperanza, *Honduras* **88 D2** 14 15N 88 10W
La Estrada = A Estrada, *Spain* **19 A1** 42 43N 8 27W
La Fayette, *U.S.A.* **77 H3** 34 42N 85 17W
La Fé, *Cuba* **88 B3** 22 2N 84 15W
La Follette, *U.S.A.* **77 G3** 36 23N 84 7W
La Grande, *U.S.A.* **82 D4** 45 20N 118 5W
La Grande →, *Canada* **70 B5** 53 50N 79 0W
La Grande Deux, Rés., *Canada* **70 B4** 53 40N 76 55W
La Grande Quatre, Rés., *Canada* **70 B5** 54 0N 73 15W
La Grande Trois, Rés., *Canada* **70 B4** 53 40N 75 10W
La Grange, *Calif., U.S.A.* **84 H6** 37 42N 120 27W
La Grange, *Ga., U.S.A.* **77 J3** 33 2N 85 2W
La Grange, *Ky., U.S.A.* **76 F3** 38 25N 85 23W
La Grange, *Tex., U.S.A.* **81 L6** 29 54N 96 52W
La Guaira, *Venezuela* **92 A5** 10 36N 66 56W
La Habana, *Cuba* **88 B3** 23 8N 82 22W
La Independencia, *Mexico* **87 D6** 16 31N 91 47W
La Isabela, *Dom. Rep.* **89 C5** 19 58N 71 2W
La Junta, *U.S.A.* **81 F3** 37 59N 103 33W
La Laguna, *Canary Is.* **22 F3** 28 28N 16 18W
La Libertad, *Guatemala* **88 C1** 16 47N 90 7W
La Libertad, *Mexico* **86 B2** 29 55N 112 41W
La Ligua, *Chile* **94 C1** 32 30S 71 16W
La Línea de la Concepción, *Spain* **19 D3** 36 15N 5 23W
La Loche, *Canada* **73 B7** 56 29N 109 26W
La Louvière, *Belgium* **15 D4** 50 27N 4 10 E
La Malbaie, *Canada* **71 C5** 47 40N 70 10W
La Mancha, *Spain* **19 C4** 39 10N 2 54W
La Martre, L., *Canada* **72 A5** 63 15N 117 55W
La Mesa, *U.S.A.* **85 N9** 32 46N 117 3W
La Misión, *Mexico* **86 A1** 32 5N 116 50W
La Moure, *U.S.A.* **80 B5** 46 21N 98 18W
La Negra, *Chile* **94 A1** 23 46S 70 18W
La Oliva, *Canary Is.* **22 F6** 28 36N 13 57W
La Orotava, *Canary Is.* **22 F3** 28 22N 16 31W
La Oroya, *Peru* **92** 11 32S 75 54W
La Palma, *Canary Is.* **22 F2** 28 40N 17 50W
La Palma, *Panama* **88 E4** 8 15N 78 0W
La Palma del Condado, *Spain* **19 D2** 37 21N 6 38W
La Paloma, *Chile* **94 C1** 30 35S 71 0W
La Pampa □, *Argentina* **94 D2** 36 50S 66 0W
La Paragua, *Venezuela* **92 B6** 6 50N 63 20W
La Paz, *Entre Ríos, Argentina* **94 C4** 30 50S 59 45W
La Paz, *San Luis, Argentina* **94 C2** 33 30S 67 20W
La Paz, *Bolivia* **92 G5** 16 20S 68 10W
La Paz, *Honduras* **88 D2** 14 20N 87 47W
La Paz, *Mexico* **86 C2** 24 10N 110 20W
La Paz Centro, *Nic.* **88 D2** 12 20N 86 41W
La Pedrera, *Colombia* **92 D5** 1 18S 69 43W
La Pérade, *Canada* **71 C5** 46 35N 72 12W
La Perouse Str., *Asia* **30 B11** 45 40N 142 0 E
La Pesca, *Mexico* **87 C5** 23 46N 97 47W
La Piedad, *Mexico* **86 C4** 20 20N 102 1W
La Pine, *U.S.A.* **82 E3** 43 40N 121 30W
La Plata, *Argentina* **94 D4** 35 0S 57 55W
La Pocatière, *Canada* **71 C5** 47 22N 70 2W
La Porte, *Ind., U.S.A.* **76 E2** 41 36N 86 43W
La Porte, *Tex., U.S.A.* **81 L7** 29 39N 95 1W
La Purísima, *Mexico* **86 B2** 26 10N 112 4W
La Push, *U.S.A.* **84 C2** 47 55N 124 38W
La Quiaca, *Argentina* **94 A2** 22 5S 65 35W
La Restinga, *Canary Is.* **22 G2** 27 38N 17 59W
La Rioja, *Argentina* **94 B2** 29 20S 67 0W
La Rioja □, *Argentina* **94 B2** 29 30S 67 0W
La Rioja □, *Spain* **19 A4** 42 20N 2 20W
La Robla, *Spain* **19 A3** 42 50N 5 41W
La Roche-en-Ardenne, *Belgium* **15 D5** 50 11N 5 35 E
La Roche-sur-Yon, *France* **18 C3** 46 40N 1 25W
La Rochelle, *France* **18 C3** 46 10N 1 9W
La Roda, *Spain* **19 C4** 39 13N 2 15W
La Romana, *Dom. Rep.* **89 C6** 18 27N 68 57W
La Ronge, *Canada* **73 B7** 55 5N 105 20W
La Rumorosa, *Mexico* **85 N10** 32 33N 116 4W
La Sabina = Sa Savina, *Spain* **22 C7** 38 44N 1 25 E
La Salle, *U.S.A.* **80 E10** 41 20N 89 6W
La Santa, *Canary Is.* **22 E6** 29 5N 13 40W
La Sarre, *Canada* **70 C4** 48 45N 79 15W
La Scie, *Canada* **71 C8** 49 57N 55 36W
La Selva Beach, *U.S.A.* **84 J5** 36 56N 121 51W
La Serena, *Chile* **94 B1** 29 55S 71 10W
La Seu d'Urgell, *Spain* **19 A6** 42 22N 1 23 E
La Seyne-sur-Mer, *France* **18 E6** 43 7N 5 52 E
La Soufrière, *St. Vincent* **89 D7** 13 20N 61 11W
La Spézia, *Italy* **18 D8** 44 7N 9 50 E
La Tagua, *Colombia* **92 C4** 0 3N 74 40W
La Tortuga, *Venezuela* **89 D6** 11 0N 65 22W
La Tuque, *Canada* **70 C5** 47 30N 72 50W
La Unión, *Chile* **96 E2** 40 10S 73 0W
La Unión, *El Salv.* **88 D2** 13 20N 87 50W
La Unión, *Mexico* **86 D4** 17 58N 101 49W
La Urbana, *Venezuela* **92 B5** 7 8N 66 56W
La Vall d'Uixó, *Spain* **19 C5** 39 49N 0 15W
La Vega, *Dom. Rep.* **89 C5** 19 20N 70 30W
La Vela de Coro, *Venezuela* **92 A5** 11 27N 69 34W
La Venta, *Mexico* **87 D6** 18 8N 94 3W
La Ventura, *Mexico* **86 C4** 24 38N 100 54W
Labe = Elbe →, *Europe* **16 B5** 53 50N 9 0 E
Labé, *Guinea* **50 F3** 11 24N 12 16W
Laberge, L., *Canada* **72 A1** 61 11N 135 12W
Labinsk, *Russia* **25 F7** 44 40N 40 48 E
Labis, *Malaysia* **39 L4** 2 22N 103 2 E
Laboulaye, *Argentina* **94 C3** 34 10S 63 30W
Labrador, *Canada* **71 B7** 53 20N 61 0W
Labrador City, *Canada* **71 B6** 52 57N 66 55W
Labrador Sea, *Atl. Oc.* **69 C14** 57 0N 54 0W
Lábrea, *Brazil* **92 E6** 7 15S 64 51W
Labuan, *Malaysia* **36 C5** 5 20N 115 14 E
Labuan, Pulau, *Malaysia* **36 C5** 5 21N 115 13 E
Labuha, *Indonesia* **37 E7** 0 30S 127 30 E
Labuhan, *Indonesia* **37 G11** 6 22S 105 50 E
Labuhanbajo, *Indonesia* **37 F6** 8 28S 120 1 E
Labuk, Telok, *Malaysia* **36 C5** 6 10N 117 50 E
Labyrinth, L., *Australia* **63 E2** 30 40S 135 11 E
Labytnangi, *Russia* **26 C7** 66 39N 66 21 E
Lac Bouchette, *Canada* **71 C5** 48 16N 72 11W
Lac Édouard, *Canada* **70 C5** 47 40N 72 16W
Lac La Biche, *Canada* **72 C6** 54 45N 111 58W
Lac la Martre = Wha Ti, *Canada* **68 B8** 63 8N 117 16W
Lac La Ronge Prov. Park, *Canada* **73 B7** 55 9N 104 41W
Lac-Mégantic, *Canada* **71 C5** 45 35N 70 53W
Lac Seul, Res., *Canada* **70 B1** 50 25N 92 30W
Lac Thien, *Vietnam* **38 F7** 12 25N 108 11 E
Lacanau, *France* **18 D3** 44 58N 1 5W
Lacantúm →, *Mexico* **87 D6** 16 36N 90 40W
Laccadive Is. = Lakshadweep Is., *Ind. Oc.* **28 H11** 10 0N 72 30 E
Lacepede B., *Australia* **63 F2** 36 40S 139 40 E
Lacepede Is., *Australia* **60 C3** 16 55S 122 0 E
Lacerdónia, *Mozam.* **55 F4** 18 3S 35 35 E
Lacey, *U.S.A.* **84 C4** 47 7N 122 49W
Lachhmangarh, *India* **42 F6** 27 50N 75 4 E
Lachi, *Pakistan* **42 C4** 33 25N 71 20 E
Lachine, *Canada* **79 A11** 45 30N 73 40W
Lachlan →, *Australia* **63 E3** 34 22S 143 55 E
Lachute, *Canada* **70 C5** 45 39N 74 21W
Lackawanna, *U.S.A.* **78 D6** 42 50N 78 50W
Lackawaxen, *U.S.A.* **79 E10** 41 29N 74 59W
Lacolle, *Canada* **79 A11** 45 5N 73 22W
Lacombe, *Canada* **72 C6** 52 30N 113 44W
Lacona, *U.S.A.* **79 C8** 43 39N 76 10W
Laconia, *U.S.A.* **79 C13** 43 32N 71 28W
Ladakh Ra., *India* **43 C8** 34 0N 78 0 E
Ladismith, *S. Africa* **56 E3** 33 28S 21 15 E
Ladnun, *India* **42 F6** 27 38N 74 25 E
Ladoga, L. = Ladozhskoye Ozero, *Russia* **24 B5** 61 15N 30 30 E
Ladozhskoye Ozero, *Russia* **24 B5** 61 15N 30 30 E
Lady Elliott I., *Australia* **62 C5** 24 7S 152 42 E
Lady Grey, *S. Africa* **56 E4** 30 43S 27 13 E
Ladybrand, *S. Africa* **56 D4** 29 9S 27 29 E
Ladysmith, *Canada* **72 D4** 49 0N 123 49W
Ladysmith, *S. Africa* **57 D4** 28 32S 29 46 E
Ladysmith, *U.S.A.* **80 C9** 45 28N 91 12W
Lae, *Papua N. G.* **64 H6** 6 40S 147 2 E
Laem Ngop, *Thailand* **39 F4** 12 10N 102 26 E
Laem Pho, *Thailand* **39 J3** 6 55N 101 19 E
Læsø, *Denmark* **9 H14** 57 15N 11 5 E
Lafayette, *Colo., U.S.A.* **80 F2** 39 58N 105 12W
Lafayette, *Ind., U.S.A.* **76 E2** 40 25N 86 54W
Lafayette, *La., U.S.A.* **81 K9** 30 14N 92 1W
Lafayette, *Tenn., U.S.A.* **77 G2** 36 31N 86 2W
Laferte →, *Canada* **72 A5** 61 53N 117 44W
Lafia, *Nigeria* **50 G7** 8 30N 8 34 E
Lafleche, *Canada* **73 D7** 49 45N 106 40W
Lagan →, *U.K.* **13 B6** 54 36N 5 55W
Lagarfljót →, *Iceland* **8 D6** 65 40N 14 18W
Lågen →, *Oppland, Norway* **9 F14** 61 8N 10 25 E
Lågen →, *Vestfold, Norway* **9 G14** 59 3N 10 3 E
Laghouat, *Algeria* **50 B6** 33 50N 2 59 E
Lagoa Vermelha, *Brazil* **95 B5** 28 13S 51 32W
Lagonoy G., *Phil.* **37 B6** 13 50N 123 50 E
Lagos, *Nigeria* **50 G6** 6 25N 3 27 E
Lagos, *Portugal* **19 D1** 37 5N 8 41W
Lagos de Moreno, *Mexico* **86 C4** 21 21N 101 55W
Lagrange, *Australia* **60 C3** 18 45S 121 43 E
Lagrange B., *Australia* **60 C3** 18 38S 121 42 E
Laguna, *Brazil* **95 B6** 28 30S 48 50W
Laguna, *U.S.A.* **83 J10** 35 2N 107 25W
Laguna Beach, *U.S.A.* **85 M9** 33 33N 117 47W
Laguna Limpia, *Argentina* **94 B4** 26 32S 59 45W
Laguna Madre, *U.S.A.* **87 B5** 27 0N 97 20W
Lagunas, *Chile* **94 A2** 21 0S 69 45W
Lagunas, *Peru* **92 E3** 5 10S 75 35W
Lahad Datu, *Malaysia* **37 D5** 5 0N 118 20 E
Lahad Datu, Teluk, *Malaysia* **37 D5** 4 50N 118 20 E
Lahan Sai, *Thailand* **38 E4** 14 25N 102 52 E
Lahanam, *Laos* **38 D5** 16 16N 105 16 E
Lahar, *India* **43 F8** 26 12N 78 57 E
Laharpur, *India* **43 F9** 27 43N 80 56 E
Lahat, *Indonesia* **36 E2** 3 45S 103 30 E
Lahewa, *Indonesia* **36 D1** 1 22N 97 12 E
Lāhījān, *Iran* **45 B6** 37 10N 50 6 E
Lahn →, *Germany* **16 C4** 50 19N 7 37 E
Laholm, *Sweden* **9 H15** 56 30N 13 2 E
Lahore, *Pakistan* **42 D6** 31 32N 74 22 E
Lahri, *Pakistan* **42 E3** 29 11N 68 13 E
Lahti, *Finland* **9 F21** 60 58N 25 40 E
Lahtis = Lahti, *Finland* **9 F21** 60 58N 25 40 E
Laï, *Chad* **51 G9** 9 25N 16 18 E
Laila = Laylá, *Si. Arabia* **46 C4** 22 10N 46 40 E
Laingsburg, *S. Africa* **56 E3** 33 9S 20 52 E
Lainio älv →, *Sweden* **8 C20** 67 35N 22 40 E
Lairg, *U.K.* **12 C4** 58 2N 4 24W
Laishui, *China* **34 E8** 39 23N 115 45 E
Laiwu, *China* **35 F9** 36 15N 117 40 E
Laixi, *China* **35 F11** 36 50N 120 31 E
Laiyang, *China* **35 F11** 36 59N 120 45 E
Laiyuan, *China* **34 E8** 39 20N 114 40 E
Laizhou, *China* **35 F10** 37 8N 119 57 E
Laizhou Wan, *China* **35 F10** 37 30N 119 30 E
Laja →, *Mexico* **86 C4** 20 55N 100 46W
Lajes, *Brazil* **95 B5** 27 48S 50 20W
Lak Sao, *Laos* **38 C5** 18 11N 104 59 E
Lakaband, *Pakistan* **42 D3** 31 2N 69 15 E
Lake Alpine, *U.S.A.* **84 G7** 38 29N 120 0W
Lake Andes, *U.S.A.* **80 D5** 43 9N 98 32W
Lake Arthur, *U.S.A.* **81 K8** 30 5N 92 41W
Lake Cargelligo, *Australia* **63 E4** 33 15S 146 22 E
Lake Charles, *U.S.A.* **81 K8** 30 14N 93 13W
Lake City, *Colo., U.S.A.* **83 G10** 38 2N 107 19W
Lake City, *Fla., U.S.A.* **77 K4** 30 11N 82 38W
Lake City, *Mich., U.S.A.* **76 C3** 44 20N 85 13W
Lake City, *Minn., U.S.A.* **80 C8** 44 27N 92 16W
Lake City, *Pa., U.S.A.* **78 D4** 42 1N 80 21W
Lake City, *S.C., U.S.A.* **77 J6** 33 52N 79 45W
Lake Cowichan, *Canada* **72 D4** 48 49N 124 3W
Lake District, *U.K.* **10 C4** 54 35N 3 20 E
Lake Elsinore, *U.S.A.* **85 M9** 33 38N 117 20W
Lake George, *U.S.A.* **79 C11** 43 26N 73 43W
Lake Grace, *Australia* **61 F2** 33 7S 118 28 E
Lake Harbour = Kimmirut, *Canada* **69 B13** 62 50N 69 50W
Lake Havasu City, *U.S.A.* **85 L12** 34 27N 114 22W
Lake Hughes, *U.S.A.* **85 L8** 34 41N 118 26W
Lake Isabella, *U.S.A.* **85 K8** 35 38N 118 28W
Lake Jackson, *U.S.A.* **81 L7** 29 3N 95 27W
Lake Junction, *U.S.A.* **82 D8** 44 35N 110 28W
Lake King, *Australia* **61 F2** 33 5S 119 45 E
Lake Lenore, *Canada* **73 C8** 52 24N 104 59W
Lake Louise, *Canada* **72 C5** 51 30N 116 10W
Lake Mead National Recreation Area, *U.S.A.* **85 K12** 36 15N 114 30W
Lake Mills, *U.S.A.* **80 D8** 43 25N 93 32W
Lake Placid, *U.S.A.* **79 B11** 44 17N 73 59W
Lake Pleasant, *U.S.A.* **79 C10** 43 28N 74 25W
Lake Providence, *U.S.A.* **81 J9** 32 48N 91 10W
Lake St. Peter, *Canada* **78 A6** 45 18N 78 2W
Lake Superior Prov. Park, *Canada* **70 C3** 47 45N 84 45W
Lake Village, *U.S.A.* **81 J9** 33 20N 91 17W
Lake Wales, *U.S.A.* **77 M5** 27 54N 81 35W
Lake Worth, *U.S.A.* **77 M5** 26 37N 80 3W
Lakefield, *Canada* **78 B6** 44 25N 78 16W
Lakehurst, *U.S.A.* **79 F10** 40 1N 74 19W
Lakeland, *Australia* **62 B3** 15 49S 144 57 E
Lakeland, *U.S.A.* **77 M5** 28 3N 81 57W
Lakemba, *Fiji* **59 D9** 18 13S 178 47W
Lakeport, *Calif., U.S.A.* **84 F4** 39 3N 122 55W
Lakeport, *Mich., U.S.A.* **78 C2** 43 7N 82 30W
Lakes Entrance, *Australia* **63 F4** 37 50S 148 0 E
Lakeside, *Ariz., U.S.A.* **83 J9** 34 9N 109 58W
Lakeside, *Calif., U.S.A.* **85 N10** 32 52N 116 55W
Lakeside, *Nebr., U.S.A.* **80 D3** 42 3N 102 26W
Lakeside, *Ohio, U.S.A.* **78 E2** 41 32N 82 46W
Lakeview, *U.S.A.* **82 E3** 42 11N 120 21W
Lakeville, *U.S.A.* **80 C8** 44 39N 93 14W
Lakewood, *Colo., U.S.A.* **80 F2** 39 44N 105 5W
Lakewood, *N.J., U.S.A.* **79 F10** 40 6N 74 13W
Lakewood, *N.Y., U.S.A.* **78 D5** 42 6N 79 19W
Lakewood, *Ohio, U.S.A.* **78 E3** 41 29N 81 48W
Lakewood, *Wash., U.S.A.* **84 C4** 47 11N 122 32W
Lakha, *India* **42 F4** 26 9N 70 54 E
Lakhaniá, *Greece* **23 D9** 35 58N 27 54 E
Lakhimpur, *India* **43 F9** 27 57N 80 46 E
Lakhnadon, *India* **43 H8** 22 36N 79 36 E
Lakhonpheng, *Laos* **38 E5** 15 54N 105 34 E
Lakhpat, *India* **42 H3** 23 48N 68 47 E
Lakin, *U.S.A.* **81 G4** 37 57N 101 15W
Lakitusaki →, *Canada* **70 B3** 54 21N 82 25W
Lakki, *Pakistan* **42 C4** 32 36N 70 55 E
Lákkoi, *Greece* **23 D5** 35 24N 23 57 E
Lakonikós Kólpos, *Greece* **21 F10** 36 40N 22 40 E
Lakor, *Indonesia* **37 F7** 8 15S 128 17 E
Lakota, *Ivory C.* **50 G4** 5 50N 5 30W
Lakota, *U.S.A.* **80 A5** 48 2N 98 21W
Laksar, *India* **42 E8** 29 46N 78 3 E
Laksefjorden, *Norway* **8 A22** 70 45N 26 50 E
Lakselv, *Norway* **8 A21** 70 2N 25 0 E
Lakshadweep Is., *Ind. Oc.* **28 H11** 10 0N 72 30 E
Lakshmanpur, *India* **43 H10** 22 58N 83 3 E
Lakshmikantapur, *India* **43 H13** 22 5N 88 20 E
Lala Ghat, *India* **41 G18** 24 30N 92 40 E
Lala Musa, *Pakistan* **42 C5** 32 40N 73 57 E
Lalago, *Tanzania* **54 C3** 3 28S 33 58 E
Lalapanzi, *Zimbabwe* **55 F3** 19 20S 30 15 E
L'Albufera, *Spain* **19 C5** 39 20N 0 27W
Lalganj, *India* **43 G11** 25 52N 85 13 E
Lalgola, *India* **43 G13** 24 25N 88 15 E
Lālī, *Iran* **45 C6** 32 21N 49 6 E
Lalibela, *Ethiopia* **46 E2** 12 2N 39 2 E
Lalin, *China* **35 B14** 45 12N 127 0 E
Lalín, *Spain* **19 A1** 42 40N 8 5W
Lalin He →, *China* **35 B13** 45 32N 125 40 E
Lalitapur = Patan, *Nepal* **41 F14** 27 40N 85 20 E
Lalitpur, *India* **43 G8** 24 42N 78 28 E
Lalkua, *India* **43 E8** 29 5N 79 31 E
Lalsot, *India* **42 F7** 26 34N 76 20 E
Lam, *Vietnam* **38 B6** 21 21N 106 31 E
Lam Pao Res., *Thailand* **38 D4** 16 50N 103 15 E
Lamaing, *Burma* **41 M20** 15 25N 97 53 E
Lamar, *Colo., U.S.A.* **80 F3** 38 5N 102 37W
Lamar, *Mo., U.S.A.* **81 G7** 37 30N 94 16W
Lamas, *Peru* **92 E3** 6 28S 76 31W
Lambaréné, *Gabon* **52 E2** 0 41S 10 12 E
Lambasa, *Fiji* **59 C8** 16 30S 179 10 E
Lambay I., *Ireland* **13 C5** 53 29N 6 1W
Lambert Glacier, *Antarctica* **5 D6** 71 0S 70 0 E
Lamberts Bay, *S. Africa* **56 E2** 32 5S 18 17 E
Lambeth, *Canada* **78 D3** 42 54N 81 18W
Lambi Kyun, *Burma* **39 G2** 10 50N 98 20 E
Lame Deer, *U.S.A.* **82 D10** 45 37N 106 40W
Lamego, *Portugal* **19 B2** 41 5N 7 52W
Lamèque, *Canada* **71 C7** 47 45N 64 38W
Lameroo, *Australia* **63 F3** 35 19S 140 33 E
Lamesa, *U.S.A.* **81 J4** 32 44N 101 58W
Lamía, *Greece* **21 E10** 38 55N 22 26 E
Lammermuir Hills, *U.K.* **12 F6** 55 50N 2 40W
Lamoille →, *U.S.A.* **79 B11** 44 38N 73 13W
Lamon B., *Phil.* **37 B6** 14 30N 122 20 E
Lamont, *Canada* **72 C6** 53 46N 112 50W
Lamont, *Calif., U.S.A.* **85 K8** 35 15N 118 55W
Lamont, *Wyo., U.S.A.* **82 E10** 42 13N 107 29W
Lampa, *Peru* **92 G4** 15 22S 70 22W
Lampang, *Thailand* **38 C2** 18 16N 99 32 E
Lampasas, *U.S.A.* **81 K5** 31 4N 98 11W
Lampazos de Naranjo, *Mexico* **86 B4** 27 2N 100 32W
Lampedusa, *Medit. S.* **20 G5** 35 36N 12 40 E
Lampeter, *U.K.* **11 E3** 52 7N 4 4W
Lampione, *Medit. S.* **20 G5** 35 33N 12 20 E
Lampman, *Canada* **73 D8** 49 25N 102 50W
Lampung □, *Indonesia* **36 F2** 5 30S 104 30 E
Lamta, *India* **43 H9** 22 8N 80 7 E
Lamu, *Kenya* **54 C5** 2 16S 40 55 E
Lamy, *U.S.A.* **83 J11** 35 29N 105 53W
Lan Xian, *China* **34 E6** 38 15N 111 35 E
Lanai, *U.S.A.* **74 H16** 20 50N 156 55W
Lanak La, *India* **43 B8** 34 27N 79 32 E
Lanak'o Shank'ou = Lanak La, *India* **43 B8** 34 27N 79 32 E
Lanark, *Canada* **79 A8** 45 1N 76 22W
Lanark, *U.K.* **12 F5** 55 40N 3 47W
Lancang Jiang →, *China* **32 D5** 21 40N 101 10 E
Lancashire □, *U.K.* **10 D5** 53 50N 2 48W
Lancaster, *Canada* **79 A10** 45 10N 74 30W
Lancaster, *U.K.* **10 C5** 54 3N 2 48W
Lancaster, *Calif., U.S.A.* **85 L8** 34 42N 118 8W
Lancaster, *Ky., U.S.A.* **76 G3** 37 37N 84 35W
Lancaster, *N.H., U.S.A.* **79 B13** 44 29N 71 34W
Lancaster, *N.Y., U.S.A.* **78 D6** 42 54N 78 40W
Lancaster, *Ohio, U.S.A.* **76 F4** 39 43N 82 36W
Lancaster, *Pa., U.S.A.* **79 F8** 40 2N 76 19W
Lancaster, *S.C., U.S.A.* **77 H5** 34 43N 80 46W
Lancaster, *Wis., U.S.A.* **80 D9** 42 51N 90 43W
Lancaster Sd., *Canada* **69 A11** 74 13N 84 0W
Lancelin, *Australia* **61 F2** 31 0S 115 18 E
Lanchow = Lanzhou, *China* **34 F2** 36 1N 103 52 E
Lanciano, *Italy* **20 C6** 42 14N 14 23 E
Lancun, *China* **35 F11** 36 25N 120 10 E
Landeck, *Austria* **16 E6** 47 9N 10 34 E
Lander, *U.S.A.* **82 E9** 42 50N 108 44W
Lander →, *Australia* **60 D5** 22 0S 132 0 E
Landes, *France* **18 D3** 44 0N 1 0W
Landi Kotal, *Pakistan* **42 B4** 34 7N 71 6 E
Landisburg, *U.S.A.* **78 F7** 40 21N 77 19W
Land's End, *U.K.* **11 G2** 50 4N 5 44W
Landsborough Cr. →, *Australia* **62 C3** 22 28S 144 35 E
Landshut, *Germany* **16 D7** 48 34N 12 8 E
Landskrona, *Sweden* **9 J15** 55 53N 12 50 E
Lanesboro, *U.S.A.* **79 E9** 41 57N 75 34W
Lanett, *U.S.A.* **77 J3** 32 52N 85 12W
Lang Qua, *Vietnam* **38 A5** 22 16N 104 27 E
Lang Shan, *China* **34 D4** 41 0N 106 30 E
Lang Suan, *Thailand* **39 H2** 9 57N 99 4 E
La'nga Co, *China* **41 D12** 30 45N 81 15 E
Langar, *Iran* **45 C9** 35 23N 60 25 E
Langara I., *Canada* **72 C2** 54 14N 133 1W
Langdon, *U.S.A.* **80 A5** 48 45N 98 22W
Langeberg, *S. Africa* **56 E3** 33 55S 21 0 E
Langeberge, *S. Africa* **56 D3** 28 15S 22 33 E
Langeland, *Denmark* **9 J14** 54 56N 10 48 E
Langenburg, *Canada* **73 C8** 50 51N 101 43W
Langholm, *U.K.* **12 F5** 55 9N 3 0W
Langjökull, *Iceland* **8 D3** 64 39N 20 12W
Langkawi, Pulau, *Malaysia* **39 J2** 6 25N 99 45 E
Langklip, *S. Africa* **56 D3** 28 12S 20 20 E
Langkon, *Malaysia* **36 C5** 6 30N 116 40 E
Langlade, *St- P. & M.* **71 C8** 46 50N 56 20W
Langley, *Canada* **84 A4** 49 7N 122 39W
Langøya, *Norway* **8 B16** 68 45N 14 50 E
Langreo, *Spain* **19 A3** 43 18N 5 40W
Langres, *France* **18 C6** 47 52N 5 20 E
Langres, Plateau de, *France* **18 C6** 47 45N 5 3 E
Langsa, *Indonesia* **36 D1** 4 30N 97 57 E
Langtry, *U.S.A.* **81 L4** 29 49N 101 34W
Langu, *Thailand* **39 J2** 6 53N 99 47 E
Languedoc, *France* **18 E5** 43 58N 3 55 E
Langxiangzhen, *China* **34 E9** 39 43N 116 8 E
Lanigan, *Canada* **73 C7** 51 51N 105 2W
Lankao, *China* **34 G8** 34 48N 114 50 E
Länkäran, *Azerbaijan* **25 G8** 38 48N 48 52 E
Lannion, *France* **18 B2** 48 46N 3 29W
L'Annonciation, *Canada* **70 C5** 46 25N 74 55W
Lansdale, *U.S.A.* **79 F9** 40 14N 75 17W
Lansdowne, *Australia* **63 E5** 31 48S 152 30 E
Lansdowne, *Canada* **79 B8** 44 24N 76 1W
Lansdowne, *India* **43 E8** 29 50N 78 41 E
Lansdowne House, *Canada* **70 B2** 52 14N 87 53W
L'Anse, *Mich., U.S.A.* **76 B1** 46 42N 88 25W
L'Anse, *Mich., U.S.A.* **80 B10** 46 45N 88 27W
L'Anse au Loup, *Canada* **71 B8** 51 32N 56 50W
L'Anse aux Meadows, *Canada* **71 B8** 51 36N 55 32W
Lansford, *U.S.A.* **79 F9** 40 50N 75 53W
Lansing, *U.S.A.* **76 D3** 42 44N 84 33W
Lanta Yai, Ko, *Thailand* **39 J2** 7 35N 99 3 E
Lantian, *China* **34 G5** 34 11N 109 20 E
Lanus, *Argentina* **94 C4** 34 44S 58 27W
Lanusei, *Italy* **20 E3** 39 52N 9 34 E
Lanzarote, *Canary Is.* **22 F6** 29 0N 13 40W
Lanzhou, *China* **34 F2** 36 1N 103 52 E
Lao Bao, *Laos* **38 D6** 16 35N 106 30 E
Laoag, *Phil.* **37 A6** 18 7N 120 34 E
Laoang, *Phil.* **37 B7** 12 32N 125 8 E
Laoha He →, *China* **35 C11** 43 25N 120 35 E
Laois □, *Ireland* **13 D4** 52 57N 7 36W
Laon, *France* **18 B5** 49 33N 3 35 E
Laona, *U.S.A.* **76 C1** 45 34N 88 40W
Laos ■, *Asia* **38 D5** 17 45N 105 0 E
Lapa, *Brazil* **95 B6** 25 46S 49 44W
Lapeer, *U.S.A.* **76 D4** 43 3N 83 19W
Lapithos, *Cyprus* **23 D12** 35 21N 33 11 E
Lapland = Lappland, *Europe* **8 B21** 68 7N 24 0 E
Laporte, *U.S.A.* **79 E8** 41 25N 76 30W

Longview

Lifudzin, Russia 30 B7 44 21N 134 58 E
Lightning Ridge, Australia 63 D4 29 22S 148 0 E
Ligonier, U.S.A. 78 F5 40 15N 79 14W
Liguria □, Italy 18 D8 44 30N 8 50 E
Ligurian Sea, Medit. S. 20 C3 43 20N 9 0 E
Lihou Reefs and Cays, Australia 62 B5 17 25S 151 40 E
Lihue, U.S.A. 74 H15 21 59N 159 23W
Lijiang, China 32 D5 26 55N 100 20 E
Likasi, Dem. Rep. of the Congo 55 E2 10 55S 26 48 E
Likoma I., Malawi 55 E3 12 3S 34 45 E
Likumburu, Tanzania 55 D4 9 43S 35 8 E
Lille, France 18 A5 50 38N 3 3 E
Lille Bælt, Denmark 9 J13 55 20N 9 45 E
Lillehammer, Norway 9 F14 61 8N 10 30 E
Lillesand, Norway 9 G13 58 15N 8 23 E
Lillian Pt., Australia 61 E4 27 40S 126 6 E
Lillooet, Canada 72 C4 50 44N 121 57W
Lillooet →, Canada 72 D4 49 15N 121 57W
Lilongwe, Malawi 55 E3 14 0S 33 48 E
Liloy, Phil. 37 C6 8 4N 122 39 E
Lim →, Bos.-H. 21 C8 43 45N 19 15 E
Lima, Indonesia 37 E7 3 37S 128 4 E
Lima, Peru 92 F3 12 0S 77 0W
Lima, Mont., U.S.A. 82 D7 44 38N 112 36W
Lima, Ohio, U.S.A. 76 E3 40 44N 84 6W
Lima →, Portugal 19 B1 41 41N 8 50W
Liman, Indonesia 37 G14 7 48S 111 45 E
Limassol, Cyprus 23 E12 34 42N 33 1 E
Limavady, U.K. 13 A5 55 3N 6 56W
Limay →, Argentina 96 D3 39 0S 68 0W
Limay Mahuida, Argentina 94 D2 37 10S 66 45W
Limbang, Brunei 36 D5 4 42N 115 6 E
Limbaži, Latvia 9 H21 57 31N 24 42 E
Limbdi, India 42 H4 22 34N 71 51 E
Limbe, Cameroon 52 D1 4 1N 9 10 E
Limburg, Germany 16 C5 50 22N 8 4 E
Limburg □, Belgium 15 C5 51 2N 5 25 E
Limburg □, Neths. 15 C5 51 20N 5 55 E
Limeira, Brazil 95 A6 22 35S 47 28W
Limerick, Ireland 13 D3 52 40N 8 37W
Limerick, U.S.A. 79 C14 43 41N 70 48W
Limerick □, Ireland 13 D3 52 30N 8 50W
Limestone, U.S.A. 78 D6 42 2N 78 38W
Limestone →, Canada 73 B10 56 31N 94 7W
Limfjorden, Denmark 9 H13 56 55N 9 0 E
Limia = Lima →, Portugal 19 B1 41 41N 8 50W
Limingen, Norway 8 D15 64 48N 13 35 E
Limmen Bight, Australia 62 A2 14 40S 135 35 E
Limmen Bight →, Australia 62 B2 15 7S 135 44 E
Límnos, Greece 21 E11 39 50N 25 5 E
Limoges, Canada 79 A9 45 20N 75 16W
Limoges, France 18 D4 45 50N 1 15 E
Limón, Costa Rica 88 E3 10 0N 83 2W
Limon, U.S.A. 80 F3 39 16N 103 41W
Limousin, France 18 D4 45 30N 1 30 E
Limoux, France 18 E5 43 4N 2 12 E
Limpopo →, Africa 57 D5 25 5S 33 30 E
Limuru, Kenya 54 C4 1 2S 36 35 E
Lin Xian, China 34 F6 37 57N 110 58 E
Linares, Chile 94 D1 35 50S 71 40W
Linares, Mexico 87 C5 24 50N 99 40W
Linares, Spain 19 C4 38 10N 3 40W
Lincheng, China 34 F8 37 25N 114 30 E
Lincoln, Argentina 94 C3 34 55S 61 30W
Lincoln, N.Z. 59 K4 43 38S 172 30 E
Lincoln, U.K. 10 D7 53 14N 0 32W
Lincoln, Calif., U.S.A. 84 G5 38 54N 121 17W
Lincoln, Ill., U.S.A. 80 E10 40 9N 89 22W
Lincoln, Kans., U.S.A. 80 F5 39 3N 98 9W
Lincoln, Maine, U.S.A. 77 C11 45 22N 68 30W
Lincoln, N.H., U.S.A. 79 B13 44 3N 71 40W
Lincoln, N. Mex., U.S.A. 83 K11 33 30N 105 23W
Lincoln, Nebr., U.S.A. 80 E6 40 49N 96 41W
Lincoln City, U.S.A. 82 D1 44 57N 124 1W
Lincoln Hav = Lincoln Sea, Arctic 4 A5 84 0N 55 0W
Lincoln Sea, Arctic 4 A5 84 0N 55 0W
Lincolnshire □, U.K. 10 D7 53 14N 0 32W
Lincolnshire Wolds, U.K. 10 D7 53 26N 0 13W
Lincolnton, U.S.A. 77 H5 35 29N 81 16W
Lind, U.S.A. 82 C4 46 58N 118 37W
Linda, U.S.A. 84 F5 39 8N 121 34W
Linden, Guyana 92 B7 6 0N 58 10W
Linden, Ala., U.S.A. 77 J2 32 18N 87 48W
Linden, Calif., U.S.A. 84 G5 38 1N 121 5W
Linden, Tex., U.S.A. 81 J7 33 1N 94 22W
Lindenhurst, U.S.A. 79 F11 40 41N 73 23W
Lindesnes, Norway 9 H12 57 58N 7 3 E
Lindhos, Greece 23 C10 36 6N 28 4 E
Lindhos, Ákra, Greece 23 C10 36 4N 28 10 E
Lindi, Tanzania 55 D4 9 58S 39 38 E
Lindi □, Tanzania 55 D4 9 40S 38 30 E
Lindi →, Dem. Rep. of the Congo 54 B2 0 33N 25 5 E
Lindsay, Canada 78 B6 44 22N 78 43W
Lindsay, Calif., U.S.A. 84 J7 36 12N 119 5W
Lindsay, Okla., U.S.A. 81 H6 34 50N 97 38W
Lindsborg, U.S.A. 80 F6 38 35N 97 40W
Linesville, U.S.A. 78 E4 41 39N 80 26W
Linfen, China 34 F6 36 3N 111 30 E
Ling Xian, China 34 F9 37 22N 116 30 E
Lingao, China 38 C7 19 56N 109 42 E
Lingayen, Phil. 37 A6 16 1N 120 14 E
Lingayen G., Phil. 37 A6 16 10N 120 15 E
Lingbi, China 35 H9 33 33N 117 33 E
Lingchuan, China 34 G7 35 45N 113 12 E
Lingen, Germany 16 B4 52 31N 7 19 E
Lingga, Indonesia 36 E2 0 12S 104 37 E
Lingga, Kepulauan, Indonesia 36 E2 0 10S 104 30 E
Lingga Arch. = Lingga, Kepulauan, Indonesia 36 E2 0 10S 104 30 E
Lingle, U.S.A. 80 D2 42 8N 104 21W
Lingqiu, China 34 E8 39 28N 114 22 E
Lingshi, China 34 F6 36 48N 111 48 E
Lingshou, China 34 E8 38 20N 114 20 E
Lingshui, China 38 C8 18 27N 110 0 E
Lingtai, China 34 G4 35 0N 107 40 E
Linguère, Senegal 50 E2 15 25N 15 5W
Lingwu, China 34 E4 38 6N 106 20 E
Lingyuan, China 35 D10 41 10N 119 15 E
Linhai, China 33 D7 28 50N 121 8 E
Linhares, Brazil 93 G10 19 25S 40 4W
Linhe, China 34 D4 40 48N 107 20 E
Linjiang, China 35 D14 41 50N 127 0 E
Linköping, Sweden 9 G16 58 28N 15 36 E
Linkou, China 35 B16 45 15N 130 18 E
Linnhe, L., U.K. 12 E3 56 36N 5 25W
Linosa, I., Medit. S. 20 G5 35 51N 12 50 E
Linqi, China 34 G7 35 45N 113 52 E
Linqing, China 34 F8 36 50N 115 42 E
Linqu, China 35 F10 36 25N 118 30 E
Linru, China 34 G7 34 11N 112 52 E
Lins, Brazil 95 A6 21 40S 49 44W
Linton, Ind., U.S.A. 76 F2 39 2N 87 10W
Linton, N. Dak., U.S.A. 80 B4 46 16N 100 14W
Lintong, China 34 G5 34 20N 109 10 E
Linwood, Canada 78 C4 43 35N 80 43W
Linxi, China 35 C10 43 36N 118 2 E
Linxia, China 32 C5 35 36N 103 10 E
Linyanti →, Africa 56 B4 17 50S 25 5 E
Linyi, China 35 G10 35 5N 118 21 E
Linz, Austria 16 D8 48 18N 14 18 E
Linzhenzhen, China 34 F5 36 30N 109 59 E
Linzi, China 35 F10 36 50N 118 20 E
Lion, G. du, France 18 E6 43 10N 4 0 E
Lionárisso, Cyprus 23 D13 35 28N 34 8 E
Lions, G. of = Lion, G. du, France 18 E6 43 10N 4 0 E
Lion's Den, Zimbabwe 55 F3 17 15S 30 5 E
Lion's Head, Canada 78 B3 44 58N 81 15W
Lipa, Phil. 37 B6 13 57N 121 10 E
Lipali, Mozam. 55 F4 15 50S 35 50 E
Lípari, Italy 20 E6 38 26N 14 58 E
Lípari, Is. = Eólie, Ís., Italy 20 E6 38 30N 14 57 E
Lipcani, Moldova 17 D14 48 14N 26 48 E
Lipetsk, Russia 24 D6 52 37N 39 35 E
Lipkany = Lipcani, Moldova 17 D14 48 14N 26 48 E
Lipovcy Manzovka, Russia 30 B6 44 12N 132 26 E
Lipovets, Ukraine 17 D15 49 12N 29 1 E
Lippe →, Germany 16 C4 51 39N 6 36 E
Lipscomb, U.S.A. 81 G4 36 14N 100 16W
Liptrap C., Australia 63 F4 38 50S 145 55 E
Lira, Uganda 54 B3 2 17N 32 57 E
Liria = Lliria, Spain 19 C5 39 37N 0 35W
Lisala, Dem. Rep. of the Congo 52 D4 2 12N 21 38 E
Lisboa, Portugal 19 C1 38 42N 9 10W
Lisbon = Lisboa, Portugal 19 C1 38 42N 9 10W
Lisbon, N. Dak., U.S.A. 80 B6 46 27N 97 41W
Lisbon, N.H., U.S.A. 79 B13 44 13N 71 55W
Lisbon, Ohio, U.S.A. 78 F4 40 46N 80 46W
Lisbon Falls, U.S.A. 77 D10 44 0N 70 4W
Lisburn, U.K. 13 B5 54 31N 6 3W
Liscannor B., Ireland 13 D2 52 55N 9 24W
Lishi, China 34 F6 37 31N 111 8 E
Lishu, China 35 C13 43 20N 124 18 E
Lisianski I., Pac. Oc. 64 E10 26 2N 174 0W
Lisichansk = Lysychansk, Ukraine 25 E6 48 55N 38 30 E
Lisieux, France 18 B4 49 10N 0 12 E
Liski, Russia 25 D6 51 3N 39 30 E
Lismore, Australia 63 D5 28 44S 153 21 E
Lismore, Ireland 13 D4 52 8N 7 55W
Lista, Norway 9 G12 58 7N 6 39 E
Lister, Mt., Antarctica 5 D11 78 0S 162 0 E
Liston, Australia 63 D5 28 39S 152 6 E
Listowel, Canada 78 C4 43 44N 80 58W
Listowel, Ireland 13 D2 52 27N 9 29W
Litani →, Lebanon 47 B4 33 20N 35 15 E
Litchfield, Calif., U.S.A. 84 E6 40 24N 120 23W
Litchfield, Conn., U.S.A. 79 E11 41 45N 73 11W
Litchfield, Ill., U.S.A. 80 F10 39 11N 89 39W
Litchfield, Minn., U.S.A. 80 C7 45 8N 94 32W
Lithgow, Australia 63 E5 33 25S 150 8 E
Líthinon, Ákra, Greece 23 E6 34 55N 24 44 E
Lithuania ■, Europe 9 J20 55 30N 24 0 E
Lititz, U.S.A. 79 F8 40 9N 76 18W
Litoměřice, Czech Rep. 16 C8 50 33N 14 10 E
Little Abaco I., Bahamas 88 A4 26 50N 77 30W
Little Barrier I., N.Z. 59 G5 36 12S 175 8 E
Little Belt Mts., U.S.A. 82 C8 46 40N 110 45W
Little Blue →, U.S.A. 80 F6 39 42N 96 41W
Little Buffalo →, Canada 72 A6 61 0N 113 46W
Little Cayman, I., Cayman Is. 88 C3 19 41N 80 3W
Little Churchill →, Canada 73 B9 57 30N 95 22W
Little Colorado →, U.S.A. 83 H8 36 12N 111 48W
Little Current, Canada 70 C3 45 55N 82 0W
Little Current →, Canada 70 B3 50 57N 84 36W
Little Falls, Minn., U.S.A. 80 C7 45 59N 94 22W
Little Falls, N.Y., U.S.A. 79 C10 43 3N 74 51W
Little Fork →, U.S.A. 80 A8 48 31N 93 35W
Little Grand Rapids, Canada 73 C9 52 0N 95 29W
Little Humboldt →, U.S.A. 82 F5 41 1N 117 43W
Little Inagua I., Bahamas 89 B5 21 40N 73 50W
Little Karoo, S. Africa 56 E3 33 45S 21 0 E
Little Lake, U.S.A. 85 K9 35 56N 117 55W
Little Laut Is. = Laut Kecil, Kepulauan, Indonesia 36 E5 4 45S 115 40 E
Little-Mecatina = Petit-Mécatina →, Canada 71 B8 50 40N 59 30W
Little Minch, U.K. 12 D2 57 35N 6 45W
Little Missouri →, U.S.A. 80 B3 47 36N 102 25W
Little Ouse →, U.K. 11 E9 52 22N 1 12 E
Little Rann, India 42 H4 23 25N 71 25 E
Little Red →, U.S.A. 81 H9 35 11N 91 27W
Little River, N.Z. 59 K4 43 45S 172 49 E
Little Rock, U.S.A. 81 H8 34 45N 92 17W
Little Ruaha →, Tanzania 54 D4 7 57S 37 53 E
Little Sable Pt., U.S.A. 76 D2 43 38N 86 33W
Little Sioux →, U.S.A. 80 E6 41 48N 96 4W
Little Smoky →, Canada 72 C5 54 44N 117 11W
Little Snake →, U.S.A. 82 F9 40 27N 108 26W
Little Valley, U.S.A. 78 D6 42 15N 78 48W
Little Wabash →, U.S.A. 76 G1 37 55N 88 5W
Little White →, U.S.A. 80 D4 43 40N 100 40W
Littlefield, U.S.A. 81 J3 33 55N 102 20W
Littlehampton, U.K. 11 G7 50 49N 0 32W
Littleton, U.S.A. 79 B13 44 18N 71 46W
Liu He →, China 35 D11 40 55N 121 35 E
Liuba, China 34 H4 33 38N 106 55 E
Liugou, China 35 D10 40 57N 118 15 E
Liuhe, China 35 C13 42 17N 125 43 E
Liukang Tenggaja = Sabalana, Kepulauan, Indonesia 37 F5 6 45S 118 50 E
Liuli, Tanzania 55 E3 11 3S 34 38 E
Liuwa Plain, Zambia 53 G4 14 20S 22 30 E
Liuzhou, China 33 D5 24 22N 109 22 E
Liuzhuang, China 35 H11 33 12N 120 18 E
Livadhia, Cyprus 23 E12 34 57N 33 38 E
Live Oak, Calif., U.S.A. 84 F5 39 17N 121 40W
Live Oak, Fla., U.S.A. 77 K4 30 18N 82 59W
Liveras, Cyprus 23 D11 35 23N 32 57 E
Livermore, U.S.A. 84 H5 37 41N 121 47W
Livermore, Mt., U.S.A. 81 K2 30 38N 104 11W
Livermore Falls, U.S.A. 77 C11 44 29N 70 11W
Liverpool, Canada 71 D7 44 5N 64 41W
Liverpool, U.K. 10 D4 53 25N 3 0W
Liverpool, U.S.A. 79 C8 43 6N 76 13W
Liverpool Bay, U.K. 10 D4 53 30N 3 20W
Liverpool Plains, Australia 63 E5 31 15S 150 15 E
Liverpool Ra., Australia 63 E5 31 50S 150 30 E
Livingston, Guatemala 88 C2 15 50N 88 50W
Livingston, U.K. 12 F5 55 54N 3 30W
Livingston, Ala., U.S.A. 77 J1 32 35N 88 11W
Livingston, Calif., U.S.A. 84 H6 37 23N 120 43W
Livingston, Mont., U.S.A. 82 D8 45 40N 110 34W
Livingston, S.C., U.S.A. 77 J5 33 32N 80 53W
Livingston, Tenn., U.S.A. 77 G3 36 23N 85 19W
Livingston, Tex., U.S.A. 81 K7 30 43N 94 56W
Livingston, L., U.S.A. 81 K7 30 50N 95 10W
Livingston Manor, U.S.A. 79 E10 41 54N 74 50W
Livingstone, Zambia 55 F2 17 46S 25 52 E
Livingstone Mts., Tanzania 55 D3 9 40S 34 20 E
Livingstonia, Malawi 55 E3 10 38S 34 5 E
Livny, Russia 24 D6 52 30N 37 30 E
Livonia, Mich., U.S.A. 76 D4 42 23N 83 23W
Livonia, N.Y., U.S.A. 78 D7 42 49N 77 40W
Livorno, Italy 20 C4 43 33N 10 19 E
Livramento, Brazil 95 C4 30 55S 55 30W
Liwale, Tanzania 55 D4 9 48S 37 58 E
Lizard I., Australia 62 A4 14 42S 145 30 E
Lizard Pt., U.K. 11 H2 49 57N 5 13W
Ljubljana, Slovenia 16 E8 46 4N 14 33 E
Ljungan →, Sweden 9 E17 62 18N 17 23 E
Ljungby, Sweden 9 H15 56 49N 13 55 E
Ljusdal, Sweden 9 F17 61 46N 16 3 E
Ljusnan →, Sweden 9 F17 61 12N 17 8 E
Ljusne, Sweden 9 F17 61 13N 17 7 E
Llancanelo, Salina, Argentina 94 D2 35 40S 69 8W
Llandeilo, U.K. 11 F4 51 53N 3 59W
Llandovery, U.K. 11 F4 51 59N 3 48W
Llandrindod Wells, U.K. 11 E4 52 14N 3 22W
Llandudno, U.K. 10 D4 53 19N 3 50W
Llanelli, U.K. 11 F3 51 41N 4 10W
Llanes, Spain 19 A3 43 25N 4 50W
Llangollen, U.K. 10 E4 52 58N 3 11W
Llanidloes, U.K. 11 E4 52 27N 3 31W
Llano, U.S.A. 81 K5 30 45N 98 41W
Llano →, U.S.A. 81 K5 30 39N 98 26W
Llano Estacado, U.S.A. 81 J3 33 30N 103 0W
Llanos, S. Amer. 92 C4 5 0N 71 35W
Llanquihue, L., Chile 96 E1 41 10S 75 50W
Llanwrtyd Wells, U.K. 11 E4 52 7N 3 38W
Llebeig, C. des, Spain 22 B9 39 33N 2 18 E
Lleida, Spain 19 B6 41 37N 0 39 E
Llentrisca, C., Spain 22 C7 38 52N 1 15 E
Llera, Mexico 87 C5 23 19N 99 1W
Lleyn Peninsula, U.K. 10 E3 52 51N 4 36W
Llico, Chile 94 C1 34 46S 72 5W
Lliria, Spain 19 C5 39 37N 0 35W
Llobregat →, Spain 19 B7 41 19N 2 9 E
Lloret de Mar, Spain 19 B7 41 41N 2 53 E
Lloyd B., Australia 62 A3 12 45S 143 27 E
Lloyd L., Canada 73 B7 57 22N 108 57W
Lloydminster, Canada 73 C7 53 17N 110 0W
Llucmajor, Spain 22 B9 39 29N 2 53 E
Llullaillaco, Volcán, S. Amer. 94 A2 24 43S 68 30W
Lo →, Vietnam 38 B5 21 18N 105 25 E
Loa, U.S.A. 83 G8 38 24N 111 39W
Loa →, Chile 94 A1 21 26S 70 41W
Loaita I., S. China Sea 36 B4 10 41N 114 25 E
Loange →, Dem. Rep. of the Congo 52 E4 4 17S 20 2 E
Lobatse, Botswana 56 D4 25 12S 25 40 E
Lobería, Argentina 94 D4 38 10S 58 40W
Lobito, Angola 53 G2 12 18S 13 35 E
Lobos, Argentina 94 D4 35 10S 59 0W
Lobos, I., Mexico 86 B2 27 15N 110 30W
Lobos, I. de, Canary Is. 22 F6 28 45N 13 50W
Loc Binh, Vietnam 38 B6 21 46N 106 54 E
Loc Ninh, Vietnam 39 G6 11 50N 106 34 E
Locarno, Switz. 18 C8 46 10N 8 47 E
Loch Baghasdail = Lochboisdale, U.K. 12 D1 57 9N 7 20W
Loch Garman = Wexford, Ireland 13 D5 52 20N 6 28W
Loch Nam Madadh = Lochmaddy, U.K. 12 D1 57 36N 7 10W
Lochaber, U.K. 12 E3 56 59N 5 1W
Locharbriggs, U.K. 12 F5 55 7N 3 35W
Lochboisdale, U.K. 12 D1 57 9N 7 20W
Loche, L. La, Canada 73 B7 56 30N 109 30W
Lochem, Neths. 15 B6 52 9N 6 26 E
Loches, France 18 C4 47 7N 1 0 E
Lochgilphead, U.K. 12 E3 56 2N 5 26W
Lochinver, U.K. 12 C3 58 9N 5 14W
Lochmaddy, U.K. 12 D1 57 36N 7 10W
Lochnagar, Australia 62 C4 23 33S 145 38 E
Lochnagar, U.K. 12 E5 56 57N 3 15W
Lochy, L., U.K. 12 E4 57 0N 4 53W
Lock, Australia 63 E2 33 34S 135 46 E
Lock Haven, U.S.A. 78 E7 41 8N 77 28W
Lockeford, U.S.A. 84 G5 38 10N 121 9W
Lockeport, Canada 71 D6 43 47N 65 4W
Lockerbie, U.K. 12 F5 55 7N 3 21W
Lockhart, Australia 63 F4 35 14S 146 40 E
Lockhart, U.S.A. 81 L6 29 53N 97 40W
Lockhart, L., Australia 61 F2 33 15S 119 3 E
Lockhart River, Australia 62 A3 12 58S 143 30 E
Lockney, U.S.A. 81 H4 34 7N 101 27W
Lockport, U.S.A. 78 C6 43 10N 78 42W
Lod, Israel 47 D3 31 57N 34 54 E
Lodeinoye Pole, Russia 24 B5 60 44N 33 33 E
Lodge Bay, Canada 71 B8 52 14N 55 51W
Lodge Grass, U.S.A. 82 D10 45 19N 107 22W
Lodgepole Cr. →, U.S.A. 80 E2 41 20N 104 30W
Lodhran, Pakistan 42 E4 29 32N 71 30 E
Lodi, Italy 18 D8 45 19N 9 30 E
Lodi, Calif., U.S.A. 84 G5 38 8N 121 16W
Lodi, Ohio, U.S.A. 78 E3 41 2N 82 0W
Lodja, Dem. Rep. of the Congo 54 C1 3 30S 23 23 E
Lodwar, Kenya 54 B4 3 10N 35 40 E
Łódź, Poland 17 C10 51 45N 19 27 E
Loei, Thailand 38 D3 17 29N 101 35 E
Loengo, Dem. Rep. of the Congo 54 C2 4 48S 26 30 E
Loeriesfontein, S. Africa 56 E2 31 0S 19 26 E
Lofoten, Norway 8 B15 68 30N 14 0 E
Logan, Iowa, U.S.A. 80 E7 41 39N 95 47W
Logan, Ohio, U.S.A. 76 F4 39 32N 82 25W
Logan, Utah, U.S.A. 82 F8 41 44N 111 50W
Logan, W. Va., U.S.A. 76 G5 37 51N 81 59W
Logan, Mt., Canada 68 B5 60 31N 140 22W
Logandale, U.S.A. 85 J12 36 36N 114 29W
Logansport, Ind., U.S.A. 76 E2 40 45N 86 22W
Logansport, La., U.S.A. 81 K8 31 58N 94 0W
Logone →, Chad 51 F9 12 6N 15 2 E
Logroño, Spain 19 A4 42 28N 2 27W
Lohardaga, India 43 H11 23 27N 84 45 E
Loharia, India 42 H6 23 45N 74 14 E
Loharu, India 42 E6 28 27N 75 49 E
Lohja, Finland 9 F21 60 12N 24 5 E
Lohri Wah →, Pakistan 42 F2 27 27N 67 37 E
Loi-kaw, Burma 41 K20 19 40N 97 17 E
Loimaa, Finland 9 F20 60 50N 23 5 E
Loir →, France 18 C3 47 33N 0 32W
Loire →, France 18 C2 47 16N 2 10W
Loja, Ecuador 92 D3 3 59S 79 16W
Loja, Spain 19 D3 37 10N 4 10W
Loji = Kawasi, Indonesia 37 E7 1 38S 127 28 E
Lokandu, Dem. Rep. of the Congo 54 C2 2 30S 25 45 E
Lokeren, Belgium 15 C3 51 6N 3 59 E
Lokichokio, Kenya 54 B3 4 19N 34 13 E
Lokitaung, Kenya 54 B4 4 12N 35 48 E
Lokkan tekojärvi, Finland 8 C22 67 55N 27 35 E
Lokoja, Nigeria 50 G7 7 47N 6 45 E
Lola, Mt., U.S.A. 84 F6 39 26N 120 22W
Loliondo, Tanzania 54 C4 2 2S 35 39 E
Lolland, Denmark 9 J14 54 45N 11 30 E
Lolo, U.S.A. 82 C6 46 45N 114 5W
Lom, Bulgaria 21 C10 43 48N 23 12 E
Lom Kao, Thailand 38 D3 16 53N 101 14 E
Lom Sak, Thailand 38 D3 16 47N 101 15 E
Loma, U.S.A. 82 C8 47 56N 110 30W
Loma Linda, U.S.A. 85 L9 34 3N 117 16W
Lomami →, Dem. Rep. of the Congo 54 B1 0 46N 24 16 E
Lomas de Zamóra, Argentina 94 C4 34 45S 58 25W
Lombadina, Australia 60 C3 16 31S 122 54 E
Lombárdia □, Italy 18 D8 45 40N 9 30 E
Lombardy = Lombárdia □, Italy 18 D8 45 40N 9 30 E
Lomblen, Indonesia 37 F6 8 30S 123 32 E
Lombok, Indonesia 36 F5 8 45S 116 30 E
Lomé, Togo 50 G6 6 9N 1 20 E
Lomela, Dem. Rep. of the Congo 52 E4 2 19S 23 15 E
Lomela →, Dem. Rep. of the Congo 52 E4 0 15S 20 40 E
Lommel, Belgium 15 C5 51 14N 5 19 E
Lomond, Canada 72 C6 50 24N 112 36W
Lomond, L., U.K. 12 E4 56 8N 4 38W
Lomphat, Cambodia 38 F6 13 30N 106 59 E
Lompobatang, Indonesia 37 F5 5 24S 119 56 E
Lompoc, U.S.A. 85 L6 34 38N 120 28W
Lomza, Poland 17 B12 53 10N 22 2 E
Loncoche, Chile 96 D2 39 20S 72 50W
Londa, India 40 M9 15 30N 74 30 E
Londiani, Kenya 54 C4 0 10S 35 33 E
London, Canada 78 D3 42 59N 81 15W
London, U.K. 11 F7 51 30N 0 3W
London, Ky., U.S.A. 76 G3 37 8N 84 5W
London, Ohio, U.S.A. 76 F4 39 53N 83 27W
London, Greater □, U.K. 11 F7 51 36N 0 5W
Londonderry, U.K. 13 B4 55 0N 7 20W
Londonderry □, U.K. 13 B4 55 0N 7 20W
Londonderry, C., Australia 60 B4 13 45S 126 55 E
Londonderry, I., Chile 96 H2 55 0S 71 0W
Londres, Argentina 96 B3 27 43S 67 7W
Londrina, Brazil 95 A5 23 18S 51 10W
Lone Pine, U.S.A. 84 J8 36 36N 118 4W
Long B., U.S.A. 77 J6 33 35N 78 45W
Long Beach, Calif., U.S.A. 85 M8 33 47N 118 11W
Long Beach, N.Y., U.S.A. 79 F11 40 35N 73 39W
Long Beach, Wash., U.S.A. 84 D2 46 21N 124 3W
Long Branch, U.S.A. 79 F11 40 18N 74 0W
Long Creek, U.S.A. 82 D4 44 43N 119 6W
Long Eaton, U.K. 10 E6 52 53N 1 15W
Long I., Australia 62 C4 22 8S 149 53 E
Long I., Bahamas 89 B4 23 20N 75 10W
Long I., Canada 70 B4 54 50N 79 20W
Long I., Ireland 13 E2 51 30N 9 34W
Long I., U.S.A. 79 F11 40 45N 73 30W
Long Island Sd., U.S.A. 79 E12 41 10N 73 0W
Long L., Canada 70 C2 49 30N 86 50W
Long Lake, U.S.A. 79 C10 43 58N 74 25W
Long Point B., Canada 78 D4 42 40N 80 10W
Long Prairie →, U.S.A. 80 C7 46 20N 94 36W
Long Pt., Canada 78 D4 42 35N 80 2W
Long Range Mts., Canada 71 C8 49 30N 57 30W
Long Reef, Australia 60 B4 14 1S 125 48 E
Long Spruce, Canada 73 B10 56 24N 94 21W
Long Str. = Longa, Proliv, Russia 4 C16 70 0N 175 0 E
Long Thanh, Vietnam 39 G6 10 47N 106 57 E
Long Xian, China 34 G4 34 55N 106 55 E
Long Xuyen, Vietnam 39 G5 10 19N 105 28 E
Longa, Proliv, Russia 4 C16 70 0N 175 0 E
Longbenton, U.K. 10 B6 55 1N 1 31W
Longboat Key, U.S.A. 77 M4 27 23N 82 39W
Longde, China 34 G4 35 30N 106 20 E
Longford, Australia 62 G4 41 32S 147 3 E
Longford, Ireland 13 C4 53 43N 7 49W
Longford □, Ireland 13 C4 53 42N 7 45W
Longguan, China 34 D8 40 45N 115 30 E
Longhua, China 35 D9 41 18N 117 45 E
Longido, Tanzania 54 C4 2 43S 36 42 E
Longiram, Indonesia 36 E5 0 5S 115 45 E
Longkou, China 35 F11 37 40N 120 18 E
Longlac, Canada 70 C2 49 45N 86 25W
Longmeadow, U.S.A. 79 D12 42 3N 72 34W
Longmont, U.S.A. 80 E2 40 10N 105 6W
Longnawan, Indonesia 36 D4 1 51N 114 55 E
Longreach, Australia 62 C3 23 28S 144 14 E
Longueuil, Canada 79 A11 45 32N 73 28W
Longview, Tex., U.S.A. 81 J7 32 30N 94 44W

Mallaig

McConaughy, L., U.S.A. 80 E4 41 14N 101 40W
McCook, U.S.A. 80 E4 40 12N 100 38W
McCreary, Canada 73 C9 50 47N 99 29W
McCullough Mt., U.S.A. 85 K11 35 35N 115 13W
McCusker →, Canada 73 B7 55 32N 108 39W
McDame, Canada 72 B3 59 44N 128 59W
McDermitt, U.S.A. 82 F5 41 59N 117 43W
McDonald, U.S.A. 78 F4 40 22N 80 14W
Macdonald, L., Australia 60 D4 23 30S 129 0 E
McDonald Is., Ind. Oc. 3 G13 53 0S 73 0 E
MacDonnell Ranges, Australia 60 D5 23 40S 133 0 E
MacDowell L., Canada 70 B1 52 15N 92 45W
Macduff, U.K. 12 D6 57 40N 2 31W
Macedonia = Makedhonía □, Greece 21 D10 40 39N 22 0 E
Macedonia, U.S.A. 78 E3 41 19N 81 31W
Macedonia ■, Europe 21 D9 41 53N 21 40 E
Maceió, Brazil 93 E11 9 40S 35 41W
Macerata, Italy 20 C5 43 18N 13 27 E
McFarland, U.S.A. 85 K7 35 41N 119 14W
McFarlane →, Canada 73 B7 59 12N 107 58W
Macfarlane, L., Australia 63 E2 32 0S 136 40 E
McGehee, U.S.A. 81 J9 33 38N 91 24W
McGill, U.S.A. 82 G6 39 23N 114 47W
Macgillycuddy's Reeks, Ireland 13 E2 51 58N 9 45W
McGraw, U.S.A. 79 D8 42 36N 76 8W
McGregor, U.S.A. 80 D9 43 1N 91 11W
McGregor Ra., Australia 63 D3 27 0S 142 45 E
Mach, Pakistan 40 E5 29 50N 67 20 E
Mâch Kowr, Iran 45 E9 25 48N 61 28 E
Machado = Jiparaná →, Brazil 92 E6 8 3S 62 52W
Machagai, Argentina 94 B3 26 56S 60 2W
Machakos, Kenya 54 C4 1 30S 37 15 E
Machala, Ecuador 92 D3 3 20S 79 57W
Machanga, Mozam. 57 C6 20 59S 35 0 E
Machattie, L., Australia 62 C2 24 50S 139 48 E
Machava, Mozam. 57 D5 25 54S 32 28 E
Machece, Mozam. 55 F4 19 15S 35 32 E
Machhu →, India 42 H4 23 6N 70 46 E
Machias, Maine, U.S.A. 77 C12 44 43N 67 28W
Machias, N.Y., U.S.A. 78 D6 42 25N 78 30W
Machichi →, Canada 73 B10 57 3N 92 6W
Machico, Madeira 22 D3 32 43N 16 44W
Machilipatnam, India 41 L12 16 12N 81 8 E
Machiques, Venezuela 92 A4 10 4N 72 34W
Machupicchu, Peru 92 F4 13 8S 72 30W
Machynlleth, U.K. 11 E4 52 35N 3 50W
McIlwraith Ra., Australia 62 A3 13 50S 143 20 E
McInnes L., Canada 73 C10 52 13N 93 45W
McIntosh, U.S.A. 80 C4 45 55N 101 21W
McIntosh L., Canada 73 B8 55 45N 105 0W
Macintosh Ra., Australia 61 E4 27 39S 125 32 E
Macintyre →, Australia 63 D5 28 37S 150 47 E
Mackay, Australia 62 C4 21 8S 149 11 E
Mackay, U.S.A. 82 E7 43 55N 113 37W
MacKay →, Canada 72 B6 57 10N 111 38W
Mackay, L., Australia 60 D4 22 30S 129 0 E
McKay Ra., Australia 60 D3 23 0S 122 30 E
McKeesport, U.S.A. 78 F5 40 21N 79 52W
McKellar, Canada 78 A5 45 30N 79 55W
McKenna, U.S.A. 84 D4 46 56N 122 33W
Mackenzie, Canada 72 B4 55 20N 123 5W
McKenzie, U.S.A. 77 G1 36 8N 88 31W
Mackenzie →, Australia 62 C4 23 38S 149 46 E
Mackenzie →, Canada 68 B6 69 10N 134 20W
McKenzie →, U.S.A. 82 D2 44 7N 123 6W
Mackenzie Bay, Canada 4 B1 69 0N 137 30W
Mackenzie City = Linden, Guyana 92 B7 6 0N 58 10W
Mackenzie Mts., Canada 68 B7 64 0N 130 0W
Mackinaw City, U.S.A. 76 C3 45 47N 84 44W
McKinlay, Australia 62 C3 21 16S 141 18 E
McKinlay →, Australia 62 C3 20 50S 141 28 E
McKinley, Mt., U.S.A. 68 B4 63 4N 151 0W
McKinley Sea, Arctic 4 A7 82 0N 0 0 E
McKinney, U.S.A. 81 J6 33 12N 96 37W
Mackinnon Road, Kenya 54 C4 3 40S 39 1 E
McKittrick, U.S.A. 85 K7 35 18N 119 37W
Macklin, Canada 73 C7 52 20N 109 56W
Macksville, Australia 63 E5 30 40S 152 56 E
McLaughlin, U.S.A. 80 C4 45 49N 100 49W
Maclean, Australia 63 D5 29 26S 153 16 E
McLean, U.S.A. 81 H4 35 14N 100 36W
McLeansboro, U.S.A. 80 F10 38 6N 88 32W
Maclear, S. Africa 57 E4 31 2S 28 23 E
Macleay →, Australia 63 E5 30 56S 153 0 E
McLennan, Canada 72 B5 55 42N 116 50W
McLeod →, Canada 72 C5 54 9N 115 44W
MacLeod, B., Canada 73 A7 62 53N 110 0W
McLeod, L., Australia 61 D1 24 9S 113 47 E
MacLeod Lake, Canada 72 C4 54 58N 123 0W
McLoughlin, Mt., U.S.A. 82 E2 42 27N 122 19W
McMechen, U.S.A. 78 G4 39 57N 80 44W
McMinnville, Oreg., U.S.A. 82 D2 45 13N 123 12W
McMinnville, Tenn., U.S.A. 77 H3 35 41N 85 46W
McMurdo Sd., Antarctica 5 D11 77 0S 170 0 E
McMurray = Fort McMurray, Canada 72 B6 56 44N 111 7W
McMurray, U.S.A. 84 B4 48 19N 122 14W
Macodoene, Mozam. 57 C6 23 32S 35 5 E
Macomb, U.S.A. 80 E9 40 27N 90 40W
Mâcon, France 18 C6 46 19N 4 50 E
Macon, Ga., U.S.A. 77 J4 32 51N 83 38W
Macon, Miss., U.S.A. 77 J1 33 7N 88 34W
Macon, Mo., U.S.A. 80 F8 39 44N 92 28W
Macossa, Mozam. 55 F3 17 55S 33 56 E
Macoun L., Canada 73 B8 56 32N 103 40W
Macovane, Mozam. 57 C6 21 30S 35 2 E
McPherson, U.S.A. 80 F6 38 22N 97 40W
McPherson Pk., U.S.A. 85 L7 34 53N 119 53W
McPherson Ra., Australia 63 D5 28 15S 153 15 E
Macquarie →, Australia 63 E4 30 5S 147 30 E
Macquarie Harbour, Australia 62 G4 42 15S 145 23 E
Macquarie Is., Pac. Oc. 64 N7 54 36S 158 55 E
MacRobertson Land, Antarctica 5 D6 71 0S 64 0 E
Macroom, Ireland 13 E3 51 54N 8 57W
MacTier, Canada 78 A5 45 9N 79 46W
Macubela, Mozam. 55 F4 16 53S 37 49 E
Macuiza, Mozam. 55 F3 18 7S 34 29 E
Macusani, Peru 92 F4 14 4S 70 29W
Macuse, Mozam. 55 F4 17 45S 37 10 E
Macuspana, Mexico 87 D6 17 46N 92 36W
Macusse, Angola 56 B3 17 48S 20 23 E
Madadeni, S. Africa 57 D5 27 43S 30 3 E
Madagascar ■, Africa 57 C8 20 0S 47 0 E
Madā'in Sālih, Si. Arabia 44 E3 26 46N 37 57 E
Madama, Niger 51 D8 22 0N 13 40 E
Madame I., Canada 71 C7 45 30N 60 58W
Madaripur, Bangla. 41 H17 23 19N 90 15 E
Madauk, Burma 41 L20 17 56N 96 52 E
Madawaska, Canada 78 A7 45 30N 78 0W
Madawaska →, Canada 78 A8 45 27N 76 21W
Madaya, Burma 41 H20 22 12N 96 10 E
Maddalena, Italy 20 D3 41 16N 9 23 E
Madeira, Atl. Oc. 22 D3 32 50N 17 0W
Madeira →, Brazil 92 D7 3 22S 58 45W
Madeleine, Îs. de la, Canada 71 C7 47 30N 61 40W
Madera, Mexico 86 B3 29 12N 108 7W
Madera, Calif., U.S.A. 84 J6 36 57N 120 3W
Madera, Pa., U.S.A. 78 F6 40 49N 78 26W
Madha, India 40 L9 18 0N 75 30 E
Madhavpur, India 42 J3 21 15N 69 58 E
Madhepura, India 43 F12 26 11N 86 23 E
Madhubani, India 43 F12 26 21N 86 7 E
Madhupur, India 43 G12 24 16N 86 39 E
Madhya Pradesh □, India 42 J8 22 50N 78 0 E
Madidi →, Bolivia 92 F5 12 32S 66 52W
Madikeri, India 40 N9 12 30N 75 45 E
Madill, U.S.A. 81 H6 34 6N 96 46W
Madimba, Dem. Rep. of the Congo 52 E3 4 58S 15 5 E
Ma'din, Syria 44 C3 35 45N 39 36 E
Madingou, Congo 52 E2 4 10S 13 33 E
Madirovalo, Madag. 57 B8 16 26S 46 32 E
Madison, Calif., U.S.A. 84 G5 38 41N 121 59W
Madison, Fla., U.S.A. 77 K4 30 28N 83 25W
Madison, Ind., U.S.A. 76 F3 38 44N 85 23W
Madison, Nebr., U.S.A. 80 E6 41 50N 97 27W
Madison, Ohio, U.S.A. 78 E3 41 46N 81 3W
Madison, S. Dak., U.S.A. 80 D6 44 0N 97 7W
Madison, Wis., U.S.A. 80 D10 43 4N 89 24W
Madison →, U.S.A. 82 D8 45 56N 111 31W
Madison Heights, U.S.A. 76 G6 37 25N 79 8W
Madisonville, Ky., U.S.A. 76 G2 37 20N 87 30W
Madisonville, Tex., U.S.A. 81 K7 30 57N 95 55W
Madista, Botswana 56 C4 21 15S 25 6 E
Madiun, Indonesia 37 G14 7 38S 111 32 E
Madoc, Canada 78 B7 44 30N 77 28W
Madona, Latvia 9 H22 56 53N 26 5 E
Madrakah, Ra's al, Oman 46 D6 19 0N 57 50 E
Madras = Chennai, India 40 N12 13 8N 80 19 E
Madras = Tamil Nadu □, India 40 P10 11 0N 77 0 E
Madras, U.S.A. 82 D3 44 38N 121 8W
Madre, L., Mexico 87 C5 25 0N 97 30W
Madre, Laguna, U.S.A. 81 M6 27 0N 97 30W
Madre, Sierra, Phil. 37 A6 17 0N 122 0 E
Madre de Dios →, Bolivia 92 F5 10 59S 66 8W
Madre de Dios, I., Chile 96 G1 50 20S 75 10W
Madre del Sur, Sierra, Mexico 87 D5 17 30N 100 0W
Madre Occidental, Sierra, Mexico 86 B3 27 0N 107 0W
Madre Oriental, Sierra, Mexico 86 C5 25 0N 100 0W
Madri, India 42 G5 24 16N 73 32 E
Madrid, Spain 19 B4 40 25N 3 45W
Madrid, U.S.A. 79 B9 44 45N 75 8W
Madura, Australia 61 F4 31 55S 127 0 E
Madura, Indonesia 37 G15 7 30S 114 0 E
Madura, Selat, Indonesia 37 G15 7 30S 113 20 E
Madurai, India 40 Q11 9 55N 78 10 E
Madurantakam, India 40 N11 12 30N 79 50 E
Mae Chan, Thailand 38 B2 20 9N 99 52 E
Mae Hong Son, Thailand 38 C2 19 16N 97 56 E
Mae Khlong →, Thailand 38 F3 13 24N 100 0 E
Mae Phrik, Thailand 38 D2 17 27N 99 7 E
Mae Ramat, Thailand 38 D2 16 58N 98 31 E
Mae Rim, Thailand 38 C2 18 54N 98 57 E
Mae Sot, Thailand 38 D2 16 43N 98 34 E
Mae Suai, Thailand 38 C2 19 39N 99 33 E
Mae Tha, Thailand 38 C2 18 28N 99 8 E
Maebashi, Japan 31 F9 36 24N 139 4 E
Maesteg, U.K. 11 F4 51 36N 3 40W
Maestra, Sierra, Cuba 88 B4 20 15N 77 0W
Maevatanana, Madag. 57 B8 16 56S 46 49 E
Mafeking = Mafikeng, S. Africa 56 D4 25 50S 25 38 E
Mafeking, Canada 73 C8 52 40N 101 10W
Mafeteng, Lesotho 56 D4 29 51S 27 15 E
Maffra, Australia 63 F4 37 53S 146 58 E
Mafia I., Tanzania 54 D4 7 45S 39 50 E
Mafikeng, S. Africa 56 D4 25 50S 25 38 E
Mafra, Brazil 95 B6 26 10S 49 55W
Mafra, Portugal 19 C1 38 55N 9 20W
Mafungabusi Plateau, Zimbabwe 55 F2 18 30S 29 8 E
Magadan, Russia 27 D16 59 38N 150 50 E
Magadi, Kenya 54 C4 1 54S 36 19 E
Magadi, L., Kenya 54 C4 1 54S 36 19 E
Magaliesburg, S. Africa 57 D4 26 0S 27 32 E
Magallanes, Estrecho de, Chile 96 G2 52 30S 75 0W
Magangué, Colombia 92 B4 9 14N 74 45W
Magdalen Is. = Madeleine, Îs. de la, Canada 71 C7 47 30N 61 40W
Magdalena, Argentina 94 D4 35 5S 57 30W
Magdalena, Bolivia 92 F6 13 13S 63 57W
Magdalena, Mexico 86 A2 30 50N 112 0W
Magdalena, U.S.A. 83 J10 34 7N 107 15W
Magdalena →, Colombia 92 A4 11 6N 74 51W
Magdalena →, Mexico 86 A2 30 40N 112 25W
Magdalena, B., Mexico 86 C2 24 30N 112 10W
Magdalena, Llano de la, Mexico 86 C2 25 0N 111 30W
Magdeburg, Germany 16 B6 52 7N 11 38 E
Magdelaine Cays, Australia 62 B5 16 33S 150 18 E
Magee, U.S.A. 81 K10 31 52N 89 44W
Magelang, Indonesia 37 G14 7 29S 110 13 E
Magellan's Str. = Magallanes, Estrecho de, Chile 96 G2 52 30S 75 0W
Magenta, L., Australia 61 F2 33 30S 119 2 E
Magerøya, Norway 8 A21 71 3N 25 40 E
Maggiore, Lago, Italy 18 D8 45 57N 8 39 E
Maghâgha, Egypt 51 C12 28 38N 30 50 E
Magherafelt, U.K. 13 B5 54 45N 6 37W
Maghreb, N. Afr. 50 B5 32 0N 4 0W
Magistralnyy, Russia 27 D11 56 16N 107 36 E
Magnetic Pole (North) = North Magnetic Pole, Canada 4 B2 77 58N 102 8W
Magnetic Pole (South) = South Magnetic Pole, Antarctica 5 C9 64 8S 138 8 E
Magnitogorsk, Russia 24 D10 53 27N 59 4 E
Magnolia, Ark., U.S.A. 81 J8 33 16N 93 14W
Magnolia, Miss., U.S.A. 81 K9 31 9N 90 28W
Magog, Canada 79 A12 45 18N 72 9W
Magoro, Uganda 54 B3 1 45N 34 12 E
Magosa = Famagusta, Cyprus 23 D12 35 8N 33 55 E
Magouládhes, Greece 23 A3 39 45N 19 42 E
Magoye, Zambia 55 F2 16 1S 27 30 E
Magozal, Mexico 87 C5 21 34N 97 59W
Magpie, L., Canada 71 B7 51 0N 64 41W
Magrath, Canada 72 D6 49 25N 112 50W
Maguarinho, C., Brazil 93 D9 0 15S 48 30W
Mağusa = Famagusta, Cyprus 23 D12 35 8N 33 55 E
Maguse L., Canada 73 A9 61 40N 95 10W
Maguse Pt., Canada 73 A10 61 20N 93 50W
Magvana, India 42 H3 23 13N 69 22 E
Magwe, Burma 41 J19 20 10N 95 0 E
Maha Sarakham, Thailand 38 D4 16 12N 103 16 E
Mahābād, Iran 44 B5 36 50N 45 45 E
Mahabharat Lekh, Nepal 43 E10 28 30N 82 0 E
Mahabo, Madag. 57 C7 20 23S 44 40 E
Mahadeo Hills, India 43 H8 22 20N 78 30 E
Mahaffey, U.S.A. 78 F6 40 53N 78 44W
Mahagi, Dem. Rep. of the Congo 54 B3 2 20N 31 0 E
Mahajamba →, Madag. 57 B8 15 33S 47 8 E
Mahajamba, Helodranon' i, Madag. 57 B8 15 24S 47 5 E
Mahajan, India 42 E5 28 48N 73 56 E
Mahajanga, Madag. 57 B8 15 40S 46 25 E
Mahajanga □, Madag. 57 B8 17 0S 47 0 E
Mahajilo →, Madag. 57 B8 19 42S 45 22 E
Mahakam →, Indonesia 36 E5 0 35S 117 17 E
Mahalapye, Botswana 56 C4 23 1S 26 51 E
Mahallāt, Iran 45 C6 33 55N 50 30 E
Māhān, Iran 45 D8 30 5N 57 18 E
Mahan →, India 43 H10 23 30N 82 50 E
Mahanadi →, India 41 J15 20 20N 86 25 E
Mahananda →, India 43 G12 25 12N 87 52 E
Mahanoro, Madag. 57 B8 19 54S 48 48 E
Mahanoy City, U.S.A. 79 F8 40 49N 76 9W
Maharashtra □, India 40 J9 20 30N 75 30 E
Mahari Mts., Tanzania 54 D3 6 20S 30 0 E
Mahasham, W. →, Egypt 47 E3 30 15N 34 10 E
Mahasolo, Madag. 57 B8 19 7S 46 22 E
Mahattat ash Shidiyah, Jordan 47 F4 29 55N 35 55 E
Mahattat 'Unayzah, Jordan 47 E4 30 30N 35 47 E
Mahaxay, Laos 38 D5 17 22N 105 12 E
Mahbubnagar, India 40 L10 16 45N 77 59 E
Mahḍah, Oman 45 E7 24 24N 55 59 E
Mahdia, Tunisia 51 A8 35 28N 11 0 E
Mahe, India 43 C8 33 10N 78 32 E
Mahendragarh, India 42 E7 28 17N 76 14 E
Mahenge, Tanzania 55 D4 8 45S 36 41 E
Maheno, N.Z. 59 L3 45 10S 170 50 E
Mahesana, India 42 H5 23 39N 72 26 E
Maheshwar, India 42 H6 22 11N 75 35 E
Mahgawan, India 43 F8 26 29N 78 37 E
Mahi →, India 42 H5 22 15N 72 55 E
Mahia Pen., N.Z. 59 H6 39 9S 177 55 E
Mahilyow, Belarus 17 B16 53 55N 30 18 E
Mahmud Kot, Pakistan 42 D4 30 16N 71 0 E
Mahnomen, U.S.A. 80 B7 47 19N 95 58W
Mahoba, India 43 G8 25 15N 79 55 E
Mahón = Maó, Spain 22 B11 39 53N 4 16 E
Mahone Bay, Canada 71 D7 44 30N 64 20W
Mahopac, U.S.A. 79 E11 41 22N 73 45W
Mahuva, India 42 J4 21 5N 71 48 E
Mai-Ndombe, L., Dem. Rep. of the Congo 52 E3 2 0S 18 20 E
Mai-Sai, Thailand 38 B2 20 20N 99 55 E
Maicurú →, Brazil 93 D8 2 14S 54 17W
Maidan Khula, Afghan. 42 C3 33 36N 69 50 E
Maidenhead, U.K. 11 F7 51 31N 0 42W
Maidstone, Canada 73 C7 53 5N 109 20W
Maidstone, U.K. 11 F8 51 16N 0 32 E
Maiduguri, Nigeria 51 F8 12 0N 13 20 E
Maihar, India 43 G9 24 16N 80 45 E
Maijdi, Bangla. 41 H17 22 48N 91 10 E
Maikala Ra., India 41 J12 22 0N 81 0 E
Mailani, India 43 E9 28 17N 80 21 E
Mailsi, Pakistan 42 E5 29 48N 72 15 E
Main →, Germany 16 C5 50 0N 8 18 E
Main →, U.K. 13 B5 54 48N 6 18W
Maine, France 18 C3 48 20N 0 15W
Maine □, U.S.A. 77 C11 45 20N 69 0W
Maine →, Ireland 13 D2 52 9N 9 45W
Maingkwan, Burma 41 F20 26 15N 96 37 E
Mainit, L., Phil. 37 C7 9 31N 125 30 E
Mainland, Orkney, U.K. 12 C5 58 59N 3 8W
Mainland, Shet., U.K. 12 A7 60 15N 1 22W
Mainoru, Australia 62 A1 14 0S 134 6 E
Mainpuri, India 43 F8 27 18N 79 4 E
Maintirano, Madag. 57 B7 18 3S 44 1 E
Mainz, Germany 16 C5 50 1N 8 14 E
Maipú, Argentina 94 D4 36 52S 57 50W
Maiquetía, Venezuela 92 A5 10 36N 66 57W
Mairabari, India 41 F18 26 30N 92 22 E
Maisi, Cuba 89 B5 20 17N 74 9W
Maisi, Pta. de, Cuba 89 B5 20 10N 74 10W
Maitland, N.S.W., Australia 63 E5 32 33S 151 36 E
Maitland, S. Austral., Australia 63 E2 34 23S 137 40 E
Maitland →, Canada 78 C3 43 45N 81 43W
Maiz, Is. del, Nic. 88 D3 12 15N 83 4W
Maizuru, Japan 31 G7 35 25N 135 22 E
Majalengka, Indonesia 37 G13 6 50S 108 13 E
Majene, Indonesia 37 E5 3 38S 118 57 E
Majorca = Mallorca, Spain 22 B10 39 30N 3 0 E
Makale, Indonesia 37 E5 3 6S 119 51 E
Makamba, Burundi 54 C2 4 8S 29 49 E
Makarikari = Makgadikgadi Salt Pans, Botswana 56 C4 20 40S 25 45 E
Makarovo, Russia 27 D11 57 40N 107 45 E
Makasar = Ujung Pandang, Indonesia 37 F5 5 10S 119 20 E
Makasar, Selat, Indonesia 37 E5 1 0S 118 20 E
Makasar, Str. of = Makasar, Selat, Indonesia 37 E5 1 0S 118 20 E
Makat, Kazakstan 25 E9 47 39N 53 19 E
Makedhonía □, Greece 21 D10 40 39N 22 0 E
Makedonija = Macedonia ■, Europe 21 D9 41 53N 21 40 E
Makena, U.S.A. 74 H16 20 39N 156 27W
Makeyevka = Makiyivka, Ukraine 25 E6 48 0N 38 0 E
Makgadikgadi Salt Pans, Botswana 56 C4 20 40S 25 45 E
Makhachkala, Russia 25 F8 43 0N 47 30 E
Makhmūr, Iraq 44 C4 35 46N 43 35 E
Makian, Indonesia 37 D7 0 20N 127 20 E
Makindu, Kenya 54 C4 2 18S 37 50 E
Makinsk, Kazakstan 26 D8 52 37N 70 26 E
Makiyivka, Ukraine 25 E6 48 0N 38 0 E
Makkah, Si. Arabia 46 C2 21 30N 39 54 E
Makkovik, Canada 71 A8 55 10N 59 10W
Makó, Hungary 17 E11 46 14N 20 33 E
Makokou, Gabon 52 D2 0 40N 12 50 E
Makongo, Dem. Rep. of the Congo 54 B2 3 25N 26 17 E
Makoro, Dem. Rep. of the Congo 54 B2 3 10N 29 59 E
Makrai, India 40 H10 22 2N 77 0 E
Makran Coast Range, Pakistan 40 G4 25 40N 64 0 E
Makrana, India 42 F6 27 2N 74 46 E
Makriyialos, Greece 23 D7 35 2N 25 59 E
Mākū, Iran 44 B5 39 15N 44 31 E
Makunda, Botswana 56 C3 22 30S 20 7 E
Makurazaki, Japan 31 J5 31 15N 130 20 E
Makurdi, Nigeria 50 G7 7 43N 8 35 E
Makūyeh, Iran 45 D7 28 7N 53 9 E
Makwassie, S. Africa 56 D4 27 17S 26 0 E
Mal B., Ireland 13 D2 52 50N 9 30W
Mala, Pta., Panama 88 E3 7 28N 80 2W
Malabar Coast, India 40 P9 11 0N 75 0 E
Malabo = Rey Malabo, Eq. Guin. 52 D1 3 45N 8 50 E
Malacca, Str. of, Indonesia 39 L3 3 0N 101 0 E
Malad City, U.S.A. 82 E7 42 12N 112 15W
Maladzyechna, Belarus 17 A14 54 20N 26 50 E
Málaga, Spain 19 D3 36 43N 4 23W
Malagarasi, Tanzania 54 D3 5 5S 30 50 E
Malagarasi →, Tanzania 54 D2 5 12S 29 47 E
Malagasy Rep. = Madagascar ■, Africa 57 C8 20 0S 47 0 E
Malahide, Ireland 13 C5 53 26N 6 9W
Malaimbandy, Madag. 57 C8 20 20S 45 36 E
Malakâl, Sudan 51 G12 9 33N 31 40 E
Malakand, Pakistan 42 B4 34 40N 71 55 E
Malakwal, Pakistan 42 C5 32 34N 73 13 E
Malamala, Indonesia 37 E6 3 21S 120 55 E
Malanda, Australia 62 B4 17 22S 145 35 E
Malang, Indonesia 37 G15 7 59S 112 45 E
Malangen, Norway 8 B18 69 24N 18 37 E
Malanje, Angola 52 F3 9 36S 16 17 E
Mälaren, Sweden 9 G17 59 30N 17 10 E
Malargüe, Argentina 94 D2 35 32S 69 30W
Malartic, Canada 70 C4 48 9N 78 9W
Malaryta, Belarus 17 C13 51 50N 24 3 E
Malatya, Turkey 25 G6 38 25N 38 20 E
Malawi ■, Africa 55 E3 11 55S 34 0 E
Malawi, L. = Nyasa, L., Africa 55 E3 12 30S 34 30 E
Malay Pen., Asia 39 J3 7 25N 100 0 E
Malaya Vishera, Russia 24 C5 58 55N 32 25 E
Malaybalay, Phil. 37 C7 8 5N 125 7 E
Malāyer, Iran 45 C6 34 19N 48 51 E
Malaysia ■, Asia 39 K4 5 0N 110 0 E
Malazgirt, Turkey 25 G7 39 10N 42 33 E
Malbon, Australia 62 C3 21 5S 140 17 E
Malbooma, Australia 63 E1 30 41S 134 11 E
Malbork, Poland 17 B10 54 3N 19 1 E
Malcolm, Australia 61 E3 28 51S 121 25 E
Malcolm, Pt., Australia 61 F3 33 48S 123 45 E
Maldah, India 43 G13 25 2N 88 9 E
Maldegem, Belgium 15 C3 51 14N 3 26 E
Malden, Mass., U.S.A. 79 D13 42 26N 71 4W
Malden, Mo., U.S.A. 81 G10 36 34N 89 57W
Malden I., Kiribati 65 H12 4 3S 155 1W
Maldives ■, Ind. Oc. 29 J11 5 0N 73 0 E
Maldonado, Uruguay 95 C5 34 59S 55 0W
Maldonado, Punta, Mexico 87 D5 16 19N 98 35W
Malé, Maldives 29 J11 4 0N 73 28 E
Malé Karpaty, Slovak Rep. 17 D9 48 30N 17 20 E
Maléa, Ákra, Greece 21 F10 36 28N 23 7 E
Malegaon, India 40 J9 20 30N 74 38 E
Malei, Mozam. 55 F4 17 12S 36 58 E
Malek Kandī, Iran 44 B5 37 9N 46 6 E
Malela, Dem. Rep. of the Congo 54 C2 4 22S 26 8 E
Malema, Mozam. 55 E4 14 57S 37 20 E
Máleme, Greece 23 D5 35 31N 23 49 E
Maleny, Australia 63 D5 26 45S 152 52 E
Malerkotla, India 42 D6 30 32N 75 58 E
Máles, Greece 23 D7 35 6N 25 35 E
Malgomaj, Sweden 8 D17 64 40N 16 30 E
Malha, Sudan 51 E11 15 8N 25 10 E
Malhargarh, India 42 G6 24 17N 74 59 E
Malheur →, U.S.A. 82 D5 44 4N 116 59W
Malheur L., U.S.A. 82 E4 43 20N 118 48W
Mali ■, Africa 50 E5 17 0N 3 0W
Mali →, Burma 41 G20 25 40N 97 40 E
Mali Kyun, Burma 38 F2 13 0N 98 20 E
Malibu, U.S.A. 85 L8 34 2N 118 41W
Maliku, Indonesia 37 E6 0 39S 123 16 E
Malili, Indonesia 37 E6 2 42S 121 6 E
Malimba, Mts., Dem. Rep. of the Congo 54 D2 7 30S 29 30 E
Malin Hd., Ireland 13 A4 55 23N 7 23W
Malin Pen., Ireland 13 A4 55 20N 7 17W
Malindi, Kenya 54 C5 3 12S 40 5 E
Malines = Mechelen, Belgium 15 C4 51 2N 4 29 E
Malino, Indonesia 37 D6 1 0N 121 0 E
Malinyi, Tanzania 55 D4 8 56S 36 0 E
Malita, Phil. 37 C7 6 19N 125 39 E
Maliwun, Burma 36 B1 10 17N 98 40 E
Maliya, India 42 H4 23 5N 70 46 E
Malkara, Turkey 21 D12 40 53N 26 53 E
Mallacoota Inlet, Australia 63 F4 37 34S 149 40 E
Mallaig, U.K. 12 D3 57 0N 5 50W

Montour Falls

Minigwal, L., *Australia* 61 E3 29 31 S 123 14 E
Minilya →, *Australia* 61 D1 23 45 S 114 0 E
Minilya Roadhouse, *Australia* 61 D1 23 55 S 114 0 E
Minipi L., *Canada* 71 B7 52 25N 60 45W
Mink L., *Canada* 72 A5 61 54N 117 40W
Minna, *Nigeria* 50 G7 9 37N 6 30 E
Minneapolis, *Kans., U.S.A.* 80 F6 39 8N 97 42W
Minneapolis, *Minn., U.S.A.* 80 C8 44 59N 93 16W
Minnedosa, *Canada* 73 C9 50 14N 99 50W
Minnesota □, *U.S.A.* 80 B8 46 0N 94 15W
Minnesota →, *U.S.A.* 80 C8 44 54N 93 9W
Minnewaukan, *U.S.A.* 80 A5 48 4N 99 15W
Minnipa, *Australia* 63 E2 32 51 S 135 9 E
Minnitaki L., *Canada* 70 C1 49 57N 92 10W
Mino, *Japan* 31 G8 35 32N 136 55 E
Miño →, *Spain* 19 A2 41 52N 8 40W
Minorca = Menorca, *Spain* 22 B11 40 0N 4 0 E
Minot, *U.S.A.* 80 A4 48 14N 101 18W
Minqin, *China* 34 E2 38 38N 103 20 E
Minsk, *Belarus* 17 B14 53 52N 27 30 E
Mińsk Mazowiecki, *Poland* 17 B11 52 10N 21 33 E
Mintabie, *Australia* 63 D1 27 15 S 133 7 E
Mintaka Pass, *Pakistan* 43 A6 37 0N 74 58 E
Minteke Daban = Mintaka Pass, *Pakistan* 43 A6 37 0N 74 58 E
Minto, *Canada* 71 C6 46 5N 66 5W
Minto, L., *Canada* 70 A5 57 13N 75 0W
Minton, *Canada* 73 D8 49 10N 104 35W
Minturn, *U.S.A.* 82 G10 39 35N 106 26W
Minusinsk, *Russia* 27 D10 53 43N 91 20 E
Minutang, *India* 41 E20 28 15N 96 30 E
Miquelon, *Canada* 70 C4 49 25N 76 27W
Miquelon, *St- P. & M.* 71 C8 47 8N 56 22W
Mīr Kūh, *Iran* 45 E8 26 22N 58 55 E
Mīr Shahdād, *Iran* 45 E8 26 15N 58 29 E
Mira, *Italy* 20 B5 45 26N 12 8 E
Mira por vos Cay, *Bahamas* 89 B5 22 9N 74 30W
Miraj, *India* 40 L9 16 50N 74 45 E
Miram Shah, *Pakistan* 42 C4 33 0N 70 2 E
Miramar, *Argentina* 94 D4 38 15 S 57 50W
Miramar, *Mozam.* 57 C6 23 50 S 35 35 E
Miramichi, *Canada* 71 C6 47 2N 65 28W
Miramichi B., *Canada* 71 C7 47 15N 65 0W
Miranda, *Brazil* 93 H7 20 10 S 56 15W
Miranda →, *Brazil* 92 G7 19 25 S 57 20W
Miranda de Ebro, *Spain* 19 A4 42 41N 2 57W
Miranda do Douro, *Portugal* 19 B2 41 30N 6 16W
Mirandópolis, *Brazil* 95 A5 21 9S 51 6W
Mirango, *Malawi* 55 E3 13 32 S 34 58 E
Mirassol, *Brazil* 95 A6 20 46 S 49 28W
Mirbāţ, *Oman* 46 D5 17 0N 54 45 E
Miri, *Malaysia* 36 D4 4 23N 113 59 E
Miriam Vale, *Australia* 62 C5 24 20 S 151 33 E
Mirim, L., *S. Amer.* 95 C5 32 45 S 52 50W
Mirnyy, *Russia* 27 C12 62 33N 113 53 E
Mirokhan, *Pakistan* 42 F3 27 46N 68 6 E
Mirond L., *Canada* 73 B8 55 6N 102 47W
Mirpur, *Pakistan* 43 C5 33 32N 73 56 E
Mirpur Batoro, *Pakistan* 42 G3 24 44N 68 16 E
Mirpur Bibiwari, *Pakistan* 42 E2 28 33N 67 44 E
Mirpur Khas, *Pakistan* 42 G3 25 30N 69 0 E
Mirpur Sakro, *Pakistan* 42 G2 24 33N 67 41 E
Mirtağ, *Turkey* 44 B4 38 23N 41 56 E
Miryang, *S. Korea* 35 G15 35 31N 128 44 E
Mirzapur, *India* 43 G10 25 10N 82 34 E
Mirzapur-cum-Vindhyachal = Mirzapur, *India* 43 G10 25 10N 82 34 E
Misantla, *Mexico* 87 D5 19 56N 96 50W
Misawa, *Japan* 30 D10 40 41N 141 24 E
Miscou I., *Canada* 71 C7 47 57N 64 31W
Mish'āb, Ra's al, *Si. Arabia* 45 D6 28 15N 48 43 E
Mishan, *China* 33 B8 45 37N 131 48 E
Mishawaka, *U.S.A.* 76 E2 41 40N 86 11W
Mishima, *Japan* 31 G9 35 10N 138 52 E
Misión, *Mexico* 85 N10 32 6N 116 53W
Misiones □, *Argentina* 95 B5 27 0S 55 0W
Misiones □, *Paraguay* 94 B4 27 0S 56 0W
Miskah, *Si. Arabia* 44 E4 24 49N 42 56 E
Miskitos, Cayos, *Nic.* 88 D3 14 26N 82 50W
Miskolc, *Hungary* 17 D11 48 7N 20 50 E
Misoke, *Dem. Rep. of the Congo* 54 C2 0 42 S 28 2 E
Misool, *Indonesia* 37 E8 1 52 S 130 10 E
Misrātah, *Libya* 51 B9 32 24N 15 3 E
Missanabie, *Canada* 70 C3 48 20N 84 6W
Missinaibi →, *Canada* 70 B3 50 43N 81 29W
Missinaibi L., *Canada* 70 C3 48 23N 83 40W
Mission, *Canada* 72 D4 49 10N 122 15W
Mission, *S. Dak., U.S.A.* 80 D4 43 18N 100 39W
Mission, *Tex., U.S.A.* 81 M5 26 13N 98 20W
Mission Beach, *Australia* 62 B4 17 53 S 146 6 E
Mission Viejo, *U.S.A.* 85 M9 33 36N 117 40W
Missisa L., *Canada* 70 B2 52 20N 85 7W
Missisicabi →, *Canada* 70 B4 51 14N 79 31W
Mississagi →, *Canada* 70 C3 46 15N 83 9W
Mississauga, *Canada* 78 C5 43 32N 79 35W
Mississippi □, *U.S.A.* 81 J10 33 0N 90 0W
Mississippi →, *U.S.A.* 81 L10 29 9N 89 15W
Mississippi L., *Canada* 79 A8 45 5N 76 10W
Mississippi River Delta, *U.S.A.* 81 L9 29 10N 89 15W
Mississippi Sd., *U.S.A.* 81 K10 30 20N 89 0W
Missoula, *U.S.A.* 82 C7 46 52N 114 1W
Missouri □, *U.S.A.* 80 F8 38 25N 92 30W
Missouri →, *U.S.A.* 80 F9 38 49N 90 7W
Missouri City, *U.S.A.* 81 L7 29 37N 95 32W
Missouri Valley, *U.S.A.* 80 E7 41 34N 95 53W
Mist, *U.S.A.* 84 E3 45 59N 123 15W
Mistassibi →, *Canada* 71 B5 48 53N 72 13W
Mistassini, *Canada* 71 C5 48 53N 72 12W
Mistassini →, *Canada* 71 C5 48 42N 72 20W
Mistassini, L., *Canada* 70 B5 51 0N 73 30W
Mistastin L., *Canada* 71 A7 55 57N 63 20W
Mistinibi, L., *Canada* 71 A7 55 56N 64 17W
Misty L., *Canada* 73 B8 58 53N 101 40W
Misurata = Misrātah, *Libya* 51 B9 32 24N 15 3 E
Mitchell, *Australia* 63 D4 26 29 S 147 58 E
Mitchell, *Canada* 78 C3 43 28N 81 12W
Mitchell, *Nebr., U.S.A.* 80 E3 41 57N 103 49W
Mitchell, *Oreg., U.S.A.* 82 D3 44 34N 120 9W
Mitchell, *S. Dak., U.S.A.* 80 D6 43 43N 98 2W
Mitchell →, *Australia* 62 B3 15 12 S 141 35 E
Mitchell, Mt., *U.S.A.* 77 H4 35 46N 82 16W
Mitchell Ranges, *Australia* 62 A2 12 49 S 135 36 E
Mitchelstown, *Ireland* 13 D3 52 15N 8 16W
Mitha Tiwana, *Pakistan* 42 C5 32 13N 72 6 E
Mithi, *Pakistan* 42 G3 24 44N 69 48 E
Mithrao, *Pakistan* 42 F3 27 28N 69 40 E
Mitilíni, *Greece* 21 E12 39 6N 26 35 E
Mito, *Japan* 31 F10 36 20N 140 30 E
Mitrovica = Kosovska Mitrovica, *Serbia, Yug.* 21 C9 42 54N 20 52 E
Mitsinjo, *Madag.* 57 B8 16 1S 45 52 E
Mitsiwa, *Eritrea* 46 D2 15 35N 39 25 E
Mitsukaidō, *Japan* 31 F9 36 1N 139 59 E
Mittagong, *Australia* 63 E5 34 28 S 150 29 E
Mitú, *Colombia* 92 C4 1 15N 70 13W
Mitumba, *Tanzania* 54 D3 7 8S 31 2 E
Mitumba, Mts., *Dem. Rep. of the Congo* 54 D2 7 0S 27 30 E
Mitwaba, *Dem. Rep. of the Congo* 55 D2 8 2S 27 17 E
Mityana, *Uganda* 54 B3 0 23N 32 2 E
Mixteco →, *Mexico* 87 D5 18 11N 98 30W
Miyagi □, *Japan* 30 E10 38 15N 140 45 E
Miyah, W. el →, *Syria* 44 C3 34 44N 39 57 E
Miyake-Jima, *Japan* 31 G9 34 5N 139 30 E
Miyako, *Japan* 30 E10 39 40N 141 59 E
Miyako-Jima, *Japan* 31 M2 24 45N 125 20 E
Miyako-Rettō, *Japan* 31 M2 24 24N 125 0 E
Miyakonojō, *Japan* 31 J5 31 40N 131 5 E
Miyani, *India* 42 J3 21 50N 69 26 E
Miyanoura-Dake, *Japan* 31 J5 30 20N 130 31 E
Miyazaki, *Japan* 31 J5 31 56N 131 30 E
Miyazaki □, *Japan* 31 H5 32 30N 131 30 E
Miyazu, *Japan* 31 G7 35 35N 135 10 E
Miyet, Bahr el = Dead Sea, *Asia* 47 D4 31 30N 35 30 E
Miyoshi, *Japan* 31 G6 34 48N 132 51 E
Miyun, *China* 34 D9 40 28N 116 50 E
Miyun Shuiku, *China* 35 D9 40 30N 117 0 E
Mizdah, *Libya* 51 B8 31 30N 13 0 E
Mizen Hd., *Cork, Ireland* 13 E2 51 27N 9 50W
Mizen Hd., *Wick., Ireland* 13 D5 52 51N 6 4W
Mizhi, *China* 34 F6 37 47N 110 12 E
Mizoram □, *India* 41 H18 23 30N 92 40 E
Mizpe Ramon, *Israel* 47 E3 30 34N 34 49 E
Mizusawa, *Japan* 30 E10 39 8N 141 8 E
Mjölby, *Sweden* 9 G16 58 20N 15 10 E
Mjøsa, *Norway* 9 F14 60 40N 11 0 E
Mkata, *Tanzania* 54 D4 5 45 S 38 20 E
Mkokotoni, *Tanzania* 54 D4 5 55 S 39 15 E
Mkomazi, *Tanzania* 54 C4 4 40 S 38 7 E
Mkomazi →, *S. Africa* 57 E5 30 12 S 30 50 E
Mkulwe, *Tanzania* 55 D3 8 37 S 32 20 E
Mkumbi, Ras, *Tanzania* 54 D4 7 38 S 39 55 E
Mkushi, *Zambia* 55 E2 14 25 S 29 15 E
Mkushi River, *Zambia* 55 E2 13 32 S 29 45 E
Mkuze, *S. Africa* 57 D5 27 10 S 32 0 E
Mladá Boleslav, *Czech Rep.* 16 C8 50 27N 14 53 E
Mlala Hills, *Tanzania* 54 D3 6 50 S 31 40 E
Mlange = Mulanje, *Malawi* 55 F4 16 2S 35 33 E
Mlanje, Pic, *Malawi* 53 H7 15 57 S 35 38 E
Mława, *Poland* 17 B11 53 9N 20 25 E
Mljet, *Croatia* 20 C7 42 43N 17 30 E
Mmabatho, *S. Africa* 56 D4 25 49 S 25 30 E
Mo i Rana, *Norway* 8 C16 66 20N 14 7 E
Moa, *Cuba* 89 B4 20 40N 74 56W
Moa, *Indonesia* 37 F7 8 0S 128 0 E
Moab, *U.S.A.* 83 G9 38 35N 109 33W
Moala, *Fiji* 59 D8 18 36 S 179 53 E
Moama, *Australia* 63 F3 36 7 S 144 46 E
Moapa, *U.S.A.* 85 J12 36 40N 114 37W
Moate, *Ireland* 13 C4 53 24N 7 44W
Moba, *Dem. Rep. of the Congo* 54 D2 7 0S 29 48 E
Mobārakābād, *Iran* 45 D7 28 24N 53 20 E
Mobaye, *C.A.R.* 52 D4 4 25N 21 5 E
Mobayi, *Dem. Rep. of the Congo* 52 D4 4 15N 21 8 E
Moberley Lake, *Canada* 72 B4 55 50N 121 44W
Moberly, *U.S.A.* 80 F8 39 25N 92 26W
Mobile, *U.S.A.* 77 K1 30 41N 88 3W
Mobile B., *U.S.A.* 77 K2 30 30N 88 0W
Mobridge, *U.S.A.* 80 C4 45 32N 100 26W
Mobutu Sese Seko, L. = Albert L., *Africa* 54 B3 1 30N 31 0 E
Moc Chau, *Vietnam* 38 B5 20 50N 104 38 E
Moc Hoa, *Vietnam* 39 G5 10 46N 105 56 E
Mocabe Kasari, *Dem. Rep. of the Congo* 55 D2 9 58 S 26 12 E
Moçambique, *Mozam.* 55 F5 15 3S 40 42 E
Moçâmedes = Namibe, *Angola* 53 H2 15 7S 12 11 E
Mocanaqua, *U.S.A.* 79 E8 41 9N 76 8W
Mochudi, *Botswana* 56 C4 24 27 S 26 7 E
Mocimboa da Praia, *Mozam.* 55 E5 11 25 S 40 20 E
Moclips, *U.S.A.* 84 C2 47 14N 124 13W
Mocoa, *Colombia* 92 C3 1 7N 76 35W
Mococa, *Brazil* 95 A6 21 28 S 47 0W
Mocorito, *Mexico* 86 B3 25 30N 107 53W
Moctezuma, *Mexico* 86 B3 29 50N 109 0W
Moctezuma →, *Mexico* 87 C5 21 59N 98 34W
Mocuba, *Mozam.* 55 F4 16 54 S 36 57 E
Mocúzari, Presa, *Mexico* 86 B3 27 10N 109 10W
Modane, *France* 18 D7 45 12N 6 40 E
Modasa, *India* 42 H5 23 30N 73 21 E
Modder →, *S. Africa* 56 D3 29 2S 24 37 E
Modderrivier, *S. Africa* 56 D3 29 2S 24 38 E
Módena, *Italy* 20 B4 44 40N 10 55 E
Modena, *U.S.A.* 83 H7 37 48N 113 56W
Modesto, *U.S.A.* 84 H6 37 39N 121 0W
Módica, *Italy* 20 F6 36 52N 14 46 E
Moe, *Australia* 63 F4 38 12 S 146 19 E
Moebase, *Mozam.* 55 F4 17 3S 38 41 E
Moengo, *Surinam* 93 B8 5 45N 54 20W
Moffat, *U.K.* 12 F5 55 21N 3 27W
Moga, *India* 42 D6 30 48N 75 8 E
Mogadishu = Muqdisho, *Somali Rep.* 46 G4 2 2N 45 25 E
Mogador = Essaouira, *Morocco* 50 B4 31 32N 9 42W
Mogalakwena →, *S. Africa* 57 C4 22 38 S 28 40 E
Mogami-Gawa →, *Japan* 30 E10 38 45N 140 0 E
Mogán, *Canary Is.* 22 G4 27 53N 15 43W
Mogaung, *Burma* 41 G20 25 20N 97 0 E
Mogi das Cruzes, *Brazil* 95 A6 23 31 S 46 11W
Mogi-Guaçu →, *Brazil* 95 A6 20 53 S 48 10W
Mogi-Mirim, *Brazil* 95 A6 22 29 S 47 0W
Mogilev = Mahilyow, *Belarus* 17 B16 53 55N 30 18 E
Mogilev-Podolskiy = Mohyliv-Podilskyy, *Ukraine* 17 D14 48 26N 27 48 E
Mogincual, *Mozam.* 55 F5 15 35 S 40 25 E
Mogocha, *Russia* 27 D12 53 40N 119 50 E
Mogok, *Burma* 41 H20 23 0N 96 40 E
Mogollon Rim, *U.S.A.* 83 J8 34 10N 110 50W
Mogumber, *Australia* 61 F2 31 2S 116 3 E
Mohács, *Hungary* 17 F10 45 58N 18 41 E
Mohales Hoek, *Lesotho* 56 E4 30 7S 27 26 E
Mohall, *U.S.A.* 80 A4 48 46N 101 31W
Moḩammadābād, *Iran* 45 B8 37 52N 59 5 E
Mohammedia, *Morocco* 50 B4 33 44N 7 21W
Mohana →, *India* 43 G11 24 43N 85 0 E
Mohanlalganj, *India* 43 F9 26 41N 80 58 E
Mohave, L., *U.S.A.* 85 K12 35 12N 114 34W
Mohawk →, *U.S.A.* 79 D11 42 47N 73 41W
Mohenjodaro, *Pakistan* 42 F3 27 19N 68 7 E
Mohicanville Reservoir, *U.S.A.* 78 F3 40 45N 82 0W
Mohoro, *Tanzania* 54 D4 8 6S 39 8 E
Mohyliv-Podilskyy, *Ukraine* 17 D14 48 26N 27 48 E
Moidart, L., *U.K.* 12 E3 56 47N 5 52W
Moira →, *Canada* 78 B7 44 21N 77 24W
Moíres, *Greece* 23 D6 35 4N 24 56 E
Moisaküla, *Estonia* 9 G21 58 3N 25 12 E
Moisie, *Canada* 71 B6 50 12N 66 1W
Moisie →, *Canada* 71 B6 50 14N 66 5W
Mojave, *U.S.A.* 85 K8 35 3N 118 10W
Mojave Desert, *U.S.A.* 85 L10 35 0N 116 30W
Mojo, *Bolivia* 94 A2 21 48 S 65 33W
Mojokerto, *Indonesia* 37 G15 7 28 S 112 26 E
Mokai, *N.Z.* 59 H5 38 32 S 175 56 E
Mokambo, *Dem. Rep. of the Congo* 55 E2 12 25 S 28 20 E
Mokameh, *India* 43 G11 25 24N 85 55 E
Mokelumne →, *U.S.A.* 84 G5 38 13N 121 28W
Mokelumne Hill, *U.S.A.* 84 G6 38 18N 120 43W
Mokhós, *Greece* 23 D7 35 16N 25 27 E
Mokhotlong, *Lesotho* 57 D4 29 22 S 29 2 E
Mokokchung, *India* 41 F19 26 15N 94 30 E
Mokp'o, *S. Korea* 35 G14 34 50N 126 25 E
Mokra Gora, *Serbia, Yug.* 21 C9 42 50N 20 30 E
Mol, *Belgium* 15 C5 51 11N 5 5 E
Molchanovo, *Russia* 26 D9 57 40N 83 50 E
Mold, *U.K.* 10 D4 53 9N 3 8W
Moldavia = Moldova ■, *Europe* 17 E15 47 0N 28 0 E
Molde, *Norway* 8 E12 62 45N 7 9 E
Moldova ■, *Europe* 17 E15 47 0N 28 0 E
Moldoveana, Vf., *Romania* 17 F13 45 36N 24 45 E
Mole →, *U.K.* 11 F7 51 24N 0 21W
Mole Creek, *Australia* 62 G4 41 34 S 146 24 E
Molepolole, *Botswana* 56 C4 24 28 S 25 28 E
Molfetta, *Italy* 20 D7 41 12N 16 36 E
Moline, *U.S.A.* 80 E9 41 30N 90 31W
Molinos, *Argentina* 94 B2 25 28 S 66 15W
Moliro, *Dem. Rep. of the Congo* 54 D3 8 12 S 30 30 E
Mollendo, *Peru* 92 G4 17 0S 72 0W
Mollerin, L., *Australia* 61 F2 30 30 S 117 35 E
Molodechno = Maladzyechna, *Belarus* 17 A14 54 20N 26 50 E
Molokai, *U.S.A.* 74 H16 21 8N 157 0W
Molong, *Australia* 63 E4 33 5S 148 54 E
Molopo →, *Africa* 56 D3 27 30 S 20 13 E
Molotov = Perm, *Russia* 24 C10 58 0N 56 10 E
Molson L., *Canada* 73 C9 54 22N 96 40W
Molteno, *S. Africa* 56 E4 31 22 S 26 22 E
Molu, *Indonesia* 37 F8 6 45 S 131 40 E
Molucca Sea, *Indonesia* 37 E6 2 0S 124 0 E
Moluccas = Maluku, *Indonesia* 37 E7 1 0S 127 0 E
Moma, *Dem. Rep. of the Congo* 54 C1 1 35 S 23 52 E
Moma, *Mozam.* 55 F4 16 47 S 39 4 E
Mombasa, *Kenya* 54 C4 4 2S 39 43 E
Mombetsu, *Japan* 30 B11 44 21N 143 22 E
Momchilgrad, *Bulgaria* 21 D11 41 33N 25 23 E
Momi, *Dem. Rep. of the Congo* 54 C2 1 42 S 27 0 E
Mompós, *Colombia* 92 B4 9 14N 74 26W
Møn, *Denmark* 9 J15 54 57N 12 20 E
Mon →, *Burma* 41 J19 20 25N 94 30 E
Mona, Canal de la, *W. Indies* 89 C6 18 30N 67 45W
Mona, Isla, *Puerto Rico* 89 C6 18 5N 67 54W
Mona, Pta., *Costa Rica* 88 E3 9 37N 82 36W
Monaca, *U.S.A.* 78 F4 40 41N 80 17W
Monaco ■, *Europe* 18 E7 43 46N 7 23 E
Monadhliath Mts., *U.K.* 12 D4 57 10N 4 4W
Monadnock, Mt., *U.S.A.* 79 D12 42 52N 72 7W
Monaghan, *Ireland* 13 B5 54 15N 6 57W
Monaghan □, *Ireland* 13 B5 54 11N 6 56W
Monahans, *U.S.A.* 81 K3 31 36N 102 54W
Monapo, *Mozam.* 55 E5 14 56 S 40 19 E
Monar, L., *U.K.* 12 D3 57 26N 5 8W
Monarch Mt., *Canada* 72 C3 51 55N 125 57W
Monashee Mts., *Canada* 72 C5 51 0N 118 43W
Monasterevin, *Ireland* 13 C4 53 8N 7 4W
Monastir = Bitola, *Macedonia* 21 D9 41 1N 21 20 E
Moncayo, Sierra del, *Spain* 19 B5 41 48N 1 50W
Monchegorsk, *Russia* 24 A5 67 54N 32 58 E
Mönchengladbach, *Germany* 16 C4 51 11N 6 27 E
Monchique, *Portugal* 19 D1 37 19N 8 38W
Moncks Corner, *U.S.A.* 77 J5 33 12N 80 1W
Monclova, *Mexico* 86 B4 26 50N 101 30W
Moncton, *Canada* 71 C7 46 7N 64 51W
Mondego →, *Portugal* 19 B1 40 9N 8 52W
Mondeodo, *Indonesia* 37 E6 3 34 S 122 9 E
Mondovì, *Italy* 18 D7 44 23N 7 49 E
Mondrain I., *Australia* 61 F3 34 9S 122 14 E
Monessen, *U.S.A.* 78 F5 40 9N 79 54W
Monett, *U.S.A.* 81 G8 36 55N 93 55W
Moneymore, *U.K.* 13 B5 54 41N 6 40W
Monforte de Lemos, *Spain* 19 A2 42 31N 7 33W
Mong Hsu, *Burma* 41 J21 21 54N 98 30 E
Mong Kung, *Burma* 41 J20 21 35N 97 35 E
Mong Nai, *Burma* 41 J20 20 32N 97 46 E
Mong Pawk, *Burma* 41 H21 22 4N 99 16 E
Mong Ton, *Burma* 41 J21 20 17N 98 45 E
Mong Wa, *Burma* 41 J22 21 26N 100 27 E
Mong Yai, *Burma* 41 H21 22 21N 98 3 E
Mongalla, *Sudan* 51 G12 5 8N 31 42 E
Mongers, L., *Australia* 61 E2 29 25 S 117 5 E
Monghyr = Munger, *India* 43 G12 25 23N 86 30 E
Mongibello = Etna, *Italy* 20 F6 37 50N 14 55 E
Mongo, *Chad* 51 F9 12 14N 18 43 E
Mongolia ■, *Asia* 27 E10 47 0N 103 0 E
Mongu, *Zambia* 53 H4 15 16 S 23 12 E
Môngua, *Angola* 56 B2 16 43 S 15 20 E
Monifieth, *U.K.* 12 E6 56 30N 2 48W
Monkey Bay, *Malawi* 55 E4 14 7S 35 1 E
Monkey Mia, *Australia* 61 E1 25 48 S 113 43 E
Monkey River, *Belize* 87 D7 16 22N 88 29W
Monkoto, *Dem. Rep. of the Congo* 52 E4 1 38 S 20 35 E
Monkton, *Canada* 78 C3 43 35N 81 5W
Monmouth, *U.K.* 11 F5 51 48N 2 42W
Monmouth, *Ill., U.S.A.* 80 E9 40 55N 90 39W
Monmouth, *Oreg., U.S.A.* 82 D2 44 51N 123 14W
Monmouthshire □, *U.K.* 11 F5 51 48N 2 54W
Mono L., *U.S.A.* 84 H7 38 1N 119 1W
Monolith, *U.S.A.* 85 K8 35 7N 118 22W
Monólithos, *Greece* 23 C9 36 7N 27 45 E
Monongahela, *U.S.A.* 78 F5 40 12N 79 56W
Monópoli, *Italy* 20 D7 40 57N 17 18 E
Monroe, *Ga., U.S.A.* 77 J4 33 47N 83 43W
Monroe, *La., U.S.A.* 81 J8 32 30N 92 7W
Monroe, *Mich., U.S.A.* 76 E4 41 55N 83 24W
Monroe, *N.C., U.S.A.* 77 H5 34 59N 80 33W
Monroe, *N.Y., U.S.A.* 79 E10 41 20N 74 11W
Monroe, *Utah, U.S.A.* 83 G7 38 38N 112 7W
Monroe, *Wash., U.S.A.* 84 C5 47 51N 121 58W
Monroe, *Wis., U.S.A.* 80 D10 42 36N 89 38W
Monroe City, *U.S.A.* 80 F9 39 39N 91 44W
Monroeton, *U.S.A.* 79 E8 41 43N 76 29W
Monroeville, *Ala., U.S.A.* 77 K2 31 31N 87 20W
Monroeville, *Pa., U.S.A.* 78 F5 40 26N 79 45W
Monrovia, *Liberia* 50 G3 6 18N 10 47W
Mons, *Belgium* 15 D3 50 27N 3 58 E
Monse, *Indonesia* 37 E6 4 0S 123 10 E
Mont-de-Marsan, *France* 18 E3 43 54N 0 31W
Mont-Joli, *Canada* 71 C6 48 37N 68 10W
Mont-Laurier, *Canada* 70 C4 46 35N 75 30W
Mont-Louis, *Canada* 71 C6 49 15N 65 44W
Mont-St-Michel, Le = Le Mont-St-Michel, *France* 18 B3 48 40N 1 30W
Mont Tremblant, Parc Recr. du, *Canada* 70 C5 46 30N 74 30W
Montagu, *S. Africa* 56 E3 33 45 S 20 8 E
Montagu I., *Antarctica* 5 B1 58 25 S 26 20W
Montague, *Canada* 71 C7 46 10N 62 39W
Montague, I., *Mexico* 86 A2 31 40N 114 56W
Montague Ra., *Australia* 61 E2 27 15 S 119 30 E
Montague Sd., *Australia* 60 B4 14 28 S 125 20 E
Montalbán, *Spain* 19 B5 40 50N 0 45W
Montalvo, *U.S.A.* 85 L7 34 15N 119 12W
Montana, *Bulgaria* 21 C10 43 27N 23 16 E
Montaña, *Peru* 92 E4 6 0S 73 0W
Montana □, *U.S.A.* 82 C9 47 0N 110 0W
Montaña Clara, I., *Canary Is.* 22 E6 29 17N 13 33W
Montargis, *France* 18 C5 47 59N 2 43 E
Montauban, *France* 18 D4 44 2N 1 21 E
Montauk, *U.S.A.* 79 E13 41 3N 71 57W
Montauk Pt., *U.S.A.* 79 E13 41 4N 71 52W
Montbéliard, *France* 18 C7 47 31N 6 48 E
Montceau-les-Mines, *France* 18 C6 46 40N 4 23 E
Montclair, *U.S.A.* 79 F10 40 49N 74 13W
Monte Albán, *Mexico* 87 D5 17 2N 96 45W
Monte Alegre, *Brazil* 93 D8 2 0S 54 0W
Monte Azul, *Brazil* 93 G10 15 9S 42 53W
Monte Bello Is., *Australia* 60 D2 20 30 S 115 45 E
Monte-Carlo, *Monaco* 18 E7 43 46N 7 23 E
Monte Caseros, *Argentina* 94 C4 30 10 S 57 50W
Monte Comán, *Argentina* 94 C2 34 40 S 67 53W
Monte Cristi, *Dom. Rep.* 89 C5 19 52N 71 39W
Monte Lindo →, *Paraguay* 94 A4 23 56 S 57 12W
Monte Patria, *Chile* 94 C1 30 42 S 70 58W
Monte Quemado, *Argentina* 94 B3 25 53 S 62 41W
Monte Rio, *U.S.A.* 84 G4 38 28N 123 0W
Monte Santu, C. di, *Italy* 20 D3 40 5N 9 44 E
Monte Vista, *U.S.A.* 83 H10 37 35N 106 9W
Monteagudo, *Argentina* 95 B5 27 14 S 54 8W
Montebello, *Canada* 70 C5 45 40N 74 55W
Montecito, *U.S.A.* 85 L7 34 26N 119 40W
Montecristo, *Italy* 20 C4 42 20N 10 19 E
Montego Bay, *Jamaica* 88 C4 18 30N 78 0W
Montélimar, *France* 18 D6 44 33N 4 45 E
Montello, *U.S.A.* 80 D10 43 48N 89 20W
Montemorelos, *Mexico* 87 B5 25 11N 99 42W
Montenegro, *Brazil* 95 B5 29 39 S 51 29W
Montenegro □, *Yugoslavia* 21 C8 42 40N 19 20 E
Montepuez, *Mozam.* 55 E4 13 8S 38 59 E
Montepuez →, *Mozam.* 55 E5 12 32 S 40 27 E
Monterey, *U.S.A.* 84 J5 36 37N 121 55W
Monterey B., *U.S.A.* 84 J5 36 45N 122 0W
Montería, *Colombia* 92 B3 8 46N 75 53W
Monteros, *Argentina* 94 B2 27 11 S 65 30W
Monterrey, *Mexico* 86 B4 25 40N 100 30W
Montes Claros, *Brazil* 93 G10 16 30 S 43 50W
Montesano, *U.S.A.* 84 D3 46 59N 123 36W
Montesilvano, *Italy* 20 C6 42 29N 14 8 E
Montevideo, *Uruguay* 95 C4 34 50 S 56 11W
Montevideo, *U.S.A.* 80 C7 44 57N 95 43W
Montezuma, *U.S.A.* 80 E8 41 35N 92 32W
Montgomery = Sahiwal, *Pakistan* 42 D5 30 45N 73 8 E
Montgomery, *U.K.* 11 E4 52 34N 3 8W
Montgomery, *Ala., U.S.A.* 77 J2 32 23N 86 19W
Montgomery, *Pa., U.S.A.* 78 E8 41 10N 76 53W
Montgomery, *W. Va., U.S.A.* 76 F5 38 11N 81 19W
Montgomery City, *U.S.A.* 80 F9 38 59N 91 30W
Monticello, *Ark., U.S.A.* 81 J9 33 38N 91 47W
Monticello, *Fla., U.S.A.* 77 K4 30 33N 83 52W
Monticello, *Ind., U.S.A.* 76 E2 40 45N 86 46W
Monticello, *Iowa, U.S.A.* 80 D9 42 15N 91 12W
Monticello, *Ky., U.S.A.* 77 G3 36 50N 84 51W
Monticello, *Minn., U.S.A.* 80 C8 45 18N 93 48W
Monticello, *Miss., U.S.A.* 81 K9 31 33N 90 7W
Monticello, *N.Y., U.S.A.* 79 E10 41 39N 74 42W
Monticello, *Utah, U.S.A.* 83 H9 37 52N 109 21W
Montijo, *Portugal* 19 C1 38 41N 8 54W
Montilla, *Spain* 19 D3 37 36N 4 40W
Montluçon, *France* 18 C5 46 22N 2 36 E
Montmagny, *Canada* 71 C5 46 58N 70 34W
Montmartre, *Canada* 73 C8 50 14N 103 27W
Montmorillon, *France* 18 C4 46 26N 0 50 E
Monto, *Australia* 62 C5 24 52 S 151 6 E
Montoro, *Spain* 19 C3 38 1N 4 27W
Montour Falls, *U.S.A.* 78 D8 42 21N 76 51W

Nanching

Mulhouse, France 18 C7 47 40N 7 20 E
Muling, China 35 B16 44 35N 130 10 E
Mull, U.K. 12 E3 56 25N 5 56W
Mull, Sound of, U.K. 12 E3 56 30N 5 50W
Mullaittivu, Sri Lanka 40 Q12 9 15N 80 49 E
Mullen, U.S.A. 80 D4 42 3N 101 1W
Mullens, U.S.A. 76 G5 37 35N 81 23W
Muller, Pegunungan, Indonesia 36 D4 0 30N 113 30 E
Mullet Pen., Ireland 13 B1 54 13N 10 2W
Mullewa, Australia 61 E2 28 29S 115 30 E
Mulligan →, Australia 62 D2 25 0S 139 0 E
Mullingar, Ireland 13 C4 53 31N 7 21W
Mullins, U.S.A. 77 H6 34 12N 79 15W
Mullumbimby, Australia 63 D5 28 30S 153 30 E
Mulobezi, Zambia 55 F2 16 45S 25 7 E
Mulroy B., Ireland 13 A4 55 15N 7 46W
Multan, Pakistan 42 D4 30 15N 71 36 E
Mulumbe, Mts., Dem. Rep. of the Congo 55 D2 8 40S 27 30 E
Mulungushi Dam, Zambia 55 E2 14 48S 28 48 E
Mulvane, U.S.A. 81 G6 37 29N 97 15W
Mumbai, India 40 K8 18 55N 72 50 E
Mumbwa, Zambia 55 F2 15 0S 27 0 E
Mun →, Thailand 38 E5 15 19N 105 30 E
Muna, Indonesia 37 F6 5 0S 122 30 E
Munabao, India 42 G4 25 45N 70 17 E
Munamagi, Estonia 9 H22 57 43N 27 4 E
München, Germany 16 D6 48 8N 11 34 E
Munchen-Gladbach = Mönchengladbach, Germany 16 C4 51 11N 6 27 E
Muncho Lake, Canada 72 B3 59 0N 125 50W
Munch'ŏn, N. Korea 35 E14 39 14N 127 19 E
Muncie, U.S.A. 76 E3 40 12N 85 23W
Muncoonie, L., Australia 62 D2 25 12S 138 40 E
Mundabbera, Australia 63 D5 25 36S 151 18 E
Munday, U.S.A. 81 J5 33 27N 99 38W
Münden, Germany 16 C5 51 25N 9 38 E
Mundiwindi, Australia 60 D3 23 47S 120 9 E
Mundo Novo, Brazil 93 F10 11 50S 40 29W
Mundra, India 42 H3 22 54N 69 48 E
Mundrabilla, Australia 61 F4 31 52S 127 51 E
Mungallala, Australia 63 D4 26 28S 147 34 E
Mungallala Cr. →, Australia 63 D4 28 53S 147 5 E
Mungana, Australia 62 B3 17 8S 144 27 E
Mungaoli, India 42 G8 24 24N 78 7 E
Mungari, Mozam. 55 F3 17 12S 33 30 E
Mungbere, Dem. Rep. of the Congo 54 B2 2 36N 28 28 E
Mungeli, India 43 H9 22 4N 81 41 E
Munger, India 43 G12 25 23N 86 30 E
Munich = München, Germany 16 D6 48 8N 11 34 E
Munising, U.S.A. 76 B2 46 25N 86 40W
Munku-Sardyk, Russia 27 D11 51 45N 100 20 E
Muñoz Gamero, Pen., Chile 96 G2 52 30S 73 5W
Munroe L., Canada 73 B9 59 13N 98 35W
Munsan, S. Korea 35 F14 37 51N 126 48 E
Münster, Germany 16 C4 51 58N 7 37 E
Munster □, Ireland 13 D3 52 18N 8 44W
Muntadgin, Australia 61 F2 31 45S 118 33 E
Muntok, Indonesia 36 E3 2 5S 105 10 E
Munyama, Zambia 55 F2 16 5S 28 31 E
Muong Et, Laos 38 B5 20 49N 104 1 E
Muong Hiem, Laos 38 B4 20 5N 103 22 E
Muong Kau, Laos 38 E5 15 6N 105 47 E
Muong Khao, Laos 38 C4 19 38N 103 32 E
Muong Liep, Laos 38 C3 18 29N 101 40 E
Muong May, Laos 38 E6 14 49N 106 56 E
Muong Nong, Laos 38 D6 16 22N 106 30 E
Muong Oua, Laos 38 C3 18 18N 101 20 E
Muong Phalane, Laos 38 D5 16 39N 105 34 E
Muong Phieng, Laos 38 C3 19 6N 101 32 E
Muong Phine, Laos 38 D6 16 32N 106 2 E
Muong Saiapoun, Laos 38 C3 18 24N 101 31 E
Muong Sen, Vietnam 38 C5 19 24N 104 8 E
Muong Soui, Laos 38 C4 19 33N 102 52 E
Muong Xia, Vietnam 38 B5 20 19N 104 50 E
Muonio, Finland 8 C20 67 57N 23 40 E
Muonionjoki →, Finland 8 C20 67 11N 23 34 E
Muping, China 35 F11 37 22N 121 36 E
Muqdisho, Somali Rep. 46 G4 2 2N 45 25 E
Mur →, Austria 17 E9 46 18N 16 52 E
Murakami, Japan 30 E9 38 14N 139 29 E
Murallón, Cerro, Chile 96 F2 49 48S 73 30W
Muranda, Rwanda 54 C2 1 52S 29 20 E
Murang'a, Kenya 54 C4 0 45S 37 9 E
Murashi, Russia 24 C8 59 30N 49 0 E
Murat →, Turkey 25 G7 38 46N 40 0 E
Muratlı, Turkey 21 D12 41 10N 27 29 E
Murayama, Japan 30 E10 38 30N 140 25 E
Murban, U.A.E. 45 F7 23 50N 53 45 E
Murchison →, Australia 61 E1 27 45S 114 0 E
Murchison, Mt., Antarctica 5 D11 73 0S 168 0 E
Murchison Falls, Uganda 54 B3 2 15N 31 30 E
Murchison Ra., Australia 62 C1 20 0S 134 10 E
Murchison Rapids, Malawi 55 F3 15 55S 34 35 E
Murcia, Spain 19 D5 38 5N 1 10W
Murcia □, Spain 19 D5 37 50N 1 30W
Murdo, U.S.A. 80 D4 43 53N 100 43W
Murdoch Pt., Australia 62 A3 14 37S 144 55 E
Mureş →, Romania 17 E11 46 15N 20 13 E
Mureşul = Mureş →, Romania 17 E11 46 15N 20 13 E
Murfreesboro, N.C., U.S.A. 77 G7 36 27N 77 6W
Murfreesboro, Tenn., U.S.A. 77 H2 35 51N 86 24W
Murgab = Murghob, Tajikistan 26 F8 38 10N 74 2 E
Murgab →, Turkmenistan 45 B9 38 18N 61 12 E
Murgenella, Australia 60 B5 11 34S 132 56 E
Murgha Kibzai, Pakistan 42 D3 30 44N 69 25 E
Murghob, Tajikistan 26 F8 38 10N 74 2 E
Murgon, Australia 63 D5 26 15S 151 54 E
Muri, India 43 H11 23 22N 85 52 E
Muria, Indonesia 37 G14 6 36S 110 53 E
Muriaé, Brazil 95 A7 21 8S 42 23W
Muriel Mine, Zimbabwe 55 F3 17 14S 30 40 E
Müritz, Germany 16 B7 53 25N 12 42 E
Murka, Kenya 54 C4 3 27S 38 0 E
Murliganj, India 43 G12 25 54N 86 59 E
Murmansk, Russia 24 A5 68 57N 33 10 E
Muro, Spain 22 B10 39 44N 3 3 E
Murom, Russia 24 C7 55 35N 42 3 E
Muroran, Japan 30 C10 42 25N 141 0 E
Muroto, Japan 31 H7 33 18N 134 9 E
Muroto-Misaki, Japan 31 H7 33 15N 134 10 E
Murphy, U.S.A. 82 E5 43 13N 116 33W
Murphys, U.S.A. 84 G6 38 8N 120 28W
Murray, Ky., U.S.A. 77 G1 36 37N 88 19W
Murray, Utah, U.S.A. 82 F8 40 40N 111 53W
Murray →, Australia 63 F2 35 20S 139 22 E
Murray, L., U.S.A. 77 H5 34 3N 81 13W
Murray Bridge, Australia 63 F2 35 6S 139 14 E
Murray Harbour, Canada 71 C7 46 0N 62 28W
Murraysburg, S. Africa 56 E3 31 58S 23 47 E
Murree, Pakistan 42 C5 33 56N 73 28 E
Murrieta, U.S.A. 85 M9 33 33N 117 13W
Murrumbidgee →, Australia 63 E3 34 43S 143 12 E
Murrumburrah, Australia 63 E4 34 32S 148 22 E
Murrurundi, Australia 63 E5 31 42S 150 51 E
Murshidabad, India 43 G13 24 11N 88 19 E
Murtle L., Canada 72 C5 52 8N 119 38W
Murtoa, Australia 63 F3 36 35S 142 28 E
Murungu, Tanzania 54 C3 4 12S 31 10 E
Mururoa, Pac. Oc. 65 K14 21 52S 138 55W
Murwara, India 43 H9 23 46N 80 28 E
Murwillumbah, Australia 63 D5 28 18S 153 27 E
Mürzzuschlag, Austria 16 E8 47 36N 15 41 E
Muş, Turkey 25 G7 38 45N 41 30 E
Mûsa, Gebel, Egypt 44 D2 28 33N 33 59 E
Musa Khel, Pakistan 42 D3 30 59N 69 52 E
Mūsá Qal'eh, Afghan. 40 C4 32 20N 64 50 E
Musaffargarh, Pakistan 40 D7 30 10N 71 10 E
Musafirkhana, India 43 F9 26 22N 81 48 E
Musala, Bulgaria 21 C10 42 13N 23 37 E
Musala, Indonesia 36 D1 1 41N 98 28 E
Musan, N. Korea 35 C15 42 12N 129 12 E
Musangu, Dem. Rep. of the Congo 55 E1 10 28S 23 55 E
Musasa, Tanzania 54 C3 3 25S 31 30 E
Musay'id, Qatar 45 E6 25 0N 51 33 E
Muscat = Masqat, Oman 46 C6 23 37N 58 36 E
Muscat & Oman = Oman ■, Asia 46 C6 23 0N 58 0 E
Muscatine, U.S.A. 80 E9 41 25N 91 3W
Musgrave Harbour, Canada 71 C9 49 27N 53 58W
Musgrave Ranges, Australia 61 E5 26 0S 132 0 E
Mushie, Dem. Rep. of the Congo 52 E3 2 56S 16 55 E
Musi →, Indonesia 36 E2 2 20S 104 56 E
Muskeg →, Canada 72 A4 60 20N 123 20W
Muskegon, U.S.A. 76 D2 43 14N 86 16W
Muskegon →, U.S.A. 76 D2 43 14N 86 21W
Muskegon Heights, U.S.A. 76 D2 43 12N 86 16W
Muskogee, U.S.A. 81 H7 35 45N 95 22W
Muskoka, L., Canada 78 B5 45 0N 79 25W
Muskwa →, Canada 72 B4 58 47N 122 48W
Muslimiyah, Syria 44 B3 36 19N 37 12 E
Musofu, Zambia 55 E2 13 30S 29 0 E
Musoma, Tanzania 54 C3 1 30S 33 48 E
Musquaro, L., Canada 71 B7 50 38N 61 5W
Musquodoboit Harbour, Canada 71 D7 44 50N 63 9W
Musselburgh, U.K. 12 F5 55 57N 3 2W
Musselshell →, U.S.A. 82 C10 47 21N 107 57W
Mussoorie, India 42 D8 30 27N 78 6 E
Mussuco, Angola 56 B2 17 2S 19 3 E
Mustafakemalpaşa, Turkey 21 D13 40 2N 28 24 E
Mustang, Nepal 43 E10 29 10N 83 55 E
Musters, L., Argentina 96 F3 45 20S 69 25W
Musudan, N. Korea 35 D15 40 50N 129 43 E
Muswellbrook, Australia 63 E5 32 16S 150 56 E
Mût, Egypt 51 C11 25 28N 28 58 E
Mut, Turkey 44 B2 36 40N 33 28 E
Mutanda, Mozam. 57 C5 21 0S 33 34 E
Mutanda, Zambia 55 E2 12 24S 26 13 E
Mutare, Zimbabwe 55 F3 18 58S 32 38 E
Muting, Indonesia 37 F10 7 23S 140 20 E
Mutoray, Russia 27 C11 60 56N 101 0 E
Mutshatsha, Dem. Rep. of the Congo 55 E1 10 35S 24 20 E
Mutsu, Japan 30 D10 41 5N 140 55 E
Mutsu-Wan, Japan 30 D10 41 5N 140 55 E
Muttaburra, Australia 62 C3 22 38S 144 29 E
Mutton I., Ireland 13 D2 52 49N 9 32W
Mutuáli, Mozam. 55 E4 14 55S 37 0 E
Muweilih, Egypt 47 E3 30 42N 34 19 E
Muy Muy, Nic. 88 D2 12 39N 85 36W
Muyinga, Burundi 54 C3 3 14S 30 33 E
Muynak, Uzbekistan 26 E6 43 44N 59 10 E
Muzaffarabad, Pakistan 43 B5 34 25N 73 30 E
Muzaffargarh, Pakistan 42 D4 30 5N 71 14 E
Muzaffarnagar, India 42 E7 29 26N 77 40 E
Muzaffarpur, India 43 F11 26 7N 85 23 E
Muzafirpur, Pakistan 42 D3 30 58N 69 9 E
Muzhi, Russia 24 A11 65 25N 64 40 E
Mvuma, Zimbabwe 55 F3 19 16S 30 30 E
Mvurwi, Zimbabwe 55 F3 17 0S 30 57 E
Mwadui, Tanzania 54 C3 3 26S 33 32 E
Mwambo, Tanzania 55 E5 10 30S 40 22 E
Mwandi, Zambia 55 F1 17 30S 24 51 E
Mwanza, Dem. Rep. of the Congo 54 D2 7 55S 26 43 E
Mwanza, Tanzania 54 C3 2 30S 32 58 E
Mwanza, Zambia 55 F1 16 58S 24 28 E
Mwanza □, Tanzania 54 C3 2 0S 33 0 E
Mwaya, Tanzania 55 D3 9 32S 33 55 E
Mweelrea, Ireland 13 C2 53 39N 9 49W
Mweka, Dem. Rep. of the Congo 52 E4 4 50S 21 34 E
Mwene-Ditu, Dem. Rep. of the Congo 52 F4 6 35S 22 27 E
Mwenezi, Zimbabwe 55 G3 21 15S 30 48 E
Mwenezi →, Mozam. 55 G3 22 40S 31 50 E
Mwenga, Dem. Rep. of the Congo 54 C2 3 1S 28 28 E
Mweru, L., Zambia 55 D2 9 0S 28 40 E
Mweza Range, Zimbabwe 55 G3 21 0S 30 0 E
Mwilambwe, Dem. Rep. of the Congo 54 D2 8 7S 25 5 E
Mwimbi, Tanzania 55 D3 8 38S 31 39 E
Mwinilunga, Zambia 55 E1 11 43S 24 25 E
My Tho, Vietnam 39 G6 10 29N 106 23 E
Myajlar, India 42 F4 26 15N 70 20 E
Myanaung, Burma 41 K19 18 18N 95 22 E
Myanmar = Burma ■, Asia 41 J20 21 0N 96 30 E
Myaungmya, Burma 41 L19 16 30N 94 40 E
Mycenæ, Greece 21 F10 37 39N 22 52 E
Myeik Kyunzu, Burma 39 G1 11 30N 97 30 E
Myers Chuck, U.S.A. 72 B2 55 44N 132 11W
Myerstown, U.S.A. 79 F8 40 22N 76 19W
Myingyan, Burma 41 J19 21 30N 95 20 E
Myitkyina, Burma 41 G20 25 24N 97 26 E
Mykines, Færoe Is. 8 E9 62 7N 7 35W
Mykolayiv, Ukraine 25 E5 46 58N 32 0 E
Mymensingh, Bangla. 41 G17 24 45N 90 24 E
Mynydd Du, U.K. 11 F4 51 52N 3 50W
Mýrdalsjökull, Iceland 8 E4 63 40N 19 6W
Myrtle Beach, U.S.A. 77 J6 33 42N 78 53W
Myrtle Creek, U.S.A. 82 E2 43 1N 123 17W
Myrtle Point, U.S.A. 82 E1 43 4N 124 8W
Myrtou, Cyprus 23 D12 35 18N 33 4 E
Mysia, Turkey 21 E12 39 50N 27 0 E
Mysore = Karnataka □, India 40 N10 13 15N 77 0 E
Mysore, India 40 N10 12 17N 76 41 E
Mystic, U.S.A. 79 E13 41 21N 71 58W
Myszków, Poland 17 C10 50 45N 19 22 E
Mytishchi, Russia 24 C6 55 50N 37 50 E
Mývatn, Iceland 8 D5 65 36N 17 0W
Mzimba, Malawi 55 E3 11 55S 33 39 E
Mzimkulu →, S. Africa 57 E5 30 44S 30 28 E
Mzimvubu →, S. Africa 57 E4 31 38S 29 33 E
Mzuzu, Malawi 55 E3 11 30S 33 55 E

N

Na Hearadh = Harris, U.K. 12 D2 57 50N 6 55W
Na Noi, Thailand 38 C3 18 19N 100 43 E
Na Phao, Laos 38 D5 17 35N 105 44 E
Na San, Vietnam 38 B5 21 12N 104 2 E
Naab →, Germany 16 D6 49 1N 12 2 E
Naantali, Finland 9 F19 60 29N 22 2 E
Naas, Ireland 13 C5 53 12N 6 40W
Nababiep, S. Africa 56 D2 29 36S 17 46 E
Nabadwip = Navadwip, India 43 H13 23 34N 88 20 E
Nabari, Japan 31 G8 34 37N 136 5 E
Nabawa, Australia 61 E1 28 30S 114 48 E
Nabberu, L., Australia 61 E3 25 50S 120 30 E
Naberezhnyye Chelny, Russia 24 C9 55 42N 52 19 E
Nabeul, Tunisia 51 A8 36 30N 10 44 E
Nabha, India 42 D7 30 26N 76 14 E
Nabīd, Iran 45 D8 29 40N 57 38 E
Nabire, Indonesia 37 E9 3 15S 135 26 E
Nabisar, Pakistan 42 G3 25 8N 69 40 E
Nabisipi →, Canada 71 B7 50 14N 62 13W
Nabiswera, Uganda 54 B3 1 27N 32 15 E
Nablus = Nābulus, West Bank 47 C4 32 14N 35 15 E
Naboomspruit, S. Africa 57 C4 24 32S 28 40 E
Nābulus, West Bank 47 C4 32 14N 35 15 E
Nacala, Mozam. 55 E5 14 31S 40 34 E
Nacala-Velha, Mozam. 55 E5 14 32S 40 34 E
Nacaome, Honduras 88 D2 13 31N 87 30W
Nacaroa, Mozam. 55 E4 14 22S 39 56 E
Naches, U.S.A. 82 C3 46 44N 120 42W
Naches →, U.S.A. 84 D6 46 38N 120 31W
Nachicapau, L., Canada 71 A6 56 40N 68 5W
Nachingwea, Tanzania 55 E4 10 23S 38 49 E
Nachna, India 42 F4 27 34N 71 41 E
Nacimiento L., U.S.A. 84 K6 35 46N 120 53W
Naco, Mexico 86 A3 31 20N 109 56W
Nacogdoches, U.S.A. 81 K7 31 36N 94 39W
Nácori Chico, Mexico 86 B3 29 39N 109 1W
Nacozari, Mexico 86 A3 30 24N 109 39W
Nadiad, India 42 H5 22 41N 72 56 E
Nador, Morocco 50 B5 35 14N 2 58W
Nadur, Malta 23 C1 36 2N 14 17 E
Nadūshan, Iran 45 C7 32 2N 53 35 E
Nadvirna, Ukraine 17 D13 48 37N 24 30 E
Nadvoitsy, Russia 24 B5 63 52N 34 14 E
Nadvornaya = Nadvirna, Ukraine 17 D13 48 37N 24 30 E
Nadym, Russia 26 C8 65 35N 72 42 E
Nadym →, Russia 26 C8 66 12N 72 0 E
Nærbø, Norway 9 G11 58 40N 5 39 E
Næstved, Denmark 9 J14 55 13N 11 44 E
Naft-e Safīd, Iran 45 D6 31 40N 49 17 E
Naftshahr, Iran 44 C5 34 0N 45 30 E
Nafud Desert = An Nafūd, Si. Arabia 44 D4 28 15N 41 0 E
Naga, Phil. 37 B6 13 38N 123 15 E
Nagahama, Japan 31 G8 35 23N 136 16 E
Nagai, Japan 30 E10 38 6N 140 2 E
Nagaland □, India 41 G19 26 0N 94 30 E
Nagano, Japan 31 F9 36 40N 138 10 E
Nagano □, Japan 31 F9 36 15N 138 0 E
Nagaoka, Japan 31 F9 37 27N 138 51 E
Nagappattinam, India 40 P11 10 46N 79 51 E
Nagar →, Bangla. 43 G13 24 27N 89 12 E
Nagar Parkar, Pakistan 42 G4 24 28N 70 46 E
Nagasaki, Japan 31 H4 32 47N 129 50 E
Nagasaki □, Japan 31 H4 32 50N 129 40 E
Nagato, Japan 31 G5 34 19N 131 5 E
Nagaur, India 42 F5 27 15N 73 45 E
Nagda, India 42 H6 23 27N 75 25 E
Nagercoil, India 40 Q10 8 12N 77 26 E
Nagina, India 43 E8 29 30N 78 30 E
Nagīneh, Iran 45 C8 34 20N 57 15 E
Nagir, Pakistan 43 A6 36 12N 74 42 E
Nagod, India 43 G9 24 34N 80 36 E
Nagoorin, Australia 62 C5 24 17S 151 15 E
Nagorno-Karabakh, Azerbaijan 25 F8 39 55N 46 45 E
Nagornyy, Russia 27 D13 55 58N 124 57 E
Nagoya, Japan 31 G8 35 10N 136 50 E
Nagpur, India 40 J11 21 8N 79 10 E
Nagua, Dom. Rep. 89 C6 19 23N 69 50W
Nagykanizsa, Hungary 17 E9 46 28N 17 0 E
Nagykörös, Hungary 17 E10 47 5N 19 48 E
Naha, Japan 31 L3 26 13N 127 42 E
Nahan, India 42 D7 30 33N 77 18 E
Nahanni Butte, Canada 72 A4 61 2N 123 31W
Nahanni Nat. Park, Canada 72 A4 61 15N 125 0W
Nahargarh, Mad. P., India 42 G6 24 10N 75 14 E
Nahargarh, Raj., India 42 G7 24 55N 76 50 E
Nahariyya, Israel 44 C2 33 1N 35 5 E
Nahāvand, Iran 45 C6 34 10N 48 22 E
Naicá, Mexico 86 B3 27 53N 105 31W
Naicam, Canada 73 C8 52 30N 104 30W
Naikoon Prov. Park, Canada 72 C2 53 55N 131 55W
Naimisharanya, India 43 F9 27 21N 80 30 E
Nain, Canada 71 A7 56 34N 61 40W
Nā'īn, Iran 45 C7 32 54N 53 0 E
Naini Tal, India 43 E8 29 30N 79 30 E
Nainpur, India 40 H12 22 30N 80 10 E
Nainwa, India 42 G6 25 46N 75 51 E
Nairn, U.K. 12 D5 57 35N 3 53W
Nairobi, Kenya 54 C4 1 17S 36 48 E
Naissaar, Estonia 9 G21 59 34N 24 29 E
Naivasha, Kenya 54 C4 0 40S 36 30 E
Naivasha, L., Kenya 54 C4 0 48S 36 20 E
Najafābād, Iran 45 C6 32 40N 51 15 E
Najd, Si. Arabia 46 B3 26 30N 42 0 E
Najibabad, India 42 E8 29 40N 78 20 E
Najin, N. Korea 35 C16 42 12N 130 15 E
Najmah, Si. Arabia 45 E6 26 42N 50 6 E
Naju, S. Korea 35 G14 35 3N 126 43 E
Nakadōri-Shima, Japan 31 H4 32 57N 129 4 E
Nakalagba, Dem. Rep. of the Congo 54 B2 2 50N 27 58 E
Nakaminato, Japan 31 F10 36 21N 140 36 E
Nakamura, Japan 31 H6 32 59N 132 56 E
Nakano, Japan 31 F9 36 45N 138 22 E
Nakano-Shima, Japan 31 K4 29 51N 129 52 E
Nakashibetsu, Japan 30 C12 43 33N 144 59 E
Nakfa, Eritrea 46 D2 16 40N 38 32 E
Nakhfar al Buşayyah, Iraq 44 D5 30 0N 46 10 E
Nakhichevan = Naxçıvan, Azerbaijan 25 G8 39 12N 45 15 E
Nakhichevan Republic = Naxçıvan □, Azerbaijan 25 G8 39 25N 45 26 E
Nakhl, Egypt 47 F2 29 55N 33 43 E
Nakhl-e Taqī, Iran 45 E7 27 28N 52 36 E
Nakhodka, Russia 27 E14 42 53N 132 54 E
Nakhon Nayok, Thailand 38 E3 14 12N 101 13 E
Nakhon Pathom, Thailand 38 F3 13 49N 100 3 E
Nakhon Phanom, Thailand 38 D5 17 23N 104 43 E
Nakhon Ratchasima, Thailand 38 E4 14 59N 102 12 E
Nakhon Sawan, Thailand 38 E3 15 35N 100 10 E
Nakhon Si Thammarat, Thailand 39 H3 8 29N 100 0 E
Nakhon Thai, Thailand 38 D3 17 5N 100 44 E
Nakhtarana, India 42 H3 23 20N 69 15 E
Nakina, Canada 70 B2 50 10N 86 40W
Nakodar, India 42 D6 31 8N 75 31 E
Nakskov, Denmark 9 J14 54 50N 11 8 E
Naktong →, S. Korea 35 G15 35 7N 128 57 E
Nakuru, Kenya 54 C4 0 15S 36 4 E
Nakuru, L., Kenya 54 C4 0 23S 36 5 E
Nakusp, Canada 72 C5 50 20N 117 45W
Nal, Pakistan 42 F2 27 40N 66 12 E
Nal →, Pakistan 42 G1 25 20N 65 30 E
Nalchik, Russia 25 F7 43 30N 43 33 E
Nalgonda, India 40 L11 17 6N 79 15 E
Nalhati, India 43 G12 24 17N 87 52 E
Naliya, India 42 H3 23 16N 68 50 E
Nallamalai Hills, India 40 M11 15 30N 78 50 E
Nam Can, Vietnam 39 H5 8 46N 104 59 E
Nam-ch'on, N. Korea 35 E14 38 15N 126 26 E
Nam Co, China 32 C4 30 30N 90 45 E
Nam Du, Hon, Vietnam 39 H5 9 41N 104 21 E
Nam Ngum Dam, Laos 38 C4 18 35N 102 34 E
Nam-Phan = Cochin China, Vietnam 39 G6 10 30N 106 0 E
Nam Phong, Thailand 38 D4 16 42N 102 52 E
Nam Tok, Thailand 38 E2 14 21N 99 4 E
Namacunde, Angola 56 B2 17 18S 15 50 E
Namacurra, Mozam. 57 B6 17 30S 36 50 E
Namak, Daryācheh-ye, Iran 45 C7 34 30N 52 0 E
Namak, Kavir-e, Iran 45 C8 34 30N 57 30 E
Namakzār, Daryācheh-ye, Iran 45 C9 34 0N 60 30 E
Namaland, Namibia 56 C2 26 0S 17 0 E
Namangan, Uzbekistan 26 E8 41 0N 71 40 E
Namapa, Mozam. 55 E4 13 43S 39 50 E
Namaqualand, S. Africa 56 E2 30 0S 17 25 E
Namasagali, Uganda 54 B3 1 2N 33 0 E
Namber, Indonesia 37 E8 1 2S 134 49 E
Nambour, Australia 63 D5 26 32S 152 58 E
Nambucca Heads, Australia 63 E5 30 37S 153 0 E
Namcha Barwa, China 32 D4 29 40N 95 10 E
Namche Bazar, Nepal 43 F12 27 51N 86 47 E
Namchonjŏm = Nam-ch'on, N. Korea 35 E14 38 15N 126 26 E
Namecunda, Mozam. 55 E4 14 54S 37 37 E
Nameponda, Mozam. 55 F4 15 50S 39 50 E
Nametil, Mozam. 55 F4 15 40S 39 21 E
Namew L., Canada 73 C8 54 14N 101 56W
Namgia, India 43 D8 31 48N 78 40 E
Namib Desert = Namibwoestyn, Namibia 56 C2 22 30S 15 0 E
Namibe, Angola 53 H2 15 7S 12 11 E
Namibe □, Angola 56 B1 16 35S 12 30 E
Namibia ■, Africa 56 C2 22 0S 18 9 E
Namibwoestyn, Namibia 56 C2 22 30S 15 0 E
Namlea, Indonesia 37 E7 3 18S 127 5 E
Namoi →, Australia 63 E4 30 12S 149 30 E
Nampa, U.S.A. 82 E5 43 34N 116 34W
Namp'o, N. Korea 35 E13 38 52N 125 10 E
Nampō-Shotō, Japan 31 J10 32 0N 140 0 E
Nampula, Mozam. 55 F4 15 6S 39 15 E
Namrole, Indonesia 37 E7 3 46S 126 46 E
Namse Shankou, China 41 E13 30 0N 82 25 E
Namsen →, Norway 8 D14 64 28N 11 37 E
Namsos, Norway 8 D14 64 29N 11 30 E
Namtsy, Russia 27 C13 62 43N 129 37 E
Namtu, Burma 41 H20 23 5N 97 28 E
Namtumbo, Tanzania 55 E4 10 30S 36 4 E
Namu, Canada 72 C3 51 52N 127 50W
Namur, Belgium 15 D4 50 27N 4 52 E
Namur □, Belgium 15 D4 50 17N 5 0 E
Namutoni, Namibia 56 B2 18 49S 16 55 E
Namwala, Zambia 55 F2 15 44S 26 30 E
Namwŏn, S. Korea 35 G14 35 23N 127 23 E
Nan, Thailand 38 C3 18 48N 100 46 E
Nan →, Thailand 38 E3 15 42N 100 9 E
Nan-ch'ang = Nanchang, China 33 D6 28 42N 115 55 E
Nanaimo, Canada 72 D4 49 10N 124 0W
Nanam, N. Korea 35 D15 41 44N 129 40 E
Nanango, Australia 63 D5 26 40S 152 0 E
Nanao, Japan 31 F8 37 0N 137 0 E
Nanchang, China 33 D6 28 42N 115 55 E
Nanching = Nanjing, China 33 C6 32 2N 118 47 E

North Knife

New Smyrna Beach, *U.S.A.* **77 L5** 29 1N 80 56W
New South Wales □, *Australia* **63 E4** 33 0S 146 0 E
New Town, *U.S.A.* **80 B3** 47 59N 102 30W
New Tredegar, *U.K.* **11 F4** 51 44N 3 16W
New Ulm, *U.S.A.* **80 C7** 44 19N 94 28W
New Waterford, *Canada* **71 C7** 46 13N 60 4W
New Westminster, *Canada* **84 A4** 49 13N 122 55W
New York, *U.S.A.* **79 F11** 40 45N 74 0W
New York □, *U.S.A.* **79 D9** 43 0N 75 0W
New York Mts., *U.S.A.* **83 J6** 35 0N 115 20W
New Zealand ■, *Oceania* **59 J6** 40 0S 176 0 E
Newaj →, *India* **42 G7** 24 24N 76 49 E
Newala, *Tanzania* **55 E4** 10 58S 39 18 E
Newark, *Del., U.S.A.* **76 F8** 39 41N 75 46W
Newark, *N.J., U.S.A.* **79 F10** 40 44N 74 10W
Newark, *N.Y., U.S.A.* **78 C7** 43 3N 77 6W
Newark, *Ohio, U.S.A.* **78 F2** 40 3N 82 24W
Newark-on-Trent, *U.K.* **10 D7** 53 5N 0 48W
Newark Valley, *U.S.A.* **79 D8** 42 14N 76 11W
Newberg, *U.S.A.* **82 D2** 45 18N 122 58W
Newberry, *Mich., U.S.A.* **76 B3** 46 21N 85 30W
Newberry, *S.C., U.S.A.* **77 H5** 34 17N 81 37W
Newberry Springs, *U.S.A.* **85 L10** 34 50N 116 41W
Newboro L., *Canada* **79 B8** 44 38N 76 20W
Newbridge = Droichead Nua, *Ireland* **13 C5** 53 11N 6 48W
Newburgh, *Canada* **78 B8** 44 19N 76 52W
Newburgh, *U.S.A.* **79 E10** 41 30N 74 1W
Newbury, *U.K.* **11 F6** 51 24N 1 20W
Newbury, *N.H., U.S.A.* **79 B12** 43 19N 72 3W
Newbury, *Vt., U.S.A.* **79 B12** 44 5N 72 4W
Newburyport, *U.S.A.* **77 D10** 42 49N 70 53W
Newcastle, *Australia* **63 E5** 33 0S 151 46 E
Newcastle, *N.B., Canada* **71 C6** 47 1N 65 38W
Newcastle, *Ont., Canada* **70 D4** 43 55N 78 35W
Newcastle, *S. Africa* **57 D4** 27 45S 29 58 E
Newcastle, *U.K.* **13 B6** 54 13N 5 54W
Newcastle, *Calif., U.S.A.* **84 G5** 38 53N 121 8W
Newcastle, *Wyo., U.S.A.* **80 D2** 43 50N 104 11W
Newcastle Emlyn, *U.K.* **11 E3** 52 2N 4 28W
Newcastle Ra., *Australia* **60 C5** 15 45S 130 15 E
Newcastle-under-Lyme, *U.K.* **10 D5** 53 1N 2 14W
Newcastle-upon-Tyne, *U.K.* **10 C6** 54 58N 1 36W
Newcastle Waters, *Australia* **62 B1** 17 30S 133 28 E
Newcastle West, *Ireland* **13 D2** 52 27N 9 3W
Newcomb, *U.S.A.* **79 C10** 43 58N 74 10W
Newcomerstown, *U.S.A.* **78 F3** 40 16N 81 36W
Newdegate, *Australia* **61 F2** 33 6S 119 0 E
Newell, *Australia* **62 B4** 16 20S 145 16 E
Newell, *U.S.A.* **80 C3** 44 43N 103 25W
Newfane, *U.S.A.* **78 C6** 43 17N 78 43W
Newfield, *U.S.A.* **79 D8** 42 18N 76 33W
Newfound L., *U.S.A.* **79 C13** 43 40N 71 47W
Newfoundland, *N. Amer.* **66 E14** 49 0N 55 0W
Newfoundland, *U.S.A.* **79 E9** 41 18N 75 19W
Newfoundland □, *Canada* **71 B8** 53 0N 58 0W
Newhall, *U.S.A.* **85 L8** 34 23N 118 32W
Newhaven, *U.K.* **11 G8** 50 47N 0 3 E
Newkirk, *U.S.A.* **81 G6** 36 53N 97 3W
Newlyn, *U.K.* **11 G2** 50 6N 5 34W
Newman, *Australia* **60 D2** 23 18S 119 45 E
Newman, *U.S.A.* **84 H5** 37 19N 121 1W
Newmarket, *Canada* **78 B5** 44 3N 79 28W
Newmarket, *Ireland* **13 D2** 52 13N 9 0W
Newmarket, *U.K.* **11 E8** 52 15N 0 25 E
Newmarket, *N.H., U.S.A.* **79 C14** 43 4N 70 56W
Newmarket, *N.H., U.S.A.* **79 C14** 43 5N 70 56W
Newnan, *U.S.A.* **77 J3** 33 23N 84 48W
Newport, *Ireland* **13 C2** 53 53N 9 33W
Newport, *I. of W., U.K.* **11 G6** 50 42N 1 17W
Newport, *Newp., U.K.* **11 F5** 51 35N 3 0W
Newport, *Ark., U.S.A.* **81 H9** 35 37N 91 16W
Newport, *Ky., U.S.A.* **76 F3** 39 5N 84 30W
Newport, *N.H., U.S.A.* **79 C12** 43 22N 72 10W
Newport, *N.Y., U.S.A.* **79 C9** 43 11N 75 1W
Newport, *Oreg., U.S.A.* **82 D1** 44 39N 124 3W
Newport, *Pa., U.S.A.* **78 F7** 40 29N 77 8W
Newport, *R.I., U.S.A.* **79 E13** 41 29N 71 19W
Newport, *Tenn., U.S.A.* **77 H4** 35 58N 83 11W
Newport, *Vt., U.S.A.* **79 B12** 44 56N 72 13W
Newport, *Wash., U.S.A.* **82 B5** 48 11N 117 3W
Newport □, *U.K.* **11 F4** 51 33N 3 1W
Newport Beach, *U.S.A.* **85 M9** 33 37N 117 56W
Newport News, *U.S.A.* **76 G7** 36 59N 76 25W
Newport Pagnell, *U.K.* **11 E7** 52 5N 0 43W
Newquay, *U.K.* **11 G2** 50 25N 5 6W
Newry, *U.K.* **13 B5** 54 11N 6 21W
Newton, *Ill., U.S.A.* **80 F10** 38 59N 88 10W
Newton, *Iowa, U.S.A.* **80 E8** 41 42N 93 3W
Newton, *Kans., U.S.A.* **81 F6** 38 3N 97 21W
Newton, *Mass., U.S.A.* **79 D13** 42 21N 71 12W
Newton, *Miss., U.S.A.* **81 J10** 32 19N 89 10W
Newton, *N.C., U.S.A.* **77 H5** 35 40N 81 13W
Newton, *N.J., U.S.A.* **79 E10** 41 3N 74 45W
Newton, *Tex., U.S.A.* **81 K8** 30 51N 93 46W
Newton Abbot, *U.K.* **11 G4** 50 32N 3 37W
Newton Aycliffe, *U.K.* **10 C6** 54 37N 1 34W
Newton Falls, *U.S.A.* **78 E4** 41 11N 80 59W
Newton Stewart, *U.K.* **12 G4** 54 57N 4 30W
Newtonmore, *U.K.* **12 D4** 57 4N 4 8W
Newtown, *U.K.* **11 E4** 52 31N 3 19W
Newtownabbey, *U.K.* **13 B6** 54 40N 5 56W
Newtownards, *U.K.* **13 B6** 54 36N 5 42W
Newtownbarry = Bunclody, *Ireland* **13 D5** 52 39N 6 40W
Newtownstewart, *U.K.* **13 B4** 54 43N 7 23W
Newville, *U.S.A.* **78 F7** 40 10N 77 24W
Neya, *Russia* **24 C7** 58 21N 43 49 E
Neyrīz, *Iran* **45 D7** 29 15N 54 19 E
Neyshābūr, *Iran* **45 B8** 36 10N 58 50 E
Nezhin = Nizhyn, *Ukraine* **25 D5** 51 5N 31 55 E
Nezperce, *U.S.A.* **82 C5** 46 14N 116 14W
Ngabang, *Indonesia* **36 D3** 0 23N 109 55 E
Ngabordamlu, Tanjung, *Indonesia* **37 F8** 6 56S 134 11 E
N'Gage, *Angola* **52 F3** 7 46S 15 16 E
Ngami Depression, *Botswana* **56 C3** 20 30S 22 46 E
Ngamo, *Zimbabwe* **55 F2** 19 3S 27 32 E
Nganglong Kangri, *China* **41 C12** 33 0N 81 0 E
Ngao, *Thailand* **38 C2** 18 46N 99 59 E
Ngaoundéré, *Cameroon* **52 C2** 7 15N 13 35 E
Ngapara, *N.Z.* **59 L3** 44 57S 170 46 E
Ngara, *Tanzania* **54 C3** 2 29S 30 40 E
Ngawi, *Indonesia* **37 G14** 7 24S 111 26 E
Ngoma, *Malawi* **55 E3** 13 8S 33 45 E
Ngomahura, *Zimbabwe* **55 G3** 20 26S 30 43 E
Ngomba, *Tanzania* **55 D3** 8 20S 32 53 E
Ngoring Hu, *China* **32 C4** 34 55N 97 5 E
Ngorongoro, *Tanzania* **54 C4** 3 11S 35 32 E
Ngozi, *Burundi* **54 C2** 2 54S 29 50 E
Ngudu, *Tanzania* **54 C3** 2 58S 33 25 E
Nguigmi, *Niger* **51 F8** 14 20N 13 20 E
Nguiu, *Australia* **60 B5** 11 46S 130 38 E
Ngukurr, *Australia* **62 A1** 14 44S 134 44 E
Ngulu Atoll, *Pac. Oc.* **37 C9** 8 0N 137 30 E
Ngunga, *Tanzania* **54 C3** 3 37S 33 37 E
Nguru, *Nigeria* **51 F8** 12 56N 10 29 E
Nguru Mts., *Tanzania* **54 D4** 6 0S 37 30 E
Nha Trang, *Vietnam* **39 F7** 12 16N 109 10 E
Nhacoongo, *Mozam.* **57 C6** 24 18S 35 14 E
Nhamaabué, *Mozam.* **55 F4** 17 25S 35 5 E
Nhamundá →, *Brazil* **93 D7** 2 12S 56 41W
Nhangutazi, L., *Mozam.* **57 C5** 24 0S 34 30 E
Nhill, *Australia* **63 F3** 36 18S 141 40 E
Nhulunbuy, *Australia* **62 A2** 12 10S 137 20 E
Nia-nia, *Dem. Rep. of the Congo* **54 B2** 1 30N 27 40 E
Niagara Falls, *Canada* **78 C5** 43 7N 79 5W
Niagara Falls, *U.S.A.* **78 C6** 43 5N 79 4W
Niagara-on-the-Lake, *Canada* **78 C5** 43 15N 79 4W
Niah, *Malaysia* **36 D4** 3 58N 113 46 E
Niamey, *Niger* **50 F6** 13 27N 2 6 E
Niangara, *Dem. Rep. of the Congo* **54 B2** 3 42N 27 50 E
Niantic, *U.S.A.* **79 E12** 41 20N 72 11W
Nias, *Indonesia* **36 D1** 1 0N 97 30 E
Niassa □, *Mozam.* **55 E4** 13 30S 36 0 E
Nibāk, *Si. Arabia* **45 E7** 24 25N 50 50 E
Nicaragua ■, *Cent. Amer.* **88 D2** 11 40N 85 30W
Nicaragua, L. de, *Nic.* **88 D2** 12 0N 85 30W
Nicastro, *Italy* **20 E7** 38 59N 16 19 E
Nice, *France* **18 E7** 43 42N 7 14 E
Niceville, *U.S.A.* **77 K2** 30 31N 86 30W
Nichicun, L., *Canada* **71 B5** 53 5N 71 0W
Nichinan, *Japan* **31 J5** 31 38N 131 23 E
Nicholás, Canal, *W. Indies* **88 B3** 23 30N 80 5W
Nicholasville, *U.S.A.* **76 G3** 37 53N 84 34W
Nichols, *U.S.A.* **79 D8** 42 1N 76 22W
Nicholson, *Australia* **60 C4** 18 2S 128 54 E
Nicholson, *U.S.A.* **79 E9** 41 37N 75 47W
Nicholson →, *Australia* **62 B2** 17 31S 139 36 E
Nicholson L., *Canada* **73 A8** 62 40N 102 40W
Nicholson Ra., *Australia* **61 E2** 27 15S 116 45 E
Nicholville, *U.S.A.* **79 B10** 44 41N 74 39W
Nicobar Is., *Ind. Oc.* **28 J13** 9 0N 93 0 E
Nicola, *Canada* **72 C4** 50 12N 120 40W
Nicolls Town, *Bahamas* **88 A4** 25 8N 78 0W
Nicosia, *Cyprus* **23 D12** 35 10N 33 25 E
Nicoya, *Costa Rica* **88 D2** 10 9N 85 27W
Nicoya, G. de, *Costa Rica* **88 E3** 10 0N 85 0W
Nicoya, Pen. de, *Costa Rica* **88 E2** 9 45N 85 40W
Nidd →, *U.K.* **10 D6** 53 59N 1 23W
Niedersachsen □, *Germany* **16 B5** 52 50N 9 0 E
Niekerkshoop, *S. Africa* **56 D3** 29 19S 22 51 E
Niemba, *Dem. Rep. of the Congo* **54 D2** 5 58S 28 24 E
Niemen = Neman →, *Lithuania* **9 J20** 55 25N 21 10 E
Nienburg, *Germany* **16 B5** 52 39N 9 13 E
Nieu Bethesda, *S. Africa* **56 E3** 31 51S 24 34 E
Nieuw Amsterdam, *Surinam* **93 B7** 5 53N 55 5W
Nieuw Nickerie, *Surinam* **93 B7** 6 0N 56 59W
Nieuwoudtville, *S. Africa* **56 E2** 31 23S 19 7 E
Nieuwpoort, *Belgium* **15 C2** 51 8N 2 45 E
Nieves, Pico de las, *Canary Is.* **22 G4** 27 57N 15 35W
Niğde, *Turkey* **25 G5** 37 58N 34 40 E
Nigel, *S. Africa* **57 D4** 26 27S 28 25 E
Niger ■, *W. Afr.* **50 E7** 17 30N 10 0 E
Niger →, *W. Afr.* **50 G7** 5 33N 6 33 E
Nigeria ■, *W. Afr.* **50 G7** 8 30N 8 0 E
Nighasin, *India* **43 E9** 28 14N 80 52 E
Nightcaps, *N.Z.* **59 L2** 45 57S 168 2 E
Nii-Jima, *Japan* **31 G9** 34 20N 139 15 E
Niigata, *Japan* **30 F9** 37 58N 139 0 E
Niigata □, *Japan* **31 F9** 37 15N 138 45 E
Niihama, *Japan* **31 H6** 33 55N 133 16 E
Niihau, *U.S.A.* **74 H14** 21 54N 160 9W
Niimi, *Japan* **31 G6** 34 59N 133 28 E
Niitsu, *Japan* **30 F9** 37 48N 139 7 E
Nijil, *Jordan* **47 E4** 30 32N 35 33 E
Nijkerk, *Neths.* **15 B5** 52 13N 5 30 E
Nijmegen, *Neths.* **15 C5** 51 50N 5 52 E
Nijverdal, *Neths.* **15 B6** 52 22N 6 28 E
Nīk Pey, *Iran* **45 B6** 36 50N 48 10 E
Nikiniki, *Indonesia* **37 F6** 9 49S 124 30 E
Nikkō, *Japan* **31 F9** 36 45N 139 35 E
Nikolayev = Mykolayiv, *Ukraine* **25 E5** 46 58N 32 0 E
Nikolayevsk, *Russia* **25 E8** 50 0N 45 35 E
Nikolayevsk-na-Amur, *Russia* **27 D15** 53 8N 140 44 E
Nikolskoye, *Russia* **27 D17** 55 12N 166 0 E
Nikopol, *Ukraine* **25 E5** 47 35N 34 25 E
Nīkshahr, *Iran* **45 E9** 26 15N 60 10 E
Nikšić, *Montenegro, Yug.* **21 C8** 42 50N 18 57 E
Nîl, Nahr en →, *Africa* **51 B12** 30 10N 31 6 E
Nîl el Abyad →, *Sudan* **51 E12** 15 38N 32 31 E
Nîl el Azraq →, *Sudan* **51 E12** 15 38N 32 31 E
Nila, *Indonesia* **37 F7** 6 44S 129 31 E
Niland, *U.S.A.* **85 M11** 33 14N 115 31W
Nile = Nîl, Nahr en →, *Africa* **51 B12** 30 10N 31 6 E
Niles, *Mich., U.S.A.* **76 E2** 41 50N 86 15W
Niles, *Ohio, U.S.A.* **78 E4** 41 11N 80 46W
Nim Ka Thana, *India* **42 F6** 27 44N 75 48 E
Nimach, *India* **42 G6** 24 30N 74 56 E
Nimbahera, *India* **42 G6** 24 37N 74 45 E
Nîmes, *France* **18 E6** 43 50N 4 23 E
Nimfaíon, Ákra = Pinnes, Ákra, *Greece* **21 D11** 40 5N 24 20 E
Nimmitabel, *Australia* **63 F4** 36 29S 149 15 E
Nīnawá, *Iraq* **44 B4** 36 25N 43 10 E
Nindigully, *Australia* **63 D4** 28 21S 148 50 E
Nineveh = Nīnawá, *Iraq* **44 B4** 36 25N 43 10 E
Ning Xian, *China* **34 G4** 35 30N 107 58 E
Ning'an, *China* **35 B15** 44 22N 129 20 E
Ningbo, *China* **33 D7** 29 51N 121 28 E
Ningcheng, *China* **35 D10** 41 32N 119 53 E
Ningjin, *China* **34 F8** 37 35N 114 57 E
Ningjing Shan, *China* **32 D4** 30 0N 98 20 E
Ningling, *China* **34 G8** 34 25N 115 22 E
Ningpo = Ningbo, *China* **33 D7** 29 51N 121 28 E
Ningqiang, *China* **34 H4** 32 47N 106 15 E
Ningshan, *China* **34 H5** 33 21N 108 21 E
Ningsia Hui A.R. = Ningxia Huizu Zizhiqu □, *China* **34 F4** 38 0N 106 0 E
Ningwu, *China* **34 E7** 39 0N 112 18 E
Ningxia Huizu Zizhiqu □, *China* **34 F4** 38 0N 106 0 E
Ningyang, *China* **34 G9** 35 47N 116 45 E
Ninh Giang, *Vietnam* **38 B6** 20 44N 106 24 E
Ninh Hoa, *Vietnam* **38 F7** 12 30N 109 7 E
Ninh Ma, *Vietnam* **38 F7** 12 48N 109 21 E
Ninove, *Belgium* **15 D4** 50 51N 4 2 E
Nioaque, *Brazil* **95 A4** 21 5S 55 50W
Niobrara, *U.S.A.* **80 D6** 42 45N 98 2W
Niobrara →, *U.S.A.* **80 D6** 42 46N 98 3W
Nioro du Sahel, *Mali* **50 E4** 15 15N 9 30W
Niort, *France* **18 C3** 46 19N 0 29W
Nipawin, *Canada* **73 C8** 53 20N 104 0W
Nipigon, *Canada* **70 C2** 49 0N 88 17W
Nipigon, L., *Canada* **70 C2** 49 50N 88 30W
Nipishish L., *Canada* **71 B7** 54 12N 60 45W
Nipissing, L., *Canada* **70 C4** 46 20N 80 0W
Nipomo, *U.S.A.* **85 K6** 35 3N 120 29W
Nipton, *U.S.A.* **85 K11** 35 28N 115 16W
Niquelândia, *Brazil* **93 F9** 14 33S 48 23W
Nīr, *Iran* **44 B5** 38 2N 47 59 E
Nirasaki, *Japan* **31 G9** 35 42N 138 27 E
Nirmal, *India* **40 K11** 19 3N 78 20 E
Nirmali, *India* **43 F12** 26 20N 86 35 E
Niš, *Serbia, Yug.* **21 C9** 43 19N 21 58 E
Nişāb, *Si. Arabia* **44 D5** 29 11N 44 43 E
Nişāb, *Yemen* **46 E4** 14 25N 46 29 E
Nishinomiya, *Japan* **31 G7** 34 45N 135 20 E
Nishino'omote, *Japan* **31 J5** 30 43N 130 59 E
Nishiwaki, *Japan* **31 G7** 34 59N 134 58 E
Niskibi →, *Canada* **70 A2** 56 29N 88 9W
Nisqually →, *U.S.A.* **84 C4** 47 6N 122 42W
Nissáki, *Greece* **23 A3** 39 43N 19 52 E
Nissum Bredning, *Denmark* **9 H13** 56 40N 8 20 E
Nistru = Dnister →, *Europe* **17 E16** 46 18N 30 17 E
Nisutlin →, *Canada* **72 A2** 60 14N 132 34W
Nitchequon, *Canada* **71 B5** 53 10N 70 58W
Niterói, *Brazil* **95 A7** 22 52S 43 0W
Nith →, *Canada* **78 C4** 43 12N 80 23W
Nith →, *U.K.* **12 F5** 55 14N 3 33W
Nitra, *Slovak Rep.* **17 D10** 48 19N 18 4 E
Nitra →, *Slovak Rep.* **17 E10** 47 46N 18 10 E
Niuafo'ou, *Tonga* **59 B11** 15 30S 175 58W
Niue, *Cook Is.* **65 J11** 19 2S 169 54W
Niut, *Indonesia* **36 D4** 0 55N 110 6 E
Niuzhuang, *China* **35 D12** 40 58N 122 28 E
Nivala, *Finland* **8 E21** 63 56N 24 57 E
Nivelles, *Belgium* **15 D4** 50 35N 4 20 E
Nivernais, *France* **18 C5** 47 15N 3 30 E
Niwas, *India* **43 H9** 23 3N 80 26 E
Nixon, *U.S.A.* **81 L6** 29 16N 97 46W
Nizamabad, *India* **40 K11** 18 45N 78 7 E
Nizamghat, *India* **41 E19** 28 20N 95 45 E
Nizhne Kolymsk, *Russia* **27 C17** 68 34N 160 55 E
Nizhnekamsk, *Russia* **24 C9** 55 38N 51 49 E
Nizhneudinsk, *Russia* **27 D10** 54 54N 99 3 E
Nizhnevartovsk, *Russia* **26 C8** 60 56N 76 38 E
Nizhniy Novgorod, *Russia* **24 C7** 56 20N 44 0 E
Nizhniy Tagil, *Russia* **24 C10** 57 55N 59 57 E
Nizhyn, *Ukraine* **25 D5** 51 5N 31 55 E
Nizip, *Turkey* **44 B3** 37 5N 37 50 E
Nízké Tatry, *Slovak Rep.* **17 D10** 48 55N 19 30 E
Njakwa, *Malawi* **55 E3** 11 1S 33 56 E
Njanji, *Zambia* **55 E3** 14 25S 31 46 E
Njinjo, *Tanzania* **55 D4** 8 48S 38 54 E
Njombe, *Tanzania* **55 D3** 9 20S 34 50 E
Njombe →, *Tanzania* **54 D4** 6 56S 35 6 E
Nkana, *Zambia* **55 E2** 12 50S 28 8 E
Nkayi, *Zimbabwe* **55 F2** 19 41S 29 20 E
Nkhotakota, *Malawi* **55 E3** 12 56S 34 15 E
Nkongsamba, *Cameroon* **52 D1** 4 55N 9 55 E
Nkurenkuru, *Namibia* **56 B2** 17 42S 18 32 E
Nmai →, *Burma* **41 G20** 25 30N 97 25 E
Noakhali = Maijdi, *Bangla.* **41 H17** 22 48N 91 10 E
Nobel, *Canada* **78 A4** 45 25N 80 6W
Nobeoka, *Japan* **31 H5** 32 36N 131 41 E
Noblesville, *U.S.A.* **76 E3** 40 3N 86 1W
Nocera Inferiore, *Italy* **20 D6** 40 44N 14 38 E
Nocona, *U.S.A.* **81 J6** 33 47N 97 44W
Noda, *Japan* **31 G9** 35 56N 139 52 E
Nogales, *Mexico* **86 A2** 31 20N 110 56W
Nogales, *U.S.A.* **83 L8** 31 20N 110 56W
Nōgata, *Japan* **31 H5** 33 48N 130 44 E
Noggerup, *Australia* **61 F2** 33 32S 116 5 E
Noginsk, *Russia* **27 C10** 64 30N 90 50 E
Nogoa →, *Australia* **62 C4** 23 40S 147 55 E
Nogoyá, *Argentina* **94 C4** 32 24S 59 48W
Nohar, *India* **42 E6** 29 11N 74 49 E
Nohta, *India* **43 H8** 23 40N 79 34 E
Noire, Mts., *France* **18 B2** 48 7N 3 28W
Noirmoutier, Î. de, *France* **18 C2** 46 58N 2 10W
Nojane, *Botswana* **56 C3** 23 15S 20 14 E
Nojima-Zaki, *Japan* **31 G9** 34 54N 139 53 E
Nok Kundi, *Pakistan* **40 E3** 28 50N 62 45 E
Nokaneng, *Botswana* **56 B3** 19 40S 22 17 E
Nokia, *Finland* **9 F20** 61 30N 23 30 E
Nokomis, *Canada* **73 C8** 51 35N 105 0W
Nokomis L., *Canada* **73 B8** 57 0N 103 0W
Nola, *C.A.R.* **52 D3** 3 35N 16 4 E
Noma Omuramba →, *Namibia* **56 B3** 18 52S 20 53 E
Nombre de Dios, *Panama* **88 E4** 9 34N 79 28W
Nome, *U.S.A.* **68 B3** 64 30N 165 25W
Nomo-Zaki, *Japan* **31 H4** 32 35N 129 44 E
Nonacho L., *Canada* **73 A7** 61 42N 109 40W
Nonda, *Australia* **62 C3** 20 40S 142 28 E
Nong Chang, *Thailand* **38 E2** 15 23N 99 51 E
Nong Het, *Laos* **38 C4** 19 29N 103 59 E
Nong Khai, *Thailand* **38 D4** 17 50N 102 46 E
Nong'an, *China* **35 B13** 44 25N 125 5 E
Nongoma, *S. Africa* **57 D5** 27 58S 31 35 E
Nonoava, *Mexico* **86 B3** 27 28N 106 44W
Nonoava →, *Mexico* **86 B3** 27 29N 106 45W
Nonthaburi, *Thailand* **38 F3** 13 51N 100 34 E
Noonamah, *Australia* **60 B5** 12 40S 131 4 E
Noord Brabant □, *Neths.* **15 C5** 51 40N 5 0 E
Noord Holland □, *Neths.* **15 B4** 52 30N 4 45 E
Noordbeveland, *Neths.* **15 C3** 51 35N 3 50 E
Noordoostpolder, *Neths.* **15 B5** 52 45N 5 45 E
Noordwijk, *Neths.* **15 B4** 52 14N 4 26 E
Nootka I., *Canada* **72 D3** 49 32N 126 42W
Nopiming Prov. Park, *Canada* **73 C9** 50 30N 95 37W
Noralee, *Canada* **72 C3** 53 59N 126 26W
Noranda = Rouyn-Noranda, *Canada* **70 C4** 48 20N 79 0W
Norco, *U.S.A.* **85 M9** 33 56N 117 33W
Nord-Kivu □, *Dem. Rep. of the Congo* **54 C2** 1 0S 29 0 E
Nord-Ostsee-Kanal, *Germany* **16 A5** 54 12N 9 32 E
Nordaustlandet, *Svalbard* **4 B9** 79 14N 23 0 E
Nordegg, *Canada* **72 C5** 52 29N 116 5W
Norderney, *Germany* **16 B4** 53 42N 7 9 E
Norderstedt, *Germany* **16 B5** 53 42N 10 1 E
Nordfjord, *Norway* **9 F11** 61 55N 5 30 E
Nordfriesische Inseln, *Germany* **16 A5** 54 40N 8 20 E
Nordhausen, *Germany* **16 C6** 51 30N 10 47 E
Norðoyar, *Færoe Is.* **8 E9** 62 17N 6 35W
Nordkapp, *Norway* **8 A21** 71 10N 25 50 E
Nordkapp, *Svalbard* **4 A9** 80 31N 20 0 E
Nordkinn = Kinnarodden, *Norway* **6 A11** 71 8N 27 40 E
Nordkinn-halvøya, *Norway* **8 A22** 70 55N 27 40 E
Nordrhein-Westfalen □, *Germany* **16 C4** 51 45N 7 30 E
Nordvik, *Russia* **27 B12** 74 2N 111 32 E
Nore →, *Ireland* **13 D4** 52 25N 6 58W
Norfolk, *Nebr., U.S.A.* **80 D6** 42 2N 97 25W
Norfolk, *Va., U.S.A.* **76 G7** 36 51N 76 17W
Norfolk □, *U.K.* **11 E8** 52 39N 0 54 E
Norfolk I., *Pac. Oc.* **64 K8** 28 58S 168 3 E
Norfork L., *U.S.A.* **81 G8** 36 15N 92 14W
Norilsk, *Russia* **27 C9** 69 20N 88 6 E
Norma, Mt., *Australia* **62 C3** 20 55S 140 42 E
Normal, *U.S.A.* **80 E10** 40 31N 88 59W
Norman, *U.S.A.* **81 H6** 35 13N 97 26W
Norman →, *Australia* **62 B3** 19 18S 141 51 E
Norman Wells, *Canada* **68 B7** 65 17N 126 51W
Normanby →, *Australia* **62 A3** 14 23S 144 10 E
Normandie, *France* **18 B4** 48 45N 0 10 E
Normandin, *Canada* **70 C5** 48 49N 72 31W
Normandy = Normandie, *France* **18 B4** 48 45N 0 10 E
Normanhurst, Mt., *Australia* **61 E3** 25 4S 122 30 E
Normanton, *Australia* **62 B3** 17 40S 141 10 E
Normétal, *Canada* **70 C4** 49 0N 79 22W
Norquay, *Canada* **73 C8** 51 53N 102 5W
Norquinco, *Argentina* **96 E2** 41 51S 70 55W
Norrbotten □, *Sweden* **8 C19** 66 30N 22 30 E
Norris Point, *Canada* **71 C8** 49 31N 57 53W
Norristown, *U.S.A.* **79 F9** 40 7N 75 21W
Norrköping, *Sweden* **9 G17** 58 37N 16 11 E
Norrland, *Sweden* **9 E16** 62 15N 15 45 E
Norrtälje, *Sweden* **9 G18** 59 46N 18 42 E
Norseman, *Australia* **61 F3** 32 8S 121 43 E
Norsk, *Russia* **27 D14** 52 30N 130 5 E
Norte, Pta. del, *Canary Is.* **22 G2** 27 51N 17 57W
Norte, Serra do, *Brazil* **92** 11 20S 59 0W
North, C., *Canada* **71 C7** 47 2N 60 20W
North Adams, *U.S.A.* **79 D11** 42 42N 73 7W
North Arm, *Canada* **72 A5** 62 0N 114 30W
North Augusta, *U.S.A.* **77 J5** 33 30N 81 59W
North Ayrshire □, *U.K.* **12 F4** 55 45N 4 44W
North Bass I., *U.S.A.* **78 E2** 41 43N 82 49W
North Battleford, *Canada* **73 C7** 52 50N 108 17W
North Bay, *Canada* **70 C4** 46 20N 79 30W
North Belcher Is., *Canada* **70 A4** 56 50N 79 50W
North Bend, *Oreg., U.S.A.* **82 E1** 43 24N 124 14W
North Bend, *Pa., U.S.A.* **78 E7** 41 20N 77 42W
North Bend, *Wash., U.S.A.* **84 C5** 47 30N 121 47W
North Bennington, *U.S.A.* **79 D11** 42 56N 73 15W
North Berwick, *U.K.* **12 E6** 56 4N 2 42W
North Berwick, *U.S.A.* **79 C14** 43 18N 70 44W
North C., *Canada* **71 C7** 47 5N 64 0W
North C., *N.Z.* **59 F4** 34 23S 173 4 E
North Canadian →, *U.S.A.* **81 H7** 35 16N 95 31W
North Canton, *U.S.A.* **78 F3** 40 53N 81 24W
North Cape = Nordkapp, *Norway* **8 A21** 71 10N 25 50 E
North Cape = Nordkapp, *Svalbard* **4 A9** 80 31N 20 0 E
North Caribou L., *Canada* **70 B1** 52 50N 90 40W
North Carolina □, *U.S.A.* **77 H6** 35 30N 80 0W
North Cascades National Park, *U.S.A.* **82 B3** 48 45N 121 10W
North Channel, *Canada* **70 C3** 46 0N 83 0W
North Channel, *U.K.* **12 F3** 55 13N 5 52W
North Charleston, *U.S.A.* **77 J6** 32 53N 79 58W
North Chicago, *U.S.A.* **76 D2** 42 19N 87 51W
North Creek, *U.S.A.* **79 C11** 43 41N 73 59W
North Dakota □, *U.S.A.* **80 B5** 47 30N 100 15W
North Downs, *U.K.* **11 F8** 51 19N 0 21 E
North East, *U.S.A.* **78 D5** 42 13N 79 50W
North East Frontier Agency = Arunachal Pradesh □, *India* **41 F19** 28 0N 95 0 E
North East Lincolnshire □, *U.K.* **10 D7** 53 34N 0 2W
North Eastern □, *Kenya* **54 B5** 1 30N 40 0 E
North Esk →, *U.K.* **12 E6** 56 46N 2 24W
North European Plain, *Europe* **6 E10** 55 0N 25 0 E
North Foreland, *U.K.* **11 F9** 51 22N 1 28 E
North Fork, *U.S.A.* **84 H7** 37 14N 119 21W
North Fork American →, *U.S.A.* **84 G5** 38 57N 120 59W
North Fork Feather →, *U.S.A.* **84 F5** 38 33N 121 30W
North Fork Grand →, *U.S.A.* **80 C3** 45 47N 102 16W
North Fork Red →, *U.S.A.* **81 H5** 34 24N 99 14W
North Frisian Is. = Nordfriesische Inseln, *Germany* **16 A5** 54 40N 8 20 E
North Gower, *Canada* **79 A9** 45 8N 75 43W
North Hd., *Australia* **61 F1** 30 14S 114 59 E
North Henik L., *Canada* **73 A9** 61 45N 97 40W
North Highlands, *U.S.A.* **84 G5** 38 40N 121 23W
North Horr, *Kenya* **54 B4** 3 20N 37 8 E
North I., *Kenya* **54 B4** 4 5N 36 5 E
North I., *N.Z.* **59 H5** 38 0S 175 0 E
North Kingsville, *U.S.A.* **78 E4** 41 54N 80 42W
North Knife →, *Canada* **73 B10** 58 53N 94 45W

Oshkosh

Ofotfjorden, *Norway* **8 B17** 68 27N 17 0 E
Ōfunato, *Japan* **30 E10** 39 4N 141 43 E
Oga, *Japan* **30 E9** 39 55N 139 50 E
Oga-Hantō, *Japan* **30 E9** 39 58N 139 47 E
Ogaden, *Ethiopia* **46 F3** 7 30N 45 30 E
Ōgaki, *Japan* **31 G8** 35 21N 136 37 E
Ogallala, *U.S.A.* **80 E4** 41 8N 101 43W
Ogasawara Gunto, *Pac. Oc.* **28 G18** 27 0N 142 0 E
Ogbomosho, *Nigeria* **50 G6** 8 1N 4 11 E
Ogden, *U.S.A.* **82 F7** 41 13N 111 58W
Ogdensburg, *U.S.A.* **79 B9** 44 42N 75 30W
Ogeechee →, *U.S.A.* **77 K5** 31 50N 81 3W
Ogilby, *U.S.A.* **85 N12** 32 49N 114 50W
Oglio →, *Italy* **20 B4** 45 2N 10 39 E
Ogmore, *Australia* **62 C4** 22 37S 149 35 E
Ogoki, *Canada* **70 B2** 51 38N 85 58W
Ogoki →, *Canada* **70 B2** 51 38N 85 57W
Ogoki L., *Canada* **70 B2** 50 50N 87 10W
Ogoki Res., *Canada* **70 B2** 50 45N 88 15W
Ogooué →, *Gabon* **52 E1** 1 0S 9 0 E
Ogowe = Ogooué →, *Gabon* **52 E1** 1 0S 9 0 E
Ogre, *Latvia* **9 H21** 56 49N 24 36 E
Ogurchinskiy, Ostrov, *Turkmenistan* **45 B7** 38 55N 53 2 E
Ohai, *N.Z.* **59 L2** 45 55S 168 0 E
Ohakune, *N.Z.* **59 H5** 39 24S 175 24 E
Ohata, *Japan* **30 D10** 41 24N 141 10 E
Ohau, L., *N.Z.* **59 L2** 44 15S 169 53 E
Ohio □, *U.S.A.* **78 F2** 40 15N 82 45W
Ohio →, *U.S.A.* **76 G1** 36 59N 89 8W
Ohře →, *Czech Rep.* **16 C8** 50 30N 14 10 E
Ohrid, *Macedonia* **21 D9** 41 8N 20 52 E
Ohridsko Jezero, *Macedonia* **21 D9** 41 8N 20 52 E
Ohrigstad, *S. Africa* **57 C5** 24 39S 30 36 E
Oiapoque, *Brazil* **93** 3 50N 51 50W
Oikou, *China* **35 E9** 38 35N 117 42 E
Oil City, *U.S.A.* **78 E5** 41 26N 79 42W
Oil Springs, *Canada* **78 D2** 42 47N 82 7W
Oildale, *U.S.A.* **85 K7** 35 25N 119 1W
Oise →, *France* **18 B5** 49 0N 2 4 E
Ōita, *Japan* **31 H5** 33 14N 131 36 E
Ōita □, *Japan* **31 H5** 33 15N 131 30 E
Oiticica, *Brazil* **93 E10** 5 3S 41 5W
Ojacaliente, *Mexico* **86 C4** 22 34N 102 15W
Ojai, *U.S.A.* **85 L7** 34 27N 119 15W
Ojinaga, *Mexico* **86 B4** 29 34N 104 25W
Ojiya, *Japan* **31 F9** 37 18N 138 48 E
Ojos del Salado, Cerro, *Argentina* **94 B2** 27 0S 68 40W
Oka →, *Russia* **24 C7** 56 20N 43 59 E
Okaba, *Indonesia* **37 F9** 8 6S 139 42 E
Okahandja, *Namibia* **56 C2** 22 0S 16 59 E
Okahukura, *N.Z.* **59 H5** 38 48S 175 14 E
Okanagan L., *Canada* **72 D5** 50 0N 119 30W
Okanogan, *U.S.A.* **82 B4** 48 22N 119 35W
Okanogan →, *U.S.A.* **82 B4** 48 6N 119 44W
Okaputa, *Namibia* **56 C2** 20 5S 17 0 E
Okara, *Pakistan* **42 D5** 30 50N 73 31 E
Okarito, *N.Z.* **59 K3** 43 15S 170 9 E
Okaukuejo, *Namibia* **56 B2** 19 10S 16 0 E
Okavango Swamps, *Botswana* **56 B3** 18 45S 22 45 E
Okaya, *Japan* **31 F9** 36 5N 138 10 E
Okayama, *Japan* **31 G6** 34 40N 133 54 E
Okayama □, *Japan* **31 G6** 35 0N 133 50 E
Okazaki, *Japan* **31 G8** 34 57N 137 10 E
Okeechobee, *U.S.A.* **77 M5** 27 15N 80 50W
Okeechobee, L., *U.S.A.* **77 M5** 27 0N 80 50W
Okefenokee Swamp, *U.S.A.* **77 K4** 30 40N 82 20W
Okehampton, *U.K.* **11 G4** 50 44N 4 0W
Okha, *India* **42 H3** 22 27N 69 4 E
Okha, *Russia* **27 D15** 53 40N 143 0 E
Okhotsk, *Russia* **27 D15** 59 20N 143 10 E
Okhotsk, Sea of, *Asia* **27 D15** 55 0N 145 0 E
Okhotskiy Perevoz, *Russia* **27 C14** 61 52N 135 35 E
Okhtyrka, *Ukraine* **25 D5** 50 25N 35 0 E
Oki-Shotō, *Japan* **31 F6** 36 5N 133 15 E
Okiep, *S. Africa* **56 D2** 29 39S 17 53 E
Okinawa □, *Japan* **31 L4** 26 40N 128 0 E
Okinawa-Guntō, *Japan* **31 L4** 26 40N 128 0 E
Okinawa-Jima, *Japan* **31 L4** 26 32N 128 0 E
Okino-erabu-Shima, *Japan* **31 L4** 27 21N 128 33 E
Oklahoma □, *U.S.A.* **81 H6** 35 20N 97 30W
Oklahoma City, *U.S.A.* **81 H6** 35 30N 97 30W
Okmulgee, *U.S.A.* **81 H7** 35 37N 95 58W
Oknitsa = Ocniţa, *Moldova* **17 D14** 48 25N 27 30 E
Okolo, *Uganda* **54 B3** 2 37N 31 8 E
Okolona, *U.S.A.* **81 J10** 34 0N 88 45W
Okotoks, *Canada* **72 C6** 50 43N 113 58W
Oksibil, *Indonesia* **37 E10** 4 59S 140 35 E
Oksovskiy, *Russia* **24 B6** 62 33N 39 57 E
Oktabrsk = Oktyabrsk, *Kazakstan* **25 E10** 49 28N 57 25 E
Oktyabrsk, *Kazakstan* **25 E10** 49 28N 57 25 E
Oktyabrskiy = Aktsyabrski, *Belarus* **17 B15** 52 38N 28 53 E
Oktyabrskiy, *Russia* **24 D9** 54 28N 53 28 E
Oktyabrskoy Revolyutsii, Ostrov, *Russia* **27 B10** 79 30N 97 0 E
Okuru, *N.Z.* **59 K2** 43 55S 168 55 E
Okushiri-Tō, *Japan* **30 C9** 42 15N 139 30 E
Okwa →, *Botswana* **56 C3** 22 30S 23 0 E
Ola, *U.S.A.* **81 H8** 35 2N 93 13W
Ólafsfjörður, *Iceland* **8 C4** 66 4N 18 39W
Ólafsvík, *Iceland* **8 D2** 64 53N 23 43W
Olancha, *U.S.A.* **85 J8** 36 17N 118 1W
Olancha Pk., *U.S.A.* **85 J8** 36 15N 118 7W
Olanchito, *Honduras* **88 C2** 15 30N 86 30W
Öland, *Sweden* **9 H17** 56 45N 16 38 E
Olary, *Australia* **63 E3** 32 18S 140 19 E
Olascoaga, *Argentina* **94 D3** 35 15S 60 39W
Olathe, *U.S.A.* **80 F7** 38 53N 94 49W
Olavarría, *Argentina* **94 D3** 36 55S 60 20W
Oława, *Poland* **17 C9** 50 57N 17 20 E
Ólbia, *Italy* **20 D3** 40 55N 9 31 E
Olcott, *U.S.A.* **78 C6** 43 20N 78 42W
Old Bahama Chan. = Bahama, Canal Viejo de, *W. Indies* **88 B4** 22 10N 77 30W
Old Baldy Pk. = San Antonio, Mt., *U.S.A.* **85 L9** 34 17N 117 38W
Old Castile = Castilla y Leon □, *Spain* **19 B3** 42 0N 5 0W
Old Crow, *Canada* **68 B6** 67 30N 139 55W
Old Dale, *U.S.A.* **85 L11** 34 8N 115 47W
Old Forge, *N.Y., U.S.A.* **79 C10** 43 43N 74 58W
Old Forge, *Pa., U.S.A.* **79 E9** 41 22N 75 45W
Old Perlican, *Canada* **71 C9** 48 5N 53 1W
Old Shinyanga, *Tanzania* **54 C3** 3 33S 33 27 E
Old Speck Mt., *U.S.A.* **79 B14** 44 34N 70 57W
Old Town, *U.S.A.* **77 C11** 44 56N 68 39W
Old Washington, *U.S.A.* **78 F3** 40 2N 81 27W
Old Wives L., *Canada* **73 C7** 50 5N 106 0W
Oldbury, *U.K.* **11 F5** 51 38N 2 33W
Oldcastle, *Ireland* **13 C4** 53 46N 7 10W
Oldeani, *Tanzania* **54 C4** 3 22S 35 35 E
Oldenburg, *Germany* **16 B5** 53 9N 8 13 E
Oldenzaal, *Neths.* **15 B6** 52 19N 6 53 E
Oldham, *U.K.* **10 D5** 53 33N 2 7W
Oldman →, *Canada* **72 D6** 49 57N 111 42W
Oldmeldrum, *U.K.* **12 D6** 57 20N 2 19W
Olds, *Canada* **72 C6** 51 50N 114 10W
Oldziyt, *Mongolia* **34 B5** 44 40N 109 1 E
Olean, *U.S.A.* **78 D6** 42 5N 78 26W
Olekma →, *Russia* **27 C13** 60 22N 120 42 E
Olekminsk, *Russia* **27 C13** 60 25N 120 30 E
Oleksandriya, *Ukraine* **17 C14** 50 37N 26 19 E
Olema, *U.S.A.* **84 G4** 38 3N 122 47W
Olenegorsk, *Russia* **24 A5** 68 9N 33 18 E
Olenek, *Russia* **27 C12** 68 28N 112 18 E
Olenek →, *Russia* **27 B13** 73 0N 120 10 E
Oléron, Î. d', *France* **18 D3** 45 55N 1 15W
Oleśnica, *Poland* **17 C9** 51 13N 17 22 E
Olevsk, *Ukraine* **17 C14** 51 12N 27 39 E
Olga, *Russia* **27 E14** 43 50N 135 14 E
Olga, L., *Canada* **70 C4** 49 47N 77 15W
Olga, Mt., *Australia* **61 E5** 25 20S 130 50 E
Olhão, *Portugal* **19 D2** 37 3N 7 48W
Olifants →, *Africa* **57 C5** 23 57S 31 58 E
Olifantshoek, *S. Africa* **56 D3** 27 57S 22 42 E
Ólimbos, Óros, *Greece* **21 D10** 40 6N 22 23 E
Olímpia, *Brazil* **95 A6** 20 44S 48 54W
Olinda, *Brazil* **93 E12** 8 1S 34 51W
Oliva, *Argentina* **94 C3** 32 0S 63 38W
Olivehurst, *U.S.A.* **84 F5** 39 6N 121 34W
Olivenza, *Spain* **19 C2** 38 41N 7 9W
Oliver, *Canada* **72 D5** 49 13N 119 37W
Oliver L., *Canada* **73 B8** 56 56N 103 22W
Ollagüe, *Chile* **94 A2** 21 15S 68 10W
Olney, *Ill., U.S.A.* **76 F1** 38 44N 88 5W
Olney, *Tex., U.S.A.* **81 J5** 33 22N 98 45W
Olomane →, *Canada* **71 B7** 50 14N 60 37W
Olomouc, *Czech Rep.* **17 D9** 49 38N 17 12 E
Olonets, *Russia* **24 B5** 61 0N 32 54 E
Olongapo, *Phil.* **37 B6** 14 50N 120 18 E
Olot, *Spain* **19 A7** 42 11N 2 30 E
Olovyannaya, *Russia* **27 D12** 50 58N 115 35 E
Oloy →, *Russia* **27 C16** 66 29N 159 29 E
Olsztyn, *Poland* **17 B11** 53 48N 20 29 E
Olt →, *Romania* **17 G13** 43 43N 24 51 E
Olteniţa, *Romania* **17 F14** 44 7N 26 42 E
Olton, *U.S.A.* **81 H3** 34 11N 102 8W
Olymbos, *Cyprus* **23 D12** 35 21N 33 45 E
Olympia, *Greece* **21 F9** 37 39N 21 39 E
Olympia, *U.S.A.* **84 D4** 47 3N 122 53W
Olympic Dam, *Australia* **63 E2** 30 30S 136 55 E
Olympic Mts., *U.S.A.* **84 C3** 47 55N 123 45W
Olympic Nat. Park, *U.S.A.* **84 C3** 47 48N 123 30W
Olympus, *Cyprus* **23 E11** 34 56N 32 52 E
Olympus, Mt. = Ólimbos, Óros, *Greece* **21 D10** 40 6N 22 23 E
Olympus, Mt. = Uludağ, *Turkey* **21 D13** 40 4N 29 13 E
Olympus, Mt., *U.S.A.* **84 C3** 47 48N 123 43W
Olyphant, *U.S.A.* **79 E9** 41 27N 75 36W
Om →, *Russia* **26 D8** 54 59N 73 22 E
Om Koi, *Thailand* **38 D2** 17 48N 98 22 E
Ōma, *Japan* **30 D10** 41 45N 141 5 E
Ōmachi, *Japan* **31 F8** 36 30N 137 50 E
Omae-Zaki, *Japan* **31 G9** 34 36N 138 14 E
Ōmagari, *Japan* **30 E10** 39 27N 140 29 E
Omagh, *U.K.* **13 B4** 54 36N 7 19W
Omagh □, *U.K.* **13 B4** 54 35N 7 15W
Omaha, *U.S.A.* **80 E7** 41 17N 95 58W
Omak, *U.S.A.* **82 B4** 48 25N 119 31W
Omalos, *Greece* **23 D5** 35 19N 23 55 E
Oman ■, *Asia* **46 C6** 23 0N 58 0 E
Oman, G. of, *Asia* **45 E8** 24 30N 58 30 E
Omaruru, *Namibia* **56 C2** 21 26S 16 0 E
Omaruru →, *Namibia* **56 C1** 22 7S 14 15 E
Omate, *Peru* **92 G4** 16 45S 71 0W
Ombai, Selat, *Indonesia* **37 F6** 8 30S 124 50 E
Omboué, *Gabon* **52 E1** 1 35S 9 15 E
Ombrone →, *Italy* **20 C4** 42 42N 11 5 E
Omdurmân, *Sudan* **51 E12** 15 40N 32 28 E
Omemee, *Canada* **78 B6** 44 18N 78 33W
Omeo, *Australia* **63 F4** 37 6S 147 36 E
Omeonga, *Dem. Rep. of the Congo* **54 C1** 3 40S 24 22 E
Ometepe, I. de, *Nic.* **88 D2** 11 32N 85 35W
Ometepec, *Mexico* **87 D5** 16 39N 98 23W
Ominato, *Japan* **30 D10** 41 17N 141 10 E
Omineca →, *Canada* **72 B4** 56 3N 124 16W
Omitara, *Namibia* **56 C2** 22 16S 18 2 E
Ōmiya, *Japan* **31 G9** 35 54N 139 38 E
Ommen, *Neths.* **15 B6** 52 31N 6 26 E
Ömnögovĭ □, *Mongolia* **34 C3** 43 15N 104 0 E
Omo →, *Ethiopia* **46 F2** 6 25N 36 10 E
Omodhos, *Cyprus* **23 E11** 34 51N 32 48 E
Omolon →, *Russia* **27 C16** 68 42N 158 36 E
Omono-Gawa →, *Japan* **30 E10** 39 46N 140 3 E
Omsk, *Russia* **26 D8** 55 0N 73 12 E
Omsukchan, *Russia* **27 C16** 62 32N 155 48 E
Ōmu, *Japan* **30 B11** 44 34N 142 58 E
Omul, Vf., *Romania* **17 F13** 45 27N 25 29 E
Ōmura, *Japan* **31 H4** 32 56N 129 57 E
Omuramba Omatako →, *Namibia* **53 H4** 17 45S 20 25 E
Ōmuta, *Japan* **31 H5** 33 5N 130 26 E
Onaga, *U.S.A.* **80 F6** 39 29N 96 10W
Onalaska, *U.S.A.* **80 D9** 43 53N 91 14W
Onancock, *U.S.A.* **76 G8** 37 43N 75 45W
Onang, *Indonesia* **37 E5** 3 2S 118 49 E
Onaping L., *Canada* **70 C3** 47 3N 81 30W
Onavas, *Mexico* **86 B3** 28 28N 109 30W
Onawa, *U.S.A.* **80 D6** 42 2N 96 6W
Oncócua, *Angola* **56 B1** 16 30S 13 25 E
Onda, *Spain* **19 C5** 39 55N 0 17W
Ondaejin, *N. Korea* **35 D15** 41 34N 129 40 E
Ondangua, *Namibia* **56 B2** 17 57S 16 4 E
Ondjiva, *Angola* **56 B2** 16 48S 15 50 E
Öndörshil, *Mongolia* **34 B5** 45 13N 108 5 E
Öndverðarnes, *Iceland* **8 D1** 64 52N 24 0W
One Tree, *Australia* **63 E3** 34 11S 144 43 E
Onega, *Russia* **24 B6** 64 0N 38 10 E
Onega →, *Russia* **24 B6** 63 58N 38 2 E
Onega, G. of = Onezhskaya Guba, *Russia* **24 B6** 64 24N 36 38 E
Onega, L. = Onezhskoye Ozero, *Russia* **24 B6** 61 44N 35 22 E
Onehunga, *N.Z.* **59 G5** 36 55S 174 48 E
Oneida, *U.S.A.* **79 C9** 43 6N 75 39W
Oneida L., *U.S.A.* **79 C9** 43 12N 75 54W
O'Neill, *U.S.A.* **80 D5** 42 27N 98 39W
Onekotan, Ostrov, *Russia* **27 E16** 49 25N 154 45 E
Onema, *Dem. Rep. of the Congo* **54 C1** 4 35S 24 30 E
Oneonta, *U.S.A.* **79 D9** 42 27N 75 4W
Oneşti, *Romania* **17 E14** 46 15N 26 45 E
Onezhskaya Guba, *Russia* **24 B6** 64 24N 36 38 E
Onezhskoye Ozero, *Russia* **24 B6** 61 44N 35 22 E
Ongarue, *N.Z.* **59 H5** 38 42S 175 19 E
Ongerup, *Australia* **61 F2** 33 58S 118 28 E
Ongjin, *N. Korea* **35 F13** 37 56N 125 21 E
Ongkharak, *Thailand* **38 E3** 14 8N 101 1 E
Ongniud Qi, *China* **35 C10** 43 0N 118 38 E
Ongoka, *Dem. Rep. of the Congo* **54 C2** 1 20S 26 0 E
Ongole, *India* **40 M12** 15 33N 80 2 E
Ongon = Havirga, *Mongolia* **34 B7** 45 41N 113 5 E
Onida, *U.S.A.* **80 C4** 44 42N 100 4W
Onilahy →, *Madag.* **57 C7** 23 34S 43 45 E
Onitsha, *Nigeria* **50 G7** 6 6N 6 42 E
Onoda, *Japan* **31 G5** 34 2N 131 25 E
Onpyŏng-ni, *S. Korea* **35 H14** 33 25N 126 55 E
Onslow, *Australia* **60 D2** 21 40S 115 12 E
Onslow B., *U.S.A.* **77 H7** 34 20N 77 15W
Ontake-San, *Japan* **31 G8** 35 53N 137 29 E
Ontario, *Calif., U.S.A.* **85 L9** 34 4N 117 39W
Ontario, *Oreg., U.S.A.* **82 D5** 44 2N 116 58W
Ontario □, *Canada* **70 B2** 48 0N 83 0W
Ontario, L., *N. Amer.* **75 B11** 43 20N 78 0W
Ontonagon, *U.S.A.* **80 B10** 46 52N 89 19W
Onyx, *U.S.A.* **85 K8** 35 41N 118 14W
Oodnadatta, *Australia* **63 D2** 27 33S 135 30 E
Ooldea, *Australia* **61 F5** 30 27S 131 50 E
Oombulgurri, *Australia* **60 C4** 15 15S 127 45 E
Oorindi, *Australia* **62 C3** 20 40S 141 1 E
Oost-Vlaanderen □, *Belgium* **15 C3** 51 5N 3 50 E
Oostende, *Belgium* **15 C2** 51 15N 2 54 E
Oosterhout, *Neths.* **15 C4** 51 39N 4 47 E
Oosterschelde →, *Neths.* **15 C4** 51 33N 4 0 E
Oosterwolde, *Neths.* **15 B6** 53 0N 6 17 E
Ootacamund = Udagamandalam, *India* **40 P10** 11 30N 76 44 E
Ootsa L., *Canada* **72 C3** 53 50N 126 2W
Opala, *Dem. Rep. of the Congo* **54 C1** 0 40S 24 20 E
Opanake, *Sri Lanka* **40 R12** 6 35N 80 40 E
Opasatika, *Canada* **70 C3** 49 30N 82 50W
Opasquia Prov. Park, *Canada* **70 B1** 53 33N 93 5W
Opava, *Czech Rep.* **17 D9** 49 57N 17 58 E
Opelika, *U.S.A.* **77 J3** 32 39N 85 23W
Opelousas, *U.S.A.* **81 K8** 30 32N 92 5W
Opémisca, L., *Canada* **70 C5** 49 56N 74 52W
Opheim, *U.S.A.* **82 B10** 48 51N 106 24W
Ophthalmia Ra., *Australia* **60 D2** 23 15S 119 30 E
Opinaca →, *Canada* **70 B4** 52 15N 78 2W
Opinaca, Rés., *Canada* **70 B4** 52 39N 76 20W
Opinnagau →, *Canada* **70 B3** 54 12N 82 25W
Opiscoteo, L., *Canada* **71 B6** 53 10N 68 10W
Opole, *Poland* **17 C9** 50 42N 17 58 E
Oporto = Porto, *Portugal* **19 B1** 41 8N 8 40W
Opotiki, *N.Z.* **59 H6** 38 1S 177 19 E
Opp, *U.S.A.* **77 K2** 31 17N 86 16W
Oppdal, *Norway* **9 E13** 62 35N 9 41 E
Opportunity, *U.S.A.* **82 C5** 47 39N 117 15W
Opua, *N.Z.* **59 F5** 35 19S 174 9 E
Opunake, *N.Z.* **59 H4** 39 26S 173 52 E
Ora, *Cyprus* **23 E12** 34 51N 33 12 E
Oracle, *U.S.A.* **83 K8** 32 37N 110 46W
Oradea, *Romania* **17 E11** 47 2N 21 58 E
Öræfajökull, *Iceland* **8 D5** 64 2N 16 39W
Orai, *India* **43 G8** 25 58N 79 30 E
Oral = Zhayyq →, *Kazakstan* **25 E9** 47 0N 51 48 E
Oral, *Kazakstan* **25 D9** 51 20N 51 20 E
Oran, *Algeria* **50 A5** 35 45N 0 39W
Orange, *Australia* **63 E4** 33 15S 149 7 E
Orange, *France* **18 D6** 44 8N 4 47 E
Orange, *Calif., U.S.A.* **85 M9** 33 47N 117 51W
Orange, *Mass., U.S.A.* **79 D12** 42 35N 72 19W
Orange, *Tex., U.S.A.* **81 K8** 30 6N 93 44W
Orange, *Va., U.S.A.* **76 F6** 38 15N 78 7W
Orange →, *S. Africa* **56 D2** 28 41S 16 28 E
Orange, C., *Brazil* **93 C8** 4 20N 51 30W
Orange Cove, *U.S.A.* **84 J7** 36 38N 119 19W
Orange Free State = Free State □, *S. Africa* **56 D4** 28 30S 27 0 E
Orange Grove, *U.S.A.* **81 M6** 27 58N 97 56W
Orange Walk, *Belize* **87 D7** 18 6N 88 33W
Orangeburg, *U.S.A.* **77 J5** 33 30N 80 52W
Orangeville, *Canada* **78 C4** 43 55N 80 5W
Oranienburg, *Germany* **16 B7** 52 45N 13 14 E
Oranje = Orange →, *S. Africa* **56 D2** 28 41S 16 28 E
Oranje Vrystaat = Free State □, *S. Africa* **56 D4** 28 30S 27 0 E
Oranjemund, *Namibia* **56 D2** 28 38S 16 29 E
Oranjerivier, *S. Africa* **56 D3** 29 40S 24 12 E
Orapa, *Botswana* **53 J5** 21 15S 25 30 E
Oras, *Phil.* **37 B7** 12 9N 125 28 E
Oraşul Stalin = Braşov, *Romania* **17 F13** 45 38N 25 35 E
Orbetello, *Italy* **20 C4** 42 27N 11 13 E
Orbisonia, *U.S.A.* **78 F7** 40 15N 77 54W
Orbost, *Australia* **63 F4** 37 40S 148 29 E
Orcas I., *U.S.A.* **84 B4** 48 42N 122 56W
Orchard City, *U.S.A.* **83 G10** 38 50N 107 58W
Orchila, I., *Venezuela* **89 D6** 11 48N 66 10W
Orcutt, *U.S.A.* **85 L6** 34 52N 120 27W
Ord, *U.S.A.* **80 E5** 41 36N 98 56W
Ord →, *Australia* **60 C4** 15 33S 128 15 E
Ord, Mt., *Australia* **60 C4** 17 20S 125 34 E
Orderville, *U.S.A.* **83 H7** 37 17N 112 38W
Ordos = Mu Us Shamo, *China* **34 E5** 39 0N 109 0 E
Ordu, *Turkey* **25 F6** 40 55N 37 53 E
Ordway, *U.S.A.* **80 F3** 38 13N 103 46W
Ordzhonikidze = Vladikavkaz, *Russia* **25 F7** 43 0N 44 35 E
Ore, *Dem. Rep. of the Congo* **54 B2** 3 17N 29 30 E
Ore Mts. = Erzgebirge, *Germany* **16 C7** 50 27N 12 55 E
Örebro, *Sweden* **9 G16** 59 20N 15 18 E
Oregon, *U.S.A.* **80 D10** 42 1N 89 20W
Oregon □, *U.S.A.* **82 E3** 44 0N 121 0W
Oregon City, *U.S.A.* **84 E4** 45 21N 122 36W
Orekhovo-Zuyevo, *Russia* **24 C6** 55 50N 38 55 E
Orel, *Russia* **24 D6** 52 57N 36 3 E
Orem, *U.S.A.* **74 B4** 40 19N 111 42W
Ören, *Turkey* **21 F12** 37 3N 27 57 E
Orenburg, *Russia* **24 D10** 51 45N 55 6 E
Orense = Ourense, *Spain* **19 A2** 42 19N 7 55W
Orepuki, *N.Z.* **59 M1** 46 19S 167 46 E
Orestiás, *Greece* **21 D12** 41 30N 26 33 E
Orestos Pereyra, *Mexico* **86 B3** 26 31N 105 40W
Orford Ness, *U.K.* **11 E9** 52 5N 1 35 E
Organos, Pta. de los, *Canary Is.* **22 F2** 28 12N 17 17W
Orgaz, *Spain* **19 C4** 39 39N 3 53W
Orgeyev = Orhei, *Moldova* **17 E15** 47 24N 28 50 E
Orhaneli, *Turkey* **21 E13** 39 54N 28 59 E
Orhangazi, *Turkey* **21 D13** 40 29N 29 18 E
Orhei, *Moldova* **17 E15** 47 24N 28 50 E
Orhon Gol →, *Mongolia* **32 A5** 50 21N 106 0 E
Oriental, Cordillera, *Colombia* **92 B4** 6 0N 73 0W
Orientale □, *Dem. Rep. of the Congo* **54 B2** 2 20N 26 0 E
Oriente, *Argentina* **94 D3** 38 44S 60 37W
Orihuela, *Spain* **19 C5** 38 7N 0 55W
Orillia, *Canada* **78 B5** 44 40N 79 24W
Orinoco →, *Venezuela* **92 B6** 9 15N 61 30W
Orion, *Canada* **73 D6** 49 27N 110 49W
Oriskany, *U.S.A.* **79 C9** 43 10N 75 20W
Orissa □, *India* **41 K14** 20 0N 84 0 E
Orissaare, *Estonia* **9 G20** 58 34N 23 5 E
Oristano, *Italy* **20 E3** 39 54N 8 36 E
Oristano, G. di, *Italy* **20 E3** 39 50N 8 29 E
Orizaba, *Mexico* **87 D5** 18 51N 97 6W
Orkanger, *Norway* **8 E13** 63 18N 9 52 E
Orkla →, *Norway* **8 E13** 63 18N 9 51 E
Orkney, *S. Africa* **56 D4** 26 58S 26 40 E
Orkney □, *U.K.* **12 B5** 59 2N 3 13W
Orkney Is., *U.K.* **12 B6** 59 0N 3 0W
Orland, *U.S.A.* **84 F4** 39 45N 122 12W
Orlando, *U.S.A.* **77 L5** 28 33N 81 23W
Orléanais, *France* **18 C5** 48 0N 2 0 E
Orléans, *France* **18 C4** 47 54N 1 52 E
Orleans, *U.S.A.* **79 B12** 44 49N 72 12W
Orléans, I. d', *Canada* **71 C5** 46 54N 70 58W
Ormara, *Pakistan* **40 G4** 25 16N 64 33 E
Ormoc, *Phil.* **37 B6** 11 0N 124 37 E
Ormond, *N.Z.* **59 H6** 38 33S 177 56 E
Ormond Beach, *U.S.A.* **77 L5** 29 17N 81 3W
Ormskirk, *U.K.* **10 D5** 53 35N 2 54W
Ormstown, *Canada* **79 A11** 45 8N 74 0W
Örnsköldsvik, *Sweden* **8 E18** 63 17N 18 40 E
Oro, *N. Korea* **35 D14** 40 1N 127 27 E
Oro →, *Mexico* **86 B3** 25 35N 105 2W
Oro Grande, *U.S.A.* **85 L9** 34 36N 117 20W
Oro Valley, *U.S.A.* **83 K8** 32 26N 110 58W
Orocué, *Colombia* **92 C4** 4 48N 71 20W
Orofino, *U.S.A.* **82 C5** 46 29N 116 15W
Orol Dengizi = Aral Sea, *Asia* **26 E7** 44 30N 60 0 E
Oromocto, *Canada* **71 C6** 45 54N 66 29W
Orono, *Canada* **78 C6** 43 59N 78 37W
Orono, *U.S.A.* **77 C11** 44 53N 68 40W
Oronsay, *U.K.* **12 E2** 56 1N 6 15W
Oroqen Zizhiqi, *China* **33 A7** 50 34N 123 43 E
Oroquieta, *Phil.* **37 C6** 8 32N 123 44 E
Orosháza, *Hungary* **17 E11** 46 32N 20 42 E
Orotukan, *Russia* **27 C16** 62 16N 151 42 E
Oroville, *Calif., U.S.A.* **84 F5** 39 31N 121 33W
Oroville, *Wash., U.S.A.* **82 B4** 48 56N 119 26W
Oroville, L., *U.S.A.* **84 F5** 39 33N 121 29W
Orroroo, *Australia* **63 E2** 32 43S 138 38 E
Orrville, *U.S.A.* **78 F3** 40 50N 81 46W
Orsha, *Belarus* **24 D5** 54 30N 30 25 E
Orsk, *Russia* **26 D6** 51 12N 58 34 E
Orşova, *Romania* **17 F12** 44 41N 22 25 E
Ortaca, *Turkey* **21 F13** 36 49N 28 45 E
Ortegal, C., *Spain* **19 A2** 43 43N 7 52W
Orthez, *France* **18 E3** 43 29N 0 48W
Ortigueira, *Spain* **19 A2** 43 40N 7 50W
Orting, *U.S.A.* **84 C4** 47 6N 122 12W
Ortles, *Italy* **18 C9** 46 31N 10 33 E
Ortón →, *Bolivia* **92 F5** 10 50S 67 0W
Ortonville, *U.S.A.* **80 C6** 45 19N 96 27W
Orūmīyeh, *Iran* **44 B5** 37 40N 45 0 E
Orūmīyeh, Daryācheh-ye, *Iran* **44 B5** 37 50N 45 30 E
Oruro, *Bolivia* **92 G5** 18 0S 67 9W
Orust, *Sweden* **9 G14** 58 10N 11 40 E
Oruzgān □, *Afghan.* **40 C5** 33 30N 66 0 E
Orvieto, *Italy* **20 C5** 42 43N 12 7 E
Orwell, *N.Y., U.S.A.* **79 C9** 43 35N 75 50W
Orwell, *Ohio, U.S.A.* **78 E4** 41 32N 80 52W
Orwell →, *U.K.* **11 F9** 51 59N 1 18 E
Orwigsburg, *U.S.A.* **79 F8** 40 38N 76 6W
Oryakhovo, *Bulgaria* **21 C10** 43 40N 23 57 E
Osa, *Russia* **24 C10** 57 17N 55 26 E
Osa, Pen. de, *Costa Rica* **88 E3** 8 0N 84 0W
Osage, *U.S.A.* **80 D8** 43 17N 92 49W
Osage →, *U.S.A.* **80 F9** 38 35N 91 57W
Osage City, *U.S.A.* **80 F7** 38 38N 95 50W
Ōsaka, *Japan* **31 G7** 34 40N 135 30 E
Osan, *S. Korea* **35 F14** 37 11N 127 4 E
Osawatomie, *U.S.A.* **80 F7** 38 31N 94 57W
Osborne, *U.S.A.* **80 F5** 39 26N 98 42W
Osceola, *Ark., U.S.A.* **81 H10** 35 42N 89 58W
Osceola, *Iowa, U.S.A.* **80 E8** 41 2N 93 46W
Oscoda, *U.S.A.* **78 B1** 44 26N 83 20W
Ösel = Saaremaa, *Estonia* **9 G20** 58 30N 22 30 E
Osgoode, *Canada* **79 A9** 45 8N 75 36W
Osh, *Kyrgyzstan* **26 E8** 40 37N 72 49 E
Oshakati, *Namibia* **53 H3** 17 45S 15 40 E
Oshawa, *Canada* **78 C6** 43 50N 78 50W
Oshkosh, *Nebr., U.S.A.* **80 E3** 41 24N 102 21W
Oshkosh, *Wis., U.S.A.* **80 C10** 44 1N 88 33W

Oshmyany

Oshmyany = Ashmyany, *Belarus* **9 J21** 54 26N 25 52 E
Oshnovīyeh, *Iran* **44 B5** 37 2N 45 6 E
Oshogbo, *Nigeria* **50 G6** 7 48N 4 37 E
Oshtorīnān, *Iran* **45 C6** 34 1N 48 38 E
Oshwe, *Dem. Rep. of the Congo* **52 E3** 3 25S 19 28 E
Osijek, *Croatia* **21 B8** 45 34N 18 41 E
Osipenko = Berdyansk, *Ukraine* **25 E6** 46 45N 36 50 E
Osipovichi = Asipovichy, *Belarus* **17 B15** 53 19N 28 33 E
Osiyan, *India* **42 F5** 26 43N 72 55 E
Osizweni, *S. Africa* **57 D5** 27 49S 30 7 E
Oskaloosa, *U.S.A.* **80 E8** 41 18N 92 39W
Oskarshamn, *Sweden* **9 H17** 57 15N 16 27 E
Oskélanéo, *Canada* **70 C4** 48 5N 75 15W
Öskemen, *Kazakstan* **26 E9** 50 0N 82 36 E
Oslo, *Norway* **9 G14** 59 55N 10 45 E
Oslofjorden, *Norway* **9 G14** 59 20N 10 35 E
Osmanabad, *India* **40 K10** 18 5N 76 10 E
Osmaniye, *Turkey* **25 G6** 37 5N 36 10 E
Osnabrück, *Germany* **16 B5** 52 17N 8 3 E
Osorio, *Brazil* **95 B5** 29 53S 50 17W
Osorno, *Chile* **96 E2** 40 25S 73 0W
Osoyoos, *Canada* **72 D5** 49 0N 119 30W
Osøyro, *Norway* **9 F11** 60 9N 5 30 E
Ospika —►, *Canada* **72 B4** 56 20N 124 0W
Osprey Reef, *Australia* **62 A4** 13 52S 146 36 E
Oss, *Neths.* **15 C5** 51 46N 5 32 E
Ossa, Mt., *Australia* **62 G4** 41 52S 146 3 E
Óssa, Óros, *Greece* **21 E10** 39 47N 22 42 E
Ossabaw I., *U.S.A.* **77 K5** 31 50N 81 5W
Ossining, *U.S.A.* **79 E11** 41 10N 73 55W
Ossipee, *U.S.A.* **79 C13** 43 41N 71 7W
Ossokmanuan L., *Canada* **71 B7** 53 25N 65 0W
Ossora, *Russia* **27 D17** 59 20N 163 13 E
Ostend = Oostende, *Belgium* **15 C2** 51 15N 2 54 E
Oster, *Ukraine* **17 C16** 50 57N 30 53 E
Osterburg, *U.S.A.* **78 F6** 40 16N 78 31W
Österdalälven, *Sweden* **9 F16** 61 30N 13 45 E
Østerdalen, *Norway* **9 F14** 61 40N 10 50 E
Östersund, *Sweden* **8 E16** 63 10N 14 38 E
Ostfriesische Inseln, *Germany* **16 B4** 53 42N 7 0 E
Ostrava, *Czech Rep.* **17 D10** 49 51N 18 18 E
Ostróda, *Poland* **17 B10** 53 42N 19 58 E
Ostroh, *Ukraine* **17 C14** 50 20N 26 30 E
Ostrołęka, *Poland* **17 B11** 53 4N 21 32 E
Ostrów Mazowiecka, *Poland* **17 B11** 52 50N 21 51 E
Ostrów Wielkopolski, *Poland* **17 C9** 51 36N 17 44 E
Ostrowiec-Świętokrzyski, *Poland* **17 C11** 50 55N 21 22 E
Ostuni, *Italy* **21 D7** 40 44N 17 35 E
Ōsumi-Kaikyō, *Japan* **31 J5** 30 55N 131 0 E
Ōsumi-Shotō, *Japan* **31 J5** 30 30N 130 0 E
Osuna, *Spain* **19 D3** 37 14N 5 8W
Oswegatchie —►, *U.S.A.* **79 B9** 44 42N 75 30W
Oswego, *U.S.A.* **79 C8** 43 27N 76 31W
Oswego —►, *U.S.A.* **79 C8** 43 27N 76 30W
Oswestry, *U.K.* **10 E4** 52 52N 3 3W
Oświęcim, *Poland* **17 C10** 50 2N 19 11 E
Otago □, *N.Z.* **59 L2** 45 15S 170 0 E
Otago Harbour, *N.Z.* **59 L3** 45 47S 170 42 E
Ōtake, *Japan* **31 G6** 34 12N 132 13 E
Otaki, *N.Z.* **59 J5** 40 45S 175 10 E
Otaru, *Japan* **30 C10** 43 10N 141 0 E
Otaru-Wan = Ishikari-Wan, *Japan* **30 C10** 43 25N 141 1 E
Otavalo, *Ecuador* **92 C3** 0 13N 78 20W
Otavi, *Namibia* **56 B2** 19 40S 17 24 E
Otchinjau, *Angola* **56 B1** 16 30S 13 56 E
Otelnuk L., *Canada* **71 A6** 56 9N 68 12W
Othello, *U.S.A.* **82 C4** 46 50N 119 10W
Otira Gorge, *N.Z.* **59 K3** 42 53S 171 33 E
Otjiwarongo, *Namibia* **56 C2** 20 30S 16 33 E
Otoineppu, *Japan* **30 B11** 44 44N 142 16 E
Otorohanga, *N.Z.* **59 H5** 38 12S 175 14 E
Otoskwin —►, *Canada* **70 B2** 52 13N 88 6W
Otra —►, *Norway* **9 G13** 58 9N 8 1 E
Otranto, *Italy* **21 D8** 40 9N 18 28 E
Otranto, C. d', *Italy* **21 D8** 40 7N 18 30 E
Otranto, Str. of, *Italy* **21 D8** 40 15N 18 40 E
Otse, *S. Africa* **56 D4** 25 2S 25 45 E
Ōtsu, *Japan* **31 G7** 35 0N 135 50 E
Ōtsuki, *Japan* **31 G9** 35 36N 138 57 E
Ottawa = Outaouais —►, *Canada* **70 C5** 45 27N 74 8W
Ottawa, *Canada* **79 A9** 45 27N 75 42W
Ottawa, *Ill., U.S.A.* **80 E10** 41 21N 88 51W
Ottawa, *Kans., U.S.A.* **80 F7** 38 37N 95 16W
Ottawa Is., *Canada* **69 C11** 59 35N 80 10W
Otter Cr. —►, *U.S.A.* **79 B11** 44 13N 73 17W
Otter L., *Canada* **73 B8** 55 35N 104 39W
Otterville, *Canada* **78 D4** 42 55N 80 36W
Ottery St. Mary, *U.K.* **11 G4** 50 44N 3 17W
Otto Beit Bridge, *Zimbabwe* **55 F2** 15 59S 28 56 E
Ottosdal, *S. Africa* **56 D4** 26 46S 25 59 E
Ottumwa, *U.S.A.* **80 E8** 41 1N 92 25W
Oturkpo, *Nigeria* **50 G7** 7 16N 8 8 E
Otway, B., *Chile* **96 G2** 53 30S 74 0W
Otway, C., *Australia* **63 F3** 38 52S 143 30 E
Otwock, *Poland* **17 B11** 52 5N 21 20 E
Ou —►, *Laos* **38 B4** 20 4N 102 13 E
Ou-Sammyaku, *Japan* **30 E10** 39 20N 140 35 E
Ouachita —►, *U.S.A.* **81 K9** 31 38N 91 49W
Ouachita, L., *U.S.A.* **81 H8** 34 34N 93 12W
Ouachita Mts., *U.S.A.* **81 H7** 34 40N 94 25W
Ouagadougou, *Burkina Faso* **50 F5** 12 25N 1 30W
Ouahran = Oran, *Algeria* **50 A5** 35 45N 0 39W
Ouallene, *Algeria* **50 D6** 24 41N 1 11 E
Ouargla, *Algeria* **50 B7** 31 59N 5 16 E
Ouarzazate, *Morocco* **50 B4** 30 55N 6 50W
Oubangi —►, *Dem. Rep. of the Congo* **52 E3** 0 30S 17 50 E
Ouddorp, *Neths.* **15 C3** 51 50N 3 57 E
Oude Rijn —►, *Neths.* **15 B4** 52 12N 4 24 E
Oudenaarde, *Belgium* **15 D3** 50 50N 3 37 E
Oudtshoorn, *S. Africa* **56 E3** 33 35S 22 14 E
Ouessant, Î. d', *France* **18 B1** 48 28N 5 6W
Ouesso, *Congo* **52 D3** 1 37N 16 5 E
Ouest, Pte. de l', *Canada* **71 C7** 49 52N 64 40W
Ouezzane, *Morocco* **50 B4** 34 51N 5 35W
Oughterard, *Ireland* **13 C2** 53 26N 9 18W
Oujda, *Morocco* **50 B5** 34 41N 1 55W
Oulainen, *Finland* **8 D21** 64 17N 24 47 E
Oulu, *Finland* **8 D21** 65 1N 25 29 E
Oulujärvi, *Finland* **8 D22** 64 25N 27 15 E
Oulujoki —►, *Finland* **8 D21** 65 1N 25 30 E
Oum Chalouba, *Chad* **51 E10** 15 48N 20 46 E
Oum Hadjer, *Chad* **51 F9** 13 18N 19 41 E
Ounasjoki —►, *Finland* **8 C21** 66 31N 25 40 E
Ounguati, *Namibia* **56 C2** 22 0S 15 46 E
Ounianga Sérir, *Chad* **51 E10** 18 54N 20 51 E
Our —►, *Lux.* **15 E6** 49 55N 6 5 E
Ouray, *U.S.A.* **83 G10** 38 1N 107 40W
Ourense, *Spain* **19 A2** 42 19N 7 55W
Ouricuri, *Brazil* **93 E10** 7 53S 40 5W
Ourinhos, *Brazil* **95 A6** 23 0S 49 54W
Ouro Fino, *Brazil* **95 A6** 22 16S 46 25W
Ouro Prêto, *Brazil* **95 A7** 20 20S 43 30W
Ourthe —►, *Belgium* **15 D5** 50 29N 5 35 E
Ouse —►, *E. Susx., U.K.* **11 G8** 50 47N 0 4 E
Ouse —►, *N. Yorks., U.K.* **10 D7** 53 44N 0 55W
Outaouais —►, *Canada* **70 C5** 45 27N 74 8W
Outardes —►, *Canada* **71 C6** 49 24N 69 30W
Outer Hebrides, *U.K.* **12 D1** 57 30N 7 40W
Outjo, *Namibia* **56 C2** 20 5S 16 7 E
Outlook, *Canada* **73 C7** 51 30N 107 0W
Outokumpu, *Finland* **8 E23** 62 43N 29 1 E
Ouyen, *Australia* **63 F3** 35 1S 142 22 E
Ovalau, *Fiji* **59 C8** 17 40S 178 48 E
Ovalle, *Chile* **94 C1** 30 33S 71 18W
Ovamboland, *Namibia* **56 B2** 18 30S 16 0 E
Overflakkee, *Neths.* **15 C4** 51 44N 4 10 E
Overijssel □, *Neths.* **15 B6** 52 25N 6 35 E
Overland Park, *U.S.A.* **80 F7** 38 55N 94 50W
Overton, *U.S.A.* **85 J12** 36 33N 114 27W
Övertorneå, *Sweden* **8 C20** 66 23N 23 38 E
Ovid, *U.S.A.* **79 D8** 42 41N 76 49W
Oviedo, *Spain* **19 A3** 43 25N 5 50W
Oviši, *Latvia* **9 H19** 57 33N 21 44 E
Ovoot, *Mongolia* **34 B7** 45 21N 113 45 E
Övör Hangay □, *Mongolia* **34 B2** 45 0N 102 30 E
Øvre Årdal, *Norway* **9 F12** 61 19N 7 48 E
Ovruch, *Ukraine* **17 C15** 51 25N 28 45 E
Owaka, *N.Z.* **59 M2** 46 27S 169 40 E
Owambo = Ovamboland, *Namibia* **56 B2** 18 30S 16 0 E
Owando, *Congo* **52 E3** 0 29S 15 55 E
Owasco L., *U.S.A.* **79 D8** 42 50N 76 31W
Owase, *Japan* **31 G8** 34 7N 136 12 E
Owatonna, *U.S.A.* **80 C8** 44 5N 93 14W
Owbeh, *Afghan.* **40 B3** 34 28N 63 10 E
Owego, *U.S.A.* **79 D8** 42 6N 76 16W
Owen Falls Dam, *Uganda* **54 B3** 0 30N 33 5 E
Owen Sound, *Canada* **78 B4** 44 35N 80 55W
Owens —►, *U.S.A.* **84 J9** 36 32N 117 59W
Owens L., *U.S.A.* **85 J9** 36 26N 117 57W
Owensboro, *U.S.A.* **76 G2** 37 46N 87 7W
Owl —►, *Canada* **73 B10** 57 51N 92 44W
Owo, *Nigeria* **50 G7** 7 10N 5 39 E
Owosso, *U.S.A.* **76 D3** 43 0N 84 10W
Owyhee, *U.S.A.* **82 F5** 41 57N 116 6W
Owyhee —►, *U.S.A.* **82 E5** 43 49N 117 2W
Owyhee, L., *U.S.A.* **82 E5** 43 38N 117 14W
Ox Mts. = Slieve Gamph, *Ireland* **13 B3** 54 6N 9 0W
Öxarfjörður, *Iceland* **8 C5** 66 15N 16 45W
Oxbow, *Canada* **73 D8** 49 14N 102 10W
Oxelösund, *Sweden* **9 G17** 58 43N 17 5 E
Oxford, *N.Z.* **59 K4** 43 18S 172 11 E
Oxford, *U.K.* **11 F6** 51 46N 1 15W
Oxford, *Mass., U.S.A.* **79 D13** 42 7N 71 52W
Oxford, *Miss., U.S.A.* **81 H10** 34 22N 89 31W
Oxford, *N.C., U.S.A.* **77 G6** 36 19N 78 35W
Oxford, *N.Y., U.S.A.* **79 D9** 42 27N 75 36W
Oxford, *Ohio, U.S.A.* **76 F3** 39 31N 84 45W
Oxford L., *Canada* **73 C9** 54 51N 95 37W
Oxfordshire □, *U.K.* **11 F6** 51 48N 1 16W
Oxnard, *U.S.A.* **85 L7** 34 12N 119 11W
Oxus = Amudarya —►, *Uzbekistan* **26 E6** 43 58N 59 34 E
Oya, *Malaysia* **36 D4** 2 55N 111 55 E
Oyama, *Japan* **31 F9** 36 18N 139 48 E
Oyem, *Gabon* **52 D2** 1 34N 11 31 E
Oyen, *Canada* **73 C6** 51 22N 110 28W
Oykel —►, *U.K.* **12 D4** 57 56N 4 26W
Oymyakon, *Russia* **27 C15** 63 25N 142 44 E
Oyo, *Nigeria* **50 G6** 7 46N 3 56 E
Oyster Bay, *U.S.A.* **79 F11** 40 52N 73 32W
Ōyübari, *Japan* **30 C11** 43 1N 142 5 E
Ozamiz, *Phil.* **37 C6** 8 15N 123 50 E
Ozark, *Ala., U.S.A.* **77 K3** 31 28N 85 39W
Ozark, *Ark., U.S.A.* **81 H8** 35 29N 93 50W
Ozark, *Mo., U.S.A.* **81 G8** 37 1N 93 12W
Ozark Plateau, *U.S.A.* **81 G9** 37 20N 91 40W
Ozarks, L. of the, *U.S.A.* **80 F8** 38 12N 92 38W
Ózd, *Hungary* **17 D11** 48 14N 20 15 E
Ozette L., *U.S.A.* **84 B2** 48 6N 124 38W
Ozona, *U.S.A.* **81 K4** 30 43N 101 12W
Ozuluama, *Mexico* **87 C5** 21 40N 97 50W

P

Pa-an, *Burma* **41 L20** 16 51N 97 40 E
Pa Mong Dam, *Thailand* **38 D4** 18 0N 102 22 E
Pa Sak —►, *Thailand* **36 B2** 15 30N 101 0 E
Paamiut = Frederikshåb, *Greenland* **4 C5** 62 0N 49 43W
Paarl, *S. Africa* **56 E2** 33 45S 18 56 E
Paauilo, *U.S.A.* **74 H17** 20 2N 155 22W
Pab Hills, *Pakistan* **42 F2** 26 30N 66 45 E
Pabbay, *U.K.* **12 D1** 57 46N 7 14W
Pabianice, *Poland* **17 C10** 51 40N 19 20 E
Pabna, *Bangla.* **41 G16** 24 1N 89 18 E
Pabo, *Uganda* **54 B3** 3 1N 32 10 E
Pacaja —►, *Brazil* **93 D8** 1 56S 50 50W
Pacaraima, Sa., *S. Amer.* **92 C6** 4 0N 62 30W
Pacasmayo, *Peru* **92 E3** 7 20S 79 35W
Pachhar, *India* **42 G7** 24 40N 77 42 E
Pachitea —►, *Peru* **92 E4** 8 46S 74 33W
Pachmarhi, *India* **43 H8** 22 28N 78 26 E
Pachpadra, *India* **40 G8** 25 58N 72 10 E
Pachuca, *Mexico* **87 C5** 20 10N 98 40W
Pacific, *Canada* **72 C3** 54 48N 128 28W
Pacific-Antarctic Ridge, *Pac. Oc.* **65 M16** 43 0S 115 0W
Pacific Grove, *U.S.A.* **84 J5** 36 38N 121 56W
Pacific Ocean, *Pac. Oc.* **65 G14** 10 0N 140 0W
Pacific Rim Nat. Park, *Canada* **84 B2** 48 40N 124 45W
Pacifica, *U.S.A.* **84 H4** 37 36N 122 30W
Pacitan, *Indonesia* **37 H14** 8 12S 111 7 E
Packwood, *U.S.A.* **84 D5** 46 36N 121 40W
Padaido, Kepulauan, *Indonesia* **37 E9** 1 5S 138 0 E
Padang, *Indonesia* **36 E2** 1 0S 100 20 E
Padang Endau, *Malaysia* **39 L4** 2 40N 103 38 E
Padangpanjang, *Indonesia* **36 E2** 0 40S 100 20 E
Padangsidempuan, *Indonesia* **36 D1** 1 30N 99 15 E
Paddle Prairie, *Canada* **72 B5** 57 57N 117 29W
Paddockwood, *Canada* **73 C7** 53 30N 105 30W
Paderborn, *Germany* **16 C5** 51 42N 8 45 E
Padma, *India* **43 G11** 24 12N 85 22 E
Pádova, *Italy* **20 B4** 45 25N 11 53 E
Padra, *India* **42 H5** 22 15N 73 7 E
Padrauna, *India* **43 F10** 26 54N 83 59 E
Padre I., *U.S.A.* **81 M6** 27 10N 97 25W
Padstow, *U.K.* **11 G3** 50 33N 4 58W
Padua = Pádova, *Italy* **20 B4** 45 25N 11 53 E
Paducah, *Ky., U.S.A.* **76 G1** 37 5N 88 37W
Paducah, *Tex., U.S.A.* **81 H4** 34 1N 100 18W
Paengnyŏng-do, *S. Korea* **35 F13** 37 57N 124 40 E
Paeroa, *N.Z.* **59 G5** 37 23S 175 41 E
Pafúri, *Mozam.* **57 C5** 22 28S 31 17 E
Pag, *Croatia* **16 F8** 44 25N 15 3 E
Pagadian, *Phil.* **37 C6** 7 55N 123 30 E
Pagai Selatan, Pulau, *Indonesia* **36 E2** 3 0S 100 15 E
Pagai Utara, Pulau, *Indonesia* **36 E2** 2 35S 100 0 E
Pagalu = Annobón, *Atl. Oc.* **49 G4** 1 25S 5 36 E
Pagara, *India* **43 G9** 24 22N 80 1 E
Pagastikós Kólpos, *Greece* **21 E10** 39 15N 23 0 E
Pagatan, *Indonesia* **36 E5** 3 33S 115 59 E
Page, *U.S.A.* **83 H8** 36 57N 111 27W
Pago Pago, *Amer. Samoa* **59 B13** 14 16S 170 43W
Pagosa Springs, *U.S.A.* **83 H10** 37 16N 107 1W
Pagwa River, *Canada* **70 B2** 50 2N 85 14W
Pahala, *U.S.A.* **74 J17** 19 12N 155 29W
Pahang —►, *Malaysia* **39 L4** 3 30N 103 9 E
Pahiatua, *N.Z.* **59 J5** 40 27S 175 50 E
Pahokee, *U.S.A.* **77 M5** 26 50N 80 40W
Pahrump, *U.S.A.* **85 J11** 36 12N 115 59W
Pahute Mesa, *U.S.A.* **84 H10** 37 20N 116 45W
Pai, *Thailand* **38 C2** 19 19N 98 27 E
Paia, *U.S.A.* **74 H16** 20 54N 156 22W
Paicines, *U.S.A.* **84 J5** 36 44N 121 17W
Paide, *Estonia* **9 G21** 58 57N 25 31 E
Paignton, *U.K.* **11 G4** 50 26N 3 35W
Päijänne, *Finland* **9 F21** 61 30N 25 30 E
Pailani, *India* **43 G9** 25 45N 80 26 E
Pailin, *Cambodia* **38 F4** 12 46N 102 36 E
Painan, *Indonesia* **36 E2** 1 21S 100 34 E
Painesville, *U.S.A.* **78 E3** 41 43N 81 15W
Paint Hills = Wemindji, *Canada* **70 B4** 53 0N 78 49W
Paint L., *Canada* **73 B9** 55 28N 97 57W
Painted Desert, *U.S.A.* **83 J8** 36 0N 111 0W
Paintsville, *U.S.A.* **76 G4** 37 49N 82 48W
País Vasco □, *Spain* **19 A4** 42 50N 2 45W
Paisley, *Canada* **78 B3** 44 18N 81 16W
Paisley, *U.K.* **12 F4** 55 50N 4 25W
Paisley, *U.S.A.* **82 E3** 42 42N 120 32W
Paita, *Peru* **92 E2** 5 11S 81 9W
Pajares, Puerto de, *Spain* **19 A3** 42 58N 5 46W
Pak Lay, *Laos* **38 C3** 18 15N 101 27 E
Pak Phanang, *Thailand* **39 H3** 8 21N 100 12 E
Pak Sane, *Laos* **38 C4** 18 22N 103 39 E
Pak Song, *Laos* **38 E6** 15 11N 106 14 E
Pakaur, *India* **43 G12** 24 38N 87 51 E
Pakenham, *Canada* **79 A8** 45 18N 76 18W
Pákhnes, *Greece* **23 D6** 35 16N 24 4 E
Pakistan ■, *Asia* **42 E4** 30 0N 70 0 E
Pakkading, *Laos* **38 C4** 18 19N 103 59 E
Pakokku, *Burma* **41 J19** 21 20N 95 0 E
Pakowki L., *Canada* **73 D6** 49 20N 111 0W
Pakpattan, *Pakistan* **42 D5** 30 25N 73 27 E
Paktīā □, *Afghan.* **40 C6** 33 0N 69 15 E
Pakwach, *Uganda* **54 B3** 2 28N 31 27 E
Pakxe, *Laos* **38 E5** 15 5N 105 52 E
Pal Lahara, *India* **43 J11** 21 27N 85 11 E
Pala, *Chad* **51 G9** 9 25N 15 5 E
Pala, *Dem. Rep. of the Congo* **54 D2** 6 45S 29 30 E
Pala, *U.S.A.* **85 M9** 33 22N 117 5W
Palabek, *Uganda* **54 B3** 3 22N 32 33 E
Palacios, *U.S.A.* **81 L6** 28 42N 96 13W
Palagruža, *Croatia* **20 C7** 42 24N 16 15 E
Palaiókastron, *Greece* **23 D8** 35 12N 26 15 E
Palaiokhóra, *Greece* **23 D5** 35 16N 23 39 E
Palam, *India* **40 K10** 19 0N 77 0 E
Palampur, *India* **42 C7** 32 10N 76 30 E
Palana, *Australia* **62 F4** 39 45S 147 55 E
Palana, *Russia* **27 D16** 59 10N 159 59 E
Palanan, *Phil.* **37 A6** 17 8N 122 29 E
Palanan Pt., *Phil.* **37 A6** 17 17N 122 30 E
Palandri, *Pakistan* **43 C5** 33 42N 73 40 E
Palanga, *Lithuania* **9 J19** 55 58N 21 3 E
Palangkaraya, *Indonesia* **36 E4** 2 16S 113 56 E
Palani Hills, *India* **40 P10** 10 14N 77 33 E
Palanpur, *India* **42 G5** 24 10N 72 25 E
Palapye, *Botswana* **56 C4** 22 30S 27 7 E
Palas, *Pakistan* **43 B5** 35 4N 73 14 E
Palashi, *India* **43 H13** 23 47N 88 15 E
Palasponga, *India* **43 J11** 21 47N 85 34 E
Palatka, *Russia* **27 C16** 60 6N 150 54 E
Palatka, *U.S.A.* **77 L5** 29 39N 81 38W
Palau ■, *Pac. Oc.* **28 J17** 7 30N 134 30 E
Palauk, *Burma* **38 F2** 13 10N 98 40 E
Palawan, *Phil.* **36 C5** 9 30N 118 30 E
Palayankottai, *India* **40 Q10** 8 45N 77 45 E
Paldiski, *Estonia* **9 G21** 59 23N 24 9 E
Paleleh, *Indonesia* **37 D6** 1 10N 121 50 E
Palembang, *Indonesia* **36 E2** 3 0S 104 50 E
Palencia, *Spain* **19 A3** 42 1N 4 34W
Palenque, *Mexico* **87 D6** 17 31N 91 58W
Paleokastrítsa, *Greece* **23 A3** 39 40N 19 41 E
Paleometokho, *Cyprus* **23 D12** 35 7N 33 11 E
Palermo, *Italy* **20 E5** 38 7N 13 22 E
Palermo, *U.S.A.* **82 G3** 39 26N 121 33W
Palestina, *Chile* **96 A3** 23 50S 69 47W
Palestine, *Asia* **47 D4** 32 0N 35 0 E
Palestine, *U.S.A.* **81 K7** 31 46N 95 38W
Paletwa, *Burma* **41 J18** 21 10N 92 50 E
Palghat, *India* **40 P10** 10 46N 76 42 E
Palgrave, Mt., *Australia* **60 D2** 23 22S 115 58 E
Pali, *India* **42 G5** 25 50N 73 20 E
Palikir, *Micronesia* **64 G7** 6 55N 158 9 E
Palioúrion, Ákra, *Greece* **21 E10** 39 57N 23 45 E
Palisades Reservoir, *U.S.A.* **82 E8** 43 20N 111 12W
Paliseul, *Belgium* **15 E5** 49 54N 5 8 E
Palitana, *India* **42 J4** 21 32N 71 49 E
Palizada, *Mexico* **87 D6** 18 18N 92 8W
Palk Bay, *Asia* **40 Q11** 9 30N 79 15 E
Palk Strait, *Asia* **40 Q11** 10 0N 79 45 E
Palkānah, *Iraq* **44 C5** 35 49N 44 26 E
Palkot, *India* **43 H11** 22 53N 84 39 E
Palla Road = Dinokwe, *Botswana* **56 C4** 23 29S 26 37 E
Pallanza = Verbánia, *Italy* **18 D8** 45 56N 8 33 E
Pallarenda, *Australia* **62 B4** 19 12S 146 46 E
Pallinup —►, *Australia* **61 F2** 34 27S 118 50 E
Pallisa, *Uganda* **54 B3** 1 12N 33 43 E
Pallu, *India* **42 E6** 28 59N 74 14 E
Palm Bay, *U.S.A.* **77 L5** 28 2N 80 35W
Palm Beach, *U.S.A.* **77 M6** 26 43N 80 2W
Palm Coast, *U.S.A.* **77 L5** 29 32N 81 10W
Palm Desert, *U.S.A.* **85 M10** 33 43N 116 22W
Palm Is., *Australia* **62 B4** 18 40S 146 35 E
Palm Springs, *U.S.A.* **85 M10** 33 50N 116 33W
Palma, *Mozam.* **55 E5** 10 46S 40 29 E
Palma, B. de, *Spain* **22 B9** 39 30N 2 39 E
Palma de Mallorca, *Spain* **22 B9** 39 35N 2 39 E
Palma Soriano, *Cuba* **88 B4** 20 15N 76 0W
Palmares, *Brazil* **93 E11** 8 41S 35 28W
Palmas, *Brazil* **95 B5** 26 29S 52 0W
Palmas, C., *Liberia* **50 H4** 4 27N 7 46W
Pálmas, G. di, *Italy* **20 E3** 39 0N 8 30 E
Palmdale, *U.S.A.* **85 L8** 34 35N 118 7W
Palmeira das Missões, *Brazil* **95 B5** 27 55S 53 17W
Palmeira dos Índios, *Brazil* **93 E11** 9 25S 36 37W
Palmer, *U.S.A.* **68 B5** 61 36N 149 7W
Palmer —►, *Australia* **62 B3** 16 0S 142 26 E
Palmer Arch., *Antarctica* **5 C17** 64 15S 65 0W
Palmer Lake, *U.S.A.* **80 F2** 39 7N 104 55W
Palmer Land, *Antarctica* **5 D18** 73 0S 63 0W
Palmerston, *Canada* **78 C4** 43 50N 80 51W
Palmerston, *N.Z.* **59 L3** 45 29S 170 43 E
Palmerston North, *N.Z.* **59 J5** 40 21S 175 39 E
Palmerton, *U.S.A.* **79 F9** 40 48N 75 37W
Palmetto, *U.S.A.* **77 M4** 27 31N 82 34W
Palmi, *Italy* **20 E6** 38 21N 15 51 E
Palmira, *Argentina* **94 C2** 32 59S 68 34W
Palmira, *Colombia* **92 C3** 3 32N 76 16W
Palmyra = Tudmur, *Syria* **44 C3** 34 36N 38 15 E
Palmyra, *Mo., U.S.A.* **80 F9** 39 48N 91 32W
Palmyra, *N.J., U.S.A.* **79 F9** 40 1N 75 1W
Palmyra, *N.Y., U.S.A.* **78 C7** 43 5N 77 18W
Palmyra, *Pa., U.S.A.* **79 F8** 40 18N 76 36W
Palmyra Is., *Pac. Oc.* **65 G11** 5 52N 162 5W
Palo Alto, *U.S.A.* **84 H4** 37 27N 122 10W
Palo Verde, *U.S.A.* **85 M12** 33 26N 114 44W
Palopo, *Indonesia* **37 E6** 3 0S 120 16 E
Palos, C. de, *Spain* **19 D5** 37 38N 0 40W
Palos Verdes, *U.S.A.* **85 M8** 33 48N 118 23W
Palos Verdes, Pt., *U.S.A.* **85 M8** 33 43N 118 26W
Palu, *Indonesia* **37 E5** 1 0S 119 52 E
Palu, *Turkey* **25 G7** 38 45N 40 0 E
Palwal, *India* **42 E7** 28 8N 77 19 E
Pamanukan, *Indonesia* **37 G12** 6 16S 107 49 E
Pamiers, *France* **18 E4** 43 7N 1 39 E
Pamir, *Tajikistan* **26 F8** 37 40N 73 0 E
Pamlico —►, *U.S.A.* **77 H7** 35 20N 76 28W
Pamlico Sd., *U.S.A.* **77 H8** 35 20N 76 0W
Pampa, *U.S.A.* **81 H4** 35 32N 100 58W
Pampa de las Salinas, *Argentina* **94 C2** 32 1S 66 58W
Pampanua, *Indonesia* **37 E6** 4 16S 120 8 E
Pampas, *Argentina* **94 D3** 35 0S 63 0W
Pampas, *Peru* **92 F4** 12 20S 74 50W
Pamplona, *Colombia* **92 B4** 7 23N 72 39W
Pamplona, *Spain* **19 A5** 42 48N 1 38W
Pampoenpoort, *S. Africa* **56 E3** 31 3S 22 40 E
Pana, *U.S.A.* **80 F10** 39 23N 89 5W
Panaca, *U.S.A.* **83 H6** 37 47N 114 23W
Panaitan, *Indonesia* **37 G11** 6 36S 105 12 E
Panaji, *India* **40 M8** 15 25N 73 50 E
Panamá, *Panama* **88 E4** 9 0N 79 25W
Panama ■, *Cent. Amer.* **88 E4** 8 48N 79 55W
Panamá, G. de, *Panama* **88 E4** 8 4N 79 20W
Panama Canal, *Panama* **88 E4** 9 10N 79 37W
Panama City, *U.S.A.* **77 K3** 30 10N 85 40W
Panamint Range, *U.S.A.* **85 J9** 36 20N 117 20W
Panamint Springs, *U.S.A.* **85 J9** 36 20N 117 28W
Panão, *Peru* **92 E3** 9 55S 75 55W
Panare, *Thailand* **39 J3** 6 51N 101 30 E
Panay, *Phil.* **37 B6** 11 10N 122 30 E
Panay, G., *Phil.* **37 B6** 11 0N 122 30 E
Pančevo, *Serbia, Yug.* **21 B9** 44 52N 20 41 E
Pandan, *Phil.* **37 B6** 11 45N 122 10 E
Pandegelang, *Indonesia* **37 G12** 6 25S 106 5 E
Pandhana, *India* **42 J7** 21 42N 76 13 E
Pandharpur, *India* **40 L9** 17 41N 75 20 E
Pando, *Uruguay* **95 C4** 34 44S 56 0W
Pando, L. = Hope, L., *Australia* **63 D2** 28 24S 139 18 E
Pandokrátor, *Greece* **23 A3** 39 45N 19 50 E
Pandora, *Costa Rica* **88 E3** 9 43N 83 3W
Panevėžys, *Lithuania* **9 J21** 55 42N 24 25 E
Panfilov, *Kazakstan* **26 E9** 44 10N 80 0 E
Pang-Long, *Burma* **41 H21** 23 11N 98 45 E
Pang-Yang, *Burma* **41 H21** 22 7N 98 48 E
Panga, *Dem. Rep. of the Congo* **54 B2** 1 52N 26 18 E
Pangalanes, Canal des, *Madag.* **57 C8** 22 48S 47 50 E
Pangani, *Tanzania* **54 D4** 5 25S 38 58 E
Pangani —►, *Tanzania* **54 D4** 5 26S 38 58 E
Pangfou = Bengbu, *China* **35 H9** 32 58N 117 20 E
Pangil, *Dem. Rep. of the Congo* **54 C2** 3 10S 26 35 E
Pangkah, Tanjung, *Indonesia* **37 G15** 6 51S 112 33 E
Pangkajene, *Indonesia* **37 E5** 4 46S 119 34 E
Pangkalanbrandan, *Indonesia* **36 D1** 4 1N 98 20 E
Pangkalanbuun, *Indonesia* **36 E4** 2 41S 111 37 E

151

153

Rzhev

Rivière-Pilote, Martinique 89 D7 14 26N 60 53W
Rivière St. Paul, Canada 71 B8 51 28N 57 45W
Rivne, Ukraine 17 C14 50 40N 26 10 E
Rivoli, Italy 18 D7 45 3N 7 31 E
Rivoli B., Australia 63 F3 37 32S 140 3 E
Riyadh = Ar Riyāḍ, Si. Arabia 46 C4 24 41N 46 42 E
Rize, Turkey 25 F7 41 0N 40 30 E
Rizhao, China 35 G10 35 25N 119 30 E
Rizokarpaso, Cyprus 23 D13 35 36N 34 23 E
Rizzuto, C., Italy 20 E7 38 53N 17 5 E
Rjukan, Norway 9 G13 59 54N 8 33 E
Road Town, Virgin Is. 89 C7 18 27N 64 37W
Roan Plateau, U.S.A. 82 G9 39 20N 109 20W
Roanne, France 18 C6 46 3N 4 4 E
Roanoke, Ala., U.S.A. 77 J3 33 9N 85 22W
Roanoke, Va., U.S.A. 76 G6 37 16N 79 56W
Roanoke —►, U.S.A. 77 H7 35 57N 76 42W
Roanoke I., U.S.A. 77 H8 35 55N 75 40W
Roanoke Rapids, U.S.A. 77 G7 36 28N 77 40W
Roatán, Honduras 88 C2 16 18N 86 35W
Robāt Sang, Iran 45 C8 35 35N 59 10 E
Robbins I., Australia 62 G4 40 42S 145 0 E
Robe, Australia 63 F2 37 11S 139 45 E
Robe —►, Australia 60 D2 21 42S 116 15 E
Robert Lee, U.S.A. 81 K4 31 54N 100 29W
Robertsdale, U.S.A. 78 F6 40 11N 78 6W
Robertsganj, India 43 G10 24 44N 83 4 E
Robertson, S. Africa 56 E2 33 46S 19 50 E
Robertson I., Antarctica 5 C18 65 15S 59 30W
Robertson Ra., Australia 60 D3 23 15S 121 0 E
Robertstown, Australia 63 E2 33 58S 139 5 E
Roberval, Canada 71 C5 48 32N 72 15W
Robeson Chan., Greenland 4 A4 82 0N 61 30W
Robesonia, U.S.A. 79 F8 40 21N 76 8W
Robinson, U.S.A. 76 F2 39 0N 87 44W
Robinson —►, Australia 62 B2 16 3S 137 16 E
Robinson Ra., Australia 61 E2 25 40S 119 0 E
Robinvale, Australia 63 E3 34 40S 142 45 E
Roblin, Canada 73 C8 51 14N 101 21W
Roboré, Bolivia 92 G7 18 10S 59 45W
Robson, Canada 72 D5 49 20N 117 41W
Robson, Mt., Canada 72 C5 53 10N 119 10W
Robstown, U.S.A. 81 M6 27 47N 97 40W
Roca, C. da, Portugal 19 C1 38 40N 9 31W
Roca Partida, I., Mexico 86 D2 19 1N 112 2W
Rocas, I., Brazil 93 D12 4 0S 34 1W
Rocha, Uruguay 95 C5 34 30S 54 25W
Rochdale, U.K. 10 D5 53 38N 2 9W
Rochefort, Belgium 15 D5 50 9N 5 12 E
Rochefort, France 18 D3 45 56N 0 57W
Rochelle, U.S.A. 80 E10 41 56N 89 4W
Rocher River, Canada 72 A6 61 23N 112 44W
Rochester, U.K. 11 F8 51 23N 0 31 E
Rochester, Ind., U.S.A. 76 E2 41 4N 86 13W
Rochester, Minn., U.S.A. 80 C8 44 1N 92 28W
Rochester, N.H., U.S.A. 79 C14 43 18N 70 59W
Rochester, N.Y., U.S.A. 78 C7 43 10N 77 37W
Rock —►, Canada 72 A3 60 7N 127 7W
Rock Creek, U.S.A. 78 E4 41 40N 80 52W
Rock Falls, U.S.A. 80 E10 41 47N 89 41W
Rock Hill, U.S.A. 77 H5 34 56N 81 1W
Rock Island, U.S.A. 80 E9 41 30N 90 34W
Rock Rapids, U.S.A. 80 D6 43 26N 96 10W
Rock Sound, Bahamas 88 B4 24 54N 76 12W
Rock Springs, Mont., U.S.A. 82 C10 46 49N 106 15W
Rock Springs, Wyo., U.S.A. 82 F9 41 35N 109 14W
Rock Valley, U.S.A. 80 D6 43 12N 96 18W
Rockall, Atl. Oc. 6 D3 57 37N 13 42W
Rockdale, Tex., U.S.A. 81 K6 30 39N 97 0W
Rockdale, Wash., U.S.A. 84 C5 47 22N 121 28W
Rockefeller Plateau, Antarctica 5 E14 80 0S 140 0W
Rockford, U.S.A. 80 D10 42 16N 89 6W
Rockglen, Canada 73 D7 49 11N 105 57W
Rockhampton, Australia 62 C5 23 22S 150 32 E
Rockingham, Australia 61 F2 32 15S 115 38 E
Rockingham, U.S.A. 77 H6 34 57N 79 46W
Rockingham B., Australia 62 B4 18 5S 146 10 E
Rocklake, U.S.A. 80 A5 48 47N 99 15W
Rockland, Canada 79 A9 45 33N 75 17W
Rockland, Idaho, U.S.A. 82 E7 42 34N 112 53W
Rockland, Maine, U.S.A. 77 C11 44 6N 69 7W
Rockland, Mich., U.S.A. 80 B10 46 44N 89 11W
Rocklin, U.S.A. 84 G5 38 48N 121 14W
Rockport, Mass., U.S.A. 79 D14 42 39N 70 37W
Rockport, Mo., U.S.A. 80 E7 40 25N 95 31W
Rockport, Tex., U.S.A. 81 L6 28 2N 97 3W
Rocksprings, U.S.A. 81 K4 30 1N 100 13W
Rockville, Conn., U.S.A. 79 E12 41 52N 72 28W
Rockville, Md., U.S.A. 76 F7 39 5N 77 9W
Rockwall, U.S.A. 81 J6 32 56N 96 28W
Rockwell City, U.S.A. 80 D7 42 24N 94 38W
Rockwood, Canada 78 C4 43 37N 80 8W
Rockwood, Maine, U.S.A. 77 C11 45 41N 69 45W
Rockwood, Tenn., U.S.A. 77 H3 35 52N 84 41W
Rocky Ford, U.S.A. 80 F3 38 3N 103 43W
Rocky Gully, Australia 61 F2 34 30S 116 57 E
Rocky Harbour, Canada 71 C8 49 36N 57 55W
Rocky Island L., Canada 70 C3 46 55N 83 0W
Rocky Lane, Canada 72 B5 58 31N 116 22W
Rocky Mount, U.S.A. 77 H7 35 57N 77 48W
Rocky Mountain House, Canada 72 C6 52 22N 114 55W
Rocky Mountain National Park, U.S.A. 82 F11 40 25N 105 45W
Rocky Mts., N. Amer. 74 C5 49 0N 115 0W
Rod, Pakistan 40 E3 28 10N 63 5 E
Rødbyhavn, Denmark 9 J14 54 39N 11 22 E
Roddickton, Canada 71 B8 50 51N 56 8W
Rodez, France 18 D5 44 21N 2 33 E
Rodhopoú, Greece 23 D5 35 34N 23 45 E
Ródhos, Greece 23 C10 36 15N 28 10 E
Rodney, Canada 78 D3 42 34N 81 41W
Rodney, C., N.Z. 59 G5 36 17S 174 50 E
Rodriguez, Ind. Oc. 3 E13 19 45S 63 20 E
Roe —►, U.K. 13 A5 55 6N 6 59W
Roebling, U.S.A. 79 F10 40 7N 74 47W
Roebourne, Australia 60 D2 20 44S 117 9 E
Roebuck B., Australia 60 C3 18 5S 122 20 E
Roermond, Neths. 15 C6 51 12N 6 0 E
Roes Welcome Sd., Canada 69 B11 65 0N 87 0W
Roeselare, Belgium 15 D3 50 57N 3 7 E
Rogachev = Ragachow, Belarus 17 B16 53 8N 30 5 E
Rogagua, L., Bolivia 92 F5 13 43S 66 50W
Rogatyn, Ukraine 17 D13 49 24N 24 36 E
Rogdhia, Greece 23 D7 35 22N 25 1 E
Rogers, U.S.A. 81 G7 36 20N 94 7W
Rogers City, U.S.A. 76 C4 45 25N 83 49W
Rogersville, Canada 71 C6 46 44N 65 26W
Roggan —►, Canada 70 B4 54 24N 79 25W
Roggan L., Canada 70 B4 54 8N 77 50W
Roggeveldberge, S. Africa 56 E3 32 10S 20 10 E
Rogoaguado, L., Bolivia 92 F5 13 0S 65 30W
Rogue —►, U.S.A. 82 E1 42 26N 124 26W
Róhda, Greece 23 A3 39 48N 19 46 E
Rohnert Park, U.S.A. 84 G4 38 16N 122 40W
Rohri, Pakistan 42 F3 27 45N 68 51 E
Rohri Canal, Pakistan 42 F3 26 15N 68 27 E
Rohtak, India 42 E7 28 55N 76 43 E
Roi Et, Thailand 38 D4 16 4N 103 40 E
Roja, Latvia 9 H20 57 29N 22 43 E
Rojas, Argentina 94 C3 34 10S 60 45W
Rojo, C., Mexico 87 C5 21 33N 97 20W
Rokan —►, Indonesia 36 D2 2 0N 100 50 E
Rokiškis, Lithuania 9 J21 55 55N 25 35 E
Rolândia, Brazil 95 A5 23 18S 51 23W
Rolla, U.S.A. 81 G9 37 57N 91 46W
Rolleston, Australia 62 C4 24 28S 148 35 E
Rollingstone, Australia 62 B4 19 2S 146 24 E
Roma, Australia 63 D4 26 32S 148 49 E
Roma, Italy 20 D5 41 54N 12 29 E
Roma, Sweden 9 H18 57 32N 18 26 E
Roma, U.S.A. 81 M5 26 25N 99 1W
Romain C., U.S.A. 77 J6 33 0N 79 22W
Romaine, Canada 71 B7 50 13N 60 40W
Romaine —►, Canada 71 B7 50 18N 63 47W
Roman, Romania 17 E14 46 57N 26 55 E
Romang, Indonesia 37 F7 7 30S 127 20 E
Români, Egypt 47 E1 30 59N 32 38 E
Romania ■, Europe 17 F12 46 0N 25 0 E
Romano, Cayo, Cuba 88 B4 22 0N 77 30W
Romanovka = Basarabeasca, Moldova 17 E15 46 21N 28 58 E
Romans-sur-Isère, France 18 D6 45 3N 5 3 E
Romblon, Phil. 37 B6 12 33N 122 17 E
Rome = Roma, Italy 20 D5 41 54N 12 29 E
Rome, Ga., U.S.A. 77 H3 34 15N 85 10W
Rome, N.Y., U.S.A. 79 C9 43 13N 75 27W
Rome, Pa., U.S.A. 79 E8 41 51N 76 21W
Romney, U.S.A. 76 F6 39 21N 78 45W
Romney Marsh, U.K. 11 F8 51 2N 0 54 E
Rømø, Denmark 9 J13 55 10N 8 30 E
Romorantin-Lanthenay, France 18 C4 47 21N 1 45 E
Romsdalen, Norway 9 E12 62 25N 7 52 E
Romsey, U.K. 11 G6 51 0N 1 29W
Ron, Vietnam 38 D6 17 53N 106 27 E
Rona, U.K. 12 D3 57 34N 5 59W
Ronan, U.S.A. 82 C6 47 32N 114 6W
Roncador, Cayos, Caribbean 88 D3 13 32N 80 4W
Roncador, Serra do, Brazil 93 F8 12 30S 52 30W
Ronda, Spain 19 D3 36 46N 5 12W
Rondane, Norway 9 F13 61 57N 9 50 E
Rondônia □, Brazil 92 F6 11 0S 63 0W
Rondonópolis, Brazil 93 G8 16 28S 54 38W
Rong, Koh, Cambodia 39 G4 10 45N 103 15 E
Ronge, L. la, Canada 73 B7 55 6N 105 17W
Rønne, Denmark 9 J16 55 6N 14 43 E
Ronne Ice Shelf, Antarctica 5 D18 78 0S 60 0W
Ronsard, C., Australia 61 D1 24 46S 113 10 E
Ronse, Belgium 15 D3 50 45N 3 35 E
Roodepoort, S. Africa 57 D4 26 11S 27 54 E
Roof Butte, U.S.A. 83 H9 36 28N 109 5W
Roorkee, India 42 E7 29 52N 77 59 E
Roosendaal, Neths. 15 C4 51 32N 4 29 E
Roosevelt, U.S.A. 82 F8 40 18N 109 59W
Roosevelt —►, Brazil 92 E6 7 35S 60 20W
Roosevelt, Mt., Canada 72 B3 58 26N 125 20W
Roosevelt I., Antarctica 5 D12 79 30S 162 0W
Roper —►, Australia 62 A2 14 43S 135 27 E
Roper Bar, Australia 62 A1 14 44S 134 44 E
Roque Pérez, Argentina 94 D4 35 25S 59 24W
Roquetas de Mar, Spain 19 D4 36 46N 2 36W
Roraima □, Brazil 92 C6 2 0N 61 30W
Roraima, Mt., Venezuela 92 B6 5 10N 60 40W
Røros, Norway 9 E14 62 35N 11 23 E
Rosa, Zambia 55 D3 9 33S 31 15 E
Rosa, L., Bahamas 89 B5 21 0N 73 30W
Rosa, Monte, Europe 18 D7 45 57N 7 53 E
Rosalia, U.S.A. 82 C5 47 14N 117 22W
Rosamond, U.S.A. 85 L8 34 52N 118 10W
Rosario, Argentina 94 C3 33 0S 60 40W
Rosário, Brazil 93 D10 3 0S 44 15W
Rosario, Baja Calif., Mexico 86 B1 30 0N 115 50W
Rosario, Sinaloa, Mexico 86 C3 23 0N 105 52W
Rosario, Paraguay 94 A4 24 30S 57 35W
Rosario de la Frontera, Argentina 94 B3 25 50S 65 0W
Rosario de Lerma, Argentina 94 A2 24 59S 65 35W
Rosario del Tala, Argentina 94 C4 32 20S 59 10W
Rosário do Sul, Brazil 95 C5 30 15S 54 55W
Rosarito, Mexico 85 N9 32 18N 117 4W
Roscoe, U.S.A. 79 E10 41 56N 74 55W
Roscommon, Ireland 13 C3 53 38N 8 11W
Roscommon □, Ireland 13 C3 53 49N 8 23W
Roscrea, Ireland 13 D4 52 57N 7 49W
Rose —►, Australia 62 A2 14 16S 135 45 E
Rose Blanche, Canada 71 C8 47 38N 58 45W
Rose Pt., Canada 72 C2 54 11N 131 39W
Rose Valley, Canada 73 C8 52 19N 103 49W
Roseau, Domin. 89 C7 15 20N 61 24W
Roseau, U.S.A. 80 A7 48 51N 95 46W
Rosebery, Australia 62 G4 41 46S 145 33 E
Rosebud, S. Dak., U.S.A. 80 D4 43 14N 100 51W
Rosebud, Tex., U.S.A. 81 K6 31 4N 96 59W
Roseburg, U.S.A. 82 E2 43 13N 123 20W
Rosedale, U.S.A. 81 J9 33 51N 91 2W
Roseland, U.S.A. 84 G4 38 25N 122 43W
Rosemary, Canada 72 C6 50 46N 112 5W
Rosenberg, U.S.A. 81 L7 29 34N 95 49W
Rosenheim, Germany 16 E7 47 51N 12 7 E
Roses, G. de, Spain 19 A7 42 10N 3 15 E
Rosetown, Canada 73 C7 51 35N 107 59W
Roseville, Calif., U.S.A. 84 G5 38 45N 121 17W
Roseville, Mich., U.S.A. 78 D2 42 30N 82 56W
Rosewood, Australia 63 D5 27 38S 152 36 E
Roshkhvār, Iran 45 C8 34 58N 59 37 E
Rosignano Maríttimo, Italy 20 C4 43 24N 10 28 E
Rosignol, Guyana 92 B7 6 15N 57 30W
Roşiori-de-Vede, Romania 17 F13 44 7N 24 59 E
Roskilde, Denmark 9 J15 55 38N 12 3 E
Roslavl, Russia 24 D5 53 57N 32 55 E
Rosmead, S. Africa 56 E4 31 29S 25 8 E
Ross, Australia 62 G4 42 2S 147 30 E
Ross, N.Z. 59 K3 42 53S 170 49 E
Ross I., Antarctica 5 D11 77 30S 168 0 E
Ross Ice Shelf, Antarctica 5 E12 80 0S 180 0 E
Ross L., U.S.A. 82 B3 48 44N 121 4W
Ross-on-Wye, U.K. 11 F5 51 54N 2 34W
Ross River, Australia 62 C1 23 44S 134 30 E
Ross River, Canada 72 A2 62 30N 131 30W
Ross Sea, Antarctica 5 D11 74 0S 178 0 E
Rossall Pt., U.K. 10 D4 53 55N 3 3W
Rossan Pt., Ireland 13 B3 54 42N 8 47W
Rossano, Italy 20 E7 39 36N 16 39 E
Rossburn, Canada 73 C8 50 40N 100 49W
Rosseau, Canada 78 A5 45 16N 79 39W
Rosseau L., Canada 78 A5 45 10N 79 35W
Rosses, The, Ireland 13 A3 55 2N 8 20W
Rossignol, L., Canada 70 B5 52 43N 73 40W
Rossignol Res., Canada 71 D6 44 12N 65 10W
Rossland, Canada 72 D5 49 6N 117 50W
Rosslare, Ireland 13 D5 52 17N 6 24W
Rosso, Mauritania 50 E2 16 40N 15 45W
Rossosh, Russia 25 D6 50 15N 39 28 E
Røssvatnet, Norway 8 D16 65 45N 14 5 E
Røst, Norway 8 C15 67 32N 12 0 E
Rosthern, Canada 73 C7 52 40N 106 20W
Rostock, Germany 16 A7 54 5N 12 8 E
Rostov, Don, Russia 25 E6 47 15N 39 45 E
Rostov, Yaroslavl, Russia 24 C6 57 14N 39 25 E
Roswell, Ga., U.S.A. 77 H3 34 2N 84 22W
Roswell, N. Mex., U.S.A. 81 J2 33 24N 104 32W
Rotan, U.S.A. 81 J4 32 51N 100 28W
Rother —►, U.K. 11 G8 50 59N 0 45 E
Rotherham, U.K. 10 D6 53 26N 1 20W
Rothes, U.K. 12 D5 57 32N 3 13W
Rothesay, Canada 71 C6 45 23N 66 0W
Rothesay, U.K. 12 F3 55 50N 5 3W
Roti, Indonesia 37 F6 10 50S 123 0 E
Roto, Australia 63 E4 33 0S 145 30 E
Rotondo Mte., France 18 E8 42 14N 9 8 E
Rotoroa, L., N.Z. 59 J4 41 55S 172 39 E
Rotorua, N.Z. 59 H6 38 9S 176 16 E
Rotorua, L., N.Z. 59 H6 38 5S 176 18 E
Rotterdam, Neths. 15 C4 51 55N 4 30 E
Rotterdam, U.S.A. 79 D10 42 48N 74 1W
Rottnest I., Australia 61 F2 32 0S 115 27 E
Rottumeroog, Neths. 15 A6 53 33N 6 34 E
Rottweil, Germany 16 D5 48 9N 8 37 E
Rotuma, Fiji 64 J9 12 25S 177 5 E
Roubaix, France 18 A5 50 40N 3 10 E
Rouen, France 18 B4 49 27N 1 4 E
Rouleau, Canada 73 C8 50 10N 104 56W
Round Mountain, U.S.A. 82 G5 38 43N 117 4W
Round Mt., Australia 63 E5 30 26S 152 16 E
Round Rock, U.S.A. 81 K6 30 31N 97 41W
Roundup, U.S.A. 82 C9 46 27N 108 33W
Rousay, U.K. 12 B5 59 10N 3 2W
Rouses Point, U.S.A. 79 B11 44 59N 73 22W
Rouseville, U.S.A. 78 E5 41 28N 79 42W
Roussillon, France 18 E5 42 30N 2 35 E
Rouxville, S. Africa 56 E4 30 25S 26 50 E
Rouyn-Noranda, Canada 70 C4 48 20N 79 0W
Rovaniemi, Finland 8 C21 66 29N 25 41 E
Rovereto, Italy 20 B4 45 53N 11 3 E
Rovigo, Italy 20 B4 45 4N 11 47 E
Rovinj, Croatia 16 F7 45 5N 13 40 E
Rovno = Rivne, Ukraine 17 C14 50 40N 26 10 E
Rovuma = Ruvuma —►, Tanzania 55 E5 10 29S 40 28 E
Row'ān, Iran 45 C6 35 8N 48 51 E
Rowena, Australia 63 D4 29 48S 148 55 E
Rowley Shoals, Australia 60 C2 17 30S 119 0 E
Roxas, Phil. 37 B6 11 36N 122 49 E
Roxboro, U.S.A. 77 G6 36 24N 78 59W
Roxburgh, N.Z. 59 L2 45 33S 169 19 E
Roxbury, U.S.A. 78 F7 40 6N 77 39W
Roy, Mont., U.S.A. 82 C9 47 20N 108 58W
Roy, N. Mex., U.S.A. 81 H2 35 57N 104 12W
Roy, Utah, U.S.A. 82 F7 41 10N 112 2W
Royal Canal, Ireland 13 C4 53 30N 7 13W
Royal Leamington Spa, U.K. 11 E6 52 18N 1 31W
Royal Tunbridge Wells, U.K. 11 F8 51 7N 0 16 E
Royan, France 18 D3 45 37N 1 2W
Royston, U.K. 11 E7 52 3N 0 0 E
Rozdilna, Ukraine 17 E16 46 50N 30 2 E
Rozhyshche, Ukraine 17 C13 50 54N 25 15 E
Rtishchevo, Russia 24 C7 52 18N 43 46 E
Ruacaná, Angola 56 B1 17 20S 14 12 E
Ruahine Ra., N.Z. 59 H6 39 55S 176 2 E
Ruapehu, N.Z. 59 H5 39 17S 175 35 E
Ruapuke I., N.Z. 59 M2 46 46S 168 31 E
Ruâq, W. —►, Egypt 47 F2 30 0N 33 49 E
Rub' al Khālī, Si. Arabia 46 D4 18 0N 48 0 E
Rubeho Mts., Tanzania 54 D4 6 50S 36 25 E
Rubha a' Mhail, U.K. 12 F2 55 56N 6 8W
Rubha Hunish, U.K. 12 D2 57 42N 6 20W
Rubha Robhanais = Lewis, Butt of, U.K. 12 C2 58 31N 6 16W
Rubicon —►, U.S.A. 84 G5 38 53N 121 4W
Rubio, Venezuela 92 B4 7 43N 72 22W
Rubtsovsk, Russia 26 D9 51 30N 81 10 E
Ruby L., U.S.A. 82 F6 40 10N 115 28W
Ruby Mts., U.S.A. 82 F6 40 30N 115 20W
Rubyvale, Australia 62 C4 23 25S 147 42 E
Rūd Sar, Iran 45 B6 37 8N 50 18 E
Rudall, Australia 63 E2 33 43S 136 17 E
Rudall —►, Australia 60 D3 22 34S 122 13 E
Rudewa, Tanzania 55 E3 10 7S 34 40 E
Rudnyy, Kazakstan 26 D7 52 57N 63 7 E
Rudolfa, Ostrov, Russia 26 A6 81 45N 58 30 E
Rudyard, U.S.A. 76 B3 46 14N 84 36W
Rufiji —►, Tanzania 54 D4 7 50S 39 15 E
Rufino, Argentina 94 C3 34 20S 62 50W
Rufunsa, Zambia 55 F2 15 4S 29 34 E
Rugby, U.K. 11 E6 52 23N 1 16W
Rugby, U.S.A. 80 A5 48 22N 100 0W
Rügen, Germany 16 A7 54 22N 13 24 E
Ruhengeri, Rwanda 54 C2 1 30S 29 36 E
Ruhnu, Estonia 9 H20 57 48N 23 15 E
Ruhr —►, Germany 16 C4 51 27N 6 43 E
Ruhuhu —►, Tanzania 55 E3 10 31S 34 34 E
Ruidoso, U.S.A. 83 K11 33 20N 105 41W
Ruivo, Pico, Madeira 22 D3 32 45N 16 56W
Rujm Tal'at al Jamā'ah, Jordan 47 E4 30 24N 35 30 E
Ruk, Pakistan 42 F3 27 50N 68 42 E
Rukhla, Pakistan 42 C4 32 27N 71 57 E
Ruki —►, Dem. Rep. of the Congo 52 E3 0 5N 18 17 E
Rukwa □, Tanzania 54 D3 7 0S 31 30 E
Rukwa, L., Tanzania 54 D3 8 0S 32 20 E
Rulhieres, C., Australia 60 B4 13 56S 127 22 E
Rum = Rhum, U.K. 12 E2 57 0N 6 20W
Rum Cay, Bahamas 89 B5 23 40N 74 58W
Rum Jungle, Australia 60 B5 13 0S 130 59 E
Rumāḥ, Si. Arabia 44 E5 25 29N 47 10 E
Rumania = Romania ■, Europe 17 F12 46 0N 25 0 E
Rumaylah, Iraq 44 D5 30 47N 47 37 E
Rumbêk, Sudan 51 G11 6 54N 29 37 E
Rumford, U.S.A. 77 C10 44 33N 70 33W
Rumia, Poland 17 A10 54 37N 18 25 E
Rumoi, Japan 30 C10 43 56N 141 39 E
Rumonge, Burundi 54 C2 3 59S 29 26 E
Rumson, U.S.A. 79 F11 40 23N 74 0W
Rumuruti, Kenya 54 B4 0 17N 36 32 E
Runan, China 34 H8 33 0N 114 30 E
Runanga, N.Z. 59 K3 42 25S 171 15 E
Runaway, C., N.Z. 59 G6 37 32S 177 59 E
Runcorn, U.K. 10 D5 53 21N 2 44W
Rundu, Namibia 53 H3 17 52S 19 43 E
Rungwa, Tanzania 54 D3 6 55S 33 32 E
Rungwa —►, Tanzania 54 D3 7 36S 31 50 E
Rungwe, Tanzania 55 D3 9 11S 33 32 E
Rungwe, Mt., Tanzania 52 F6 9 8S 33 40 E
Runton Ra., Australia 60 D3 23 31S 123 6 E
Ruoqiang, China 32 C3 38 55N 88 10 E
Rupa, India 41 F18 27 15N 92 21 E
Rupar, India 42 D7 31 2N 76 38 E
Rupat, Indonesia 36 D2 1 45N 101 40 E
Rupen —►, India 42 H4 23 28N 71 31 E
Rupert, U.S.A. 82 E7 42 37N 113 41W
Rupert —►, Canada 70 B4 51 29N 78 45W
Rupert B., Canada 70 B4 51 35N 79 0W
Rupert House = Waskaganish, Canada 70 B4 51 30N 78 40W
Rupsa, India 43 J12 21 37N 87 1 E
Rurrenabaque, Bolivia 92 F5 14 30S 67 32W
Rusambo, Zimbabwe 55 F3 16 30S 32 4 E
Rusape, Zimbabwe 55 F3 18 35S 32 8 E
Ruschuk = Ruse, Bulgaria 21 C12 43 48N 25 59 E
Ruse, Bulgaria 21 C12 43 48N 25 59 E
Rush, Ireland 13 C5 53 31N 6 6W
Rushan, China 35 F11 36 56N 121 30 E
Rushden, U.K. 11 E7 52 18N 0 35W
Rushmore, Mt., U.S.A. 80 D3 43 53N 103 28W
Rushville, Ill., U.S.A. 80 E9 40 7N 90 34W
Rushville, Ind., U.S.A. 76 F3 39 37N 85 27W
Rushville, Nebr., U.S.A. 80 D3 42 43N 102 28W
Russas, Brazil 93 D11 4 55S 37 50W
Russell, Canada 73 C8 50 50N 101 20W
Russell, Kans., U.S.A. 80 F5 38 54N 98 52W
Russell, N.Y., U.S.A. 79 B9 44 27N 75 9W
Russell, Pa., U.S.A. 78 E5 41 56N 79 8W
Russell L., Man., Canada 73 B8 56 15N 101 30W
Russell L., N.W.T., Canada 72 A5 63 5N 115 44W
Russellkonda, India 41 K14 19 57N 84 42 E
Russellville, Ala., U.S.A. 77 H2 34 30N 87 44W
Russellville, Ark., U.S.A. 81 H8 35 17N 93 8W
Russellville, Ky., U.S.A. 77 G2 36 51N 86 53W
Russia ■, Eurasia 27 C11 62 0N 105 0 E
Russian —►, U.S.A. 84 G3 38 27N 123 8W
Russkoye Ustie, Russia 4 B15 71 0N 149 0 E
Rustam, Pakistan 42 B5 34 25N 72 13 E
Rustam Shahr, Pakistan 42 F2 26 58N 66 6 E
Rustavi, Georgia 25 F8 41 30N 45 0 E
Rustenburg, S. Africa 56 D4 25 41S 27 14 E
Ruston, U.S.A. 81 J8 32 32N 92 38W
Rutana, Burundi 54 C3 3 55S 30 0 E
Ruteng, Indonesia 37 F6 8 35S 120 30 E
Ruth, U.S.A. 78 C2 43 42N 82 45W
Rutherford, U.S.A. 84 G4 38 26N 122 24W
Rutland, U.S.A. 79 C12 43 37N 72 58W
Rutland □, U.K. 11 E7 52 38N 0 40W
Rutland Water, U.K. 11 E7 52 39N 0 38W
Rutledge —►, Canada 73 A6 61 4N 112 0W
Rutledge L., Canada 73 A6 61 33N 110 47W
Rutshuru, Dem. Rep. of the Congo 54 C2 1 13S 29 25 E
Ruvu, Tanzania 54 D4 6 49S 38 43 E
Ruvu —►, Tanzania 54 D4 6 23S 38 52 E
Ruvuma □, Tanzania 55 E4 10 20S 36 0 E
Ruvuma —►, Tanzania 55 E5 10 29S 40 28 E
Ruwais, U.A.E. 45 E7 24 5N 52 50 E
Ruwenzori, Africa 54 B2 0 30N 29 55 E
Ruyigi, Burundi 54 C3 3 29S 30 15 E
Ružomberok, Slovak Rep. 17 D10 49 3N 19 17 E
Rwanda ■, Africa 54 C3 2 0S 30 0 E
Ryan, L., U.K. 12 G3 55 0N 5 2W
Ryazan, Russia 24 D6 54 40N 39 40 E
Ryazhsk, Russia 24 D7 53 45N 40 3 E
Rybache = Rybachye, Kazakstan 26 E9 46 40N 81 20 E
Rybachiy Poluostrov, Russia 24 A5 69 43N 32 0 E
Rybachye = Ysyk-Köl, Kyrgyzstan 28 E11 42 26N 76 12 E
Rybachye, Kazakstan 26 E9 46 40N 81 20 E
Rybinsk, Russia 24 C6 58 5N 38 50 E
Rybinskoye Vdkhr., Russia 24 C6 58 30N 38 25 E
Rybnitsa = Râbniţa, Moldova 17 E15 47 45N 29 0 E
Rycroft, Canada 72 B5 55 45N 118 40W
Ryde, U.K. 11 G6 50 43N 1 9W
Ryderwood, U.S.A. 84 D3 46 23N 123 3W
Rye, U.K. 11 G8 50 57N 0 45 E
Rye —►, U.K. 10 C7 54 11N 0 44W
Rye Bay, U.K. 11 G8 50 52N 0 49 E
Rye Patch Reservoir, U.S.A. 82 F4 40 28N 118 19W
Ryegate, U.S.A. 82 C9 46 18N 109 15W
Ryley, Canada 72 C6 53 17N 112 26W
Rylstone, Australia 63 E4 32 46S 149 58 E
Ryōtsu, Japan 30 E9 38 5N 138 26 E
Rypin, Poland 17 B10 53 3N 19 25 E
Ryūgasaki, Japan 31 G10 35 54N 140 11 E
Ryūkyū Is. = Ryūkyū-rettō, Japan 31 M3 26 0N 126 0 E
Ryūkyū-rettō, Japan 31 M3 26 0N 126 0 E
Rzeszów, Poland 17 C11 50 5N 21 58 E
Rzhev, Russia 24 C5 56 20N 34 20 E

S

Sa, *Thailand* **38 C3** 18 34N 100 45 E
Sa Canal, *Spain* **22 C7** 38 51N 1 23 E
Sa Conillera, *Spain* **22 C7** 38 59N 1 13 E
Sa Dec, *Vietnam* **39 G5** 10 20N 105 46 E
Sa Dragonera, *Spain* **22 B9** 39 35N 2 19 E
Sa Mesquida, *Spain* **22 B11** 39 55N 4 16 E
Sa Savina, *Spain* **22 C7** 38 44N 1 25 E
Sa'ādatābād, *Fārs, Iran* **45 D7** 30 10N 53 5 E
Sa'ādatābād, *Hormozgān, Iran* **45 D7** 28 3N 55 53 E
Sa'ādatābād, *Kermān, Iran* **45 D7** 29 40N 55 51 E
Saale →, *Germany* **16 C6** 51 56N 11 54 E
Saalfeld, *Germany* **16 C6** 50 38N 11 21 E
Saar →, *Europe* **18 B7** 49 41N 6 32 E
Saarbrücken, *Germany* **16 D4** 49 14N 6 59 E
Saaremaa, *Estonia* **9 G20** 58 30N 22 30 E
Saarijärvi, *Finland* **9 E21** 62 43N 25 16 E
Saariselkä, *Finland* **8 B23** 68 16N 28 15 E
Sab 'Ābar, *Syria* **44 C3** 33 46N 37 41 E
Saba, *W. Indies* **89 C7** 17 42N 63 26W
Šabac, *Serbia, Yug.* **21 B8** 44 48N 19 42 E
Sabadell, *Spain* **19 B7** 41 28N 2 7 E
Sabah □, *Malaysia* **36 C5** 6 0N 117 0 E
Sabak Bernam, *Malaysia* **39 L3** 3 46N 100 58 E
Sabalān, Kūhhā-ye, *Iran* **44 B5** 38 15N 47 45 E
Sabalana, Kepulauan, *Indonesia* **37 F5** 6 45S 118 50 E
Sábana de la Mar, *Dom. Rep.* **89 C6** 19 7N 69 24W
Sábanalarga, *Colombia* **92 A4** 10 38N 74 55W
Sabang, *Indonesia* **36 C1** 5 50N 95 15 E
Sabará, *Brazil* **93 G10** 19 55S 43 46W
Sabarmati →, *India* **42 H5** 22 18N 72 22 E
Sabattis, *U.S.A.* **79 B10** 44 6N 74 40W
Saberania, *Indonesia* **37 E9** 2 5S 138 18 E
Sabhah, *Libya* **51 C8** 27 9N 14 29 E
Sabi →, *India* **42 E7** 28 29N 76 44 E
Sabie, *S. Africa* **57 D5** 25 10S 30 48 E
Sabinal, *Mexico* **86 A3** 30 58N 107 25W
Sabinal, *U.S.A.* **81 L5** 29 19N 99 28W
Sabinas, *Mexico* **86 B4** 27 50N 101 10W
Sabinas →, *Mexico* **86 B4** 27 37N 100 42W
Sabinas Hidalgo, *Mexico* **86 B4** 26 33N 100 10W
Sabine →, *U.S.A.* **81 L8** 29 59N 93 47W
Sabine L., *U.S.A.* **81 L8** 29 53N 93 51W
Sabine Pass, *U.S.A.* **81 L8** 29 44N 93 54W
Sabinsville, *U.S.A.* **78 E7** 41 52N 77 31W
Sabkhet el Bardawîl, *Egypt* **47 D2** 31 10N 33 15 E
Sablayan, *Phil.* **37 B6** 12 50N 120 50 E
Sable, *Canada* **71 A6** 55 30N 68 21W
Sable, C., *Canada* **71 D6** 43 29N 65 38W
Sable, C., *U.S.A.* **75 E10** 25 9N 81 8W
Sable I., *Canada* **71 D8** 44 0N 60 0W
Sabrina Coast, *Antarctica* **5 C9** 68 0S 120 0 E
Sabulubbek, *Indonesia* **36 E1** 1 36S 98 40 E
Sabzevār, *Iran* **45 B8** 36 15N 57 40 E
Sabzvārān, *Iran* **45 D8** 28 45N 57 50 E
Sac City, *U.S.A.* **80 D7** 42 25N 95 0W
Săcele, *Romania* **17 F13** 45 37N 25 41 E
Sachigo →, *Canada* **70 A2** 55 6N 88 58W
Sachigo, L., *Canada* **70 B1** 53 50N 92 12W
Sachsen □, *Germany* **16 C7** 50 55N 13 10 E
Sachsen-Anhalt □, *Germany* **16 C7** 52 0N 12 0 E
Sackets Harbor, *U.S.A.* **79 C8** 43 57N 76 7W
Sackville, *Canada* **71 C7** 45 54N 64 22W
Saco, *Maine, U.S.A.* **77 D10** 43 30N 70 27W
Saco, *Mont., U.S.A.* **82 B10** 48 28N 107 21W
Sacramento, *U.S.A.* **84 G5** 38 35N 121 29W
Sacramento →, *U.S.A.* **84 G5** 38 3N 121 56W
Sacramento Mts., *U.S.A.* **83 K11** 32 30N 105 30W
Sacramento Valley, *U.S.A.* **84 G5** 39 30N 122 0W
Sada-Misaki, *Japan* **31 H6** 33 20N 132 1 E
Sadabad, *India* **42 F8** 27 27N 78 3 E
Sadani, *Tanzania* **54 D4** 5 58S 38 35 E
Sadao, *Thailand* **39 J3** 6 38N 100 26 E
Sadd el Aali, *Egypt* **51 D12** 23 54N 32 54 E
Saddle Mt., *U.S.A.* **84 E3** 45 58N 123 41W
Sadimi, *Dem. Rep. of the Congo* **55 D1** 9 25S 23 32 E
Sado, *Japan* **30 F9** 38 0N 138 25 E
Sadon, *Burma* **41 G20** 25 28N 97 55 E
Sadra, *India* **42 H5** 23 21N 72 43 E
Sadri, *India* **42 G5** 25 11N 73 26 E
Sæby, *Denmark* **9 H14** 57 21N 10 30 E
Saegertown, *U.S.A.* **78 E4** 41 43N 80 9W
Şafājah, *Si. Arabia* **44 E3** 26 25N 39 0 E
Säffle, *Sweden* **9 G15** 59 8N 12 55 E
Safford, *U.S.A.* **83 K9** 32 50N 109 43W
Saffron Walden, *U.K.* **11 E8** 52 1N 0 16 E
Safi, *Morocco* **50 B4** 32 18N 9 20W
Şafīābād, *Iran* **45 B8** 36 45N 57 58 E
Safid Dasht, *Iran* **45 C6** 33 27N 48 11 E
Safīd Kūh, *Afghan.* **40 B3** 34 45N 63 0 E
Safid Rūd →, *Iran* **45 B6** 37 23N 50 11 E
Safipur, *India* **43 F9** 26 44N 80 21 E
Safwān, *Iraq* **44 D5** 30 7N 47 43 E
Sag Harbor, *U.S.A.* **79 F12** 41 0N 72 18W
Saga, *Japan* **31 H5** 33 15N 130 16 E
Saga □, *Japan* **31 H5** 33 15N 130 20 E
Sagae, *Japan* **30 E10** 38 22N 140 17 E
Sagamore, *U.S.A.* **78 F5** 40 46N 79 14W
Sagar, *India* **40 M9** 14 14N 75 6 E
Sagar, *Mad. P., India* **43 H8** 23 50N 78 44 E
Sagara, L., *Tanzania* **54 D3** 5 20S 31 0 E
Saginaw, *U.S.A.* **76 D4** 43 26N 83 56W
Saginaw →, *U.S.A.* **76 D4** 43 39N 83 51W
Saginaw B., *U.S.A.* **76 D4** 43 50N 83 40W
Saglouc = Salluit, *Canada* **69 B12** 62 14N 75 38W
Sagō-ri, *S. Korea* **35 G14** 35 25N 126 49 E
Sagua la Grande, *Cuba* **88 B3** 22 50N 80 10W
Saguache, *U.S.A.* **83 G10** 38 5N 106 8W
Saguaro Nat. Park, *U.S.A.* **83 K8** 32 12N 110 38W
Saguenay →, *Canada* **71 C5** 48 22N 71 0W
Sagunt, *Spain* **19 C5** 39 42N 0 18W
Sagunto = Sagunt, *Spain* **19 C5** 39 42N 0 18W
Sagwara, *India* **42 H6** 23 41N 74 1 E
Sahagún, *Spain* **19 A3** 42 18N 5 2W
Saḩam al Jawlān, *Syria* **47 C4** 32 45N 35 55 E
Sahand, Kūh-e, *Iran* **44 B5** 37 44N 46 27 E
Sahara, *Africa* **50 D6** 23 0N 5 0 E
Saharan Atlas = Saharien, Atlas, *Algeria* **50 B6** 33 30N 1 0 E
Saharanpur, *India* **42 E7** 29 58N 77 33 E
Saharien, Atlas, *Algeria* **50 B6** 33 30N 1 0 E
Saharsa, *India* **43 G12** 25 53N 86 36 E
Sahasinaka, *Madag.* **57 C8** 21 49S 47 49 E
Sahaswan, *India* **43 E8** 28 5N 78 45 E
Sahel, *Africa* **50 E5** 16 0N 5 0 E
Sahibganj, *India* **43 G12** 25 12N 87 40 E
Sāḩilīyah, *Iraq* **44 C4** 33 43N 42 42 E
Sahiwal, *Pakistan* **42 D5** 30 45N 73 8 E
Şaḩneh, *Iran* **44 C5** 34 29N 47 41 E
Sahuaripa, *Mexico* **86 B3** 29 0N 109 13W
Sahuarita, *U.S.A.* **83 L8** 31 57N 110 58W
Sahuayo, *Mexico* **86 C4** 20 4N 102 43W
Sai →, *India* **43 G10** 25 39N 82 47 E
Sai Buri, *Thailand* **39 J3** 6 43N 101 45 E
Sa'id Bundas, *Sudan* **51 G10** 8 24N 24 48 E
Sa'īdābād, *Kermān, Iran* **45 D7** 29 30N 55 45 E
Sa'īdābād, *Semnān, Iran* **45 B7** 36 8N 54 11 E
Sa'īdīyeh, *Iran* **45 B6** 36 20N 48 55 E
Saidpur, *Bangla.* **41 G16** 25 48N 89 0 E
Saidpur, *India* **43 G10** 25 33N 83 11 E
Saidu, *Pakistan* **43 B5** 34 43N 72 24 E
Saigon = Phanh Bho Ho Chi Minh, *Vietnam* **39 G6** 10 58N 106 40 E
Saijō, *Japan* **31 H6** 33 55N 133 11 E
Saikhoa Ghat, *India* **41 F19** 27 50N 95 40 E
Saiki, *Japan* **31 H5** 32 58N 131 51 E
Sailana, *India* **42 H6** 23 28N 74 55 E
Sailolof, *Indonesia* **37 E8** 1 7S 130 46 E
Saimaa, *Finland* **9 F23** 61 15N 28 15 E
Şa'īn Dezh, *Iran* **44 B5** 36 40N 46 25 E
St. Abb's Head, *U.K.* **12 F6** 55 55N 2 8W
St. Alban's, *Canada* **71 C8** 47 51N 55 50W
St. Albans, *U.K.* **11 F7** 51 45N 0 19W
St. Albans, *Vt., U.S.A.* **79 B11** 44 49N 73 5W
St. Albans, *W. Va., U.S.A.* **76 F5** 38 23N 81 50W
St. Alban's Head, *U.K.* **11 G5** 50 34N 2 4W
St. Albert, *Canada* **72 C6** 53 37N 113 32W
St. Andrew's, *Canada* **71 C8** 47 45N 59 15W
St. Andrews, *U.K.* **12 E6** 56 20N 2 47W
St-Anicet, *Canada* **79 A10** 45 8N 74 22W
St. Ann B., *Canada* **71 C7** 46 22N 60 25W
St. Ann's Bay, *Jamaica* **88 C4** 18 26N 77 15W
St. Anthony, *Canada* **71 B8** 51 22N 55 35W
St. Anthony, *U.S.A.* **82 E8** 43 58N 111 41W
St. Antoine, *Canada* **71 C7** 46 22N 64 45W
St. Arnaud, *Australia* **63 F3** 36 40S 143 16 E
St-Augustin →, *Canada* **71 B8** 51 16N 58 40W
St-Augustin-Saguenay, *Canada* **71 B8** 51 13N 58 38W
St. Augustine, *U.S.A.* **77 L5** 29 54N 81 19W
St. Austell, *U.K.* **11 G3** 50 20N 4 47W
St. Barbe, *Canada* **71 B8** 51 12N 56 46W
St-Barthélemy, *W. Indies* **89 C7** 17 50N 62 50W
St. Bees Hd., *U.K.* **10 C4** 54 31N 3 38W
St. Bride's, *Canada* **71 C9** 46 56N 54 10W
St. Brides B., *U.K.* **11 F2** 51 49N 5 9W
St-Brieuc, *France* **18 B2** 48 30N 2 46W
St. Catharines, *Canada* **78 C5** 43 10N 79 15W
St. Catherines I., *U.S.A.* **77 K5** 31 40N 81 10W
St. Catherine's Pt., *U.K.* **11 G6** 50 34N 1 18W
St-Chamond, *France* **18 D6** 45 28N 4 31 E
St. Charles, *Ill., U.S.A.* **76 E1** 41 54N 88 19W
St. Charles, *Mo., U.S.A.* **80 F9** 38 47N 90 29W
St. Charles, *Va., U.S.A.* **76 F7** 36 48N 83 4W
St. Christopher-Nevis = St. Kitts & Nevis ■, *W. Indies* **89 C7** 17 20N 62 40W
St. Clair, *Mich., U.S.A.* **78 D2** 42 50N 82 30W
St. Clair, *Pa., U.S.A.* **79 F8** 40 43N 76 12W
St. Clair →, *U.S.A.* **78 D2** 42 38N 82 31W
St. Clair, L., *Canada* **70 D3** 42 30N 82 45W
St. Clair, L., *U.S.A.* **78 D2** 42 27N 82 39W
St. Clairsville, *U.S.A.* **78 F4** 40 5N 80 54W
St. Claude, *Canada* **73 D9** 49 40N 98 20W
St-Clet, *Canada* **79 A10** 45 21N 74 13W
St. Cloud, *Fla., U.S.A.* **77 L5** 28 15N 81 17W
St. Cloud, *Minn., U.S.A.* **80 C7** 45 34N 94 10W
St. Cricq, C., *Australia* **61 E1** 25 17S 113 6 E
St. Croix, *Virgin Is.* **89 C7** 17 45N 64 45W
St. Croix →, *U.S.A.* **80 C8** 44 45N 92 48W
St. Croix Falls, *U.S.A.* **80 C8** 45 24N 92 38W
St. David's, *Canada* **71 C8** 48 12N 58 52W
St. David's, *U.K.* **11 F2** 51 53N 5 16W
St. David's Head, *U.K.* **11 F2** 51 54N 5 19W
St-Denis, *France* **18 B5** 48 56N 2 22 E
St-Dizier, *France* **18 B6** 48 38N 4 56 E
St. Elias, Mt., *U.S.A.* **68 B5** 60 18N 140 56W
St. Elias Mts., *Canada* **72 A1** 60 33N 139 28W
St. Elias Mts., *U.S.A.* **68 C6** 60 0N 138 0W
St-Étienne, *France* **18 D6** 45 27N 4 22 E
St. Eugène, *Canada* **79 A10** 45 30N 74 28W
St. Eustatius, *W. Indies* **89 C7** 17 20N 63 0W
St-Félicien, *Canada* **70 C5** 48 40N 72 25W
St-Flour, *France* **18 D5** 45 2N 3 6 E
St. Francis, *U.S.A.* **80 F4** 39 47N 101 48W
St. Francis →, *U.S.A.* **81 H9** 34 38N 90 36W
St. Francis, C., *S. Africa* **56 E3** 34 14S 24 49 E
St. Francisville, *U.S.A.* **81 K9** 30 47N 91 23W
St-François, L., *Canada* **79 A10** 45 10N 74 22W
St-Gabriel, *Canada* **70 C5** 46 17N 73 24W
St. Gallen = Sankt Gallen, *Switz.* **18 C8** 47 26N 9 22 E
St-Gaudens, *France* **18 E4** 43 6N 0 44 E
St. George, *Australia* **63 D4** 28 1S 148 30 E
St. George, *Canada* **71 C6** 45 11N 66 50W
St. George, *S.C., U.S.A.* **77 J5** 33 11N 80 35W
St. George, *Utah, U.S.A.* **83 H7** 37 6N 113 35W
St. George, C., *Canada* **71 C8** 48 30N 59 16W
St. George, C., *U.S.A.* **77 L3** 29 40N 85 5W
St. George Ra., *Australia* **60 C4** 18 40S 125 0 E
St. George's, *Canada* **71 C8** 48 26N 58 31W
St-Georges, *Canada* **71 C5** 46 8N 70 40W
St. George's, *Grenada* **89 D7** 12 5N 61 43W
St. George's B., *Canada* **71 C8** 48 24N 58 53W
St. Georges Basin, *N.S.W., Australia* **63 F5** 35 7S 150 36 E
St. Georges Basin, *W. Austral., Australia* **60 C4** 15 23S 125 2 E
St. George's Channel, *Europe* **13 E6** 52 0N 6 0W
St. Georges Hd., *Australia* **63 F5** 35 12S 150 42 E
St. Gotthard P. = San Gottardo, P. del, *Switz.* **18 C8** 46 33N 8 33 E
St. Helena, *U.S.A.* **82 G2** 38 30N 122 28W
St. Helena ■, *Atl. Oc.* **49 H3** 15 55S 5 44W
St. Helena, Mt., *U.S.A.* **84 G4** 38 40N 122 36W
St. Helena B., *S. Africa* **56 E2** 32 40S 18 10 E
St. Helens, *Australia* **62 G4** 41 20S 148 15 E
St. Helens, *U.K.* **10 D5** 53 27N 2 44W
St. Helens, *U.S.A.* **84 E4** 45 52N 122 48W
St. Helens, Mt., *U.S.A.* **84 D4** 46 12N 122 12W
St. Helier, *U.K.* **11 H5** 49 10N 2 7W
St-Hubert, *Belgium* **15 D5** 50 2N 5 23 E
St-Hyacinthe, *Canada* **70 C5** 45 40N 72 58W
St. Ignace, *U.S.A.* **76 C3** 45 52N 84 44W
St. Ignace I., *Canada* **70 C2** 48 45N 88 0W
St. Ignatius, *U.S.A.* **82 C6** 47 19N 114 6W
St. Ives, *U.K.* **11 G2** 50 12N 5 30W
St. James, *U.S.A.* **80 D7** 43 59N 94 38W
St-Jean →, *Canada* **71 B7** 50 17N 64 20W
St-Jean, L., *Canada* **71 C5** 48 40N 72 0W
St-Jean-Port-Joli, *Canada* **71 C5** 47 15N 70 13W
St-Jean-sur-Richelieu, *Canada* **79 A11** 45 20N 73 20W
St-Jérôme, *Canada* **70 C5** 45 47N 74 0W
St. John, *Canada* **71 C6** 45 20N 66 8W
St. John, *U.S.A.* **81 G5** 38 0N 98 46W
St. John →, *U.S.A.* **77 C12** 45 12N 66 5W
St. John, C., *Canada* **71 C8** 50 0N 55 32W
St. John's, *Antigua* **89 C7** 17 6N 61 51W
St. John's, *Canada* **71 C9** 47 35N 52 40W
St. Johns, *Ariz., U.S.A.* **83 J9** 34 30N 109 22W
St. Johns, *Mich., U.S.A.* **76 D3** 43 0N 84 33W
St. Johns →, *U.S.A.* **77 K5** 30 24N 81 24W
St. John's Pt., *Ireland* **13 B3** 54 34N 8 27W
St. Johnsbury, *U.S.A.* **79 B12** 44 25N 72 1W
St. Johnsville, *U.S.A.* **79 D10** 43 0N 74 43W
St. Joseph, *La., U.S.A.* **81 K9** 31 55N 91 14W
St. Joseph, *Mich., U.S.A.* **75 B9** 42 6N 86 29W
St. Joseph, *Mo., U.S.A.* **80 F7** 39 46N 94 50W
St. Joseph →, *U.S.A.* **76 D2** 42 7N 86 29W
St. Joseph, I., *Canada* **70 C3** 46 12N 83 58W
St. Joseph, L., *Canada* **70 B1** 51 10N 90 35W
St-Jovite, *Canada* **70 C5** 46 8N 74 38W
St. Kilda, *N.Z.* **59 L3** 45 53S 170 31 E
St. Kitts & Nevis ■, *W. Indies* **89 C7** 17 20N 62 40W
St. Laurent, *Canada* **73 C9** 50 25N 97 58W
St. Lawrence, *Australia* **62 C4** 22 16S 149 31 E
St. Lawrence, *Canada* **71 C8** 46 54N 55 23W
St. Lawrence →, *Canada* **71 C6** 49 30N 66 0W
St. Lawrence, Gulf of, *Canada* **71 C7** 48 25N 62 0W
St. Lawrence I., *U.S.A.* **68 B3** 63 30N 170 30W
St. Leonard, *Canada* **71 C6** 47 12N 67 58W
St. Lewis →, *Canada* **71 B8** 52 26N 56 11W
St-Lô, *France* **18 B3** 49 7N 1 5W
St. Louis, *Senegal* **50 E2** 16 8N 16 27W
St. Louis, *U.S.A.* **80 F9** 38 37N 90 12W
St. Louis →, *U.S.A.* **80 B8** 47 15N 92 45W
St. Lucia ■, *W. Indies* **89 D7** 14 0N 60 50W
St. Lucia, L., *S. Africa* **57 D5** 28 5S 32 30 E
St. Lucia Channel, *W. Indies* **89 D7** 14 15N 61 0W
St. Maarten, *W. Indies* **89 C7** 18 0N 63 5W
St. Magnus B., *U.K.* **12 A7** 60 25N 1 35W
St-Malo, *France* **18 B2** 48 39N 2 1W
St-Marc, *Haiti* **89 C5** 19 10N 72 41W
St. Maries, *U.S.A.* **82 C5** 47 19N 116 35W
St-Martin, *W. Indies* **89 C7** 18 0N 63 0W
St. Martin, L., *Canada* **73 C9** 51 40N 98 30W
St. Mary Pk., *Australia* **63 E2** 31 32S 138 34 E
St. Marys, *Australia* **62 G4** 41 35S 148 11 E
St. Marys, *Canada* **78 C3** 43 20N 81 10W
St. Mary's, *Corn., U.K.* **11 H1** 49 55N 6 18W
St. Mary's, *Orkney, U.K.* **12 C6** 58 54N 2 54W
St. Marys, *Ga., U.S.A.* **77 K5** 30 44N 81 33W
St. Marys, *Pa., U.S.A.* **78 E6** 41 26N 78 34W
St. Mary's, C., *Canada* **71 C9** 46 50N 54 12W
St. Mary's B., *Canada* **71 C9** 46 50N 53 50W
St. Marys Bay, *Canada* **71 D6** 44 25N 66 10W
St-Mathieu, Pte., *France* **18 B1** 48 20N 4 45W
St. Matthew I., *U.S.A.* **68 B2** 60 24N 172 42W
St. Matthews, I. = Zadetkyi Kyun, *Burma* **39 H2** 10 0N 98 25 E
St-Maurice →, *Canada* **70 C5** 46 21N 72 31W
St-Nazaire, *France* **18 C2** 47 17N 2 12W
St. Neots, *U.K.* **11 E7** 52 14N 0 15W
St-Niklaas, *Belgium* **15 C4** 51 10N 4 8 E
St-Omer, *France* **18 A5** 50 45N 2 15 E
St-Pamphile, *Canada* **71 C6** 46 58N 69 48W
St. Pascal, *Canada* **71 C6** 47 32N 69 48W
St. Paul, *Canada* **72 C6** 54 0N 111 17W
St. Paul, *Minn., U.S.A.* **80 C8** 44 57N 93 6W
St. Paul, *Nebr., U.S.A.* **80 E5** 41 13N 98 27W
St-Paul →, *Canada* **71 B8** 51 27N 57 42W
St. Paul, I., *Ind. Oc.* **3 F13** 38 55S 77 34 E
St. Paul I., *Canada* **71 C7** 47 12N 60 9W
St. Peter, *U.S.A.* **80 C8** 44 20N 93 57W
St. Peter Port, *U.K.* **11 H5** 49 26N 2 33W
St. Peters, *N.S., Canada* **71 C7** 45 40N 60 53W
St. Peters, *P.E.I., Canada* **71 C7** 46 25N 62 35W
St. Petersburg = Sankt-Peterburg, *Russia* **24 C5** 59 55N 30 20 E
St. Petersburg, *U.S.A.* **77 M4** 27 46N 82 39W
St-Pie, *Canada* **79 A12** 45 30N 72 54W
St-Pierre, *St- P. & M.* **71 C8** 46 46N 56 12W
St-Pierre, L., *Canada* **70 C5** 46 12N 72 52W
St-Pierre et Miquelon □, *St- P. & M.* **71 C8** 46 55N 56 10W
St. Quentin, *Canada* **71 C6** 47 30N 67 23W
St-Quentin, *France* **18 B5** 49 50N 3 16 E
St. Regis, *U.S.A.* **82 C6** 47 18N 115 6W
St. Sebastien, Tanjon' i, *Madag.* **57 A8** 12 26S 48 44 E
St-Siméon, *Canada* **71 C6** 47 51N 69 54W
St. Simons I., *U.S.A.* **77 K5** 31 12N 81 15W
St. Simons Island, *U.S.A.* **77 K5** 31 9N 81 22W
St. Stephen, *Canada* **71 C6** 45 16N 67 17W
St. Thomas, *Canada* **78 D3** 42 45N 81 10W
St. Thomas I., *Virgin Is.* **89 C7** 18 20N 64 55W
St-Tite, *Canada* **70 C5** 46 45N 72 34W
St-Tropez, *France* **18 E7** 43 17N 6 38 E
St. Troud = St. Truiden, *Belgium* **15 D5** 50 48N 5 10 E
St. Truiden, *Belgium* **15 D5** 50 48N 5 10 E
St. Vincent, G., *Australia* **63 F2** 35 0S 138 0 E
St. Vincent & the Grenadines ■, *W. Indies* **89 D7** 13 0N 61 10W
St. Vincent Passage, *W. Indies* **89 D7** 13 30N 61 0W
St-Vith, *Belgium* **15 D6** 50 17N 6 9 E
St. Walburg, *Canada* **73 C7** 53 39N 109 12W
Ste-Agathe-des-Monts, *Canada* **70 C5** 46 3N 74 17W
Ste-Anne, L., *Canada* **71 B6** 50 0N 67 42W
Ste-Anne-des-Monts, *Canada* **71 C6** 49 8N 66 30W
Ste. Genevieve, *U.S.A.* **80 G9** 37 59N 90 2W
Ste-Marguerite →, *Canada* **71 B6** 50 9N 66 36W
Ste-Marie, *Martinique* **89 D7** 14 48N 61 1W
Ste-Marie de la Madeleine, *Canada* **71 C5** 46 26N 71 0W
Ste-Rose, *Guadeloupe* **89 C7** 16 20N 61 45W
Ste. Rose du Lac, *Canada* **73 C9** 51 4N 99 30W
Saintes, *France* **18 D3** 45 45N 0 37W
Saintes, I. des, *Guadeloupe* **89 C7** 15 50N 61 35W
Saintfield, *U.K.* **13 B6** 54 28N 5 49W
Sainthiya, *India* **43 H12** 23 57N 87 40 E
Saintonge, *France* **18 D3** 45 40N 0 50W
Saipan, *Pac. Oc.* **64 F6** 15 12N 145 45 E
Sairang, *India* **41 H18** 23 50N 92 45 E
Sairecábur, Cerro, *Bolivia* **94 A2** 22 43S 67 54W
Saitama □, *Japan* **31 F9** 36 25N 139 30 E
Saiyid, *Pakistan* **42 C5** 33 7N 73 2 E
Sajama, *Bolivia* **92 G5** 18 7S 69 0W
Sajószentpéter, *Hungary* **17 D11** 48 12N 20 44 E
Sajum, *India* **43 C8** 33 20N 79 0 E
Sak →, *S. Africa* **56 E3** 30 52S 20 25 E
Sakai, *Japan* **31 G7** 34 30N 135 30 E
Sakaide, *Japan* **31 G6** 34 15N 133 50 E
Sakaiminato, *Japan* **31 G6** 35 38N 133 11 E
Sakākah, *Si. Arabia* **44 D4** 30 0N 40 8 E
Sakakawea, L., *U.S.A.* **80 B4** 47 30N 101 25W
Sakami →, *Canada* **70 B4** 53 40N 76 40W
Sakami, L., *Canada* **70 B4** 53 15N 77 0W
Sakania, *Dem. Rep. of the Congo* **55 E2** 12 43S 28 30 E
Sakarya, *Turkey* **25 F5** 40 48N 30 25 E
Sakashima-Guntō, *Japan* **31 M2** 24 46N 124 0 E
Sakata, *Japan* **30 E9** 38 55N 139 50 E
Sakchu, *N. Korea* **35 D13** 40 23N 125 2 E
Sakeny →, *Madag.* **57 C8** 20 0S 45 25 E
Sakha □, *Russia* **27 C14** 66 0N 130 0 E
Sakhalin, *Russia* **27 D15** 51 0N 143 0 E
Sakhalinskiy Zaliv, *Russia* **27 D15** 54 0N 141 0 E
Šakiai, *Lithuania* **9 J20** 54 59N 23 2 E
Sakon Nakhon, *Thailand* **38 D5** 17 10N 104 9 E
Sakrand, *Pakistan* **42 F3** 26 10N 68 15 E
Sakri, *India* **43 F12** 26 13N 86 5 E
Sakrivier, *S. Africa* **56 E3** 30 54S 20 28 E
Sakti, *India* **43 H10** 22 2N 82 58 E
Sakuma, *Japan* **31 G8** 35 3N 137 49 E
Sakurai, *Japan* **31 G7** 34 30N 135 51 E
Sala, *Sweden* **9 G17** 59 58N 16 35 E
Sala Consilina, *Italy* **20 D6** 40 23N 15 36 E
Sala-y-Gómez, *Pac. Oc.* **65 K17** 26 28S 105 28W
Salaberry-de-Valleyfield, *Canada* **79 A10** 45 15N 74 8W
Saladas, *Argentina* **94 B4** 28 15S 58 40W
Saladillo, *Argentina* **94 D4** 35 40S 59 55W
Salado →, *Buenos Aires, Argentina* **94 D4** 35 44S 57 22W
Salado →, *La Pampa, Argentina* **96 D3** 37 30S 67 0W
Salado →, *Santa Fe, Argentina* **94 C3** 31 40S 60 41W
Salado →, *Mexico* **81 M5** 26 52N 99 19W
Salaga, *Ghana* **50 G5** 8 31N 0 31W
Sālah, *Syria* **47 C5** 32 40N 36 45 E
Sálakhos, *Greece* **23 C9** 36 17N 27 57 E
Salālah, *Oman* **46 D5** 16 56N 53 59 E
Salamanca, *Chile* **94 C1** 31 46S 70 59W
Salamanca, *Spain* **19 B3** 40 58N 5 39W
Salamanca, *U.S.A.* **78 D6** 42 10N 78 43W
Salāmatābād, *Iran* **44 C5** 35 39N 47 50 E
Salamis, *Cyprus* **23 D12** 35 11N 33 54 E
Salamis, *Greece* **21 F10** 37 56N 23 30 E
Salar de Atacama, *Chile* **94 A2** 23 30S 68 25W
Salar de Uyuni, *Bolivia* **92 H5** 20 30S 67 45W
Salatiga, *Indonesia* **37 G14** 7 19S 110 30 E
Salavat, *Russia* **24 D10** 53 21N 55 55 E
Salaverry, *Peru* **92 E3** 8 15S 79 0W
Salawati, *Indonesia* **37 E8** 1 7S 130 52 E
Salaya, *India* **42 H3** 22 19N 69 35 E
Salayar, *Indonesia* **37 F6** 6 7S 120 30 E
Salcombe, *U.K.* **11 G4** 50 14N 3 47W
Saldanha, *S. Africa* **56 E2** 33 0S 17 58 E
Saldanha B., *S. Africa* **56 E2** 33 6S 18 0 E
Saldus, *Latvia* **9 H20** 56 38N 22 30 E
Sale, *Australia* **63 F4** 38 6S 147 6 E
Salé, *Morocco* **50 B4** 34 3N 6 48W
Sale, *U.K.* **10 D5** 53 26N 2 19W
Salekhard, *Russia* **26 C7** 66 30N 66 35 E
Salem, *India* **40 P11** 11 40N 78 11 E
Salem, *Ill., U.S.A.* **76 F1** 38 38N 88 57W
Salem, *Ind., U.S.A.* **76 F2** 38 36N 86 6W
Salem, *Mass., U.S.A.* **79 D14** 42 31N 70 53W
Salem, *Mo., U.S.A.* **81 G9** 37 39N 91 32W
Salem, *N.H., U.S.A.* **79 D13** 42 45N 71 12W
Salem, *N.J., U.S.A.* **76 F8** 39 34N 75 28W
Salem, *N.Y., U.S.A.* **79 C11** 43 10N 73 20W
Salem, *Ohio, U.S.A.* **78 F4** 40 54N 80 52W
Salem, *Oreg., U.S.A.* **82 D2** 44 56N 123 2W
Salem, *S. Dak., U.S.A.* **80 D6** 43 44N 97 23W
Salem, *Va., U.S.A.* **76 G5** 37 18N 80 3W
Salerno, *Italy* **20 D6** 40 41N 14 47 E
Salford, *U.K.* **10 D5** 53 30N 2 18W
Salgótarján, *Hungary* **17 D10** 48 5N 19 47 E
Salgueiro, *Brazil* **93 E11** 8 4S 39 6W
Salibabu, *Indonesia* **37 D7** 3 51N 126 40 E
Salida, *U.S.A.* **74 C5** 38 32N 106 0W
Salihli, *Turkey* **21 E13** 38 28N 28 8 E
Salihorsk, *Belarus* **17 B14** 52 51N 27 27 E
Salima, *Malawi* **53 G6** 13 47S 34 28 E
Salina, *Italy* **20 E6** 38 34N 14 50 E
Salina, *Kans., U.S.A.* **80 F6** 38 50N 97 37W
Salina, *Utah, U.S.A.* **83 G8** 38 58N 111 51W
Salina Cruz, *Mexico* **87 D5** 16 10N 95 10W
Salinas, *Brazil* **93 G10** 16 10S 42 10W
Salinas, *Chile* **94 A2** 23 31S 69 29W
Salinas, *Ecuador* **92 D2** 2 10S 80 58W
Salinas, *U.S.A.* **84 J5** 36 40N 121 39W
Salinas →, *Guatemala* **87 D6** 16 28N 90 31W
Salinas →, *U.S.A.* **84 J5** 36 45N 121 48W
Salinas, B. de, *Nic.* **88 D2** 11 4N 85 45W
Salinas, Pampa de las, *Argentina* **94 C2** 31 58S 66 42W
Salinas Ambargasta, *Argentina* **94 B3** 29 0S 65 0W

Solfonn

Síkinos, Greece 21 F11 36 40N 25 8 E
Sikkani Chief →, Canada 72 B4 57 47N 122 15W
Sikkim □, India 41 F16 27 50N 88 30 E
Sikotu-Ko, Japan 30 C10 42 45N 141 25 E
Sil →, Spain 19 A2 42 27N 7 43W
Silacayoapan, Mexico 87 D5 17 30N 98 9W
Silawad, India 42 J6 21 54N 74 54 E
Silchar, India 41 G18 24 49N 92 48 E
Siler City, U.S.A. 77 H6 35 44N 79 28W
Silesia = Śląsk, Poland 16 C9 51 0N 16 30 E
Silgarhi Doti, Nepal 43 E9 29 15N 81 0 E
Silghat, India 41 F18 26 35N 93 0 E
Silifke, Turkey 25 G5 36 22N 33 58 E
Siliguri = Shiliguri, India 41 F16 26 45N 88 25 E
Siling Co, China 32 C3 31 50N 89 20 E
Silistra, Bulgaria 21 B12 44 6N 27 19 E
Silivri, Turkey 21 D13 41 4N 28 14 E
Siljan, Sweden 9 F16 60 55N 14 45 E
Silkeborg, Denmark 9 H13 56 10N 9 32 E
Silkwood, Australia 62 B4 17 45S 146 2 E
Sillajhuay, Cordillera, Chile 92 G5 19 46S 68 40W
Sillamäe, Estonia 9 G22 59 24N 27 45 E
Silloth, U.K. 10 C4 54 52N 3 23W
Siloam Springs, U.S.A. 81 G7 36 11N 94 32W
Silsbee, U.S.A. 81 K7 30 21N 94 11W
Šilutė, Lithuania 9 J19 55 21N 21 33 E
Silva Porto = Kuito, Angola 53 G3 12 22S 16 55 E
Silvani, India 43 H8 23 18N 78 25 E
Silver City, U.S.A. 83 K9 32 46N 108 17W
Silver Cr. →, U.S.A. 82 E4 43 16N 119 13W
Silver Creek, U.S.A. 78 D5 42 33N 79 10W
Silver L., U.S.A. 84 G6 38 39N 120 6W
Silver Lake, Calif., U.S.A. 85 K10 35 21N 116 7W
Silver Lake, Oreg., U.S.A. 82 E3 43 8N 121 3W
Silver Streams, S. Africa 56 D3 28 20S 23 33 E
Silverton, Colo., U.S.A. 83 H10 37 49N 107 40W
Silverton, Tex., U.S.A. 81 H4 34 28N 101 19W
Silvies →, U.S.A. 82 E4 43 34N 119 2W
Simaltala, India 43 G12 24 43N 86 33 E
Simanggang = Bandar Sri Aman, Malaysia 36 D4 1 15N 111 32 E
Simard, L., Canada 70 C4 47 40N 78 40W
Simav, Turkey 21 E13 39 4N 28 58 E
Simba, Tanzania 54 C4 2 10S 37 36 E
Simbirsk, Russia 24 D8 54 20N 48 25 E
Simbo, Tanzania 54 C2 4 51S 29 41 E
Simcoe, Canada 78 D4 42 50N 80 20W
Simcoe, L., Canada 78 B5 44 25N 79 20W
Simdega, India 43 H11 22 37N 84 31 E
Simeria, Romania 17 F12 45 51N 23 1 E
Simeulue, Indonesia 36 D1 2 45N 95 45 E
Simferopol, Ukraine 25 F5 44 55N 34 3 E
Sími, Greece 21 F12 36 35N 27 50 E
Simi Valley, U.S.A. 85 L8 34 16N 118 47W
Simikot, Nepal 43 E9 30 0N 81 50 E
Simla, India 42 D7 31 2N 77 9 E
Simmie, Canada 73 D7 49 56N 108 6W
Simmler, U.S.A. 85 K7 35 21N 119 59W
Simojoki →, Finland 8 D21 65 35N 25 1 E
Simojovel, Mexico 87 D6 17 12N 92 38W
Simonette →, Canada 72 B5 55 9N 118 15W
Simonstown, S. Africa 56 E2 34 14S 18 26 E
Simplonpass, Switz. 18 C8 46 15N 8 3 E
Simpson Desert, Australia 62 D2 25 0S 137 0 E
Simpson Pen., Canada 69 B11 68 34N 88 45W
Simpungdong, N. Korea 35 D15 40 56N 129 29 E
Simrishamn, Sweden 9 J16 55 33N 14 22 E
Simsbury, U.S.A. 79 E12 41 53N 72 48W
Simushir, Ostrov, Russia 27 E16 46 50N 152 30 E
Sin Cowe I., S. China Sea 36 C4 9 53N 114 19 E
Sinabang, Indonesia 36 D1 2 30N 96 24 E
Sinadogo, Somali Rep. 46 F4 5 50N 47 0 E
Sinai = Es Sînâ', Egypt 47 F3 29 0N 34 0 E
Sinai, Mt. = Mûsa, Gebel, Egypt 44 D2 28 33N 33 59 E
Sinai Peninsula, Egypt 47 F3 29 30N 34 0 E
Sinaloa □, Mexico 86 C3 25 0N 107 30W
Sinaloa de Leyva, Mexico 86 B3 25 50N 108 20W
Sinarádhes, Greece 23 A3 39 34N 19 51 E
Sincelejo, Colombia 92 B3 9 18N 75 24W
Sinch'ang, N. Korea 35 D15 40 7N 128 28 E
Sinchang-ni, N. Korea 35 E14 39 24N 126 8 E
Sinclair, U.S.A. 82 F10 41 47N 107 7W
Sinclair Mills, Canada 72 C4 54 5N 121 40W
Sinclair's B., U.K. 12 C5 58 31N 3 5W
Sinclairville, U.S.A. 78 D5 42 16N 79 16W
Sincorá, Serra do, Brazil 93 F10 13 30S 41 0W
Sind, Pakistan 42 G3 26 0N 68 30 E
Sind □, Pakistan 42 G3 26 0N 69 0 E
Sind →, India 43 F8 26 26N 79 13 E
Sind →, Jammu & Kashmir, India 43 B6 34 18N 74 45 E
Sind Sagar Doab, Pakistan 42 D4 32 0N 71 30 E
Sindangan, Phil. 37 C6 8 10N 123 5 E
Sindangbarang, Indonesia 37 G12 7 27S 107 1 E
Sinde, Zambia 55 F2 17 28S 25 51 E
Sindri, India 43 H12 23 45N 86 42 E
Sines, Portugal 19 D1 37 56N 8 51W
Sines, C. de, Portugal 19 D1 37 58N 8 53W
Sineu, Spain 22 B10 39 38N 3 1 E
Sing Buri, Thailand 38 E3 14 53N 100 25 E
Singa, Sudan 51 F12 13 10N 33 57 E
Singapore ■, Asia 39 M4 1 17N 103 51 E
Singapore, Straits of, Asia 39 M5 1 15N 104 0 E
Singaraja, Indonesia 36 F5 8 6S 115 10 E
Singida, Tanzania 54 C3 4 49S 34 48 E
Singida □, Tanzania 54 D3 6 0S 34 30 E
Singitikós Kólpos, Greece 21 D11 40 6N 24 0 E
Singkaling Hkamti, Burma 41 G19 26 0N 95 39 E
Singkang, Indonesia 37 E6 4 8S 120 1 E
Singkawang, Indonesia 36 D3 1 0N 108 57 E
Singkep, Indonesia 36 E2 0 30S 104 25 E
Singleton, Australia 63 E5 32 33S 151 0 E
Singleton, Mt., N. Terr., Australia 60 D5 22 0S 130 46 E
Singleton, Mt., W. Austral., Australia 61 E2 29 27S 117 15 E
Singoli, India 42 G6 25 0N 75 22 E
Singora = Songkhla, Thailand 39 J3 7 13N 100 37 E
Singosan, N. Korea 35 E14 38 52N 127 25 E
Sinhung, N. Korea 35 D14 40 11N 127 34 E
Sînî □, Egypt 47 F3 30 0N 34 0 E
Sinjai, Indonesia 37 F6 5 7S 120 20 E
Sinjār, Iraq 44 B4 36 19N 41 52 E
Sinkat, Sudan 51 E13 18 55N 36 49 E
Sinkiang Uighur = Xinjiang Uygur Zizhiqu □, China 32 C3 42 0N 86 0 E
Sinmak, N. Korea 35 E14 38 25N 126 14 E
Sinnamary, Fr. Guiana 93 B8 5 25N 53 0W
Sinni →, Italy 20 D7 40 8N 16 41 E
Sinop, Turkey 25 F6 42 1N 35 11 E
Sinor, India 42 J5 21 55N 73 20 E
Sinp'o, N. Korea 35 E15 40 0N 128 13 E
Sinsk, Russia 27 C13 61 8N 126 48 E
Sintang, Indonesia 36 D4 0 5N 111 35 E
Sinton, U.S.A. 81 L6 28 2N 97 31W
Sintra, Portugal 19 C1 38 47N 9 25W
Sinŭiju, N. Korea 35 D13 40 5N 124 24 E
Siocon, Phil. 37 C6 7 40N 122 10 E
Siófok, Hungary 17 E10 46 54N 18 3 E
Sioma, Zambia 56 B3 16 25S 23 28 E
Sion, Switz. 18 C7 46 14N 7 20 E
Sion Mills, U.K. 13 B4 54 48N 7 29W
Sioux City, U.S.A. 80 D6 42 30N 96 24W
Sioux Falls, U.S.A. 80 D6 43 33N 96 44W
Sioux Lookout, Canada 70 B1 50 10N 91 50W
Sioux Narrows, Canada 73 D10 49 25N 94 10W
Siping, China 35 C13 43 8N 124 21 E
Sipiwesk L., Canada 73 B9 55 5N 97 35W
Sipra →, India 42 H6 23 55N 75 28 E
Sipura, Indonesia 36 E1 2 18S 99 40 E
Siquia →, Nic. 88 D3 12 10N 84 20W
Siquijor, Phil. 37 C6 9 12N 123 35 E
Siquirres, Costa Rica 88 D3 10 6N 83 30W
Şīr Banī Yās, U.A.E. 45 E7 24 19N 52 37 E
Sir Edward Pellew Group, Australia 62 B2 15 40S 137 10 E
Sir Graham Moore Is., Australia 60 B4 13 53S 126 34 E
Sir James MacBrien, Mt., Canada 68 B7 62 8N 127 40W
Sira →, Norway 9 G12 58 23N 6 34 E
Siracusa, Italy 20 F6 37 4N 15 17 E
Sirajganj, Bangla. 43 G13 24 25N 89 47 E
Sirathu, India 43 G9 25 39N 81 19 E
Sīrdān, Iran 45 B6 36 39N 49 12 E
Sirdaryo = Syrdarya →, Kazakstan 26 E7 46 3N 61 0 E
Siren, U.S.A. 80 C8 45 47N 92 24W
Sirer, Spain 22 C7 38 56N 1 22 E
Siret →, Romania 17 F14 45 24N 28 1 E
Sirghāyā, Syria 47 B5 33 51N 36 8 E
Sirmaur, India 43 G9 24 51N 81 23 E
Sirohi, India 42 G5 24 52N 72 53 E
Sironj, India 42 G7 24 5N 77 39 E
Síros, Greece 21 F11 37 28N 24 57 E
Sirretta Pk., U.S.A. 85 K8 35 56N 118 19W
Sīrrī, Iran 45 E7 25 55N 54 32 E
Sirsa, India 42 E6 29 33N 75 4 E
Sirsa →, India 43 F8 26 51N 79 4 E
Sisak, Croatia 16 F9 45 30N 16 21 E
Sisaket, Thailand 38 E5 15 8N 104 23 E
Sishen, S. Africa 56 D3 27 47S 22 59 E
Sishui, Henan, China 34 G7 34 48N 113 15 E
Sishui, Shandong, China 35 G9 35 42N 117 18 E
Sisipuk L., Canada 73 B8 55 45N 101 50W
Sisophon, Cambodia 38 F4 13 38N 102 59 E
Sisseton, U.S.A. 80 C6 45 40N 97 3W
Sīstān, Asia 45 D9 30 50N 61 0 E
Sīstān, Daryācheh-ye, Iran 40 D2 31 0N 61 0 E
Sīstān va Balūchestān □, Iran 45 E9 27 0N 62 0 E
Sisters, U.S.A. 82 D3 44 18N 121 33W
Siswa Bazar, India 43 F10 27 9N 83 46 E
Sitamarhi, India 43 F11 26 37N 85 30 E
Sitapur, India 43 F9 27 38N 80 45 E
Siteki, Swaziland 57 D5 26 32S 31 58 E
Sitges, Spain 19 B6 41 17N 1 47 E
Sitía, Greece 23 D8 35 13N 26 6 E
Sitka, U.S.A. 72 B1 57 3N 135 20W
Sitoti, Botswana 56 C3 23 15S 23 40 E
Sittang Myit →, Burma 41 L20 17 20N 96 45 E
Sittard, Neths. 15 C5 51 0N 5 52 E
Sittingbourne, U.K. 11 F8 51 21N 0 45 E
Sittwe, Burma 41 J18 20 18N 92 45 E
Situbondo, Indonesia 37 G16 7 42S 114 0 E
Siuna, Nic. 88 D3 13 37N 84 45W
Siuri, India 43 H12 23 50N 87 34 E
Sīvand, Iran 45 D7 30 5N 52 55 E
Sivas, Turkey 25 G6 39 43N 36 58 E
Siverek, Turkey 44 B3 37 50N 39 19 E
Sivomaskinskiy, Russia 24 A11 66 40N 62 35 E
Sivrihisar, Turkey 25 G5 39 30N 31 35 E
Sîwa, Egypt 51 C11 29 11N 25 31 E
Siwa Oasis, Egypt 48 D6 29 10N 25 30 E
Siwalik Range, Nepal 43 F10 28 0N 83 0 E
Siwan, India 43 F11 26 13N 84 21 E
Siwana, India 42 G5 25 38N 72 25 E
Sixmilebridge, Ireland 13 D3 52 44N 8 46W
Sixth Cataract, Sudan 51 E12 16 20N 32 42 E
Siziwang Qi, China 34 D6 41 25N 111 40 E
Sjælland, Denmark 9 J14 55 30N 11 30 E
Sjumen = Shumen, Bulgaria 21 C12 43 18N 26 55 E
Skadarsko Jezero, Montenegro, Yug. 21 C8 42 10N 19 20 E
Skaftafell, Iceland 8 D5 64 1N 17 0W
Skagafjörður, Iceland 8 D4 65 54N 19 35W
Skagastølstindane, Norway 9 F12 61 28N 7 52 E
Skagaströnd, Iceland 8 D3 65 50N 20 19W
Skagen, Denmark 9 H14 57 43N 10 35 E
Skagerrak, Denmark 9 H13 57 30N 9 0 E
Skagit →, U.S.A. 84 B4 48 23N 122 22W
Skagway, U.S.A. 68 C6 59 28N 135 19W
Skala-Podilska, Ukraine 17 D14 48 50N 26 15 E
Skala Podolskaya = Skala-Podilska, Ukraine 17 D14 48 50N 26 15 E
Skalat, Ukraine 17 D13 49 23N 25 55 E
Skåne, Sweden 9 J15 55 59N 13 30 E
Skaneateles, U.S.A. 79 D8 42 57N 76 26W
Skaneateles L., U.S.A. 79 D8 42 51N 76 22W
Skara, Sweden 9 G15 58 25N 13 30 E
Skardu, Pakistan 43 B6 35 20N 75 44 E
Skarżysko-Kamienna, Poland 17 C11 51 7N 20 52 E
Skeena →, Canada 72 C2 54 9N 130 5W
Skeena Mts., Canada 72 B3 56 40N 128 30W
Skegness, U.K. 10 D8 53 9N 0 20 E
Skeldon, Guyana 92 B7 5 55N 57 20W
Skellefte älv →, Sweden 8 D19 64 45N 21 10 E
Skellefteå, Sweden 8 D19 64 45N 20 50 E
Skelleftehamn, Sweden 8 D19 64 40N 21 9 E
Skerries, The, U.K. 10 D3 53 25N 4 36W
Ski, Norway 9 G14 59 43N 10 52 E
Skiathos, Greece 21 E10 39 12N 23 30 E
Skibbereen, Ireland 13 E2 51 33N 9 16W
Skiddaw, U.K. 10 C4 54 39N 3 9W
Skidegate, Canada 72 C2 53 15N 132 1W
Skien, Norway 9 G13 59 12N 9 35 E
Skierniewice, Poland 17 C11 51 58N 20 10 E
Skikda, Algeria 50 A7 36 50N 6 58 E
Skilloura, Cyprus 23 D12 35 14N 33 10 E
Skipton, U.K. 10 D5 53 58N 2 3W
Skirmish Pt., Australia 62 A1 11 59S 134 17 E
Skíros, Greece 21 E11 38 55N 24 34 E
Skive, Denmark 9 H13 56 33N 9 2 E
Skjálfandafljót →, Iceland 8 D5 65 59N 17 25W
Skjálfandi, Iceland 8 C5 66 5N 17 30W
Skoghall, Sweden 9 G15 59 20N 13 30 E
Skole, Ukraine 17 D12 49 3N 23 30 E
Skópelos, Greece 21 E10 39 9N 23 47 E
Skopí, Greece 23 D8 35 11N 26 2 E
Skopje, Macedonia 21 C9 42 1N 21 26 E
Skövde, Sweden 9 G15 58 24N 13 50 E
Skovorodino, Russia 27 D13 54 0N 124 0 E
Skowhegan, U.S.A. 77 C11 44 46N 69 43W
Skull, Ireland 13 E2 51 32N 9 34W
Skunk →, U.S.A. 80 E9 40 42N 91 7W
Skuodas, Lithuania 9 H19 56 16N 21 33 E
Skvyra, Ukraine 17 D15 49 44N 29 40 E
Skye, U.K. 12 D2 57 15N 6 10W
Skykomish, U.S.A. 82 C3 47 42N 121 22W
Skyros = Skíros, Greece 21 E11 38 55N 24 34 E
Slættaratindur, Færoe Is. 8 E9 62 18N 7 1W
Slagelse, Denmark 9 J14 55 23N 11 19 E
Slamet, Indonesia 37 G13 7 16S 109 8 E
Slaney →, Ireland 13 D5 52 26N 6 33W
Śląsk, Poland 16 C9 51 0N 16 30 E
Slate Is., Canada 70 C2 48 40N 87 0W
Slatina, Romania 17 F13 44 28N 24 22 E
Slatington, U.S.A. 79 F9 40 45N 75 37W
Slaton, U.S.A. 81 J4 33 26N 101 39W
Slave →, Canada 72 A6 61 18N 113 39W
Slave Coast, W. Afr. 50 G6 6 0N 2 30 E
Slave Lake, Canada 72 B6 55 17N 114 43W
Slave Pt., Canada 72 A5 61 11N 115 56W
Slavgorod, Russia 26 D8 53 1N 78 37 E
Slavonski Brod, Croatia 21 B8 45 11N 18 1 E
Slavuta, Ukraine 17 C14 50 15N 27 2 E
Slavyanka, Russia 30 C5 42 53N 131 21 E
Slavyansk = Slovyansk, Ukraine 25 E6 48 55N 37 36 E
Slawharad, Belarus 17 B16 53 27N 31 0 E
Sleaford, U.K. 10 D7 53 0N 0 24W
Sleaford B., Australia 63 E2 34 55S 135 45 E
Sleat, Sd. of, U.K. 12 D3 57 5N 5 47W
Sleeper Is., Canada 69 C11 58 30N 81 0W
Sleepy Eye, U.S.A. 80 C7 44 18N 94 43W
Slemon L., Canada 72 A5 63 13N 116 4W
Slide Mt., U.S.A. 79 E10 42 0N 74 25W
Slidell, U.S.A. 81 K10 30 17N 89 47W
Sliema, Malta 23 D2 35 54N 14 30 E
Slieve Aughty, Ireland 13 C3 53 4N 8 30W
Slieve Bloom, Ireland 13 C4 53 4N 7 40W
Slieve Donard, U.K. 13 B6 54 11N 5 55W
Slieve Gamph, Ireland 13 B3 54 6N 9 0W
Slieve Gullion, U.K. 13 B5 54 7N 6 26W
Slieve Mish, Ireland 13 D2 52 12N 9 50W
Slievenamon, Ireland 13 D4 52 25N 7 34W
Sligeach = Sligo, Ireland 13 B3 54 16N 8 28W
Sligo, Ireland 13 B3 54 16N 8 28W
Sligo, U.S.A. 78 E5 41 6N 79 29W
Sligo □, Ireland 13 B3 54 8N 8 42W
Sligo B., Ireland 13 B3 54 18N 8 40W
Slippery Rock, U.S.A. 78 E4 41 3N 80 3W
Slite, Sweden 9 H18 57 42N 18 48 E
Sliven, Bulgaria 21 C12 42 42N 26 19 E
Sloan, U.S.A. 85 K11 35 57N 115 13W
Sloansville, U.S.A. 79 D10 42 45N 74 22W
Slobodskoy, Russia 24 C9 58 40N 50 6 E
Slobozia, Romania 17 F14 44 34N 27 23 E
Slocan, Canada 72 D5 49 48N 117 28W
Slonim, Belarus 17 B13 53 4N 25 19 E
Slough, U.K. 11 F7 51 30N 0 36W
Slough □, U.K. 11 F7 51 30N 0 36W
Sloughhouse, U.S.A. 84 G5 38 26N 121 12W
Slovak Rep. ■, Europe 17 D10 48 30N 20 0 E
Slovakia = Slovak Rep. ■, Europe 17 D10 48 30N 20 0 E
Slovakian Ore Mts. = Slovenské Rudohorie, Slovak Rep. 17 D10 48 45N 20 0 E
Slovenia ■, Europe 16 F8 45 58N 14 30 E
Slovenija = Slovenia ■, Europe 16 F8 45 58N 14 30 E
Slovenské Rudohorie, Slovak Rep. 17 D10 48 45N 20 0 E
Slovyansk, Ukraine 25 E6 48 55N 37 36 E
Sluch →, Ukraine 17 C14 51 37N 26 38 E
Sluis, Neths. 15 C3 51 18N 3 23 E
Słupsk, Poland 17 A9 54 30N 17 3 E
Slurry, S. Africa 56 D4 25 49S 25 42 E
Slutsk, Belarus 17 B14 53 2N 27 31 E
Slyne Hd., Ireland 13 C1 53 25N 10 10W
Slyudyanka, Russia 27 D11 51 40N 103 40 E
Småland, Sweden 9 H16 57 15N 15 25 E
Smalltree L., Canada 73 A8 61 0N 105 0W
Smallwood Res., Canada 71 B7 54 0N 64 0W
Smara, Morocco 50 B4 32 9N 8 16W
Smarhon, Belarus 17 A14 54 20N 26 24 E
Smartt Syndicate Dam, S. Africa 56 E3 30 45S 23 10 E
Smartville, U.S.A. 84 F5 39 13N 121 18W
Smeaton, Canada 73 C8 53 30N 104 49W
Smederevo, Serbia, Yug. 21 B9 44 40N 20 57 E
Smerwick Harbour, Ireland 13 D1 52 12N 10 23W
Smethport, U.S.A. 78 E6 41 49N 78 27W
Smidovich, Russia 27 E14 48 36N 133 49 E
Smith, Canada 72 B6 55 10N 114 0W
Smith Center, U.S.A. 80 F5 39 47N 98 47W
Smith Sund, Greenland 4 B4 78 30N 74 0W
Smithburne →, Australia 62 B3 17 3S 140 57 E
Smithers, Canada 72 C3 54 45N 127 10W
Smithfield, S. Africa 57 E4 30 9S 26 30 E
Smithfield, N.C., U.S.A. 77 H6 35 31N 78 21W
Smithfield, Utah, U.S.A. 82 F8 41 50N 111 50W
Smiths Falls, Canada 79 B9 44 55N 76 0W
Smithton, Australia 62 G4 40 53S 145 6 E
Smithville, Canada 78 C5 43 6N 79 33W
Smithville, U.S.A. 81 K6 30 1N 97 10W
Smoky →, Canada 72 B5 56 10N 117 21W
Smoky Bay, Australia 63 E1 32 22S 134 13 E
Smoky Hill →, U.S.A. 80 F6 39 4N 96 48W
Smoky Hills, U.S.A. 80 F5 39 15N 99 30W
Smoky Lake, Canada 72 C6 54 10N 112 30W
Smøla, Norway 8 E13 63 23N 8 3 E
Smolensk, Russia 24 D5 54 45N 32 5 E
Smolikas, Óros, Greece 21 D9 40 9N 20 58 E
Smolyan, Bulgaria 21 D11 41 36N 24 38 E
Smooth Rock Falls, Canada 70 C3 49 17N 81 37W
Smoothstone L., Canada 73 C7 54 40N 106 50W
Smorgon = Smarhon, Belarus 17 A14 54 20N 26 24 E
Smyrna = İzmir, Turkey 21 E12 38 25N 27 8 E
Smyrna, U.S.A. 76 F8 39 18N 75 36W
Snæfell, Iceland 8 D6 64 48N 15 34W
Snaefell, U.K. 10 C3 54 16N 4 27W
Snæfellsjökull, Iceland 8 D2 64 49N 23 46W
Snake →, U.S.A. 82 C4 46 12N 119 2W
Snake I., Australia 63 F4 38 47S 146 33 E
Snake Range, U.S.A. 82 G6 39 0N 114 20W
Snake River Plain, U.S.A. 82 E7 42 50N 114 0W
Snåsavatnet, Norway 8 D14 64 12N 12 0 E
Sneek, Neths. 15 A5 53 2N 5 40 E
Sneeuberge, S. Africa 56 E3 31 46S 24 20 E
Snelling, U.S.A. 84 H6 37 31N 120 26W
Sněžka, Europe 16 C8 50 41N 15 50 E
Snizort, L., U.K. 12 D2 57 33N 6 28W
Snøhetta, Norway 9 E13 62 19N 9 16 E
Snohomish, U.S.A. 84 C4 47 55N 122 6W
Snoul, Cambodia 39 F6 12 4N 106 26 E
Snow Hill, U.S.A. 76 F8 38 11N 75 24W
Snow Lake, Canada 73 C8 54 52N 100 3W
Snow Mt., Calif., U.S.A. 84 F4 39 23N 122 45W
Snow Mt., Maine, U.S.A. 79 A14 45 18N 70 48W
Snow Shoe, U.S.A. 78 E7 41 2N 77 57W
Snowbird L., Canada 73 A8 60 45N 103 0W
Snowdon, U.K. 10 D3 53 4N 4 5W
Snowdrift →, Canada 73 A6 62 24N 110 44W
Snowflake, U.S.A. 83 J8 34 30N 110 5W
Snowshoe Pk., U.S.A. 82 B6 48 13N 115 41W
Snowtown, Australia 63 E2 33 46S 138 14 E
Snowville, U.S.A. 82 F7 41 58N 112 43W
Snowy →, Australia 63 F4 37 46S 148 30 E
Snowy Mt., U.S.A. 79 C10 43 42N 74 23W
Snowy Mts., Australia 63 F4 36 30S 148 20 E
Snug Corner, Bahamas 89 B5 22 33N 73 52W
Snyatyn, Ukraine 17 D13 48 27N 25 38 E
Snyder, Okla., U.S.A. 81 H5 34 40N 98 57W
Snyder, Tex., U.S.A. 81 J4 32 44N 100 55W
Soahanina, Madag. 57 B7 18 42S 44 13 E
Soalala, Madag. 57 B8 16 6S 45 20 E
Soan →, Pakistan 42 C4 33 1N 71 44 E
Soanierana-Ivongo, Madag. 57 B8 16 55S 49 35 E
Sobat, Nahr →, Sudan 51 G12 9 22N 31 33 E
Sobhapur, India 42 H8 22 47N 78 17 E
Sobradinho, Reprêsa de, Brazil 93 E10 9 30S 42 0 E
Sobral, Brazil 93 D10 3 50S 40 20W
Soc Trang, Vietnam 39 H5 9 37N 105 50 E
Socastee, U.S.A. 77 J6 33 41N 79 1W
Soch'e = Shache, China 32 C2 38 20N 77 10 E
Sochi, Russia 25 F6 43 35N 39 40 E
Société, Is. de la, Pac. Oc. 65 J12 17 0S 151 0W
Society Is. = Société, Is. de la, Pac. Oc. 65 J12 17 0S 151 0W
Socompa, Portezuelo de, Chile 94 A2 24 27S 68 18W
Socorro, N. Mex., U.S.A. 83 J10 34 4N 106 54W
Socorro, Tex., U.S.A. 83 L10 31 39N 106 18W
Socorro, I., Mexico 86 D2 18 45N 110 58W
Socotra, Ind. Oc. 46 E5 12 30N 54 0 E
Soda L., U.S.A. 83 J5 35 10N 116 4W
Soda Plains, India 43 B8 35 30N 79 0 E
Soda Springs, U.S.A. 82 E8 42 39N 111 36W
Sodankylä, Finland 8 C22 67 29N 26 40 E
Soddy-Daisy, U.S.A. 77 H3 35 17N 85 10W
Söderhamn, Sweden 9 F17 61 18N 17 10 E
Söderköping, Sweden 9 G17 58 31N 16 20 E
Södermanland, Sweden 9 G17 58 56N 16 55 E
Södertälje, Sweden 9 G17 59 12N 17 39 E
Sodiri, Sudan 51 F11 14 27N 29 0 E
Sodus, U.S.A. 78 C7 43 14N 77 4W
Soekmekaar, S. Africa 57 C4 23 30S 29 55 E
Soest, Neths. 15 B5 52 9N 5 19 E
Sofia = Sofiya, Bulgaria 21 C10 42 45N 23 20 E
Sofia →, Madag. 57 B8 15 27S 47 23 E
Sofiya, Bulgaria 21 C10 42 45N 23 20 E
Sōfu-Gan, Japan 31 K10 29 49N 140 21 E
Sogamoso, Colombia 92 B4 5 43N 72 56W
Sogār, Iran 45 E8 25 53N 58 6 E
Sogndalsfjøra, Norway 9 F12 61 14N 7 5 E
Søgne, Norway 9 G12 58 5N 7 48 E
Sognefjorden, Norway 9 F11 61 10N 5 50 E
Sŏgwipo, S. Korea 35 H14 33 13N 126 34 E
Soh, Iran 45 C6 33 26N 51 27 E
Sohâg, Egypt 51 C12 26 33N 31 43 E
Sohagpur, India 42 H8 22 42N 78 12 E
Sŏhori, N. Korea 35 D15 40 7N 128 23 E
Soignies, Belgium 15 D4 50 35N 4 5 E
Soissons, France 18 B5 49 25N 3 19 E
Sōja, Japan 31 G6 34 40N 133 45 E
Sojat, India 42 G5 25 55N 73 45 E
Sokal, Ukraine 17 C13 50 31N 24 15 E
Söke, Turkey 21 F12 37 48N 27 28 E
Sokelo, Dem. Rep. of the Congo 55 D1 9 55S 24 36 E
Sokhumi, Georgia 25 F7 43 0N 41 0 E
Sokodé, Togo 50 G6 9 0N 1 11 E
Sokol, Russia 24 C7 59 30N 40 5 E
Sokółka, Poland 17 B12 53 25N 23 30 E
Sokołów Podlaski, Poland 17 B12 52 25N 22 15 E
Sokoto, Nigeria 50 F7 13 2N 5 16 E
Sol Iletsk, Russia 24 D10 51 10N 55 0 E
Solai, Kenya 54 B4 0 2N 36 12 E
Solan, India 42 D7 30 55N 77 7 E
Solano, Phil. 37 A6 16 31N 121 15 E
Solapur, India 40 L9 17 43N 75 56 E
Soldotna, U.S.A. 68 B4 60 29N 151 3W
Soléa □, Cyprus 23 D12 35 5N 33 4 E
Soledad, Colombia 92 A4 10 55N 74 46W
Soledad, U.S.A. 84 J5 36 26N 121 20W
Soledad, Venezuela 92 B6 8 10N 63 34W
Solent, The, U.K. 11 G6 50 45N 1 25W
Solfonn, Norway 9 F12 60 2N 6 57 E

Vestfjorden

Vestfjorden, Norway 8 C15 67 55N 14 0 E
Vestmannaeyjar, Iceland 8 E3 63 27N 20 15W
Vestspitsbergen, Svalbard 4 B8 78 40N 17 0 E
Vestvågøy, Norway 8 B15 68 18N 13 50 E
Vesuvio, Italy 20 D6 40 49N 14 26 E
Vesuvius, Mt. = Vesuvio, Italy 20 D6 40 49N 14 26 E
Veszprém, Hungary 17 E9 47 8N 17 57 E
Vetlanda, Sweden 9 H16 57 24N 15 3 E
Vetlugu →, Russia 24 C8 56 36N 46 4 E
Vettore, Mte., Italy 20 C5 42 49N 13 16 E
Veurne, Belgium 15 C2 51 5N 2 40 E
Veys, Iran 45 D6 31 30N 49 0 E
Vezhen, Bulgaria 21 C11 42 50N 24 20 E
Vi Thanh, Vietnam 39 H5 9 42N 105 26 E
Viacha, Bolivia 92 G5 16 39S 68 18W
Viamão, Brazil 95 C5 30 5S 51 0W
Viana, Brazil 93 D10 3 13S 44 55W
Viana do Alentejo, Portugal 19 C2 38 17N 7 59W
Viana do Castelo, Portugal 19 B1 41 42N 8 50W
Vianden, Lux. 15 E6 49 56N 6 12 E
Vianópolis, Brazil 93 G9 16 40S 48 35W
Viaréggio, Italy 20 C4 43 52N 10 14 E
Vibo Valéntia, Italy 20 E7 38 40N 16 6 E
Viborg, Denmark 9 H13 56 27N 9 23 E
Vic, Spain 19 B7 41 58N 2 19 E
Vicenza, Italy 20 B4 45 33N 11 33 E
Vich = Vic, Spain 19 B7 41 58N 2 19 E
Vichada →, Colombia 92 C5 4 55N 67 50W
Vichy, France 18 C5 46 9N 3 26 E
Vicksburg, Ariz., U.S.A. 85 M13 33 45N 113 45W
Vicksburg, Miss., U.S.A. 81 J9 32 21N 90 53W
Victor, India 42 J4 21 0N 71 30 E
Victor, U.S.A. 78 D7 42 58N 77 24W
Victor Harbor, Australia 63 F2 35 30S 138 37 E
Victoria = Labuan, Malaysia 36 C5 5 20N 115 14 E
Victoria, Argentina 94 C3 32 40S 60 10W
Victoria, Canada 72 D4 48 30N 123 25W
Victoria, Chile 96 D2 38 13S 72 20W
Victoria, Malta 23 C1 36 2N 14 14 E
Victoria, Kans., U.S.A. 80 F5 38 52N 99 9W
Victoria, Tex., U.S.A. 81 L6 28 48N 97 0W
Victoria □, Australia 63 F3 37 0S 144 0 E
Victoria →, Australia 60 C4 15 10S 129 40 E
Victoria, Grand L., Canada 70 C4 47 31N 77 30W
Victoria, L., Africa 54 C3 1 0S 33 0 E
Victoria, L., Australia 63 E3 33 57S 141 15 E
Victoria Beach, Canada 73 C9 50 40N 96 35W
Victoria de Durango = Durango, Mexico 86 C4 24 3N 104 39W
Victoria de las Tunas, Cuba 88 B4 20 58N 76 59W
Victoria Falls, Zimbabwe 55 F2 17 58S 25 52 E
Victoria Harbour, Canada 78 B5 44 45N 79 45W
Victoria I., Canada 68 A8 71 0N 111 0W
Victoria L., Canada 71 C8 48 20N 57 27W
Victoria Ld., Antarctica 5 D11 75 0S 160 0 E
Victoria Nile →, Uganda 54 B3 2 14N 31 26 E
Victoria River, Australia 60 C5 16 25S 131 0 E
Victoria Str., Canada 68 B9 69 30N 100 0W
Victoria Taungdeik, Burma 41 J18 21 15N 93 55 E
Victoria West, S. Africa 56 E3 31 25S 23 4 E
Victoriaville, Canada 71 C5 46 4N 71 56W
Victorica, Argentina 94 D2 36 20S 65 30W
Victorville, U.S.A. 85 L9 34 32N 117 18W
Vicuña, Chile 94 C1 30 0S 70 50W
Vicuña Mackenna, Argentina 94 C3 33 53S 64 25W
Vidal, U.S.A. 85 L12 34 7N 114 31W
Vidal Junction, U.S.A. 85 L12 34 11N 114 34W
Vidalia, U.S.A. 77 J4 32 13N 82 25W
Vídho, Greece 23 A3 39 38N 19 55 E
Vidin, Bulgaria 21 C10 43 59N 22 50 E
Vidisha, India 42 H7 23 28N 77 53 E
Vidzy, Belarus 9 J22 55 23N 26 37 E
Viedma, Argentina 96 E4 40 50S 63 0W
Viedma, L., Argentina 96 F2 49 30S 72 30W
Vielsalm, Belgium 15 D5 50 17N 5 54 E
Vienna = Wien, Austria 16 D9 48 12N 16 22 E
Vienna, Ill., U.S.A. 81 G10 37 25N 88 54W
Vienna, Mo., U.S.A. 80 F9 38 11N 91 57W
Vienne, France 18 D6 45 31N 4 53 E
Vienne →, France 18 C4 47 13N 0 5 E
Vientiane, Laos 38 D4 17 58N 102 36 E
Vientos, Paso de los, Caribbean 89 C5 20 0N 74 0W
Vierzon, France 18 C5 47 13N 2 5 E
Vietnam ■, Asia 38 C6 19 0N 106 0 E
Vigan, Phil. 37 A6 17 35N 120 28 E
Vigévano, Italy 18 D8 45 19N 8 51 E
Vigia, Brazil 93 D9 0 50S 48 5W
Vigía Chico, Mexico 87 D7 19 46N 87 35W
Víglas, Ákra, Greece 23 D9 35 54N 27 51 E
Vigo, Spain 19 A1 42 12N 8 41W
Vihowa, Pakistan 42 D4 31 8N 70 30 E
Vihowa →, Pakistan 42 D4 31 8N 70 41 E
Vijayawada, India 41 L12 16 31N 80 39 E
Vík, Iceland 8 E4 63 25N 19 1W
Vikeke, Indonesia 37 F7 8 52S 126 23 E
Viking, Canada 72 C6 53 7N 111 50W
Vikna, Norway 8 D14 64 55N 10 58 E
Vila da Maganja, Mozam. 55 F4 17 18S 37 30 E
Vila de João Belo = Xai-Xai, Mozam. 57 D5 25 6S 33 31 E
Vila do Bispo, Portugal 19 D1 37 5N 8 53W
Vila do Chibuto, Mozam. 57 C5 24 40S 33 33 E
Vila Franca de Xira, Portugal 19 C1 38 57N 8 59W
Vila Gamito, Mozam. 55 E3 14 12S 33 0 E
Vila Gomes da Costa, Mozam. 57 C5 24 20S 33 37 E
Vila Machado, Mozam. 55 F3 19 15S 34 14 E
Vila Mouzinho, Mozam. 55 E3 14 48S 34 25 E
Vila Nova de Gaia, Portugal 19 B1 41 8N 8 37W
Vila Real, Portugal 19 B2 41 17N 7 48W
Vila-real de los Infantes, Spain 19 C5 39 55N 0 3W
Vila Real de Santo António, Portugal 19 D2 37 10N 7 28W
Vila Vasco da Gama, Mozam. 55 E3 14 54S 32 14 E
Vila Velha, Brazil 95 A7 20 20S 40 17W
Vilagarcía de Arousa, Spain 19 A1 42 34N 8 46W
Vilaine →, France 18 C2 47 30N 2 27W
Vilanandro, Tanjona, Madag. 57 B7 16 11S 44 27 E
Vilanculos, Mozam. 57 C6 22 1S 35 17 E
Vilanova i la Geltrú, Spain 19 B6 41 13N 1 40 E
Vileyka, Belarus 17 A14 54 30N 26 53 E
Vilhelmina, Sweden 8 D17 64 35N 16 39 E
Vilhena, Brazil 92 F6 12 40S 60 5W
Viliga, Russia 27 C16 61 36N 156 56 E
Viliya →, Lithuania 9 J21 55 8N 24 16 E
Viljandi, Estonia 9 G21 58 28N 25 30 E
Vilkitskogo, Proliv, Russia 27 B11 78 0N 103 0 E
Vilkovo = Vylkove, Ukraine 17 F15 45 28N 29 32 E
Villa Abecia, Bolivia 94 A2 21 0S 68 18W
Villa Ahumada, Mexico 86 A3 30 38N 106 30W
Villa Ana, Argentina 94 B4 28 28S 59 40W
Villa Ángela, Argentina 94 B3 27 34S 60 45W
Villa Bella, Bolivia 92 F5 10 25S 65 22W
Villa Bens = Tarfaya, Morocco 50 C3 27 55N 12 55W
Villa Cañás, Argentina 94 C3 34 0S 61 35W
Villa Cisneros = Dakhla, W. Sahara 50 D2 23 50N 15 53W
Villa Colón, Argentina 94 C2 31 38S 68 20W
Villa Constitución, Argentina 94 C3 33 15S 60 20W
Villa de María, Argentina 94 B3 29 55S 63 43W
Villa Dolores, Argentina 94 C2 31 58S 65 15W
Villa Frontera, Mexico 86 B4 26 56N 101 27W
Villa Guillermina, Argentina 94 B4 28 15S 59 29W
Villa Hayes, Paraguay 94 B4 25 5S 57 20W
Villa Iris, Argentina 94 D3 38 12S 63 12W
Villa Juárez, Mexico 86 B4 27 37N 100 44W
Villa María, Argentina 94 C3 32 20S 63 10W
Villa Mazán, Argentina 94 B2 28 40S 66 30W
Villa Montes, Bolivia 94 A3 21 10S 63 30W
Villa Ocampo, Argentina 94 B4 28 30S 59 20W
Villa Ocampo, Mexico 86 B3 26 29N 105 30W
Villa Ojo de Agua, Argentina 94 B3 29 30S 63 44W
Villa San José, Argentina 94 C4 32 12S 58 15W
Villa San Martín, Argentina 94 B3 28 15S 64 9W
Villa Unión, Mexico 86 C3 23 12N 106 14W
Villacarlos, Spain 22 B11 39 53N 4 17 E
Villacarrillo, Spain 19 C4 38 7N 3 3W
Villach, Austria 16 E7 46 37N 13 51 E
Villafranca de los Caballeros, Spain 22 B10 39 34N 3 25 E
Villagrán, Mexico 87 C5 24 29N 99 29W
Villaguay, Argentina 94 C4 32 0S 59 0W
Villahermosa, Mexico 87 D6 17 59N 92 55W
Villajoyosa, Spain 19 C5 38 30N 0 12W
Villalba, Spain 19 A2 43 26N 7 40W
Villanueva, U.S.A. 81 H2 35 16N 105 22W
Villanueva de la Serena, Spain 19 C3 38 59N 5 50W
Villanueva y Geltrú = Vilanova i la Geltrú, Spain 19 B6 41 13N 1 40 E
Villarreal = Vila-real de los Infantes, Spain 19 C5 39 55N 0 3W
Villarrica, Chile 96 D2 39 15S 72 15W
Villarrica, Paraguay 94 B4 25 40S 56 30W
Villarrobledo, Spain 19 C4 39 18N 2 36W
Villavicencio, Argentina 94 C2 32 28S 69 0W
Villavicencio, Colombia 92 C4 4 9N 73 37W
Villaviciosa, Spain 19 A3 43 32N 5 27W
Villazón, Bolivia 94 A2 22 0S 65 35W
Ville-Marie, Canada 70 C4 47 20N 79 30W
Ville Platte, U.S.A. 81 K8 30 41N 92 17W
Villena, Spain 19 C5 38 39N 0 52W
Villeneuve-d'Ascq, France 18 A5 50 38N 3 9 E
Villeneuve-sur-Lot, France 18 D4 44 24N 0 42 E
Villiers, S. Africa 57 D4 27 2S 28 36 E
Villingen-Schwenningen, Germany 16 D5 48 3N 8 26 E
Vilna, Canada 72 C6 54 7N 111 55W
Vilnius, Lithuania 9 J21 54 38N 25 19 E
Vilvoorde, Belgium 15 D4 50 56N 4 26 E
Vilyuy →, Russia 27 C13 64 24N 126 26 E
Vilyuysk, Russia 27 C13 63 40N 121 35 E
Viña del Mar, Chile 94 C1 33 0S 71 30W
Vinarós, Spain 19 B6 40 30N 0 27 E
Vincennes, U.S.A. 76 F2 38 41N 87 32W
Vincent, U.S.A. 85 L8 34 33N 118 11W
Vinchina, Argentina 94 B2 28 45S 68 15W
Vindelälven →, Sweden 8 E18 63 55N 19 50 E
Vindeln, Sweden 8 D18 64 12N 19 43 E
Vindhya Ra., India 42 H7 22 50N 77 0 E
Vineland, U.S.A. 76 F8 39 29N 75 2W
Vinh, Vietnam 38 C5 18 45N 105 38 E
Vinh Linh, Vietnam 38 D6 17 4N 107 2 E
Vinh Long, Vietnam 39 G5 10 16N 105 57 E
Vinita, U.S.A. 81 G7 36 39N 95 9W
Vinkovci, Croatia 21 B8 45 19N 18 48 E
Vinnitsa = Vinnytsya, Ukraine 17 D15 49 15N 28 30 E
Vinnytsya, Ukraine 17 D15 49 15N 28 30 E
Vinton, Calif., U.S.A. 84 F6 39 48N 120 10W
Vinton, Iowa, U.S.A. 80 D8 42 10N 92 1W
Vinton, La., U.S.A. 81 K8 30 11N 93 35W
Virac, Phil. 37 B6 13 30N 124 20 E
Virachei, Cambodia 38 F6 13 59N 106 49 E
Virago Sd., Canada 72 C2 54 0N 132 30W
Viramgam, India 42 H5 23 5N 72 0 E
Viranşehir, Turkey 44 B3 37 13N 39 45 E
Virawah, Pakistan 42 G4 24 31N 70 46 E
Virden, Canada 73 D8 49 50N 100 56W
Vire, France 18 B3 48 50N 0 53W
Vírgenes, C., Argentina 96 G3 52 19S 68 21W
Virgin →, U.S.A. 83 H6 36 28N 114 21W
Virgin Gorda, Virgin Is. 89 C7 18 30N 64 26W
Virgin Is. (British) ■, W. Indies 89 C7 18 30N 64 30W
Virgin Is. (U.S.) ■, W. Indies 89 C7 18 20N 65 0W
Virginia, S. Africa 56 D4 28 8S 26 55 E
Virginia, U.S.A. 80 B8 47 31N 92 32W
Virginia □, U.S.A. 76 G7 37 30N 78 45W
Virginia Beach, U.S.A. 76 G8 36 51N 75 59W
Virginia City, Mont., U.S.A. 82 D8 45 18N 111 56W
Virginia City, Nev., U.S.A. 84 F7 39 19N 119 39W
Virginia Falls, Canada 72 A3 61 38N 125 42W
Virginiatown, Canada 70 C4 48 9N 79 36W
Viroqua, U.S.A. 80 D9 43 34N 90 53W
Virovitica, Croatia 20 B7 45 51N 17 21 E
Virpur, India 42 J4 21 51N 70 42 E
Virton, Belgium 15 E5 49 35N 5 32 E
Virudunagar, India 40 Q10 9 30N 77 58 E
Vis, Croatia 20 C7 43 4N 16 10 E
Visalia, U.S.A. 84 J7 36 20N 119 18W
Visayan Sea, Phil. 37 B6 11 30N 123 30 E
Visby, Sweden 9 H18 57 37N 18 18 E
Viscount Melville Sd., Canada 4 B2 74 10N 108 0W
Visé, Belgium 15 D5 50 44N 5 41 E
Višegrad, Bos.-H. 21 C8 43 47N 19 17 E
Viseu, Brazil 93 D9 1 10S 46 5W
Viseu, Portugal 19 B2 40 40N 7 55W
Vishakhapatnam, India 41 L13 17 45N 83 20 E
Visnagar, India 42 H5 23 45N 72 32 E
Viso, Mte., Italy 18 D7 44 38N 7 5 E
Visokoi I., Antarctica 5 B1 56 43S 27 15W
Vista, U.S.A. 85 M9 33 12N 117 14W
Vistula = Wisła →, Poland 17 A10 54 22N 18 55 E
Vitebsk = Vitsyebsk, Belarus 24 C5 55 10N 30 15 E
Viterbo, Italy 20 C5 42 25N 12 6 E
Viti Levu, Fiji 59 C7 17 30S 177 30 E
Vitigudino, Spain 19 B2 41 1N 6 26W
Vitim, Russia 27 D12 59 28N 112 35 E
Vitim →, Russia 27 D12 59 26N 112 34 E
Vitória, Brazil 93 H10 20 20S 40 22W
Vitória da Conquista, Brazil 93 F10 14 51S 40 51W
Vitória de São Antão, Brazil 93 E11 8 10S 35 20W
Vitoria-Gasteiz, Spain 19 A4 42 50N 2 41W
Vitsyebsk, Belarus 24 C5 55 10N 30 15 E
Vittória, Italy 20 F6 36 57N 14 32 E
Vittório Véneto, Italy 20 B5 45 59N 12 18 E
Viveiro, Spain 19 A2 43 39N 7 38W
Vivian, U.S.A. 81 J8 32 53N 93 59W
Vizcaíno, Desierto de, Mexico 86 B2 27 40N 113 50W
Vizcaíno, Sierra, Mexico 86 B2 27 30N 114 0W
Vize, Turkey 21 D12 41 34N 27 45 E
Vizianagaram, India 41 K13 18 6N 83 30 E
Vjosa →, Albania 21 D8 40 37N 19 24 E
Vlaardingen, Neths. 15 C4 51 55N 4 21 E
Vladikavkaz, Russia 25 F7 43 0N 44 35 E
Vladimir, Russia 24 C7 56 15N 40 30 E
Vladimir Volynskiy = Volodymyr-Volynskyy, Ukraine 17 C13 50 50N 24 18 E
Vladivostok, Russia 27 E14 43 10N 131 53 E
Vlieland, Neths. 15 A4 53 16N 4 55 E
Vlissingen, Neths. 15 C3 51 26N 3 34 E
Vlóra, Albania 21 D8 40 32N 19 28 E
Vltava →, Czech Rep. 16 D8 50 21N 14 30 E
Vo Dat, Vietnam 39 G6 11 9N 107 31 E
Voe, U.K. 12 A7 60 21N 1 16W
Vogelkop = Doberai, Jazirah, Indonesia 37 E8 1 25S 133 0 E
Vogelsberg, Germany 16 C5 50 31N 9 12 E
Voghera, Italy 18 D8 44 59N 9 1 E
Vohibinany, Madag. 57 B8 18 49S 49 4 E
Vohimarina = Iharana, Madag. 57 A9 13 25S 50 0 E
Vohimena, Tanjon' i, Madag. 57 D8 25 36S 45 8 E
Vohipeno, Madag. 57 C8 22 22S 47 51 E
Voi, Kenya 54 C4 3 25S 38 32 E
Voiron, France 18 D6 45 22N 5 35 E
Voisey B., Canada 71 A7 56 15N 61 50W
Vojmsjön, Sweden 8 D17 64 55N 16 40 E
Vojvodina □, Serbia, Yug. 21 B9 45 20N 20 0 E
Volborg, U.S.A. 80 C2 45 51N 105 41W
Volcano Is. = Kazan-Rettō, Pac. Oc. 64 E6 25 0N 141 0 E
Volda, Norway 9 E12 62 9N 6 5 E
Volga →, Russia 25 E8 46 0N 48 30 E
Volga Hts. = Privolzhskaya Vozvyshennost, Russia 25 D8 51 0N 46 0 E
Volgodonsk, Russia 25 E7 47 33N 42 5 E
Volgograd, Russia 25 E7 48 40N 44 25 E
Volgogradskoye Vdkhr., Russia 25 E8 50 0N 45 20 E
Volkhov →, Russia 24 B5 60 8N 32 20 E
Volkovysk = Vawkavysk, Belarus 17 B13 53 9N 24 30 E
Volksrust, S. Africa 57 D4 27 24S 29 53 E
Volochanka, Russia 27 B10 71 0N 94 28 E
Volodymyr-Volynskyy, Ukraine 17 C13 50 50N 24 18 E
Vologda, Russia 24 C6 59 10N 39 45 E
Vólos, Greece 21 E10 39 24N 22 59 E
Volovets, Ukraine 17 D12 48 43N 23 11 E
Volozhin = Valozhyn, Belarus 17 A14 54 3N 26 30 E
Volsk, Russia 24 D8 52 5N 47 22 E
Volta →, Ghana 48 F4 5 46N 0 41 E
Volta, L., Ghana 50 G6 7 30N 0 0 E
Volta Redonda, Brazil 95 A7 22 31S 44 5W
Voltaire, C., Australia 60 B4 14 16S 125 35 E
Volterra, Italy 20 C4 43 24N 10 51 E
Volturno →, Italy 20 D5 41 1N 13 55 E
Volzhskiy, Russia 25 E7 48 56N 44 46 E
Vondrozo, Madag. 57 C8 22 49S 47 20 E
Vopnafjörður, Iceland 8 D6 65 45N 14 50W
Vóriai Sporádhes, Greece 21 E10 39 15N 23 30 E
Vorkuta, Russia 24 A11 67 48N 64 20 E
Vormsi, Estonia 9 G20 59 1N 23 13 E
Voronezh, Russia 25 D6 51 40N 39 10 E
Voroshilovgrad = Luhansk, Ukraine 25 E6 48 38N 39 15 E
Voroshilovsk = Alchevsk, Ukraine 25 E6 48 30N 38 45 E
Võrts Järv, Estonia 9 G22 58 16N 26 3 E
Võru, Estonia 9 H22 57 48N 26 54 E
Vosges, France 18 B7 48 20N 7 10 E
Voss, Norway 9 F12 60 38N 6 26 E
Vostok I., Kiribati 65 J12 10 5S 152 23W
Votkinsk, Russia 24 C9 57 0N 53 55 E
Votkinskoye Vdkhr., Russia 24 C10 57 22N 55 12 E
Votsuri-Shima, Japan 31 M1 25 45N 123 29 E
Vouga →, Portugal 19 B1 40 41N 8 40W
Voúxa, Ákra, Greece 23 D5 35 37N 23 32 E
Vozhe, Ozero, Russia 24 B6 60 45N 39 0 E
Voznesensk, Ukraine 25 E5 47 35N 31 21 E
Voznesenye, Russia 24 B6 61 0N 35 28 E
Vrangelya, Ostrov, Russia 27 B19 71 0N 180 0 E
Vranje, Serbia, Yug. 21 C9 42 34N 21 54 E
Vratsa, Bulgaria 21 C10 43 15N 23 30 E
Vrbas →, Bos.-H. 20 B7 45 8N 17 29 E
Vrede, S. Africa 57 D4 27 24S 29 6 E
Vredefort, S. Africa 56 D4 27 0S 27 22 E
Vredenburg, S. Africa 56 E2 32 56S 18 0 E
Vredendal, S. Africa 56 E2 31 41S 18 35 E
Vrindavan, India 42 F7 27 37N 77 40 E
Vríses, Greece 23 D6 35 23N 24 13 E
Vršac, Serbia, Yug. 21 B9 45 8N 21 20 E
Vryburg, S. Africa 56 D3 26 55S 24 45 E
Vryheid, S. Africa 57 D5 27 45S 30 47 E
Vu Liet, Vietnam 38 C5 18 43N 105 23 E
Vukovar, Croatia 21 B8 45 21N 18 59 E
Vulcan, Canada 72 C6 50 25N 113 15W
Vulcan, Romania 17 F12 45 23N 23 17 E
Vulcaneşti, Moldova 17 F15 45 41N 28 18 E
Vulcano, Italy 20 E6 38 24N 14 58 E
Vulkaneshty = Vulcaneşti, Moldova 17 F15 45 41N 28 18 E
Vunduzi →, Mozam. 55 F3 18 56S 34 1 E
Vung Tau, Vietnam 39 G6 10 21N 107 4 E
Vyatka = Kirov, Russia 24 C8 58 35N 49 40 E
Vyatka →, Russia 24 C9 55 37N 51 28 E
Vyatskiye Polyany, Russia 24 C9 56 14N 51 5 E
Vyazemskiy, Russia 27 E14 47 32N 134 45 E
Vyazma, Russia 24 C5 55 10N 34 15 E
Vyborg, Russia 24 B4 60 43N 28 47 E
Vychegda →, Russia 24 B8 61 18N 46 36 E
Vychodné Beskydy, Europe 17 D11 49 20N 22 0 E
Vyg-ozero, Russia 24 B5 63 47N 34 29 E
Vylkove, Ukraine 17 F15 45 28N 29 32 E
Vynohradiv, Ukraine 17 D12 48 9N 23 2 E
Vyrnwy, L., U.K. 10 E4 52 48N 3 31W
Vyshniy Volochek, Russia 24 C5 57 30N 34 30 E
Vyškov, Czech Rep. 17 D9 49 17N 17 0 E
Vytegra, Russia 24 B6 61 0N 36 27 E

W

W.A.C. Bennett Dam, Canada 72 B4 56 2N 122 6W
Waal →, Neths. 15 C5 51 37N 5 0 E
Waalwijk, Neths. 15 C5 51 42N 5 4 E
Wabana, Canada 71 C9 47 40N 53 0W
Wabasca →, Canada 72 B5 58 22N 115 20W
Wabasca-Desmarais, Canada 72 B6 55 57N 113 56W
Wabash, U.S.A. 76 E3 40 48N 85 49W
Wabash →, U.S.A. 76 G1 37 48N 88 2W
Wabigoon L., Canada 73 D10 49 44N 92 44W
Wabowden, Canada 73 C9 54 55N 98 38W
Wabuk Pt., Canada 70 A2 55 20N 85 5W
Wabush, Canada 71 B6 52 55N 66 52W
Waco, U.S.A. 81 K6 31 33N 97 9W
Waconichi, L., Canada 70 B5 50 8N 74 0W
Wad Hamid, Sudan 51 E12 16 30N 32 45 E
Wâd Medanî, Sudan 51 F12 14 28N 33 30 E
Wad Thana, Pakistan 42 F2 27 22N 66 23 E
Wadai, Africa 48 E5 12 0N 19 0 E
Wadayama, Japan 31 G7 35 19N 134 52 E
Waddeneilanden, Neths. 15 A5 53 20N 5 10 E
Waddenzee, Neths. 15 A5 53 6N 5 10 E
Waddington, U.S.A. 79 B9 44 52N 75 12W
Waddington, Mt., Canada 72 C3 51 23N 125 15W
Waddy Pt., Australia 63 C5 24 58S 153 21 E
Wadebridge, U.K. 11 G3 50 31N 4 51W
Wadena, Canada 73 C8 51 57N 103 47W
Wadena, U.S.A. 80 B7 46 26N 95 8W
Wadeye, Australia 60 B4 14 28S 129 52 E
Wadhams, Canada 72 C3 51 30N 127 30W
Wādī as Sīr, Jordan 47 D4 31 56N 35 49 E
Wadi Halfa, Sudan 51 D12 21 53N 31 19 E
Wadsworth, Nev., U.S.A. 82 G4 39 38N 119 17W
Wadsworth, Ohio, U.S.A. 78 E3 41 2N 81 44W
Waegwan, S. Korea 35 G15 35 59N 128 23 E
Wafangdian, China 35 E11 39 38N 121 58 E
Wafrah, Si. Arabia 44 D5 28 33N 47 56 E
Wageningen, Neths. 15 C5 51 58N 5 40 E
Wager B., Canada 69 B11 65 26N 88 40W
Wagga Wagga, Australia 63 F4 35 7S 147 24 E
Waghete, Indonesia 37 E9 4 10S 135 50 E
Wagin, Australia 61 F2 33 17S 117 25 E
Wagner, U.S.A. 80 D5 43 5N 98 18W
Wagon Mound, U.S.A. 81 G2 36 1N 104 42W
Wagoner, U.S.A. 81 H7 35 58N 95 22W
Wah, Pakistan 42 C5 33 45N 72 40 E
Wahai, Indonesia 37 E7 2 48S 129 35 E
Wahiawa, U.S.A. 74 H15 21 30N 158 2W
Wâḥid, Egypt 47 E1 30 48N 32 21 E
Wahnai, Afghan. 42 C1 32 40N 65 50 E
Wahoo, U.S.A. 80 E6 41 13N 96 37W
Wahpeton, U.S.A. 80 B6 46 16N 96 36W
Wai, Koh, Cambodia 39 H4 9 55N 102 55 E
Waiau →, N.Z. 59 K4 42 47S 173 22 E
Waibeem, Indonesia 37 E8 0 30S 132 59 E
Waigeo, Indonesia 37 E8 0 20S 130 40 E
Waihi, N.Z. 59 G5 37 23S 175 52 E
Waihou →, N.Z. 59 G5 37 15S 175 40 E
Waika, Dem. Rep. of the Congo 54 C2 2 22S 25 42 E
Waikabubak, Indonesia 37 F5 9 45S 119 25 E
Waikari, N.Z. 59 K4 42 58S 172 41 E
Waikato →, N.Z. 59 G5 37 23S 174 43 E
Waikerie, Australia 63 E3 34 9S 140 0 E
Waikokopu, N.Z. 59 H6 39 3S 177 52 E
Waikouaiti, N.Z. 59 L3 45 36S 170 41 E
Wailuku, U.S.A. 74 H16 20 53N 156 30W
Waimakariri →, N.Z. 59 K4 43 24S 172 42 E
Waimate, N.Z. 59 L3 44 45S 171 3 E
Wainganga →, India 40 K11 18 50N 79 55 E
Waingapu, Indonesia 37 F6 9 35S 120 11 E
Waini →, Guyana 92 B7 8 20N 59 50W
Wainwright, Canada 73 C6 52 50N 110 50W
Waiouru, N.Z. 59 H5 39 28S 175 41 E
Waipara, N.Z. 59 K4 43 3S 172 46 E
Waipawa, N.Z. 59 H6 39 56S 176 38 E
Waipiro, N.Z. 59 H7 38 2S 178 22 E
Waipu, N.Z. 59 F5 35 59S 174 29 E
Waipukurau, N.Z. 59 J6 40 1S 176 33 E
Wairakei, N.Z. 59 H6 38 37S 176 6 E
Wairarapa, L., N.Z. 59 J5 41 14S 175 15 E
Wairoa, N.Z. 59 H6 39 3S 177 25 E
Waitaki →, N.Z. 59 L3 44 56S 171 7 E
Waitara, N.Z. 59 H5 38 59S 174 15 E
Waitsburg, U.S.A. 82 C5 46 16N 118 9W
Waiuku, N.Z. 59 G5 37 15S 174 45 E
Wajima, Japan 31 F8 37 30N 137 0 E
Wajir, Kenya 54 B5 1 42N 40 5 E
Wakasa, Japan 31 G7 35 20N 134 24 E
Wakasa-Wan, Japan 31 G7 35 40N 135 30 E
Wakatipu, L., N.Z. 59 L2 45 5S 168 33 E
Wakaw, Canada 73 C7 52 39N 105 44W
Wakayama, Japan 31 G7 34 15N 135 15 E
Wakayama □, Japan 31 H7 33 50N 135 30 E
Wake Forest, U.S.A. 77 H6 35 59N 78 30W

West Indies

West Indies, Cent. Amer. 89 D7 15 0N 65 0W
West Jordan, U.S.A. 82 F8 40 36N 111 56W
West Lorne, Canada 78 D3 42 36N 81 36W
West Lothian □, U.K. 12 F5 55 54N 3 36W
West Lunga →, Zambia 55 E1 13 6S 24 39 E
West Memphis, U.S.A. 81 H9 35 9N 90 11W
West Midlands □, U.K. 11 E6 52 26N 2 0W
West Mifflin, U.S.A. 78 F5 40 22N 79 52W
West Milton, U.S.A. 78 E8 41 1N 76 50W
West Monroe, U.S.A. 81 J8 32 31N 92 9W
West Newton, U.S.A. 78 F5 40 14N 79 46W
West Nicholson, Zimbabwe 55 G2 21 2S 29 20 E
West Palm Beach, U.S.A. 77 M5 26 43N 80 3W
West Plains, U.S.A. 81 G9 36 44N 91 51W
West Point, N.Y., U.S.A. 79 E11 41 24N 73 58W
West Point, Nebr., U.S.A. 80 E6 41 51N 96 43W
West Point, Va., U.S.A. 76 G7 37 32N 76 48W
West Pt. = Ouest, Pte. de l', Canada 71 C7 49 52N 64 40W
West Pt., Australia 63 F2 35 1S 135 56 E
West Road →, Canada 72 C4 53 18N 122 53W
West Rutland, U.S.A. 75 B12 43 38N 73 5W
West Schelde = Westerschelde →, Neths. 15 C3 51 25N 3 25 E
West Seneca, U.S.A. 78 D6 42 51N 78 48W
West Siberian Plain, Russia 28 C11 62 0N 75 0 E
West Sussex □, U.K. 11 G7 50 55N 0 30W
West-Terschelling, Neths. 15 A5 53 22N 5 13 E
West Valley City, U.S.A. 82 F8 40 42N 111 57W
West Virginia □, U.S.A. 76 F5 38 45N 80 30W
West-Vlaanderen □, Belgium 15 D2 51 0N 3 0 E
West Walker →, U.S.A. 84 G7 38 54N 119 9W
West Wyalong, Australia 63 E4 33 56S 147 10 E
West Yellowstone, U.S.A. 82 D8 44 40N 111 6W
West Yorkshire □, U.K. 10 D6 53 45N 1 40W
Westall Pt., Australia 63 E1 32 55S 134 4 E
Westbrook, U.S.A. 77 D10 43 41N 70 22W
Westbury, Australia 62 G4 41 30S 146 51 E
Westby, U.S.A. 80 A2 48 52N 104 3W
Westend, U.S.A. 85 K9 35 42N 117 24W
Westerland, Germany 16 A5 54 54N 8 17 E
Westerly, U.S.A. 79 E13 41 22N 71 50W
Western □, Kenya 54 B3 0 30N 34 30 E
Western □, Uganda 54 B3 1 45N 31 30 E
Western □, Zambia 55 F1 15 15S 24 30 E
Western Australia □, Australia 61 E2 25 0S 118 0 E
Western Cape □, S. Africa 56 E3 34 0S 20 0 E
Western Dvina = Daugava →, Latvia 9 H21 57 4N 24 3 E
Western Ghats, India 40 N9 14 0N 75 0 E
Western Isles □, U.K. 12 D1 57 30N 7 10W
Western Sahara ■, Africa 50 D3 25 0N 13 0W
Western Samoa ■, Pac. Oc. 59 B13 14 0S 172 0W
Westernport, U.S.A. 76 F6 39 29N 79 3W
Westerschelde →, Neths. 15 C3 51 25N 3 25 E
Westerwald, Germany 16 C4 50 38N 7 56 E
Westfield, Mass., U.S.A. 79 D12 42 7N 72 45W
Westfield, N.Y., U.S.A. 78 D5 42 20N 79 35W
Westfield, Pa., U.S.A. 78 E7 41 55N 77 32W
Westhill, U.K. 12 D6 57 9N 2 19W
Westhope, U.S.A. 80 A4 48 55N 101 1W
Westland Bight, N.Z. 59 K3 42 55S 170 5 E
Westlock, Canada 72 C6 54 9N 113 55W
Westmar, Australia 63 D4 27 55S 149 44 E
Westmeath □, Ireland 13 C4 53 33N 7 34W
Westminster, U.S.A. 76 F7 39 34N 76 59W
Westmont, U.S.A. 78 F6 40 19N 78 58W
Westmorland, U.S.A. 85 M11 33 2N 115 37W
Weston, Oreg., U.S.A. 82 D4 45 49N 118 26W
Weston, W. Va., U.S.A. 76 F5 39 2N 80 28W
Weston I., Canada 70 B4 52 33N 79 36W
Weston-super-Mare, U.K. 11 F5 51 21N 2 58W
Westover, U.S.A. 78 F6 40 45N 78 40W
Westport, Canada 79 B8 44 40N 76 25W
Westport, Ireland 13 C2 53 48N 9 31W
Westport, N.Z. 59 J3 41 46S 171 37 E
Westport, N.Y., U.S.A. 79 B11 44 11N 73 26W
Westport, Oreg., U.S.A. 84 D3 46 8N 123 23W
Westport, Wash., U.S.A. 84 D2 46 53N 124 6W
Westray, Canada 73 C8 53 36N 101 24W
Westray, U.K. 12 B5 59 18N 3 0W
Westree, Canada 70 C3 47 26N 81 34W
Westville, U.S.A. 84 F6 39 8N 120 42W
Westwood, U.S.A. 82 F3 40 18N 121 0W
Wetar, Indonesia 37 F7 7 30S 126 30 E
Wetaskiwin, Canada 72 C6 52 55N 113 24W
Wete, Tanzania 52 F7 5 4S 39 43 E
Wetherby, U.K. 10 D6 53 56N 1 23W
Wethersfield, U.S.A. 79 E12 41 42N 72 40W
Wetteren, Belgium 15 D3 51 0N 3 53 E
Wetzlar, Germany 16 C5 50 32N 8 31 E
Wewoka, U.S.A. 81 H6 35 9N 96 30W
Wexford, Ireland 13 D5 52 20N 6 28W
Wexford □, Ireland 13 D5 52 20N 6 25W
Wexford Harbour, Ireland 13 D5 52 20N 6 25W
Weyburn, Canada 73 D8 49 40N 103 50W
Weymouth, Canada 71 D6 44 30N 66 1W
Weymouth, U.K. 11 G5 50 37N 2 28W
Weymouth, U.S.A. 79 D14 42 13N 70 58W
Weymouth, C., Australia 62 A3 12 37S 143 27 E
Wha Ti, Canada 68 B8 63 8N 117 16W
Whakatane, N.Z. 59 G6 37 57S 177 1 E
Whale →, Canada 71 A6 58 15N 67 40W
Whale Cove, Canada 73 A10 62 11N 92 36W
Whales, B. of, Antarctica 5 D12 78 0S 165 0W
Whalsay, U.K. 12 A8 60 22N 0 59W
Whangamomona, N.Z. 59 H5 39 8S 174 44 E
Whangarei, N.Z. 59 F5 35 43S 174 21 E
Whangarei Harb., N.Z. 59 F5 35 45S 174 28 E
Wharfe →, U.K. 10 D6 53 51N 1 9W
Wharfedale, U.K. 10 C5 54 6N 2 1W
Wharton, N.J., U.S.A. 79 F10 40 54N 74 35W
Wharton, Pa., U.S.A. 78 E6 41 31N 78 1W
Wharton, Tex., U.S.A. 81 L6 29 19N 96 6W
Wheatland, Calif., U.S.A. 84 F5 39 1N 121 25W
Wheatland, Wyo., U.S.A. 80 D2 42 3N 104 58W
Wheatley, Ont., Canada 78 D2 42 6N 82 27W
Wheatley, Ont., Canada 78 D2 42 6N 82 27W
Wheaton, Md., U.S.A. 76 F7 39 3N 77 3W
Wheaton, Minn., U.S.A. 80 C6 45 48N 96 30W
Wheelbarrow Pk., U.S.A. 84 H10 37 26N 116 5W
Wheeler, Oreg., U.S.A. 82 D2 45 41N 123 53W
Wheeler, Tex., U.S.A. 81 H4 35 27N 100 16W
Wheeler →, Canada 71 A6 57 2N 67 13W
Wheeler L., U.S.A. 77 H2 34 48N 87 23W
Wheeler Pk., N. Mex., U.S.A. 83 H11 36 34N 105 25W
Wheeler Pk., Nev., U.S.A. 83 G6 38 57N 114 15W
Wheeler Ridge, U.S.A. 85 L8 35 0N 118 57W
Wheeling, U.S.A. 78 F4 40 4N 80 43W
Whernside, U.K. 10 C5 54 14N 2 24W
Whiskey Jack L., Canada 73 B8 58 23N 101 55W
Whistleduck Cr. →, Australia 62 C2 20 15S 135 18 E
Whistler, Canada 72 C4 50 7N 122 58W
Whitby, Canada 78 C6 43 52N 78 56W
Whitby, U.K. 10 C7 54 29N 0 37W
White →, Ark., U.S.A. 81 J9 33 57N 91 5W
White →, Ind., U.S.A. 76 F2 38 25N 87 45W
White →, S. Dak., U.S.A. 80 D5 43 42N 99 27W
White →, Tex., U.S.A. 81 J4 33 14N 100 56W
White →, Utah, U.S.A. 82 F9 40 4N 109 41W
White →, Vt., U.S.A. 79 C12 43 37N 72 20W
White →, Wash., U.S.A. 84 C4 47 12N 122 15W
White, L., Australia 60 D4 21 9S 128 56 E
White B., Canada 71 C8 50 0N 56 35W
White Bird, U.S.A. 82 D5 45 46N 116 18W
White Butte, U.S.A. 80 B3 46 23N 103 18W
White City, U.S.A. 82 E2 42 26N 122 51W
White Cliffs, Australia 63 E3 30 50S 143 10 E
White Hall, U.S.A. 80 F9 39 26N 90 24W
White Haven, U.S.A. 79 E9 41 4N 75 47W
White Horse, Vale of, U.K. 11 F6 51 37N 1 30W
White I., N.Z. 59 G6 37 30S 177 13 E
White L., Canada 79 A8 45 18N 76 31W
White L., U.S.A. 81 L8 29 44N 92 30W
White Mountain Peak, U.S.A. 83 G4 37 38N 118 15W
White Mts., Calif., U.S.A. 84 H8 37 30N 118 15W
White Mts., N.H., U.S.A. 75 B12 44 15N 71 15W
White Mts., N.H., U.S.A. 76 C10 44 10N 71 20W
White Nile = Nîl el Abyad →, Sudan 51 E12 15 38N 32 31 E
White Otter L., Canada 70 C1 49 5N 91 55W
White Pass, U.S.A. 84 D5 46 38N 121 24W
White Plains, U.S.A. 79 E11 41 2N 73 46W
White River, Canada 70 C2 48 35N 85 20W
White River, S. Africa 57 D5 25 20S 31 0 E
White River, U.S.A. 80 D4 43 34N 100 45W
White Rock, Canada 84 A4 49 2N 122 48W
White Russia = Belarus ■, Europe 17 B14 53 30N 27 0 E
White Sea = Beloye More, Russia 24 A6 66 30N 38 0 E
White Sulphur Springs, Mont., U.S.A. 82 C8 46 33N 110 54W
White Sulphur Springs, W. Va., U.S.A. 76 G5 37 48N 80 18W
White Swan, U.S.A. 84 D6 46 23N 120 44W
Whitecliffs, N.Z. 59 K3 43 26S 171 55 E
Whitecourt, Canada 72 C5 54 10N 115 45W
Whiteface Mt., U.S.A. 79 B11 44 22N 73 54W
Whitefield, U.S.A. 79 B13 44 23N 71 37W
Whitefish, U.S.A. 82 B6 48 25N 114 20W
Whitefish L., Canada 73 A7 62 41N 106 48W
Whitefish Point, U.S.A. 76 B3 46 45N 84 59W
Whitegull, L., Canada 71 A7 55 27N 64 17W
Whitehall, Mich., U.S.A. 76 D2 43 24N 86 21W
Whitehall, Mont., U.S.A. 82 D7 45 52N 112 6W
Whitehall, N.Y., U.S.A. 79 C11 43 33N 73 24W
Whitehall, Wis., U.S.A. 80 C9 44 22N 91 19W
Whitehaven, U.K. 10 C4 54 33N 3 35W
Whitehorse, Canada 72 A1 60 43N 135 3W
Whitemark, Australia 62 G4 40 7S 148 3 E
Whiteriver, U.S.A. 83 K9 33 50N 109 58W
Whitesand →, Canada 72 A5 60 9N 115 45W
Whitesboro, N.Y., U.S.A. 79 C9 43 7N 75 18W
Whitesboro, Tex., U.S.A. 81 J6 33 39N 96 54W
Whiteshell Prov. Park, Canada 73 D9 50 0N 95 40W
Whitesville, U.S.A. 78 D7 42 2N 77 46W
Whiteville, U.S.A. 77 H6 34 20N 78 42W
Whitewater, U.S.A. 76 D1 42 50N 88 44W
Whitewater Baldy, U.S.A. 83 K9 33 20N 108 39W
Whitewater L., Canada 70 B2 50 50N 89 10W
Whitewood, Australia 62 C3 21 28S 143 30 E
Whitewood, Canada 73 C8 50 20N 102 20W
Whithorn, U.K. 12 G4 54 44N 4 26W
Whitianga, N.Z. 59 G5 36 47S 175 41 E
Whitman, U.S.A. 79 D14 42 5N 70 56W
Whitney, Canada 78 A6 45 31N 78 14W
Whitney, Mt., U.S.A. 84 J8 36 35N 118 18W
Whitney Point, U.S.A. 79 D9 42 20N 75 58W
Whitstable, U.K. 11 F9 51 21N 1 3 E
Whitsunday I., Australia 62 C4 20 15S 149 4 E
Whittier, U.S.A. 85 M8 33 58N 118 3W
Whittlesea, Australia 63 F4 37 27S 145 9 E
Wholdaia L., Canada 73 A8 60 43N 104 20W
Whyalla, Australia 63 E2 33 2S 137 30 E
Wiarton, Canada 78 B3 44 40N 81 10W
Wiay, U.K. 12 D1 57 24N 7 13W
Wibaux, U.S.A. 80 B2 46 59N 104 11W
Wichian Buri, Thailand 38 E3 15 39N 101 7 E
Wichita, U.S.A. 81 G6 37 42N 97 20W
Wichita Falls, U.S.A. 81 J5 33 54N 98 30W
Wick, U.K. 12 C5 58 26N 3 5W
Wicked Pt., Canada 78 C7 43 52N 77 15W
Wickenburg, U.S.A. 83 K7 33 58N 112 44W
Wickepin, Australia 61 F2 32 50S 117 30 E
Wickham, Australia 60 D2 20 42S 117 11 E
Wickham, C., Australia 62 F3 39 35S 143 57 E
Wickliffe, U.S.A. 78 E3 41 36N 81 28W
Wicklow, Ireland 13 D5 52 59N 6 3W
Wicklow □, Ireland 13 D5 52 57N 6 25W
Wicklow Hd., Ireland 13 D6 52 58N 6 0W
Wicklow Mts., Ireland 13 C5 52 58N 6 26W
Widgeegoara Cr. →, Australia 63 D4 28 51S 146 34 E
Widgiemooltha, Australia 61 F3 31 30S 121 34 E
Widnes, U.K. 10 D5 53 23N 2 45W
Wieluń, Poland 17 C10 51 15N 18 34 E
Wien, Austria 16 D9 48 12N 16 22 E
Wiener Neustadt, Austria 16 E9 47 49N 16 16 E
Wiesbaden, Germany 16 C5 50 4N 8 14 E
Wigan, U.K. 10 D5 53 33N 2 38W
Wiggins, Colo., U.S.A. 80 E2 40 14N 104 4W
Wiggins, Miss., U.S.A. 81 K10 30 51N 89 8W
Wight, I. of □, U.K. 11 G6 50 40N 1 20W
Wigston, U.K. 11 E6 52 35N 1 6W
Wigton, U.K. 10 C4 54 50N 3 10W
Wigtown, U.K. 12 G4 54 53N 4 27W
Wigtown B., U.K. 12 G4 54 46N 4 15W
Wilber, U.S.A. 80 E6 40 29N 96 58W
Wilberforce, Canada 78 A6 45 2N 78 13W
Wilberforce, C., Australia 62 A2 11 54S 136 35 E
Wilburton, U.S.A. 81 H7 34 55N 95 19W
Wilcannia, Australia 63 E3 31 30S 143 26 E
Wilcox, U.S.A. 78 E6 41 35N 78 41W
Wildrose, U.S.A. 85 J9 36 14N 117 11W
Wildspitze, Austria 16 E6 46 53N 10 53 E
Wilge →, S. Africa 57 D4 27 3S 28 20 E
Wilhelm II Coast, Antarctica 5 C7 68 0S 90 0 E
Wilhelmshaven, Germany 16 B5 53 31N 8 7 E
Wilhelmstal, Namibia 56 C2 21 58S 16 21 E
Wilkes-Barre, U.S.A. 79 E9 41 15N 75 53W
Wilkie, Canada 73 C7 52 27N 108 42W
Wilkinsburg, U.S.A. 78 F5 40 26N 79 53W
Wilkinson Lakes, Australia 61 E5 29 40S 132 39 E
Willandra Creek →, Australia 63 E4 33 22S 145 52 E
Willapa B., U.S.A. 82 C2 46 40N 124 0W
Willapa Hills, U.S.A. 84 D3 46 35N 123 25W
Willard, N.Y., U.S.A. 78 D8 42 40N 76 50W
Willard, Ohio, U.S.A. 78 E2 41 3N 82 44W
Willcox, U.S.A. 83 K9 32 15N 109 50W
Willemstad, Neth. Ant. 89 D6 12 5N 69 0W
Willet, U.S.A. 79 D9 42 28N 75 55W
William →, Canada 73 B7 59 8N 109 19W
William 'Bill' Dannely Res., U.S.A. 77 J2 32 10N 87 10W
William Creek, Australia 63 D2 28 58S 136 22 E
Williams, Australia 61 F2 33 2S 116 52 E
Williams, Ariz., U.S.A. 83 J7 35 15N 112 11W
Williams, Calif., U.S.A. 84 F4 39 9N 122 9W
Williams Harbour, Canada 71 B8 52 33N 55 47W
Williams Lake, Canada 72 C4 52 10N 122 10W
Williamsburg, Ky., U.S.A. 77 G3 36 44N 84 10W
Williamsburg, Pa., U.S.A. 78 F6 40 28N 78 12W
Williamsburg, Va., U.S.A. 76 G7 37 17N 76 44W
Williamson, N.Y., U.S.A. 78 C7 43 14N 77 11W
Williamson, W. Va., U.S.A. 76 G4 37 41N 82 17W
Williamsport, U.S.A. 78 E7 41 15N 77 0W
Williamston, U.S.A. 77 H7 35 51N 77 4W
Williamstown, Australia 63 F3 37 51S 144 52 E
Williamstown, Ky., U.S.A. 76 F3 38 38N 84 34W
Williamstown, Mass., U.S.A. 79 D11 42 41N 73 12W
Williamstown, N.Y., U.S.A. 79 C9 43 26N 75 53W
Willimantic, U.S.A. 79 E12 41 43N 72 13W
Willingboro, U.S.A. 76 E8 40 3N 74 54W
Willis Group, Australia 62 B5 16 18S 150 0 E
Williston, S. Africa 56 E3 31 20S 20 53 E
Williston, Fla., U.S.A. 77 L4 29 23N 82 27W
Williston, N. Dak., U.S.A. 80 A3 48 9N 103 37W
Williston L., Canada 72 B4 56 0N 124 0W
Willits, U.S.A. 82 G2 39 25N 123 21W
Willmar, U.S.A. 80 C7 45 7N 95 3W
Willoughby, U.S.A. 78 E3 41 39N 81 24W
Willow Bunch, Canada 73 D7 49 20N 105 35W
Willow L., Canada 72 A5 62 10N 119 8W
Willow Wall, The, China 35 C12 42 10N 122 0 E
Willowick, U.S.A. 78 E3 41 38N 81 28W
Willowlake →, Canada 72 A4 62 42N 123 8W
Willowmore, S. Africa 56 E3 33 15S 23 30 E
Willows, U.S.A. 84 F4 39 31N 122 12W
Willowvale = Gatyana, S. Africa 57 E4 32 16S 28 31 E
Wills, L., Australia 60 D4 21 25S 128 51 E
Wills Cr. →, Australia 62 C3 22 43S 140 2 E
Willsboro, U.S.A. 79 B11 44 21N 73 24W
Willunga, Australia 63 F2 35 15S 138 30 E
Wilmette, U.S.A. 76 D2 42 5N 87 42W
Wilmington, Australia 63 E2 32 39S 138 7 E
Wilmington, Del., U.S.A. 76 F8 39 45N 75 33W
Wilmington, N.C., U.S.A. 77 H7 34 14N 77 55W
Wilmington, Ohio, U.S.A. 76 F4 39 27N 83 50W
Wilmington, Vt., U.S.A. 79 D12 42 52N 72 52W
Wilmslow, U.K. 10 D5 53 19N 2 13W
Wilpena →, Australia 63 E2 31 25S 139 29 E
Wilsall, U.S.A. 82 D8 45 59N 110 38W
Wilson, N.C., U.S.A. 77 H7 35 44N 77 55W
Wilson, N.Y., U.S.A. 78 C6 43 19N 78 50W
Wilson, Pa., U.S.A. 79 F9 40 41N 75 15W
Wilson →, Australia 60 C4 16 48S 128 16 E
Wilson Bluff, Australia 61 F4 31 41S 129 0 E
Wilson Inlet, Australia 61 G2 35 0S 117 22 E
Wilsons Promontory, Australia 63 F4 38 55S 146 25 E
Wilton, U.S.A. 80 B4 47 10N 100 47W
Wilton →, Australia 62 A1 14 45S 134 33 E
Wiltshire □, U.K. 11 F6 51 18N 1 53W
Wiltz, Lux. 15 E5 49 57N 5 55 E
Wiluna, Australia 61 E3 26 36S 120 14 E
Wimborne Minster, U.K. 11 G6 50 48N 1 59W
Wimmera →, Australia 63 F3 36 8S 141 56 E
Winam G., Kenya 54 C3 0 20S 34 15 E
Winburg, S. Africa 56 D4 28 30S 27 2 E
Winchendon, U.S.A. 79 D12 42 41N 72 3W
Winchester, U.K. 11 F6 51 4N 1 18W
Winchester, Conn., U.S.A. 79 E11 41 53N 73 9W
Winchester, Idaho, U.S.A. 82 C5 46 14N 116 38W
Winchester, Ind., U.S.A. 76 E3 40 10N 84 59W
Winchester, Ky., U.S.A. 76 G3 38 0N 84 11W
Winchester, N.H., U.S.A. 79 D12 42 46N 72 23W
Winchester, Nev., U.S.A. 85 J11 36 6N 115 10W
Winchester, Tenn., U.S.A. 77 H2 35 11N 86 7W
Winchester, Va., U.S.A. 76 F6 39 11N 78 10W
Wind →, U.S.A. 82 E9 43 12N 108 12W
Wind River Range, U.S.A. 82 E9 43 0N 109 30W
Windau = Ventspils, Latvia 9 H19 57 25N 21 32 E
Windber, U.S.A. 78 F6 40 14N 78 50W
Winder, U.S.A. 77 J4 34 0N 83 45W
Windermere, Cumb., U.K. 10 C5 54 23N 2 55W
Windermere, Cumb., U.K. 10 C5 54 22N 2 56W
Windhoek, Namibia 56 C2 22 35S 17 4 E
Windom, U.S.A. 80 D7 43 52N 95 7W
Windorah, Australia 62 D3 25 24S 142 36 E
Window Rock, U.S.A. 83 J9 35 41N 109 3W
Windrush →, U.K. 11 F6 51 43N 1 24W
Windsor, Australia 63 E5 33 37S 150 50 E
Windsor, N.S., Canada 71 D7 44 59N 64 5W
Windsor, Ont., Canada 78 D2 42 18N 83 0W
Windsor, U.K. 11 F7 51 29N 0 36W
Windsor, Colo., U.S.A. 80 E2 40 29N 104 54W
Windsor, Conn., U.S.A. 79 E12 41 50N 72 39W
Windsor, Mo., U.S.A. 80 F8 38 32N 93 31W
Windsor, N.Y., U.S.A. 79 D9 42 5N 75 37W
Windsor, Vt., U.S.A. 79 C12 43 29N 72 24W
Windsor & Maidenhead □, U.K. 11 F7 51 29N 0 40W
Windsorton, S. Africa 56 D3 28 16S 24 44 E
Windward Is., W. Indies 89 D7 13 0N 61 0W
Windward Passage = Vientos, Paso de los, Caribbean 89 C5 20 0N 74 0W
Winefred L., Canada 73 B6 55 30N 110 30W
Winfield, U.S.A. 81 G6 37 15N 96 59W
Wingate Mts., Australia 60 B5 14 25S 130 40 E
Wingham, Australia 63 E5 31 48S 152 22 E
Wingham, Canada 78 C3 43 55N 81 20W
Winisk, Canada 70 A2 55 20N 85 15W
Winisk →, Canada 70 A2 55 17N 85 5W
Winisk L., Canada 70 B2 52 55N 87 22W
Wink, U.S.A. 81 K3 31 45N 103 9W
Winkler, Canada 73 D9 49 10N 97 56W
Winlock, U.S.A. 84 D4 46 30N 122 56W
Winnebago, L., U.S.A. 76 D1 44 0N 88 26W
Winnecke Cr. →, Australia 60 C5 18 35S 131 34 E
Winnemucca, U.S.A. 82 F5 40 58N 117 44W
Winnemucca L., U.S.A. 82 F4 40 7N 119 21W
Winnett, U.S.A. 82 C9 47 0N 108 21W
Winnfield, U.S.A. 81 K8 31 56N 92 38W
Winnibigoshish, L., U.S.A. 80 B7 47 27N 94 13W
Winnipeg, Canada 73 D9 49 54N 97 9W
Winnipeg →, Canada 73 C9 50 38N 96 19W
Winnipeg, L., Canada 73 C9 52 0N 97 0W
Winnipeg Beach, Canada 73 C9 50 30N 96 58W
Winnipegosis, Canada 73 C9 51 39N 99 55W
Winnipegosis L., Canada 73 C9 52 30N 100 0W
Winnipesaukee, L., U.S.A. 79 C13 43 38N 71 21W
Winnisquam L., U.S.A. 79 C13 43 33N 71 31W
Winnsboro, La., U.S.A. 81 J9 32 10N 91 43W
Winnsboro, S.C., U.S.A. 77 H5 34 23N 81 5W
Winnsboro, Tex., U.S.A. 81 J7 32 58N 95 17W
Winokapau, L., Canada 71 B7 53 15N 62 50W
Winona, Minn., U.S.A. 80 C9 44 3N 91 39W
Winona, Miss., U.S.A. 81 J10 33 29N 89 44W
Winooski, U.S.A. 79 B11 44 29N 73 11W
Winooski →, U.S.A. 79 B11 44 32N 73 17W
Winschoten, Neths. 15 A7 53 9N 7 3 E
Winsford, U.K. 10 D5 53 12N 2 31W
Winslow, Ariz., U.S.A. 83 J8 35 2N 110 42W
Winslow, Wash., U.S.A. 84 C4 47 38N 122 31W
Winsted, U.S.A. 79 E11 41 55N 73 4W
Winston-Salem, U.S.A. 77 G5 36 6N 80 15W
Winter Garden, U.S.A. 77 L5 28 34N 81 35W
Winter Haven, U.S.A. 77 M5 28 1N 81 44W
Winter Park, U.S.A. 77 L5 28 36N 81 20W
Winterhaven, U.S.A. 85 N12 32 47N 114 39W
Winters, U.S.A. 84 G5 38 32N 121 58W
Wintersville, U.S.A. 78 F4 40 23N 80 42W
Winterswijk, Neths. 15 C6 51 58N 6 43 E
Winterthur, Switz. 18 C8 47 30N 8 44 E
Winthrop, U.S.A. 82 B3 48 28N 120 10W
Winton, Australia 62 C3 22 24S 143 3 E
Winton, N.Z. 59 M2 46 8S 168 20 E
Wirrulla, Australia 63 E1 32 24S 134 31 E
Wisbech, U.K. 11 E8 52 41N 0 9 E
Wisconsin □, U.S.A. 80 C10 44 45N 89 30W
Wisconsin →, U.S.A. 80 D9 43 0N 91 15W
Wisconsin Rapids, U.S.A. 80 C10 44 23N 89 49W
Wisdom, U.S.A. 82 D7 45 37N 113 27W
Wishaw, U.K. 12 F5 55 46N 3 54W
Wishek, U.S.A. 80 B5 46 16N 99 33W
Wisła →, Poland 17 A10 54 22N 18 55 E
Wismar, Germany 16 B6 53 54N 11 29 E
Wisner, U.S.A. 80 E6 41 59N 96 55W
Witbank, S. Africa 57 D4 25 51S 29 14 E
Witdraai, S. Africa 56 D3 26 58S 20 48 E
Witham, U.K. 11 F8 51 48N 0 40 E
Witham →, U.K. 10 E7 52 59N 0 2W
Withernsea, U.K. 10 D8 53 44N 0 1 E
Witney, U.K. 11 F6 51 47N 1 28W
Witnossob →, Namibia 56 D3 26 55S 20 37 E
Wittenberge, Germany 16 B6 53 0N 11 45 E
Wittenoom, Australia 60 D2 22 15S 118 20 E
Wkra →, Poland 17 B11 52 27N 20 44 E
Wlingi, Indonesia 37 H15 8 5S 112 25 E
Włocławek, Poland 17 B10 52 40N 19 3 E
Włodawa, Poland 17 C12 51 33N 23 31 E
Woburn, U.S.A. 79 D13 42 29N 71 9W
Wodian, China 34 H7 32 50N 112 35 E
Wokam, Indonesia 37 F8 5 45S 134 28 E
Woking, U.K. 11 F7 51 19N 0 34W
Wokingham □, U.K. 11 F7 51 25N 0 51W
Wolf →, Canada 72 A2 60 17N 132 33W
Wolf Creek, U.S.A. 82 C7 47 0N 112 4W
Wolf L., Canada 72 A2 60 24N 131 40W
Wolf Point, U.S.A. 80 A2 48 5N 105 39W
Wolfe I., Canada 79 B8 44 7N 76 20W
Wolfeboro, U.S.A. 79 C13 43 35N 71 13W
Wolfsberg, Austria 16 E8 46 50N 14 52 E
Wolfsburg, Germany 16 B6 52 25N 10 48 E
Wolin, Poland 16 B8 53 50N 14 37 E
Wollaston, Is., Chile 96 H3 55 40S 67 30W
Wollaston L., Canada 73 B8 58 7N 103 10W
Wollaston Lake, Canada 73 B8 58 3N 103 33W
Wollaston Pen., Canada 68 B8 69 30N 115 0W
Wollongong, Australia 63 E5 34 25S 150 54 E
Wolmaransstad, S. Africa 56 D4 27 12S 25 59 E
Wolseley, S. Africa 56 E2 33 26S 19 7 E
Wolsey, U.S.A. 80 C5 44 24N 98 28W
Wolstenholme, C., Canada 66 C12 62 35N 77 30W
Wolvega, Neths. 15 B6 52 52N 6 0 E
Wolverhampton, U.K. 11 E5 52 35N 2 7W
Wondai, Australia 63 D5 26 20S 151 49 E
Wongalarroo L., Australia 63 E3 31 32S 144 0 E
Wongan Hills, Australia 61 F2 30 51S 116 37 E
Wŏnju, S. Korea 35 F14 37 22N 127 58 E
Wonosari, Indonesia 37 G14 7 58S 110 36 E
Wonosobo, Indonesia 37 G13 7 22S 109 54 E
Wonowon, Canada 72 B4 56 44N 121 48W
Wŏnsan, N. Korea 35 E14 39 11N 127 27 E
Wonthaggi, Australia 63 F4 38 37S 145 37 E
Wood Buffalo Nat. Park, Canada 72 B6 59 0N 113 41W
Wood Is., Australia 60 C3 16 24S 123 19 E
Wood L., Canada 73 B8 55 17N 103 17W
Woodah I., Australia 62 A2 13 27S 136 10 E
Woodbourne, U.S.A. 79 E10 41 46N 74 36W
Woodbridge, Canada 78 C5 43 47N 79 36W
Woodbridge, U.K. 11 E9 52 6N 1 20 E
Woodburn, U.S.A. 82 D2 45 9N 122 51W
Woodenbong, Australia 63 D5 28 24S 152 39 E

Yezd

World: Regions in the News

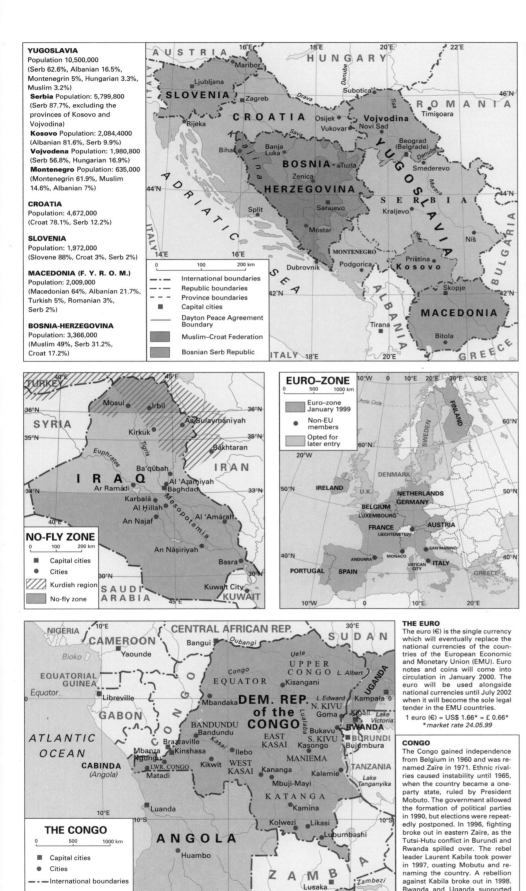

Legend (Former Yugoslavia map)
- — · — · — International boundaries
- — · · — · · — Republic boundaries
- — — — — Province boundaries
- ■ Capital cities
- Dayton Peace Agreement Boundary
- Muslim–Croat Federation
- Bosnian Serb Republic

FORMER YUGOSLAVIA AND KOSOVO

The former Yugoslavia, a federation of six republics, split apart in 1991–2. Fearing Serb domination, Croatia, Slovenia, Macedonia and Bosnia-Herzegovina declared themselves independent. This left two states, Serbia and Montenegro, to continue as Yugoslavia. The presence in Croatia and Bosnia-Herzegovina of Orthodox Christian Serbs, Roman Catholic Croats, and Muslims led to civil war and "ethnic cleansing." In 1995, the war ended when the Dayton Peace Accord affirmed Bosnia-Herzegovina as a single state partitioned into a Muslim-Croat Federation and a Serbian Republic.

But the status of Kosovo, a former autonomous Yugoslav region, remained unresolved. Kosovo's autonomy had been abolished in 1989 and the Albanian-speaking, Muslim Kosovars were forced to accept direct Serbian rule. After 1995, support grew for the rebel Kosovo Liberation Army. The Serbs hit back and thousands of Kosovars were forced to flee their homes. In March 1999, NATO launched an aerial offensive against Serbia in an attempt to halt the "ethnic cleansing." A Serb military withdrawal from Kosovo was finally agreed in June.

KOSOVO
- ■ Capital city
- • Other towns
- — · — · — International boundaries

NO-FLY ZONE (map)
- ■ Capital cities
- • Cities
- Kurdish region
- No-fly zone

EURO–ZONE (map)
- Euro–zone January 1999
- • Non-EU members
- Opted for later entry

THE EURO

The euro (€) is the single currency which will eventually replace the national currencies of the countries of the European Economic and Monetary Union (EMU). Euro notes and coins will come into circulation in January 2000. The euro will be used alongside national currencies until July 2002 when it will become the sole legal tender in the EMU countries.

1 euro (€) = US$ 1.66* = £ 0.66*
*market rate 24.05.99

THE NEAR EAST
- — · — · — 1949 Armistice Line
- ———— 1974 Cease–fire Line
- Efrata ● Main Jewish settlements in the West Bank and Gaza Strip
- Halhul ● Main Palestinian Arab towns in the West Bank and Gaza Strip
- ■ Capital cities

THE CONGO (map)
- ■ Capital cities
- • Cities
- — · — · — International boundaries
- Neighboring countries involved in the conflict in the Congo

CONGO

The Congo gained independence from Belgium in 1960 and was re-named Zaïre in 1971. Ethnic rivalries caused instability until 1965, when the country became a one-party state, ruled by President Mobuto. The government allowed the formation of political parties in 1990, but elections were repeatedly postponed. In 1996, fighting broke out in eastern Zaïre, as the Tutsi-Hutu conflict in Burundi and Rwanda spilled over. The rebel leader Laurent Kabila took power in 1997, ousting Mobutu and renaming the country. A rebellion against Kabila broke out in 1998. Rwanda and Uganda supported the rebels, while Angola, Chad, Namibia and Zimbabwe sent troops to assist Kabila.

MAP PROJECTIONS

MAP PROJECTIONS

A map projection is the systematic depiction on a plane surface of the imaginary lines of latitude or longitude from a globe of the earth. This network of lines is called the graticule and forms the framework upon which an accurate depiction of the earth is made. The map graticule, which is the basis of any map, is constructed sometimes by graphical means, but often by using mathematical formulae to give the intersections of the graticule plotted as x and y co-ordinates. The choice between projections is based upon which properties the cartographer wishes the map to possess, the map scale and also the extent of the area to be mapped. Since the globe is three dimensional, it is not possible to depict its surface on a two dimensional plane without distortion. Preservation of one of the basic properties listed below can only be secured at the expense of the others and the choice of projection is often a compromise solution.

Correct Area
In these projections the areas from the globe are to scale on the map. For example, if you look at the diagram at the top right, areas of 10° x 10° are shown from the equator to the poles. The proportion of this area at the extremities are approximately 11:1. An equal area projection will retain that proportion in its portrayal of those areas. This is particularly useful in the mapping of densities and distributions. Projections with this property are termed **Equal Area, Equivalent or Homolographic.**

Correct Distance
In these projections the scale is correct along the meridians, or in the case of the Azimuthal Equidistant scale is true along any line drawn from the centre of the projection. They are called **Equidistant.**

Correct Shape
This property can only be true within small areas as it is achieved only by having a uniform scale distortion along both x and y axes of the projection. The projections are called **Conformal or Orthomorphic.**

In order to minimise the distortions at the edges of some projections, central portions of them are often selected for atlas maps. Below are listed some of the major types of projection.

Latitude and Longitude

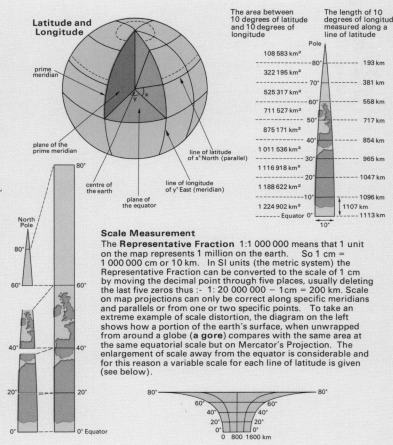

The area between 10 degrees of latitude and 10 degrees of longitude		The length of 10 degrees of longitude measured along a line of latitude
	Pole	
108 583 km²	80°	193 km
322 195 km²	70°	381 km
525 317 km²	60°	558 km
711 527 km²	50°	717 km
875 171 km²	40°	854 km
1 011 536 km²	30°	965 km
1 116 918 km²	20°	1047 km
1 188 622 km²	10°	1096 km
1 224 902 km²	Equator 0°	1107 km
	10°	1113 km

Scale Measurement
The **Representative Fraction** 1:1 000 000 means that 1 unit on the map represents 1 million on the earth. So 1 cm = 1 000 000 cm or 10 km. In SI units (the metric system) the Representative Fraction can be converted to the scale of 1 cm by moving the decimal point through five places, usually deleting the last five zeros thus :- 1: 20 000 000 — 1cm = 200 km. Scale on map projections can only be correct along specific meridians and parallels or from one or two specific points. To take an extreme example of scale distortion, the diagram on the left shows how a portion of the earth's surface, when unwrapped from around a globe (**a gore**) compares with the same area at the same equatorial scale but on Mercator's Projection. The enlargement of scale away from the equator is considerable and for this reason a variable scale for each line of latitude is given (see below).

0 800 1600 km

AZIMUTHAL OR ZENITHAL PROJECTIONS

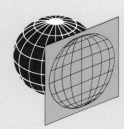

These are constructed by the projection of part of the graticule from the globe onto a plane tangential to any single point on it. This plane may be tangential to the equator (**equatorial case**), the poles (**polar case**) or any other point (**oblique case**). Any straight line drawn from the point at which the plane touches the globe is the shortest distance from that point and is known as a **great circle**. In its **Gnomonic** construction *any* straight line on the map is a great circle, but there is great exaggeration towards the edges and this reduces its general uses. There are five different ways of transferring the graticule onto the plane and these are shown on the right. The central diagram below shows how the graticules vary, using the polar case as the example.

Equidistant   **Equal-Area**   **Orthographic**   **Gnomonic**   **Stereographic (conformal)**

Oblique Case

The plane touches the globe at any point between the equator and poles. The oblique orthographic uses the distortion in azimuthal projections away from the centre to give a graphic depiction of the earth as seen from any desired point in space. It can also be used in both Polar and Equatorial cases. It is used not only for the earth but also for the moon and planets.

Polar Case

The polar case is the simplest to construct and the diagram below shows the differing effects of all five methods of construction comparing their coverage, distortion etc., using North America as the example.

Equatorial Case

The example shown here is Lambert's Equivalent Azimuthal. It is the only projection which is both equal area and where bearing is true from the centre.

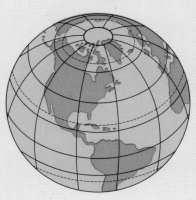

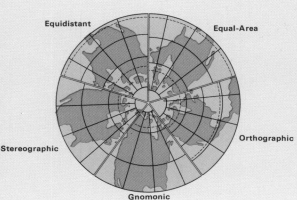

Equidistant   Equal-Area

Stereographic   Orthographic

Gnomonic

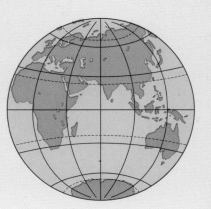